THE CAMBRIDGE
ENCYCLOPEDIA OF
THE ENGLISH
LANGUAGE

Published by the Press Syndicate of the University of Cambridge
The Pitt Building, Trumpington Street, Cambridge CB2 1RP
40 West 20th Street, New York, NY 10011-4211, USA
10 Stamford Road, Oakleigh, Melbourne 3166, Australia

First published in 1995
Reprinted in 1996
First paperback printing 1997

Printed in the United Kingdom at the University Press, Cambridge
Colour origination by Saxon Photolitho Ltd, Norwich

A catalogue record for this book is available from the British Library

Library of Congress Cataloguing-in-Publication Data

Crystal, David.   1941–
The Cambridge encyclopedia of the English language / David Crystal.
p.   cm.
Includes bibliographical references (p.   ) and indexes.
ISBN 0 521 40179 8 (hc)
1. English language—Handbooks, manuals, etc.   I. Title
PE1072.C68   1995
420—dc20   94–23918   CIP

ISBN 0 521 40179 8 hardback
ISBN 0 521 59655 6 paperback

Library of Congress Cataloguing-in-Publication Data for paperback version applied for

Design: Roger Walker
Maps and diagrams: European Map Graphics Limited
Picture research: Paula Granados and Anne Priestley
Jacket: Unit 18 Photography and Ian Garstka Graphic Design
Typeset in Adobe Garamond and Frutiger

THE CAMBRIDGE
ENCYCLOPEDIA OF
THE ENGLISH
LANGUAGE

DAVID CRYSTAL

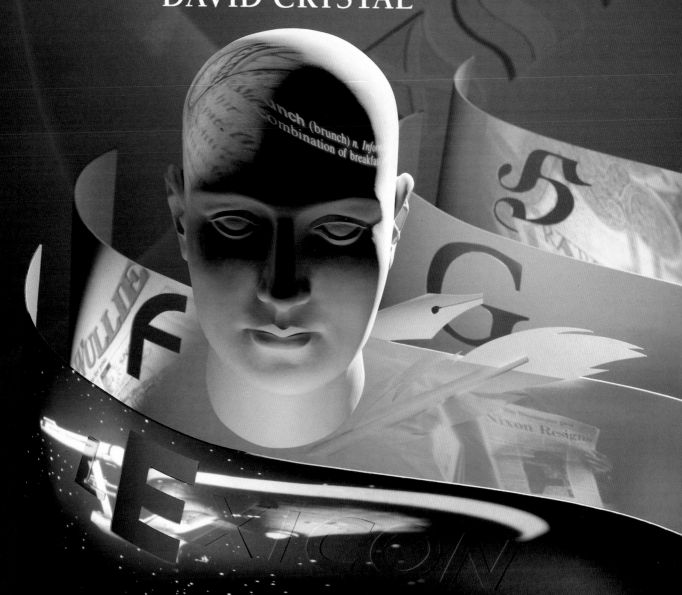

CONTENTS

PREFACE

A book about the English language – or about any individual language – is a daring enterprise, for it has as many perceptive critics as there are fluent readers. The language as a whole belongs to no one, yet everyone owns a part of it, has an interest in it, and has an opinion about it. Moreover, whenever people begin to talk about their own language, they all have something to offer – favourite words or sayings, dialect anecdotes and observations, usage likes and dislikes. Individual linguistic memories, experiences, and abilities enable everyone to make a personal contribution to language chat. In a sense, we are all truly equal when we participate – even though this democratic vision is disturbed by the widely-shared perception that some (notably, those who have learned the terminology of language study) are more equal than others.

The stories of English

That is why the metaphor of 'the story' (as in 'the story of English') is somewhat misleading. There is no one 'story' of English. There are innumerable individual stories. And even if we look for broad narrative themes, there are several dimensions competing for our attention. For example, there is the structural story – the way the sounds, grammar, and vocabulary of the language have evolved. There is the social story – the way the language has come to serve a multiplicity of functions in society. There is the literary story – the way writers have evoked the power, range, and beauty of the language to express new orders of meaning. And there is the chronological story – apparently the most straightforward, though even here it is not possible to give a simple account, in terms of a beginning, middle, and end. There is no single beginning to the story of English, but several, with waves of Anglo-Saxon invaders arriving in various locations, and laying the foundations of later dialect difference. There is no single middle, but several, with the language diverging early on in England and Scotland, then much later taking different paths in Britain, North America, and elsewhere. And, as we observe the increasingly diverse directions in which English is currently moving around the world, there is certainly no single end.

A traveller's guide

The biggest problem in compiling this book, accordingly, was what order to impose upon the mass of material which presents itself for inclusion. I have started with history, moved on to structure, and concluded with use. But it might have been otherwise, and I have written the six parts so that it is possible for readers to begin with any one of them and move in any direction. The same principle was applied to the structure of each part. While there is a certain logic of exposition in some topics (such as Part I, the history of English), there is none in others (such as Part V, the account of major regional or social varieties). In all cases, therefore, chapters, and sections within chapters, have been planned as self-contained entities, with relevant conceptual underpinning provided by the frequent use of cross-references.

The basic unit of organization in the book is the double-page spread. Sentences never cross turn-over pages, and the vast majority of topics are treated within the constraints of a single spread. I have tried to ensure that it will be possible for readers to dip into this book at any point, and find a coherent treatment of a topic in a single opening. There is too much in any language for the information to be assimilated in a continuous reading, and this is especially so in the case of English, with its lengthy history and vast range of use; and while some may wish to read this book 'from left to right', I suspect most will prefer to make more leisurely excursions over a period of time – more a casual stroll than a guided tour. The double-page spread approach is designed for that kind of traveller. Indeed, the metaphor of travelling is far more suitable for this book than the metaphor of story-telling.

Treatment and coverage

I have kept several criteria in mind while writing *CEEL* (pronounced 'seal', as we have come to call it). I have tried to find a balance between talking about the language and letting the language speak for itself. Most spreads distinguish between an expository overview and detailed examples (largely through the typographic convention of main text vs panels). Then within each spread, I have tried to provide examples of the wonder which can be found when we begin to look carefully at the language. All languages are fascinating, beautiful, full of surprises, moving, awesome, fun. I hope I have succeeded in provoking at least one of these responses on every page. I would be disappointed if, after any opening, a reader did not feel to some extent entertained, as well as informed.

Obviously it has all been a personal selection. The hardest part, in fact, was the choosing. Once I had decided on a topic for a spread, I would collect material relating to it from as many sources as I could find. I would write the opening perspective, and then look at all the material to find textual and pictorial illustrations. Invariably I had enough material to fill several spreads, and choosing what to put in and what to leave out was always painful. The moral is plain. There are several other possible encyclopedic worlds.

Wider horizons

In particular, there has not been space to go into the many applications of English language studies in proper detail. I touch upon some of these areas in Part VI, but the aim of that part is not to be comprehensive, but simply to illustrate the various directions that applied language studies can take. There are many other horizons which can only be approached by using systematic information about the language, but this book does not try to reach them. However, in view of its special place in the history of language study, I do try to reach out in the direction of literature as often as possible, and it is perhaps worth drawing attention to the way that literary examples are dispersed throughout the book. I have always been strongly

opposed to the great divide which traditionally separates 'lang' and 'lit'. It seemed to me that it would only reinforce that divide if I were to include a separate chapter called something like 'literary language', so I have not done so – a position which is discussed towards the end of Chapter 22. Many pages, accordingly, display a literary presence – sometimes by way of stylistic comment, often through extensive quotation.

Acknowledgements

If an enterprise of this kind has succeeded, it is because its author has managed to balance on the shoulders of many others, without too often falling off. I owe a particular debt of gratitude to Professor Whitney Bolton, of Rutgers University, who read the whole text of the book and offered innumerable valuable comments and suggestions. I must thank Dr Andy Orchard and Professor David Burnley for their advice on several points in the Old and Middle English chapters. And a number of other scholars or organizations have helped me find the best illustration of a particular topic: these points of contact are acknowledged formally at the end of the book, but I would want to record personal thanks to Henry G. Burger, Lou Burnard, Kenneth Cameron, Jack Chambers, Vinod Dubey, Leslie Dunkling, Charles Jones, Kevin Kiernan, Edwin D. Lawson, Geoffrey Leech, Valerie Luckins, Angus McIntosh, Chrissie Maher, Chris Upward, Maggie Vance, and Lyn Wendon. Anne Rowlands helped me compile the indexes. It is perhaps unusual to thank a journal, but I have to acknowledge an enormous debt to *English Today*, and thus to its editor, Tom McArthur, for bringing together such a valuable collection of English-language material. For anyone who wishes to maintain a healthy English language lifestyle, I prescribe the reading of *ET* three times a day after meals.

The book has been a real collaboration with in-house staff at Cambridge University Press, and involved many planning meetings both in Cambridge and Holyhead, over a period of some three years. It is therefore a real pleasure to acknowledge the roles of Geoff Staff and Clare Orchard, who managed and coordinated the project at Cambridge, Paula Granados and Anne Priestley, who carried out the picture research, and Carol-June Cassidy, who read the text from the point of view of American English. I have much enjoyed collaborating once again with Roger Walker, whose design experience will be evident on every page. I am especially grateful to Adrian du Plessis, director of Cambridge Reference, for his personal interest and encouragement from the earliest days of this project. And, in a different sense of in-house, I thank my wife, Hilary, whose editorial comments have greatly improved the clarity of the text, and whose role in relation to the book's planning and production has been so great that it defies any attempt at conventional expression.

David Crystal
Holyhead, October 1994

Preface to the paperback edition

I have been delighted by the enthusiastic reception given to the appearance of *CEEL*, which has permitted the early production of a paperback edition. For this edition I have taken the opportunity of correcting a number of typographical errors which slipped through in the first printing, and have made a number of small textual modifications in response to points made by readers and reviewers. The only major authorial change affects Chapter 7, where I have brought the table of world English statistics up to date, using 1995 population estimates; this has also involved a rewriting of the associated commentary.

Several other changes have affected later sections of that chapter, largely as a consequence of the rapidly growing position of English throughout the world. Indeed, since the text of *CEEL* was completed, in 1994, this topic has attracted greatly increased media attention, with the millennium providing the excuse for fresh discussion of 'the future of English'. A related publication, *English as a Global Language* (Cambridge University Press, 1997), has enabled me to deal with this issue in proper depth, supplementing the historical story outlined in the first part of Chapter 7 with a fuller account of contemporary developments (such as the role of English on the Internet) than it has been possible to present in the present book.

This preface gives me an opportunity to thank the many readers of the first edition who have sent in facts, comments, and anecdotes about the way English is used in various parts of the world. These are far too numerous and extensive to be easily included in a book like *CEEL*, but they have all been carefully filed, and it is my hope that before too long there will be an opportunity to use this information as part of an archive about the English language, whose absence (referred to at the end of the book) I continue to lament.

David Crystal
Holyhead, February 1997

1 · MODELLING ENGLISH

An essential early step in the study of a language is to model it. A 'model', in this context, is not a three-dimensional miniature replica: this book does not devote its space to techniques of moulding the English language in Play-Doh®, Meccano®, or Lego®. To model the English language is, rather, to provide an abstract representation of its central characteristics, so that it becomes easier to see how it is structured and used.

Two models provide this first perspective. The first, shown below, breaks the structure of English down into a series of components; and these will be used to organize the exposition throughout Parts II to IV. On the facing page, there is a model of the uses of English; and this will be used as a perspective for Parts I and V. The omnicurious eye of the English linguist surveys the whole scene, in ways which are examined in Part VI.

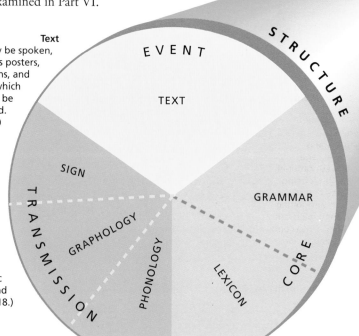

Text
A coherent, self-contained unit of discourse. Texts, which may be spoken, written, or signed, vary greatly in size, from such tiny units as posters, captions, and bus tickets, to such large units as novels, sermons, and conversations. They provide the frame of reference within which grammatical, lexical, and other features of English can be identified and interpreted. (See Part V, §19.)

Sign
A visual language used chiefly by people who are deaf. This book refers only to those signing systems which have been devised to represent aspects of English structure, such as its spelling, grammar, or vocabulary. (See §23.)

Graphology
The writing system of a language. Graphological (or orthographic) study has two main aspects: the visual segments of the written language, which take the form of vowels, consonants, punctuation marks, and certain typographical features; and the various patterns of graphic design, such as spacing and layout, which add structure and meaning to stretches of written text. (See Part IV, §18.)

Phonology
The pronunciation system of a language. Phonological study has two main aspects: the sound segments of the spoken language, which take the form of vowels and consonants; and the various patterns of intonation, rhythm, and tone of voice, which add structure and meaning to stretches of speech. (See Part IV, §17.)

Lexicon
The vocabulary of a language. Lexical study is a wide-ranging domain, involving such diverse areas as the sense relationships between words, the use of abbreviations, puns, and euphemisms, and the compilation of dictionaries. (See Part II.)

Grammar
The system of rules governing the construction of sentences. Grammatical study is usually divided into two main aspects: *syntax*, dealing with the structure and connection of sentences; and *morphology*, dealing with the structure and formation of words. (See Part III.)

BUT IS IT ART?

Just occasionally, someone tries to visualize language in a way which goes beyond the purely diagrammatic. This print was made by art students as part of their degree. They were asked to attend lectures from different university courses, and then present an abstract design which reflected their perception of the topic. As may perhaps be immediately obvious, this design is the result of their attending a lecture on the structure of the English language, given by the present author. The design's asymmetries well represent the irregularities and erratic research paths which are so much a part of English language study. (Equally, of course, they could represent the structural disorganization of the lecturer.)

Social variation

Society affects a language, in the sense that any important aspect of social structure and function is likely to have a distinctive linguistic counterpart. People belong to different social classes, perform different social roles, and carry on different occupations. Their use of language is affected by their sex, age, ethnic group, and educational background. English is being increasingly affected by all these factors, because its developing role as a world language is bringing it more and more into contact with new cultures and social systems. (See Part V, §21.)

Personal variation

People affect a language, in the sense that an individual's conscious or unconscious choices and preferences can result in a distinctive or even unique style. Such variations in self-expression are most noticeable in those areas of language use where great care is being taken, such as in literature and humour. But the uniqueness of individuals, arising out of differences in their memory, personality, intelligence, social background, and personal experience, makes distinctiveness of style inevitable in everyone. (See Part V, §22.)

USE

TEMPORAL VARIATION
LONG TERM — SHORT TERM

SOCIAL VARIATION

REGIONAL VARIATION

PERSONAL VARIATION

Temporal variation

Time affects a language, both in the long term and short term, giving rise to several highly distinctive processes and varieties.

Long term: English has changed throughout the centuries, as can be seen from such clearly distinguishable linguistic periods as Old English, Middle English, and Elizabethan English. Language change is an inevitable and continuing process, whose study is chiefly carried on by philologists and historical linguists. (See Part I.)

Short term: English changes within the history of a single person. This is most noticeable while children are acquiring their mother tongue, but it is also seen when people learn a foreign language, develop their style as adult speakers or writers, and, sometimes, find that their linguistic abilities are lost or seriously impaired through injury or disease. Psycholinguists study language learning and loss, as do several other professionals, notably speech therapists and language teachers. (See Part VI, §23.)

Regional variation

Geography affects language, both within a country and between countries, giving rise to regional accents and dialects, and to the pidgins and creoles which emerged around the world whenever English first came into contact with other languages. *Intranational* regional varieties have been observed within English from its earliest days, as seen in such labels as 'Northern', 'London', and 'Scottish'. *International* varieties are more recent in origin, as seen in such labels as 'American', 'Australian', and 'Indian'. Regional language variation is studied by sociolinguists, geographical linguists, dialectologists, and others, the actual designation depending on the focus and emphasis of the study. (See §7 and Part V, §20.)

WHY STUDY THE ENGLISH LANGUAGE?

Because it's fascinating

It is remarkable how often the language turns up as a topic of interest in daily conversation – whether it is a question about accents and dialects, a comment about usage and standards, or simply curiosity about a word's origins and history.

Because it's important

The dominant role of English as a world language forces it upon our attention in a way that no language has ever done before. As English becomes the chief means of communication between nations, it is crucial to ensure that it is taught accurately and efficiently, and to study changes in its structure and use.

Because it's fun

One of the most popular leisure pursuits is to play with the English language – with its words, sounds, spellings, and structures. Crosswords, Scrabble®, media word shows, and many other quizzes and guessing games keep millions happily occupied every day, teasing their linguistic brain centres and sending them running to their dictionaries.

Because it's beautiful

Each language has its unique beauty and power, as seen to best effect in the works of its great orators and writers. We can see the 1,000-year-old history of English writing only through the glass of language, and anything we learn about English as a language can serve to increase our appreciation of its oratory and literature.

Because it's useful

Getting the language right is a major issue in almost every corner of society. No one wants to be accused of ambiguity and obscurity, or find themselves talking or writing at cross-purposes. The more we know about the language the more chance we shall have of success, whether we are advertisers, politicians, priests, journalists, doctors, lawyers – or just ordinary people at home, trying to understand and be understood.

Because it's there

English, more than any other language, has attracted the interest of professional linguists. It has been analysed in dozens of different ways, as part of the linguist's aim of devising a theory about the nature of language in general. The study of the English language, in this way, becomes a branch of linguistics – English linguistics.

PART I
The history of English

The history of English is a fascinating field of study in its own right, but it also provides a valuable perspective for the contemporary study of the language, and thus makes an appropriate opening section for this book. The historical account promotes a sense of identity and continuity, and enables us to find coherence in many of the fluctuations and conflicts of present-day English language use. Above all, it satisfies the deep-rooted sense of curiosity we have about our linguistic heritage. People like to be aware of their linguistic roots.

We begin as close to the beginning as we can get, using the summary accounts of early chronicles to determine the language's continental origins (§2). The Anglo-Saxon corpus of poetry and prose, dating from around the 7th century, provides the first opportunity to examine the linguistic evidence. §3 outlines the characteristics of Old English texts, and gives a brief account of the sounds, spellings, grammar, and vocabulary which they display. A similar account is given of the Middle English period (§4), beginning with the effects on the language of the French invasion and concluding with a discussion of the origins of Standard English. At all points, special attention is paid to the historical and cultural setting to which texts relate, and to the character of the leading literary works, such as *Beowulf* and *The Canterbury Tales*.

The Early Modern English period (§5) begins with the English of Caxton and the Renaissance, continues with that of Shakespeare and the King James Bible, and ends with the landmark publication of Johnson's *Dictionary*. A recurring theme is the extent and variety of language change during this period. The next section, on Modern English (§6), follows the course of further language change, examines the nature of early grammars, traces the development of new varieties and attitudes in America, and finds in literature, especially in the novel, an invaluable linguistic mirror. Several present-day usage controversies turn out to have their origins during this period. By the end of §6, we are within living memory.

The final section (§7) looks at what has happened to the English language in the present century, and in particular at its increasing presence worldwide. The approach is again historical, tracing the way English has travelled to the United States, Canada, Africa, Australia, South and South-East Asia, and several other parts of the globe. The section reviews the concept of World English, examines the statistics of usage, and discusses the problems of intelligibility and identity which arise when a language achieves such widespread use. The notion of Standard English, seen from both national and international perspectives, turns out to be of special importance. Part I then concludes with some thoughts about the future of the language, and about the relationships which have grown up (sometimes amicable, sometimes antagonistic) between English and other languages.

◄ A map of Anglo-Saxon England taken from Edmund Gibson's 1692 edition of the Anglo-Saxon Chronicle. The Latin caption (top left) explains that the map shows the places mentioned in the Chronicle and in Old English literature.

2 · THE ORIGINS OF ENGLISH

'To Aëtius, thrice consul, the groans of the Britons.' Thus, according to the Anglo-Saxon historian, the Venerable Bede, began the letter written to the Roman consul by some of the Celtic people who had survived the ferocious invasions of the Scots and Picts in the early decades of the 5th century. 'The barbarians drive us to the sea. The sea drives us back towards the barbarians. Between them we are exposed to two sorts of death: we are either slain or drowned.'

The plea fell on deaf ears. Although the Romans had sent assistance in the past, they were now fully occupied by their own wars with Bledla and Attila, kings of the Huns. The attacks from the north continued, and the British were forced to look elsewhere for help. Bede gives a succinct and sober account of what then took place.

They consulted what was to be done, and where they should seek assistance to prevent or repel the cruel and frequent incursions of the northern nations; and they all agreed with their King Vortigern to call over to their aid, from parts beyond the sea, the Saxon nation…

In the year of our Lord 449… the nation of the Angles, or Saxons, being invited by the aforesaid king, arrived in Britain with three long ships, and had a place assigned them to reside in by the same king, in the eastern part of the island, that they might thus appear to be fighting for their country, whilst their real intentions were to enslave it. Accordingly they engaged with the enemy, who were come from the north to give battle, and obtained the victory; which, being known at home in their own country, as also the fertility of the country, and the cowardice of the Britons, a more considerable fleet was quickly sent over, bringing a still greater number of men, which, being added to the former, made up an invincible army…

Bede describes the invaders as belonging to the three most powerful nations of Germany – the Saxons, the Angles, and the Jutes. The first group to arrive came from Jutland, in the northern part of modern Denmark, and were led, according to the chroniclers, by

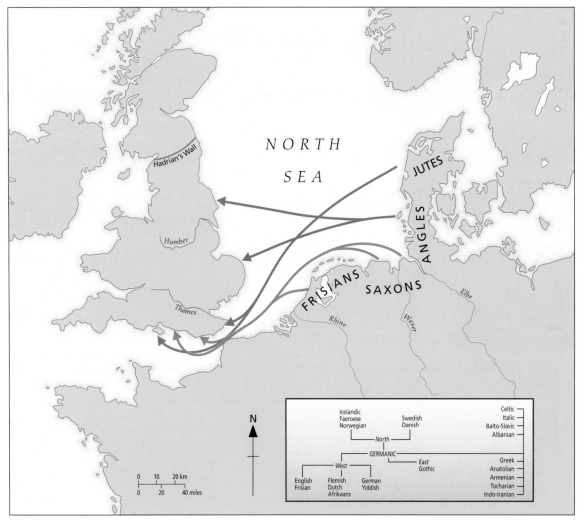

The homelands of the Germanic invaders, according to Bede, and the direction of their invasions. Little is known about the exact locations of the tribes. The Jutes may have had settlements further south, and links with the Frisians to the west. The Angles may have lived further into Germany. The linguistic differences between these groups, likewise, are matters for speculation. The various dialects of Old English (p. 28) plainly relate to the areas in which the invaders settled, but there are too few texts to make serious comparison possible.

English is a member of the western branch of the Germanic family of languages. It is closest in structure to Frisian – though hardly anything is known about the ancient Frisians and their role in the invasions of Britain. Germanic is a branch of the Indo-European language family.

two Jutish brothers, Hengist and Horsa. They landed at Ebbsfleet in the Isle of Thanet, and settled in the areas now known as Kent, the Isle of Wight, and parts of Hampshire. The Angles came from the south of the Danish peninsula, and entered Britain much later, along the eastern coast, settling in parts of Mercia, Northumbria (the land to the north of the Humber, where in 547 they established a kingdom), and what is now East Anglia. The Saxons came from an area further south and west, along the coast of the North Sea, and from 477 settled in various parts of southern and south-eastern Britain. The chroniclers talk about groups of East, West, and South Saxons – distinctions which are reflected in the later names of Essex, Wessex, and Sussex. The name Middlesex suggests that there were Middle Saxons too. Bede's account takes up the story:

In a short time, swarms of the aforesaid nations came over the island, and they began to increase so much that they became terrible to the natives themselves who had invited them. Then, having on a sudden entered into league with the Picts, whom they had by this time expelled by the force of their arms, they began to turn their weapons against their confederates.

The Anglo-Saxon Chronicle (see p.15), compiled over a century later than Bede under Alfred the Great, gives a grim catalogue of disasters for the Britons.

457· In this year Hengest and Æsc fought against the Britons at a place which is called Crecganford [Crayford, Kent] and

A page from one of the manuscripts of Bede's *Ecclesiastical History*. The language is Latin.

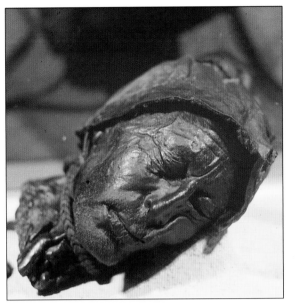

The remarkably preserved body of a man, found in a peat bog in Denmark. Over 500 such remains have been found throughout northern Europe, many in the area formerly occupied by the Germanic tribes. The person has been murdered, possibly as a sacrificial victim to the Earth goddess. The Roman historian Tacitus wrote of the tribes in his *Germania*, and at one point mentions a group of tribes including the Eudoses and the Anglii: 'These tribes are protected by forests and rivers, nor is there anything noteworthy about them individually, except that they worship in common Nerthus, or Mother Earth, and conceive her as intervening in human affairs, and riding in procession through the cities of men.' (Trans. M. Hutton, 1914.)

there slew four thousand men; and the Britons then forsook Kent and fled to London in great terror.

465· In this year Hengest and Æsc fought against the Welsh near Wippedesfleot and there slew twelve Welsh nobles; and one of the thanes, whose name was Wipped, was slain there.

473· In this year Hengest and Aesc fought against the Welsh and captured innumerable spoils, and the Welsh fled from the English as one flies from fire.

The fighting went on for several decades, but the imposition of Anglo-Saxon power was never in doubt. Over a period of about a hundred years, further bands of immigrants continued to arrive, and Anglo-Saxon settlements spread to all areas apart from the highlands of the west and north. By the end of the 5th century, the foundation was established for the emergence of the English language.

THE NAME OF THE LANGUAGE

With scant respect for priorities, the Germanic invaders called the native Celts *wealas* ('foreigners'), from which the name Welsh is derived. The Celts called the invaders 'Saxons', regardless of their tribe, and this practice was followed by the early Latin writers. By the end of the 6th century, however, the term *Angli* ('Angles') was in use – as early as 601, a king of Kent, Æthelbert, is called *rex Anglorum* ('King of the Angles') – and during the 7th century *Angli* or *Anglia* (for the country) became the usual Latin names. Old English *Engle* derives from this usage, and the name of the language found in Old English texts is from the outset referred to as *Englisc* (the *sc* spelling representing the sound *sh*, /ʃ/). References to the name of the country as *Englaland* ('land of the Angles'), from which came *England*, do not appear until *c.* 1000.

The Northumbrian monk, Bede, or Bæda, known as the Venerable Bede. Born at Monkton on Tyne in *c.* 673, he was taken at the age of 7 to the new monastery at Wearmouth, moving in 682 to the sister monastery at Jarrow, where he worked as a writer and teacher. He died in 735, and was buried at Jarrow. His masterpiece, the *Historia Ecclesiastica Gentis Anglorum* ('Ecclesiastical History of the English Nation'), was begun in his later years, and finished in 731. Its focus is the growth of Christianity in England, but its scope is much wider, and it is recognized as the most valuable source we have for early English history. Written in Latin, an Old English translation was made in the reign of Alfred the Great.

3 · OLD ENGLISH

THE EARLY PERIOD

Before the Anglo-Saxon invasions (§2), the language (or languages) spoken by the native inhabitants of the British Isles belonged to the Celtic family, introduced by a people who had come to the islands around the middle of the first millennium BC. Many of these settlers were, in turn, eventually subjugated by the Romans, who arrived in 43 BC. But by 410 the Roman armies had gone, withdrawn to help defend their Empire in Europe. After a millennium of settlement by speakers of Celtic, and half a millennium by speakers of Latin, what effect did this have on the language spoken by the arriving Anglo-Saxons?

Celtic borrowings

There is, surprisingly, very little Celtic influence – or perhaps it is not so surprising, given the savage way in which the Celtic communities were destroyed or pushed back into the areas we now know as Cornwall, Wales, Cumbria, and the Scottish borders. Some Celts (or Romano-Celts) doubtless remained in the east and south, perhaps as slaves, perhaps intermarrying, but their identity would after a few generations have been lost within Anglo-Saxon society. Whatever we might expect from such a period of cultural contact, the Celtic language of Roman Britain influenced Old English hardly at all.

Only a handful of Celtic words were borrowed at the time, and a few have survived into modern English, sometimes in regional dialect use: *crag, cumb* 'deep valley', *binn* 'bin', *carr* 'rock', *dunn* 'grey, dun', *brock* 'badger', and *torr* 'peak'. Others include *bannoc* 'piece', *rice* 'rule', *gafeluc* 'small spear', *bratt* 'cloak', *luh* 'lake', *dry* 'sorcerer', and *clucge* 'bell'. A few Celtic words of this period ultimately come from Latin, brought in by the Irish missionaries: these include *assen* 'ass', *ancor* 'hermit', *stær* 'history', and possibly *cross*. But there cannot be more than two dozen loan words in all. And there are even very few Celtic-based place names (p. 141) in what is now southern and eastern England. They include such river names as *Thames, Avon* 'river', *Don, Exe, Usk*, and *Wye*. Town names include *Dover* 'water', *Eccles* 'church', *Bray* 'hill', *London* (a tribal name), *Kent* (meaning unknown), and the use of *caer* 'fortified place' (as in *Carlisle*) and *pen* 'head, top, hill' (as in *Pendle*).

Latin loans

Latin has been a major influence on English throughout its history (pp. 24, 48, 60, §9), and there is evidence of its role from the earliest moments of contact. The Roman army and merchants gave new names to many local objects and experiences, and introduced several fresh concepts. About half of the new words were to do with plants, animals, food and drink, and household items: Old English *pise* 'pea', *plante* 'plant', *win* 'wine', *cyse* 'cheese', *catte* 'cat', *cetel* 'kettle', *disc* 'dish', *candel* 'candle'. Other important clusters of words related to clothing (*belt* 'belt', *cemes* 'shirt', *sutere* 'shoemaker'), buildings and settlements (*tigle* 'tile', *weall* 'wall', *ceaster* 'city', *stræt* 'road'), military and legal institutions (*wic* 'camp', *diht* 'saying', *scrifan* 'decree'), commerce (*mangian* 'trade', *ceapian* 'buy', *pund* 'pound'), and religion (*mæsse* 'Mass', *munuc* 'monk', *mynster* 'minster').

Whether the Latin words were already used by the Anglo-Saxon tribes on the continent of Europe, or were introduced from within Britain, is not always clear (though a detailed analysis of the sound changes they display can help, p. 19), but the total number of Latin words present in English at the very beginning of the Anglo-Saxon period is not large – less than 200. Although Vulgar Latin (the variety of spoken Latin used throughout the Empire) must have continued in use – at least, as an official language – for some years after the Roman army left, for some reason it did not take root in Britain as it had so readily done in Continental Europe. Some commentators see in this the first sign of an Anglo-Saxon monolingual mentality.

A reconstruction of Anglo-Saxon huts at West Stow, Suffolk. Each hut is some 15–20 feet (5–6 m) in length.

RUNES

Old English was first written in the runic alphabet. This alphabet was used in northern Europe – in Scandinavia, present-day Germany, and the British Isles – and it has been preserved in about 4,000 inscriptions and a few manuscripts. It dates from around the 3rd century AD. No one knows exactly where the alphabet came from, but it seems to be a development of one of the alphabets of southern Europe, probably the Roman, which runes resemble closely.

The common runic alphabet found throughout the area consisted of 24 letters. It can be written horizontally in either direction. Each letter had a name, and the alphabet as a whole was called by the name of its first six letters, the *futhorc* (in the same way as the word *alphabet* comes from Greek *alpha* + *beta*). The version found in Britain used extra letters to cope with the range of sounds found in Old English; in its most developed form, in 9th-century Northumbria, it

consisted of 31 symbols.

The inscriptions in Old English are found on weapons, jewellery, monuments, and other artefacts, and date largely from the 5th or 6th centuries AD, the earliest (at Caistor-by-Norwich) possibly being late 4th century. They often say simply who made or owned the object. Most of the large rune stones say little more than 'X raised this stone in memory of Y', and often the message is unclear.

The meaning of *rune*

What *rune* (OE *run*) means is debatable. There is a long-standing tradition which attributes to it such senses as 'whisper', 'mystery', and 'secret', suggesting that the symbols were originally used for magical or mystical rituals. Such associations were certainly present in the way the pagan Vikings (and possibly the Continental Germans) used the corresponding

word, but there is no evidence that they were present in Old English. Current research suggests that the word *run* had been thoroughly assimilated into Anglo-Saxon Christianity, and meant simply 'sharing of knowledge or thoughts'. Any extension to the world of magic and superstition is not part of the native tradition. Modern English *rune* is not even a survival of the Old English word, but a later borrowing from Norse via Latin.

For the modern, magical sense of *rune* we are therefore indebted to the Scandinavian and not the Anglo-Saxon tradition. It is this sense which surfaced in the 19th century in a variety of esoteric publications, and which lives on in the popular and fantastic imagination of the 20th, perhaps most famously in the writing of Tolkien (p. 185). (After C. E. Fell, 1991.)

THE OLD ENGLISH RUNIC ALPHABET

This list gives the names of the symbols in Old English, and their meanings (where these are known). It does not give the many variant shapes which can be found in the different inscriptions. The symbols consist mainly of intersecting straight lines, showing their purpose for engraving on stone, wood, metal, or bone. Manuscript uses of runes do exist in a few early poems (notably in four passages where the name of Cynewulf is represented), and in the solutions to some of the riddles in the *Exeter Book* (p. 12), and are in evidence until the 11th century, especially in the north, but there are very few of them.

Rune	Anglo-Saxon	Name	Meaning (where known)
	f	feoh	cattle, wealth
	u	ür	bison (aurochs)
	þ	þorn	thorn
	o	ōs	god/mouth
	r	rād	journey/riding
	c	cen	torch
	g[j]	giefu	gift
	w	wyn	joy
	h	hægl	hail
	n	nied	necessity/trouble
	i	is	ice
	j	gear	year
	ʒ	ēoh	yew
	p	peor	?
	x	eolh	?sedge
	s	sigel	sun
	t	tiw/tir	Tiw (a god)
	b	beorc	birch
	e	eoh	horse
	m	man	man
	l	lagu	water/sea
	ng	ing	Ing (a hero)
	oe	eþel	land/estate
	d	dæg	day
	a	ac	oak
	æ	æsc	ash
	y	yr	bow
	ea	ear	?earth
	g [ɣ]	gar	spear
	k	calc	?sandal/chalice/chalk
	k̄		(name unknown)

EARLY INSCRIPTIONS

There are less than 30 clear runic inscriptions in Old English, some containing only a single name. The two most famous examples both date from the 8th century, and represent the Northumbrian dialect (p. 28). Both inscriptions make some use of the Roman alphabet as well.

• The Ruthwell Cross, near Dumfries, Scotland, is 16 feet (5 m) high. Its faces contain panels depicting events in the life of Christ and the early Church, as well as carvings of birds and beasts, and lines of runes around the edges are similar to part of the Old English poem 'The Dream of the Rood' (*rood* = 'cross') in the *Vercelli Book*. A glossed extract is shown below (there are no spaces between the words in the original inscription; also some scholars transcribe 'blood' as *blodi*).

ᛁᚳ ᚦᚫᚢ ᛗᛁᚦ   ᛒᛚᚪᚠᚪ ᛒᛁᚾᛏᛗᛗᛁᚻ
ic wæs miþ   blodæ bistemid
I was with blood bedewed

• The Franks Casket is a richly carved whalebone box, illustrating mythological and religious scenes, not all of which can be interpreted. The picture shows the panel with the Adoration of the Magi alongside the Germanic legend of Wayland (Weland) the Smith. The inscriptions are partly in Old English, and partly in Latin.

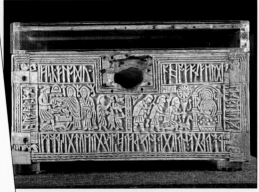

The box first came to light in the 19th century, owned by a farmer from Auzon, France. It is named after Sir Augustus Wollaston Franks, through whom it came to be deposited in the British Museum. One side was missing, but it later came into the possession of the Bargello Museum, Florence, and a cast was made of it, so that the box in the British Museum now appears complete.

THE AUGUSTINIAN MISSION

It would be a considerable overstatement to suggest (as one sometimes reads) that St Augustine brought Christianity to Britain. This religion had already arrived through the Roman invasion, and in the 4th century had actually been given official status in the Roman Empire. It was a Briton, St Patrick, who converted Ireland in the early 5th century; and a goodly number of early Welsh saints' names are remembered in place names beginning with *Llan* ('church [of]'). The story of St Alban (said to have been martyred in 305 near the city of Verulam, modern St Albans) is recounted in detail by Bede.

Augustine's task was more specific: to convert the Anglo-Saxons. He had been prior of the monastery of St Andrew in Rome, before being chosen by Pope Gregory for the mission. He and his companions arrived in the Isle of Thanet, to be met by Æthelberht, king of Kent, and they must have been heartily relieved to find that his wife was already a (Celtic) Christian. They were given leave to live and preach in Canterbury, and within a year the king himself was converted. Three bishoprics were established by the end of the decade, with Augustine as archbishop at Canterbury, Justus as bishop at Rochester, and Mellitus at London, as bishop of the East Saxons.

It took some time for this early success to become consolidated. Following Augustine's death (604/5) there was much tension over religious practices between the Roman Christians and their Celtic counterparts, who had lived in isolation from Rome for so long. Matters came to a head in the conflict over the date of Easter, resolved (in favour of Rome) at the Synod of Whitby in 664.

Part of the difficulty in developing the faith must have been linguistic: according to Bede, it was nearly 50 years before Anglo-Saxon was being used as a missionary tongue. King Egbert of Kent in 664 had to make a special plea to ensure that an Anglo-Saxon speaking bishop was appointed, 'so that with a prelate of his own nation and language, the king and his subjects might be more perfectly instructed in the words and mysteries of the faith'. This was the first expression of an issue which would be raised again several hundred years later in English language history (p. 61).

THE OLD ENGLISH CORPUS

There is a 'dark age' between the arrival of the Anglo-Saxons and the first Old English manuscripts. A few scattered inscriptions in the language date from the 5th and 6th centuries, written in the runic alphabet which the invaders brought with them (p. 9), but these give very little information about what the language was like. The literary age began only after the arrival of the Roman missionaries, led by Augustine, who came to Kent in AD 597. The rapid growth of monastic centres led to large numbers of Latin manuscripts being produced, especially of the Bible and other religious texts.

Because of this increasingly literary climate, Old English manuscripts also began to be written – much earlier, indeed, than the earliest vernacular texts from other north European countries. The first texts, dating from around 700, are glossaries of Latin words translated into Old English, and a few early inscriptions and poems. But very little material remains from this period. Doubtless many manuscripts were burned during the 8th-century Viking invasions (p. 25). The chief literary work of the period, the heroic poem *Beowulf*, survives in a single copy, made around 1,000 – possibly some 250 years after it was composed (though the question of its composition date is highly controversial). There are a number of short poems, again almost entirely preserved in late manuscripts, over half of them concerned with Christian subjects – legends of the saints, extracts from the Bible, and devotional pieces. Several others reflect the Germanic tradition, dealing with such topics as war, travelling, patriotism, and celebration. Most extant Old English texts were written in the period following the reign of King Alfred (849–99), who arranged for many Latin works to be translated – including Bede's *Ecclesiastical History* (p. 7). But the total corpus is extremely small. The number of words in the corpus of Old English compiled at the University of Toronto, which contains all the texts (but not all the alternative manuscripts of a text), is only 3.5 million – the equivalent of about 30 medium-sized modern novels. Only *c.* 5 per cent of this total (*c.* 30,000 lines) is poetry.

THE GREGORIAN PUN

In Bede there is an account of St Gregory's first meeting with the inhabitants of England. Gregory, evidently a punster of some ability, himself asked to be sent to Britain as a missionary, but the pope of the time refused – presumably because of Gregory's social position, the son of a senator and former prefect of the city. When Gregory became pope himself (590), he sent Augustine to do the job for him. Bede tells the story at the end of his account of Gregory's life (Book 2, Ch. 1).

Nor is the account of St Gregory, which has been handed down to us by the tradition of our ancestors, to be passed by in silence, in relation to his motives for taking such interest in the salvation of our nation [Britain]. It is reported that, some merchants, having just arrived at Rome on a certain day, exposed many things for sale in the market-place, and an abundance of people resorted thither to buy: Gregory himself went with the rest, and, among other things, some boys were set to sale, their bodies white, their countenances beautiful, and their hair very fine. Having viewed them, he asked, as is said, from what country or nation they were brought? and was told, from the island of Britain, whose inhabitants were of such personal appearance. He again inquired whether those islanders were Christians, or still involved in the errors of paganism? and was informed that they were pagans. Then, fetching a deep sigh from the bottom of his heart, 'Alas! what pity,' said he, 'that the author of darkness is possessed of men of such fair countenances; and that being remarkable for such graceful aspects, their minds should be void of inward grace.' He therefore again asked, what was the name of that nation? and was answered, that they were called Angles. 'Right,' said he, 'for they have an Angelic face, and it becomes such to be co-heirs with the Angels in heaven. What is the name,' proceeded he, 'of the province from which they are brought?' It was replied, that the natives of that province were called Deiri. 'Truly they are *De ira*,' said he, 'withdrawn from wrath, and called to the mercy of Christ. How is the king of that province called?' They told him his name was Ælla; and he, alluding to the name, said, 'Hallelujah, the praise of God the Creator must be sung in those parts.' (Trans. J. Stevens, 1723.)

SAINT AUGUSTINE

SAINT GREGORY

HWÆT WE GARDE-
What!   We Spear-Danes'

na.   in gear-dagum. þeod-cyninga
in yore-days,   tribe-kings'

þrym ge-frunon huða æþelingas ellen
glory heard,   how the leaders   courage

fremedon. Oft scyld scefing sceaþena
accomplished. Often Scyld, Scef's son, from enemies'

þreatum monegum mægþum meodo-setla
bands,   from many tribes   mead-benches

of-teah egsode eorl syððan ærest wearð
seized, terrorised earl[s], since   first he was

fea-sceaft funden he þæs frofre gebad
destitute found;   he its   relief knew,

weox under wolcnum weorð-myndum þah.
grew under skies,   in honours   throve,

oð þæt him æghwylc þara   ymb-sittendra
until   to him each   of the   neighbours

ofer hron-rade hyran scolde gomban
over whale-road submit must,   tribute

gyldan þæt wæs god cyning. ðæm eafera wæs
yield;   that was good king!   To him heir   was

æfter cenned geong in geardum þone god
after born   young in dwellings,   him God

sende folce to frofre fyren–ðearfe on-
sent   to folk for solace; intense misery

geat þ   hie ær   drugon aldor-[le]ase. lange
saw when they before felt   leaderless   a long

hwile him   þæs lif-frea wuldres wealdend
while; to them for it Life-Lord, glory's   Ruler

worold-are for-geaf. beowulf wæs breme
world honour gave,   Beow   was famed,

blæd   wide   sprang scyldes eafera scede-
renown widely sprang of Scyld's heir Danish

landum in. Swa sceal [geong g]uma gode
lands   in. So   shall young man   by good [deeds]

ge-wyrcean fromum feoh-giftum. on fæder
ensure,   by fine   fee-gifts   in father's …

(After
J. Zupitza,
1882. Trans.
J. Porter, 1991.)

THE *SCOP'S* TALE

This opening page of the *Beowulf* text is taken from the text now lodged in the British Library, London (manuscript reference, Cotton Vitellius A. xv). The manuscript is a copy made in *c.* 1000, but it was damaged by a fire at the Cottonian Library in 1731, hence the odd shape to the page. The name of the poet, or *scop*, whose version is found here is not known, nor is it clear when the work was first composed: one scholarly tradition assigns it to the 8th century; another to a somewhat later date.

This is the first great narrative poem in English. It is a heroic tale about a 6th-century Scandinavian hero, Beowulf, who comes to the aid of the Danish king Hrothgar. Hrothgar's retinue is under daily attack from a monstrous troll, Grendel, at the hall of Heorot ('Hart') in Denmark (located possibly on the site of modern Leire, near Copenhagen). Beowulf travels from Geatland, in southern Sweden, and after a great fight kills the monster, and in a second fight the monster's vengeful mother. Beowulf returns home, recounts his story, and is later made king of the Geats, ruling for 50 years. There, as an old man, he kills a dragon in a fight that leads to his own death.

This plot summary does no justice to the depth of meaning and stylistic impact of the work. Apart from its lauding of courage, heroic defiance, loyalty to one's lord, and other Germanic values, *Beowulf* introduces elements of a thoroughly Christian perspective, and there are many dramatic undercurrents and ironies. The monster is a classical figure in Germanic tradition, but it is also said to be a descendant of Cain, and a product of hell and the devil. The contrast between earthly success and mortality is a recurrent theme. While Beowulf is being feted in Hrothgar's court, the poet alludes to disastrous events which will one day affect the Geats, providing a note of doom that counterpoints the triumphal events of the narrative. The poem is full of dramatic contrasts of this kind.

Whether the poem is a product of oral improvisation or is a more consciously contrived literary work has been a bone of scholarly contention. Many of its striking features, in particular its alliterative rhythmical formulae (p. 23), are those we would associate with oral composition, for they would be a valuable aid to memorization; on the other hand, modern scholars have drawn attention to the patterned complexity of its narrative structure, its metrical control, and its lexical richness, suggesting a literary process of composition (p. 23). The critic W. P. Ker expressed one view, in *The Dark Ages* (1904), that *Beowulf* is a 'book to be read' – but if so it is one which makes maximum use of a style which must originally have evolved for use in oral poetry. (For an account of some modern investigative techniques, see p. 437.)

THE EARLIEST ENGLISH LITERATURE

As with foreign languages, there is never complete agreement about the best way of translating Old English texts; nor is there unanimity about the best way of editing them. The extracts on these and adjacent pages are here to illustrate the range and character of the literature of the period, but they also show the varied editorial practice which exists. Some editors have tried to make their text resemble the original manuscript as closely as possible; others have produced a modernized version.

About the need for editing, there is no doubt. To print a facsimile of Old English texts would be to make them unreadable to all but the specialist. There is plenty of scope for editorial intervention. Scribal habits of capitalization, punctuation, paragraphing, word spacing, and word division were diverse and inconsistent, and order needs to be imposed. There are no poetic line divisions in the manuscript of *Beowulf*, for example (p. 11), and these have to be added.

Nonetheless, editorial practices vary greatly in the way texts are made consistent. Some editors silently correct scribal errors; others draw attention to them in parentheses. Missing letters at the edge of a torn or burned manuscript may be restored, or their omission may be indicated by special symbols. Some editions add an indication of vowel length. Some replace outmoded letters (p. 16) by modern equivalents. Poetic half-lines may or may not be recognized (both practices are shown below). And editors vary in the attention they pay to the existence of alternative readings in different copies of a manuscript.

An important feature, which can add a great deal to the 'alien' appearance of a text, is whether the scribe's orthographic abbreviations are retained, or are expanded. In some texts, for example, þ is used as the abbreviation for *þæt* or for *þþ*, 7 for the various forms of *and*, and the tilde (~) marks an expansion, usually to a following nasal. (For later scribal conventions, see p. 40.)

The Battle of Maldon was fought in August 991. A Viking fleet had sailed up the estuary of the River Blackwater to the island of Northey, near Maldon in Essex. Their passage across the river (now called Southey Creek) was opposed by Byrhtnoth, ealdorman of Essex, and his household. The poem, which lacks a beginning and end in the extant manuscript, tells of how the English reject the Viking demand for tribute, then allow them safe passage across the causeway from Northey, to enable a battle to take place. This turned out to be an unfortunate decision:

THE BATTLE OF MALDON

Byrhtþold maþelode, bord hafenode—
se þæs eald ʒeneat—æsc acþehte;
he ful baldlice beornas lærde:
'Hiʒe sceal þe heardra, heorte þe cenre,
mod sceal þe mare, þe ure mæʒen lytlað.
Her lið ure ealdor eall forheapen,
ʒod on ʒreote. A mæʒ ʒnornian
se ðe nu fram þis piʒpleʒan þendan þenceð.
Ic eom frod feores. Fram ic ne pille,
ac ic me be healfe minum hlaforde,
be spa leofan men licʒan þence.'
Spa hi Æþelʒares bearn ealle bylde
ʒodric to ʒuþe. Oft he ʒar forlet,
pælspere pindan on þa picinʒas;
spa he on þam folce fyrmest eode,
heop 7 hynde, oð þæt he on hilde ʒecranc.

Byrhtwold spoke; he grasped his shield—
he was an old follower—he shook the ash spear;
very boldly he exhorted the warriors:
'Courage shall be the fiercer, heart the bolder,
spirit the greater, as our strength lessens.
Here lies our chief all hewn down,
a noble man in the dust. He has cause ever to mourn
who intends now to turn from this war-play.
I am advanced in years. I will not hence,
but I by the side of my lord,
by so dear a man, intend to lie.'
Likewise, Godric, the son of Æthelgar, exhorted them all
to the battle. Often he let the spear fly,
the deadly spear speed away among the Vikings;
as he went out in the forefront of the army,
he hewed and struck, until he perished in the battle.

some of the English flee the field, Byrhtnoth is killed, and the remaining loyal soldiers die heroically. The extract [left] is from the last few lines of the extant text, when Byrhtwold, an old warrior, expresses the heroism which it is the purpose of the poem to commemorate.

The ford which led to the mainland, now built up into a causeway, is shown in the picture. It is only some 77 yards (70 m) long, which would thus enable the English and Viking leaders to shout their demands to each other – an exchange which is dramatically recorded in the poem.

HOW DO TWELVE BECOME FIVE?

Wer sæt æt wine   mid his wifum twam
ond his twegen suno   ond his twa dohtor,
swase gesweostor,   ond hyra suno twegen,
freolico frumbearn;   fæder wæs þær inne
þara æþelinga   æghwæðres mid,
eam ond nefa.   Ealra wæron fife
eorla ond idesa   insittendra.

A man sat at wine with his two wives
and his two sons and his two daughters,
beloved sisters, and their two sons,
noble first-born; the father was in there
of both of those princes,
the uncle and the nephew. In all there were five
lords and ladies sitting in there.

This is one of the 95 poetic riddles (some of which date from the 8th century) in the *Exeter Book*, a late 10th-century compilation of secular and religious poetry. By 1072 it belonged to Bishop Leofric of Exeter, who bequeathed it to his cathedral. The solution to the riddle comes from the Book of Genesis, where it is said that Lot's two daughters lay with him, and each bore him a son.

THE RUNE POEM

Each stanza of this poem begins with the name of the rune printed alongside (p. 9). The poem would have been passed on orally, the rhythm and alliteration making it easy to remember, in much the same way as children today learn 'Thirty days hath September'.

Feoh byþ frofur fira gehwylcum—
sceal ðeah manna gehwylc miclun hyt dælan
gif he wile for Drihtne domes hleotan.

Ur byþ anmod 7 oferhyrned,
felafrecne deor, feohteþ mid hornum,
mære morstapa: þ is modig wuht!

Þorn byþ ðearle scearp, ðegna gehwylcum
anfeng ys yfyl, ungemetun reþe
manna gehwylcun ðe him mid resteð.

Os byþ ordfruma ælcre spræce,
wisdomes wraþu and witena frofur
and eorla gehwam eadnys and tohiht.

Rad byþ on recyde rinca gehwylcum
sefte, and swiþhwæt ðam ðe sitteþ onufan
meare mægenheardum ofer milpaþas.

Cen byþ cwicera gehwam cuþ on fyre,
blac and beorhtlic, byrneþ oftust
ðær hi æþelingas inne restaþ.

Wealth is a joy to every man—
but every man must share it well
if he wishes to gain glory in the sight of the Lord.

Aurochs is fierce, with gigantic horns,
a very savage animal, it fights with horns,
a well-known moor-stepper: it is a creature of
courage!

Thorn is very sharp, harmful to every man
who seizes it, unsuitably severe
to every man who rests on it.

Mouth is the creator of all speech,
a supporter of wisdom and comfort of wise men,
and a blessing and hope to every man.

Journey is to every warrior in the hall
pleasant, and bitingly tough to him who sits
on a mighty steed over the mile-paths.

Torch is to every living thing known by its fire;
bright and brilliant, it burns most often
where the princes take their rest within.

Old English poetic manuscripts contained no titles. Titles such as *Beowulf* or *The Seafarer* have been added by editors, usually in the 19th century. Most of the poetry is also anonymous, the chief exceptions being the few lines known to be by Cædmon (p. 20) and four poems containing the name of Cynewulf woven in runes into the texts as an acrostic (p. 398), so that readers could pray for him. We know more of the prose authors, who included King Alfred, Archbishop Wulfstan, and Abbot Ælfric, but even here most of the surviving material, as in the Anglo-Saxon Chronicle (p. 14), is anonymous.

THE OPENING LINES OF *THE SEAFARER*

Mæg ic be me sylfum soðgied wrecan,
siþas secgan, hu ic geswincdagum
earfoðhwile oft þrowade,
bitre breostceare gebiden hæbbe,
gecunnad in ceole cearselda fela,
atol yþa gewealc.

Can I about myself true-poem utter,
of journeys tell, how I in toilsome-days
hardship-times often suffered
bitter heart-sorrow have endured,
come to know on ship many sorrow-halls
cruel rolling of waves.

FROM *THE DREAM OF THE ROOD*

Þæt wæs geara iu— ic þæt gyta geman—
þæt ic wæs aheawen holtes on ende
astyred of stefne minum. Genaman me ðær
strange feondas,
geworhton him þær to wæfersyne, heton me
heora wergas hebban;
bæron me þær beornas on eaxlum, oð ðæt hie me
on beorg asetton;
gefæstnodon me þær feondas genoge. Geseah ic
þa Frean mancynnes
efstan elne micle, þæt he me wolde on gestigan.

That was very long ago— I remember it still—
that I was cut down at the forest's edge
stirred from my root. Strong enemies took me there,
made me into a spectacle there for themselves, ordered
me to lift up their criminals;
men carried me there on shoulders, until they set me on
a hill;
many enemies fastened me there. I saw then the Lord of
mankind
hastening with great courage, that he intended to climb
on me.

FROM ALFRED WITH LOVE

Ælfred kyning hateð gretan Wærferþ biscep his wordum luflice ond freondlice…

King Alfred sends his greetings to Bishop Werferth in his own words, in love and friendship…

In the preface to his translation of Gregory's *Cura Pastoralis* ('Pastoral Care'), made *c.* 893, Alfred contrasts the early days of English Christianity with his own time, for which the destruction caused by the Vikings would have been largely to blame (p. 25). This book was part of a great programme of learning which Alfred inaugurated in an effort to repair the damage, organizing the translation of major texts which previously had been available only in Latin. Most of the surviving manuscripts of Old English are 10th-century in origin, and must owe their existence to the success of this programme.
   The preface continues:

I want to let you know that it has often occurred to me to think what wise men there once were throughout England… and how people once used to come here from abroad in search of wisdom and learning – and how nowadays we would have to get it abroad (if we were to have it at all). Learning had so declined in England that there were very few people this side of the Humber who could understand their service-books in English, let alone translate a letter out of Latin into English – and I don't imagine there were many north of the Humber, either. There were so few of them that I cannot think of even a single one south of the Thames at the time when I came to the throne. Thanks be to almighty God that we now have any supply of teachers. (Trans. A. G. Rigg.)

The opening lines of *The Seafarer*, from the *Exeter Book*.

455 Her Hengest 7 Horsa fuhton wiþ Wyrt georne þam cyninge, in þaere stowe þe is gecueden Agæles þrep, 7 his broþur Horsan man ofslog. 7 æfter þam Hengest feng [to] rice 7 Æsc his sunu.

455 In this year Hengest and Horsa fought against King Vortigern at a place which is called Agælesþrep [Aylesford], and his brother Horsa was slain. And after that Hengest succeeded to the kingdom and Æsc, his son.

457 Her Hengest 7 Æsc fuhton wiþ Brettas in þære stowe þe is ge cueden Crecgan ford, 7 þær ofslogon .IIII. wera, 7 þa Brettas þa forleton Cent lond, 7 mid micle ege flugon to Lunden byrg.

457 In this year Hengest and Æsc fought against the Britons at a place which is called Crecganford [Crayford], and there slew four thousand men; and the Britons then forsook Kent and fled to London in great terror.

465 Her Hengest 7 Æsc gefuhton wið Walas neah Wippedes fleote, 7 þær .XII. Wilisce aldor menn ofslogon, 7 hiera þegn an þær wearþ ofslægen, þam wæs noma Wipped.

465 In this year Hengest and Æsc fought against the Welsh near Wippedesfleot and there slew twelve Welsh nobles; and one of their thanes, whose name was Wipped, was slain there.

473 Her Hengest 7 Æsc gefuhton wiþ Walas, 7 genamon un arimedlico here reaf, 7 þa Walas flugon þa Englan swa fyr.

473 In this year Hengest and Æsc fought against the Welsh and captured innumerable spoils, and the Welsh fled from the English like fire.

477 Her cuom Ælle on Breten lond, 7 his .III. suna. Cymen, 7 Wlencing, 7 Cissa. mid .III. scipum, on þa stowe þe is nemned Cymenes ora, 7 þær ofslogon monige Wealas, 7 sume on fleame bedrifon on þone wudu þe is genemned Andredes leage.

477 In this year Ælle came to Britain and his three sons Cymen, Wlencing, and Cissa with three ships at the place which is called Cymenesora [The Owers to the south of Selsey Bill], and there they slew many Welsh and drove some to flight into the wood which is called Andredesleag [Sussex Weald].

485 Her Ælle gefeaht wiþ Walas neah Meare rædes burnan stæðe.

485 In this year Ælle fought against the Welsh near the bank of [the stream] Mearcrædesburna.

488 Her Æsc feng to rice, 7 was .XXIIII. wintra Cantwara cyning.

488 In this year Æsc succeeded to the kingdom, and was king of the people of Kent twenty-four years.

(After C. Plummer, 1892. Trans. G. N. Garmonsway, 1972.)

SOURCES OF THE CHRONICLE

The Anglo-Saxon Chronicle is not a single text, but a compilation from several sources which differ in date and place of origin. It takes the form of a year-by-year diary, with some years warranting extensive comment, some a bare line or two, and many nothing at all. Most ancient European chronicles were kept in Latin, but the present work is distinctive for its use of Old English – and also for the vast time-span it covers, from year 1 (the birth of Christ) to various dates in the 11th or 12th century.

There are seven surviving chronicle manuscripts, six of which are completely in Old English, the seventh partly in Latin. Scholars have given each text a distinguishing letter name, but they are more commonly known by the name of their source location or that of an early owner.

- Text A[1]: the *Parker Chronicle*. This is the oldest manuscript, written in a single hand from the beginning to 891, then kept up to date in 13 or 14 other hands up to 1070. Its name derives from a former owner, Matthew Parker, Archbishop of Canterbury (1504–75). It is sometimes called the *Winchester Chronicle*, because its 9th-century subject-matter was compiled at Winchester, being later transferred to Canterbury. This is the version from which the facing extract is taken.
- Text A[2]: Fragments of an 11th-century copy of the *Parker Chronicle*, almost completely destroyed in the same Cottonian Library fire that damaged *Beowulf* (p. 11).
- Texts B and C: the *Abingdon Chronicles*. Two West Saxon versions: the first (B), extending to year 977, was copied c. 1000, and kept at Canterbury without additions; the second (C), extending to 1066, is a mid-11th century copy which was kept up to date.
- Text D: the *Worcester Chronicle*. A text, with northern material added, which was sent to the diocese of Worcester. It was written in the mid-11th century, and kept up to date until 1079.
- Text E: the *Peterborough Chronicle*; also called the *Laud Chronicle*, after Archbishop William Laud (1573–1645). This version, copied at Peterborough in a single hand until 1121, extends as far as 1154.
- Text F: the bilingual *Canterbury Epitome*. This is a version of E in Latin and English, written in Canterbury c. 1100.

The Easter Tables

The text opposite shows the years 455 to 490 from Text E, and deals with the events soon after the arrival of the Anglo-Saxons (p. 7). In this part of the Chronicle, the scribe has written a series of years on separate lines, assuming that a single line would suffice for each year. (He missed out year 468, and had to insert it afterwards – an interesting example of how scribal errors can be made.)

The Chronicles are not all like this. They change in style as they develop, and lose their list-like appearance. Many of the later entries, especially those written by contemporaries, contain a great deal of narrative, and take on the character of literary essays under their year headings.

The listing technique shown in the illustration is one which originated with the *Easter Tables*, drawn up to help the clergy determine the date of the feast in any year. A page consisted of a sequence of long horizontal lines. Each line began with a year number, which was followed by several columns of astronomical data (e.g. movements of the Sun and Moon), and the results of the calculation. Of particular relevance was the space left at the end of each line, which was used to write short notes about events to help distinguish the years from each other (such as 'In this year Cnut became king'). The Chronicles grew out of this tradition, but as the intention changed, and they became more like historical records, these end-of-line notes took up more space than was expected, and the scribe had to make room where he could find it. This is why some of the entries in the illustration appear opposite several year numbers.

OLD ENGLISH LETTERS

Although there is much in common between Old and Modern English, it is the differences which strike us most forcibly when we first encounter edited Anglo-Saxon texts. The editors have done a great deal to make the texts more accessible to present-day readers, by introducing modern conventions of word spaces, punctuation, capitalization, and line division (p. 12), but there are certain features of the original spelling which are usually retained, and it is these which make the language look alien. Learning to interpret the distinctive symbols of Old English is therefore an essential first step.

Old English texts were written on parchment or vellum. The first manuscripts were in the Roman alphabet, using a half-uncial, minuscule script (p. 258) brought over by Irish missionaries: a good example is Bede's *Ecclesiastical History*, illustrated on p. 7. The rounded letter shapes of this script later developed into the more angular and cursive style (called the *insular script*), which was the usual form of writing until the 11th century.

The Old English alphabet was very similar to the one still in use, though any modern eye looking at the original manuscripts would be immediately struck by the absence of capital letters.

• A few of the letters were different in shape. There was an elongated shape for *s*, for example. Modern letter *g* appeared as ȝ, often called 'yogh' (for its sound, see p. 18). A few other letter-shapes, such as *e*, *f*, and *r*, also look rather different.

London, British Library, MS Cotton Tiberius A. xv, fol. 60v. The first five lines of glossed text are transcribed in the panel to the right.

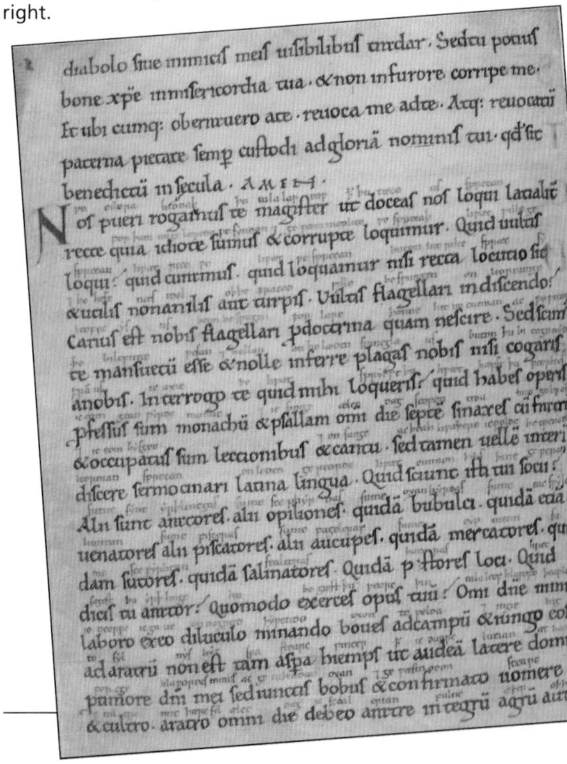

• Several modern letters will not be seen: *j* is usually spelled with a ȝ, *v* with an *f*; *q*, *x*, and *z* are very rarely used.

• *w* was written using a runic symbol, 'wynn', ƿ, which can still be seen printed in older editions of Old English texts (p. 12). Modern editions use *w*. Variant forms using *u* or *uu* are sometimes found, especially in early texts.

• *æ* was called 'ash', a name borrowed from the runic alphabet (p. 9), though the symbol is an adaptation of Latin *ae*, which it gradually replaced during the 8th century. Its sound was somewhere between [a] and [e] (p. 18).

ÆLFRIC'S *COLLOQUY*

The *Colloquy* is one of the earliest English educational documents. Colloquies were a standard technique of instruction in the monastic schools of Europe, and were especially used for teaching Latin. Ælfric's *Colloquy* takes the form of a conversation between a teacher and a young monk, and deals largely with the daily tasks of the monk's companions in the school and of the monk's own life there. The work is of considerable historical interest for the picture it provides of the life of ordinary people in Anglo-Saxon society. It is also of great linguistic interest as, in one of the four surviving manuscripts (Cotton Tiberius A.iii, shown below left), someone has added glosses in Old English above the lines. This was almost certainly a later teacher, rather than a pupil or Ælfric himself – though the point has been much debated.

Little is known about Ælfric. He was born c. 955, and died c. 1020. He was a monk at Winchester, and he became Abbot of Eynsham in c. 1005. His other writing includes many homilies, saints' lives, and a *Latin Grammar* for which later scholars gave him the title of 'Grammaticus'. He is widely regarded as one of the greatest writers of Old English prose. Certainly, his *Colloquy* is

remarkable for the liveliness and realism, tinged with humour, of the dialogue.

The *Colloquy* shows two writing styles. The Latin uses Carolingian minuscule (p. 258), whereas the Old English is in an older style (as shown by such features as the rounded *a*, the insular *s*, the dotted *y*, and the use of *yogh*). Note the early punctuation system, especially the form for the question mark in the Latin text. A period is used to end sentences, and also in some places where we would nowadays use a comma.

The Old English shows typical features of late West Saxon (p. 28), and probably dates from the first half of the 11th century. Basic punctuation has been added to the above transcript, as an aid for the modern reader – but as the text is a gloss, rather than a coherent narrative, the sentences do not always run smoothly. The gloss is almost complete in these opening lines, but there are several omitted words later in the *Colloquy*.

In this transcript, each turn in the dialogue is placed on a new line. Abbreviated forms marked by a tilde in the manuscript have been expanded in square brackets, but 7 (for *et*) has been left. The transcript does not show the dot over the y.

ƿe cildra biddaþ þe, eala lareoþ, þ[æt] þu tæce us sprecan forþam unȝelærede ƿe syndon 7 ȝepæmmodlice ƿe sprecaþ.

hƿæt ƿille ȝe sprecan?

hƿæt rece ƿe hƿæt ƿe sprecan, buton hit riht spræc sy 7 behefe, næs idel oþþe fracod.

ƿille bespunȝen on leornunȝe?

leofre ys us beon bespunȝen for lare þænne hit ne cunnan.

Nos pueri rogamus te magister ut doceas nos loqui latialit[er] recte quia idiote sumus & corrupte loquimur.
Quid uultis loqui?
Quid curamus. quid loquamur nisi recta locutio sit & utilis, non anilis aut turpis.
Uultis flagellari in discendo?
Carius est nobis flagellari p[ro] doctrina quam nescire.

We boys ask you, master, that you teach us to speak Latin correctly, because we are ignorant and we speak ungrammatically.
What do you want to speak?
What do we care what we speak, as long as the speech is correct and useful, not foolish or base.
Are you ready to be beaten while you learn?
We would rather be beaten for our teaching than not to know it.

• þ was called 'thorn', both the name and symbol being borrowed from the runic alphabet. It represented either of the 'th' sounds [θ] or [ð] (p. 18). This symbol and ð (see below) were in fact interchangeable: a scribe might use first one, then the other, in the same manuscript – though thorn became commoner in the later Old English period. (A *th* spelling was also sporadically used at the very beginning of the Old English period, presumably reflecting Irish influence, but it was quickly replaced by the new symbols.)

• ð was called 'that' in Anglo-Saxon times, though the name given to it by 19th-century editors is 'eth' (pronounced as in the first syllable of *weather*, see p. 18). The origin of this symbol is obscure, though it may be an adaptation of an early Irish letter.

• Numbers were written only in Roman symbols (as can be seen in the dates of the Anglo-Saxon Chronicle, p. 14). Arabic numerals came much later.

The standard Old English alphabet thus had the following 24 letters:

a, æ, b, c, d, e, f, g, h, i, k, l, m, n, o, p, r, s, t, þ, ð, u, w, y

Several of these letters were used in combinations (*digraphs*) to represent single sound units, in much the same way as do several modern forms, such as *th* and *ea* (as in *meat*).

One other point about spelling should be noted. There was a great deal of variation, reflecting the different preferences of individual scribes, as well as regional attempts to capture local sounds precisely. Practices also varied over time. But even with a single scribe in a single place at a single time, there could be variation, as can be seen from the existence of several variant forms in manuscripts such as *Beowulf*. The spelling became much more regular by the time of Ælfric (in the late 10th century), but this was a temporary state of affairs. Change was on the horizon, in the form of new Continental scribal practices, an inevitable graphic consequence of 1066 (p. 40).

THE LINDISFARNE GOSPELS

A page from the Lindisfarne Gospels, written at the monastery on the island of Lindisfarne (also called Holy Island), two miles off the Northumberland coast in NE England, and linked to the mainland by a causeway at low tide. The text was written c. 700, if we can trust the brief biographical note added in a space on one of the later pages (fol. 259). This says that Eadfrith, Bishop of Lindisfarne (in office, 698–721), wrote the book, that Æthelwald, Bishop of Lindisfarne (in office, 724–40), bound it, and that Billfrith made an outer casing for it, which he decorated with precious stones. The text is now in the British Museum, but the gems no longer survive.

The illustration shows the opening of Matthew 1.18. This verse was held to be the real beginning of this Gospel, as the preceding verses contained only genealogical material, hence the richness of the illumination at this point. The page is of considerable artistic interest because of its mixture of Irish, Germanic, and Byzantine motifs; but it is also of great graphological interest, as it displays several styles of writing (§18).

The rubric above the monogram is in uncials. The four lines of text below are in ornamental capitals, with elaborate links between some letters to save space. The first line of the Gospel text has been left unfinished. Between the lines is an Old English gloss written in an insular script by a Northumbrian scribe in the 10th century.

Incipit euangelium secundum mattheum
Christi autem generatio sic
erat cvm esset desponsata
mater eius Maria Iosebh.

onginneð godspell æft~ matheus
Cristes soðlice cynnreccenise ɪ cneuresu-
　　suæ ɪ ðus
wæs mið ðy wæs biwoedded ɪ beboden ɪ
befeastnad ɪ betaht
moder his

(The glossator is using several Old English words to express one in Latin; these are linked using the abbreviation for Latin *uel* ('or'): ɪ. He also sometimes adds further explanatory comments, in the margins. For the use of ~, see p. 12.)

The beginning of the Gospel according to Matthew Now the birth of Jesus Christ was in this wise. When Mary his mother had been betrothed to Joseph…

(After P. H. Blair, 1977.)

OLD ENGLISH SOUNDS

How do we know what Old English sounded like? The unhelpful answer is that we do not. In later periods, we can rely on accounts by contemporary writers (p. 69) – but there is none of this in Old English. The best we can do is make a series of informed guesses, based on a set of separate criteria (see below), and hope that the results are sufficiently similar to warrant some general conclusions. A great deal of scholarship has been devoted to this issue, and we now have a fair degree of certainty about how most of the sounds were pronounced. If an Anglo-Saxon were available, using the information on these pages we could probably communicate intelligibly.

We would have to get used to each other's accent, of course, in much the same way as modern speakers (unused, say, to Geordie or Cockney speech) need to do. There is no reason to suppose that there was any less phonetic variation in

Anglo-Saxon times than there is today, and the symbols opposite should not be interpreted too narrowly. To say that Old English *æ* was pronounced as an open front vowel (p. 238) is sufficient to distinguish it from *e* and other vowels, but it does not tell us the exact vowel quality which would have been used.

The evidence

There are four main types of evidence used in deducing the sound values of Old English letters.

• *Alphabetical logic* We know a great deal about how the letters of the Roman alphabet were pronounced, and it seems reasonable to assume that, when the missionaries adapted this alphabet to Old English, they tried to do so in a consistent and logical way. The letter representing the sound of *m* in Latin would have been used to represent the same sound in English. Likewise, if they found it necessary to find a new letter, this must have been because they felt no Latin letters were suitable (as in the case of the new symbol *æ*).

Similarly, a great deal of information comes from the way variations of regional accent and changes over time are shown in the spelling of Old English texts. The

GETTING IT RIGHT

Generations of Old English students have pored over tables such as this one, in an effort to work out the 'sound' of the language. Many must have identified during their university days with the students of Ælfric (p. 16), caring not so much about what they said, as long as they said it right. But the analogy is only a partial one: 20th-century university tutors of Old English would not, on the whole, beat their charges.

Letter	Example and its meaning	IPA symbol	Modern example
æ	sæt 'sat'	[æ]	Southern BrE sat
ǣ	dǣd 'deed'	[ɛː]	French bête
a	mann 'man'	[ɒ][1]	AmE hot
	dagas 'days'	[ɑ]	German Land
ā	hām 'home'	[ɑː]	father
c	cyrice 'church'	[tʃ][2]	church
	cēne 'bold'	[k]	keen
cg	ecg 'edge'	[dʒ]	edge
e	settan 'set'	[ɛ]	set
ē	he 'he'	[eː]	German Leben
ea	earm 'arm'	[æə]	as for [æ], [ɛː],
ēa	eare 'ear'	[ɛːə]	[e], [eː],
eo	eorl 'nobleman'	[eə]	followed by the
ēo	beor 'beer'	[eːə]	first syllable of about
f	æfre 'ever'	[v][3]	ever
	fīf 'five'	[f]	fife
g	gyt 'get'	[j][2]	yet
	fugol 'bird'	[ɣ][4]	colloq. German sagen
	gān 'go'	[g]	go
h	heofon 'heaven'	[h][5]	heaven
	niht 'night'	[ç][6]	German ich
	brōhte 'brought'	[x][7]	German brachte
i	sittan 'sit'	[i]	sit
ī	wīd 'wide'	[iː]	weed
o	monn 'man'	[ɒ][1]	AmE hot
	God 'God'	[ɔ]	BrE hot
ō	god 'good'	[oː]	German Sohn
s	rīsan 'rise'	[z][8]	rise
	hūs 'house'	[s]	house
sc	scip 'ship'	[ʃ]	ship
þ, ð	ōþer, ōðer 'other'	[ð][8]	other
	þurh, ðurh 'through'	[θ]	through
u	ful 'full'	[u]	full
ū	hūs 'house'	[uː]	goose
y	wynn 'joy'	[y]	German Würde
ȳ	rȳman 'make way'	[yː]	German Güte

A birch of the type used in medieval monastic schools.

Notes
Some of the sounds are restricted to certain contexts.

1 before m, n, n(g)
2 before/after i, and often æ, e, y
3 between voiced sounds
4 between back vowels
5 initially
6 after æ, e, i, y
7 after a, o, u
8 between vowels

The following riddle (No. 86 in the *Exeter Book* (p. 12)) illustrates the use of this transcription in a continuous piece of writing.

(After R. Quirk, V. Adams, & D. Davy, 1975.)

Wiht cwōm gangan   þǣr weras sǣton
[wiçt kwoːm gɒngɑn   θɛːr wɛrɑs sɛːton]

monige on mæðle,   mōde snottre;
[mɒnijə ɔn mæðlə   moːdə snɒtrə]

hæfde ān ēage   ond ēaran twā
[hævdə ɑːn ɛːəjə   ɒnd ɛːərɑn twɑː]

ond twēgen fēt,   twelf hund hēafda,
[ɒnd tweːjən feːt   twelf hund hɛːəvdɑ]

hrycg ond wombe   ond honda twa
[hrydʒ ɒnd wɒmbə   ɒnd hɒndə twɑː]

earmas ond eaxle,   ānne swēoran
[ɛːərmɑs ɒnd æəkslə   ɑːnːə sweːərɑn]

ond sīdan twā.   Saga hwæt ic hātte!
[ɒnd siːdɑn twɑː   sɑɣɑ hwæt itʃ hɑːtːə]

scribes generally tried to write words down to show the way they were spoken. They were not in a culture where there were arbitrary rules for standardized spelling (though rigorous conventions were maintained in certain abbeys), so we are not faced with such problems as silent letters: the *w* of *writan*, the ancestor of *write*, was pronounced. Old English is, accordingly, much more 'phonetic' than Modern English (p. 272).

• *Comparative reconstruction* We can work backwards from later states of the language to make deductions about how Old English must have sounded. Several of the sounds of Modern English (especially dialect forms) are likely to have close similarities with those of Old English. It is unlikely that there is any real difference in the way most of the consonants were pronounced then and now. The chief problems are the vowels, whose values are always more difficult to pinpoint (p. 237).

• *Sound changes* We know a great deal about the kinds of sound change which take place as language progresses. It is therefore possible to propose a particular sound value for an Old English letter different from the one in existence today, as long as we are able to give a plausible explanation for the change. For example, the Old English equivalent to *it* was *hit*. If we claim that the *h* was pronounced, we have to assume that people stopped pronouncing it at a later stage in the language. Is this a likely sound change? Given that the dropping of *h* in unstressed pronouns is something that happens regularly today (*I saw 'im*), it would seem so.

• *Poetic evidence* The way in which poets make words rhyme or alliterate can provide important clues about the way the sound system works. So can the rhythmical patterns of lines of verse, which can show the way a word was stressed, and thus indicate what value to give to a vowel appearing in an unstressed syllable – a critical matter in the late Old English period (p. 32).

Complications

There are many pitfalls to trap the unwary philologist. Scribes could be very inconsistent. They were also prone to error. But of course we do not know in advance whether an idiosyncratic form in a manuscript is in fact an error or a deliberate attempt to represent an ongoing sound change or a regionalism. A great deal of detailed comparative work may be required before we can be sure.

The absence of universal spelling rules can also pose a problem, as there was no necessity for scribes to be consistent, and many were not (p. 10). Manuscripts can vary in their use of þ and ð (p. 16), single or double consonants (*s* or *ss*, *d* or *dd*), and several groups of vowels (notably, *i*, *y*, and *ie*). At one point we might find *hit*, and at another, *hyt*; *gyldan* 'pay' might be spelled *gieldan*; *þær* might be *þar*. Such difficulties, it must be appreciated, contribute only to the fortitude and motivation of the true Old English phonologist. *Hiȝe sceal þe heardra, heorte þe cenre* (p. 12).

ANCIENT MUTATIONS

Some English word pairs showing the effects of a phonological change which took place over 1,200 years ago.

goose – geese
tooth – teeth
man – men
mouse – mice
hale – health
doom – deem
full – fill
whole – heal
fall – fell (vb.)
blood – bleed
foul – filth
long – length
broad – breadth
old – elder

THE FIRST VOWEL SHIFT

We can say one thing with certainty about the accent of the Anglo-Saxon invaders after they arrived in Britain: it changed. We know this because the words which emerged in Old English out of the Germanic spoken on the Continent (p. 6) looked (and therefore sounded) very different from their later counterparts in the early days of German. What happened to cause such a difference?

A related observation arises out of the way some Latin words were borrowed into Old English without a change in their vowel, whereas others did change. Latin *caseus* became *cyse* 'cheese' in Old English, but *castellum* became *castel* 'village'. In the first case, the *a* vowel changed; in the second case, it did not. There are many similar examples. What happened to cause such a difference?

i-mutation

The explanation is now a well-established part of Germanic philology. It asserts that the Old English vowels changed in quality between the time the Anglo-Saxons left the Continent and the time Old English was first written down. By examining hundreds of cases, it is possible to establish a pattern in the way this change took place.

In Germanic there were many words where a vowel in a stressed syllable was immediately followed by a high front vowel ([i]) or vowel-like sound ([j]) in the next syllable. The plural of **fōt* is

thought to have been **fōtiz*, with the stress on *fō*. For some reason (see below), the quality of this high front sound caused the preceding vowel to change (mutate). In the case of **fōt*, the *ō* became *ē*, which ultimately came to be pronounced [i:], as in modern *feet*. The *-iz* ending dropped away, for once the plural was being shown by the e vowel, it was unnecessary to have an ending as well. *Fēt* therefore emerged as an irregular noun in English – though the process which gave rise to it was perfectly regular, affecting hundreds of cases.

This process has come to be called *i*-mutation, or *i*-umlaut (a German term meaning 'sound alteration'). It is thought to have taken place during the 7th century. There is no sign of the vowels continuing to change in this way in later periods. The process also explains the Latin example above: *caseus* must have been borrowed very early into English, before the time that *i*-mutation was operating, as its vowel has been affected (in this case, the *a* has become *y*); *castellum*, however, must have been borrowed after the time when *i*-mutation stopped taking place, as its *a* vowel has remained in *castel*.

i-mutation is a kind of 'vowel harmony' – a very natural process which affects many modern languages. People, it seems, readily fall into the habit of making one vowel in a word sound more like another in the same word, and this is what happened in 7th-century Old English. All back vowels in the context described above were changed into front vowels – and all short front

vowels and diphthongs were affected, too, being articulated even further forward and higher (with the exception of [i], of course, which is already as far forward and as high in the mouth as any vowel can be).

There are a few exceptions and complications, which analysts still puzzle over, but the general effect on the language was immense, as this sound change applied to the most frequently occurring word classes, all of which had *i* sounds in their inflectional endings. This is why we have in Modern English such pairs as *food / feed* (from the addition of an **-ian* verb-forming suffix in Germanic), as well as *strong / strength* and several others (from the addition of an **-iþ* adjective-forming suffix). Not all the forms affected by *i*-mutation have survived into Modern English, though. In Old English, the plural of *book* was *bec*, but this has not come through into Modern English as *beek*: the forces of analogy (p. 200) have taken over, and caused a change to the regular *books*.

We do not know why *i*-mutation operated when it did. What was it that made 7th-century Anglo-Saxons start pronouncing their vowels in this way? And why did the process not affect all cases of *i* in a following suffix (words ending in *-ing*, for example, were not affected)? This phonological detective story is by no means over.

The asterisk marks a hypothetical form.

SOME FEATURES OF OLD ENGLISH GRAMMAR

THE CÆDMON STORY

Old English prose provides the clearest way in to analysing the grammar of the language (the poetry, as can be seen from the extracts on pp. 12–13, is much more compressed and intricate). This extract is from an Old English translation of Bede's *Ecclesiastical History* (Book 4, Ch. 24). It tells the story of Cædmon, the unlettered cowherd who became England's first Christian poet, sometime in the late 7th century. The translation dates from the late 9th century. (The actual text of Cædmon's hymn is given on p. 29.)

To modern eyes and ears, Old English grammar (for grammatical terminology, see Part III) provides a fascinating mixture of the familiar and the unfamiliar. The word order is much more varied than it would be in Modern English, but there are several places where it is strikingly similar. Adjectives usually go before their nouns, as do prepositions, articles, and other grammatical words, just as they do today. Sometimes, whole sentences are identical in the order of words, or nearly so, as can be seen from the word-for-word translation in the Cædmon text below. The main syntactic differences affect the placing of the verb, which quite often appears before the subject, and also at the very end of the clause – a noticeable feature of this particular story.

In Modern English, word order is relatively fixed. The reason Old English order could vary so much is that the relationships between the parts of the sentence were signalled by other means. Like other Germanic languages, Old English was *inflected*: the job a word did in the sentence was signalled by the kind of ending it had. Today, most of these inflections have died away, leaving the modern reader with the major task of getting used to the word endings, in order to understand the Old English texts. It is necessary to learn the different forms taken by the verbs, nouns, pronouns, adjectives, and the definite article. The irregular verbs, which change their form from present to past tense, are a particular problem (as they continue to be, for foreign learners), because there are so many more of them. Nonetheless, it should be plain from reading the glosses to the Cædmon extract that present-day English speakers already have a 'feel' for Old English grammar. (Long vowel marks (p. 16) are added in the notes below, as an aid to pronunciation.)

---

wæs he se mon in weoruldhade geseted oð þa tide þe he
Was he the man in secular life   settled   until the time that he

wæs gelyfdre   ylde; ond he næfre nænig leoð geleornode, ond he
was of-advanced age; and he never any   poem learned,   and he

for þon oft   in gebeorscipe, þonne þær wæs blisse intinga
therefore often at banquet,   when   there was of-joy occasion

gedemed, þæt heo ealle sceolden þurh endebyrdnesse be hearpan
decided,   that they all   should   by   arrangement   with harp

5 singan, þonne he geseah þa hearpan him nealecan, þonne aras he
to sing, when he saw   the harp   him approach, then   arose he

for scome from þæm symble, ond ham eode to his huse. þa   he
for shame from the   feast,   and home went to his house. When he

þæt þa sumre tide dyde, þæt he forlet þæt hus   þæs
that a certain time did,   that he left   the house of the

gebeorscipes, ond ut   wæs gongende to neata   scipene,
banquet,   and out was going   to of-cattle stall

þara   heord him wæs þære neahte beboden; þa   he ða þær
of which keeping him was that night entrusted; when he   there

10 in gelimplice tide his leomu on reste gesette ond onslepte,
at suitable   time his limbs at rest set   and fell asleep,

þa   stod him sum   mon æt   þurh swefn, ond hine halette
then stood him a certain man beside in   dream, and him hailed

ond grette, ond hine be his noman nemnde, 'Cedmon, sing me
and greeted, and him by his name   called.   'Cædmon, sing me

hwæthwugu.' þa   ondswarede he, ond cwæð, 'Ne con ic noht
something.'   Then answered   he, and said,   'Not can I nothing

singan; ond ic for þon of   þeossum gebeorscipe ut   eode ond hider
sing;   and I for that from this   banquet   out went and hither

15 gewat, for þon ic naht   singan ne cuðe.'   Eft   he cwæð,
came, because I nothing to sing not knew how.' Again he spoke,

se ðe   wið hine sprecende wæs, 'Hwæðre þu meaht me
he that with him speaking   was, 'However you can   for-me

singan.' þa   cwæð he, 'Hwæt sceal ic singan?' Cwæð he, 'Sing
sing.'   Then said   he, 'What shall I sing?'   Said he, 'Sing

me frumsceaft.' þa   he ða þas andsware onfeng, þa   ongon he
me creation.'   When he this answer   received, then began he

sona   singan in herenesse Godes Scyppendes, þa   fers
immediately to sing in praise   of God Creator,   those verses

20 ond þa   word þe   he næfre gehyrde…
and those words that he never had heard…

WORD ORDER

The varying forms of nouns, adjectives, and articles tell us how the parts of the clause relate to each other. In Modern English, the difference between (i) and (ii) is a matter of word order:

(i) *the woman saw the man*
(ii) *the man saw the woman*

In Old English, the two sentences would be:

(i) *sēo cwēn geseah þone guman*
(ii) *se guma geseah þā cwēn.*

The nominative feminine form *seo* in (i) has changed to an accusative form, *þā*, in (ii). Similarly, the accusative masculine form *þone* in (i) has become a nominative *se* in (ii).

It is thus always clear who is doing what to whom, regardless of the order in which the noun phrases appear: *þone guman geseah sēo cwēn* has the same meaning as (i).

WÆS HE SE MON…

wæs

The past tense of the verb 'be' has changed little since Old English times, apart from the loss of the plural ending.

- *wæs* 'was' 1st/3rd sg.
  wære 'were' 2nd sg.
  wæron 'were' 1st/2nd/3rd pl.

The present tense forms, however, show several differences. To begin with, Old English had two sets of words expressing the notion of 'be', one parallel to Latin *esse* and the other to Latin *fui*.

- *wesan*
  eom 1st sg.
  eart 2nd sg.
  is 3rd sg.
  sind(on) 1st/2nd/3rd pl.
- *bēon*
  bēo 1st sg.
  bist 2nd sg.
  bið 3rd sg.
  bēoð 1st/2nd/3rd pl.

There were also subjunctive, imperative, and participial forms of both verbs.

There seem to have been several differences in the way the two sets of verbs were used, though there is insufficient evidence to draw up hard-and-fast rules. The *bēon* forms were preferred in habitual and repetitive contexts, and especially when there was a future implication. Ælfric's *Latin Grammar* actually equates *eom, eart, is* to Latin *sum, es,* *est,* and *bēo, bist, bið* to *erō, eris, erit.* There is a clear example of this difference in one of the Homilies, where the speaker addresses the Holy Trinity:

ðu ðe æfre wære, and æfre bist, and nu eart, an ælmihtig God… *you who always were, and ever will be, and now are, one almighty God…*

---

hē

The personal pronoun system had more members than we find in Modern English, and several of them are well illustrated in this extract (the numbers below refer to lines). Modern equivalent forms are given below, but these do not capture the way in which the pronouns were used in Old English, where gender is grammatical (p. 209): for example, *bōc* 'book' is feminine, and would be referred to as *heo* 'she', whereas *mægden* 'girl' is neuter, and would be referred to as *hit*. (This list gives the standard forms found in late West Saxon (p. 28), and ignores spelling variations.)

- *ic* (13) 'I' nom.
  mē (16) 'me' acc./dat.
  mīn 'my, mine' gen.
- *wē* 'we' nom.
  ūs 'us' acc./dat.
  ūre 'our(s)' gen.
- *þū* (16) 'thou' (sg.) nom.
  þē 'thee' acc./dat.
  þīn 'thy, thine' gen.
- *gē* 'ye' (pl.) nom.
  ēōw 'you' acc./dat.
  ēōwer 'your(s)' gen.
- *hē* (1) 'he' nom.
  hine (11) 'him' acc.
  his (6) 'his' gen.
  him (5) '(to) him' dat.
- *hēō* 'she' nom.
  hī 'her' acc.
  hire 'her(s)' gen.
  hire '(to) her' dat.
- *hit* 'it' nom./acc.
  his 'its' gen.
  him '(to) it' dat.
- *hī/hēō* 'they/them' nom./acc.
  hira 'their(s)' gen.
  him '(to) them' dat.

In addition, the language showed the remains of a 'dual' personal pronoun system, but only in the 1st and 2nd persons. The 1st person form meant 'we two' (nom. *wit*, acc./dat. *unc*, gen. *uncer*); the 2nd person form 'you two' (nom. *git*, acc./dat. *inc*, gen. *incer*). This disappeared by the 13th century.

There are obvious correspondences with the modern pronouns in most cases, but not between the old and modern sets of 3rd person plural forms. The West Saxon forms were supplanted by Scandinavian forms some time after the Norman Conquest, perhaps because people felt they needed to make a clear difference in pronunciation between the 3rd person singular and plural forms – *him*, in particular, must have been a source of confusion. Whatever the reason, Viking influence prevailed, and the modern English forms now begin with *th-*. (For the special problem of *she*, see p. 43.)

---

se

Old English nouns may be masculine, feminine, or neuter, regardless of the biological sex of their referents. They also appear in nominative, accusative, genitive, and dative forms (p. 202), depending on their function in the clause. The nominative masculine form of the definite article, *se*, is seen here with *mon* (a common spelling for *man*); the equivalent feminine form, *sēō*, would be found with *hearpe* 'harp'; and the equivalent neuter form, *þæt*, would be found with *hūs*. Other forms of the article can be seen in the extract – though it should be noted that articles are not used as much as they would be in Modern English, as can be seen from 'in dream' (11) and other such cases:

- *þā* The acc. sg. form of *sēō*, following the preposition *oð* 'until' (1), or as object of the verb (5, 7). It also appears as the acc. pl. of *þæt* (19, 20).
- *þǣm* (6) The dat. sg. of *þæt*, following the preposition *from*.
- *þæs* (7) The gen. sg. of *þæt*.

ABBREVIATIONS

acc.	accusative case
dat.	dative case
gen.	genitive case
nom.	nominative case
pl.	plural
sg.	singular
1st	1st person
2nd	2nd person
3rd	3rd person

… geseted

There are three main kinds of Modern English verbs (p. 204), and all three can be traced back to Old English.

1 Those forming their past tense by adding *-ed* to the root form of the present tense: *jump/jumped*. Then as now, the majority of verbs are of this type.
2 Those forming their past tense by changing a vowel in the root form of the present tense: *see/saw*. These are called *vocalic* or 'strong' verbs in Old English grammars, and the patterned changes in vowel quality which they display are described as *vowel gradation* or *ablaut*.
3 Wholly irregular forms, such as *can, will*, and *be* (see above).

Verb inflections

The modern verb has very few inflectional endings. Past tense for regular verbs is marked by the *-ed* suffix in all persons; and in the present tense only the 3rd person singular is distinctive (*-s*). Old English made far more distinctions, as can be seen from the following paradigm (variation between different classes of verbs is not shown):

Present tense
ic lufie 'I love'
þū lufast 'you (sg.) love'
hē/hēō/hit lufað 'he/she/it loves'
wē, gē, hī lufiað 'we/you (pl.)/they love'

Past tense
ic lufode 'I loved'
þū lufodest 'you (sg.) loved'
hē/hēō/hit lufode 'he/she/it loved'
wē/gē/hī lufodon 'we/you (pl.)/they loved'

Some of the present tense endings weakened and disappeared soon after the Old English period. But the 2nd and 3rd person singular forms stayed on, developing into the familiar *-est* and *-eth* forms of Middle English (*lovest, loveth*). Their later development is described on p. 44.

There were several other distinctive inflectional features of the Old English verb:

- The infinitive (p. 204): *-an* or *-ian* was added to the root. Examples in the Cædmon text include *singan* 'to sing' and *nealecan* '(to) approach' (5). The infinitive of 'love' was *lufian*. The use of a suffix to mark the infinitive was lost during the Middle English period, and the particle *to* came to be used as an alternative marker.
- The *-ing* form (p. 204): the equivalent form was *-end(e)*. Examples in the text are *gongende* (8) 'going' and *sprecende* (16) 'speaking'. This form hardly survives the beginning of the Middle English period, being replaced by the *-ing(e)* ending which in Old English had been restricted to nouns.
- The *-ed* form (p. 204): this shows the same kind of vowel changes and endings we see today, but it also had a special prefix, *ge-* (as in all other West Germanic languages): the form is well represented in the Cædmon text, being a past narrative – see *geseted* 'settled' (1), *geleornode* 'learned' (2), etc. It stays well into Middle English, but is lost by *c.* 1500, apart from in archaisms (such as *yclept* 'called').
- The subjunctive (p. 216): unlike in Modern English, this mood was systematically used, but it had far fewer endings than the indicative. It can be seen especially in subordinate clauses expressing a subjective attitude. Plural forms in both present and past tenses have a distinctive *-en* ending. An example in the text is *sceolden* 'should' (4).

OLD ENGLISH VOCABULARY

The vocabulary of Old English presents a mixed picture, to those encountering it for the first time. The majority of the words in the Cædmon extract (p. 20) are very close to Modern English – once we allow for the unfamiliar spelling (p. 16) and the unexpected inflections (p. 21) – whereas those in the poetic texts (p. 12) are not. In the Cædmon text we would have little difficulty recognizing *singan* as *sing* or *stōd* as *stood*; and *ondswarede* is quite close to *answered*, *onslepte* to *asleep*, and *geleornode* to *learned*. Omitting the *ge-* prefix helps enormously, making *-seted* more like *seated*, *-seah* like *saw*, and *-hyrde* like *heard*. Most of the prepositions and pronouns are identical in form (though not always in meaning): *for, from, in, æt* ('at'), *he, him, his*.

On the other hand, some of the words look very strange, because they have since disappeared from the language. In the Cædmon extract these include *gelimplice* 'suitable', *neata* 'cattle', *swefn* 'dream', *beboden* 'entrusted', and *frumsceaft* 'creation', as well as some of the grammatical words, such as *se* 'the' (p. 21). These examples also illustrate the chief characteristic of the Old English lexicon, the readiness to build up words from a number of parts – a feature which has stayed with English ever since (p. 128). Frequent use is made of prefixes and suffixes, and compound words are everywhere in evidence. The meaning of these words often emerges quite quickly, once their parts are identified. Thus, *endebyrdnesse* is a combination of *ende* 'end' + *byrd* 'birth, rank' + *-ness*, which conveys the meaning of 'arrangement', or (in the present context) of people 'taking their turn'. *Gebeorscipe* seems to have nothing to do with 'banquet' until we see that it is basically 'beer' + 'ship'.

Particular care must be taken with words which look familiar, but whose meaning is different in Modern English. An Anglo-Saxon *wīf* was any woman, married or not. A *fugol* 'fowl' was any bird, not just a farmyard one. *Sōna* (*soon*) meant 'immediately', not 'in a little while'; *won* (*wan*) meant 'dark', not 'pale'; and *fæst* (*fast*) meant 'firm, fixed', not 'rapidly'. These are 'false friends', when translating out of Old English.

WORD-BUILDING

The way Old English vocabulary builds up through the processes of affixation and compounding can be seen by tracing the way a basic form is used throughout the lexicon.

(Only a selection of forms is given, and only one possible meaning of each form.)

gān/gangan 'go'

gang journey

Compounding
æftergengness succession
ciricgang churchgoing
forliggang adultery
gangewīfre spider ('go' + 'weaver')
gangpytt privy
hindergenga crab
sægenga sea-goer

Prefixation
beganga inhabitant
begangan visit
bīgengere worker
foregān go before
forgān pass over
forþgān go forth
ingān go in
ingang entrance
niþergān descend
ofergān pass over
ofergenga traveller
ofgān demand
ongān approach
oþgān go away
tōgān go into
þurhgān go through
undergān undergo
upgān go up
upgang rising
ūtgān go out
ūtgang exit
wiþgān go against
ymbgān go round
(After D. Kastovsky, 1992.)

Not all Old English prefixes have come down into Modern English. Among those which have been lost are *ge-* (p. 21), *oþ-* ('away'), *niþe-* ('down'), and *ymb-* ('around'). There is a memorial to *tō-* in *today, towards*, and *together*.

SELF-EXPLAINING COMPOUNDS

gōdspel < *gōd* 'good' + *spel* 'tidings': gospel
sunnandæg < *sunnan* 'sun's' + *dæg* 'day': Sunday
stæfcræft < *stæf* 'letters' + *cræft* 'craft': grammar
mynstermann < *mynster* 'monastery' + *mann* 'man': monk
frumweorc < *frum* 'beginning' + *weorc* 'work': creation
eorþcræft < *eorþ* 'earth' + *cræft* 'craft': geometry
rōdfæstnian < *rōd* 'cross' + *fæstnian* 'fasten': crucify
dægred < *dæg* 'day' + *red* 'red': dawn
lēohtfæt < *lēoht* 'light' + *fæt* 'vessel': lamp
tīdymbwlātend < *tīd* 'time' + *ymb* 'about' + *wlātend* 'gaze': astronomer

THE WHOLE STORY

The root form *hāl* is used in Old English as the basis of six words; and the process continues into Modern English, where a further nine words are in evidence (plus many more compounds, such as *whole-food* and *health-farm*).

The diagram also shows a related set of etymologies. Old Norse *heill* and Old English *hāl* both come from the same Germanic root. Much later, the Scandinavian development also affected English.
(After W. F. Bolton, 1982.)

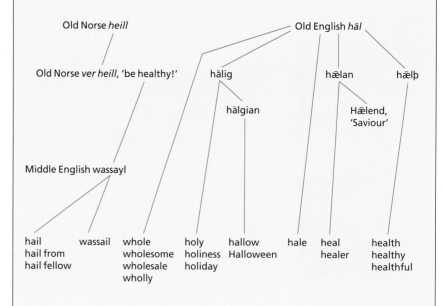

Kennings

It is in the poetry (pp. 11–13) that we find the most remarkable coinages. The genre abounds in the use of vivid figurative descriptions known as *kennings* (a term from Old Norse poetic treatises). Kennings describe things indirectly, allusively, and often in compounds. Their meaning is not self-evident; there has been a leap of imagination, and this needs to be interpreted. Sometimes the interpretation is easy to make; sometimes it is obscure, and a source of critical debate. Famous kennings include *hronrād* 'whale-road' for the sea, *bānhūs* 'bone-house' for a person's body, and *beadolēoma* 'battle light' for a sword. Often, phrases are used as well as compound words: God, for example, is described as *heofonrīces weard* 'guardian of heaven's kingdom' and as *moncynnes weard* 'guardian of mankind'. Some elements are particularly productive. There are over 100 compounds involving the word *mōd* ('mood', used in Old English for a wide range of attitudes, such as 'spirit, courage, pride, arrogance'): they include *mōdcræft* 'intelligence', *glædmōdnes* 'kindness', *mōdcearu* 'sorrow of soul', and *mādmōd* 'folly'.

Kennings are sometimes a problem to interpret because the frequency of synonyms in Old English makes it difficult to distinguish nuances of meaning. There are some 20 terms for 'man' in *Beowulf*, for example, such as *rinc*, *guma*, *secg*, and *beorn*, and it is not always easy to see why one is used and not another. When these words are used in compounds, the complications increase. *Beado-rinc* and *dryht-guma* are both translatable as 'warrior', but would there be a noticeable difference in meaning if the second elements were exchanged? A careful analysis of all the contexts in which each element is used in Old English can often give clues (and is now increasingly practicable, §24), but this option is of course unavailable when the item is rare. And items are often rare. There may be

only a single instance of a word in a text, or even in Old English as a whole. There are 903 noun compounds in *Beowulf*; according to one study (A. G. Brodeur, 1959); but of these, 578 are used only once, and 518 of them are known only from this poem. In such circumstances, establishing the precise meaning of an expression becomes very difficult.

Kennings were often chosen to satisfy the need for alliteration in a line, or to help the metrical structure (p. 415): there is perhaps no particular reason for having *sincgyfan* 'giver of treasure' at one point in *Beowulf* (l. 1342) and *goldgyfan* 'giver of gold' at another (l. 2652), other than the need to alliterate with a following word beginning with *s* in the first case and beginning with *g* in the second. But kennings also allowed a considerable compression of meaning, and a great deal of study has been devoted to teasing out the various associations and ironies which come from using a particular form. A good example is *anpaðas* 'one + paths', a route along which only one person may pass at a time. This meaning sounds innocuous enough, but to the Anglo-Saxon mind such paths provided difficult fighting conditions, and there must have been a connotation of danger. The word is used in *Beowulf* (l. 1410) at the point where the hero and his followers are approaching the monster's lair. Their route leads them along *enge ānpaðas* 'narrow lone paths', where there would have been an ever-present risk of ambush.

Beowulf stands out as a poem which makes great use of compounds: there are over a thousand of them, comprising a third of all words in the text. Many of these words, and of the elements they contain, are not known outside of poetry. Some, indeed, might have been archaisms. But most are there because of their picturesque and vivid character, adding considerable variety to the descriptions of battles, seafaring, the court, and fellowship in Anglo-Saxon times.

THE CRUEL SEA

sǣ, *mere*, *brim*, *lagu*, *wæter*, *fām* ('foam'), *wǣg* ('wave')...

The Icelandic linguists, such as Snorri Sturluson (13th century), distinguished several types of poetic expression. The literalness of *wǣgflota* 'wave-floater' for a ship might be distinguished from the more metaphorical *wǣghengest* 'wave-steed'. Various levels of figurativeness can be seen in the following list of compounds for 'sea' – a dozen out of the 50 or more known from Old English literature. Several use one of the 'sea' synonyms listed above.

seolbæþ seal + bath
ȳþageswing waves + surge
fisceseþel fish + home
strēamgewinn waters + strife
hwælweg whale + way
sǣwylm sea + welling
swanrād swan + road
brimstrēam ocean + stream
merestrēam lake + stream
wæterflōd water + flood
drencflōd drowning + flood
bæþweg bath + way

LEXICAL INVASIONS

The history of early English vocabulary is one of repeated invasions, with newcomers to the islands bringing their own language with them, and leaving a fair amount of its vocabulary behind when they left or were assimilated. In the Anglo-Saxon period, there were two major influences of this kind – one to do with this world, the other to do with the next.

The effect of Latin

The focus on the next world arrived first, in the form of the Christian missionaries from Ireland and Rome (p. 10). Not only did they introduce literacy, they brought with them a huge Latin vocabulary. The Anglo-Saxons had of course already encountered Latin as used by the Continental Roman armies and the Romano-British, but only a few Vulgar Latin words had come into Old English as a result (p. 8). By contrast, the missionary influence resulted in hundreds of new words coming into the language, and motivated many derived forms. The new vocabulary was mainly to do with the Church and its services, theology, and learning, but there were also many biological, domestic, and general words, most of which have survived in Modern English. At the same time, many Old English words were given new, 'Christian' meanings under missionary influence. *Heaven, hell, God, Gospel, Easter, Holy Ghost, sin,* and several others were semantically refashioned at the time.

The loans came in over a long time scale, and differed in character. Up to *c.* 1000, many continued to arrive from spoken Latin, and these tended to relate more to everyday, practical matters. After *c.* 1000, following the rebirth of learning associated with King Alfred (p. 13) and the 10th-century Benedictine monastic revival, the vocabulary came from classical written sources, and is much more scholarly and technical. Sometimes, even, the Latin ending would be retained in the loan word, instead of being replaced by the relevant Old English ending: an example is *acoluthus* 'acolyte', which first appears in one of Ælfric's works as *acolitus*. Many of these learned words (such as *collectaneum* and *epactas*) did not survive – though several (*fenestra* and *bibliotheca* are instances) were to be reincarnated some time later in a second stage of classical borrowing (p. 48).

THE KIRKDALE INSCRIPTION

The best surviving example of an inscribed Anglo-Saxon sundial, now placed above the south porch of the church at Kirkdale, North Yorkshire. The inscription reads as follows:

Left panel

✠ ORM GAMAL / SVNA BOHTE S(AN)C(TV)S / GREGORIVS MIN / STERÐONNE HI / T WES ÆL TOBRO /

Right panel

CAN 7 TOFALAN 7 HE / HIT LET MACAN NEWAN FROM / GRUNDE XPE 7 S(AN)C(TV)S GREGORI / VS IN EADWARD DAGVM C(I)NG / 7 (I)N TOSTI DAGVM EORL ✠

Centre panel

✠ ÞIS IS DÆGES SOLMERCA ✠ / ÆT ILCVM TIDE / ✠ 7 HAWARÐ ME WROHTE 7 BRAND PR̄S

Orm, son of Gamal, bought St Gregory's church when it was all ruined and tumbled down and he caused it to be built afresh from the foundation (in honour of) Christ and St Gregory in the days of King Edward and in the days of Earl Tosti.
This is the day's sun-marking at every hour. And Hawarð made me, and Brand, priest (?)

Tostig, brother of Harold Godwineson, became earl of Northumbria in 1055, and died in 1066, so the dial belongs to that decade.

The text shows an interesting mix of influences, with the Latin saint's name alongside Old Norse personal names, and Latin *minster* alongside Germanic *tobrocan*.

AND A FEW MORE LATIN LOANS…

abbot, accent, alb, alms, anchor, angel, antichrist, ark, cancer, candle, canon, canticle, cap, cedar, celandine, cell, chalice, chest, cloister, cucumber, cypress, deacon, dirge, elephant, fever, fig, font, giant, ginger, history, idol, laurel, lentil, litany, lobster, lovage, marshmallow, martyr, master, mat, nocturn, noon, oyster, paper, periwinkle, place, plaster, pope, priest, prime, prophet, psalm, pumice, purple, radish, relic, rule, scorpion, scrofula, shrine, sock, synagogue, temple, tiger, title, tunic

EARLY LATIN LOANS (BEFORE 1000)

Ecclesiastical

abbadissa > *abudesse* 'abbess'
altar > *alter* 'altar'
apostolus > *apostol* 'apostle'
culpa > *cylpe* 'fault'
missa > *mæsse* 'Mass'
nonnus > *nonne* 'monk'
offerre > *offrian* 'sacrifice'
praedicare > *predician* 'preach'
scola > *scol* 'school'
versus > *fers* 'verse' (used in the Cædmon extract, p. 20, l. 19)

General

calendae > *calend* 'month'
cavellum > *caul* 'basket'
epistula > *epistol* 'letter'
fenestra > *fenester* 'window'
lilium > *lilie* 'lily'
organum > *orgel* 'organ'
picus > *pic* 'pike'
planta > *plant* 'plant'
rosa > *rose* 'rose'
studere > *studdian* 'take care of'

LATE LATIN LOANS (AFTER 1000)

Ecclesiastical

apostata > *apostata* 'apostate'
chrisma > *crisma* 'chrism'
clericus > *cleric* 'clerk'
credo > *creda* 'creed'
crucem > *cruc* 'cross'
daemon > *demon* 'demon'
discipulus > *discipul* 'disciple'
paradisus > *paradis* 'paradise'
prior > *prior* 'prior'
sabbatum > *sabbat* 'sabbath'

General

bibliotheca > *biblioþece* 'library'
chorus > *chor* 'choir, chorus'
declinare > *declinian* 'decline'
delphinus > *delfin* 'dolphin'
grammatica > *grammatic* 'grammar'
hymnus > *ymen* 'hymn'
mechanicus > *mechanisc* 'mechanical'
persicum > *persic* 'peach'
philosophus > *philosoph* 'philosopher'
scutula > *scutel* 'scuttle, dish'

The effect of Norse

The second big linguistic invasion came as a result of the Viking raids on Britain, which began in AD 787 and continued at intervals for some 200 years. Regular settlement began in the mid-9th century, and within a few years the Danes controlled most of eastern England. They were prevented from further gains by their defeat in 878 at Ethandun (p. 26). By the Treaty of Wedmore (886) the Danes agreed to settle only in the north-east third of the country – east of a line running roughly from Chester to London – an area that was subject to Danish law, and which thus became known as the *Danelaw*. In 991, a further invasion brought a series of victories for the Danish army (including the Battle of Maldon, p. 12), and resulted in the English king, Æthelred, being forced into exile, and the Danes seizing the throne. England then stayed under Danish rule for 25 years.

The linguistic result of this prolonged period of contact was threefold. A large number of settlements with Danish names appeared in England. There was a marked increase in personal names of Scandinavian origin (p. 26). And many general words entered the language, nearly 1,000 eventually becoming part of Standard English. Only *c*. 150 of these words appear in Old English manuscripts, the earliest in the treaty between Alfred and Guthrum, and in the northern manuscripts of the Anglo-Saxon Chronicle (D and E, p. 15). They include *landing, score, beck, fellow, take, husting,* and *steersman,* as well as many words which did not survive in later English (mostly terms to do with Danish law and culture, which died away after the Norman Conquest). The vast majority of loans do not begin to appear until the early 12th century (p. 48). These include many of our modern words which use [sk-] sounds (an Old Norse feature), such as *skirt, sky,* and *skin,* as well as most of the words listed below.

The closeness of the contact between the Anglo-Saxons and the Danish settlers is clearly shown by the extensive borrowings. Some of the commonest words in Modern English came into the language at that time, such as *both, same, get,* and *give.* Even the personal pronoun system was affected (p. 21), with *they, them,* and *their* replacing the earlier forms. And – the most remarkable invasion of all – Old Norse influenced the verb *to be.* The replacement of *sindon* (p. 21) by *are* is almost certainly the result of Scandinavian influence, as is the spread of the 3rd person singular -s ending in the present tense in other verbs (p. 44).

SCANDINAVIAN PLACE NAMES

Scandinavian parish names in England, related to the boundary line of the Danelaw.

There are over 1,500 such place names (p. 141) in England, especially in Yorkshire and Lincolnshire. Over 600 end in *-by*, the Scandinavian word for 'farm' or 'town' – *Derby, Grimsby, Rugby, Naseby*, etc. Many of the remainder end in *-thorp* ('village'), as in *Althorp, Astonthorpe,* and *Linthorpe; -thwaite* ('clearing'), as in *Braithwaite, Applethwaite,* and *Storthwaite;* and *-toft* ('homestead'), as in *Lowestoft, Eastoft,* and *Sandtoft.* The *-by* ending is almost entirely confined to the area of the Danelaw, supporting a theory of Scandinavian origin, despite the existence of the word *by* 'dwelling' in Old English. (After P. H. Sawyer, 1962.)

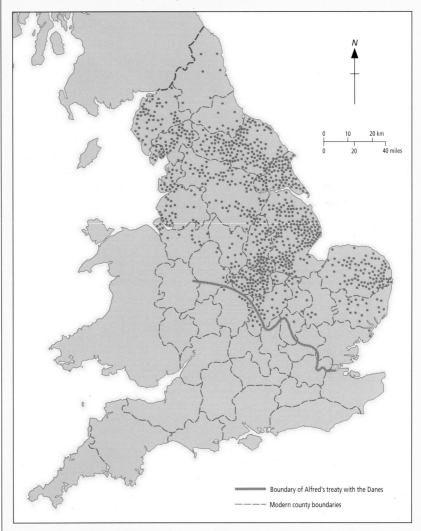

Boundary of Alfred's treaty with the Danes

Modern county boundaries

◄ A signpost in North Yorkshire acts as a Danish memorial.

AND A FEW MORE NORSE LOANS...

again, anger, awkward, bag, band, bank, birth, brink, bull, cake, call, clip, crawl, crook, die, dirt, dregs, egg, flat, fog, freckle, gap, gasp, get, guess, happy, husband, ill, keel, kid, knife, law, leg, loan, low, muggy, neck, odd, outlaw, race, raise, ransack, reindeer, rid, root, rugged, scant, scare, scowl, scrap, seat, seem, silver, sister, skill, skirt, sly, smile, snub, sprint, steak, take, thrift, Thursday, tight, trust, want, weak, window

THE OTHER WHITE HORSE

This figure was carved to commemorate the victory of King Alfred over the Danes at the Battle of Ethandun (878), modern Edington, Wiltshire. It was a decisive battle. As the Anglo-Saxon Chronicle puts it:

King Alfred… went from these camps to Iley Oak, and one day later to Edington; and there he fought against the entire host, and put it to flight, and pursued it up to the fortification [probably Chippenham], and laid siege there for a fortnight; and then the host gave him preliminary hostages and solemn oaths that they would leave his kingdom, and promised him in addition that their king would receive baptism; and they fulfilled this promise…

The Edington horse (known locally as the Bratton or Westbury horse) may be less well known to modern tourists than its prehistoric counterpart at Uffington in Berkshire, but it is far more important to English history.

SCANDINAVIAN PERSONAL NAMES

The distribution of English family names (p. 149) ending in -son, such as *Davidson*, *Jackson*, and *Henderson*. The figures give the number of different surnames which are thought to have come from each county. The Scandinavian influence in the north and east is very clear, especially in Yorkshire and north Lincolnshire, where over 60 per cent of personal names in early Middle English records show Scandinavian influence.

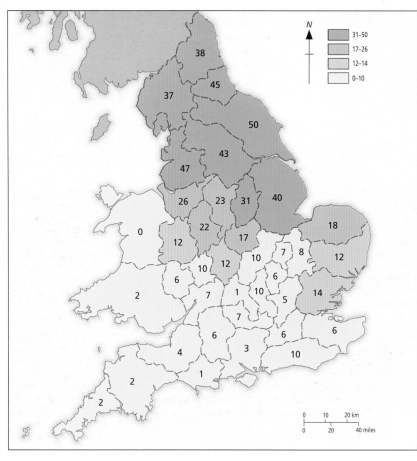

SURVIVAL OF THE FITTEST?

With two cultures in such close contact for so long, a large number of duplicate words must have arisen, both Old Norse (ON) and Old English (OE) providing ways of describing the same objects or situations. It is hardly ever possible in such cases to explain why one word proves to be fitter than another to survive. All we know is that there is evidence of three subsequent developments.

ON 1 OE 0

Sometimes the Scandinavian word was kept. This is what happened with *egg* vs *ey* (OE), *sister* vs *sweostor* (OE), *silver* vs *seolfor* (OE), and many more.

ON 0 OE 1

In other cases, the Old English word stayed, as in *path* vs *reike* (ON), *sorrow* vs *site* (ON), *swell* vs *bolnen* (ON), and also many more.

The linguistic situation must have been quite confusing at times, especially when people travelled about the country, and were uncertain about which form to use (as shown by William Caxton's famous story about the words for 'egg', p. 58).

ON 1 OE 1

In several cases, both words have been retained. For this to happen, of course, the two words would need to develop a useful difference in meaning. These cases include:

ON	OE
dike	ditch
hale	whole (p. 22)
raise	rise
scrub	shrub
sick	ill
skill	craft
skin	hide
skirt	shirt

In many cases, one form has become standard, and the other kept in a regional dialect:

garth	yard
kirk	church
laup	leap
nay	no
trigg	true

Vocabulary then and now

It should be plain from pp. 22–3 that there are many differences between the way vocabulary was used in Old English and the way it is used today. The Anglo-Saxons' preference for expressions which are synonymous, or nearly so, far exceeds that found in Modern English, as does their ingenuity in the use of compounds. The absence of a wide-ranging vocabulary of loan words also forced them to rely on a process of lexical construction using native elements, which produced much larger 'families' of morphologically related words than are typical of English now.

A great deal of the more sophisticated lexicon, we must also conclude, was consciously created, as can be seen from the many *loan translations* (or *calques*) which were introduced in the later period. Calques are lexical items which are translated part-by-part into another language. The process is unusual in Modern English – an example is *superman*, which is a translation of German *Übermensch*. In late Old English, by contrast, calques are very common, as can be seen from the following examples.

praepositio 'preposition' > *foresetnys*
coniunctio 'joining' > *geðeodnys*
episcopatus 'episcopate' > *biscophad*
significatio 'signification' > *getacnung*
unicornis 'unicorn' > *anhorn*
aspergere 'sprinkle' > *onstregdan*
inebriare 'make drunk' > *indrencan*
trinitas 'trinity' > *þriness*
contradictio 'contradiction' > *wiðcwedennis*
comparativus 'comparative' > *wiðmetendlic*

Ælfric is one who used them widely in his writing, especially when developing the terminology of his *Grammar* (p. 16).

Wiðmetennis

A final comparison. There are, it is thought, around 24,000 different lexical items (§8) in the Old English corpus. This lexicon, however, is fundamentally different from the one we find in Modern English. About 85 per cent of Old English words are no longer in use. Moreover, only 3 per cent of the words in Old English are loan words, compared with over 70 per cent today. Old English vocabulary was thus profoundly Germanic, in a way that is no longer the case. Nearly half of Modern English general vocabulary comes from Latin or French, as a result of the huge influx of words in the Middle English period (p. 46). And the readiness to absorb foreign elements has given the modern language a remarkable etymological variety which was totally lacking in Old English. It is this situation, indeed, which latter-day Anglo-Saxonist language reformers find intolerable (p. 125).

FRENCH BEFORE 1066

French vocabulary influenced Middle English so markedly after the Norman Conquest (p. 30) that it is easy to ignore the fact that French loan words can be found in Old English too. Indeed, it would be surprising if there had been no such influence, given the close contacts which had grown up in the 10th and 11th centuries. The monastic revival (p. 24), in particular, had started in France, and many English monks must have studied there.

Above all, there was close contact between the two cultures following the exile to Normandy of Edward the Confessor, the son of Æthelred II (the *unræd*, or 'ill-advised') and Emma, daughter of the Duke of Normandy. Edward lived there for 25 years, returning to England in 1041 with many French courtiers. When he succeeded to the throne, several of the French nobles were given high positions – a source of considerable grievance among their Anglo-Saxon counterparts.

Whatever the political consequences of these events, the linguistic consequences were a handful of French loan words, among them *capun* 'capon', *servian* 'serve', *bacun* 'bacon', *arblast* 'weapon', *prisun* 'prison', *castel* 'castle', and *cancelere* 'chancellor'. Some words gave rise to related forms, notably *prud* 'proud', whose derivatives included *prutness* 'pride' and *ofer-* *prut* 'haughty' (compare earlier *ofermod*, p. 22).

Old Saxon

One other language provided a small number of loan words – that spoken by the Saxons who had remained on the continent of Europe. It is known that copies of Old Saxon texts were being made in southern England during the 10th century. A personage known as John the Old Saxon helped Alfred in his educational reforms. There also exists a passage translated in the 9th century from Old Saxon and embedded within the Old English poem *Genesis* (and known as *Genesis B*). In it we find such forms as *hearra* 'lord', *sima* 'chain', *landscipe* 'region', *heodæg* 'today', and a few others, all of which are thought to be Old Saxon. These words had no real effect on later English, but they do illustrate the readiness of the Anglo-Saxons to take lexical material from all available sources – a feature which has characterized the language ever since.

EDWARDVS REX. ANGLIÆ

THE LORD'S PRAYER

The predominantly Germanic character of Old English vocabulary is well illustrated by the standard version of the 'Our Father'. (Long vowels are shown, as an aid to pronunciation: see p. 18.)

Fæder ūre,
þū þe eart on heofonum,
sī þīn nama gehālgod.
Tō becume þīn rīce.
Gewurþe ðīn willa on eorðan swā swā on heofonum.
Ūrne gedæghwāmlīcan hlāf syle ūs tō dæg.
And forgyf ūs ūre gyltas, swā swā wē forgyfað ūrum gyltendum.
And ne gelæd þū ūs on costnunge,
ac ālȳs ūs of yfele. Amen

OLD ENGLISH DIALECTS

The Old English texts which have survived come from several parts of the country, and from the way they are written they provide evidence of dialects. As there was no standardized system of spelling (p. 16), scribes tended to spell words as they sounded; but because everyone used the same Latin-based alphabetic system, there was an underlying consistency, and it is possible to use the spellings to work out dialect differences. For example, in the south-east, the word for 'evil' was written *efel*, whereas in other places it was *yfel*, suggesting that the latter vowel was unrounded and more open (p. 238). Hundreds of such spelling differences exist.

Most of the Old English corpus is written in the West Saxon dialect (see map), reflecting the political and cultural importance of this area in the 10th century. Dialects from other areas are very sparsely represented, with only about a dozen texts of any substance – inscriptions, charters, glosses, and verse fragments – spread over a 300-year period. Nonetheless, Old English scholars have found a few diagnostic features which enable us to identify dialect areas.

The historical setting

The major areas are traditionally thought to relate to the settlements of the invading tribes, with their different linguistic backgrounds; but what happened in the 300 years after the invasions is obscure. There is evidence of at least 12 kingdoms in England by the year 600. Seven are traditionally called the *Anglo-Saxon Heptarchy* (Northumbria, Mercia, East Anglia, Kent, Essex, Sussex, Wessex), but it is difficult to know what realities underlie such a grouping. From a linguistic point of view, only three kingdoms emerged with enough power for there to be clear dialectal consequences: Northumbria, in the 7th century, then Mercia, and by the 9th century Wessex, the latter emerging under King Egbert (ruled 802–39). These three areas, along with Kent (whose early importance is suggested by the Augustine story, p. 10) have led to the recognition of four major dialects in Old English.

To talk about regional dialects at all is somewhat daring, given that the areas are so approximate, and the texts are so few. Indeed, regional definition may not be the best approach, given the political and religious situation of the time. Social and literary factors may have been paramount. Because the writing of manuscripts was in the hands of monastic copyists, and copies (as well as the copyists) travelled between centres, dialect features would appear outside a particular geographical region. The use of a 'koiné' of poetic conventions may have been widespread. Manuscripts with 'mixed' dialect features are thus common.

The chief dialect areas of Old English. The map also shows some of the more important Anglo-Saxon kingdoms known from the early period, and their approximate locations.

DIALECT SIGNPOSTS

Old English dialectology is a complex subject, full of meticulous description, cautious generalization, tabulated exception, and (given the limited evidence) controlled frustration. There are no single indicators which will definitively locate a text. Rather, dialect work involves comparing a large number of possible diagnostic signposts, and drawing a conclusion on the basis of the direction to which most of them seem to be pointing. Given the realities of scribal error and dialect mixture, it is not uncommon to find a text pointing in several directions at once.

Some examples of signposts:

• If you see a manuscript form with the spelling *ie*, this is likely to be a West Saxon text, with the symbol representing a diphthong. In other dialects there would be a pure vowel. Example: 'yet' would be *giet* in West Saxon, but *get* elsewhere.

• If you see an *o* before a nasal consonant (*m, n, ng*), it is probably a Northumbrian or Mercian text. (Compare the Scots pronunciation of *mon* for *man* today.) Example: 'land' would be *land* in West Saxon and Kentish, but *lond* further north.

• If you see the personal pronouns *mec, usic, þec,* and *eowic* instead of *me, us, þe,* and *eow* (p. 20), the text is likely to be Northumbrian or Mercian. Example: see the *Lord's Prayer* on p. 27.

The chief dialect divisions

The area originally occupied by the Angles gave rise to two main dialects:

• *Northumbrian* was spoken north of a line running approximately between the Humber and Mersey rivers. It extended into the eastern lowlands of present-day Scotland, where it confronted the Celtic language of the Strathclyde Britons. A period of Northumbrian political power in the late 7th century made the north a cultural centre, with several monasteries (notably, Wearmouth and Jarrow) and the work of Bede pre-eminent. Most of the earliest Old English texts (7th–8th century) are Northumbrian, as a result. They include Cædmon's Hymn (see opposite), Bede's Death Song, the Ruthwell Cross and the Franks Casket inscriptions (p. 9), a short poem known as the *Leiden Riddle*, a few glosses, and the 6,000 or so names of people and places in Bede's *Ecclesiastical History* (p. 7).

• *Mercian* was spoken in the Midlands, roughly between the River Thames and the River Humber, and as far west as the boundary with present-day Wales. Very few linguistic remains exist, presumably because of the destructive influence of the Vikings. The chief texts are various charters, a famous gloss to the Vespasian Psalter, and a few other Latin glossaries. The chief period of Mercian power was the early 8th century, but many later West Saxon texts show the influence of Mercian, partly because several scholars from this area (e.g. Werferth) were enlisted by King Alfred to help the literary renaissance he inspired.

• *Kentish*, spoken in the area of Jutish settlement, was used mainly in present-day Kent and the Isle of Wight. There is very little extant material – a few charters of the 8th–9th centuries, a psalm, a hymn, and sporadic glosses. Scholars have also made some further deductions about this dialect from the way it developed in Middle English (p. 50), where there is more material.

• The rest of England, south of the Thames and west as far as Cornwall (where Celtic was also spoken) was settled by (West) Saxons, and became known as Wessex. Most of the Old English corpus is written in the Wessex dialect, *West Saxon*, because it was this kingdom, under King Alfred, which became the leading political and cultural force at the end of the 9th century. However, it is one of the ironies of English linguistic history that modern Standard English is descended not from West Saxon, but from Mercian, which was the dialect spoken in the area around London when that city became powerful in the Middle Ages (pp. 41, 50).

CÆDMON'S HYMN

The version of Cædmon's hymn (p. 20) usually printed is in literary late West Saxon, and the text here is from an 11th-century manuscript. However, a Northumbrian version has also survived in an 8th-century manuscript, which is thus very close to the language Bede himself must have used. The differences are very evident, though in only one case (l. 3) does an important variant reading occur.

West Saxon	**Northumbrian**
Nu we sceolan herigean heofonrices weard,	Nu scylun hergan hefaenricaes uard,
metodes mihte ⁊ his modgeþanc,	metudæs maecti end his modgidanc,
wera wuldorfæder, swa he wuldres gehwæs,	uerc uuldurfadur, sue he uundra gihuaes,
ece drihten, ord onstealde.	eci dryctin, or astelidæ.
He æres[t] gescop eorðan bearnum,	He aerist scop aelda barnum,
heofon to rofe, halig scyppend;	heben til hrofe, haleg scepen;
þa middangeard moncynnes weard,	tha middungeard moncynnes uard,
ece drihten, æfter teode,	eci dryctin, æfter tiadæ,
firum foldan, frea ælmihtig.	firum foldu, frea allmectig.

Now we shall praise the keeper of the heavenly kingdom,
the power of the lord of destiny and his imagination,
the glorious father of men,
the deeds of the glorious father, } *when of every glorious thing*
he, the eternal lord, ordained the beginning.
He first shaped for the children of earth
the heaven as a roof, the holy creator;
then the guardian of mankind, the eternal lord,
afterwards made middle-earth;
the almighty lord (made) land for living beings.

WS fæder ure þu þe eart on heofonum
No. fader urer ðu art in heofnu(m)
Me. feder ure þu eart in heofenum
  'father our thou (which) art in heaven'

The opening line from a West Saxon (WS, late 11th century), Northumbrian (No., late 10th century), and Mercian (Me., early 10th century) version of the Lord's Prayer illustrates two of the important dialect features of Old English. (After T. E. Toon, 1992.)

• 'father' The original Germanic vowel has come forward in WS, and even further forward in Me., but has stayed back in No.
• 'art' WS and Me. have developed a diphthong before [r] and a following consonant. This has not happened in No., where the vowel has stayed low, and also moved further back.

This extract also shows how not all the variations found in a comparison of manuscripts should be interpreted as dialectal.

• The use of letter 'eth' rather than 'thorn' in the words for 'thou' is not a dialect matter, as these symbols were often interchangeable (p.16).
• It is not possible to read much into the different spellings of the unstressed syllable of 'heaven', as the sound quality would have been indeterminate (just as it is in Modern English) and the spelling unsystematic.
• There is insufficient dialect evidence in the Old English corpus to draw any firm conclusions from the grammatical variations.

Of course, when we first examine a manuscript, we have to work such things out for ourselves. We are not given the information in advance. Every variant form is a possible signpost. Finding out which lead somewhere and which do not is what makes Old English dialectology so engrossing. And the story is by no means over, for there are many dialect questions which remain to be answered.

4 · MIDDLE ENGLISH

The year 1066 marks the beginning of a new social and linguistic era in Britain, but it does not actually identify the boundary between Old and Middle English. It was a long time before the effects of the Norman invasion worked their way into the language, and Old English continued to be used meanwhile. Even a century later, texts were still being composed in the West Saxon variety that had developed in the years following the reign of King Alfred (p. 29).

The period we call Middle English runs from the beginning of the 12th century until the middle of the 15th. It is a difficult period to define and discuss, largely because of the changes taking place between the much more distinctive and identifiable worlds of Old English (§3) and Modern English (§§5–6). The manuscripts give an impression of considerable linguistic variety and rapid transition. Also, the gradual decay of Anglo-Saxon traditions and literary practices, overlapping with the sudden emergence of French and Latin literacy, gives much of this period an elusive and unfocused character. It is not until 1400 that a clear focus emerges, in the work of Chaucer, but by then the period is almost over. Chaucer himself, indeed, is more often seen as a forerunner of Modern English poetry than as a climax to Middle English.

The rise of French

The main influence on English was, of course, French – strictly, Norman French, the language introduced to Britain by the invader. Following William of Normandy's accession, French was rapidly established in the corridors of power. French-speaking barons were appointed, who brought over their own retinues. Soon after, French-speaking abbots and bishops were in place. Lanfranc, Abbot of St Stephen's at Caen, was made Archbishop of Canterbury as early as 1070. Within 20 years of the invasion, almost all the religious houses were under French-speaking superiors, and several new foundations were solely French. Large numbers of French merchants and craftsmen crossed the Channel to take advantage of the commercial opportunities provided by the new regime. And aristocratic links remained strong with Normandy, where the nobles kept their estates.

Doubtless bilingualism quickly flourished among those who crossed the social divide – English people learning French in order to gain advantages from the aristocracy, and baronial staff learning English as part of the daily contact with local communities. But there is hardly any sign of English being used among the new hierarchy – a situation which was to continue for over a century.

DOMESDAY

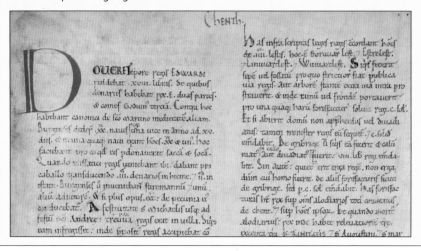

A detail from the opening folio of Great Domesday, the larger of the two volumes which make up the Domesday Book, the survey of English land compiled by William I in 1086. It is written in Latin, but it is of value to the English language historian for the information it provides about English personal names and (to a lesser extent) place names. The spelling, however, is troublesome, for the scribes used Latin conventions which were an inadequate means of representing English sounds.

OUI, THREE KINGS

Most of the Anglo-Norman kings were unable to communicate at all in English – though it is said some used it for swearing. However, by the end of the 14th century, the situation had changed. Richard II addressed the people in English during the Peasants' Revolt (1381). Henry IV's speeches at Richard's deposition were made in English. And Henry's will was written in English (1413) – the first royal will to be so.

William I (1066–87) spent about half his reign in France, in at least five of those years not visiting England at all; according to the chronicler Ordericus Vitalis, he tried to learn English at the age of 43, but gave up.

William II (1087–1100) spent about half his reign in France; his knowledge of English is not known.

Henry I (1100–35) spent nearly half his reign in France, often several years at a time; the only king to have an English wife until Edward IV (1461–83), he may have known some English.

And later?

Stephen (1135–54) was kept in England through civil strife (p. 33); his knowledge of English is not known.

Henry II (1154–89) spent a total of 20 years in France; he understood English, but did not speak it.

Richard I (1189–99) spent only a few months in England; he probably spoke no English.

John (1199–1216) lived mainly in England after 1204; the extent of his English is not known.

William I

William II

Henry I

The rise of English

During the 12th century, English became more widely used among the upper classes, and there was an enormous amount of intermarriage with English people. The largely monolingual French-speaking court was not typical of the rest of the country. Richard Fitz Neal's *Dialogus de Scaccario* ('A Dialogue on the Exchequer'), written in 1177, reports:

Now that the English and Normans have been dwelling together, marrying and giving in marriage, the two nations have become so mixed that it is scarcely possible today, speaking of free men, to tell who is English, who of Norman race.

By the end of the 12th century, contemporary accounts suggest that some children of the nobility spoke English as a mother tongue, and had to be taught French in school. French continued to be used in Parliament, the courts, and in public proceedings, but we know that translations into English increased in frequency throughout the period, as did the number of handbooks written for the teaching of French.

From 1204, a different political climate emerged. King John of England came into conflict with King Philip of France, and was obliged to give up control of Normandy. The English nobility lost their estates in France, and antagonism grew between the two countries, leading ultimately to the Hundred Years War (1337–1453). The status of French diminished as a spirit of English nationalism grew, culminating in the Barons' War (1264–5). In 1362, English was used for the first time at the opening of Parliament. By about 1425 it appears that English was widely used in England, in writing as well as in speech.

Reasons for survival

How had the language managed to survive the French invasion? After all, Celtic had not survived the Anglo-Saxon invasions 500 years before (p. 8). Evidently the English language in the 11th century was too well established for it to be supplanted by another language. Unlike Celtic, it had a considerable written literature and a strong oral tradition. It would have taken several hundred years of French immigration, and large numbers of immigrants, to have changed things – but the good relations between England and France lasted for only 150 years, and some historians have estimated that the number of Normans in the country may have been as low as 2 per cent of the total population.

This 150 years, nonetheless, is something of a 'dark age' in the history of the language. There is hardly any written evidence of English, and we can thus only speculate about what was happening to the language during that period. Judging by the documents which have survived, it seems that French was the language of government, law, administration, literature, and the Church, with Latin also used in administration, education, and worship. The position of English becomes clearer in the 13th century, when we find an increasing number of sermons, prayers, romances, songs, and other documents. Finally, in the 14th century, we have the major achievements of Middle English literature, culminating in the writing of Geoffrey Chaucer (p. 38).

THE ONOMASTIC CONQUEST

A modern drawing of Southampton, Hampshire, c. 1500. At that time, one of the two most important streets of the town was called French Street (it is the middle of the three thoroughfares running north–south), evidently a location for many French merchants and settlers. Several other towns in the south showed early influence of French settlement.

One way of trying to plot French influence in the period is through the analysis of baptismal names (see the discussion of onomastics, p. 140). Native pre-Conquest names were chiefly West Germanic (p. 6), but showed the influence of Scandinavian in the Danelaw, and also of Celtic in the border areas – *Godwine, Egbert, Alfred, Wulfric, Haraldr, Eadric*, and the like. Within a century of the Conquest, most of these had been replaced by such names as *John, Peter, Simon*, and *Stephen*. A Canterbury survey made in the 1160s shows that 75 per cent of the men had Continental names. And the history of English naming has reflected this influence ever since.

ALL UNDERSTAND THE ENGLISH TONGUE

Contemporary writers sometimes provide insights into the linguistic state of the nation. A much-quoted example is from William of Nassyngton's *Speculum Vitae* or *Mirror of Life* (c. 1325). Although some who have lived at court do know French, he says, nobody now knows only French. Everyone, whatever their learning, knows English. (For grammatical endings, see p. 44; spelling conventions, see p. 40. The extract uses two earlier English symbols (p. 14): thorn, þ, later replaced by *th*, and yogh, ȝ, later replaced by *y*. Modern *u* is written *v*, and vice versa.)

In English tonge I schal ȝow telle,
ȝif ȝe wyth me so longe wil dwelle.
No Latyn wil I speke no [*nor*] waste,
But English, þat men vse mast [*most*],
Þat can eche [*each*] man vnderstande,
Þat is born in Ingelande;
For þat langage is most chewyd [*shown*]
Os [*as*] wel among lered [*learned*] os lewyd [*unlearned*].
Latyn, as I trowe [*believe*] can nane [*know none*]
But þo [*except those*] þat haueth it in scole tane [*school taken*],
And somme can [*some know*] Frensche and no Latyn,
þat vsed han [*have*] cowrt [*court*] and dwellen þerein,
And somme can of Latyn a party [*part*]
Þat can of Frensche but febly [*feebly*];
And somme vnderstonde wel Englysch,
Þat can noþer [*neither*] Latyn nor Frankys [*Frankish, i.e. French*].
Boþe lered and lewed, olde and ȝonge,
Alle vnderstonden english tonge.

THE TRANSITION FROM OLD ENGLISH

A fundamental change in the structure of English took place during the 11th and 12th centuries – one without precedent in the history of the language, and without parallel thereafter. Grammatical relationships in Old English had been expressed chiefly by the use of inflectional endings (p. 20). In Middle English, they came to be expressed (as they are today) chiefly by word order. Why did this change take place? Few subjects in the history of English have attracted so much speculation.

The decay of inflections

About one fact there is no doubt. There are clear signs during the Old English period of the decay of the inflectional system. The surviving texts suggest that the change started in the north of the country, and slowly spread south. Several of the old endings are still present in the 12th-century text of the *Peterborough Chronicle* opposite, but they are not used with much consistency, and they no longer seem to play an important role in conveying meaning.

But why did the Old English inflectional endings decay? The most obvious explanation is that it became increasingly difficult to hear them, because of the way words had come to be stressed during the evolution of the Germanic languages (p. 6). The ancestor language of Germanic, Indo-European, had a 'free' system of accentuation, in which the stress within a word moved according to intricate rules (p. 248). In Germanic, this system changed, and most words came to carry the main stress on their first syllable. This is the system found throughout Old English. As always, there were exceptions – the *ge-* prefix, for example (p. 21), is never stressed.

Having the main stress at the beginning of a word can readily give rise to an auditory problem at the end. This is especially so when there are several endings which are phonetically very similar, such as *-en*, *-on*, and *-an*. In rapid conversational speech it would have been difficult to distinguish them. The situation is not too far removed from that which still obtains in Modern English, where people often make such forms as *-ible* and *-able* (*visible*, *washable*) or *Belgian* and *Belgium* sound the same. This 'neutralization' of vowel qualities undoubtedly affected the Old English system.

The contact situation

However, auditory confusion cannot be the sole reason. Other Germanic languages had a strong initial stress, too, yet they retained their inflectional system (as is still seen in modern German). Why was the change so much greater in English? Some scholars cite the Viking settlement as the decisive factor (p. 25). During the period of the Danelaw, they argue, the contact between English and Scandinavian would have led to the emergence of a pidgin-like variety of speech between the two cultures, and perhaps even eventually to a kind of creole which was used as a lingua franca (p. 344). As with pidgins everywhere, there would have been a loss of word endings, and greater reliance on word order. Gradually, this pattern would have spread until it affected the whole of the East Midlands area – from which Standard English was eventually to emerge (p. 50). At the very least, they conclude, this situation would have accelerated the process of inflectional decay – and may even have started it.

Whether such arguments are valid depends on how far we believe that the speakers of Old English and Old Norse were unable to understand each other at the time, and this is largely a matter of speculation. Perhaps there existed a considerable degree of mutual intelligibility, given that the two languages had diverged only a few hundred years before. The roots of many words were the same, and in the Icelandic sagas it is said that the Vikings and the English could understand each other. Whatever the case, we can tell from the surviving Middle English texts that the Danelaw was a much more progressive area, linguistically speaking, than the rest of the country. Change which began here affected southern areas later. Some form of Viking influence cannot easily be dismissed.

As inflections decayed, so the reliance on word order became critical, resulting in a grammatical system which is very similar to that found today. There is no sign in the *Peterborough Chronicle* extract of the Old English tendency to put the object before the verb, for example (p. 44). The Subject–Verb–Object order, already a noticeable feature of Old English, has become firmly established by the beginning of the Middle English period.

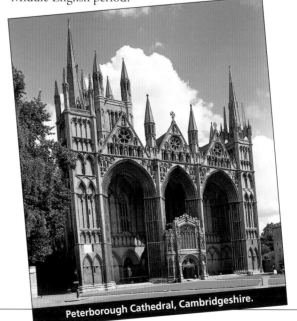

Peterborough Cathedral, Cambridgeshire.

INFLECTIONAL CARRYING POWER

This is a list of the most important endings in Old English regular nouns and verbs (p. 20), along with one lexical example of each. All endings which consisted of just a vowel, or a vowel plus nasal, disappeared from the language during the Middle English period. The only endings to survive were the ones with greater carrying power – the high-pitched *-s* forms (*kings, king's, lovest*), the *-th* forms (*loveth*, later replaced by *-s*, p. 44), and the distinctive *-ende* of the participle (later replaced by *-ing*, p. 45) and past tense.

Nouns
(*cyning* 'king', *scip* 'ship', *glof* 'glove', *guma* 'man')

-e, -n (acc. sg.) *glofe, guman*
-es, -e, -n (gen. sg.) *cyninges, glofe, guman*
-e, -n (dat. sg.) *cyninge, guman*
-as, -u, -a (nom. pl.) *cyningas, scipu, glofa*
-n, -as, -u, -a (acc. pl.) *guman, cyningas, scipu, glofa*
-a, -ena, (gen. pl.) *cyninga, glofa, gumena*
-um (dat. pl.) *cyningum, glofum, gumum*

Verbs
(*fremman* 'perform', *lufian* 'love', *deman* 'judge')

-e (1 sg. pres. ind.)
 fremme, lufie, deme
-est, -ast, -st (2 sg. pres. ind.)
 fremest, lufast, demst
-eð, -að, -ð (3 sg. pres. ind.)
 fremeð, lufað, demð
-að (1–3 pl. pres. ind.)
 fremmað, lufiað, demað
-e (1–3 sg. pres. subj.)
 fremme, lufie, deme
-en (1–3 pl. pres. subj.)
 fremmen, lufien, demen
-de (1 & 3 sg. past ind.)
 fremede, lufode, demde
-dest (2 sg. past ind.)
 fremedest, lufodest, demdest
-don (1–3 pl. past ind.)
 fremedon, lufodon, demdon
-de (1–3 sg. past subj.)
 fremede, lufode, demde
-den (1–3 pl. past subj.)
 fremeden, lufoden, demden
-ende (pres. part.)
 fremmende, lufiende, demende

Abbreviations (see Part III)
acc. accusative; *dat.* dative; *gen.* genitive; *ind.* indicative; *nom.* nominative; *part.* participle; *pl.* plural; *pres.* present tense; *sg.* singular; *subj.* subjunctive; *1, 2, 3* 1st, 2nd, 3rd person.

THE *PETERBOROUGH CHRONICLE*

We are fortunate to have the later years of the Anglo-Saxon Chronicle (p. 14), which continues to the middle of the 12th century, to illustrate this period of change. In 1116, most of the monastery at Peterborough was destroyed by fire, along with many manuscripts. The monks immediately began to replace the writings which had been lost. They borrowed the text of the Chronicle from another monastery, copied it out, and then carried on writing the history themselves. They continued until 1131, but then the writing stopped – doubtless because of the chaotic conditions of civil war which existed in the reign of King Stephen, some of which are described in the extract below.

This extract is from the Chronicle when it begins again in 1154, after the death of Stephen, adding several events from the intervening years. The language is now quite different. Despite points of similarity with the previous work, the overall impression is that the writer is starting again, using vocabulary and grammatical patterns which reflect the language of his time and locality, and inventing fresh spelling conventions to cope with new sounds. The extract has been set out in a word-for-word translation, but (unlike the Old English extract about Cædmon on p. 20), it is no longer necessary to add a free translation as well. Apart from a few phrases, the language now seems much closer to Modern English.

The later material from the *Peterborough Chronicle* looks back towards Old English and ahead towards Middle English. Scholars have indeed argued at length about whether it is best to call it 'late Old English' or 'early Middle English'. Some stress the archaic features of the text, pointing to similarities with the West Saxon dialect of Old English (p. 29); others stress the differences, and consider it to be the earliest surviving Middle English text. The Chronicle illustrates very clearly the difficulty of drawing a sharp boundary between different stages in the development of a language. But it does not take much longer before the uncertainty is resolved. Other texts from the 12th century confirm the new direction in which the language was moving; and within a century of the close of the Chronicle, there is no doubt that a major change has taken place in the structure of English. (The first twelve lines of the illustration are transcribed and translated below.)

Oxford, Bodleian Library, MS Laud Misc. 636, fol. 89 v.

[Me dide   cnotted strenges abuton here] hæued and
[One placed knotted cords   about   their] head   and

uurythen it ðat it gæde   to þe hærnes. Hi diden
twisted   it that it entered to the brains.   They put

heom in quarterne þar   nadres and snakes and pades
them in cell   where adders and snakes and toads

wæron inne, and drapen heom swa. Sume hi   diden in
were   in,   and killed them so. Some they put   in

5 crucethus,   ðat is in an ceste þat was scort, and nareu,
torture-box,   that is in a chest that was short, and narrow,

and undep, and dide scærpe stanes þerinne, and
and shallow, and put sharp   stones therein, and

þrengde þe man þær-inne, ðat him bræcon   alle þe limes.
pressed the man therein,   that   they broke all the limbs.

In mani of þe castles wæron lof   and grin, ðat
In many of the castles were   headband and halter, that

wæron rachenteges ðat twa oþer thre men hadden onoh
were   fetters   that two or three men had   enough

10 to bæron onne; þat was sua maced, ðat is fæstned to an
to bear   one; that was so made,   that is fastened to a

beom, and diden an scærp iren abuton þa mannes throte
beam, and put   a sharp iron about the man's   throat

and his hals, ðat he ne myhte nowiderwardes, ne   sitten
and his neck, that he not might in no direction,   neither sit

ne lien ne slepen, oc bæron al ðat iren. Mani
nor lie nor sleep, but bear   all that iron. Many

þusen hi drapen mid   hungær.
thousand they killed by means of hunger.

15 I ne can   ne I ne mai tellen alle þe wunder ne alle þe
I not know nor I not can tell   all the atrocities nor all the

pines ðat hi diden wreccemen   on   þis land, and ðat
cruelties that they did to wretched people in this land, and that

lastede þa xix wintre wile Stephne was king, and æure   it was
lasted   the 19 winters while Stephen   was king, and always it was

uuerse and uuerse.
worse   and worse.

THE MIDDLE ENGLISH CORPUS

The Middle English period has a much richer documentation than is found in Old English (p. 10). This is partly the result of the post-Conquest political situation. The newly centralized monarchy commissioned national and local surveys, beginning with the Domesday Book (p. 30), and there is a marked increase in the number of public and private documents – mandates, charters, contracts, tax-rolls, and other administrative or judicial papers. However, the early material is of limited value to those interested in the linguistic history of English because it is largely written in Latin or French, and the only relevant data which can be extracted relate to English place and personal names (§10). Most religious publication falls into the same category, with Latin maintaining its presence throughout the period as the official language of the Church. A major difference from Old English is the absence of a continuing tradition of historical writing in the native language, as in the Anglo-Saxon Chronicle – a function which Latin supplanted, and which was not revived until the 15th century.

Material in English appears as a trickle in the 13th century, but within 150 years it has become a flood. In the early period, we see a great deal of religious prose writing, in the form of homilies, tracts, lives of the saints, and other aids to devotion and meditation. Sometimes a text was written with a specific readership in mind; the *Ancrene Riwle* ('Anchorites' Guide'), for example, was compiled by a spiritual director for three noblewomen who had abandoned the world to live as anchoresses. During the 14th century, there is a marked increase in the number of translated writings from French and Latin, and of texts for teaching these languages (p. 31). Guild records, proclamations, proverbs, dialogues, allegories, and letters illustrate the diverse range of new styles and genres. Towards the end of the century, the translations of the Bible inspired by John Wycliff appear amid considerable controversy, and the associated movement produces many manuscripts (p. 54). Finally, in the 1430s, there is a vast output in English from the office of the London Chancery scribes, which strongly influenced the development of a standard written language (p. 41).

The poetic puzzle

Poetry presents a puzzle. The Anglo-Saxon poetic tradition apparently dies out in the 11th century, to reappear patchily in the 13th. A lengthy poetic history of Britain known as *Laȝamon's Brut* (p. 36) is one of the earliest works to survive from Middle English, and in the 14th century come the important texts of *Piers Plowman* and *Sir Gawain and the Green Knight* (p. 37). What is surprising is that the alliterative Old English style (p. 23) is still present in all these works, despite an apparent break in poetic continuity of at least a hundred years. The conundrum has generated much discussion. Perhaps the alliterative technique was retained through prose: several Middle English prose texts are strongly alliterative, and it is sometimes difficult to tell from a manuscript which genre (poetry or prose) a piece belongs to, because the line divisions are not shown. Perhaps the Old English style survived through the medium of oral transmission. Or perhaps it is simply that most poetic manuscripts have been lost.

Middle English poetry was inevitably much influenced by French literary traditions, both in content and style. One of the earliest examples is the 13th-century verse-contest known as *The Owl and the Nightingale* (p. 36). Later works include romances in the French style, secular lyrics, bestiaries, ballads, biblical poetry, Christian legends, hymns, prayers, and

 Ælfric abbod, þe we Alquin hoteþ, he was bocare, and þe fif bec wende, Genesis, Exodus, Vtronomius, Numerus, Leuiticus. þurh þeos weren ilærde ure leoden on Englisc. þet weren þeos biscopes þe bodeden Cristendom: Wilfrid of Ripum, Iohan of Beoferlai, Cuþbert of Dunholme, Oswald of Wireceastre, Egwin of Heoueshame, Ældelm of Malmesburi, Swithun, Æþelwold, Aidan, Biern of Wincæstre, Paulin of Rofecæstre, S. Dunston, and S. Ælfeih of Cantoreburi. þeos lærden ure leodan on Englisc. Næs deorc heore liht, ac hit fæire glod. Nu is þeo leore forleten, and þet folc is forloren…

elegies. The mystical dream-vision, popular in Italy and France, is well illustrated by the poem modern editors have called *Pearl*, in which the writer recalls the death of his two-year-old daughter, who then acts as his spiritual comforter. Drama also begins to make its presence felt, in the form of dialogues, pageants, and the famous cycles of mystery plays (p. 58).

Much of Middle English literature is of unknown authorship, but by the end of the period this situation has changed. Among the prominent names which emerge in the latter part of the 14th century are John Gower, William Langland, John Wycliff, and Geoffrey Chaucer, and some time later John Lydgate, Thomas Malory, William Caxton, and the poets who are collectively known as the Scottish Chaucerians (p. 53). Rather than a somewhat random collection of interesting texts, there is now a major body of 'literature', in the modern sense. It is this which provides the final part of the bridge between Middle and Early Modern English (§5).

Abbot Ælfric, whom we call Alquin, he was a writer, and translated five books, Genesis, Exodus, Deuteronomy, Numbers, Leviticus. Through these our people were taught in English. These were the bishops who preached Christianity: Wilfrid of Ripum, Iohan of Beoferlai, Cuthbert of Dunholme, Oswald of Wireceastre, Egwin of Heoueshame, Ældelm of Malmesburi, Swithun, Æthelwold, Aidan, Biern of Wincæstre, Paulin of Rofecæstre, S. Dunston, and S. Ælfeih of Cantoreburi. These taught our people in English. Their light was not dark, and it shone brightly. Now is this knowledge abandoned, and the people damned…

JOHN OF TREVISA

The Cornishman John of Trevisa (d. 1402), who became an Oxford scholar and clergyman, made in 1387 a translation of Ranulf Higden's Latin *Polychronicon* – so called because it was the chronicle of many ages, from the Creation to 1352. At one point, Higden reviews the language teaching situation in England, and gives two reasons for the decline of the mother tongue.

On ys for chyldern in scole, aȝenes þe vsage and manere of al oþer nacions, buþ compelled for to leue here oune longage, and for to construe here lessons and here þinges a Freynsch, and habbeþ suþthe þe Normans come furst into Engelond. Also gentil men children buþ ytauȝt for to speke Freynsch fram tyme þat a buþ yrokked in here cradel, and conneþ speke and playe wiþ a child hys brouch; and oplondysch men wol lykne hamsylf to gentil men, and fondeþ wiþ gret bysynes for to speke Freynsch, for to be more ytold of.

One [reason] is that children in school, contrary to the usage and custom of all other nations, are compelled to abandon their own language, and to carry on their lessons and their affairs in French, and have done since the Normans first came to England. Also the children of gentlemen are taught to speak French from the time that they are rocked in their cradle, and learn to speak and play with a child's trinket; and rustic men will make themselves like gentlemen, and seek with great industry to speak French, to be more highly thought of.

At this point, John of Trevisa adds the following:

Þys manere was moche y-vsed tofore þe furste moreyn, and ys seþthe somdel ychaunged. For Iohan Cornwal, a mayster of gramere, chayngede þe lore in gramerscole and construccion of Freynsch into Englysch; and Richard Pencrych lurnede þat manere techyng of hym, and oþer men of Pencrych, so þat now, þe ȝer of oure Lord a þousond þre hondred foure score and fyue, of þe secunde kyng Richard after þe Conquest nyne, in al þe gramerscoles of Engelond childern leueþ Frensch, and construeþ and lurneþ an Englysch, and habbeþ þerby avauntage in on syde, and desavantauge yn anoþer. Here avauntage ys þat a lurneþ here gramer yn lasse tyme þan childern wer ywoned to do. Desavauntage ys þat now childern of gramerscole conneþ no more Frensch þan can here lift heele, and þat ys harm for ham and a scholle passe þe se and trauayle in strange londes, and in meny caas also. Also gentil men habbeþ now moche yleft for to teche here childern Frensch.

Plus ça change…

This practice was much used before the first plague, and has since been somewhat changed. For John Cornwall, a teacher of grammar, changed the teaching in grammar school and the construing of French into English; and Richard Penkridge learned that method of teaching from him, and other men from Penkridge, so that now, AD 1385, the ninth year of the reign of the second King Richard after the Conquest, in all the grammar schools of England children abandon French, and compose and learn in English, and have thereby an advantage on the one hand, and a disadvantage on the other. The advantage is that they learn their grammar in less time than children used to do. The disadvantage is that nowadays children at grammar school know no more French than their left heel, and that is a misfortune for them if they should cross the sea and travel in foreign countries, and in other such circumstances. Also, gentlemen have now largely abandoned teaching their children French.

A PASTON LETTER

This is an extract from one of the collection of letters written by members of the Norfolk family of Paston during the 15th century. There are over a thousand items in the collection, dealing with everything from legal matters to domestic gossip, and written throughout in a natural and often vivid style. Most of the collection is now in the British Museum. The present example comes from a letter written 'in hast[e]' by Margaret Paston to her husband John on 19 May 1448, Trinity Sunday evening.

Ryght worshipfull husbond, I recomaund me to you, and prey yow to wete that on Friday last passed before noon, the parson of Oxened beyng at messe in oure parossh chirche, evyn atte levacion of the sakeryng, Jamys Gloys hadde ben in the toune and come homward by Wymondams gate. And Wymondam stod in his gate, and John Norwode his man stod by hym, and Thomas Hawys his othir man stod in the strete by the canell side. And Jamys Gloys come wyth his hatte on his hede betwen bothe his men, as he was wont of custome to do. And whanne Gloys was ayenst Wymondham, he seid thus: 'Covere thy heed!' And Gloys seid ageyn, 'So I shall for the.' And whanne Gloys was forther passed by the space of iii or iiii strede, Wymondham drew owt his dagger and seid, 'Shalt thow so, knave?' And therwith Gloys turned hym, and drewe owt his dagger and defendet hym, fleyng into my moderis place; and Wymondham and his man Hawys kest stonys and dreve Gloys into my moderis place, and Hawys folwyd into my moderis place and kest a ston as meche as a forthyng lof into the halle after Gloys, and than ran owt of the place ageyn. And Gloys folwyd owt and stod wythowt the gate, and thanne Wymondham called Gloys thef and seid he shuld dye, and Gloys seid he lyed and called hym charl, and bad hym come hym self or ell the best man he hadde, and Gloys wold answere hym on for on. And thanne Haweys ran into Wymondhams place and feched a spere and a swerd, and toke his maister his swerd. And wyth the noise of this asaut and affray my modir and I come owt of the chirche from the sakeryng, and I bad Gloys go into my moderis place ageyn, and so he dede. And thanne Wymondham called my moder and me strong hores, and seid the Pastons and alle her kyn were [*hole in paper*]… seid he lyed, knave and charl as he was. And he had meche large langage, as ye shall knowe herafter by mowthe.

My dear husband, I commend myself to you, and want you to know that, last Friday before noon, the parson of Oxnead was saying Mass in our parish church, and at the very moment of elevating the host, James Gloys, who had been in town, was coming home past Wyndham's gate. And Wyndham was standing in his gateway with his man John Norwood by his side, and his other man, Thomas Hawes, was standing in the street by the gutter. And James Gloys came with his hat on his head between both his men, as he usually did. And when Gloys was opposite Wyndham, Wyndham said 'Cover your head!' And Gloys retorted, 'So I shall for you!' And when Gloys had gone on three or four strides, Wyndham drew out his dagger and said, 'Will you, indeed, knave?' And with that Gloys turned on him, and drew out his dagger and defended himself, fleeing into my mother's place; and Wyndham and his man Hawes threw stones and drove Gloys into my mother's house, and Hawes followed into my mother's and threw a stone as big as a farthing-loaf into the hall at Gloys, and then ran out of the place again. And Gloys followed him out and stood outside the gate, and then Wyndham called Gloys a thief and said he had to die, and Gloys said he lied and called him a peasant, and told him to come himself or else the best man he had, and Gloys would answer him, one against one. And then Hawes ran into Wyndham's place and fetched a spear and a sword, and gave his master his sword. And at the noise of this attack and uproar my mother and I came out of the church from the sacrament, and I told Gloys to go into my mother's again, and he did so. And then Wyndham called my mother and me wicked whores, and said the Pastons and all her kin were (…) said he lied, knave and peasant that he was. And he had a great deal of broad language, as you shall hear later by word of mouth.

Such a story could have appeared in any modern tabloid. (The hole in the paper is fortuitous, and is unlikely to be an 'expletive deleted'.) The experience shocked Margaret, who 'wolde not for xl *li*. have suyche another trouble' ('wouldn't have another such disturbance happen for £40').

THE OWL AND THE NIGHTINGALE

This is the first example to appear in English of the debate verse form which was so popular in Europe during the 12th and 13th centuries. In the poem, the two speakers argue their views in the manner of a lawsuit. The work has become famous for its humour and irony, and for the lively way in which the characters of the two birds are portrayed. It displays a French-inspired scheme of four-beat lines in rhyming couplets. Its authorship has not been established, though the dialect represented is southern, and it was probably composed *c.* 1200. From a reference in the poem to a Master Nicholas of Guildford (who the birds agree should judge the debate), that area of Surrey has been suggested as a possible source. The following extracts are of the opening lines, and part of one of the nightingale's diatribes.

Ich was in one sumere dale,	*I was in a summer valley,*
In one suþe diȝele hale,	*In a very hidden corner,*
Iherde ich holde grete tale	*I heard holding a great argument*
An hule and one niȝtingale.	*An owl and a nightingale.*
Þat plait was stif an starc an strong,	*The dispute was fierce and violent and strong,*
Sum-wile softe an lud among;	*Sometimes soft and loud at intervals;*
An eiþer aȝen oþer sval,	*And each swelled in anger against the other,*
An let þat vuele mod ut al.	*And let out their bad temper.*
An eiþer seide of oþeres custe	*And each said of the other's qualities*
Þat alre-worste þat hi wuste …	*The worst things that they knew …*
An þu tukest wroþe an vuele,	*And you ill-treat cruelly and badly,*
Whar þu miȝt, over-smale fuȝele …	*Wherever you can, very small birds …*
Þu art lodlich to biholde,	*You are hateful to behold,*
An þu art loþ in monie volde;	*And you are hateful in many ways;*
Þi bodi is short, þi swore is smal,	*Your body is short, your neck is small,*
Grettere is þin heued þan þu al;	*Your head is bigger than the rest of you;*
Þin eȝene boþ colblake an brode,	*Your eyes both charcoal-black and wide,*
Riȝt swo ho weren ipeint mid wode …	*Just like they were painted with woad….*

THE CUCKOO SONG

This well-known song is one of several secular lyrics dating from *c.* 1225. It is one of a very few such lyrics which have musical notation in the manuscript (as well as an alternative religious text in Latin).

Svmer is icumen in,	*Summer has come in,*
Lhude sing cuccu!	*Loudly sing, cuckoo!*
Groweþ sed and bloweþ med	*The seed grows and the*
And springþ þe wde nu.	* meadow bursts into flower*
Sing cuccu!	*And the wood springs up now.*
	Sing, cuckoo!
Awe bleteþ after lomb,	*The ewe bleats after the lamb,*
Lhouþ after calue cu,	*The cow lows after the calf.*
Bulluc sterteþ, bucke uerteþ.	*The bullock leaps, the buck farts.*
Murie sing cuccu!	*Merry sing, cuckoo!*
Cuccu, cuccu,	*Cuckoo, cuckoo,*
Wel singes þu cuccu.	*You sing well, cuckoo.*
Ne swik þu nauer nu!	*Never cease you now!*

LAȜAMON'S BRUT

This is a poem of *c.* 16,000 lines telling the history of Britain from the landing of Brutus (the *Brut* of the title, the reputed founder of the Britons) to the last Saxon victory over the Britons in 689. It uses an alliterative line, showing the influence of Old English (p.11), and many of its themes reflect those of earlier Germanic times; but the approach was also much influenced by French chivalric romances. The text actually uses as a source a French verse chronicle, *Roman de Brut*, made by the 12th-century Anglo-Norman author, Wace.

Little is known of Laȝamon (modern spelling, Layamon), other than what he tells us in the opening lines of the work – that he was a parish priest of Ernleȝe (modern Areley Kings, Worcestershire). There are two extant manuscripts, both dating from the first half of the 13th century, and separated in time by about a generation. This has given scholars a rare chance to make a comparison, to see if the two versions throw some light on the way the language could have changed during that time.

The poem is written in long lines, divided into half-line groups, and a great deal of use is made of alliteration, rhyme, and other phonological features which give the units their structure (p. 415). A surprising feature of the text is that, despite being written 150 years after the Conquest, it has very few French loan words. It is likely that the poem's subject matter, much concerned with battles within the epic tradition, motivated Laȝamon to use an older vocabulary, associated more with the Old English period. However, there are no kennings in the text (p. 23). The later version also contains rather more French loans, suggesting that the scribe was to some extent trying to modernize the language. (Extracts and translation from N. Blake, 1992.)

Earlier version

Nu haueð Vortigernes cun Aurilien aquald.
nu þu ært al ane of aðele þine cunne.
Ah ne hope þu to ræde of heom þat liggeð dede.
ah þenc of þe seolðen seolðen þe beoð ȝiueþe.
for selde he aswint þe to him-seolue þencheð.
þv scalt wurðen god king & gumenene lauerd.
& þu to þere mid-nihte wepne þine cnihtes.
þat we i þan morȝen-liht mæȝen come forð-riht.

Later version

Nou haueþ Vortigerne his cun Aurelie acwelled.
nou hart þou al one of alle þine kunne.
Ac ne hope þou to reade of ham þat liggeþ deade.
ac þench ou þou miht þi-seolf þine kinedom werie.
for sealde he aswint þat to him-seolue tresteþ.
þou salt worþe god king and steorne þorh alle þing.
And þou at þare midniht wepne þine cnihtes.
þat þou at þan moreliht maȝe be a-redi to þe fiht.

Now that Vortigern's family has killed Aurilie,
you are the sole survivor of your family.
But do not expect any support from him who lies dead.
Put your trust in yourself that help is granted you,
for seldom is he disappointed who puts his trust in
* himself.*
You will become a worthy king and ruler of people.
And arm your followers at midnight
so that we may advance in the morning.

SIR GAWAIN AND THE GREEN KNIGHT

This story from Arthurian legend is an account of two adventures – the arrival of a green knight at Arthur's court and the challenge he issues, and the temptation of Sir Gawain, who takes up the challenge at the green knight's chapel. The story was probably written towards the end of the 14th century, and shows the influence of the French courtly tradition. The poem is written in a West Midland dialect, and there is some evidence from the language that it originated in south Lancashire. The manuscript, which contains three other poems written in the same neat angular hand, is now in the British Library. In the present extract, the editors have added modern capitalization and punctuation. (After J. R. R. Tolkien & E. V. Gordon, 1925.)

Siþen þe sege and þe assaut watȝ sesed at Troye,
Þe borȝ brittened and brent to brondeȝ and askeȝ,
Þe tulk þat þe trammes of tresoun þer wroȝt
Watȝ tried for his tricherie, þe trewest on erthe:
Hit watȝ Ennias þe athel and his highe kynde,
Þat siþen depreced prouinces, and patrounes bicome
Welneȝe of al þe wele in þe West Iles.
Fro riche Romulus to Rome ricchis hym swyþe,
With gret bobbaunce þat burȝe he biges vpon fyrst,
And neuenes hit his aune nome, as hit now hat;
Tirius to Tuskan and teldes bigynnes,
Langaberde in Lumbardie lyftes vp homes,
And fer ouer þe French flod Felix Brutus
On mony bonkkes ful brode Bretayn he setteȝ
                    with wynne,
Where werre and wrake and wonder
Bi syþeȝ hatȝ wont þerinne,
And oft boþe blysse and blunder
Ful skete hatȝ skyfted synne.

Ande quen þis Bretayn watȝ bigged bi þis burn rych,
Bolde bredden þerinne, baret þat lofden,
In mony turned tyme tene þat wroȝten.
Mo ferlyes on þis folde han fallen here oft
Þen in any oþer þat I wot, syn þat ilk tyme.
Bot of alle þat here bult of Bretaygne kynges
Ay watȝ Arthur þe hendest, as I haf herde telle.

Since the siege and the assault came to an end in Troy,
The city destroyed and burnt to brands and ashes,
The man who there devised the devices of treason
Was tried for his treachery, the truest on earth:
It was the noble Aeneas and his noble kindred
Who later subjugated provinces, and became lords
Of almost all the wealth in the Western Isles.
When noble Romulus quickly makes his way to Rome,
With great pomp that city he builds up first,
And names it with his own name, as it is now called;
Tirius founds buildings in Tuscany,
Langaberde builds up dwellings in Lombardy,
And far over the English Channel Felix Brutus
Upon many broad hillsides founds Britain with joy,

Where fighting and distress and wondrous deeds
At times have been found therein
And often both happiness and sadness
Have since then quickly alternated.

And when this Britain was founded by this noble man,
Bold men multiplied there, who loved fighting,
In many a later time who brought about harm.
More marvels in this land have often happened here
Than in any other that I know of, since that same time.
But of all of Britain's kings who dwelled here
Always was Arthur the noblest, as I have heard tell.

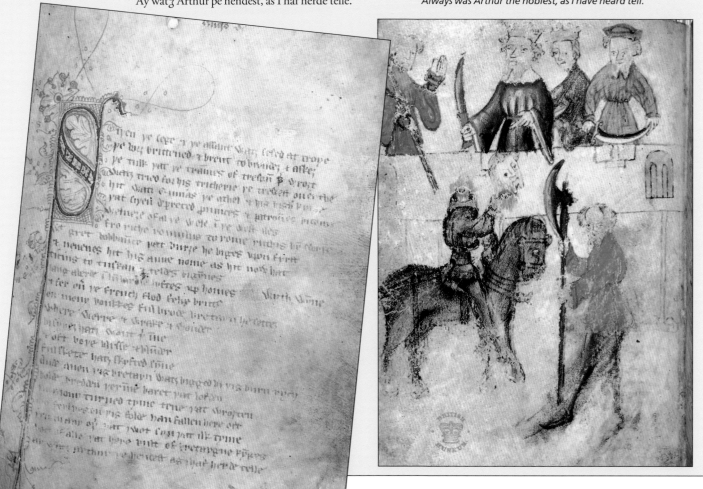

THE CHAUCERIAN ACHIEVEMENT

The tiny voice of this book can add nothing to the critical acclaim which has been given to Chaucer's poetic and narrative achievements, or to his insights into medieval attitudes and society; but it can affirm with some conviction the importance of his work to any history of the language. It is partly a matter of quantity – one complete edition prints over 43,000 lines of poetry, as well as two major prose works – but more crucial is the breadth and variety of his language, which ranges from the polished complexity of high-flown rhetoric to the natural simplicity of domestic chat. No previous author had shown such a range, and Chaucer's writing – in addition to its literary merits – is thus unique in the evidence it has provided about the state of medieval grammar, vocabulary, and pronunciation.

Chaucer's best-known work, *The Canterbury Tales*, is not of course a guide to the spoken language of the time: it is a variety of the written language which has been carefully crafted. It uses a regular metrical structure and rhyme scheme – itself a departure from the free rhythms and alliteration of much earlier poetry (p. 36). It contains many variations in word order, dictated by the demands of the prosody. There are also frequent literary allusions and turns of phrase which make the text difficult to follow. What has impressed readers so much is that, despite the constraints, Chaucer has managed to capture so vividly the intriguing characters of the speakers, and to reflect so naturally the colloquial features of their speech. In no other author, indeed, is there better support for the view that there is an underlying correspondence between the natural rhythm of English poetry and that of English everyday conversation (p. 412).

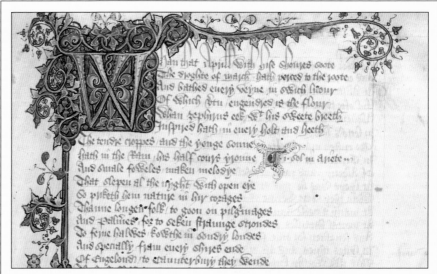

Whan that Aprille with hise shoures soote
When April with its sweet showers
'hwan θat 'aːprɪl ˌwɪθ hɪs 'ʃuːrəs 'soːtə

The droghte of March hath perced to the roote
has pierced the drought of March to the root
θə 'drʊxt of 'marʧ haθ 'persəd ˌtoː ðə 'roːtə

And bathed every veyne in swich licour
and bathed every vein in such liquid
and 'baːðəd 'ɛːvrɪ 'vɛɪn ɪn 'swɪʧ lɪ'kuːr

Of which vertu engendred is the flour
from which strength the flower is engendered;
of 'hwɪʧ vɛr'tiu enˈʤendred ˌɪs θə 'fluːr

5 Whan Zephirus eek with his sweete breeth
When Zephirus also with his sweet breath
hwan ˌzɛfɪ'rʊs ɛːk ˌwɪθ hɪs 'sweːtə 'breːθ

Inspired hath in euery holt and heeth
has breathed upon in every woodland and heath
ɪn'spiːrəd 'haθ ɪn 'ɛːvrɪ 'hɔlt and 'heːθ

The tendre croppes and the yonge sonne
the tender shoots, and the young sun
θə 'tɛndər 'krɔppəs ˌand ðə 'jʊŋgə 'sʊnnə

Hath in the Ram his half cours yronne
has run his half-course in the Ram,
'haθ ɪn ðə 'ram hɪs 'half 'kʊrs ɪ'rʊnnə

And smale fowules maken melodye
and small birds make melody
and 'smaːlə 'fuːləs 'maːkən ˌmɛloˈdiːə

10 That slepen al the nyght with open eye
that sleep all night with open eye
θat 'sleːpən 'aːl ðə 'niʧt wɪθ 'ɔːpən 'iːə

So priketh hem nature in hir corages
(so nature pricks them in their hearts);
sɔː 'prɪkəθ 'hem naːˈtiur ɪn 'hɪr kʊ'raːʤəs

Thanne longen folk to goon on pilgrimages…
then people long to go on pilgrimages…
θan 'lɔːŋgən 'fɔlk toː 'goːn ɔn ˌpɪlgrɪ'maːʤəs

(Phonetic transcription after A. C. Gimson, 1962.)

GEOFFREY CHAUCER (?1345–1400)

Chaucer provides us with an unparalleled insight into the speech and manners of medieval London, from gutter to court. Very little is known of his life, and what biographical information there is gives us no hint of his role as a writer.

He was born in the early or mid-1340s, the son of John Chaucer, a London vintner, who had some standing at court. In 1357 Geoffrey became a page in the service of the wife of Lionel, Duke of Clarence, and later joined the household of King Edward III. He served in the French campaign, was taken prisoner, and ransomed. In the mid-1360s he married the daughter of Sir Payne Roet, Philippa, through whose sister he was later linked by marriage to John of Gaunt.

By 1368 he was one of the king's esquires. He travelled widely on diplomatic missions abroad

during the 1370s, notably to Italy, and received several official appointments. In 1382 he was made comptroller of the Petty Customs, and in 1386 was elected a knight of the shire for Kent. He then lost his offices, probably as part of the political strife surrounding the authority of the young King Richard II, and fell into debt. In 1389, when Richard came of age, Chaucer was appointed Clerk of the King's Works, but in 1391 left this post, becoming deputy forester at Petherton in Somerset. In 1399 he took a lease of a house in the garden of Westminster Abbey, and died the following year. He was buried in the Abbey, and it is through this that part of the building came to be known as Poets' Corner.

His first poetry is the elegaic love-vision, *The Book of the Duchess*, written *c.* 1370 to commemorate the death of the wife of John of Gaunt. Other important works are the translation of part

of the French *Roman de la Rose*, the allegorical *Parliament of Fowls*, the love-vision *The House of Fame*, and the unfinished legendary, *The Legend of Good Women* – a tribute to classical heroines who suffered out of devotion to their lovers. His longest romance, *Troilus and Criseyde*, is the crowning work of his middle period. His visits to Italy were a major influence on both the style and content of his writing, as can be seen throughout the 24 stories of *The Canterbury Tales*. These, written over a period of at least a decade, but left unfinished, have been a continuing source of scholarly debate over their order and dating. No original manuscripts in Chaucer's hand have survived, but there are many copies of his works – over 80 of the *Tales* – which have kept generations of editors busy in the task of identifying and eradicating errors.

POETRY FOR THE EAR

'**D**elightful', 'enchanting', and 'beguiling' are just some of the terms critics have used to express their feelings about the opening lines of the Prologue to *The Canterbury Tales*. The lines unquestionably demonstrate Chaucer's great skill in poetic description, for, when we look carefully at their grammatical structure, they ought not to generate such responses at all. On the face of it, it is improbable that a term like 'enchanting' would ever be used of a sentence which begins with a four-line subordinate clause with a coordinate clause inside it, and which is immediately followed by a six-line subordinate clause with two more coordinate clauses inside it, and which also includes a relative clause and a parenthetical clause, before it reaches the main clause. Sentences with multiple embeddings (p. 227), such as the one you have just read, are not usu-

ally described as 'enchanting'. The fact that we not only cope with Chaucer's sentence but have the aural impression that it flows along so smoothly and simply is a tribute to his poetic genius.

The lines work partly because of the rhyme, which organizes the meaning into units that our auditory memory can easily assimilate, and partly because of the metre, which adds pace and control to the reading. The long sequence of clauses, identifying first one aspect of the time of year, then another, also promotes a leisurely, story-telling atmosphere which anticipates the vast scale of the work to follow. It is as if the poet were asking us, through the syntax and prosody, whether we are sitting comfortably, before he begins. As some critics have put it, it is poetry for the ear rather than for the eye.

The artifice of the grammar of these opening lines

can also be seen in several points of detail. The normal order of clause elements is reversed in l. 11 and l. 12 (verb before subject), and in l. 2 (object before verb). The normal order of phrase elements is reversed in l. 1 (adjective after noun) and l. 6 (auxiliary verb after main verb). As a further aid to the metre, we see an extra particle brought into the opening line (*Whan **that** Aprille …*) and a prefix added to a past participle in l. 8 (*yronne*). These were some of the stylistic options available to Chaucer at the time: it would have been perfectly possible for him to have written *Whan Aprille* and *ronne*. The existence of variant forms in a language is of considerable poetic value, providing the writer with options to suit different metrical contexts – if *also* or *better* will not fit a line, then *als* and *bet* might – to ensure the verse 'does not fail' (see below). A modern poet might similarly enjoy the freedom of choice

between *happier* and *more happy*, or between *all work, all the work*, and *all of the work*.

The way in which Chaucer can capture the natural features of colloquial speech is not well illustrated by the *Prologue* – at least, not until towards the end, when the Host starts to speak. The following extract, from *The Summoner's Tale* (ll. 2202–6) provides a better example:

'Ey, Goddes mooder', quod she, 'Blisful mayde!
Is ther oght elles? telle me feithfully.'
'Madame,' quod he, 'how thynke ye herby?'
'How that me thynketh?' quod she, 'so God me speede,
I seye, a cherl hath doon a cherles deede.'

('Ee, God's mother', said she, 'Blissful maiden! Is there anything else? Tell me faithfully.' 'Madame', said he, 'What do you think about that?' 'What do I think about it?' said she, 'so God help me, I say a churl

has done a churl's deed.') Here we see the way in which Chaucer keeps a dialogue going, with quickfire questions and answers within the verse structure. The words are uncomplicated, mostly just one syllable long. The passage also shows one of his favourite stylistic tricks, the use of a rhyming tag with a natural conversational rhythm to it: *so God me speede* – like his use elsewhere of *as I gesse* ('as I guess') and many other such 'comment clauses' (p. 229). Other important characteristics of conversation are seen in the example, such as the 'I said/he said' pattern still found in narrative today, as well as an exclamation, an oath, and the use of direct address (*Madame*). Along with a goodly store of vulgarisms and name-calling – *for Goddes bones, by Seinte Loy, olde fool, by my feith* – these features demonstrate why Chaucer's conversational poetry is so distinctive and so real.

SOME LESSER-KNOWN EXTRACTS

These two extracts further illustrate the variety of Chaucer's writing. The first is the opening of the scientific discourse he wrote in c. 1391 for 'little Lewis, my son', *A Treatise on the Astrolabe* (an early instrument for observing the position and altitudes of celestial bodies). The second is the opening of his 'ABC', an early poem in which the first letter of each verse follows the order of the letters of the alphabet. It was possibly written in the mid-1360s for devotional use by Blanche, the first wife of John of Gaunt.

Lyte Lowys my sone, I aperceyve wel by certeyne evydences thyn abilite to lerne sciences touching nombres and proporciouns; and as wel considre I thy besy praier [*anxious prayer*] in special to lerne the tretys of the Astrelabie. Than [*then*] for as moche [*much*] as a philosofre saith, 'he wrappeth him in his frend, that condescendith to the rightfulle praiers of his frend,' therfore have I yeven the [*given thee*] a suffisant Astrelabie as for oure orizonte [*horizon*], compowned [*constructed*] after the latitude of Oxenforde [*Oxford*]; upon which, by mediacioun [*mediation*] of this litel tretys, I purpose to teche the [*thee*] a certein nombre of conclusions aperteynyng to the same instrument. I seie a certein of conclusions, for thre [*three*] causes. The first cause is this: truste wel that alle the conclusions that han [*have*] be founde, or ellys possibly might be founde in so noble an instrument as is an Astrelabie ben [*are*] unknowe parfitly [*perfectly*] to eny mortal man in this regioun, as I

suppose. Another cause is this, that sothly [*truly*] in any tretis of the Astrelabie that I have seyn, there be somme conclusions that wol [*will*] not in alle thinges parformen her bihestes [*fulfil their promise*]; and somme of hem ben to [*them are too*] harde to thy tendir age to conceyve.

Almighty and al merciable queene,
To whom that al this world fleeth for socour [*help*],
To have relees of sinne, of sorwe, and teene [*hurt*],
Glorious virgine, of alle floures flour [*flower of all flowers*]
To thee I flee, confounded in errour.
Help and releeve, thou mighti debonayre [*gracious one*],
Have mercy on my perilous langour [*affliction*]!
Venquisshed me hath my cruel adversaire.

Bountee so fix hath in thin [*thy*] herte his tente,
That wel I wot [*know*] thou wolt [*will*] my socour bee;
Thou canst not warne [*refuse*] him that with good entente
Axeth [*asks for*] thin helpe, thin herte is ay [*always*] so free [*generous*].
Thou art largesse of pleyn felicitee [*absolute bliss*],
Haven of refut [*refuge*], of quiete, and of reste.
Loo (*Lo*), how that theeves sevene [*the seven deadly sins*] chasen mee!
Help, lady bright, er that [*before*] my ship tobreste [*is wrecked*]!

THE -e QUESTION

The chief difficulty in trying to read Chaucer's verse aloud in its original pronunciation is knowing when to sound the -e which appears at the end of so many words (p. 32). The opening lines of the *Tales* provide several examples: do we add a 'weak' ending to *soote, droghte, roote, sweete, melodye*, and others? The transcription given suggests that we do, in most cases, but is this transcription the only one?

Final -e was certainly on its way out of the language at this time, and a generation or so later it would be completely gone. But in Chaucer's time, there would have been considerable variation. Older speakers might keep it; younger ones drop it. Or perhaps the -e would be kept in careful recitation style. It would almost certainly be elided (p. 247) before a vowel, as in *droghte* (l. 2). And when it represented an earlier inflectional ending (and not a later spelling idiosyncrasy), it would probably have been pronounced. But many cases cannot be resolved so easily.

Scholars are divided on the issue, some recommending the pronunciation in doubtful instances, others rejecting it. That Chaucer himself was aware of the importance of metrical regularity is suggested by his request to Apollo (in *The House of Fame*, l. 1098) to guide him in making his poetry pleasing, 'Though som vers fayle in a sillable' ('Though some lines fail in a syllable'). But no one has yet found a foolproof way of determining Chaucer's prosodic intentions, and different readings continue to be heard.

MIDDLE ENGLISH SPELLING

What is immediately noticeable from the range of texts illustrated in the preceding pages is the extraordinary diversity of Middle English spelling – far greater than that found in Old English (p. 16). Students who are new to the period quickly learn the skill of glossary delving – encountering a variant spelling in an edited text (e.g. *naure, næure, ner, neure*), then trawling through the back of the book to track down what it is a variant of (in this case, of *neuer* 'never'). A good editor makes the job easy, by providing copious cross-references. Some words have a dozen or more variants.

This situation results from a combination of historical, linguistic, and social factors. The sociolinguistic impact of the French invasion, the continuation of the processes of sound change which began in Anglo-Saxon times, and the considerable growth and movement in population during the medieval period, especially in the south-east of the country, all helped to influence the shape of the writing system. The change is quite dramatic. There is a marked contrast between the diverse and idiosyncratic forms used at the beginning of the period and the highly regularized system of spelling which begins to appear in the 15th century, in the work of the Chancery scribes and William Caxton (p. 56).

Some textual features

The text of the *Peterborough Chronicle* (p. 33), dating from the very beginning of the period, shows some of the important features of Middle English spelling. The Old English runic symbols are still in use, but there is some inconsistency. The *-th* spelling makes a sporadic appearance for *þ*. The symbol *ƿ* is used in the manuscript, but this has been represented on p. 33 by *w* (as is usual in modern editions of these texts). *uu* is also a common spelling for this sound; the word for 'wretched people', for example, is spelled both ways in the illustration (ll. 11, 14). The letter *g* is used for a sound which most other texts of the time spell with *ȝ*. There is some alternation between *æ* and *a*. In addition, *u* is used where we would now find *v*, in such words as *gyuen* 'give' and *æure* 'ever'.

Because of the spelling, several words look stranger than they really are. An example is *wreccemen*, which would have been pronounced like *wretch-man* (but with the *w* sounded), and is thus very close to modern *wretched*. *Cyrceiærd* likewise would have been close to the modern pronunciation of *churchyard*, because the two *c* spellings each represented a *ch* sound, and *i* stood for the same sound as modern *y*. And *altegædere* is not far from *altogether*, nor *læiden* from *laid*.

MIGHT **IS RIGHT**

The various spellings of *might* clearly illustrate the way grammatical, dialectal, and scribal variants complicate the study of Middle English texts. All the following are listed in one standard collection of early extracts (B. Dickins & R. M. Wilson, 1951).

maht   miȝtte
mahte   mihhte
mayht   mihte
micht   mist
michtis mithe
micthe mouthe
miȝt   myht
miȝte   myhte
miȝten myhtes
miȝtest myhtestu

Some of the variation can be explained by grammatical context (e.g. the *-est* endings for the 2nd person singular). Some is probably due

to scribal error (e.g. *mayht*). A good example of a dialectal variant is *micht*, which suggests an origin in the north-east (compare modern Scots *nicht* 'not'). However, by the time of William Caxton (p. 56), many of the variations had died out, and Caxton's own use of the *myght* spelling proved to be a major influence on the emergence of the modern form.

Fader oure þat is ī heuen.
blessid be þi name to neuen.
Come to us þi kyngdome.
In heuen ⁊ erth þi wille be done.
oure ilk day bred g"unt vs to day.
and oure mysdedes forgyue vs ay.
als we do hom þt trespasus
right so haue merci vpon us.
and lede vs ī no foundynge.
bot shild vs fro al wicked tinge.
    amen.

(After C. Jones, 1972.)

SOME MANUSCRIPT FEATURES

This is an extract from a 14th-century manuscript – a translation of the Lord's Prayer used in *The Lay Folk's Mass Book*. It is written in *book hand*, a script which was widely used during the Middle English period.

• Old English thorn (*þ*) is used, but written identically to *y* (see further, p. 41): compare the first symbol of *þi* (l. 2) with the last symbol of *day* (l. 5) in the manuscript. *þ* is beginning to be replaced by *th*, as in *erthe* (l. 4).
• The yogh (*ȝ*) and ash (*æ*) symbols have been replaced by *g* (as in *forgyue*, l. 6) and *a* (as in *fader*, l.1), respectively. There is an unusual replacement for Old English *þ*, seen in *wille* (l. 4). The new symbols show the influence of the Carolingian script widely used in Continental Europe (p. 258).
• The long s symbols, also found in Carolingian script, are used in such words as *blessid* (l. 2). There is a later example in the extract from Shakespeare (p. 63). The shape continued to be used in print until the 18th century.
• Some of the symbols are beginning to take on a modern appearance, compared with their earlier use in insular script (p.16). A long downward stroke is no longer used in *r* (*erth*, l. 4). The top of *f* now ascends above the general level of the line (*forgyue*, l. 6), and the ascender in *t* now goes through the crossbar (*right*, l. 8). As a result, these symbols are much

easier to distinguish than they were in Old English.
• Several abbreviations are used, including a line suspended above a symbol to show a missing *n* (l. 1), a superscript standing for *ra* (l. 5), and a shorthand form of *and* (l. 4).
• There is no real punctuation. A mark resembling a period is used after most lines, but its function is unclear.

Minim confusion

Texts of this period show a problem known as *minim confusion* (p. 261). A *minim* is a short vertical stroke of the pen, as in the *i* of *is* (l. 1) or *þi* (l. 2). Several letters were formed by a sequence of such strokes – *u, n, m, v*, and sometimes *w* (*uu*). Because scribes did not usually leave space between different letters, any word which contained these letters in adjacent positions would be difficult to read. A sequence of six minims could be read as *mni, imu, inni*, and several other possibilities. Compare the *m* of *merci* (l. 8) with the *un* of *foundynge* (l. 9). Because there were so many possible ambiguities, Norman scribes introduced the Carolingian convention of writing the minims representing *u* as an *o*, whenever a sequence of two or three other minims followed (as in *come*, l. 3). No new pronunciation is implied by this change. As with the later dotting of *i*, and the reshaping of the tops of *m* and *n*, there was a purely graphic reason for it – to help keep different letters apart.

NORMAN INFLUENCE

As the period progressed, so the spelling changed. The Norman scribes listened to the English they heard around them, and began to spell it according to the conventions they had previously used for French, such as *qu* for *cw* (*queen* for *cwen*). They brought in *gh* (instead of *h*) in such words as *night* and *enough*, and *ch* (instead of *c*) in such words as *church*. They used *ou* for *u* (as in *house*). They began to use *c* before *e* (instead of *s*) in such words as *cercle* ('circle') and *cell*. And because the letter *u* was written in a very similar way to *v*, *n*, and *m* (see opposite), words containing a sequence of these letters were difficult to read; they therefore often replaced the *u* with an *o*, in such cases as *come*, *love*, *one*, and *son*. *k* and *z* came to be increasingly used, as did *j* (a visually more distinct form of *i*). And one pair of letters came to be used in complementary ways: *v* at the beginning of a word (*vnder*), and *u* in the middle (whether consonant or vowel, as in *haue*). By the beginning of the 15th century, English spelling was a mixture of two systems, Old English and French. The consequences plague English learners still (p. 274).

YE OLDE LETTERS

How did *the* become *ye* in *Ye Olde Tea Shoppe* and other such institutions?

Of the four Old English letters, only thorn (þ) continued to be much used throughout the Middle English period, eventually being replaced by *th*. However, scribal practice altered during that time, and the symbol took on a new shape (see illustration opposite), becoming so like a *y* that some writers actually added a dot above the symbol to help distinguish it. This new shape was used in such grammatical words as *the*, *thou*, and *that*, and was often abbreviated (e.g. as *ye*, *yt*).

The writing of þe 'the' as *ye* continued in some manuscript styles until the 19th century, by which time people had long forgotten the original letter shape and the 'th' sound it once represented. They saw the letter as a *y*, gave it the expected modern value, and pronounced the word as 'ye' – a usage still found today in such mock-archaic contexts as pub names (*Ye Olde Fighting Cocks*), shoppe names, and comic dialogue (see further, p. 185).

THE CHANCERY LINE

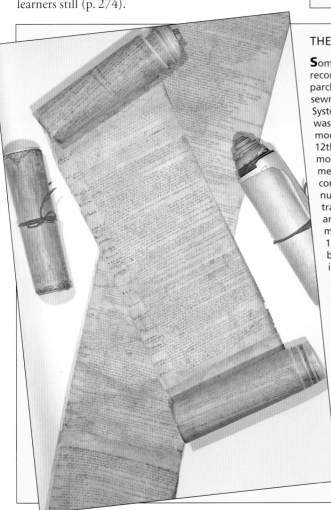

Some of the royal Chancery records, kept on skins of parchment which were then sewn together and rolled up. Systematic record-keeping was an essential part of the monarchy's attempt in the 12th century to develop more effective government. At first the Chancery consisted of a small number of scribes who travelled with the king and prepared his documents; but during the 13th century they came to be permanently located in Westminster.

The importance of the Chancery is its role in fostering the standardization of English, in handwriting, spelling, and grammatical forms. The 'Chancery hand' developed in Italy in the 13th century, and spread to London via France. From *c.* 1430 a vast number of documents emerged. Careful analysis of the manuscripts in the Early Chancery Proceedings has shown that the clerks imposed a great deal of order on the wide range of spellings which existed at the time, and that the choices they made are very largely the ones which have since become standard. The genealogy of modern Standard English goes back to Chancery, not Chaucer.

Although other varieties of English had achieved some degree of standardization, they were soon overtaken by the quantity of material which emerged from the Chancery office. When Caxton established his press, also in Westminster (1476), 'Chancery Standard' already carried enormous prestige. It is perhaps not surprising, then, that it is this set of practices which, associated with the authority of the court and fostered by the power of the press, eventually exercised such influence around the country – though not all Chancery features were retained by the printing-houses.

An example of Chancery influence is its choice of *such*, as opposed to *sich*, *sych*, *seche*, *swiche*, and other variants. *Can*, *could*, *shall*, *should*, and other grammatical words were also given their modern form here. Moreover, there are clear differences between Chancery Standard (CS) and Chaucer's spelling preferences (p. 38) – for example, *not* (CS) for *nat*, *but* (CS) for *bot*, *gaf* (CS) for *yaf* ('gave'), *thes(e)* (CS) for *thise*, and *thorough* (CS) for *thurch* ('through').

Chancery Standard does not derive from the language and style found in the works of Chaucer and Gower, and other major literary figures, therefore; and it took a while before Chancery features emerged in literary texts. Rather, it is a quite distinct variety, showing the influence of the Central and East Midland dialects (p. 50), as well as features associated with London. This mixture is not surprising, given that we know large numbers of people were attracted to the London area from the Midlands in the 15th century. But it does give the Midland dialect area a somewhat larger role in the shaping of modern Standard English than was traditionally thought to be the case (p. 54).

MIDDLE ENGLISH SOUNDS

At the same time as new letter shapes and preferences were emerging (pp. 40–1), there was a continual process of change affecting the way the language was pronounced. The result is a degree of complex interaction between the writing and sound systems which has no parallel in the history of English. It is not possible for these pages to provide a systematic description, but they can at least indicate the general character of the pronunciation developments throughout the period. For those interested in the history of spelling (p. 274), especially, it is a particularly important time, as this is when many rules and idiosyncrasies of the modern system were introduced.

New spelling conventions

Several consonant sounds came to be spelled differently, especially because of French influence. For example, Old English *sc* /ʃ/ is gradually replaced by *sh* or *sch* (*scip* becomes *ship*), though some dialects use *s*, *ss* or *x*. Old English *c* /ʧ/ is replaced by *ch* or *cch* (as in *church*), and the voiced equivalent /ʤ/, previously spelled as *cg* or *gg*, becomes *dg* (as in *bridge*).

New conventions for showing long and short vowels also developed. Increasingly, long vowel sounds came to be marked with an extra vowel letter, as in *see* (earlier *sē*) and *booc* (earlier *bōc*). Short vowels were identified by consonant doubling, in cases where there might otherwise be confusion, as in *sitting* vs *siting*. This convention became available once it was no longer needed to mark the lengthened consonants which had been present in Old English, but lost in early Middle English.

A similar redeployment of graphic resources followed the loss of the unstressed vowels that originally distinguished inflectional endings, as in *stane* 'stone' (p. 39). Although the final /ə/ sound disappeared, the *-e* spelling remained, and it gradually came to be used to show that the preceding vowel was long. This is the origin of the modern spelling 'rule' about 'silent e' in such words as *name* and *nose* (p. 272). The availability of such a useful and frequent letter also motivated its use in other parts of the system: for example, it marked the consonantal use of *u* (*haue*) and the affricate use of *g* (*rage* vs *rag*), and it helped distinguish such modern pairs as *tease*/*teas* and *to*/*toe*.

New pronunciations

Several sounds altered during the early Middle English period. Some took on a different value; some disappeared altogether. In particular, there was a restructuring of the Old English vowel system (p.18). The original diphthongs became pure vowels, and new diphthongs emerged. Some of the new units arose when certain consonants at the end of a syllable came to be pronounced in a vowel-like manner – an example is *wei* 'way', from Old English *weg*. French loan words also introduced new diphthongs, in the form of /ɔi/ and /ʊi/ – unusual sounds for English, and the ancestors of modern /ɔi/ in *joy*, *point*, etc.

Several of the pure vowels also changed their values. For example, in most parts of the country (except the north), Old English /ɑː/ came to be articulated higher at the back of the mouth, as is shown by such spelling changes as *ban* becoming *bon* 'bone' or *swa* becoming *so*. Northern speech followed its own course in several other areas too (p. 50); for example, several of the new diphthongs were far more evident in the south, being replaced by pure vowels in the north (*light* vs *licht*).

An interesting change happened to [h]. This sound appeared before a consonant at the beginning of many Old English words, such as *hring* 'ring' and *hnecca* 'neck'. It was lost early on in the Middle English period – the first sign of the process of 'aitch-dropping' which is still with us today. The loss of *h* before a vowel began some time later, producing variations in usage which continued into the 16th century. Middle English manuscripts show many examples of an *h* absent where it should be present (*adde* for *had*, *eld* for *held*) or present where it should be absent (*ham* for *am*, *his* for *is*). The influence of spelling (and doubtless the prescriptive tradition in schools) led to the *h*-forms being later

---

SOUND SYSTEM 1350–1400

By 1400 the sound system emerging in the south-east of the country (as used by the Chancery and Chaucer) would have had the following inventory. (There is continuing controversy over the number and phonetic quality of the diphthongs.)

The spelling shown in the examples is in many cases just one of several possibilities. The asterisk identifies emerging phonemes (see above).

Consonants

p, b	*p*in, *b*it
t , d	*t*ente, *d*art
k , g	*k*in, *g*ood
ʧ	*ch*irche 'church'
ʤ	bri*gg*e 'bridge'
m, n, ŋ*	*m*ake, *n*ame, so*ng*
l, r	*l*ay, *r*age
w, j	*w*eep, *y*elwe 'yellow'
f, v*	*f*ool, *v*ertu 'virtue'
s, z*	*s*ore, *Z*ephirus
θ, ð	*th*ank, *th*e
h	*h*appen

Long vowels

iː	r*y*den
eː	sw*ee*te
ɛː	h*ee*th
ɑː	n*a*me
uː	h*ou*re
oː	g*oo*d
ɔː	h*o*ly

Short vowels

ɪ	th*i*s
ɛ	m*e*n
a	c*a*n
ə	*a*boute (in unstressed syllables)
ʊ	b*u*t
ɔ	*o*ft

Diphthongs

æɪ	d*ay*
ɔɪ*	j*oy*e
ʊɪ*	j*oi*nen 'join'
ɪʊ	n*ew*e
ɛʊ	f*ew*e 'few'
aʊ	l*aw*e
ɔʊ	gr*ow*e

THE ORMULUM

Ȝiss boc iss nemmnedd
  Orrmulum, forrþi þatt
  Orrm itt wrohhte.

This book is called Ormulum, because Orm wrote it.

Little else is known about the author. The opening lines of the Dedication (see below) tell us that he has a brother, Walter, who is also an Augustinian canon. The text is c.1180, and the dialect is probably north Midland. It is a series of homilies, intended to be read aloud. Over 10,000 full lines survive, and this (according to the contents) may be only about an eighth of the projected work.

Orm's work is of interest not for its poetic style (a series of 15-syllable lines, meticulously kept, but with little ornament) nor especially for its content, which has attracted such epithets as 'intolerably diffuse' and 'tedious'. Its significance is the idiosyncratic orthography, and in particular his system of consonant doubling. He has tried to devise a foolproof way of helping his intended readers, so that they make no mistakes when reading aloud.

Orm's basic rule is to double a consonant after a short vowel in a closed syllable – a principle he implements scrupulously. His concern has been of great value to linguists, providing a major source of evidence about the length of vowels in early Middle English. He is very aware of what he is doing, and evidently quite proud of his system: indeed, at one point in his Dedication he warns future copyists to make sure they get his double lettering system right. No wonder that some have called him the first English spelling reformer.

Nu broþerr Wallterr,
  broþerr min, affterr þe
  flæshess kinde,
Annd broþerr min i
  Crisstenndom þurrh ful
  luht annd þurrh trowwþe
  …

Now brother Walter, my brother, after the manner of the flesh and my brother in Christianity through baptism and through faith…

restored in many words in Received Pronunciation (though not in such Romance loans as *honour*), and thus to the present-day situation where the use of /h-/ is socially diagnostic (p. 319).

New contrasts

In a few cases, new contrastive units (phonemes, p. 236) emerged. The /v/ sound became much more important, because of its use in French loan words, and began to distinguish pairs of words, as it does today (*feel* vs *veal*). Although both [f] and [v] sounds are found in Old English, the language did not use them to differentiate words. Similarly, French influence caused /s/ and /z/ to become contrastive (*zeal* vs *seal*). And the *ng* sound /ŋ/ at the end of a word also began to distinguish meanings at this time (*thing* vs *thin*). In Old English, this sound had always been followed by a /g/ – *cyning* 'king', for example, was /kyniŋg/. However the /g/ died away at the end of the Old English period, leaving /ŋ/ as the sole distinguishing unit.

The study of Middle English phonology is made increasingly difficult (and fascinating) by the intricate dialect situation (p. 50). On the one hand, a letter might be given different pronunciations depending on the dialect area in which it appears; an example is the letter *y*, which for a while represented an unrounded sound quality in the south and a rounded sound quality in the north. On the other hand, a sound might be given different spellings depending on the dialect area in which it appears; an example here is Old English /x/, spelled in the middle of words as *gh* in the south, and as *ch* in the north (*night* vs *nicht*). Finally, we should note the continuing need for analytical caution because spelling was not standardized. Problems of authorial idiosyncrasy and copyist error abound, contributing to both the complex character of the period and the moral fibre of its students.

THE *SHE* PUZZLE

Plotting the way sounds and words changed between Old and Middle English can be an intriguing business, and one which cannot always be resolved, as the story of *she* illustrates. There is a fairly obvious relationship between most of the Old English pronouns (p. 20) and their Modern English equivalents. But what is the link between *hēo* and *she*? The question has attracted several answers, and remains controversial.

• The simplest solution is to argue that there was a series of sound changes by which *hēo* gradually changed into *she*.

1 Sometime between Old and Middle English, the diphthong altered, the first element becoming shorter and losing its stress. [he:ə] thus became [hjo:].

2 The [hj] element then came to be articulated closer to the palate, as [ç], in much the same way as happens to modern English *huge*.

3 [ç] then became [ʃ], to give the modern consonant.

There are certain facts in favour of this theory (the preferred explanation). Spellings such as *scho* are found in very early Middle English in the north. Also, a similar development took place in a few place names, such as Old Norse *Hjaltland* becoming modern *Shetland*. The main argument against the theory is that there is no clear evidence for Step 3 elsewhere in English at any time – apart from in these few foreign place names. Is it plausible to propose a sound change which affected only one word? Also, we are still left with the problem of getting from [o:] to [e:], which is required in order to produce the modern sound of *she*. For this, we have to assume a process such as analogy – perhaps the vowel of *she* being influenced by that of *he*. But there is no clear evidence for this.

• Alternative theories argue that *hēo* comes from *sēo*, the feminine form of the definite article. The simplest version postulates similar sound changes to the above, giving [sjo:] as a result. This is a short, plausible step away from [ʃo:]. However, we are still left with the question of why the [o:] vowel became [e:].

• A third argument also begins with *sēo*, but takes a different phonological route. Sometime after the Conquest, we have a lot of evidence to show that the sound of *ēo* [e:ə] changed to become close to *ē* [e:]. This would have had the effect of making the words *heo* and *hē* sound the same; and as this process began to operate, it must have been quite disconcerting. People would have been unclear whether someone was saying *he* or *she*. In these circumstances, there would be a need to find a way of keeping the two words apart; and the suggestion is that *sēo* filled this need.

Why *sēo*? There is a close semantic link between personal and demonstrative pronouns in many languages, and it can be seen in Old English too, where *sēo* meant 'that' as well as 'the'. We can see the closeness in the text on p. 20 (l. 16), where the masculine form *se* 'the' is used as 'the one', and is glossed as 'he'. The same could apply to *sēo* in its relation to *hēo*. It would be very natural to use the phonetic distinctiveness of the former to help sort out the ambiguity of the latter. All that would then be needed was a further consonant change from [s] to [ʃ], as the vowel is already on course for its modern sound.

The problem here is in this last step. How can [s] become [ʃ] in front of an [e:] vowel? It would be the equivalent of a change from *same* to *shame*. To get from [s] to [ʃ], there needs to be some intervening sound which 'pulls' the s in the direction of the more palatal sound [ʃ]. The obvious candidate is [j], itself a palatal sound, but the whole point of this third argument is that there is no [j] left in *hēo*. The possibility of a [j] developing disappeared when we argued that *ēo* became [e:].

The origins of *she* thus remain one of the unsolved puzzles in the history of English.

MEDIEVAL LINGUISTIC CURIOS

The name *Stanley*, along with its abbreviated form *Stan*, is quite unusual from a phonological point of view. It is an ancient aristocratic name, found throughout the Middle English period, and the family name of the earls of Derby. It means 'stony field' – presumably an earlier place name. What makes the name interesting is that it did not follow the normal pattern of sound change which affected the long *ā* vowel in Old English: *stān* became *stōn* in early Middle English, which became modern *stone* – just like *bān* 'bone', *hām* 'home', and many others. But the Old English spelling was preserved in the proper name (presumably because of the influence of northern dialects, p. 50), so that we have *Stanley* rather than *Stonely Holloway*.

Interesting things happened in Middle English to the velar fricative /x/, spelled *h* and then *gh*, at the end of a word. It came to be pronounced /f/ in some words (e.g. *enough*, *tough*), but it was lost in others (*through*, *plough*). In one word, both changes took place, giving the modern doublet of *dough*, where the /x/ was lost, and *duff*, where it became /f/. The latter is found now only in such forms as *plum-duff*, a type of pudding, and (possibly) *duffer* ('man of dough'?).

MIDDLE ENGLISH GRAMMAR

What happened to English grammar, following the decay of the Old English inflectional system (p. 32)? An important preliminary point is to appreciate that – as we would expect from the way language change operates – the loss of inflections was not a sudden nor a universal process. Their disappearance can be traced throughout the whole of the Middle English period, affecting different parts of the country at different times. Moreover, the switch from a synthetic to an analytic type of grammar is not the whole story of Middle English: there were independent changes taking place simultaneously in other parts of the grammatical system, and these also need to be considered.

From word ending to word order

None of this gainsays the observation that the most important grammatical development was the establishment of fixed patterns of word order to express the relationship between clause elements. There was already a tendency towards Subject–Verb–Object (SVO) order in Old English (p. 20), and this was now consolidated in some constructions and extended to others. The *Peterborough Chronicle* illustration on p. 33 shows how the earlier verb-final pattern continued to make itself felt, especially when the subject was short (such as a pronoun or a single noun).

ræueden hi	*robbed they*
forbaren hi	*spared they*
was corn dære	*was corn dear*

and other departures from modern word order are apparent in that text:

ne næure hethen men werse ne diden
nor never heathen men worse not did

Variations of this kind continue to be in evidence even at the end of the Middle English period, especially when prompted by the demands of poetic metre, as shown by such Chaucerian examples as *inspired hath* and *so priketh hem nature* (p. 39). Nonetheless, the underlying trend towards SVO is inexorable. The Chronicle uses SVO much more regularly than did the West Saxon texts of a few years before (the contrast is especially noticeable in subordinate clauses), and SVO is by far the dominant order in Chaucer.

Prepositions became particularly critical when noun endings were lost. For example, where Old English would have said *þæm scipum*, with a 'dative' ending on both the words for 'the' and 'ship', Middle English came to say *to the shippes*, using a preposition and the common plural ending. The only noun case to survive into Modern English was the genitive ('s or s' in writing) – a relic which continued to present problems

in later centuries (p. 203). Some of the personal pronouns also kept the old dative form: *he* vs *him*, *she* vs *her*, etc.

The endings of the verb remained close to those of Old English during this period. Most verbs would have had the following forms, illustrated here in Chaucer's English for *turnen* 'turn', and ignoring certain dialect differences, such as the northern use of *-es* instead of *-eth*. (Alternative forms are shown in parentheses.)

	Present tense	*Past tense*
(I)	turn(e)	turned(e)
(thou)	turnest	turnedest
(he/she/it)	turneth	turned(e)
(we/you/they)	turne(n)	turned(en)

The final simplification to the modern system (p. 204), where we have only *turn* and *turns* in the present tense, and *turned* throughout the past, took place after the Middle English period.

PLOTTING CHANGES IN WORD ORDER

We can see the gradual way in which new patterns of word order developed in Middle English by looking at the range of constructions in a text. There is considerable variety at the beginning of the period, and progressively less as we approach Early Modern English. One study examined over 1,500 full lines from the late 12th-century *Ormulum* (p. 42) to determine the order of Subject, Verb, and Object (SVO) elements: 1,697 clauses were analysed, and the chief results are shown here in chart form (after R. A. Palmatier, 1969).

The overall SVO statement order is striking, but there are many inversions. A closer analysis shows some interesting features.

• Most VS variation is in main clauses: 97 per cent of subordinate clauses have SV order, but only 67 per cent of main clauses.
• VS is especially likely in certain syntactic contexts. If a negative word or an indirect object appear at the front of a clause, then the VS order seems to be obligatory. If the clause begins with an adverb, it is very likely – in 57 per cent of all VS cases, an adverb precedes.

Ne shall he drinnkenn
Nor shall he drink
Forrþi wass mikell wræche sett
Thus great punishment was set

• OV figures also need to be broken down. If the O is a pronoun, it is just as likely to appear before the V as after it (51 per cent vs 49 per cent). However, if the O is a noun, it is unusual for it to appear before the V (18 per cent vs 82 per cent). This is the same pattern as that noted above in the *Peterborough Chronicle*.

After all this counting, we are only at the beginning of our search for explanations. What is it about an adverb which prompts a VS inversion? Adverbs of time, place, and negation seem to be particularly influential. Why does one part of the clause change at a different rate from another? Although the OV pattern becomes VO quite early on, the VS pattern remains strong in some contexts until Early Modern English, when SV statement order became normal almost everywhere.

These are the kinds of questions investigated by Middle English scholars. Special cases of inversion in statements remain in Modern English, of course, such as the use of *said he* in narrative. Negative adverbs still require inversion (*Hardly had he left*, *Never have I heard*). And in poetry, we may well find such cases as *Tomorrow shall I leave* (used as a statement) or *There would he stay*. In these examples we are glimpsing the word order preferences of a thousand years ago.

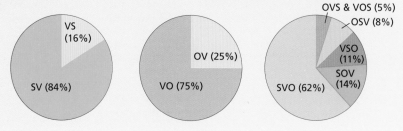

New features of English grammar

The Middle English period is particularly interesting because it shows where several important features of Modern English grammar have come from. It also provides a useful perspective for present-day arguments about English usage, as a number of the issues which have been condemned as 20th-century sloppiness are well in evidence from the earliest times.

POSTMODIFYING GENITIVE

This construction employs *of* instead of the genitive case in the noun phrase: we now say *the back of the house*, not **the house's back* (p. 202). The *of* pattern was hardly used in late Old English, but by late Middle English over 80 per cent of all genitive constructions were of this kind. The influence of the parallel French construction in *de* may have been a factor in moving this change forward so quickly. The genitive ending stayed much longer in poetry, where it gave the poet a useful metrical alternative. As in Modern English, the inflectional genitive remained with personal nouns (*the boy's book*).

The 'group genitive' (as in *the Duke of York's hat*) also emerged at this time, replacing a construction where the two noun phrases were separated (*the Duke's hat, of York*). Again, the development was a gradual one, affecting some types of phrase before others: in Chaucer, for example, *God of Loves servantz* exists alongside *Wyves Tale of Bath*. There are also instances of the replacement of the genitive ending by a possessive pronoun (*The Man of Lawe his Tale*). This became more common in Early Modern English, before it died out, and fuelled an argument, still sometimes found today, that the *'s* ending is a reduced form of the pronoun *his* (p. 203).

NEGATION

A noticeable feature of the Chronicle extract (p. 33) is the continuing use of the Old English construction involving 'double' or 'triple' negatives. These need to be correctly interpreted: there should be no temptation to 'cancel out' their meaning, using the mathematical rule that 'two negatives make a positive'. Despite the efforts of modern prescriptivists (p. 366), this has never been how the negation system has worked in English. The principle shown in the earliest English texts is simple: extra negative words increase the emphasis, making the negative meaning stronger. It is not clear just how emphatic the *ne* element is in the Chronicle examples, but the cumulative effect is not in doubt.

ne hadden nan more to gyuen
(they) had no more to give
for nan ne wæs o þe land
for there was none in the land

During the Middle English period, the situation simplified. The Old English double negative (*ne … naht*) was much used in the early part of the period, but by the end just one form (*nat* or *not*) was marking negation, and *ne* was being dropped before other negative words. This is the situation later adopted in Standard English; but the emphatic principle remained in nonstandard varieties, and is still with us (p. 326).

MARKING THE INFINITIVE

In Old English, the infinitive was shown by an inflectional ending *-(i)an* (p. 20). As this decayed, the particle *to* began to take over. Originally a preposition, *to* developed a function as a purpose marker ('in order to'), but then lost all its semantic content, acting solely as a sign of the infinitive. A construction using *for to*, again with a purposive meaning, developed in early Middle English, but this also lost its semantic force, ending up only as a useful metrical alternative in poetry. Chaucer uses both forms in *The Canterbury Tales*:

Thanne longen folk *to goon* on pilgrimages
And palmeres *for to seken* straunge strondes…

As soon as *to* begins to be used as an infinitive marker, we find it separated from its verb. As early as the 13th century, adverbs and pronouns were inserted, as in *for to him reade* 'to advise him' (Laʒamon's *Brut*), and quite lengthy constructions were at times introduced, as in this example from a 15th-century bishop, Reginald Pecock:

for to freely and in no weye of his owne dette or of eny oþer mannys dette to ʒeve and paie eny reward…
(*The Reule of Crysten Religioun*)

Many such examples show that infinitive-splitting is by no means an unnatural process in English, as prescriptivists argue, and certainly not a modern phenomenon (p. 195).

FOUNDATIONS

The Middle English period laid the foundation for the later emergence of several important constructions. Chief among these was the progressive form (as in *I am running*), which was used much more frequently towards the end of the period, especially in northern texts. Its use then increased dramatically in Early Modern English.

The modern progressive requires an auxiliary verb (a form of *be*), and this function also emerged during the period (p. 225). For a while *have* and *be* competed for the expression of perfect aspect: in *The Canterbury Tales*, for example, we find instances of both *ben entred* ('are entered') and *han entred* ('have entered'), each in contexts expressing past time. This situation was full of potential ambiguity, as *be* was also used in passive constructions (p. 204). The problem was resolved when *have* came to be used for perfective aspect, and *be* for the passive and progressive. At the same time, *do* also developed its function as an 'empty' form in questions (*does he know?*) and negation (*I didn't go*). And the modal verbs (*will, shall, may, might, can*, etc.) took on fresh functions. Their meaning had already begun to overlap with that of the subjunctive in late Old English, and once verbs lost their endings, modals were the only way in which such meanings as possibility and necessity could be expressed.
(After O. Fischer, 1992.)

NEW PRONOUN FORMS

In the Middle English period, the entire third-person plural pronoun system is gradually replaced by Scandinavian forms. The Old English system used forms beginning with *h-* (p. 21). The Scandinavian forms beginning with *þ-* appeared first in northern dialects, and moved slowly south. Some parts of the system moved faster than others: the nominative was usually the first form to be affected, followed by the genitive. *þei* arrived in London during the 14th century, and was used systematically by Chaucer, alongside *her(e)* or *hir(e)* for the genitive, and *hem* for other cases. During the 15th century, *their* became the norm, and by the beginning of the 16th century *them* had followed it.

No *th-*
Me dide cnotted strenges abuton *here* hæued…
Hi diden *heom* in quarterne
One placed knotted cords about their head…
They put them in a cell…
(12th century, *Peterborough Chronicle*)

Mixed *th-*
Eten and drounken and maden *hem* glad…
Hoere paradis *hy* nomen here
And nou *þey* lien in helle ifere…
[they] ate and drank and enjoyed themselves
Their paradise they received here
And now they lie in hell together…
(13th-century poem)

Nominative *th-* established
And pilgrimes were *they* alle…
So hadde I spoken with *hem* everichon [everyone]
That I was of *hir* felaweshipe anon
(late 14th century, *The Canterbury Tales*)

All *th-* established
And alle other that be understanding and fyndyng ony defaute, I requyre and pray *them* of *theyre* charyte to correcte and amende hit; and so doyng *they* shal deserve thanke and meryte of God…
(late 15th century, William Caxton, Prologue to *Knight of the Tower*)

MIDDLE ENGLISH VOCABULARY

The vocabulary of the *Peterborough Chronicle* (p. 32) is not typical of the Middle English period as a whole. Despite the fact that it was written almost a century after the Conquest, there is little sign of the French vocabulary which was to be the distinctive characteristic of the era. The Chronicle vocabulary is still typical of what would have appeared in literary West Saxon – predominantly Germanic, with an admixture of Latin and Scandinavian (p. 24). Several of its words have since dropped from the language – for example, we no longer use *pines* 'cruelties', or *namen* 'took'. And of the words which are still found today, several have altered meanings: *wonder* could mean 'atrocities' as well as 'marvels', and *flesh* had the general sense of 'meat'. Such 'false friends' are always a problem in reading a Middle English text because of their misleading similarity to the modern words.

The French factor

French influence became increasingly evident in English manuscripts of the 13th century (p. 31). It has been estimated that some 10,000 French words came into English at that time – many previously borrowed from more distant sources (such as *alkali* from Arabic). These words were largely to do with the mechanisms of law and administration, but they also included words from such fields as medicine, art, and fashion. Many of the new words were quite ordinary, everyday terms. Over 70 per cent were nouns. A large number were abstract terms, constructed using such new French affixes as *con-, trans-, pre-, -ance, -tion*, and *-ment*. About three-quarters of all these French loans are still in the language today.

As new words arrived, there were many cases where they duplicated words that had already existed in English from Anglo-Saxon times. In such cases, there were two outcomes. Either one word would supplant the other; or both would co-exist, but develop slightly different meanings. The first outcome was very common, in most cases the French word replacing an Old English equivalent; for example, *leod* gave way to *people*, *wlitig* to *beautiful*, and *stow* (n.) to *place*. Hundreds of Old English words were lost in this way. But at the same time, Old English and French words often both survived with different senses or connotations, such as *doom* (OE) and *judgment* (F), *hearty* (OE) and *cordial* (F), and *house* (OE) and *mansion* (F) (p. 124). Sometimes pairs of words were used, one glossing the other: *for routhe and for pitie* is a Chaucerian example, and legal terminology often developed coordinations of this kind (p. 374). Bilingual word lists were compiled as early as the mid-13th century to aid intelligibility between English and French.

COURTLY FRENCH LOANS

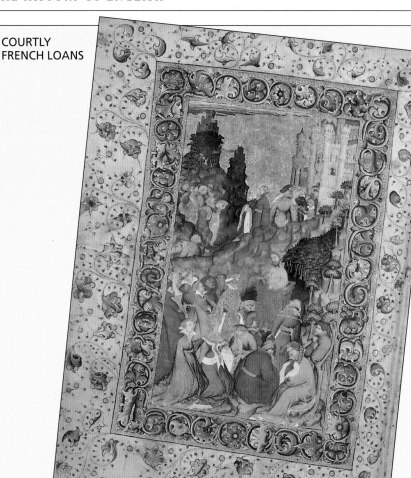

A miniature of *c.* 1400, showing Chaucer reading his works aloud to a group of nobles and their ladies. The words from French which would have been entering the language during Chaucer's lifetime were rather different in character from those which arrived in the early Middle English period. The French of the Norman conquerors was a northern dialect of the language, and this dominated the English scene for 200 years (p. 30). By the 12th century, however, Paris had come to be established as the centre of influence in France, and new loan words began to arrive from the dialect of that area.

As the Parisian court grew in prestige, so Parisian French became the prestige dialect. It is this variety of French which in due course would have been taught in quality schools in England, with the earlier English-influenced varieties of French considered uneducated and perhaps a bit of a joke (if this is the correct interpretation of Chaucer's remark about the Prioress, who learned her French at the Benedictine nunnery in Stratford, Middlesex):

And Frenssh she spak ful faire and fetisly
   [*gracefully*],
After the scole [*school*] of Stratford atte
   Bowe,
For Frenssh of Parys was to hire unknowe
   [*her unknown*].

From a lexical point of view, it is important to note these dialect differences, as otherwise it is not possible to explain certain spelling variants. There are several pairs of loan words affected (though not all have survived in Modern English):

Norman French	Parisian French
calange (1225)	challenge (1300)
canchelers (1066)	chanceleres (1300)
wile (1154)	guile (1225)
warrant (1225)	guarantee (1624)
warden (1225)	guardian (1466)
reward (1315)	regard (1430)
conveie (1375)	convoy (1425)
lealte (1300)	loialte (1400)
prisun (1121)	prison (1225)
gaol (1163)	jail (1209)

The central French spellings post-date the Norman ones. The situation is not always clear, partly because of the uncertainties of English spelling practices at the time (p. 40); but there is enough evidence to show that there were two distinct stages of borrowing from French in early Middle English. (After D. Burnley, 1992.)

FRENCH INFLUENCE ON THE ENGLISH LEXICON

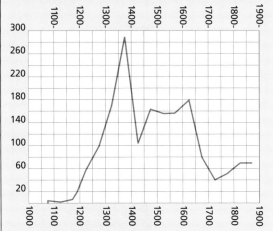

This diagram shows the varying rate at which French words have come into English since late Anglo-Saxon times, based on the entries in a historical dictionary showing the date at which an item is first used in an English text. The rate of French borrowing reaches a peak in the second half of the 14th century.

Such global figures need to be taken cautiously, for they hide several kinds of variation. In the early Middle English period, for example, there was a greater incidence of French loan words in courtly poetry, they were more common in the south of the country, and they were much more likely in works which were translations from French. By the end of the period, however, there is no doubting the extent to which they had permeated the language. Using Chaucer as a yardstick, in the 858 lines of the Prologue to *The Canterbury Tales*, there are nearly 500 different French loans.

A TOUCH OF CLASSE

Almost all the English words to do with the aristocracy and their servants are of French origin (though the meaning of these words in medieval times was often rather different from what it is today). The chief examples are *baron, count(ess), courtier, duchess, duke, marchioness, marquis, noble, page, peer, prince, princess, squire,* and *viscount(ess). King, queen, lord, lady, knight,* and *earl* are the Anglo-Saxon exceptions.

Similarly, the names of all the best-known precious stones are French: *amethyst, diamond, emerald, garnet, pearl, ruby, sapphire, topaz, turquoise.*

SOME FRENCH LOANS IN MIDDLE ENGLISH

Administration
authority, bailiff, baron, chamberlain, chancellor, constable, coroner, council, court, crown, duke, empire, exchequer, government, liberty, majesty, manor, mayor, messenger, minister, noble, palace, parliament, peasant, prince, realm, reign, revenue, royal, servant, sir, sovereign, squire, statute, tax, traitor, treason, treasurer, treaty, tyrant, vassal, warden

Law
accuse, adultery, advocate, arrest, arson, assault, assize, attorney, bail, bar, blame, chattels, convict, crime, decree, depose, estate, evidence, executor, felon, fine, fraud, heir, indictment, inquest, jail, judge, jury, justice, larceny, legacy, libel, pardon, perjury, plaintiff, plea, prison, punishment, sue, summons, trespass, verdict, warrant

Religion
abbey, anoint, baptism, cardinal, cathedral, chant, chaplain, charity, clergy, communion, confess, convent, creator, crucifix, divine, faith, friar, heresy, homily, immortality, incense, mercy, miracle, novice, ordain, parson, penance, prayer, prelate, priory, religion, repent, sacrament, sacrilege, saint, salvation, saviour, schism, sermon, solemn, temptation, theology, trinity, vicar, virgin, virtue

Military
ambush, archer, army, barbican, battle, besiege, captain, combat, defend, enemy, garrison, guard, hauberk, lance, lieutenant, moat, navy, peace, portcullis, retreat, sergeant, siege, soldier, spy, vanquish

Food and drink
appetite, bacon, beef, biscuit, clove, confection, cream, cruet, date, dinner, feast, fig, fruit, fry, grape, gravy, gruel, herb, jelly, lemon, lettuce, mackerel, mince, mustard, mutton, olive, orange, oyster, pigeon, plate, pork, poultry, raisin, repast, roast, salad, salmon, sardine, saucer, sausage, sole, spice, stew, sturgeon, sugar, supper, tart, taste, toast, treacle, tripe, veal, venison, vinegar

Fashion
apparel, attire, boots, brooch, buckle, button, cape, chemise, cloak, collar, diamond, dress, embroidery, emerald, ermine, fashion, frock, fur, garment, garter, gown, jewel, lace, mitten, ornament, pearl, petticoat, pleat, robe, satin, taffeta, tassel, train, veil, wardrobe

Leisure and the arts
art, beauty, carol, chess, colour, conversation, courser, dalliance, dance, falcon, fool, harness, image, jollity, joust, juggler, kennel, lay, leisure, literature, lute, melody, minstrel, music, noun, painting, palfrey, paper, parchment, park, partridge, pavilion, pen, pheasant, poet, preface, prose, recreation, rein, retrieve, revel, rhyme, romance, sculpture, spaniel, stable, stallion, story, tabor, terrier, title, tournament, tragedy, trot, vellum, volume

Science and learning
alkali, anatomy, arsenic, calendar, clause, copy, gender, geometry, gout, grammar, jaundice, leper, logic, medicine, metal, noun, ointment, pain, physician, plague, pleurisy, poison, pulse, sphere, square, stomach, study, sulphur, surgeon, treatise

The home
basin, blanket, bucket, ceiling, cellar, chair, chamber, chandelier, chimney, closet, couch, counterpane, curtain, cushion, garret, joist, kennel, lamp, lantern, latch, lattice, pantry, parlour, pillar, porch, quilt, scullery, towel, tower, turret

General nouns
action, adventure, affection, age, air, city, coast, comfort, country, courage, courtesy, cruelty, debt, deceit, dozen, envy, error, face, fault, flower, forest, grief, honour, hour, joy, labour, manner, marriage, mischief, mountain, noise, number, ocean, opinion, order, pair, people, person, piece, point, poverty, power, quality, rage, reason, river, scandal, season, sign, sound, spirit, substance, task, tavern, unity, vision

General adjectives
active, amorous, blue, brown, calm, certain, clear, common, cruel, curious, eager, easy, final, foreign, gay, gentle, honest, horrible, large, mean, natural, nice, original, perfect, poor, precious, probable, real, rude, safe, scarce, scarlet, second, simple, single, solid, special, strange, sudden, sure, usual

General verbs
advise, allow, arrange, carry, change, close, continue, cry, deceive, delay, enjoy, enter, form, grant, inform, join, marry, move, obey, pass, pay, please, prefer, prove, push, quit, receive, refuse, remember, reply, satisfy, save, serve, suppose, travel, trip, wait, waste

Turns of phrase
by heart, come to a head, do homage, do justice to, have mercy on, hold one's peace, make complaint, on the point of, take leave, take pity on

The role of Latin

French is the most dominant influence on the growth of Middle English vocabulary (p. 46), but it is by no means the only one. During the 14th and 15th centuries several thousand words came into the language directly from Latin (though it is often difficult to exclude an arrival route via French). Most of these words were professional or technical terms, belonging to such fields as religion, medicine, law, and literature. They also included many words which were borrowed by a writer in a deliberate attempt to produce a 'high' style. Only a very small number of these 'aureate terms' entered the language, however (e.g. *meditation, oriental, prolixity*). The vast majority died almost as soon as they were born (e.g. *abusion, sempitern, tenebrous*).

The simultaneous borrowing of French and Latin words led to a highly distinctive feature of Modern English vocabulary – sets of three items all expressing the same fundamental notion but differing slightly in meaning or style, such as *kingly / royal / regal* and *rise / mount / ascend* (p. 124). The Old English word is usually the more popular one, with the French word more literary, and the Latin word more learned.

Other sources

The effects of the Scandinavian invasions also made themselves felt during this period. Although the chief period of borrowing must have been much earlier, relatively few Scandinavian loans appear in Old English, and most do not come to be used in manuscripts until well into the 13th century, and then mainly in northern areas where Danish settlement was heaviest. A list is given in the section on Old English (p. 25).

Several other languages also supplied a sprinkling of new words at this time, though not all survived. Contact with the Low Countries brought *poll* ('head'), *doten* ('be foolish'), *bouse* ('drink deeply'), and *skipper* ('ship's master'), resulting from commercial and maritime links with the Dutch. Other loans included *cork* (Spanish), *marmalade* (Portuguese), *sable* (Russian), *lough* (Irish), and many words from Arabic, especially to do with the sciences (*saffron, admiral, mattress, algebra, alkali, zenith*). In most cases, the words arrived after they had travelled through other countries (and languages), often entering English via French. A good example is the vocabulary of chess (*chess, rook, check, mate*), which came directly from French, but which is ultimately Persian.

The effect of all this borrowing on the balance of words in the English lexicon was dramatic. In early Middle English, over 90 per cent of words (lexical types, p. 123) were of native English origin. By the end of the Middle English period this proportion had fallen to around 75 per cent.

SOME LATIN LOANS IN MIDDLE ENGLISH

Administration and law
alias, arbitrator, client, conspiracy, conviction, custody, gratis, homicide, implement, incumbent, legal, legitimate, memorandum, pauper, prosecute, proviso, summary, suppress, testify, testimony

Science and learning
abacus, allegory, etcetera, comet, contradiction, desk, diaphragm, discuss, dislocate, equator, essence, explicit, formal, genius, history, index, inferior, innumerable, intellect, item, library, ligament, magnify, major, mechanical, minor, neuter, notary, prosody, recipe, scribe, simile, solar, tincture

Religion
collect, diocese, immortal, incarnate, infinite, limbo, magnificat, mediator, memento, missal, pulpit, requiem, rosary, scripture, tract

General
admit, adjacent, collision, combine, conclude, conductor, contempt, depression, distract, exclude, expedition, gesture, imaginary, include, incredible, individual, infancy, interest, interrupt, lucrative, lunatic, moderate, necessary, nervous, ornate, picture, popular, private, quiet, reject, solitary, spacious, subjugate, substitute, temperate, tolerance, ulcer

---

THE WYCLIFFITE BIBLE

The authorship of the Bible translation attributed to John Wycliff (d. 1384) is uncertain. Because of the unorthodox nature of Wycliff's opinions, the early manuscripts of his writings were widely destroyed. Also, his followers included several scholars who helped him carry out the task of translation. But there is no doubt that the inspiration for the work came from Wycliff himself, who was particularly concerned that lay people should be able to read the Bible in their own language. The first translation, using the Latin version of St Jerome, was made between 1380 and 1384.

Wycliff's method was to rely greatly on glossing the Latin text, seeking where possible to preserve the original style. As a consequence, there are over a thousand Latin words whose use in English is first recorded in his translation. Almost any extract shows the influence of Latin vocabulary, either directly imported, or known through French, and these items are in italics below.

And it was don, in tho daies: a *maundement* went out fro the *emperrour* august: that al the world schulde be *discryued* / this first *discryvynge* was made of siryn *iustice* of sirie / and alle men wenten to make *professioun* eche in to his owne *citee* / Ioseph wente up fro galilee, fro the *citee* nazareth, in to iudee, in to a *cite* of davith that is clepid bethleem, for that he was of the hous and of the *meynee* of davith, that he schulde knowleche with marie, his wiif that was weddid to hym, and was greet with child / ... ye schuln fynde a yunge child wlappid in clothis: and leide in a *cracche* / and *sudeynli* there was made with the *aungel* a *multitude* of heuenli knyghthod: heriynge god and seiynge / *glorie* be in the highist thingis to god: and in erthe *pees* be to men of good wille. (From Luke 2.1–14.)

The burning of John Wycliff's bones, 41 years after his death.

LEXICAL IMPRESSIONS

One way of developing a sense of the extensiveness of foreign borrowing during Middle English is to take a text and identify the loan words – using the *Oxford English Dictionary* or a more specialized etymological work (p. 136). If this were done for the early Middle English *Peterborough Chronicle* extract (p. 33), very few such words would be identified. The only items which have no antecedents in Old English are Scandinavian *hærnes* (l. 2), *drapen* (l. 4), and *rachenteges* (l. 9), and Latin *crucethus* (l. 5).

By contrast, the following extracts, both taken from late Middle English texts, and containing similar subject matter, show the major impact of borrowing (all loans are italicized).

• Scandinavian loans include *get*, *wayk*, *haile*, *sterne*, *ball*, *birth*, and *fro*.
• Words directly from French include *empryce*, *riall*, *spyce*, *cristall*, *soverayne*, and *flour*.
• Words from Latin via French include *sapience*, *reverence*, *magnificence*, *science*, and *suffragane*.

The second passage has a large number of distinctively Latin words – an example of the 'aureate diction' consciously employed by several authors in the late Middle English period and beyond (p. 61). These include *imperatrice*, *mediatrice*, *salvatrice*, *virginall*. *pulcritud*, and *celsitud*.
(After D. Burnley, 1992.)

The Canterbury Tales
(from the Prologue of *The Prioress's Tale*)

O mooder Mayde! o mayde Mooder free!
O bussh un*brent brennynge* in Moyses sighte,
That *ravyshedest* doun *fro* the *Deitee*
Thurgh thyn *humblesse* the Goost that in th'alighte,
Of whos *vertu*, whan he thyn herte lighte
Conceyved was the Fadres *sapience*,
Help me to telle it in thy *reverence*!

Lady, thy *bountee*, thy *magnificence*,
Thy *vertu*, and thy grete *humylitee*,
Ther may no tonge *expresse* in no *science*;
For somtyme, Lady, er men *praye* to thee,
Thou goost biforn of thy *benyngnytee*,
And *getest* us the lyght, of thy *preyere*,
To *gyden* us unto thy Sone so deere.

My konnyng is so *wayk*, o blisful Queene,
For to *declare* thy grete worthynesse
That I ne may the weighte nat *susteene*;
But as a child of twelf month oold, or lesse,
That kan unnethes any word *expresse*,
Right so fare I, and therfore I yow *preye*,
Gydeth my song that I shal of yow seye.

From a poem by William Dunbar (p. 53)

Empryce of *prys*, *imperatrice*,
Bricht *polist precious* stane;
Victrice of *vyce*, hie *genitrice*
Of Jhesu lord *soverayne*;
Our wys *pavys fro enemys*
Agane the Feyndis *trayne*;
Oratrice, *mediatrice*, *salvatrice*,
To God gret *suffragane*;
Ave Maria, *gracia plena*:
Haile, *sterne*, *meridiane*;
Spyce, *flour delice* of *paradys*
That *baire* the *gloryus grayne*.

Imperiall wall, *place palestrall*
Of *peirles pulcritud*;
Tryumphale hall, hie *trone regall*
Of Godis *celsitud*;
Hospitall riall, the lord of all
Thy *closet* did *include*;
Bricht *ball cristall*, *ros virginall*
Fulfillit of *angell* fude.
Ave Maria, *gracia plena*:
Thy *birth* has with his blude
Fra fall *mortall originall*
Us *raunsound* on the rude.

NEW WORD FORMATION

Loan words were by no means the only way in which the vocabulary of Middle English increased. The processes of word formation which were already established in Old English continued to be used, and were extended in various ways.

Compounding
The poetic compounds of Old English (p. 23) declined dramatically at the beginning of the Middle English period. There are over a thousand compounds in *Beowulf*, but Laȝamon's *Brut*, also an alliterative poem (p. 36), and ten times as long, has only around 800. Nonetheless, some types of compounding did continue to produce new words: noun examples include *bagpipe*, *birthday*, *blackberry*, *craftsman*, *grandfather*, *highway*, and *schoolmaster*. New compounds in -*er* were especially frequent in the 14th century: *bricklayer*, *housekeeper*, *moneymaker*, *soothsayer*. Compounds of the type *he-lamb* date from *c.* 1300. Adjective examples from the period include *lukewarm*, *moth-eaten*, *new-born*, and *red-hot*. Phrasal verbs (p. 212) also increased in frequency, sometimes coexisting with an earlier prefixed form, as in the case of *go out* (alongside *outgo*) and *fall by* (alongside *bifallen*).

Affixation
Only a few of the Old English prefixes (p. 22) continued into Middle English, but the system was supplemented by several new items from French and Latin, and the range of suffixes also increased (p. 46). New words formed include *authoress*, *consecration*, *duckling*, *forgetful*, *greenish*, *manhood*, *napkin*, *uncover*, *unknowable*, *withdraw*, and *wizard*. By no means all of the new formations were to stay in the language: for example, a different suffix eventually replaced several words ending in -*ship* (such as *boldship*, *cleanship*, and *kindship*), and several of the items which began life using *with*- were eventually replaced, such as *withsay* (renounce), *withspeak* (contradict), and *withset* (resist).

A sense of the range of words which came into the language through prefixation can be seen in the following selection of *dis*-items found in Chaucer (only one meaning is given in each case). The list also illustrates some of the suffixes typical of the time.

disavauncen set back
disaventure misadventure
disblamen exonerate
disceyven deceive
dischevele dishevelled
disclaunderen slander
discomfit discomfited
disconfiture discomfiture
disconfort discomfort
disconforten discourage
discorden disagree
discoveren uncover
discuren discover
disdeinous disdainful
disencresen decrease
disese discomfort
disesen trouble
disesperate desperate
disfigurat disguised
disgysen disguise
dishonest dishonourable
disobeysaunt disobedient
displesaunce displeasure
displesaunt displeasing
disposicioun disposition
disseveraunce separation
disrewlely irregularly
distemperaunce inclemency
dissolucioun dissoluteness

THE FAMOUS WORD PAIRS

No account of Middle English vocabulary would be complete without a reference to the famous culinary lexical pairs (often attributed to Sir Walter Scott) which resulted from the influx of Romance words.

Old English	French
ox	beef
sheep	mutton
calf	veal
deer	venison
pig, swine	pork

There are many other examples:

begin	commence
child	infant
doom	judgment
freedom	liberty
happiness	felicity
hearty	cordial
help	aid
hide	conceal
holy	saintly
love	charity
meal	repast
stench	aroma
wedding	marriage
wish	desire

MIDDLE ENGLISH DIALECTS

The main dialect divisions traditionally recognized in Middle English broadly correspond to those found in Old English (p. 28), but scholars have given different names to some of the dialects, and there has been one important development. *Kentish* remains the same, but West Saxon is now referred to as *Southern*, and Northumbrian as *Northern*. The Mercian dialect area has split in two: there is now an eastern dialect (*East Midland*) and a western one (*West Midland*). And the East Anglian region is sometimes separately distinguished. The map shows the traditional picture; but the result of a great deal of modern research (as illustrated opposite) has demonstrated that there is an enormous amount of oversimplification in such displays.

What evidence is there for dialect difference? The evidence lies in the distinctive words, grammar, and spellings found in the manuscripts. The way verb endings change is one of the main diagnostic features:

• The *-ing* participle ending (as in Modern English *running*) appears as *-and(e)* in Northern; as *-end(e)* in parts of the East Midlands; as *-ind(e)* in parts of the West Midlands; and as *-ing* elsewhere.

• The *-th* ending (as in *goeth*) appears as *-s* in Northern and throughout most of the north Midland area – a form which ultimately becomes standard.

• The verb ending used in the present tense with plural forms such as *we* and *they* also varies: it is *-es* in Northern and the northern parts of the East Midlands; *-eth* in Southern, Kentish, and the southern parts of the West Midlands; and *-en* elsewhere. (None of these endings has survived in Modern English.)

There were several other reliable indicators, apart from verbs:

• *They*, *their*, and *them* are found in Northern and the West Midlands, but they appear as *his*, *here*, and *hem* in the south – at least until towards the end of the Middle English period (p. 45).

• *Shall*, *should*, and a few other words appear without an *h* in Northern and Kentish (as *sal*, etc.), but keep it elsewhere.

• There are several distinctive uses of individual vowels and consonants. *Stane* in the north corresponds to *stone* in the south; *for* in the north Midlands to *vor* in the south; *kirk* in the north to *church* in the south; and so on. But in each case, we must remember, what we mean by 'north' and 'south' differs: there is no single, neat dividing line.

There are of course many manuscripts where it is not easy to determine the dialect. Sometimes the spellings of a text seems to reflect a mixture of dialects, perhaps because an author (or scribe) lived in a boundary area, or had moved about the country. Quite often,

an author is not particularly consistent – as would be likely to happen in a period when sounds and spellings were changing so rapidly (p. 32) and texts were being copied repeatedly. Sometimes, most of the forms reflect one dialect, and there is a scattering of forms from another – suggesting that the person who was copying the manuscript came from a different part of the country from the original author. And analysts need always to be watchful for the possibility that a form in a manuscript never had any linguistic existence at all – in other words, the copyist made a mistake.

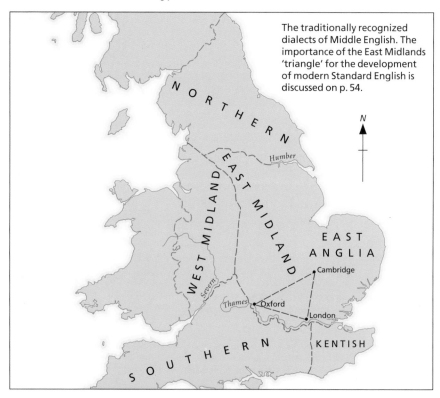

The traditionally recognized dialects of Middle English. The importance of the East Midlands 'triangle' for the development of modern Standard English is discussed on p. 54.

FOXED

Sometimes, sounds from different dialects have survived in alternative forms of a word in Modern English. *Fox* has an /f/, reflecting its Northern/ Midlands origins. *Vixen* has a /v/, reflecting its origins as a Southern word. In origin a feminine form of *fox* (compare German *Füchsin*), forms in *fixen(e)* are recorded from the early 15th century, both for the animal and (later) for its sense of a 'quarrelsome woman', and can be found until the early 17th century. The *v-* forms then become standard, but it is not known why this preference prevailed.

DIALECT REALITIES

The true complexity of the Middle English dialect situation was demonstrated in the 1980s by the atlas material of the Middle English Dialect Survey, based at the University of Edinburgh. The approach assumes that scribes were consistent in their methods of spelling, and that it is possible to examine orthographic variants to determine the dialect origins of a manuscript, quite independently of the sounds which the letters are thought to convey. The Survey plotted the distribution of the variants on maps, such as this one which gives over 500 instances of *church* and *kirk* from the first half of the 15th century. It shows clearly that *kirk* is northern and *church* is southern; but it also shows what is often ignored, that *kirk* was being used much further south than the traditional boundary suggests.

Moreover, there are some forms (such as *cherche*) which cut across the dialect boundaries, and interesting 'pockets' of usage where a particular spelling is popular.

Because some manuscripts (such as wills and charters) are definitely known to come from a certain place, it is possible to use the norms seen in such material as a yardstick against which texts of unknown provenance can be assessed. With enough 'anchor' points, it is often possible to fit an unlocalized text into the pattern displayed by a localized one. It is important, in such an approach, to make the timespan of the enquiry as narrow as possible, otherwise variation due to historical change is likely to interfere.

Dialect complexity of this order is only to be expected. Modern dialect surveys show it (§20), and there is no reason for the dialects of Middle English to be any different.

(After A. M. McIntosh, M. L. Samuels, & M. Benskin, 1986.)

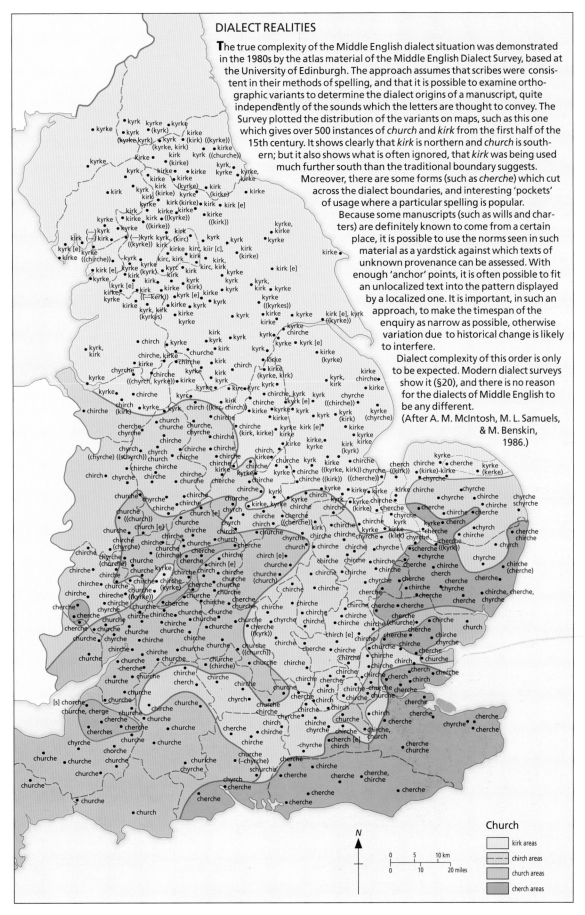

Church

- kirk areas
- chirch areas
- church areas
- cherch areas

N

| 0 | 5 | 10 km |
| 0 | 10 | 20 miles |

SYSTEM OR ERROR?

Betidde a time in litel quile
Iacob went walcande bi þe Ile
He sagh apon þe wateres reme
Chaf fletande come wiþ þe
    streme
Of þat siȝt wex he fulle bliþe
And tille his sones talde hit
    squyþe

It came to pass after a short
    while
Jacob went walking by the Nile
He saw upon the water's realm
Chaff come floating with the
    stream
That sight made him very glad
And he quickly told his sons
    about it

This extract from the late 13th-century biblical poem, *Cursor Mundi* (from the Fairfax text in the Bodleian Library, Oxford), illustrates one of the historical dialectologist's problems. Features such as *quile* (for 'while'), *walcande* ('walking'), and *talde* ('told') indicate that the text is Northern; and this is confirmed by the same features appearing elsewhere in the text. The *a* for *o*, for example, is found in *haly*, *fra*, *ga*, *lange*, *hame*, *name*, and many other words; and a corresponding set of *o* spellings appears in a Midland version of the text (such as the one held at Trinity College, Cambridge).

But in one line, we find this:

In goddes name and so we salle

So, with the same long vowel as the other words, ought to appear with an *a*, perhaps as *swa*. Why doesn't it? There are only two explanations. Either *so* is an exception to the rule, or it is a scribal error. If the former, we must find a reason – something in the adjacent sounds which might plausibly have caused the change to *o*, in just this case. There seems to be no such reason. Rather more likely is the second explanation. The scribe could have been copying out this text from a southern one in which the *o* vowel was used throughout, and 'translating' the spellings into the northern dialect of his readers as he went along; but at this point he made a slip. Support for this view would come from other slips of a similar kind – and indeed, we find the same scribe writing western *con* for eastern *can* a few lines earlier.

(After C. Jones, 1972.)

MIDDLE SCOTS

Students of the Middle English period have tradition-ally focused on the dialect situation in England, and especially on those areas in which the standard lan-guage was later to develop (p. 54). This has led to a neglect of what was taking place in Scotland at the time, where the language was being influenced by a different set of factors, and developing its own distinc-tive character.

From the outset, the region had its own linguistic history. After the 5th-century invasions, what is now the north-east of England and the south-east of Scot-land came to be occupied by the Angles, which led to the emergence of the Northumbrian dialect of Old English (p. 28). During the Anglo-Saxon period, most of Scotland was Celtic-speaking (chiefly the variety known as Gaelic), but the number of English speakers in the southern part of the country increased greatly in the 11th century, following the Norman Conquest. Many English noblemen became refugees and fled north, where they were welcomed by the Scots King Malcolm Canmore (reigned 1058–93). During the 12th century, the movement north continued, with southern families being invited to settle in the area by King David I (reigned 1124–53) – notably in the new chartered royal estates known as *burhs* (such as Aberdeen and Edinburgh). These places were largely English-speaking, and gradually English spread through the whole lowlands area, with Gaelic remain-ing beyond the Highland line. The English calendar replaced the Celtic one, and the Anglo-Norman feudal system replaced traditional patterns of land holding. Eventually, French became the language of the Scot-tish court. In 1295 there was a formal treaty between Scotland and France, renewed several times in the fol-lowing 200 years. As in England, Latin was used for administration and in the Church (p. 30).

This Scots English became increasingly different from the English used in England, especially in pro-nunciation and vocabulary, and many of these differ-ences are still found today (p. 328).

• In pronunciation, there was the use of *ch* in the middle of such words as *nicht* ('night'). A distinction was made between the first sound of *witch* and *which*. The vowel in such words as *guid* ('good') tended to be longer and produced further forward in the mouth than it was in southern English. A distinctive spelling difference is the use of *quh-* where southern English wrote *wh-* (*quhan, quhile*, etc.).
• There were some distinctive grammatical features, such as the past tense ending *-it* (*wantit* for *wanted*), forms for expressing negation (*nae, nocht, -na*), and *ane* as the indefinite article (for *a/an*).

• A number of loan words arrived which did not enter the language further south (for those that did, see p. 47). Examples from French include *bonny* ('beauti-ful, handsome'), *fash* ('to bother'), and *asbet* (a serving dish). *Callan* ('lad'), *mutchkin* ('quarter pint'), and *cowk* ('retch') were among those which arrived from Dutch, with whom Scottish merchants traded. Words from Gaelic included *clachan* ('hamlet'), *ingle* ('hearth fire'), and *strath* ('wide valley'). Several legal and administrative terms came in from Latin, such as *dominie* ('schoolmaster') and *fugie* ('runaway').

THE LANGUAGE OF GOLF

The Scottish origins of golf are there in the vocabulary. *Golf* itself is recorded in Scots English from the late 15th century, and various spellings suggest a pronunciation without an /l/, including *gouff*, *goiff*, *goff*, and *gowff*. The origins of the word are obscure. It is commonly thought to be a Dutch loanword, from *colf*, the name of a stick or club used in various striking games of the time, but there is no definite evidence.

Other golf-related terms which first appear in Scots English are *caddie* (from French *cadet*, 'cadet') and *links* (a development of an Old English word meaning 'rising ground'). These words have joined *scone*, *croon*, *croup*, and several others to give Modern English its Middle Scots lexical legacy (p. 329).

The golf course at St Andrews, Scotland.

THE BRUCE

The earliest surviving work to be written entirely in Scots English after the Conquest is a historical poem by John Barbour (1325?–95), archdeacon of Aberdeen. It was a Scottish national epic, a mixture of romance and chronicle, dealing with 'The Actes and Life of the most Victorious Con-queror, Robert Bruce King of Scotland'. It was completed in 1376, taking up 20 books, and is preserved in manuscripts of a century later.

This extract is from the siege of Berwick (1319).

Thar mycht men se a felloune sicht:
With staffing, stoking, and striking
Thar maid thai sturdy defending,
For with gret strynth of men the þet
Thai defendit, and stude tharat,
Magré thair fais, quhill the nycht
Gert thame on bath halfis leif the ficht.

There might men see a grim sight:
With hitting [with staffs], stabbing, and
  striking
There they made an obstinate defence
For with a great force of men the gate
They defended, and stood there,
In spite of their foes, until the night
Caused them on both sides to stop fighting

Rise and fall

By the end of the 13th century, the English of Scotland and that of England had markedly diverged. A major social factor had been the split between the nations which followed Edward I of England's attempt at annexation, and the subsequent long period of conflict. From 1424, the Scottish Parliament wrote its statutes in English. By the late Middle Ages, Middle Scots had evolved as far from Old English as had the Middle English of England, and in a different direction. It is often said that the two varieties were as far apart as, say, Danish and Swedish are today – largely mutually intelligible, but capable of supporting national identities. As a result, some writers on the period refer to the two varieties as distinct 'languages' – and continue to do so when discussing modern Scots. The term 'Scottis' (as opposed to the previously used 'Inglis') comes to be used in the late 15th century. The period as a whole (*Older Scots*) tends to be divided into *Early Scots* (1100–1450) and *Middle Scots* (1450–1700).

From the end of the 14th century to the beginning of the 17th, there was a flowering of literature in Scots – a period which reached its peak in the poetry of the 15th-century *makars* ('makers'), such as Robert Henryson, William Dunbar, and Gavin Douglas. Southern English literature exercised considerable influence, especially the poetry of Chaucer, to such an extent that this group is often called the 'Scottish Chaucerians'. Scots also increasingly replaced Latin as an administrative language, and came to be widely used in sermons, diaries, letters, and other private and public literature. By the end of the century it had effectively established itself as a regional standard.

This course of development altered during the 16th century, as Scots fell progressively under the influence of the strongly emerging Standard English of the south. Southern words and spellings became increasingly evident in Scottish writing, and printers began to anglicize material presented to them in Scots. The main factor was the uniting of the crowns of Scotland and England in 1603, and the move to London of James VI and the Scottish court – a move which led in due course to the adoption among the upper classes of southern English norms of speech. As James I of England, the new king ordered that the Authorized Version of the Bible (p. 64) be used in Scotland, thus spreading further the influence of the southern standard as a prestige form. There is very little sign of a distinctive variety of Scots in published material at the end of the 17th century. However, Scots English was not fated to become extinct: its later history is reviewed on pp. 328–33.

THE MAKARS

The leading poets of Scotland from *c.* 1425 to *c.* 1550 are usually grouped together as the 'Scottish Chaucerians', because of the way they were influenced by the themes and verse style of Chaucer (p. 38). In fact, their poetry shows a mixture of influences, ranging from a courtly 'aureate' style, full of Latinate diction, to forceful abuse (flyting) in Scots vernacular. *The Tretis of the Twa Mariit Wemen and the Wedo* – a conversation between two married women and a widow – illustrates something of this range. The poem is by William Dunbar (*c.* 1460–*c.* 1520), who was employed at the Scottish court. It parodies the high style of the literary pastoral, and juxtaposes earthy comments in colloquial Scots, as the women talk about their husbands.

I saw thre gay ladeis sit in ane grein arbeir
    [*arbour*]
All grathit [*decked*] into garlandis of freshe
    gudlie flouris;

So glitterit as the gold wer thair glorius gilt
    tressis,
Quhill [*While*] all the gressis [*grass*] did
    gleme of the glaid hewis;
Kemmit [*combed*] was thair cleir hair, and
    curiouslie shed
Attour thair shulderis doun shyre [*clear*],
    shyning full bricht…

I have ane wallirag [*sloven*], ane worme,
    ane auld wobat [*caterpillar*] carle
A waistit wolroun [*boar*], na worth but
    wordis to clatter;
Ane bumbart [*driveller*], ane dron bee, ane
    bag full of flewme,
Ane skabbit skarth [*scurvy cormorant*], ane
    scorpioun, ane scutarde behind;
To see him scart [*scratch*] his awin skyn grit
    scunner [*disgust*] I think.

The meaning of all the words in this passage is not entirely clear – but their sound leaves no doubt about their intent. The /sk-/ sequence is particularly notable (p. 251).

AN EFFORT 'TO REFORM AN ERROUR'

The Scots were well aware of what was happening to their language, as is clear from this story, told by Alexander Hume in his *Orthographie and Congruitie of the Britan Tongue*, written *c.* 1617, and intended for use in Scottish schools. He is defending the Scots spelling *quh-* for *wh-* against some unsympathetic English colleagues. Despite the *quh-* spellings put into the mouths of the English, the passage is full of southernisms, such as *laughed* (which has no *ch*, and uses the *-ed* inflection) and *a* or *an* (instead of *ane*). It shows how much influence southern English had exercised on Scots by this time – even on a staunch defender.

…to reform an errour bred in the south, and now usurped be our ignorant printeres, I wil tel quhat befel my-self quhen I was in the south with a special gud frende of myne. Ther rease [*rose*], upon sum accident, quhither [*whether*] quho, quhen, quhat, etc., sould be symbolized with q or w, a hoat [*hot*] disputation betuene him and me. After manie conflictes (for we oft encountered), we met be chance, in the citie of baeth [*Bath*], with a doctour of divinitie of both our acquentance. He invited us to denner. At table my antagonist, to bring the question on foot amangs his awn condisciples, began that I was becum an heretik, and the doctour spering [*asking*] how, ansuered that I denyed quho to be spelled with a w, but with qu. Be quhat reason? quod the Doctour. Here, I beginning to lay my grundes of labial, dental, and guttural soundes and symboles, he snapped me on this hand and he on that, that the doctour had mikle a doe to win me room for a syllogisme. Then (said I) a labial letter can not symboliz a guttural syllab [*syllable*]. But w is a labial letter, quho a guttural sound. And therfoer w can not symboliz quho, nor noe syllab of that nature. Here the doctour staying them again (for al barked at ones), the proposition, said he, I understand; the assumption is Scottish, and the conclusion false. Quherat al laughed, as if I had bene dryven from al replye, and I fretted to see a frivolouse jest goe for a solid ansuer.

A NEW NATION

In 1604 James made a speech to his first Parliament, in which he declared his intentions to rule a single nation:

I am the Husband and the whole Isle is my lawfull Wife; I am the Head and it is my Body; I am the Shepherd and it is my flocke; I hope therefore no man will be so unreasonable as to think that I that am a Christian King under the Gospel should be a polygamist and husband to two wives; that I being the Head should have a divided and monstrous Body.

In such circumstances, two written standards could not possibly co-exist. What is remarkable is that Scots was able to survive the court's move to London, the Union of Parliaments a century later (1707), and a great deal of later ridicule levelled at those who continued to use 'Scotticisms', to surface again in the 20th century.

THE ORIGINS OF STANDARD ENGLISH

The variety which we now call Standard English (p. 110) is the result of a combination of influences, the most important of which do not emerge until the Middle English period. There is no direct connection between West Saxon, the written standard of Old English (p. 28), and the modern standard. The political heart of the country moved from Winchester to London after the Conquest, and the major linguistic trends during Middle English increasingly relate to the development of the capital as a social, political, and commercial centre. A written standard English began to emerge during the 15th century and, following the detailed study of the dialect characteristics of the period, it is now possible to isolate several factors which contributed to its identity (after M. L. Samuels, 1963).

• A regionally standardized literary language appeared in the last part of the 14th century, based on the dialects of the Central Midland counties, especially Northamptonshire, Huntingdonshire, and Bedfordshire. This is chiefly found in the large number of Wycliffite manuscripts which have survived (p. 48), including sermons, tracts, prayers, poems, and the different versions of the Wycliff Bible, as well as several secular works. The Lollards spread this variety widely, even into south-west England, thus increasing its status as a standard. In the long term, it was unable to compete with the quantity of material emanating from the capital; but its Central Midland origins are nonetheless noteworthy (see below).

• The growth of a standard from the London area can be seen by the mid-14th century. Although London was very much a dialectal hybrid (with the City influenced by the Essex dialect, and Westminster, some distance further west, showing the influence of Middlesex), patterns of standardization gradually appear. There is a small group of manuscripts, written prior to 1370, which are noted for their uniformity of spelling. A later and much larger group of diverse manuscripts include the work of Chaucer and Langland. These texts in their different ways represent London English of around 1400, but the amount of variation they display suggests that they cannot be called a standard, in any strict sense. Not even Chaucer's writing, traditionally thought to be a precursor of modern Standard English, exercised a specific influence on the form this standard took – nor is it likely that poetic usage would ever influence general usage in any real way (p. 412). It can hardly be doubted, though, that Chaucer's literary standing would have greatly added to the prestige associated with written language in the London dialect.

• The most significant factor must have been the emergence of London as the political and commercial centre of the country. In particular the influence of the administrative offices of the London Chancery (p. 41) is now thought to have been critical, especially after c. 1430. Vast amounts of manuscript copying took place within the London area, and standards of practice emerged among the Chancery scribes. These practices then influenced the many individual scribes who worked privately, and eventually all kinds of material, including literary texts, were affected. It would not have taken long for a widespread standardization to be current. When Caxton set up his press in Westminster (p. 56), and chose local London speech as his norm, the lasting influence of his Chancery Lane neighbours was assured.

These observations add up to the claim that the main influence on the standard language was the Central Midlands area, several of whose linguistic features eventually influenced the shape of Chancery Standard. That the central area could exercise such influence is suggested by a number of contemporary comments, as well as by deductions based on social history. John of Trevisa, translating Higden's *Polychronicon* (p. 35) in

DIALECT ROUTES

A map of 14th-century roads, based on an original by Richard Gough, showing the most important routes in and out of London – notably, the Great North Road and Watling Street, leading to the Central Midlands. No other part of the country had better communications with the capital. If people were to bring their dialects to London in ever-increasing numbers, most would travel along these roads.

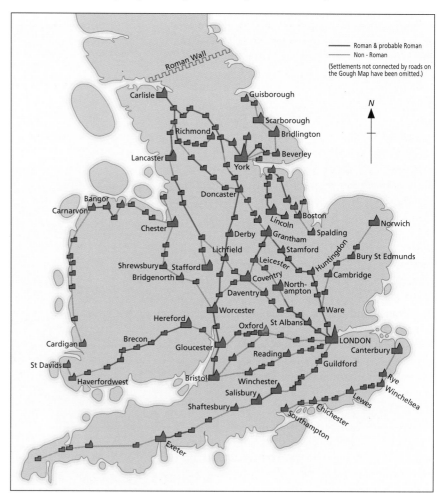

*c.*1387, identifies its function as a communication 'bridge' between north and south:

for men of þe est wiþ men of þe west, as it were vndir þe same partie of heuene, acordeþ more in sownynge of speche [pronunciation] þan men of þe norþ wiþ men of þe souþ; þerfore it is þat Mercii [Mercians], þat beeþ men of myddel Engelond, as it were parteners of þe endes, vnderstondeþ bettre þe side langages, norþerne and souþerne, þan norþerne and souþerne vnderstondeþ eiþer oþer.

By way of social considerations, we have evidence of a marked population shift in the 14th century. In the earlier part of that century, immigration to the London area was highest from the East Midlands counties of Norfolk, Essex, and Hertfordshire, but it later increased dramatically from such Central Midlands counties as Leicestershire, Northamptonshire, and Bedfordshire. As a result, the London dialect came to display many of the linguistic features of Midland writing.

These observations bring a fresh perspective to the traditional map of Middle English dialects (p. 50), where no recognition is given to a Central Midlands area, and where special attention is paid to an East Midlands 'triangle' bounded by London, Cambridge, and (on the borders with Southern) Oxford – an area of high population, containing the main social and political centre, and the main seats of learning. This was a wealthy agricultural region, and the centre of the growing wool trade. Its role in promoting the importance of the south-east in the Middle Ages is clear. However, the findings of present-day historical dialectology suggest that its linguistic influence was far less important than that of the area further west.

The final factor in the emergence of a southern literary standard was the development of printing (p. 56). This resulted in the spread of a single norm over most of the country, so much so that during the 15th century it becomes increasingly difficult to determine on internal linguistic grounds the dialect in which a literary work is written – apart from the northern dialects, such as Scots, which retained their written identity longer (p. 52). People now begin to make value judgments about other dialects. In the Towneley Plays (p. 58), Mak the sheep-stealer masquerades as a person of importance, and adopts a southern accent. John of Trevisa comments that northern speech is 'scharp, slitting, and frotynge and vnschape' ('shrill, cutting, and grating and ill-formed'), giving as one of the reasons that northerners live far away from the court. And in *The Arte of English Poesie*, attributed to George Puttenham (*c.* 1520–90), the aspiring poet is advised to use 'the usuall speach of the Court, and that of London and the shires lying about London within lx. myles, and not much above'. There was never to be total uniformity, but the forerunner of Standard English undoubtedly existed by the end of the 15th century.

THE GREAT VOWEL SHIFT

Why does the sound system used in Chaucer's time (p. 38) seem so different from that found in Shakespeare's (p. 25)? Why is Chaucer so much more difficult to read than Caxton, less than a century later? The answer to both these questions lies in a major change in pronunciation which took place at the very end of the Middle English period. Chaucer probably heard it beginning, but it did not take proper effect until the early decades of the 15th century. Because of the way the vowel system of the language was fundamentally affected, the change has been called the *Great Vowel Shift*.

The changes affected the seven long vowels in the language (p. 42), shown in Figure A on a cardinal vowel diagram (p. 238). Each vowel changed its sound quality, but the distinction between one vowel and the next was maintained. (The two front vowels /eː/ and /ɛː/ did merge as /iː/, but not until the 18th century.) In two cases, just a single move was involved (B3, B4); in others, the movement had further consequences which sometimes took 200 years to work themselves out. It is

the first main stage in this development which is usually referred to as the 'shift'.

Push-me, pull-you
The traditional view is that the series of changes was connected, a move in one of the vowels causing a move in another, and so on throughout the system, with each vowel 'keeping its distance' from its neighbour. However, there is a long-standing dispute over which vowel moved first.

• In one view, the /iː/ vowel was the first to change (becoming a diphthong), which left a 'space' into which the next vowel came, 'pulling' other vowels upwards in a chain reaction (Figure C).
• Alternatively, the /ɑː/ vowel was the first to move (further forwards), 'pushing' the next vowel upwards, and starting off a different chain reaction (Figure D). The problem with this view is finding a reason for the back vowel movement, once /ɑː/ is used to start the front vowel chain reaction.

Whether we favour pushing or pulling, we seem to be dealing with a sound change that is simple and symmetrical. The vowels appear to be moving 'in pairs', with the same things

happening at the front and the back of the mouth. A great deal of evidence has been used to support this interpretation, in the form of the order in which new spellings appeared (such as *ei* for /iː/), the use of new rhymes, and the descriptions of contemporary writers.

In the 1980s, as more textual evidence and dialect survey material became available, the simplicity of this explanation was called into question. Some scholars now doubt the connectedness of the changes, either in whole or in part. Some think that there were two separate chain-like movements which belonged to different parts of the country, but which came together in certain texts – two 'small' vowel shifts (raising and diphthongization) rather than one 'big' one. The sifting of the textual evidence, it seems, has hardly begun, and suddenly what was for so long an uncontroversial issue has become an open question. It is one of many reanalyses which are ongoing, as scholars get to grips with the data being provided by the major Middle English surveys. It is an exciting time for linguistic medievalists.

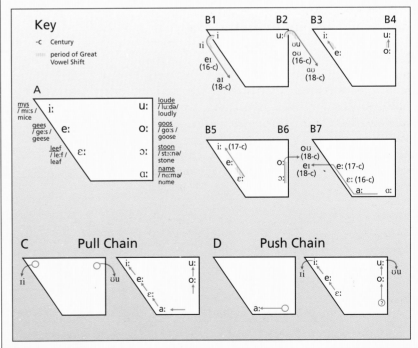

5 · EARLY MODERN ENGLISH

There is no doubt that an Early Modern English period needs to be recognized in the history of English. The jump from Middle English to Modern English would be too great without it. Between the time of Chaucer and the time of Johnson, roughly 1400 to 1800, the language continues to change in quite noticeable ways, and there are many points of difference with modern usage. By the end of the 18th century, however, very few linguistic differences remain. Reading a Jane Austen novel does not require the same kind of effort or editorial elaboration as is needed to understand Shakespeare (p. 76).

There is no consensus about when the Early Modern English period begins. Some opt for an early date, 1400–50, just after Chaucer and the beginning of the pronunciation shift which identifies a major intelligibility barrier between Middle and Modern English (p. 55). Some opt for a late date, around 1500, after the effects of the printing revolution had become well established. But it is the advent of printing itself which many consider to be the key factor, and this section accordingly begins in 1476, when William Caxton set up his press in Westminster.

The new invention gave an unprecedented impetus to the formation of a standard language and the study of its properties. Apart from its role in fostering norms of spelling and punctuation, the availability of printing provided more opportunities for people to write, and gave their works much wider circulation. As a result, more texts of the period have survived. Within the following 150 years, it is estimated that nearly 20,000 books appeared. The story of English thus becomes more definite in the 16th century, with more evidence available about the way the language was developing, both in the texts themselves, and in a growing number of observations dealing with such areas as grammar, vocabulary, writing system, and style. In that century, scholars seriously got down to talking *about* their language (p. 61).

THE FIRST ENGLISH PRINTER

William Caxton was born in Kent, and by 1438 is known to have been apprenticed to a London textile dealer, or mercer. This suggests a birthdate any time between 1415 and 1424. He went to Bruges during the early 1440s, where he prospered as a mercer, and in 1462 was appointed governor of the English trading company there, the Merchant Adventurers.

In 1469 he began work on his first translation, a French account of the Trojan Wars, and two years later received the patronage of Margaret, Duchess of Burgundy, which enabled him to complete it. In 1471 he travelled to Cologne, where he stayed for 18 months, and learned the technique of printing. Back in Bruges he collaborated with the Flemish calligrapher Colard Mansion to set up a press, and in late 1473 or early 1474 put through his 700-page translation of *The Recuyell* [French *recueil* 'compilation'] *of the Historyes of Troye*, the first book printed in English. Returning to England, in 1476 he set up his wooden press in a shop somewhere within the precincts of Westminster Abbey, to be near the court.

He published nearly 80 items, several in more than one edition. We know very little about how long he

The earliest known representation of a printing office: *La grante danse macabre* (1499), with death coming to take wicked printers away.

took to translate or print a work, despite the details he provides in his prologues and epilogues, because we do not know how conditions changed as he and his staff grew in experience. We do not even know how many presses he had, or whether he worked on more than one book at a time. Evidently, some works were produced quite slowly; others very rapidly. For example, it took him about seven weeks to print *Cordial* (1479) – a book of 74 leaves with 28/29 lines per page; but in 1483, a book of 115 leaves with 38 lines per page (*Festial*) was completed in just 24 days.

After his death, his business was taken over by his assistant, Wynkyn de Worde, who in 1500 moved the press to Fleet Street in London – from the court to the city – and a new era in printing began.

Caxton shows his handiwork to Edward IV at the almonry, Westminster.

THE ADVERTISEMENT

> ℑf it plese onẏ man ſpirituel oꝛ temporel to bẏe onẏ pẏes of two and thꝛe comemoꝛacōs of ſaliſburi vſe enprẏntid after the foꝛme of this preſēt lettre whiche ben wel and truly correct, late hẏm come to weſtmoꝛneſter in to the almoneſrẏe at the reed pale and he ſhal haue them good chepe ⁖
>
> ### Supplico ſtet cedula

If it plese ony man spirituel or temporel to bye ony pyes of two and thre comemoracions of Salisburi Use enpryntid after the forme of this present lettre, whiche ben wel and truly correct, late hym come to Westmonester in to the Almonesrye at the Reed Pale and he shal have them good chepe. *Supplico sted cedula*.

The 'pye' which was for sale was the *Ordinale*, a book of Latin liturgical directions also printed by Caxton in *c.* 1477, and evidently in the same typeface ('forme'). A pye was a collection of rules showing how to act liturgically on a day when there was more than one office, or 'commemoration'. The 'Salisburi Use' was the widely practised form of the liturgy originally developed at Salisbury Cathedral. The commemorations are to the Virgin Mary and the saints. The last sentence tells the audience that a printed book will be cheap (that is, compared with the price of a copied manuscript). The shop in the almonry at Westminster was within the Abbey precincts. The significance of Caxton's sign, the Red Pale, is unknown: it may have been on the shop already, before he rented it. Someone has glossed the Latin, for the benefit of the less well educated.

The first printed works

We know of 103 separate items printed by Caxton, several of which are different editions of the same work. They can be grouped into four categories (after N. Blake, 1969):

- His own translations, such as *The Recuyell of the Historyes of Troy* and *The Knight of the Tower*. This is the largest category, its prologues and epilogues providing a great deal of information about Caxton's aims as a publisher.
- Works of the courtly poets of 1350–1450 – chiefly, Chaucer, Gower, and Lydgate – and including two editions of *The Canterbury Tales*. Caxton's concentration on these authors shows him aware of the fashionable demand for an 'elevated' style of writing.
- Prose works in English, also including many translations, such as Chaucer's *Boethius*, Trevisa's *Polychronicon* (p. 35), and Malory's *Morte Darthur* (p. 58).
- A miscellaneous group of works, probably produced for particular clients. They include books of indulgences, statutes, phrase books, devotional pieces, and a Latin grammar.

A TIME OF CHANGE

From the epilogue to *Charles the Great*, the 'first Cristen Kyng of Fraunce':

The whyche werke was fynysshed in the reducyng of hit into Englysshe the xviii day of Juyn the second yere of Kyng Rychard the Thyrd and the yere of Our Lord MCCCClxxxv, and emprynted the fyrst day of Decembre the same yere of Our Lord and the fyrst yere of Kyng Harry the Seventh.

In the meantime, there had been the Battle of Bosworth: 22 August 1485.

WITHOUT WHOM . . .

A page from the first English printed book, *The Recuyell of the Historyes of Troy*. In the prologue, Caxton tells of his debt to the Duchess of Burgundy, and adds some interesting remarks about his own background.

And afterward whan I rememberyd my self of my symplenes and vnperfightnes that I had in bothe langages, that is to wete [*namely*] in Frenshe and in Englisshe, for in France was I neuer, and was born & lerned myn Englissh in Kente in the Weeld, where I doubte not is spoken as brode and rude Englissh as is in ony place of Englond; & haue contynued by the space of xxx yere for the most parte in the contres [*countries*] of Braband, Flandres, Holand, and Zeland; and thus when alle thyse thynges cam tofore me aftyr that Y had made and wretyn a fyue or six quayers [*books*], Y fyll in dispayr of thys werke and purposid no more to haue contynuyd therin, and tho [*those*] quayers leyd apart; and in two yere aftyr laboured no more in thys werke. And was fully in wyll to haue lefte hyt tyll on a tyme hit fortuned that the ryght redoughted lady, my Lady Margarete . . . sente for me to speke wyth her good grace of dyuerce maters. Among the whyche Y lete her Hyenes haue knowleche of the forsayd begynnyng of thys werke, whiche anone comanded me to shewe the sayd v or vi quayers to her sayd grace. And whan she had seen hem, anone she fonde [*found*] a defaute in myn Englissh whiche sche comanded me to amende and moreouer comanded me straytli to contynue and make an ende of the resydue than not translated . . .

This book was printed in Bruges. The first book Caxton printed in England was *The Dictes or Sayengis of the Philosophres* (1477), translated from French by the second Earl Rivers.

CAXTON'S PROBLEM

Caxton was a merchant, not a linguist or a literary scholar. Faced with the task of translation, he had to deal with several major problems:

- Should he use foreign words in his translation or replace them by native English words?
- Which variety of English should he follow, given the existence of major regional differences?
- Which literary style should be used as a model? Chaucer? Or something less 'ornate'?
- How should the language be spelled and punctuated, given the scribal variations of the previous centuries?
- In publishing native writers, should he change their language to make it more widely understood?

If the books were to sell, the language they contained had to be understood throughout the country; but, as he complained, how could he satisfy everyone? A famous extract from one of his prologues gives a vivid account of the size of the problem. If even a simple little word like *eggs* cannot be universally understood, what hope was there for him?

Caxton made his decisions, as did other publishers of the time, and in due course a consensus arose (p. 66). His own work is in fact extremely inconsistent. It is not until nearly a century later that there is uniformity in the appearance of printed texts – and indeed some matters (such as the use of the apostrophe) never settle down at all (p. 203).

THE 'EGG' STORY

And also my lorde abbot of westmynster ded [*did*] do shewe to me late certayn euydences [*documents*] wryton in olde englysshe for to reduce it in to our englysshe now vsid [*used*] / And certaynly it was wreton in suche wyse that it was more lyke to dutche [*German*] than englysshe I coude not reduce ne brynge it to be vnderstonden / And certaynly our langage now vsed varyeth ferre from that. whiche was vsed and spoken whan I was borne / For we englysshe men / ben [*are*] borne vnder the domynacyon of the mone. [*moon*] whiche is neuer stedfaste / but euer wauerynge / wexynge one season / and waneth & dyscreaseth another season / And that comyn englysshe that is spoken in one shyre varyeth from a nother. In so moche that in my dayes happened that certayn marchauntes were in a shippe in tamyse [*Thames*] for to haue sayled ouer the see into zelande / and for lacke of wynde thei taryed atte forlond. [*headland*] and wente to lande for to refreshe them And one of theym named sheffelde a mercer cam into an hows and axed [*asked*] for mete. and specyally he axyd after eggys And the good wyf answerde. that she coude speke no frenshe. And the marchaunt was angry. for he also coude speke no frenshe. but wold haue hadde egges / and she vnderstode hym not / And thenne at laste a nother sayd that he wolde haue eyren / then the good wyf sayd that she vnderstod hym wel / Loo what sholde a man in thyse dayes now wryte. egges or eyren / certaynly it is harde to playse euery man / by cause of dyuersite & chaunge of langage.

Sheffield's problem arose because *egges* was a northern form, a development from Old Norse, whereas *eyren* was a southern form, a development from Old English. The passage also shows some of Caxton's spelling inconsistencies and his idiosyncratic use of punctuation and capital letters. (Prologue to Virgil's *Booke of Eneydos*, c. 1490, with modern punctuation.)

TRANSITIONAL TEXTS

Several authors and texts illustrate the linguistic transition from Middle to Early Modern English. They include the great prose romance translated by Sir Thomas Malory, the *Morte Darthur*, published by Caxton in 1485, and the cycles of miracle and mystery plays, preserved in several 15th-century manuscripts. There are still many points of grammar, spelling, and vocabulary which cause difficulty to the 20th-century reader, but overall the language is familiar and intelligible, and is often used in modern presentations with little editorial intervention.

MYSTERY PLAYS

The miracle and mystery plays of medieval Europe were plays on biblical subjects, performed in cycles on special religious occasions such as the feast of Corpus Christi. The extract below is from the 32-play *Towneley Cycle* (so called because the manuscript once belonged to the library of Towneley Hall in Lancashire), and thought to have been the text for the plays performed at Wakefield in West Yorkshire.

Some of the plays have been acclaimed for the dramatically interesting way in which they develop their plot and characters, adding an extra dimension to the religious subject-matter. A case in point is the *Second Shepherds' Play*, which has been called the earliest surviving English comedy. The extract is from the episode where the shepherds visit Mak, the sheep-stealer, in his house, and find their sheep wrapped up as a baby in a cradle. Of stylistic note is the lively conversational rhythm of the dialogue and the humorous use of rhyme. Of grammatical note is the northern dialect *-s* ending on the third person singular present tense (p. 65).

FIRST SHEPHERD: Gaf ye the chyld any thyng?
SECOND SHEPHERD: I trow not oone farthyng.
THIRD SHEPHERD: Fast agane will I flyng,
          Abyde ye me there.
     Mak, take it to no grefe if I com to thi barne [*child*].
MAK: Nay, thou dos me greatt reprefe, and fowll has thou farne [*behaved*].
THIRD SHEPHERD: The child will it not grefe, that lytyll day starne [*star*].
     Mak, with your leyfe, let me gyf youre barne
          Bot sex pence.
MAK: Nay, do way: he slepys.
THIRD SHEPHERD: Me thynk he pepys.
MAK: When he wakyns he wepys.
     I pray you go hence.
THIRD SHEPHERD: Gyf me lefe hym to kys, and lyft up the clowtt.
     What the dewill is this? He has a long snowte.

The sheep-stealing scene from the Hijinx Theatre 1993 production of *In the Bleak Mid Winter* by Charles Way, with Richard Berry as Zac, Firenza Guidi as Miriam, Helen Gwyn as Gill, and David Murray as Mak.

THE QUEST OF THE HOLY GRAIL

The author of the work traditionally called the *Morte Darthur* calls himself Thomas Malory, a knight, who was in prison when he did most of the writing (1469–70). His identity is controversial, the leading candidate being Sir Thomas Malory of Newbold Revell in Warwickshire (1393?–1471), who served in France under the Earl of Warwick.

The extract is from Chapter 8 of Book XIII of Caxton's edition, and shows several of the features characteristic of his work (p. 57). There is the use of the slash mark as the main feature of punctuation, but with little system in its use: it can mark the end of a sentence (but not always), a major grammatical boundary within a sentence (but not all of them), or just a pause. The capital letter, likewise, appears unexpectedly (Wold) and inconsistently (in Quene and Launcelot). A great deal of editorial intervention is needed to provide a readily intelligible text; but in most other respects the grammar and vocabulary are accessible, and the narrative appealing – as Caxton puts it in his prologue: full of 'noble actes, feates of armes of chyvalrye, prowesse, hardynesse, humanyte, love, curtosye and veray gentylnesse, wyth many wonderful hystoryes and adventures'.

Thenne after the seruyse [*service*] was done / the kyng Wold wete [*wished to know*] how many had vndertake the queste of the holy graylle / and to accompte them he prayed them all [*he prayed them all to count themselves*] / Thenne fond they by the tale [*count*] an honderd and fyfty / and alle were knyghtes of the table round / And thenne they putte on their helmes and departed / and recommaunded them all holy [*entirely*] vnto the Quene / and there was wepynge and grete sorowe / Thenne the Quene departed in to her chamber / and helde her / that no man shold perceyue her grete sorowes / whanne syre Launcelot myst the quene / he wente tyl her chamber / And when she sawe hym / she cryed aloude / O launcelot / launcelot ye haue bitrayed me / and putte me to the deth for to leue thus my lord A madame I praye yow be not displeased / for I shall come ageyne as soone as I may with my worship / Allas sayd she that euer I sawe yow / but he that suffred vpon the crosse for all mankynde he be vnto yow good conduyte and saufte [*protection*] / and alle the hole felaushyp / Ryght soo departed Launcelot / & fond his felaushyp that abode [*awaited*] his comyng / and so they mounted on their horses / and rode thorou the strete of Camelot / and there was wepynge of ryche and poure / and the kyng tourned awey and myghte not speke for wepynge /

THE AGE OF BIBLES

The King James Bible, also known as the Authorized Version of the Bible, published in 1611, exercised enormous influence on the development of the language (p. 64); but it was itself influenced by several existing versions, all produced during the 16th century. The motivation for these bibles lay in the religious controversies of the day (Luther's protest at Wittenburg took place in 1517). Accordingly, they display great variation, not only in theological slant and stylistic level, but also in typography, presentation, editorial matter, and mode of presentation. For the historical linguist, the range and frequency of editions provides an unparalleled opportunity to view the development of the language at that time. Because they are all translations of the same core set of texts, the different versions can throw special light on changes in orthography, grammar, and vocabulary throughout the period.

The cover of the Great Bible

TYNDALE'S POPULAR VOICE

I had perceaved by experyence, how that it was impossible to stablysh the laye people in any truth, excepte the scripture were playnly layde before their eyes in their mother tonge, that they might se the processe, ordre and meaninge of the texte…

Tyndale's aim to translate for the people can be seen in the colloquial style of many passages:

1 But the serpent was sotyller than all the beastes of the felde which ye LORde God had made, and sayd unto the woman. Ah syr [*sure*], that God hath sayd, ye shall not eate of all maner trees in the garden. 2 And the woman sayd unto the serpent, of the frute of the trees in the garden we may eate, 3 but of the frute of the tree that is in the myddes of the garden (sayd God) se that we eate not, and se that ye touch it not: lest ye dye. 4 Then sayd the serpent unto the woman: tush ye shall not dye: 5 But God doth knowe, that whensoever ye shulde eate of it, youre eyes shuld be opened and ye sholde be as God and knowe both good and evell. 6 And the woman sawe that it was a good tree to eate of and lustie [*desirable*] unto the eyes and a plesant tre for to make wyse. And toke of the frute of it and ate, and gaue unto hir husband also with her, and he ate. 7 And the eyes of both of them were opened, that they understode how that they were naked. Than they sowed fygge leves togedder and made them apurns [*aprons*]. (Genesis 3.1–7)

TYNDALE'S INFLUENCE

It has been estimated that about 80 per cent of the text of the Authorized Version shows the influence of Tyndale. The Beatitudes is a good example: the differences are minor, and the number of words in the two passages (Matthew 5.1–10) almost identical.

Tyndale	Authorized Version
1 When he sawe the people, he went vp into a mountayne, and when he was set, his disciples came to hym, 2 and he opened hys mouthe, and taught them sayinge: 3 Blessed are the povre in sprete: for theirs is the kyngdome of heven. 4 Blessed are they that morne: for they shalbe conforted. 5 Blessed are the meke: for they shall inheret the erth. 6 Blessed are they which honger and thurst for rightewesnes: for they shalbe filled. 7 Blessed are the mercifull: for they shall obteyne mercy. 8 Blessed are the pure in herte: for they shall se God. 9 Blessed are the peacemakers: for they shalbe called the chyldren of God. 10 Blessed are they which suffre persecucion for rightwesnes sake: for theirs ys the kyngdome of heuen.	1 And seeing the multitudes, he went vp into a mountaine: and when he was set, his disciples came vnto him. 2 And he opened his mouth, and taught them, saying, 3 Blessed are the poore in spirit: for theirs is the kingdome of heauen. 4 Blessed are they that mourne: for they shall be comforted. 5 Blessed are the meeke: for they shall inherit the earth. 6 Blessed are they which doe hunger and thirst after righteousnesse: for they shall be filled. 7 Blessed are the mercifull: for they shall obtaine mercie. 8 Blessed are the pure in heart: for they shall see God. 9 Blessed are the peacemakers: for they shall bee called the children of God. 10 Blessed are they which are persecuted for righteousnesse sake: for theirs is the kingdome of heauen.

THE CHIEF 16TH-CENTURY TRANSLATIONS

William Tyndale (c. 1494–1536)
Tyndale's New Testament of 1525, revised in 1534, was the first English vernacular text to be printed (in Cologne), and the basis for most subsequent versions. He was a strong proponent of the view that people should be able to read the Bible in their own language.

Miles Coverdale (?1488–1569)
Coverdale's text of 1535, published at Cologne, was the first complete Bible to be printed in English. It was a translation from German.

Matthew's Bible (1537)
This complete Bible was the first to be printed in England. The text is attributed to Thomas Matthew, Chamberlain of Colchester, but it was compiled by John Rogers, a friend of Tyndale's. It is based largely on Tyndale's work, with some use of Coverdale.

The Great Bible (1539)
This text, so-called because of its physical size, was the first of many official versions for use in Protestant England. A copy would be placed in every parish church in the country. It is a revision of Matthew's Bible by Coverdale. Because Archbishop Thomas Cranmer wrote a preface to it, the work became widely known as 'Cranmer's Bible'.

The Geneva Bible (1560)
This translation was produced by English Protestant exiles during the reign of Queen Mary. It was the first English Bible in roman type.

The Bishops' Bible (1568)
This revised version of the Great Bible became the official version of the Church in 1571, and was used by the scholars working on the Authorized Version (p. 64).

The Douai-Rheims Bible (1609–10)
This translation was issued by Roman Catholic priests in exile in Europe. The Rheims New Testament first appeared in 1582, and the remaining text was produced from Douai in 1609. Based on the Latin Vulgate, it was used by English Catholics for the next century.

ENGLISH DURING THE RENAISSANCE

During the 16th century there was a flood of new publications in English, prompted by a renewed interest in the classical languages and literatures, and in the rapidly developing fields of science, medicine, and the arts. This period, from the time of Caxton until around 1650, was later to be called the 'Renaissance', and it included the Reformation, the discoveries of Copernicus, and the European exploration of Africa and the Americas. The effects of these fresh perspectives on the English language were immediate, far-reaching, and controversial.

The focus of interest was vocabulary. There were no words in the language to talk accurately about the new concepts, techniques, and inventions which were coming from Europe, and so writers began to borrow them. Most of the words which entered the language at the time were taken from Latin, with a good number from Greek, French, Italian, Spanish, and Portuguese. Then, as the period of world-wide exploration got under way, words came into English from over 50 other languages, including several indigenous languages of North America, Africa, and Asia. Some words came into English directly; others came by way of an intermediate language. Many came indirectly from Latin or Italian via French.

Some writers, such as Thomas Elyot, went out of their way to find new words, in order (as they saw it) to 'enrich' the language. They saw their role as enabling the new learning to be brought within the reach of the English public – whether this was access to the old classical texts, or to the new fields of science, technology, and medicine. There were many translations of classical works during the 16th century, and thousands of Latin or Greek terms were introduced, as translators searched for an English equivalent and could not find one. Some, indeed, felt that English was in any case not an appropriate vehicle for the expression of the new learning. English, in this view, did not compare well with the tried and tested standards of Latin or Greek, especially in such fields as theology or medicine. It was a language fit for the street, but not for the library.

Then as now, the influx of foreign vocabulary attracted bitter criticism, and people leaped to the language's defence. Purists opposed the new 'inkhorn' terms, condemning them for obscurity and for interfering with the development of native English vocabulary. Some writers (notably, the poet Edmund Spenser) attempted to revive obsolete English words instead – what were sometimes called 'Chaucerisms' – and to make use of little-known words from English dialects. *Algate* ('always'), *sicker* ('certainly'), and *yblent*

('confused') are examples (p. 125). The scholar John Cheke used English equivalents for classical terms whenever he could, such as *crossed* for 'crucified' and *gainrising* for 'resurrection' (p. 124).

The increase in foreign borrowings is the most distinctive linguistic sign of the Renaissance in English. Purist opinion did not, in the event, stem the influx of new words – nor has it ever, in the history of this language.

SOME RENAISSANCE LOAN WORDS IN ENGLISH

From Latin and Greek
absurdity, adapt, agile, alienate, allusion, anachronism, anonymous, appropriate, assassinate, atmosphere, autograph, benefit, capsule, catastrophe, chaos, climax, conspicuous, contradictory, crisis, criterion, critic, delirium, denunciation, disability, disrespect, emancipate, emphasis, encyclopedia, enthusiasm, epilepsy, eradicate, exact, exaggerate, excavate, excursion, exist, expectation, expensive, explain, external, extinguish, fact, glottis, habitual, halo, harass, idiosyncrasy, immaturity, impersonal, inclemency, jocular, larynx, lexicon, lunar, malignant, monopoly, monosyllable, necessitate, obstruction, pancreas, parasite, parenthesis, pathetic, pneumonia, relaxation, relevant, scheme, skeleton, soda, species, system, tactics, temperature, tendon, thermometer, tibia, tonic, transcribe, ulna, utopian, vacuum, virus

From or via French
alloy, anatomy, battery, bayonet, bigot, bizarre, chocolate, colonel, comrade, detail, docility, duel, entrance, equip, explore, grotesque, invite, moustache, muscle, naturalize, passport, pioneer, probability, progress, shock, surpass, ticket, tomato, vase, vogue, volunteer

From or via Italian
argosy, balcony, ballot, cameo, carnival, concerto, cupola, design, fuse, giraffe, grotto, lottery, macaroni, opera, piazza, portico, rocket, solo, sonata, sonnet, soprano, stanza, stucco, trill, violin, volcano

From or via Spanish and Portuguese
alligator, anchovy, apricot, armada, banana, barricade, bravado, cannibal, canoe, cockroach, cocoa, corral, desperado, embargo, guitar, hammock, hurricane, maize, mosquito, mulatto, negro, potato, port (wine), rusk, sombrero, tank, tobacco, yam

From other languages
bamboo (Malay), bazaar (Persian), caravan (Persian), coffee (Turkish), cruise (Dutch), curry (Tamil), easel (Dutch), flannel (Welsh), guru (Hindi), harem (Arabic), horde (Turkish), keelhaul (Dutch), ketchup (Malay), kiosk (Turkish), knapsack (Dutch), landscape (Dutch), pariah (Tamil), raccoon (Algonquian), rouble (Russian), sago (Malay), sheikh (Arabic), shekel (Hebrew), shogun (Japanese), troll (Norwegian), trousers (Irish Gaelic), turban (Persian), wampum (Algonquian), yacht (Dutch), yoghurt (Turkish)

EXPLAIN THYSELF

The inventors of neologisms were well aware of the need to explain their coinages. One strategy was to pair a new word with a familiar equivalent, such as *persist and continue*, and *animate or gyue courage to*. Another was to expound a meaning at greater length, as does Sir Thomas Elyot in introducing *encyclopedia*:

in an oratour is required to be a heape of all manner of lernyng: whiche of some is called the worlde of science: of other the circle of doctrine / whiche is in one worde of greeke *Encyclopedia*.

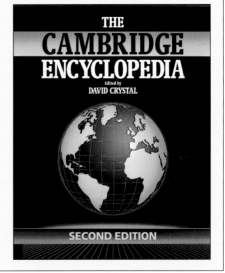

THE INKHORN CONTROVERSY

Monetary metaphors were especially popular in the 16th-century controversy over the use of foreign words in English. Supporters use such terms as 'enrich' and 'credit'; opponents talk about 'bankruptcy' and 'counterfeiting'.

FOR

Thomas Elyot (c. 1490– 1546)
I am constraind to vsurpe a latine word callyng it *Maturitie*: whiche worde though it be strange and darke / yet by declaring the vertue in a fewe mo wordes / the name ones [*once*] brought in custome / shall be as facile to vnderstande as other wordes late commen out of Italy and France / and made denizins amonge vs. ... And this I do nowe remembre for the necessary augmentation of our langage. (*The boke named the Gouernour*, 1531.)

George Pettie (1548–89)
Wherefore I marueile how our english tongue hath crackt it [*its*] credite, that it may not borrow of the Latine as well as other tongues: and if it haue broken, it is but of late, for it is not vnknowen to all men how many woordes we haue fetcht from thence within these fewe yeeres, which if they should be all counted inkpot termes, I know not how we should speake any thing without blacking our mouthes with inke: for what woord can be more plaine then this word *plaine*, and yet what can come more neere to the Latine? (Preface to *The ciuile conuersation of M. Steeuen Guazzo*, 1581.)

The impossibility of the purist ideal, as Pettie points out, is well illustrated by such passages, which all contain several words of non-Germanic origin (such as *bankrupt* and, indeed, the word *pure* itself).

AGAINST

Thomas Wilson (?1528–81)
Among all other lessons this should first be learned, that wee never affect any straunge ynkehorne termes, but to speake as is commonly received: neither seeking to be over fine, nor yet living over-carelesse, using our speeche as most men doe, and ordering our wittes as the fewest have done. Some seeke so far for outlandish English, that they forget altogether their mothers language. And I dare sweare this, if some of their mothers were alive, thei were not able to tell what they say; and yet these fine English clerkes will say, they speake in their mother tongue, if a man should charge them for counterfeiting the Kings English. (*The Arte of Rhetorique*, 1553.)

John Cheke (1514–57)
I am of this opinion that our tung shold be written cleane and pure, vnmixt and vnmangeled with borowing of other tunges, wherein if we take not heed bi tijm, euer borowing and neuer payeng, she shall be fain to keep her house as bankrupt. For then doth our tung naturallie and praisablie vtter her meaning, when she bouroweth no counterfeitness of other tunges to attire her self withall ... (*Letter to Thomas Hoby*, 1557.)

WORSHIPFULL SIR

The rhetorician Thomas Wilson was one of the most ferocious critics of the new Latinate vocabulary emerging in England. In *The Arte of Rhetorique* he cites a letter written (he claims) by a Lincolnshire gentleman asking for assistance in obtaining a vacant benefice. It is likely that the letter is a parody, Wilson's own concoction, but the words he uses seem to be genuine, and in most cases are attested elsewhere. The following extract illustrates its style:

Ponderyng expendyng [*weighing*], and reuolutyng [*revolving*] with my self your ingent [*enormous*] affabilitee, and ingenious capacitee, for mundane affaires: I cannot but celebrate and extolle your magnificall dexteritee, aboue all other. For how could you haue adepted [*acquired*] suche illustrate prerogatiue [*illustrious preeminence*], and dominicall [*lordly*] superioritee, if the fecunditee of your ingenie [*intellectual powers*] had not been so fertile, and wounderfull pregnaunt. Now therefore beeyng accersited [*summoned*], to suche splendent renoume, and dignitee splendidious: I doubt not but you will adiuuate [*help*] such poore adnichilate [*destitute*] orphanes, as whilome ware condisciples [*schoolfellows*] with you, and of antique familiarite in Lincolnshire.

What is noteworthy is that several of these new Latinate words have since entered the language (e.g. *ingenious*, *capacity*, *mundane*, *celebrate*, *extol*, *dexterity*). By contrast, most of the native coinages invented by contemporary writers as alternatives to Latin loans have failed to survive. An example is the set of terms proposed by Ralph Lever in his *Arte of Reason, rightly termed, Witcraft* (1573) for the study of logic. They include such Latin equivalents as *endsay* ('conclusio'), *ifsay* ('propositio conditionalis'), *naysay* ('negatio'), *saywhat* ('definitio'), *shewsay* ('propositio'), and *yeasay* ('affirmatio'). Though most of Lever's coinages had no future, a few of his forms emerged independently in regional use (especially *naysay(er)* and *yeasay(er)*). All of them intriguingly anticipate Newspeak (p. 135).

DERUNCINATED WORDS

cohibit ('restrain'), *deruncinate* ('weed'), *eximious* ('excellent'), *illecebrous* ('delicate'), *suppeditate* ('supply')…

During the Renaissance, many words were coined which did not survive. What is interesting, but little understood, is why some words were retained while others were not. For example, both *impede* and *expede* were introduced during this period, but only the former has survived. *Demit* ('send away') has been replaced by *dismiss*, though the parallel items *commit* and *transmit* have remained; and *disadorn* and *disaccustom* have been lost, though *disagree* and *disabuse* have been kept. In Wilson's letter, from which an extract is quoted above, most of the new Latin words survived, but *obtestate* and *fatigate* did not. In certain cases, the existence of perfectly satisfactory words in the language for a particular concept militated against the introduction of a further item: what need of *aspectable*, when we already have *visible*? It is mostly impossible to say why one word lived and another died.

NEW FORMATIONS

The influx of foreign words was the most noticeable aspect of lexical growth; but throughout the period the vocabulary was steadily expanding in other ways. Far more new words in fact came into English by adding prefixes and suffixes, or by forming new compounds (p. 128). It is also important to note the use of the process of word-class conversion, much encountered in Shakespeare (p. 63).

Prefixation
bedaub, counterstroke, disabuse, disrobe, endear, forename, interlink, nonsense, submarine, uncivilized, uncomfortable

Suffixation
blandishment, changeful, considerable, delightfulness, drizzling, frequenter, gloomy, immaturity, laughable, lunatical, murmurous

Compounding
chap-fallen, commander-in-chief, Frenchwoman, heaven-sent, laughing-stock, pincushion, pine-cone, rosewood, spoonwort

Conversion
Noun from verb: invite, laugh, scratch
Verb from noun: gossip, launder, season ('Season your admiration for a while…')

ENGLISH RECOGNIZED

The controversy over which kind of English lexicon to use should not be allowed to obscure the fact that English was now widely accepted as the language of learning. At the beginning of the 16th century, the situation had been very different, with Latin still established as the normal language of scholarship. All over Europe, vernaculars were criticized as crude, limited, and immature – fit for popular literature, but little else.

Richard Mulcaster (?1530–1611), headmaster of Merchant Taylors' School, was a leading supporter of the capabilities and value of the mother tongue in all subjects:

I do not think that anie language, be it whatsoever, is better able to utter all arguments, either with more pith, or greater planesse, than our English tung is, if the English utterer be as skilfull in the matter, which he is to utter: as the foren utterer is… I love Rome, but London better, I favor Italie, but England more, I honor the Latin, but I worship the English.

By the end of the 16th century, the matter was resolved. English became the language of learning.

THE INFLUENCE OF SHAKESPEARE

All textbooks on the history of English agree that the two most important influences on the development of the language during the final decades of the Renaissance are the works of William Shakespeare (1564–1616) and the King James Bible of 1611 (p. 64). 'Influence' does not here refer to the way these works use language in a beautiful or memorable way. Extracts from both sources predominate in any collection of English quotations; but the present section is not primarily concerned with issues of aesthetic excellence or quotability (p. 184). 'To be or not to be' is a quotation, but it is unimportant in discussing the development of the language's grammar or vocabulary. On the other hand, Shakespeare's use of *obscene* (in *Richard II*) is not part of any especially memorable quotation, but it is the first recorded use of this word in English. And even though he may not have been the very first to use it (some Shakespearean 'firsts', such as *puppi-dogges*, will undoubtedly have been present in the spoken language already), his usage would have been influential in developing popular awareness of it, and thus increasing its circulation.

The Shakespearean impact on the language was chiefly in the area of the lexicon, as the examples on these pages suggest. His work, however, also provides countless instances of the way English was developing at the time, and illustrations from his poems and plays are unavoidable in any discussion of contemporary pronunciation (p. 69), word formation, syntax (p. 70), or language use (p. 71). In return, the studies of Renaissance language in general have contributed many insights into Shakespeare's own use of language.

THE NEW GLOBE

An architect's model of the International Shakespeare Globe Centre, due for completion in spring 1995.

The first wooden structure opened in 1599, but was burned down in 1613 – it is said, by a spark from a cannon during a performance of *Henry VIII*. Although immediately rebuilt, the theatre was closed by the Puritans in 1642, and subsequently demolished.

The reconstruction was the brainchild of American actor-director Sam Wanamaker who died in December 1993, aged 74. The Globe Playhouse Trust was formed in 1970, but building work on the site, some 500 yards from the original location, did not begin until 1989. Elizabethan building techniques have been used to create a replica of the oak-framed theatre, based on contemporary sketches and records. The aim of the project is to restore an appreciation of Shakespeare's works as they were first performed. When complete, the Globe will have a capacity of 1,500, including 300 standing in the theatre's open yard, and will mount plays in the style of Elizabethan drama, and in the setting described simply and effectively in the Prologue to *Henry V* as a 'wooden O'.

WILLIAM SHAKESPEARE (1564–1616)

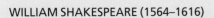

Shakespeare was born in Stratford-upon-Avon, Warwickshire, the son of John Shakespeare, a glover, and Mary Arden, of farming stock. Much uncertainty surrounds his early life. He was the eldest of three sons, and there were four daughters. Educated at the local grammar school, in 1582 he married Anne Hathaway, from a local farming family. Their children were Susanna (1583) and twins Hamnet and Judith (1585).

In about 1591 he moved to London and became an actor. The first evidence of his association with the stage is in 1594, when he was acting with the Lord Chamberlain's company of players, later 'the King's Men'. When the company built the Globe theatre, he became a partner, living modestly in a house in Silver Street until c. 1606, then moving near the Globe. He returned to Stratford c. 1610, living as a country gentleman at his house, New Place. His will was made in March 1616 (p. 149), a few months before he died, and he was buried at Stratford.

The modern era of Shakespearean scholarship has long been noted for its meticulous investigation of the text, chronology, and authorship of the plays, and of the theatrical, literary, and socio-historical contexts which gave rise to them. To all this has now been added a comparatively small but rapidly growing contribution from linguistically-inspired approaches such as stylistics, pragmatics, sociolinguistics, and computational linguistics (pp. 63, 153). Of particular interest is the extent to which the remaining controversial questions of authorship (such as *Henry VI Part I* and *Two Noble Kinsmen*) can be illuminated using modern stylostatistical and computational techniques (pp. 266, 423).

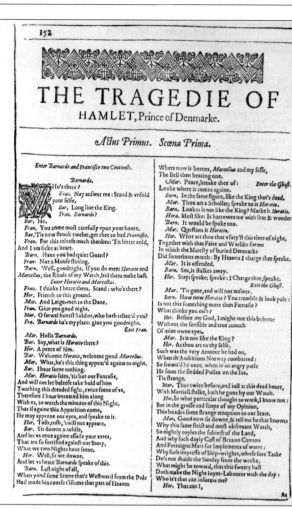

A page from the First Folio, the first complete edition of Shakespeare's plays, published in 1623.

LEXICAL FIRSTS

• There are many words first recorded in Shakespeare which have survived into Modern English. Some examples:

accommodation, assassination, barefaced, countless, courtship, dislocate, dwindle, eventful, fancy-free, lack-lustre, laughable, premeditated, submerged

• There are also many words first recorded in Shakespeare which have not survived. About a third of all his Latinate neologisms fall into this category. Some examples:

abruption, appertainments, cadent, exsufflicate, persistive, protractive, questrist, soilure, tortive, ungenitured, unplausive, vastidity

GRAMMATICAL CONVERSIONS

One of the consequences of the falling away of inflectional endings in English (p. 44) was a marked growth in the process of grammatical conversion – the use of one word class with the function of another (p. 129) – and this became particularly noticeable during the later Renaissance period, especially in dramatic writing. Contemporary rhetoricians called it *anthimeria*. Shakespeare made copious use of it, and was especially fond of making verbs from nouns.

Season your admiration for a while…
It *out-herods* Herod…
No more shall trenching war *channel* her fields…
Grace me no grace, nor *uncle* me no uncle…
Julius Caesar, / Who at Phillipi the good Brutus *ghosted*…
Destruction straight shall *dog* them at the heels…
I am *proverbed* with a grandsire phrase…

DIVERSE HYPHENATIONS

Any study of Shakespeare's lexicon would be inadequate if it did not draw attention to his use of hyphenated compounds. Many of these (such as *hugger-mugger*) are uniquely and recognizably his, and they thus form an uncertain category between those neologisms in his writing which have survived into the modern language and those which have died (see above). It is their structural diversity which is so noticeable, as is suggested by this set of examples from *King John* (each occurs in the play just once):

Arch-heretique	Canker-sorrow	ill-tuned	sinne-conceiuing
baby-eyes	faire-play	kindred-action	smooth-fac'd
bare-pickt	giant-world	ore-look'd	thin-bestained
Basilisco-like	halfe-blowne	pale-visag'd	vile-concluded
breake-vow	heauen-mouing	pell-mell	widow-comfort

(After W. F. Bolton, 1992.)

SUCH KNAVERY

One approach to Shakespeare's linguistic creativity takes an everyday concept and shows the imaginative range of the expressions used to convey it. Even the commonest notions display a remarkable variety, as shown by this collection of insulting phrases using the word *knave*.

wrangling knave; foul knave; Fortune's knave; fantastical knave; naughty knave; Sir knave; arrant knave; a devilish knave; lousy knave; lunatic knave; muddy knave; unthrifty knave; a thin-faced knave; a subtle knave; beastly knave; untaught knaves; bacon-fed knaves; gorbellied knaves; crafty knaves; lazy knaves; most unjust knave; most villainous knave; thou most untoward knave; poor gallant knave; base notorious knave; scurvy, lousy knave; a counterfeit cowardly knave; arrant, malmsy-nose knave; scurvy railing knave; rascally yea-forsooth knave; stubborn ancient knave; jealous rascally knave; poor cuckoldy knave; a pestilent complete knave; foul-mouthed and caluminous knave; sly and constant knave; a slipper and subtle knave; shrewd knave and unhappy; a young knave and begging; knaves that smell of sweat; shrewd and knavish sprite; knave very voluble; little better than false knaves; the lying'st knave in Christendom; the rascally, scauld, beggarly, lousy, pragging knave; scurvy, doting, foolish knave; whoreson beetle-headed, flap-ear'd knave; poor, decayed, ingenius, foolish, rascally knave; base, proud, shallow, beggarly, three-suited, hundred-pound, filthy worsted-stocking knave.
(After W. J. Hill & C. J. Öttchen, 1991.)

IDIOMATIC EXPRESSIONS

The jump from quotation to everyday idiom is sometimes not great, as the following examples illustrate. All were introduced by Shakespeare, and have become part of the idiomatic expression of the modern language (though sometimes with an altered meaning).

what the dickens
(*The Merry Wives of Windsor*, III.ii)
beggars all description
(*Antony and Cleopatra*, II.ii)
a foregone conclusion
(*Othello*, III.iii)
hoist with his own petard
(*Hamlet*, III.iv)
in my mind's eye
(*Hamlet*, I.ii)
caviare to the general
(*Hamlet*, II.ii)
it's Greek to me
(*Julius Caesar*, I.ii)
salad days
(*Antony and Cleopatra*, I.v)
play fast and loose
(*Antony and Cleopatra*, IV.xii)
a tower of strength
(*Richard III*, V.iii)
make a virtue of necessity
(*Pericles*, I.iii)
dance attendance
(*Henry VIII*, V.ii)
cold comfort
(*King John*, V.vii)
at one fell swoop
(*Macbeth*, IV.iii)
to the manner born
(*Hamlet*, I.iv)
brevity is the soul of wit
(*Hamlet*, II.ii)
hold the mirror up to nature
(*Hamlet*, III.ii)
I must be cruel only to be kind
(*Hamlet*, III.iv)
all our yesterdays
(*Macbeth*, V.v)
with bated breath
(*Merchant of Venice*, I.iii)
love is blind
(*Merchant of Venice*, II.vi)
as good luck would have it
(*The Merry Wives of Windsor*, III.v)

THE KING JAMES BIBLE

In the year that Shakespeare retired from writing for the stage, 1611, the 'Authorized Version' or King James Bible was published. It was never in fact authorized by any parliamentary process, but its title-page states that it was appointed to be read in churches throughout the kingdom, and in this way its influence on the population, and on the language at large, was to be far-reaching.

The origins of the work are well-documented. On his journey from Edinburgh to London in 1603, King James was presented with the 'Millenary Petition', in which 750 reformers from within the Church of England requested a new translation of the Bible. In a conference the following year, the King proposed a panel of university scholars who would carry out a preliminary translation, and this would then be submitted to the bishops for revision. The 54 translators were divided into six 'companies', each working on a separate section of the Bible. The preliminary version took four years, and the final revision a further nine months. The first edition, printed in an elegant black-letter type, appeared two years later.

The panel followed a number of guidelines. Translators were to use the Bishops' Bible where possible (p. 59), but were permitted to consult Tyndale and other earlier versions if necessary (and in fact they did so to a considerable extent). They were to preserve recognized chapter divisions and proper names, and to avoid lengthy marginal notes. Translations by any one member of the group were to be approved by the other members, and each company was to send its material to the others for final agreement. Disagreements were to be formally discussed, and external opinions sought if required. Never had there been such a translation by committee.

Committee documents are often faceless and uninspiring, with character and individuality swamped by the waves of revision required to achieve consensus. That this project proved to be so successful must have been due to the intellectual quality and personal enthusiasm of the panel members, which comes across strongly in their Preface to the work. They show themselves well aware of the dangers of consensus language:

An other thing we thinke good to admonish thee of (gentle Reader) that wee haue not tyed our selues to an vniformitie of phrasing, or to an identitie of words, as some peraduenture would wish that we had done, because they obserue, that some learned men

some where, haue beene as exact as they could that way...That we should expresse the same notion in the same particular word; as for example, if we translate the Hebrew or Greeke word once by *Purpose*, neuer to call it *Intent*; if one where *Iourneying*, neuer *Traveiling*; if one where *Thinke*, never *Suppose*; if one where *Paine*, neuer *Ache*; if one where *Ioy*, neuer *Gladnesse*, etc. Thus to minse the matter, wee thought to sauour more of curiositie then wisedome, and that rather it would breed scorne in the Atheist, then bring profite to the godly Reader. For is the kingdome of God become words or syllables? why should wee be in bondage to them if we may be free, vse one precisely when wee may vse another no lesse fit, as commodiously?

There were other important emphases in the work which contributed to its effectiveness. The translators were consciously conservative, and frequently introduced archaism and traditional readings, especially from Tyndale and Coverdale (p. 59). The resonances of the past were strong in their choices. And perhaps most important of all, they listened to final drafts of the translation being read aloud, verse by verse, in order to assess their rhythm and balance. It is, *par excellence*, a preachers' Bible.

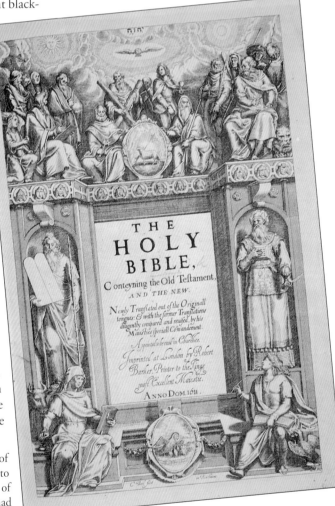

The title-page of the King James Bible.

A conservative style

The style of the King James Bible is much more conservative than that found in Shakespeare. As the translators say in their Preface, their aim was not to make a new translation, 'but to make a good one better, or out of many good ones, one principall good one'. They aimed for a dignified, not a popular style, and often opted for older forms of the language, when modern alternatives were available. Their text therefore does not contain large numbers of new words, as Shakespeare's plays did (p. 63). One estimate finds in it only about 8,000 different words, which is less than half of the Shakespearean total (p. 123).

Similarly, the King James Bible looks backwards in its grammar, and preserves many of the forms and constructions which were falling out of use elsewhere. Some of these features are as follows:

• Many irregular verbs are found in their older forms: examples include *digged* ('dug'), *gat* ('got') and *gotten*, *bare* ('bore'), *spake* ('spoke'), *clave* ('cleft'), *holpen* ('helped'), and *wist* ('knew'). Other archaic forms are also found, such as *brethren*, *kine*, and *twain*.

• Older word orders are still in use, such as *follow thou me*, *speak ye unto*, *cakes unleavened*, and *things eternal*. In particular, the modern use of *do* with negatives and in questions is missing: we find *they knew him not* instead of *they did not know him*. By contrast, both old and new constructions are used in Shakespeare, and the *do* construction became standard by about 1700.

• The third person singular of the present tense of verbs is always *-(e)th*. In other texts of the period, it is being replaced by *-s* – a northern form which was moving south in the 16th century (p. 50), and which is often found in Shakespeare (along with the *-eth* ending).

• The second person plural pronouns were changing during this period (p. 71). Originally, *ye* was the subject form, and *you* was the form used as object or after a preposition. This distinction is preserved in the Bible, as can be seen in such examples as *Ye cannot serve God and Mammon. Therefore I say unto you...* But in most writing, by the end of the 16th century, *you* was already being used for *ye*, which disappeared from standard English in the late 17th century (apart from in some poetic and religious use).

• *His* is used for *its*, as in *if the salt has lost his savour, wherewith shall it be salted*. Although *its* is recorded as early as the end of the 16th century, it does not become general until 100 years later. Similarly, the modern use of the genitive was still not established, as can be seen in such usages as *for Jesus Christ his sake*.

• Several prepositions have different uses from today. *Of*, in particular, is widespread: *the zeal of* ('for') *thine house*, *tempted of* ('by') *Satan*, *went forth of* ('from') *the Arke*. Other examples include *in* ('at') *a good old age*, *taken to* (as a) *wife*, and *like as* ('like', 'as') *the sand of the sea*.

• *An* is used before many nouns begining with *h-* in a stressed syllable, such as *an hundred, an helpe, an harlot*. This usage, begun by Wycliff, is still to be found as late as the 19th century.

Thomas Cranmer
(1489–1556)

TWO SAMPLE TEXTS

The first extract represents the 1611 printing, apart from the replacement of long 's' by s; the second extract is from a 19th-century printing, with modernized spelling and punctuation, which is closer to the versions that most people see today.

Luke 15.29–32

And he answering said to his father, Loe, these many yeeres doe I serue thee, neither transgressed I at any time thy commandement, and yet thou neuer gauest mee a kid, that I might make merry with my friends: But as soone as this thy sonne was come, which hath deuored thy liuing with harlots, thou hast killed for him the fatted calfe. And he said vnto him, Sonne, thou art euer with me, and all that I haue is thine. It was meete that we should make merry, and be glad: for this thy brother was dead, and is aliue againe: and was lost, and is found.

Genesis 27.10–22

And he lighted upon a certain place, and tarried there all night, because the sun set: and he took of the stones of that place, and put them for his pillows, and lay down in that place to sleep.

And he dreamed, and behold a ladder set upon the earth, and the top of it reached to heaven: and behold the angels of God ascending and descending on it.

And behold, the Lord stood above it, and said, I am the Lord God of Abraham thy father, and the God of Isaac: the land whereon thou liest, to thee will I give it, and to thy seed:

And thy seed shall be as the dust of the earth; and thou shalt spread abroad to the west, and to the east, and to the north, and to the south: and in thee, and in thy seed, shall all the families of the earth be blessed.

THE BOOK OF COMMON PRAYER

A related influential text was the Prayer Book, which appeared in 1549 with the full title of *The Booke of the Common Prayer and administracion of the Sacramentes, and other Rites and Ceremonies after the Use of the Churche of England*. It provided a single order of public worship to be followed throughout the country. The first edition was compiled by a group of bishops and scholars led by the Archbishop of Canterbury (Thomas Cranmer), and radically revised, after its controversial reception, in 1552. A later revision, generally known as the 1662 Book (from the date of enforcement of its use), substituted the text of the King James Bible, and introduced a degree of linguistic modernization. This version continued as the only official text in the Church of England until the adoption of an alternative liturgy in contemporary language at the end of the 1970s (p. 403).

The Prayer Book is responsible for a great deal of the vernacular idiom of English prayer, such as 'As it was in the beginning, is now, and ever shall be: world without end. Amen', 'Lord have mercy upon us', 'be amongst you and remain with you always'. A few of its phrases (such as *holy wedlock*) have achieved broader currency, and a much larger number have achieved the status of quotations:

Read, mark, learn, and inwardly digest (*Collect, 2nd Sunday in Advent*)
Renounce the devil and all his works (*Public Baptism*)
Wilt thou have this woman to thy wedded wife? (*Solemnization of Matrimony*)
earth to earth, ashes to ashes, dust to dust (*The Burial of the Dead*)

THE EMERGING ORTHOGRAPHIC SYSTEM

Even a generation after Caxton (p. 56), the English writing system remained in a highly inconsistent state. Although there were clear signs of standardization, as the conventions adopted by the Chancery scribes became increasingly influential (p. 54), there was still a considerable lack of uniformity in spelling and punctuation. This can be seen not only between printed and handwritten texts, or between the practices of different printers, but within the work of an individual printer or author. Caxton, for example, in a single passage (p. 57) has both *booke* and *boke*, and *axyd* and *axed*, and uses double letters and final *-e* in a fairly haphazard fashion (*hadde*, *wel*, *whiche*). There is a comparable randomness in the work of his immediate successors; and a century later, spelling variation is still much in evidence: *fellow*, for example, might appear as *felow*, *felowe*, *fallow*, *fallowe*, and several other forms. It is this situation which motivated teacher and scholar Richard Mulcaster, in the first part of his *Elementarie* (1582), 'to find out the right writing of ours'.

There were many unfavourable comments about the chaotic nature of the writing system at the time, and printers in particular came in for a great deal of criticism. Alexander Gil, headmaster of St Paul's, writing in 1619, argues that 'corruption in writing originated with the printing of our books, I lay all the blame for our chaotic spelling on the last'. The printers were blamed for a variety of reasons. Many of them were foreigners, who introduced their native conventions at will, and who were uncertain of orthographic traditions in English. Proofreading was not always carried out by educated people, so that errors were promulgated. Because there was only a limited amount of type, arbitrary spellings were often introduced. And arbitrariness also crept in when printers altered spelling (such as adding or deleting a final *-e*) in order to make a line of words end neatly at the right-hand margin.

It is difficult to evaluate the justice of these charges, in the absence of explicit statements from the printers, or detailed studies of the way orthographic consistency developed in their books. It should be borne in mind that several of the critics had an axe to grind, in the form of their own system of reformed spelling or method of teaching. But there is no doubt that, throughout the early decades of the 17th century, the English writing system was widely perceived to be in a mess. Although many authors wrote with fair consistency in systems of their own devising, there was no generally recognized standard.

A SUPERFLUITY OF LETTERS

John Hart, in *The opening of the unreasonable writing of our Inglish toung* (1551), discusses 'the divers vices and corruptions which use (or better abuse) maintaineth in our writing'. One of his vices is 'superfluite' – the use of 'more letters than the pronunciation neadeth of voices'. He accepts that an extra letter is sometimes useful (such as to mark a long vowel), but in many cases the reason for the letter is, in his view, an irrelevance. A particular case in point was the attempt to show etymology (p. 136) in the spelling, especially in words which had come from Latin, either directly or via French: this had led to such practices as the use of a *b* in *debt* and *doubt*, an *o* in *people*, an *s* in *baptism*, and a *d* in *adventure*. Another was the use of different letters to show the difference between homophones, such as *sunne* and *sonne*.

The arguments for and against such practices were much debated at the time. Some scholars insisted that an indication of etymology was highly desirable; others that it was wholly irrelevant. Some argued that homophone distinctions would help to avoid ambiguity in writing; others that they were unnecessary, as context would solve the problem in much the same way as it generally does in speech. In the event, all these positions exercised some influence on orthographic practice, contributing to the unpredictability of the modern spelling system.

THE FIRST REFORMERS

Then, as now (p. 276), several commentators thought that the best solution to the problem of unsystematic spelling was radical reform on phonetic lines. Hart's *Orthographie* (1569) presented one such system, as did William Bullokar's *Booke at Large, for the Amendment of Orthographie for English Speech* (1580). Bullokar uses an alphabet of 37 letters, in which the traditional forms are supplemented by several diacritics. This, he hopes, will receive more favour than the earlier approaches, which in his view overused new symbols. However, there were many, such as Richard Mulcaster, who were strongly opposed to any new alphabets, preferring to stay with traditional orthography, but used in a more principled way. It is their views which eventually triumphed.

Bullokar's proposed alphabet, from *A Short Introduction or guiding to print, write, and reade Inglish speech* (1580). There are eight vowels, four 'half vowels' (*l, r, m, n*) (compare semi-vowels, p. 242), and 25 consonants. His consonant proposals include a written distinction between voiced and voiceless *th*, and a separate symbol for *ch*. His use of diacritics can be seen in his 'rule to understand this table following', which assigns names to old and new letters.

Growing regularization

Mulcaster's own views did a great deal to hasten the growth of regularization at the end of the 16th century. His *Elementarie* provided a table listing recommended spellings for nearly 9,000 words, and influenced a generation of orthoepists (pronunciation teachers) and grammarians. Several other works of the period focused on the writing system, and a climate emerged which fostered standardization – at least in print (manuscript practices took much longer to conform).

Vowels especially came to be spelled in a more predictable way. There was increased use of a double-vowel convention (as in *soon*) or a silent *-e* (as in *name*) to mark length; and a doubled consonant within a word became a more predictable sign of a preceding short vowel (*sitting*) – though there continued to be some uncertainty over what should happen at the end of a word (*bed* and *glad*, but *well* and *glasse*). Then, in the 1630s, one of the most noticeable variations in medieval English came to be standardized: the use of *u* and *v*. These symbols were at first interchangeable (p. 41), and then positionally distinguished (with *v* used initially and *u* medially in a word); they later followed Continental practice and adopted fixed phonetic values, with *v* representing a consonant and *u* a vowel. A similar standardization affected *j* (earlier a variant form of *i*) and *i*.

During the 17th century, an increasing number of spelling guides came to be published, which inevitably influenced printing practice. Children's schoolbooks began to contain lists of homophones (such as *made* and *maid*) and irregular spellings, which had to be learned by heart. And a considerable pressure for standardization followed the arrival of the first dictionaries (from 1604, p. 72). By the middle of the century, printing conventions had become highly regularized, and the gulf established between the forms of speech and their written representation. The modern system, in which irregular spellings can be explained but not predicted, had arrived. The period of social tolerance of variant spellings came to an end; and as 18th-century notions of correctness emerged (p. 72), poor spelling became increasingly stigmatized.

CAPITALIZATION

Hart recommended his readers to use a capital letter at the beginning of every sentence, proper name, and important common noun. By the early 17th century, the practice had extended to titles (*Sir, Lady*), forms of address (*Father, Mistris*), and personified nouns (*Nature*). Emphasized words and phrases would also attract a capital. By the beginning of the 18th century, the influence of Continental books had caused this practice to be extended still further (e.g. to the names of the branches of knowledge), and it was not long before some writers began using a capital for any noun that they felt to be important. Books appeared in which all or most nouns were given an initial capital (as is done systematically in modern German) – perhaps for aesthetic reasons, or perhaps because printers were uncertain about which nouns to capitalize, and so capitalized them all.

The fashion was at its height in the later 17th century, and continued into the 18th. The manuscripts of Butler, Traherne, Swift, and Pope are full of initial capitals. However, the later 18th-century grammarians were not amused by this apparent lack of order and discipline in the written language. In their view, the proliferation of capitals was unnecessary, and causing the loss of a useful potential distinction. Their rules brought a dramatic reduction in the types of noun permitted to take a capital letter (p. 122).

An extract from Jonathan Swift's *Baucis and Philemon* (1706), showing almost every noun capitalized. (After P. J. Croft, 1973.)

In antient Time, as Story tells
The Saints would often leave their Cells,
And strole about, but hide their Quality,
To try the People's Hospitality.

  It happen'd on a Winter's night,
As Authors of the Legend write
Two Brother-Hermits, Saints by Trade
Taking their Tour in Masquerade
Came to a Village hard by Rixham
Ragged, and not a Groat betwixt'em.
It rain'd as hard as it could pour,
Yet they were forc't to walk an Hour
From House to House, wett to the Skin
Before one Soul would let 'em in.
They call'd at ev'ry Dore; Good People,
My Comrade's Blind, and I'm a Creeple
Here we ly starving in the Street
'Twould grieve a Body's Heart to see't;
No Christian would turn out a Beast
In such a dreadfull Night at least;
Give us but Straw, and let us Ly
In yonder Barn to keep us dry.
Thus in the Strolers usuall Cant
They beg'd Relief which none would grant;

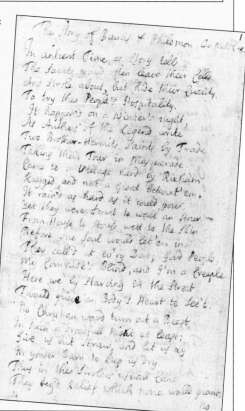

IN FAVOUR OF CAPITALS

The American statesman and scientist, Benjamin Franklin (1706–90), had a keen interest in the English language, and especially in its typography (having been a printer in his youth). In a letter to Noah Webster (p. 80), written in 1789, he mourns the passing of the age of noun capitalization.

In examining the English books that were printed between the restoration and the accession of George the Second [1660–1727], we may observe, that all substantives were begun with a capital, in which we imitated our mother tongue, the German. This was more particularly useful to those who were not well acquainted with the English, there being such a prodigious number of our words that are both verbs and substantives, and spelt in the same manner, though often accented differently in pronunciation. This method has, by the fancy of printers, of late years been entirely laid aside; from an idea, that suppressing the capitals shews the character to greater advantage; those letters, prominent above the line, disturbing its even, regular appearance. The effect of this change is so considerable, that a learned man of France, who used to read our books, though not perfectly acquainted with our language, in conversation with me on the subject of our authors, attributed the greater obscurity he found in our modern books, compared with those of the period above mentioned, to a change of style for the worse in our writers; of which mistake I convinced him, by marking for him each substantive with a capital, in a paragraph, which he then easily understood, though before he could not comprehend it. This shews the inconvenience of that pretended improvement.

RENAISSANCE PUNCTUATION

The basis of the modern punctuation system emerged during the Renaissance. Caxton was heir to a graphic tradition which was limited, unclear, and inconsistent. In common with classical models, the symbols were used rhetorically (p. 278), showing readers where to breathe, how long to pause, and how to introduce emphasis and rhythmical balance into their speech. Even so, there was a great deal of idiosyncrasy and arbitrariness in their use, and attempts to find a neat correlation between punctuation and prosody in Early Modern English texts have never succeeded.

The chief symbols were the *virgule*, or oblique stroke (/), found in both short and long forms; the *period* (.), found at various heights; and the *colon* (:). There is no correspondence with modern uses. In Caxton, the virgule variously had the function of a modern comma, period, or semi-colon; it fell out of use in the 16th century, and was largely replaced by the comma. The period was often used where today we would have a comma (as in the closing lines of the 'egg' text, p. 57). The colon had a broad range of rhetorical functions, and was not restricted to introducing a list or summary, as it is now.

John Hart (p. 66) had a great deal to say about both the rhetorical and grammatical functions of 'pointing'. He distinguished the period ('point'), colon ('joint'), comma, question mark ('asker'), exclamation mark ('wonderer'), parentheses ('clozer'), square brackets ('notes'), apostrophe ('tourner'), hyphen ('joiner'), diaresis ('sondrer'), and capital ('great') letters. His detailed account greatly influenced the way grammarians and printers dealt with this area, and punctuation marks in books came to be more widely used as a result.

Other marks emerged in English Renaissance printing. The *semi-colon* (also called a *comma-colon*, *hemi-colon*, or *sub-colon*) came into use during the 16th century, and for a while was used interchangeably with the colon. 'Turned double commas', later called *quotation marks* or *inverted commas*, made their appearance to open direct speech, and some time afterwards double raised commas were brought in to close it. But not only did new symbols emerge; older symbols developed new uses. In the 18th century, for example, the apostrophe (p. 283) extended its range, first marking the genitive singular of nouns, then the genitive plural. There was also a much heavier use of the comma than is typical today, as the extract from Benjamin Franklin illustrates (p. 67). By the end of the Early Modern English period, the modern punctuation system was in most respects established.

QUOTE... UNQUOTE

Joshua Steele includes this letter as an Appendix to his treatise on *The Melody and Measure of Speech* (1775). Because he is thinking of it as a quotation, he encloses the whole thing in double inverted commas, following the conventions current at that time. Each new line is opened by these commas, with just one pair of raised commas to mark the close. An interesting feature is the inclusion of the date within the quotation.

[93]

TO THE AUTHOR OF THE TREATISE ON THE MELODY AND MEASURE OF SPEECH.

" May 14, 1775.

" YOU have inclosed my remarks, which are too long; but
" as you desired them soon, I had not time to make them
" shorter. I am glad that you are to give your system to the
" public. * * * * * As to the queries and observations I sent
" you formerly, and have now sent you, you may make what
" use of them you think proper; and if they contribute in the
" least to make more compleat so ingenious a performance, I
" shall think they do me honour.

EDITING THE TEXT

A modern edition of a Renaissance text may introduce several differences in punctuation which affect the way the passage is to be interpreted (and, in the case of drama, how the actor should present it). Whether the emendations help or hinder is a matter for discussion; but the first thing is to be aware that they exist. The following extract from *King Lear* illustrates the issue (I.i.55–61). The first version is from the First Folio (1623); the second is from the New Penguin edition (1972).

GONERILL: Sir, I loue you more than words can weild ye matter,
　Deerer then eye-sight, space, and libertie,
　Beyond what can be valewed, rich or rare,
　No lesse then life, with grace, health, beauty, honor:
　As much as Childe ere lou'd, or Father found.
　A loue that makes breath poore, and speech vnable,
　Beyond all manner of so much I loue you.

GONERILL: Sir, I love you more than word can wield the matter,
　Dearer than eyesight, space, and liberty,
　Beyond what can be valued rich or rare,
　No less than life, with grace, health, beauty, honour,
　As much as child e'er loved or father found;
　A love that makes breath poor and speech unable;
　Beyond all manner of 'so much' I love you.

There are several differences which could lead to an interesting argument.

• Does the removal of the comma after *valewed* (l. 3) alter the meaning of the phrase *rich or rare* (to mean 'what can be valued as rich or rare' rather than 'no matter how rich or rare')?
• Does the replacement of the colon after *honor* (l. 4) by a comma reduce the dramatic impact of the pause following the list of nouns?
• Does the removal of the comma after *lou'd* (l. 5) lessen the force of the contrast between *Childe* and *Father*? Similarly, is its removal desirable after *poore* in the next line?
• Does the replacement of the period after *found* (l. 5) by a semi-colon reduce the summarizing prominence of the final two lines?

(After G. Ronberg, 1992.)

PAUSAL PRECISION

Many writers of the time draw attention to the rhetorical role of punctuation marks, often computing pausal values with mathematical precision. An example is Simon Daines, in *Orthoepia Anglicana* (1640), who defines the period in this way:

The *Period*... is altogether used at the end of every speech or sentence,... and signifies *conclusion*. The pause or distance of speaking hereto appropriate is sometime more, sometime lesse: for... when in the middle of a line it cuts off any integrall part of a complete Tractate [*treatise*], which goes not on with the same, but begins a new line, it requireth double the time of pause, that it doth when the treatise persists in the same line: being then foure times as long as a *Colon*, which in the same line is but twice.

SOUND CHANGES

The pronunciation changes which took place during Early Modern English have been studied in considerable detail. Not only is there a great deal of literary evidence, derived from the rhymes and rhythms of poetry, there are also detailed accounts of contemporary pronunciation from phoneticians and spelling reformers. The changes were many and complex. The effects of the Great Vowel Shift (p. 55) were still slowly working their way through the sound system, and several other important developments were in progress.

A GREAT FEAST OF LANGUAGES

Dramatists can provide a source of insight into contemporary pronunciation, partly because of their use of rhymes and word-play, but also because of what they make their characters say. A famous Shakespearean example is in *Love's Labour's Lost* (V.i.15), where the schoolmaster Holofernes complains about Don Armado's pronunciation.

I abhor such fanatical phantasimes, such insociable and point-devise companions; such rackers of orthography, as to speak 'dout' fine, when he should say 'doubt'; 'det' when he should pronounce 'debt' – d, e, b, t, not d, e, t. He clepeth [*calls*] a calf 'cauf', half 'hauf'; neighbour vocatur [*is called*] 'nebour'; 'neigh' abbreviated 'ne'. This is abhominable – which he would call 'abbominable'.

There were evidently two styles of pronunciation current in the late 16th century, and there is no doubt about which the schoolmaster prefers – the more conservative one, which most closely reflects the spelling (p. 66).

SOUND DESCRIPTION

The precision with which some writers could describe the sounds of English is well illustrated by this extract from John Wallis's account of [n] in his *Treatise on Speech* (1st edition, 1653). (Translated from the Latin by J. A. Kemp, 1972.)

For there is a difference between the sound of the letter *n* in the words *thin, sin, in,* and that in *thing, think, sing, single, sink, ink, lynx,* etc. Similarly in *hand, band, ran* the *n* is not the same as it is in *hang, bank, rank,* etc....In the former of each of these two groups the pronunciation of *n* always involves the tip of the tongue striking the front of the palate, near the roots of the upper teeth; whereas in the latter the tip of the tongue is normally moved down to the roots of the lower teeth, and the back of the tongue is raised up to the back of the palate, blocking the sound at this point.

Precision indeed – and in 1653!

NEW SOURCES OF VARIATION

Some of the most important pronunciation indicators of present-day regional and social variation emerged during this period.

• The distinction in modern British Received Pronunciation (RP, p. 245) between *cut* (*son, run,* etc.) and *put* (*pull, wolf,* etc.) developed in the 17th century. Previously, both types of word had a high, back, rounded vowel /ʊ/–the quality heard in modern *put*. This quality remained in certain phonetic contexts (e.g. preceded by a labial consonant, as in *full, wolf, put*), but elsewhere the vowel became more open and lost its rounding, resulting in /ʌ/. In due course, pairs of words began to be contrasted using these qualities (such as *look* vs *luck*), and a new phonemic distinction emerged (p. 236). However, the change was ignored in many regions, with people continuing to use /ʊ/ in both types of word, and this is now one of the chief means of telling whether someone has been brought up in the North of England.

• Throughout this period, /r/ was sounded before consonants and at the end of a word, as is suggested by the way it has been preserved in modern spelling (*jar, corn, fire,* etc.). It stopped being pronounced in RP during the 18th century, with various effects on the preceding vowel: sometimes the vowel became a diphthong (as in *peer* and *bear*); sometimes it lengthened (as in *barn, corn,* and *clerk*). The RP change proved to be something of an exception: most British and American regional accents retained the /r/, and the discrepancy between sound and spelling later became a focus of purist criticism (p. 365).

• Two new consonants emerged during this period. The [ŋ] sound in such words as *sing* was pronounced in Middle English, but always followed by [g] or [k], so that it never had any independent status as a phoneme. By the early 17th century, this final [-g] was no longer being pronounced in RP, leaving /ŋ/ as a separate contrastive unit. Soon after, 'g-dropping' became a social issue (p. 77).

• The /ʒ/ phoneme also emerged in the 17th century, a development of /zj/ – in much the same way as in Modern English a rapid pronunciation of *was your* readily results in a coalescence of the two sounds. The change chiefly affected such words as *occasion* and *vision, measure* and *pleasure,* and later appeared in final position in such loan words as *beige* and *garage.* The French overtones of the sound are a source of controversy still, as when people argue the case of /gəˈrɑːʒ/ vs /ˈgærɪdʒ/.

THE TONGUE THAT SHAKESPEARE SPOKE

Now o'er the one half-world
nəu oːer ðə wʏn haːf wʏrld
Nature seems dead, and wicked dreams abuse
neːtər siːmz ded ənd wɪkɪd dreːmz əbjuːz
The curtain'd sleep; now witchcraft celebrates
ðə kʏrteɪnd sliːp nəu wɪtʃkraft selɪbreːts
Pale Hecate's offerings; and wither'd murder,
peːl hekəts ʊfərɪŋz ənd wɪðərd mʏrdər
Alarum'd by his sentinel, the wolf,
əlarəmd bəi hɪz sentɪnəl ðə wʊlf
Whose howl's his watch, thus with his stealthy pace,
huːz həulz hɪz watʃ ðʏs wɪθ hɪz steltθɪ peːs
With Tarquin's ravishing strides, towards his design
wɪθ tarkwɪnz rævɪʃɪŋ strəidz tuːərdz hɪz dɪzəin
Moves like a ghost.
muːvz ləik ə goːst.

(*Macbeth,* II. i. 49–56, transcription by A. C. Gimson; for phonetic symbols, see §17.)

STRESS SHIFTS

Many words could be heard with a different stress pattern from the one found today.

• First syllable stressed: *antique, **convenient**, **distinct**, **entire**, **extreme**, **July**.*
• Second syllable stressed: *ad**vertise**, cha**racter**, demon**strate**, si**nister**.*
• Final syllable stressed: *aspect, expert, paramount, parent, yesterday.*

Secondary stress (p. 248) also often differed: for example, at one time *academy* had such a stress on its third syllable (so that it was rhythmically like *helicopter*). Many poetic rhymes do not make sense until this extra stress (and its effect on the vowel) is taken into account: Donne rhymes *make us one* and *propagation*, and Shakespeare *never die* and *memory.*

It is in fact difficult to be definite about word stress during this period. There was an unusual amount of variation, because native stress patterning (which tended to put the stress on the root syllable of a word) was in competition with the pattern heard in Romance loan-words (which tended to put the stress on a syllable at or near the end of a word). Stress might also vary depending on the position in which a word appeared in a sentence or metrical line. *Complete,* for example, has a stress on its first syllable in 'A thousand complete courses of the Sun' (*Troilus and Cressida*), but on the second in 'never complete' (*Timon of Athens*).

How do we know?

The clearest evidence comes from the way words are used in poetry, where a predictable metre or rhyme forces a pronunciation upon us. Also, grammarians began to describe accentuation in their accounts of the language – though they did not always agree with each other. Indeed, disputes about stress seem to have been just as strong then as they are today. One writer (Robert Nares, in 1784) criticizes Dr Johnson for recommending such forms as *bombast* and *carmine* instead of *bombast* and *carmine,* and complains about 'barbarous and unpleasing sounds . . . which no ear can hear without being offended'.

EARLY MODERN ENGLISH GRAMMAR

The major shifts in English grammatical structure were over by the time of the Renaissance (p. 44); but even a casual glance at texts from the period shows that many important changes were continuing to take place, although of a more limited kind. For example, several features of verb use show differences from today: 'My life is run his compass', says Cassius (*Julius Caesar*, V.iii.25), where today we should say *has run* – and this sentence also illustrates one of the pronoun uses typical of the time. Constructions involving a double negative (*I cannot go no further*) were commonplace; there are still signs of impersonal verbs (*me thinks he did*); and during the period a number of verb inflections (e.g. *pleaseth, know'st, spake*) fell out of standard use (for other examples, see pp. 63, 65).

There were also significant stylistic developments in sentence structure (p. 214). In Caxton and Malory, the sentences tend to be loose and linear, with repeated *and* or *then* coordination, and a limited amount of subordination, mostly introduced by *which* or *that*. Here is a typical sentence, taken from Caxton's prologue to the *Golden Legend* (for other extracts, see pp. 57–8).

And I shal praye for them vnto Almyghty God that he of his benygne grace rewarde them etc., and that it prouffyte to alle them that shal rede or here it redde, and may encreace in them vertue and expelle vyce and synne that by the ensaumple of the holy sayntes amende theyr lyuyng here in thys shorte lyf that by their merytes they and I may come to everlastyng lyf and blysse in heuen.

The influence of Latin syntactic style on English became marked in the 16th century. Cicero in particular was much imitated. There is a more complex use of subordination, and a search for rhetorical contrast and balance, as is shown by this extract from William Camden's *Remaines Concerning Britain* (1605):

As for the *Monosyllables* so rife in our tongue which were not so originally, although they are vnfitting for verses and measures, yet are they most fit for expressing briefly the first conceipts of the minde, or *Intentionalia* as they call them in schooles: so that we can set downe more matter in fewer lines, than any other language.

The awkwardness or uncertainty which a modern reader often feels in reading early Renaissance prose is chiefly a consequence of the way writers were beginning to explore the potential of the language for complex sentence construction (p. 226). There was conscious experimentation with new grammatical patterns, supported by an increasingly standardized punctuation system (p. 68). New conjunctions emerged: *because*, for example, first appears in Chaucer, but *for (that)* remained the normal way of expressing cause

until the early 17th century. Participial constructions became extremely common, and added greatly to the length of sentences which, in the more complex writers, might run to 20 lines or more. In the early period, such sentences often appear incomplete or ill-formed to modern eyes (failing in concord, for example, or displaying an unattached subordinate clause); but it is important to appreciate that at the time such variability was normal. By the 17th century, however, highly sophisticated and carefully crafted sentences, following a variety of Latin models, were commonplace, as can be seen in the writing of John Lyly, Philip Sidney, and John Milton.

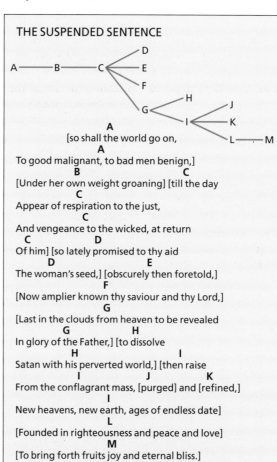

THE SUSPENDED SENTENCE

[so shall the world go on,
   A
To good malignant, to bad men benign,]
   B   C
[Under her own weight groaning] [till the day
   C
Appear of respiration to the just,
   C
And vengeance to the wicked, at return
   C   D
Of him] [so lately promised to thy aid
   D   E
The woman's seed,] [obscurely then foretold,]
   F
[Now amplier known thy saviour and thy Lord,]
   G
[Last in the clouds from heaven to be revealed
   G   H
In glory of the Father,] [to dissolve
   H   I
Satan with his perverted world,] [then raise
   I   J   K
From the conflagrant mass, [purged] and [refined,]
   I
New heavens, new earth, ages of endless date]
   L
[Founded in righteousness and peace and love]
   M
[To bring forth fruits joy and eternal bliss.]

The controlled complexity of sentence construction is well illustrated by this extract from Milton's *Paradise Lost* (XII.537–51), in which archangel Michael concludes his account of the future of mankind. The diagram shows the formal balance involved. Each clause is identified by a capital letter (A–M). At each level of subordination there is a cluster of clauses, but only the last clause in each cluster (C, G, I, L) acts as a starting-point for further structural development. The effect is rather like a series of waves of meaning – as one critic has put it, 'surge follows surge in the relentless tide of Michael's vision' – until we reach the final clause (M), syntactically dependent on the opening clause (A), six levels of structure away. Constructions which display such a marked delay in grammatical and semantic resolution are often described as 'suspended sentences'. (After T. N. Corns, 1990.)

SAY YOU SO? I DO

One of the most important syntactic developments of this period concerned the use of *do* as an auxiliary verb (p. 212). The differences from modern usage can be seen in such interrogative and negative sentences as *Says she so?* and *Believe him not*, where today we would introduce a *do*-form (*Does she say so?*, *Do not believe him*). By Shakespeare's time, it was possible to use *do* in these sentences, but it was not obligatory. Also, *do* could be used in a declarative affirmative sentence without conveying any extra emphasis, again unlike today, as in 'they do offend our sight' (*Henry V*, IV.vi.56), which means no more than 'they offend our sight'.

During the period, it became increasingly usual to insert *do*-forms into negative and interrogative sentences, and to omit them from declarative affirmative ones (except in cases of emphasis). In one study of this topic, only c. 20 per cent of interrogative sentences used *do*-forms in 1500, whereas over 90 per cent did so by 1700. The graph shows the steady growth of *do*-forms in one of these contexts: affirmative questions (such as *Do they know?*). (After A. Ellegård, 1953.)

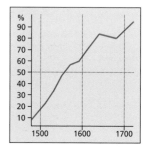

The thou/you question

The second person pronoun system of Renaissance English has been the subject of much investigation – not simply because the forms provide an obvious point of contrast with Modern English, but because they perform a central role in the expression of personal relationships, and are thus crucial to any study of contemporary drama. Understanding the Early Modern English functions of *thou* (*thee, thine, thy, thyself*) and *you* (*ye, yours, your, yourself*) can be critical in interpreting the emotions of the characters, as well as their varying attitudes towards each other during the course of a play.

The chief stages in the development of the system were as follows:

• In Old English (p. 20), *thou* (and its related forms) was used for addressing one person; *ye* (and its related forms) for more than one. Within these categories, *thou* and *ye* were used as clause subject, *thee* and *you* as object.

• During Middle English, *ye/you* came to be used as a polite singular form alongside *thou/thee*, a situation which was probably influenced by French *vous* vs *tu*.

• During Early Modern English, the distinction between subject and object uses of *ye* and *you* gradually disappeared, and *you* became the norm in all grammatical functions and social situations. *Ye* continued in use, but by the end of the 16th century it was restricted to archaic, religious, or literary contexts. By 1700, the *thou* forms were also largely restricted in this way.

The Renaissance system

By the time of Shakespeare, *you* had developed the number ambiguity it retains today, being used for either singular or plural; but in the singular it also had a role as an alternative to *thou/thee*. It was used by people of lower rank or status to those above them (such as ordinary people to nobles, children to parents, servants to masters, nobles to the monarch), and was also the standard way for the upper classes to talk to each other. By contrast, *thou/thee* were used by people of higher rank to those beneath them, and by the lower classes to each other; also, in elevated poetic style, in addressing God, and in talking to witches, ghosts, and other supernatural beings. There were also some special cases: for example, a husband might address his wife as *thou*, and she reply with *you*.

Of particular interest are those cases where an extra emotional element entered the situation, and the use of *thou* or *you* broke the expected conventions. *Thou* commonly expressed special intimacy or affection; *you*, formality, politeness, and distance. *Thou* could also be used, even by an inferior to a superior, to express such feelings as anger and contempt (as in the biblical text on p. 65). The use of *thou* to a person of equal rank could thus easily count as an insult, as Sir Toby Belch well knows when he advises Sir Andrew Aguecheek on how to write a challenge to 'the Count's youth' (Viola): 'if thou thou'st him some thrice, it shall not be amiss' (*Twelfth Night*, III.ii.42), himself using a demeaning *thou* in a speech situation where the norm is *you*. Likewise, the use of *you* when *thou* was expected (such as from master to servant) would also require special explanation.

WHY *THOU*, TO GOD?

We might have expected the deity to be addressed as *You* in Early Modern English, given such descriptions as 'king', 'father', and 'most high'. In fact, during this period he is always addressed as *Thou*. This may be because the usage was consciously archaic – a recollection of the early Middle English situation when *Thou* would have been the only possible form of address in the singular. Alternatively, the usage may show the influence of the first Bible translators (p. 59), who were following languages that distinguished second person singular and plural pronouns (as in Latin *tu* vs *vos*). As God would have been referred to by the singular pronoun in these languages, this practice may have influenced the choice of *Thou* in English, even in an age when a singular *you* would have been possible.

PURE PROPER UNTO ONE

By the middle of the 17th century, *thou* was disappearing from standard usage; but it was kept alive by members of the emerging Society of Friends, or Quakers, who disapproved of the way singular *you* had come to be part of social etiquette, and who accordingly used *thou* forms to everyone. This usage, it was felt, was closer to the way Christ and his disciples spoke, avoided unnecessary social distinction, and was grammatically more exact, being a 'particular, single, pure proper unto one'. The singular use of *you*, by contrast, was considered a corruption, a form of worldly honour, to be shunned along with all other empty social customs. The point was forcibly made by one of the first Quakers, Richard Farnsworth, in *The Pure Language of the Spirit of Truth* (1655), from which the above quotation also comes: 'That which cannot bear thee and thou to a single person, what sort soever, is exalted proud flesh, and is accursed'.

The use of *thou* forms often brought angry reactions, especially from those in authority who still sensed the words' former association with 'lower' speech situations, and found them objectionable. At one point in his *Journal*, George Fox recalls that Friends were 'in danger many times of our lives, and often beaten, for using those words to some proud men, who would say, "Thou'st 'thou' me, thou ill-bred clown", as though their breeding lay in saying "you" to a singular'.

Switching between *thou* and *you* is so common in some texts that it may appear to lack purpose. However, if we adopt a sociolinguistic perspective, readings of considerable interest can result, as can be seen in the following Shakespearian examples.

• In the opening scene of *King Lear*, Lear's daughters address him as *you*, and he addresses Goneril and Regan as *thou* (as would be expected); but his opening remark to his 'best' daughter, Cordelia conveys special respect: 'what can you say…'. Then, when he is displeased by her response, he switches to an angry *thy*: 'But goes thy heart with this?'

• Hamlet uses *thou* to the Ghost throughout Act I, as is normal in addressing spirits, but changes to *you* in the closet scene (III.iv), presumably because his doubts about the identity of the Ghost have been removed. The *you* is now one of respect of son to father.

• The murderers of Clarence in *Richard III* (I.iv) address him as *you*, and he addresses them separately as *thou*. But his speech threatening God's vengeance provokes an angry retort, and their pronoun alters with their mood: 'And that same Vengeance doth he hurl on thee'.

• In *Henry VI Part 3* (III.ii), Edward IV is trying to persuade a reluctant Lady Gray to be his queen. At one point, after a sequence in which the King uses only *thou* forms, her evasion provokes him to an irritated *you* response – but he soon regains his composure:

EDWARD: Sweet widow, by my state I swear to thee
I speak no more than what my soul intends,
And that is to enjoy thee for my love.
LADY GRAY: And that is more than I will yield unto.
I know I am too mean to be your queen,
And yet too good to be your concubine.
EDWARD: You cavil, widow – I did mean my queen.
LADY GRAY: 'Twill grieve your grace my sons should call you father.
EDWARD: No more than when my daughters call thee mother.

THE SEARCH FOR STABILITY

The great age of Elizabethan literature brought an unprecedented breadth and inventiveness in the use of English, especially in the area of vocabulary (p. 60). It has been estimated that the period between 1530 and the Restoration (1660) displayed the fastest lexical growth in the history of the language. Nearly half of the new words were borrowings from the many cultures with which English was coming into contact; the remainder were different types of word formation using native resources. There was also a great deal of semantic change, as old words acquired new senses – a factor particularly noticed by those involved in the production of religious texts. The authors of the revised edition of the Book of Common Prayer (1662) comment that most of their alterations to the 1552 version were made 'for the more proper expressing of some words or phrases of ancient usage, in terms more suitable to the language of the present times'.

This unprecedented growth brought with it unprecedented uncertainty. By the end of the 17th century there was a widespread feeling of unease about the direction in which the language was moving. Many critics felt that English was changing too quickly and randomly, and applied such terms to it as 'unruly', 'corrupt', 'unrefined', and 'barbarous'. A particular area of concern was the lack of consistency in spelling or punctuation (pp. 66–9): at one extreme, there were people who spelled as they spoke (such as *sartinly* for *certainly*); at the other, there were those who took pains to reflect Classical etymology in their spelling (often mistakenly, such as by adding an *s* to *island* or a *c* to *scissors*). There was also a fear that foreign words and neologisms were entering the language in an uncontrolled way. The critics could see no order in the lexical inventiveness of the Elizabethan dramatists. Many of Shakespeare's new words had become part of the language, but many had not (p. 63), and it was unclear how such anomalies should be dealt with.

Contemporary linguistic fashions and trends provided no solace. John Dryden, in *Defence of the Epilogue* (1672) complains about those 'who corrupt our English Idiom by mixing it too much with French'. Joseph Addison, in a *Spectator* essay (4 August 1711), complains about the use of contracted forms, which has 'untuned our Language, and clogged it with Consonants': he cites such contractions as *mayn't* and *won't*, as well as such abbreviations as *rep* (*reputation*) and *ult* (*ultimate*). Daniel Defoe, in *An Essay upon Projects* (1697), complains about the 'inundation' of swearwords in the language of his time, and hopes that the introduction of an Academy might stem what he calls a 'Frenzy of the Tongue, a Vomit of the Brain'. Fifteen years later, Jonathan Swift takes up the challenge.

A
Table Alphabeticall, conteyning and teaching the true vvriting, and vnderftanding of hard vfuall Englifh wordes, borrowed from the Hebrew, Greeke, Latine, or French. &c.

With the interpretation thereof by *plaine Englifh words, gathered for the benefit & helpe of Ladies, Gentlewomen, or any other vnskilfull perfons.*

Whereby they may the more eafilie and better vnderftand many hard Englifh wordes, vvhich they fhall heare or read in Scriptures, Sermons, or elfwhere, and alfo be made able to vfe the fame aptly themfelues.

Legere, et non intelligere, neglegere eft.
As good not read, as not to vnderftand.

AT LONDON,
Printed by I. R. for Edmund Weauer, & are to be fold at his fhop at the great North doore of Paules Church.
1 6 0 4.

THE FIRST SYNONYM DICTIONARY

An important step forward in organizing the English lexicon took place when Robert Cawdrey published the first 'dictionary of hard words' in 1604. *A Table Alphabeticall* contained glosses for 3,000 'hard vsuall English wordes', such as *abbettors*, glossed as 'counsellors', and *abbreuiat*, glossed as 'to shorten, or make short'. It was a commercial success, and was followed by several other compilations on similar lines.

LEXICAL SUMMITS

The peak of vocabulary growth in the Renaissance period is clearly shown by this graph, which is based on a count of items appearing in an abridged version of the *Oxford English Dictionary* (p. 443). Graphs of this kind must not be interpreted too precisely, however. Because of the bias adopted by the *OED* (as stated in its original Preface) towards 'great English writers', the lexicon of many 'ordinary' texts of the Early Modern English period is not fully taken into account. Several studies have shown that quite a large number of words and senses are not included in the *OED*, and that its first citations can often be antedated by many years. A German investigator of the period, Jürgen Schäfer, has estimated that, if all types of correction are taken into account, the total number of discrepancies in the *OED* database might be as many as half a million. Graphs such as the above are thus likely to be serious underestimates of the true lexical resources of Early Modern English; the late 15th century, in particular, is thought to be poorly represented. But the general impression of lexical growth conveyed by the graph is reasonable enough, and certainly corresponds to any intuitive sense of what was happening throughout this period.
(After T. Nevalainen, forthcoming 1996.)

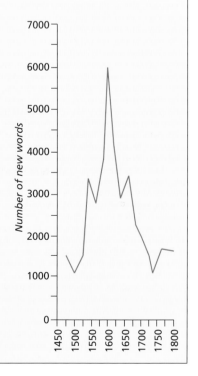

The Academy issue

Authors such as Swift were deeply worried about the speed at which the language was changing. Without proper controls, would their work still be intelligible in a generation or so? In 'A Proposal for Correcting, Improving and Ascertaining the English Tongue' (1712), Swift presented his case:

if it [English] were once refined to a certain Standard, perhaps there might be Ways found out to fix it for ever; or at least till we are invaded and made a Conquest by some other State; and even then our best Writings might probably be preserved with Care, and grow in Esteem, and the Authors have a Chance for Immortality.

He submitted his proposal to the Earl of Oxford:

My Lord; I do here, in the Name of all the Learned and Polite Persons of the Nation, complain to Your LORDSHIP, as *First Minister*, that our Language is extremely imperfect; that its daily Improvements are by no means in proportion to its daily Corruptions; that the Pretenders to polish and refine it, have chiefly multiplied Abuses and Absurdities; and, that in many Instances, it offends against every Part of Grammar.

Swift attacked in all directions: he was against Restoration licentiousness, the sloppiness of the young nobility, the abbreviations used by poets, the spelling proposals which tried to reflect speech, the fashionable slang of university people – 'illiterate Court-Fops, half-witted Poets, and University-Boys'. His solution was to follow the example of the French (whose Academy was founded in 1635):

a free judicious Choice should be made of such Persons, as are generally allowed to be best qualified for such a Work, without any regard to Quality, Party, or Profession. These, to a certain Number at least, should assemble at some appointed Time and Place, and fix on Rules by which they design to proceed. ...what I have most at Heart is, that some Method should be thought on for *ascertaining* and *fixing* our Language for ever, after such Alterations are made in it as shall be thought requisite. For I am of Opinion, that it is better a Language should not be wholly perfect, than that it should be perpetually changing...

Swift was not the first person to propose an Academy for English: Dryden and Defoe had also done so. But even though the idea attracted a great deal of interest, it never got off the ground. Many saw that language cannot be kept static, and that standards always change. Dr Johnson was one who derided the notion:

When we see men grow old and die at a certain time one after another, we laugh at the elixir that promises to prolong life to a thousand years; and with equal justice may the lexicographer be derided, who being able to produce no example of a nation that has preserved their words and phrases from mutability, shall imagine that his dictionary can embalm his language, and secure it from corruption and decay ...

Neither Britain nor the United States (p. 81) chose the Academy solution; and although the idea has been raised at intervals ever since, it has never found widespread support within those nations.

The debate about language corruption in the 17th century did, however, focus public attention on the existence of a problem and the need for a solution. If the language needed protection, or at least consistency and stability, these could be provided by dictionaries, grammars, spelling guides, and pronunciation manuals. Standards of correctness would thereby emerge, which all could follow. It was Johnson himself who put the first part of this solution into place (p. 74).

THE SCIENTIFIC APPROACH

The sense of chaos and confusion which surrounded the language was attacked in several ways. Some scholars proposed radical systems of spelling reform (p. 66). Some, such as the mathematician Bishop John Wilkins (1614–72) tried to develop a logical alternative to English, which would do away with all irregularity – one of the first attempts at a universal language.

When the Royal Society for the Promotion of Natural Knowledge was founded in 1660, a scientific approach was proposed. A group of its members formed a committee to 'improve the English tongue, particularly for philosophic [i.e. scientific] purposes'. The aim was to develop a plain, objective style, without rhetoric and classical vocabulary, which would be more suitable to scientific expression. The committee achieved no consensus, and did not exist for long, but a 'naked, natural way of speaking; positive expressions; clear senses' was said to have been a hallmark of the founder members' style. This group was the nearest Britain ever came to having an Academy.

An allegorical engraving by Hollar, representing the foundation of the Royal Society (from Bishop Sprat's *History of the Royal Society*). Fame crowns the bust of Charles II, 'Royal Author and Patron'. On the right sits Francis Bacon, 'Artium Instaurator' (Renewer of the Arts); on the left is Lord Brouncker, the first president. Scientific instruments and books surround them.

THE SOUTH AFRICAN EXCEPTION

The only part of the English-speaking world which has ever set up an Academy is South Africa. 'The English Academy of Southern Africa' was established in 1961, and promotes 'the effective use of English as a dynamic language in Southern Africa'. Based in Johannesburg, it arranges lectures and conferences, administers prizes, participates in national bodies, and dispenses language information. It also operates an English advisory service, popularly known as 'Grammar-phone'.

JOHNSON'S DICTIONARY

It were a thing verie praiseworthie… if som one well learned and as laborious a man, wold gather all the words which we vse in our English tung… into one dictionarie.

Thus wrote Richard Mulcaster (p. 66) in 1582. Apart from the occasional collection of a few thousand 'hard words' (p. 72), the task was not attempted until 1721, when Nathaniel Bailey published his *Universal Etymological English Dictionary*. Bailey's entries are fuller, compared with the glosses in the hard-word books, and there are more of them (as many as 60,000, in the 1736 edition), but his definitions lack illustrative support, and he gives little guidance about usage.

It was not until Samuel Johnson completed *A Dictionary of the English Language* in 1755 that the lexicon received its first authoritative treatment. Over a seven-year period, Johnson wrote the definitions of *c.* 40,000 words, illustrating their use from the best authors since the time of the Elizabethans (but excluding his own contemporaries). Although he has fewer entries than Bailey, his selection is more wide-ranging, and his lexicological treatment is far more discriminating and sophisticated. The book, according to his biographer Boswell, 'conferred stability' on the language – and at least with respect to spelling (where most of Johnson's choices are found in modern practice), this seems to be so.

A stained-glass feature in Johnson's house, 17 Gough Square, off Fleet Street, London, where he lived from 1748 to 1759, and thus where most of the *Dictionary* was compiled. The house was rescued from demolition in 1911, refurbished during the 1980s, and is now a Johnson museum.

The alphabetical section of Johnson's *Dictionary* is preceded by a famous Preface, in which he outlines his aims and procedures:

> When I took the first survey of my undertaking, I found our speech copious without order, and energetick without rules: wherever I turned my view, there was perplexity to be disentangled, and confusion to be regulated… Having therefore no assistance but from general grammar, I applied myself to the perusal of our writers; and noting whatever might be of use to ascertain or illustrate any word or phrase, accumulated in time the materials of a dictionary, which, by degrees, I reduced to method…

The preliminaries also include a short history of the language, with long extracts from earlier authors, and a grammar, much influenced by the work of John Wallis (p. 69), with sections on orthography and prosody. But it is in the Preface, often anthologized as an independent text, that we find an unprecedented statement of the theoretical basis of a dictionary project. The statement is notable for its awareness of the realities of the lexicographer's task, and also for its descriptive intention (p. 442) – an interesting change of opinion from the prescriptive attitudes Johnson expressed in his 1747 *Dictionary* plan. There he had written: 'The chief intent… is to preserve the purity and ascertain the meaning of our English idiom'. The Preface, by contrast, stresses that his aim is to 'not form, but register the language'; and it is this principle which introduces a new era in lexicography.

SOME JOHNSONIAN DEFINITIONS

There are not many truly idiosyncratic definitions in the *Dictionary*, but some have become famous.

LEXICOGRAPHER A writer of dictionaries; a harmless drudge, that busies himself in tracing the original, and detailing the signification of words.

EXCISE A hateful tax levied upon commodities, and adjudged not by the common judges of property, but wretches hired by those to whom excise is paid.

OATS A grain, which in England is generally given to horses, but in Scotland supports the people.

PATRON One who countenances, supports or protects. Commonly a wretch who supports with insolence, and is paid with flattery.

PENSION An allowance made to anyone without an equivalent. In England it is generally understood to mean pay given to a state hireling for treason to his country.

And which political party did Johnson support?

TORY One who adheres to the antient constitution of the state, and the apostolical hierarchy of the church of England, opposed to a *whig*.

WHIG 2. The name of a faction.

His definitions sometimes got him into trouble. He was threatened with libel over *excise*, and much lampooned over *pension* (after accepting one himself in 1762).

SAMUEL JOHNSON (1709–84)

Johnson was born in Lichfield, Staffordshire, the son of a provincial bookseller. He studied for a while at Oxford, but lack of money caused him to leave after a year. He became a teacher and writer, moving to London in 1737, where he wrote for *The Gentleman's Magazine*. He also helped catalogue the library of the Earl of Oxford.

He produced an outline for his *Dictionary* in 1746, a contract was signed, and the first of his amanuenses began work on midsummer day of that year. A more fully elaborated *Plan of a Dictionary of the English Language* appeared a year later. It took him some three years to read his source works and mark the citations to be used. These were then copied by his amanuenses onto slips of paper, and filed alphabetically. Once all slips were collated, he began to draft his definitions. The first sheets were printed in 1750, beginning with letter A. The work was complete by 1754, and an edition of 2,000 copies appeared the following year, priced £4 10s. There was soon a second edition, published in 165 weekly sections at sixpence each; and a fourth edition, much revised, appeared in 1773. The book dominated the dictionary market for decades, and appeared in several editions for much of the next century.

After the *Dictionary*, Johnson continued as a literary journalist, and received financial security from a pension granted by George III. He met his biographer, James Boswell, in 1763, and in 1764 founded the Literary Club, where many of his famous conversations took place. Later works included an eight-volume edition of Shakespeare's plays and a ten-volume *Lives of the Most Eminent English Poets*. He was granted an honorary doctorate by Trinity College Dublin in 1765, and again by Oxford in 1775, and thus received the title by which he has come to be most widely known: Dr Johnson.

E T E

will not obey, who, to get rid of his rider, riſes mightily before; and while his forehand is yet in the air, yerks furiouſly with his hind legs. *Farrier's Dict.*

ESTRE'ATE. *n. ſ.* [*extractum*, Latin.] The true copy of an original writing: for example, of amerciaments or penalties, ſet down in the rolls of a court, to be levied by the bailiff, or other officer, of every man for his offence. A law term. *Cowel.*

ESTRE'PEMENT. *n. ſ.* [of the French word *eſtre, ier.*] Spoil made by the tenant for term of life upon any lands or woods, to the prejudice of him in the reverſion. *Cowel.*

E'STRICH. *n. ſ.* [commonly written *oſtrich.*] The largeſt of birds.

To be furious,
Is to be frighted out of fear; and, in that mood,
The dove will peck the *eſtridge*. *Shak Anth. and Cleopatra.*

The peacock, not at thy command, aſſumes
His glorious train; nor *eſtrich* her rare plumes. *Sandys.*

E'STUARY. *n. ſ.* [*æſtuarium*, Latin.] An arm of the ſea; the mouth of a lake or river in which the tide reciprocates; a frith.

To E'STUATE. *v. a.* [*æſtuo*, Latin.] To ſwell and fall reciprocally; to boil; to be in a ſtate of violent commotion. *Dict.*

ESTUA'TION. *n. ſ.* [from *æſtuo*, Latin.] The ſtate of boiling; reciprocation of riſe and fall; agitation; commotion.

Rivers and lakes, that want fermenting parts at the bottom, are not excited unto *eſtuations*; therefore ſome ſeas flow higher than others. *Brown's Vulgar Errours, b.* vii. *c.* 13.

The motion of the will is accompanied with a ſenſible commotion of the ſpirits, and an *eſtuation* of the blood. *Norris.*

E'STURE. *n. ſ.* [*æſtus*, Latin.] Violence; commotion.

The ſeas retain
Not only their outrageous *eſture* there,
But ſupernatural miſchief they expire. *Chapman's Odyſſey.*

E'SURIENT. *adj.* [*eſuriens*, Latin.] Hungry; voracious. *Dict.*

E'SURINE. *adj.* [*eſurio*, Latin.] Corroding; eating.

Over much piercing is the air of Hampſtead, in which ſort of air there is always ſomething *eſurine* and acid. *Wiſeman.*

ETC. A contraction of the two Latin words *et cætera*, which ſignifies *and ſo on*; *and the reſt*; *and others of the like kind.*

To ETCH. *v. a.* [*etizen*, German.]

1. A way uſed in making of prints, by drawing with a proper needle upon a copper-plate, covered over with a ground of wax, &c. and well blacked with the ſmoke of a link, in order to take off the figure of the drawing or print; which having its backſide tinctured with white lead, will, by running over the ſtrucken out lines with a ſtift, impreſs the exact figure on the black or red ground; which figure is afterwards with needles drawn deeper quite through the ground, and all the ſhadows and hatchings put in; and then a wax border being made all round the plate, there is poured on a ſufficient quantity of well tempered *aqua fortis*, which, inſinuating into the ſtrokes made by the needles, uſually eats, in about half an hour, into the figure of the print or drawing on the copper plate. *Harris.*

2. To ſcetch; to draw; to delineate [unleſs this word be miſtaken by *Locke* for *eke.*]

There are many empty terms to be found in ſome learned writers, to which they had recourſe to *etch* out their ſyſtems. *Locke.*

3. [This word is evidently miſtaken by *Ray* for *edge.*] To move forwards towards one ſide.

When we lie long awake in the night, we are not able to reſt one quarter of an hour without ſhifting of ſides, or at leaſt *etching* this way and that way, more or leſs. *Ray.*

ETCH. *n. ſ.* A country word, of which I know not the meaning.

When they ſow their *etch* crops, they ſprinkle a pound or two of clover on an acre. *Mortimer's Huſbandry.*

Where you find dunging of land makes it rank, lay dung upon the *etch*, and ſow it with barley. *Mortimer's Huſbandry.*

ETE'RNAL. *adj.* [*æternus*, Latin.]

1. Without beginning or end.

The *eternal* God is thy refuge. *Deut.* xxxiii. 27.

2. Without beginning.

It is a queſtion quite different from our having an idea of eternity, to know whether there were any real being, whoſe duration has been *eternal*. *Locke.*

3. Without end; endleſs; immortal.

Thou know'ſt that Banquo and his Fleance lives.
—But in them nature's copy's not *eternal*. *Shakeſ. Macbeth.*

4. Perpetual; conſtant; unintermitting.

Burnt off'rings morn and ev'ning ſhall be thine,
And fires *eternal* in thy temple ſhine. *Dryd. Knight's Tale.*

5. Unchangeable.

Hobbes believed the *eternal* truths which he oppoſed. *Dryd.*

ETE'RNAL. *n. ſ.* [*eternel*, French.] One of the appellations of the Godhead.

That law whereby the *eternal* himſelf doth work. *Hooker.*

The *eternal*, to prevent ſuch horrid fray,
Hung out of heav'n his golden ſcales. *Milton.*

ETE'RNALIST. *n. ſ.* [*æternus*, Latin.] One that holds the paſt exiſtence of the world infinite.

E T H

I would aſk the *eternaliſts* what mark is there that they could expect or deſire of the novelty of a world, that is not found in this? Or what mark is there of eternity that is found in this? *Burnet's Theory of the Earth.*

To ETE'RNALISE. *v. a.* [from *eternal.*] To make eternal. *Dict.*

ETE'RNALLY. *adv.* [from *eternal.*]

1. Without beginning or end.

2. Unchangeably; invariably.

That which is morally good, or evil, at any time, or in any caſe, muſt be alſo *eternally* and unchangeably ſo, with relation to that time and to that caſe. *South's Sermons.*

3. Perpetually; without intermiſſion.

Bear me, ſome god, to Baja's gentle ſeats,
Or cover me in Umbria's green retreats,
Where weſtern gales *eternally* reſide,
And all the ſeaſons laviſh all their pride. *Addiſon.*

ETE'RNE. *adj.* [*æternus*, Latin.] Eternal; perpetual; endleſs.

The Cyclops hammers fall
On Mars his armour forg'd for proof *eterne*. *Shak. Hamlet.*

ETE'RNITY. *n. ſ.* [*æternitas*, Latin.]

1. Duration without beginning or end.

In this ground his precious root
Still lives, which, when weak time ſhall be pour'd out
Into *eternity*, and circular joys
Dancing an endleſs round, again ſhall riſe. *Craſhaw.*

Thy immortal rhyme
Makes this one ſhort point of time,
To fill up half the orb of round *eternity*. *Cowley.*

By repeating the idea of any length of duration which we have in our minds, with all the endleſs addition of number, we come by the idea of *eternity*. *Locke.*

2. Duration without end.

Beyond is all abyſs,
Eternity, whoſe end no eye can reach! *Milt. Parad. Loſt.*

Eternity, thou pleaſing, dreadful thought!
Through what variety of untried being,
Through what new ſcenes and changes muſt we paſs. *Add.*

To ETE'RNIZE. *v. a.* [*æterno*, Latin.]

1. To make endleſs; to perpetuate.

I with two fair gifts
Created him endow'd; with happineſs,
And immortality: that fondly loſt,
This other ſerv'd but to *eternize* woe. *Milton's Parad. Loſt.*

2. To make for ever famous; to immortalize.

Mankind by all means ſeeking to *eternize* himſelf, ſo much the more as he is near his end, doth it by ſpeeches and writings. *Sidney.*

And well beſeems all knights of noble name,
That covet in th' immortal book of fame
To be *eternized*, that ſame to haunt. *Fairy Queen, b.* i.

I might relate of thouſands, and their names
Eternize here on earth; but thoſe elect
Angels, contented with their fame in heav'n,
Seek not the praiſe of men. *Milton's Paradiſe Loſt, b.* vi.

The four great monarchies have been celebrated by the writings of many famous men, who have *eternized* their fame, and thereby their own. *Temple.*

Both of them are ſet on fire by the great actions of heroes, and both endeavour to *eternize* them. *Dryden's Dufreſnoy.*

Hence came its name, in that the grateful Jove
Hath *eterniz'd* the glory of his love. *Creech's Manilius.*

E'THER. *n. ſ.* [*æther*, Latin; αἰθήρ.]

1. An element more fine and ſubtle than air; air refined or ſublimed.

If any one ſhould ſuppoſe that *ether*, like our air, may contain particles which endeavour to recede from one another; for I do not know what this *ether* is; and that its particles are exceedingly ſmaller than thoſe of air, or even than thoſe of light, the exceeding ſmallneſs of its particles may contribute to the greatneſs of the force, by which thoſe particles may recede from one another. *Newton's Opt.*

The parts of other bodies are held together by the eternal preſſure of the *ether*, and can have no other conceivable cauſe of their coheſion and union. *Locke.*

2. The matter of the higheſt regions above.

There fields of light and liquid *ether* flow,
Purg'd from the pond'rous dregs of earth below. *Dryden.*

ETHE'REAL. *adj.* [from *ether.*]

1. Formed of ether.

Man feels me, when I preſs th' *ethereal* plains. *Dryden.*

2. Celeſtial; heavenly.

Go, heav'nly gueſt, *ethereal* meſſenger,
Sent from whoſe ſov'reign goodneſs I adore. *Milton.*

Thrones and imperial pow'rs, offspring of heav'n,
Ethereal virtues! *Milton's Paradiſe Loſt, b.* ii. *l.* 311.

Such as theſe, being in good part freed from the entanglements of ſenſe and body, are employed, like the ſpirits above, in contemplating the Divine Wiſdom in the works of nature; a kind of anticipation of the *ethereal* happineſs and employment. *Glanv. Apol.*

Vaſt

THE JOHNSONIAN METHOD

'Thus have I laboured by settling the orthography, displaying the analogy, regulating the structures, and ascertaining the signification of *English* words, to perform all the parts of a faithful lexicographer…'

This page illustrates several features of the approach Johnson outlines in his Preface:

- Most of the definitions are succinct, appropriate, and consistent between entries, as can be seen from the *eternal* series.
- He pays special attention to the different senses of a word – five, in the case of *eternal*. (In the entry on *take*, no less than 124 uses are distinguished.)
- There is a copious use of quotations to support a definition – *c.* 116,000 in all. These are generally taken from dead authors so as not to be 'misled by partiality'.
- He follows the usage of his sources in arriving at his definitions, even if he thinks his sources are incorrect, as shown by sense 3 of *etch* (verb).
- He routinely identifies parts of speech.
- He shows the most strongly stressed syllable in a headword by an accent.
- There is an openness of approach, nicely illustrated by his entry on *etch* (noun): 'A country word, of which I know not the meaning'.
- Following the tradition established by Ephraim Chambers and other encyclopedists of his age, he includes topical explanations of some words, as seen in *etch* (verb), sense 1.
- A wide range of ordinary words (*estuary*, etc.) are included alongside technical terms (*estrepement*, *ether*) – though he apologizes in his Preface for his limited coverage of specialized fields.

Although very well received at the time, the *Dictionary* was later to receive a great deal of criticism.

- It includes, in the 'hard-words' tradition, many cumbersome Latinate forms, such as *cubiculary*, *estuation*, *esurine*, and *incompossibility*, whose status within English was doubtful.
- His citations are highly selective, chosen more for their literary or moral value than for their linguistic clarity. Half of all his quotations come from just seven sources – Shakespeare, Dryden, Milton, Addison, Bacon, Pope, and the Bible.
- Several of his definitions use difficult words (a problem he acknowledges in his Preface), such as *reciprocates* in *estuary*. A famous example is *cough* (noun), 'A convulsion of the lungs, vellicated by some sharp serosity'.
- Several of his definitions have become famous for their subjectivity (see p. 74).
- In the end, he ran out of space, and had to leave out about half the quotations he had collected. This caused a certain unevenness of treatment; in particular, words at the beginning of the alphabet were much more generously illustrated.

But despite these weaknesses, Johnson's *Dictionary* was the first attempt at a truly principled lexicography. It portrayed the complexity of the lexicon and of English usage more accurately than ever before; and his quotations initiated a practice which has informed English dictionaries ever since.

Imperceptibly, during the 18th century, English loses the most noticeable remaining features of structural difference which distance the Early Modern English period from us. By the end of that century, with but a few exceptions, the spelling, punctuation, and grammar are very close to what they are today. If we take an essay of William Hazlitt (1778–1830) or a novel of Jane Austen (1775–1817), for example, we can read for pages before a point of linguistic difference might make us pause. We would find the vocabulary somewhat unfamiliar in places, the idiom occasionally unusual or old-fashioned, the style elegant or quaint, and we might feel that the language was in some indefinable way characteristic of a previous age; but we do not need to consult a special edition or historical dictionary at every turn in order to understand the text. Jane Austen makes demands of our modern English linguistic intuitions which seem little different from those required by Catherine Cookson or P. D. James.

However, despite this apparent continuity, the language at the end of the 18th century is by no means identical to what we find today. Many words, though spelled the same, had a different meaning. If we had tape recordings of the time, we would also notice several differences in pronunciation, especially in the way words were stressed (p. 69). And an uninformed modern intuition would achieve only a superficial reading of the literary texts of the period. In reading a novel of the 1990s, we can make an immediate linguistic response to the social and stylistic nuances introduced into the text, because we are part of its age: we recognize the differences between formality and informality, or educated and uneducated; and we can sense when someone is being jocular, ironic, risqué, archaic, or insincere. We can easily miss such nuances in the writing of the early 19th century, especially in those works which take the manners of contemporary society as their subject. This world is linguistically more removed from us than at first it may appear.

SEEING BENEATH THE SURFACE

Emma Woodhouse, handsome, clever, and rich, with a comfortable home and happy disposition, seemed to unite some of the best blessings of existence; and had lived nearly twenty-one years in the world with very little to distress or vex her.

She was the youngest of the two daughters of a most affectionate, indulgent father; and had, in consequence of her sister's marriage, been mistress of his house from a very early period. Her mother had died too long ago for her to have more than an indistinct remembrance of her caresses; and her place had been supplied by an excellent woman as governess, who had fallen little short of a mother in affection…

Thus begins Jane Austen's *Emma*, published in 1816. To the modern reader, its language presents no unexpected difficulties. We might be struck by the use of *handsome* (used more commonly today with male reference), or by *youngest* referring only to two; but neither of these points is likely to disturb our smooth comprehension of these opening lines.

Early 19th-century English can, however, deceive in its apparent familiarity. There are hundreds of instances where words have changed their meaning, often in highly subtle ways. For example, in the middle of a long and somewhat erratic monologue, Emma's garrulous acquaintance Miss Bates describes a reaction to some baked apples:

'"Oh!", said he, directly, "there is nothing in the way of fruit half so good, and these are the finest-looking home-baked apples I ever saw in my life." That, you know, was so very – And I am sure, by his manner, it was no compliment ...' (*Emma*, Ch. 27)

It is easy to let the speaker carry us on past this point, so that we do not notice the existence of the problem: if the first comment means anything at all, it is surely a compliment, yet Miss Bates seems to be denying it. The apparent contradiction is resolved when we know that *compliment* had an additional sense in Austen's time, which it has since lost: it could mean simply 'polite or conventional praise'. What Miss Bates means is 'It wasn't just flattery'.

We do not always note such difference in usage, because the context often enables us to see the intended sense. Here are some other instances from the novels where usage has changed in a subtle way (after K. C. Phillips, 1970, who also provides an index and page references):

• 'the supposed inmate of Mansfield Parsonage': *inmate* had not yet developed its sense of someone occupying a prison or institution.
• '[she] had neither beauty, genius, accomplishment, nor manner': *genius* did not yet have its modern sense of 'outstanding intellectual quality'.
• 'her regard had all the warmth of first attachment': *regard* had a much stronger sense of 'affection'.
• 'She was now in an irritation as violent from delight as...': *irritation* could be caused by a pleasurable emotion.
• 'three or four Officers were lounging together': *lounge* meant 'stroll', not 'lie carelessly on a chair'.

A number of differences are of a more idiomatic kind, where the substitution of one element produces the modern equivalent:

• whatever the *event* of ('outcome')
• caught in the *fact* ('act')
• made her first *essay* ('attempt')
• she saw her *in idea* ('in her mind's eye')
• Emma well knew *by character* ('by repute')
• the prospect...was highly *grateful* to her ('gratifying')
• Suppose you *speak for* tea ('order')

Grammatical trends

Jane Austen would have arrived at school (Abbey School, in Reading) at a time when Lowth's *Grammar* was well established, and a second generation of 'young ladies' (p. 78) was having its tenets instilled into them. That she was much concerned about correctness in grammar is suggested by the way she often changed her own grammatical usage in later editions of her novels. For example, at one point in *Pride and Prejudice*, she wrote 'the tables were broke up', but later emended the verb to *broken*.

That she was also aware of the social role of grammar is evident from many pieces of her dialogue, where nonstandard usage is seen as a mark of vulgarity, and good grammar as a sign of good breeding. Thus, Emma is surprised at the linguistic standard of the letter from the yeoman farmer, Robert Martin (who, in her opinion, is 'plain' and 'clownish'), when he proposes marriage to Harriet Smith:

The style of the letter was much above her expectation. There were not merely no grammatical errors, but as a composition it would not have disgraced a gentleman.

The following examples from Austen's novels illustrate some of the distinctive grammatical features of early 19th-century English, compared with today (Part III). There are differences in (1) tense usage, (2) auxiliary verbs (compare the Early Modern English practice, p. 70), (3) irregular verbs, (4) articles, (5) contracted forms, (6) prepositions, (7) adverbs, and (8) the comparative (also shown in the quotation from *Emma* on p. 76). All the examples come from the usage of educated characters in the novels, or are part of Austen's own narrative. (Uneducated characters have an identifiable grammar and lexicon of their own.)

(1) I am so glad we *are got* acquainted.
    So, you *are come* at last!
(2) What *say you* to the day?
    she *doubted not*…
(3) Fanny *shrunk* back…
    and much was *ate*…
(4) It is *a nothing* of a part…
    to be taken *into the account*…
(5) *Will not it* be a good plan?
    It would quite shock you…*would not it*?
(6) he told me *in* our journey…
    She was small *of* her age.
(7) I stood for a minute, feeling *dreadfully*.
    It is really very *well* for a novel.
(8) the *properest* manner…
    the *richest* of the two…

MY DEAR JAMES

In Letter VIII of his *Grammar of the English Language in a Series of Letters* (1829), William Cobbett advises his son James (aged 14) on the problems of irregular verbs. Most of his list of nearly 200 verbs recommends past tenses which are identical with present-day usage, but there are a few differences:

to bend	I bended
to light	I light
to sink	I sunk
to stink	I stunk

A number of past participles also differ:

chide	chidden
loaded	loaden
sat	sitten
shot	shotten
slid	slidden
snow	snown
spit	spitten

However, Cobbett does not list all the variations which were found at the time, and some of his recommendations are of questionable validity. *Sat*, for instance, was much used as a past tense form in the early 19th century, but he does not mention it. And several other forms occur in the Jane Austen novels, such as a past tense *sprung* for *sprang*, and a past participle *drank* for *drunk*. He is also uncertain about the best form to recommend for *sting*, giving both *stung* and *stang* as past tenses.

Usage of these old strong verbs (p. 21) was evidently very mixed at the time in polite society, and it was only during the 19th century that grammarians managed in most cases to resolve the variation (though leaving a residue of uncertainty, p. 204). On the other hand, there was no doubt about the nonstandard status of some usages: Jane Austen allows only servants and other uneducated people to use such 'barbarous' (in the words of Lowth) constructions as *have went*, *had took*, or *should have gave* (all spoken by Lucy Steele in *Sense and Sensibility*).

RULES TO BE OBSERVED

In 1774, the year before Jane Austen was born, John Walker published his *Pronouncing Dictionary of English*, with the aim of doing for pronunciation what Johnson had done for vocabulary (p. 74) and Lowth for grammar (p. 79). The book is a valuable information source about contemporary sound change, attitudes to pronunciation, and differences in usage between then and now. It also looks at major regional accents, and provides 'rules to be observed by the natives of Scotland, Ireland, and London, for avoiding their respective peculiarities'.

• Letter *r* 'is never silent', though 'particularly in London, the *r* in *lard* … is pronounced so much in the throat as to be little more than the middle or Italian *a*, lengthened into *laad*…'.
• The *s* in the prefix *dis* 'ought always to be pronounced as *z*, when it is not under the accent…', as in *dismay* and *dismiss*.
• When the letters *au* 'are followed by *n* and another consonant, they change to the second sound of *a*, heard in *far*', as in *haunt* and *laundry*.
• Several words are accented differently: *cement* (noun) has a stress on the first syllable; *balcony* on the middle; *prefix* (verb) on the last.
• 'The aspirate *h* is often sunk, particularly in the capital, where we do not find the least distinction of sound between *while* and *wile*…'.
• He notes that 'our best speakers do not invariably pronounce the participial *ing*, so as to rhyme with *sing*', and recommends that *ing* should be used, but allows an exception where there is an *-ng* ending in the root (as in *singing*).

SAT UPON

Hospitable Host. "Does any gentleman say pudden?"
Precise Guest. "No, sir. No *gentleman* says *pudden*."

THE RISE OF PRESCRIPTIVE GRAMMAR

The second half of the 18th century differs fundamentally from our own age in its attitudes towards English. The middle of the century had seen the culmination of the first major effort to impose order on the language, in the form of Johnson's *Dictionary* (p. 74). With spelling and lexicon now being handled in an increasingly systematic way, attention turned to grammar, and the first attempts to define this field in its own right began to appear.

Treatises on aspects of grammar are known from the 16th century. The dramatist Ben Jonson wrote *An English Grammar…for the Benefit of all Strangers, out of his Observation of the English Language now Spoken, and in Use*, published posthumously in 1640. John Wallis's *Grammatica Linguae Anglicanae* (Grammar of the English Language, 1653) was written 'because there is clearly a great demand for it from foreigners, who want to be able to understand the various important works which are written in our tongue' (which is why he, as others of his time, wrote in Latin). And Johnson, largely following Wallis, added a grammatical sketch at the front of his dictionary.

Which authority?

From the outset, however, there were fundamental differences of opinion about which way to proceed, and which authority to follow. Jonson (in his essay, 'Timber: or, Discoveries', 1640) is in no doubt about where to look for models of usage (*Custome*):

Custome, is the most certaine Mistresse of Language, as the publicke stampe makes the current money. But wee must not be too frequent with the mint, every day coyning…Yet when I name Custome, I understand not the vulgar Custome: For that were a precept no lesse dangerous to Language, then life, if wee should speake or live after the manners of the vulgar: But that I call Custome of speech, which is the consent of the Learned; as Custome of life, which is the consent of the good.

Wallis, on the other hand, writing in his Preface about suitable models of structure, is strong in his criticism of Jonson and other grammarians hitherto:

They all forced English too rigidly into the mould of Latin (a mistake which nearly everyone makes in descriptions of other modern languages too), giving many useless rules about the cases, genders and declensions of nouns, the tenses, moods and conjugations of verbs, the government of nouns and verbs, and other things of that kind, which have no bearing on our language, and which confuse and obscure matters instead of elucidating them.

These positions, and their opposites, were restated and adopted anew in the 1760s, which marks the beginning of a new period of interest and involvement in English grammar. Over 200 works on grammar and rhetoric appeared between 1750 and 1800. The most influential was undoubtedly Bishop Robert Lowth's *Short Introduction to English Grammar* (1762) – the inspiration for an even more widely-used book, Lindley Murray's *English Grammar* (1794). Both grammars went through many editions in the years following their publication, and had enormous influence on school practices, especially in the USA. This is evident even in the comments of those who disapproved of them. Thomas de Quincey, writing in *Blackwood's Magazine* in April 1839, condemns a number of 'inferior attempts to illustrate the language', and ends his list with Murray's:

This book, full of atrocious blunders…reigns despotically through the young ladies' schools, from the Orkneys to the Cornish Scillys.

It would have taken only a generation for any intellectual despotism to become firmly entrenched – and it is thus not surprising to see dogmatic attitudes towards grammar routinely appearing in early 19th-century magazines, letters, and novels (such as Jane Austen's, p. 76).

William Hazlitt (1778–1830)

A CASE OF RAGE AND VEXATION

By way of justifying his remark about 'blunders', De Quincey refers to the views of William Hazlitt, which had been forcibly expressed in an essay on English grammar in *The Atlas* some years before (15 March 1829). Hazlitt's attack on the way grammarians talk about cases in English (p. 202) well illustrates his position:

it is roundly asserted that there are *six cases* (why not seven?) in the English language; and a case is defined to be a peculiar termination or inflection added to a noun to show its position in the sentence. Now in the Latin language there are no doubt a number of cases, inasmuch as there are a number of inflections; and for the same reason (if words have a meaning) in the English language

there are none, or only one, the genitive; because if we except this, there is no inflection or variety whatever in the terminations. Thus to instance in the present noun – A case, Of a case, To a case, A case, O case, From a case – they tell you that the word *case* is here its own nominative, genitive, dative, accusative, vocative, and ablative, though the deuce of any case – that is, inflection of the noun – is there in the case. Nevertheless, many a pedagogue would swear till he was black in the face that it is so; and would lie awake many a restless night boiling with rage and vexation that any one should be so lost to shame and reason as to suspect that there is here also a distinction without a difference.

And he comments:

If a system were made in burlesque and purposely to call into question and expose its own nakedness, it could not go beyond this, which is gravely taught in all seminaries, and patiently learnt by all school-boys as an exercise and discipline of the intellectual faculties… All this might be excusable as a prejudice or oversight; but then why persist in it in the thirty-eighth edition of a standard book published by the great firm in Paternoster-row?

He is referring, of course, to Lindley Murray's grammar, published by Longman.

Traditional grammar

The books by Lowth and Murray, and those which they influenced, contain the origins of most of the grammatical controversies which continue to attract attention today (p. 194). This is the period which gave rise to the concept of 'traditional grammar' (as 20th-century linguists would one day call it), and in which the rules of 'correct' grammatical usage were first drawn up. It was a time when the subject was debated at length, with philosophical, logical, aesthetic, historical, and occasionally linguistic reasons proposed for adopting one position rather than another. Most fiercely argued was the question of whether grammars and dictionaries should *reflect* usage, describing and analysing current practice, or should *evaluate* usage, by prescribing certain forms as correct and proscribing others as incorrect. During the last decades of the 18th century, the latter position was the influential one. But at all times these rules were as forcefully attacked as they were authoritatively formulated. Thus, we find Bishop Lowth saying in 1762:

The principal design of a Grammar of any Language is to teach us to express ourselves with propriety in that Language; and to enable us to judge of every phrase and form of construction, whether it be right or not.

And we have the scientist Joseph Priestley saying in *The Rudiments of English Grammar* (1761):

Our grammarians appear to me to have acted precipitately… It must be allowed, that the custom of speaking is the original and only just standard of any language.

This was the chief controversy in the 1760s, and it remains with us today (p. 192).

Robert Lowth (1710–87)

Lowth, born in Winchester, Hampshire, was both scholar and clergyman. In 1742 he became Professor of Poetry at Oxford, and in 1766 Bishop of St David's and of Oxford. He was consecrated Bishop of London in 1777. Apart from his *Grammar*, he was known for his work on Hebrew poetry, especially as it appears in the Old Testament.

Lindley Murray (1745–1826)

Murray was born in Swatara Creek, Pennsylvania. He trained as a lawyer, and had a highly successful practice in New York. In 1784 he retired to England, because of ill health, and lived near York. Apart from his *Grammar*, he wrote other books on English, as well as religious works.

CORRUPTION EVERYWHERE

Lowth's 'short introduction' contained less than 200 pages, but in it there are hundreds of examples of what he felt to be corrupt grammar. It is important to note that these examples are not taken from the speech or writing of the uneducated, or even of the reasonably well-educated, but from 'the politest part of the nation, and …our most approved authors'. Lowth is talking about Shakespeare, Milton, Pope, Swift, all of whom in his opinion 'offend'.

His procedure has been imitated for over 200 years: 'to lay down rules, and to illustrate them by examples'. These examples, moreover, are of two kinds, so that 'beside shewing what is right, the matter may be further explained by pointing out what is wrong'.

In illustrating Lowth, we simultaneously illustrate Murray, who copies extensively from him. An example is the condemnation of the double negative construction (p. 194), where Murray uses exactly the same words as Lowth:

Two negatives in English destroy one another, or are equivalent to an affirmative.

And here is Lowth identifying what was to become one of the most famous shibboleths of traditional grammar: 'Never put a preposition at the end of a sentence'. His tone here is in fact much less condemnatory than that of his imitators a generation later.

The preposition is often separated from the Relative which it governs, and joined to the Verb at the end of the Sentence, or of some member of it: as, 'Horace is an author, *whom* I am much delighted *with*'…This is an idiom, which our language is strongly inclined to: it prevails in common conversation, and suits very well with the familiar style in writing: but the placing of the Preposition before the Relative is more graceful, as well as more perspicuous; and agrees much better with the solemn and elevated style.

His list of bad examples includes the following:

'*Who* servest thou *under*?'
Shakespear, Hen.V.
'*Who* do you speak *to*?' As you like it….
'We are still much at a loss, *who* civil power belongs *to*.'
Locke.

A SHORT

INTRODUCTION

TO

ENGLISH GRAMMAR:

WITH

CRITICAL NOTES.

A NEW EDITION, CORRECTED.

Nam ipfum *Latine* loqui, eſt illud quidem in magna laude ponendum ; ſed non tam fua fponte, quam quod eſt a plerifque neglectum. Non enim tam præclarum eſt ſcire *Latine*, quam turpe neſcire; neque tam id mihi oratoris boni, quam civis *Romani*, proprium videtur.   CICERO.

PRINTED FOR THE BOOKSELLERS.

M DCC LXXXVII.

And he adds:

In all these places, it ought to be *whom*.

There is irony, of course (if his usage is not deliberate), in that Lowth himself commits the error he is criticizing. But whether deliberate or not, in this case Murray would have none of it. His version of Lowth's sentence silently corrects its grammar: 'This is an idiom to which our language is strongly inclined'!

NEW NATION, NEW THEMES

The linguistic issues and developments which had preoccupied British scholars in the first half of the 18th century were to hold the attention of American scholars in the second. A gap of 33 years separates the grammars of Lowth and Murray (p. 79), and a similar period separates Johnson's *Dictionary* (p. 74) from Noah Webster's *Dissertations on the English Language* (1789). In this work, Webster proposed the institution of an 'American standard'. It was partly a matter of honour 'as an independent nation…to have a system of our own, in language as well as government'; it was partly a matter of common sense, because in England 'the taste of her writers is already corrupted, and her language on the decline'; and it was partly a matter of practicality, England being at 'too great a distance to be our model'. This national or 'federal' language was inevitable, because the exploration of the new continent would bring many new words into the language, which Britain would not share; but it also needed fostering. Spelling reform, he concluded, would be a major step in that direction: 'a difference between the English orthography and the American…is an object of vast political consequence'.

Although Webster went through a period in which he advocated radical reform, the position he finally adopted was a fairly moderate one. In the Preface to his first lexicographical venture, *A Compendious Dictionary of the English Language* (1806), he writes:

No great change should be made at once, nor should any change be made which violates established principles, creates great inconvenience, or obliterates the radicals of the language. But gradual changes to accommodate the written to the spoken language, when they occasion none of those evils, and especially when they purify words from corruptions, improve the regular analogies of a language and illustrate etymology, are not only proper, but indispensable.

This dictionary was no small achievement: it contained *c.* 28,000 words, as well as encyclopedic information (such as population figures). However, it received a mixed reception: despite its inclusion of new American vocabulary, many were offended by the way Webster attacked Johnson's *Dictionary* (he objected in particular to its difficult words, its vulgarisms, and its excessive use of quotations) and by his evident ambition to surpass Johnson's achievement. His recommended spellings were also treated with suspicion, as were some of his pronunciations. Critics pointed to inconsistencies in the way he tried to justify his proposals. If the *u* in *labour* is to be omitted because it is not used in *laborious*, why not omit the *u* of *curious* because it is not used in *curiosity*? And why not keep *-re*, given the links between *centre* and *central*, *theatre* and *theatrical*, and many others?

WEBSTER'S PROBLEM

The following words are among those spelled *-our* in Johnson's *Dictionary*:

anterieur, ardour, armour, behaviour, clamour, colour, dishonour, emperour, errour, fervour, flavour, governour, harbour, honour, horrour, humour, inferiour, interiour, labour, neighbour, odour, oratour, parlour, rancour, rumour, saviour, splendour, superiour, terrour, tremour, valour, vapour, warriour

The following are some of those spelled with *-or*:

actor, auditor, author, captor, collector, conductor, creditor, director, doctor, editor, elector, equator, exterior, factor, inspector, junior, languor, liquor, manor, mediator, mirror, motor, pastor, posterior, professor, protector, rector, sculptor, sector, senator, senior, stupor, tailor, torpor, tutor

Given the inconsistency in the list (e.g. *interior* vs *exterior*), it is not surprising to find Webster, and Worcester after him (p. 82), opting to dispense with the distinction altogether.

THE BLUE-BACKED SPELLER

The *American Spelling Book* was first published in 1783 as Part 1 of *A Grammatical Institute of the English Language* (Part 2, a grammar, appeared in 1784, and Part 3, a reader, in 1785). Within the next 60 years this book, in its distinctive blue cover, went through over 250 printings, and had several revised editions. Undoubtedly the most popular schoolbook ever published, it was selling a million copies a year in the 1850s – and in a total US population of only *c.* 23 million.

In the introduction to the speller, Webster follows British spelling norms, and cites Johnson's *Dictionary* as his guide. He even goes so far as to denounce those spelling reformers who 'alter the spellings of words, by expunging the superfluous letters', such as *favor*.

Within a few years, however, he had changed his mind. At first he planned a radically different phonetic alphabet, but when this received little support he developed a more moderate solution, avoiding

the introduction of any new letters (apart from a few 'trifling alterations', such as diacritics and ligatures). These proposals, first advocated in a 1789 essay, were based instead on 'the omission of all superfluous and silent letters' (e.g. *bred* for *bread*) and on the 'substitution of a character that has a certain definite sound, for one that is more vague and indeterminate' (e.g. *greeve* for *grieve*).

The major revision of the speller in 1804 contained his first proposals, deleting *u* from words ending in *-our* (e.g. *favor*) and *-k* from those ending in *-ick* (e.g. *music*). His full range of proposals was published in his *Compendious Dictionary* of 1806; they included *-er* for *-re* (e.g. *theater*) *-se* for *-ce* (e.g. *defense*), *-k* for *-que* (e.g. *check*), and single *l* before a suffix, depending on the stress (*traveling* vs *excelling*). These changes are now familiar because they were to become standard features of US spelling. Several others, such as the dropping of final *e* (as in *definit* and *examin*) or of silent letters (as in *fether* and *ile*) never caught on.

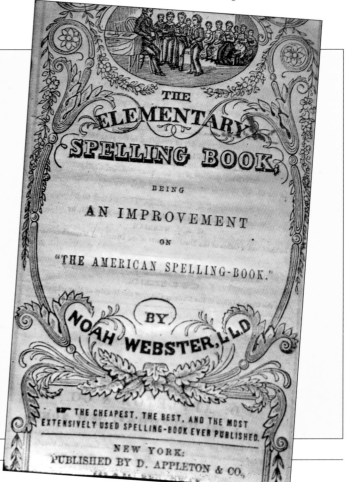

THE
ELEMENTARY
SPELLING BOOK;
BEING
AN IMPROVEMENT
ON
"THE AMERICAN SPELLING-BOOK."
BY
NOAH WEBSTER, LL.D.

☞ THE CHEAPEST, THE BEST, AND THE MOST EXTENSIVELY USED SPELLING-BOOK EVER PUBLISHED.

NEW YORK:
PUBLISHED BY D. APPLETON & CO.

Webster's

In 1828 appeared *An American Dictionary of the English Language*, in two volumes, containing some 70,000 words. The work greatly improved the coverage of scientific and technical terms, as well as terms to do with American culture and institutions (such as *congress* and *plantation*), and added a great deal of encyclopedic information. A new feature was the introduction of Webster's own etymologies – though the speculative nature of many of these was an early source of unwelcome criticism. The spellings were somewhat more conservative than those used in the 1806 book. Its pronunciations were generally provincial in character – those of Webster's own New England.

The label 'American' in the title is more a reflection of the works of American authors referred to than of its uniquely American lexicon. Indeed, at one point Webster observed (though not with any great accuracy) that 'there were not fifty words in all which were used in America and not in England'. On the other hand, nearly half of the words he did include are not to be found in Johnson's *Dictionary*, which added considerable force to his claim that he was giving lexicography a fresh direction.

Despite its weaknesses and its critics, the *American Dictionary* made Webster a household name in the USA. It was fiercely attacked in Britain for its Americanism, especially in matters of spelling and usage; but the work was crucial in giving to US English an identity and status comparable to that given to the British English lexicon by Dr Johnson. Indeed, it is difficult to appreciate today the impact which 'Webster's' made at the time, and just how authoritative the book was perceived to be. Two contemporary quotations are quite clear on the point. One is from a letter sent to Webster by the principal of a New York high school in 1827 – a year before the dictionary actually appeared:

Your Dictionary, Sir, is the best book of the kind that has been published since the flood. As soon as it is published, I will lay it on my table, and tell my pupils, 'That is your canon; follow that, and no other book'.

The other, some years later (1854), was sent to the publishers by the Superintendent of Common Schools in the state of Maine:

Nationality of language is a stronger bond of union than constitutional compromises or commercial affiliations. Your Dictionaries afford every facility for a national standard.

The later history of Webster's dictionary is reviewed on p. 442.

NOAH WEBSTER (1758–1843)

Webster was born in West Hartford, Connecticut. He graduated from Yale in 1778, having served briefly in the US War of Independence. He then worked as a teacher, clerk, and lawyer; and it was during his time as a teacher that he became dissatisfied with the texts which were available, especially with their lack of a distinctively American perspective. After publishing his speller, grammar, and reader (1783–5), he spent a great deal of time travelling and lobbying, partly to support himself, and partly to obtain support for his ideas as well as protection for his writing (there being no copyright law at that time). In 1798 he moved to New Haven, Connecticut, where he became active in local politics, and later helped to found academic institutions, notably Amherst College in Massachusetts. He began his dictionary work in 1800, and 25 years later, following a year's research in European libraries, he finished the text of the *American Dictionary* in Cambridge, England. It finally appeared in 1828, when he was 70.

AN AMERICAN ACADEMY

The concept of an Academy as a means of regulating the language was debated in the USA as well as in Britain (p. 73). A proposal for an 'American Society of Language' was made as early as 1774. In 1780, Congress received a letter hoping that it would form 'the first public institution for refining, correcting, and ascertaining the English language', and a bill for the incorporation of a national academy was actually introduced into Congress in 1806, but unsuccessfully. The short-lived Philological Society of New York, formed in 1788, and with Webster a prominent member, also had the aim of 'ascertaining and improving the American tongue'.

It was not until 1820, in New York City, that an American Academy of Language and Belles Lettres was finally launched, with John Quincy Adams as president. Its aim was 'to promote the purity and uniformity of the English language', and it had plans for a dictionary – though of a rather different kind from Webster's, for the members strongly disapproved of American neologisms. However, after only two years, having received little support from government or public, the group broke up.

THE ORIGINAL AMERICANISM

John Witherspoon was a Scottish minister who emigrated to America in 1768, becoming president of the College of New Jersey (now Princeton University). An enthusiastic supporter of the American colonists, he was the only clergyman to sign the Declaration of Independence. His place in English linguistic history is assured as the first to use the term *Americanism* – a way of speaking 'peculiar to this country' – in an essay on English in America, written in 1781.

John Witherspoon (1723–94)

THE FIRST DICTIONARY WAR

Webster's *American Dictionary* cost $20 – an expensive item, and with a first edition of only 2,500 copies, it was not a commercial success. Webster actually had to borrow money to help pay the printer's bill. A single-volume abridged version was therefore proposed, and Joseph Worcester (1784–1865), widely known as a textbook writer, was employed to edit it. The new edition appeared in 1829.

A year later, Worcester published a dictionary of his own, *A Comprehensive Pronouncing and Explanatory Dictionary of the English Language* – a work which was more conservative in spelling than Webster's, contained no etymologies, and presented a more cultivated level of pronunciation. Although Worcester had planned his dictionary before working for Webster, its appearance brought criticisms of plagiarism, and antagonism grew after the publication of a larger edition in 1846 under the title of *A Universal and Critical Dictionary of the English Language*, whose English edition had on its title-page 'Compiled from the Materials of Noah Webster, LL.D., by Joseph E. Worcester'. As a new edition of Webster's *Dictionary* had appeared in 1841, this fuelled the opposition between the two lexicographers and their supporters. It was not just a marketing battle between rival

publishers; different lexicographical principles were at stake. Webster's unequivocal Americanism was in marked contrast with Worcester's lexical conservatism, with his choice of a more refined pronunciation, and with his preference for established (British) usage in spellings.

The war of the dictionaries lasted until the 1860s, long after Webster's death (1843), and is now remembered more for the antagonistic pamphleteering and general unpleasantness of its rival marketing campaigns than for its contribution to lexicographical thought. The last engagement of the war took place when Worcester's major work, *A Dictionary of the English Language* (1860) appeared, with 104,000 entries, many illustrative quotations, synonym essays, and traditional spellings. The work was very well received, but it was overtaken by the 1864 edition of Webster, which introduced some of Worcester's innovatory features, and contained a total revision of the etymologies by a German scholar, C. A. F. Mahn. This revision, now called *A Dictionary of the English Language* (and known in lexicography as the Webster-Mahn), won the day. The US Government Printing Office adopted it the same year, and Webster's spellings were used in its first Style Manual of 1887. The dictionary war was over. (But there was to be a second dictionary war, a century later: see p. 442.)

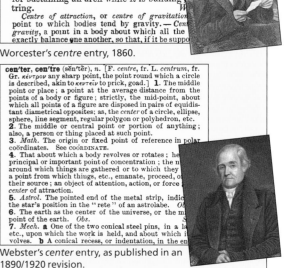

CĔN'TRE (sĕn'tẹr), *n.* [Gr. κέντρον; L. *centrum*; It. & Sp. *centro*; Fr. *centre.*]
1. (*Geom.*) A point equally distant from the extremities of a line, from every part of the circumference of a circle, or the surface of a sphere.
☞ The *centre* of any plane curve is a point in the plane of the curve which bisects every straight line drawn through it and terminated by the curve. The *centre* of a regular polygon is a point equally distant from all its vertices. The *centre* of any surf... point which bisects all straight lines drawn t... it and terminated by the surface. *Eliot.*
2. The middle point of any thing; the... dle; as, "The *centre* of an army or of a ...
3. (*Arch.*) A framework, usually of ti... for sustaining an arch while it is building ... tring.
Centre of attraction, or *centre of gravitation* point to which bodies tend by gravity. — *Cen... gravity,* a point in a body about which all the exactly balance **one** another, so that, if it be suppo...

Worcester's centre *entry, 1860.*

cen'ter, cen'tre (sĕn'tẹr), *n.* [F. *centre,* fr. L. *centrum,* fr. Gr. κέντρον any sharp point, the point round which a circle is described, akin to κεντεῖν to prick, goad.] **1.** The middle point or place; a point at the average distance from the points of a body or figure; strictly, the mid-point, about which all points of a figure are disposed in pairs of equidistant diametrical opposites; as, the *center* of a circle, ellipse, sphere, line segment, regular polygon or polyhedron, etc.
2. The middle or central point or portion of anything; also, a person or thing placed at such point.
3. *Math.* The origin or fixed point of reference in polar coördinates. See coördinate.
4. That about which a body revolves or rotates; he... principal or important point of concentration; the n... around which things are gathered or to which they ... a point from which things, etc., emanate, proceed, o... their source; an object of attention, action, or force ... *center* of attraction.
5. *Astrol.* The pointed end of the metal strip, indic... the star's position in the "rete" of an astrolabe. *Ob...*
6. The earth as the center of the universe, or the m... point of the earth. *Obs.*
7. *Mech.* **a** One of the two conical steel pins, in a l... etc., upon which the work is held, and about which i... volves. **b** A conical recess, or indentation, in the en...

Webster's center *entry, as published in an 1890/1920 revision.*

THE AGE OF DICTIONARIES

The first half of the 19th century was remarkable for the number of dictionaries which appeared on both sides of the Atlantic. Joseph Worcester provides a catalogue of English dictionaries at the beginning of his 1860 edition, and identifies 64 items published in England since Johnson's *Dictionary* (1755) and a further 30 items in America since the first Webster compilation (1806) – almost one a year. These were all general dictionaries: in addition there were over 200 specialized dictionaries and glossaries, as well as over 30 encyclopedias, showing how compilers were under pressure to keep up with the increases in knowledge and terminology that stemmed from the Industrial Revolution, progress in science and medicine, and fresh philological perspectives. The world was not to see such an explosion of dictionaries and reference works again until the 1980s (p. 444).

A DECADE OF DICTIONARIES AND ENCYCLOPEDIAS

1840 J. S. Henslow, *A Dictionary of Botanical Terms.*
1840 William Humble, *Dictionary of Geology and Mineralogy.*
1840 Samuel Maunder, *Scientific and Literary Treasury.*
1840 B. H. Smart, *Smart's Pronouncing Dictionary of the English Language.*
1841 R. H. Dana, Jr, *Dictionary of Sea Terms.*
1841 Walter F. Hook, *Church Dictionary.*
1841 Edward Scudamore, *A Dictionary of Terms in Use in the Arts and Sciences.*
1841 Noah Webster, *An American Dictionary of the English Language* (new edition).
1842 John Y. Akerman, *A Glossary of Provincial Words in Use in Wiltshire.*
1842 William Brande, *A Dictionary of Science, Literature, and Art.*
1842 William Carpenter, *A Comprehensive Dictionary of English Synonymes* (3rd edition).
1842 G. Francis, *The Dictionary of the Arts, Sciences, and Manufactures.*
1842 John C. Loudon, *Encyclopædia of Trees and Shrubs.*
1842 Gibbons Merle, *The Domestic Dictionary and Housekeeper's Manual.*
1842 Macvey Napier, *Encyclopædia Britannica* (7th edition)
1843 John Bouvier, *A Law Dictionary, adapted to the Constitution and Laws of the United States, and of the several States.*
1843 William Goodhugh and William C. Taylor, *The Pictorial Dictionary of the Holy Bible.*
1843 William Waterston, *A Cyclopædia of Commerce.*
1844 E. S. N. Campbell, *A Dictionary of Military Science.*
1844 Joseph Gwilt, *An Encylopædia of Architecture.*
1844 Richard D. Hoblyn, *A Dictionary of the Terms used in Medicine and the Collateral Sciences.*
1844 Cuthbert W. Johnson, *The Farmer's Encyclopædia and Dictionary of Rural Affairs.*
1844 John Kitto, *A Cyclopædia of Biblical Literature.*
1844 Alexander Reid, *A Dictionary of the English Language.*
1844 Thomas Webster, *An Encyclopædia of Domestic Economy.*
1845 William Bowles, *An Explanatory and Phonographic Pronouncing Dictionary of the English Language.*
1845 Shirley Palmer, *A Pentaglot Dictionary of Anatomy, Physiology, Pathology, Practical Medicine, Surgery, &c.*
1845 John Platts, *A Dictionary of English Synonymes.*
1845 Noah Webster, *A Dictionary of the English Language* (university abridged edition).
1846 William Bowles, *A Phonographic Pronouncing Dictionary* (abridged).
1846 John T. Brockett, *A Glossary of North Country Words.*
1846 Robert Eden, *Churchman's Theological Dictionary* (2nd edition).
1846 B. F. Graham, *English Synonymes.*
1846 James O. Halliwell, *A Dictionary of Archaic and Provincial Words.*
1846 J. E. Worcester, *A Universal and Critical Dictionary of the English Language.*
1847 H. Fox Talbot, *English Etymologies.*
1847 Robert Sullivan, *A Dictionary of the English Language.*
1848 John R. Bartlett, *Dictionary of Americanisms.*
1848 John Boag, *The Imperial Lexicon of the English Language.*
1848 Arthur B. Evans, *Leicestershire Words.*
1848 Samuel Maunder, *Treasury of Natural History, or Popular Dictionary of Animated Nature.*
1849 Anonymous, *A Glossary of Words used in Teesdale, Durham.*
1849 J. R. Beard, *The People's Dictionary of the Bible.*
1849 John Craig, *A New, Universal, Etymological, Technological, and Pronouncing Dictionary of the English Language.*
1849 John Eadie, *Biblical Cyclopædia.*
1850 Alexander Burrill, *A Law Dictionary and Glossary.*

AMERICAN IDENTITIES

Around the turn of the 19th century in America there was fierce intellectual debate about the direction the new country was taking. Of particular concern was the slow emergence of American literature compared with what was seen to be happening in Europe (the age of Wordsworth, Scott, and Goethe). Despite the well-established genres of sermons, journals, letters, histories, practical manuals, descriptions of America, and political pamphlets, from a literary point of view the post-revolutionary period was, as Ralph Waldo Emerson later described it, singularly 'barren'. According to one commentator, George Tucker, writing in 1813, Britain's population of 18 million was producing up to a thousand new books a year, whereas America's six million could manage only 20. And in 1823, another public figure, Charles J. Ingersoll, drew attention to the continuing intellectual dependence of America on Britain, citing the way American presses were printing a flood of editions of British books and magazines. Perhaps as many as half

a million of Scott's novels had been printed there by that time, and dozens of American towns were being given such names as Waverley and Ivanhoe (p. 144).

The lack of works by recognized literary figures is one reason for the limited lexical growth suggested by Webster and others (p. 81). Thousands of new words were being coined all over America, of course, but they were not reaching a wide public through large book sales, and domestic sources of usage did not appeal to those lexicographers who wished to emulate Johnson by using prestigious literary quotations (p. 75). Times would change, as the works of Washington Irving, James Fenimore Cooper, Edgar Allan Poe, and of Emerson himself would demonstrate. By the middle of the century, we have the first edition of *Leaves of Grass* (1855) by Walt Whitman, an author who calls for a literature free from European influence, and Harriet Beecher Stowe's *Uncle Tom's Cabin*, the best-selling novel of the 19th century. And in this later work would appear the results of the vast tide of lexical innovation which was already, in those early decades, transforming the linguistic identity of the new nation.

AN INTERNATIONAL STANDARD

The resonances of Abraham Lincoln's speech at the dedication of the Gettysburg Civil War cemetery (19 November 1863) have travelled far beyond its time and country. Its sentiments are memorably nationalistic, but there is nothing in its vocabulary, grammar, or rhetorical style to show that it is American in origin. This is standard English, transcending national boundaries, and evidently well established by mid-century. It is important not to disregard the existence of this genre, on both sides of the Atlantic, when paying attention to American and Victorian (p. 86) linguistic distinctiveness.

Fourscore and seven years ago our fathers brought forth on this continent a new nation, conceived in liberty and dedicated to the proposition that all men are created equal. Now we are engaged in a great civil war, testing whether that nation, or any nation so conceived and so dedicated, can long endure. We are met on a great battle field of that war. We have come to dedicate a portion of that field as a final resting-place for those who here gave their lives that that nation might live. It is altogether fitting and proper that we should do this. But, in a larger sense, we cannot dedicate – we cannot consecrate – we cannot hallow – this ground. The brave men, living and dead, who struggled here, have consecrated it far above our poor power to add or detract. The world will little note, nor long remember what we say here, but it can never forget what they did here. It is for us the living, rather, to be dedicated here to the unfinished work which they who fought here have thus far so nobly advanced. It is rather for us to be here dedicated to the great task remaining before us – that from these honored dead we take increased devotion to that cause for which they gave the last full measure of devotion; that we here highly resolve that these dead shall not have died in vain; that this nation, under God, shall have a new birth of freedom, and that government of the people, by the people, for the people, shall not perish from the earth.

AMERICA TALKING

The new American vocabulary of the 19th century came from a mixture of sources. Spanish and Native American words were especially influential, but also many older English words came to be used with new senses or in new phrases. The opening up of the West was one major factor in lexical expansion; the arrival of waves of immigrants, towards the end of the century, was another (p. 94).

bronco (1850), cattle town (1881), chaps (1870), corral (1829), cowpoke (1880), dogie (1888), dude (1883), lariat (1831), lasso (1819), maverick (1867), ranch (1808), range (1835), roundup (1876), rustler (1882), six shooter (1844), stampede (1843), tenderfoot (1849), trail boss (1890)

The Melting Pot

This phrase, the title of Israel Zangwill's 1909 successful play, itself became part of the new lexicon, and well summarizes the effect on American English of thousands of new words and phrases from German, Italian, Yiddish, and other European languages, as well as the jargon of the immigration process. Not everything was pleasant. In particular, there was a marked increase in the number of offensive racial labels.

delicatessen (1893), Hunk (1896), kike (1880s), kindergarten (1862), naturalization papers (1856), Polack (1879), spaghetti (1880s), spiel (1894), tutti-frutti (1876), wop (1890s).

(After S. B. Flexner, 1976.)

THE COW BOY COOK.

MYTH OR REALITY?

brave (1819), firewater (1817) Great Spirit (1790), Indian Agency (1822), medicine dance (1805), peace pipe (1860), reservation (1789), smoke signal (1873)

These words represent a fairly late stage of development in the lexicon of Native American affairs. Many native words entered the language during the period of first encounter: for example, *moccasin, papoose, powwow, wigwam,* and *tomahawk*

are all 17th-century borrowings.
In the later period, many of the words put into the mouths of native people were invented or popularized by white authors who imagined that this was how 'Indians' ought to talk. Examples include *How!* (as a greeting), *heap big,* and *Great White Father. Happy Hunting Ground* is known from Washington Irving (1837); *paleface, war path,* and *war paint* are from James Fenimore Cooper (1820s). Myth or reality, they became part of the American lexicon nonetheless.

BREAKING THE RULES

By the 1860s, the American spelling system had become so established that writers dared to play about with it, and several made nation-wide reputations from doing so. Artemus Ward and Josh Billings were leading proponents of a comic-spelling genre which was extremely popular in the later decades of the century. Its homespun wit and down-to-earth sentiments were expressed in a style which seemed to reflect the sounds and rhythms of local speech. Both writers used an intuitive semi-phonetic system. Neither of them bothered much about consistency (e.g. *to* is spelled *tew*, *tu*, or *2*; *fun* appears as both *fun* and *phun*), but the simple combination of informal non-standard forms with a subject-matter normally associated with formal Standard English was evidently enough to guarantee success.

It is perhaps not surprising that people who had only recently come to recognize their own literary standards should begin to laugh at those who had not. But these writers should not be seen in isolation.

They were capitalizing on an important genre of dialect writing which had emerged in American literature during the 1840s, seen at its most successful in *Uncle Tom's Cabin* (1851–2), and on a trend in comic writing where southern speakers, especially blacks, were portrayed as uneducated or as figures of fun. Dialect vocabulary and grammar (*hain't*, *saw* for *seen*, etc.) were used as well as mis-spelling, though it was the spelling which created the impact.

The British writer, John Camden Hotten, in an 1865 essay introducing the works of Artemus Ward, thought to explain the man's remarkable appeal as part of an American tradition of 'mixing of sacred with secular matters':

incongruity of ideas is carried to a much greater extent in American humour than it is in our own; and it is this mental exaggeration, this odd mixture of widely different thoughts, that distinguishes Yankee from English fun…

It was the linguistic incongruity, however, which was the key to the success of both Ward and Billings. Rewrite their material into Standard English, and – as Billings originally realized – much of its effect is lost.

JOSH BILLINGS

Josh Billings was the pseudonym of Henry Wheeler Shaw (1818–85). Born in Lanesboro, Massachusetts, he settled in Poughkeepsie, New York, as a land dealer, and began to write in his 40s. His famous 'Essay on the Mule', when first published in *The Poughkeepsian*, attracted little interest. He then saw a piece by Artemus Ward, and 'translated' his Essay into the same kind of grotesque spelling, as 'An Essa on the Muel'. It was an immediate success, and he became a national figure in the years after the Civil War, known especially for his rustic philosophizing:

It is better to know less than to know so much that ain't so.

Abraham Lincoln commented: 'Next to William Shakespeare Josh Billings was the greatest judge of human nature the world has ever seen' – and read his aphorisms to the Cabinet.

Billings' style did not escape criticism. Mark Twain thought the bad spelling got in the way of the wisdom, which had real value in its own right. And Shaw himself seems to have had some reservations about it. In 'Answers to Personal Letters' (1873), he remarked:

I adopted it in a moment ov karlassness …There is just az mutch joke in bad spelling az thare iz in looking kross-eyed, and no more…like other sinners who ask for forgiveness and keep rite on sinning, i now ask the world tew forgiv me and I will promis not tew reform.

People did, and Shaw didn't. In 1873 he was hardly half way through a 10-year series of burlesque pieces, *Josh Billings' Farmer's Allminax*. An 1868 aphorism best sums up his approach (from 'Josh Billings on Ice'):

I hold that a man has just as mutch rite tew spel a word as it is pronounced, as he has tew pronounce it the way it ain't spelt.

JOSH BILLINGS: HIS SAYINGS

Chastity iz like an isikel. if it onse melts that's the last ov it.

After awl ced and dun the gran sekret of winning is tew win.

It iz tru that welth won't maik a man vartuous, but i notis thare ain't ennyboddy who wants tew be poor jist for the purpiss ov being good.

Humin natur is the same all over the world, cept in Nu England, and thar its akordin tu sarcumstances.

Akordin tu skripter thar will be just about as many Kammills in heavin as rich men.

Koliding

The word 'kolide,' used bi ralerode men, haz an indefinit meaning tew menny folks. Thru the kindness of a nere and dear frend, i am able tew translate the wurd so that enny man ken understand it at onst. The term 'kolide' is used tew explain the sarkumstanse ov 2 trains ov cars triing tew pass each uther on a single trak. It is ced that it never yet haz bin did suckcessfully, hence a 'kolide.'

The mule

The mule is haf hoss, and haf Jackass, and then kums to a full stop, natur diskovering her mistake. Tha weigh more, akordin tu their heft, than enny other kreetur, except a crow-bar. Tha kant hear enny quicker, not further than the hoss, yet their ears are big enuff for snow shoes. You kan trust them with enny one whose life aint worth enny more than the mules.

ARTEMUS WARD

Artemus Ward was the pseudonym of Charles Farrar Browne (1834–67) – a printer's apprentice who became a journalist, then a professional humorist. The character he created was presented as the manager of an itinerant sideshow who 'sounds off' in articles and letters on all kinds of topics, using a style which is full of puns and bad spellings. His lectures, full of word-play and throw-away remarks, always delivered in a grave, melancholy manner, brought him fame throughout the USA as well as abroad. He was in poor health for many years, and his early death was mourned throughout the country.

ARTEMUS WARD TO THE PRINCE OF WALES

FRIEND WALES, – You remember me. I saw you in Canady a few years ago. I remember you too. I seldim forgit a person.

I hearn of your marrige to the Printcis Alexandry, & ment ter writ you a congratoolatory letter at the time, but I've bin bildin a barn this summer, & hain't had no time to write letters to folks. Excoos me.

Numeris changes has tooken place since we met in the body politic. The body politic, in fack, is sick. I sumtimes think it has got biles, friend Wales.

In my country, we've got a war, while your country, in conjunktion with Cap'n Sems of the *Alobarmy*, manetanes a nootrol position!...

Yes, Sir, we've got a war, and the troo Patrit has to make sacrifisses, you bet. I have alreddy given two cousins to the war, & I stand reddy to sacrifiss my wife's brother ruther'n not see the rebelyin krusht. And if wuss cums to wuss I'll shed ev'ry drop of blud my able-bodid relations has got to prosekoot the war. I think sumbody oughter be prosekooted, & it may as well be the war as any body else. When I git a goakin [joking] fit onto me it's no use to try ter stop me.

You hearn about the draft, friend Wales, no doubt. It caus'd sum squirmin', but it was fairly conducted, I think, for it hit all classes...

We hain't got any daily paper in our town, but we've got a female sewin circle, which ansers the same purpuss, and we wasn't long in suspents as to who was drafted...

"Artemus Ward"

TWO DIALECT GIANTS

The American comic writers were writing for an audience who by the 1860s were well used to seeing a written representation of nonstandard speech. In particular, most of those who laughed at Billings or Ward would have read *Uncle Tom's Cabin*, published in 1851–2 as a series of instalments in the abolitionist journal, *National Era*. In 1852 it appeared in book form, and sold 300,000 copies in America during its first year, with huge (though heavily pirated) sales in Britain.

The linguistic conventions used by Stowe in many ways presage the essays of Billings and Ward, and these in turn anticipate the style of dialect writing which reached its peak in the novels of Mark Twain (who knew Billings' work well). Twain's use of orthography is sophisticated, consistently distinguishing several speech varieties. Nonetheless, throughout all these literary representations there is an inevitable shaping, selectivity, and simplification, resulting in a stereotype which, for many, has replaced reality (pp. 96, 346).

'I'm glad Mas'r did n't go off this morning, as he looked to,' said Tom; 'that ar hurt me more than sellin', it did. Mebbe it might have been natural for him, but 't would have come desp't hard on me, as has known him from a baby; but I've seen Mas'r, and I begin ter feel sort o' reconciled to the Lord's will now. ...

(*Uncle Tom's Cabin*, 1851–2, Ch. 7.)

Looky here – didn't de line pull loose en de raf' go a hummin' down de river, en leave you en de canoe behine in de fog?...En didn't you whoop....You answer me dat.'

(*Huckleberry Finn*, 1884, Ch. 15.)

VARIETY AWARENESS

One of the most interesting features of the 19th century is the way consciousness was raised about the nature and use of language. The compilation of dictionaries, grammars, spelling books, and pronunciation manuals in the second half of the 18th century had focused attention on standard forms in an unprecedented manner (pp. 72, 78). With widespread standardization came an increased sensitivity on the part of 'ordinary' users of the language to the range of varieties which existed, and to the social nuances attached to different usages. There was also an increased readiness on the part of authors to experiment with the language (p. 84), and in particular to find new techniques of expression for the range of diverse 'voices' which the emerging genre of the novel permitted. As Charles Dickens put it, in an essay on 'Saxon English' in *Household Words* (1858): 'if a man wishes to write for all, he must know how to use the speech of all'.

Also important were the discoveries at the end of the 18th century about the historical relationship between Sanskrit, Greek, and Latin, which ushered in the age of comparative philology. This subject brought fresh perspectives to the study of language, especially in relation to questions of etymology (§10) and the role of classical models. It stimulated arguments about the nature of language change, correctness in usage, and methods of teaching. Innumerable societies and journals were founded to study such subjects as local dialects, the history of language, vocabulary reform (p. 125), spelling reform (p. 276), and shorthand, or to debate the future of English. The Romantic movement in particular promoted a special interest in the way ordinary people spoke, and there was a growing sense of the distance between linguistic scholarship and language reality. The American poet Walt Whitman, in an essay on American slang for *The North American Review* (1885), summed it up like this:

Language, be it remembered, is not an abstract construction of the learned, or of dictionary-makers, but is something arising out of the work, needs, ties, joys, affections, tastes, of long generations of humanity, and has its bases broad and low, close to the ground. Its final decisions are made by the masses, people nearest the concrete, having most to do with actual land and sea. It impermeates all, the past as well as the present, and is the grandest triumph of the human intellect.

LANGUAGE ATTITUDES

• Mrs Durbeyfield habitually spoke the dialect; her daughter, who had passed the Sixth Standard in the National School under a London-trained mistress, spoke two languages; the dialect at home, more or less; ordinary English abroad and to persons of quality.
(Thomas Hardy, *Tess of the Durbervilles*, 1891, Ch. 3.)

• Lord Derby was very punctilious in his pronunciation of English, though his son talked a Lancashire patois. Lord Derby would insolently correct Lord Granville across the House of Lords. Lord Granville always said 'wropped up' – 'wrapped' Lord Derby would say in a tone clear to the reporters.
(Benjamin Disraeli, *Reminiscences.*)

• I did so like your long handsome note four or five days ago. I do so thank you for your kindness. There! there are 2 sentences with 'so' in them not followed by 'as', as Mr Gaskell says they ought to be. I will make them one grammatical sentence, & have done. I am so much obliged to you as to be incapable of expressing my obligation but by saying that I am always – Yours most truly, E. C. Gaskell
(*Letters*, 1854.)

• Let another thing also be remembered. We must distinguish between the English which we speak, and that which we write. Many expressions are not only tolerated but required in conversation, which are not usually put on paper. Thus, for instance, everyone says *can't* for *cannot*, *won't* for *will not*, *isn't* for *is not*, in conversation; but we seldom see these contractions in books, except where a conversation is related.
(Henry Alford, *The Queen's English*, 1869, Point 94.)

Some of the best evidence for the increased awareness of language issues in the 19th century comes from the way writers and cartoonists begin to satirize them. This dialogue was reprinted in a late Victorian anthology called *Mr. Punch in Society*. (See further, p. 195.)

Visitor. "I've just to make my first call on Mrs. Johnson."
Lady of the House. "So glad, dear. Poor thing, she's glad to know *anyone!*"

THE LATEST THING IN CRIME

(A Dialogue of the Present Day)

SCENE – *Mrs. Featherston's Drawing-room.*
Mrs. Thistledown discovered calling.

Mrs. Thistledown (taking up a novel on a side-table). "The Romance of a Plumber," by Paul Poshley. My dear Flossie, you *don't* mean to tell me you read *that* man?
Mrs. Featherston. I haven't had time to do more than dip into it as yet. But why, Ida? *Oughtn't* I to read him?
Ida. Well, from something Mr. Pinceney told me the other day – but really it's too bad to repeat such things. One never knows, there *may* be nothing in it.
Flossie. Still, you might just as well *tell* me, Ida! Of course I should never dream –
Ida. After all, I don't suppose there's any secret about it. It seems, from what Mr. Pinceney says, that this Mr. Poshley – you must *promise* not to say I told you –

Flossie. Of course – of course. But do go on, Ida. What *does* Mr. Poshley do?
Ida. Well, it appears he *splits his infinitives.*
Flossie (horrified). Oh, not *really*? But how *cruel* of him! Why, I met him at the Dragnetts' only last week, and he didn't look at *all* that kind of person!
Ida. I'm afraid there's no doubt about it. It's perfectly notorious. And of course any one who once takes to *that* –
Flossie. Yes, indeed. *Quite* hopeless. At least, I *suppose* so. Isn't it?
Ida. Mr Pinceney seemed to think so.
Flossie. How sad! But can't anything be *done*, Ida? Isn't there any law to punish him? By the bye, how *do* you split – what is it? – infinitudes?
Ida. My dear, I thought you knew. I really didn't like to ask any questions.
Flossie. Well, whatever it is, I shall tell Mudies not to send me anything more of his. I *don't* think one ought to encourage such persons.

(From *Mr. Punch in Society*, c. 1870.)

The language of science

English scientific and technical vocabulary had been growing steadily since the Renaissance (p. 60), but the 19th century saw an unprecedented growth in this domain, while the lexicon incorporated the consequences of the Industrial Revolution and the accompanying period of scientific exploration. Significant discoveries and theories, such as Faraday's on electricity, or Darwin's on evolution, achieved widespread publicity, and introduced new nomenclatures and styles of expression to an ever-curious public. By the end of the century, there was a recognizable variety of scientific English (p. 372), shaped by the observations of grammarians, the expectations of the burgeoning scientific societies, and the style guides of the new academic journals. Both 'scientific' and 'technical' are recognized as major lexical dimensions in the 1888 Preface to the *New English Dictionary* (p. 443).

SCIENTIFIC DISCOURSE

Michael Faraday (1791–1867) giving a Friday Evening Discourse at the Royal Institution in Albemarle Street, London (founded in 1799 by Benjamin Thompson, Count Rumford). The Prince Consort is in the audience.

These discourses, along with a series of Christmas lectures for children, were begun in 1826 as part of a concern to make science accessible. In the 1990s the Institution continues to provide a forum where, as its annual Proceedings state, 'non-specialists may meet the leading scientists of our time and hear their latest discoveries explained in everyday language'.

Keeping pace with the growth in scientific societies must have been difficult, in Faraday's time. The 1830s, for example, began in Britain with the formation of the Geographical Society of London (1830), the British Association for the Advancement of Science (1831), and the Provincial Medical and Surgical Association (1832, later called the British Medical Association). In the USA, the following decade saw the American Statistical Association (1839), the American Medical Association (1847), and the American Association for the Advancement of Science (1848). By the end of the century, in America alone, over 50 national councils, societies, or associations had been founded, dealing with scientific subjects as diverse as entomology, dentistry, and engineering.

The most prominent requisite to a lecturer, though perhaps not really the most important, is a good delivery; for though to all true philosophers science and nature will have charms innumerable in every dress, yet I am sorry to say that the generality of mankind cannot accompany us one short hour unless the path is strewed with flowers.
…With respect to the action of the lecturer, it is requisite that he have some, though it does not here bear the importance that it does in other branches of oratory; for though I know of no other species of delivery that requires less motion, yet I would by no means have a lecturer glued to the table or screwed to the floor. He must by all means appear as a body distinct and separate from the things around him, and must have some motion apart from that which they possess. (Letter from Faraday to Benjamin Abbott, 11 June 1813. See p. 293.)

NOMENCLATURE

Any examination of the growth of scientific vocabulary in the 19th century would find that some sciences are conspicuously under-represented, for the simple reason that their foundations had been laid much earlier. Most of the basic terms of anatomy, for example, had been introduced by the end of the 17th century, as had a great deal of mathematical terminology. On the other hand, from the end of the 18th century rapid progress in chemistry, physics, and biology led to such major lexical developments as the nomenclature of chemical elements and compounds, and the Linnaean system of classification in natural history (p. 372). The dates given below are those of the first recorded usage, as given in the *Oxford English Dictionary*. (After T. H. Savory, 1967.)

Science names

biology	1802
petrology	1807
taxonomy	1828
morphology	1830
palaeontology	1838
ethnology	1842
gynaecology	1847
histology	1847
carcinology	1852
embryology	1859

Chemistry

tellurium	1800
sodium	1807
strontium	1808
platinum	1812
silicon	1817
caffeine	1830
chloroform	1848
sucrose	1862
cocaine	1874
argon	1895

Physics

sonometer	1808
centigrade	1812
altimeter	1847
ohm	1861
ampère	1861
colorimeter	1863
joule	1882
voltmeter	1882
watt	1882
electron	1891

Biology

photosynthesis	1804
flagellum	1807
chlorophyll	1810
spermatozoon	1830
bacterium	1847
diatom	1854
leucocyte	1870
symbiosis	1877
mitosis	1882
chromosome	1890

Geology

apatite	1803
cretaceous	1832
pliocene	1833
Jurassic	1833
Cambrian	1836
mesozoic	1840
triassic	1841
oligocene	1859
bauxite	1868
Ordovician	1887

Medicine

gastritis	1806
laryngitis	1822
kleptomania	1830
cirrhosis	1839
neuritis	1840
haemophilia	1854
diphtheria	1857
aphasia	1867
claustrophobia	1879
beri beri	1879

LITERARY VOICES

WILLIAM WORDSWORTH (1770–1850)

The principal object, then, proposed in these Poems, was to choose incidents and situations from common life, and to relate or describe them throughout, as far as was possible, in a selection of language really used by men, and, at the same time, to throw over them a certain colouring of the imagination, whereby ordinary things should be presented to the mind in an unusual aspect…Humble and rustic life was generally chosen…because such men hourly communicate with the best objects from which the best part of language is originally derived; and because, from their rank in society and the sameness and narrow circle of their intercourse, being less under the influence of social vanity, they convey their feelings and notions in simple and unelaborated expressions. Accordingly, such a language, arising out of repeated experience and regular feelings, is a more permanent, and a far more philosophical language, than that which is frequently substituted for it by Poets, who think that they are conferring honour upon themselves and their art in proportion as they separate themselves from the sympathies of men, and indulge in arbitrary and capricious habits of expression, in order to furnish food for fickle tastes and fickle appetites of their own creation. (Preface to the second edition of the *Lyrical Ballads*, 1800.)

> Glad sight wherever new with old
> Is joined through some dear
>   homeborn tie;
> The life of all that we behold
> Depends upon that mystery.
> Vain is the glory of the sky,
> The beauty vain of field and
>   grove,
> Unless, while with admiring eye
> We gaze, we also learn to love.
> (Poem, 1845)

WALTER SCOTT (1771–1832)

Scotch was a language which we have heard spoken by the learnd and the wise & witty & the accomplished and which had not a trace of vulgarity in it but on the contrary sounded rather graceful and genteel. You remember how well Mrs Murray Keith – the late Lady Dumfries – my poor mother & other ladies of that day spoke their native language – it was different from the English as the Venetian is from the Tuscan dialect of Italy but it never occurd to any one that the Scottish any more than the Venetian was more vulgar than those who spoke the purer and more classical – But that is all gone and the remembrance will be drownd with us the elders of this existing generation. (*Letters*, VII.83)

> 'It would have cost him sae little fash,' she said to herself; 'for I hae seen his pen gang as fast ower the paper, as ever it did ower the water when it was in the grey goose's wing. Wae's me! maybe he may be badly – but then my father wad likely hae said something about it – Or maybe he may hae taen the rue, and kensna how to let me wot of his change of mind. He needna be at muckle fash about it'… (Jeanie, thinking about Butler, in *The Heart of Midlothian*, 1818, Border edition, pp. 592–3.)

WILLIAM MAKEPEACE THACKERAY (1811–63)

I think Mr Dickens has in many things quite a divine genius so to speak, and certain notes in his song are so delightful and admirable that I should never think of trying to imitate him, only hold my tongue and admire him. I quarrel with his Art in many respects: which I don't think represents Nature duly; for instance Micawber appears to me an exaggeration of a man, as his name is of a name. It is delightful and makes me laugh: but it is no more a real man than my friend Punch is: and in so far I protest against him…holding that the Art of Novels *is* to represent Nature: to convey as strongly as possible the sentiment of reality – in a tragedy or a poem or a lofty drama you aim at producing different emotions; the figures moving, and their words sounding, heroically: but in a drawing-room drama a coat is a coat and a poker a poker; and must be nothing else according to my ethics, not an embroidered tunic, not a great red-hot instrument like the Pantomine weapon. (*Letters*, Vol. 2, p. 772.)

> Whenever he spoke (which he did almost always), he took care to produce the very finest and longest words of which the vocabulary gave him the use; rightly judging, that it was as cheap to employ a handsome, large, and sonorous epithet, as to use a little stingy one.
>   Thus he would say to George in school, 'I observed on my return home from taking the indulgence of an evening's scientific conversation with my excellent friend Dr Bulders – a true archaeologian,…that the windows of your venerated grandfather's almost princely mansion in Russell Square were illuminated as if for the purposes of festivity. Am I right in my conjecture, that Mr Osborne entertained a society of chosen spirits round his sumptuous board last night?' (Rev. Veal, in *Vanity Fair*, 1847–8, ed. Tillotson, p. 545.)

THOMAS HARDY (1840–1928)

An author may be said to fairly convey the spirit of intelligent peasant talk if he retains the idiom, compass, and characteristic expressions, although he may not encumber the page with obsolete pronunciations of the purely English words, and with mispronunciations of those derived from Latin and Greek. In the printing of standard speech hardly any phonetic principle at all is observed; and if a writer attempts to exhibit on paper the precise accents of a rustic speaker he disturbs the proper balance of a true representation by unduly insisting upon the grotesque element; thus directing attention to a point of inferior interest, and diverting it from the speaker's meaning, which is by far the chief concern where the aim is to depict the men and their natures rather than their dialect forms. (*The Athenaeum*, 30 November 1878.)

> 'O, they never look at anything that folks like we can understand,' the carter continued, by way of passing the time. 'On'y foreign tongues used in the days of the Tower of Babel, when no two families spoke alike. They read that sort of thing as fast as a night-hawk will whir. 'Tis all learning there – nothing but learning, except religion. And that's learning too, for I never could understand it. Yes, 'tis a serious-minded place. Not but there's wenches in the streets o' nights.
>   You know, I suppose, that they raise pa'sons there like radishes in a bed? And though it do take – how many years, Bob? – five years to turn a lirriping hobble-de-hoy chap into a solemn preaching man with no corrupt passions, they'll do it, if it can be done, and polish un off like the workmen they be, and turn un out wi' a long face, and a long black coat and waistcoat, and a religious collar and hat, same as they used to wear in the Scriptures, so that his own mother wouldn't know un sometimes.' (Description of the people of Christminster, in *Jude the Obscure*, 1895, Ch. 3.)

THE LANGUAGES OF DICKENS

Nowhere is the range of 19th-century social, regional, occupational, and personal variation in the use of language more fully illustrated than in the novels and sketches of Charles Dickens (1812–70). His characters not only speak for themselves; Dickens often explicitly draws our attention to their speech, identifying the stylistic basis of the comic effect. (For further examples, see p. 254.)

A detail of 'Dickens's Dream', by Robert William Buss.

The law

'Did he say, for instance,' added Brass, in a kind of comfortable, cosy tone – 'I don't assert that he did say so, mind; I only ask you, to refresh your memory – did he say, for instance, that he was a stranger in London – that it was not his humour or within his ability to give any references – that he felt we had a right to require them – and that, in case anything should happen to him, at any time, he particularly desired that whatever property he had upon the premises should be considered mine, as some slight recompense for the trouble and annoyance I should sustain – and were you, in short,' added Brass, still more comfortably and cosily than before, 'were you induced to accept him on my behalf, as a tenant, upon those conditions?' 'Certainly not,' replied Dick. (*The Old Curiosity Shop*, 1840–1, Ch. 35.)

Religion

'I say, my friends,' pursues Mr Chadband,… 'why can we not fly? Is it because we are calculated to walk? It is. Could we walk, my friends, without strength? We could not. What should we do without strength, my friends? Our legs would refuse to bear us, our knees would double up, our ankles would turn over, and we should come to the ground. Then from whence, my friends, in a human point of view, do we derive the strength that is necessary to our limbs? Is it,' says Chadband, glancing over the table, 'from bread in various forms, from butter which is churned from the milk which is yielded unto us by the cow, from the eggs which are laid by the fowl, from ham, from tongue, from sausage, and from such like? It is. Then let us partake of the good things which are set before us!'

The persecutors denied that there was any particular gift in Mr Chadband's piling verbose flights of stairs, one upon another, after this fashion. But this can only be received as proof of their determination to persecute, since it must be within everybody's experience, that the Chadband style of oratory is widely received and much admired. (*Bleak House*, 1852–3, Ch. 19.)

IDIOSYNCRASIES

Now, Mrs Piper – what have you got to say about this?

Why, Mrs Piper has a good deal to say, chiefly in parentheses and without punctuation, but not much to tell. Mrs Piper lives in the court (which her husband is a cabinet-maker), and it has long been well beknown among the neighbours (counting from the day next but one before the half-baptizing of Alexander James Piper aged eighteen months and four days old on accounts of not being expected to live such was the sufferings gentlemen of that child in his gums) as the Plaintive – so Mrs Piper insists on calling the deceased – was reported to have sold himself. Thinks it was the Plaintive's air in which that report originatin in. See the Plaintive often and considered as his air was feariocious and not to be allowed to go about some children being timid (and if doubted hoping Mrs Perkins may be brought forard for she is here and will do credit to her husband and herself and family). (*Bleak House*, Ch. 11.)

MRS GAMP, AUTHOR

The idiosyncratic speech of Mrs Gamp in *Martin Chuzzlewit* (1843–4) was evidently one of Dickens's own favourite creations, if we may judge by the frequency with which she appears in the novel – and also outside it. In his biography (Book VI, Ch. 1), Dickens's confidant John Forster tells the story of how, to help raise money for a benefit fund for Leigh Hunt, Dickens proposed to turn his character into an author, in 'an Account of a late Expedition into the North, for an Amateur Theatrical Benefit, written by Mrs Gamp (who was an eyewitness)'. The story was abandoned after a few pages, but Forster includes what Dickens wrote, commenting, 'There are so many friends of Mrs Gamp who will rejoice at this unexpected visit from her'.

The piece, a pastiche in its own right, makes much of Mrs Gamp's erratic syntax and distinctive articulation, in which several sounds (especially /z/ and /s/) come out as [dʒ], usually spelled *g* (sometimes *dg* or *j*).

Mrs Harris, wen I see that little willain bodily before me, it give me such a turn that I was all in a tremble. If I hadn't lost my umbreller in the cab, I must have done him a injury with it! Oh the bragian little traitor!… Oh the aggravation of that Dougladge! Mrs Harris, if I hadn't apologiged to Mr Wilson, and put a little bottle to my lips which was in my pocket for the journay, and which it is very rare indeed I have about me, I could not have abared the sight of him – there, Mrs Harris! I could not! – I must have tore him, or have give way and fainted.

' Mrs Gamp proposes a toast' by Phiz (Hablot Knight Browne).

IN LIVING MEMORY

Thomas Hardy died in 1928. George Bernard Shaw, who was 14 when Dickens died, lived until 1950 (pp. 88–9). As we enter the 20th century, there is a sense in which the 'history of English' ceases to be a helpful notion, and the boundary blurs between the present section and later parts of this book. It hardly seems to be 'history' when we can make direct contact with the pronunciation, grammar, vocabulary, and attitudes to language of the early decades of the present century, simply by talking to people whose language was shaped then. Moreover, it is difficult to think of a period as constituting a part of the history of the language when its speech and writing seem to be almost identical with what we find today.

The overwhelming impression is certainly one of continuity. Any differences we may notice in pronunciation, grammar, or vocabulary seem to be occasional and superficial, and tend to be described as 'old-fashioned' rather than (somewhat more distantly) as 'archaic' (p. 185). There is even an uncomfortable sense of *déja vu* about the issues which were being discussed two generations ago. A glance at newspapers or government reports after the turn of the century shows that the same concerns about language were being expressed then as now: standards of English had evidently reached an unprecedented low point in schools, and adult usage was deteriorating so rapidly that there was little hope for the future of the language.

Ongoing change

At the same time, we should not underestimate the linguistic differences between grandchild and grandparent – and indeed, many a domestic argument between the generations must have been fuelled by changes which *have* taken place in the language during the past 75 years.

• Vocabulary, as always, has been the chief index of change. Apart from the rapid growth in standard English vocabulary, associated with such areas as technological development and the emergence of the 'permissive society', there are many differences between the slang of previous decades and that of today (p. 182), and the dialect surveys have drawn our attention to the speed at which the regional vocabulary known to older generations has disappeared (p. 318).

• Earlier pronunciation norms can be heard in the 'broader' regional accents of many older people, or the more open vowel qualities of the early BBC presenters, several of whom are accessible through archive recordings. An example of change in the educated standard can be deduced from Daniel Jones's *The Pronunciation of English* (1919), where he describes the British pronunciation of the vowel in such words as *lord* /ɔ:/ as 'intermediate between open back rounded and half-open back rounded' (p. 240). This is rather different from the present-day quality of this vowel, which is articulated higher in the mouth. According to Jones's description, *lord* must have sounded similar to the way *lard* is pronounced now.

LEXICALYSED

Any area of the lexicon will demonstrate the routine and ongoing nature of lexical change. 'Getting drunk' is a notion which seems to have been particularly fruitful in the 20th century – as indeed it was in the 19th. The dates given are of the earliest recorded instance in historical dictionaries. Multi-word idioms are not listed. (After S. B. Flexner, 1976.)

pifflicated	1900s
lit	1900
ginned	1900
ossified	1901
pot-eyed	1901
saturated	1902
petrified	1903
tanked	1905
blotto	1905
shellacked	1905
rosey	1905
spifflicated	1906
slopped	1907
jingled	1908
bunned	1908
orie-eyed	1910
piped	1912
plastered	1912
polluted	1912
organized	1914
gassed	1915
hooted	1915
aped	1915
jugged	1919
canned	1920s
juiced	1920s
fried	1920s
buried	1920s
potted	1922
illuminated	1926
crocked	1927
lubricated	1927
stinko	1927
wall-eyed	1927
busted	1928
flooey	1930
rum-dum	1931
bombed	1940s
shit-faced	1940s
looped	1940s
swacked	1941
sloshed	1950s
boxed	1950s
zonked	1950s
crashed	1950s
clobbered	1951

VOICES FROM THE PAST

Thomas Edison's phonograph, patented in 1877, has enabled us to hear tiny extracts of English from speakers born in the age of Napoleon. The voice of Florence Nightingale (1820–1910) (inset) is one of those preserved in a recording housed at the Science Museum in London. The picture shows a public demonstration of the phonograph at the Paris International Exposition of 1889.

• There are major differences in language awareness and attitude. A century of prescriptive grammar, rigorously taught in schools (p. 78), inevitably left its mark on linguistic sensibilities then in a way that is not found now. Indeed, prescriptivism left its mark in other ways too, as one senior citizen emphatically pointed out, reacting in 1983 to a BBC language programme devoted to the split infinitive (p. 195) and other usage topics:

The reason why the older generation feel so strongly about English grammar is that we were severely punished if we didn't obey the rules! One split infinitive, one whack; two split infinitives, two whacks; and so on.

Another correspondent, his junior by 50 years or more, contented himself with a four-word letter, and thereby identified a linguistic generation gap whose consequences are still being sorted out (p. 190):

What's a split infinitive?

• Most of the grammatical controversies which come from the prescriptive tradition have to do with making a choice between alternative usages already in the language, and do not reflect any real issues of language change. However, English grammar has not stood still,

during the present century. It continues to change, in numerous small ways, sometimes attracting attention, sometimes not. Many of these points are identified at relevant places in Part III.

• There have been significant changes in the pragmatics of the language (p. 286) – in particular, in what counts as acceptable public linguistic behaviour. The norms of interaction have altered, as shown by differences in such diverse areas as the use of first names, personal titles, taboo words, greeting formulae, and the conventions of letter-writing. A vast gulf separates the generations in their expectations about conversational etiquette.

• The most important developments in the language during the present century have been the emergence of new varieties, both national and international. Some, such as computing and broadcasting, are completely novel; others, such as religious English and journalese, have been affected by social change (Part V). Above all, there are the new regional varieties of English which have come into prominence throughout the world. Their place in any future history of the language is assured, and only a separate section can do justice to them now (§7).

TIMES CHANGE

I can only just remember the time, in the very early twenties, when a typical boy-and-girl conversation might have run: '*He*: May I call you by your christian name? *She*: If you like. *He*: Er – what *is* your christian name?' Since that time the use of christian names by U-speakers has been continually increasing. In the thirties, it was quite customary for a member of a *partie carée* [a party consisting of two men and two women] going to a dance who was unknown to the other three to be introduced by the christian name alone (or, often, just as *John Smith* or *Jane Smith*, without prefix). In the War the use of christian names increased still further; it was often the custom for a man at the head of a large section of girls to call them all by their christian names, while they called him *Mr. X—*. (A. S. C. Ross, 1956. For U and non-U, see p. 364.)

PRONUNCIATION PREFERENCES

Some of the results of the *Longman Pronunciation Dictionary* survey, carried out in 1988–9 at University College London. It took the form of a postal questionnaire covering 90 words with controversial pronunciation. People from a variety of educated backgrounds were asked to choose which of two pronunciations they preferred. The analysis showed that in many cases their choice was significantly affected by age. (For other examples of alternative pronunciations, see p. 255.) (After J. C. Wells, 1989.)

Key:
1 Age over 66 (born before 1923)
2 Age 41–65 (born 1923–47)
3 Age 26–40 (born 1948–62)
4 Age under 25 (born since 1962)

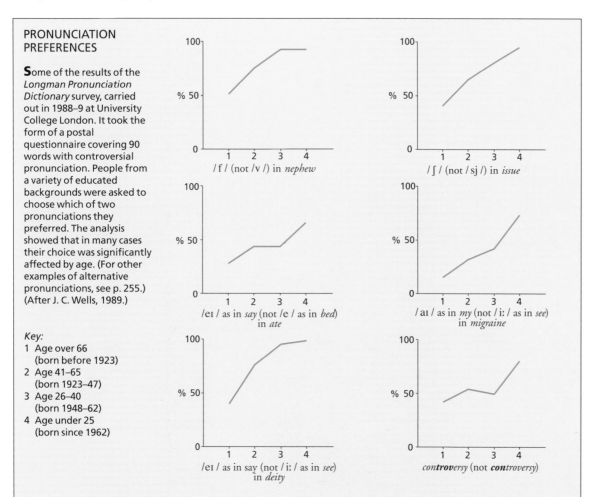

/ f / (not / v /) in *nephew*

/ ʃ / (not / sj /) in *issue*

/ eɪ / as in *say* (not / e / as in *bed*) in *ate*

/ aɪ / as in *my* (not / iː / as in *see*) in *migraine*

/ eɪ / as in say (not / iː / as in *see*) in *deity*

controversy (not *controversy*)

SOME THINGS DON'T CHANGE

Sentiments such as the following, notwithstanding its date of origin, are timeless. This one is dated 1921, but it could be 1991 – or 1891 (p. 367).

Come into a London elementary school and see what it is that the children need most. You will notice, first of all, that, in the human sense, our boys and girls are almost inarticulate. They can make noises, but they cannot speak. Linger in the playground and listen to the talk and shouts of the boys; listen to the girls screaming at their play – listen especially to them as they 'play at schools'; you can barely recognise your native language.... Ask a boy to tell you something – anything, about a book, or a game, or a place, and he will struggle convulsively among words like a fly in a jam-dish. (G. Sampson, *English for the English*, 1921.)

7·WORLD ENGLISH

The first significant step in the progress of English towards its status as a world language (p. 106) took place in the last decades of the 16th century. At that time, the number of mother-tongue English speakers in the world is thought to have been between five and seven million, almost all of them living within the British Isles. Between the end of the reign of Elizabeth I (1588) and the beginning of the reign of Elizabeth II (1952), this figure increased almost fiftyfold, to around 250 million, the majority (around four-fifths) living outside the British Isles. Most of these people were, and continue to be, Americans, and it is in 16th-century North America that we find a fresh dimension being added to the history of the language.

The New World

The first expedition from England to the New World was commissioned by Walter Raleigh in 1584, and proved to be a failure. A group of explorers landed near Roanoke Island, in what is today North Carolina, and established a small settlement. Conflict with the native people followed, and it proved necessary for a ship to return to England for help and supplies. By the time these arrived, in 1590, none of the original group of settlers could be found. The mystery of their disappearance has never been solved.

The first permanent English settlement dates from 1607, when an expedition arrived in Chesapeake Bay. The colonists called their settlement Jamestown (after James I) and the area Virginia (after the 'Virgin Queen', Elizabeth). Further settlements quickly followed along the coast, and also on the nearby islands, such as Bermuda. Then, in November 1620, the first group of Puritans, 35 members of the English Separatist Church, arrived on the *Mayflower* in the company of 67 other settlers. Prevented by storms from reaching Virginia, they landed at Cape Cod Bay, and established a settlement at what is now Plymouth, Massachusetts.

The group was extremely mixed, ranging in age from young children to people in their 50s, and with diverse regional, social, and occupational backgrounds. What the 'Pilgrim Fathers' (as they were later called) had in common was their search for a land where they could found a new religious kingdom free from persecution and 'purified' from the church practices they had experienced in England. It was a successful settlement, and by 1640 about 25,000 immigrants had come to the area.

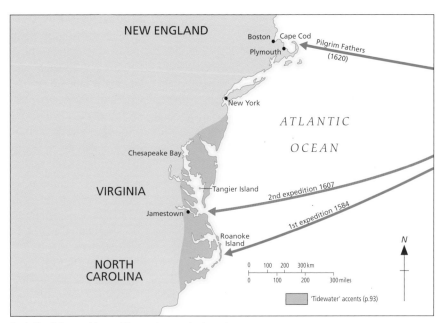

Early English-speaking settlement areas in America.

THE LIVING MUSEUM

Plimoth Plantation, a re-creation at Plymouth, Massachusetts, of the colonists' first settlement. The life of the settlers is portrayed as closely as possible – including a reconstruction of the way they probably spoke.

DIALECT DIFFERENCES

The two settlements – one in Virginia, to the south; the other to the north, in present-day New England – had different linguistic consequences. The southern colonists came mainly from England's 'West Country' – such counties as Somerset and Gloucestershire – and brought with them its characteristic accent, with its 'Zummerzet' voicing of *s* sounds, and the *r* strongly pronounced after vowels. Echoes of this accent can still be heard in the speech of communities living in some of the isolated valleys and islands in the area, such as Tangier Island in Chesapeake Bay. These 'Tidewater' accents, as they are called, have changed somewhat over the past 300 years, but not as rapidly (because of the relative isolation of the speakers) as elsewhere in the country. They are sometimes said to be the closest we will ever get to the sound of Shakespearean English (p. 69).

By contrast, many of the Plymouth colonists came from counties in the east of England – in particular, Lincolnshire, Nottinghamshire, Essex, Kent, and London, with some from the Midlands, and a few from further afield. The eastern accents were rather different – notably, lacking an *r* after vowels, as in present-day Received Pronunciation (RP, p. 365) – and they proved to be the dominant influence in this area. The tendency 'not to pronounce the *r*' is still a feature of the speech of people from New England.

Other features of the language of 17th-century England have their correlates in modern American speech, such as the short, 'flat' *a* vowel in such words as *dance*, where RP developed the 'long' *a* (p. 307). British English also came to pronounce such words as *not* with lip-rounding, whereas in the USA the earlier unrounded vowel (found as *nat* in Chaucer, for example) remained. Several older words or meanings became part of the US standard, such as *mad* 'angry' and *fall* 'autumn', as well as many dialect words; *scallion* 'spring onion', for example, originally from northern England, is commonly used throughout the USA. A phrase such as *I guess*, which is often condemned as an Americanism by British purists, can in fact be traced back to Middle English (p. 39).

During the 17th century, new shiploads of immigrants brought an increasing variety of linguistic backgrounds. Pennsylvania, for example, came to be settled mainly by Quakers whose origins were mostly in the Midlands and the north of England. People speaking very different kinds of English thus found themselves living alongside each other, as the 'middle' Atlantic areas (New York, in particular) became the focus of settlement. As a consequence, the sharp divisions between regional dialects gradually began to blur. The concept of the 'melting pot' must have applied very early on to immigrant accents.

In the 18th century, there was a vast wave of immigration from northern Ireland. The Irish had been migrating to America from around 1600, but the main movements took place during the 1720s, when around 50,000 Irish and Scots-Irish immigrants arrived (p. 338). By the time independence was declared (1776), it is thought that no less than one in seven of the colonial population was Scots-Irish. Many stayed along the coast, especially in the area of Philadelphia, but most moved inland through the mountains in search of land. They were seen as frontier people, with an accent which at the time was described as 'broad'. The opening up of the south and west was largely due to the pioneering spirit of this group of settlers.

By the time of the first census, in 1790, the population of the country was around 4 million, most of whom lived along the Atlantic coast. A century later, after the opening up of the west, the population numbered over 50 million, spread throughout the continent. The accent which emerged can now be heard all over the so-called Sunbelt (from Virginia to southern California), and is the accent most commonly associated with present-day American speech (p. 312).

MYLES STANDISH (1584–1656)

From the point of view of dialect background, Captain Myles Standish was exceptional – the only Pilgrim to come from the Isle of Man. A soldier who had fought in the Netherlands, he served as the military leader of the colonists at Plymouth, and later acted as assistant governor and colony treasurer.

In reviewing the individual history of each of the colonists, a patchwork quilt of dialects emerges. Standish's wife, Barbara, came from Ormskirk, in Lancashire. William Bradford, the first governor of the colony, came from a town on the Yorkshire/Lincolnshire boundary; his wife, Alice, came from Somerset. Nicholas Snow came from London; his wife, Constance, came from Gloucestershire. However, none of the provincial features of accent or grammar which we might associate with these dialects prevailed in New England. It was the speech of the eastern part of England which is the ancestor of the norm in this part of the USA. (After M. Wakelin, 1986.)

DAVY CROCKETT (1786–1836)

The legendary frontiersman, born in Tennessee, came from a family of Scots-Irish immigrants. The son of a backwoods farmer, he became known through fighting in the Creek War (1813–15). He then entered politics, and served in both the Tennessee legislature and the US House of Representatives. He was killed at the battle of the Alamo, after joining the forces fighting the Mexicans in Texas. The heroic myths about him grew during his political campaigns, when he was known for his vigorous and humorous speeches, and were fuelled by many folk epic publications, to which he may himself have contributed. He has signed this picture: 'I am happy to acknowledge this to be the only correct likeness that has been taken of me'.

Linguistic diversity

It was not only England which influenced the directions that the English language was to take in America. The Spanish had occupied large parts of the west and south-west. The French were present in the northern territories, around the St Lawrence River, and throughout the middle regions (French Louisiana) as far as the Gulf of Mexico. The Dutch were in New York (originally New Amsterdam) and the surrounding area. Large numbers of Germans began to arrive at the end of the 17th century, settling mainly in Pennsylvania and its hinterland. In addition, there were increasing numbers of Africans entering the south, as a result of the slave trade, and this dramatically increased in the 18th century: a population of little more than 2,500 black slaves in 1700 had become about 100,000 by 1775, far outnumbering the southern whites.

From the outset, the cosmopolitan nature of American life had its effect on the language (and especially on its vocabulary and practices of naming). Any US biographical dictionary will contain such typical 'American' names as (German) *Eisenhower, Rockefeller, Chrysler*, and *Studebaker*, and (Italian) *Capone, DiMaggio, Sinatra*, and *Valentino*. Likewise, the etymological diversity of modern place names (p. 144) can be seen in (Dutch) *Bronx, Yonkers*, and *Harlem*, (French) *Maine, Detroit*, and *Louisville*, and (Spanish) *El Paso, San Francisco*, and *Toledo*. For a further example of the nation's multilingual history, see the account of states' names on p. 145.

GIVE ME YOUR TIRED...

The 19th century saw a massive increase in American immigration, as people fled the results of revolution, poverty, and famine in Europe. Large numbers of Irish came following the potato famine in the 1840s. Germans and Italians came, escaping the consequences of the failed 1848 revolutions. And, as the century wore on, there were increasing numbers of Central European Jews, especially fleeing from the pogroms of the 1880s. In the first two decades of the present century, immigrants were entering the USA at an average of three quarters of a million a year.

The mood of the time was captured by the writer Emma Lazarus (1849–87), whose sonnet to the Statue of Liberty, 'The New Colossus', expressed her belief in America as a refuge for the oppressed. Inscribed on a plaque inside the pedestal for the Statue, its famous final lines read:

Give me your tired, your poor,
Your huddled masses, yearning to breathe free,
The wretched refuse of your teeming shore.
Send these, the homeless, tempest-tost to me,
I lift my lamp beside the golden door!

Entering a New World by C. J. Staniland, 1892.

DIALECT AREAS

The later population movements across America largely preserved the dialect distinctions which arose out of the early patterns of settlement. The New England people moved west into the region of the Great Lakes; the southerners moved along the Gulf Coast and into Texas; and the midlanders spread throughout the whole of the vast, mid-western area, across the Mississippi and ultimately into California. The dialect picture was never a neat one, because of widespread north–south movements within the country, and the continuing inflow of immigrants from different parts of the world. There are many mixed dialect areas, and pockets of unexpected dialect forms. But the main divisions of north, midland, and south are still demonstrable today (p. 312).

Canada

The first English-language contact with Canada was as early as 1497, when John Cabot reached Newfoundland; but English migration along the Atlantic coast did not develop until a century later, when the farming, fishing, and fur-trading industries attracted English-speaking settlers. There was ongoing conflict with the French, whose presence dated from the explorations of Jacques Cartier in the 1520s; but this came to an end when the French claims were gradually surrendered during the 18th century, following their defeat in Queen Anne's War (1702–13) and the French and Indian War (1754–63). During the 1750s thousands of French settlers were deported from Acadia (modern Nova Scotia), and were replaced by settlers from New England. The numbers were then further increased by many coming directly from England, Ireland, and Scotland (whose earlier interest in the country is reflected in the name *Nova Scotia* 'New Scotland').

The next major development followed the Declaration of Independence in 1776. Loyalist supporters of Britain (the 'United Empire Loyalists') found themselves unable to stay in the new United States, and most left for Canada, settling first in what is now Nova Scotia, then moving to New Brunswick and further inland. They were soon followed by many thousands (the so-called 'late Loyalists') who were attracted by the cheapness of land, especially in the area known as Upper Canada (above Montreal and north of the Great Lakes). Within 50 years, the population of this province had reached 100,000.

Modern Canadian English has a great deal in common with the English spoken in the rest of North America, and people who live outside the region often find the two varieties difficult to distinguish. Why the similarity exists has been the subject of some debate. On the one hand, it might always have been there, with early Canadian English deriving from the same kind of mixture of British English dialects as that which produced the original New England speech (p. 93). On the other hand, the similarity might have emerged through force of numbers, with the dialects of the many 19th-century American immigrants swamping what may have been a more distinctive variety. The linguistic situation, under either hypothesis, would have been extremely heterogeneous.

Despite the similarities between Canadian and US English, there is no identity between them; however, there is no simple statement which can differentiate them. The chief differences are described on pp. 340–3.

The map shows the general direction of English-speaking immigration into Canada. An interesting development took place in the Maritime Provinces, which attracted many people from New England. The area did not retain the *r*-less accent which had been the chief New England characteristic (p. 93), but began to sound the *r* (in such words as *bar* and *cart*). The change may well have been influenced by the arrival of large numbers of *r*-users from the British Isles, but its widespread adoption suggests that these early Canadians were already sensing a need to sound different from their US neighbours. Ironically, the *r* feature would later lose its value as an identity marker, once it became the norm for US English.

LAKELAND

Most of Canada's lakes (outside of Quebec) have been named according to the English pattern: *Rawhide Lake*, *Elliot Lake*, and *Quirke Lake*, for example, are all to be found in southern Ontario. But a few miles further south we find *Lake Huron*, with the generic term preceding. Why is it not *Huron Lake*? The answer lies in the considerable influence of French throughout the early period of exploration. The French pattern, seen in such Quebec names as *Lac Dumont* and *Lac du Fils*, has been used in all the Great Lakes (and certain others, such as *Lake Winnipeg*).

French also influenced the general vocabulary. Most of the words which entered English in those early days seem to have come from French, or from American Indian languages via French, such as *Esquimaux* (1548), *canoe* (1576), *caribou* (1665), and the vocabulary of the fur trade and its pioneers. The

name of the country itself has such an origin: *Canada* is recorded in the journal of the French explorer Jacques Cartier in 1535 as the name of one of the Indian kingdoms along the Saguenay River (though the Iroquoian word he encountered, *kanata*, probably meant no more than 'village').

BLACK ENGLISH

During the early years of American settlement (p. 92), a highly distinctive form of English was emerging in the islands of the West Indies and the southern part of the mainland, spoken by the incoming black population. This was a consequence of the importation of African slaves to work on the sugar plantations, a practice started by the Spanish as early as 1517. From the early 17th century, ships from Europe travelled to the West African coast, where they exchanged cheap goods for black slaves. The slaves were shipped in barbarous conditions to the Caribbean islands and the American coast, where they were in turn exchanged for such commodities as sugar, rum, and molasses. The ships then returned to England, completing an 'Atlantic triangle' of journeys, and the process began again. The first 20 African slaves arrived in Virginia on a Dutch ship in 1619. By the time of the American Revolution (1776) their numbers had grown to half a million, and there were over 4 million by the time slavery was abolished, at the end of the US Civil War (1865).

The policy of the slave-traders was to bring people of different language backgrounds together in the ships, to make it difficult for groups to plot rebellion. The result was the growth of several pidgin forms of communication (p. 346), and in particular a pidgin between the slaves and the sailors, many of whom spoke English. Once arrived in the Caribbean, this pidgin English continued to act as a major means of communication between the black population and the new landowners, and among the blacks themselves. Then, when their children were born, the pidgin gradually began to be used as a mother tongue, producing the first black creole speech in the region.

It is this creole English which rapidly came to be used throughout the southern plantations, and in many of the coastal towns and islands. At the same time, standard British English was becoming a prestige variety throughout the area, as a consequence of the emerging political influence of Britain. Creolized forms of French, Spanish, and Portuguese were also emerging in and around the Caribbean, and some of these interacted with both the creole and the standard varieties of English. The Caribbean islands thus came to develop a remarkably diverse range of varieties of English, reflecting their individual political and cultural histories, with the various creolized forms displaying the influence of the standard language to different degrees. Moreover, West Indian speech did not stay within the Caribbean islands, but moved well outside, with large communities eventually found in Canada, the USA, and Britain. As we might expect, these new locations fostered the emergence of new varieties. There are now major differences between the speech of those living in London, for example (most of whom have never been to the West Indies) and their counterparts in the Caribbean. We shall examine the chief features of this unique range of varieties on pp. 342–5.

(p. 92) ... (p. 346) ... pp. 342–5.

THE COLONIAL LEGACY

The other languages which came to the Caribbean as a result of colonialism have left their mark on the English of the region. French and Spanish are especially evident.

Spanish

Loans include *armadillo*, *cascadura* (a fish), *sancoche* (a soup-like dish), and *paca* (a rodent). Loans from native American languages via Spanish include *chicle* (Aztec), *iguana* (Arawak), and *manatee* (Carib).

French

Loans from French include *flamboyant* (a tree), *ramier* (a pigeon), *fete* (a house-party or picnic), and *macommere* (a godmother, a close female friend, or an effeminate man).

Several words are associated with particular islands. For example, a *parang* is a house-to-house serenade at Chrstmas-time, found in Trinidad and Tobago. A *punta* is a vigorous group dance associated with Belize. A *douillete* is a traditional costume found in Dominica and St Lucia.

In addition, the names of people, places, and events often display early Romance influence:

Dimanche Gras The climax of the Carnival season in Trinidad and Tobago.
La Rose The flower festival held in St Lucia on 31 August.
Basseterre Capital of St Kitts.
Vieux Fort Town in St Lucia.
Trinidad Island name (Spanish for 'trinity').

(After J. Allsopp, 1992.)

CLOSE CONTACTS

Restaurant in Mayaquez, Puerto Rico. The West Indies is unusual in that it brings American and British varieties of English into close proximity. Puerto Rico became part of the USA following the Spanish–American War in 1898. Donuts is one of the consequences.

American and British English are also juxtaposed on the nearby Virgin Islands. The British presence in the islands dates from the arrival of English planters in 1666. The US islands were bought from Denmark in 1917.

The growth of Black English Vernacular

In the USA, vernacular varieties of Black English have come to be a particular focus of attention in recent years (see the linguistic outline on pp. 344–7). The history of these varieties is complex, controversial, and only partly understood. Records of the early speech forms are sparse. It is unclear, for example, exactly how much influence black speech has had on the pronunciation of southern whites. According to some linguists, generations of close contact resulted in the families of the slave-owners picking up some of the speech habits of their servants, which gradually developed into the distinctive southern 'drawl'. Information is clearer from the mid-19th century, when the abolitionist movement focused national attention on blacks' civil rights, and sympathetic representations of Black English began to appear in literary works, such as those by Harriet Beecher Stowe and Mark Twain (p. 85).

Following the widespread movement to the industrial cities of the northern states in the late 19th century, black culture became known throughout the country, especially for its music. The linguistic result was a large influx of new, informal vocabulary into general use, as whites picked up the lively speech patterns of those who sang, played, and danced – from the early spirituals, through the many forms of jazz and blues, to later fashions in rapping, soul music, and break-dancing. At the same time, there was a growth in educational opportunities for black people, and an increasing involvement in political and professional roles. The civil rights movement in the 1960s had its linguistic as well as its political successes, with schools being obliged to take account of the distinctive character of Black English Vernacular, following the successful outcome of a test case at Ann Arbor, Michigan, in 1977.

In the 1980s, the public use of many expressions in the language for talking about this group of people was radically constrained by those maintaining a doctrine of political correctness (p. 177). The current respectability of *African-American* (which dates from the 1860s) has replaced such forms as *Afro-American*, *Africo-American*, *Afro* (all in evidence from the 1830s), *coloured* (preferred in the period after the Civil War), *negro* (preferred after the 1880s, and with a capital *N* some 50 years later), and *black/Black* (which became the preferred form during the 1960s, and is still the commonest use). *Black* is now often proscribed, and language conflicts have grown as people strive to find fresh forms of expression lacking the pejorative connotations they sense in earlier usage.

OLD AND NEW ATTITUDES

The African-American presence in the USA has made a substantial impact on English vocabulary. Until the mid-19th century, most of this lexicon reflected the status and conditions of slavery, a great deal of it consisting of insult and invective. Increasingly thereafter, the language showed the efforts to move towards a better order. The following examples have early 19th-century sources:

slave driver (1807) an overseer of slaves; later used for any harsh or demanding employer.
Uncle (1820s) white term of address for an elderly black male (p. 156).
negro thief (1827) someone who helped a slave escape.
nigger lover (1830s) (white slang term for) an abolitionist.
poor white trash (1833) (slave term for) whites willing to do slave work.
free papers (1838) a document given to freed slaves as proof of their status.

By contrast, much of the vocabulary of the 1960s has a positive or confident ring: *black power*, *freedom march*, *soul brother*, as well as such catch phrases as *Tell it like it is!* and *Black is beautiful!* (After S. B. Flexner, 1976.)

SITTING IN

An anti-segregation *sit-in* outside an American public building. The term became popular in the early 1960s when black students sat at places reserved for whites in restaurants, bus stations, theatres, and other public locations. Other terms were soon formed on analogy, such as *pray-in*, in support of the movement, *play-in*, and *swim-in* (in segregated leisure areas), and by the end of the decade the -*in* suffix was being used in all kinds of contexts, extending well beyond the protest movement (*love-in*, *teach-in*, *be-in*).

I HAVE A DREAM

Dr Martin Luther King, Jr, making his famous speech at the Lincoln Memorial on 28 August 1963, at the end of the 'March on Washington' in support of black civil rights. Its words have since become a rhetorical symbol of the civil rights movement in the USA.

I have a dream that one day on the red hills of Georgia the sons of former slaves and the sons of former slave-owners will be able to sit down together at the table of brotherhood...

I have a dream that my four little children will one day live in a nation where they will not be judged by the colour of their skin...

Dr King was awarded the Nobel Peace Prize in 1964. He was assassinated on 4 April 1968. His birthday (15 January), celebrated on the third Monday in January, has been a federal legal public holiday since 1986.

THE SOUTHERN HEMISPHERE

Towards the end of the 18th century, the continuing process of British world exploration established the English language in the southern hemisphere. The numbers of speakers have never been very large, by comparison with those in the northern hemisphere, but the varieties of English which have emerged are comparably distinctive. Also, the political and cultural situations of each country present the linguist with different issues from those encountered in the history of the language in North America.

Australia

Australia was visited by James Cook in 1770, and within 20 years Britain had established its first penal colony at Sydney, thus relieving the pressure on the overcrowded prisons in England. About 130,000 prisoners were transported during the 50 years after the arrival of the 'first fleet' in 1788. 'Free' settlers, as they were called, also began to enter the country from the very beginning, but they did not achieve substantial numbers until the mid-19th century. From then on, immigration rapidly increased. By 1850, the population of Australia was about 400,000, and by 1900 nearly 4 million. Today, it is over 17 million.

The British Isles provided the main source of settlers, and thus the main influence on the language. Many of the convicts came from London and Ireland (especially following the 1798 Irish rebellion), and features of Cockney and Irish English can be traced in the speech patterns heard in Australia today. Several words commonly thought of as Australian started out in Britain, and may still be heard locally in British dialects, such as *cobber*, *tucker* (compare *tuck shop*), and *joker* ('person'). On the other hand, the variety contains many expressions which have originated in Australia (including a number from Aboriginal languages), and in recent years the influence of American English has been noticeable, so that the country now has a very mixed lexical character (p. 352).

A major issue in Australian social history has been the question of identity. There has long been a tension between the preservation of British cultural values and the promotion of Australian independence. Many inhabitants have favoured the maintenance and development of cultural continuity with Britain; many others have come to reject this tradition, instead advocating nationalism, or some kind of internationalism (but without a British focus). The linguistic consequences of this issue can be clearly seen in the patterns of present-day usage variation (pp. 350–3).

SERIOUS DRAWBACKS

The first fleet into Botany Bay carried 717 prisoners and nearly 300 officials, guards, and their families, starting a system of convict settlement which lasted until 1840. The picture shows a group of convicts in Tasmania, made to walk 30 miles carrying 56 lb weights. One linguistic consequence, often remarked upon by early visitors to Australia, was the frequency of swearing, which soon began to affect the free settlers. Charles Darwin, visiting Sydney on *The Beagle* in 1835, commented on the 'serious drawbacks' which affected the comfort of a colonial official's life, particularly citing the way convict servants exposed children to 'the vilest expressions'. The reduced force of *bloody* in Australian English (p. 172) is doubtless a long-term effect of its high frequency of use within the original population.

ABORIGINAL INFLUENCES

Neither the Aborigines of Australia nor the Maori of New Zealand were very numerous when the Europeans arrived – perhaps 200,000 of each race at the beginning of the 19th century. The Aborigines were nomadic, contact was occasional, and there were many language differences, with over 200 languages in use at the time. As a result, only a few Aboriginal words came into English, most of them being plant and animal names, such as *kangaroo* and *koala* (p. 352). On the other hand, about a third of Australian place names (p. 353) are unmistakably Aboriginal: *Mooloogool, Pannawonica, Gnaraloo, Konnongorring, Koolyanobbing, Widgiemooltha*.

THE OLD ORDER CHANGETH

In October 1992, Australia's prime minister Paul Keating and Queen Elizabeth II formalized an agreement that Australian citizens would no longer be nominated for the receipt of UK honours. The change had begun in 1975, when the government of Gough Whitlam established the Order of Australia as an alternative award. The move ended an imperial tradition of over 200 years, and symbolized the emergence of a new kind of relationship between the two countries.

NEW ZEALAND

In New Zealand (Maori name, *Aotearoa*), the story of English started later and moved more slowly. Captain Cook charted the islands in 1769–70, and European whalers and traders began to settle there in the 1790s, expanding developments already taking place in Australia. Christian missionary work began among the Maori from *c.* 1814. However, the official colony was not established until 1840, following the Treaty of Waitangi between Maori chiefs and the British Crown. There was then a rapid increase in European immigration – from around 2,000 in 1840 to 25,000 by 1850, and to three-quarters of a million by 1900. As early as the turn of the century, visitors to the country were making comments on the emergence of a New Zealand accent. The total population in 1990 was nearly 3.4 million.

Three strands of New Zealand's social history in the present century have had especial linguistic consequences. First, in comparison with Australia, there has been a stronger sense of the historical relationship with Britain, and a greater sympathy for British values and institutions. This has led to a more widespread conservatism, especially in relation to accents (p. 298). Secondly, there has been a growing sense of national identity, and in particular an emphasis on the differences between New Zealand and Australia. This has drawn attention to differences in the accents of the two countries, and motivated the use of distinctive New Zealand vocabulary. Thirdly, there has been a fresh concern to take account of the rights and needs of the Maori people, who now form some 12 per cent of the population. This has resulted in an increased awareness (and, to some extent, use) of Maori words in New Zealand English. The linguistic effects of all these trends are described on pp. 354–5.

READ ALL ABOUT IT

The front page of the first issue of *The Lyttelton Times*, published on 11 January 1851 in 'a colony a few days old', and giving news of the first four ships to land at the settlement. 'New Zealandisms' (italicized below) were in evidence from the very first issue.

Of the five cows landed from the ships, three have died, Mr Brittan's by falling over the cliff, Mr Fitzgerald's and Mr Phillips's by eating *tutu*.

The immediate choosing of the town acre *sections* has been a most important and useful measure.

tutu (usually pronounced /tuːt/) a poisonous local shrub
section a city building plot

(After G. W. Turner, 1966.)

Dunedin Cathedral

COLONIAL ENTERPRISE

During the 1830s several British colonization schemes were proposed, notably the New Zealand Company, founded in 1838 under the influence of British colonial statesman Edward Gibbon Wakefield (1796–1862). These 'Wakefield settlements', promoted during the 1840s, were at Wellington, New Plymouth, Wanganui, Nelson, Otago, and Canterbury. The Otago settlement (1848), based at Dunedin, was organized by the Scottish Free Church, and Scots influence is evident from the many Scottish names in the area, such as *Invercargill, Oban, Bannockburn,* and *Dunedin* itself (an anglicized spelling of the Gaelic name for Edinburgh). The Scottish influence is also thought responsible for the pronunciation of *r* after vowels in parts of the Southland and Otago areas – the 'Southland burr'.

Edward Gibbon Wakefield

THE Lyttelton Times

Vol. I. No. 1.   SATURDAY, JANUARY 11, 1851.   PRICE SIXPENCE.

SOUTH AFRICA

Although Dutch colonists arrived in the Cape as early as 1652, British involvement in the region dates only from 1795, during the Napoleonic Wars, when an expeditionary force invaded. British control was established in 1806, and a policy of settlement began in earnest in 1820, when some 5,000 British were given land in the eastern Cape. English was made the official language of the region in 1822, and there was an attempt to anglicize the large Afrikaans-speaking population. English became the language of law, education, and most other aspects of public life. Further British settlements followed in the 1840s and 1850s, especially in Natal, and there was a massive influx of Europeans after the development of the gold and diamond areas in the Witwatersrand in the 1870s. Nearly half a million immigrants, many of them English-speaking, arrived in the country during the last quarter of the 19th century.

The English language history of the region thus has many strands. There was initially a certain amount of regional dialect variation among the different groups of British settlers, with the speech of the London area prominent in the Cape, and Midlands and northern British speech strongly represented in Natal; but in due course a more homogeneous accent emerged – an accent that shares many similarities with the accents of Australia, which was also being settled during this period (p. 98). At the same time, English was being used as a second language by the Afrikaans speakers, and many of the Dutch colonists took this variety with them on the Great Trek of 1836, as they moved north to escape British rule. An African variety of English also developed, spoken by the black population, who had learned the language mainly in mission schools, and which was influenced in different ways by the various local African language backgrounds. In addition, English came to be used, along with Afrikaans and often other languages, by those with an ethnically mixed background (Coloureds); and it was also adopted by the many immigrants from India, who arrived in the country from around 1860.

South African English has thus come to comprise a range of varieties, but from a social point of view they can be grouped together in contrast to the use of Afrikaans, and they do display certain common features (described on p. 356). English has always been a minority language in South Africa. Afrikaans, which was given official status in 1925, is the first language of the majority of whites, including those formerly in power, and acts as an important symbol of identity for those of Afrikaner background. It is also the first language of most of the Coloured popula-

tion. English is used by the remaining whites (of mainly British background) and by increasing numbers of the majority black population (blacks outnumber whites by over four to one). There is thus a linguistic side to the political divisions which have marked South African society in recent decades: Afrikaans was perceived by the black majority as the language of authority and repression; English was perceived by the white government as the language of protest and self-determination. Many blacks see English as a means of achieving an international voice, and uniting themselves with other black communities.

On the other hand, the contemporary situation regarding the use of English is more complex than any simple opposition suggests. For the white authorities, too, English was important as a means of international communication, and 'upwardly mobile' Afrikaners became increasingly bilingual, with fluent command of an English that often resembles the British-based variety. The public statements by South African politicians, seen on world television, illustrate this ability. As a result, a continuum of accents exists, ranging from those which are strongly influenced by Afrikaans to those which are very close to Received Pronunciation (p. 357); and there are corresponding variations in grammar and vocabulary. Such complexity is inevitable in a country where the overriding issue is social and political status, and people have striven to maintain their deeply held feelings of national and ethnic identity in the face of opposition.

EARLY WORDS

Many of the words which are distinctive to South African English appear very early in the history of the country, as is evident from the files of the Rhodes University research programme for a Dictionary of South African English on Historical Principles. Among the earliest are:

dagga (1670) 'cannabis'
Hottentot (1677)
brak (1731) 'brackish'
kaross (1731) 'skin blanket'
tronk (1732) 'prison'
boer (1776)
aardvark (1786)

In a count of over 2,500 lexical items in the dictionary files in 1988, nearly half (48 per cent) were of Dutch Afrikaans origin, followed by English (29 per cent), Bantu languages (11 per cent), and a few others (such as Khoisan and Malay). There are signs in the 1990s that African languages are already beginning to make an increasing impact. An account of the types of vocabulary originating in South Africa is given on p. 357. (After J. Branford & W. Branford, 1991.)

TAXI!

It is just after four in the morning and the streets of Soweto are already filled with roaring Zola Budds and zooming Mary Deckers flying up and down.

This 1990 report in the local *Weekly Mail* is in fact about

taxicabs, not runners, and is a citation in the fourth edition of *A Dictionary of South African English* (1991). The reference is to South-African-born athlete Zola Budd, controversially selected for the British Olympic squad

at the 1984 Los Angeles games. She was involved in an incident which led to US athlete Mary Decker falling during the 3000 m. Presumably it was the mixture of speed and competitiveness that motivated the conversion of the names to vehicular nouns.

SOUTH ASIA

In terms of numbers of English speakers, the Indian subcontinent ranks third in the world, after the USA and UK. This is largely due to the special position which the language has come to hold in India itself, where it has been estimated that some 4 per cent of the people (over 30 million in 1994) now make regular use of English. There are also considerable numbers of English speakers elsewhere in the region, which comprises six countries (India, Bangladesh, Pakistan, Sri Lanka, Nepal, Bhutan) that together hold about a fifth of the world's population. The variety which has emerged throughout the subcontinent is known as South Asian English. It is less than 200 years old, but it is already one of the most distinctive varieties in the English-speaking world (see p. 360).

The origins of South Asian English lie in Britain. The first regular British contact with the subcontinent came in 1600 with the formation of the British East India Company – a group of London merchants who were granted a trading monopoly in the area by Queen Elizabeth I. It established its first trading station at Surat in 1612, and by the end of the century others were in existence at Madras, Bombay, and Calcutta. During the 18th century, it overcame competition from other European nations, especially France. As the power of the Mughal emperors declined, the Company's influence grew, and in 1765 it took over the revenue management of Bengal. Following a period of financial indiscipline among Company servants, the 1784 India Act established a Board of Control responsible to the British Parliament, and in 1858, after the Indian Mutiny, the Company was abolished and its powers handed over to the Crown.

During the period of British sovereignty (the *Raj*), from 1765 until independence in 1947, English gradually became the medium of administration and education throughout the subcontinent. The language question attracted special attention during the early 19th century, when colonial administrators debated the kind of educational policy which should be introduced. A recognized turning-point was Lord William Bentinck's acceptance of a Minute, written by Thomas Macaulay in 1835, which proposed the introduction of an English educational system in India. When the universities of Bombay, Calcutta, and Madras were established in 1857, English became the primary medium of instruction, thereby guaranteeing its status and steady growth during the next century.

INFLUENTIAL VIEW

Thomas Macaulay (1800–59) began a four-year period of service on the Supreme Council of India in 1834. His famous Minute presented the case for a new English subculture in the region:

I think it is clear…that we ought to employ them [our funds] in teaching what is best worth knowing; that English is better worth knowing than Sanscrit or Arabic; that the natives are desirous to be taught English, and are not desirous to be taught Sanscrit or Arabic;…that it is possible to make natives of this country thoroughly good English scholars; and that to this end our efforts ought to be directed.

The climate of opinion which led to this Minute had been much influenced by the views of the religious and social reformer Ram Mohan Roy (1772–1833). In the 1820s he had proposed the introduction of a Western educational curriculum, arguing that instruction in English was essential if Indians were to have access to European scientific knowledge.

Though this view became official policy, Macaulay's Minute was highly controversial at the time, and laid the foundation of the linguistic disputes which were to become increasingly bitter after independence.

THE STATUS OF ENGLISH

In India, English is now recognized as an 'associate' official language, with Hindi the official language. It is also recognized as the official language of four states (Manipur, Meghalaya, Nagaland, Tripura) and eight Union territories. In Pakistan, it is an associated official language. It has no official status in the other countries of South Asia, but throughout the region it is universally used as the medium of international communication.

In India, the bitter conflict between the supporters of English, Hindi, and regional languages led in the 1960s to the 'three language formula', in which English was introduced as the chief alternative to the local state language (typically Hindi in the north and a regional language in the south). English has, as a consequence, retained its standing within Indian society, continuing to be used within the legal system, government administration, secondary and higher education, the armed forces, the media, business, and tourism. In the Dravidian-speaking areas of the south, it is widely preferred to Hindi as a lingua franca.

Since the 1960s, much attention has focused on what has been called the ongoing 'Indianization' of English. The novelist R. K. Narayan (1906–) is one who has addressed the issue:

The English language, through sheer resilience and mobility, is now undergoing a process of Indianization in the same manner as it adopted US citizenship over a century ago, with the difference that it is the major language there but here one of the fifteen listed in the Indian Constitution.

And the critic K. R. S. Iyengar (1908–) has remarked:

Indian writing in English is but one of the voices in which India speaks. It is a new voice, no doubt, but it is as much Indian as others. The point is controversial, and is reflected in controversies in other parts of the world, where the growth of the English language is perceived as a threat as well as a blessing (p. 114). There is no doubt, however, about the emerging structural identity of Indian English, or about the growth of a recognized body of Indian English literature (p. 360). (After B. B. Kachru, 1983.)

COLONIAL AFRICA

Despite several centuries of European trade with African nations, by the end of the 18th century only the Dutch at the Cape had established a permanent settlement (p. 100). However, by 1914 colonial ambitions on the part of Britain, France, Germany, Portugal, Italy, and Belgium had resulted in the whole continent (apart from Liberia and Ethiopia) being divided into colonial territories. After the two World Wars there was a repartitioning of the region, with the confiscation of German and Italian territories. Most of the countries created by this partition achieved independence in or after the 1960s, and the Organization of African Unity pledged itself to maintain existing boundaries.

West Africa

The English began to visit West Africa at the end of the 15th century, and soon after we find sporadic references to the use of the language as a lingua franca in some coastal settlements. By the beginning of the 19th century, the increase in commerce and anti-slave-trade activities had brought English to the whole West African coast. With hundreds of local languages to contend with, a particular feature of the region was the rise of several English-based pidgins and creoles, used alongside the standard varieties of colonial officials, missionaries, soldiers, and traders. Some of the linguistic features of this highly complex language area are described on pp. 361–2.

East Africa

Although English ships had visited the area from the end of the 16th century, systematic interest began only in the 1850s, with the expeditions to the interior of such British explorers as Richard Burton (1821–90), David Livingstone (1813–73), and John Speke (1827–64). The Imperial British East Africa Company was founded in 1888, and soon afterwards a system of colonial protectorates became established, as other European nations (Germany, France, and Italy) vied with Britain for territorial control. Five modern states, each with a history of British rule, gave English official status when they gained independence in the 1960s, and Zimbabwe followed suit in 1980.

The kinds of English which developed in these countries were very different from those found in West Africa. Large numbers of British emigrants settled in

---

ENGLISH IN WEST AFRICA

British varieties developed especially in five countries, each of which now gives English official status.

Sierra Leone In the 1780s, philanthropists in Britain bought land to establish a settlement for freed slaves, the first groups arriving from England, Nova Scotia, and Jamaica. The settlement became a Crown Colony in 1808, and was then used as a base for anti-slave-trading squadrons, whose operations eventually brought some 60,000 'recaptives' to the country. The chief form of communication was an English-based creole, Krio (p. 349), and this rapidly spread along the West African coast. The hinterland was declared a British protectorate in 1896; and the country received its independence in 1961. Its population had grown to over 4 million by 1991, most of whom can use Krio.

Ghana (formerly **Gold Coast**) Following a successful British expedition against the Ashanti to protect trading interests, the southern Gold Coast was declared a Crown Colony in 1874. The modern state was created in 1957 by the union of this colony and the adjacent British Togoland trust territory, which had been mandated to Britain after World War 1. Ghana was the first Commonwealth country to achieve independence, in 1960. Its population was over 15 million in 1991, about a million of whom use English as a second language.

Gambia English trading along the Gambia River dates from the early 17th century. A period of conflict with France was followed in 1816 by the establishment of Bathurst (modern Banjul) as a British base for anti-slaver activities. The country became a Crown Colony in 1843, an independent member of the Commonwealth in 1965, and a republic in 1970. It had a populat- ion approaching 900,000 in 1991. Krio is widely used as a lingua franca.

Nigeria After a period of early 19th-century British exploration of the interior, a British colony was founded at Lagos in 1861. This amalgamated with other southern and northern territories to form a single country in 1914, and it received independence in 1960. Its population in 1991 was 88.5 million.

Cameroon Explored by the Portuguese, Spanish, Dutch, and British, this region became a German protectorate in 1884, and was divided between France and Britain in 1919. After some uncertainty, the two areas merged as a single country in 1972, with both French and English remaining as official languages. It is a highly multilingual region, with a 1991 population of nearly 12 million. It is thus a country in which contact languages have flourished, notably Cameroon Pidgin, spoken by about half the population (see also p. 359).

There was also an American influence in the region.

Liberia Africa's oldest republic was founded in 1822 through the activities of the American Colonization Society, which wished to establish a homeland for former slaves. Within 50 years it received some 13,000 black Americans, as well as some 6,000 slaves recaptured at sea. The settlement became a republic in 1847, and adopted a constitution based on that of the USA. It managed to retain its independence despite pressure from European countries during the 19th-century 'scramble for Africa'. Its population in 1991 was some 2.5 million. Links with US Black English (p. 96) are still very evident.

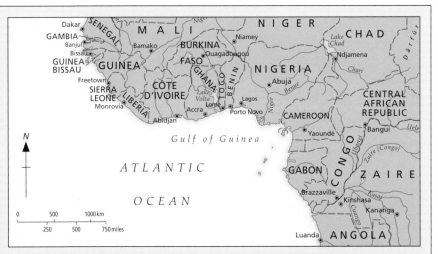

the area, producing a class of expatriates and African-born whites (farmers, doctors, university lecturers, etc.) which never emerged in the environmentally less hospitable West African territories. A British model was introduced early on into schools, reinforcing the exposure to British English brought by the many missionary groups around the turn of the century. The result was a variety of mother-tongue English which has more in common with what is heard in South Africa or Australia than in Nigeria or Ghana. The South African connection is especially noticeable in the countries to the south, and is presumably due to the influence of Afrikaans-speaking immigrants and the shared history of contact with Bantu languages.

The rapid emergence of a settled population who used British English as a first language had two important effects. First, it provided a strong model for Africans to learn as a second language. These would soon form the majority of English users in the region, living mainly in the cities and larger towns. Secondly, with standard English becoming widespread as a lingua franca (and with Swahili also available in this role) there was little motivation for the development of the pidgin varieties of English, which are such a noticeable characteristic of West African countries.

ENGLISH IN EAST AFRICA

British English has played a major role in the development of six East African states, where it has come to be widely used in government, the courts, schools, the media, and other public domains. It has also been adopted elsewhere in the region as a medium of international communication, such as in Ethiopia and Somalia.

Kenya A British colony from 1920, this country became independent in 1963, following a decade of unrest (the Mau Mau rebellion). English was then made the official language, but Swahili replaced it in 1974. The country had some 25 million people in 1991.

Tanzania (formerly **Zanzibar** and **Tanganyika**) Zanzibar became a British protectorate in 1890, and Britain received a mandate for Tanganyika in 1919. The first East African country to gain independence (1961), its population was over 24 million in 1991. English was a joint official language with Swahili until 1967, then lost its status (p. 114).

Uganda The Uganda kingdoms were united as a British protectorate between 1893 and 1903, and the country received its independence in 1962. Its population was around 17 million in 1991. English is the sole official language, but Swahili is widely used as a lingua franca.

Malawi (formerly **Nyasaland**) The area became a British colony in 1907, and received its independence in 1964. Its population was around 9 million in 1991. English is an official language along with Chewa.

Zambia (formerly **Northern Rhodesia**) At first administered by the British South Africa Company, the country became a British protectorate in 1924, and received its independence in 1964. Its population was around 8.5 million in 1991. English is the official language.

Zimbabwe (formerly **Southern Rhodesia**) Also administered by the British South Africa Company, it became a British colony in 1923. Colonists' opposition to independence under African rule led to a Unilateral Declaration of Independence (UDI) by the white-dominated government in 1965. Power was eventually transferred to the African majority, and the country achieved its independence in 1980. Its population was around 9.5 million in 1991. English is the official language.

The different political histories of the East African countries makes it difficult to generalize about the use of English in the region. For example, the fact that Tanzania was German colonial territory until World War 1 led to the promotion of Swahili as a lingua franca, and English is less widely used in the various public domains there than in the other countries of the region. Attitudes towards English also varied in the years following independence, as the countries strove to establish their national identities, and adopted different political stances towards Britain. Nonetheless, several common structural features can be identified (p. 362), and there are a number of sociolinguistic parallels, as can be seen in the table.

(After I. F. Hancock & R. Angogo, 1984.)

SOME DOMAINS OF ENGLISH USE IN SIX EAST AFRICAN STATES

	Kenya	Tanzania	Uganda	Zambia	Malawi	Zimbabwe
Official status	No	No	Yes	Yes	Yes	Yes
High court	Yes	Yes	Yes	Yes	Yes	Yes
Parliament	Yes	No	Yes	Yes	Yes	Yes
Civil service	Yes	No	Yes	Yes	Yes	Yes
Secondary school	Yes	Yes	Yes	Yes	Yes	Yes
Primary school	Yes	No	Yes	Yes	Yes	Yes
Radio	Yes	No	Yes	Yes	Yes	Yes
Newspapers	Yes	Yes	Yes	Yes	Yes	Yes
Advertising	Yes	Yes	Yes	Yes	Yes	Yes
Road signs	Yes	No	Yes	Yes	Yes	Yes
Shop & vehicle signs	Yes	Yes	Yes	Yes	Yes	Yes
Business & correspondence	Yes	Yes	Yes	Yes	Yes	Yes

Yes = English used   No = English not used

SOUTH-EAST ASIA AND THE SOUTH PACIFIC

The territories in and to the west of the South Pacific display an interesting mixture of British and American English. British influence began through the voyages of English sailors at the end of the 18th century, notably the journeys of Captain Cook in the 1770s. The London Missionary Society sent its workers to the islands of the South Pacific 50 years later. In south-east Asia, the development of a British colonial empire grew from the work of Stamford Raffles, an administrator in the British East India company, who established centres in Penang and Java, and in 1819 founded Singapore. Hong Kong island was ceded to Britain in 1842 by the Treaty of Nanking, at the end of the first Opium War, and Kowloon was added to it in 1860; the New Territories, which form the largest part of the colony, were leased from China in 1898 for 99 years. Towards the end of the 19th century, several territories in the region became British

protectorates, the administration of some being later taken over by Australia and New Zealand.

The main American presence emerged after the Spanish-American War of 1898, from which the USA received the island of Guam (and Puerto Rico in the Caribbean, p. 96) and sovereignty over the Philippines. Hawaii was annexed at that time also, after a period of increasing US influence. In the 1940s, the US invasion of Japanese-held Pacific islands was followed after World War 2 by several areas being made the responsibility of the USA as United Nations Trust Territories (p. 105). The Philippines became independent in 1946, but the influence of American English remains strong. And as this country has by far the largest population of the English-speaking states in the region, it makes a significant contribution to the world total for users of English as a second language (p. 109).

DIFFERENT PATHS

English inevitably and rapidly became the language of power in the British territories of SE Asia. The East India Company settlement at Penang (1786) was followed by one at Singapore (1819) and another at Malacca (1824). Within a few months, the population of Singapore had grown to over 5,000, and by the time the Federated Malay States were brought together as a Crown Colony (1867), English had come to be established throughout the region as the medium of law and administration, and was being increasingly used in other contexts. A famous example is the English-language daily newspaper, *The Straits Times*, which began publication in 1845.

The introduction of a British educational system exposed learners to a standard British English model very early on. English-medium schools began in Penang in 1816, with senior teaching staff routinely brought in from Britain. Although at the outset these schools were attended by only a tiny percentage of the population, numbers increased during the 19th century as waves of Chinese and Indian immigrants entered the area. English rapidly became the language of professional advancement and the chief literary language. Soon after the turn of the century, higher education through the medium of English was also introduced. The language thus became a prestige lingua franca among those who had received an English education and who had thereby entered professional society.

In such a multilingual area, it is not surprising to find the British English model being influenced by local factors, leading to the emergence of regionally distinctive varieties. The Chinese background of many students was probably one such factor, influencing the way English was routinely used in schools. Another was the presence of many teachers of English from India, using a spoken variety that was already diverging from the British standard (p. 101). However, despite the common colonial history of the region, a single variety of 'South-east Asian English' has not emerged. The political histories of Singapore and Malaysia, especially since independence, have been too divergent for this to happen; and the socio-linguistic situation in Hong Kong is unique (p. 105).

SINGAPORE

In the 1950s a bilingual educational system was introduced in Singapore, with English used as a unifying and utilitarian medium alongside Chinese, Malay, or Tamil. However, English remained the language of government and the legal system, and retained its importance in education and the media. Its use has also been steadily increasing among the general population. In a 1975 survey, only 27 per cent of people over age 40 claimed to understand English, whereas among 15–20-year-olds, the proportion was over 87 per cent. There is also evidence of quite widespread use in family settings. In such an environment, therefore, it is not surprising that a local variety ('Singaporean English') should have begun to emerge (p. 363).

MALAYSIA

The situation is very different in Malaysia where, following independence (1957), Bahasa Malaysia was adopted as the national language, and the role of English accordingly became more restricted. Malay-medium education was introduced, with English an obligatory subject but increasingly being seen as of value for international rather than intra-national purposes – more a foreign language than a second language. The traditional prestige attached to English still exists, for many speakers, but the general sociolinguistic situation is not one which motivates the continuing emergence of a permanent variety of 'Malaysian English'.

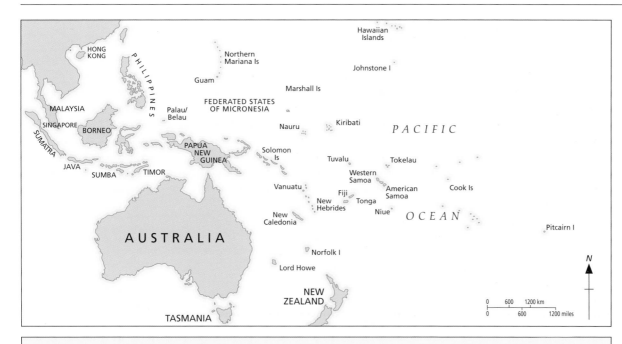

ENGLISH IN SE ASIA AND THE SOUTH PACIFIC

Country	First English speakers	First formal status	Present status
American Samoa	British missionaries, 1830	US treaty, 1878	Territory of USA
Belau (or Palau)	US invasion, 1944 (Japanese mandate, 1920)	Part of US Trust Territory of the Pacific Is, 1947	Republic, 1981
Cook Is	Capt. Cook, 1770s	British protectorate, 1888	New Zealand dependency, 1901
Fiji	Capt. Cook, 1774	British colony, 1874	Independence, 1970
Guam	Sporadic	Ceded by Spain to USA after Spanish–American War, 1898	Territory of USA
Hawaii	Capt. Cook, 1778 (named Sandwich Is) US missionaries, 1820	Under US protection, 1851; annexed by USA, 1898	Admitted as 50th US State, 1959
Hong Kong	Sporadic	Ceded by China to Britain, 1842	British colony (until 1997)
Kiribati	British sailors, 1765	British protectorate (as part of Gilbert & Ellice Is), 1892	Independence, 1979
Malaysia	Penang settlement, 1786	British colony of the Straits Settlements, 1826	Independence, 1957
Marshall Is	US invasion, 1944 (Japanese mandate, 1920)	Part of US Trust Territory of the Pacific Is, 1947	Independence, 1990
Micronesia, Federated States of	US invasion, 1944 (Japanese mandate, 1920)	Part of US Trust Territory of the Pacific Is, 1947	Independence, 1990
Nauru	British sailors, 1798	Australian mandate, 1919 (German administration, 1888)	Independence, 1968
Niue	Capt. Cook, 1774 British missionaries, 1830	British protectorate, 1900	New Zealand dependency, 1901
Norfolk I	Capt. Cook, 1774	British penal settlement (via Australia), 1788	Territory of Australia, 1913
Northern Mariana Is	Sporadic	US mandate, 1947	Independence, 1990
Papua New Guinea	British sailors, 1793	British protectorate, 1884; Australian mandate, 1920	Independence, 1975
Philippines	Sporadic	Ceded to USA after Spanish–American War, 1898	Independence, 1946
Pitcairn I	British sailors, 1767; occupied by *Bounty* mutineers, 1790	Jurisdiction of British High Commissioner, 1898	British colony (part of Fiji, 1952–70)
Singapore	British settlement, 1819	One of the Straits Settlements, 1826	Independence, 1965
Solomon Is	Sporadic	British protectorate, 1893–9	Independence, 1978
Tokelau	British sailors, 1760s	British protectorate, 1889	New Zealand territory, 1925
Tonga	Capt. Cook, 1773 (named Friendly Is)	British protectorate, 1899	Independence, 1970
Tuvalu	British missionaries, 1860s	British protectorate (as part of Gilbert & Ellis Is), 1892	Independence, 1978
Vanuatu	Capt. Cook, 1774	Anglo-French administration as New Hebrides, 1906	Independence, 1980
Western Samoa	British missionaries, 1830s	New Zealand mandate, 1919	Independence, 1962

HONG KONG

English has always had a limited use in the territory, associated with government or military administration, law, business, and the media. Chinese (Cantonese) is the mother-tongue of over 98 per cent of the population. However, in recent years there has been a major increase in educational provision, with 1992 estimates suggesting that over a quarter of the population now have some competence in English. English and Chinese have joint official status, but Chinese predominates in most speech situations, often with a great deal of code-mixing (p. 115). There is considerable uncertainty surrounding the future role of English, after the 1997 transfer of power.

THE PHILIPPINES

• At the Ateneo alumni homecoming, I saw so many old faces and new teeth.
• There is a restaurant in Ongpin that specializes in noodles with American flavor. It is called Miami Vice.
• The Land Transportation Commission (LTC) wages war on smoke belchers. Riding in a smoking car is hazardous to your health. Smoking in a car is even more dangerous.

These extracts from a humorous column in *The Manila Chronicle* (15 January 1987) plainly show the effect of nearly a century of US cultural and linguistic influence in the Philippines. Apart from local Filipino allusions, British English readers would notice *alumni* and *car*, as well as the spelling of *flavor*. (After A. B. Gonzalez, 1991.)

A WORLD LANGUAGE

The movement of English around the world began with the pioneering voyages to the Americas, Asia, and the Antipodes (pp. 92–101), continued with the 19th-century colonial developments in Africa and the South Pacific (pp. 102–5), and took a significant further step when it was adopted in the 20th century as an official or semi-official language by many newly-independent states (p. 110). English is now the dominant or official language in over 60 countries (see the table on p. 109), and is represented in every continent and in the three major oceans – Atlantic (e.g. St Helena), Indian (e.g. Seychelles), and Pacific (e.g. Hawaii). It is this spread of representation which makes the application of the term 'world language' a reality.

The present-day world status of English is primarily the result of two factors: the expansion of British colonial power, which peaked towards the end of the 19th century, and the emergence of the United States as the leading economic power of the 20th century. It is the latter factor which continues to explain the position of the English language today (much to the discomfiture of some in Britain who find the loss of historical linguistic preeminence unpalatable). The USA contains nearly four times as many English mother-tongue (EMT) speakers as the next most important EMT nation (the UK), and these two countries comprise 70 per cent of all EMT speakers in the world (excluding creole varieties: see the table on p. 109). Such dominance, with its political and economic underpinnings, gives the Americans a controlling interest in the way the language is likely to develop.

With over 60 political and cultural histories to consider, it is difficult to find safe generalizations about the range of social functions with which English has come to be identified. General statements about the structure of the language are somewhat easier to make (§20). The problem is not so much in relation to those countries where English is a first language, and where by definition it is available for all communicative situations, but for those where it has status as a second or foreign language, and where its role is often defined by a conscious process of language planning, and not by the natural course of linguistic evolution. Sociolinguistic generalization is especially a problem in those countries where English is used simultaneously as a first and a second language (e.g. Canada), or where a history of language contact has produced a legacy of language conflict (e.g. India).

WHY ENGLISH?

If English is not your mother-tongue, why should you want to learn it, or give it special status in your country? There are seven kinds of answer given to this question.

Historical reasons
Because of the legacy of British or American imperialism, the country's main institutions may carry out their proceedings in English. These include the governing body (e.g. parliament), government agencies, the civil service (at least at senior levels), the law courts, national religious bodies, the schools, and higher educational institutions, along with their related publications (textbooks, proceedings, records, etc.).

Internal political reasons
Whether a country has imperial antecedents or not, English may have a role in providing a neutral means of communication between its different ethnic groups. A distinctive local variety of English may also become a symbol of national unity or emerging nationhood. The use of English in newspapers, on radio, or on television, adds a further dimension.

External economic reasons
The USA's dominant economic position acts as a magnet for international business and trade, and organizations wishing to develop international markets are thus under considerable pressure to work with English. The tourist and advertising industries are particularly English-dependent, but any multinational business will wish to establish offices in the major English-speaking countries.

Practical reasons
English is the language of international air traffic control, and is currently developing its role in international maritime, policing, and emergency services (p. 390). It is the chief language of international business and academic conferences, and the leading language of international tourism.

Intellectual reasons
Most of the scientific, technological, and academic information in the world is expressed in English, and over 80 per cent of all the information stored in electronic retrieval systems is in English. Closely related to this is the concern to have access to the philosophical, cultural, religious, and literary history of Western Europe, either directly or through the medium of an English translation. In most parts of the world, the only way most people have access to such authors as Goethe or Dante is through English. Latin performed a similar role in Western Europe for over a thousand years.

Entertainment reasons
English is the main language of popular music, and permeates popular culture and its associated advertising. It is also the main language of satellite broadcasting, home computers, and video games, as well as of such international illegal activities as pornography and drugs.

Some wrong reasons
It is sometimes thought that English has achieved its worldwide status because of its intrinsic linguistic features. People have claimed that it is inherently a more logical or more beautiful language than others, easier to pronounce, simpler in grammatical structure, or larger in vocabulary. This kind of reasoning is the consequence of unthinking chauvinism or naive linguistic thinking: there are no objective standards of logic or beauty to compare different languages, and questions of phonetic, grammatical, or lexical complexity are never capable of simple answers. For example, English may not have many inflectional endings (which is what most people are thinking of when they talk about English as grammatically 'simple', p. 190), but it has a highly complex syntax; and the number of endings has no bearing on whether a language becomes used worldwide (as can be seen from the former success of Latin). Languages rise and fall in world esteem for many kinds of reasons – political, economic, social, religious, literary – but linguistic reasons do not rank highly among them.

AN OLD STORY

Some of the reasons that people give for learning English are by no means new, as the following quotation illustrates:

I have undertaken to write a grammar of this language [English] because there is clearly a great demand for it from foreigners, who want to be able to understand the various important works which are written in our tongue. For instance there are many people, particularly foreign theologians, whose great ambition is to study Practical Theology, as it is normally taught in our tradition…But it is not only theological works; all kinds of literature are widely available in English editions, and, without boasting, it can be said that there is scarcely any worthwhile body of knowledge which has not been recorded today, adequately at least, in the English language.

This is an extract translated from the Latin preface to John Wallis's *Grammatica Linguae Anglicanae* (Grammar of the English Language), published in 1765 (p. 78). Little has changed – apart from the choice of theology as the lead example.

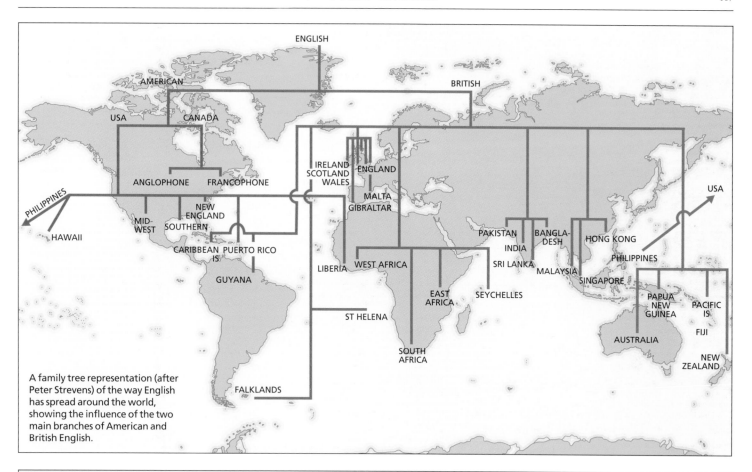

A family tree representation (after Peter Strevens) of the way English has spread around the world, showing the influence of the two main branches of American and British English.

THE THREE CIRCLES

The spread of English around the world has been visualized as three concentric circles, representing different ways in which the language has been acquired and is currently used.

• The *inner circle* refers to the traditional bases of English, where it is the primary language: it includes the USA, UK, Ireland, Canada, Australia, and New Zealand.

• The *outer* or *extended circle* involves the earlier phases of the spread of English in non-native settings, where the language has become part of a country's chief institutions, and plays an important 'second language' role in a multilingual setting: it includes Singapore, India, Malawi, and over 50 other territories (p. 109).

• The *expanding circle* involves those nations which recognize the importance of English as an international language, though they do not have a history of colonization by members of the inner circle, nor have they given English any special status in their language policy. It includes China, Japan, Israel, Greece, Poland, and (as the name of this circle suggests) a steadily increasing number of other states. In these areas, English is taught as a foreign language.

As with all linguistic models, the distinctions are not watertight. Some countries (e.g. South Africa, Malaysia) display a socio-linguistic situation which contains a mixture of second and foreign language features. Some (e.g. Tanzania, Kenya) have changed their language policy since independence, no longer according English official status. Some (e.g. Papua New Guinea, Nigeria) use varieties of English whose status as a first or foreign language is not always clear (p. 108). The value of the model is the attention it draws to the different historical and social issues raised by the notion of world English, and (when comprehensive lists are drawn up, with population totals) its indication of trends in the language's growth. (After B. B. Kachru, 1985.)

Figures refer to populations of English speakers

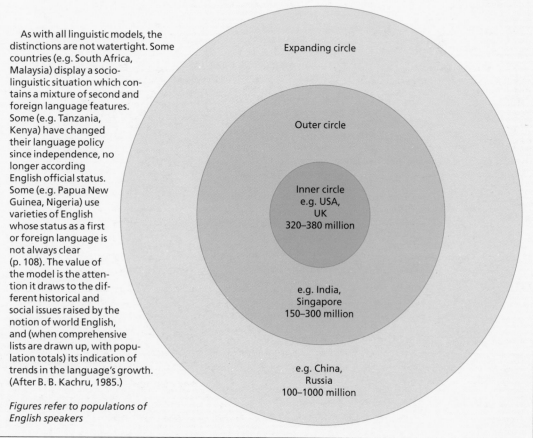

Expanding circle

Outer circle

Inner circle
e.g. USA,
UK
320–380 million

e.g. India,
Singapore
150–300 million

e.g. China,
Russia
100–1000 million

HOW MANY MILLIONS?

The table on p. 109 shows 75 territories in which English has held or continues to hold a special place. In two instances, it groups territories which have a population of less than 10,000: 'UK islands' (Guernsey, Jersey, Man) and 'Other dependencies', the latter including the territories administered by Australia (Norfolk I, Christmas I, Cocos Is), New Zealand (Niue, Tokelau), and the UK (Anguilla, Falkland Is, Pitcairn I, Turks & Caicos Is). No account has been taken in the table of those who have learned English as a foreign language in countries where it has no special place (e.g. China, Germany).

To have a 'special place' can mean various things. Sometimes English is an official or joint official language of a state, its status being defined by law, as in the case of India, Ireland, or Canada. Sometimes it may be the sole or dominant language for historical reasons, as in the case of the USA or the UK (in neither country is it defined legally as an official national language: see p. 107, 115). In a few cases, such as Kenya and Tanzania, English has lost the formal status it once had, though it still plays an important role in the community. In many cases, its standing is less certain, coexisting with other local languages in a relationship which

shifts with time and social function. But in all cases, the population is living in an environment in which the English language is routinely in evidence, publicly accessible in varying degrees, and part of the nation's recent or present identity.

Tables of this kind contain all kinds of hidden assumptions, and have to be carefully interpreted.

• Column 2 gives the 1995 population estimate of each country – in other words, the total number of people who are in theory routinely exposed to English. The grand total, rounded up, is 2,025 million – equivalent, in 1997 (assuming a world population rate of increase of 1.7 per cent per annum) to 2,090 million, which is well over a third of the world's population.

• Column 3 gives a percentage estimate of those who have learned English as a first language (L1). This is translated into totals in Column 4, which shows a grand total of some 337 million. This result needs some interpretation. It could be increased if we were able to include L1 figures for every country (and some reference books do cite as many as 450 million); however, in many places (shown by a question mark) it simply is not known how many L1 speakers there are. On the other hand, the grand total could be decreased if we were to exclude all the cases where

countries use a creole or creolized pidgin (p. 346); these cases, marked with (c), amount to some 6 million. If we do exclude them, we end up with an L1 total of around 330 million (which is commonly cited).

• Column 5 gives a percentage estimate of those who have learned English as a second language (L2). In some cases (e.g. India) this figure is the result of careful thought by linguists who have studied the sociolinguistic situation. In most cases, however, no such evaluation has taken place, and all that is available is an estimate based on relevant social considerations. The present table has taken as a guideline the percentage of people over the age of 25 who have completed secondary education or higher, and who are thus likely to have English at a reasonable standard. (This percentage excludes any L1 speakers listed in Column 3.) All uncertain percentages, and their related totals in Column 6, are preceded by a question mark, to show their doubtful status.

• Column 5 also includes speakers of pidgin/creole varieties of English (as a second language) – hence the high estimates in such countries as Nigeria. The linguistic justification for this approach is that these are varieties of English (as opposed to, say, French), and are usually related to standard English along a con-

tinuum. On the other hand, because the ends of this continuum may not be mutually intelligible, it could be argued that pidgin/creole totals should not be included – in which case, some 50/60 million speakers should be subtracted from the L2 total below. Countries where this is an issue are marked with (c).

• The grand total of L2 speakers is around 235 million – a much lower figure than that commonly cited in accounts of world English, where 300 or 350 million are common estimates. However, we can, if we wish, reach this larger total by relaxing the criterion of what it takes to count as a 'speaker of English'. In seven countries, even a small increase in the percentages given would make a big difference: India, Pakistan, Ghana, Nigeria, Malaysia, Philippines, and Tanzania. These seven had a combined total of over 1,300 million people in 1995. If we allow only 5 per cent of these to have some command of English, we immediately exceed 300 million. The more limited a command of English we allow to be acceptable, the more this figure can be inflated. Whether we wish to inflate the figures, of course, depends on factors which go well beyond the linguistic.

A SHORT GLOSSARY OF EL TERMS

The world of World English (WE), and especially of English Language Teaching (ELT) is full of acronyms (p. 120).

EAP (*English for Academic Purposes*) >> **ESP**

EFL (*English as a Foreign Language*) English seen in the context of countries where it is not the mother tongue and has no special status, such as Japan, France, Egypt, and Brazil. Well over half the countries of the world fall into this category (the 'expanding circle', p.107).

EGP (*English for General Purposes*) >> **ESP**

EIL (*English as an International Language*) The use of English for purposes of international communication. The notion is especially relevant among professional people who do not have the language as a mother tongue (e.g. the business, scientific, political, and academic communities).

ENL (*English as a Native Language*) >> **L1**

EOP (*English for Occupational Purposes*) A course whose content is determined by the specific needs of learners practising a particular occupation (e.g. working with instructional manuals).

ESL (*English as a Second Language*) English in countries where it holds special status as a medium of communication (the 'outer circle', p. 107). The term has also been applied to the English of immigrants and other foreigners who live within a country where English is the first language.

ESP (*English for Special Purposes*) A course whose content is determined by the professional needs of the learner. It contrasts with *English for General Purposes*, where the aim is to establish a general level of proficiency. Several areas have been recognized, such as *English for Academic Purposes* and *English for Science and Technology*.

EST (*English for Science and Technology*) >> **ESP**

L1 (*first language*) The language first acquired by a child (also called a *mother tongue* or *native language*) or preferred in a multilingual situation. The latter context may not be identical to the former: for example, the children of many European emigrants to the USA have come to use English as a first language in the latter sense, though it is not their mother tongue.

L2 (*second language*) A language which is not a person's mother tongue, but which is used in order to meet a communicative need. A country may choose to designate a language as an official second language for its population, or give it some other kind of special status (as shown in the table opposite).

L3 (*third language*) An additional language used to meet a special communicative need. This notion is not as widespread as L1 and L2.

LSP (*Language for Special/Specific Purposes*) A language course designed to meet a predictable and specific range of commu-

nicative needs, such as scientists, doctors, lawyers, or air traffic controllers.

MT (*mother tongue*) >> **L1**

NL (*native language*) >> **L1**

NNL (*non-native language*) A language which people use other than their mother tongue.

NNV (*non-native variety*) A variety of English which has developed in a country or region where it is not used as a mother tongue, such as Indian English.

TEFL (*Teaching English as a Foreign Language*) >> **EFL**

TEIL (*Teaching English as an International Language*) >> **EIL**

TESL (*Teaching English as a Second Language*) >> **ESL**

TESOL (*Teaching English to Speakers of Other Languages*) The teaching of English to anyone who does not have it as a mother tongue. The notion developed in the USA, but TESOL operations are now found in many countries. There is no distinction between *second* and *foreign*, as is generally found in British language-teaching contexts.

Country	Pop (1995)	% L1	Total L1	% L2	Total L2	Country	Pop (1995)	% L1	Total L1	% L2	Total L2
American Samoa	58,000	4	2,000	96	56,000	Nauru	10,000	8	800	?90	? 9,400
Antigua & Barbuda	64,000	95 (c)	61,000	4	2,000	Nepal	20,093,000	?	?	?30	? 5,927,000
Australia	18,025,000	85	15,316,000	12	2,084,000	New Zealand	3,568,000	95	3,396,000	?4	? 150,000
Bahamas	276,000	90 (c)	250,000	9	25,000	Nigeria	95,434,000	?	?	?45 (c)	? 43,000,000
Bangladesh	120,093,000	?	?	?3	? 3,100,000	N Marianas	58,000	5 (c)	3,000	?86 (c)	? 50,000
Barbados	265,000	100 (c)	265,000	—	—	Pakistan	140,497,000	?	?	?11	? 16,000,000
Belize	216,000	65 (c)	135,000	?12	? 30,000	Palau	17,000	?3	? 500	?96	? 16,300
Bermuda	61,000	95	60,000	?	?	Papua New Guinea	4,302,000	3 (c)	120,000	?65 (c)	? 2,800,000
Bhutan	1,200,000	?	?	?5	? 60,000	Philippines	70,011,000	?0.0002	? 15,000	52	36,400,000
Botswana	1,549,000	?	?	?4	? 620,000	Puerto Rico	3,725,000	?3	? 110,000	47	1,746,000
British Virgin Is	18,000	95 (c)	17,000	?	?	Rwanda	7,855,000	?	?	?0.003	? 24,000
Brunei	291,000	3	10,000	?36	? 104,000	St Kitts	39,000	100 (c)	39,000	—	—
Cameroon	13,233,000	?	?	50 (c)	6,600,000	St Lucia	143,000	20	29,000	?15	? 22,000
Canada	29,463,000	63	19,700,000	?20	? 6,000,000	St Vincent & Grenadines	112,000	99 (c)	111,000	—	—
Cayman Is	29,000	100	29,000	—	—	Seychelles	75,000	3	2,000	?15	? 11,000
Cook Is	19,000	?5	? 1,000	?12	? 2,000	Sierra Leone	4,509,000	?10 (c)	? 450,000	?85 (c)	? 3,830,000
Dominica	72,000	4	3,000	?16	? 12,000	Singapore	2,989,000	?10	? 300,000	?35	? 1,046,000
Fiji	791,000	?1	? 5,000	?20	? 160,000	Solomon Is	382,000	?0.005 (c)	? 2,000	35 (c)	135,000
Gambia	1,115,000	?	?	?3 (c)	? 33,000	South Africa	41,465,000	9	3,600,000	?24	? 10,000,000
Ghana	16,472,000	?	?	?7 (c)	? 1,153,000	Sri Lanka	18,090,000	?0.005	? 10,000	?10	? 1,850,000
Gibraltar	28,000	90	25,000	?7	? 2,000	Suriname	430,000	?60 (c)	? 258,000	?35 (c)	? 150,000
Grenada	92,000	99 (c)	91,000	—	—	Swaziland	913,000	?	?	?4	? 40,000
Guam	149,000	37	56,000	?62	? 92,000	Tanzania	28,072,000	?	?	?11	? 3,000,000
Guyana	770,000	90 (c)	700,000	?4	? 30,000	Tonga	100,000	?	?	?30	? 30,000
Hong Kong	6,205,000	2	125,000	?30	? 1,860,000	Trinidad & Tobago	1,265,000	95 (c)	1,200,000	?	?
India	935,744,000	?0.0003	? 320,000	?4	? 37,000,000	Tuvalu	9,000	?	?	6	600
Ireland	3,590,000	95	3,400,000	?5	? 190,000	Uganda	18,659,000	?	?	?11	? 2,000,000
Jamaica	2,520,000	95 (c)	2,400,000	?2	? 50,000	United Kingdom	58,586,000	97	56,990,000	2	1,110,000
Kenya	28,626,000	?	?	?9	? 2,576,000	UK Islands	218,000	99	217,000	—	—
Kiribati	80,000	?	?	?25	? 20,000	United States	263,057,000	86	226,710,000	11	30,000,000
Lesotho	2,050,000	?	?	?24	? 488,000	US Virgin Is	98,000	80 (c)	79,000	?10	? 10,000
Liberia	2,380,000	?2	? 60,000	?84 (c)	? 2,000,000	Vanuatu	168,000	?2	? 2,000	?95 (c)	? 160,000
Malawi	9,939,000	?	?	?5	? 517,000	Western Samoa	166,000	?0.006	? 1,000	?52	? 86,000
Malaysia	19,948,000	2	375,000	30	5,984,000	Zambia	9,456,000	?0.005	? 50,000	?11	? 1,000,000
Malta	370,000	2	8,000	?23	? 86,000	Zimbabwe	11,261,000	?2	? 250,000	?30	? 3,300,000
Marshall Is	56,000	?	?	?50	? 28,000	Other dependencies	30,000	60	18,000	40	12,000
Mauritius	1,128,000	?0.002	2,000	?15	? 167,000						
Micronesia	105,000	?4	? 4,000	?18	? 15,000						
Montserrat	11,000	100 (c)	11,000	—	—	**Totals**	2,024,614,000		337,407,300		235,351,300
Namibia	1,651,000	?0.008	? 13,000	?18	? 300,000						

Note: As suggested on p. 108, a table of this kind is a reflection of historical/political reality only. It does not reflect the sociolinguistic realities of the way English is being used in the modern world as a foreign language. In such a world, the role of English in such countries as Sweden and Denmark is much more pervasive than it is in, say, Nepal and Namibia. To make a language 'official', as happened to English in Rwanda in 1996, may not mean very much in real terms. Indeed, it is increasingly suggested that the distinction between 'second' and 'foreign' language, or between 'outer' and 'expanding' circles (p. 107) is less relevant now than it used to be. And certainly, the next generation will see world English totals dramatically influenced by factors which will apply just as much to China, Japan, Russia, Indonesia, and Brazil (where there are huge potential 'foreign language' populations) as to India, Nigeria, and the other countries listed above.

STANDARD ENGLISH

It is difficult to know what to expect, when a language develops a worldwide presence to the extent that English has (p. 108). There are no precedents for such a geographical spread or for so many speakers. Moreover, the speed at which it has all happened is unprecedented: although the history of world English can be traced back 400 years (p. 92), the current growth spurt in the language has a history of less than 40 years. There has never been such an increase in independent states (UN membership has more than doubled since 1960) nor such a growth in world population (from 2.5 thousand million in 1950 to 5.4 thousand million in 1992). How will English fare (how would *any* language fare?), faced with such responsibilities and having to respond to such pressures?

The two chief issues – internationalism and identity – raise an immediate problem, because they conflict. In the former case, a nation looks out from itself at the world as a whole, and tries to define its needs in relation to that world. In the latter case, a nation looks within itself at the structure of its society and the psychology of its people, and tries to define its needs in relation to its sense of national identity. Corresponding linguistic issues automatically arise.

• Internationalism implies intelligibility. If the reason for any nation wishing to promote English is to give it access to what the broader English-speaking world has to offer, then it is crucial for its people to be able to understand the English of that world, and to be understood in their turn. In short, internationalism demands an agreed standard – in grammar, vocabulary, spelling, pronunciation, and conventions of use.

• Identity implies individuality. If a nation wishes to preserve its uniqueness or to establish its presence, and to avoid being an anonymous ingredient in a cultural melting-pot, then it must search for ways of expressing its difference from the rest of the world. Flags, uniforms, and other such symbols will have their place, but nothing will be so naturally and universally present as a national language – or, if there is none, a national variety of an international language. In short, in the context of English, identity demands linguistic distinctiveness – in grammar, vocabulary, spelling, pronunciation, or conventions of language use.

The future of the English language (p. 112) depends on how the tension between these two principles will be resolved.

WHAT IS STANDARD ENGLISH?

Since the 1980s, the notion of 'standard' has come to the fore in public debate about the English language. At national level, in several countries (but especially in the UK), the concern has focused on the devising of an acceptable national curriculum for English in primary and secondary education. At international level, the focus has been on the question of which national standards to use in teaching English as a foreign language. In both contexts, however, before sensible decisions can be made about how to introduce Standard English or teach it, there is a need for clear understanding about what it actually is. The cautious opening of the entry on Standard English (SE) in *The Oxford Companion to the English Language* (1992), written by the editor Tom McArthur, suggests that we may be entering a minefield:

a widely used term that resists easy definition but is used as if most educated people nonetheless know precisely what it refers to...

Disentangling the issues is best done first at national level, where the issues have been around a long time, and are reasonably well understood. (For the early history of Standard English, see p. 54.)

Towards a definition
From the dozens of definitions available in the literature on English, we may extract five essential characteristics.

• SE is a *variety* of English – a distinctive combination of linguistic features with a particular role to play. Some people call it a 'dialect' of English – and so it is, but of a rather special kind, for it has no local base (p. 298). There is nothing in the grammar and vocabulary of a piece of SE to tell us which part of a country it comes from.

• The linguistic features of SE are chiefly matters of grammar, vocabulary, and orthography (spelling and punctuation). It is important to note that SE is not a matter of pronunciation: SE is spoken in a wide variety of accents (including, of course, any prestige accent a country may have, such as British RP, p. 365).

• SE is the variety of English which carries most prestige within a country. 'Prestige' is a social concept, whereby some people have high standing in the eyes of others, whether this derives from social class, material success, political strength, popular acclaim, or educational background. The English that these people choose to use will, by this very fact, become the standard within their community. In the words of one US linguist, SE is 'the English used by the powerful' (James Sledd).

• The prestige attached to SE is recognized by adult members of the community, and this motivates them to recommend SE as a desirable educational target. It is the variety which is used as the norm of communication by the community's leading institutions, such as its government, law courts, and media. It is therefore the variety which is likely to be the most widely disseminated among the public. It will, accordingly, be widely understood – though not to the same extent by everyone, and with varying comprehension of some of its features (thus motivating the demands of the 'plain English' campaigns, p. 176). It may or may not be liked.

• Although SE is widely understood, it is not widely produced. Only a minority of people within a country (e.g. radio newscasters) actually use it when they talk. Most people speak a variety of regional English, or an admixture of standard and regional Englishes, and reserve such labels as 'BBC English' or 'the Queen's English' for what they perceive to be a 'pure' SE. Similarly, when they write – itself a minority activity – the consistent use of SE is required only in certain tasks (such as a letter to a newspaper, but not necessarily to a close friend). More than anywhere else, SE is to be found in print.

On this basis, we may define the Standard English of an English-speaking country as a minority variety (identified chiefly by its vocabulary, grammar, and orthography) which carries most prestige and is most widely understood.

ENGLISH WHAT IS WROTE

18 APRIL 1993

More than just talking proper

Randolph Quirk argues Standard English is about words and meanings, not accents

Whenever there is a public debate about English in schools, newspapers resort to 'clever' headlines in which they use nonstandard forms. This example, from *The Independent*, was one of many which appeared in Britain during the 1992–3 debate on the National Curriculum for state primary and secondary schools. Of course, it stands out only because the rest of the paper is in Standard English.

THE CIRCLE OF WORLD ENGLISH

One way of representing the unity and diversity of the English-speaking world (from T. McArthur, 1987). At the centre is placed the notion of World English, conceived as a 'common core'. Around it are placed the various regional or national standards, either established or becoming established ('standardizing'). On the outside are examples of the wide range of popular Englishes which exist. Each boundary line could provoke an argument, as the author acknowledges, but the overall perspective is illuminating. A small selection of heads of state or government symbolizes the way Standard English is used worldwide in public roles.

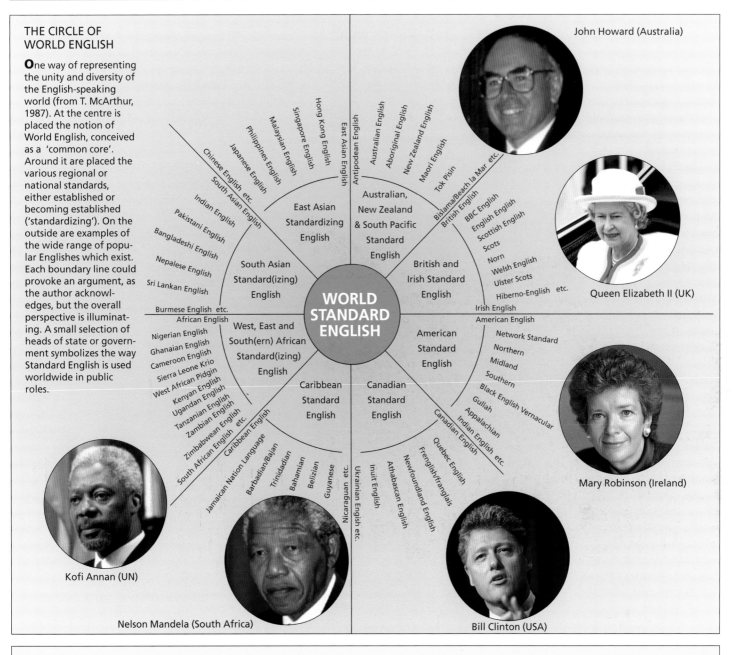

John Howard (Australia)

Queen Elizabeth II (UK)

Mary Robinson (Ireland)

Bill Clinton (USA)

Nelson Mandela (South Africa)

Kofi Annan (UN)

WORLD STANDARD ENGLISH?

If we read the newspapers or listen to the newscasters around the English-speaking world, we will quickly develop the impression that there is a World Standard English (WSE), acting as a strongly unifying force among the vast range of variation which exists. There is a great deal of evidence to support this impression, and models such as the 'World English circle' above formally represent it. However, it is misleading in several respects. A totally uniform, regionally neutral, and unarguably prestigious variety does not yet exist worldwide.

• Each country where English is a first language is aware of its linguistic identity, and is anxious to preserve it from the influence of others. New Zealanders do not want to be Australians; Canadians do not want to be 'Americans'; and *Americanism* is perceived as a danger signal by usage guardians everywhere (except in the USA) (p. 310).

• All other countries can be grouped into those which follow American English, those which follow British English, and those (e.g. Canada) where there is a mixture of influences (p. 107). One of the most noticeable features of this divided usage is spelling. In certain domains, such as computing and medicine, US spellings are becoming increasingly widespread (*program*, *disk*, *pediatrics*), but we are a long way from uniformity (p. 307).

• A great deal of lexical distinctiveness can be observed in the specialized terms of local politics, business, culture, and natural history, and in the 'domestic' columns of national newspapers (such as Want Ads); this is illustrated in detail in §20. There is also a certain amount of grammatical distinctiveness, especially between US and UK English.

• The notion of a 'standard pronunciation' is useful in the international setting of English as a second or foreign language (p. 108), but here too there is more than one teaching model – chiefly, British Received Pronunciation and US General American (p.307).

• The question of prestige is not easy to determine, at an international level, because of the different national histories which coexist. Would it be more prestigious for a report from an international body to appear in British or American spelling? Should it refer to *cars* or *automobiles*? What image do its authors wish to convey? Decisions about such matters are made in innumerable contexts every day. It will take time before the world sees a consensus, and only time will tell whether this consensus will display the domination of a present-day variety of English or the development of a new, composite variety (p. 113).

THE FUTURE OF ENGLISH

There is no linguistic subject more prone to emotional rhetoric or wild exaggeration than the future of the English language. Heights of optimism compete with depths of pessimism. Among the optimists we may cite the German philologist Jakob Grimm, who addressed the point in a lecture published in 1852:

Of all modern languages, not one has acquired such great strength and vigour as the English…[it] may be called justly a LANGUAGE OF THE WORLD: and seems, like the English nation, to be destined to reign in future with still more extensive sway over all parts of the globe.

In the late Victorian period, estimates of the numbers of mother-tongue English speakers living a century thereafter (i.e. today) often reached astronomical heights. One writer, in an issue of *The Phonetic Journal* (13 September 1873) calculated (with hopeful precision) that by the year 2000 this total would be 1,837,286,153 – an estimate which, with the benefit of hindsight, can be seen to be in error by a factor of six (p.109). Such totals were commonplace in the heady atmosphere which accompanied the climax of British and American colonial expansion.

By contrast, there were the pessimists, predicting that within a century the English language would be in fragments. Here we may cite the British philologist Henry Sweet, who wrote in 1877:

by that time [a century hence] England, America, and Australia will be speaking mutually unintelligible languages, owing to their independent changes of pronunciation.

The same point had been made nearly a century before by Noah Webster, in his *Dissertations on the English Language* (1789). Webster thought that such a development would be 'necessary and unavoidable', and would result in 'a language in North America, as different from the future language of England, as the modern Dutch, Danish and Swedish are from the German, or from one another'. From Webster's pro-American point of view, of course (p. 81), this would not have been such a bad thing.

Neither Grimm nor Sweet proved to be accurate prophets. English has indeed become a world language, but it is by no means everywhere and it is by no means always welcome. And English has indeed developed many spoken varieties, but these are by no means mutually unintelligible. Perhaps the only safe generalization to be made is that predictions about the future of English have a habit of being wrong.

WAS HE RIGHT?

In a paper written in 1970 for a conference in Luxembourg organized by the London-based Institute of Linguists, Randolph Quirk, then Quain Professor of English at University College London, engaged in a speculation about the future. His paper was called 'English in twenty years'.

I must base my speculation about [the future role of English] upon assumptions outside linguistics, and my assumptions are these: that Britain will become more and more closely involved with continental Europe, economically, intellectually and politically; and that English will retain in the next 20 years the degree of prestige it has enjoyed in continental Europe in the past 20 years. Whether this prestige rests upon the achievements of Carnaby Street or Cape Kennedy, on the fame of jump jets or junkies, on Canadian nickel or Australian fruit, on happenings at MIT or LSE, is beside the point. On these assumptions I would confidently predict that English will retain its prominent place in Europe, though without these assumptions, I should not be nearly as confident. One could in fact go further and predict that English will actually increase its currency, above all for purposes of trade, but also in scientific communication and in the everyday matters of popular culture – for example, through Eurovision. And all this even in the European countries whose mother tongue is so important a language as German or French. Already *Le Monde* produces a weekly edition in English, and much of German industry regards English as the main language of export promotion: with Britain's increasing involvement in Europe between now and 1990, English can scarcely be expected to become less relevant in France and Germany. In the rather smaller language communities of Europe, of course, the place of English is likely to affect the daily lives of the people still more closely, and cases like the day-to-day factory use of English by the Swedish ball-bearing firm SKF are likely to multiply. Already the medium for more than half the world's scientific writing and popular entertainment by radio, TV and film alike, English has a momentum which only a cultural cataclysm plus an abyss of much more than 20 years in width could seriously hamper. Given something more like a cultural boost, we may expect present uses of English to expand so that by 1990 everyone in Europe may be using, or be exposed to, English for some part of every day.

If all this seems very easy, let the reader now write a corresponding paragraph predicting the role of English in 2020.

ONE LANGUAGE OR MANY?

There are two competing pressures currently influencing the development of English (p. 110): one acts to maintain international intelligibility, promoting a uniform World Standard English; the other acts to preserve national identity, promoting a diverse set of Regional Standard Englishes.

The drive for intelligibility

The pressure for international intelligibility is very strong, and may by now be unstoppable. International travel, satellite broadcasting, world press and television, world stock markets, multinational corporations, intergovernmental agencies, and many other institutions have guaranteed a situation of daily contact for hundreds of millions of English speakers who together represent every major variety. Historical loyalties (e.g. to Britain) have been largely replaced by pragmatic, utilitarian reasoning. If using British English can sell goods and services, then let British English be used. If it needs American English, then so be it. And let either or others be employed as occasion demands.

It is not surprising, in such a climate, to find a core of English grammar, vocabulary, and orthography already in widespread use, at least in print (p. 110). There is, however, still some way to go before the world arrives at a level of uniform usage which will guarantee international intelligibility at levels comparable to those found intranationally. Breakdowns in communication due to differences in idiom, vocabulary, or grammar are common enough, even between British and American English (p. 306), and differences in regional accent can be devastating.

The drive for identity

The pressure to foster national identity is also very strong, and the signs are that divergence is increasing. The 1990s has seen no reduction in the number of conflicts which involve regions trying to establish their independence, and one consequence of successful nationalism is the early adoption of speech forms marking a linguistic distance between the new nation and its colonial antecedents. Two local factors readily foster this distancing.

It is inevitable, first of all, that when English is in close contact with other languages it will adopt some of the characteristics of those languages, especially their vocabulary and prosody. The latter, in particular, can be a major source of local variety identity, as is heard in the distinctive stress-timed rhythm of Indian or Caribbean English, or the rising intonations of Australian and New Zealand English (p. 249).

Secondly, the fact that English is found all over the world means that it will be used to express an unparalleled range of fauna, flora, and cultural features.

Each English-speaking country will accordingly find itself with thousands of words to express its local character. Whether we view these words as part of a world standard or a regional standard will depend chiefly on the extent to which the world at large is interested in the notions they express. Thus, in South African English *apartheid* and *impala* have become part of World Standard English, whereas *dorp* ('small town or village') and *bredie* ('type of stew') have not. The words most resistant to world standardization will be those which already have equivalents in Standard British or American English, such as *outwith* (Scots, 'outside') or *godown* (Indian 'warehouse').

Compromise?

There may be a natural balance which the language will eventually achieve. A nationalistic climate may cause a variety to move in a particular direction away from its source standard, but may then be pulled back when moderates within the community find it increasingly difficult to understand what is being said. An example of this actually happening was reported in 1985 by Alan Maley, at the time the British Council Representative in South India:

Mrs Indira Gandhi was prompted to write to her Ministry of Education not so long ago to complain of falling standards of English in India, reportedly after attending an international meeting at which she had been unable to understand the contribution of the Indian delegate (speaking in English).

The features of Indian English which gave Mrs Gandhi a problem are well-recognized (p. 360). Whether her reaction was representative and influential remains to be seen.

WHICH WORLD STANDARD?

How could a more uniform World Standard English arise? There are three main possibilities.
• A current variety could gradually come to be adopted by the leading international institutions, and emerge as the world standard. American English already seems to have made considerable progress in this direction.
• The different varieties of English could gradually merge, to produce a new variety which is like none of those that currently exist. An example is the kind of English commonly heard in the corridors of power of the European Community, and called 'Euro-English'.
• A fresh variety could be created, based on a set of assumptions about those aspects of English which are most useful for international purposes. An example is the proposal in the early 1980s to develop a 'nuclear' kind of English which would include only the most communicative features of grammar and vocabulary.

A TRIDIALECTAL FUTURE?

Wherever World Standard English eventually comes from, a new *bidialectism* (the ability to use two dialects of a language) is sure to emerge. And because many people are already bidialectal (knowing their national standard and a regional dialect), *tridialectism* is likely to be the norm.

We have lunch with friends. We use a variety of English influenced by the dialect of the region in which we live.

We go to a commercial fair in Birmingham, England. We talk to the sales representatives using British Standard English.

We are on holiday in Egypt, and meet up with people from other English-speaking countries. We talk together in World Standard English.

THREATENING ENGLISH

As English extends worldwide, its presence is widely viewed as beneficial. Aims such as international intelligibility and national identity (p. 110) are positive-sounding and forward-looking. But there is another side to the coin, for English is not always welcome. Its presence may generate antagonism, especially when it is perceived to interfere with the character or use of local languages. Nationalistic movements may totally reject it – and not always peacefully.

Three forms of antagonism

• There is always mutual influence as languages come into contact with each other. English itself has a long history of borrowing from other languages (§§3–5), and is always ready to increase its lexicon through the acquisition of loan words (p. 126). When other languages borrow heavily from English, however, the local reaction may be far less positive. People may complain about the excessive influence of English on their language, and their country may even try to legislate against it (as in France). Such activities may be passionately pursued, though any success is likely to be limited to restricted domains, such as official publications or committee dictionaries.

• Lexical invasion is feared because it is seen as the thin end of a wedge. Linguistic history contains several examples of English supplanting other languages – Cumbric, Cornish, Norn, Manx, most North American Indian languages, most Australian Aboriginal languages. Gaelic, Welsh, Maori, and Hawaiian struggle to retain their identity. A reaction can take place, as people become increasingly conscious of the rights of minorities, but the atmosphere is inevitably one of uncertainty and mistrust. Small countries feel particularly threatened, even if they do not have an English colonial history, as with Denmark and Iceland. On this topic, the language is emotive. 'Did English murder Irish?' asks one journal headline. 'Is English killing off other languages?' asks another.

• English may be rejected as an official language because of its associations with colonial history. This has happened several times in recent years. In Tanzania, English was jointly official with Swahili until 1967, when the latter became sole official language. In 1974, Kenya also replaced English by Swahili as the official language. In Malaysia the National Language Act of 1967 disestablished English as a joint official language, giving sole status to Malay. In India, the role of English in relation to Hindi and other regional languages is a continuing source of controversy (p. 101).

VORSPRUNG DURCH ANGLISTIK

Several studies in the 1980s have shown a rapid rise in the frequency with which English loan words appear in foreign language publications. According to one analyst, Broder Carstensen, there was a fivefold increase in the number of Anglicisms in German newspapers during the 1980s. Advertising copywriters especially have a liking for English technical vocabulary.

One researcher analysed the frequency of English loan words in German car advertising between 1987 and 1990, using 569 brochures and model descriptions relating to the 30 most important makes of car on the German market. In 8,458 pages analysed, there were 7,190 nouns from English. The table shows the 75 Anglicisms occurring more than 20 times in the corpus. (After S. A. Vesterhus, 1991.)

The five most frequent users of English loan words were all Japanese: Mitsubishi, Daihatsu, Nissan, Suzuki, and Honda.

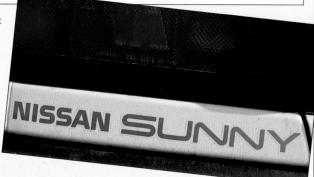

Anglicisms	Refs	Anglicisms	Refs	Anglicisms	Refs	Anglicisms	Refs
Design	411	Motor-		Touch	62	T-bar-roof	29
Cockpit	387	management	114	Trend	62	Low end torque	28
Spoiler	297	Rush-hour	112	Memory	55	Boom	26
Styling	256	Leasing	109	Offroader	54	Full cover	
Limit	233	City	107	Open air feeling	52	(wheel trim)	26
Star	218	Mix	103	Understanding	49	Make-up	
Display	205	Team	100	Recycling	46	(mirror)	26
Power	199	High-tech	99	Overdrive	43	Silent shaft	26
Know-how	191	Box	96	Spotlight	42	Torque-sensory	25
Output	188	Computer	93	Transfer	40	Award	24
Tuning	179	Stop and Go	89	Roadster	39	Dolby	24
Twin-Cam-		Kit	86	Sound	39	Allrounder	23
Motor	167	Bestseller	83	Autoreverse	38	Intercooler	23
Dummy	163	Look	80	Check	37	Keycode	23
Airbag	151	Top	80	Equalizer	35	Overboost	22
Check-Control	143	Kickdown	78	Crash	34	Pickup	21
Fading	134	Set	76	Drive	33	Coating	20
Hardtop	132	Show	73	Hi-Fi-Pack	31	Recorder	20
Handling	127	Highlight	70	Choke	30	Synthesizer	20
Color	123	Injection	67	Killer	30		

NO SURRENDER

The basis of any independent government is a national language, and we can no longer continue aping our former colonizers . . . Those who feel they cannot do without English can as well pack up and go. (President Jomo Kenyatta, Nairobi, 1974.)

SURRENDER

In January 1989, officials in Osaka, the largest city in the Kinki district of west-central Japan, announced that the word *Kinki* would no longer be used overseas because 'in English this word means odd, unusual, and some other things'. The alternative name for the region, *Kansai*, was to be used instead. As a result, the new *Kinki Research Complex* changed its name to the *Kansai Research Complex*. Other candidates for change: the English-language tourist magazine *Kinki* and the luggage logo *Kinki Nippon Tourist*.

ENGLISH THREATENED

The example of Kenya on the facing page shows that, while English itself often poses a threat, it can also itself be threatened. This development is perhaps unsurprising in countries where English acts as a second or foreign language, but we might not expect to find it within the 'inner circle' of countries where it has traditionally been a first language (p. 107). The threat to a first-language environment is nonetheless perceived as real, and can come from two directions.

• Standard English users in the community may become worried by the spread of a nonstandard variety, especially one which shows a mixture of linguistic influences. Code-mixing takes place to some degree everywhere that English is spoken alongside another language, and is a normal feature of bilingualism. The mixed varieties are given blended names to show their origins, such as *Japlish*, *Swedlish*, *Anglikaans*, *Angleutsch*, *Wenglish* (*Welsh* + *English*), and *Tex-Mex*.

Some situations prompt pairs of names in order to show different levels of dominance by the contributing languages, as in the case of *Spanglish* and *Englañol* or *Frenglish* and *Franglais*. It is unusual to see any of these varieties in writing, but some are very widely spoken. They have received only limited linguistic study.

• English speakers may also feel threatened by the substantial growth of an immigrant language in their country. Normally, the gradual process of immigration results in the process of language shift, with second and third generations of non-English-speaking immigrants adopting the language of their host state. However, in one country, the USA, the growth in the number of Hispanic speakers has prompted a major protectionist movement, (*US English*), an ensuing reaction (*English Plus*), and a sociolinguistic controversy of unprecedented proportions.

THE ENGLISH LANGUAGE AMENDMENT

Although English has been the dominant language of the USA since independence, it has never been legally recognized as official. Until recently, this has rarely been an issue. But in the early 1980s a movement developed in America as a reaction to the perceived dramatic growth of Spanish in certain parts of the country (such as Florida, the south-western states, and New York City). Large numbers of Hispanic immigrants were felt to be altering the balance of society, and there was alarm that one day English might lose its leading role.

In 1981 Senator S. I. Hayakawa proposed a constitutional amendment to make English the official language of the United States – the *English Language Amendment* (ELA). His measure failed, but the spirit behind it evidently struck a public nerve, for in 1983 *US English* was founded to take the idea forward. This body saw English as the only way to integrate US ethnic diversity, and saw an ELA as the only way to safeguard the future of English. The movement gathered considerable support, and currently has over a million members. By 1996, 23 states had made English their official language; and an 'official English' bill was actually passed by the House of Representatives that year, though the dissolution of Congress stopped its further progress.

From the outset, *US English* was bitterly attacked by many who saw it as a white supremacist movement which would in due course deny ethnic minorities their linguistic rights. The organization was widely condemned for its perceived chauvinism by leading organizations in linguistics and language teaching. One consequence was the formation in 1987 of an alternative pressure group, *English Plus*, to encourage American bilingualism – English 'plus' one or more other languages. Its members proposed their own amendment, the *Cultural Rights Amendment*, to ensure that ethnic and linguistic diversity in the USA would be celebrated and used as a national resource rather than condemned and suppressed.

The issues surrounding the ELA have long ceased to be matters of fact. There are claims of hidden agendas on both sides. There are real fears and deeply entrenched attitudes. In those parts of the country where the Hispanic presence is strongest, there are profound anxieties about the future of traditional English values and resources. Equally profound are the doubts of those who believe that an inevitable consequence of an ELA will be increased discrimination against language minorities. Their fear is that, one day, active bilingualism will be condemned as unAmerican.

The biggest problem now facing either side, in seeking success for their amendments, is the diversity of positions which have been adopted by the individual US states. With each side watching the other like hawks, and organizing opposition to any legal moves, it is difficult at present to see a way in which the dispute might be resolved. The compilation of accurate sociolinguistic statistics will certainly help. There is currently some dispute about the numbers of Hispanic immigrants, and the extent to which they are turning to English. Some studies suggest that up to 75 per cent of second-generation Hispanics follow the normal course of language shift and become bilingual or monolingual English. If this is so, the motivation for the debate will, in due course, simply disappear.

GREETINGS FROM PLANET EARTH

The US space shuttle *Discovery*, in its English-language livery, suggesting the eventual emergence of an 'outermost circle' to add to the three already found on Earth (p. 107). Or perhaps we will one day need to recognize several 'exterior circles', if the message sent with the Voyager project to the outer planets ever yields communicative fruit. *Voyager 1*, launched in 1977 on a trajectory which eventually took it into outer space, contained a message in English from an Austrian, Kurt Waldheim.

As the Secretary-General of the United Nations, an organization of 147 member states who represent almost all of the human inhabitants of the planet Earth, I send greetings on behalf of the people of our planet...

The first seeds, perhaps, of Solar System Standard English.

PART II

English vocabulary

Vocabulary is the Everest of a language. There is no larger task than to look for order among the hundreds of thousands of words which comprise the lexicon. There may be many *greater* tasks – working out a coherent grammatical system is certainly one – but nothing beats lexical study for sheer quantity and range.

Questions of size and scope are thus the first to be addressed in Part II. How big is the lexicon of English? How many words do any of us know? And how do we calculate size, with such an amorphous phenomenon? Defining the basic unit to be counted turns out to be an unexpected difficulty, and the important notion of a lexeme is introduced, which Part II relies upon greatly. We examine some of the other difficulties, such as the status of abbreviations and proper names, and draw some tentative conclusions.

Where does the vastness of the lexicon come from? We look at the question of sources. There is an important balance – not to say tension – between the stock of native words and the avalanche of foreign borrowings into English over the centuries. The use of prefixes, suffixes, compounding, and other processes of word-building turns out to play a crucial part in English vocabulary growth. We make a separate study of lexical creativity, which introduces a range of interesting processes, some sounding quite technical (portmanteaux,

reduplicatives, neologisms), others with a much more appealing resonance (nonsense-words, nonce-words).

We then turn to the detailed study of lexical history – to etymology, and the processes of semantic change. A major part of this section is devoted to one of the most fascinating topics in popular linguistic enquiry: the history of names – place-names, first names, surnames, nicknames, and much more. This is followed by a careful examination of the structure of the lexicon. Lexemes are grouped into semantic fields, and the relationships between them are plotted. We look at dictionaries and thesauri, synonyms and antonyms, collocations and idioms, and several other central concepts. A fuller account of lexical reference books, however, is left to Part VI.

Part II concludes by taking a series of slices through the lexical cake. We look at some of the ways in which words can be 'loaded', and introduce such notions as connotations, taboo words, jargon, doublespeak, and political correctness. We capture some of the ways in which the language is most alive, in the form of catch phrases, vogue words, slang, slogans, and graffiti. And we end by a sympathetic look at language which is dead or dying – at quotations, archaisms, and clichés. A few 'last' words round off the treatment of what is the largest component of the English language structure.

◀ An impressive collection of the English lexicon – but even this library represents only a fraction of the lexical resources of the worldwide spoken and written language.

The term *lexicon* is known in English from the early 17th century, when it referred to a book containing a selection of a language's words and meanings, arranged in alphabetical order. The term itself comes from Greek *lexis* 'word'. It is still used today in this word-book meaning, but it has also taken on a more abstract sense, especially within linguistics, referring to the total stock of meaningful units in a language – not only the words and idioms, but also the parts of words which express meaning, such as the prefixes and suffixes. This is how the term is used throughout the present book.

To study the lexicon of English, accordingly, is to study all aspects of the vocabulary of the language – how words are formed, how they have developed over time, how they are used now, how they relate in meaning to each other, and how they are handled in dictionaries and other word books. It is a study which is carried on by *lexicologists*, who are thus practising *lexicology*. If lexicologists choose to write a dictionary, they are known as *lexicographers*, and their calling is *lexicography* (§11). The two pairs of terms are closely related, but there is no symmetry between them. Lexicographers need to have had some training in lexicology, if they are to come up with good dictionaries. On the other hand, one can be a good lexicologist without ever having written a dictionary at all.

LEXEMES

What shall we call the units of meaning which appear as the headwords in an English dictionary? The tradition is to call them *words*, and for the most part this familiar designation will do. We think of ourselves as 'looking a word up in the dictionary'. However, in a serious study of the lexicon we need to be rather more precise than this, because when we refer to a dictionary we actually do something rather more subtle, without consciously thinking about it.

• We encounter the sentence *It was fibrillating*, and conclude that we need help to understand it. But we do not in fact look up *fibrillating* in the dictionary. We look up *fibrillate*. We 'know' that this is the important unit, and we disregard the ending. Similarly, we would have disregarded the endings if we had come across *fibrillated* or *fibrillates*. What shall we call *fibrillate*, then? It is a word, certainly, but at the same time it is something more than a word. It is the unit of meaning which lies behind the words *fibrillating*, *fibrillated*, and *fibrillates*.

• We encounter the sentence *It was raining cats and dogs*, and (perhaps because we are foreign, and meeting the phrase for the first time) need to look it up. We know the meaning of the words *rain*, *cats*, and *dogs*, but this does not seem to help. Evidently the meaning of the whole phrase is different from the combined meanings of the constituent words. What shall we call *rain cats and dogs*, then? The usual solution is to call it an idiom, but an idiom is a unit of meaning larger than the single word.

• We encounter the sentence *Come in*. Again, we have a unit of meaning which is larger than a single word, but this phrase hardly seems to have enough lexical meat in it to be called an idiom. There are thousands of such multi-word verbs in English (p. 212), so the issue is important. What shall we call *come in*, then? This unit of meaning can hardly be called a word, as its constituents are themselves words.

The term which has been introduced to handle all these cases is *lexeme* (or *lexical item*). A lexeme is a unit of lexical meaning, which exists regardless of any inflectional endings it may have or the number of words it may contain. Thus, *fibrillate*, *rain cats and dogs*, and *come in* are all lexemes, as are *elephant*, *jog*, *cholesterol*, *happiness*, *put up with*, *face the music*, and hundreds of thousands of other meaningful items in English. The headwords in a dictionary are all lexemes, and lexemes are the focus of interest in the rest of this section.

On the writing of grammars • Doublespeak at large • The tentative female
English as a decorative language • The redoubtable Roget

WHAT COUNTS AS A WORD?

The cover of the periodical *English Today* poses a question of considerable theoretical and practical significance. Usually, people look at the spaces in a piece of writing, and think that they are enough to decide the matter. So, the first sentence of this paragraph, we would all agree, contains 16 words. Unfortunately for lexicologists, word space is not an infallible guide, as the cover examples show.

• Hyphens complicate matters: shall we count *eat-as-much-as-you-like* as a single word? or *Highs-Lows*?

• The absence of hyphens complicates matters: is *Value for Money* truly three separate words?

• Unusual compounds complicate matters: shall we count *FLYAWAY* and *CITYSPRINT* as single words?

• Abbreviations complicate matters: are *BA* and *BCal* one word or two?

Several other kinds of difficulty can be given.

• Meaning complicates matters: *bear* (the animal) and *bear* (to carry) are plainly different words, but are *lock* (on a door) and *lock* (in a canal) different words? Is *high* in *high tea*, *high priest*, and *high season* the same word?

• Usage complicates matters: people sometimes write *flowerpot*, sometimes *flower pot*, and sometimes *flower-pot*.

• Idioms complicate matters: if we insist that a word should have a clear meaning, then how many words are there in *get my act together* and *get my own back*?

Problems of this kind mean that it is always wise to take word estimates cautiously, especially when evaluating the competing claims about coverage made by English dictionaries. Equally, the problems present an interesting challenge to lexicologists, as they get to grips with their task.

HOW LARGE IS THE ENGLISH LEXICON?

The two biggest dictionaries suggest around half a million lexemes – a total approached by the unabridged *Webster's Third New International* (which claimed over 450,000 entries in 1961) and by the integrated edition of the *Oxford English Dictionary* (which claimed over 500,000 entries in 1992). The true figure is undoubtedly a great deal higher.

A comparison of these two dictionaries – or of any other group of dictionaries of comparable size – shows a remarkable lack of identity between headword lists. In the sample analysed here (see right), the *Webster* and *Oxford* dictionaries have only 21 headwords in common out of a possible 57 – less than two-fifths. If this pattern were continued, their combined lexicon would exceed three-quarters of a million.

Discrepancies are usually caused by differing editorial emphases. The *Oxford* has far more historical references and British dialect items than does the *Webster*, which in turn has far more local American items. On the other hand, neither work would claim to be comprehensive in its coverage of the vocabulary of the 'new Englishes' (Part V) in such parts of the world as India, Singapore, and Nigeria, where thousands of new lexemes are coming into the language. And because the tradition in lexicography is to use the written language as the test for inclusion (p. 442), much local spoken nonstandard vocabulary will be omitted. There must be thousands of slang expressions currently in common use which have never been recorded, such as all the lexemes which express the concept of 'being drunk' – *canned, blotto, squiffy, jagged, paralytic, smashed*, etc.

Even if we restrict the issue to standard vocabulary, there are many items which could be included as part of the lexicon, but which are not usually found in a dictionary. There are some half a million abbreviated forms in English (p. 120), many of which have a clear lexical status (*BA, FBI, NATO*, etc.); and fauna and flora also provide a vast lexical resource. For example, there are apparently some million insects already described, with several million more awaiting description. This means that there must be at least a million designations enabling English-speaking entomologists to talk about their subject. Should all of these be allowed into the word-count as well?

It is difficult to see how even a conservative estimate of English vocabulary could go much below a million lexemes. More radical accounts, allowing in all of scientific nomenclature, could easily double this figure. Only a small fraction of these totals, of course, is learned by any one of us (p. 123).

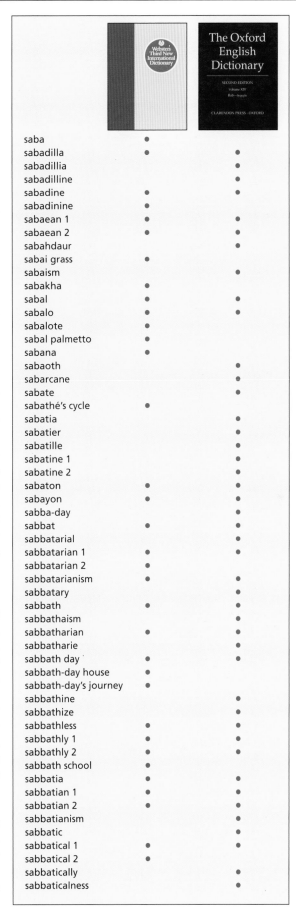

THE SUPERDICTIONARY

This comparison of the boldface items listed in two unabridged dictionaries shows the surprisingly limited extent of their overlap; and if we looked in addition for correspondence between senses, the extent of the discrepancy would be even greater. Nor is this the whole of the English lexicon at this point in the alphabet. Reference to *Chambers English Dictionary* (a much shorter work) brings to light another five items – *saba* (in a different sense from the one given in *Webster*), *sabahan, sabbath-breach, sabbath-breaker*, and *sabbath- breaking*. Reference to Willis's *Dictionary of the Flowering Plants and Ferns* (8th edn) gives *sabalaceae, sabalacineae, sabaudia, sabaudiella, sabazia, sabbata*, and three senses of *sabbatia*. We have reached over 70 items now, with many other specialist dictionaries left to consult – but will anyone ever have enough time and motivation to consult them all, for the entire alphabet, and thus arrive at a truly complete superdictionary? Until someone (or, we must suppose, an electronic something) does, estimates about the size of the English lexicon will remain pure guesswork.

The dictionaries handle the capitalization of lexemes in different ways, and several items are variable in their use of capital letters. To avoid complicating the issue, no capitals are shown in the table. Alternative spellings, likewise (e.g. *sabaean* and *sabean*) have been ignored, as have optional hyphenations (e.g. in *sabbath day*).

ABBREVIATIONS

Abbreviations, one of the most noticeable features of present-day English linguistic life, would form a major part of any superdictionary. Often thought to be an exclusively modern habit, the fashion for abbreviations can be traced back over 150 years. In 1839, a writer in the New York *Evening Tatler* comments on what he calls 'the initial language ... a species of spoken shorthand, which is getting into very general use among loafers and gentlemen of the fancy, besides Editors, to whom it saves much trouble in writing ...'. He was referring to *OK* ('all correct'), *PDQ* ('pretty damn quick') – two which have lasted – *GT* ('gone to Texas'), *LL* ('liver loafers'), and many other forms introduced, often with a humorous or satirical intent, by society people.

The fashionable use of abbreviation – a kind of society slang – comes and goes in waves, though it is never totally absent. In the present century, however, it has been eclipsed by the emergence of abbreviations in science, technology, and other special fields, such as cricket, baseball, drug trafficking, the armed forces, and the media. The reasons for using abbreviated forms are obvious enough. One is the desire for linguistic economy – the same motivation which makes us want to criticise someone who uses two words where one will do (see p. 180). Succinctness and precision are highly valued, and abbreviations can contribute greatly to a concise style. They also help to convey a sense of social identity: to use an abbreviated form is to be 'in the know' – part of the social group to which the abbreviation belongs. Computer buffs the world over will be recognized by their fluent talk of *ROM* and *RAM*, of *DOS* and *WYSIWYG*. You are no buff if you are unable to use such forms, or need to look them up (respectively, 'read-only memory', 'random-access memory', 'disk operating system', and 'what you see is what you get'). It would only irritate computer-literate colleagues and waste time or space (and thus money) if a computer-literate person pedantically expanded every abbreviated form. And the same applies to those abbreviations which have entered everyday speech. It would be strange indeed to hear someone routinely expanding *BBC, NATO, USA, AIDS*, and all the other common abbreviations of contemporary English. Indeed, sometimes (as with *radar* and *AIDS*), the unabbreviated form may be so specialized that it is unknown to most people – a point not missed by the compilers of quiz games, who regularly catch people out with a well-known (sic) abbreviation. As a test, try *UNESCO* and *UNICEF, AAA, SAM* and *GI* (context: military), or *DDT* and *TNT* (context: chemistry). (See foot of facing page for answers, if required.)

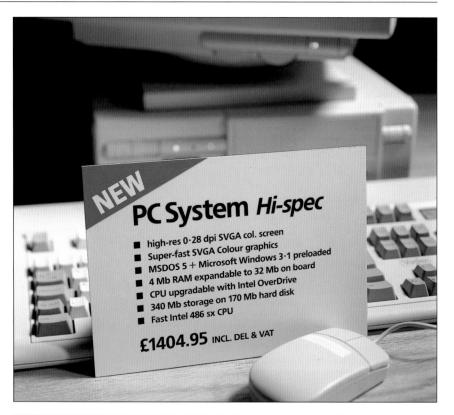

TYPES OF ABBREVIATION

Initialisms
Items which are spoken as individual letters, such as *BBC, DJ, MP, EEC,* e.g., and *USA*; also called alphabetisms. The vast majority of abbreviations fall into this category. Not all use only the first letters of the constituent words: *PhD*, for example, uses the first two letters of the word *philosophy*, and *GHQ* and *TV* take a letter from the middle of the word.

Acronyms
Initialisms which are pronounced as single words, such as *NATO, laser, UNESCO*, and *SALT* (talks). Such items would never have periods separating the letters – a contrast with initialisms, where punctuation is often present (especially in older styles of English). However, some linguists do not recognize a sharp distinction between acronyms and initialisms, but use the former term for both.

Clipping
A part of a word which serves for the whole, such as *ad* and *phone*. These examples illustrate the two chief types: the first part is kept (the commoner type, as in *demo, exam, pub, Gill*), and the last part is kept (as in *bus, plane*). Sometimes a middle part is kept, as in *fridge* and *flu*. There are also several clippings which retain material from more than one part of the word, such as *maths* (UK), *gents*, and *specs*. *Turps* is a curiosity, in the way it adds an -s. Several clipped forms also show adaptation, such as *fries* (from *French fried potatoes*), *Betty* (from *Elizabeth*), and *Bill* (from *William*).

Blends
A word which is made out of the shortened forms of two other words, such as *brunch* (breakfast + lunch), *heliport* (helicopter + airport), *smog* (smoke + fog), and *Eurovision* (European + television). Scientific terms frequently make use of blending (as in the case of *bionic*), as do brand names (a device which cleaned your teeth while you used the phone might be called *Teledent*) and fashionable neologisms (p. 130).

Awkward cases
Abbreviations which do not fall clearly into the above four categories. Some forms can be used either as initialisms or acronyms (*UFO* – 'U F O' or 'you-foe'). Some mix these types in the one word (*CDROM*, pronounced 'see-dee-rom'). Some can form part of a larger word, using affixes (*ex-JP*, *pro-BBC*, *ICBMs*). Some are used only in writing (*Mr, St* – always pronounced in full in speech).

Facetious forms
TGIF Thank God It's Friday

CMG Call Me God (properly, 'Companion of St Michael and St George')

KCMG Kindly Call Me God (properly, 'Knight Commander of St Michael and St George')

GCMG God Calls Me God (properly, 'Grand Cross of St Michael and St George') and above all

AAAAAA Association for the Alleviation of Asinine Abbreviations and Absurd Acronyms (actually listed in the Gale Dictionary described on the facing page).

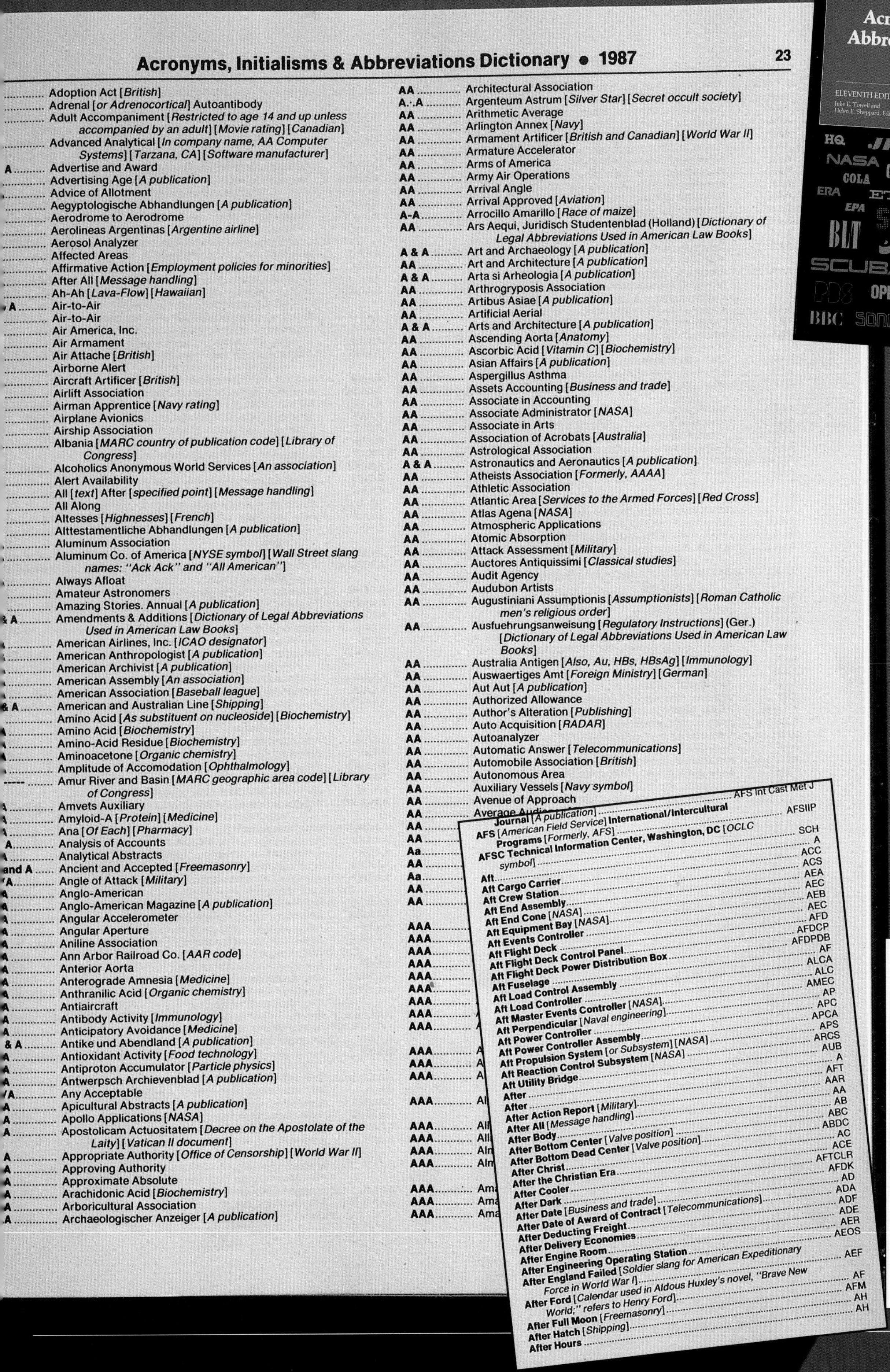

Acronyms, Initialisms & Abbreviations Dictionary ● 1987   23

.....	Adoption Act [British]
.....	Adrenal [or Adrenocortical] Autoantibody
.....	Adult Accompaniment [Restricted to age 14 and up unless accompanied by an adult] [Movie rating] [Canadian]
.....	Advanced Analytical [In company name, AA Computer Systems] [Tarzana, CA] [Software manufacturer]
A	Advertise and Award
.....	Advertising Age [A publication]
.....	Advice of Allotment
.....	Aegyptologische Abhandlungen [A publication]
.....	Aerodrome to Aerodrome
.....	Aerolineas Argentinas [Argentine airline]
.....	Aerosol Analyzer
.....	Affected Areas
.....	Affirmative Action [Employment policies for minorities]
.....	After All [Message handling]
.....	Ah-Ah [Lava-Flow] [Hawaiian]
A	Air-to-Air
.....	Air-to-Air
.....	Air America, Inc.
.....	Air Armament
.....	Air Attache [British]
.....	Airborne Alert
.....	Aircraft Artificer [British]
.....	Airlift Association
.....	Airman Apprentice [Navy rating]
.....	Airplane Avionics
.....	Airship Association
.....	Albania [MARC country of publication code] [Library of Congress]
.....	Alcoholics Anonymous World Services [An association]
.....	Alert Availability
.....	All [text] After [specified point] [Message handling]
.....	All Along
.....	Altesses [Highnesses] [French]
.....	Alttestamentliche Abhandlungen [A publication]
.....	Aluminum Association
.....	Aluminum Co. of America [NYSE symbol] [Wall Street slang names: "Ack Ack" and "All American"]
.....	Always Afloat
.....	Amateur Astronomers
.....	Amazing Stories. Annual [A publication]
& A	Amendments & Additions [Dictionary of Legal Abbreviations Used in American Law Books]
.....	American Airlines, Inc. [ICAO designator]
.....	American Anthropologist [A publication]
.....	American Archivist [A publication]
.....	American Assembly [An association]
.....	American Association [Baseball league]
& A	American and Australian Line [Shipping]
.....	Amino Acid [As substituent on nucleoside] [Biochemistry]
.....	Amino Acid [Biochemistry]
.....	Amino-Acid Residue [Biochemistry]
.....	Aminoacetone [Organic chemistry]
.....	Amplitude of Accomodation [Ophthalmology]
----	Amur River and Basin [MARC geographic area code] [Library of Congress]
.....	Amvets Auxiliary
.....	Amyloid-A [Protein] [Medicine]
.....	Ana [Of Each] [Pharmacy]
A.	Analysis of Accounts
.....	Analytical Abstracts
and A	Ancient and Accepted [Freemasonry]
A	Angle of Attack [Military]
.....	Anglo-American
.....	Anglo-American Magazine [A publication]
.....	Angular Accelerometer
.....	Angular Aperture
.....	Aniline Association
.....	Ann Arbor Railroad Co. [AAR code]
.....	Anterior Aorta
.....	Anterograde Amnesia [Medicine]
.....	Anthranilic Acid [Organic chemistry]
.....	Antiaircraft
.....	Antibody Activity [Immunology]
.....	Anticipatory Avoidance [Medicine]
& A	Antike und Abendland [A publication]
.....	Antioxidant Activity [Food technology]
.....	Antiproton Accumulator [Particle physics]
.....	Antwerpsch Archievenblad [A publication]
A	Any Acceptable
.....	Apicultural Abstracts [A publication]
.....	Apollo Applications [NASA]
A	Apostolicam Actuositatem [Decree on the Apostolate of the Laity] [Vatican II document]
.....	Appropriate Authority [Office of Censorship] [World War II]
.....	Approving Authority
.....	Approximate Absolute
.....	Arachidonic Acid [Biochemistry]
.....	Arboricultural Association
.....	Archaeologischer Anzeiger [A publication]

AA	Architectural Association
A∴A	Argenteum Astrum [Silver Star] [Secret occult society]
AA	Arithmetic Average
AA	Arlington Annex [Navy]
AA	Armament Artificer [British and Canadian] [World War II]
AA	Armature Accelerator
AA	Arms of America
AA	Army Air Operations
AA	Arrival Angle
AA	Arrival Approved [Aviation]
A-A	Arrocillo Amarillo [Race of maize]
AA	Ars Aequi, Juridisch Studentenblad (Holland) [Dictionary of Legal Abbreviations Used in American Law Books]
A & A	Art and Archaeology [A publication]
AA	Art and Architecture [A publication]
A & A	Arta si Arheologia [A publication]
AA	Arthrogryposis Association
AA	Artibus Asiae [A publication]
AA	Artificial Aerial
A & A	Arts and Architecture [A publication]
AA	Ascending Aorta [Anatomy]
AA	Ascorbic Acid [Vitamin C] [Biochemistry]
AA	Asian Affairs [A publication]
AA	Aspergillus Asthma
AA	Assets Accounting [Business and trade]
AA	Associate in Accounting
AA	Associate Administrator [NASA]
AA	Associate in Arts
AA	Association of Acrobats [Australia]
AA	Astrological Association
A & A	Astronautics and Aeronautics [A publication]
AA	Atheists Association [Formerly, AAAA]
AA	Athletic Association
AA	Atlantic Area [Services to the Armed Forces] [Red Cross]
AA	Atlas Agena [NASA]
AA	Atmospheric Applications
AA	Atomic Absorption
AA	Attack Assessment [Military]
AA	Auctores Antiquissimi [Classical studies]
AA	Audit Agency
AA	Audubon Artists
AA	Augustiniani Assumptionis [Assumptionists] [Roman Catholic men's religious order]
AA	Ausfuehrungsanweisung [Regulatory Instructions] (Ger.) [Dictionary of Legal Abbreviations Used in American Law Books]
AA	Australia Antigen [Also, Au, HBs, HBsAg] [Immunology]
AA	Auswaertiges Amt [Foreign Ministry] [German]
AA	Aut Aut [A publication]
AA	Authorized Allowance
AA	Author's Alteration [Publishing]
AA	Auto Acquisition [RADAR]
AA	Autoanalyzer
AA	Automatic Answer [Telecommunications]
AA	Automobile Association [British]
AA	Autonomous Area
AA	Auxiliary Vessels [Navy symbol]
AA	Avenue of Approach
AA	Average Audi...

The overlapping inset list (AFS / Aft entries):

	Journal [A publication] International/Intercultural
AFS	[American Field Service] ..... AFSIIP
AAA	Programs [Formerly, AFS]
	AFSC Technical Information Center, Washington, DC [OCLC symbol] ..... SCH
Aa.	Aft ..... A
Aa.	Aft Cargo Carrier ..... ACC
AA	Aft Crew Station ..... ACS
AA	Aft End Assembly ..... AEA
	Aft End Cone [NASA] ..... AEC
	Aft Equipment Bay [NASA] ..... AEB
AAA	Aft Events Controller ..... AEC
AAA	Aft Flight Deck ..... AFD
AAA	Aft Flight Deck Control Panel ..... AFDCP
AAA	Aft Flight Deck Power Distribution Box ..... AFDPDB
AAA	Aft Fuselage ..... AF
AAA	Aft Load Control Assembly ..... ALCA
AAA	Aft Load Controller ..... ALC
AAA	Aft Master Events Controller [NASA] ..... AMEC
AAA	Aft Perpendicular [Naval engineering] ..... AP
AAA	Aft Power Controller ..... APC
AAA	Aft Power Controller Assembly ..... APCA
AAA	Aft Propulsion System [or Subsystem] [NASA] ..... APS
AAA	Aft Reaction Control Subsystem [NASA] ..... ARCS
AAA	Aft Utility Bridge ..... AUB
	Aft ..... A
AAA	After ..... AFT
AAA	Af... ..... AAR
	Af... ..... AA
AAA	After ..... AB
AAA	After Action Report [Military] ..... ABC
AAA	After All [Message handling] ..... ABDC
AAA	After Body ..... AC
AAA	After Bottom Center [Valve position] ..... ACE
	After Bottom Dead Center [Valve position] ..... AFTCLR
AAA	After Christ ..... AFDK
AAA	After the Christian Era ..... AD
AAA	After Cooler ..... ADA
AAA	After Dark [Business and trade] ..... ADF
AAA	After Date [Telecommunications] ..... ADE
AAA	After Date of Award of Contract ..... AER
	After Deducting Freight ..... AEOS
	After Delivery Economies
	After Engine Room
	After Engineering Operating Station ..... AEF
	After England Failed [Soldier slang for American Expeditionary Force in World War I]
	After Ford [Calendar used in Aldous Huxley's novel, "Brave New World;" refers to Henry Ford] ..... AF
	After Full Moon [Freemasonry] ..... AFM
	After Hatch [Shipping] ..... AH
	After Hours ..... AH

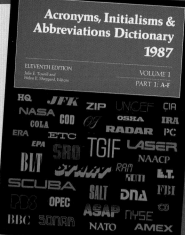

ACCUMULATING ABBREVIATIONS

Ask someone how many abbreviations there are in English, and the reply tends to be in the low thousands – perhaps five or ten. Such impressions have been fostered by the short lists of abbreviations tucked away at the back of dictionaries, or occasionally published as separate guides to specialized fields. The truth is somewhat different. The *Acronyms, Initialisms & Abbreviations Dictionary* published by the Gale Research Company contained over 400,000 entries in its 11th edition (1987). The top illustration shows part of a page towards the beginning of the alphabet – some of the 178 entries listed for AA. Below is a section from the *Reverse Dictionary* —to be used if you know the full form but do not know the abbreviation.

Test Answers (see facing page)

UNESCO United Nations Educational, Scientific, and Cultural Organization

UNICEF United Nations International Children's Emergency Fund (now the United Nations Children's Fund)

AAA anti-aircraft artillery (or 'triple A')

SAM surface-to-air missile

GI Government Issue

DDT dichlorodiphenyltrichloroethane

TNT trinitrotoluene

PROPER NAMES

Are proper names part of the English lexicon? Should all words beginning with a capital letter be excluded from a vocabulary count of the language? One answer is hidden within a piece of old music-hall repartee:

A: I say, I say, I say. I can speak French.
B: You can speak French? I didn't know that. Let me hear you speak French.
A: Paris, Calais, Jean-Paul Sartre, Charles de Gaulle …

The audience laughs, which indicates that they sense an anomaly here. And indeed, there is an intuitive difference between such words as *table* and *sleep*, on the one hand, and *Paris* and *Sartre*, on the other. We do not usually count the latter as true vocabulary. If it were otherwise, we could call ourselves lexically fluent whenever we toured in a foreign country, and got to know its towns, streets, and shop names.

However, proper names cannot be so easily dismissed. There is a sense in which they *are* part of the learning of a language. If French speakers learn English, they have to learn to replace *Londres* by *London*, and Greeks have to replace *Joannis* by *John*. There are rules of pronunciation which have to be followed, and rules of grammar which apply to proper names in a special way (p. 208). There are names which form part of the idiomatic history of an English-speaking community, such as *Billy the Kid, The Times, William the Conqueror, The Mayflower, Phi Beta Kappa*, and *Woolworth's*. And there are names which have taken on an additional sense, such as *Fleet Street* (= 'the British press'), *The White House* (= 'the US government'), and *Fido* (= 'any dog'). A general encyclopedia contains thousands of such cases.

Nor does the use of an initial capital help much in deciding if a word should be in the lexicon. In many cases, there is uncertainty as to whether a word should be capitalized or not. Should it be *Bible* or *bible, Sun* or *sun, National Park* or *national park, Heaven* or *heaven, Communist Party* or *communist party* (or *Communist party*)? Reference books vary in their practices. Thus, *Chambers Biographical Dictionary* has people receiving the 'Nobel prize for physics', whereas the *Encyclopaedia Britannica* has them receiving the 'Nobel Prize for Physics'. There are thousands of these cases, too.

We have to conclude that English proper names are on the boundary of the lexicon. Some of them are so closely bound up with the way meaning is structured in the language that it would be difficult to exclude them from any superdictionary. They are felt to 'belong' to the language, and often have a language-specific form (e.g. *Christmas, January, the Moon, the*

Falklands). Others are felt to be independent of English – or any other language – and would seem to be more at home in an encyclopedia (e.g. *Alpha Centauri, Diplodocus, Helen Keller*). Allowing in just a proportion of the proper names, though, considerably increases the size of the lexicon.

The symbol of American commercial theatre – Broadway. The proper name has a more general meaning.

WHAT DOES WIGAN MEAN?

Listed below are a number of places which always begin with a capital letter, and would thus be considered to be proper names. In each case, though, there is something 'lexical' about them, in that they seem to have a meaning which exists over and above the reference they have to a particular location. In each case, people who know the location can ask 'What does —— mean?' and expect general agreement about the reply. By contrast, it does not make sense to ask, say, 'What does Wigan mean?' – Wigan being a town in Lancashire, England – expecting an agreed response from British people (though of course it is perfectly possible to have privately intelligible associations about Wigan – or anywhere). There is one Wigan-like intruder in the following list (see foot of facing page for answer, if required).

Black Hole (of Calcutta)
Broadway
Dartmoor
East End
Fort Knox
Greenwich Village
Hyde Park Corner
Iron Curtain
Madison Avenue
Mason-Dixon Line
Mayfair
Number 10
Pearl Harbor
Scotland Yard
Soho
Third World
West Bank (Middle East)
West End
Wrexham

TO CAP OR NOT TO CAP

(below left) Part of an entry from the 1992 edition of *The Cambridge Encyclopedia*, showing the capitalization policy. (below right) The same entry re-set in a capitalization style similar to that used in *The Chambers Biographical Dictionary*.

Howe, Sir (Richard Edward) Geoffrey (1926–) British Conservative statesman, educated at Winchester and Cambridge. He was called to the Bar in 1952 and became an MP in 1964. Knighted in 1970, he became Solicitor-General (1970–2), Minister for Trade and Consumer Affairs (1972–4), Chancellor of the Exchequer (1979–1983), and Foreign Secretary (1983–9). In 1989 he was made Deputy Prime Minister, Lord President of the Council, and Leader of the House of Commons, but resigned

Howe, Sir (Richard Edward) Geoffrey (1926–) British Conservative statesman, educated at Winchester and Cambridge. He was called to the bar in 1952 and became an MP in 1964. Knighted in 1970, he became solicitor-general (1970–2), minister for trade and consumer affairs (1972–4), Chancellor of the Exchequer (1979–1983), and foreign secretary (1983–9). In 1989 he was made deputy prime minister, lord president of the Council, and leader of the House of Commons, but resigned

HOW LARGE IS YOUR LEXICON?

There seems to be no more agreement about the size of an English speaker's vocabulary than there is about the total number of lexemes (p. 118) in the language. Much depends on a person's hobbies and educational background. Someone who reads several novels a week is obviously going to pick up a rather larger vocabulary than someone whose daily reading is restricted to the telephone directory. And a degree in a subject like chemistry or botany will result in an enormous increase in vocabulary, given that so much of the lexicon is made up of scientific terms. Averages, then, mean very little. Such figures as 10–12,000 (for someone who has just left school) and 20–25,000 (for a college graduate) are often cited in the media – but are totally lacking in research credibility.

Apart from anything else, there must always be *two* totals given when presenting the size of a person's vocabulary: one reflecting *active* vocabulary (lexemes actively used in speech or writing) and the other reflecting *passive* vocabulary (lexemes known but not used). Neither figure is easy to arrive at. It is often remarkably difficult to be sure whether one actually uses or knows a lexeme. In the sample listed below (right), do you know the lexeme *cableway*, or do you just think you know it? Are you sure you use *cab-rank* or *cabstand*, and not *taxi-rank* or *taxi stand*? It is wise to include a category of uncertain cases, when doing lexeme counts, hence the three columns of known and used vocabulary in the table.

This world-famous page from *Reader's Digest* has persuaded several generations of readers to take an interest in their vocabulary. The column has been running since 1945.

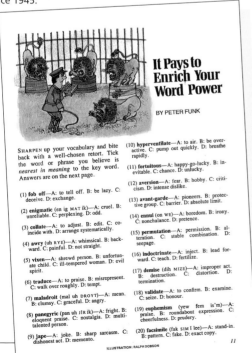

For anyone with the time and energy, it would be perfectly possible to go through a medium-sized dictionary (of *c.* 100,000 entries) and mark it up in this way. However, most people wishing to live an otherwise normal life will prefer to opt for a small sample – say, 1per cent (20 pages from a 2,000-page book, but taken from several parts of the alphabet), which gives quite a good first approximation. An office secretary, a businesswoman (and a voracious reader), and a lecturer all carried out this exercise: their active totals (respectively) were 31,500, 63,000, and 56,250; their passive totals were 38,300, 73,350, and 76,250 – an average increase of 25 per cent.

HOW MANY WORDS IN SHAKESPEARE?

'**S**hakespeare had one of the largest vocabularies of any English writer, some 30,000 words' (from the BBC television series, *The Story of English*, 1986). This is a commonly quoted figure, deriving from Marvin Spevack's multi-volume *Complete and Systematic Concordance to the Works of Shakespeare* (1968–80), which lists 29,066 different words and 884,647 words in all.

However, before we can interpret such figures, we need to ask what is meant by 'different words'. The Concordance counts different text types – for example, all instances of *goes* would be counted together, as would all instances of *going*, and all instances of *gone*. But to count these as three different words is of limited value when talking about vocabulary size in a literary context, where we are trying to develop a sense of an author's expressive breadth. An approach which counts lexemes (p.118) captures this insight more efficiently: all instances of *goes*, *going*, and *gone* would then be placed under the single heading, *GO*. But when this is done, the size of Shakespeare's lexicon takes a sudden and dramatic fall, to less than 20,000.

Part of one person's vocabulary judgments, showing three levels of decision-making.
● = items are known/used.

	KNOWN			USED		
	Well	Vaguely	Not	Often	Occasionally	Never
cablese		●				
cable stitch	●			●		
cable television	●				●	
cable vision		●				●
cableway			●			●
cabman		●				●
cabob			●			●
Caboc			●			●
cabochon (noun)			●			●
cabochon (adverb)			●			●
caboodle	●				●	
caboose		●				●
cabotage			●			●
cab-rank			●	●		
cabriole			●			●
cabriolet			●			●
cabstand	●					●

SCRABBLING FOR WORDS

Increasing your word power does not necessarily involve the learning of long words. There are 106 two-letter words listed in the official word-lists for Scrabble® published by Chambers, and 18 four-letter words using the letter Q. Few people could say what they all mean, without special preparation.

AA AD AE AH AI AM AN AR AS AT
AW AX AY BA BE BO BY CH DA DI
DO EA EE EF EH EL EM EN ER ES
EX FA FY GI GO GU HA HE HI HO

ID IF IN IO IS IT JO KA KO KY LA
LI LO MA ME MI MO MU MY NA
NE NO NU NY OB OD OE OF OH
OI OM ON OO OP OR OS OU OW
OX OY PA PI PO RE SH SI SO ST TA
TE TI TO UG UM UN UP UR US UT
WE WO XI YE YO YU ZO

AQUA QADI QATS QUAD QUAG
QUAT QUAY QUEP QUEY QUID
QUIM QUIN QUIP QUIT QUIZ QUOD
QUOP SUQS

Test Answer (see facing page): Wrexham

9 · THE SOURCES OF THE LEXICON

How is it possible to see order in the vocabulary of English, if there are a million or more lexemes to deal with (§8)? A common approach looks at origins, and asks: Where have the items in the lexicon come from?

NATIVE VOCABULARY

Many lexemes have always been there – in the sense that they arrived with the Germanic invaders, and have never fallen out of use (§1). The Anglo-Saxon lexical character continues to dominate everyday conversation, whether it be grammatical words (*in, on, be, that*), lexical words (*father, love, name*), or affixes (*mis-, un-, -ness, -less*). Although Anglo-Saxon lexemes comprise only a relatively small part of the total modern lexicon, they provide almost all the most frequently used words in the language. In the million-word Brown University corpus of written American English (p. 438), the 100 most frequently used items are almost all Anglo-Saxon. The exceptions are a few Scandinavian loans (such as *they* and *are*); there is nothing from Romance sources until items 105 (*just*) and 107 (*people*).

THE COMMON CORE

The diagram used by the first editor of the *Oxford English Dictionary*, James Murray, in the section called 'General Explanations' which preceded Volume 1 (1888): 'the English Vocabulary contains a nucleus or central mass of many thousand words whose "Anglicity" is unquestioned; some of them only literary, some of them only colloquial, the great majority at once literary and colloquial, – they are the *Common Words* of the language'. Just how common they are can be judged from this list of examples:

Parts of the body: hand, foot, arm, eye, heart, chin, bone.
Natural landscape: land, field, meadow, hedge, hill, wood, oak.
Domestic Life: house, home, stool, door, floor, weave, knit.
Calendar: sun, moon, day, month, year.
Animals: horse, cow, sheep, dog, hen, goat, swine, fish.
Common adjectives: black, white, wide, long, good, dark.
Common verbs: fly, drink, swim, help, come, see, eat, sit, send, sell, think, love, say, be, do, go, shove, kiss, have, live.

The fact that most of these words are short and concrete has often been noted as a major stylistic feature of the Anglo-Saxon lexicon. Some may be surprised that the 'four-letter words' do not figure in the list; but neither *fuck* nor *cunt* are recorded in Old English (though *shit*, *turd*, and *arse* are).

LEXICAL TWINS AND TRIPLETS

A good way of developing a feel for the Anglo-Saxon element in the lexicon is to place Old English lexemes alongside later French or Latin borrowings. Disregarding any differences of meaning, the later forms are usually more formal, careful, bookish, or polite.

Old English	French	Latin
guts	courage	
clothes	attire	
climb		ascend
sweat	perspire	
happiness		felicity
house	mansion	
wish	desire	
weariness		lassitude

There are also several 'lexical triplets', in which French and Latin forms have both joined an original Old English item. The readiness of English to acquire near-synonyms has been an important factor in the development of the stylistic versatility of the modern language.

Old English	French	Latin
rise	mount	ascend
ask	question	interrogate
fast	firm	secure
kingly	royal	regal
holy	sacred	consecrated
fire	flame	conflagration

ORWELL, *et al.*

George Orwell (1903–50) held strong views about what he perceived to be a modern trend to replace Anglo-Saxon words by classical ones. He writes in his essay *Politics and the English Language* (1946):

'Bad writers, and especially scientific, political and sociological writers, are nearly always haunted by the notion that Latin or Greek words are grander than Saxon ones, and unnecessary words like *expedite, ameliorate, predict, extraneous, deracinated, clandestine, subaqueous* and hundreds of others constantly gain ground from their Anglo-Saxon opposite numbers …

I am going to translate a passage of good English into modern English of the worst sort. Here is a well-known verse from Ecclesiastes:

I returned, and saw under the sun, that the race is not to the swift, nor the battle to the strong, neither yet bread to the wise, nor yet riches to men of understanding, nor yet favour to men of skill; but time and chance happeneth to them all.

Here it is in modern English:

Objective consideration of contemporary phenomena compels the conclusion that success or failure in competitive activities exhibits no tendency to be commensurate with innate capacity, but that a considerable element of the unpredictable must inevitably be taken into account.'

He comments: 'This is a parody, but not a very gross one …'

The English humanist John Cheke (1514–57), expressed a similarly strong opinion 'that our own tung shold be written cleane and pure, vnmixt and vnmangeled with borrowing of other tunges' (letter to Thomas Hoby, 1561). Thus, in his translation of the Bible he replaced *lunatic* by *mooned, centurion* by *hundreder, prophet* by *foresayer, crucified* by *crossed*, and *resurrection* by *gainrising*. Three hundred years later, his sentiments would be given unequivocal support in the writing of William Barnes (see facing page).

SAXONMANIA

Many writers – among them, Charles Dickens, Thomas Hardy, Gerard Manley Hopkins, and George Orwell – have enthused about the supposed 'purity' of Anglo-Saxon vocabulary, but never was this enthusiasm so strong as in the 19th century, as part of the English Romantic movement. In the case of the Dorsetshire poet, William Barnes (1801–86), the concern became an obsession.

Barnes left school at 15, then studied Classics privately, developing a fascination with philology. He opened a school, and in his 40s became a country parson. He is best known for his several books of poems written in the Dorset dialect, but his other writing includes an Anglo-Saxon primer, *An Outline of English Speech-Craft* (1878), whose title aptly reflects his story.

Barnes' aim was to promote a kind of English purified of alien (that is, non-Germanic) borrowings. In particular, the removal of French, Latin, and Greek words would, he felt, make the language more accessible and intelligible. There would

be a psychological benefit, too, as English came to reassert its identity with its Germanic origins.

What made his approach so distinctive was his creativity. Not only did he use surviving Anglo-Saxon lexemes in place of foreign ones, he did not hesitate to resuscitate long-dead Anglo-Saxonisms, or to devise completely new lexemes using Anglo-Saxon roots. Thus, he resurrected Old English *inwit* for *conscience*, and coined such forms as *birdlore* for *ornithology* and *matewording* for *synonym*. Contemporary lexicographers, however, paid him little attention. A tiny number of his coinages found their way into the *Oxford English Dictionary* (such as *speechcraft* for *grammar*, and *starlore* for *astronomy*), but the vast majority were ignored, and are now likely to be encountered only in the pages of wordbooks like this one.

So I unto my selfe alone will sing;
The woods shall to me answer, and my eccho ring.

The serenity of the refrain from Edmund Spenser's 'Epithalamion' (1595) is reflected in John Constable's painting ('The Hay Wain', 1821).

E.K., the anonymous author of an Epistle preceding Spenser's first major work, 'The Shepheardes Calander' (1579), draws attention to a critical feature of the poet's style:

'it is one special prayse, of many whych are dew to this poete, that he hath laboured to restore, as to theyr rightfull heritage, such good and naturall English words as have ben long time out of use and almost cleare disherited...'

E.K. goes on to lament what has happened to English, and is particularly scathing of those authors who in his view have

'patched up the holes with peces and rags of other languages, borrowing here of the French, there of the Italian, every where of the Latine... so now they have made our English tongue a gallimaufray or hodgepodge of al other speches.'

In this he is at one with Barnes and Orwell.

THE LEXICAL CONQUEST

A sequence from the Bayeux Tapestry, depicting the Norman invasion of England, and thus symbolizing the most significant change of direction in the history of English vocabulary. By 1400 about 10,000 new lexemes had come into the language from French, and several thousand more had entered from Latin. By the end of the Middle English period, the surviving Old English lexicon was already in the minority.

The tapestry, a linen band 231 feet long and 19.5 inches wide (70 m by 50 cm), is now displayed in the specially-designed Bayeux Tapestry Museum at the William the Conqueror Centre, Bayeux. The events are summarized in a Latin narrative. The sequence dis-

played here shows the arrival of the Normans on the English coast. The text says 'Here the horses are disembarking from the ships and here the knights have hurried off to [Hastings]'.

ANGLISH

What would have happened to the lexicon had William the Conqueror been conquered? A possible answer was given by British humorist Paul Jennings in a 1966 edition of *Punch* celebrating the 900th anniversary of the Norman Conquest. Here is the opening lines of a famous soliloquy, turned (apart from *outrageous*) into 'Anglish':

To be, or not to be: that is the ask-thing:
Is't higher-thinking in the brain to bear
The slings and arrows of outrageous dooming
Or to take weapons 'gainst a sea of bothers
And by againstwork end them?

Barnes himself created thousands of neologisms. The following dozen examples captures their flavour:

booklore literature
breaksome fragile
folkdom democracy
forewit prudence
gleeman musician
hareling leveret
hearsomeness obedience
loreless ignorant
outgate exit
soothfastness veracity
water-giver reservoir
yeartide anniversary

FOREIGN BORROWINGS

When one language takes lexemes from another, the new items are usually called *loan words* or *borrowings* – though neither term is really appropriate, as the receiving language does not give them back. English, perhaps more than any other language, is an insatiable borrower. Whereas the speakers of some languages take pains to exclude foreign words from their lexicons, English seems always to have welcomed them. Over 120 languages are on record as sources of its present-day vocabulary, and the locations of contact are found all over the world.

The borrowing began even before the Anglo-Saxons arrived (§3). There are very few Celtic loans during that period, but the influence of Latin is strong, especially after the arrival of Christianity (e.g. *bishop, church, priest, school, giant, lobster, purple, plant*). The Viking invasions alone resulted in about 2,000 Scandinavian words coming into English (e.g. *dirt, egg, kid, leg, skin, sky, window*). After the Norman Conquest, the influx of words from the continent of Europe, especially French, doubled the size of the lexicon to over 100,000 items (p. 46–7). By the end of the Renaissance, the growth in classically-derived vocabulary, especially from Latin, had doubled the size of the lexicon again. While these periods represent the peaks of borrowing activity in the history of English, there was no reduction in the underlying trend during later centuries.

Since the 1950s, a fresh wave of borrowing has been taking place, which eventually may exceed the totals encountered in the Middle English period. The emergence of English as a world language (§7) has promoted regular contact with an unprecedented number of languages and cultures, and the borrowings have shown an immediate and dramatic upturn. New fauna and flora, political groups and institutions, landscape features, industrial products, foodstuffs, inventions, leisure activities, and other forms of behaviour have all generated thousands of new lexemes – and continue to do so. The growth of local nationalism has had its effect, too, with people seeking fresh lexical ways of showing their local identity within the undifferentiated domain of international Standard English.

Of course, not all the new items will be widely intelligible. In the late 1980s, alongside *intifada, perestroika*, and *glasnost* we find *pryzhok* (Russian, 'leap'), *visagiste* (French, 'beautician'), and *zaitech* (Japanese, 'large-scale company financial speculation') – all found in English newspapers and periodicals. Several of the items in the world map are of this kind, requiring an up-to-date dictionary before one can be sure what they mean. But that is always the way of it, with loan words.

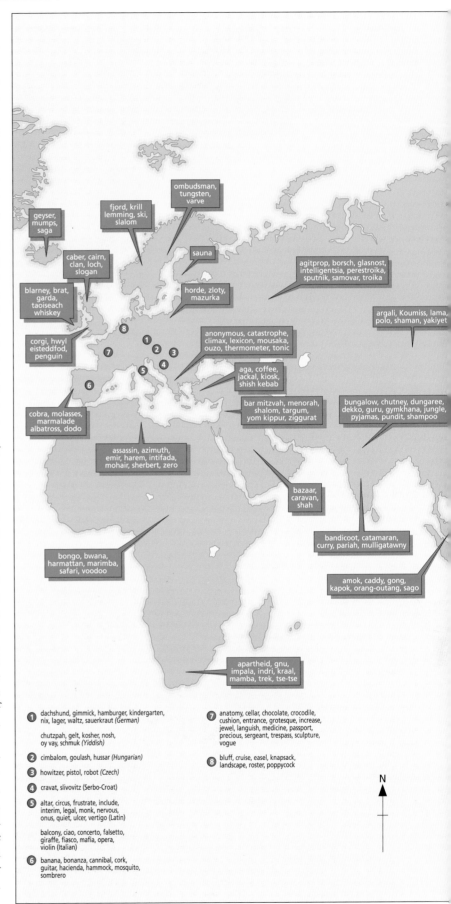

ombudsman, tungsten, varve

fjord, krill, lemming, ski, slalom

geyser, mumps, saga

caber, cairn, clan, loch, slogan

sauna

agitprop, borsch, glasnost, intelligentsia, perestroika, sputnik, samovar, troika

blarney, brat, garda, taoiseach, whiskey

horde, zloty, mazurka

argali, Koumiss, lama, polo, shaman, yakiyet

corgi, hwyl, eisteddfod, penguin

anonymous, catastrophe, climax, lexicon, mousaka, ouzo, thermometer, tonic

aga, coffee, jackal, kiosk, shish kebab

bungalow, chutney, dungaree, dekko, guru, gymkhana, jungle, pyjamas, pundit, shampoo

cobra, molasses, marmalade, albatross, dodo

bar mitzvah, menorah, shalom, targum, yom kippur, ziggurat

assassin, azimuth, emir, harem, intifada, mohair, sherbert, zero

bazaar, caravan, shah

bandicoot, catamaran, curry, pariah, mulligatawny

bongo, bwana, harmattan, marimba, safari, voodoo

amok, caddy, gong, kapok, orang-outang, sago

apartheid, gnu, impala, indri, kraal, mamba, trek, tse-tse

1 dachshund, gimmick, hamburger, kindergarten, nix, lager, waltz, sauerkraut (*German*)

chutzpah, gelt, kosher, nosh, oy vay, schmuk (*Yiddish*)

2 cimbalom, goulash, hussar (*Hungarian*)

3 howitzer, pistol, robot (*Czech*)

4 cravat, slivovitz (*Serbo-Croat*)

5 altar, circus, frustrate, include, interim, legal, monk, nervous, onus, quiet, ulcer, vertigo (*Latin*)

balcony, ciao, concerto, falsetto, giraffe, fiasco, mafia, opera, violin (*Italian*)

6 banana, bonanza, cannibal, cork, guitar, hacienda, hammock, mosquito, sombrero

7 anatomy, cellar, chocolate, crocodile, cushion, entrance, grotesque, increase, jewel, languish, medicine, passport, precious, sergeant, trespass, sculpture, vogue

8 bluff, cruise, easel, knapsack, landscape, roster, poppycock

N

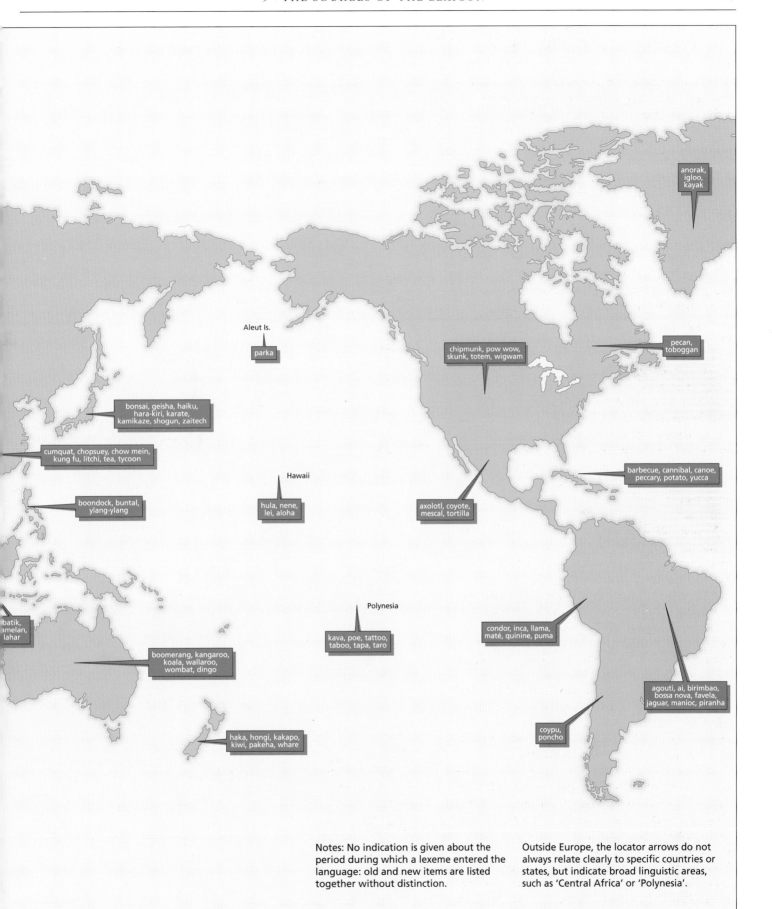

anorak, igloo, kayak

parka

Aleut Is.

chipmunk, pow wow, skunk, totem, wigwam

pecan, toboggan

bonsai, geisha, haiku, hara-kiri, karate, kamikaze, shogun, zaitech

cumquat, chopsuey, chow mein, kung fu, litchi, tea, tycoon

Hawaii

barbecue, cannibal, canoe, peccary, potato, yucca

boondock, buntal, ylang-ylang

hula, nene, lei, aloha

axolotl, coyote, mescal, tortilla

batik, gamelan, lahar

Polynesia

kava, poe, tattoo, taboo, tapa, taro

condor, inca, llama, maté, quinine, puma

boomerang, kangaroo, koala, wallaroo, wombat, dingo

agouti, ai, birimbao, bossa nova, favela, jaguar, manioc, piranha

haka, hongi, kakapo, kiwi, pakeha, whare

coypu, poncho

Notes: No indication is given about the period during which a lexeme entered the language: old and new items are listed together without distinction.

Outside Europe, the locator arrows do not always relate clearly to specific countries or states, but indicate broad linguistic areas, such as 'Central Africa' or 'Polynesia'.

LEXICAL STRUCTURE

Most English vocabulary arises by making new lexemes out of old ones – either by adding an affix to previously existing forms, altering their word class, or combining them to produce compounds. These processes of construction are of interest to grammarians as well as lexicologists, and much of what is involved in word structure will be reviewed on other pages (§14). But the importance of word-formation to the development of the lexicon is second to none, and accordingly the matter needs to be reviewed in this section also. After all, almost *any* lexeme, whether Anglo-Saxon or foreign, can be given an affix, change its word class, or help make a compound. Alongside the Anglo-Saxon root in *kingly*, for example, we have the French root in *royally* and the Latin root in *regally*. There is no elitism here. The processes of affixation, conversion, and compounding are all great levellers.

AFFIXATION

There are three possible types of affix (p.198): those which occur before the root or stem of a word (*prefixes*), those which occur after (*suffixes*), and those which occur within (*infixes*). English does not have affixes in large numbers – only about 50 common prefixes, somewhat fewer common suffixes, and no clear instances of infixes. But these limited resources are used in a complex and productive way, as older children sense when they play with such forms as *antidisestablishmentarianism*. Not all affixes have a strong creative potential, of course: the Old English *-th* ending, for example (found in *warmth*, *length*, *depth*, *width*, *sixth*, and a few other items), is hardly ever used now to create new words – though *zeroth* and *coolth* are interesting exceptions. On the other hand, there are tens of thousands of lexemes which either exist or are awaiting creation through the use of the ending *-ness*.

A SAMPLING OF SUFFIXES

-tion, -ship, -ness, -able, -ery, -ese, -ling, -like, -let, -esque, -ette, -ess, -ism, -ite, -ish

These are some of the commonly occurring English suffixes. A number of them have a meaning which is fairly easy to state: *-ess*, for example, means 'female of' (*lioness*). Some have several meanings: *-ette* can mean 'female of' (*usherette*), 'small version of' (*kitchenette*), or 'substitute for' (*leatherette*). Some have a highly abstract meaning, difficult to define precisely: one of the meanings of *-ery* is 'the quality or state of having a particular trait' (*snobbery*).

Suffixes do more than alter the meaning of the word to which they are attached. Many of them also change the word's grammatical status – for example, the *-ify* ending turns the noun *beauty* into the verb *beautify*, and the *-ing* ending turns the concrete noun *farm* into the abstract one *farming*. In this respect, suffixes differ from prefixes, which rarely cause words to change their class, and are thus best discussed under the heading of grammar. A complete list of suffixes, accordingly, is given in the section on morphology, p. 198.

AND NO INFIXES?

Many languages make great use of infixes – affixes which are placed within the stem of a word to express such notions as tense, number, or gender. English has no system of infixes, but people do from time to time coin words into which other forms have been inserted. This happens quite commonly while swearing or being emphatic, as in *absobloominglutely* and *kangabloodyroo*. In one case, someone was heard to insert an affix as well as a word: I don't like *intebloodyminillectuals*. On the whole, though, such forms as **compseudoputer* or **sarsemicastic* are not possible constructions in current English.

57 VARIETIES OF PREFIX

This list gives all the common prefixes in English – though not all the variant forms. The prefix *in-*, for example, becomes *il-* before words beginning with /l/ (as in *illiberal*). Nor does the list include scientific and technical items which are commonly used in compounds, such as *bio-*, *Euro-*, and *techno-* (see facing page).

Some prefixes appear more than once in the list because they have more than one meaning. There is a difference between *unexpected* (which means simply 'not expected') and *unwrap* (which adds the specific sense of reversing a previous action).

Negation
a- -theist, -moral
dis- -obey, -believe
in- -complete, -decisive
non- -smoker, -medical
un- -wise, -helpful

Reversal
de- -frost, -fraud

dis- -connect, -infect
un- -do, -mask

Disparaging
mal- -treat, -function
mis- -hear, -lead
pseudo- -intellectual

Size or degree
arch- -duke, -enemy
co- -habit, -pilot
hyper- -market, -card
mega- -loan, -merger
mini- -skirt, -bus
out- -class, -run
over- -worked, -flow
sub- -normal, -conscious
super- -market, -man
sur- -tax, -charge
ultra- -modern, -sound
under- -charge, -play
vice- -chair, -president

Orientation
anti- -clockwise, -social
auto- -suggestion, -biography
contra- -indicate, -flow
counter- -clockwise, -act
pro- -socialist, -consul

Location and distance
extra- -terrestrial, -mural
fore- -shore, -leg
inter- -marry, -play
intra- -venous, -national

pan- -African, -American
super- -script, -structure
tele- -scope, -phone
trans- -plant, -atlantic

Time and order
ex- -husband, -president
fore- -warn, -shadow
neo- -Gothic, -classical
paleo- -lithic, -botany
post- -war, -modern
pre- -school, -marital
proto- -type, -European
re- -cycle, -new

Number
bi- -cycle, -lingual
demi- -god, -tasse
di- -oxide, -graph
mono- -rail, -plane
multi- -racial, -purpose
poly- -technic, -gamy
semi- -circle, -detached
tri- -maran, -pod
uni- -sex, -cycle

Grammatical conversion
Verb to Adjective
a- -stride, -board
Noun to Verb
be- -friend, -witch
en- -flame, -danger

WILL IT BURN?

There are several lexemes beginning with *in-* where the prefix has a locative or intensifying meaning, such as *inflate* and *ingredient*. Because *in-* also has a negative meaning, however – as with *infrequent* and *ingratitude* – ambiguity is sometimes possible. The famous case is *inflammable*, which derives from *inflame* – that is, an inflammable object *will* burn. However, because so many people have interpreted the form to mean 'non-flame' – that is, it will *not* burn – there has been a gradual change in usage. These days, objects tend to be identified using the contrast of *flammable* vs *nonflammable* (or *inflammable* vs *noninflammable*).

CONVERSION

Lexemes can be made to change their word class without the addition of an affix – a process known as *conversion*. The items chiefly produced in this way are nouns, adjectives, and verbs – especially the verbs which come from nouns (e.g. *to bottle*) and the nouns which come from verbs (e.g. *a doubt*). Not all the senses of a lexeme are usually carried through into the derived form, however. The noun *paper* has several meanings, such as 'newspaper', 'wallpaper', and 'academic article'. The verb *to paper* relates only to the second of these. Lecturers and editors may paper their rooms, but not their audiences or readers.

THE CONVERTED

Verb to noun
a swim/hit/cheat/
   bore/show-off/
   drive-in

Adjective to noun
a bitter/natural/final/
   monthly/regular/wet

Noun to verb
to bottle/catalogue/oil/
   brake/referee/bicycle

Adjective to verb
to dirty/empty/dry/
   calm down/sober up

Noun to adjective
it's cotton/brick /
   reproduction

Grammatical word to noun
too many *ifs* and *buts*
that's a *must*
the *how* and the *why*

Affix to noun
ologies and isms

Phrase to noun
a has-been/free-for-all/
   also-ran/down-and-
   out

Grammatical word to verb
to *down* tools/to *up* and
   do it

THE ATHENS OF THE NORTH

Thus Edinburgh was once described in a travel magazine. Given this picture, most readers would notice only the architectural point being made. The alert linguist, however, would additionally note that here we have an instance of a further type of conversion – the switch from proper noun to common noun. Proper nouns do not normally allow the use of the article (p.208): we do not say **I went to an Athens* or **I saw the Athens*. But given the meaning of 'a member of the class typified by the proper noun', the conversion is indeed possible, as also seen in *He's a real Jeremiah* and *She has several Picassos*. The processes involved in this kind of conversion would be analysed under the heading of grammar.

COMPOUNDS

A compound is a unit of vocabulary which consists of more than one lexical stem. On the surface, there appear to be two (or more) lexemes present, but in fact the parts are functioning as a single item, which has its own meaning and grammar. So, *flower-pot* does not refer to a flower and a pot, but to a single object. It is pronounced as a unit, with a single main stress, and it is used grammatically as a unit – its plural, for example, is *flower-pots*, and not **flowers-pots*.

The unity of *flower-pot* is also signalled by the orthography, but this is not a foolproof criterion. If the two parts are linked by a hyphen, as here, or are printed without a space ('solid'), as in *flowerpot*, then there is no difficulty. But the form *flower pot* will also be found, and in such cases, to be sure we have a compound (and not just a sequence of two independent words), we need to look carefully at the meaning of the sequence and the way it is grammatically used. This question turns up especially in American English, which uses fewer hyphens than does British English.

Compounds are most readily classified into types based on the kind of grammatical meaning they represent. *Earthquake*, for example, can be paraphrased as 'the earth quakes', and the relation of *earth* to *quake* is that of subject to verb. Similarly, a *crybaby* is also subject + verb ('the baby cries'), despite its back-to-front appearance. *Scarecrow* is verb + object ('scares crows'). Some involve slightly trickier grammatical relations, such as *playgoer*, *windmill*, *goldfish*, and *homesick*. A list of grammatical types (including the analysis of these examples) is given in the section on syntax, p. 220.

ANGLO-COMPOUND-O-MATICS

There is an interesting formation in which one of the elements does not occur as a separate word. These forms are usually classical in origin, and are linked to the other element of the compound by a linking vowel, usually *-o-*, but sometimes *-a-* or *-i-*. They are traditionally found in the domains of science and scholarship, but in recent years some have become productive in everyday contexts too, especially in advertising and commerce.

First element

agri-   -culture, -business
bio-   -data, -technology
micro-   -chip, -electronics
Euro-   -money, -feebleness
psycho-   -logy, -analysis
techno-   -phobia, -stress

Second element

-aholic   work-, comput-
-athon   mar-, swim-, read-
-matic   coffee-, wash-o-
-rama   sports-a-, plant-o-

Such forms might well be analysed as affixes, but for the fact that their meaning is much more like that of an element in a compound. *Euromoney*, for example, means 'European money'; *biodata* means 'biological data'; *swimathon* means 'swimming marathon'.

UNUSUAL STRUCTURES

Affixation, conversion, and compounding are the three major types of word-formation (pp. 128–9); but these by no means exhaust the methods of lexical construction available in English. A complete description of these methods would have to take into account the different kinds of abbreviation (p. 120), as well as the ingenious techniques illustrated below.

BACK-FORMATIONS

It is common in English to form a new lexeme by adding a prefix or a suffix to an old one (p. 128). From *happy* we get *unhappy*; from *inspect* we get *inspector*. Every so often, however, the process works the other way round, and a shorter word is derived from a longer one by deleting an imagined affix. *Editor*, for example, looks as if it comes from *edit*, whereas in fact the noun was in the language first. Similarly, *television* gave rise to *televise*, *double-glazing* preceded *double-glaze*, and *baby-sitter* preceded *baby-sit*. Such forms are known as *back-formations*.

Each year sees a new crop of back-formations. Some are coined because they meet a real need, as when a group of speech therapists in Reading in the 1970s felt they needed a new verb to describe what they did – to *therap*. Some are playful formations, as when a tidy person is described as *couth*, *kempt*, or *shevelled*. Back-formations often attract criticism when they first appear, as happened in the late 1980s to *explete* (to use an *expletive*) and *accreditate* (from *accreditation*).

ALL GRAMS MINIMUM 20 MINUTES

This ad appeared in a London magazine in 1986 – one of the earliest published instances of the new form, from *telegram*. Gram seems to have established itself as a useful generic term for kissagrams, strippagrams, gorillagrams, and much more. It might be better now to analyse it as a type of clipping (p. 120).

REDUPLICATIVES

An interesting type of lexeme is one which contains two identical or very similar constituents: a *reduplicative*. Items with identical spoken constituents, such as *goody-goody* and *din-din*, are rare. What is normal is for a single vowel or consonant to change between the first constituent and the second, such as *see-saw* and *walkie-talkie*.

Reduplicatives are used in a variety of ways. Some simply imitate sounds: *ding-dong*, *bow-wow* (p. 250). Some suggest alternative movements: *flip-flop*, *ping-pong*. Some are disparaging: *dilly-dally*, *wishy-washy*. And some intensify meaning: *teeny-weeny*, *tip-top*. Reduplication is not a major means of creating lexemes in English, but it is perhaps the most unusual one.

BLENDS

A lexical blend, as its name suggests, takes two lexemes which overlap in form, and welds them together to make one (p. 120). Enough of each lexeme is usually retained so that the elements are recognizable. Here are some long-standing examples, and a few novelties from recent publications.

motor + hotel = motel
breakfast + lunch = brunch
helicopter + airport = heliport
smoke + fog = smog
advertisement + editorial = advertorial
Channel + Tunnel = Chunnel
Oxford + Cambridge = Oxbridge

Yale + Harvard = Yarvard
slang + language = slanguage
guess + estimate = guesstimate
square + aerial = squaerial
toys + cartoons = toytoons
breath + analyser = breathalyser
affluence + influenza = affluenza
information + commercials = infomercials
dock + condominium = dockominium

In most cases, the second element is the one which controls the meaning of the whole. So, *brunch* is a kind of lunch, not a kind of breakfast – which is why the lexeme is *brunch* and not, say, **lunkfast*. Similarly, a *toytoon* is a kind of cartoon (one which generates a series of shop toys), not a kind of toy.

Blending seems to have increased in popularity in the 1980s, being increasingly used in commercial and advertising contexts. Products are *sportsational*, *swimsational*, and *sexsational*. TV provides *dramacons*, *docufantasies*, and *rockumentaries*. The forms are felt to be eye-catching and exciting; but how many of them will still be around in a decade remains an open question.

EURO TUNNEL

PORTMANTEAUX

In *Through the Looking Glass, and What Alice Found There* (1871), Lewis Carroll has the egotistical linguistic philosopher, Humpty Dumpty, deal with the question of blends. He calls them *portmanteau words* – a term which has since achieved some currency in linguistic studies.

'You seem very clever at explaining words, Sir', said Alice. 'Would you kindly tell me the meaning of the poem called "Jabberwocky"?'

'Let's hear it,' said Humpty Dumpty. 'I can explain all the poems that ever were invented – and a good many that haven't been invented just yet.'

This sounded very hopeful, so Alice repeated the first verse:

> 'Twas brillig, and the slithy toves
> Did gyre and gimble in the wabe:
> All mimsy were the borogoves,
> And the mome raths outgrabe.

'That's enough to begin with,' Humpty Dumpty interrupted: 'there are plenty of hard words there. "*Brillig*" means four o'clock in the afternoon – the time when you begin *broiling* things for dinner.'

'That'll do very well,' said Alice: 'and "*slithy*"?'

'Well, "*slithy*" means "lithe and slimy." "Lithe" is the same as "active." You see it's like a portmanteau – there are two meanings packed up into one word.'

'I see it now,' Alice remarked thoughtfully: 'and what are "*toves*"?' . . .

'Well, "*toves*" are something like badgers – they're something like lizards – and they're something like corkscrews.'

'They must be very curious-looking creatures.'

'They are that,' said Humpty Dumpty: 'also they make their nests under sundials – also they live on cheese.'

TALKING NONSENSE

'**P**rofessor' Stanley Unwin, British stage and film comic personality, renowned in the 1960s for the fluent neologistic style of his academic opinions. The humour cannot be totally captured by writing the words down. The comic effect depends not just on his bizarre lexical creations but on the way these are uttered deadpan using a perfectly routine conversational style.

In his autobiography, *Deep Joy* (1984), someone describes him as 'The gentleman who gets his words all intertwingled' – an accurate enough summary of anyone who speaks like this:

(*On addressing the United Nations*) O joyful peoplodes! Quick vizzy intercapitoles, round table and freedom talkit with genuine friendly eyebold gleam…

(*On boxing*) Oh the self destructibold of the human beale, while we dig in the pokky for a ringside seal towards his fateful and cheer for a bashy-ho. Tutty tutty.

NONSENSE WORDS

Supercalifragilisticexpialidocious

Not all coinages have to mean something before they can achieve currency – as this example from the Walt Disney film *Mary Poppins* illustrates. Sung by Julie Andrews in the title role, it is probably the most famous nonsense word of the century. However, it is by no means the longest nonsense word to appear in a book or script. That accolade probably belongs to James Joyce, one of whose 100-letter blends is given below. It is one of ten linguistic thunderclaps in *Finnegans Wake*, symbolizing the great fall of Tim Finnegan from his ladder (p. 134). Humpty Dumpty is part of it.

Bothallchoractorschumminaroundgansumuminarumdrumstrumtruminahumptadumpwaultopoofoolooderamaunsturnup!

FAMILIARITY MARKERS

Sometimes an abbreviation and an affix combine, producing a lexeme which is highly informal in tone, and often used as part of the slang of a close-knit social group. The most important affixes which work in this way are *-y*, *-o*, *-er*, and *-s*.

-y/-ie telly, baddy, goalie, auntie, daddy, Julie, Billy (and many other familiar forms of first names)

-o ammo, aggro (British English, 'aggravation'), arvo (Australian English, 'afternoon'), weirdo

-er footer ('football'), fresher ('freshman'), boner ('blunder'), rugger (all chiefly found in British English)

-s Moms, Debs, Gramps, bananas ('mad')

-eroo crackeroo, sockeroo (Australian English, as in *It disappeared right up the crackeroo*)

The affixes themselves may combine, to produce such forms as *fatso*, *tootsies*, *the willies*, *starkers* ('stark naked'), and *preggers* ('pregnant'). The forms in *-ers* are especially associated with English upper-class slang of the period between the two World Wars: *Pass the champers to Momsie, Daffers old sport* (rough translation: 'Pass the champagne to Mother, Daphne dear').

LEXICAL CREATION

Anglo-Saxon forms, borrowings, and the use of affixes account for most of what appears within the English lexicon, but they do not tell the whole story. People do some creative, even bizarre things with vocabulary, from time to time, and a fascinating topic in lexicology is to examine just what they get up to. The general term for a newly-created lexeme is a *coinage*; but in technical usage a distinction can be drawn between *nonce words* and *neologisms*.

A nonce word (from the 16th-century phrase *for the nonce*, meaning 'for the once') is a lexeme created for temporary use, to solve an immediate problem of communication. Someone attempting to describe the excess water on a road after a storm was heard to call it a *fluddle* – she meant something bigger than a puddle but smaller than a flood. The newborn lexeme was forgotten (except by a passing linguist) almost as soon as it was spoken. It was obvious from the jocularly apologetic way in which the person spoke that she did not consider *fluddle* to be a 'proper' word at all. There was no intention to propose it for inclusion in a dictionary. As far as she was concerned, it was simply that there seemed to be no word in the language for what she wanted to say, so she made one up, for the nonce. In everyday conversation, people create nonce-words like this all the time.

But there is never any way of predicting the future, with language. Who knows, perhaps the English-speaking world has been waiting decades for someone to coin just this lexeme. It would only take a newspaper to seize on it, or for it to be referred to in an encyclopedia, and within days (or months) it could be on everyone's lips. Registers of new words would start referring to it, and within five years or so it would have gathered enough written citations for it to be a serious candidate for inclusion in all the major dictionaries. It would then have become a neologism – literally, a 'new word' in the language.

A neologism stays new until people start to use it without thinking, or alternatively until it falls out of fashion, and they stop using it altogether. But there is never any way of telling which neologisms will stay and which will go. *Blurb*, coined in 1907 by the American humorist Gelett Burgess (1866–1951), proved to meet a need, and is an established lexeme now. On the other hand, his coinage of *gubble*, 'to indulge in meaningless conversation', never caught on. Lexical history contains thousands of such cases. In the 16th century – a great age of neologisms (p. 60) – we find *disaccustom* and *disacquaint* alongside *disabuse* and *disagree*. Why did the first two neologisms disappear and the last two survive? We also find *effectual, effectuous, effectful, effectuating*, and *effective*. Why did only two of the five forms survive, and why those two, in particular? The lexicon is full of such mysteries.

F IS FOR FLUDDLE

Now that you have been introduced to *fluddle*, will you start using it? Is it truly useful? Or is it just a little too marginal, or jocular, for your taste? Five years after the first appearance of this book, we should know.

THINGUMMYBOB AND WHATSISNAME

It is by no means clear how we should spell most of the items in the following list – and accordingly they tend to be omitted from dictionaries, whose focus is generally on the written language. They are nonetheless an important element in the English lexicon, providing speakers with a signal that they are unable to retrieve a lexeme – either because it has slipped their mind, or perhaps because there is a lexical gap in the language. Such nonsense words occur in many variant forms and pronunciations, just some of which are recorded here.

deeleebob
deeleebobber
diddleebob
diddleydo
diddleything
diddleythingy
dingus
dingdong
dingy
dooda
doodad
doohickey
gadget
geega
gewgaw
gimmick
gizmo
goodie
hootenanny
lookit
oojamaflop
thingamabob
thingamabobbit
thingamajig
thingummy

thingummybob
thingy
thingybob
whatchacallem
whatchacalit
whatchamacallit
whatever
whatsisname
whatsit
whatsits
whatnot
whosis
whosit
whosits
widget

In addition, those with sharp ears (for such forms are often said very rapidly) will hear many idiosyncratic items – such as *gobsocket*, *jiminycricket*, and this splendid blend (from a professor of linguistics, no less) *thingummycallit*.

BAGONIZING

However many words there are in English (p.119), the total will be small compared with those which do not yet exist. Native speakers, however, seem to have a mania for trying to fill lexical gaps. If a word does not exist to express a concept, there is no shortage of people very ready to invent one. Following a ten-minute programme about neologisms on BBC Radio 4 in 1990, over 1,000 proposals were sent in for new English lexemes. Here are a dozen of the more ingenious creations.

aginda a pre-conference drink
circumtreeviation the tendency of a dog on a leash to want to walk past poles and trees on the opposite side to its owner
blinksync the guarantee that, in any group photo, there will always be at least one person whose eyes are closed
fagony a smoker's cough
footbrawl physical violence associated with the game of soccer
litterate said of people who care about litter
illitterate said of people who do not care about litter
catfrontation the cause of nightly noise when you live in a neighbourhood full of cats
polygrouch someone who complains about everything
kellogulation what happens to your breakfast cereal when you are called away by a 15-minute phone call, just after you have poured milk on it
potspot that part of the toilet seat which causes the phone to ring the moment you sit on it
hicgap the time that elapses between when hiccups go away and when you suddenly realise that they have

– and, of course

leximania a compulsive desire to invent new words

Bagonize: to wait anxiously for your suitcase to appear on the baggage carousel (coined by Neil McNicholas).

THE GREAT ENCYCLOPEDIATHON

Reliable comparative statistics are not yet available, but there does seem to have been a trend towards the increased use of affixes as a means of word-formation in English in the last decade or so. The trend looks set to continue.

The picture shows a sponsored reading aloud of the whole of *The Cambridge Encyclopedia* in ten hours by a team of over 300 people at the Ucheldre Centre in Holyhead, N Wales in August 1992. The organizers might have called it *Encyclopedia-aid*, but they chose *Encyclopediathon*. By the time the occasion was over, several other novelty lexemes had been coined, including:

encyclopedialicious
encyclopediaboom
encyclopediarama
encyclopediaspeak
encyclopediarism.

It was an honest occasion, in aid of charity, and so fortunately there was no *encyclopediagate*.

LOADSALEXEMES

Loadsamoney, an informal label for someone who flaunts wealth, first came to notice in the mid-1980s as the name of a character invented by British alternative comedian Harry Enfield. It caught on, and was given a boost in May 1988, when Labour Party leader Neil Kinnock used it to label the Conservative government's policy of encouraging the creation of wealth for its own sake. Journalists began referring to a *loadsamoney mentality* and the *loadsamoney economy*, and gradually the prefix began to take on a life of its own. Later that year we find in various newspapers *loadsasermons, loadsaglasnost, loadsaspace,* and *loadsapeople*.

Several affixes seem to have found new life in the 1980s. *Mega-*, for example, was used with dozens of forms, such as *-trendy, -sulk, -worry, -terror, -plan, -bid, -brand,* and *-city*. The suffixing use of *-friendly* was found not only with *user-* (its original usage), but also with *audience-, customer-, environment-, farmer-, girl-, nature-,* and many more. *Sexism* brought a host of other *-isms*, such as *weightism, heightism,* and *ageism*. *Rambo*-based coinages included *Ramboesque* and *Ramboistic*. *Band-aid* gave birth to *Sport-aid* and *Nurse-aid*. And the Watergate affair of the mid-1970s lived on linguistically, *-gate* continuing to attach itself to almost any proper noun where there may be a hint of wicked goings-on, as in *Irangate, Lloydsgate,* and the remarkable *Gospelgate* (for the wrongdoings of US televangelists).

LITERARY NEOLOGIZING

The more creative the language context, the more likely we are to encounter lexical experiments, and find ourselves faced with unusual neologisms. The stretching and breaking of the rules governing lexical structure, for whatever reason, is characteristic of several contexts, notably humour (p. 408), theology (p. 403), and informal conversation (p. 400), but the most complex, intriguing, and exciting instances come from the language of literature.

These pages illustrate the range of neologisms used by several modern authors, with pride of place given to the chief oneiroparonomastician (or 'dream-pun-namer' – the term is Anthony Burgess's), James Joyce. Joyce himself called *Finnegans Wake* 'the last word in stolentelling', a remark which seems to recognize that the extraordinary lexical coinages in his novel have their roots in perfectly everyday language. Certainly, it is our grass-roots linguistic awareness which enables us to disentangle some of the layers of meaning in a Joycean neologism. However, untutored native intuition will not sort everything out, as considerable use is also made of elements from foreign languages and a wide range of classical allusions.

The style largely depends on the mechanisms involved in the simple pun (p. 408), but whereas puns generally rely for their effect on a single play on words, it is usual for Joyce's forms to involve several layers of meaning, forming a complex network of allusions which relate to the characters, events, and themes of the book as a whole. There is also a similarity to the 'portmanteau' words of Lewis Carroll (p. 131), though Carroll never tried to pack as much meaning into a portmanteau as Joyce routinely did.

JOYCEAN JABBERWOCKY

In *Joysprick* (1973), Anthony Burgess presents an illuminating analysis of the linguistic processes involved in the development of what he calls Joyce's 'jabberwocky'. These successive drafts (a-c) of *Finnegans Wake*, published in the 1920s, show that the style is carefully engineered, despite its apparent randomness and spontaneity. Each version introduces extra connotations, puns, and allusions, and a growing intricacy of lexical structure. The version which appears in the book (d) is included for comparison.

(a) Tell me, tell me, how could she cam through all her fellows, the daredevil? Linking one and knocking the next and polling in and petering out and clyding by in the eastway. Who was the first that ever burst? Some one it was, whoever you are. Tinker, tailor, soldier, sailor, Paul Pry or polish man. That's the thing I always want to know.

(b) Tell me, tell me, how could she cam through all her fellows, the neckar she was, the diveline? Linking one and knocking the next, tapping a flank and tipping a jutty and palling in and petering out and clyding by on her eastway. Wai-whou was the first that ever burst? Someone he was, whoever they were, in a tactic attack or in single combat. Tinker, tailor, soldier, sailor, Paul Pry or polishman. That's the thing I always want to know.

(c) Tell me, tell me, how cam she camlin through all her fellows, the neckar she was, the diveline? Linking one and knocking the next, tapting a flank and tipting a jutty and palling in and pietaring out and clyding by on her eastway. Waiwhou was the first thurever burst? Someone he was, whuebra they were, in a tactic attack or in single combat. Tinker, tilar, souldrer, salor, Pieman Peace or Polistamann. That's the thing I always want to know.

(d) Tell me, tell me, how cam she camlin through all her fellows, the neckar she was, the diveline? Casting her perils before our swains from Fonte-in-Monte to Tidingtown and from Tidingtown tilhavet. Linking one and knocking the next, tapting a flank and tipting a jutty and palling in and pietaring out and clyding by on her eastway. Waiwhou was the first thurever burst? Someone he was, whuebra they were, in a tactic attack or in single combat. Tinker, tilar, souldrer, salor, Pieman Peace or Polistaman. That's the thing I'm elways on edge to esk.

James Joyce (1882–1941)

ECHECHOHOES OF JOYCE

A good way of developing an understanding of how Joyce's neologisms work is to try to imitate them, or parody them.

Burgess suggests a game to fill long winter evenings. In response to an instruction to 'punbaptise the names of the months from the viewpoint of a confirmed drunkard', he gives us:

Ginyouvery
Pubyoumerry
Parch
Grapeswill
Tray
Juinp
Droolie
Sawdust
Siptumbler
Actsober
Newwinebar
Descendbeer

And a rather more complex example:

Construct a sentence in Joycean oneiroglot, with at least five long subordinate clauses and three or four parentheses. The subject shall be the origin of the legend of Martin Luther's six toes on the left foot. Present Luther as both a bird and a musical instrument.

To bigsing mitt (and there are some of sinminstral hexacordiality who have cheeped Nine! Nine! to so supernumerapodical a valgar halluxination of their Herro) it was harpbuzzing tags when, achording to Fussboden and Sexfanger, the gamut and spinet of it was (A! O! says Rholy with his Alfa Romega) that funf went into sox and Queen Kway was half dousin to her sixther, so that our truetone orchestinian luter (may his bother martins swallow rondines and roundels of chelidons and their oves be eaved on the belfriars) deptargmined not to be housesmartined by his frival sinxters (Ping! wint the strongs of the eadg be guitarnberg), put hexes on his hocks and said sex is funf, which is why he aspiered to a dietty of worms and married anon (Moineau! Consparrocy!) after he had strummed his naughntytoo frets on the door (fish can nosh tenders) and was eggscomeinacrated.

Neologistic compounds

Joycean lexicoining is but one of the several techniques described in earlier pages available to any author who wishes to neologize. For example, there may be a novel use of affixes:

> Altarwise by owl-light in the half-way house
> The gentleman lay graveward with his furies;
> (Dylan Thomas, 'Altarwise by Owl-light', 1935–6)

or an unusual word-class conversion:

> we slipped thro' the frenchwindows
> and arminarmed across the lawn
> (Roger McGough, 'The Fish', 1967)

But innovative compounds are particularly widespread, and deserve special space.

The staid set of compound lexemes illustrated on p. 129 does not even begin to capture the exuberant inventiveness which can be seen in English literature from its earliest days. Old English was dominated by its creative compounding (p. 23), as seen in such forms as *hronrad* 'sea' (literally, 'whale-road'), and, much later, Shakespeare made considerable use of neologistic compounds: *pity-pleading eyes* and *oak-cleaving thunderbolts*. Sometimes several items are joined in a compound-like way:

> a base, proud, shallow, beggerly, three-suited-hundred-pound, filthy woosted-stocking knave, a Lilly-livered, action-taking, whoreson, glasse-gazing super-seruiceable finicall Rogue   (*King Lear*, II.ii.15)

It is not a great remove from here to the Joycean juxtapositions of *Ulysses*, 1922:

> a broadshouldered deepchested stronglimbed frankeyed redhaired freely freckled shaggy-bearded widemouthed largenosed longheaded deepvoiced barekneed brawnyhanded hairy-legged ruddyfaced sinewyarmed hero.

or to the lexical creations of Gerard Manley Hopkins, mixing hyphenated and solid forms:

> This darksome burn, horseback brown,
> His rollrock highroad roaring down . . .
> A windpuff-bonnet of fawn-froth
> Turns and twindles over the broth . . .
> ('Inversnaid', 1881)

Of course, simply to print a series of words without spaces between them is hardly to create a compound, except at a most superficial level. A real compound acts as a grammatical unit, has a unified stress pattern, and has a meaning which is in some way different from the sum of its parts (p. 129). Many literary compounds do none of this, and have a solely graphic appeal, as in this later line from Roger McGough's poem:

> then you tookoff your other glove

There is perhaps a phonetic implication in such forms, suggestive of a difference in rhythm or speed of utterance when read aloud; but there is no grammatical or semantic change involved. A different kind of point is being made: to break graphic convention for its own sake reinforces the iconoclastic, irreverent tone with which the Liverpool Poets of the 1960s came to be identified.

THE ICINGBUS

the littleman
with the hunchbackedback
creptto his feet
to offer his seat
to the blindlady

people gettingoff
steered carefully around
the black mound
of his back
as they would a pregnantbelly

the littleman
completely unaware
of the embarrassment behind
watched as the blindlady
fingered out her fare

*   *   *

muchlove later he suggested
that instead
ofa wedding-cake they shouldhave a miniaturebus
made outof icing but she laughed
andsaid that buses werefor travelling in
and notfor eating and besides
you cant taste shapes.   (Roger McGough, 1967)

A painting of the Liverpool Poets, 1985, by Peter Edwards: (from left to right) Adrian Henry (1932–), Roger McGough (1937–), and Brian Patten (1946–).

ORWELLIAN COMPOUNDSPEAK

times 3.12.83 reporting bb dayorder doubleplusgood refs unpersons rewrite fullwise upsub antefiling

This Newspeak message, sent for re-editing to Winston Smith, in George Orwell's *Nineteen Eighty-Four*, is given the following Oldspeak (standard English) translation:

The reporting of Big Brother's Order for the Day in The Times of December 3rd 1983 is extremely unsatisfactory and makes references to non-existent persons. Rewrite it in full and submit your draft to higher authority before filing.

Newspeak uses three kinds of word: the 'A vocabulary' consists of everyday items; the 'B vocabulary' is ideological; and the 'C vocabulary' contains technical terms. The B vocabulary comprises only compound words. Orwell describes it as 'a sort of verbal shorthand, often packing whole ranges of ideas into a few syllables'. Its aim is 'to impose a desirable mental attitude upon the person using them'. Examples include:

doublethink, goodthink, oldthink, crimethink, oldspeak, speakwrite, thoughtcrime, sexcrime, prolefeed, dayorder, blackwhite, duckspeak.

These forms could be inflected in the usual way. For example, *goodthink* ('orthodoxy' in Oldspeak), could generate *goodthinking, goodthinkful, goodthinkwise, goodthinker,* and *goodthinked*

(there are no irregular forms in Newspeak). Other terms in Newspeak are not so much compounds as blends, involving fragments of either or both of the constituent lexemes (p. 130):

Pornsec ('Pornography Section'), *Ficdep* ('Fiction Department'), *Recdep* ('Records Department'), *thinkpol* ('Thought Police').

The novel gives the impression that there are hundreds of such forms. Indeed, one of the characters (Syme) is engaged in the enormous task of compiling the Eleventh Edition of the Newspeak Dictionary. In fact, there are only a few dozen Newspeak terms mentioned in the novel and its Appendix, though several of them are used repeatedly.

10 · ETYMOLOGY

Etymology is the study of lexical history. It investigates the origins of individual lexemes (p.118), the affinities they have had to each other, and how they have changed in meaning and in form to reach their present state. The subject exercises a remarkable popular fascination. People readily ask where a word comes from, and are prepared to speculate at length about its origins. Why is the drink *punch* so-called? How could *silly* once have meant 'blessed', or *sly* have meant 'wise', or *treacle* have meant 'wild animal'? There is also an inevitable curiosity when it is known that two apparently unrelated words have the same origins. How can it be that *glamour* and *grammar* were once the same word, or *salary* and *sausage*? Etymology has important links with questions of folklore: why, for example, is it the stork which brings babies? And the continuing popularity of books on 'Naming your Child' suggests the decision-making role that the subject can play. People, in short, like to know where words come from, whether they be personal names, place names, common nouns, idioms, abbreviations, proverbs, or any other recognized lexical domain. In this book, there need be no apology for a section on etymology.

Arguing etymologically

During a discussion, reference to a word's earlier meaning can often influence the way an argument proceeds. In a recent debate on the way history should be taught in schools – whether the focus should be on 'facts' or 'methods' – a supporter of the latter position referred to the 'real' meaning of *history* as 'investigation' or 'learning by enquiry', as this was what was meant by Greek *historia*, from which the modern term derives. Several people were swayed by the point, and referred to it throughout the debate. When Sigmund Freud was investigating hysteria, he encountered resistance from his colleagues, who argued that, because the term *hysteria* derived from the Greek word for 'womb', the concept of male hysteria was a contradiction in terms.

Both these cases illustrate what has been called the *etymological fallacy* – the view that an earlier meaning of a lexeme, or its original meaning, is its 'true' or 'correct' one. The fallacy is evident when it is realised that most common lexemes have experienced several changes in meaning during their history. *Nice*, for example, earlier meant 'fastidious', and before that 'foolish' or 'simple', and if we trace it back to the equivalent Latin form, *nescius*, the meaning is 'ignorant' (from *ne* 'not' + *scire* 'know'). Should we therefore say that the true meaning of *nice* is 'fastidious', 'foolish', or 'ignorant'? The 'original' meaning of the lexeme is, of course, unknowable: *sci-* derives from a root probably

ETYMOLOGICAL ANSWERS

• *punch* Despite a widely held view to the contrary, the name of the drink has nothing to do with the effect that the mixture can have on the drinker. The recipe originated in India, and the name comes from the Hindi word for 'five', because there were five ingredients involved (spirit, water, lemon-juice, sugar, and spice).

• *sly* The word came into Middle English from Scandinavian, where the dominant meaning was 'cunning', with its implication of special knowledge or wisdom. *Sly* is also related to *sleight* 'dexterity' and *slay* (originally, 'dexterous with the hammer').

• *salary* and *sausage* *Salary* came into English via French from Latin, where *salarium* meant 'salt-money' (given to the soldiers to buy salt). *Sausage* also came via French from Latin, where *salsicium* was something made from salted meat. Salt is the common element, seen also in *sauce* and *salad*.

• *grammar* and *glamour* *Grammar* is the older form, recorded since the early 14th century, coming into English via Old French and Latin, and ultimately from Greek, where *grammata* meant 'letters'. To the illiterate, *grammar* quickly came to be identified with the mysterious domain of the scholar, and thus developed the sense of 'learning' (in general), and then of 'the incomprehensible', and even of 'black magic'. Much later, in 18th-century Scottish English, a form appears which is spelled with an *l* (a common sound

change, p. 245), and which retains its magical sense. Robert Burns links the two words, referring to gypsies who 'deal in glamour' and those who are 'deep-read in hell's black grammar' (1781). Soon after, *glamour* developed the sense of 'enchantment' or 'charm', and by the mid-19th century we find its current sense of 'alluring charm' – an association which for most people (though not for this author) is missing from the modern term, *grammar*.

• *treacle* The term was formerly used for a medicinal compound widely used as an antidote against poisoning. It came into Middle English as *triacle* from French, and ultimately via Latin from Greek, where *theriake* had the meaning of 'antidote against the bite of a wild beast'. *Theriake*, in turn, is derived from *therion*, a diminutive form of *ther*, the word for 'wild animal'. The modern substance was called *treacle* in the UK (US molasses) because of its similar appearance to the original medicinal compound.

• *storks and babies* In Middle High German, the related term *Storch* had the basic meaning of 'stick', specifically referring to such objects as a fishing rod, a tree stump, and – in a 15th-century Austrian medical treatise – the male appendage (*des Mannes Storch*). Once the bird was nicknamed 'a stick', it would not have taken long for the *double entendre* to have generated the now familiar piece of folklore. (After W. Lockwood, 1976.)

The history of *silly*, showing the way pejorative senses have developed since the 17th century. (After G. Hughes, 1988.)

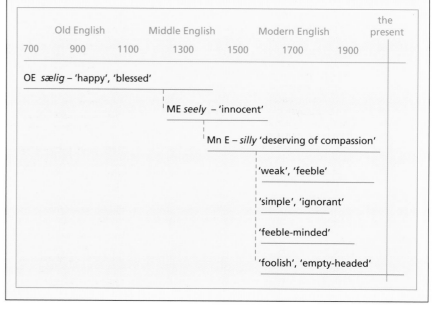

meaning 'cut' in Indo-European; but no one has any idea of what meanings existed before that.

The sense of a modern lexeme depends on the way it is used now, and not on its semantic antecedents, which are often multiple and obscure. To argue etymologically is to impale oneself on the horns of several dilemmas. Fascinating as etymologies are, in debate they can only be a rhetorical cheat.

Semantic fields

Etymology has traditionally focused on the study of individual lexemes, tracing their earlier forms (*etymons*). Often, as in the case of *grammar* and *glamour*, pairs of related forms (*doublets*) would be investigated. Contemporary etymological studies tend to adopt a broader perspective, looking at the relationships between whole sets of lexemes belonging to a particular area of meaning, or *semantic field* (p. 154). Examples of two such fields are illustrated here, showing the periods during which relevant lexemes entered the language. Neither example is complete in its lexical coverage, but it is nonetheless possible to see broad trends in the way each field has developed. There is also a certain intrinsic interest in seeing groups of lexemes set out in this way.

A HISTORICAL MENU

The evolution of terms for food and drink is an interesting reflection of the history of cultural contact between English-speaking countries and the rest of the world. (After G. Hughes, 1988.)

	Food	**Drink**
	tacos, quiche, schwarma	
	pizza, osso bucco	
1900	paella, tuna, goulash	
	hamburger, mousse, borscht	Coca Cola
	grapefruit, éclair, chips	soda water
	bouillabaisse, mayonnaise	
	ravioli, crêpes, consommé	riesling
1800	spaghetti, soufflé, bechamel	tequila
	ice cream	
	kipper, chowder	
	sandwich, jam	seltzer
	meringue, hors d'oeuvre	whisky
	welsh rabbit	
1700	avocado, paté	gin
	muffin	port
	vanilla, mincemeat, pasta	champagne
	salmagundi	brandy
	yoghurt, kedgeree	sherbet
1600	omelette, litchi, tomato, curry	tea, sherry
	chocolate	
	banana, macaroni, caviar, pilav	coffee
	anchovy, maize	
	potato, turkey	
	artichoke, scone	sillabub
1500	marchpane (marzipan)	
	whiting, offal, melon	
	pineapple, mushroom	
	salmon, partridge	
Middle	venison, pheasant	muscatel
English	crisp, cream, bacon	rhenish
	biscuit, oyster	(rhine wine)
	toast, pastry, jelly	claret
	ham, veal, mustard	
	beef, mutton, brawn	
	sauce, potage	
	broth, herring	
	meat, cheese	ale
Old	cucumber, mussel	beer
English	butter, fish	wine
	bread	water

ECONOMIC HISTORY

This presentation of the semantic field of economic terms distinguishes two types of lexeme. The first column lists items which have always carried an economic sense, such as *tax* and *cheque*. The second column lists items where an economic sense has been added to a general term, as with *loan* and *cheap* (in these cases, the date given is that of the emergence of the economic meaning).

The development of the field shows an interesting shift in the growth of the two categories. Until about 1400, the vocabulary largely belongs to the first column. From about 1550 to 1700 the growth is mainly in the second column, indicating a major increase in items which have developed a specialized economic meaning.

It is interesting to observe that the vocabulary of the economy in recent times is rather different from that associated with science and technology, where neologisms (p. 132) predominate. Rather than invent new terms, we seem for the most part to have adapted familiar ones to talk about the economy, perhaps reflecting the increasingly central role which monetary matters play in our lives. There is, certainly, an immediate meaningfulness and accessibility about such terms as *inflation*, *demand*, and *consumption*, deriving from their established general uses, which would be missing if these notions had been expressed neologistically. (After G. Hughes, 1988.)

	Original economic sense	Date of earliest specialized economic sense
900	fee, buy	
950	yield, rich	
1000	fellow, guild	
1050		
1100		
1150		
1200	tally, tithe	
1250		pay, wealth
1300	account, control, thrift usury, debt, exchequer	sell, price, rent
1350	money, bargain, salary tax, exchange	wage, customs
1400	broker, magnate redeem, mercenary expense, levy	company, save, bill
1450	staple, commodity revenue	loan, charge
1500	farm, excise, duty	bribe, market, cheap
1550	monopoly, trade mark	bank, chattel, interest (usury), purchase (n.), trade, traffic, credit, finance, goodwill, dues
1600	capitalist, cash, tariff commerce, pre-emption	embezzle, fortune, profit, dividend, share, income invest, corporation, industry
1650	jobber	concession, workhouse, factory
1700	cheque	consumption, demand, economy, fund, note, stock interest, bull, bear, luxury, security, concern
1750	capitalist scab	budget, business, currency, draft stock exchange
1800	exploitation trade union	exploit, speculate/or, firm, strike crash, depression
1850	entrepreneur	inflation, blackleg, limited (liability), nationalization
1900	boom (n.), devaluation	cartel, dole, welfare, slump (n.), recession
1950	reschedule	

SEMANTIC CHANGE

Everyone knows that words can change their meaning. We do not need to have taken a course in semantics to hold a view about what has happened to *gay* since the 1960s. Some strongly disapprove of the new meaning which this lexeme has developed; some welcome it; but all native speakers of English recognize that there has been a change, and are able to talk about it. Semantic change is a fact of life. And those who have had to study older works of literature, such as a Shakespeare play, will need no reminding of how much of the vocabulary has been affected by such changes.

Linguists have distinguished several kinds of semantic change. Four particularly important categories are given below (for other types and examples, see the sections on euphemism (p. 172), cliché (p. 186), and figurative language (p. 421), and the various dimensions of 'political correctness' discussed on p. 177).

• *Extension* or *generalization*. A lexeme widens its meaning. Numerous examples of this process have occurred in the religious field, where *office*, *doctrine*, *novice*, and many other terms have taken on a more general, secular range of meanings.

• *Narrowing* or *specialization*. A lexeme becomes more specialized in meaning. *Engine* was formerly used in a general sense of 'mechanical contrivance' (especially of war and torture), but since the Industrial Revolution it has come to mean 'mechanical source of power'. Several of the terms of economics (p. 137) also show specialization.

• *Amelioration* A lexeme develops a positive sense of approval. *Revolutionary*, once associated in the capitalist mind with an undesirable overthrowing of the status quo, is now widely used by advertisers as a signal of desirable novelty. *Lean* no longer brings to mind emaciation but athleticism and good looks.

• *Pejoration* or *deterioration*. A lexeme develops a negative sense of disapproval. Middle English *villein* neutrally described a serf, whereas Modern English *villain* is by no means neutral. Similarly, *junta* has acquired a sinister, dictatorial sense, and *lewd* (originally, 'of the laity') has developed a sense of sexual impropriety.

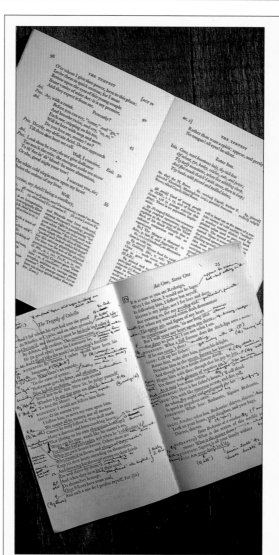

EVIDENCE

The lower example is from a student's notes on *Othello* and graphically illustrates the linguistic distance which exists between Shakespeare's vocabulary and that of the 20th century. Some of the notes are to do with bibliographical matters (the Qs and F refer to alternative readings in the various printings of the text), but several identify important points of semantic change (e.g. *peculiar* 'particular', *timorous* 'terrifying').

The upper example makes the same point, but rather more neatly. It is from the Arden Shakespeare edition of *The Tempest*, edited by Frank Kermode.

COWBOY

This is an interesting example of how a lexeme can have its meaning deteriorate in several directions at once. *Cowboy* originally developed quite positive connotations, with its romantic associations of the Wild West. To these have now been added a number of distinctly negative overtones in certain regional varieties.
• In British English, it can mean an incompetent or irresponsible workman or business: *cowboy plumbers, cowboy double-glazing firm.*
• In Northern Ireland, it can mean a member of a sectarian gang.
• In American English, it can mean an automobile driver who does not follow the rules of the road or a factory worker who does more than the piece-work norms set by his union or fellow-workers.

FOR BETTER OR WORSE?

Whether you view the 'homosexual' meaning of *gay* as a semantic change for the better (amelioration) or worse (deterioration) depends on factors that are more to do with personal taste and morality than with language. Because of this, lexical change can often be controversial.

Shop names frequently extend lexical meaning in controversial ways. *Salon*, once a term belonging to the French aristocratic social scene, may now be found in all kinds of contexts which have nothing at all to do with the aristocracy or elegant social interaction,

such as cosmetics, hairdressing, and what in inner-city side-streets is euphemistically referred to as 'relaxation'. *Parlour*, formerly a part of a monastery or convent used for conversation, has developed a similar range of street meanings. People who would never dream of entering a *relaxation parlour*

would see in this term a prime example of lexical deterioration – but those leaving such a parlour probably would not. The purr-words (p. 171) of the property developer and commercial advertiser repeatedly provoke contradictory reactions in this way.

FOLK ETYMOLOGY

When people hear a foreign or unfamiliar word for the first time, they try to make sense of it by relating it to words they know well. They guess what it must mean – and often guess wrongly. However, if enough people make the same wrong guess, the error can become part of the language. Such erroneous forms are called *folk* or *popular etymologies*.

Bridegroom provides a good example. What has a groom got to do with getting married? Is he going to 'groom' the bride, in some way? Or perhaps he is responsible for horses to carry him and his bride off into the sunset? The true explanation is more prosaic. The Middle English form was *bridgome*, which goes back to Old English *brydguma*, from 'bride' + *guma* 'man'. However, *gome* died out during the Middle English period. By the 16th century its meaning was no longer apparent, and it came to be popularly replaced by a similar-sounding word, *grome*, 'serving lad'. This later developed the sense of 'servant having the care of horses', which is the dominant sense today. But *bridegroom* never meant anything more than 'bride's man'.

Here are a few other folk etymologies:

• *sparrow-grass* A popular name for *asparagus* – though this vegetable has nothing to do with sparrows.

• *cockroach* The name came from Spanish *cucuracha*, the first part of which must have been particularly obscure to English ears. There is no connection with *cock*.

• *helpmate* The form comes from a Bible translation of Genesis 2.18, when God said 'I will make him a help meet for him'. *Meet* in this context is an adjective, meaning 'suitable'; but the popular view preferred to take the word as a form of *mate*.

• *salt-cellar* In Old French, a *salier* was a salt-box. When the word came into English, the connection with salt was evidently not clear, and people started calling the object a *salt-saler*. The modern form has no connection with a cellar.

The first part of *sirloin* is simply derived from the French word *sur* 'above'. The form must have greatly puzzled the people of the early Middle English period. Unused to French, they etymologized the form to *sir*, and then thought up a legend to make sense of it (the story of the English king who found this joint of meat so splendid that he gave it a knighthood).

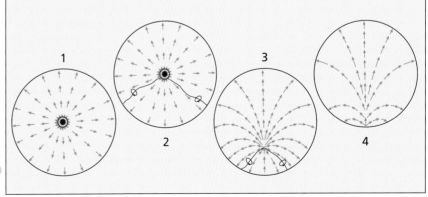

PHYSICIST NEOLOGIST

I know the exact moment when I decided to make the word 'boojum' an internationally accepted scientific term.

Thus begins the opening chapter of David Mermin's book, *Boojums All the Way Through: Communicating Science in a Prosaic Age* (1990). The year was 1976, and he was returning from a symposium on the discovery of the superfluid phases of liquid helium-3. Superfluids, he explains, are liquids in which currents can flow for ever, without succumbing to the frictional drag that causes currents in ordinary fluids to die away. Helium-3 is an 'anisotropic' liquid – one whose atomic structure in any little region points along a particular line. The structure is especially noticeable in one of its phases, and at the symposium the question was discussed of how the lines in this phase would arrange themselves in a spherical drop of the liquid.

A theoretical pattern, elegant in its symmetry, is shown in Figure 1 below. Figure 2 shows what happens as a vortex line (the long funnel of a little whirlpool) connects the point of convergence of the lines to the surface of the drop. The vortices draw the convergence point to the surface (Figure 3), resulting in a final pattern, shown in Figure 4, where the symmetry has collapsed, and the lines radiate from a point on the surface.

What should this new pattern be called? Mermin was reminded of Lewis Carroll's poem 'The Hunting of the Snark', where the last lines are 'He had softly and suddenly vanished away / For the Snark was a Boojum, you see'. As the symmetrical pattern in the liquid drop had indeed 'softly and suddenly vanished away', the term seemed highly appropriate.

In his book, Mermin tells the story of the difficulties he faced in getting his term accepted. It is rare for any new lexeme to attach itself to the lexicon without repercussions, and this is what he found. Each lexeme has to elbow its way in, and find an acceptable place in the semantic field to which it belongs. Its existence will probably affect the definition of established lexemes. And people may object to the new lexeme on a whole variety of grounds, such as that it is not needed, or that other terms are better suited, or that

they simply do not like the sound of it. These difficulties are compounded in a scientific subject, where there is an understandable conservatism, in the interests of maintaining intelligibility (p. 372), and where terminological proposals are subjected to detailed peer-group scrutiny.

In the end, the term did come to be recognized, but not without a great deal of effort. The proposal was first recorded as part of the published symposium discussion, but in quotation marks (as we would expect). Mermin then gave a paper a few months later in which he used the term several times. It was published in the proceedings, and appeared in the index. He then used the term at several other conferences.

A burst of correspondence followed between Mermin and the editor of a scientific journal to whom a paper had been submitted which included the term. The editor objected to *boojum* on the grounds that it would not be sufficiently known to the international scientific community to justify its inclusion. Mermin responded by giving a definition ('any surface point singularity the motion of which can catalyze the decay of a supercurrent') and pointing out that the lexical item as such was already in the dictionary. However, the editor was not swayed, and the term was rejected.

Mermin continued his efforts, writing a further article for another leading physics journal, and adding a note on the etymological background. The submission led to an in-depth dialogue with one of the journal's editorial team, and this time it was finally allowed to appear. As part of the discussion, there was a debate about which plural form to use: should it be *booja*, *boojum*, or *boojums*? They settled on the last. And in 1978 a paper appeared which contained *boojums* in its title, and which used the term throughout without apology (as the name of Mermin's book indicates: 'boojums all the way through').

Boojum therefore emerged in print within a couple of years of its creation, to join such fashionable physics terms as *quark*, *hedgehog*, and *charm*. Whatever its future in physics, its place in etymological history is assured. It is unusual to find the gestation and birth of a lexeme given such a detailed tabulation.

NAMES

One of the most popular aspects of etymology is the history of names – those words or phrases which uniquely identify persons, animals, places, concepts, or things. A 'proper name', as grammar books often call it (p. 208), presents an entity as an individual instance, and not as an anonymous member of a class (a 'common noun'). *The Beatles, Llanfairpwllgwyngyll, A Clockwork Orange*, and *Peter Rabbit* are uniquely located in space and time, and are thus names, in this sense; whereas *group, village, novel*, and *rabbit* have multiple and open-ended reference, and are thus common nouns. In English, names are generally identified by being printed with an initial capital letter; but this convention cannot always be trusted: should we write *the church* or *the Church? the president* or *the President?* (p. 122).

There seems to be a universal and deep-rooted drive to give individual names to things. People, places, pets, and houses are among the most obvious categories, but anything with which we have a special relationship is likely to be named. In a 1990 edition of the BBC Radio 4 series *English Now*, over 1,000 listeners sent in information about the things they named at home: the list included cars, yachts, word processors, wheelbarrows, washing machines, kitchen implements, house plants, and toothbrushes. Institutions also readily name their products, most obviously for purposes of identification and marketing (as in the case of brand names, book titles, paint colours, and roses), but also as a way of maintaining a tradition (as in the case of British locomotives, many of which are identified by name as well as number).

The science which studies names is called *onomastics* (also *onomatology*). Among its branches are the study of personal names (*anthroponomastics*) and place names (*toponomastics*, or *toponymy*). These days the subject deals with far more than etymology, and investigates a wide range of social, psychological, and legal questions. Why do names come into fashion and go out of fashion? What factors affect the success of a name? What controls limit the use of a name? Why are people so sensitive about their names? Names research is an open-ended and complex domain, and one which is particularly greedy of the researcher's time – as anyone can quickly discover, simply by asking people why they gave their house the name it has. But few other areas of linguistic study prove to be so riveting, or focus so directly on the personal and emotional aspects of language.

Place names

The names people give to the countries, districts, topographical features, settlements, streets, and houses in which they live constitute one of the most established domains of onomastics. It is not difficult to see why this should be so. Place names can provide a unique source of information about a society's history, structure, customs, and values. Often, a place name is the only record of a person's existence or of a historical event. Pada, Cippa, Cynehild, and Gip are known only from their linguistic memorials in (respectively) Paddington, Chippenham, Kenilworth, and Ipswich. Gallowtree Gate in Leicester and Pillory Lane in London are toponymic reminders of the sanctions of a previous age.

RUNNYMEDE

The place where King John met the English Barons in 1215, and sealed the Magna Carta, has one of the most familiar names in the history of England. But why did the meeting take place there? The name itself provides a clue. *Runnymede* means 'meadow at Runy', and *Runy* originally meant 'island where a council is held'. Evidently this locality had an ancient history of use for important meetings.

There are many other examples of names which refer to meeting-places. *Spelhoe* in Northumberland means 'speech hill', and *Skyrack* in Yorkshire is the 'oak where the shire meets'. Similar etymologies underlie *Spetchley* in Worcestershire ('speech glade'), *Spellbrook* in Hertfordshire, *Matlock* in Derbyshire ('oak at which a meeting is held'), and *Mottistone* in the Isle of Wight ('speaker's stone').

NAMING PLACES

To understand how places come to be named, it is helpful to put ourselves in the position of the Anglo-Saxon invaders of the 5th century, faced with vast tracts of unnamed Britain. How would *you* set about the task of identifying where people live and what they do there? This is what the Anglo-Saxons did.

• In some cases, they took over a name already in use by the inhabitants they found there. Several river names, in particular, are Celtic, such as *Thames*, *Avon*, *Wye*, and *Ouse*. These were often used to help form the names of settlements, such as *Taunton* (on the R. Tone) and *Wilton* (on the R. Wylie). It is remarkable that so few such names remain.

• They also kept some of the place names introduced by the Romans during their period of occupation (AD 43–*c.* 400). There are over 200 modern British place names which have Roman origins, notably those ending in -*port*, -*chester*, or -*street*.

• Families or tribal groups would settle in a locality, which would then become known by the head person's name. Examples include *Reading* ('place of Reada's people'), *Dagenham* ('Dacca's homestead'), and those cited on the facing page. There are thousands of these place names – in the patriarchal society of the time, of course, mostly referring to males (but there are several exceptions, such as *Bamburgh*, from the 7th century Queen Bebba).

• Names relating to religious beliefs and practices, both pagan and Christian, are well represented. *Harrow*, *Weedon*, and *Alkham* all contain Old English words relating to heathen temples or idols. *Westminster*, *Whitchurch*, and *St Ives* all contain Christian elements. Some names are of uncertain status: *Gadshill* in Kent could refer to either a pagan or the Christian god.

• The largest number of place names relate to topography – to the coastline, hills, rivers, woods, trees, stones, fields, and other physical features. The variety of names to do with hills and valleys is especially understandable, when we remember that the Anglo-Saxons came from one of the flattest areas in Europe, and would have been particularly attentive to the identification value of even quite gentle slopes and mounds.

TOPOGRAPHICAL ELEMENTS IN ENGLISH PLACE NAMES

SILBURY HILL

Hills and slopes
bank, barrow, borough, breck, cam, cliff, crook, down, edge, head, hill, how, hurst, ley, ling, lith, mond, over, pen, ridge, side , tor

Examples:
Barrow, Blackdown, Longridge, Redcliff, Thornborough, Windhill

LANGSTROTHDALE CHASE

Valleys and hollows
bottom, clough, combe, dale, den, ditch, glen, grave, hole, hope, slade

Examples:
Cowdale, Denton, Greenslade, Hoole, Longbottom, Thorncombe

WOODCOTE

Woods and groves
bear, carr, derry, fen, frith, greave, grove, heath, holt, lea, moor, oak, rise, scough, shaw, tree, well, with, wold, wood

Examples:
Blackheath, Hazlewood, Oakley, Southwold, Staplegrove

Rivers and streams
batch, beck, brook, burn, ey, fleet, font, ford, keld, lade, lake, latch, marsh, mere, mouth, ore, pool, rith, wade, water, well

Examples:
Broadwater, Fishlake, Mersey, Rushbrooke, Saltburn

LAKE BUTTERMERE

Dwellings and farms
barton, berwick, biggin, bold, by, cote, ham, hampstead, hamton, house, scale, sett, stall, thorpe, toft, ton, wick

Examples:
Fishwick, Newham, Potterton, Westby, Woodthorpe

WHITBY

General locations and routes
bridge, ford, gate, ing, mark, path, stead, stoke, stow, street, sty, way

Examples:
Epping, Horsepath, Longford, Ridgeway, Stonebridge, Streetly

BRADFORD-ON-AVON

INVERNESS

Coastline features
ey, holme, hulme, hythe, naze, ness, port, sea

Examples:
Bardsey, Greenhithe, Sheerness, Southport, Southsea

NR WIDECOMBE

Fields and clearings
combe, croft, den, ergh, field, ham, haugh, hay, ing, land, lease, lock, meadow, rick, ridding, rode, shot, side, thwaite, wardine, worth, worthy

Examples:
Applethwaite, Cowden, Smallworthy, Southworth, Wethersfield

BEAMINSTER

Buildings and stones
brough, burton, caster, church, cross, kirk, mill, minster, stain, stone, wark

Examples:
Crossthwaite, Felixkirk, Newminster, Staines, Whitchurch

Notes
• *These elements are all found in many different spellings. Old English* beorg *'hill, mound', for example, turns up as* bar-, berg-, -ber, -berry, -borough, *and* -burgh. *Only one form is given above (*Thornborough*).*

• *Several items have the same form, but differ in meaning because they come from different words in Old English. For example,* -ey *has developed in different ways from the two words* ea *'river' and* eg *'island'. It is not always easy deciding which is the relevant meaning in a given place name.*

• *The table does not distinguish between forms which appear in different parts of a place name. Old English* leah *'forest, glade', for example, sometimes appears at the beginning of a name (*Lee- *or* Leigh-*), sometimes at the end (*-leigh, -ley*), and sometimes alone (*Leigh*).*
(After K. Cameron, 1961.)

Successful place-name research puts several academic disciplines to work. Palaeography and philology (p. 436) are needed to decode the names in maps and manuscripts, and to work out the subtle relationship between sounds and spellings. History, archaeology, and sociology are needed to provide plausible contexts for the interpretations proposed by linguistic research. A knowledge of the relevant source languages is obviously critical. And a healthy scepticism is invariably beneficial.

The scepticism is required because place names are often not what they seem. There is probably little doubt that *Highwood* or *Ridgeway* mean what they appear to mean. But several modern forms no longer have the meaning they once had: a *field*, for example, is often now an enclosed piece of land, but the word referred only to a piece of open country in Anglo-Saxon times. Even more confusing are the cases where originally different forms have come out as identical in modern English: there are several places called *Aston*, and the meaning is usually 'eastern farmstead', but in certain localities (such as *Cold Aston* in Gloucestershire) the meaning is 'farmstead by ash trees'. There is also the opposite case, where the same form has developed several spellings, sometimes because of dialect differences in pronunciation, sometimes because of the new spelling practices introduced by Norman French scribes after the Conquest: there is no etymological difference between *Northwich*, *Northwick*, and *Norwich*, which all come from the Old English words meaning 'northern dwelling-place'. Great care is needed if wrong conclusions are not to be drawn, and in regrettably many instances an original form or meaning cannot be proposed with any conviction.

MANUSCRIPT SOURCES

The *Domesday Book*, compiled by 1086, provides the earliest recorded spelling of most English village and parish names. These spellings have to be viewed critically, however, because the French scribes naturally transcribed many of the Old English pronunciations using their own writing system. Also, unfamiliarity with the names inevitably led to errors.

Earlier sources include the 'Guide to Geography' of Ptolemy, dating from *c.* 150, and a few other Latin sources and inscriptions. The Old English period has a large number of charters, wills, and other legal documents containing place names, as well as the invaluable *Anglo-Saxon Chronicle* (p. 14). As the documents are often preserved in copies made several centuries later, the risk of copyist error must always be borne in mind.

Sources from the Middle English period include the Pipe Rolls, dating from the mid-12th century, which contain the yearly accounts of the sheriffs for each county. Along with various other legal and administrative documents of the time, they list thousands of local names, and are important for the information they provide about people as well as places (p. 149).

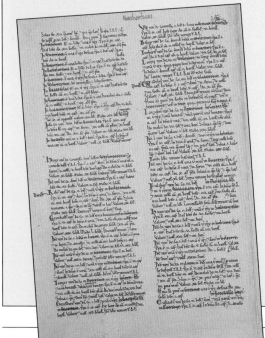

One of the earliest-known detailed maps of Britain, containing a great deal of information about medieval place names. It was compiled *c.* 1250 for the *Chronica Maiora* of the English Benedictine chronicler, Matthew Paris of St Albans (died 1259). It is now in the British Library.

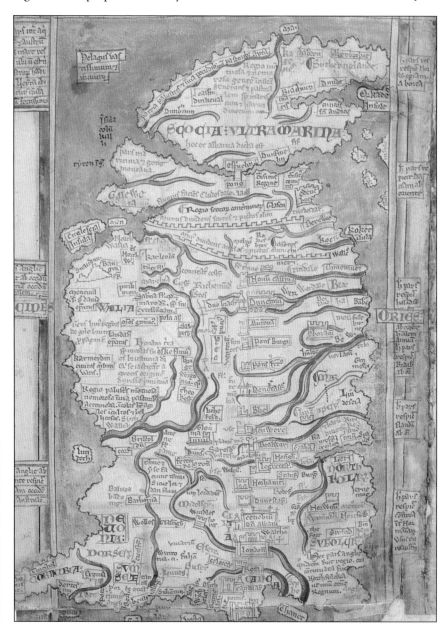

BRITISH COUNTY NAMES

This is an etymological glossary of the county names of Great Britain recognized by the 1972 local government reorganization. It excludes those where the meaning of the name is self-evident, as in the case of *Highland* and *Borders*. Several etymologies are uncertain or controversial, especially those marked (?).

1 *Shetland* 'hilt land'
2 *Grampian* unknown origin
3 *Tayside* 'silent river' or 'powerful river'
4 *Fife* 'territory of Vip' (?)
5 *Lothian* '(territory of) Leudonus'
6 *Strathclyde* 'valley of the Clyde' (the 'cleansing one')
7 *Dumfries* 'woodland stronghold' *Galloway* '(territory of) the stranger-Gaels'
8 *Northumberland* 'land of those dwelling north of the Humber'
9 *Tyne* 'water, river' *Wear* 'river'
10 *Durham* 'island with a hill'
11 *Cleveland* 'hilly land'
12 *Yorkshire* 'place of Eburos'
13 *Humberside* 'side of the good river'
14 *Lincoln* '(Roman) colony at Lindo' ('lake place')
15 *Derby* 'village where there are deer'
16 *Nottingham* 'homestead of Snot's people'
17 *Leicester* '(Roman) fort of the Ligore people'
18 *Northampton* 'northern home farm'
19 *Cambridge* 'bridge over the river Granta'
20 *Norfolk* 'northern people'
21 *Suffolk* 'southern people'
22 *Bedford* 'Beda's ford'
23 *Hertford* 'hart ford'
24 *Essex* '(territory of) the East Saxons'
25 *London* '(territory of) Londinos' ('the bold one')(?)
26 *Kent* 'land on the border' (?)
27 *Surrey* 'southern district'
28 *Sussex* '(territory of) the South Saxons'

29 *Buckingham* 'riverside land of Bucca's people'
30 *Berkshire* 'county of the wood of Barroc' ('hilly place')
31 *Wight* 'place of the division' (of the sea) (?)
32 *Hampshire* 'county of Southampton' ('southern home farm')
33 *Oxford* 'ford used by oxen'
34 *Wiltshire* 'county around Wilton' ('farm on the river Wylie')
35 *Dorset* '(territory of the) settlers around Dorn' ('Dorchester')
36 *Somerset* '(territory of the) settlers around Somerton' ('summer dwelling')
37 *Devon* '(territory of) the Dumnonii' ('the deep ones', probably miners)
38 *Cornwall* '(territory of) Britons of the Cornovii' ('promontory people')
39 *Scilly* unknown origin
40 *Avon* 'river'
41 *Gloucester* '(Roman) fort at Glevum' ('bright place')
42 *Gwent* 'favoured place'
43 *Glamorgan* '(Prince) Morgan's shore'
44 *Hereford* 'army ford' *Worcester* '(Roman) fort of the Wigora'
45 *Powys* 'provincial place'
46 *Dyfed* '(territory of) the Demetae'
47 *Gwynedd* '(territory of) Cunedda' (5th-century leader)
48 *Clwyd* 'hurdle' (? on river)
49 *Shropshire* 'county of Shrewsbury' ('fortified place of the scrubland region')
50 *Warwick* 'dwellings by a weir'
51 *Stafford* 'ford beside a landing-place'
52 *Cheshire* 'county of Chester' (Roman 'fort')
53 *Merseyside* '(side of the) boundary river'
54 *Manchester* '(Roman) fort at Mamucium'
55 *Lancashire* '(Roman) fort on the Lune' ('health-giving river')
56 *Cumbria* 'territory of the Welsh'
57 *Man* 'land of Mananan' (an Irish god)
58 *Orkney* 'whale island' (?)

(After J. Field, 1980.)

ENGLISH PLACE NAMES IN THE NEW WORLD

A notable feature of early British toponyms (p. 140), is the absence of commemorative personal names. The Anglo-Saxons readily named places after the chief person who lived there, but rarely used the name of a famous person from elsewhere. Even the greatest of Anglo-Saxon kings, Alfred, receives no major place-name memorial – though several localities stressing the role rather than the person did follow his reign (*Kingston, Kingswood,* etc.). Saints provide a few exceptions, as in the case of *St Albans*. It must be the self-effacing English character. Not the done thing.

Things have not much changed in Britain: there seems to be no town or village in England with a sovereign's name since the Conquest (though there is no such reluctance to give a monarchical name to humbler locations, such as parks, streets, and railway stations). But, as with modern tourism, when the English travel abroad, they act in very different ways. In the USA, there is a *Jamestown* in Arkansas, California, Kentucky, and several other states, along with numerous cases of *Charleston, Williamsburg, Georgetown,* and *Victoria.* There are well over 100 cities and townships (and a state) with the name of *Washington. Carolina, Maryland, Fredericksburg, Columbus, Louisiana, Napoleonville, Carson, Coolidge, Lincoln,* and *Monroe* recall a variety of rulers, pioneers, and statesmen. Australia, similarly, has *Victoria, Tasmania, Cooktown,* the *Flinders Ranges,* the *Gibson Desert,* and such colonial secretaries as *Newcastle, Bathurst, Kimberley, Normanby,* and *Hobart.* All over the New World, famous people are commemorated in ways that are thoroughly alien within Britain.

The names used by the English-speaking countries of the world are remarkable in their diversity.
• The environment is used in much the same way as in early Britain, but the meaning of the names is usually transparent: *Twin Peaks, Salt Lake City, Kangaroo Bluff, Table Mountain, Little Rock, Crooked Creek, Swan River.*
• Local native names are much in evidence: *Saratoga, Tallahassie,* and *Oklahoma* from American Indian languages; *Paramatta, Kalgoorlie,* and *Woomera* from Aboriginal languages; *Wanganui, Tauranga,* and *Akaroa* from Maori.
• Inspirational names have been imported from the Old World: *Paris, Berlin, London, Athens, Memphis, Hertford.* Several have a modifier: *New London, New Norfolk.*
• Important events or feelings are recorded: *Cape Catastrophe, Waterlooville, Encounter Bay, Hope Valley, Fort Defiance, Fog Bay, Hard Luck Creek.*
• The language of the settlers has been a major influence: Spanish in *Los Angeles, Sacramento,* and *San Francisco;* French in *Montréal, Baton Rouge,* and *Le Roy.*
• Many names have been chosen for their literary associations (*Longfellow, Hiawatha, Ivanhoe, Elsinore*) and many for their romantic sound (*Meadowvale, Sunnyhurst, Arcadia, Rosebud*).
• Pedestrian descriptions abound, as they did in early England: there are hundreds of *Newtowns, Newports, Mount Pleasants,* and *Greenvilles* around the English-speaking world. *North Bay, South Island, Bridgeport, Center Point,* and *Hill City* suggest a singular lack of imagination – or perhaps simply pioneer fatigue.
• By contrast, many names display a wild and vivid inventiveness: *Hot Coffee* (Mississippi), *Knuckles* (Kentucky), and *Difficult* (Tennessee). *Tesnus* (Texas) is spelled backwards to avoid a clash with an already existing *Sunset* in the same state. *Truth or Consequences* (New Mexico) changed its name from *Hot Springs* under the influence of a radio game show.

SHAKESPEARE COUNTRY

Rulers, statesmen, explorers, soldiers, and sailors are the ones usually chosen to name important places. Artists, writers, and composers are conspicuous by their absence. Several of Shakespeare's characters, such as *Viola* and *Othello,* have come to name small towns in the USA, but Shakespeare himself has been largely avoided. There is a *Shakespeare Island* in Canada, and a small town called *Shakespeare* near Stratford, Ontario. And yet, if a new city was to be built in the middle of the Australian outback, would it feel right to propose its name as *Shakespeare* – or, for that matter, *Chaucer, Britten, Elgar,* or *Constable*?

Shakespeare, Ontario, 1989.

JAMES COOK (1728–79)

Captain Cook named thousands of localities during his voyages between 1768 and 1779. His names included the *Society Islands* (after the Royal Society, which had sponsored his expedition) and many of the coastal features of New Zealand and Australia. He frequently chose names belonging to contemporary British personalities, such as *Halifax* and *Grafton.* Many others were based on his observations of the physical environment (*Smoky Cape, Botany Bay*) or on events to do with the journey (*Weary Bay, Thirsty Sound*). *Mount Cook* in New Zealand, the *Cook Strait,* and the *Cook Islands* are among the few localities which carry his own name.

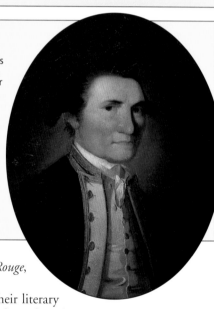

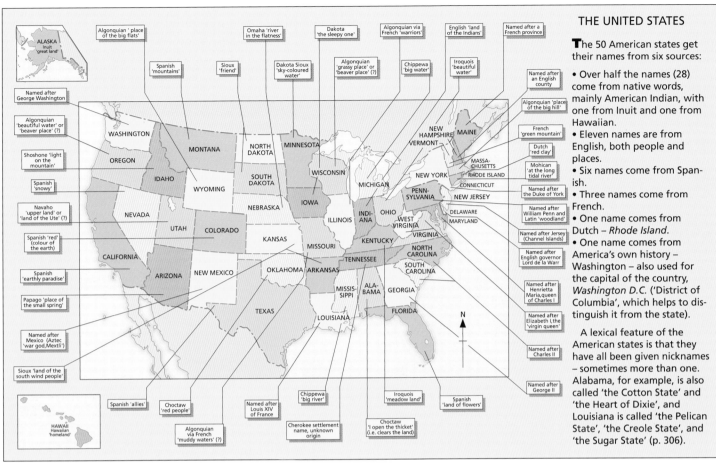

THE UNITED STATES

The 50 American states get their names from six sources:

• Over half the names (28) come from native words, mainly American Indian, with one from Inuit and one from Hawaiian.

• Eleven names are from English, both people and places.

• Six names come from Spanish.

• Three names come from French.

• One name comes from Dutch – *Rhode Island*.

• One name comes from America's own history – Washington – also used for the capital of the country, *Washington D.C.* ('District of Columbia', which helps to distinguish it from the state).

A lexical feature of the American states is that they have all been given nicknames – sometimes more than one. Alabama, for example, is also called 'the Cotton State' and 'the Heart of Dixie', and Louisiana is called 'the Pelican State', 'the Creole State', and 'the Sugar State' (p. 306).

A typical mix of New World place names, seen here on Cape Breton Island, and along the coastline of Nova Scotia, Canada. American Indian, English, and French names all rub shoulders. The evidence of Scottish immigration is clearly to be seen in such names as *Loch Lomond* and *Inverness*.

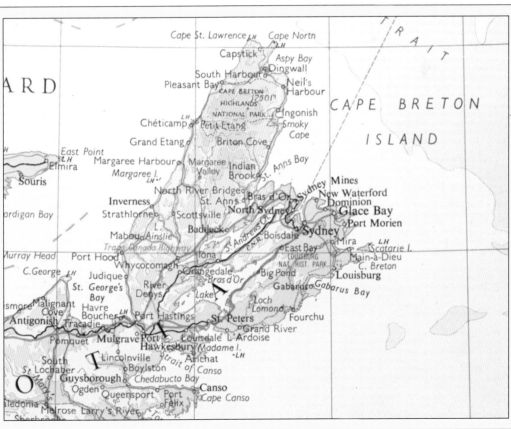

Street-wise

The names of pubs, shops, houses, alleys, centres, markets, parks, promenades, and quaysides, along with the dozens of other locutions available in English to describe 'the street where we live', provide a rich supply of data for the place-name enthusiast. Each English pub sign, for example, has a story to tell, and can give a fascinating glimpse of social history. *The Bible and Crown* was a Cavalier drinking-toast. *The Rising Sun* was a heraldic allusion (to the arms of the House of York). *The Flying Bull* derives from stagecoach names. Each house name, too, tells a personal story, as amply demonstrated by the thousands of records in the files of the Names Society, which has collected house names in over 45 languages (L. Dunkling, 1974). Why *Cobwebs*? Not what the word suggests, but an acronym –

'Currently Owned by the Woolwich Equitable Building Society'. Why *Hysteria*? Next door to a house called *Wisteria*. Why *Thistledew*? Derived from 'This'll do'.

Street names are particularly intriguing, partly because of the evidence they provide about social history, and partly because of their continuing social associations. People will often take note of the name before deciding to buy a house in a particular street. Many refuse to live in a *Street* at all, but prefer *Avenue, Chase, Crescent, Drive, Gardens, Villas, Close*, or some other substitute word. Local government offices often receive requests to change a street name, and a considerable amount of time can be devoted to choosing the names in a new area of housing development. As so often in place-name studies, social issues outrank etymological ones.

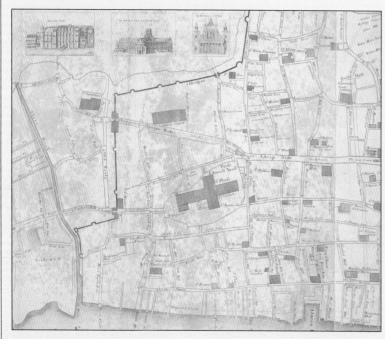

WILLIAM PENN (1644–1718)

The founder of Pennsylvania, the son of Admiral Sir William Penn, after whom the state was named. The younger Penn himself named and planned *Philadelphia* ('brotherly love'). Because of his Quaker beliefs, he did not want to name each street after the most important person who lived in it (as was the existing practice). People, in his view, were equal before God. He therefore introduced a numbering system, using the geometrical layout of the city as a guide. East–West streets were called *First Street, Second Street*, and so on. North–South streets were given names from nature, such as *Walnut Street* and *Pine Street*. Many other towns adopted the system, with the result that American city centre nomenclature is now very different from its British counterpart. There is no UK idiom corresponding to such US elliptical expressions as 'First and Vine' (for the intersection of First Street and Vine Street).

CITY STREETS

Part of a plan of the City of London, taken from John Leake's *An exact surveigh of the streets lanes and churches contained within the ruines of the city of London*, published in 1667, after the Great Fire of 1666. Studies of London's streets date from the 16th century, and there are now several name guides and dictionaries. While the etymologies are sometimes controversial, they are always interesting – and surprisingly little known.

Downing Street Named after the soldier and diplomat, Sir George Downing (c. 1623–84), who held a lease on the land.
Kingsway Named for King Edward VII (reigned 1901–10).
Oxford Street Named after Edward Harley, second Earl of Oxford, who

owned the land in the early 18th century.
Piccadilly Named after the ruffed lace collars (known as *pickadills*) popular in the early 17th century. According to one theory, these collars were particularly associated with a certain tailor, whose house came to be dubbed *Pickadilly Hall*. The name later transferred to its locality.
Regent Street Named after the Prince Regent who in 1820 became George IV.
Shaftesbury Avenue Named after Anthony Ashley Cooper, seventh Earl of Shaftesbury (1801–85), the factory reformer and philanthropist.
Soho Originally a hunting-cry, and perhaps the name of an inn in the area.
Strand The 'shore' of the Thames.
Tottenham Court Road 'the court of Totta's village'.

THE ENGLISH PLACE-NAME SOCIETY

For over half a century, there has been a society devoted to the study of English place names. It is the English Place-Name Society, founded in 1923 at the suggestion of Allan Mawer, at the time Baines Professor of English Language at the University of Liverpool. The Society had an ambitious aim: to carry out research into all the place names of England, and to publish its surveys, county by county.

Mawer became the first Director of the Society, which moved with him to University College London in 1929. After his death in 1942, the Society found a home first in Reading, then in Cambridge (1946), then back in University College (1951), finally in 1967 moving its chief office to its present location, the University of Nottingham, where it came under the direction of Professor Kenneth Cameron.

The Society aimed to publish a volume a year, and although this programme was given a setback by the Second World War, 66 volumes had appeared by 1992. A further five were then in the pipeline, including the complete survey of Rutland, and further volumes on Shropshire and Norfolk. Research continues into several other areas, a journal regularly appears, and there are plans for more surveys.

As the reports of its Secretaries show, the history of the Society is a remarkable story of enthusiasm, loyalty, and scholarship. It has always been precariously housed, with resources barely adequate for its work. Several other countries have well-funded institutes devoted to place-name study (such as those in Scandinavia). By contrast, the volumes of the English Society have always been produced on a shoestring. The British Academy has been particularly supportive, as has Nottingham University, but the support of the Society's members has also been crucial, in enabling the Society to achieve so much in such a relatively short time. (See also p. 446).

LIFF, THE UNIVERSE, AND EVERYTHING

Place names often reflect and influence the way society behaves, and are thus a ready butt of comedy and satire. In any country, a name can immediately bring to mind a social milieu, or convey a stereotype of it. In London Mayfair sits uneasily alongside Wapping, as does Brooklyn Heights alongside Brownsville in New York City.

Add social nuance to the etymological histories of many place names, which have led to recognizable phonetic associations with other words in the language, and to the symbolic potential of certain sound sequences (p. 250), and we have the situation which allows a book such as *The Meaning of Liff* to appear. Written in 1983 by Douglas Adams, the author of *The Hitch Hiker's Guide to the Galaxy*, and John Lloyd, it perfectly illustrates the evocative power of English place names. However, the authors evidently have, deep down, by their own admission, a serious purpose: to remedy some of the lexical deficiencies of the language (p. 133) by making use of the place names, which, as their preface points out, 'spend their time doing nothing but loafing about on signposts pointing at places'. Here are some examples from A to H.

Ahenny (adj.) The way people stand when examining other people's book-shelves.
Amersham (n.) The sneeze which tickles but never comes.
Banff (adj.) Pertaining to, or descriptive of, that kind of facial expression which is impossible to achieve except when having a passport photograph taken.
Clun (n.) A leg which has gone to sleep and has to be hauled around after you.
Detchant (n.) That part of a hymn (usually a few notes at the end of a verse) where the tune goes so high or so low that you suddenly have to change octaves to accommodate it.
Duleek (n.) Sudden realisation, as you lie in bed, waiting for the alarm to go off, that it should have gone off an hour ago.
Ely (n.) The first, tiniest inkling you get that something, somewhere, has gone terribly wrong.
Ewelme (n., vb.) The smile bestowed on you by an air hostess.
Goole (n.) The puddle on the bar into which the barman puts your change.
Happle (vb.) To annoy people by finishing their sentences for them and then telling them what they really meant to say (cf. p. 295).
Hoff (vb.) To deny indignantly something which is palpably true.

NAMES-RACE

The names of the major physical features of the far side of the moon bring together the domains of toponymy and anthroponymy (p. 140). The surnames of astronauts, astronomers, and other scientists predominate, alongside the occasional name of a project (*Apollo*) or place (*Moscoviense* – Latin 'Moscow'). It is certainly possible to see the history of the lunar space-race in the distinctive surnames. By contrast, there is very little sign of the romantic Latin descriptions (such as *Mare Nubium* – 'Sea of Clouds') with which the facing side of the moon has so long been identified.

WHERE NAMES GIVE WAY TO NUMBERS

This beautiful object goes by the name of NGC 6302. NGC stands for *New General Catalogue*, a listing of 7840 nebulae made by the Danish astronomer Johan Dreyer in 1888. An earlier catalogue, compiled by Frenchman Charles Messier, lists objects using Messier's initial and a serial number: the so-called *Crab Nebula*, for example, is *M1*. Several other catalogues provide names in this way. With so many objects in the sky to be identified, numerical listing is the only practicable method.

Certain nebulae, galaxies, and clusters can also be identified in other ways, with reference to the constellation or large-scale star pattern in which they appear. *Centaurus A*, for example, refers to the first radio source to be found within the constellation of Centaurus. Greek letters are also used as identifiers, as in *Alpha Centauri*.

Descriptive labels are used for a small number of well-known stellar objects, based on their fancied resemblance to terrestrial phenomena. Examples are the *Crab Nebula* and the *Ring Nebula*. This approach, ancient in origin, provided the original names of the constellations, and is most widely recognized in the signs of the Zodiac.

PERSONAL NAMES

There is no linguistic impropriety more likely to irritate people than a mis-spelling of their name; and nothing more likely to fascinate them than an account of their name's origins. Very few, however, know where their name comes from, though etymological awareness of first names often accompanies pregnancy. The study of personal names, in any case, suffers from the same kind of research difficulties as does the study of place names (p. 140). The earlier forms of a name are often uncertain. Scribes may have introduced errors while copying from one manuscript to another, or different dialect pronunciations may have led to divergent spellings of the same name. The social pressure to use a standard spelling, moreover, did not emerge until the 18th century, and earlier writers saw no problem in spelling a person's name in a variety of ways. In one study, over 130 variants of the name *Mainwaring* were found among the parchments belonging to that family. Nonetheless, thanks to over a century of academic study of personal names, a great deal of reliable information now exists, and is available for consultation in name dictionaries.

The question of what counts as a name is not a simple one to answer. Variations involving a single letter may be considered minor or major: *Steven* is usually considered the same name as *Stephen* (but 'spelled with a v') and *Catherine* as *Katherine*; but *Christine* is less clearly the same as *Christina*, and *Francis* is certainly not the same as *Frances*. Many names have more substantial variants – shortened forms (*Beth*, *Pete*), forms with endings marking familiarity (*Davy*, *Mikey*), and pet forms, technically called *hypocoristics* (*Nell*, *Jojo*). There is no problem with *Pete* being felt to be the 'same' name as *Peter*, but is *Beth* always felt to be the same as *Elizabeth*?

Personal names in English are generally classified into three types. The *first name* (or *given name*, formerly often called the *Christian name*) is distinguished from the *surname* (or *family name*), and both of these from the *middle name(s)*, where present. In the early Middle Ages, there were only first names. Surnames came later – additional names used to aid identification between people who had the same given name (the term is from French *sur + nom*, and is found in English from the 14th century). The practice of using one or more middle names did not emerge until the 17th century, and there were soon divergences between Britain and the USA. The American fashion was to use the middle name, routinely reducing it to an initial letter, as in *William P. Knott*. The British fashion was either to ignore the middle name, or to keep it in full, especially when it was needed to maintain a family tradition, or to distinguish otherwise identical names. In Welsh English, for example, one might hear a *John Arthur Jones* being differentiated from a *John Bryn Jones*, with the middle name acting as a kind of surname (and the true surname often elided, with people talking familiarly about 'John Arthur' and 'John Bryn'). Sequences of middle names are also to be found, especially when a family finds itself having to remember particular relatives or ancestors, or when religious or other practices intervene (such as adding a saint's name). Eccentricity abounds: there are several cases of parents giving their child 26 names, each beginning with a different letter of the alphabet.

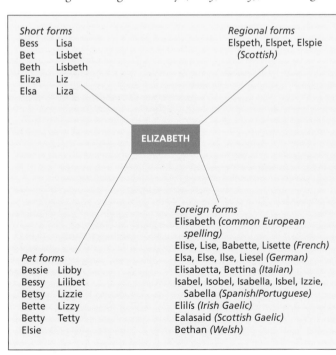

Short forms		Regional forms
Bess	Lisa	Elspeth, Elspet, Elspie
Bet	Lisbet	(Scottish)
Beth	Lisbeth	
Eliza	Liz	
Elsa	Liza	

ELIZABETH

Foreign forms
Elisabeth *(common European spelling)*
Elise, Lise, Babette, Lisette *(French)*
Elsa, Else, Ilse, Liesel *(German)*
Elisabetta, Bettina *(Italian)*
Isabel, Isobel, Isabella, Isbel, Izzie, Sabella *(Spanish/Portuguese)*
Elilís *(Irish Gaelic)*
Ealasaid *(Scottish Gaelic)*
Bethan *(Welsh)*

Pet forms
Bessie	Libby
Bessy	Lilibet
Betsy	Lizzie
Bette	Lizzy
Betty	Tetty
Elsie	

ELIZABETHAN FAMILY

Elizabeth is an ancient name, appearing in the Old Testament as the name of Aaron's wife, and in the New Testament as the mother of John the Baptist. Its Hebrew meaning is not entirely clear, but *Elisheba* might be interpreted as 'oath of God' or 'God is perfection'. Its role in both Jewish and Christian traditions made it a very common name in Europe. In Britain, its popularity grew after the reign of Elizabeth I, and it became one of the top three girl's names (along with *Mary* and *Ann*) for 300 years.

The name has developed many variants and shortened forms, as can be seen from the figure. It is normally spelled with an 's' on the continent of Europe, but this spelling has now entered English-speaking areas also, along with such European forms as *Elise* and *Lisette*. These variations raise a major issue of classification. If two people were to examine all the names related to *Elizabeth*, would they agree that they are variants of the one name, or would they think of some forms as different names? And which foreign equivalents are now so nativized that they would be considered English names?

Elizabeth began to lose favour around the turn of the present century, and has not been in the top 20 girl's names since then. This is rather surprising, especially in Britain, as it is the name of two of the best-known British women of the century, Elizabeth Bowes-Lyon, who became the wife of King George VI, and her daughter, who became Queen Elizabeth II.

Envoi
'People always grow up like their names. It took me thirty years to work off the effects of being called Eric. If I wanted a girl to grow up beautiful I'd call her Elizabeth ... ' (Letters of George Orwell, originally Eric Blair).

SHAKESPEARE'S SIGNATURES

The spelling variation found in personal names is well illustrated by the corpus of six signatures known to come from the hand of William Shakespeare. They are all found in documents dated between 1612 and 1616. The last three belong to pages 1, 2 and 3 of his will (25 March 1616), which was written shortly before his death; the hand is slightly shaky, and the signatures do not end confidently. There is a great deal of variation between each example,

both in the form of the letters, and in the abbreviations used. (The parentheses enclose letters which seem to be absent.) With less well-known names, such variants would present serious problems of identification.

(1) Will(ia)m Shakp(er)
(2) William Shakspe(r)
(3) W(illia)m Shaksper
(4) William Shakspere
(5) Willi(a)m Shakspere
(6) William Shakspeare

Types of surname

Most surnames can be classified from an etymological point of view into one of four types.

• They derive from a place name or general topographical location, identifying where a person has come from. This is by far the largest class of names. Examples: *Norman, Moor, Hall, Chesterfield, Street, Wood.*

• They represent an occupation – also a large class of names. Examples: *Cook, Taylor, Clark, Smith, Turner, Cooper.*

• They express kinship, the relationship to a parent or ancestor being shown by the word-ending. A first name may also be used without any special ending. Examples: *Johnson, Robertson, Watkins, Nicholas, Thomas.*

• They are nicknames, expressing some physical, moral, or other characteristic. Examples: *Long, Little, Moody, Fox, Brown, Young, Rich.*

PLAYING WITH SURNAMES

The comic possibilities of English surnames have always attracted the writer, as can be seen in the cast lists of any comedy by Shakespeare or Sheridan, or the characters of Charles Dickens or Mervyn Peake:
Bottom, Flute, Starveling, Snout...
Absolute, Languish, Malaprop, O'Trigger...
Pardiggle, Skimpole, Snagsby, Bucket...
Deadyawn, Flannelcat, Prunesquallor, Flay...

The verses below also continue an ancient tradition of word-play. They are a small part of a work by one James Smith, published in Ernest Weekley's *The Romance of Names* (1914).

Men once were surnamed from their
      shape or estate
   (You all may from History worm it);
There was Lewis the Bulky, and Henry the
      Great,
   John Lackland, and Peter the Hermit.

But now, when the door-plates of Misters
      and Dames
   Are read, each so constantly varies
From the owner's trade, figure, and
      calling, surnames
   Seem given by the rule of contraries.

Mr Box, though provoked, never doubles
      his fist,
   Mr Burns, in his grate, has no fuel;
Mr Playfair won't catch me at hazard or
      whist,
   Mr Coward was wing'd in a duel.
Mr Wise is a dunce, Mr King is a whig,
   Mr Coffin's uncommonly sprightly,
And huge Mr Little broke down in a gig,
   While driving fat Mrs Golightly.

Mr Barker's as mute as a fish in the sea,
   Mr Miles never moves on a journey;
Mr Gotobed sits up till half-after three,
   Mr Makepeace was bred an attorney.
Mr Gardiner can't tell a flower from a
      root,
   Mr Wilde with timidity draws back,
Mr Ryder performs all his journeys on foot,
   Mr Foote all his journeys on horseback.

MEDIEVAL SURNAMES

An extract from one of the medieval Hundred Rolls, part of the list compiled for Sussex (Arundel). Such rolls provide an excellent source of information about the early history of personal names. The following names have been taken from various 13th-century lists, with one of its modern equivalents (and, where needed, an explanation) given in parentheses.

Baldwin le Bocher (Butcher)
William de Paris (Parish)
Richard le Paumer (Palmer –
   someone who had made a
   pilgrimage to the Holy Land)

William le Boteler (Butler – a
   bottle-maker)
John de Cruce (Cross – someone who
   lived near an outdoor cross)
Henry le Waleys (Walsh – the
   western Celtic 'foreigner')
Thomas le Clerc (Clark)
Alexander de Leycestre (Lester)
Reginald le Blond (Blunt)
John Rex (King)
William Neuman (Newman – a
   newcomer to the area)
Stephen Cornevaleis (Cornwallis)

Not all medieval names remain productive in modern times. Examples of such dead surnames can be seen in the occupational names of *Stephen le Hatter* and *Henry le Wimpler.*

Types of first name

There is no agreed way of classifying first names, but we can distinguish several types on etymological grounds.

• They may identify a particular physical characteristic: *Kevin* ('handsome at birth'), *Maurice* ('dark-skinned, Moorish'), *Adam* ('red complexion'). Within this category we might also include very general descriptions, such as *Charles* ('man'), *Thomas* ('twin').

• They may relate to a time or place of origin, or to a type of activity: *Barbara* ('foreign'), *Francis* ('Frenchman'), *Noel* ('Christmas'), *George* ('farmer').

• They often express a real or desirable characteristic: *Peter* ('rock'), *Agnes* ('pure'), *Alexander* ('defender of men'), *Hilary* ('cheerful'), *Stephen* ('crown').

• They can express a parent's feelings: *Amy* ('loved'), *Abigail* ('father rejoices'), *Lucy* ('light'), *Benjamin* ('son of my right hand').

• Some names are authors' inventions. They may have an etymological meaning (as with Shakespeare's *Miranda*, in *The Tempest*, which means 'fit to be admired') or they may have no obvious meaning at all (as with *Wendy*, devised by J. M. Barrie on the basis of a child's coinage, *fwendy-wendy*, and used in *Peter Pan* (1904)).

• Many names contain an element derived from Hebrew *Jehovah* or other designations for 'God': *John, Jonathan, Josephine, Joan, Gabriel, Jeremy, Emanuel, Elizabeth.*

• Names are often taken from plants, gemstones, and other natural objects: *Susan* ('lily'), *Fern, Holly, Rosemary, Ruby, Crystal.* This practice was very popular in the 19th century.

• Surnames may emerge as first names – another common 19th-century practice: *Baron, Beverley, Fletcher, Maxwell.* Many of these names were originally place names (p. 141): *Clifford* ('ford near a slope'), *Douglas* (a Celtic river name, 'dark water'), *Shirley* ('bright clearing').

• Some names have a particular linguistic structure, which becomes especially noticeable when the names are in fashion. The prefixes *De-, La-,* and *Sha-* are common African-American elements, for example: *Dejuan, Deshawn, Ladonna, Latisha, Shakirra, Shafaye.* Several endings, such as *-ene, -ette, -elle, -ona,* and *-ice,* occur frequently in contemporary feminine forms: *Jolene, Marlene, Charlene, Darlene …*

• Several names are of obscure or unknown origin: *Antony, Arthur, Belinda, Mary.*

NAMING FASHIONS

There is no doubt that there are fashions in naming. In a particular year, one boy in three and one girl in five are given one of the 10 top first names. We all 'know' which names within our culture are old-fashioned (*Herbert, Percy, Nellie, May*), and which are modern (*Karen, Joanne, Craig, Darren*). But why do names come and go?

• Traditionally, members of the British royal family have been influential in the UK, as shown by the popularity of such names as *William* and *George*. This influence now seems to be waning: *Elizabeth, Philip, Charles,* and *Diana* have caused no upsurge in the use of these names in recent years. Neither *Charles* nor *Diana* figure in even the top 50 names in the 1985 lists for England and Wales, for example, despite the popular acclaim which surrounded their marriage just four years previously.

• Names with religious associations form a major group. They include Old Testament names (*Joseph, Ruth, Eve, David*), New Testament names (*Mark, John, Mary*), saints' names (*Teresa, Bernardette, Francis, Dominic*), and especially the names of patron saints (*George, David, Andrew, Patrick*). We find the same influences among English-speaking immigrants whose origins lie outside of the Judaeo-Christian tradition: *Krishna, Arjun, Sanjay, Shakti, Kanti* (from Hindu tradition), *Surinder, Rupinder* (from Sikhism), and *Muhammad, Abdallah* (from Islam).

• Literature can have a marked influence, as seen in the history of use surrounding *Alice* (after Lewis Carroll), *Justine* (after Lawrence Durrell), and *Rhett* (after Margaret Mitchell's *Gone With the Wind*). Surprisingly, Shakespeare's character names have been little used. How many people do you know called *Portia, Romeo, Cordelia,* or *Hamlet*?

• Film, television, and popular music are undoubtedly the dominant contemporary influences, with people using the names of the stars (*Marlon, Marilyn, Cary, Kylie, Elvis*) or the characters they create.

• Some names attract disapproval in particular traditions (and approval in others): for example, Protestant names such as *Luther* and *Calvin* would not usually be found in Roman Catholic households (though this association is less strong among African-Americans).

There are also certain names which are almost universally avoided in English-speaking countries because of their taboo status (*Judas, Adolf, Lucifer*).

Agatha Christie

Some names have but a single resonance. Most people know only one *Agatha* – Christie (1891–1975). Other personality-dominant first names include *Raquel* (Welch), *Dustin* (Hoffman), and *Errol* (Flynn). Some sources may not be real: *Linus* for most people is a cartoon character (from *Peanuts*), though perhaps not for chemists (*Linus Pauling*).

Prince Albert

The name *Albert* grew enormously in popularity towards the end of the 19th century, as a consequence of the marriage of Queen Victoria to Prince Albert. It does not appear in the list of the top 50 names in 1800, but it had reached the top 10 by 1900. Surprisingly, *Victoria* was never intensively used in the 19th century, probably because of the special respect in which this Queen was held, though it became popular during the 1940s.

Kylie Minogue

Some names are regionally distinctive. *Kylie* is an Australian name, but it began to become popular in Britain in the late 1980s as a result of the fame of Australian actress and singer, Kylie Minogue (1969 –). The meaning of the name is obscure: it may derive from an Aboriginal word for 'boomerang', or be an adaptation of another name, such as *Kyle* or *Kelly*.

Data sources

The lists given below, which do not give all the variant spellings, are based on a diverse range of information sources. They include British parish registers, probably the most important source of early names. Modern names can be traced through the yearly indexes of the various birth registry offices. A popular source is the birth announcement columns published by national newspapers (though inevitably these lists are socio-economically biased). And name specialists have carried out many surveys of their own, such as compiling lists of students at various universities in English-speaking parts of the world. One unpublished survey, by C. V. Appleton, takes as its scope every first name used by the Smiths of England and Wales since 1837.

Most studies to date have focused on Britain and the USA, but information is slowly accumulating about naming habits in other countries, and ethnic differences are now being more seriously addressed. A significant proportion of the people of Britain and the USA have non-English-speaking backgrounds, and the naming fashions of their original countries are often included in modern name surveys. *A Dictionary of First Names* (1990), by Patrick Hanks and Flavia Hodges, provides supplements on the common names of the Arab world and the subcontinent of India. They are names about which most white Anglo-Saxons have no clear intuitions, even to the extent of recognizing whether they belong to boys or to girls – Arabic names such as *Kamal* ('perfection'), *Khalid* ('eternal'), *Mahmud* ('praiseworthy'), and *Mansur* ('victorious'); Indian names such as *Ravi* ('sun'), *Rama* ('pleasing'), *Vasu* ('bright'), and *Vishwanath* ('lord of all').

TOP TEN FIRST NAMES

	1700	1800	1900	1925	1950	mid-1960s	mid-1970s	mid-1980s
Girls in England and Wales	Mary	Mary	Florence	Joan	Susan	Tracey	Claire	Sarah
	Elizabeth	Ann	Mary	Mary	Linda	Deborah	Sarah	Claire
	Ann	Elizabeth	Alice	Joyce	Christine	Julie	Nicola	Emma
	Sarah	Sarah	Annie	Margaret	Margaret	Karen	Emma	Laura
	Jane	Jane	Elsie	Dorothy	Carol	Susan	Joanne	Rebecca
	Margaret	Hannah	Edith	Doris	Jennifer	Alison	Helen	Gemma
	Susan	Susan	Elizabeth	Kathleen	Janet	Jacqueline	Rachel	Rachel
	Martha	Martha	Doris	Irene	Patricia	Helen	Lisa	Kelly
	Hannah	Margaret	Dorothy	Betty	Barbara	Amanda	Rebecca	Victoria
	Catherine	Charlotte	Ethel	Eileen	Ann	Sharon	Karen	Katharine
Boys in England and Wales	John	William	William	John	David	Paul	Stephen	Christopher
	William	John	John	William	John	David	Mark	Matthew
	Thomas	Thomas	George	George	Peter	Andrew	Paul	David
	Richard	James	Thomas	James	Michael	Stephen	Andrew	James
	James	George	Charles	Ronald	Alan	Mark	David	Daniel
	Robert	Joseph	Frederick	Robert	Robert	Michael	Richard	Andrew
	Joseph	Richard	Arthur	Kenneth	Stephen	Ian	Matthew	Steven
	Edward	Henry	James	Frederick	Paul	Gary	Daniel	Michael
	Henry	Robert	Albert	Thomas	Brian	Robert	Christopher	Mark
	George	Charles	Ernest	Albert	Graham	Richard	Darren	Paul

	1875	1900	1925	1950	1960	1970	mid-1980s (white)	mid-1980s (non-white)
Girls in the USA	Mary	Mary	Mary	Linda	Mary	Michelle	Jennifer	Tiffany
	Anna	Ruth	Barbara	Mary	Deborah	Jennifer	Sarah	Ashley
	Elizabeth	Helen	Dorothy	Patricia	Karen	Kimberly	Jessica	Latoya
	Emma	Margaret	Betty	Susan	Susan	Lisa	Ashley	Crystal
	Alice	Elizabeth	Ruth	Deborah	Linda	Tracy	Amanda	Erica
	Edith	Dorothy	Margaret	Kathleen	Patricia	Kelly	Megan	Danielle
	Florence	Catherine	Helen	Barbara	Kimberly	Nicole	Nicole	Jennifer
	May	Mildred	Elizabeth	Nancy	Catherine	Angela	Katherine	Ebony
	Helen	Frances	Jean	Sharon	Cynthia	Pamela	Lindsey	Jessica
	Katharine	Alice	Ann	Karen	Lori	Christine	Stephanie	Candice
Boys in the USA	William	John	Robert	Robert	Michael	Michael	Michael	Michael
	John	William	John	Michael	David	Robert	Christopher	Christopher
	Charles	Charles	William	James	Robert	David	Matthew	Brandon
	Harry	Robert	James	John	James	James	Joshua	Anthony
	James	Joseph	Charles	David	John	John	David	James
	George	James	Richard	William	Mark	Jeffrey	Daniel	Robert
	Frank	George	George	Thomas	Steven	Steven	Ryan	Marcus
	Robert	Samuel	Donald	Richard	Thomas	Christopher	Andrew	David
	Joseph	Thomas	Joseph	Gary	William	Brian	Brian	Brian
	Thomas	Arthur	Edward	Charles	Joseph	Mark	John	Jason

Nicknames

The word *nickname* is first recorded in the 15th century: 'an eke name' (Old English *eke*, 'also') was an extra or additional name used to express such attitudes as familiarity, affection, and ridicule. Nicknames are usually applied to people, but places and things can have them too. All the US States have nicknames (p. 145), as do many tourist and business areas (*Costa Brava* in Spain, *Silicon Valley* in California), cities (*Motown* for Detroit), countries (*The Emerald Isle* for Ireland), and astronomical bodies (*Red Planet* for Mars). There are even nicknames based on nicknames, such as *Costa Geriatrica* for the coastal towns in southern England where many retired elderly people live. Among the objects which have been given nicknames are flags (*Jolly Roger*), newspapers (*The Thunderer* for *The Times* of London), symphonies (*Eroica*), and clocks (*Big Ben*). A nickname can also have several applications: the *Big Bang* may have happened at the beginning of the universe, but it also occurred at the moment of deregulation in the City of London Stock Exchange in October 1986.

Personal nicknames are commonest among children, but any closely-knit group will generate nicknames (such as the members of a family, sports team, or army unit). People who tend to be nicknamed are special friends or enemies, those in authority (teachers, officers, politicians), and anyone who has achieved notoriety (especially criminals). It is an important index of intimacy when we feel comfortable in using someone's nickname to their face. Some nicknames have come to be associated with particular surnames: *Chalky* goes with *White*, *Nobby* with *Clark*, *Spider* with *Webb*, and *Spud* with *Murphy*. Some first names, likewise, have standard nicknames: *Chuck* (Charles), *Menace* (Dennis), *Spike* (Michael). Hair colour (*Ginger*) or absence (*Baldy*), spectacles (*Four-Eyes*), size (*Tubby*), and other features of physique or behaviour have long been a prime source.

Pseudonyms

Many people adopt a name other than their original name for a particular purpose – perhaps to convey an image of some kind, to avoid an unpleasant association, to make their identity more memorable, to hide their identity, or simply to make their name more pronounceable or easier to spell. Terminology varies, but *pseudonym*, *pen-name*, *nom de plume*, *stage-name*, *byname*, *alias*, and *allonym* have all been used, with different nuances, to identify the practice. While the option is available to anyone, certain professions attract the use of pseudonyms – notably, authors, actors, and media personalities. Among famous writers who used pen-names are the Brontë sisters, Charlotte, Emily, and Anne (*Currer*, *Ellis*, and *Acton Bell*), Charles Dodgson (*Lewis Carroll*), and Charles Dickens (*Boz*). Stage-names have three main methods of derivation – they may change a surname only (*Fred Astaire* from *Frederick Austerlitz*), a first name only (*Kim Novak* from *Marilyn Novak*), or the whole name (*Boris Karloff* from *William Henry Pratt*, *Cliff Richard* from *Harold Roger Webb*, *John Wayne* from *Marion Michael Morrison*). Single-item names are also known: *Twiggy* (*Lesley Hornby*), *Madonna* (*Madonna Louise Ciccone*).

ONOMASTIC UNIQUENESS

President Andrew Jackson (1767–1845), seventh president of the USA, known as *Old Hickory*, whose strong-willed administration gave him his nickname (a tree known for its tough wood).

From time to time someone is given a nickname, in this way, which remains unique to that person. There is only one *Merry Monarch* (Charles II), one *Capability Brown* (Lancelot Brown, 18th-century landscape-gardener), one *Iron Duke* (the Duke of Wellington), and one *Old Hickory*.

Personal names abound in idiosyncrasy. The telescoping of certain British surnames is a well-known feature which defies predictability: there is no way in which anyone could guess the pronunciation of *Marjoribanks* as 'Marshbanks', of *Featherstonehaugh* as 'Fanshaw', or of *Cholmondley* as 'Chumley'. Social, not linguistic, tuition is what is required in such cases.

THE LANGUAGE OF VALENTINES

An extract from a page of St Valentine's Day greetings, taken from *The Independent on Sunday* on 14 February 1993. Probably on no other occasion is the practice of idiosyncratic nicknaming taken to such great extremes. The entries are also notable for their use of bizarre and deviant linguistic features operating at all levels of language (p.400).

WATCH OUT SCHNOOTER Mr Sniperty Snooperty is after you. All my love Sausage.

SCMALISON, carling chemist contemplates coupling with languid linguist.

RITA FROM THE HEELANDS love you still yobread.

KAREN, LOVE YOU loads, your white Wooly Ram.

FIRST, MEWSING; then courting; now ingling; love, C.

THE SWEETIEST kiss I can give you after a shooting star.

IN PLAY RUB Mooma Vooma ook ook R.

KITBAG Six smashing years, love you more, Div.

PETER IS YUMMY, the coley was scrummy, muffet.

LESLIE LOVE YOU more as Mrs M. JCx.

HAPPINESS IS two size six and twelve paws.

WENDY. Happy Valentines Love Mark and Rover. ARF.

ALISON, tie your shoelaces to my shoelaces. Love you always Dave.

DEAR CRED, the mother-ship loves you.

PERFECT IS amazing your amazing love beb.

PUDSO I STILL fancy you love from pert.

MARY, over here at last, with me for ever. Andrew.

IAN sausages for ever. Love cold footed mole.

ELBOW, ILY, IILWY, YMMW. Festive 50 No1 1990.

ALL MY LOVE Cuddly Chops, from Kevin Costner.

LOVING YOU, MY puppy. Is the most wonderful emotion I possess. Yours always, your Bondigowee.

STINKY VAMP, you're my little love Bubble, Kevin.

COME DOWN FROM THAT fence and sip the wine, no need to call me Terence, just be mine.

TO TEEB, with love from the far shores. USA Dobbins Inc.

BOAT EVANS you bring out the be(a)st in me Hunky man.

MAUREEN DARLING WIFE our magic continues to tingle and blossom I love you James.

DEAR LADY JANE, the red robin loves you.

SYLVIA Tenth year. Still care. Still there. Toge.

FROM AFAR? Secret squirrel feeder will always be loved & missed.

TOOTS CHESHAM The slide, the rain finding you. I love you, Chris.

IRENE THINKING OF you, all my love always, Glyn.

TANT VOTRE IMAGE à jamais chère habite en ce coeur tout à vous.

DOLLY DONUT, my love for you grows each day. I am the luckiest man in the world to have you for my wife. 42R.

FREDDIE, YOU CAN STICK your fingers in my chocolate heart any time you donnerstag pet.

MUMMY 2B, you're the top! Love Daddy 2b.

RATFINK weely weely wuv yoo tonz fwom woooo!

DARLING KIRSTY, CLOSER together, though perceptions still differ. All my love, Simon.

JAY first March too long love now. Gee.

SNOWBALL YOU STILL warm this Hippo's heart.

JAN TATTERED and torn but not forlorn. Love Alan, Derek, Graham.

MY NISH, one kish is all, I wish.

I LOVE YOU G Happy valentines Love E.

WINDOWS, SHIPS, FROGS, all could make your valentine.

MINIMUS MUM, I love you, Dads.

GOOD MORNING Squeaky mouse Happy Valentines love Bear.

SPARKLES I LOVE YOU HUGS and kisses Peter.

S.W., I LOVE you madly. Be mine forever, S.P.

CLAIRE T-of-B in admiration Manqué Puzzle.

TO TWEETIE PIE from   Bear... let's snog.

BUZZY BEE – Love from mine to yours.

RSK I love you even more. We will make great things in 93 and onto Down Under.

SOUNDS (FE)MALE

When first names are given a phonological analysis (p. 236), some interesting differences emerge between males and females. It seems the sexes do not sound the same. The results reported below were derived from an analysis of 1,667 entries in a dictionary of English first names, but the claims can easily be checked against the lists of popular names given on p. 37.

• Female first names tend to be longer than males, in terms of the number of syllables they contain. Males are much more likely to have a monosyllabic first name (*Bob, Jim, Fred, Frank, John*), and much less likely to have a name of three or more syllables (*Christopher, Nicholas*). By contrast, there are few monosyllabic female names in the list (*Ann, Joan, May*), and many of them are trisyllabic or longer (*Katharine, Elizabeth, Amanda, Victoria*).

• 95 per cent of male names have a firrst syllable which is strongly stressed, whereas only 75 per cent of female names show this pattern. It is not difficult to think of female names which begin with an un-stressed syllable (*Patricia, Elizabeth, Amanda, Rebecca, Michelle*), but male names are few and far between (*Jerome, Demetrius*). In fact, none of the popular British male names in the past 75 years has had an unstressed initial syllable – and only three American names.

• The stressed syllables of female names tend to make much more use of the high front vowel /i/, such as *Lisa, Tina, Celia, Maxine*, and the archetypal *Fifi* and *Mimi*. Male names in /i/ are far less common (*Steve, Keith, Peter*).

• Female pet names tend to be longer than male. A bisyllabic pet name could be either male or female, but a monosyllabic one is much more likely to be male. *Jackie* could be either sex, but *Jack* is male. Several other pairs share this expectancy, such as *Bill/Billie* and *Bob/Bobbie*.

• Female names are much more likely to end in a (spoken) vowel, as with *Linda, Tracey, Patricia, Deborah, Mary, Barbara*. If not a vowel, the last sound will very likely be a continuant (p. 242), especially a nasal (*Jean, Kathleen, Sharon, Ann*). By contrast, plosives are much more likely to be found in male endings (*Bob, David, Dick, Jock*). Interesting comparative questions arise. Is *Kate* more male-sounding than *Kath* or *Katie* or *Katherine*? Nothing is more likely to generate controversy.

It is of course difficult, perhaps impossible, to explain these trends. Could the sound-symbolic associations of /i/ (p. 250), such as smallness and brightness, explain the bias of that vowel? Can we relate the trend towards use of an initial stressed syllable to greater masculine aggressiveness? One thing is sure: it is much more difficult to generalize safely about female names. Popular

male names are used much more predictably. There are several male names which have appeared on every list of the top 20 names in recent times (e.g. *John, David*), but no one female name appears on all lists. People are much readier to be inventive and different with female names.

Whatever the explanations, it would appear that a name such as *Sabrina* is as clear-cut a 'feminine' name as we are likely to find: it has more than two syllables, an un-stressed first syllable, and a strong /i/ vowel. Another example is *Christine*, judged by men to be the most sexy female name, in one US survey. By contrast, *Bob* is a highly 'masculine' name. Such conclusions shed some light on the way comedians and scriptwriters obtain comic effects, simply by selecting an inappropriate name. Why else would British comedian Rowan Atkinson, in one of his series, call a pretty girl in soldier's uniform *Bob*, or the British satirical programme *Spitting Image* advise its listeners to 'pretend your name is Keith' (in *The Chicken Song*, Virgin Records, 1986)?
(After A. Cutler, J. McQueen & K. Robinson, 1990.)

Proportions of male names and female names with one, two, three, and four/five syllables

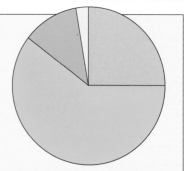

Male names Number of syllables

	1: 24.3%
	2: 60.2%
	3: 13.4%
	4/5: 2.1%

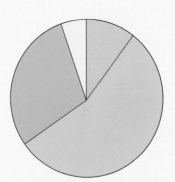

Female names Number of syllables

	1: 9.7%
	2: 54.2%
	3: 29.1%
	4/5: 7%

I'FAITH, KATE

When Henry V of England meets Princess Katherine of France (in Shakespeare's *Henry V*, 5.ii), he calls her both *Katherine* and *Kate*. But he uses *Katherine* only with a pre-ceding attribute – usually *fair*, but also *dear*, *la plus belle*, and *Queen of all* – each a strongly female collo-cation. When Henry uses a straight-forward vocative, it is *Kate* – an appropriate pet form, perhaps, from a 'plain king' who knows 'no ways to mince it in love', and who speaks to her as a 'plain soldier'.

Kenneth Branagh as Henry and Emma Thompson as Katherine in a scene from Henry V *(1989)*

OBJECT NAMES

In principle, we can give an individual name to any entity or concept; in practice, we do this in a very selective way. There seems to be an intuitive scale of 'nameability' which motivates us to name things on the basis of their closeness or relevance to our lives. People and the places where they live are at the top of this scale. Animals come next – but those animals which we treat as pets (dogs, cats, rabbits, budgerigars, etc.) are much more likely to receive individual names than are the 'lower animals'. We do not tend to give personal names to spiders, slugs, and snakes – though there is a 9-year-old-boy exception to every rule, and people have been known to develop all kinds of personal relationships with friendly insects (such as the English student in a foreign bedsit who dubbed her daily visiting cockroach *Arnold Schwarzenegger*). Objects which move us about in groups are also relatively high on this scale: we regularly name locomotives, aeroplanes, buses, and boats. (Curiously, our personal chariots – our automobiles, bicycles, motorcycles, and skateboards – are much less frequently named.) Items of special value or usefulness, such as washing-machines and wheelbarrows, also receive names. At the other end of the scale, we do not normally name objects which are easily replaced, or which have only an incidental role in our lives, such as pencils, stones, and hedges.

It is important to appreciate the variety of reasons which lead us to name things. Pride, affection, and nostalgia combine with such hard-nosed factors as practicability, recognizability, memorability, and saleability. Many objects, such as locomotives and coloured paints, are unambiguously identifiable through their number, code, or formula. They do not 'need' personalized names, but they are often named nonetheless. And if a category of objects becomes of special human relevance, it will attract a set of individual names, as we see in the case of food and drink (potatoes, apples, cocktails), personal products (lipsticks, perfumes, deodorants), and hobbies (roses, orchids, birds). The extent of the phenomenon must be appreciated: for example there are over 7,500 names in use for the 6,000 cultivars listed in the *National Apple Register of the United Kingdom* (1971). It is perhaps not surprising, then, to find that several countries have name societies which promote an interest in onomastic studies (p. 140).

LOCOMOTIVE NAMES

Most of the larger British steam locomotives have been given individual names – a practice which dates from the earliest railway days. George Stephenson's *Rocket* (1829) takes its place alongside such contemporary names as *Novelty*, *Locomotion*, and *Catch Me Who Can*. Often, series of names have been devised on a single theme, such as castles, counties, or universities. Some names have come to be particularly well known, either because of the records they achieved or the routes they travelled, as in the case of the *Flying Scotsman*, the *Mancunian*, the *Mallard*, and the *Welsh Dragon*. The naming of locomotives remains, however, a distinctively British practice.

The *Rocket*

COLOUR CHARTS

Part of the *Atlas of the Munsell Color System*, devised by the American artist Albert Henry Munsell in 1915. This was the most successful of many early attempts to construct a logical basis for colour systems. Standard methods of notation have been devised to identify the thousands of distinctions which can be recognized: for example, in one system a particular sample of emerald green is identifiable by the formula 5.0G 6.7/11.2 (which refers to values for hue and chroma).

Paint manufacturers tend not to present their customers with formulae, but prefer such appealing and memorable (albeit arbitrary) labels as *Serenade*, *Monte Carlo*, *Buttercup*, and *Forget-Me-Not*. However, these names vary greatly in their relationship to visual reality: *Pastel Green* and *Silver Grey* are intuitively meaningful (though the paint shades vary greatly between manufacturers who use these names); *Water Lily* and *Cornflower* are plausibly recognizable; *Early Dawn* and *Morning Sun* are doubtfully predictable; and *Nocturne* and *Sonata* have no visual basis at all (the names being chosen because of their semantic relevance to a series of colours which the manufacturer has called 'New Harmonies'). (See also p. 171.)

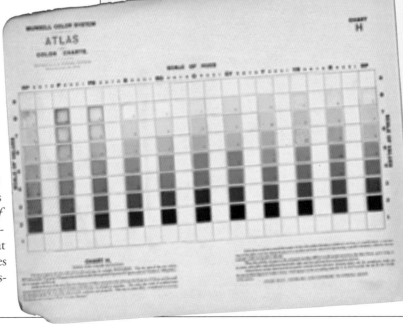

Names into words

In this section we have been looking at the many ways in which elements of the English language have been used in the formation of names. It closes with a brief look at the opposite process – where names are used in the formation of new lexemes. When a personal name is used in this way, it is known as an *eponym*, and the process as *eponymy*. Confusingly, the same term is also sometimes used for the derived form. So, the name of the French acrobat Jules *Léotard* (1842-70) as well as the close-fitting one-piece costume which he introduced in his circus act could both be referred to as *eponyms*. Similarly, lexemes which are derived from place names, as well as the place names themselves, are often known as *toponyms* (p. 140).

EPONYMOUS WORDS

Pavlova A meringue topped with cream and fruit. Source: Anna Pavlova (1885–1931), Russian ballerina. The concoction was devised by Australian chefs, reflecting her popularity during a tour of Australia and New Zealand.

volt The unit of electrical potential difference and electromotive force. Source: Italian physicist *Alessandro Volta* (1745–1827), the inventor of the electric battery.

Crufts The annual British dog show. Source: British dog breeder and showman *Charles Cruft* (1852–1939), who organized his first show in 1886.

cardigan A knitted jacket fastened with buttons, first worn during the Crimean War as protection against the cold winters. Source: English cavalry officer James Thomas Brudenell, *seventh Earl of Cardigan* (1797–1868), who led the 'Charge of the Light Brigade' at Balaclava (1854).

maverick An independent person who refuses to conform. Source: US pioneer *Samuel Augustus Maverick* (1803–70), who did not brand his calves.

nicotine Chemical compound, known for its presence in tobacco. Source: French diplomat and scholar *Jean Nicot* (1530–1600), who introduced tobacco into France.

teddy bear A soft toy in the shape of a bear. Source: US president *Theodore Roosevelt* (1858–1919), whose nickname was *Teddy*. The usage emerged after a cartoon showed Roosevelt, known as a bear-hunter, sparing the life of a bear cub.

magnolia A genus of shrubs and trees with large showy flowers. Source: French botanist *Pierre Magnol* (1638–1715), known for his system of plant classification.

EPONYMOUS HERO(IN)ES

Fictitious or mythical people can also be eponymous: *He's a real Romeo; What a Scrooge!*

atlas: Greek Titan, Atlas.
Cinderella: fairy tale character.
herculean: Greek god, Hercules.
Jekyll and Hyde: characters in a novel by Robert Louis Stevenson.
June: Roman goddess, Juno.
keeping up with the Joneses: characters in a US comic strip (1913).
man Friday: character in Daniel Defoe's *Robinson Crusoe*.
mentor: Mentor, a character in Homer's *Odyssey*.
quixotic: hero of Cervantes' novel, *Don Quixote de la Mancha*.
Romeo: character in Shakespeare's *Romeo and Juliet*.
Scrooge: character in Dickens' story, *A Christmas Carol*.
Shylock: character in Shakespeare's *Merchant of Venice*.
Thursday: Norse god, Thor.

EPONYMOUS PLACES

Place names are a common source of lexemes.

alsatian: Alsace, France.
balaclava: Balaclava, Crimea.
bikini: Bikini Atoll, Marshall Islands.
bourbon: Bourbon County, Kentucky.
Brussels sprouts: Brussels, Belgium.
champagne: Champagne, France.
conga: Congo, Africa.
copper: Cyprus.
currant: Corinth, Greece.
denim: Nîmes, France (originally, *serge de Nim*).
dollar: St Joachimsthal, Bohemia (which minted silver coins called *joachimstalers*, shortened to *thalers*, hence *dollars*).
duffle coat: Duffel, Antwerp.
gauze: Gaza, Israel.
gypsy: Egypt.
hamburger: Hamburg, Germany.
jeans: Genoa, Italy.
jersey: Jersey, Channel Islands.
kaolin: Kao-ling, China.
labrador: Labrador, Canada.
lesbian: Lesbos, Aegean island.
marathon: Marathon, Greece.
mayonnaise: Mahón, Minorca.
mazurka: Mazowia, Poland.
muslin: Mosul, Iraq.
pheasant: Phasis, Georgia.
pistol: Pistoia, Italy.
rugby: Rugby (School), UK.
sardine: Sardinia.
sherry: Jerez, Spain.
suede: Sweden.
tangerine: Tangier.
turquoise: Turkey.
tuxedo: Tuxedo Park Country Club, New York.
Venetian blind: Venice, Italy.

11 · THE STRUCTURE OF THE LEXICON

In seeking guidance about the lexicon of a language, no book is more widely used or appreciated than the traditional dictionary (p. 442). Its alphabetical organization is - once we have learned how to spell – straightforwardly efficient, and its sense-by-sense entry structure is sensible and succinct. We might be forgiven, therefore, for thinking that the dictionary contains everything we would ever want to know about lexemes (p. 118). Such a belief, however, would be quite wrong. Conventional dictionaries contain very little information about the way the lexicon is structured.

When we talk about the 'structure' of the lexicon, we are referring to the network of meaning relationships which bind lexemes together – what is known as its *semantic structure*. No lexeme exists in splendid isolation. As soon as we think of one (say, *uncle*), a series of others come to mind. Some of these lexemes help to define *uncle* (*brother*, *father*, *mother*), others relate to it closely in meaning (*aunt*, *cousin*, *nephew*, *niece*), others have a looser semantic connection (*relatives*, *family*, *visit*, *outing*), and there may be figurative or literary uses (*Uncle Sam*, *Uncle Tom Cobleigh*), as well as a few personal or idiosyncratic associations (*birthday*, *funeral*, *loony*). If we mentally probe all aspects of the semantic network which surrounds *uncle*, we shall soon build up a large number of connections. But if we look at a dictionary entry for *uncle*, we shall see very few of our intuitions represented there. Some works give the bare minimum of information: 'brother of a father or mother', says one; and at *aunt*, 'sister of a father or mother'. Nowhere in this particular book are we told of the meaning relationship which binds these two nouns, despite the alphabetical distance which divorces them.

When we study semantic structure, we are trying to expound all the relationships of meaning that relate lexemes to each other. However, because of the size and complexity of the English lexicon, very little of this structure has been described. There have been a few theoretical accounts introducing such basic notions as synonymy and antonymy (p. 164), some attempts at general classification, and the detailed investigation of some small areas of meaning. We now know broadly what kinds of lexical relationship exist; but the descriptive task remains. The following pages can only be illustrative, therefore, and can do little more than indicate the size of the task facing those who wish to get to grips with lexical structure.

B24 *nouns & verbs* : **the eye in detail**

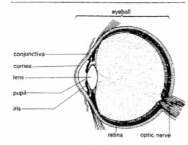

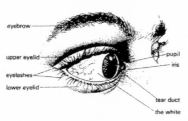

the eye

eyebrow [C] the line of hairs above each of the two human eyes: *He has very thick dark eyebrows; they make him look fierce.*
eyelid [C] one of the pieces of covering skin which can move down to close each eye: *Fish do not have eyelids and some creatures have more than one on each eye. He blinked his eyelids to clear his eyes.*
eyelash [C] one of the small hairs of which a number grow from the edge of each eyelid in humans and most hairy animals: *The eyelashes keep dust from the eyes. I have an eyelash in my eye; it's hurting my eye.*
eyeball [C] the whole of the eye, including the part inside the head, which forms a more or less round ball
pupil [C] the small black round opening which can grow larger or smaller in the middle of the coloured part of the eye, through which light passes
iris [C] the round coloured part of the eye which surrounds the pupil
white [C] the white part of the eye around the iris, which shows all the time in the human eye, but is usually hidden in animals: *The whites of his eyes were bloodshot from lack of sleep. The frightened horse showed the whites of its eyes.*
blink 1 [T1; I0] to shut and open (the eyes) quickly, usu because of strong light, surprise, tears, etc: *She blinked (her eyes) in surprise.* **2** [I0](*fig*) (of distant lights) to seem to be unsteady; seem to go rapidly on and off: *The ship's lights blinked at us across the water.* **3** [T1; I0] *AmE* to wink **4** [C] an act of blinking: *The blink of an eye.*
wink 1 [T1; I0] to shut and open (one eye) quickly, sometimes with quick slight movement of the head, to show friendliness, amusement, a shared secret, etc: *He winked his left eye. She winked at him and smiled.* **2** [C] an act of doing this: *He gave a friendly wink.*

B25 *nouns* : **kinds of noses** [C]

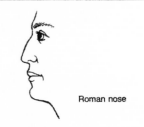

Roman nose

Roman nose a nose that curves out near the top at the bridge

retroussé nose

retroussé nose a nose that is turned back at the lower end

snub nose

snub nose a nose that is short and flat with the end turned back

---

SEMANTIC FIELDS

A fruitful notion in investigating lexical structure is the *semantic* or *lexical field* – a named area of meaning in which lexemes interrelate and define each other in specific ways. Think, for example, of all the lexemes we know to do with 'fruit', or 'parts of the body', or 'vehicles', or 'buildings', or 'colour'. We shall have no difficulty assigning *banana, nostril, lorry, town hall,* and *scarlet* to their respective fields. To what extent is it possible to assign all the lexemes in English to a semantic field in an unambiguous way?

The task is not as straightforward as it might appear, for several reasons. Some lexemes seem to belong to fields which are very difficult to define, or which are vague – to what field should *noise* or *difficult* belong? Some seem to belong to more than one field – does *orange* belong to 'fruit' or 'colour'? And some lexemes seem to fall midway between two fields – does *tomato* belong to 'fruit' or 'vegetable'? There is also the ques-

tion of how best to define a semantic field: shall we say that *tractor* belongs to the field of 'agricultural vehicles', 'land vehicles', or just 'vehicles'? is *flavour* part of the semantic field of 'taste', or *taste* part of the semantic field of 'flavour', or are both members of some broader semantic field, such as 'sensation'?

These are typical of the problems which keep semanticists in work, as they try to relate the neatness of their analytical categories to the fuzziness of the real world. At the same time, the existence of these difficulties must not hide the fact that a very large number of lexemes can be grouped together into fields and subfields in a fairly clear-cut way. That these accounts are illuminating can be seen from their growing use in such domains as foreign language teaching and speech therapy, where it has proved helpful to present learners with sets of related lexemes, rather than with a series of randomly chosen items (p. 434). And young children, too, learn much of their vocabulary by bringing lexemes together in this way (p. 424).

THE STYLISTIC FACTOR

Some of the lexemes belonging to the semantic field of 'madness', so arranged that it is possible to see differences in their stylistic type (p. 394). At the top of the circle are the items which are literary, academic, or technical in character; at the bottom are the colloquialisms. Items on the left are somewhat dated or archaic; those on the right are relatively recent in origin. The

stylistically neutral lexeme which identifies the field as a whole is placed in the centre.

This kind of perspective is essential if we wish to see order in the long lists of lexemes found in a thesaurus (p. 158). When we are linking items in the lexicon, we need to take account of the stylistic level at which they operate. From a structural semantic point of view, the opposite of *sane* is *insane*, not *bonkers*.

(After G. Hughes, 1988.)

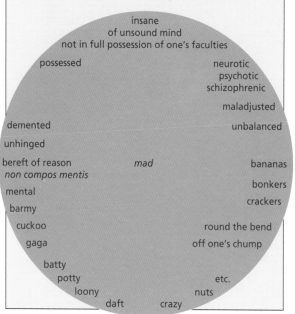

insane
of unsound mind
not in full possession of one's faculties

possessed

neurotic
psychotic
schizophrenic

maladjusted

demented

unbalanced

unhinged

bereft of reason
non compos mentis

mad

bananas

bonkers

mental

crackers

barmy

cuckoo

round the bend

gaga

off one's chump

batty

potty

etc.

loony

nuts

daft

crazy

THE VOCABULARY OF WINE

Wine appreciation is an interesting semantic field, because its lexemes are largely figurative applications from other fields. Terms which we would normally associate with music, textiles, food, physique, personality, morality, and behaviour rub shoulders with terms from colour, chemistry, botany, and nutrition. Because the topic is so subjective, the lexicon plays a critical role. The relationships between the lexemes define the contrasts of taste which the wine enthusiast seeks to identify. To learn about wine is first to learn how to talk about wine. This can be seen in the following definitions, taken from a popular introduction.

bland Implies lack of character, too mild.
crisp Firm, brisk, refreshing, zestful. Indicates good level of acidity, particularly in dry whites.
dry In relation to wine always means not sweet; sugar fully fermented out.
finesse An abstract qualitative term

related to refinement, elegance.
firm Sound constitution, positive. A desirable quality on the palate.
flabby Soft, feeble, lacking acidity on the palate.
flat The next stage after flabby, well beyond bland. Total lack of vigour on nose and on palate; lack of acidity; oxidation.
heavy Over-endowed with alcohol, more than full bodied; clumsy, lacking finesse.
meaty Rich 'chunky' nose, almost chewable flavour.
piquant A high-toned, over-fragrant, fruity nose verging on sharp, usually confirmed by an over-acidic end taste.
pricked Distinctly sharper

than piquant. Acetic smell, tart. An irremediable fault.
sharp Acidity on the nose and palate somewhere between piquant and pricked. Usually indicating a fault.
sinewy Lean, muscular on the palate. Usually a wine of some potential.
stringy A texture: on the thin and scrawny side, lacking equability.
supple Texture, balance: pleasant combination of vigour and harmony.
tart Sharp, nose catching, tongue curling.
velvety A textural description: silky, smooth, a certain opulence on the palate.

(After M. Broadbent, 1983.)

THE THESAURUS

The notion of semantic fields (p. 157) suggests that there may be other possible approaches to lexicography than the traditional one using alphabetical order. The *thesaurus* is such an alternative. Thesauri are based on the notion of grouping lexemes thematically – a notion which can be traced back to 16th-century schemes for the classification of all human knowledge. Francis Bacon (1561–1626) and John Wilkins (1614–72), in particular, wrote essays which outlined a way of dividing everything into a small number of major areas, each being progressively subclassified until all concepts are dealt with in their appropriate place. Such attempts at a universal hierarchy fell out of favour until the 19th century, when scientific interest in taxonomy became a dominant feature of the age, and the botanical metaphor of the tree came to be applied to language as well as to natural history.

Roget's *Thesaurus*

The influence of natural history is evident in the work which pioneered the thesaurus as we know it today. Roget's *Thesaurus*, first published in 1852, divides the lexicon into six main areas: abstract relations, space, the material world, the intellect, volition, and sentient/moral powers. Each area is then progressively subclassified, giving a total of 1,000 semantic categories. In his Introduction, Roget explains his aim and method:

The present Work is intended to supply, with respect to the English language, a desideratum hitherto unsupplied in any language; namely, a collection of the words it contains and of the idiomatic combinations peculiar to it, arranged, not in the alphabetical order as they are in a Dictionary, but according to the *ideas* which they express … The principle by which I have been guided in framing my verbal classification is the same as that which is employed in the various departments of Natural History. Thus the sectional divisions I have formed, correspond to Natural Families in Botany and Zoology, and the filiation of words presents a network analogous to the natural filiation of plants or animals.

Roget assumed that his readers would be able to find their way through the Thesaurus by working intuitively down through his classifications. He added a short alphabetical index, but it was left to his son, John Lewis Roget, to develop this in the 1879 edition into a major feature of the book. In modern editions, the index takes up as many pages as does the thematic classification, and is the way into the work which most people use.

New thematic models

A thesaurus acts as a complement to the traditional dictionary: in a dictionary, we have a lexeme in mind, and wish to check on its meaning or use; by contrast,

PETER MARK ROGET (1779–1869)

It is now nearly fifty years since I first projected a system of verbal classification similar to that on which the present Work is founded. Conceiving that such a compilation might help to supply my own deficiencies, I had, in the year 1805, completed a classed catalogue of words on a small scale …

Roget was born in Soho, London, the son of the pastor at the French Protestant church in Threadneedle Street. He studied at Edinburgh University, and became a doctor by the age of 19. In 1804 he was appointed physician to the Manchester Infirmary, and it was there that he began to collect material for his thesaurus. In 1808 he moved to London, where he held various medical posts, and was active in helping to found London University. He also became the first Fullerian Professor of Physiology at the Russell Institution. He wrote a great deal, on a wide range of subjects, and contributed to many encyclopedias and journals. He became a fellow of the Royal College of Physicians, and also of the Royal Society, where he eventually took up the post of Secretary (1827–49). He retired as a doctor in 1840, but continued to work at diverse projects – including a calculating machine and a pocket chessboard.

He started again on the thesaurus project in 1849, retirement from his Royal Society post having given him the spare time he needed. After three years of intensive work, the book was published, and was a remarkable success, with 28 editions published by the time of his death. He died at the age of 91 at West Malvern in Worcestershire. His son, John Lewis Roget, took over as editor, and *his* son, Samuel Romilly Roget, continued the family editorial connection until Longmans, Green & Co purchased the copyright from him in 1952. Modern editions show the influence of the 1962 revision by Cambridge scholar Robert Dutch, which reorganized the layout and headings, and introduced keywords in italics. The most recent edition, edited by Betty Kirkpatrick, appeared in 1987.

WORD-FINDERS

In the *Chambers Thesaurus* (1991) clusters of sense-related items are arranged in alphabetical order. Several 'family word-finder' books are organized in this way.

silhouette *n.* configuration, delineation, form, outline, shadow-figure, shadowgraph, shape.

silky *adj.* fine, satiny, silken, sleek, smooth, soft, velvety.

silly *adj.* absurd, addled, asinine, benumbed, bird-brained, brainless, childish, cuckoo, daft, dazed, dopey, drippy, fatuous, feather-brained, flighty, foolhardy, foolish, frivolous, gaga, giddy, groggy, hen-witted, idiotic, illogical, immature, imprudent, inane, inappropriate, inept, irrational, irresponsible, meaningless, mindless, muzzy, pointless, preposterous, puerile, ridiculous, scatter-brained, senseless, spoony, stunned, stupefied, stupid, unwise, witless.

   antonyms collected, mature, sane, sensible, wise.

n. clot, dope, duffer, goose, half-wit, ignoramus, ninny, silly-billy, simpleton, twit, wally.

in a thesaurus we have a meaning in mind, and wish to check on the lexemes available to express it. A thesaurus such as Roget's, however, has obvious limitations. It does not provide any definitions: if we do not know the meaning of a lexeme in the thesaurus, we still need to look it up in a dictionary. It says nothing about the stylistic levels at which the lexemes are used: formal and informal items rub shoulders, as do items belonging to technical, professional, domestic, regional, and other varieties (Part V). There is no principled basis to the way lexemes are organized within entry paragraphs. And the traditional thesaurus is limited, for reasons of practicability, to the more commonly occurring lexemes: users are often left with the feeling that, even though no lexeme is listed for the meaning they have in mind, one may nonetheless exist, but have been omitted by accident. In recent years, efforts have begun to be made to reduce these limitations, some using new techniques of visual illustration, others aided by the vastly increased storage and retrieval power of the computer (p. 436).

ANOTHER WORD FOR *news*?

Two ways of finding the answer to this question are illustrated below. The first is from general to particular, identifying that *news* is a matter of the intellect, to do with communication, and moreover with a particular mode of communication. The second is to go to the index, where the various meanings of *news* are identified, and be sent directly to the relevant section (529). Most people use the latter method as the quickest way of answering a specific query; but the former method has its uses, too, when we are trying to develop a sense of the range of vocabulary available to express a concept.

Some of the noun entries for *news* are illustrated, taken from two editions of Roget: Dutch (1962) and Kirkpatrick (1987). It is interesting to compare the entries in detail, to see how the vocabulary has changed and developed during the intervening period. The general headings are those of the 1987 edition.

THE VISUAL DICTIONARY

A picture from the *Macmillan Visual Dictionary* (1992), showing the way a detailed illustration can add meaning to what would otherwise be a random listing of terms:

lintel, trefoil, pier, portal, tympanum, etc. The approach is obviously limited by the extent to which items can be clearly drawn, and so the book is largely composed of nouns. However, with over 800 pages of diagrams covering 600 subjects, it is an informative guide to the use of some 25,000 terms.

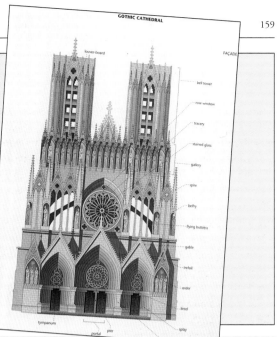

GOTHIC CATHEDRAL

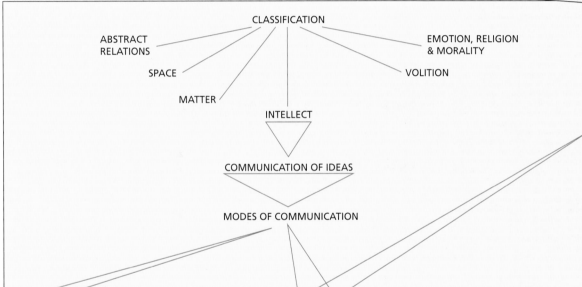

CLASSIFICATION

ABSTRACT RELATIONS

EMOTION, RELIGION & MORALITY

SPACE

VOLITION

MATTER

INTELLECT

COMMUNICATION OF IDEAS

MODES OF COMMUNICATION

529 News

N. *news*, good n.; bad news 509n. *disappointment*; tidings, glad t.; gospel, evangel 973n. *religion*; budget of news, packet of n., newspacket, despatches, diplomatic bag; intelligence, report, despatch, word, advice; piece of information, something to tell, titbit, flash 524n. *information*; bulletin, communiqué, hand-out; newspaper report, press notice; fresh news, stirring n., latest n., stop-press n.; sensation, scoop; old news, stale n.; copy, filler; yarn, story, old s.; tall s.; broadcast, telecast, newscast, newsreel 528n. *publicity*; news-value.
rumour, unverified news, unconfirmed report; flying rumour, fame; hearsay, gossip, gup, talk, talk of the town, tittle-tattle 584n. *chat*; scandal 926n. *calumny*; noise, cry, buzz, bruit; false report, hoax, canard; grape-vine; kite-flying.

message, oral m., word of mouth, word, advice, tip 524n. *information*; communication 547n. *signal*; marconigram, wireless message, radiogram, cablegram, cable, telegram, wire, lettergram 531n. *telecommunication*; letter, postcard, letters, despatches 588n. *correspondence*; ring, phone-call; errand, embassy 751n. *commission*.
newsmonger, quidnunc, gossip, talker 584n. *interlocutor*; tattler, chatterer; scandalmonger 926n. *defamer*; retailer of news, newspedlar; newsman, news-hound, news reporter, reporter, sob-sister, special correspondent 589n. *author*; newsboy, news-agent, newsvendor.

(Dutch, 1962)

529 News

N. *news*, good n., no news is good n.; bad news 509 *disappointment*; tidings, glad t.; gospel, evangel 973 *religion*; dispatches, diplomatic bag; intelligence, report, dispatch, word, intimation, advice; piece of information, something to tell, titbit 524 *information*; bulletin, communiqué, handout, press release; newspaper report, press notice; news item, news flash 531 *broadcast*; fresh news, stirring n., hot n., latest n., stop-press n.; sensation, scoop, exclusive; old news, stale n.; copy, filler; yarn, story, old s., tall s.; newscast, newsreel 528 *publicity*; news value, news-worthiness.
rumour, unverified news, unconfirmed report; flying rumour, fame; on dit, hearsay, gossip, gup, talk, talk of the town, tittle-tattle 584 *chat*; scandal 926 *calumny*; whisper, buzz, noise, bruit; false report, hoax, canard; grapevine, bush telegraph; kite-flying.

message, oral m., word of mouth, word, advice, tip 524 *information*; communication 547 *signal*; wireless message, radiogram, cablegram, cable, telegram, telemessage, wire, fax, electronic mail 531 *telecommunication*; postcard, pc, note, letters, dispatches 588 *correspondence*, 531 *postal communications*; ring, phone call, buzz, tinkle; errand, embassy 751 *commission*.
news reporter, newspaperman or -woman, reporter, cub r., journalist, correspondent, legman, stringer 589 *author*; gentleman or lady of the press, pressman or -woman, press representative 524 *informant*; newsreader, newscaster 531 *broadcaster*; newsmonger, quidnunc, gossip, tittle-tattler, talker 584 *interlocutor*; tattler, chatterer; muckraker, scandalmonger 926 *defamer*; retailer of news 528 *publicizer*; newsagent, newsvendor, newspaper boy or girl.

(Kirkpatrick, 1987)

newness
originality 21 n.
beginning 68 n.
newness 126 n.
new poor
unlucky person 731 n.
poor person 801 n.
news
topic 452 n.
information 524 n.
news 529 n.
broadcast 531 n.
important matter 638 n.
news agency
informant 524 n.
news blackout
prohibition 757 n.
newsagent
tradespeople 794 n.
newscast
publication 528 n.
news 529 n.
newscaster
news reporter 529 n.
broadcaster 531 n.
news flash
news 529 n.
broadcast 531 n.
newsletter
publicity 528 n.
the press 528 n.
newsmonger
news reporter 529 n.
newspaper
the press 528 n.
reading matter 589 n.
(Index: Kirkpatrick, 1987)

LEXICAL STRUCTURE

One way of imposing order on the thousands of lexemes which make up the English vocabulary is to group them into semantic fields (p. 157). But how are these fields structured? How exactly do the lexemes within a field relate to each other? It is obvious from dictionary definitions and thesaurus groupings that some lexemes do 'belong together'. How can we define what this 'belonging together' consists of?

A well-established model of lexical structure makes us think of lexemes as being related along two intersecting dimensions, as shown in the figure (right).

• On the horizontal dimension, we sense the relationships between lexemes in a *sequence*. There is a certain mutual expectancy between the main lexemes in the sentence *It writhed on the ground in excruciating pain.* Our linguistic intuition tells us that *excruciating* tends to occur with *pain*, *agony*, and a few other lexemes, and not with *joy*, *ignorance*, and most other nouns in the language. Likewise, *writhe* and *agony* commonly co-occur, as do *writhe* and *ground*. 'Horizontal' expectancies of this kind are known as *collocations*, or *selectional restrictions*. *Excruciating*, we can say, 'selects' or 'collocates with' *pain*.

• On the vertical dimension, we sense the way in which one lexeme can *substitute* for another, and relate to it in meaning. If the sentence were *My auntie has bought a red automobile*, we can focus on any one of the lexemes, and replace it. We might replace *bought* by a lexeme of similar meaning (a *synonym*), such as *purchased*; or by one of contrasting meaning (an *antonym*), such as *sold*. We might replace *automobile* by a lexeme of more specific meaning (a *hyponym*), such as *Ford*, or by one of more general meaning (a *hypernym*), such as *vehicle*. Or, of course, we might replace *automobile* by a lexeme which has nothing to do with it in meaning at all, such as *dress* or *pencil*. The predictable links between lexemes are called *sense relations*, and they are at the core of any account of lexical structure (p. 164).

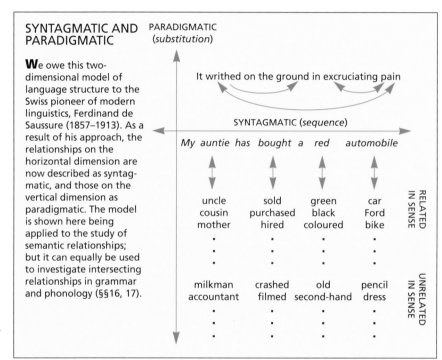

SYNTAGMATIC AND PARADIGMATIC

We owe this two-dimensional model of language structure to the Swiss pioneer of modern linguistics, Ferdinand de Saussure (1857–1913). As a result of his approach, the relationships on the horizontal dimension are now described as syntagmatic, and those on the vertical dimension as paradigmatic. The model is shown here being applied to the study of semantic relationships; but it can equally be used to investigate intersecting relationships in grammar and phonology (§§16, 17).

PARADIGMATIC *(substitution)*

It writhed on the ground in excruciating pain

SYNTAGMATIC *(sequence)*

My auntie has bought a red automobile

uncle	sold	green	car
cousin	purchased	black	Ford
mother	hired	coloured	bike
·	·	·	·
milkman	crashed	old	pencil
accountant	filmed	second-hand	dress
·	·	·	·

RELATED IN SENSE

UNRELATED IN SENSE

```
40359 03 US  89 ns the beautiful, classy woman has long been a Hollywood staple, a disturbing change has taken place in the characte
40180 02 WAF 90 ost of it produced locally. Maize is more important as a staple among the ethnic groups in the southern savanna than
40180 02 WAF 90 on the branching habit, and petiole colour. Cassava is a staple among the ethnic groups of southern Ghana particular
30055 09 UK  02 he foul reek of the surrounding swamp. In one of these a staple and chain, with a quantity of gnawed bones, showed w
00218 09 UK  01 ungry Umballa, and were among the mile-wide green of the staple crops.<para> He was a white-bearded and affable eld
30113 08 AUS 80 esting thing about the group is that many of them form a staple diet for Aboriginal people, while others which look
00078 08 UK  66 mount.<para>     That claret was considered a part of the staple diet, even of the or- dinary man, is clear from the
30113 08 AUS 80 to the camels later on, and stuck with what was to be my staple diet: brown rice, lentils, garlic, curry, oil, panca
40135 07 UK  88 water.<para>     It was a simple frugal life. The African staple diet was a solid, stodgy porridge, called sazda, mad
40180 02 WAF 90 portant item of diet in institutions. Where it becomes a staple diet it is important that the whole grain is eaten t
43021 04 UK  87 <para>   3.''There was no real labour aristocracy in the staple export trades- coal and the main branches of textile
00116 02 UK  59 all, while for some distance south of it rice is not the staple food of the inhabitants. The climate in the rice reg
42075 07 UK  73 here, but none fits exactly. This substance was Israel's staple food in an area where both rainfall and other condit
40180 02 WAF 90 hat in much of West Africa, they are still the preferred staple food ,among most of the inhabitants of the forest zon
40180 02 WAF 90 rridge or added to <ff>other cereals as meal. It is the staple food of many semi-Bantu tribes of northern Nigeria.
40075 07 UK  73 here, but none fits exactly. This substance was Israel's staple food for 40 years, ceasing abruptly when they entere
10116 02 UK  59 nd) crop but more usually in water. The ripe seed is the staple food in many Eastern countries. It is not, however,
40180 02 WAF 90 rn and Millet, in the northern parts of Ghana. It is the staple food in Senegal, parts of the Ivory Coast, Gambia, S
40135 07 UK  88 On the compound they were never desperately short of the staple foods, though it was more difficult when sanctions w
60465 04 UK  89  maltreated that the country is now desperately short of staple foods.<para>  <tab>Food self-sufficiency went long a
40100 04 US  34 all groups. Hunting and fishing must still have provided staple foods. Arrow-heads indeed are =   surprisingly rare
00091 09 US  71 tied, and the twisted rope was fastened to a strong iron staple in a heavy wooden beam above, near the fireplace. He
```

Investigating collocations

The print-out of *staple* on p. 160 illustrates two useful concepts in the study of collocations: there is a central lexeme, or *node*, surrounded by a fixed amount of language – the *span* within which the search for collocations takes place. The span shown in that example is quite large, allowing 10 or so words on either side of the node: often, collocational studies look only at the lexemes which are immediately adjacent to a node, or at those which fall within three or four places on either side of it. For common lexemes, we need to examine quite a wide span, and to look at many examples of use, in order for clear lexical patterns to emerge. Computational help is essential in such cases.

ON LINE

The remarkable collocational range of an everyday lexeme. There are nearly 150 predictable contexts for *line*, which can be grouped into 30 or so senses. Traditional dictionary entries do not give this kind of information.

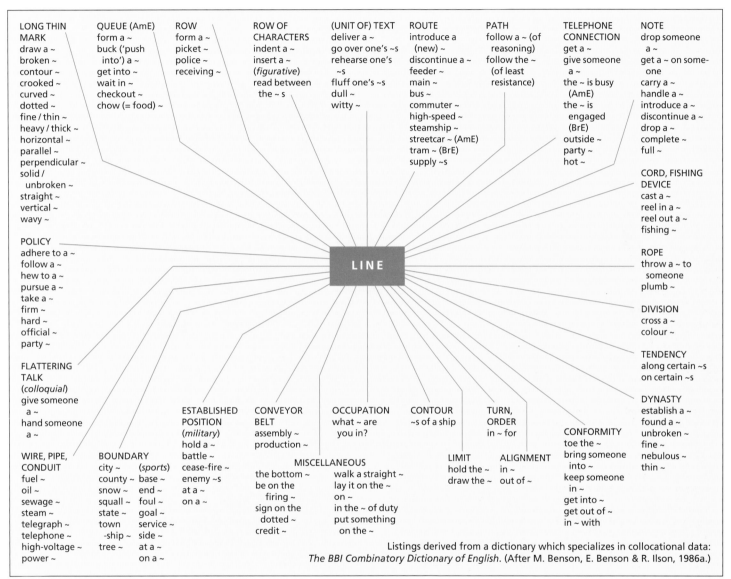

LONG THIN MARK
draw a ~
broken ~
contour ~
crooked ~
curved ~
dotted ~
fine / thin ~
heavy / thick ~
horizontal ~
parallel ~
perpendicular ~
solid / unbroken ~
straight ~
vertical ~
wavy ~

QUEUE (AmE)
form a ~
buck ('push into') a ~
get into ~
wait in ~
checkout ~
chow (= food) ~

ROW
form a ~
picket ~
police ~
receiving ~

ROW OF CHARACTERS
indent a ~
insert a ~
(*figurative*)
read between the ~ s

(UNIT OF) TEXT
deliver a ~
go over one's ~s
rehearse one's ~s
fluff one's ~s
dull ~
witty ~

ROUTE
introduce a (new) ~
discontinue a ~
feeder ~
main ~
bus ~
commuter ~
high-speed ~
steamship ~
streetcar ~ (AmE)
tram ~ (BrE)
supply ~s

PATH
follow a ~ (of reasoning)
follow the ~ (of least resistance)

TELEPHONE CONNECTION
get a ~
give someone a ~
the ~ is busy (AmE)
the ~ is engaged (BrE)
outside ~
party ~
hot ~

NOTE
drop someone a ~
get a ~ on someone
carry a ~
handle a ~
introduce a ~
discontinue a ~
drop a ~
complete ~
full ~

POLICY
adhere to a ~
follow a ~
hew to a ~
pursue a ~
take a ~
firm ~
hard ~
official ~
party ~

CORD, FISHING DEVICE
cast a ~
reel in a ~
reel out a ~
fishing ~

ROPE
throw a ~ to someone
plumb ~

LINE

DIVISION
cross a ~
colour ~

FLATTERING TALK (*colloquial*)
give someone a ~
hand someone a ~

TENDENCY
along certain ~s
on certain ~s

DYNASTY
establish a ~
found a ~
unbroken ~
fine ~
nebulous ~
thin ~

WIRE, PIPE, CONDUIT
fuel ~
oil ~
sewage ~
steam ~
telegraph ~
telephone ~
high-voltage ~
power ~

BOUNDARY
city ~
county ~
snow ~
squall ~
state ~
town
  -ship ~
tree ~

(*sports*)
base ~
end ~
foul ~
goal ~
service ~
side ~
at a ~
on a ~

ESTABLISHED POSITION (*military*)
hold a ~
battle ~
cease-fire ~
enemy ~s
at a ~
on a ~

CONVEYOR BELT
assembly ~
production ~

MISCELLANEOUS
the bottom ~
be on the firing ~
sign on the dotted ~
credit ~

OCCUPATION
what ~ are you in?

walk a straight ~
lay it on the ~
on ~
in the ~ of duty
put something on the ~

CONTOUR
~s of a ship

LIMIT
hold the ~
draw the ~

TURN, ORDER
in ~ for

ALIGNMENT
in ~
out of ~

CONFORMITY
toe the ~
bring someone into ~
keep someone in ~
get into ~
get out of ~
in ~ with

Listings derived from a dictionary which specializes in collocational data: *The BBI Combinatory Dictionary of English.* (After M. Benson, E. Benson & R. Ilson, 1986a.)

WHAT MAY WE DO TO A DICTUM?

The panel on the opposite page begins:

The purpose of this dictum...

However, it did not start life like that. The first draft of this sentence was:

This dictum, — ed by the British linguist, J. R. Firth...

I puzzled for some time over which verb to collocate with *dictum*. Do we *coin* a dictum, or *formulate* one, or *present* one, or *announce* one? *Made, given,* and *used* seemed tame or not quite right. *Propounded, pronounced,* and *promulgated* seemed too official. *Delivered, voiced, advanced, introduced, adumbrated,* and several other verbs all came to mind, but added distracting nuances for the neutral meaning I wished to express. Is there a standard collocation in English?

Dictionaries exist to provide remedies for failed intuitions. Unfortunately, I could find no example of a transitive verb governing *dictum.* The *Oxford English Dictionary* provided only an instance of *adduce* in a legal context. An informant test on half-a-dozen people brought no consensus – only more verbs (*mooted,* *framed, exclaimed...*). I cut my temporal losses, and changed the construction.

The point of this anecdote is twofold: it provides a further warning against complacency, when dealing with usage (p. 196); and it highlights a typical difficulty in the study of collocations. Textbooks and teaching materials are full of the clear cases of lexical collocation, where intuition is in no doubt. We do not have trouble with *quench my —, auspicious —, spick and —,* and many other such sequences. But there are an uncertain (and I suspect large) number of cases where usage is not established, and where any of us with confidence can become an arbiter of usage, if we so choose. If I had written, 'This dictum, coined by J. R. Firth', would anyone have noticed?

Predicting lexemes

The notion of collocation (p.160) focuses our attention on the extent to which lexemes come together randomly or predictably. Often, a sequence of lexemes is governed by chance – that is, by factors which are controlled by an individual speaker, and not by tendencies in the language as a whole. For example, the sentence *I like —* gives us no clue about which lexeme will come next. Almost anything that exists can be liked. It is up to the individual to choose. Such sequences as *(I) like potatoes* or *like films* are said to be 'free combinations' of lexemes. They are not collocations, because there is no mutual expectancy between the items. Thousands of lexical juxtapositions in everyday speech and writing fall into this category.

By contrast, the lexical items involved in a collocation are always to some degree mutually predictable, occurring regardless of the interests or personality of the individual user. All mature native speakers use such sequences as *commit a murder* and not, say, *commit a task*, even though the sense of 'carry out' would be applicable in the latter case. And everyone says *monumental ignorance*, not *monumental brilliance*. Collocations may occur, moreover, with apparent disregard for the observable situation to which they relate: we may be *green with envy*, and a book may have a *purple passage*, even though no colour is evident on the face or page. Collocations cannot be predicted from a knowledge of the world. *Coffee* with milk may look *sepia, hazel, beige, buff, fawn, khaki, bronze, copper, amber*, and various other shades of *brown*; but we normally call it *white*.

All that is required, for a sequence of lexemes to be described as a collocation, is for one item to 'call up' another, to some extent, in the mind of a native speaker. Sometimes the predictability is weak: *heavy* collocates with quite a diverse range of items (*loss, wear, traffic, burden, defeat*, etc.), as does *line* on p.161. Sometimes the predictability is strong: *auspicious* collocates only with *occasion*, and a few other closely-related items (*event, moment*, etc.); *circuit* collocates with *break/broken, close(d), integrated, printed, short, make*, a few figurative expressions to do with travelling (e.g. *lecture, rodeo, talk-show*), but little more. However, when sequences are so highly predictable that they allow little or no change in their lexical elements (as with *spick and span* or *run amok*), it is not very illuminating to analyse them as collocations. Such minimally varying sequences are usually referred to as *fixed expressions*, or *idioms*, and require a separate analysis.

BLANKETY —

This collocation has been used as a euphemism since the mid-19th century, but it received a new lease of life from the popular British television game show, *Blankety Blank*, in the 1980s. The aim of the game was simple: participants were presented with a phrase in which one of the items was left blank, and they had to guess which was the missing lexeme. The game relied on people's everyday knowledge of collocations, and was perhaps so successful for that reason. Unlike some games, where intellectual or physical strength is a prerequisite for success, *Blankety Blank* relied only on a universal linguistic skill – our intuitive sense of 'which word comes next'. It was the most egalitarian of games.

ASSOCIATIVE RESPONSES

It is important to distinguish between collocations and associative responses. A lexeme might bring to mind all kinds of 'free associations'. If I ask you to say the first word which comes into your head when I say *whiskey*, you might respond with *Scotch, soda, dog* (because *Whiskey* is the name of your dog), or *Fred* (because Fred is someone you know who drinks a lot of whiskey); but only the first two are collocations – linguistically predictable sequences known by mature English language users. The last two are idiosyncratic, and have to be interpreted to make sense. Psychotherapists are often particularly interested in associations of this kind, believing that these can throw light on what is going on in a person's unconscious mind.

The table gives the set of associative responses made in 1952 by a group of American students to the item *city*. The list shows several personal associations (e.g. *Rochester, Minneapolis*), several collocations of varying degrees of predictability (e.g. *hall, square, block, traffic*), and several items which from a linguistic point of view would be free combinations (e.g. *here, people, large, noise*). Surprisingly, some of the most central collocations of *city* are not in the list – notably, *capital*.
(After L. Postman & G. Keppel, 1970.)

City No.	Response	Total
1	town	353
2	Minneapolis	121
3	state	74
4	country	69
5	square	64
6	people	32
7	street	32
8	St. Paul	24
9	building(s)	22
10	block(s)	20
11	big	15
12	New York	12
13	house(s)	11
14	large	10
15	light(s)	9
16	noise	8
17	farm	7
18	village	7
19	block	5
20	Chicago	5
21	dirty	5
22	busy	4
23	hall	4
24	traffic	4
25	dirt	3
26	dump	3
27	home	3
28	round	3
29	water	3
30	car(s)	2
31	day	2
32	here	2
33	live	2
34	man	2
35	parks	2
36	place	2
37	smoke	2
38	streetcar	2
39	towers	2
40–92	(*f*=1)	

Ames, bustle, club, concrete, cop, county, court, crowds, dark, Des Moines, downtown, Duluth, dust, Excelsior, excitement, factory, Faribault, fun, gas, hard, high, hinge, life, map, Memphis, metropolis, Milwaukee, Montevideo, New Orleans, ocean, pig, pipe, plant, population, Preston, Rochester, RR, rural, school, Seattle, sidewalk, sin, site, skyscrapers, snow, stand, suburb, subway, triangle, urban, vast, wells, window

IDIOMS

Two central features identify an idiom. The meaning of the idiomatic expression cannot be deduced by examining the meanings of the constituent lexemes. And the expression is fixed, both grammatically (p. 216) and lexically. Thus, *put a sock in it!* means 'stop talking', and it is not possible to replace any of the lexemes and retain the idiomatic meaning. *Put a stocking in it* or *put a sock on it* must be interpreted literally or not at all.

It is easy to forget just how many idiomatic constructions a lexeme can enter into. The following list of idiomatic uses of *hand*, adapted from the *Longman Dictionary of English Idioms* (1979), makes no claim to completeness.

at first hand
at second hand
a bird in the hand…
bite the hand that feeds him
bound/tied hand and foot

cap in hand
close at hand
come the heavy hand
cross my hand with silver
a dab hand
fight hand to hand
force my hand
a free hand
to get/keep my hand in
give/lend me a hand
give her the glad hand
go/be hand in hand
hand in glove
hand it to me on a plate
hand over fist
have/take a hand in it
have me eating out of her hand
have him in the palm of my hand
have to hand it to her
hold your hand ('support')
in hand
an iron hand in a velvet glove
know it like the back of my hand
lift a hand/finger
live from hand to mouth
off hand
an old hand
on every hand
on hand

on the one hand…
out of hand
put/dip his hand into his pocket
put/lay my hands on it
his left hand doesn't know what his right hand's doing
put my hand to the plough
raise/lift my hand against us
his right hand (man)
rule them with an iron hand
see the hand/finger of God in…
show/reveal your hand
stay your hand
strengthen your hand
take it in hand
throw his hand in
to hand ('within reach')
try your hand
turn/set/put your hand to
the upper/whip hand
wait on me hand and foot
with a heavy hand
with a high hand
with an open hand
with one hand tied behind my back
catch red-handed.

It is important to note that the plural form enters into a

quite different set of idioms:
all hands to the pump
at your hands
my bare hands
change hands
the devil finds work for idle hands
get my hands on…
our hands are tied
hands down
hands up!
I've only got one pair of hands
have clean hands
have my hands full
have his blood on my hands
in good hands
keep your hands off
lay my hands on it
many hands make light work
on/off her hands
out of my hands
play into his hands
shake hands
a show of hands
sit on their hands
soil/dirty our hands
take my life in my hands
take the law into our own hands
throw up my hands (in horror)
wash my hands of…

Lexical phrases

We can find other patterns within lexical sequences, apart from the free combinations, idioms, and kinds of collocation described in preceding pages. In particular, there are the specially assembled sequences of items which have been called (amongst other names) *sentence stems, composite forms,* or *lexical phrases.* (This field of study is fairly recent, so terminology is not yet fixed.) To adopt the last of these terms: *lexical phrases* are rather like the prefabricated components used in building a house or a computer. They are chunks of language in which all the items have been pre-assembled. Hundreds of such phrases exist, of varying length and complexity, such as *it seems to me…, would you mind…, on the one hand… on the other hand…,* and *… lived happily ever after.* Some resemble formulae: *let me start by Xing a/the Y* (e.g. *making the point, asking a question*) or *the Xer you Y, the Aer you B* (e.g. *the longer you wait, the angrier you get*). Such phrases are used frequently in both speech and writing, but they are especially important in conversation, where they perform a number of roles – for instance, expressing agreement, summing up an argument, introducing an example, or changing a topic. The full analysis of interactional functions of this kind, involving reference to phonological and grammatical factors as well as lexical ones, forms part of the study of *pragmatics* (p. 286).

TYPES OF LEXICAL PHRASE

One study of lexical phrases groups them into four main types.

Polywords
Short phrases which function very much like individual lexemes. They cannot be varied, and their parts cannot be separated.

in a nutshell
by the way
so to speak
so far so good
once and for all

Institutionalized expressions
Units of sentence length, functioning as separate utterances. Like polywords, they are invariable, and their parts cannot be separated. They include proverbs, aphorisms, and other quotable utterances (§12).

How do you do?
Have a nice day.
Give me a break.
Long time no see.
You can fool some of the people some of the time.

Phrasal constraints
These are phrases which allow some degree of variation; they are usually quite short.

as I was — (saying, mentioning)
good — (morning, night)
a — ago (day, long time)
as far as I — (can see, know)

Sentence builders
Phrases which provide the framework for whole sentences; they allow considerable variation.

not only… but also…
my point is that…
I'm a great believer in…
that reminds me of…
let me begin by…

Phrases from any of these categories may be used to perform the same social (or 'pragmatic') function. For example, the function of leave-taking can be expressed by a polyword (*so long*), an institutionalized expression (*have a nice day*), or a phrasal constraint (*see you later*). Further examples of pragmatic functions are given on p. 288. (After J. R. Nattinger & J. S. DeCarrico, 1992.)

CREATIVE COLLOCATIONS

Many of Dylan Thomas's poetic effects rely on a deliberate breaking of collocational conventions, especially between adjective and noun, as can be seen in this extract from 'After the Funeral', 1939.

Her flesh was meek as milk,
   but this skyward statue
With the wild breast and
   blessed and giant skull
Is carved from her in a room
   with a wet window
In a fiercely mourning house
   in a crooked year.
I know her scrubbed and sour
   humble hands
Lie with religion in their
   cramp, her threadbare
Whisper in a damp word, her
   wits drilled hollow,
Her fist of a face died
   clenched on a round
   pain…

Wet window, humble hands, and (possibly) *mourning house* are col-locations with some degree of expectancy. *Skyward statue* and *giant skull* are unusual, but at least they can be readily interpreted. *Crooked year, threadbare whisper, damp word,* and *round pain* go well beyond our expectations, and force us to search for meanings. Critics of Thomas's verse are divided over whether coherent meanings can be found for such juxtapositions.

The breaking of collocational norms is found not only in poetry, but also in humour and religion. It is easy enough to raise a sitcom laugh with such lexical sequences as *a herd of traffic wardens,* or *I can hear neighing; it must be your mother.* And prayers such as 'Litany for the Ghetto' present a theography (p. 368, 403) in which the divine and the human are lexically juxtaposed:

O God, who hangs on street corners, who tastes the grace of cheap wine and the sting of the needle,
Help us to touch you…

Investigating sense relations

We have a sense relation when we feel that lexemes (p. 118) relate to each other in meaning. If we pick any two lexemes at random from a dictionary, it is unlikely that they will bear any meaningful relationship to each other. There is nothing which obviously relates *echo* and *mayonnaise*, or *obedient* and *rainbow*. But we would feel otherwise if we picked out *wide* and *narrow* or *trumpet* and *bassoon*. What, then, are the chief types of lexical sense relation?

Synonyms (Greek 'same' + 'name')

Synonyms are lexemes which have the same meaning – a definition which sounds straightforward enough. However, when we think about it, the notion of synonymy is really rather curious – for why *should* a language have more than one lexeme to express a particular meaning? One lexeme per meaning ought to be sufficient.

In fact, there may be no lexemes which have exactly the same meaning. It is usually possible to find some nuance which separates them, or a context in which one of the lexemes can appear but the other(s) cannot.

• There may be a dialect difference: *autumn* and *fall* are synonymous, but the former is British English and the latter is American (p. 308); *sandwich* and *butty* are synonymous in Britain, but the former is standard and the latter is regional.

• There may be a stylistic difference: *insane* and *loony* are synonymous, but the former is formal and the latter is informal (p. 157); *salt* and *sodium chloride* are synonymous, but the former is everyday and the latter is technical.

• There may be a collocational difference (p. 160): *rancid* and *rotten* are synonymous, but the former is used only of *butter* or *bacon*; *kingly*, *royal*, and *regal* are synonymous (p. 124), but the *mail* has to be *royal* in the UK.

• There may be a difference of emotional feeling, or connotation: *youth* and *youngster* are synonymous, but youths are less pleasant than youngsters.

These are not the only ways in which synonyms can be differentiated, but the examples are enough to make the basic point: there may be no such thing as a pair of 'perfect synonyms' – lexemes which could substitute for each other in all possible locations. Slight but detectable differences are invariably present. However, for most practical purposes, these differences can be ignored: *enough/sufficient*, *perplexed/bewildered*, and *cherubic/angelic* are so close in meaning that they can safely be described as synonyms.

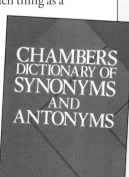

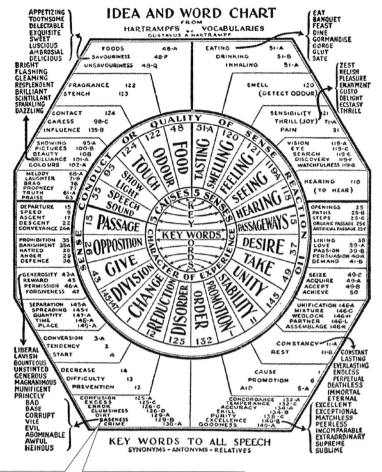

seduce, draw into evil

Victimise
frame, foist an imposition (colloq.)
plant, frame (colloq.)
sell, betray
victimise, dupe

Betray
betray, victimise treacherously

Conspire
abet, aid criminally
apostatise, desert principles
cabal, plot
connive, abet
conspire, concert in crime

impish, mischievous
injurious, bad, unjust
maleficient, mischievous
mischievous, bad
naughty, perverse, bad

Depraved
abandoned, dissolute
bad, wicked
corrupt, bad
criminal, wicked
debased, corrupt
depraved, debased
dishonest, discreditable
dissolute, wicked
felonious, criminal
ill, evil
immoral, corrupt

The idea and word chart from *Hartrampf's Vocabularies* (1929) – an early attempt to plot basic sense relations. The twelve word-pairs are claimed to 'underlie the fundamental qualities in all ideas'. To use the chart, the enquirer chooses a key-word (e.g. DISORDER), finds the required vocabulary heading, and goes to the page number. That page gives lists of lexemes, each with a synonym, and cross-references to opposite and associated items. An extract from the page for *crime* is illustrative.

DICTIONARIES OF SYNONYMS

A synonym dictionary is more tightly constrained than a thesaurus (p.158). The entries are shorter and the number of items less wide-ranging. Such dictionaries usually give some guidance about antonyms, too.

This extract from the *Chambers Dictionary of Synonyms and Antonyms* shows how synonyms are available for all lexemes in the language, not just those which are literary, distinctive, or difficult. It also shows that multi-word lexemes can also be synonyms.

eventually *adv.* after all, at last, at length, finally, sooner or later, subsequently, ultimately.

ever *adv.* always, at all, at all times, at any time, constantly, continually, endlessly, evermore, for ever, in any case, in any circumstances, on any account, perpetually. *antonym* never.

everlasting *adj.* constant, endless, eternal, immortal, imperishable, indestructible, infinite, never-ending, permanent, perpetual, timeless, undying. *antonyms* temporary, transient.

everybody *n.* all and sundry, each one, everyone, one and all, the whole world.

Antonyms (Greek 'opposite' + 'name')

Antonyms are lexemes which are opposite in meaning – again a definition which sounds straightforward, until we begin to think about what is meant by 'opposite'. Unlike synonymy (where there is doubt about whether true synonyms exist at all), antonymy very definitely exists – and, moreover, exists in several forms.

• There are opposites such as *large/small*, *happy/sad*, and *wet/dry*. These are items (adjectives) which are capable of comparison; they do not refer to absolute qualities. We can say that something is *very wet* or *quite dry*, or *wetter* or *drier* than something else. Opposites of this kind are called *gradable antonyms*. It is as if there is a scale of wetness/dryness, with *wet* at one end and *dry* at the other.

• There are opposites such as *single/married*, *first/last*, and *alive/dead*. These are not gradable opposites: there is no scale of 'aliveness' or 'firstness'. In such cases, if one of the pair of lexemes applies, the other does not. To be alive is not to be dead; and to be dead is not to be alive. The items complement each other in their meaning, and are thus known as *complementary antonyms*.

• There are antonyms such as *over/under*, *buy/sell*, and *wife/husband*. These antonyms are mutually dependent on each other. There cannot be a wife without a husband. We cannot buy something without something being sold. This type of oppositeness, where one item presupposes the other, is called *converseness*. The lexemes are *converse terms*.

All these lexemes have a common feature: they can all be used in the question–answer exchange 'What is the opposite of X? Y.' In this respect, they are different from the vast majority of lexemes in the language, which have no opposites at all. It simply does not make sense to ask 'What is the opposite of rainbow? or of chemistry? or of sandwich?'.

The other point to note is that there is usually an intuitive certainty about the relationship between the lexemes. We 'know' that X is the opposite of Y, in these cases. This is what distinguishes antonymy from other, vaguer kinds of oppositeness, where the concepts may be opposed but the lexemes are not. For example, *big* and *large* are very similar in meaning, as are *little* and *small*, but the antonym of *little* is *big*, and of *large* is *small*. *Large* is not the antonym of *little*, even though they are conceptually opposed. And the same point applies to more extensive sets of lexemes. In relation to the concept of 'awkwardness', for example, we find such terms as *awkward*, *clumsy*, *gawky*, and *ungainly*, on the one hand, and *skilful*, *dexterous*, *adroit*, and *deft*, on the other. But it is not possible to pair these off as antonyms in any obvious way: any of the first set could be seen as the opposite of any of the second. The concepts are in opposition, certainly, but there are no pairs of antonyms.

One of the pairs of drawings by the American illustrator Joan Hanson in her children's book *Antonyms* (1972).

Create **Destroy**

KEEPING TRACK OF ANTONYMS

The shutter aperture may be made larger or smaller by changing the foil area...
To us and to every nation of the Free World, rich or poor...
New panels are exchanged for the old...
Am I right, am I wrong?

These extracts are taken from a 25-million-word corpus of American English – a collection of 550 texts of varying sizes compiled by the American Printing House for the Blind. They show one of the most important features of antonymic use: antonym pairs frequently co-occur in the same sentence. They often appear close together, linked by a single conjunction, or function 'in parallel', within identical constructions in different parts of the sentence.

The table shows an analysis of some of the antonyms found in the corpus. The top line of the first column tells us that there were 4,981 occurrences of *bad* in the corpus, and the third column that there were 25,147 occurrences of *good*. The fifth column gives the number of sentences in which both adjectives occur, 516. The sixth column estimates the number of sentences which would be expected to have this happen by chance (81.7), and the seventh column gives the ratio of observed to expected co-occurrences. In the case of *bad/good*, the observed frequency is 6.3 times more than what would be expected by chance. The final column then estimates the probability of this happening. The result for *black/white* is especially striking, but all of the co-occurrences are statistically significant.

(After J. S. Justeson & S. M. Katz, 1992.)

Number of occurrences in the corpus				Co-occurrences in the same sentence			
				Observed	Expected	Ratio	Probability
4981	bad	25147	good	516	81.7	6.3	3.36×10^{-237}
11470	big	28360	little	483	212.0	2.3	3.13×10^{-59}
9842	black	11698	white	1226	75.0	16.3	1.55×10^{-1046}
2174	bottom	6061	top	198	8.6	23.1	8.47×10^{-195}
2203	clean	1143	dirty	22	1.6	13.4	7.73×10^{-18}
5259	cold	4036	hot	204	13.8	14.7	1.51×10^{-161}
5716	dark	8123	light	306	30.3	10.1	4.86×10^{-195}
4662	deep	501	shallow	19	1.5	12.5	4.13×10^{-15}
2500	dry	1501	wet	68	2.4	27.8	9.56×10^{-73}
3866	easy	7921	hard	43	19.9	2.2	4.68×10^{-6}
2507	empty	7386	full	44	12.1	3.6	8.84×10^{-13}
11985	far	5851	near	121	45.7	2.6	9.77×10^{-21}
3228	fast	2263	slow	61	4.7	12.8	1.24×10^{-45}
15915	few	25640	many	487	265.9	1.8	3.62×10^{-35}
32866	first	17439	last	764	373.6	2.0	4.38×10^{-73}
3668	happy	1176	sad	20	2.8	7.1	2.32×10^{-11}
7921	hard	2345	soft	76	12.1	6.3	2.31×10^{-35}
4004	heavy	8123	light	105	21.2	5.0	3.57×10^{-39}
11016	high	4195	low	293	30.1	9.7	1.14×10^{-182}

Hyponyms (Greek 'under' + 'name')

Hyponymy is a less familiar term to most people than either synonymy or antonymy (p. 164), but it refers to a much more important sense relation. It describes what happens when we say 'An X is a kind of Y' – *A daffodil is a kind of flower*, or simply, *A daffodil is a flower*. The relationship between the lexemes can best be shown in the form of a tree diagram, where the more general term is placed at the top, and the more specific terms are placed underneath. In the present example, *daffodil* is one of many lexemes which are all 'included' within *flower*.

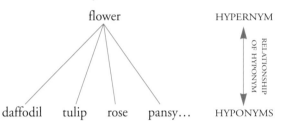

The included items, as the etymology suggests, are the *hyponyms*. The lexeme at the top is the *superordinate* term, or *hypernym* (Greek 'above' + 'name').

Hyponymy is particularly important to linguists because it is the core relationship within a dictionary. The most illuminating way of defining a lexeme is to provide a hypernym along with various distinguishing features – an approach to definition whose history can be traced back to Aristotle. For example, a *majorette* is 'a girl' (the hypernym) 'who twirls a baton and accompanies a marching band'. It is usually possible to trace a hierarchical path through a dictionary, following the hypernyms as they become increasingly abstract, until we arrive at such general notions (*essence*, *being*,

existence) that clear sense-relations between the lexemes no longer exist. At any point along this path, a lexeme can be seen to have a hyponymic relationship with everything above it, though we usually take seriously only those involving successive levels. So, in answer to the question, 'What is Gorgonzola?', the expected answer is 'a kind of cheese'. If someone does not know exactly what Gorgonzola is, 'a kind of food' would be an acceptable first approximation; but to go higher in the hierarchy of abstraction by saying 'a kind of substance' or 'a sort of thing' would not.

MISSING HYPERNYMS

There are many lexemes which belong to no hypernym. If we try the formula 'X is a kind of Y' on such items as chaos, nightclub, interesting, and balloon, we shall be unable to assign any hypernym other than a vague general term, such as state, place, or thing. Dictionaries grope for better alternatives, but not always successfully: balloon, for example, is variously described as a bag, ball, pouch, and toy. Abstract nouns are especially difficult, in this respect, and verbs and adjectives are more awkward still. Also, the level of abstraction of a lexeme may be difficult to determine. Is noise a kind of sound or sound a kind of noise? When the answer is 'neither', some other way of analysing the sense relation must be found, such as by using the notion of synonymy (p. 164) or incompatibility (see facing page).

HYPONYMIC HIERARCHIES

Eventually, all classifications and definitions lead inexorably to some basic notion of BEING. Roget's Thesaurus, Part 1, Section 1, is entitled simply EXISTENCE (p. 158). The figure shows what happens if we follow a set of lexemes through a dictionary, being guided only by the hypernyms. Only one of the senses is quoted in each case, and only one of the many possible paths. The further down the page we travel, the less easy it becomes to find clear hypernyms.

If we read the figure in the reverse direction, the point is reinforced. Thus, there are a limited number of items which can answer the question 'What can be a cheese?' and 'What can be food?'. These questions make sense. But such questions as 'What can be a material?' or 'What can be a substance? cannot be given a coherent linguistic interpretation.

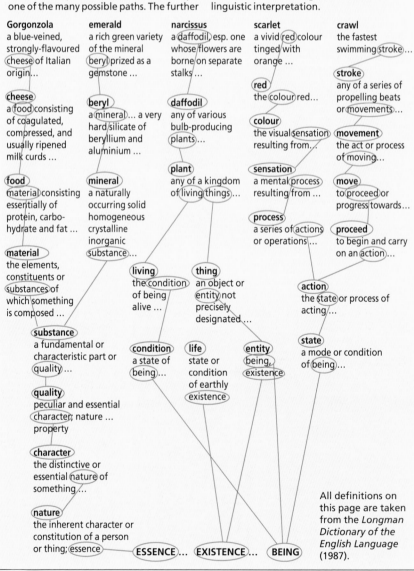

All definitions on this page are taken from the *Longman Dictionary of the English Language* (1987).

Incompatibles

When we want to include one meaning within another, we talk about hyponymy. When we want to exclude one meaning from another, we talk about incompatibility. Under this heading are grouped sets of lexemes which are mutually exclusive members of the same superordinate category. *Daffodil, tulip, rose,* and *pansy,* shown on the facing page, are examples, because they are all hyponyms of the same hypernym (*flower*). What this means can be seen by comparing these two sentences:

I am thinking of a single flower and it is a daffodil
    and a rose.

I am thinking of a single flower and it is a daffodil
    and a prizewinner.

The first sentence fails to make sense because *daffodil* and *rose* are incompatible. The second sentence succeeds because *daffodil* and *prizewinner* are not; they are compatible. Here is another pair of examples – this time, using adjectives:

I am thinking of an object which is painted in a
    single colour, and it is red and yellow.

I am thinking of an object which is painted in a
    single colour, and it is red and dirty.

Again, there is a problem with the first sentence, because *red* and *yellow* are both hyponyms under *colour*. *Red* and *dirty*, however, do not belong to the same set, and can be used together without difficulty.

Learning about sets of hyponyms is an important feature of lexical acquisition (p. 430). To begin with, we may have no idea how to differentiate them. All we may know is that the lexemes relate to the same hypernym. An example is *crocodile* and *alligator*. Most people know that these are types of *reptile*, but are still unclear about how to tell them apart. Similar difficulties can be encountered within any semantic field: there is no doubt that *second cousin* and *cousin once removed* are types of *relative*, or that *trumpet* and *flugelhorn* are types of *musical instrument*, but for many people that is as far as they are able to go without a reference book.

MUSICAL RELATIONS

The most familiar examples of the interaction between hyponymy and incompatibility are the classifications of objects and organisms which we learn as part of our basic education. The largest domain is that of natural history, where organisms are grouped into their presumed evolutionary relationships – the distinctions between species, genus, family, order, class, phylum (for animals) or division (for plants), and kingdom (p. 372).

The instruments of the modern symphony orchestra provide another example. These are traditionally divided into four types – woodwind, brass, percussion, and strings – and that is how we see them in the concert hall. However, it has long been known that this classification is not entirely satisfactory: it is difficult to place certain instruments under these headings, and the labels are sometimes misleading. For example, some woodwind instruments can be made of metal (such as saxophones), and some brass instruments can be made of wood (such as alphorns).

The standard classification in modern musicology is different, and derives from the work of Erich von Hornbostel and Kurt Sachs, published in 1914. Instruments are now divided into five types, according to the physical characteristics of the sound source – the vibrating agent.

• **aerophones** In this group, the sound is generated by air. They include the brass, reed, and woodwind instruments.

• **chordophones** In this group, the sound is generated by one or more strings. They include the stringed instruments and most keyboard instruments.

• **idiophones** In this group, the sound is generated by the body of the instrument itself. They include several percussion instruments, such as bells and the triangle, as well as the musical saw, and a few others.

• **membranophones** In this group, the sound is generated by a stretched membrane. They include the various kinds of drum, as well as such items as the kazoo and tambourine.

• **electrophones** In this group, the sound is generated by non-acoustic devices, such as oscillators. They include synthesizers and electric guitars.

Although the aim of any new classification is conceptual rather than linguistic, there are always consequences for the way the language is used. The arrival of a new level within the lexical hierarchy for talking about instruments alters the way we express ourselves. In the traditional classification, there is no problem with saying this:

I can play every kind of brass instrument,
    but I can't play any woodwind.

But in the modern classification, we cannot say this:

I can play every kind of aerophone, but I
    can't play any woodwind.

If we wish to enter into a conversation in this area, we need to do more than just 'learn the terminology'. We have to learn how the terminology is organized. And this means learning how the lexemes interrelate in terms of hyponymy and incompatibility. Without an awareness of the lexical structure of the field, we quite literally 'don't know what we're talking about'.

SHOWING OUR TRUE COLOURS

The way the linguistic world fails to correspond to the physical world is well illustrated by the use of the lexeme *colour*. A physical account recognizes *red, yellow,* and *blue* as primary colours, and *green, violet,* and *orange* as their complementaries. In a large box of paints, several dozen colours will be found, including *black, white, grey, brown,* and a number of increasingly fine discriminations (*lilac, mauve, purple, indigo,* etc.).

In language, what is considered to be a hyponym of *colour* depends very much on the context.

• In the field of snooker, the *colours* exclude *red*.

The *coloured* balls can be played only after a red ball has been potted.

• By contrast, in the field of health (for Caucasians), *colour* can mean *only* red, or at least pink (in *the colour came back to his cheeks*).

• In publishing, a book printed in black type on white paper is not considered to be in colour. Yet if blue, say, is introduced to add interest to the page, this is called

using a second colour (*black* being the 'first' colour).

• In the field of South African racial relations, coloured excludes black and white.

• In the cinema and on television, there is a contrast between films made in colour (as in Technicolor) and in black-and-white. Camera film and television sets, too, are categorized in this way.

Other sense relations

Notions such as synonymy and hyponymy (pp. 164–7) are fundamental to semantic analysis, because they express basic logical relationships which are represented widely throughout the lexicon. Certain other kinds of meaning relationship, however, are much less widespread, applying to restricted sets of lexemes. Three such categories are illustrated below: parts/wholes, hierarchies, and series.

PARTS AND WHOLES

The relationship between *wheel* and *car*, or *sleeve* and *jacket*, illustrates a further kind of sense relation – that between *part* and *whole*. The relationship is not as obvious as it may seem: in particular, there is a strong tendency for the relationship to be acceptable only between adjacent items in a chain of more than two items. Thus, a *door* is a part of a *house* and a *house* is a part of a *village*, but it would be most unusual to say that a *door* is a part of a *village*. On the other hand, certain chains do permit a relationship between non-adjacent items: a *cuff* is a part of a *sleeve* which is part of a *shirt* – but also, a *cuff* is a part of a *shirt*. Why some chains permit this and others do not is unclear.

There are several other refinements to the part-whole issue, some of which have attracted the attention of philosophers as well as linguists. One distinction has been drawn between those parts which are an essential feature of an entity and those which are optional: an *arm* is an essential feature of a (normal) male body, whereas a *beard* is not. There is also an uncertain boundary between allowing something to be a 'part' at all, as opposed to an 'attribute': may we consider a stout person's girth to be a part of the body?

Part–whole relations can be seen in many areas of the lexicon.

- Clothing: zip, button, hem, collar, lining, cuff
- Food: stalk, leaf, root, husk, shell, bone, seed
- Vehicle: wheel, brakes, engine, door, steering wheel
- Animal: hoof, mane, leg, feather, claw, tail
- Container: top, lid, door, side, handle, back
- House: bathroom, bedroom, kitchen, roof, window, door

HIERARCHIES

A lexical hierarchy is a graded series of lexemes in which each item holds a particular rank, being 'higher' or 'lower' than adjacent items. The sequence *corporal–sergeant–lieutenant* is part of one such hierarchy. The relationship between *corporal* and *sergeant* is not one of synonymy (they are not the same in meaning), nor antonymy (they are not opposites), nor hyponymy (a *corporal* is not a kind of *sergeant*, or vice versa). It is really one of incompatibility, but of a rather special kind: the relationship between *corporal* and *sergeant* is not like that between *clarinet* and *oboe*. *Sergeant* is 'higher' than *corporal*, whereas neither of the instruments can be said to outrank the other (though soloists of either instrument might disagree).

Several lexical domains are organized as hierarchies. They often reflect relationships between people, as in the case of military ranks or church seniority: *priest– bishop– archbishop…* Notions of quantity are also important, especially in relation to units of measurement: *second– minute–hour…* Some hierarchies also represent levels of abstraction, as can be seen in the levels of grammar identified on p. 217.

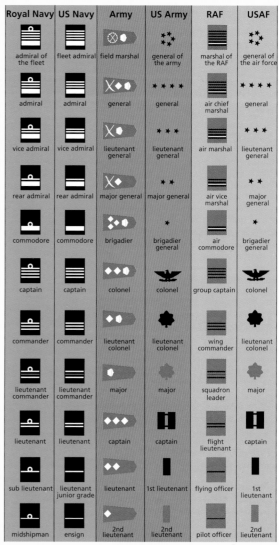

The hierarchy of military ranks, showing the differences between British and American usage.

Royal Navy	US Navy	Army	US Army	RAF	USAF
admiral of the fleet	fleet admiral	field marshal	general of the army	marshal of the RAF	general of the air force
admiral	admiral	general	general	air chief marshal	general
vice admiral	vice admiral	lieutenant general	lieutenant general	air marshal	lieutenant general
rear admiral	rear admiral	major general	major general	air vice marshal	major general
commodore	commodore	brigadier	brigadier general	air commodore	brigadier general
captain	captain	colonel	colonel	group captain	colonel
commander	commander	lieutenant colonel	lieutenant colonel	wing commander	lieutenant colonel
lieutenant commander	lieutenant commander	major	major	squadron leader	major
lieutenant	lieutenant	captain	captain	flight lieutenant	captain
sub lieutenant	lieutenant junior grade	lieutenant	1st lieutenant	flying officer	1st lieutenant
midshipman	ensign	2nd lieutenant	2nd lieutenant	pilot officer	2nd lieutenant

SERIES

The number system is unique, in the lexicon of a language, because its items are members of an open-ended series in which the place of each item is defined by mathematical rules. We might be tempted to refer to such items as *one*, *two*, *three*, *four*… as a hierarchy, like military ranks, but the number system is different: from a lexical point of view, 2 is not always 'higher' than 1.

There are other lexical series which are not open-ended. The commonest examples are the days of the week and the months of the year, which are *cyclical* in character: we reach the end of the series then we start again.

A calendar illustrates three types of lexical series: dates, days, and months

WHO IS NUMBER 1?

In *The Prisoner*, British cult television series of the 1960s, Patrick McGoohan finds himself trapped in a village where everyone has a number. Number 2 is in charge, but subordinate to a hidden Number 1.

Making sense

This section has examined the main ways in which the English lexicon is structured. It has been an investigation of what we mean when we say that something 'makes sense'. But there is one notion which we still need to recognize before this investigation is complete: the *definition*. A definition is the linguistic mechanism which brings everything together. It is a special type of sentence which relates all the relevant aspects of a lexeme's meaning, enabling us to understand it. Definitions are listed in dictionaries, sometimes using a full sentence (*A dress is a piece of clothing which…*), sometimes in an abbreviated form (*dress: a piece of clothing which…*).

The basic structure of a definitional sentence has been known since the time of Aristotle, who distinguished two factors: a general category to which a word belongs, and the specific features or attributes which distinguish that word from related words. Thus, *a cow is an animal which moos* is a childlike attempt at a definition, but this might be sufficient to distinguish it from *a dog is an animal which barks*. In these cases, *animal* is the more general term (the hypernym, p. 166), and *mooing* and *barking* are the distinguished attributes. In mature definitions, several attributes may be required, often involving both formal distinguishing features (e.g. a cow has four legs, horns, a tail) and functional ones (e.g. a cow gives milk, lives in a field, does not give rides). It can also be quite a task working out the essential attributes needed in a definition, as the *factory* example (below) illustrates; and the theoretical problems of working with definitions have kept several generations of linguistic philosophers happily occupied.

WHAT'S A FACTORY?

When someone asks a question like this (a child, a foreigner, a politician), there are two ways of answering. One way is to find a factory and point to it. The other way, which is generally more practicable, is to attempt a definition of the word *factory*. The first approach, which identifies the word's *reference* in the outside world, is of limited interest to linguists. The second, which gives the *sense* of the word in English, is central to linguistic enquiry.

But how do we define *factory*? The first task is to examine the way in which the word is used in spoken or written English. This is in fact what lexicographers do when they write their dictionary entries. But as *factory* can be used in all kinds of contexts, it is still necessary to make a selection, to decide which attributes are essential to the definition and which are not. Dictionaries do not always agree on this matter, as the following definitions show.

factory
• a building or set of buildings where the production of goods or processing of raw materials takes place (*Longman Dictionary of the English Language*)
• a large building or group of buildings where goods are made in large quantities, usually with the use of machines (*Collins Cobuild English Language Dictionary*)
• a place where goods are manufactured (*Chambers English Dictionary*)
• a building or buildings containing plant or equipment for manufacturing machinery or goods (*Concise Oxford Dictionary*)

Five main elements emerge from a comparison of these definitions (along with the definition of *manufacture* in

Chambers: 'make, usually by machinery and on a large scale').

• the more general term is *place*, more specifically, *building or buildings*.
• things are *made* or *manufactured*, more specifically (according to one of the definitions) *produced and processed*.
• the things which are made are *goods*, but (in one case) *raw materials* and (in another case) *machinery* are distinguished separately from the category of *goods*.
• the *goods* are made with *machines*, in one case described as *plant or equipment*.
• the building is *large*, and in one case the goods are said to be made in *large* quantities.

On this basis, a 'minimalist' definition of factory would be:

A large building in which machines make goods in quantity.

A children's dictionary comes near to this:

a large building or group of buildings where goods are made (*Childcraft Dictionary*)

And a dictionary for foreign learners of English gives a two-level definition:

a building or group of buildings where goods are made, especially in great quantities by machines.
(*Longman Dictionary of Contemporary English*)

It is easy to see how an oversimplified or careless definition can be misleading. In one reported case, a mother replied to her young child that a factory was 'a place where you make things'. The child then later referred to her kitchen as a factory! Indeed, on the basis of this response, it could be argued that none of the above books mentions the salient point, which is that the manufactured goods are for sale.

SEMANTIC FUZZINESS

Definitions are not always as precise as we would like them to be, largely because the entities and events which we want to talk about in the real world are not always clear and determinate. It is not possible to give a watertight definition of *factory* in everyday language. How large is *large*? Can a small building never be a factory? *Must* it contain machines? One of the dictionaries actually builds this uncertainty into its definition: 'especially in great quantities by machines'.

For the most part, such 'hedges' do not matter. We tolerate a great deal of imprecision in daily interaction. Only in special cases, such as an Act of Parliament or a legal conflict (p. 374), is it necessary to be truly precise, and to give a definition to such notions as 'large'.

There are many areas of lexical fuzziness: when does a *booklet* become a *book*? or a *hill* become a *mountain*? or a *village* become a *town*? or a *discussion* become a *dispute*? In relation to attributes, how essential is the feature 'able to fly' for *bird* (allowing for ostriches and penguins)? or 'having a handle' for *cup* (allowing for paper cups and egg cups)? The more abstract the notion, the more difficult it is to arrive at a watertight lexical definition.

Everyday language contains many expressions which introduce imprecision into what we say: *typically, roughly, practically, in the region of, thereabouts, well nigh, within an ace of, verging on, virtually, perhaps, usually, invariably, sort of*, etc. They are also found in technical and scientific discussion, which often uses such expressions as *there are perhaps 1,500 such cases a year*. It is too easy to dismiss all fuzzy expressions as manifestations of sloppiness in thought or speech. Rather, by enabling us to get the gist of a point across, or to focus on a major issue, they can play an important role in efficient communication.

12 · LEXICAL DIMENSIONS

The English lexicon is so vast and varied that it is impossible to classify it into neat categories. It is not like a cake, which we can cut up into distinct slices. A single lexeme (p. 118) simultaneously contains information relating to several linguistic dimensions: when it came into English (the historical dimension), how it is formed (the structural dimension), whether it is in standard use or restricted to a dialect (the regional dimension), whether it carries resonances of gender, class, formality, or ethnicity (the social dimension), whether it has special status in such domains as science, religion, or law (the occupational dimension), and much more. The lexicon is a particularly sensitive index of historical, social, and technological change. As a consequence, vocabulary is a relevant aspect of the discussion in many parts of this book, but especially in the historical, regional, and social sections (Parts I, V).

We conclude Part II by surveying several routine ways in which the lexicon plays a role in our lives – sometimes quietly and unconsciously, sometimes aggressively and controversially. One important role will be conspicuous by its absence: the humorous use of lexical items, which receives separate treatment in §22.

THE LOADED LEXICON

Most of our discussion about the lexicon has been taken up with the dictionary meaning of lexemes – what is often called their *denotation*. A denotation is the objective relationship between a lexeme and the reality to which it refers: so, the denotation of *spectacles* is the object which balances on our nose in front of the eyes; and the denotation of *purple* is a colour with certain definable physical characteristics. A denotation identifies the central aspect of lexical meaning, which everyone would agree about – hence, the concept of a 'dictionary definition'.

By contrast, *connotation* refers to the personal aspect of lexical meaning – often, the emotional associations which a lexeme incidentally brings to mind. So, for many people, *bus* has such connotations as 'cheapness' and 'convenience'; for others, 'discomfort' and 'inconvenience'; for many children, it connotes 'school'; and for many American adults, in this connection, it has a political overtone (because of the 1960s policy in the USA of 'bussing' children to school as a means of promoting social integration in ethnically divided urban communities). Connotations vary according to the experience of individuals, and (unlike collocations, p. 160) are to some degree unpredictable. On the other hand, because people do have some common experiences, many lexemes in the language have connotations which would be shared by large groups of speakers. Among the widely-recognized connotations of *city*, for example, are 'bustle', 'crowds', 'dust', 'excitement', 'fun', and 'sin' (see p. 162).

When a lexeme is highly charged with connotations, we commonly refer to it as 'loaded'. The language of politics and religion is full of such loaded expressions: *capitalist, fascism, radical, federalism, democracy, bureaucracy, politician; priest, dogma, pagan, orthodox, sect, heresy, fundamentalist*. The language of science and law, on the other hand, attempts (not always successfully) to avoid vocabulary which is highly connotative. In general, the more a domain or topic is controversial, the more it will contain loaded vocabulary, providing people with the lexical ammunition they need to reinforce their point of view.

ALL THE RIGHT CONNOTATIONS . . .

residence, dwelling, luxury, substantial, spacious, quiet, potential, benefit, views, well-appointed, well-screened, desirable, landscaped, select, prestige position, attractive, refurbished, restored, mature, character, unspoilt, tasteful, well-proportioned, individual, well-stocked, convenient, modernized, immaculate, magnificent opportunity . . .

RECEPTION AREAS AND FACILITIES
The approach to Osborne Court is via an elegant stairway, through double doors into a glass vestibule. A secured door entry system gives access to the impressive main reception hall with marble flooring and period decor. The main staircase is of polished hardwood with turned handrail and spindles, and an eight-person lift offers a less exacting route to the upper levels. The staircase and upstairs corridors are fitted with heavy duty Axminster carpet, whilst the decor maintains the building's Italian theme.

The atmosphere as a whole is of sumptuous elegance recalling the grandeur of another age.

THE APARTMENTS
Each of the apartments at Osborne Court is individual in nature, and efforts are being made where possible to accommodate purchasers' own selections from appointed suppliers on a range of fittings. The apartments themselves have been designed to provide optimum space with interesting aspects, and layouts to meet the needs of modern day living.

Entrance halls are generally spacious providing a comfortable area in which to receive guests, and they afford an impressive introduction to the apartments. Living rooms are of generous proportions with ceiling height accentuated by moulded plaster coving. Lighting to these main rooms includes both wall and ceiling

---

CONNOTATIVE FUNCTIONS

Connotations can play an important role in explaining the way in which lexemes are used. A group of synonyms, for example, cannot by definition (p. 164) be distinguished in terms of their denotation, but they usually display noticeable differences of connotation, as in the case of *car, automobile, runabout, buggy, banger, bus, hot rod, jalopy, old crock, racer,* and so on. Indeed, in describing an unconventional design, the connotations may become critical marketing considerations (p. 388).

Connotations are also an important means of conveying personal attitude and point of view. Bertrand Russell, on a BBC Brains Trust programme some years ago, gave a perfect illustration of this when he 'conjugated' the following 'irregular verb':

I am firm.
You are obstinate.
He is a pig-headed fool.

The idea prompted the British periodical, *The New Statesman*, to set a competition for its readers. Here are some of the published entries.

I am sparkling.
You are unusually talkative.
He is drunk.

I am a creative writer.
You have a journalistic flair.
He is a prosperous hack.

I day dream.
You are an escapist.
He ought to see a psychiatrist.

Many other triplets could be devised: slender/thin/skinny, frank/blunt/insolent, overweight/plump/fat...

SNARLING AND PURRING

The American writer on semantics, S. I. Hayakawa (1906–), distinguished between 'snarl' words and 'purr' words, when discussing connotations. To take his examples: the sentence *You filthy scum* is little more than a verbal snarl, whereas *You're the sweetest girl in all the world* is the linguistic equivalent of a feline purr or canine tail wag. There is little objective content (denotation) in either sentence.

The most ferocious snarl words raise distinct issues, and are best discussed separately under such headings as *invective* and *taboo* (p. 172). But there are many other words which carry negative or unfavourable connotations, as well as many which carry positive or favourable ones. Often these contrast, as in the distinction between *a youngster* and *a youth*:

A group of youngsters stood on the street corner.
A group of youths stood on the street corner.

You might well chat to the first group, as you passed them by; you might well avoid eye contact with the second. Similarly, *politicians* are somewhat less respectable than *statesmen* and *states-women*, as are *lodgers* compared with *paying guests*, *plots* compared with *plans*, and *papists* compared with *Catholics*.

A random selection of snarl words includes *terrorist*, *exploitation*, *steam-roller* (vb.), *skulk*, *nag*, *clammy*, *clique*, *loafing*, *politicking*, and *pontificate*. Among the purr words of the language are *comrade*, *enterprise*, *freedom*, *patriot*, *colourful*, *compact*, *partnership*, *jolly*, *green*, and *environment*. People will often disagree over whether a lexeme snarls or purrs, as in the case of *curiosity*, *hanging*, *communist*, *civil servant*, *republican*, and *ambitious*.

Part of the problem of studying connotations is that they readily change with the passage of time (p. 138). *Lewd* once meant simply 'of the laity', 'uneducated', but along with its change of meaning has come a distinctly negative tone. *Gentle*, which comes from a word meaning 'clan' or 'people', now has very positive associations. It is particularly difficult keeping track of the way connotations respond to short-term changes in fashion and social status – which is one reason why it is so difficult to make sense of 'political correctness' (p. 177).

COLOUR VITAMINS

The symbolic or psychological associations of colours have a long history. In the 12th century, a colour sequence for the liturgical year in the Roman Catholic Church was outlined by Pope Innocent III, and continues to be used today. For example, red vestments are used at Pentecost or for the feasts of martyrs, the colour representing tongues of fire and the shedding of blood; black vestments are the colour of mourning; violet vestments represent the mitigation of black, in Advent and Lent; and green is the 'neutral' colour, used 'in ordinary time', when there is no special period or feast-day being celebrated. These and certain other colours (notably white, blue, gold, and rose) are also often used symbolically in many medieval religious paintings.

In modern times, the psychological associations of colours, and thus the connotations of colour vocabulary, continue to be exploited in a wide range of contexts, such as in the description of paint shades (p. 154), advertising language, and techniques of self-imaging. The *Color Me Beautiful* system is a good example within the last category. This consultancy was founded by Carole Jackson in the USA in 1974, and now has branches in many parts of the world. Its aim is to help women discover their natural beauty through colour, using the metaphor of the four seasons. In much the same way as each season presents a distinct array of colours, a person's colouring is said to be in harmony with one of these palettes, and advice is given about how to enhance these natural colours, and about how to choose additional colours (of make-up and clothing). There are 11 key 'colour vitamins', and these are related to a range of positive (+) and negative (–) attributes.

red
+ up-beat, confident, assertive, exciting
– aggressive, domineering, bossy, threatening

pink
+ feminine, gentle, accessible, non-threatening
– pathetic, unimportant, safe, under-confident

blue
+ peaceful, trustworthy, constant, orderly
– 'holier than thou', tiresome, predictable, conservative

brown
+ earthy, homely, gregarious
– safe, boring, unsophisticated

yellow
+ cheerful, hopeful, active, uninhibited
– impulsive, tiresome, whirlwind, volatile

green
+ self-reliant, tenacious, nurturing, dependable
– boring, stubborn, risk-averse, predictable

orange
+ vital, funny, enthusiastic, sociable, uninhibited
– superficial, common, faddist, giddy

violet
+ imaginative, sensitive, intuitive, unusual, unselfish
– weird, impractical, immature, superior

grey
+ respectable, neutral, balanced
– non-committal, deceptive, uncertain, safe

black
+ formal, sophisticated, mysterious, strong
– mournful, aloof, negative, lifeless

white
+ pure, clean, fresh, futuristic
– clinical, 'colourless', cold, neutral

(After M. Spillane, 1991.)

SPRINGS

The range of colours recommended for Springs (note the unusual countable noun, p. 209). Carole Jackson advises: 'peach, apricot, salmon, and coral, as well as all peachy pinks, are for Spring…'
(After C. Jackson, 1980.)

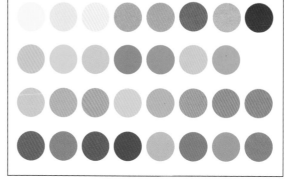

Taboo

A few dozen lexemes comprise the special category of *taboo* language – items which people avoid using in polite society, either because they believe them harmful or feel them embarrassing or offensive. The possibility of harm may be genuinely thought to exist, in the case of notions to do with death and the supernatural, or there may be merely a vague discomfort deriving from a half-believed superstition. Embarrassment tends to be associated with the sexual act and its consequences. Offensiveness relates to the various substances exuded by the body, and to the different forms of physical, mental, and social abnormality. Words associated with certain other topics may also be called taboo, from time to time, because society is sensitive to them. During the *recession* of the early 1990s, newspapers would talk about 'the R word', and after the 1991 Maastricht conference would refer to the proposed *federalism* of the European Community as 'the F word'. For some people, indeed, all jargon is taboo (p. 174).

The prohibition on use may be explicit, as in the law courts ('contempt of court'), the Houses of Parliament ('unparliamentary language'), and the broadcasting media (words officially banned until after a certain time in the evening, so that children are less likely to be exposed to them). More commonly, it is a tacit understanding between people, which occasionally becomes explicit in the form of a comment, correction, or sanction (such as a parental rebuke). The comment may be directed to oneself ('Pardon my French') or to others ('Ladies present'), and may be jocular ('Wash your mouth out') or serious ('God forgive me for swearing').

There are various ways of avoiding a taboo item. One is to replace it by a more technical term, as commonly happens in medicine (e.g. *anus, genitalia, vagina, penis*). Another, common in older writing, is to part-spell the item (*f—k, bl——*). The everyday method is to employ an expression which refers to the taboo topic in a vague or indirect way – a *euphemism*. English has thousands of euphemistic expressions, of which these are a tiny sample:

casket (coffin), fall asleep (die), push up the daisies (be dead), the ultimate sacrifice (be killed), under the weather (ill), after a long illness (cancer), not all there (mentally subnormal), little girl's room (toilet), spend a penny (urinate), be economical with the truth (lie), adult video (pornography), let you go (sack), industrial action (strike), in the family way (pregnant), expectorate (spit), tired and emotional (drunk).

GORDON BENNETT

A list of euphemisms involving the word *God*, and the year of their earliest recorded use in the *Oxford English Dictionary*, would begin with *gog* (1350s), *cokk* (1386), *cod* (1569), and include such later forms as *gosh* (1743), *golly* (1743), *gracious* (1760s), *by George* (1842), *Drat* (= God rot) (1844), *Doggone* (= God-Damn (1851), and *Great Scott* (1884). Many pronunciation variants can be found, over the centuries, such as *adad, bedad, begad, begar, begob, dod, gar, ged, gom, gosse, gud, gum, icod,* and *igad*. *Gordon Bennett* and *Gordon Highlanders* are more recent coinages.

All swear words generate euphemisms, sooner or later, and the stronger the taboo, the larger the number of avoidance forms. The number of euphemistic expressions based on *God* is quite impressive, but the strongest taboo word, *cunt*, has accumulated around 700 forms.
(After G. Hughes, 1991.)

TABOO USAGE

It is difficult to generalize about the usage of taboo words. They express varying degrees of force, and no two are exactly the same with respect to the way they are grammatically used. It may seem strange to think of taboo words as following grammatical rules, but they do. *Damn*, for example, cannot be used with a preceding personal pronoun (**You damn!*) and *arse* cannot be followed by one (**Arse you!*); *fart* cannot be followed by *off* or *it*; *bugger*, however, can be used in all four of these contexts. Taboo words, moreover, vary in their ability to be used as nouns, verbs, adjectives, and adverbs, or to form part of compounds. *Shit* is a versatile term, in this respect.

It is also difficult to define the 'tabooness' of a taboo word. *Shit*, for example (represented as *S* in the display), includes a great deal more than its central, literal sense of 'excrement' (as in *have a shit*). It has several figurative and idiomatic uses, which vary greatly in rhetorical force, from insult and rudeness to intimacy and solidarity, and it merges with an interesting range of euphemistic and jocular forms. The usage display is already complex, but it is by no means complete, because of the problem of keeping track of the way such forms are used among social dialects and subcultures.

S
'excrement'
(plural *the Ss* 'diarrhoea')

POSITIVE

general emotive response (wonder, sympathy, embarrassment, etc.)
Aw S!, a cute little S,
S a brick!,
Shee-y-it, She-it, Sh-i-i-i-t!,
Hot S!, S-hot,
Tough S!

hard cheese,
tough cheddar,
stiff biscuits,
etc.

drugs (cannabis, etc.)
want some S?,
S was scarce,
good S for sale,
clean white S

EUPHEMISTIC
Shivers! Sugar!
Shoot! Shute!
Shucks! Sherbert!

DIALECT/JOCULAR
shite, shice, sheiss(e)

NEGATIVE

personal abuse
he's a regular/little/first-class S,
they're Ss, on my S-list,
S-arse/-bag/-breeches/-face/-
hawk/-head/-heel/-hole/
-house/-poke/-pot,
S-kicker (AmE 'rustic')

dirty activities
S-work ('menial housework'),
S-kickers (AmE, 'heavy work-boots')

negation
not give a S, ain't worth a S, ain't got S,
don't tell them S

trouble
be in the S, been through a lot of S, be in S street, S out of luck, take a lot of S, when the S flies, when the S hits the fan, up S creek (without a paddle), S on someone from a great height

fear
S scared, S oneself, S bricks, scared S-less, beat/fuck/kick/knock the S out of someone, give one the Ss

deception/tease
are you S-ting me?, No S!

nastiness
that's a S-ty thing to say, in a S-ty mood, it's S-ting down outside

rubbish   shirty
load of S, all that S, shoot the S, don't give me any S, full of S, he thinks the Zodiacs are S

bull-S,
chicken-S

bull,
chicken droppings,
etc.

Swearing

We need to draw a clear distinction between the language of taboo, the language of abuse (*invective*), and the language of swearing. The three may overlap or coincide: to call someone a *shit* is to use a taboo word as a term of abuse, and if said with enough emotional force would be considered an act of swearing. But there is no necessary identity. *Piss* is a taboo word which is not usually employed on its own as invective or as a swear word. *Wimp* is a term of abuse which is neither a taboo word nor a swear word. And *heck* is a swear word which is neither taboo nor invective. Yet other distinctions are often drawn, some being given legal definition, and invoking sanctions in certain circumstances. Probably the commonest notions are *obscenity*, which involves the expression of indecent sexuality – 'dirty' or 'rude' words; *blasphemy*, which shows contempt or lack of reverence specifically towards God or gods; and *profanity*, which has a wider range, including irreverent reference to holy things or people (such as, in Christianity, the cross or the saints). However, despite these distinctions, the term *swearing* is often used as a general label for all kinds of 'foul-mouthed' language, whatever its purpose.

In a narrower sense, swearing refers to the strongly emotive use of a taboo word or phrase. 'Use' is perhaps too weak. Swearing is an outburst, an explosion, which gives relief to surges of emotional energy. It is a substitute for an aggressive bodily response, and can be aimed either at people or at objects (as when our head makes inadvertent contact with a low roof beam). Its forcefulness is reflected in its use of short, sharp sounds (p. 251) and emphatic rhythms. Its function is to express a wide range of emotions, from mild annoyance through strong frustration to seething anger, and not to make sense. Indeed, if we look closely at swearing formulae, we may find no meaning at all: *fucking hell* and other such phrases are, literally, nonsense.

However, the view of swearing as an emotional phenomenon is itself too narrow. Swearing has important social functions. It can mark social distance, as when a group of youths display their contempt for social conventions by swearing loudly in public or writing obscene graffiti on walls. And it can mark social solidarity, as when a group develops identical swearing habits. It is important to appreciate, in this respect, that swearing is universal. Everyone swears – though the mild expletive use of *sugar* or *golly* by one person would probably not be considered as swearing by someone whose normal imprecation is *sonofabitch* or *motherfucker*.

When we join a new social group, it seems we are much influenced by its swearing norms. Swearing is contagious. In one study, the swearing patterns of zoologists during an expedition to the Arctic were observed by a psychologist. She noted that when the members of the group were relaxed, there was a noticeable increase in the amount of social ('one of the gang') swearing. This, the commonest swearing pattern, always depended for its effect upon an audience being present, and varied in intensity according to the swearing habits of the participants – social swearing diminished all round if a non-swearer was present. Annoyance swearing was different: this occurred as a reaction to stress, regardless of audience, and became more frequent as conditions became more difficult. However, when a situation was extremely stressful, there was no swearing at all, not even of the annoyance type. One of the psychologist's conclusions was that swearing is a sign that a stressful situation is bearable, and indeed may be a factor in helping to reduce stress. It raises the interesting hypothesis that those who swear suffer less from stress than those who do not. (After H. E. Ross, 1960.)

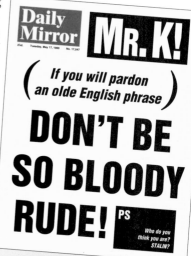

This was a daring front page, for a British newspaper in 1960.

TO B— OR NOT TO —— THAT IS THE *BLOODY* QUESTION

TO-NIGHT'S "PYGMALION," IN WHICH MRS. PATRICK CAMPBELL IS EXPECTED TO CAUSE THE GREATEST THEATRICAL SENSATION FOR YEARS

On 28 May 1714, Jonathan Swift commented, in one of his letters to Stella, that 'it was bloody hot walking today'. Almost exactly 200 years later, the *Daily Sketch* of 11 April 1914 used the above headline to report a sensation, when Mrs Patrick Campbell had to say the line 'Not bloody likely' for the opening of Shaw's *Pygmalion*, thus using a word which 'is certainly not used in decent society'. (For the full report, see p. 383). Indeed, public outrage at even the hint of the word had caused Gilbert and Sullivan in 1887 to alter the spelling of their opera *Ruddygore* to *Ruddigore*.

The literal use of the word can be traced back to Old English, and was common in Elizabethan drama: 'O most bloody sight' (*Julius Caesar*, III.2) is one of many Shakespearian quotations. Its later use as an intensifier (with the basic meaning of 'very') has never been satisfactorily explained. One theory has associated it with the rowdy behaviour of the 'young bloods' of the Restoration period; another

(rather more likely) claims a figurative development, meaning 'the blood is up' (so that *bloody drunk* would mean 'ready for a fight'). There are several popular etymologies (p. 139) deriving the word from *by Our Lady* or from *God's blood*. Perhaps the association of the word with uncouth behaviour, plus the popular belief that it might be profane, gradually led to its being used by the lower classes as a swearword. It had certainly begun to fall from grace in Britain by the end of the 18th century, when it was recorded as part of underworld slang, and dictionaries began to refer to it as 'vulgar'. It was definitely a common swear-word by the early 19th century, called a 'horrid word', and printed as b——y.

The word became a major social issue only in Britain. It never gained popularity in America, and in Australia it became so frequent that it quickly lost its pejorative associations. The 'great Australian adjective', as it was called

towards the end of the 19th century, ceased to be regarded as swearing by the 1940s, and was often heard in respectable settings. This contrasts with the situation at the time in Britain, where the Lord Chamberlain's office was still excising the word from plays submitted to it, and people were being fined for using the word in public. But times were changing, and indeed *The Times* printed it in full in 1941 (in a poem containing the line 'I really loathe the bloody Hun'). The word's progress towards renewed respectability has been steady since then, though Prince Charles' comment in 1989 that English 'is taught so bloody badly' received less publicity for what he said than for the way he said it. The associations of some 200 years die hard, and many people never use the word in public, feel embarrassed if someone does so, and (in Britain) complain to the BBC if they hear it on air before 9 pm.

Jargon

Jargon is itself a loaded word (p. 170). One dictionary defines it, neatly and neutrally, as 'the technical vocabulary or idiom of a special activity or group', but this sense is almost completely overshadowed by another: 'obscure and often pretentious language marked by a roundabout way of expression and use of long words'. For most people, it is this second sense which is at the front of their minds when they think about jargon. Jargon is said to be a *bad* use of language, something to be avoided at all costs. No one ever describes it in positive terms ('that was a delightful piece of rousing jargon'). Nor does one usually admit to using it oneself: the myth is that jargon is something only *other* people employ.

The up side

The reality is that everyone uses jargon. It is an essential part of the network of occupations and pursuits which make up society. All jobs present an element of jargon, which workers learn as they develop their expertise. All hobbies require mastery of a jargon. All sports and games have their jargon. Each society grouping has its jargon. The phenomenon turns out to be universal – and valuable. It is the jargon element which, in a job, can promote economy and precision of expression, and thus help make life easier for the workers. It is also the chief linguistic element which shows professional awareness ('know-how') and social togetherness ('shop-talk').

When we have learned to command it, jargon is something we readily take pleasure in, whether the subject area is motorcycles, knitting, cricket, baseball, computers, or wine. It can add pace, variety, and humour to speech – as when, with an important event approaching, we might slip into NASA-speak, and talk about *countdown, all systems go*, and *lift-off*. We enjoy the mutual showing-off which stems from a fluent use of terminology, and we enjoy the in-jokes which shared linguistic experience permits. Moreover, we are jealous of this knowledge. We are quick to demean anyone who tries to be part of our group without being prepared to take on its jargon. And we resent it when some other group, sensing our lack of linguistic awareness, refuses to let us in.

The down side

If jargon is so essential a part of our lives, why then has it had such a bad press? The most important reason stems from the way jargon can exclude as well as include. We may not be too concerned if we find ourselves faced with an impenetrable wall of jargon when the subject matter has little perceived relevance to our everyday lives, as in the case of hydrology or linguistics. But when the subject matter is one where we feel implicated, and think we have a right to know, and the speaker uses words which act as a barrier to our under-

standing, then we start to complain; and if we suspect that the obfuscation is deliberate policy, we unreservedly condemn, labelling it *gobbledegook* and calling down public derision upon it.

No area is sacrosanct, but advertising, political, and military statements have been especially criticised in recent years by the various campaigns for Plain English (p. 376). In these domains, the extent to which people are prepared to use jargon to hide realities is a ready source of amusement, disbelief, and horror. A lie is a lie, which can be only temporarily hidden by calling it an 'inoperative statement' or 'an instance of plausible deniability'. Nor can a nuclear plant explosion be suppressed for long behind such phrases as 'energetic disassembly', 'abnormal evolution', or 'plant transient'.

While condemning unnecessary or obscuring jargon in others, we should not forget to look out for it in ourselves. It is so easy to 'slip into' jargon, without realizing that our own listeners/readers do not understand. It is also temptingly easy to slip some jargon into our expression, to *ensure* that others do not understand. And it is just as easy to begin using jargon which we ourselves do not understand. The motivation to do such apparently perverse things is not difficult to grasp. People like to be 'in', to be part of an intellectual or technical elite; and the use of jargon, whether understood or not, is a badge of membership. Jargon, also, can provide a lazy way into a group or an easy way of hiding uncertainties and inadequacies: when terminology slips plausibly from the tongue, it is not essential for the brain to keep up. Indeed, it is commonly asserted that politicians and civil servants have developed this skill to professional levels. And certainly, faced with a telling or awkward question, and the need to say something acceptable in public, slipping into jargon becomes a simple way out, and can soon develop into a bad habit. It is a short step, then, to jargon's first cousin, cliché (p. 186).

AMAZE YOUR FRIENDS

The way jargon enters into our lives, often without our even noticing it, can be seen in this short selection of published examples (from W. Nash, 1993).

• … smells interestingly of flowers and curiously of bath salts, but has tropical fruit on the palate, with rough sauvignon blanc edges absent, except perhaps on the finish

• His breast of chicken with tarragon and girolles goes back to the classic French repertoire: the skin of the fowl crisped to gold, oderiferously swathed in a thick, creamy sauce …

• … Labour has to establish its credentials as the party of economic growth, and hang the recession round the neck of the Government's monetary and fiscal stewardship.

• A mere yard off the fairway at the fourth, he could only hack out from the clinging Bermuda rough, three putts adding up to a six. Much the same happened at the par-five sixth for another six.

A famous jargonizer

Literary examples show that jargon is by no means only a modern phenomenon. Here, Hamlet takes issue with Osric over the pretentious use of *carriages* – a term more appropriately used, in Hamlet's estimation, for guns (*cannon*) than for swords.

Osric: The king, sir, hath wager'd with him six Barbary horses: against the which he has imponed, as I take it, six French rapiers and poniards, with their assigns, as girdle, hangers, and so; three of the carriages, in faith, are very dear to fancy, very responsive to the hilts, most delicate carriages, of very liberal conceit.

Hamlet : What call you the carriages?

Horatio (aside to Hamlet): I knew you must be edified by the margent ['margin'] ere you had done.

Osric: The carriages, sir, are the hangers.

Hamlet: The phrase would be more german to the matter, if we could carry cannon by our sides: I would it might be hangers until then.

(*Hamlet* V.ii)

FIGHTING BACK

When people get fed up with obscure or unnecessary jargon, there at first seems very little they can do about it. Below are a few examples of the way some people have chosen to counter-attack using the weapons of satire and parody. On p. 176 is an account of the way one organization has successfully orchestrated a much more ambitious campaign.

Q

To be, or the contrary? Whether the former or the latter be preferable would seem to admit of some difference of opinion; the answer in the present case being of an affirmative or of a negative character according as to whether one elects on the one hand to mentally suffer the disfavour of fortune, albeit in an extreme degree, or on the other to boldly envisage adverse conditions in the prospect of bringing them to a conclusion. The condition of sleep is similar to, if not indistinguishable from, that of death; and with the addition of finality the former might be considered identical with the latter; so that in this connection it might be argued with regard to sleep that, could the addition be effected, a termination would be put to the endurance of a multiplicity of inconveniences, not to mention a number of downright evils incidental to our fallen humanity, and thus a consummation achieved of a most gratifying nature.

(According to Arthur Quiller-Couch, 1916.)

CARSPEAK: A SHOPPER'S GUIDE

specimen, a: a very large, very, very shiny, long-nosed motor car with leather seats.

must be seen: a fairly large, shiny car with a host of extras; alt., a rather peculiar foreign model that you might hesitate to buy because of the rumours you have heard.

host of extras: (usu. in conn. with *must be seen*), a sun-roof, stereo speakers, badge bar, and a horn that plays the opening strains of 'Dixie'.

one careful, lady owner: boringly sedate and reliable; unscratched, over-hoovered, taken through the car-wash once a week; called Belinda.

snip, a: a vehicle priced at £50–£100 below the sum the vendor originally thought of, because the reading on the mileometer is suspect, because the alternator is *in articulo mortis* (called, in the trade, 'dead dodgy') and because he needs to get this car off his forecourt in order to make room for *a specimen*.

good runner, a: a vehicle which has not had the benefit of *one careful, lady owner*. It will do you no credit at the Country Club, but will trundle you round the houses well enough. Sometimes abbreviated to *a runner*, in which case it may not be good enough to trundle you all the way round *all* the houses, because it *needs some attention*.

needs some attention: (usu. in conn. with *runner*), needs a new gearbox, clutch, offside rear wing panel, windscreen wiper motor, doorlock and window crank on driver's side; otherwise, in A1 condition.

(According to W. Nash, 1993.)

THE FOLKLORE ARTICLE RECONSTITUTION KIT

This aid to academic article writing was circulated anonymously in the 1970s by a disaffected folklore scholar. Anyone wishing to produce an acceptable paper for a folklore journal, the author contends, has simply to construct sentences from the columns below, in the sequence A-B-C-D.

A	B	C	D
1 Obviously,	1 a large proportion of intercultural communicative coordination	1 must utilize and be functionally interwoven with	1 Propp's basic formulation.
2 On the other hand,	2 a constant flow of field-collected input ordinates	2 maximizes the probability of project success while minimizing cross-cultural shock elements in	2 the anticipated epistemological repercussions.
3 From the intercultural standpoint,	3 the characterization of critically co-optive criteria	3 adds explicit performance contours to	3 improved subcultural compatibility-testing.
4 Similarly,	4 initiation of basic charismatic subculture development	4 necessitates that coagulative measures be applied to	4 all deeper structuralistic conceptualization.
5 As Lévi-Strauss contends,	5 our fully integrated field program	5 requires considerable further performance analysis and computer studies to arrive at	5 any communicatively-programmed computer techniques.
6 In this regard,	6 any exponential Folklife coefficient	6 is holistically compounded, in the context of	6 the profound meaning of *The Raw and the Cooked*.
7 Based on my own field-work in Guatemala,	7 further and associated contradictory elements	7 presents a valuable challenge showing the necessity for	7 our hedonic Folklife perspectives over a given time-period.
8 For example,	8 the incorporation of agonistic cultural constraints	8 recognizes the importance of other disciplines, while taking into account	8 any normative concept of the linguistic / holistic continuum.
9 Thus, within given parameters,	9 my proposed independent structuralistic concept	9 effects a significant implementation of	9 the total configurational rationale.
10 In respect to essential departmental goals,	10 a primary interrelationship between systems and/or subsystems logistics	10 adds overwhelming Folkloristic significance to	10 *Krapp's Last Tape*.

The Doublespeak campaign

During the 1970s in the USA, there was a marked increase in concern about the way jargon was being used to confuse or deceive by people in power. In 1971, the National Council of Teachers of English passed two resolutions on language.

On Dishonest and Inhumane Uses of Language

That the National Council of Teachers of English find means to study dishonest and inhumane uses of language and literature by advertisers, to bring offenses to public attention, and to propose classroom techniques for preparing children to cope with commercial propaganda.

On the Relation of Language to Public Policy

That the National Council of Teachers of English find means to study the relation of language to public policy, to keep track of, publicize, and combat semantic distortion by public officials, candidates for office, political commentators, and all those who transmit through the mass media.

In 1973 the Council decided on its way forward, forming a Committee on Public Doublespeak – a blend of *newspeak + doublethink* from Orwell's *Nineteen Eighty-Four* (p. 135). The Committee focused on classroom activities and on professional awareness, publishing a newsletter (later, the *Quarterly Review of Doublespeak*) and other materials; but its highest public profile came with the birth of the annual Doublespeak Awards in 1974.

So what is doublespeak? In the view of the Committee Chair, it is 'language which pretends to communicate, but really doesn't. It is language which makes the bad seem good, the negative seem positive, the unpleasant appear attractive, or at least tolerable. It is language which avoids or shifts responsibility, language which is at variance with its real or its purported meaning. It is language which conceals or prevents thought' (W. Lutz, 1987). It is stressed that such language is not the product of carelessness or sloppy thinking; rather, it is the result of clear thinking. The claim is that this language has been carefully designed to change reality and to mislead.

Judging by the media attention given to the annual awards, the emergence of similar societies in other countries, the growth in public awareness of the problem, and the way in which many organizations have responded positively to the demand for 'plain English' (p. 376), the campaign to date has been remarkably successful. But, in view of the examples which continue to be cited in the yearly award ceremonies, no one is suggesting that the problem is anywhere near being solved.

AIR SUPPORT

The winner of the first Doublespeak Award in 1974 was Colonel Opfer, the United States Air Force press officer in Cambodia. After a US bombing raid, he told reporters: 'You always write it's bombing, bombing, bombing. It's not bombing! It's air support!'

AND SOME OTHER WINNERS

• 1977 The Pentagon and the Energy Research and Development Administration, for explaining that the neutron bomb was 'an efficient nuclear weapon that eliminates an enemy with a minimum degree of damage to friendly territory'.

• 1979 The nuclear power industry, for the euphemisms devised in relation to the incident at Three Mile Island, when an explosion was called 'energetic disassembly', a fire 'rapid oxidation', a reactor accident a 'normal aberration', and plutonium contamination 'infiltration'.

• 1984 The US Department of State, for announcing that in reports on the status of human rights in other countries, the word *killing* would in future be replaced by 'unlawful or arbitrary deprivation of life'.

THE GOLDEN BULL AWARDS

These are the British equivalent of the Doublespeak Awards, organized by the Plain English Campaign and the National Consumer Council.

The first plaque was given in 1982 to the author of Section 38 of the Criminal Justice Act, for writing as follows:

(4) An enactment in which section 31 (6) and (7) of the Criminal Law Act 1977 (pre-1949 enactments) produced the same fine or maximum fine for different convictions shall be treated for the purposes of this section as if there were omitted from it so much of it as before 29th July 1977...

The use of 'plain English' involves much more than an avoidance of unnecessary jargon, but must take into account questions of grammar and typography, as this example shows. The issues raised by such examples are therefore discussed later in this book (p. 376).

THE ORWELL AWARDS

It should not always be bad news. While the thrust of the Doublespeak campaign has been directed against language misuse, there have also been efforts to reward those who have helped to direct public attention to the issues, and who themselves use language well.

The Orwell Awards were introduced by the National Council of Teachers of English to recognize a work which has made an outstanding contribution to the critical analysis of public discourse. The first award was given in 1975 to David Wise for his book *The Politics of Lying*. Particularly appropriate to this section was the award given to Dwight Bolinger's book, *Language, the Loaded Weapon* (1980).

A similar concern to develop positive initiatives is found in the UK, where in 1990 the Plain English Campaign introduced the Crystal Mark scheme to recognize clarity in written documents (p. 376). The choice of this title, it is believed, does not derive from the name of any linguistics author living or dead.

Political correctness

Some of the most loaded words in the language are those associated with the way society talks about itself, and especially about groups of people whom it perceives to be disadvantaged or oppressed. The most sensitive domains are to do with race, gender, sexual affinity, ecology, and (physical or mental) personal development. During the 1980s, an increasing number of people became concerned to eradicate what they saw to be prejudice (especially language prejudice) in these areas. The label *racialist* was already known from the turn of the century, and *racist* from the 1930s. *Sexist* was added in the 1960s, and followed by a series of other *-ist* terms which focussed on real or imagined areas of linguistic discrimination. Many of the critics were members of progressive or activist groups (e.g. advocates of minority rights), especially in universities, and thus, as the movement grew, attracting hard-line extremists alongside moderates, it drew down upon itself the antagonism of conservative academics and journalists. By the 1990s, this hard-line linguistic orthodoxy was being referred to, pejoratively, as *political correctness (PC)*.

Anyone who used vocabulary held to be 'politically incorrect' risked severe condemnation by PC activists. Organizations, fearful of public criticism and litigation, went out of their way to avoid using language which might be construed as offensive. The word *black*, for example, was felt to be so sensitive that some banned its use in all possible contexts (including such instances as *blackboard* and the *black pieces* in chess). The generic use of *man* was widely attacked (p. 368). *Mentally handicapped* people were to become people *with learning difficulties*. *Disabled* people were to be *differently abled*. *Third World* countries were to be *developing nations*. All but the most beautiful or handsome were *aesthetically challenged*. And in the academic literary world there would need to be safeguards against the unhealthy influence wielded by such *DWEMs* ('Dead White European Males') as Shakespeare, Goethe, and Molière.

Critical reaction

In the early 1990s, many people reacted strongly to what they saw as a trend towards terminological absurdity. The inflexible condemnation of 'incorrect' vocabulary reminded some of the 'thought police' of futuristic novels. Newspaper headlines contained references to 'McCarthyism' and 'the end of academic freedom of speech'. And certainly, there were cases cited of academics who had criticised the PC position being labelled racist or sexist, and losing their courses or their case for promotion. According to a writer in the *New York Times* (July, 1991), PC had become 'a lethal weapon for silencing anyone whose ideas you don't like'. It was, according to an *Economist* editorial of the time, 'the most pernicious form of intolerance'.

The arguments continue. Critics of PC believe that the search for a 'caring' lexicon is pointless, as long as the inequalities which the language reflects do not change. Proponents of PC argue that the use of language itself helps to perpetuate these inequalities. At present, the speed at which fashions change in the use of PC terms suggests that it is not so easy to manipulate language as the reformers think. Dissatisfaction over one term tends to spread to its replacement, as has been seen with such sequences as *negro* to *black* to *Afro-American* to *African-American*. Above all, it is very difficult to ascertain just how far linguistic attitudes are generally held. In one 1991 survey of black Americans, carried out in the USA by the black-oriented Joint Center for Political and Economic Studies, over 70 per cent of blacks said they preferred to be called *black*, notwithstanding the supposed contemporary vogue for the politically-correct *African-American*.

Political correctness has become one of the most contentious issues on the US socio-political scene in recent years, and attitudes continue to harden. Those who adopt a PC line typically do so with an aggressiveness which creates antagonism even among those who might themselves be concerned about traditional labels. However, extreme positions quickly attract ridicule, and it is not surprising to find several publications in the 1990s beginning to satirise them. It may yet be humour which will restore a balanced perspective to the debate.

INTELLECTUAL CHALLENGE

The image of 'Little Stephen', for 25 years the logo of the British charity Mencap, which represents mentally-handicapped people. In 1992 Mencap launched a new campaign to promote a more positive image, using pictures of real people and a fresh slogan 'Making the most of life'.

There was controversy, however, when Mencap decided not to change the name *mental handicap*. The opposition came from critics who felt that this was a term of insult, implying that these people were unable to help themselves. Alternative names proposed, said to be more positive, included *people with learning difficulties* and the *intellectually challenged*.

Mencap's director of marketing said at the time: 'A change in name is not going to make any difference to the problems people face. The general public – the people whose attitudes we need to change – do not recognise "learning difficulty" as mental handicap. It is only a matter of time before even the most right-on expression becomes a term of abuse. It has been the same since people talked about village idiots, and "learning difficulties" is no exception. Children are already calling each other LDs as an insult'.

Such points, however, did not persuade those seeking linguistic change, who continue their campaign. As for the parents of people with a learning disability, they seemed to be for or against change in very similar numbers. The arguments have been bitter and long-running. Arguments which involve issues of political correctness always are.

mencap
making the most of life

-ISTS AND -ISMS

Suffixes (p. 198) mark the areas which cause greatest concern. In each case, the label identifies one way in which people can discriminate against others by using language which is demeaning or offensive.

Sexist: discrimination against one sex, typically men against women.
Racist: discrimination against a race, typically whites against blacks.
Ableist: discrimination by the able-bodied against those with physical or mental difficulties.
Ageist: discrimination against those of a particular age, typically the very young or the very old.
Heightist: discrimination against those of a certain height, typically against very short people.

Other such labels have been proposed, such as *fattyist* or *weightist* (against fat people) and *heterosexist* (against homosexuals of either sex), and the list has been extended in many ways, especially by those who have little sympathy with the PC frame of mind. *Alphabetist*, for example, was proposed in 1987 to label discrimination against someone on the grounds of alphabetical order. If your name begins with an A, you are advantaged (e.g. in a pile of job applications); if with Z, you are not.

THE LIVING LEXICON

We know that something is alive when we see it move; and language is no exception. Spoken language, in particular, is always on the move; and the more alive a language is, the more we see it change, as it adapts to new demands and circumstances. English, by this criterion, is in the forefront of living languages.

In reality, of course, this way of putting it is somewhat misleading. It is not language, as such, which adapts and changes. Only people do that. And it is people who, as they try to communicate fresh thoughts and feelings, and look for new ways of making an impact on each other, explore and stretch the limits of the lexicon. This section examines some of the main areas of vocabulary where we are likely to find this energy and life most clearly displayed. (For other examples of the 'life' of language, see Part V.)

Catch phrases

In catch phrases, we see the spoken language 'on the wing'. As the name suggests, a catch phrase is simply a phrase which is so appealing that people take pleasure in using it. It comes to be on everyone's lips, for a while. In some cases, a phrase comes and goes within a few weeks. More usually, it stays for a few years. And, every now and then, it stays in use for decades, at least among older people. It is even possible for catch phrases to be so useful that they become permanent additions to the language, in the form of rather self-conscious and often jocular expressions whose origins people may have long forgotten. Anyone who says (or adapts) *A man's gotta do what a man's gotta do*, *They went thataway*, or *This town isn't big enough for both of us* is 'recalling' the catch phrases of a generation of cowboy Western films, now several decades old – though it is unlikely that anyone could now recollect where they first heard them.

Catch phrases, typically, are not like these last examples, but have a clearly identifiable source. However, to identify them, we need to be part of the culture which gave rise to them. The catch phrases currently echoing around Australia are unlikely to be recognized in Britain or the USA (and vice versa), unless they have managed to capture international attention through the media. The cinema has been the chief 20th-century medium, in this respect. It is probable that most native speakers of English will know the following examples, though not everyone will be able to identify their sources with certainty (*see foot of facing page, if needed*).

What's up, doc?
Here's another fine mess you've gotten me into.
You cannot be serious!

CATCH STRUCTURES

The grammatical structure of a catch phrase may become popular in its own right. A famous case occurs in the opening text of *Star Trek*: *to boldly go where no man has gone before*. This construction is often transferred to other contexts, retaining *boldly* between *to* and the verb (p. 195), but altering the chief meaning-carrying lexemes: *to boldly split infinitives where no man has split before* is one (somewhat abstruse) instance, heard at a conference on English usage in the 1980s

Courtesy of Paramount Pictures

Here's looking at you, kid.
Phone home.
May the Force be with you!

On the other hand, many examples will have a much more 'local' response. Most people in Britain will know (and many will have used) such TV catch phrases as the following, though few English speakers in other countries will have much of an intuition about them.

Pass Used in the sense 'I don't know, ask me another' in both the BBC TV quiz game *Mastermind* and the US TV show *Password*. It is said by contestants who are unable to answer one question and who wish to move onto the next as quickly as possible before they run out of time.

Gissa job 'Give us a job' – a Liverpool dialect form of 'Give us (=me) a job', used by the unemployed character Yosser in Alan Bleasdale's TV play, *Boys from the Black Stuff* (1982).

Evenin' all 'Good evening, all', typically spoken in a mock-Cockney pronunciation (with final /g/ omitted and a vowel-like version of /l/). The greeting was used in the 1950s by the TV character PC Dixon in the series about a London policeman, *Dixon of Dock Green*, and is still widespread.

Most American viewers, on the other hand, would have no trouble recognizing

Here's Johnny Used at the beginning of the US TV chat programme, *The Johnny Carson Show*, to welcome the host. It is echoed by the insane character played by Jack Nicholson as he axes through the door at the climax of the film *The Shining*.

Very interesting Spoken in a mock German accent, with a lengthened 'meditative' first vowel, by the 'German soldier' on *Rowan and Martin's Laugh-In*, shown on US TV in the 1960s–70s. He would be seen peering at other characters through foliage and commenting on their idiocy.

The transatlantic situation is not a symmetrical one, however. Far more American films and shows are seen in Britain than move in the other direction. Thus, most British people would have no trouble with *Who loves ya, baby?* (from *Kojak*) or *Hi-yo, Silver* (from *The Lone Ranger*), and many other catch phrases from television series. *The 64-dollar* (later, *64-thousand dollar*) *question* is used in Britain without hesitation (and without any replacement of the word *dollar*). It is distinctly more unusual for a British catch-phrase to take off in the USA – though the *Monty Python* series first shown on British TV had some impact in the 1980s, with such phrases as *And now for something completely different*, and *Nudge nudge, wink wink, say no more*.

It is not just the media which generates catch phrases, of course. Anyone in the public domain can – wittingly or unwittingly – be the source of one. Politicians provide one breeding-ground, as illustrated by *You never had it so good*, found both in the USA (as the slogan of the Democratic Party in the 1952 presidential election) and the UK (by Harold Macmillan in 1957: *most of our people have never had it so good*). Sports personalities provide another: a famous case is *We wuz robbed*, attributed to Joe Jacobs, the manager of boxing heavyweight Max Schmeling, who lost on points to Jack Sharkey in 1932. Generals, admirals, singers, archbishops, judges, the British Royal Family – indeed, anyone who is likely to attract the public eye, and be quoted in the press – can, if they say the right words at the right time, find themselves taking up residence in a *Dictionary of Catch Phrases*. And if what they say is truly memorable, it might even be a *Dictionary of Quotations* (p. 184).

MYTHICAL CATCH PHRASES

Me Tarzan, you Jane is not to be found in any of the Tarzan films, though Tarzan and Jane do greet each other elliptically in some productions. Nor did Sherlock Holmes ever say *Elementary, my dear Watson* in any of the books by Conan Doyle (though it does appear in a film). Catch phrases are often adapted and renewed with scant regard for accuracy.

VOGUE WORDS

Vogue words, as the name suggests, are lexemes which take on a fashionable or cult status within the language as a whole, or among the members of a particular group (such as teachers, government ministers, or teenagers). They are similar in many ways to catch phrases (which might, indeed, be called *vogue phrases*), but vogue words usually lack the specific sources which can be found for most catch phrases.

Vogue words do not suddenly appear, but grow gradually and unobtrusively, until one day we are aware that everybody is using them.

Vogue words are not the same as neologisms (p. 130). A lexeme which has been in the language for years may become a vogue word – as happened to *absolutely* in the late 1980s, which came to be used as an emphatic substitute for 'yes I agree'. A neologism must have a certain popularity, of course, otherwise it would not become part of the language at all; but only a few neologisms become so popular that they could be called 'vogue'.

To become a vogue word, something extra has to happen – a word has to be taken up and used with extra frequency by large numbers of people, and must be extended to contexts beyond the one which originally gave rise to it (as when *gridlock*, a term describing a type of unmoving traffic jam, is applied to other forms of impasse, such as the positions in an argument). The term *buzz word* is also used to describe such a development, and in some ways is a more appropriate term, with its suggestion of excitement, activity, and change – the features of any fashion.

The use of affixes (p. 128) has come to be an important feature of vogue words in recent years. The *-gate* of *Watergate* has retained its popularity into the 1990s, producing hundreds of expressions (*Cartergate, Hollywoodgate, Dallasgate, Dianagate, Camillagate*, etc). *Euro-* in the early 1990s also achieved vogue status, being attached to almost anything which had – or could be given – a European Community application (*Eurowisdom, Eurocrat, Eurodollar, Euromess*, etc.). Other examples of vogue affixes which emerged during the 1980s include *-athon* (p. 131), *mega-, -aid, -speak*, and all the *-isms* and *-ists* (p. 177).

The trouble with vogue words is that they are transient and unpredictable. At the time of writing (1993), the vogue words of the 1980s (*Yuppie* and its friends, *glasnost, perestroika, Rambo*, etc.) are still in use, but have been overtaken by the fresh tones of the 1990s (*double whammy, virtual reality*, etc.). And by the time this book appears, most of these may well have lost their vogue, and been replaced. To be up-to-date with examples of vogue words, in fact, you will have to put this book down, go out-and-about, and listen.

Catch phrase origins (see facing page)

Bugs Bunny
Oliver Hardy, of *Laurel and Hardy*
John McEnroe
Humphrey Bogart, in *Casablanca*
ET, in *ET*
Various characters in *Star Wars*

Slogans

Originally, the word *slogan* was used to describe the battle-cry or rallying-cry of a Scottish clan. Today, the application is different, but the intention behind modern slogans is much the same – to form a forceful, catchy, mind-grabbing utterance which will rally people, in this case to buy something, or to behave in a certain way. Indeed, the force of the hard sell with which some slogans are placed before the public would no doubt have received the enthusiastic approval of any ancient Highlander.

In their linguistic structure, slogans are very like proverbs (p. 184). Sentences tend to be short, with a strong rhythm:

Safety First
Beanz Meanz Heinz
Ban the Bomb
Walls Have Ears

They often have a balanced structure, especially if they get at all lengthy:

Make love, not war
When you need aspirin, drink Disprin

There can be striking use of figurative language:

Terylene keeps its promises
Switch on the sunshine (Kellogg's cereal)

Frequent use is made of alliteration (p. 415) and rhyme ('jingles'):

Guinness is good for you
Electrolux brings luxury to life
Drinka pinta milka day
Put a tiger in your tank (Exxon/Esso)
You'll wonder where the yellow went
    When you brush your teeth with Pepsodent

And several mimic a conversational style:

It's fingerlickin' good (Kentucky Fried Chicken)
I bet (s)he drinks Carling Black Label
That'll do nicely (American Express).

As these examples suggest, slogans are used for far more than advertising commercial products, but are an essential part of all campaigns – political, safety, protest, health, environmental, and so on. Indeed, one of the first steps in any campaign is to think up a good slogan, and some companies run regular competitions to obtain fresh ideas from the public. Invent a successful slogan today, and (who knows?) it could be Sun City for you tomorrow.

 BP Britain at its best.

THE ULTIMATE DRIVING MACHINE

CENTRAL HEATING *for* KIDS

hygena

Simply beautiful. And beautifully simple.

 **IBERIA** ᗷ **Nikon SPORT OPTICS**
AIRLINES OF SPAIN
WARM TO THE EXPERIENCE.   *You'll never see things quite the same again.*™

KYOMI
WORKS WITH YOUR BODY, NOT AGAINST IT.

 *Leica*  **TROY-BILT**®
The freedom to see   *An American Legend Caring For The Land.*®

Yᴏᴜ CAN BE SURE OF Sʜᴇʟʟ

 American Sunflower Seed Bureau
FOR A HEALTHY APPETITE

Leading the way to the USA.

TWA

Graffiti

The word *graffito* originally referred to a drawing or inscription scratched on an ancient wall, such as those which have been found at Pompeii. In the present century, the name has come to be used for any spontaneous and unauthorized writing or drawing on walls, vehicles, and other public places. It is typically obscene or political in character, but a great deal of humour and popular wisdom can also be found, which has formed the basis of several collections by folklorists and humorists.

Graffiti are often occasional, in character, responding to current events and preoccupations, such as an election or a famous scandal. Most graffiti, however, bear no relation to a particular time or place. The same themes recur, over the years, as do some of the favourite formulae of the graffiti-writers. For example, there must by now be thousands of variants of the *X rules OK* structure, said to have begun as a British soccer boast (*Arsenal rules, OK?*). A small sample from one paperback collection illustrates this sub-genre in action (N. Rees, 1981):

> *Apathy rules, oh dear.*
> *Examples rule, e.g.*
> *Einstein rules relatively, OK.*
> *Bureaucracy rules OK*
> *   OK*
> *   OK*

Several other general characteristics can also be observed.

• There is a great deal of straightforward praise or invective, for or against particular gangs, religious groups, political parties, protest groups, etc. The group's symbols or logos often play a prominent role in the design.

• Likewise, a large amount of space is devoted to obscenity and dirty jokes in general, as is only to be expected from data which originates on lavatory walls.

• A common tactic is to respond to a well-known quotation or slogan. Biblical quotations are frequently used (*Faith can move mountains. She's a big girl*) as are commercial slogans (*I thought that an innuendo was an Italian suppository until I discovered Smirnoff*).

• Graffiti dialogues also exist, as writers react to each other.

> *Be alert.*
> *Your country needs lerts.*
> *– No, Britain has got enough lerts now, thank you.*
> *Be aloof.*
> *– No, really, be alert. There's safety in numbers.*

• Puns and word play abound. These are usually of the category that might charitably be described as execrable (*Quasimodo – that name rings a bell*), but they are sometimes highly ingenious – in this case, playing with the words of a once popular song ('Miss Otis regrets she's unable to lunch today'):

> *LIFT UNDER REPAIR – USE OTHER LIFT.*
> *This Otis regrets it's unable to lift today.*

WHO WUZ HERE?

Two of the longest-standing graffiti are *Kilroy* and *Chad*, both of World War 2 origin, and still being drawn around the world in the 1990s.

Kilroy
Kilroy began in America. He may have been a Massachusetts shipyard inspector, James Kilroy, who in 1941 was marking the phrase on equipment to show he had checked it. Or he may have been a Sergeant Francis Kilroy whose arrival at a Florida air base was anticipated by the notice *Kilroy will be here next week*. Several other theories exist, and the truth may never be known.

Chad
Chad (also known as *Mr Chad*) appeared in Britain early in the War, always accompanied by a standard phrase of the type *What, no —?*. He turns up, often under a different name, in several countries (e.g. *Clem*, in Canada). Again, many explanations have been proposed, both for the drawing and for the name. A popular view is that the face grew out of a diagram, such as that of an alternating wave form, which could have been part of a lecture to military personnel.

The name *Chad* was chiefly Royal Air Force; *Private Snoops* was the Army equivalent, and *The Watcher* was often found in the Navy. Theories about its origins are also highly speculative: they include the view that it derives from the name of a forces lecture centre (*Chadwick House*), and that it comes from the name of a 1940s' film (*Chad Hannah*).

Slang

Slang, according to the American poet, Carl Sandburg (1878–1967) is 'language which takes off its coat, spits on its hands – and goes to work'. The *Oxford English Dictionary* provides a more judicious account: 'language of a highly colloquial type, considered as below the level of educated standard speech, and consisting either of new words or of current words employed in some special sense'. In a related definition, it also describes slang as 'language of a low or vulgar type' and 'the special vocabulary or phraseology of a particular calling or profession'. This sums up the paradox of slang very well. People look down on it, but can hardly avoid using it, for everyone has some 'calling or profession', even if the 'call' is only to watch football, collect stamps, or go drinking. There is upper-class slang alongside lower-class slang, the slang of doctors and of lawyers, the slang of footballers and philatelists, as well as the slang which cuts across social class and occupation, available to anyone as the most colloquial variety of language (p. 290). The word 'most' is important. *Let's have a drink* is colloquial, but not slang. *Let's dip the bill* (Raymond Chandler, *The Big Sleep*), which means the same thing, is both.

The complexity of slang is immediately apparent when we examine its varied functions (see right). If forced to choose the primary function of slang from Eric Partridge's list, it would have to be number 13 (and its complement, 14). 'The chief use of slang', it has been wisely said, 'is to show that you're one of the gang' – and, in Chandler's novels, literally so. Slang is one of the chief markers of in-group identity. As such, it comes very close to jargon (p. 174).

THE USES OF SLANG

According to the British lexicographer, Eric Partridge (1894–1979), people use slang for any of at least 15 reasons:

1 In sheer high spirits, by the young in heart as well as by the young in years; 'just for the fun of the thing'; in playfulness or waggishness.
2 As an exercise either in wit and ingenuity or in humour. (The motive behind this is usually self-display or snobbishness, emulation or responsiveness, delight in virtuosity.)
3 To be 'different', to be novel.
4 To be picturesque (either positively or – as in the wish to avoid insipidity – negatively).
5 To be unmistakeably arresting, even startling.
6 To escape from clichés, or to be brief and concise. (Actuated by impatience with existing terms.)
7 To enrich the language. (This deliberateness is rare save among the well-educated, Cockneys forming the most notable exception; it is literary rather than spontaneous.)
8 To lend an air of solidity, concreteness, to the abstract; of earthiness to the idealistic; of immediacy and appositeness to the remote. (In the cultured the effort is usually premeditated, while in the uncultured it is almost always unconscious when it is not rather subconscious.)
9a To lessen the sting of, or on the other hand to give additional point to, a refusal, a rejection, a recantation;
9b To reduce, perhaps also to disperse, the solemnity, the pomposity, the excessive seriousness of a conversation (or of a piece of writing);
9c To soften the tragedy, to lighten or to 'prettify' the inevitability of death or madness, or to mask the ugliness or the pity of profound turpitude (e.g. treachery, ingratitude); and/or thus to enable the speaker or his auditor or both to endure, to 'carry on'.
10 To speak or write down to an inferior, or to amuse a superior public; or merely to be on a colloquial level with either one's audience or one's subject matter.
11 For ease of social intercourse. (Not to be confused or merged with the preceding.)
12 To induce either friendliness or intimacy of a deep or a durable kind. (Same remark.)
13 To show that one belongs to a certain school, trade, or profession, artistic or intellectual set, or social class; in brief, to be 'in the swim' or to establish contact.
14 Hence, to show or prove that someone is *not* 'in the swim'.
15 To be secret – not understood by those around one. (Children, students, lovers, members of political secret societies, and criminals in or out of prison, innocent persons in prison, are the chief exponents.)
(From *Slang: Today and Yesterday*, 1933, Ch. 2.)

CLASSY TALK

The upper-class dialogues of Wodehouse are not usually obscure, though here the quasi-legal phrase *in durance vile* ('in awful confinement') might give pause.

She lugged the poor wench off to Blandings, and she's been there ever since, practically in durance vile, her every movement watched. But this Myra seems to be a sensible, level-headed girl, because, learning from her spies that Lady C was to go to Shrewsbury for a hair-do and wouldn't be around till dinner time, she phoned Bill that she would be free that day and would nip up to London and marry him.
(P.G. Wodehouse, *Service With a Smile*, 1961.)

EARLY AUSSIE

An adapted extract from one of the slang vocabulary lists (for early 20th-century Australian) compiled by Eric Partridge (1933).

canary A convict (c. 1820–1900).
clinah, cliner A sweetheart (from Yiddish, c. 1900).
cobber A friend or mate (c. 1895).
cossie Swimming costume (c. 1920).
derry A grudge (c. 1896).
dilly-bag A shopping or utility bag (c. 1885).
dingbat An officer's servant (*dingo* + *batman*, World War 1).
dinkum Good, true (c. 1900).
drum Correct information (c. 1912).

RHYMING SLANG

Best-known for its use by London Cockneys, these unusual formations are little recorded before the mid-19th-century. Probably originating as part of a criminal argot, the underworld associations have now largely disappeared.

apples and pears stairs
artful dodger lodger
Cain and Abel table
Chalk Farm arm
Gawd forbids kids
Hampstead Heath teeth
I suppose nose
lean and lurch church
mince pie eye
north and south mouth
read and write fight
tit for tat hat
trouble and strife wife

TOUGH GUY TALK

She's a grifter, shamus. I'm a grifter. We're all grifters. So we sell each other out for a nickel. Okey. See can you make me. … I haven't pulled anything in here … I came in talking two C's. That's still the price. I come because I thought I'd get a take it or leave it, one right gee to another. Now you're waving cops at me. You oughta be ashamed of yourself.

(Raymond Chandler, *The Big Sleep*, 1939, Ch. 25.)

Gloss (for amateurs):
grifter small-time criminal
shamus private detective
C 100-dollar note
gee man (first letter of *guy*)

ARGOT

There is a close link between slang and *argot*, the special language of a secretive social group. In this piece of literary invention, context is cleverly used to aid the reader.

Our pockets were full of deng, so there was no real need from the point of view of crasting any more pretty polly to tolchock some old veck in an alley and viddy him swim in his blood while we counted the takings and divided by four, nor to do the ultra-violent on some shivering starry grey-haired ptitsa in a shop and go smecking off with the till's guts. But, as they say, money isn't everything.
(Anthony Burgess, *A Clockwork Orange*, 1962, Ch. 1.)

[Facsimile dictionary pages]

PROVINCE OF BACCHUS   **664**

character of Providence : coll. : 1856, Emerson (O.E.D.).

province of Bacchus. Drunkenness : Oxford University : ca. 1820–40. Egan's Grose.

provost. A garrison or other cell for short-sentence prisoners : military coll. (— 1890) >, ca. 1905, S.E. ; ob. Abbr. *provost-cell*.

prow. A bumpkin : naval : ca. 1800–90. ? ex ob. *prow*, good, worthy.

prowl. To womanise : low coll. : late C. 17–20. B.E., as *proling* [sic]. (Like a wild beast for meat : cf. *mutton*, q.v.)—2. To wait for 'the ghost to walk' : theatrical : from ca. 1870 ; ob. See *ghost*.—3. To go about, looking for something to steal : c. (— 1887). Baumann.

Prowler, Hugh. A generalised (? low) coll. nickname for a thief, a highwayman : mid-C. 16–17. Tusser, 'For fear of Hugh Prowler get home with the rest.'

proxime. Proxime accessit : coll. abbr. (schools', universities') : 1896. O.E.D.

Pru, the. The Prudential insurance company : insurance : late C. 19–20. Collinson.

pruff. Sturdy : Winchester College : from ca. 1870. Ex *proof against pain*. Pascoe, 1881, 'Deprive a Wykehamist of words . . . such as quill . . . pruff . . . cad . . . and his vocabulary becomes limited.'

prugg(e). A female partner ; a doxy : C. 17 : either (low) s. or c. Nares (1822) ; Halliwell (1847). Prob. cognate with *prig* and perhaps with *prog*, qq.v.

prunella, leather and. This misquotation of Pope's *leather or prunella* has been misapplied to mean something to which one is completely indifferent. (Fowler.)

Prunella, Mr ; or prunella. A clergyman : late C. 18–mid-19. Grose, 1st ed. Clergymen's, like barristers', gowns were formerly made from this strong (silk, later) worsted stuff.

Prussian blue, my. An endearment : ca. 1815–70, though app. not recorded before 1837, Dickens, ' "Vell, my Prooshan Blue," responded the son.' Punning the colour ; ex the tremendous popularity of the Prussians after Waterloo : cf. the old toast,

---

1909 condemned by the O.E.D. as illiterate ; by 1920 (so I infer from W.) it was no worse coll. ; by 1930, it was S.E., for the orig. co *toe-may-in* had disappeared,—the author (*ho dictu !*) has never even heard it. Cf. *potomain*

pu-pu. A variant of *pooh-pooh*.

pub. A public-house (see **public**, n.) : H., in his first ed. : s. >, ca. 1890 Anon., *The Siliad*, ca. 1871, 'All the great and the minor pubs.'—2. See *P.B.*

pub (always **pub it**). To frequent ' pubs ' 1889, Jerome K. Jerome. Ex preceding.

pub-crawl ; esp. **do a p.-c.** A liquori grination from bar to bar : from not later th Hence *pub-crawler*, *pub-crawling* : from

pubes. An incorrect pl. of *pubis*, a p innominate bone : from ca. 1840.—2. correct for *pubis*, the pubic bone : 1872

pubis. A mistake for *pubes*, the h region : from ca. 1680. O.E.D.

public. A public-house : coll. : 1709 warden's account (O.E.D.) ; ob. S woman keeps an inn, then ? interrupt A public, in a prim way, replied Blan q.v.

public, adj. In, of, a public-house : C. 18–20. Ex preceding.

public buildings, inspector of. loafer : from ca. 1850 ; ob. Hence, of work : from ca. 1860 ; † by 1930

public ledger. A harlot : low : very ob. 'Because like that paper, all parties,' Grose, 2nd ed. Pu *Public Ledger* (of Philadelphia, 18 the Public Register.

public line, something in the. tualler : coll. Dickens, who, in 18 or, at the least, gave currency to— on *the public business*.

public man. A bankrupt : ca Bal., 1811. Perhaps suggested woman (Fr. *femme publique*), a harlo

***public patterer.** A ' swell m mobsman) who, pretending to be preacher, harangues in the open a crowd for his confederates to rob : 1910. H., 3rd ed., 1864. See *patt*

public-room men. ' In modern

PUCKER

Prudential men, or **men of the Prudential.** Officers in the Special Branch of the R.N.V.R. Naval : 1939–45. With a pun on the Prudential insurance company. (P-G-R.)

prune is short for *Prune*, P/O. John Moore, in *The Observer*, Oct. 4, 1942, ' "Lost anybody?" "Some prune who thought he could beat up the searchlights" ' ; B., 1942.

prune, v. To adjust or otherwise tinker with (a ship's engines) : Naval : since ca. 1930. (P-G-R.)

Prune, P/O ; in speech, **Pilot Officer Prune.** 'A pilot who takes unnecessary risks, and generally loses his neck through his *prunery*' and ' "P/O Prune" is the title bestowed upon a pilot who has several "prangs" on his record' (H. & P.) : R.A.F. : since ca. 1935. He is a constant emblematic monitory figure in the pages of *The R.A.F. Journal*. Not unconnected with the impracticality of 'prunes and prisms'. Created, Jackson tells us, by S/Ldr Anthony Armstrong and L.A.C.W. Hooper ('Raff').

prune-juice. Hard liquor : since ca. 1935. (Richard Gordon, *Doctor and Son*, 1953.)

Prussian Guard. A flea : Army : 1914–18. 'Dignity and Impudence.'—2. In the game of House, a card : rhyming s. : C. 20.

psych. A 'psychological' bet, one made on a hunch : Australian two-up players' : since ca. 1930. (Lawson Glassop, *Lucky Palmer*, 1949.)

***psyche man.** See **front man**.

psychedelia. 'Drugs, flashing lights, sound, colour, movies, dance—usually experienced simultaneously' (Peter Fryer in *The Observer* colour supplement, Dec. 3, 1967) : drug addicts' and hippies' : since early 1967. Ex *psychedelic* (cf. drug, e.g. LSD) ...

A MONUMENT TO SLANG

The speed at which slang moves can be sensed by tracing the natural history of what many regard as the greatest publication on slang: Eric Partridge's *Dictionary of Slang and Unconventional English*. This monumental work first appeared in 1937, with the sub-heading *Colloquialisms and Catch-phrases, Solecisms and Catachreses, Nicknames, Vulgarisms, and such Americanisms as have been naturalized*. The second edition (1938) contained a substantial Addendum. The third edition appeared in 1948 with a much longer Addendum, largely consisting of new items from World War 2. By the time of the fifth edition (1960), the new material had run to 100,000 words, and justified separate publication as a supplementary volume. There is now an integrated edition.

An extract from both volumes is shown, illustrating the first compilation, as well as the additional information discovered. Every page of the work shows its social, historical, and geographical range, and the meticulous care with which the author approached his task. It was a real labour of love, for Partridge was no salaried academic, but a free-lance enthusiast. Although he lacked the means available to the *Oxford English Dictionary* to give full authentication to all his historical observations on slang, his work was the first major collection of evidence about the development of a genre which the first editors of the *OED* had almost completely ignored. The *Dictionary* was well received at the time, though when librarians discovered that it had 'those words' in it, many banned it from their shelves, and it is still often available only on restricted loan.

The *Dictionary* confirmed Partridge in his chosen career. In, 'Genesis of a Lexicographer', he wrote:

Although I have linguistic interests other than lexicography and etymology, and shall, I hope, be able to indulge myself in expressing them, yet, being a passably honest man, I am bound to admit the justice of the charge, 'Once a lexicographer, always a lexicographer'. There are worse fates.

GODFATHER IV: THE DICTIONARY

Lexicography is not usually thought of as a dangerous profession – though opinions might change after reading Partridge's account of data sources for *A Dictionary of the Underworld, British and American* (1949).

Only a little of the underworld material that came to me direct was in written form, professional criminals being, with the exception of confidence tricksters ('con men'), notoriously inept with the pen, even 'penmen' or 'scratchers' being useless – outside of forgery. Luckily, famous criminals have employed 'ghosts', and they and other criminals have frequently been tapped by journalists and authors; prison chaplains and governors, or wardens, are, to coin a phrase, mines of information; police officers, especially detectives, pick up many words and phrases; tramps and hoboes, whether ex-professional or amateur, tend much more than criminals to write of their experiences; special investigators into prostitution and the drug-traffic – that is, those of them who take their work seriously and are engaged therein for long periods – learn much of the cant (the philologists' term for 'language of the underworld') used by the purveyors and their customers; police-court proceedings are occasionally helpful. That is an incomplete though not a grossly inadequate list of the more accessible sources available to a researcher into cant.

But he who deals, or professes to deal, directly with the underworld has to be very careful. Criminals are naturally suspicious of a stranger: and usually they either withhold information or supply 'phoney' material…. More than one British, and more than one American, journalist and social worker and philologist have had their legs pulled.

The book took Partridge 13 years to complete. How he avoided having more than just his leg pulled throughout this time is difficult to imagine.

THE DYING AND DEAD LEXICON

Words can come alive overnight (as happened to *sputnik*, on 4 October 1957); but they take decades to die. Indeed, deciding that a word is dead is by no means easy. For when *is* a word dead? Presumably, when no one uses it any more. But when can we be sure that people are no longer using a word? How much time should we allow to go by before we can say that a word has stopped being *obsolescent* (in occasional use by a few) and has come to be *obsolete* (used by no one)? In the case of the standard lexicon, we might have to wait for a whole generation to pass away, before an inquest would return anything other than an open verdict. In the case of small-group slang, a word may be born and die within weeks or months.

We can rarely observe the birth of a word (but see p. 139), and never its death – something of a problem, of course, for anyone interested in (lexical) natural history. On the other hand, there are several clues which tell us that a word is dying, and several corners of the lexicon which demonstrate the changelessness that we associate with death.

Quotations

A quotation is a fragment of socially-embalmed language. It is language which has been placed on a pedestal, freely available for anyone to use, but readily sensitive to abuse. An error (*misquotation*) may not always be noticed, but if it is, there is a real risk of peer-group derision. Anything which someone has said or written can be a quotation, but the term usually refers to those instances which have become 'famous' over the years. Both *To be or not to be* and *Let me see one* are extracts from *Hamlet*, but only the former has come to be treated as quotation.

It can be useful to distinguish quotations from catch phrases (p. 178). By definition, the utterances which fall within both of these categories have impact and are memorable, and most can be traced to a specific source. Catch phrases are, indeed, a species of quotation. But there are important differences. Catch phrases tend to be of spoken origin, very short, subject to variation, relatively trivial in subject matter, and popular for only a short period. Quotations tend to be of written origin, indeterminate in length, highly restricted in the contexts where they may be used, semantically more profound, and capable of standing the test of time. There is a colloquial tone to the former, and a literary tone to the latter. There is no identity.

Sometimes, especially with political utterances, it is possible to see shifting between the categories. Harold Macmillan's *never had it so good* (p. 179) began life as a quotation, became a catch phrase variant, and the variant is now a quotation again. But when an utterance finally settles down as a quotation, there is no longer any capability for change. We might even consider it as a linguistic specimen, to be collected in the manner of a natural history or anatomy museum. Such catalogues, indeed, do exist, in the form of dictionaries of quotations. However, the analogy with death can be taken only so far before it too becomes moribund. Unlike an anatomical specimen in formaldehyde (horror films aside), a quotation may still exercise a strong and lively pragmatic effect (p. 286).

ON MYTHS AND MEN

Many quotations have become so well-known that they have entered the standard language, with their origins all but forgotten. How many now know that *the best-laid schemes of mice and men* is a quotation from Robert Burns' poem *To a Mouse*, or that *all hell broke loose* is from Milton's *Paradise Lost*? (*Of mice and men* is in fact a double quotation, as it was also used by John Steinbeck as the title of a novel). Several Shakespearian and Biblical quotations have entered the language in this way (pp. 63, 64).

Quite often, a quotation is adapted in the process. An example is *Ours not to reason why*, which is an adaptation of *Theirs not to reason why*, from Tennyson's *The Charge of the Light Brigade* (1854). Sometimes, more subtle processes are at work. In 1981, British Conservative politician Norman Tebbitt included in a speech a reference to his father's search for employment, using the words *He got on his bike and looked for work*. The media headlined it with the older colloquialism *On your bike* ('Go away'), and today it is this phrase which most people would confidently assert to be what Mr Tebbitt said. Like Topsy, the story just 'grow'd'.

SO WHO WAS TOPSY?

'**H**ave you ever heard anything about God, Topsy?'
The child looked bewildered, but grinned as usual.
'Do you know who made you?'
'Nobody, as I knows on,' said the child, with a short laugh. The idea appeared to amuse her considerably; for her eyes twinkled, and she added,—
'I spect I grow'd. Don't think nobody never made me.'
(Harriet Beecher Stowe, *Uncle Tom's Cabin*, 1851–2, Ch. 20.)

PROVERBS

Proverbial expressions have been given a variety of labels: *adages*, *dictums*, *maxims*, *mottoes*, *precepts*, *saws*, *truisms*. The terms all convey the notion of a piece of traditional wisdom, handed down by previous generations. In most cases, the origin of a proverb is unknown.

The effectiveness of a proverb lies largely in its brevity and directness. The syntax is simple, the images vivid, and the allusions domestic, and thus easy to understand. Memorability is aided through the use of alliteration, rhythm, and rhyme (p. 415). These points can all be identified in the following selection.

General
Children should be seen and not heard.
Still waters run deep.
Once bitten, twice shy.
Look before you leap.
A cat may look at a king.
An apple a day keeps the doctor away.
A friend in need is a friend indeed.
Every little helps.
Curiosity killed the cat.
Ask no questions, hear no lies.
It never rains but it pours.
The pen is mightier than the sword.

Scottish
Fuils and bairns never ken when they're weel aff. ('Fools and children never know when they're well off')
Ye canna tak clean water out o a foul wall. ('You can't take clean water out of a foul well')
Muckle whistlin but little redd land. ('Much whistling but little ploughed land')
There's aye some water whar the stirkie drouns. ('There's always some water where the steer drowns')
(From D. Murison, 1981.)

American
There's no such thing as a horse that can't be rode or a cowboy that can't be throwed.
Another day, another dollar.
Nothing is certain except death and taxes.
A friend in power is a friend lost.
The wheel that does the squeaking is the one that gets the grease.
The big possum walks just before dawn.
Every man must skin his own skunk.
Never trust a fellow that wears a suit.
Puttin' feathers on a buzzard don't make it no eagle.
Too many Eskimos, too few seals.
(From W. Mieder, 1992.)

Archaisms

An archaism is a feature of an older state of the language which continues to be used while retaining the aura of its past. Grammar and the lexicon provide the chief examples, though older pronunciations will from time to time be heard, and archaic spellings seen. The clearest cases are those which are separated by a substantial time-gap, notably those dating from Middle and Early Modern English (Part I).

• Lexical items include *behold, damsel, ere* ('before'), *fain* ('rather'), *hither, oft, quoth, smite, unto, wight* ('person'), *wot* ('know'), *yonder, varlet, forsooth, sire.*
• Grammatical features include present-tense verb endings (*-est, -eth*) and their irregular forms (*wilt, shouldst,* etc.), contracted forms (*'tis, 'twas, 'gainst, e'en* ('even'), *ne'er, o'er*), past tenses (*spake, clothèd*), pronouns such as *thou* and *ye*, and vocative (p. 220) constructions beginning with *O.*

The hunter of archaisms will find them in an unexpectedly diverse range of contexts. Most obviously, they are used in many historical novels, plays, poems, and films about such topics as King Arthur or Robin Hood. Novelists who have used archaic language in a careful way include Walter Scott in *Ivanhoe* and William Thackeray in *Esmond.* In poetry, Spenser and Milton were influential in maintaining an archaic tradition of usage (p. 125). Children's historical stories also tend to use them, albeit in a somewhat stereotyped manner. Archaisms can be found in religious and legal settings (p. 371, 374), in nursery rhymes and fairy tales, and (if the product warrants it) in trade names and commercial advertising. Rural dialects often retain words which have gone out of use in the standard language. And many older elements, such as *thorpe* ('village') and *lea* ('wood'), are preserved in place names (p. 140).

FORM !

" Good Heavens ! What a swell! What is it ? Tea-fight ? Wedding breakfast ? "

" Oh no ; only going to my tailor's. *Must* be decently dressed when I go to see *him*. He's so beastly critical ! "

UNCOMMONLY DATED

Not all archaisms are ancient. Many items evoke Victorian or Edwardian times, and include a great deal of slang (p. 182) and social usage, as well as outmoded technical names and notions. In such cases as the following, we may prefer to give them a less definite label, such as *old-fashioned* or *dated*.

beau	beastly
esquire	gov'nor
blest	(father)
(if I know)	grandpapa
bodice	luncheon
breeches	parlour
brougham	pray (sit
capital!	down)
civil (of you)	rotter
confound you!	spiffing
damnable	uncommon
(cheek)	(nice)
deuced	wireless

The stereotyped nature of archaic language in children's comic strips about historical characters can be seen in this piece from *Beano* (13 May 1939). The occasional *forsooth, varlet, zounds,* or *gadzooks* has been deemed enough to give such characters a historical identity.

© D.C. Thomson & Co. Ltd.

THUS WROTE ISILDUR THEREIN

The Great Ring shall go now to be an heirloom of the North Kingdom; but records of it shall be left in Gondor, where also dwell the heirs of Elendil, lest a time come when the memory of these great matters shall grow dim. It was hot when I first took it, hot as a glede, and my hand was scorched, so that I doubt if ever again I shall be free of the pain of it. Yet even as I write it is cooled, and it seemeth to shrink, though it loseth neither its beauty nor its shape. Already the writing upon it, which at first was as clear as red flame, fadeth and is now only barely to be read…
(J. R. R. Tolkien, *The Lord of the Rings*, 1954–5, Part I, Ch. 2.)

J. R. R. Tolkien (1892–1973)

IN THE OLD STYLE

Archaic spellings and styles of writing immediately add an extra layer of meaning to a text, whether it be a pub sign or a poem.

In that open field
If you do not come too close, if you do not
        come too close,
On a summer midnight, you can hear the music
Of the weak pipe and the little drum
And see them dancing around the bonfire
The association of man and woman
In daunsinge, signifying matrimonie –
A dignified and commodious sacrament.
Two and two, necessarye coniunction,
Holding eche other by the hand or the arm
Which betokeneth concorde…
(T. S. Eliot, *East Coker*, 1944.)

Clichés

In clichés we see fragments of language apparently dying, yet unable to die. Clichés emerge when expressions outlive their usefulness as conveyors of information. They are dying not from underuse, as with the gradual disappearance of old-fashioned words (p. 185), but from overuse. Such phrases as *at this moment in time* and *every Tom, Dick, and Harry*, it is said, have come to be so frequently used that they have lost their power to inform, to enliven, to mean. They have become trite, hackneyed expressions. And yet they survive, in a kind of living death, because people continue to use them, despite complaints and criticisms. They are, in effect, lexical zombies.

Why do clichés receive such a bad press? Because, in the view of the critics, it is the cliché-user who is the zombie. To use expressions which have been largely emptied of meaning implies that the user is someone who cannot be bothered to be fresh, clear, careful, or precise, or possibly someone who wishes to avoid clarity and precision. The suggestion is that such people are at best lazy or unimaginative, at worst careless or deceitful. In the case of learnèd clichés, perhaps they also wish to impress, to show off.

But clichés have their defenders, who point out that many of the expressions cited as clichés (such as those listed below) have a value. Indeed, their value is precisely the ability to express what the critics condemn. If we wish to be lazy or routine in our thinking, if we wish to avoid saying anything precise, then clichés are what we need. Such wishes are commonplace. It is not possible to be fresh and imaginative all the time. Life is full of occasions when a serious conversation is simply too difficult, or too energetic, and we gratefully fall back on clichés. They can fill an awkward gap in a conversation; and there is no denying that there are some conversations which we would rather not have. In such circumstances, clichés are an admirable lexical life-jacket. The passing remarks as people recognize each other in the street but with no time to stop, the self-conscious politeness of strangers on a train, the forced interactions at cocktail parties, or the desperate platitudes which follow a funeral: these are the kinds of occasion which give clichés their right to be.

No one would be satisfied with clichés when we expect something better from a speaker or writer. A politician who answers a direct question with clichés can expect to be attacked or satirized. A student who answers a teacher's question with a cliché is, we hope, not going to get away with it. Likewise, we complain if we encounter poems, essays, or radio talks filled with clichés. But a blanket condemnation of all clichés is as futile as unthinking acceptance.

The need for a flexible view of cliché is reinforced by a collage of quotations from various places in Walter Redfern's book, *Clichés and Coinages* (1989). Clichés, he argues, are 'bad, indispensable, sometimes good'. On the one hand, they are 'comfortable', 'Musak of the mind', 'a labour-saving device', 'a line of least resistance'. On the other hand, they 'stop us thinking of nothing', and provide 'social lubrication', 'verbal caulking', 'useful padding'. But, whether we like them or not, one thing is certain: 'They are highly contagious, and there is no known immunity, except possibly silence … and even that only conceals the infection.'

IN A NUTSHELL

If I may venture an opinion, when all is said and done, it would ill become me to suggest that I should come down like a ton of bricks, as large as life and twice as natural, and make a mountain out of a molehill on this issue. From time immemorial, in point of fact, the object of the exercise, as sure as eggs are eggs, has been, first and foremost, to take the bull by the horns and spell it out loud and clear. At the end of the day, the point of the exercise is to tell it like it is, lay it on the line, put it on the table – putting it in a nutshell, drop a bombshell and get down to the nitty-gritty, the bottom line. I think I can honestly say, without fear or favour, that I have left no stone unturned, kept my nose firmly to the grindstone, and stuck to my last, lock stock and barrel, hook line and sinker. This is not to beat about the bush or upset the apple-cart, but to give the green light to the calm before the storm, to hit the nail on the head, to bite the bullet, and thus at the drop of a hat to snatch victory from the jaws of defeat.

That's it. Take it or leave it. On your own head be it. All good things must come to an end. I must love you and leave you. I kid you not. Don't call us, we'll call you. And I don't mean maybe.

Am I right or am I right?

NEITHER RHYME NOR REASON

All of the following items have been taken from published lists of 'clichés' in usage manuals. What is immediately apparent is that such lists combine very different kinds of expressions. It is doubtful whether everyone would agree that they are all clichés, and, if they did, which items should be the most penalized.

to add insult to injury
much of a muchness
a blessing in disguise
to leave no stone unturned
dead as a doornail
like a bat out of hell
she who must be obeyed
twelve good men and true
c'est la vie
sick as a parrot
I tell a lie
in this day and age
warts and all
a memory like a sieve
the fair sex
be that as it may
from time immemorial
it takes all sorts

The arbitrary way in which usage books operate can be readily illustrated. In one such book, the items in the first list below are considered useful idiomatic phrases; the items in the second list are said to be clichés. (From *The Right Word at the Right Time*, Readers' Digest, 1985.)

a bone of contention
the old school tie
in the heat of the moment
a house of cards
to take someone down a peg
    or two
a wild-goose chase

the burden of proof
the happy couple
in no uncertain terms
a tissue of lies
to throw the book at some-
    one
a last-ditch attempt

Plus ça change, plus c'est la même chose. Know what I mean?

The words won't lie down

This quotation is from Dylan Thomas – or, at least, from a television dramatization of his last illness – and it acts as an effective epitaph to this part of the Encyclopedia. Whatever else we may say about the lexicon, and whatever we call the units (*words, lexemes, lexical items, idioms* …), it is undoubtedly the area of language which is most difficult to systematize and control. Its size, range, and variability are both an attraction and a hindrance. It comprises the largest part of the forms and structures which make up a language. As a consequence, the present section is inevitably the largest in the encyclopedia.

The words will not lie down. Even if we left them alone, they would not, for vocabulary grows, changes, and dies without anyone being in charge. There is no Minister for the Lexicon, and in countries which do have an Academy with responsibility for the language, vocabulary rules (*au Quai*, for example, p. 181) with a bland disregard for the pronouncements of academics, politicians, and pedants. It is the most anarchic area of language.

But we do not leave words alone. We do not even let them rest in peace. There are linguistic resurrectionists, who try to revive words that have been dead for centuries – such as the Anglo-Saxon enthusiasts (p. 124). There are reincarnationists, who recall the previous existence of a word, and let it influence their lives (p. 125). There are revolutionaries, who are trying to change the lexical world today, and even that is too late (p. 177). There are resuscitators, who assail the letter-columns of publications with pleas to preserve past usage; redeemers, who believe that all words can be saved; and retributionists, who believe that, for some words, hanging's too good for 'em. A few, well-intentioned souls think that the government should legalize lexical euthanasia.

Lastly, there are the linguistic necrologists, who should be given the last word in any treatment of the lexicon. These are the people who collect last words and pore over them, attributing to them a fascination which no other quotations could possibly possess. The utterances are a source of pathos, humour, irony, joy, bewilderment, sadness – indeed, all possible human emotions. They provide an apposite coda to any study of the lexicon.

LAST WORDS

It has all been very interesting.
(Mary Wortley Montagu, 1762)

It would really be more than the English could stand if another century began and I were still alive. I am dying as I have lived – beyond my means.
(Oscar Wilde, 1900)

I've had eighteen straight whiskies, I think that's the record … After 39 years, this is all I've done.
(Dylan Thomas, 1953)

Make the world better.
(Lucy Stone, suffragist, 1893)

Now I'll have eine kleine pause.
(Kathleen Ferrier, 1953)

Go on, get out! Last words are for fools who haven't said enough.
(Karl Marx, 1883)

Does nobody understand?
(James Joyce, 1941)

On the whole, I'd rather be in Philadelphia.
(W. C. Fields, 1946)

The rest is silence.
(Hamlet)

If this is dying, I don't think much of it.
(Lytton Strachey, 1932)

I am about to, or I am going to, die. Either expression is used.
(Dominique Bouhours, grammarian, 1702)

(From J. Green, 1979.)

LEXICAL GHOST STORIES

A ghost word is one which has never existed in real life, but which nonetheless turns up in a dictionary. It often happens because lexicographers are human, and make mistakes. An error in copying, typing, programming, or filing can easily lead to a false spelling or hyphenation, and sometimes even a completely fictitious item. Once the dictionary has appeared, however, its 'authority' will then make readers assume that the form is genuine. Some people may begin to use it. Certainly other lexicographers will notice it, and it may then find its way into other dictionaries.

Such was the history of *dord*. In the early 1930s, the office preparing the second edition of *Webster's New International Dictionary* (p. 442) held a file of abbreviations, one of which was 'D or d' for *density*. When the work was published, in 1934, the item appeared as *Dord*, and given the meaning 'density'. Before long, the word was appearing in other dictionaries too.

This is a somewhat unusual case, but fictitious forms are certainly not rare. It is very easy for a lexicographer to imagine that a form exists, and to slip it into a dictionary, even though it may never have been used. Is there such a word as *antiparliamentarianism*? The *Oxford English Dictionary* gives evidence only of *antiparliamentarian*. Our intuitions very readily create these potential words.

Scientific terms have been particularly prone to ghost treatment, and none more so than medical terms. One study cites over a dozen nonstandard approximations for the disease whose standard name is *myelofibrosis*. And the field of speech pathology is well known for the uncertainty of its terminology. Someone suffering from a serious difficulty in pronunciation, for example, might be described as manifesting an *articulation disorder*, *articulatory handicap*, *articulatory defect*, *articulation syndrome*, *misarticulation*, or any of over a dozen other words or phrases. Dictionaries of speech pathology do not agree about which terms to include as legitimate alternatives, and in the absence of lexical research there is no guarantee that the terms a particular dictionary selects are the most commonly used ones – or, indeed, whether there is anyone out there using them at all.

has a fascination for
d be "Railways have
"He is fascinated by

the rescuers had co
have been saved.".
been saved".

d result" - what's
ult"?

egotiating table" -
le into it every ti
put a table?

Never ever". We use
was that in Never
He was jeered" for
ily Telegraph, no
his one.

hope I have not g
teacher, by the wa
but all the abov
ature of my blood
g point.

Pet hate - less fu FEWER -

"less buses"
people
etc
etc

and one battle long - since lost

SPLIT INFINITIVES.

ear Sir, Help! What is this
modern craze for prefixing the
word "missing" with "gone"?
One hears it continually on T.V.
and radio! Surely someone
"is missing" — "gone missing" is
tautology?

words!)
"
nsequently
"
ild (ugh!)
"

y of
ently
nt,
on

Wo
HA
NOE

GLISH NOW' REQUEST FOR
DAY 18TH FEBRUARY 1988

sage which makes my
is that of the word "conv
as used by sports commenta
For instance :— "He played con
or "He scored a convincing go
What on earth does this mea

15TH Feb 1988

ar David Crystal, you will see from my address that I am BASED about
ifty KILOMMETERS from London. BASICALLY my wife SORT OF told me
about your programme and I understood you have GIVEN THE GO AHEAD
to listeners to write in about what they find most HORRENDOUS about spoken
English on the TRANNY or the BOX.
Preye-merrily give become increasingly concerned that
English is AT RISK but UP UNTIL now have refrained from writing
to you about it. Perhaps the deterioration is no DIFFERENT to what
it was in the past but spoken English does seem to be increasingly in an
VUNNRABLE (sic) SITUATION — one hopes only TEMPO RARE "
HOPEFULLY one's comments may reach some HIGH RANKING official
who will be able to SORT OUT such conTROVersy before it
escalates.
HAVING SAID THAT IN THE FINAL ANALYSIS
AND AT THE END OF THE DAY, THAT'S WHAT
IT'S ALL ABOUT!

r general.
She lives in the central area-r of th
He works in the area-r of horses. (W
I enjoyed a soprano aria-r in the St
There was an armada-r of ships in Ma
I felt a sense of awe-r and wonder.
The electric cinema-r in London. sta
A Cortina-r or some car like it.
He has good data-r about X-Rays.
The drama-r of deteriorating homes
You listen to Drama-r on R
d
he

18. 2
ENGLISH NOW
Thurs. 11.50 am LW

.... It makes my
blood boil —
to hear} LESS
read}
when it should
be FEWER.

London,

Dear Sirs
I would appreciate your v
about why so many eminent author
of English, who must know better, sh
gravitate so abjectly to the regretta
tendency that if enough idiots say
something wrong it becomes right;
instead of endeavouring to educate
se same idiots into some apprecia
he beauty found by using the ma
des of meaning in our very versa
guage.

The Presenter,
"English Now,"
Radio 4.

Dear Sir,
A few weeks ago, on "English Now," you
asked listeners what it was in English usage which
particularly irritated them. I should like to reply:
1) The worst offender is the habitual use of
"hopefully", which should be an adverb meaning "in a
hopeful manner" and instead is used wrongly by 99%
of broadcasters to mean "I hope", "it is hoped" etc.
How can "hopefully" possibly be better than "I hope"?
Its use is particularly bad when used in a sentence
like, "Hopefully, this will not always happen...."
(How can 'this' be 'hopeful'?) Is there no possibility that this idiotic mis-use of a word can be
stopped?
2) Another irritation is a matter of pronunciation;
the use of "thi sevening" instead of "this evening"
I know that some slight liaison cannot be avoided
between the two words, but you must be aware that
every broadcaster now actually emphasises it to such
an extent that it is deliberately pronounced as
"sevening". Weather forecasters seemed to lead the
field here!
3) More generally, I long for a return to some good
old-fashioned four-letter words on the media! Have
no fear, I don't mean those words, but broadcasters
invariably now seem to believe that they must avoid

21st February, 1988

Mr. David Crystal,
English Now,
BBC London,
W1A 1AA

Dear Mr. Crystal,
I welcome the return of your series.
You asked for examples of bad English that "make
our blood boil". I should like to oblige with
the following:

1. Pleonastic use of the subordinating
   conjunction "that" after a parenthesis, e.g.,
   "He said that, if it was raining, that he
   would not go". This locution is frequently
   heard now, even from educated people, but
   to my knowledge no-one has drawn attention
   to it.
2. Phrases like "... unfair to we old people".
   Mind you, I have heard the speaker make up
   for it by saying in the very next sentence
   "Us old people don't like it"!
3. Sentences using the perfect infinitive
   where the present one would be correct, e.g.,
   "He would have liked to have done it" for
   "He would have liked to do it" (or, with a

7. "Negotiating table" - Why bring
   table into it every time? Can no-
   without a table?
8. "Never ever". We used to say "Ne
   or was that in Never Ever Land?
9. "He was jeered" for "He was jeere
   Daily Telegraph, no less, often pe
   this one.

I hope I have not given you too man
t a teacher, by the way, or in the aca
rld, but all the above solecisms raise
erature of my blood, though not, perha
ling point.

PART III
English grammar

The central role of grammar in the study of language has become an established tenet of modern linguistics; but outside the hallowed linguistic halls the status of the subject has in recent decades been the subject of much controversy. The pendulum has moved dramatically – from a time when few people questioned the place of grammatical knowledge as an essential element of a person's education to one when few people tried to defend it. Currently, there is a definite although erratic movement in the reverse direction, towards a position which once again recognizes the importance of grammar in general education – though this is not the same position the pendulum held in the 1950s, when it started its unprecedented swing.

Part III therefore has a historical slant to it. It opens with an account of the various beliefs and attitudes which people hold about grammatical study, drawing an essential distinction between 'knowing grammar' and 'knowing about grammar'. It then gives an account of what was involved in traditional grammar, which dom-inated the study of the subject for the best part of 200 years, and investigates some of the leading shibboleths of prescriptive grammar. This leads to a consideration of current trends, and of the differences between ancient and modern approaches to grammar.

The remainder of Part III is devoted to a systematic presentation of the main areas of English grammar. It begins with morphology, the study of word structure, looking in particular at the various word-endings which have a role to play in expressing grammatical relationships. In §15 the important concept of the 'word class' (or 'part of speech') is presented, and we identify the most important of these classes in English, as well as some of the less important ones. Finally §16, the largest section in Part III, gives an account of the main aspects of syntax, the study of sentence structure. This is too vast a domain to be comprehensively covered in a book such as this, but the section does look systematically at a wide range of basic syntactic notions, and illustrates them from several areas of usage, from spontaneous informal conversation to established written literature.

◀ Some of the thousands of letters about English grammar sent in by listeners to the BBC Radio 4 series, English Now (see further, p. 194).

13 · GRAMMATICAL MYTHOLOGY

The study of grammar goes back to the time of the ancient Greeks, Romans, and Indians, and from its earliest days has caught the interest of the learned and the wise. As a result the subject has developed around itself a hallowed, scholarly, and somewhat mysterious atmosphere. In the popular mind, grammar has become difficult and distant, removed from real life, and practised chiefly by a race of shadowy people ('grammarians') whose technical apparatus and terminology require a lengthy novitiate before it can be mastered. The associated mythology has grown with time, and is now pervasive and deep-rooted. Millions of people believe that they are failures at grammar, say that they have forgotten it, or deny that they know any grammar at all – in each case using their grammar convincingly to make their point. It is such a shame, because the fundamental point about grammar is so very important and so very simple.

A matter of making sense

It is all to do with making sense. The fundamental purpose of language is to make sense – to communicate intelligibly. But if we are to do this, we need to share a single system of communication. It would be no use if one person were using Japanese and the other were using Arabic, or one knew only Morse code and the other knew only semaphore. The rules controlling the way a communication system works are known as its grammar, and both sender and recipient need to use the same grammar if they are to understand each other. If there is no grammar, there can be no effective communication. It is as simple as that.

We can see this by dipping into the vocabulary of English, and trying to do without grammar. The lexicon has been investigated in Part II. With its hundreds of thousands of words, it is certainly the most prominent aspect of the language; yet without grammar the value of this remarkable resource becomes so limited as to be almost worthless. We might believe that 'making sense' is a matter of vocabulary – that meaning lies in the lexicon. This is certainly the superficial impression we receive whenever we use a dictionary, and 'look up a meaning'. However, all the lexicon provides is a sense of a word's meaning potential – its semantic possibilities (p. 118). To draw out this potential we need to add grammar. A dictionary does this unobtrusively, through its definitions and citations (p. 156). When we use a dictionary, we are being fed grammar all the time, without realizing it.

THE MYTH OF SIMPLICITY

This advertisement (minus the name of the firm who produced it) appeared in a foreign Sunday paper a few years ago. It represents one of the most pervasive myths about a language – that grammar is needed for writing, but not for speech.

'English...has a grammar of great simplicity and flexibility', wrote the authors of *The Story of English* (on p. 47) – a book, based on a BBC television series, which became a best-seller in the 1980s. This kind of statement is often made by those who identify the complexity of a language with the number of word-endings it has – an unfortunate legacy of the Latin influence on English grammar (p. 192). The reality can be seen in the three kilos of paper comprising *A Comprehensive Grammar of the English Language* (1985). Non-native speakers of English who have spent several years learning the grammar to an advanced level have little sympathy with the view that English grammar is 'simple'. (Flexibility is a different matter: see p. 233.)

BASIC ENGLISH COURSE

20 lessons

We teach you how to speak so there's not much grammar.

TAKE A WORD, ANY WORD...

If meaning resides only in a word, you will be able to understand the following utterance without difficulty:

Table.

The problem, of course, is that too many possibilities come to mind. The speaker might have intended any of the following, which are just some of the senses of this word:

- A piece of furniture.
- An array of figures.
- A group of people.
- An occasion of eating.
- A negotiating session.

The task, you might conclude, is unfair. It is impossible to say which sense is intended without being given any context. 'Put the word into a context', you might say, 'and then I can tell you what it means'. But to put a word into its linguistic context is to put it into a sentence. And putting it into a sentence is to add grammar.

- The table has a broken leg.
- There are three columns in the table.
- We make up a bridge table each week.
- I'll tell you all at table.
- They've come to the peace table.

There would be a similar problem even if the possible senses were restricted to the first one. If the only meaning of table were 'piece of furniture', it would still be unclear what the speaker

was talking about. Is the utterance simply identifying a table, or saying that something has happened to one, or asking us to put something on one? There are so many possibilities, and again, only by putting the word into context will it become clear which one is meant.

I see a table.
The table is broken.
The paint is on the table.
I'm going to table the motion.

With utterances such as these, matters are becoming clearer. We have put the word into a sentence. We have added some grammar. We are beginning to make sense.

'TO KNOW' OR 'TO KNOW ABOUT'

Much mythology stems from a confusion between 'knowing grammar' and 'knowing about grammar'. Two very different types of knowledge are involved.

• If you have reached this point on the page and understood what you have read, you must 'know' English grammar. You may not agree with what I say, or like the way I say it, but you are certainly able to construe what it is I have said. Knowing grammar, in this sense, is a facility which developed with little conscious effort when we were young children. As adults, we learn to put words together in the right order, and add the right endings. Moreover, we have the ability to recognize certain types of error, and know how to correct them. If sentence the am writing I now contains major errors, you are likely to immediately notice them. However, to be able to diagnose the problems with such a sentence, you must 'know English grammar' (at least, to that extent).

• All of this is an unconscious process. By contrast, 'knowing about' English grammar is a conscious, reflective process. It means being able to talk about what it is we are able to do when we construct sentences – to describe what the rules are, and what happens when they fail to apply. It is not difficult to point to the errors in the previous paragraph; but it *is* difficult to describe precisely what they are, and to state the rules which have been broken. If you are able to do this (using such terms as 'word order', 'noun', and 'definite article'), then you 'know about English grammar' (at least, to that extent).

Fluent native speakers of English quite often say that they 'don't know' any grammar, or that foreigners speak English better than they do. One way of making sense of such comments, which at first seem nonsensical, is to apply the above distinction. It is certainly true that many foreigners can talk about English grammar more confidently than native speakers can, because foreign learners have usually acquired their knowledge in a conscious way. It is also true that many native speakers have little or no ability to describe their own grammatical knowledge, either because they have never been taught to do so, or because the potential fascination of this task has been stifled by poor teaching methods. The pedagogical quest has long been to find ways of developing a person's 'knowledge about' grammar which are both enlivening and rewarding, and it continues to be an important goal of contemporary educational linguistics.

'WELL, MARY ANNE?'

Charles Dickens pulls no punches when he finds an opportunity to satirize the grammatical tradition which held such power in British schools during the early 19th century (p.193). For example, in *The Old Curiosity Shop* (1840–1) he describes Mrs Jarley's efforts to attract visitors from boarding-schools to her waxworks 'by altering the face and costume of Mr Grimaldi as clown to represent Mr Lindley Murray as he appeared when engaged in the composition of his English Grammar' (Ch. 29).

In *Our Mutual Friend* (1864–5, Book 2, Ch. 1) he uses an extended example to satirize the way prescriptive grammarians would tend to look for faults in everyday expressions. The schoolteacher, Miss Peecher, has just been speaking to Mr Headstone, whom she secretly loves, and Charley Hexam. They have just left, and Mary Anne, her favourite pupil, who now assists her in her household, wants to say something:

The pupil had been, in her state of pupilage, so imbued with the class-custom of stretching out an arm, as if to hail a cab or omnibus, whenever she found she had an observation on hand to offer to Miss Peecher, that she often did it in their domestic relations; and she did it now.

'Well, Mary Anne?' said Miss Peecher.

'If you please, ma'am, Hexam said they were going to see his sister.'

'But that can't be, I think,' returned Miss Peecher: 'because Mr Headstone can have no business with *her*.'

Mary Anne again hailed.

'Well, Mary Anne?'

'If you please, ma'am, perhaps it's Hexam's business?'

'That may be,' said Miss Peecher. 'I didn't think of that. Not that it matters at all.'

Mary Anne again hailed.

'Well, Mary Anne?'

'They say she's very handsome.'

'Oh, Mary Anne, Mary Anne!' returned Miss Peecher, slightly colouring and shaking her head, a little out of humour; 'how often have I told you not to use that vague expression, not to speak in that general way? When you say *they* say, what do you mean? Part of speech, They?'

Mary Anne hooked her right arm behind her in her left hand, as being under examination, and replied:

'Personal pronoun.'

'Person, They?'

'Third person.'

'Number, They?'

'Plural number.'

'Then how many do you mean, Mary Anne? Two? Or more?'

'I beg your pardon, ma'am,' said Mary Anne, disconcerted now she came to think of it; 'but I don't know that I mean more than her brother himself.' As she said it, she unhooked her arm.

'I felt convinced of it,' returned Miss Peecher, smiling again. 'Now pray, Mary Anne, be careful another time. He says is very different from They say, remember. Difference between He says and They say? Give it me.'

Mary Anne immediately hooked her right arm behind her in her left hand – an attitude absolutely necessary to the situation – and replied: 'One is indicative mood, present tense, third person singular, verb active to say. Other is indicative mood, present tense, third person plural, verb active to say.'

'Why verb active, Mary Anne?'

'Because it takes a pronoun after it in the objective case, Miss Peecher.'

'Very good indeed,' remarked Miss Peecher, with encouragement. 'In fact, could not be better. Don't forget to apply it, another time, Mary Anne.'

WHY STUDY GRAMMAR?

• 'Because it's there'. People are constantly curious about the world in which they live, and wish to understand it and (as with mountains) master it. Grammar is no different from any other domain of knowledge in this respect.
• But more than mountains, language is involved with almost everything we do as human beings. We cannot live without language. To understand the linguistic dimension of our existence would be no mean achievement. And grammar is the fundamental organizing principle of language.
• Our grammatical ability is extraordinary. It is probably the most creative ability we have. There is no limit to what we can say or write, yet all of this potential is controlled by a finite number of rules. How is this done?
• Nonetheless, our language can let us down. We encounter ambiguity, imprecision, and unintelligible speech or writing. To deal with these problems, we need to put grammar under the microscope, and work out what went wrong. This is especially critical when children are learning to emulate the standards used by educated adult members of their community.
• Learning about English grammar provides a basis for learning other languages. Much of the apparatus we need to study English turns out to be of general usefulness. Other languages have clauses, tenses, and adjectives too. And the differences they display will be all the clearer if we have first grasped what is unique to our mother tongue.
• After studying grammar, we should be more alert to the strength, flexibility, and variety of our language, and thus be in a better position to use it and to evaluate others' use of it. Whether our own usage in fact improves, as a result, is less predictable. Our *awareness* must improve, but turning that awareness into better practice – by speaking and writing more effectively – requires an additional set of skills. Even after a course on car mechanics, we can still drive carelessly.

TRADITIONAL GRAMMAR

The study of English grammar may have its share of mythology (p. 190), but many people have unhappy memories of an early close encounter with the subject which was certainly no myth. 'Dry', 'boring', 'pointless', and 'irrelevant' are just some of the critical adjectives which have been used. To anyone coming to the subject fresh in the 1990s, and reflecting on the positive reasons which motivate grammatical enquiry (p. 191), these attitudes might appear puzzling. An explanation can, however, be found, deriving from the approach to language study which developed in the middle of the 18th century (p. 78), and which led to the first influential generation of what were later called *traditional* English grammars.

The tradition that these grammars represent developed rapidly in the 19th century and was strongly in evidence even in the 1960s. Well over a thousand such grammars came to be published throughout the English-speaking world, and many went through dozens of printings. For example, J. C. Nesfield, the British author of a highly successful series on English grammar and composition, produced *English Grammar: Past and Present* in 1898; it was continuing to sell in its 25th edition in 1961. Nor has the tradition died. New versions of old grammars continue to appear in the 1990s, though printed now in a glossy livery and modern typography which belies their content.

Hallmarks

Two chief hallmarks of the traditional era account for much of the negative reaction which can arise when people talk about the subject of grammar.

• Traditional grammars insisted that only certain styles of English were worth studying – in particular, the more formal language used by the best orators and writers. Textual samples selected for analysis or commentary were typically erudite and sophisticated, commonly taken from literary, religious, or scholarly sources. Informal styles of speech were ignored, or condemned as incorrect. This meant that the language which most children used and heard around them received no positive reinforcement in grammar lessons. To many, accordingly, the subject became distant and unreal.

• Traditional English grammars also treated their subject in a highly abstruse way, describing grammatical patterns through the use of an analytical apparatus which derived from Latin grammars. The technique went under various names (such as *parsing*, *clause analysis*, and *diagramming*) but the end result was the same: students had to master a classification system

and terminology which was alien to English, and apply it correctly to an array of sentences which, very often, were chosen for their difficulty. To many, accordingly, the subject seemed arbitrary and arcane.

None of this amounts to a criticism of the task of grammatical analysis as such: after all, this task defines modern linguistics as much as it does traditional grammar. But whereas modern linguists take pains to set up their rules following a careful analysis of the way the English language actually works, traditional grammarians assumed that all relevant grammatical distinctions and standards of use could be obtained by automatically applying the categories and practices of Latin grammar. This was a false assumption, but it is one we cannot ignore, for grammarians of the 1990s are the inheritors of the distortions and limitations imposed on English by two centuries of a Latinate perspective, and have to find ways of dealing with them.

N.B. – CANDIDATES MUST NOT BREAK UP THEIR ANSWERS INTO SCATTERED PIECES. GREAT IMPORTANCE WILL BE ATTACHED TO CLEARNESS AND ACCURACY OF EXPRESSION AND STYLE.

I.—LANGUAGE

(*Not more than* **seven** *of these* **ten** *questions are to be attempted.*)

1. Explain carefully what is meant by the term "grammar." Give the chief divisions of "grammar," with definitions and examples.
2. Comment on the following statements:–
   a) "To reform Modern English spelling would be to destroy the life-history of many of our words."
   (b) "The spelling of Modern English is little better than a chaos."
3. At what periods, and under what conditions, have Latin words been introduced into English directly or indirectly? Give examples.
4. Derive and explain:– *Matriculate, parliament, isle, alderman, mayor, cricket*; and mention some derivatives from and some cognates with these words.
5. What is meant by "relative pronouns"? Differentiate the uses of the relative pronouns in Modern English, giving instances of each.
6. Write notes on the following words:– *worse, nearer, but, it, songstress, riches, alms, ye, first, Wednesday.*
7. Classify adverbs, according to their origin and formation, with instances.
8. How are (i) infinitives, and (ii) participles distinguished from the other parts of verbs? Write down and discuss six sentences illustrating the various uses of (i) the Infinitive and (ii) the Present Participle.
9. What is meant by "defective verbs"? Discuss the conjugation of any *three*.
10. "To make a revolution every day is the nature of the sun, because of that necessary course which God hath ordained it, from which it cannot swerve but by a faculty from that voice which first did give it motion."
    (i) Analyse this sentence; (ii) underline the words of Latin origin.

A TESTING TIME

The English language paper which was set as part of the London Matriculation examination for senior pupils in June 1899.

Although traditional grammar was the orthodoxy, not everyone approved of it, as this writer demonstrated:

Grammar as a separate subject inevitably means definitions and difficulties. My ears still recall the voices of Standard IV boys filling the air with their sweet jargoning as they chanted definitions of relative pronouns, mood and prepositions... What happens when grammar is treated as a separate subject can be best illustrated by an example. Recently the girls in the Lower Fifth of a County Secondary School had to analyse this passage: *We can only have the highest happiness, such as goes along with being a great man, by having wide thoughts, and much feeling for the rest of the world as well as ourselves; and this sort of happiness often brings so much pain with it, that we can only tell it from pain by its being what we would choose before everything else, because our souls see it is good.* (Romola.) Really, it is nothing short of an outrage that girls of fourteen and fifteen should have such exercises inflicted on them ... The exercise is so far from exceptional that the unfortunate girls have a book full of similar passages and have to dissect one each week. Surely no one will pretend that such exercises have any purpose, intellectual or emotional, useful or ornamental. The one effect they certainly achieve is to make the victims hate English with peculiar intensity.
(G. Sampson, 1921.)

A SERIOUS SUBJECT

English grammar has generally been perceived and practised as a highly serious subject of study, with the aim of continuing the tradition which began with Classical Greek authors, and which was held to have reached its heights in the work of such stylists as Cicero. The focus was always on the written language and on the elimination of what was considered to be grammatical error or infelicity. Rules of grammar were strictly defined and rigorously enforced, either by physical punishment or (as in the case of such young ladies as Mary Anne, p. 191) through social sanction. No one was exempt, not even the highest in the land, as William Cobbett's letters demonstrate.

The atmosphere of many grammar classes was, as a consequence, one of uncertainty and trepidation. Because a large number of the grammatical rules stemmed from the arbitrary decisions of the first grammarians, and lacked a solid basis in the English language, the only safety for the student lay in learning by rote, not by reason. 'Parsing' (p. 197) became an end in itself: it was satisfactory to have correctly identified the parts of a sentence, and unnecessary to ask what this procedure proved. The prospect of a grammar class being enjoyable was rare – though we do sometimes hear stories of teachers who were able to make the subject come alive. For most young people, the aim was to satisfy their teacher or their examiners, then to leave school and forget about grammar as quickly as possible.

Unfortunately, society would never permit school-leavers such friendly oblivion. The distance between the rules in their grammar books and the way they actually spoke was so great that for the rest of their lives they would find themselves burdened with a sense of linguistic inferiority. This is the real source of such notions, widely held among native speakers of English, that they do not speak 'correct English', or that foreigners speak the language 'better' than they do (p. 191). Additionally, the fact that a minority of students, through hard work or good fortune, did manage to master the intricacies of traditional grammar, and thereby were perceived to be educated, gave them a vested interest in preserving these norms, and in imposing them on anyone over whom they later found themselves to be in control. For schoolchildren, secretaries, and subordinates of all kinds, the use of split infinitives was one of several sure signs of social linguistic inadequacy (p. 195), and their avoidance a mark of successful upward mobility.

GUARDING THE GUARDIANS

Towards the end of William Cobbett's *English Grammar* (1829), there is a series of lessons 'intended to prevent statesmen from using false grammar, and from writing in an awkward manner'. He takes his examples from speeches made by Lord Castlereagh, the Duke of Wellington, the Prince Regent, and others. Here is what he has to say about one sentence used by 'the first Commoner of England', the Speaker of the House of Commons:

2. The subjects which have occupied our attention have been more numerous, more various and more important than are usually submitted to the consideration of Parliament in the same Session.

It is difficult to say what is meant, in Paragraph No. 2, by the word *various*. The speaker had already said, that the *subjects* were more *numerous*, which was quite enough; for they necessarily *differed* from each other, or they were one and the same; and, therefore, the word *various* can in this place have no meaning at all, unless it mean that the subjects were *variegated* in themselves, which would be only one degree above sheer nonsense.

Next comes the '*than are*' without a nominative case. Chambermaids, indeed, write in this way, and in such a case, 'the dear unintelligible scrawl' is, as the young rake says in the play, 'ten thousand times more *charming*' than correct writing; but, from a Speaker in his robes, we might have expected 'than *those which* are usually submitted.'

And what does the Speaker mean by 'in *the same* Session?' He may mean 'in *one and the same* Session;' but, what business had the word *same* there at all? Could he not have said, 'during *one* Session, or during a *single* Session?'

Comment
Cobbett pulls no punches and is scared of nobody. One of his letters to his son James (p. 77) is headed 'Errors and Nonsense in a King's Speech'. The condemnations are an interesting mixture of personal taste (coloured also by Cobbett's political opinions), acute observation, and common sense, but always filtered through the prescriptive grammatical tradition, to which he regularly alludes.

Not all of his arrows are wide of the mark: he often pinpoints a real ambiguity or lack of clarity, thereby anticipating by over a century the methods of Sir Ernest Gowers and the Plain English campaigners (p. 376). But, the average person might well think, if people of such eminence as the King and the Prime Minister are perceived to make such gross errors, after presumably receiving a comprehensive grammatical education, what chance is there for the rest of us? The same question might be asked after reading Lowth's or Murray's criticisms of Shakespeare's grammar (p. 79). One of the ironies of the prescriptive approach is that its universal censoriousness promotes the very scepticism about grammatical correctness which it was designed to eradicate.

PRESCRIPTIVE GRAMMAR

Traditional grammar reflects the approach to language known as *prescriptivism* (p. 366) – the view that one variety of a language has an inherently higher value than others and ought to be the norm for the whole of the speech community. A distinction is often drawn between *prescriptive rules*, which state usages considered to be acceptable, and *proscriptive rules*, which state usages to be avoided – grammatical 'do's and don'ts'. In fact the 'Thou Shalt Not' tradition predominates, with most recommendations being phrased negatively.

A GRAMMATICAL TOP TEN

This table lists the 'top ten' complaints about grammar found in a survey of letters written to the BBC Radio 4 series *English Now* in 1986. One programme asked listeners to send in a list of the three points of grammatical usage they most disliked, as well as the three they most liked. The writers were also asked to give their age. Over a thousand letters arrived.

Of those writers who did mention their age, the vast majority were over 50. Many were over 70. Hardly anyone responded to the request for 'usages liked'. On the other hand, only a few obediently restricted themselves to just three points under 'usages disliked'. Several letters were over four pages long, full of detailed complaints. The longest contained a list of over 200 split infinitives which the listener had carefully noted over a period of a month.

The language of most letters was intemperate and extreme, talking about 'pet hates', and using apocalyptic metaphors to describe the writers' feelings. The dozen reactions listed below are typical, and perhaps help to explain why it is so difficult to make progress in any debate about, for example, a grammatical curriculum in schools. Grammar, for some reason, raises the most deep-rooted of hackles.

abomination	appal
blood boil	cringe
drive me wild	grate
grind my teeth	horrified
irritant	pain to my ear
prostitution	shudder

Many listeners felt that they were observing something new in the language – a trend of the permissive 1980s, or perhaps the particular result of slackness at the BBC itself. However, the usage issues on these pages have a much longer history: for example, many are referred to by Dean Alford in *The Queen's English* (1869), long before the BBC was born, and several go back another century or more. That is the way of it with grammatical shibboleths: they do not readily die.

Complaint

1 *I* should not be used in *between you and I*. The pronoun should be *me* after a preposition, as in *Give it to me* (p. 203).

2 Split infinitives should not be used (see facing page).

3 *Only* should be next to the word to which it relates. People should not say *I only saw Jane* when they mean *I saw only Jane*.

4 *None* should never be followed by a plural verb. It should be *None was left on the table*, not *None were left on the table*.

5 *Different(ly)* should be followed by *from* and not by *to* or *than*.

6 A sentence should not end with a preposition. We should say *That was the clerk to whom I gave the money*, and not *That was the clerk I gave the money to*.

7 People should say *I shall/ you will/he will* when they are referring to future time, not *I will/you shall/he shall*.

8 *Hopefully* should not be used at the beginning of a sentence as in *Hopefully, Mary will win the race*.

9 *Whom* should be used, not *who*, in such sentences as *That is the man whom you saw*. The pronoun is the object of the verb *saw*, and should be in the objective case (p. 203).

10 Double negatives should be avoided, as in *They haven't done nothing*.

Comment

This is an interesting instance of the effect traditional grammatical attitudes can have on intuitions. Many educated people are unconsciously aware of the way these grammars have criticized *me* in other constructions, recommending *It is I* instead of *It is me* (p. 203). They have a vague feeling that *I* is somehow the more polite form, and thus begin to use it in places where it would not normally go.

The context usually makes it obvious which sense is intended. It is wise to be careful in writing, where ambiguity can arise; but spoken usage is hardly ever ambiguous, because *only* is always linked with the next word that carries a strong stress. Note the difference between *I only saw JANE* (and no one else) and *I only SAW Jane* (I didn't talk to her).

Traditional grammars see *none* as a singular form (= 'no one'), which should therefore take a singular verb. But usage has been influenced by the plural meaning of *none*, especially when followed by a plural noun. *None of the books were left on the table* means 'They were not on the table'. Concord (p. 221) is often affected by meaning in this way.

Traditional grammarians were impressed by the meaning of the first syllable of this word in Latin (*dis-* = 'from'), and argued that the historical meaning was the correct one (p. 136). But *to* has come to be the more frequent British usage, perhaps because of the influence of *similar to*, *opposed to*, etc. *Than* is often objected to in Britain because of its supposed connection with American English (p. 441).

This usage was probably first introduced by John Dryden in the 17th century, and shows the influence of Latin grammar, where prepositions usually preceded nouns. It has never reflected colloquial practice in English, though in formal English the prescriptive rule tends to be followed (p. 367). To alter someone's practice can be dangerous, as in Winston Churchill's famous reaction to secretarial changes made to his usage: 'This is the sort of English up with which I will not put'.

Traditional grammars have tried to regularize the use of these auxiliary verbs (p. 212) since the 18th century, but it is doubtful whether the words ever followed the neat usage patterns recommended. Certainly there has been a tendency to replace *shall* by *will* for well over a century. It is now hardly ever used in American, Irish, or Scots English, and is becoming increasingly less common in other varieties. Usages such as *I'll be thirty next week* are now in the majority.

This is a fairly modern usage, so the fact that it has attracted such criticism shows that the prescriptive tradition is alive and well. People argue that it is the speaker, not Mary, who is being hopeful in this example, and so a better construction would be *It is hoped that* or *I hope that*. But *hopefully* is one of hundreds of adverbs which are used in this way (*frankly*, *naturally*, etc.), and this general pattern has prevailed. It is unclear why *hopefully* has been singled out for criticism.

The *whom* construction has developed very formal overtones, and in informal speech people often replace it by *who*, or drop the relative pronoun altogether: *That's the man you saw*. It remains the norm for formal writing. Note that a stylistic clash would occur if the informal contracted verb were used with the formal relative pronoun: *That's the man whom you saw*.

This construction is no longer acceptable in Standard English, though it was normal in earlier periods of the language (p. 70). It is now common in nonstandard speech throughout the world. Traditional grammarians condemn it on logical grounds – that the two negatives cancel each other out, as minus signs would in mathematics. However, in nonstandard usage a different criterion applies: here, extra negative forms add emphasis. *They haven't done nothing* means 'They really haven't done anything' and not 'They have done something'.

THE SPLIT INFINITIVE STORY

Traditional grammars have long objected to the insertion of an adverb between the particle and the infinitive form of a verb, as in *to definitely ask*. *To ask* makes a grammatical unit, they argue, and the two parts should stay together. The fact that there was no precedent for separating them in Latin (which formed its infinitives, such as *amare* 'to love', using a word-ending) made the usage particularly unappealing.

The extent to which people inveighed against the split infinitive in the 19th century was remarkable. It was considered a solecism of the worst kind (p. 86). Henry Fowler refers scathingly to 'the non-split diehard' – 'bogy-haunted creatures… who would as soon be caught putting knives in their mouths as splitting an infinitive'. A famous example is reported in Andrew Lang's *Life of Sir Stafford Northcote*, the British statesman who was much involved in foreign affairs in the 1860s. Lang describes how the British government was prepared to make several concessions in negotiating a treaty with the United States, but 'telegraphed that in the wording of the treaty it would under no circumstances endure the insertion of an adverb between the preposition *to*… and the verb'.

George Bernard Shaw

If you do not immediately suppress the person who takes it upon himself to lay down the law almost every day in your columns on the subject of literary composition, I will give up the *Chronicle*. The man is a pedant, an ignoramus, an idiot and a self-advertising duffer… Your fatuous specialist…is now beginning to rebuke 'second-rate' newspapers for using such phrases as 'to suddenly go' and 'to boldly say'. I ask you, Sir, to put this man out…without interfering with his perfect freedom of choice between 'to suddenly go', 'to go suddenly' and 'suddenly to go'…Set him adrift and try an intelligent Newfoundland dog in his place. (Letter to the *Chronicle*, 1892.)

T. R. Lounsbury

More than twenty years ago the late Fitzedward Hall…showed conclusively that the practice of inserting words between the preposition and the infinitive went back to the fourteenth century, and that to a greater or less degree it has prevailed in every century since. (*The Standard of Usage in English*, 1908.)

Hall's catalogue of examples, with some supplementation by Lounsbury, came from a galaxy of writers, including Wycliff, Tyndale, Coleridge, Donne ('specially addicted to the usage'), Goldsmith, George Eliot, Burns, and Browning.

Macaulay, in revising an article in 1843, even changed 'in order fully to appreciate' to 'in order to fully appreciate'. (W. H. Mittins, *et al.*, *Attitudes to English Usage*, 1970.)

H. W. Fowler

The English-speaking world may be divided into (1) those who neither know nor care what a split infinitive is; (2) those who do not know, but care very much; (3) those who know and condemn; (4) those who know and approve; and (5) those who know and distinguish…. Those who neither know nor care are the vast majority, and are a happy folk, to be envied by most of the minority classes…

We will split infinitives sooner than be ambiguous or artificial. (*A Dictionary of Modern English Usage*, 1926.)

Otto Jespersen

This name is misleading, for the preposition *to* no more belongs to the infinitive as a necessary part of it, than the definite article belongs to the substantive, and no one would think of calling *the good man* a split substantive. (*Essentials of English Grammar*, 1933.)

Stephen Leacock

Many of our actual verbs are in themselves split infinitives, as when we say *to undertake* or *to overthrow*…Many of us who write books are quite willing to split an 'infinitive' or to half split it or to quite split it according to effect. We might even be willing to sometimes so completely, in order to gain a particular effect, split the infinitive as to practically but quite consciously run the risk of leaving the *to* as far behind as the last caboose of a broken freight train. (*How to Write*, 1944.)

Ernest Gowers

It is a bad rule; it increases the difficulty of writing clearly and makes for ambiguity by inducing writers to place adverbs in unnatural and even misleading positions. *A recent visit to Greece has convinced me that the modern Englishman fails completely to recognise that…* Does the modern Englishman completely fail to recognise, or does he fail to completely recognise?… The reader has to guess and he ought never to have to guess…

Nor is this all. The split infinitive taboo, leading as it does to the putting of adverbs in awkward places, is so potent that it produces an impulse to put them there even though there is not really any question of avoiding a split infinitive. I have myself been taken to task by a correspondent for splitting an infinitive because I wrote 'I gratefully record'. He was, no doubt, under the influence of the taboo to an exceptional extent. But sufferers from the same malady in a milder form can be found on every hand…The split infinitive bogy is having such a devastating effect that people are beginning to feel that it must be wrong to put an adverb between any auxiliary and any part of a verb, or between any preposition and any part of a verb. (*The Complete Plain Words*, 1954.)

Barbara Strang

Fussing about split infinitives is one of the more tiresome pastimes invented by nineteenth century grammarians. (*Modern English Structure*, 1962.)

David Crystal

To boldly go has one big thing in its favour. It is following the natural rhythm of English – the te-tum te-tum rhythm favoured by Shakespeare and which is the mainstay of our poetic tradition. If the scriptwriter had written *boldly to go*, the two weak syllables would have come together, and this would have sounded jerky. If he had written *to go boldly*, he would have ended up with two strong syllables together, which sounds ponderous. *To boldly go* is rhythmically very neat. The *Star Trek* scriptwriter hasn't really been linguistically bold at all. (*Who Cares About English Usage?*, 1984.)

Reader's Digest

Bear in mind that purists do still object to the split infinitive. If you refuse to pander to this irrational objection of theirs, and if you are unconcerned that people might think you know no better, then by all means split your infinitives. But remember the possible consequences: your reader or listener may give less credit to your arguments (because he thinks of you as a careless speaker or writer), or he may simply lose the thread of your argument entirely (because he has been distracted by your grammatical 'error').

At the same time, it is also inadvisable to wrench a sentence into ambiguity or ugliness simply in order to avoid splitting an infinitive. Doing this can cause equal distraction in your reader or listener, or it might once again reduce his regard for your views – as being those of a pedant this time, rather than of an ignoramus. The best course may be to skirt such a predicament altogether, and simply recast your sentence, wording it in an entirely different way. (*The Right Word at the Right Time*, 1985.)

THE 20TH-CENTURY LEGACY

From the outset, the prescriptive approach to English grammar had its critics, some of whom were prepared to castigate the Latinate tradition in the strongest language, responding to what they saw as excessive authoritarianism in the early grammars (p. 78). By the beginning of the 20th century, however, the extreme positions had moderated somewhat. Many traditional grammarians, while continuing to operate happily within a Latinate descriptive framework, began to accept that the influence of contemporary usage could not be completely ignored, and became more pragmatic in their approach. At the same time, there were signs of an increasing respect for the value of the kind of disciplined approach to grammatical study which the Latinate framework represented. As the comments on pp. 194–5 illustrate, it is unusual today to see an author unreservedly condemning a traditionally disputed point of English usage – though blanket condemnation is still commonplace in letters of complaint about usage sent to newspapers and radio feedback shows.

LOOK IT UP IN FOWLER

Fowler's *Dictionary of Modern English Usage* (1926) has long acted as a bible for those concerned with questions of disputed usage. The book was planned in association with his younger brother, Francis George, who had collaborated 20 years previously on their first influential work on usage, *The King's English* (1906). However, Francis died in 1918, having contracted tuberculosis in the trenches of World War 1, and it was left to Henry to complete the book. It is a large, alphabetically organized list of entries on points of grammar, pronunciation, spelling, punctuation, vocabulary, and style. Often referred to in the revered tones which one associates with bibles, it is the apotheosis of the prescriptive approach (p. 194).

Prescriptive in his aims Fowler certainly is, but he contrasts with 19th-century grammatical authors by the way he combines a respect for tradition with a readiness to debunk the worst excesses of purism, and – most unusually for the prescriptive tradition – underpins his remarks with an elegant blend of humour and common sense. For example, he had no time for the distortions imposed on English by Latinate grammars. His entry on *case* judges these grammarians to be:

guilty, of flogging the minds of English children with terms and notions that are essential to the understanding of Greek and Latin syntax, but have no bearing on English.

On the other hand, in a *Society for Pure English Tract* (No. 26) he defends the role that traditional language study has played in shaping contemporary consciousness.

Whether or not it is regrettable that we English have for centuries been taught what little grammar we know on Latin traditions, have we not now to recognize that the iron has entered into our souls, that our grammatical conscience has by this time a Latin element inextricably compounded in it, if not predominant?

The remnants of this conscience are with older people still. How far younger people continue to be influenced by it, after the reduced emphasis on grammar teaching in many schools since the 1960s, is not at all clear. Generations of people have now passed through school without ever having been introduced to basic grammatical terminology, and who are unaware of what many of the traditional shibboleths are all about (p. 194). On the other hand, the Latinate influence on analysis is profound, and goes much deeper than the occasional dispute about usage. With some areas of grammar, such as the verb, where the Latin model has caused English tense forms to multiply well beyond necessity, Fowler's point has certainly to be granted.

Henry Watson Fowler (1858–1933)

HOW MANY TENSES?

How many tenses of the verb are there in English? If your automatic reaction is to say 'three, at least' – past, present, and future – you are showing the influence of the Latinate grammatical tradition. If you go for a larger number, adding such labels as perfect and pluperfect, this tradition is even more deep-rooted within you. Twenty or more tense forms are set up in some traditional grammars.

An example is *A Higher English Grammar* by Llewelyn Tipping, first published in 1927, and with a dozen reprintings to its credit by the 1960s. This is strongly Latinate in character. Nouns are given five cases, and solemnly listed: nominative (*king*), vocative (*O king*), genitive (*king's*), dative (*king*), and accusative (*king*). Over 40 forms of the verb in its various tenses and moods are recognized.

To see the extent to which this is a distortion of the way English works, we must be sure of how the word *tense* was used in traditional grammar. Tense was thought of as the grammatical expression of time, and identified by a particular set of endings on the verb. In Latin there were present-tense endings (*amo, amas, amat...*'I love, you love, he/she/it loves...'), future tense endings (*amabo, amabis, amabit...*'I will/shall love, you will/shall love, he/she/it will/shall love...'), perfect tense endings (*amavi, amavisti, amavit...*'I loved, you loved, he/she/it loved...'), and several others marking different tense forms.

English, by contrast, has only one inflectional form to express time: the past tense marker (typically *-ed*), as in *walked, jumped,* and *saw.* There is therefore a two-way tense contrast in English: *I walk* vs *I walked* – present tense vs past tense. English has no future tense ending, but uses a wide range of other techniques to express future time (such as *will/shall, be going to, be about to,* and future adverbs. The linguistic facts are uncontroversial. However, people find it extremely difficult to drop the notion of 'future tense' (and related notions, such as imperfect, future perfect, and pluperfect tenses) from their mental vocabulary, and to look for other ways of talking about the grammatical realities of the English verb.

THE MAIN BRANCHES OF GRAMMAR

The field of grammar is often divided into two domains: *morphology* and *syntax*. The former focuses on the structure of words, dealing with such matters as inflectional endings and the way words can be built up out of smaller units (§14); the latter focuses on the structure of sentences (§16).

Modern grammars display a major shift in emphasis from that found in traditional grammars. A large part of a traditional grammar was devoted to aspects of morphology – though not using this label, which is a term from linguistics. The traditional term was *accidence* (from Latin *accidentia*, 'things which befall'), defined in Nesfield's *Grammar* as 'the collective name for all those changes that are incidental to certain parts of speech'. Thus, accidence dealt with such matters as the number, gender, and case of

nouns, and the voice, mood, number, person, and tense of verbs, as well as the question of their classification into regular and irregular types.

Most of a traditional grammar was given over to accidence, following the Latin model. Although in Nesfield syntactic matters are to be found throughout the book, only two chapters are officially assigned to the subject, and these are largely devoted to the techniques of clause analysis and the parsing of parts of speech. By contrast, most of a modern grammar of English is given over to syntax. There is relatively little in the language to be accounted for under the heading of inflectional morphology, and in some grammars the notion of morphology is dispensed with altogether, its concerns being handled as the 'syntax of the word'.

WHY?

SYNTAX: from Latin *syntaxis*, and earlier from Greek *syn* + *tassein* 'together + arrange'. The term is quite often used in a figurative way. Article titles encountered in the 1990s include 'the syntax of cooking' and 'the syntax of sex'.

MORPHOLOGY: ultimately from Greek *morphē* 'form' + *logos* 'word'. The term is also used in other contexts; in biology, for example, it refers to the form and structure of animals and plants.

NEW GRAMMAR...

The chapter headings in S. Greenbaum & R. Quirk's *A Student's Grammar of the English Language* (1990).

 1 The English language.
 2 A general framework.
 3 Verbs and auxiliaries.
 4 The semantics of the verb phrase.
 5 Nouns and determiners.
 6 Pronouns.
 7 Adjectives and adverbs.
 8 The semantics and grammar of adverbials.
 9 Prepositions and prepositional phrases.
10 The simple sentence.
11 Sentence types and discourse functions.
12 Pro-forms and ellipsis.
13 Coordination.
14 The complex sentence.
15 Syntactic and semantic functions of subordinate clauses.
16 Complementation of

verbs and adjectives.
17 The noun phrase.
18 Theme, focus, and information processing.
19 From sentence to text.

There are some clear parallels with traditional grammar, especially the opening treatment of word classes (Chs. 1–9), but over half the book is explicitly devoted to syntax, and a substantial part of the early chapters deals with syntactic matters too.

The approach which this grammar represents falls well within the European tradition of grammatical analysis, but it would be a mistake to think that all modern grammars look like this. In particular, many grammars which show the

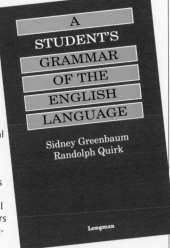

influence of contemporary linguistic theory reverse this order of treatment, beginning with a systematic exposition of syntactic matters, leaving matters of word classification and morphology to the end.

...FOR OLD

The chapter headings in Part I ('Modern English Grammar') of J. C. Nesfield's *English Grammar Past and Present* (1898).

 1 Analytical outline: general definitions.
 2 Nouns.
 3 Adjectives.
 4 Pronouns.
 5 Verbs.
 6 Adverbs.
 7 Prepositions.
 8 Conjunctions.
 9 Interjections.
10 Analysis of sentences.
11 The same word used as different parts of speech.
12 Syntax.
13 Punctuation, or the right use of stops.

The minor role played by syntax is to be noted, by comparison with its major role in modern grammars.

PARSING

Parsing played an important role in traditional grammar teaching. The procedure involved stating the part of speech (Latin *pars*) to which a word belonged, and giving certain details about it. Latin grammars used to ask *Quae pars orationis?* 'What part of speech?' (See further, §15.)
• *Noun*: state the number, gender, and case, and say

why the noun is in that case.
• *Adjective*: state kind of adjective, degree, and what word it qualifies.
• *Pronoun*: state kind of pronoun, number, person, gender, and case, and why it is in that case.
• *Verb*: state kind of verb (whether weak or strong, p. 21), transitive or intransitive, voice, mood, tense, number, person, the subject with which it agrees, and the

object it governs.
• *Adverb*: state kind of adverb, degree, and what word it modifies.
• *Preposition*: state the word it governs.
• *Conjunction*: state kind (coordinating, subordinating) and what it joins.
• *Interjection*: state that it is an interjection.

AN EXAMPLE

I go would be parsed as follows (after L. Tipping, 1927):

I Personal pronoun, first person, singular, nominative case, subject of verb *go*.

go Verb, strong, intransitive, indicative mood, present tense, first person singular, agreeing with its subject *I*.

Well done, Mary Anne! (p. 191)

The categories reflect the way Latin grammar worked, with its complex inflectional morphology, and also the method used in learning it (translation to and from English). As very few of these types of word-ending remain in English, the technique of parsing is no longer seen as having much relevance. More sophisticated forms of sentence analysis have replaced it (§16).

Morphology, the study of the structure of words, cuts across the division of this book into Lexicon (Part II) and Grammar (Part III). For English, it means devising ways of describing the properties of such disparate items as *a, horses, took, indescribable, washing machine*, and *antidisestablishmentarianism*. A widely-recognized approach divides the field into two domains: *lexical* or *derivational morphology* studies the way in which new items of vocabulary can be built up out of combinations of elements (as in the case of *in-describ-able*); *inflectional morphology* studies the way words vary in their form in order to express a grammatical contrast (as in the case of *horses*, where the ending marks plurality). The processes of lexical word-formation are described in §9. In the present section, we examine the processes of inflection.

An essential first step is to be able to describe the elements (or *morphemes*) out of which words can be constructed.

- Many words cannot be broken down into grammatical parts: *boy, a, yes, person, elephant, problem*. These words are said to consist only of a *base* form (some grammars refer to this as the *root* or *stem*). All we can do, in such cases, is describe what the words mean (see Part III) and how they are pronounced or spelled – such as the number of syllables they have, or the pattern of vowels and consonants they display (see Part IV).
- English permits the addition of meaningful, dependent elements both before and after the base form: these are called *affixes*. Affixes which precede the base are *prefixes*; those which follow it are *suffixes*. The possibility of affixes occurring within the base (*infixes*) is considered on p. 128.
- Prefixes in English have a purely lexical role, allowing the construction of a large number of new words: *un-, de-, anti-, super-*, etc. They are described as part of word-formation on p. 128.
- Suffixes in English are of two kinds. Most are purely lexical, their primary function being to change the meaning of the base form: examples of these *derivational suffixes* include *-ness, -ship*, and *-able*. A few are purely grammatical, their role being to show how the word must be used in a sentence: examples here include plural *-s*, past tense *-ed*, and comparative *-er*. Elements of this second type, which have no lexical meaning, are the *inflectional suffixes* (or simply, *inflections*) of the language.

The derivational field of a single word (from J. Tournier, 1985).

Inflections are a quite distinct group, always occurring at the very end of a word (*graces, disgraced*), and following the derivational suffixes if there are any. If there were several instances of *gracelessness* to be talked about, we could say (admittedly, not with any great elegance) *gracelessnesses*.

Tournier's detailed study also includes extremely full listings of the derivational affixes in English. There are a surprisingly large number of them: excluding variant forms, he gives 386 prefixes and 322 suffixes. The latter total includes dozens of forms which are rare in everyday conversation (except among specialists), such as *-acea, -ectomy, -gynous, -mancy*, and *-ploid*.

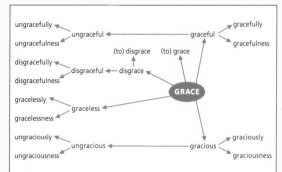

Affixes of this kind come and go: *-nik*, for example, is a development in English which became highly productive in the late 1950s, following the launch of *Sputnik 1*, and such subsequent operations as the launch of a dog into space (*pupnik, woofnik, muttnik*, etc.) and the failure of a US satellite (*Yanknik, dudnik, stallnik*, etc.). This usage seems to have died out in the early 1960s. A related suffix, with citations since the 1940s, and seen in *beatnik* and similar uses (*beachnik, filmnik, jazznik*, etc.), was productive into the early 1970s, but seems to have since died out (after L. Bauer, 1983).

Inflectional suffixes, by contrast, do not come and go. There have been no changes in the system since the Early Modern English period (§5).

TYPES OF SUFFIX

This table shows the commonest English suffixes, though not all the variant forms (e.g. *-ible* for *-able*). The list of inflectional categories is complete; the list of derivational suffixes has been limited to 50.

Inflectional suffixes
noun plural, e.g. *-s* (p. 201)
genitive case, e.g. *-'s* (p. 202)
3rd person singular, e.g. *-s* (p. 204)
past tense, e.g. *-ed* (p. 212)
contracted negative *-n't* (pp. 205, 212)
objective pronoun, e.g. *him* (pp. 203, 210)
-ing form or present participle (p. 204)
-ed form or past participle (p. 204)
-er comparison (pp. 199, 211)
-est comparison (pp. 199, 211)

Derivational suffixes
Abstract-noun-makers (p. 209)
-age frontage, mileage
-dom officialdom, stardom

-ery drudgery, slavery
-ful cupful, spoonful
-hood brotherhood, girlhood
-ing farming, panelling
-ism idealism, racism
-ocracy aristocracy
-ship friendship, membership

Concrete-noun-makers
-eer engineer, racketeer
-er teenager, cooker
-ess waitress, lioness
-ette kitchenette, usherette
-let booklet, piglet
-ling duckling, underling
-ster gangster, gamester

Adverb-makers (p. 211)
-ly quickly, happily
-ward(s) northwards, onwards
-wise clockwise, lengthwise

Verb-makers (p. 212)
-ate orchestrate, chlorinate
-en deafen, ripen
-ify beautify, certify
-ize/-ise modernize, advertise

Adjective-/noun-makers (p. 211)
-ese Chinese, Portuguese

-(i)an republican, Parisian
-ist socialist, loyalist
-ite socialite, Luddite

Nouns from verbs
-age breakage, wastage
-al refusal, revival
-ant informant, lubricant
-ation exploration, education
-ee payee, absentee
-er writer, driver
-ing building, clothing
-ment amazement, equipment
-or actor, supervisor

Nouns from adjectives
-ity rapidity, falsity
-ness happiness, kindness

Adjectives from nouns
-ed pointed, blue-eyed
-esque Kafkaesque
-ful useful, successful
-ic atomic, Celtic
-(i)al editorial, accidental
-ish foolish, Swedish
-less careless, childless
-ly friendly, cowardly
-ous ambitious, desirous
-y sandy, hairy

Adjectives from verbs
-able drinkable, washable
-ive attractive, explosive

ADJECTIVES

Inflections provide one of the ways in which the quality expressed by an adjective (p. 211) can be compared. The comparison can be to the same degree, to a higher degree, or to a lower degree.

• The base form of the adjective is called the *absolute* form: *big, happy.*

The inflections identify two steps in the expression of a higher degree.

• Adding *-er* produces the *comparative* form: *bigger, happier.*
• Adding *-est* produces the *superlative* form: *biggest, happiest.*

There are no inflectional ways of expressing the same or lower degrees in English. These notions are expressed syntactically, using *as… as* (for the same degree: *X is as big as Y*) and *less* or *least* for lower degrees (*X is less interested than Y, Z is the least interested of all*).

There is also a syntactic (often called a *periphrastic*) way of expressing higher degree, through the use of *more* (for the comparative) and *most* (for the superlative): *A is more beautiful than B* and *C is the most beautiful of all.*

THE LONG AND THE SHORT OF IT

The availability of two ways of expressing higher degree raises a usage question: which form should be used with any particular adjective? The answer is largely to do with how long the adjective is.

• Adjectives of one syllable usually take the inflectional form: *big, thin, small, long, fat, red.* But there are exceptions: *real, right,* and *wrong* do not allow **realler, *wrongest,* etc. Nor do participles (p. 204) allow an inflection when they are used as adjectives: *That's the most burnt piece of toast I've ever seen* (not **the burntest*).

• Adjectives of three syllables or more use only the periphrastic form: we do not say **beautifuller* or **interestingest.* But here too there are exceptions: for example, a few three-syllable adjectives which begin with *un-* do allow the inflection, as in the case of *unhealthier* and *unhappiest.*

• The chief problem arises with two-syllable adjectives, many of which permit both forms of comparison: *That's a quieter/more quiet place.* A few, such as *proper* and *eager,* are straightforward: they do not allow the inflection at all. Others, such as many adjectives ending in *-y, -er,* and *-le,* favour it: *happier, cleverer,* and *gentlest* are commoner than *more/most happy,* etc., but the choice is often made on stylistic grounds. In the previous sentence, for example, there is little to choose between *commoner* and *more common* except the rhythm and the immediate context (*commoner* avoids an inelegant clash with the use of *more* two words later).

TESTING COMPARISON

An item from a screening test designed to assess the language ability of 3- to 5-year-old children. This particular item tries to elicit the child's awareness of comparative and superlative forms. The speech and language therapist uses a structured prompt, while pointing appropriately to the picture:

This boy is little, this one is big, this one is even – and this one is the – .

(After S. Armstrong & M. Ainley, 1990.)

IRREGULARS

There are very few irregular comparative forms, but the ones there are do occur quite frequently.

• *Better* and *best* are the comparison forms of *good; worse* and *worst* are the comparison forms of *bad.*
• *Far* has two forms: *further/furthest* and *farther/farthest* (the latter pair being less common, and mainly used to express physical distance, as in *farthest north*).
• *Old* has regular forms (*older/oldest*) and also an irregular use (*elder/eldest*) when talking about family members.
• Some adverbs (p. 211) also allow inflectional comparison (e.g. *soonest*), but most adverbs are compared periphrastically: *more frankly, most willingly.*

POETICAL SUPERLATIVES

In his *Sketches by Boz* (1836–7), Charles Dickens notes a popular use of the superlative form by 'the poetical young gentleman'.

When the poetical young gentleman makes use of adjectives, they are all superlatives. Everything is of the grandest, greatest, noblest, mightiest, loftiest; or the lowest, meanest, obscurest, vilest, and most pitiful. He knows no medium: for enthusiasm is the soul of poetry; and who so enthusiastic as a poetical young gentleman? 'Mr Milkwash,' says a young lady as she unlocks her album to receive the young gentleman's original contribution, 'how very silent you are! I think you must be in love.' 'Love!' cries the poetical young gentleman, starting up from his seat by the fire and terrifying the cat who scampers off at full speed, 'Love! that burning consuming passion; that ardour of the soul, that fierce glowing of the heart. Love! The withering blighting influence of hope misplaced and affection slighted. Love did you say! Ha! ha! ha!'

With this, the poetical young gentleman laughs a laugh belonging only to poets and Mr O. Smith of the Adelphi Theatre, and sits down, pen in hand, to throw off a page or two of verse in the biting, semi-atheistical demoniac style, which, like the poetical young gentleman himself, is full of sound and fury, signifying nothing.

WHITER THAN WHITEST

Commercial advertising provides fertile soil for adjective inflections.

The brightest knits in town

WASHES CLEANER THAN ANY OTHER MACHINE.

THE RESULT: SMOOTHER, FIRMER SKIN

ENGLAND'S FINEST BONE CHINA

THE TASTIEST FISH

THE PURER WAY TO ADD FLAVOUR

The latest in gas cooking

DECORATING? Check with us first for all the latest tools and tips

better, bolder, brighter than ever!

NOUNS: NUMBER

Most nouns (p. 208) have both a singular and a plural form, expressing a contrast between 'one' and 'more than one', and these are known as *variable* nouns. A small group of cases do not have a number contrast – the *invariable* nouns (p. 201). Most variable nouns change from singular to plural in a wholly predictable way, usually described simply as 'adding an *-s*' (though the reality is not so straightforward). This is the *regular* plural form, as seen in *cats, oboes, eggs, pterodactyls, grammars*, and thousands more words. By contrast, there are only a few hundred nouns with an *irregular* plural form – though it is these which attract the interest of the grammarian, as they are the ones which lead to difficulties in language learning, and cry out for explanation. Why *doesn't* Standard English (SE) say *mouses, childs*, and *foots*?

ONE OR MORE THAN ONE?

In most cases, the distinction between singular and plural corresponds to that between 'one' and 'more than one', but there are exceptions. The picture shows a large number of objects growing on a tree: if we describe what we see as *foliage*, we use a singular; if we say we see *leaves*, we use a plural. But the number of objects is the same in each case. Similarly, *wheat* is grammatically singular and *oats* is grammatically plural, but the distinction is not apparent to the combine harvester.

ADDING AN -S?

In speech
The *-s* ending is pronounced in any of three possible ways, depending on the nature of the sound at the end of the singular noun. (An identical set of rules applies to other uses of an /-s/ inflection: pp. 202, 204.)

• If the noun ends in an /s/-like sound (a *sibilant*, p. 262) – /s/, /z/, /ʃ/, /ʒ/, /tʃ/, and /dʒ/ – it is followed by an extra syllable, /ɪz/, as in *buses, phrases, dishes, beaches, sledges*, and (for /ʒ/, some pronunciations of) *mirages*.
• All other nouns ending in a voiceless consonant add /s/, as in *cups, pots, sacks, scruffs, growths*.
• All other nouns ending in a voiced consonant or a vowel (including *r*-coloured vowels, p. 237) add /z/, as in *cubs, rods, bags, graves, tithes, farms, guns, rings, pools, cars, players, bees, foes, zoos*, etc.

In writing
The spelling rules are more complex. The vast majority of nouns in the language simply add an *-s*. This includes those nouns where the singular form ends in a 'silent *-e*', such as *plate*. But there are several types of exception (p. 272).

• The ending is *-es* if there is no silent *-e*, and the noun ends in *-s, -z, -x, -ch*, and *-sh* (all representing sibilants), as in *buses, buzzes, boxes, bitches, bushes*.
• If the noun ends in *-o*, the plural is spelled *-os* in most cases (as in *studios, zoos, pianos, solos, radios, kilos*), but there are a few nouns which require *-oes* (as in *potatoes, dominoes, heroes, tomatoes*), and some allow both (as in *volcano(e)s, cargo(e)s, motto(e)s*), though modern usage seems to be slowly moving towards the *-os* norm.
• If a common noun (p. 208) ends in *-y*, with a preceding consonant, the *-y* is replaced by *-i*, and *-es* is added, as in *skies, flies*. If there is only a preceding vowel, the *-y* stays (as in *ways, boys*), as it does in proper nouns (*old and new Germanys, the three Marys*).
• There are several unusual cases, such as consonant doubling (*quizzes, fezzes*), the use of apostrophes after a letter name (*cross your t's*) or a number (*3's*), especially in British English, and doubling a letter in some written abbreviations, as in *pp.* ('pages'), *exx.* ('examples'), and *ll.* ('lines').

EXCEPTIONAL PLURALS

There are several groups of native English words which display exceptional plural forms. Although we cannot say why these particular words did not follow the regular pattern, it is at least often possible to see why they have their distinctive form by referring to the types of plural formation found in Old English or Germanic (p. 8).

• Seven nouns change their vowel (a process known as *mutation*, or *umlaut*, p. 19): *man > men, foot > feet, goose > geese, mouse > mice, woman > women, tooth > teeth, louse > lice*. The change does not take place when there is a derived sense, as when *louse* refers to a person (*you louses!*) or *mouse* to a character (*we've hired three Mickey Mouses this month*).
• Four nouns add *-en*, in two cases changing the vowel sound as well: *ox > oxen, aurochs > aurochsen, child > children, brother > brethren*. The use of /-n/ as a plural marker was a feature of an important class of Old English nouns. Several other family words showed this ending in Middle English, such as *doughtren* ('daughters') and *sustren* ('sisters'), both found in Chaucer.
• A few nouns change their final fricative consonant (p. 243) as well as adding /z/. Some change /-f/ to /-v/, as in *wives, loaves*, and *halves*. The spelling reflects a change which took place in Old English, where /f/ was voiced between vowels (the plural of *hlaf* 'loaf' was *hlafas*). Some change /-θ/ to /-ð/, as in *booths* and *mouths. House* is unique, with /-s/ changing to /-z/ in *houses*.

In several cases, usage is uncertain: *dwarf, hoof, scarf*, and *wharf* will be found with both /-fs/ and /-vz/, and spelled accordingly (e.g. both *scarfs* and *scarves*); *truth, oath, sheath, wreath*, and (especially in American English) *youth* will be found with both /-θs/ and /-ðz/, but both spelled in the same way, *-ths* (much to the frustration of the foreign learner). Exceptions to the exceptions include *still lifes* and the Toronto ice-hockey team, the *Maple Leafs*.

A vowel diagram (p. 238) showing the way the high front position of the tongue (in the vowel of the hypothetical Germanic plural suffix */-iz/) once 'pulled' the vowel of the associated noun in its direction (p. 19). The effect can still be seen relating the singular and plural forms of the surviving nouns. Several other nouns were also affected at the time (such as *bēc*, plural of *bōc* 'book' in Old English), though the mutated forms have not survived in Modern English.

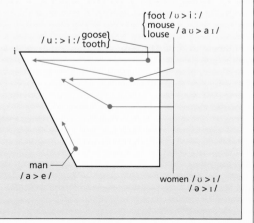

NOUNS OF FOREIGN ORIGIN

Nouns which have been borrowed from foreign languages pose a particular problem. Some have adopted the regular plural ending: *They sang another two choruses* (not **chori*). Some have kept the original foreign plural: *More crises to deal with* (not **crisises*). And some permit both: *What lovely cactuses/cacti!*

There are no rules. People have to learn which form to use as they meet the words for the first time, and must become aware of variations in usage. Where there is a choice, the classical plural is usually the more technical, learned, or formal, as in the case of *formulas* vs *formulae* or *curriculums* vs *curricula*. Sometimes, alternative plurals have even developed different senses, as in the case of (spirit) *mediums* vs (mass) *media*, or *appendixes* (in bodies or books) vs *appendices* (only in books). The table (right) shows the main types of foreign plural formation.

Source / ending	Native plural	Foreign plural	Both plurals
Latin *-us*	*+ -es* apparatus, campus, circus, sinus, virus	*> -i* stimulus, bacillus, locus, alumnus	focus, fungus, cactus, terminus, syllabus, radius
Latin/Greek *-a*	*+ -s* area, dilemma, drama	*> -ae* alumna, alga, larva	antenna, formula, nebula, vertebra
Latin *-um*	*+ -s* album, museum, premium	*> -a* bacterium, erratum, desideratum	aquarium, maximum, medium, podium, referendum, forum
Latin *-ex*, *-ix*	*+ -es* suffix, prefix	*> -ices* codex, spadex, fornix	index, appendix, apex, vortex, matrix
Greek *-is*	*+ -es* metropolis, clitoris, glottis	*> -es* analysis, basis, crisis, oasis, synopsis	
Greek *-on*	*+ -s* electron, proton, neutron, horizon	*> -a* criterion, entozoon, phenomenon	automaton, polyhedron
French *-eau*	*+ -s* Cointreau	*> -eaux* gateau	bureau, tableau, plateau, chateau
Italian *-o*	*+ -s* solo, soprano, portico, piccolo, supremo	*> -i* timpano, graffito, mafioso	virtuoso, tempo, libretto, allegro, scherzo
Hebrew nouns	*+ -s/-es*	*> -im* moshav, midrash	kibbutz, cherub, seraph

INVARIABLE NOUNS

Many nouns do not show a contrast between singular and plural: the *invariable* nouns. These are usually classified into two types: those used only in the singular, and those used only in the plural.

Singular-only nouns

• Proper names (p. 208), such as *Francis* and *York*. SE does not allow (except possibly in jest) **Yorks are nice places*.
• Names of subjects, diseases, and games, such as *physics, mumps, billiards*. SE does not allow **Physics are fun*. These nouns can mislead, because their *-s* ending makes them look plural. Some have singular and plural uses: compare *Darts is easy* and *Your darts are broken*.
• Nouns in a noncount use (p. 209): *music, homework, snow*. SE does not allow **I like musics*. If the noun is used in a countable way, a plural is normal: compare *They make beer* and *They had two beers*.

Plural-only nouns

• Names of 'two-part' items, such as *scissors, binoculars, jeans*. SE does not allow **Your jeans is dry*.
• A few dozen nouns ending in *-s*, such as *amends, annals, auspices, congratulations, dregs, outskirts, remains, thanks, tropics*. In such cases, either there is no singular form in SE (**An outskirt of the city*) or the singular gives a different sense (as in *dregs of beer* vs *He's a dreg!* – British slang, 'worthless person').
• A few nouns which look singular but are always plural: *vermin, livestock, cattle, poultry, people, folk*, and *police*. SE does not allow **The police is outside*.

Double-plural nouns

Several animal names have two plurals. There is the regular plural, adding an *-s*, and there is a 'zero' plural form, with no ending at all.

I have two *rabbits*.

They've been shooting *rabbit*.

There is a clear difference in meaning. If the animals are being thought of as individuals, the plural form is used. If they are a category of game, they have a zero plural. The professional hunter goes *shootin' duck*, never *ducks*. And visitors to the local pond *feed the ducks*, never *feed the duck* – unless, of course, the pond contains only one.

Words without end

A few nouns have the same form for both singular and plural, even though they are semantically variable, allowing a difference between 'one' and 'more than one'. In such sentences as *I like your sheep*, only the context enables us to know which meaning is intended. *That sheep* or *those sheep* would resolve the matter, as would observation of the relevant field. Like *sheep* are the names of some animals (e.g. *deer, salmon*) and nationalities (e.g. *Portuguese, Swiss*), several nouns expressing quantity (e.g. *quid* – British slang, '£', *p* 'pence'), and a few others (e.g. *aircraft, offspring, series, species*).

SOME CONTROVERSIAL NOUNS

• *Data* causes a usage problem. This word was once found only as a plural, but is now often used as a singular, especially in computing and other scientific contexts: *Much of this data needs to be questioned* (rather than *Many of these data need to be questioned*). This use continues to attract criticism from those who were brought up on the older pattern. The singular function is still not totally established, in fact, as many who say *this data* baulk at saying *a data* or *two data*. American English seems to be ahead of British, in this respect.

• With a small group of nouns usually ending in *-s*, people sometimes argue over whether they should be used as singulars or plurals: *The headquarters is nearby* vs *...are nearby*. In such cases, either form is possible depending on the intended meaning. The singular suggests the idea of a single entity, whereas the plural emphasizes that the entity is made up of individual units. Other such nouns include *barracks, steelworks*, and *kennels*.

• *Dice* (meaning 'a marked cube used in games of chance') is now used (like *sheep*) both as a singular and a plural: *The dice is on the table* refers to one, *... are on the table* refers to more than one. The singular usage, known from the 14th century, is now found only in the idiom *The die is cast*. However, purists anxious to preserve the original distinction continue to recommend the use of *a die* whenever a single cube is on the table.

NOUNS: CASE

There are only two cases left in Modern English (p. 21): a *common* case, where the noun has no ending at all, and the *genitive*. The genitive is formed by adding an *-s* to the singular form of the noun. In writing, this appears with a preceding apostrophe (p. 283, the 'apostrophe *s*'): *the cat's food*. With most plural forms, an *-s* ending is already present, so the written form just adds a following sign (the *'s* apostrophe'): *the cats' food*. In a few irregular plural instances, *'s* is used (as in *the men's books*). In speech, there is no difference in pronunciation between *cat's* and *cats'*.

The chief meaning of the genitive case is possession: *the cat's food*. But the case is used to express several other meanings too. The notion of origin is present in *the traveller's story*. There is description in *a summer's day*. A period is measured in *three months' leave*. And the form can express the idea of the noun either doing the action or receiving the action: in *the hostage's application*, the hostage is the one who applies; in *the hostage's release*, the hostage is the one who is released.

There is a close similarity between a noun in the genitive case and the same noun preceded by *of* (the *of-genitive*): *the ship's name = the name of the ship*. The choice is largely based on factors of gender and style. Personal nouns and the higher animals (p. 209) tend to take the genitive ending; inanimate nouns take the *of-*genitive. Thus we find *Hilary's book* rather than **the book of Hilary*, but *a part of the difficulty* rather than **the difficulty's part*. The genitive case is also used with many nouns of special human relevance (*my life's aim, the body's needs*). But the *of-* form is used for titles (*The Duke of Kent*) – always allowing for cases of contrived informality (*England's Queen*).

KEEPING UP WITH THE JONES'(S)

Not all singular nouns can add a genitive ending. There are a few instances where the only signal is the apostrophe. This is what happens with Greek names of more than one syllable and ending in -s: *Socrates' bust*, not usually *Socrates's bust*. Names ending in /-z/ vary in their usage: we find both *Dickens's novels* and *Dickens' novels, Jesus's name* and *Jesus' name*. With the shorter form, the implied extra syllable can still be pronounced: *Dickens'* could be /ˈdɪkɪnz/ or /ˈdɪkɪnzɪz/.

POSSESSIVE POETRY

'**T**he Possessive Case', a poem by Lisel Mueller (1977), in addition to its intriguing semantic juxtapositions, provides an interesting corpus for testing hypotheses about the use of the two forms of genitive.

Your father's mustache
My brother's keeper
La plume de ma tante
Le monocle de mon oncle
His Master's Voice
Son of a bitch
Charley's Aunt
Lady Chatterley's Lover
   The Prince of Wales
   The Duchess of Windsor
   The Count of Monte Cristo
   The Emperor of Ice Cream
   The Marquis de Sade
   The Queen of the Night
      Mozart's Requiem
      Beethoven's Ninth
      Bach's B-Minor Mass
      Schubert's Unfinished
      Krapp's Last Tape
      Custer's Last Stand
      Howards End
      Finnegans Wake
         The March of Time
         The Ides of March
         The Auroras of Autumn
         The winter of our discontent
         The hounds of spring
         The Hound of Heaven
     Dante's Inferno
     Vergil's Aeneid
     Homer's Iliad
  The Fall of the City
  The Decline of the West
  The Birth of a Nation
The Declaration of Independence
The ride of Paul Revere
The Pledge of Allegiance
The Spirit of '76
   The Age of Reason
   The Century of the Common Man
   The Psychopathology of Everyday Life
      Portnoy's Complaint
      Whistler's Mother
      The Sweetheart of Sigma Chi
      The whore of Babylon
      The Bride of Frankenstein
      The French Lieutenant's Woman
         A Room of One's Own
         Bluebeard's Castle
         Plato's cave
         Santa's workshop
         Noah's ark
         The House of the Seven Gables
     The Dance of the Seven Veils
     Anitra's Dance
     The Moor's Pavane
     My Papa's Waltz
Your father's mustache

THE ABERRANT APOSTROPHE

The apostrophe was introduced into English from French in the 16th century (p. 68), and became widespread during the 17th; but there was much uncertainty about its use, even until the middle of the 19th century. Not only did it mark the omission of letters (as in *can't*), it was often used before a plural ending, especially when the noun was a loan word ending in a vowel (as in *the two comma's*, which even today many people feel 'needs' an apostrophe). By the 18th century, it was being regularly used as a genitive marker in the singular, representing (according to the most likely theory) the omission of the letter *e* from the ending of the former genitive case *-es* (p. 44). Later, the usage extended to the genitive plural, but even at the beginning of the 19th century there was inconsistency over whether constructions such as *the girls' dresses* should contain an apostrophe (because no letter was being 'left out').

Later that century, printers and grammarians tried to lay down rules saying when the apostrophe should be used. Unfortunately, with such a long period of varying usage to consider, the rules which they devised were arbitrary and incomplete, and it proved impossible to establish a totally logical set of principles. For example, the apostrophe was allowed to mark possession in nouns (*girl's*) but not in pronouns (*hers*), and even this rule had exceptions (*one's*).

Around the turn of the century, the apostrophe began to be dropped from the names of many British banks and large businesses (e.g. *Lloyds*, *Harrods*).

Today in the UK, it is almost always omitted in shop signs, placards, and other notices. It varies greatly in place names: *St Ann's Bay* in Jamaica contrasts with *St Anns Bay* in Cape Breton Island, according to the *Britannica Atlas*. The bias is definitely towards omission: of the several hundred names of the *St Ann's* type in the *Britannica*, two-thirds have no apostrophe. In shopping centres we find *Ladies wear* and *Mans shop*. On the other hand, the 1993 New York City subway map gives *St. Patrick's Cathedral* and *Grant's Tomb*.

Many modern sign-writers and typographical designers leave the apostrophe out because they think it looks fussy and old-fashioned; and in most cases its omission causes no ambiguity, as the context makes it clear whether the *-s* ending refers to number or case, and whether it expresses a singular or a plural genitive meaning. However, there are undoubtedly many occasions when the availability of the apostrophe expresses a valuable written distinction, and there is strong pedagogical pressure on children to maintain its use, especially in the USA.

As a result of changing attitudes and practices, some people nowadays feel unsure about the correct use of the apostrophe, and add it before anything they sense to be an *-s* ending, such as a plural or a third person singular: **We sell fresh pie's*, **Everyone like's our chips*. These usages are universally condemned by educated writers, but the uncertainty is understandable, given the long and confused history of this punctuation mark in English (see further, p. 283).

NEW IMAGES FOR OLD

The covers of the 1935 edition of *Chambers's Encyclopaedia* and their 1993 *English Dictionary*, showing the loss of the apostrophe and extra syllable. The change took place, after great heart-searching, in the 1960s. The firm's 1966 catalogue has the apostrophe; their 1969 issue does not.

Today most public names do not use the apostrophe, though some businesses consciously continue with it as part of an image of tradition, reliability, and other such values. In a 1992 issue of a popular British magazine, less than 10 per cent of the trade names ending in a genitive used an apostrophe, and most of those which did so had no choice in the matter because their names already ended in a sibilant (p. 243), as in *Ross's*. For such names, the only alternative is to avoid the genitive ending altogether – which is actually a popular strategy nowadays (e.g. *John Lewis*, instead of *Lewis's*).

PRONOUNS: CASE

Personal pronouns (p. 210) have a genitive form, as have nouns, but they also have an *objective* form, which nouns no longer have. This form is chiefly used when the pronoun is the object of a clause (as in *He saw me*) and when it is governed by a preposition (as in *He gave it to me*). The term *objective* reflects this function, and replaces the older term *accusative*, favoured by traditional grammar (p.192), which was more appropriate for Latin. Similarly, when a pronoun is the subject of a clause, it is said to be in the *subjective* (formerly, *nominative*) case.

Five pronouns show this distinction: *I/me*, *we/us*, *he/him*, *she/her*, and *they/them*. *Who* also has an objective form (*whom*) as well as a genitive form (*whose* = 'of whom/which'). The other pronouns have genitive forms, too, traditionally described as the *possessive* pronouns: *my/mine*, *our(s)*, *his*, *her(s)*, *its*, *their(s)*, and *your(s)*, The alternatives identify two constructions, in which the pronoun can either accompany a noun or stand alone: *That is her book* vs *That book is hers*.

GOODNESS GRACIOUS ! !

The objective case has long been a focus of prescriptive discontent (p. 194).

• In certain contexts, it is used where the Latin-influenced grammatical tradition recommends the subjective:

Who's there? It's me.
She's as tall as him.
Ted and me went by bus.

These usages attract varying degrees of criticism in a formal setting. *Me* as a single-word reply is now used by almost everyone, and attracts little comment (despite the publicity it received in the song sung by Peter Sellers and Sophia Loren in the film *The Millionairess*). The *X and me* type of construction, however, is often criticized, especially when speakers reverse the normal order of politeness, and put the pronoun first: *Me and Ted went by bus*.

Ironically, as a result of the long-standing criticism of *me* and other objective forms, there is now a widespread sensitivity about their use, and this has led people to avoid them, even in parts of the clause where their use would be grammatically correct:

Between you and I...(p. 194)
He asked Mike and I to do it.

• There is also uncertainty over the correct form in sentences such as *It's no use my/me asking her*. Older grammars analyse words like *asking* as 'verbal nouns', or *gerunds*, and insist on the use of the possessive pronoun (*my*, etc.) or the genitive form of a noun: *John's asking me*. Modern grammars do not use the term gerund: *asking* in this example would be analysed as a verb (the *-ing* form, p. 204), as can be seen from the way it takes an object, *him*. The possessive is the preferred usage in a formal style, especially if the item is a pronoun or a short, personal noun phrase. The alternative is more common in informal styles.

VERBS

The forms of a *regular* lexical verb (p. 212) can be predicted by rules. An *irregular* lexical verb is one where some of the forms are unpredictable. There are thousands of regular verbs in Modern English, but less than 300 irregular ones. Many irregular forms are surviving members of the highly developed system of 'strong' verb classes found in Old English (p. 21).

Regular verbs appear in four forms, each playing a different role in the clause (p. 220).

• The *base form* – a form with no endings, as listed in a dictionary (in one of its uses called the *infinitive form*): *go, see, remember, provide.*
• The *-s form*, made by adding an *-(e)s* ending to the base (sometimes with a spelling change), used for the third person singular in the present tense: *he/she/it sees.* The pronunciation of this ending varies, depending on the preceding sound, as already described with reference to nouns (p. 200): /-s/, as in *looks, chops,* and *jumps;* /-z/, as in *tries, goes,* and *reminds;* and /-ɪz/, as in *passes, rushes,* and *buzzes. Does* and *says* are exceptions, in that they change their pronunciation when the ending is added: /dʌz/ not */duːz/ and /sez/ not */seɪz/ (except sometimes in reading aloud).
• The *-ing form*, or *-ing participle*, made by adding *-ing* to the base (often with a spelling change): *running, jumping, going.* In traditional grammar, this would be called the *present participle;* but as the form is by no means restricted to expressing present time (as in *He was going*), this term is not used by many modern grammarians.
• The *-ed form*, made by adding *-ed* to the base (often with a spelling change). This ending is found in the *past form* and in the *-ed participle form.* The past form has just one use: to express the past tense, as in *I kicked the ball.* The *-ed* participle form has four uses: to help express a past aspect (as in *I've kicked the ball,* p. 225); to help express the passive voice (as in *The ball was kicked,* p. 225); in certain types of subordinate clause and to begin a clause (as in *Kicked and battered, I hobbled off the field,* p. 226); and as an adjective (as in *the cooked meal,* p. 211). The *-ed* participle form would have been called the *past participle* in traditional grammar, but as its use is not restricted to past time (as in *I will be asked*) this label also tends to be avoided in modern grammar.

Irregular verbs make their *-s* form and *-ing* form by adding an ending to the base, in the same way as regular verbs do. But they have either an unpredictable past tense, or an unpredictable *-ed* participle form, or both. Many irregular verbs therefore appear in five forms, instead of the usual four.

THE IRREGULAR VERBS

There are two main features of irregular lexical verbs, both of which pose routine problems for young children and foreign learners (p. 428):

• Most irregular verbs change the vowel of the base to make their past or *-ed* participle forms. This process is known as vowel *gradation* (p. 21): *meet > met* (not **meeted*), *take > took* (not **taked*).
• The *-ed* ending is never used in a regular way, and is often not used at all, as in *cut, met, won: I have cut* (not **I have cutted*), *It was won* (not **It was winned*).

Using these features, it is possible to group irregular verbs into seven broad classes.

Class 1
About 20 verbs whose only irregular feature is the ending used for both their past and *-ed* participle forms: *have > had, send > sent.*
Class 2
About 10 verbs whose past tense is regular, but whose *-ed* participle form has an *-n* ending, as well as a variant form in *-ed: mow > mown* or *mowed, swell > swollen* or *swelled.*

Class 3
About 40 verbs which have the same ending for the past and *-ed* participle forms, but this is irregular; they also change the vowel of the base form: *keep > kept, sleep > slept, sell > sold.*
Class 4
About 75 verbs which have an *-n* ending for the *-ed* participle form, and an irregular past form; they also change the vowel of the base form: *blow > blew > blown, take > took > taken, see > saw > seen.*
Class 5
About 40 verbs which have the same form throughout, as in *cut, let, shut: I shut the door* (now), *I shut the door* (last week), *I have shut the door.*
Class 6
About 70 verbs which have no ending, but use the same form for both past tense and *-ed* participle; they also change the vowel of the base form: *spin > spun, sit > sat, stand > stood.*
Class 7
About 25 verbs, forming the most irregular type. There is no ending; the past and *-ed* participle forms differ; and the vowels change with each form: *swim > swam > swum, come > came > come, go > went > gone.*

A BURNING QUESTION

Several irregular verbs (of Class 2) have alternative *-ed* forms, one regular (with *-ed*), the other irregular (with *-t*). They include:

burned	burnt
learned	learnt
smelled	smelt
spelled	spelt
spilled	spilt
spoiled	spoilt

The straw burned or The straw burnt?

Burnt straw or burned straw?

The *-t* ending is rare in American English (p. 441). In British English, however, there is a great deal of usage variation, and it makes an interesting question to ask whether some of this could be patterned, expressing a subtle difference in meaning between the two forms.

The close comparison of examples suggests that the *-ed* form may be more likely when the duration of an action is being emphasized. Something which has happened once, which has taken up very little time, or which focuses on the result of a process rather than on the process itself may be more likely to attract the *-t* ending. The following examples can be used to test this hypothesis. Do they feel different?

The heather burned for days.
The burnt heather looked awful.

The torturer burned my arm.
I burnt my arm against the stove.

We've always burned wood in that stove.
I saw a piece of burnt wood in the shed.

The drink burned in my throat.
(It was whiskey.)
The drink burnt my throat.
(It was acid.)

Sometimes the context does not bear one or other of the above interpretations, which could explain why in this next example (which seems to require a long period of time) the first sentence is more likely than the second.

They burned with desire for each other.
?They burnt with desire for each other.

However, on many occasions the choice may well be random, because the verb or context does not motivate the drawing of such semantic distinctions, as in the case of *I spelled/spelt it with an e.* And at the other extreme, there are some collocations (p. 160) which permit little or no variation, as in the adjectival *burnt sienna, burnt almonds, burnt offering, burnt toast,* and T. S. Eliot's poem *Burnt Norton.*

ADDING AN -ED?

In speech

The -ed ending of regular verbs is pronounced in any of three possible ways, depending on the nature of the sound at the end of the base form. (A similar set of rules applies to way the /-s/ inflection is pronounced: see p. 200.)

• If the verb ends in a /t/ or /d/ (an *alveolar*, p. 243), it is followed by an extra syllable, /ɪd/, as in *wanted, boarded*. This form has several pronunciation variants around the world; for example, it is pronounced /əd/ in South Africa.
• All other verbs ending in a voiceless consonant add /t/, as in *stopped* /stɒpt/, *boxed* /bɒkst/.
• All other verbs ending in a voiced consonant or a vowel (including *r*-coloured vowels, p. 237) add /d/, as in *robed, died, barred*.

In writing

The spelling rules are more complex, and show several regional variations between British and American English. The chief patterns are as follows:

• If the base form ends in a 'silent -e', this -e is dropped before -ed (and also before the -ing ending), as in *typed*, not **typeed* (or **typeing*). Most verbs ending in *-ye, -oe, -ie, -nge*, and a few others, lose the -e before -ed (but keep it before -ing), as in *dyed* (but *dyeing*), *singed* (but *singeing*). This allows such contrasts as *singing* and *singeing* to be distinguished.
• A single consonant letter at the end of the base is doubled before -ed (and also before -ing), if the preceding vowel carries a stress and is spelt with a single letter: *jogged* (*jogging*), *permitted* (*permitting*). This doubling does not usually happen when the preceding vowel is unstressed (*enter* > *entered, entering*) or is written with two letters (*greet* > *greeted, greeting*).
• Some final consonants are exceptions to this rule, allowing a double conso-

nant even when the preceding vowel is unstressed. This is normal practice in British English, but American English also permits the use of a single consonant (though frequency varies, in the following cases). The chief instances are *-l, -m(me)*, and some verbs in *-p*:

Always in BrE, often in AmE	Never in BrE, often in AmE
signalled	signaled
diagrammed	diagramed
kidnapper	kidnaper

Verbs ending in a vowel + -c spell the doubling with -ck, as in *panicked*. However, when the base ends in a vowel + -s, there is great variation in usage, with some publishers insisting on a double consonant, and others avoiding it: *focussed* vs *focused, biassed* vs *biased*. The present book uses a single -s- in such words.
• As with nouns (p. 200), if the verb ends in -y, with a preceding consonant, the -y is replaced by -i, and -ed is added, as in *cried, tried*. If there is a preceding vowel, the -y usually remains (as in *stayed*). The same rule applies to the -s ending too: *cries, tries*. One difference from nouns is that the -y stays in cases where an -ing ending is used: *crying, trying*.
• Even more than with nouns, there are exceptions to the exceptions. So, if a -y verb is preceded by -a-, the -y is replaced, as in *paid* and *laid*. And if a verb ending in -ie adds -ing, the -ie changes to -y, as in *dying* and *tying*. When a word ends in a silent consonant, it is not doubled, as in *crocheted* and *hurrahed*. In the present tense, there are such exceptions as *does* and *goes*, where an -e- has been added. And there are a few forms which present variation in usage, such as *ageing* and *aging, arcked* and *arced*, or *verandahed* and *verandah'd* (see further, p. 274).

TO LIGHTNING

Lightning used as a verb (*It thundered and lightninged all night*) seems to be the only exception to the rule that -ing can be added to the base to produce an -ing form. We do not say **It was thundering and lightninging all night*, but keep the verb unchanged: *It was thundering and lightning all night*. However, this is such an unusual form for English that many people find it uncomfortable, and prefer to rephrase their sentence rather than say it or write it.

RELAYING CARPETS AND MESSAGES

relayed or *relaid*?

relaid or *relayed*?

Spelling can be a critical factor in distinguishing verb meanings. A message is *relayed*, but a carpet is *relaid*. The first is a verb, to *relay*, which has been derived from the noun *relay*; the second is a verb based on *lay*. The first uses the regular -y spelling, but the second shares the exceptional -ed spelling of *lay* (*laid*).

---

n't

The contracted form of the negative word *not* is used as an inflection with some verbs. The ones which allow this are the auxiliary verbs (p. 212), most of which can thus appear in two negative forms:

does not	doesn't
is not	isn't

In some cases, the form of the verb is altered:

will not	won't
shall not	shan't
were not	weren't
do not	don't
	/dəʊnt/, not /duːnt/

Some auxiliaries do not permit the ending in Standard English, notably **amn't* (though it will be heard in Irish English, for example). Some usages are dated (*mayn't, usedn't*). But the major contrast is with lexical verbs, which never allow the contracted form: **sitn't, *walkedn't*.

15 · WORD CLASSES

Traditional grammars of English, following an approach which can be traced back to Latin (§13), agreed that there were eight parts of speech in English: the noun, pronoun, adjective, verb, adverb, preposition, conjunction, and interjection. Some books paid separate attention to the participle; some additionally mentioned the article. But none was in any doubt that the definition of the parts of speech was an essential first step in learning about English grammar.

Why is it necessary to talk about parts of speech at all? The main reason is to be able to make general and economical statements about the way the words of the language behave. It is only a matter of common sense to generalize, when we notice that a set of words all work in the same way. In a simple case, we observe such sentences as

> It is in the box.
> It is near the fence.
> It is on the horse.
> It is by the table.
> It is under the car.
> It is for the book.

and note the identity of structure. In each instance, there is an item preceding *the* which seems to have the same sort of function, expressing some kind of proximity relationship between *it* (whatever that is) and the following words. Rather than talk about each of these items individually, it makes sense to group them together into a single category. Latin had words with the same function, which the grammarians called *prepositions* (from *prae* + *positio* 'placing in front' – that is, in front of a noun), and modern English grammars have happily continued to use the term.

Modern grammarians are happy because this is one of the areas where Latin and English grammar seem to behave in a similar way. The notion of preposition is a particularly useful one for describing English (p. 213). However, there is less happiness when people try to apply the old part-of-speech labels to English words that do not have a clear counterpart in Latin (such as *the*, *shall*, or the *to* in *to go*), or when they use definitions of the parts of speech that prove difficult to work with. Indeed, when linguists began to look closely at English grammatical structure in the 1940s and 1950s, they encountered so many problems of identification and definition that the term *part of speech* soon fell out of favour, *word class* being introduced instead. Word classes *are* equivalent to parts of speech, but defined according to strictly linguistic criteria.

THE TRADITIONAL DEFINITIONS

The definitions found in traditional grammars vary between authors, but they share a vagueness and inconsistency of approach which has not endeared them to modern linguists. A set of definitions and examples (from Nesfield, 1898: see p. 197) is given below, along with a note of the chief difficulties they present to anyone wanting to make a precise description of English grammar. The general intent behind the traditional definitions is clear enough; but several are insufficiently general to apply to all instances, and the lack of formal detail about their morphology (§14) or syntax (§16) makes them difficult to apply consistently.

Definitions

A noun is a word used for naming some person or thing.
Examples: *man, house, Paris, height*

Comments

The notional definition is difficult to work with; some grammars add a separate reference to places, but even that excludes many nouns which could not easily be described as 'persons, places, and things', such as abstract qualities (*beauty*) and actions (*a thump*). No reference is made to morphology or syntax (see p. 208).

An adjective is a word used to qualify a noun...to restrict the application of a noun by adding something to its meaning.
Examples: *fine, brave, three, the*

The definition is too broad and vague, as it allows a wide range of elements (e.g. *the, my, all*) which have very different grammatical properties, and even nouns in certain types of construction (e.g. *her brother the butcher*) do not seem to be excluded. No reference is made to morphology or syntax (see p. 211).

A pronoun is a word used instead of a noun or noun-equivalent [i.e. a word which is acting as a noun].
Examples: *this, who, mine*

The definition is almost there, but it has to be altered in one basic respect: pronouns are used instead of noun *phrases* (p. 222), not just nouns. *He* refers to the whole of the phrase *the big lion*, not just the word *lion* (we cannot say **the big he*). Nothing is said about morphology or syntax (see p. 210).

A verb is a word used for saying something about some person or thing.
Examples: *make, know, buy, sleep*

On this definition, there is little difference between a verb and an adjective (above). Some grammars prefer to talk about 'doing words' or 'action words', but this seems to exclude the many *state* verbs, such as *know*, *remember*, and *be*. No reference is made to morphology or syntax (see p. 212).

An adverb is a word used to qualify any part of speech except a noun or pronoun.
Examples: *today, often, slowly, very*

This is an advance on the more usual definition, in which adverbs are said to qualify (or 'modify') verbs – which is inadequate for such words as *very* and *however*. Even so, the definition leaks, as it hardly applies to interjections, and examples such as *the very man* and *slovenly me* have to be thought about. Nothing is really said about morphology or syntax (p. 211).

A preposition is a word placed before a noun or noun-equivalent to show in what relation the person or thing stands to something else.
Examples: *on, to, about, beyond*

This is a good start, as it gives a clear syntactic criterion. The definition needs tightening up, though, as prepositions really go before noun phrases, rather than just nouns, and may also be used in other parts of the sentence (p. 213). As with nouns above, more than just persons and things are involved.

A conjunction is a word used to join words or phrases together, or one clause to another clause.
Examples: *and, before, as well as*

This captures the essential point about conjunctions, but it also needs some tightening up, as prepositions might also be said to have a joining function (*the man in the garden*). A lot depends on exactly what is being joined (p. 213).

An interjection is a word or sound thrown into a sentence to express some feeling of the mind.
Examples: *Oh!, Bravo!, Fie!*

This is vaguer than it need be, for elsewhere Nesfield acknowledges the essential point, that interjections do not enter into the construction of sentences. Despite the emotional function of these words, they still need to be considered as part of sentence classification (p. 213).

CLASS CONSCIOUSNESS

It is not possible to tell which word class a word belongs to just by looking at it. We need to look carefully at how it behaves in a sentence. The word *brown*, for example, has three grammatical uses:

• As an adjective, when it is used in such contexts as *I bought a brown car* and *My arms are brown*.
• As a noun, when it is used in such contexts as *I pocketed the brown*.
• As a verb, when it is used in such contexts as *The toast has browned nicely*.

Some words have even more uses. *Round* has five, as adjective, noun, verb, adverb, and preposition.

A round table.

The yacht rounded the buoy.

Round the corner came a fire engine.

It's your round.

Walking round to the shops.

IDENTIFYING WORD CLASSES

A word class is a group of words which, from a grammatical point of view, behave in the same way. In theory, this means two things.

• The words are the same morphologically (§14): they show which class they belong to by using the same endings. For example, verbs add such inflectional endings as *-ing* and *-s* (p. 204); they can also be identified by various lexical endings, such as *-ize* and *-ify* (p. 198).
• The words are the same syntactically (§16): they show which class they belong to by being used in the same way within a sentence. For example, adjectives can appear between *the* and a noun, or immediately after a form of *be*: *the happy cat*, *the cat is happy*.

The task of word class identification is an interesting one for linguists, as it is not always obvious which are the best criteria to use. For example, when trying to decide what can be called a noun in English (p. 208), there are several possible criteria, each of which identifies a particular group of words. One criterion is the use of a plural ending. This includes *cats*, *dogs*, *horses*, and thousands of other words; but it excludes many words which do not have a plural form, such as *sheep*, *police*, *information*, and *John*. Another possible criterion is the use of a distinctive noun-making suffix, such as *-hood* or *-tion*. This includes *information*, *boyhood*, and thousands of words; but it excludes thousands of others which do not have such an ending.

At the same time, we sense that certain criteria have nothing to do with nouns at all. For example, the use of a comparative or superlative ending (p. 199) does not seem relevant in dealing with such words as *cat* and *dog*: we do not say **catter* or **doggest*. A different group of words can be identified using that criterion – those we call adjectives.

Some criteria, although in principle applicable to nouns, seem to identify such a limited group of words that they are of little real value. An example is the use of the genitive case, which has a marked preference for animate nouns (p. 202), as in *the boy's back* but not **the house's back*. Although it is a relevant criterion, which contributes to our sense of what makes a 'typical' noun, it is not a very useful distinguishing feature, because it excludes so many words that are definitely nouns according to other criteria.

Traditional grammar did not have the same interest in studying the actual linguistic behaviour of word classes. It assumed that the criteria which worked well for Latin would also work for English (p. 192), and it used definitions of the parts of speech which related more to their supposed meaning than to the way they worked in sentences. Neither of these practices has proved to be of much help in the description of English.

SOME NEW WORD CLASSES

When we look carefully at the way words behave in sentences, the differences can strike us as much as the similarities. Many words, indeed, turn out to be unique. For example, there is no other word in the language which has exactly the same formal properties as *house*, with its idiosyncratic way of forming a plural (p. 200). Likewise, there are features of the formal behaviour of *children*, *good*, *lightning*, *say*, *will*, and *do* (all identified in §14) which no other word in the language shares. Idiosyncrasies of this kind are usually disregarded when dealing with word classes. *House* is still classified as a noun, albeit a slightly individual one.

This approach brings to light several important groups of words in English which are syntactically so distinctive that they demand separate recognition – which means finding a new name for them. Here are three examples of these 'new' word classes.

• *Determiners* A group of words which can be used instead of *the* and *a* in the noun phrase, expressing such notions as quantity, number, possession, and definiteness. Examples include *some*, *much*, *that*, and *my*. Traditional grammars would call these adjectives.
• *Conjuncts* A group of words whose function is to relate (or 'conjoin') independent grammatical units, such as clauses, sentences, and paragraphs. Examples include *however*, *meanwhile*, *otherwise*, and *namely*. Traditional grammars would call these adverbs.
• *Auxiliaries* A group of words whose function is to assist the main verb in a clause to express several basic grammatical contrasts, such as of person, number, and tense. Examples include *have*, *can*, *do*, and *was*. Traditional grammars sometimes recognized these as a separate class of 'defective verbs'.

HOW NOUN-LIKE IS *PARIS*?

Modern grammars recognize that the largest word classes are convenient fictions, to some degree. All the words in a proposed class are seen to be sharing some features, but few share all of them. For example, there are four important features often suggested for nouns (p. 208):

A They are words which can be the head of a noun phrase.
B They are words which can be the subject of a clause.
C They are words which can have a plural form.
D They are words which display a suffix such as *-tion* or *-hood*.

The more criteria a word satisfies, the more 'noun-like' it is.

Deprivation is an 'excellent' noun, because it satisfies all four criteria:

A I hate the terrible deprivation.
B Deprivation is increasing.
C The deprivations were awful.
D depriva*tion*

On the other hand, *Paris* is much less typical.

A Unlikely (apart from cases where it becomes a common noun, as in *The Paris I used to know*: see p. 208).
B Paris is a capital city.
C Unlikely (again, apart from special cases, such as *How many Parises do you know?*).
D None.

THE CLASS OF NOUNS

When we look at the way nouns behave, we find that the following factors are involved:

- *Syntactic structure* (§16): a noun is the chief item (or 'head') of a noun phrase (p. 222), as in *the new **telephones***. It is often preceded by one of a small class of determiners (p. 207), such as *the* or *some*.
- *Syntactic function* (§16): a noun functions as the subject, object, or complement of a clause (p. 220), as in ***Apples** are popular*, *I like **apples***, *Those objects are **apples***.
- *Grammatical morphology* (§14): a noun can change its form to express a contrast in singular/plural number or to mark the genitive case (p. 202), as in *cat/cats/cat's/cats'*.
- *Lexical morphology* (§14): a noun can be formed by adding one of a small list of suffixes (e.g. *-age*, *-ment*, *-tion*) to a verb, an adjective, or another noun.

In parsing nouns (p. 197), traditional grammar insisted on noting gender as well as number and case. Modern grammars disregard this criterion, recognizing that gender has no grammatical role in English. They do however find good grammatical reasons for respecting the importance of several other traditional contrasts, especially *proper* vs *common*, and *abstract* vs *concrete*, and have developed the contrast between *mass* and *count* nouns into a major dimension of sub-classification.

THE MAIN SUBCLASSES

Nouns can be grouped into six main classes. The first division is into *proper* and *common* nouns. Common nouns can then be divided into *count* and *noncount* types. And both of these can be further divided into *concrete* and *abstract* types.

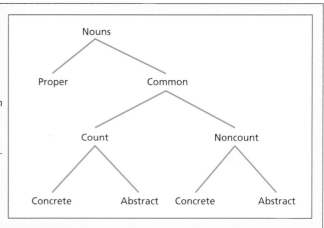

SUFFIXES THAT FORM NOUNS

	Abstract nouns			Concrete nouns	
Suffix	Add to	Example	Suffix	Add to	Example
-age	Noun	mileage	-ant	Verb	contestant
-age	Verb	wastage	-ee	Verb	referee
-al	Verb	refusal	-eer	Noun	profiteer
-(a)tion	Verb	exploitation	-er	Noun	villager
-dom	Noun	kingdom	-er	Verb	writer
-(e)ry	Noun	slavery	-ese	Noun/Adj.	Chinese
-ful	Noun	spoonful	-ess	Noun	waitress
-hood	Noun	boyhood	-ette	Noun	kitchenette
-ing	Noun	carpeting	-(i)an	Noun/Adj.	Parisian
-ing	Verb	building	-ist	Noun/Adj.	loyalist
-ism	Noun	idealism	-ite	Noun/Adj.	socialite
-ity	Adjective	rapidity	-let	Noun	booklet
-ment	Verb	amazement	-ling	Noun	duckling
-ness	Adjective	kindness	-or	Verb	survivor
-ocracy	Noun	democracy	-ster	Noun	gangster
-ship	Noun	friendship			

PROPER AND COMMON NOUNS

***P**roper nouns* are names of specific people, places, times, occasions, events, publications, and so on. They differ from common nouns in three main ways.

- Proper nouns can stand alone as a clause element (p.220, as in *I like London*, *Fred is here*, *Today is Tuesday*), whereas only certain common nouns can (*Chess is fun*, but **Egg is bad*, **Book is red*, **I see cat*, etc.).
- Proper nouns do not usually allow a plural (**Londons*, **Freds*, **Everests*), whereas most common nouns do (*books*, *eggs*, *pens*, but **musics*).
- Proper nouns are not usually used with determiners (p. 207) (**a London*, **the Fred*, **some France*), whereas common nouns are (*a book*, *the music*, *some bread*). In some circumstances, proper nouns can behave like common nouns:

Look at all those Smiths.
I used to know a Mary Jones.
I hate Mondays.

    Proper nouns are written with an initial capital letter. But not all words with initial capitals are proper nouns – as in the ironic *That's a Big Deal!* (p. 278). Also, there is sometimes uncertainty as to whether a word should be considered proper or common: is it *the moon* or *the Moon*? This issue has important consequences when it comes to deciding the size of the lexicon (p.122).

THE THE HAGUE

A proper noun is a single word, but many proper names consist of more than one word: *John Smith*, *King's College*. In these cases, the words work together as a single unit.
    Names like *The Hague* look as if they are being used with the definite article, but *The* is part of the name in such cases. It cannot be omitted, changed, or separated: we cannot say **Hague*, **A Hague*, **The The Hague*, or **The beautiful Hague*.

COUNT AND NON-COUNT NOUNS

Common nouns can be divided into two types. *Count* nouns refer to individual, countable entities, such as *books*, *eggs*, and *horses*. *Noncount* nouns refer to an undifferentiated mass or notion, such as *butter*, *music*, and *advice*. Noncount nouns are also known as *mass* nouns. There are clear grammatical differences between them.

• Count nouns cannot stand alone in the singular (**Book is red*); noncount nouns can (*Chess is fun*).
• Count nouns allow a plural (*books*, *eggs*); noncount nouns do not (**musics*).
• Count nouns occur in the singular with *a* (*a book*); noncount nouns with *some*

(*some music*). Both types can occur with *the* (*the book / the music*).

Some nouns can be either count or noncount, depending on their meaning. *Cake*, for example, is a count noun in this sentence:

Would you like a cake?

but a noncount noun in this one:

Do you like cake?

There are many such pairs.

The lights were amazing.
Light travels very fast.

I've bought some bricks.
It's built of brick.

I've had some odd experiences.
I've not had much experience.

A — OF KITTENS

Many noncount nouns have an equivalent countable expression using such words as *piece* or *bit* (*partitive* or *collective* nouns) followed by *of*:

luck	a piece of luck
grass	a blade of grass
bread	a loaf of bread

A common quiz question is to find the special collective term which describes

such groups of things: *a **flock** of sheep*, *a **pride** of lions*. English has some highly specialized (but nowadays rarely used) collective nouns, especially for animals. The item which fills the gap above is one of them – *a **kindle** of kittens*. Other colourful collectives are:

an exaltation of larks
a muster of peacocks
a plump of waterfowl
a rout of wolves
a skulk of foxes

ABSTRACT AND CONCRETE NOUNS

Both count and noncount nouns can be divided further into *abstract* and *concrete* types (p.198). Concrete nouns refer to entities which can be observed and measured, such as *book*, *car*, *elephant*, and *butter*. Abstract nouns refer to unobservable notions, such as *difficulty*, *idea*, *certainty*, and *remark*. The distinction seems straightforward, but in fact it can be quite difficult deciding whether a word is being used in a purely abstract or concrete way. Nouns such as *structure*, *version*, and *music* permit both abstract and concrete interpretations.

GENDER

In many languages (such as Latin and French), nouns can be grouped into types, based on the kind of endings they have, or on the way they pattern with other words in the noun phrase, and these types are known as *gender classes*. For example, in German, when nouns appear as subject of a clause, one type is preceded by *der* ('the'), and these are called *masculine*. Another type is preceded by *die* ('the'), and these are called *feminine*. Those preceded by *das* ('the') form a third type, and these are called *neuter*. This is a classification of *grammatical gender*: it may or may not reflect the biological sex of the entities involved (their *natural gender*). For example, in German one word for 'girl' (*das Mädchen*) is neuter.

English has nothing like this. It has no grammatical gender; but it does have ways of identifying natural gender. We can distinguish *animate* beings from *inanimate* entities, *personal* from *nonpersonal* beings, and *male* from *female* sexes. It is chiefly done by using pronouns, which correlate with nouns in precise ways:

• *Inanimate* nouns (*box*, *advice*) pattern only with *it* and *which*.

Here is a box. *It* is the box *which* was in the street.

• *Animate* nouns make varying use of *he/she* and *who*, and are divided into personal and nonpersonal types.

Here is a man. *He* is the man *who* was in the street.
Here is a woman. *She* is the woman *who* was in the street.

• *Personal* animate nouns refer to males and females, and pattern with *he/she/who*, as in the above examples, and also in such pairs as *host/hostess* and *prince/princess*, where the noun ending makes the gender clear. Some nouns can be either 'he' or 'she' (they have *dual gender*), such as *artist*, *cook*, *cousin*, and *singer*.

Your cousin is a singer, isn't he/she?

• *Nonpersonal* animate nouns refer to animals. Most take *it/which*, but those with a special place in human society take *he/she/who*, and some even have distinct male/female forms: *bull/cow*, *dog/bitch*,

tiger/tigress. The 'lower animals' (*ant*, *cod*, etc.) do not normally take *he/she*, though an enthusiast for ants (or cod) might well exclaim:

Isn't he/she lovely?

This is invariably an emotional identification, of course, given the difficulty of identifying the true sex in such cases.

• In British English, *collective* nouns, such as *committee*, *government*, *team*, *army*, and *family*, can take either *it/which* or *they/who*, depending on the point of view involved. The singular stresses the impersonal unity of the group; the plural the personal individuality of its members (p. 201).

The committee which has met…It is concerned…
The committee who have met…They are concerned…

Plural forms are far less common in American English: *government*, for example, almost always takes a singular verb in the USA.

The topic of gender raises sensitive usage questions that go beyond grammatical issues; these are discussed on pp. 368–9.

FORTY-TWO

Many nouns are given variable gender, depending on whether they are thought of in an intimate way. Vehicles and countries are often called *she* as well as *it* (*She can reach 60 in 5 seconds*; *France has increased her exports*). Pets are often *he* or *she*. A crying baby may become *it*.

It is not obvious why some entities are readily personified while others are not. Nor is it obvious why most entities are given female personifications. It is not simply a matter of feminine stereotypes, for *she* is used in aggressive and angry situations as well as in affectionate ones: guns, tanks, and trucks which won't go remain *she*. The only consistently male trend in personification which the author has heard in recent years is in computing, where word processors and other devices are widely given male pet names and pronouns. Why this should be so is beyond him, though the reason is doubtless somewhere within the answer given by the (male) super-computer Deep Thought to the Ultimate Question, and quoted above as the heading to this item.

'There is an answer?' said Fook with breathless excitement.
'A simple answer?' added Lunkwill.
'Yes,' said Deep Thought. 'Life, the Universe, and Everything. There is an answer. But,' he added, 'I'll have to think about it.'
(Douglas Adams, *The Hitch Hiker's Guide to the Galaxy*, 1979.)

THE CLASS OF PRONOUNS

Pronouns are words which stand for a noun (Latin *pro* = 'for'), a whole noun phrase (p. 222), or several noun phrases. They can also refer directly to some aspect of the situation surrounding the speaker or writer. In each case, the meaning expressed is much less specific than that found in phrases containing nouns.

• Replacing a noun: *I've got a red **hat** and Jane's got a brown **one**.*
• Replacing a noun phrase: ***My uncle Fred**'s just arrived. **He**'s quite tired.*
• Referring to a very general concept which includes the meaning of many possible noun phrases: *I can see **someone** in the distance* (where *someone* includes men, women, boys, girls, soldiers, etc.).

• Referring to some unspecified event of the situation: (pointing) *Look at **that**! He's going to crash.*

Pronouns carry out a similar range of functions to nouns and noun phrases (p. 208) – for example, they can appear as subject, object, or complement of the clause (***She** saw me, **That**'s you*). However, they differ from nouns chiefly in not usually permitting modification (*a big car*, but not **a big it*), and in expressing a distinctive set of contrasts.

• Some pronouns have separate cases for subject and object functions, as in *I* vs *me*, *who* vs *whom* (p. 203).
• Some show a contrast between personal and nonpersonal gender and between male and female (p. 209): *he/she* vs *it*, *who* vs *which*. (For the issues raised by gender, see p. 368.)
• Some distinguish singular and plural number, but not by adding an *-s* (p. 200), as in *I* vs *we*, *he* vs *they*.
• Some have different persons: *I* vs *you* vs *he/she/it*.

ME, MYSELF, I

If people know anything at all about pronouns, it is usually about the personal pronouns, which occur more frequently than any other type. They are called 'personal' because they refer to the people involved in the act of communication.

• The *first person* involved refers to the speaker(s) or writer(s) of the message: *I, me, my, mine, myself; we, us, our(s), ourselves*
• The *second person* refers to the addressee(s), excluding speaker(s) or writer(s): *you, your(s), yourself/-selves*
• The *third person* refers to 'third parties', i.e. excluding the speaker(s), writer(s), and addressee(s): *he, him, his, himself; she, her(s), herself; it, its, itself; they, them, their(s), themselves. It* is included, even though it refers to nonpersonal entities, because it behaves in the same way as the others.

There are a few additional personal pronouns. A *thou* series (*thee, thy, thyself, thine*) is still sometimes found in religious use (p. 371), and in some rural British dialects. There are also some nonstandard forms, such as *youse* in northern USA, Ireland, and parts of Britain (e.g. Liverpool, Glasgow). Southern USA has the plural *you-all* or *y'all*.

Special uses
The above roles are the usual ones; but there are also a few special uses.

• *We* can refer to a single person in the 'royal' or 'editorial' *we*: *We are not amused.*
• *We* can refer to the addressee, especially when talking 'down': *How are we today?* (nurse to patient).
• *We* can refer to a third party: *We're in a bad mood today* (secretary about boss).
• *You* and *they* can refer to people in general, or to some group within society: *You never can tell, They keep putting fares up.*
• *It* can be used to refer in a general way to time, distance, or life in general: *Isn't it a shame? It's lovely out.*

TYPES OF PRONOUN

There are many kinds of word which can act as a pronoun, but they express different kinds of meaning, and they do not all follow the same grammatical rules. This means that different subclasses of pronoun have to be recognized. The first three subclasses below are sometimes grouped together as the *central* pronouns, because they all express contrasts of person, gender, and number.

• *Personal pronouns* are the main means of identifying speakers, addressees, and others: *I, you, he, she, it, we, they*.
• *Reflexive pronouns*, always ending in *-self* or *-selves* (*myself*, etc.), 'reflect' the meaning of a noun or pronoun elsewhere in the clause: *They washed **themselves**.*
• *Possessive pronouns* express ownership, and appear in two forms. *My, your*, etc. are used as determiners (p. 207) in the noun phrase, as in *my car, her bike. Mine, yours*, etc. are used on their own, as in *This is mine, Hers is over there*.

There are several other subclasses.
• *Reciprocal pronouns* are used to express a 'two-way' relationship: *each other, one another*.

• *Interrogative pronouns* are used to ask questions about personal and non-personal nouns: *who?, whom?, whose?, which?, what?*
• *Relative pronouns* (*who, whom, whose, which, that*) are used to link a subordinate clause (p. 226) to the head of the noun phrase, as in *That's the book **which** caused the trouble.*
• *Demonstrative pronouns* (*this/these, that/those*) express a contrast between 'near' and 'distant', as in *Take this one here, not that one over there.* They also have a range of extended uses: for example, *this* may be used to introduce a new topic in familiar speech (*I saw this girl . . .*), and *that* may express a negative attitude (*That Roger!*).
• *Indefinite pronouns* express a notion of quantity. There are two main types. *Compound pronouns* consist of two elements: *every-, some-, any-,* or *no-* + *-one, -body,* or *-thing*, as in *someone* and *anything. Of-pronouns* consist of several forms which may appear alone or be followed by *of* (*I've eaten all the cake / all of the cake*). Their meanings range from the 'universal' sense of *all* and *both* to the 'negative' sense of *none* and *few*. Other items in this class include *each, much, many, more, most, less, fewer, some,* and *neither*.

WHICH WAY

What and *which* permit a contrast between definite and indefinite meaning.

***What** road shall we take?* (indefinite: an open choice)

***Which** road shall we take?* (definite: we are choosing from a small number of alternatives)

THE CLASS OF ADJECTIVES

Words which express some feature or quality of a noun or pronoun are traditionally known as adjectives. To decide if a word is an adjective, several criteria are available.

• An adjective can occur immediately before a noun: *a big house*. This is called the adjective's *attributive* function.
• An adjective can occur alone after forms of the verb *be*. *The house was big*. This is the adjective's *predicative* function.
• An adjective can be immediately preceded by *very* and other *intensifying* words: *very big, terribly nice*.
• An adjective can be compared (p. 199): *bigger/biggest, more/most beautiful*.
• Many adjectives permit the addition of *-ly* to form an adverb (see below): *sad > sadly*.

To count as an adjective, a word must be able to function in both attributive and predicative positions. The vast majority of adjectives are like this, and these form the *central* class of adjectives. Words which can appear in only one or other of these positions are *peripheral* adjectives. They include *utter* and *loath*: we can say *utter nonsense*, but not *the nonsense is utter*; and *the man was loath to leave*, but not *the loath man*.

ADJECTIVE SUFFIXES

Many adjectives (e.g. *big, thin*) have no distinctive ending, but there are a few suffixes (p. 198) which typically signal that a word is an adjective.

Suffix	Add to	Result	Suffix	Add to	Result
-able	Verb	washable	-less	Noun	restless
-al	Noun	musical	-like	Noun	childlike
-ed	Noun	ragged	-ly	Noun	friendly
-esque	Noun	romanesque	-ous	Noun	desirous
-ful	Noun	hopeful	-some	Noun	bothersome
-ic	Noun	heroic	-worthy	Noun	praiseworthy
-ish	Noun	foolish	-y	Noun	sandy
-ive	Verb	effective			

ADJECTIVE OR NOT?

The adjective is a good example of a word class with fuzzy edges. Some words are much more adjective-like than others.

• *Numerals*, such as *four* and *forty*, share some of the properties of central adjectives, but not others. They can occur before a noun and after *be* (*the four cats, She's four*), but cannot compare or take *-ly* (**fourer, *fourly*).
• Words ending in *-ed* or *-ing* could be either an adjective or a form of a verb (p. 204). In *the interesting problem*, we see an adjective; in *We are interesting them in the problem*, we see the *-ing* form of a verb. Sometimes there is ambiguity: *She is calculating*.
• Words which are normally used as nouns may appear in the position associated with adjectives: *the garden party*. They are no longer strictly nouns, because (for example) they have lost their capacity to pluralize: we cannot say **the gardens party*. On the other hand, they are not strictly adjectives either, because (for example) they cannot compare: we cannot say **the gardenest party*. They form a 'mixed' word class.

THE CLASS OF ADVERBS

The adverb is the most heterogeneous of all the word classes in English grammar. Over the years, words have been assigned to it which perform a wide variety of functions within the sentence. Traditional grammar (§13) included under this heading not only such items as *quickly* and *soon*, which are representative of large groups of words, but also such idiosyncratic items as *no, not,* and *the* (as in *the sooner the better*) – largely, one supposes, because there was no other class to which they could easily be assigned. Modern grammars try to make adverbs less of a 'dustbin' class by identifying their main functions and setting up subclasses to handle the most divergent types.

Adverbs have two chief uses. Most can act as an element of clause structure (an *adverbial*, p. 220), usually relating directly to the meaning of the verb (as in *We're leaving tonight*), but often to some other element of the clause or to the clause as a whole (as in *Morally, he should resign*). Some adverbs affect the meaning of an adjacent word or phrase by attaching themselves to it, as in *very anxiously* and *quite a party* or *the day before* and *someone else* . These clausal and phrasal functions are discussed further on pp. 221–2.

TYPES OF ADVERB

Most adverbs are fairly easy to recognize because they are formed by adding an *-ly* suffix to an adjective, as in *quickly* and *happily*. Less obvious are the following:

• Adverbs which have no distinctive element, such as *just* and *soon*, or compound adverbs, such as *somehow* and *whereby*.
• A few other endings which mark a word as an adverb, used especially in informal speech: *new-style, earthwards, clockwise, sideways, sailor-fashion*. Coinages such as *physics-wise* are very common in American English.
Because adverbs work along with adverb phrases and clauses to perform their range of functions, they are discussed under the heading of adverbial on p. 221.

AND IT'S THERE!

Now Smith passes *beautifully* to Gray, who heads it *very firmly* and *deliberately* to Pritchard, who pushes it *nimbly* towards the post…

Sports commentary is one of several varieties which greatly rely on adverbs for their effect. In this football match between Wimbledon and Blackburn Rovers (29 March 1994), Wimbledon's Dean Holdsworth and John Scales watch the ball go past Blackburn's keeper Tim Flowers.

THE CLASS OF VERBS

A sentence may contain a single verb, or it may use a cluster of verbs which work together as a verb phrase (p. 224): *I **saw** an elephant, You **didn't see** one, They **couldn't have seen** one.* The last two examples show a *main verb* (a form of *see* in each case) accompanied by one or more *auxiliary verbs*. There can be up to four auxiliaries, all going in front of the main verb, though constructions using all four are unusual: *They **must have been being** advised by the government.*

Three classes of verb can occur within the verb phrase.

• *Lexical verbs* (also called *full verbs*) are those with a meaning that can be clearly and independently identified (e.g. in a dictionary), such as *run, jump, walk, want, cogitate*. They act as main verbs.
• *Modal verbs* convey a range of judgments about the likelihood of events; they function only as auxiliary verbs, expressing meanings which are much less definable, focused, and independent than those of lexical verbs. There are nine verbs in this subclass: *can, could, may, might, will, would, shall, should*, and *must*, with *dare, need, ought to*, and *used to* having a very similar function.
• *Primary verbs* can function either as main verbs or as auxiliary verbs. There are just three of them: *be, have*, and *do*.

Main verb use:
They **are** happy. She **has** a dog. They **do** sums.
Auxiliary verb use:
They **are** going. She **has** seen it. **Do** they go?

Finite and nonfinite

The forms of the verb (p. 204), and the phrases they are part of, are usually classified into two broad types, based on the kind of contrast in meaning they express. The notion of *finiteness* is the traditional way of classifying the differences. This term suggests that verbs can be 'limited' in some way, and this is in fact what happens when different kinds of endings are used.

• The *finite* forms are those which limit the verb to a particular number, tense, person, or mood. For example, when the *-s* form is used, the verb is limited to the third person singular of the present tense, as in *goes* and *runs*. If there is a series of verbs in the verb phrase, the finite verb is always the first, as in *I **was** being asked.*
• The *nonfinite* forms do not limit the verb in this way. For example, when the *-ing* form is used, the verb can be referring to any number, tense, person, or mood:

I'm *leaving* (first person, singular, present)
They're *leaving* (third person, plural, present)
He was *leaving* (third person, singular, past)
We might be *leaving* tomorrow (first person, plural, future, tentative)

As these examples show, a nonfinite form of the verb stays the same in a clause, regardless of the grammatical variation taking place alongside it.

Auxiliary verbs						Main verb
						advise
					is	*advising*
				has	*been*	*advising*
			must	*have*	*been*	*advising*
(rare)	*must*	*have*	*been*	*being*		*advised*

AUXILIARY VERBS

Auxiliary (or 'helping') verbs assist the main verb in a clause to express several basic grammatical contrasts, such as in person, number, and tense. They do not follow the same grammatical rules as main verbs, which is why they must be considered as a separate class.

• Auxiliaries can be used before the word *not*; main verbs (in modern English) cannot. We can change *I might go* into *I might not go*, but we cannot change *I saw it* into **I saw not it*.
• The contracted form *n't* (p. 205) can be attached to almost all auxiliaries; this is not possible with main verbs (apart from *be* and

have). We can say *can't* and *won't*, but not **walkn't* or **jumpn't*.
• The first auxiliary in a verb phrase has a distinctive role, as it can be used before the subject in order to ask a question; this is not possible with main verbs. We can say *Have they gone home?*, but not **Saw they a car?*

The auxiliary class can itself be divided into two subclasses:

• The primary verbs have *-s* forms; the modals do not. We find *is, has*, and *does*, but not **mays, *wills*, or **musts*.
• The primary verbs have nonfinite forms; the modals do not. We find *to have, having*, and *had*, but not **to may, *maying*, or **mayed*.

TRANSITIVITY

The choice of the verb actually determines, to a large extent, what other elements can be used in the clause (p. 220). Once we have 'picked' our verb, certain other things are likely to happen.

• If we pick *go*, we can stop the clause there, without fear of being ungrammatical: *The cat's going*. Verbs of this type, which can be used without an object, have long been called *intransitive verbs*.

• If we pick *enjoy*, another element has to follow. We cannot say **The cat's enjoying*. It has to be *The cat's enjoying something*, with the object present.

SOME COMMON TRANSITIVES

bring	keep
carry	like
desire	make
find	need
get	use

SOME COMMON INTRANSITIVES

appear	happen
die	lie
digress	matter
fall	rise
go	wait

Verbs which require an object are traditionally known as *transitive verbs*.

FINITE CONTRASTS

The finite forms of the verb are the *-s* form, the past form, and some uses of the base form (p. 204). The nonfinite forms show no variation.

Finite forms
• Show a contrast in tense: *She works in London* vs *She worked in London.*
• Show a contrast in number and person: *he works* vs *they work; I am* vs *you are.*
• Allow the expression of facts, possibilities, wishes, and other contrasts of mood: *They suggested that the papers **be** delivered by hand. They **were**.*

Nonfinite forms
There are three nonfinite forms of the verb:
• The *-ing* participle: *I'm leaving.*
• The *-ed* participle: *I've asked, They were asked.*
• The base form used as an infinitive: *They might **see**, He wants **to see**.*

MULTI-WORD VERBS

Some verbs consist of more than one word (and are thus better described as lexemes (p. 118). The most common type consists of a verb followed by one or more *particles: come in, sit down, drink up, put up with*. The particles are either spatial adverbs (e.g. *aback, ahead*, and *away*), prepositions (e.g. *at, for, from*), or words which in other contexts can act either as adverbs or as prepositions (e.g. *by, down, in*).

Verbs which use adverb particles are often called *phrasal verbs*, with those taking prepositional particles being distinguished as *prepositional verbs*. In some grammars, however, the term *phrasal verb* is used for both. Whatever the terminology, one fact is clear: the number of multi-word verbs in the language has grown remarkably, especially in the present century (p. 118), and they constitute one of the most distinctive features of English syntax.

THE CLASS OF PREPOSITIONS

A preposition expresses a relationship of meaning between two parts of a sentence, most often showing how the two parts are related in space or time: *We sat on the bench*, *They left at three*. Most of the common prepositions consist of only one word; they have no distinctive ending, and do not vary. Several prepositions consist of more than one word.

• Single-word prepositions include: *about, at, before, by, down, for, from, in, of, on, out, over, round, since, through, to, under, up, with.*

• Multi-word prepositions include: (two words) *ahead of, because of, due to, instead of, near to*; (three words) *as far as, by means of, in accordance with, in spite of, on behalf of*. The words in these prepositions do not vary freely, as they would in other circumstances. *In spite of,* for example, cannot change to *out spite of or **in spite for.*

Several prepositions are restricted in their frequency of use, especially such foreign borrowings as *anti, circa, versus,* and *vis-à-vis. Unto* is archaic, and used only in religious contexts. There are also some dialect uses, such as *towards* (British) vs *toward* (American), *outwith* (Scots, 'except'), and *while* (Yorkshire, 'until').

PREPOSITIONAL MEANINGS

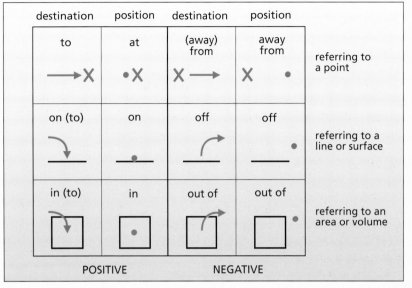

Most prepositions can be used in several different ways. *Over*, for example, is found in the sense of position (*The picture was over the door*), movement across (*They climbed over the wall*), accompanying circumstances (*We'll talk over dinner*), orientation to the speaker (*They live over the road*), and other meanings. Other types of meaning include time (e.g. *during the* night), cause (e.g. *because of the fog*), method (e.g. *with a spoon*), and possession (*a pianist of talent*). In addition, there are many figurative uses involving prepositions: *He's in a hole* may literally mean what it says, or it may not. The diagram shows the chief prepositions which express spatial meanings (after R. Quirk, *et al.,* 1985).

THE CLASS OF CONJUNCTIONS

Conjunctions are items which join clauses or parts of clauses together. There are two ways in which this can be done: through *coordination* and *subordination* (p. 226). There are thus two types of conjunction:

• *Coordinating conjunctions* link units which have the same status in the sentence, such as two clauses, two noun phrases, or two adjectives. The chief items are *and, or,* and *but,* and there are a few 'pairs', such as *neither... nor.* These conjunctions signal such meanings as addition and sequence (*and*), the expression of alternatives (*or*), and contrast (*but*). Coordination with *and* and *or* could continue indefinitely: *We were wet and dirty and tired and hungry and...*

• *Subordinating conjunctions* join units which do not have the same grammatical status in the sentence. The typical case is when one clause is subordinated to another, as in *We went out when the rain stopped.* Here, the main clause (*We went out*) is joined to the subordinate clause (*the rain stopped*) by the conjunction *when.* Subordinating conjunctions far outnumber coordinating ones, and several consist of more than one word.

SOME SUBORDINATE MEANINGS

There are over a dozen types of meaning expressed by subordinating conjunctions. Here are some of them.

• Time: *I stayed until you left.*
• Place: *I'll know where you are.*
• Condition: *We'll get wet if it rains.*
• Concession: *He was there, though the bus was late.*
• Purpose: *She wrote in order to get her money back.*
• Reason: *I can't buy it because it's expensive.*

The compound subordinating conjunctions boldly introducing the first and last paragraphs are an important means of identifying the linguistic structure of complex legal documents.

AND INTERJECTIONS?

We can make a wide range of emotional noises which stand in for sentences, such as *Eh?, Oy!, Huh?, Tut-tut!, Coo!,* and *Yuk!* The important point to note is that they are standing in for *sentences,* not words, as the punctuation marks indicate. They are therefore better treated as a type of sentence (a minor sentence, p. 216) rather than as a word class.

16 · THE STRUCTURE OF SENTENCES

The study of sentence structure is called *syntax*, and because there is so little variation in the grammatical structure of English words (§14), a syntactic analysis forms the dominant element in a modern English grammar. The area thus provides the main point of contrast with traditional grammars (§13), which because of their Latinate origins paid little attention to the syntactic properties of sentences.

Sentences

The sentence is probably the most familiar of all grammatical terms. We are introduced to it in our early school years, if not before, and it quickly becomes part of our linguistic awareness. We imagine we speak in sentences, and we teach children to write in them, making sure that they put in all the periods. It might therefore be thought that sentences are easy things to identify and define. The opposite turns out to be the case.

Those who learned some traditional grammar will remember the old definition of a sentence as 'a complete expression of a single thought'. Unfortunately, this *notional* approach is too vague to be of much help. There are many sentences which seem to express a single thought, but which are not complete, by traditional standards:

Lovely day!   Taxi!   Nice one!   Tennis?

There are also many sentences which are complete, but express more than one thought:

For his birthday, Ben wants a bike, a computer game, and a visit to the theme park.

The *formal* approach to English grammar, by contrast, tries to avoid these kinds of difficulty by describing the way in which sentences are constructed – the patterns of words they contain. It is an approach which can lead to some surprises, especially when we look carefully at what happens in everyday speech.

SPOKEN AND WRITTEN SYNTAX

One of the legacies of traditional grammar is the view that the spoken language has 'less' grammar because it does not 'follow the rules' which are found in writing (p. 192). There are indeed many differences between the two types of communication (p. 291), and some of the most important of these are to do with the notion of a sentence. Putting it at its simplest: Do we speak in sentences? The answer is that we do, but the kind of sentence organization we find in speech is rather different from that found in writing, as the first transcript below shows.

When we are writing, we usually have time to make notes, plan ahead, pause, reflect, change our mind, start again, revise, proof-read, and generally polish the language until we have reached a level which satisfies us. The reader sees only the finished product. But in everyday conversation, there is no time for such things to happen. We do not have the opportunity to plan what we want to say, and we have to allow for false starts, interruptions, second thoughts, words on the tip of the tongue, and a host of other disturbances which take place while we are in full flow.

Extracts of informal spoken conversation look weird in print, because it is not possible to show all the melody, stress, and tone of voice which made the speaker sound perfectly natural in context; but it does show how spoken grammar differs from written. Punctuating the material in such a transcript is not easy, as can be seen by the second version below, where an attempt has been made to cut out hesitations and false starts, and to identify possible sentences. The use of *and* in particular makes it difficult to work out where one sentence ends and the next begins. Readers who doubt the seriousness of this problem might care to pencil in their own impressions about where the sentences end, and then compare their decisions with those shown below. There will be several discrepancies.

Find the sentence

As this is a transcript of speech, there are no capital letters. Major pauses are shown by –, and units of rhythm by /. (After D. Crystal & D. Davy, 1975.)

we had our breakfast in the kitchen / - and then we sort of did what we liked / and er got ready to go out / we usually went out quite soon after that / - erm the children were always up / at the crack of dawn / with the farmer / - and they went in the milking sheds / and helped him feed the pigs / and all this / you know we didn't see the children / – and er then we used to go out / we - we had super weather / – absolutely super / - and so we went to a beach / usually for er but by about four o'clock it we were hot and we had to come off the beach / - so we'd generally go for a tea somewhere / just in case supper was delayed you know / and then we'd get back / and the children would go straight back on to the farm / and have ponies / their own children had ponies / and they'd come up and put them on the ponies' backs / and er - and the milking it was milking time / and really we were committed to getting back for milking time /

We had our breakfast in the kitchen, and then we did what we liked, and got ready to go out.
We usually went out quite soon after that.
The children were always up at the crack of dawn with the farmer, and they went into the milking sheds and helped him feed the pigs.
We didn't see the children.
And then we used to go out.
We had super weather, absolutely super.
And so we went to a beach, but by about four o'clock we were hot and we had to come off the beach.
So we'd generally go for a tea somewhere, just in case supper was delayed.
And then we'd get back, and the children would go straight back on to the farm, and have ponies.
Their own children had ponies, and they'd come up and put them on the ponies' backs.
And it was milking time, and really we were committed to getting back for milking time.

WORD ORDER

Word order is at the heart of syntax, and most of English grammar is taken up with the rules governing the order in which words, and clusters of words, can appear. The importance of this domain can be seen from the following set of examples, where the meaning of the sentence alters fundamentally once the order varies.

Dog chases postman. / Postman chases dog.
They are outside. / Are they outside?
Only I saw Mary. / I saw only Mary.

Naturally, I got up. / I got up naturally (*not awkwardly*).
Show me the last three pages (*of one book*). / Show me the three last pages (*of three books*).
The man with a dog saw me. / The man saw me with a dog.

There are also many rules forbidding us to put words in a certain order. Mother-tongue speakers never think twice about them, because they unconsciously learned these rules as children. But the rules are there, nonetheless, making us use the first of the following alternatives, not the second (the asterisk shows that the sentence is unacceptable).

I walked to town. / *I to town walked.
Hardly had I left… / *Hardly I had left…
That's a fine old house. / *That's an old fine house.
John and I saw her. / *I and John saw her.
She switched it on. / *She switched on it.

Mother-tongue speakers instinctively know that the first is correct, and the second is not; but explaining why this is so to anyone who asks (such as a foreign learner) is a specialist task, which requires a professional approach if it is to succeed.

Three general points apply to any English sentence.

• Sentences are constructed according to a system of rules, known by all the adult mother-tongue speakers of the language, and summarized in a grammar. A sentence formed in this way is said to be *grammatical*.

• Sentences are the largest constructions to which the rules of grammar apply. (The formation of larger units, such as paragraphs, is discussed on p. 232.) This means that, before we can satisfactorily carry out the task of identifying sentences, we need to know something about grammatical analysis. Once we have worked our way through a good English grammar, we know what the possible sentences are, because the grammar has told us.

• Sentences are constructions which can be used on their own – units of meaning which seem to 'make sense' by themselves. This is an ancient and plausible criterion, but it is never a straightforward one. For example, if we apply it to the sentences in the extract opposite, we find that we need to do some editing to make it work. *We didn't see the children* poses no problem; but *We usually went out quite soon after that* does, for we have to 'fill out' the meaning of *that* with reference to what has gone before. Also, to make the sentences in the extract sound truly 'self-contained', we have to find a way of dealing with the conjunctions which appear at the beginning of several of them – perhaps by analysing some as dispensable 'thinking' noises rather than as true conjunctions with a genuine linking function (p. 227). The problem turns out to be quite a complex one – and typical of the intriguing questions which arise when we begin the investigation of syntax.

AND NOW FOR SOMETHING COMPLETELY DIFFERENT

A sentence is something which begins with a capital letter and ends with a full stop? This traditional definition, which applies only to the written language, is faulty on three counts.

• We have to allow for question marks and exclamation marks as well (as in the first sentence of this caption).
• Punctuation is often not used in writing, and yet we still know when a construction is a sentence. Many advertisements, public notices, newspaper headlines, and legal documents lack punctuation marks.
• People disagree about the best way to punctuate a text. In particular, some manuals of style say we should never end a sentence before such words as *and* or *but*, and this rule is often taught in schools. Its source lies in the uncontrolled way in which young children use *and* in their early written work, reflecting its frequency in natural conversation. But there are other manuals which accept that authors often do begin sentences in this way (usually to emphasize a contrast in meaning), and these do not condemn the usage. It is a regular feature of the style of the present author, who finds it on occasion a much more dramatic and rhythmical way of drawing a contrast than to use the various alternatives available. To replace *but* by *however* two sentences above, for example, would be to slow down the movement of the paragraph quite noticeably – in his view an unnecessary change of pace in a piece of text which wishes to make its point quickly and economically.

Magazine covers destroy any simple definition of sentences in terms of initial capital letters and final full stops. Here we have a sentence which is all capital letters, and four others where an unusual use of capitals has replaced conventional punctuation.

THE END OF THE BEGINNING

Winston Churchill, according to the Chambers *Biographical Dictionary*, 'the last of the classic orators with a supreme command of English'.

The quotation is from the end of the third and the opening of the fourth paragraph of Book 1 of *The History of the Second World War*. The succinct, dramatic effectiveness of the contrast should silence for ever those who unthinkingly condemn the use of a sentence-initial conjunction as 'bad style'. But it won't.

To those Frenchmen – and there were many in high authority – who had fought and suffered in 1870 it seemed almost a miracle that France should have emerged victorious from the incomparably more terrible struggle which had just ended. All their lives they had dwelt in fear of the German Empire. They remembered the preventive war which Bismarck had sought to wage in 1875; they remembered the brutal threat which had driven Declassé from office in 1905; they had quaked at the Moroccan menace in 1906, at the Bosnian dispute of 1908, and at the Agadir crisis of 1911. The Kaiser's 'mailed fist' and 'shining armour' speeches might be received with ridicule in England and America: they sounded a knell of horrible reality in the hearts of the French. For fifty years almost they had lived under the terror of the German arms. Now, at the price of their life-blood, the long oppression had been rolled away. Surely here at last was peace and safety. With one passionate spasm the French people cried 'Never again!'

But the future was heavy with foreboding…

TYPES OF SENTENCE

It is obvious, as we look through the pages of a novel, or a daily newspaper, that there must be a large number of sentence patterns in English. What is less obvious is that these can be grouped into two main types, on the basis of whether they are formed in a regular or an irregular way. Regular sentences are often referred to as *major sentences*; irregular ones as *minor sentences*.

Major sentences

The major sentences are in the vast majority. All the sentences in this book, apart from the headings and some of the examples, are of this type. Essentially, they are sentences which can be broken down into a specific and predictable pattern of elements. The following examples show some of the possibilities.

The visitor	brought	a book	for you.
I	gave	the letter	to Mary.
Mary	saw	Jane	today.

We need a term to describe 'patterns of elements' of this type, and many grammars use *clause* for the purpose. Sentences which consist of just one clause (pattern of elements) are said to be *simple sentences*. Sentences which can be immediately analysed into more than one clause are *multiple sentences* (described further on p. 227).

SIMPLE AND MULTIPLE SENTENCES

The difference between simple and multiple sentences can be seen in the following two examples:

A book has fallen on John's foot.
A book has fallen on John's foot and a book has fallen on Mary's foot.

The same clause pattern turns up twice in the second sentence; the only difference between them is the lexical change (the change of name). Indeed, it is possible to imagine a sentence in which this clause pattern is used repeatedly, with innumerable books falling on innumerable feet, and just the name changing each time. As long as the speaker kept adding *and...and ...and...*, or some other linking word, the sentence could continue indefinitely.

The diagram summarizes the two possibilities.

```
              sentence (simple)
                     |
                     |
                  clause

              sentence (multiple)
                    /\
                   /  \
                  /  : \
                 /   :  \
      clause + linking word + clause...
```

MINOR SENTENCES

Minor sentences are not constructed in a regular way. They use abnormal patterns which cannot be clearly analysed into a sequence of clause elements, as can major sentences. There are only a few minor sentence types, but instances of each type are frequently used in everyday conversation and when conversations are represented in fiction. They are also common in certain types of written language, such as notices, headlines, labels, advertisements, subheadings, and other settings where a message is presented as a 'block'.

Minor sentences do not follow all the rules of grammar. For example, in a major sentence the verbs can change their persons: *How do you manage?* > *How does he manage?* But the greeting *How do you do?* is a minor sentence, and we cannot change the person to *How does he do?* (without changing the sense into something quite different). Nor can we change the tense and ask *How did you do?* The sentence has to be learned as a whole, and used as an idiom (p.162).

It will be seen from this example that some types of minor sentence look quite complex – so much so that on a first impression they might be thought to be displaying a major pattern. But in each case there is something 'odd' about them. For example, one type uses an archaic verb form (the subjunctive) to express wishes, as in *God save the Queen!* and *Heaven forbid!* Another type uses question words idiosyncratically: *How come she's gone out?* These are minor sentences because it is not possible to introduce the full range of normal grammatical changes into their structure, to produce such forms as *God saves the Queen* or *God doesn't save the Queen*. Only major sentences allow systematic variations of this kind.

SOME MINOR SENTENCE TYPES

• Formulae for stereotyped social situations, such as *Hello*, *How do you do?*, *Thanks*, and *Cheers!*
• Emotional or functional noises (traditionally called *interjections*), many of which do not follow the normal pronunciation patterns of the language, such as *Eh?*, *Ugh!*, *Ow!*, *Tut tut*, and *Shh!*
• Proverbs or pithy sayings (*aphorisms*, p. 163), such as *Easy come, easy go* or *Least said, soonest mended*.
• Abbreviated forms, such as are used in postcards, instructions, or commentaries, as in *Wish you were here*, *Mix well*, and *One lap more*.
• Words and phrases used as exclamations, questions, and commands, such as *Nice day!*, *Taxi?*, and *All aboard!*

LEVELS OF SENTENCE STRUCTURE

Major sentences can be very simple (*I love you*), but they have the potential to contain a great deal of grammatical structure, as is evident from almost every instance on this page. Literature, oratory, and other sophisticated forms of communication provide particularly striking examples of sentence complexity (p. 70). To demonstrate the order which controls this complexity, all grammars work with the idea of 'levels' of organization.

A 'level' is a way of recognizing the fact that a sentence is not a simple linear string of items. Rather, items are grouped together into units, which then work as wholes in relation to other units. Adult native-speakers do not have to be told that these units exist: they 'know' that they do, subconsciously, as a result of learning the language. (They may not be able to describe the elements they sense to be present, of course, for that is a more conscious task – the difference between 'knowing about' rather than just 'knowing' language, p. 191.)

The sentence *The big dogs enjoyed their unexpected bones* quickly yields evidence of a hierarchy of levels of organization. The smallest level of this hierarchy hardly needs an explanation. If asked to divide this sentence into its parts, most people would immediately identify the seven words. But this is not the whole story.

• Four of these words contain smaller units: *dog + -s, enjoy + -ed, un- + expect + -ed*, and *bone + -s*. The use of suffixes and prefixes shows that there is a level of structure within the word (the *morphological* level, §14).

• The first three words, and the last three, both combine into larger units: *the big dogs* and *their unexpected bones*. These larger units are called *phrases*, and they show that there is a level of structure between the word and the sentence.

• It would be possible to make the sentence bigger by linking it to a similar sequence of words: *The big dogs enjoyed their unexpected bones, and the little puppies liked the scraps.* The sentence now consists of two clauses (p. 216), showing that there can be a further level of structure between the phrase and the sentence.

These four levels – word, phrase, clause, sentence – comprise the grammatical hierarchy summarized in the figure (above), which also gives further examples of the units which operate at each level. The figure also suggests the possibility of a level of grammatical organization which is larger than the sentence: this is discussed on p. 232 and in §19.

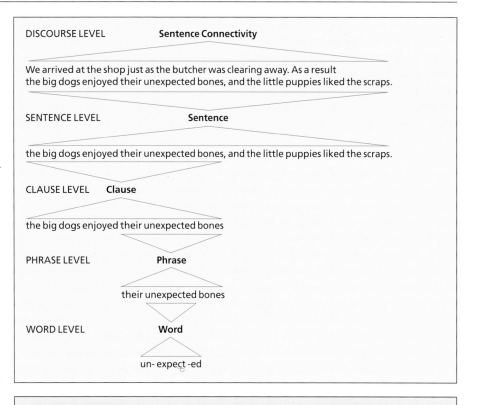

DISCOURSE LEVEL — **Sentence Connectivity**

We arrived at the shop just as the butcher was clearing away. As a result the big dogs enjoyed their unexpected bones, and the little puppies liked the scraps.

SENTENCE LEVEL — **Sentence**

the big dogs enjoyed their unexpected bones, and the little puppies liked the scraps.

CLAUSE LEVEL — **Clause**

the big dogs enjoyed their unexpected bones

PHRASE LEVEL — **Phrase**

their unexpected bones

WORD LEVEL — **Word**

un- expect -ed

FINDING GRAMMATICAL UNITS

The following sentences are taken from the regularized monologue on p. 214.

We usually went out quite soon after that. The children were always up at the crack of dawn with the farmer, and they went into the milking sheds and helped him feed the pigs. We didn't see the children. So we'd generally go for a tea somewhere, just in case supper was delayed.

Clause level
The conjunctions and other linking words have been omitted below. Note that the subject of *helped* has to be understood from the previous clause, as has the subject of *feed*. *Helped him feed the pigs* presents a problem of analysis, as some grammarians would take this construction as a single clause.

we usually went out quite soon after that
the children were always up at the crack of dawn with the farmer
they went into the milking sheds
helped him
feed the pigs
we didn't see the children

we'd generally go for a tea somewhere
just in case supper was delayed

Phrase level
Only multi-word phrases are listed below. However, it is important to note that in this approach the notion of *phrase* also extends to single words, as long as they are potentially expandable into a larger unit: for example, *supper* is considered an example of a *noun phrase* (p. 222) because it could be expanded into *our supper, the big supper*, etc. Grammarians can spend hours debating the merits and demerits of such decisions. The point shows that even a simple instruction as 'find the phrases' raises interesting questions of analysis. Similarly, there are issues over the analysis of clauses (see above) and words (see below).

went out
quite soon
after that
the children
were…up
at the crack of dawn
with the farmer
into the milking sheds
the pigs
didn't see
'd…go
for a tea
in case

was delayed

Word level
The existence of several irregular forms makes the analysis of word structure more complex than may appear at first sight: *went*, for example, is the past tense of *go*, and can thus be analysed as *go + -ed*.

usual*ly* (a derivational suffix, p. 211)
went (an irregular past tense form, p. 204)
child*ren* (the changed vowel of *child* is not apparent in the written form)
were (another irregular past tense form)
milk*ing* (a derivational suffix, p. 208)
sheds (*milking sheds* can also be analysed as a compound word, p. 129)
help*ed*
him (objective form of *he*, p. 203)
pigs
did*n't* (*did* is another irregular past tense form)
we*'d*
general*ly* (another derivational suffix)
somewhere (a compound form, p. 129)
was (another irregular past tense form)
delay*ed*

SENTENCE FUNCTIONS

Traditional grammars recognized four types of sentence function: *statement*, *question*, *command*, and *exclamation*. Some modern grammars, especially those which work within a framework of speech acts (p. 290), recognize a much larger range of functions. Even if we restrict ourselves to the four 'classical' types, though, there are certain refinements which need to be introduced. In particular, the notion of 'question' covers several different kinds of construction; the sentences called 'commands' express other kinds of meaning in addition to commanding; the notion of 'exclamation' is unacceptably vague; and there is an important sentence type (the 'echo' utterance) which fits into none of these four categories.

STATEMENTS

Almost all the sentences used in this book are statements. A statement is a sentence whose primary purpose is to 'state' – to convey information. Two criteria usually apply:

• The clause contains a subject (p. 220) – though in informal conversation this is sometimes omitted.

(I) Beg (your) pardon?
(I) Told you so.
(It) Looks like rain.

• The subject precedes the verb. Here too there are a few exceptions, such as when the clause begins with *hardly*, *barely*, or other 'negative' words.

Hardly had we left when it started to rain. (*not* *Hardly we had left…)

These sentences are traditionally said to have a *declarative* structure – a structure which 'declares' or 'makes something known'.

QUESTIONS

Questions are sentences which seek information. They fall into three main types, depending on the kind of reply they expect, and on how they are constructed. Sentences formed in these ways are said to have an *interrogative* structure – a structure which 'interrogates'.

• *Yes–no questions* allow an affirmative or negative reply – often just 'yes' or 'no'. The subject follows the auxiliary verb (p. 207).

Are they ready?
Is the plumber here?

In addition, a questioning tone of voice (p. 248) can turn a statement into a *yes–no* question. These questions have the structure of a declarative sentence, and only the question-mark shows their function in writing.

Mary's outside?
You've bought a new car?

• *Wh-questions* allow a reply from a wide range of possibilities. They begin with a question word, such as *what*, *why*, *where*, or *who*.

Where are you going?
Why don't they answer?

• *Alternative questions* require a reply which relates to the options given in the interrogative sentence. They always contain the connecting word *or*.

Will you be travelling by train or by bus?

EXCLAMATORY QUESTIONS

Some sentences resemble questions in their structure, but are actually being used as exclamations. They express the speaker's strong feelings, and ask the hearer to agree. Despite the presence of a negative element, they are strongly positive in meaning.

Hasn't she grown!
Wasn't it marvellous!

Often, both positive and negative forms of the sentence can be used, with very little difference in meaning. In such cases, the auxiliary verb and the subject are usually strongly stressed.

Wasn't he angry!
Was he angry! (I'll say he was!)

RHETORICAL QUESTIONS

These sentences also resemble questions in their structure, but they are used as if they were emphatic statements. The speaker does not expect an answer.

Who cares?
How should I know?
What difference does it make?

Public speakers, politicians, poets, and all who give monologues quite often use rhetorical questions as a means of making a dramatic point.

Is man an ape or an angel? (Disraeli)

There is always the risk, of course, in a public speech, that a member of the audience will choose to reply, in the pause which follows.
    Poets tend to self-question more than others:

Do I wake or sleep? (Keats)

but we are all prone to it:

Now, shall I stop here or add another sentence?

TAG QUESTIONS

Sometimes the interrogative structure is left to the end of the sentence, in the form of a *tag question*, which expects a *yes/no* kind of reply.

It's there, isn't it?
She's not in, is she?

The *n't* ending of some tag questions is replaced by *not* in formal English. In legal cross-examination we might hear:

They left early, did they not?

This usage is conversationally normal in some regional dialects, such as northern British and Irish.
    If we change the intonation (p. 248), we alter the meaning of a tag question. In many dialects, when the melody is rising, the sentence is 'asking'; when it is falling, the sentence is 'telling'. In writing, the punctuation can indicate the difference:

They're not in, are they?
    (I really want to know)
They're not in, are they!
    (I told you so)

But in speech this contrast can be unclear, prompting the complaint 'Are you asking me or telling me?'

Tag questions are illustrated further on p. 299.

TAGS, EH?

Informal English uses a few words which perform the same function as tag questions. They include *eh?*, *OK?*, and *right?* Dialects often have a distinctive form, such as Canadian *eh?* or Welsh *ay?* (pronounced [aɪ]). A joke told by Welsh singer and entertainer Max Boyce relies on this last example:

How do people in Bangor spell *Mississippi*?
M, ay? double s, ay? double s, ay? double p, ay?

DIRECTIVES

Directives are sentences which instruct someone to do something. They are often called commands, but this term is misleading. Commanding is just one of the many uses of directive sentences.

- Commanding: Sit down!
- Inviting: Have a drink.
- Warning: Mind your head!
- Pleading: Help me!
- Suggesting: Let's walk.
- Advising: Take an aspirin.
- Instructing: Turn left.
- Permitting: Help yourself.
- Requesting: Open the window, please.
- Meditating: Let me see.
- Expressing good wishes: Have a nice day!
- Expressing an imprecation: Go to hell!

In each case, the verb is in its basic form, with no endings (p. 204), and there is usually no subject element present. Structures of this type are called *imperatives* – from Latin *imperare* 'to command'.

Some directives do not use the basic pattern:

- They allow a subject, with a strong stress:

You be quiet!
Nobody move!

- They begin with *let*, followed by a subject:

Let me see.
Let us pray.
Let's go.

- They begin with *do* or *don't*:

Do come in.
Don't laugh.
Do not leave.

BUY NOW! PAY LATER!

Advertisements rely a great deal on imperative sentences. But not every verb can be used in a directive way, and there are several restrictions on the use of those which can. In particular, many verbs which express a state, rather than an activity, cannot be used as directives: we can say *Buy a new car* but not **Need a new car*. Nor may we use an imperative form of a verb along with a past time reference: we can say *Buy tomorrow!* but not **Buy yesterday!*

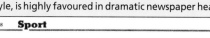

EXCLAMATIONS

Exclamations are sentences which show that a person has been impressed or roused by something. They often take the form of a single word or short phrase – a minor sentence (p. 216) such as *Gosh!*, *Oh dear!*, or *Of all the nerve!* But exclamations can have a major sentence status too, with a structure which

differentiates them from statements, questions, and directives.

- Their first element begins with *what* or *how*, and is followed by a subject and a verb, in that order:

What a lovely day it is!
What a mess they've made!
How nice they look!

- They also occur frequently in a reduced form, using only the first element:

What a lovely day!
What a mess!
How nice!

Sentences of this kind are said to possess an *exclamative* structure.

Exclamatives with subject and verb inverted are possible, but rare. They can sometimes be found in literary or mock-dramatic contexts:

How often have I cursed that terrible day!

The abbreviated exclamation, with its succinct and punchy style, is highly favoured in dramatic newspaper headlines.

ECHOES

The traditional classification of major sentences into statements, questions, commands (or directives), and exclamations ignores one other type of sentence: the *echo sentence*. It is used only in dialogue, and its purpose is to confirm, question, or clarify what the previous speaker has just said.

The essential feature of an echo utterance is that it reflects the structure of the preceding sentence, which it repeats in whole or in part. All types of sentence can be echoed.

Statements

A: John didn't like the film.
B: He didn't what?

Questions

A: Have you got my knife?
B: Have I got your wife?

Directives

A: Sit down here.
B: Down there?

Exclamations

A: What a lovely day!
B: What a lovely day, indeed!

Echoes sometimes sound impolite, unless accompanied by an apologetic 'softening' phrase, such as *I'm sorry* or *I beg your pardon*. This is most noticeable with the question *What did you say?*, which is often shortened to *What?* A common parental plea to children focuses on this form, often considered to be bad manners: *Don't say 'What?', say 'Pardon (me)'.*

INTELLIGENT ECHOES

In the film version of the novel *Being There*, by Jerzy Kosinski, Peter Sellers played the role of a simpleton gardener who repeats (in a slow, almost meditative style) what other people say to him. The result is that he is thought to be highly intelligent.

A similar strategy is not uncommon in life off the screen. For example, if we find ourselves out of our depth in a conversation, it is possible to convey an intelligent impression by occasionally echoing parts of what the other people are saying. Once, the present author was even congratulated by a town councillor for having such sensible ideas, when all he had been able to do was repeat, at irregular intervals, fragments of what had emerged in the councillor's own monologue.

CLAUSE ELEMENTS

All clauses are made up out of elements, each expressing a particular kind of meaning. Traditional grammars recognized two main elements, which they called the *subject* and the *predicate*. These make a useful starting-point for sentence analysis, but the predicate heading needs to be analysed further, in order to distinguish several very different kinds of construction. The present grammatical analysis recognizes five types of clause element, all of which appear in the following sentence:

That cyclist / has called / Dave / a fool / twice.

• The first element in this clause is the subject (S). The subject usually identifies the theme or topic of the clause. We are evidently talking about a cyclist.
• The second element is the verb (V). The verb expresses a wide range of meanings, such as actions, sensations, or states of being. Here we are talking about the action of calling, performed by the cyclist.
• The third element is the object (O). Objects identify who or what has been directly affected by the action of the verb. Here we are talking about Dave, who is the object of the cyclist's attention.
• The fourth element is the complement (C). Complements give further information about another clause element. Here, *a fool* adds to the meaning of *Dave* – Dave *is* a fool (according to the cyclist).
• The fifth element is the adverbial (A). Adverbials usually add extra information about the situation, such as the time of an action, its location, or its manner of being performed. Here, we are talking about the frequency of the calling. The cyclist was plainly very upset.

In Modern English, in about 90 per cent of the clauses which contain a subject, verb, and object, the subject precedes the verb, and the verb precedes the object. The language was not always like this (p. 44), and there are several important types of exception, notably in questions (p. 218).

ELEMENTS AND WORDS

As the examples on this and the previous page suggest, a clause element is not the same as a word. An element may be a single word, or several words. The following sentences each contain a subject, verb, and object, but there are varying numbers of words.

I	saw	Fred.
My uncle	has seen	Fred.
All the kids	know	dear old Fred.

VOCATIVES

A vocative (from Latin *vocare* 'to call') is a name used for the person(s) to whom a sentence is addressed. It may be there to attract attention (as in *Mike, phone for you*), or to express a particular social relationship or personal attitude (as in *Doctor, I need a tonic* or *Leave it alone, imbecile!*). In traditional grammar (p. 192), it was claimed to be a distinct noun 'case', and glossed by the word *O* – a usage now found only in religious contexts (*O God, who…*).

• The vocative is an optional element: it can be added to or removed from a sentence without affecting the rest of the construction.
• It may occur in various positions in a sentence, as in *(John) I'd like auntie (John) to be here (John)*.
• It is not an element of clause structure like subject or verb.
A vocative belongs to a whole sentence, however many clauses it contains, as in *Mary, come in, sit down, and tell me what happened.*

MY LORDS, LADIES, AND GENTLEMEN…

Vocatives can be of several kinds.

• Names, with or without titles: *David, Mrs Smith*.
• Family labels: *mum, uncle*.
• Markers of status or respect: *sir, my Lord*.
• Labels for occupations: *waiter, nurse*.
• Evaluative labels: *darling, pig, dear*.
• General labels: *lads, ladies and gentlemen*.
• The pronoun *you* (an extremely impolite use): *You, where's the phone?*
• Certain kinds of clause: *Come out, come out, whoever you are!*
• Some vocatives can be expanded: *old man, you fat fraud!*

ANALYSING COMPOUNDS

sunrise
'the sun rises' (S + V)

oil well
'the well contains oil' (S + O)

scarecrow
'it scares crows' (V + O)

Compounds are an important part of the lexicon (p. 129), but they can be usefully classified into types based on the kind of grammatical meaning they represent. *Popcorn*, for example, can be paraphrased as 'the corn pops', and the relation of *corn* to *pops* is that of subject to verb. The order of the elements (as in this example) does not necessarily correspond to that found in a grammatical sentence. A list of the chief grammatical relations involved follows.

Nouns
Subject + verb
sunrise, headache, hangman, popcorn, washing machine, working party, dancing girl
Verb + object
haircut, tax-payer, scarecrow, crime report, chewing-gum, window-cleaner, sightseeing
Verb + adverbial
living-room ('live in a room') playgoer ('go to a play')
Subject + object
motorcycle, windmill, oil well, gaslight, doorknob, table leg, postman,

chairperson
Subject + complement
('X.is Y' or 'X is like/for Y')
oak tree, handyman, darkroom, flypaper, goldfish, birdcage, tissue paper, blackboard

Adjectives
Verb + object
man-eating, breathtaking
Verb + adverbial
law-abiding, handmade, typewritten, widespread
Verbless
homesick, camera-ready, rock-hard, Franco-German

CLAUSE TYPES

Clause elements combine into a very small number of patterns. In fact, most sentences can be analysed into one of only seven basic clause types, each minimally consisting of two, three, or four elements:

S + V: I / yawned.
S + V + O: I / opened / the door.
S + V + C: I / am / ready.
S + V + A: I / went / to London.
S + V + O + O: I / gave / him / a pen.
S + V + O + C: I / got / my shoes / wet.
S + V + O + A: I / put / the box / on the floor.

There are a few other kinds of construction which can be derived from these basic types. They include directives (p. 219) and various kinds of elliptical sentences (p. 228).

• The subject usually appears before the verb in statements, and after the first verb in questions.
The boy yawned.
Are *you* going?
• The subject controls whether the verb is singular or plural in the third person of the present tense (p. 204).
She looks fine. *They* look fine.
• The subject controls the form of certain objects and complements:
I shaved *myself*. They shaved *themselves*.
• Some pronouns (p. 203) have a distinctive form when used as a subject:
I can see her. *She* can see me.
• Subjects can be noun phrases (including single nouns), pronouns, or certain kinds of subordinate clause (p. 226):
The train was late. *Mary* went home.
Beer, crisps, and cheese are for sale.
I like fishing. *What he said* was funny. (i.e. *It* was funny.)
• In this analysis, a series of noun phrases is analysed as a single clause element, not as a sequence of different elements. There is only *one* subject recognized per clause.

• Object elements usually follow the subject and verb in a clause. There are two types: *direct* and *indirect*. The direct object is the common one, typically referring to some person or thing directly affected by the action expressed by the verb.
The child lost *her ball*. I remember *the occasion*.
• The indirect object typically refers to an animate being which is the recipient of the action. In these cases, a direct object is usually present in the clause as well.
She gave *the dog* a stroke. I told *them* my news.
In these constructions, the indirect object precedes the direct. In such clauses as *I gave my paper **to the boy***, the order is reversed.
• Some pronouns (p. 203) have a distinctive form when used as an object:
She saw *him*. They asked *me*.
• Objects can be noun phrases (including single nouns), pronouns, or certain kinds of subordinate clause (p. 226):
I saw *our new house*. We asked *Fred*. Now hear *this*.
She said *I'd been foolish*. (i.e. She said *this*.)
• As with subjects, a set of connected noun phrases is analysed as a single element, in this analysis: *He saw **a cat, a dog, and a cow*** is S + V + O.

• The verb plays a central role in clause structure. It is the most obligatory of all the clause elements, as can be seen from such clauses as

That farmer	drinks	beer	by the bucketful.
S	V	O	A

We can omit the adverbial (*That farmer drinks beer*), the object (*That farmer drinks by the bucketful*), and even the subject, in casual style (*Drinks beer by the bucketful*, nodding in his direction), but we cannot omit the verb (**That farmer beer by the bucketful*). There is just one type of exception – 'verbless' clauses

such as *If possible* (i.e. if it is possible), *arrive early*.
• The verb element must be a verb phrase (including a single verb):
The bus *is coming*. The dog *ate* the crisps. I'*m* sorry.
In this analysis, only one verb element is allowed per clause, though this may consist of a sequence of auxiliary verbs as well as a main verb (p. 207), all of which combine to express a single grammatical meaning.
• The choice of verb largely determines what other elements are used in the clause, such as whether an object is present or not (p. 212).

• Complements express a meaning which *adds* to that of another clause element – either the subject (the *subject complement*) or the object (the *object complement*).
• A subject complement usually follows the subject and verb. The verb is most often a form of *be*, but it may also be one of a few other verbs that are able to link complements to their subjects in meaning. These are called *copular* ('linking') verbs.
She *is* a doctor. The bull *became* angry. (i.e. It *was* angry.)
The tune *sounds* lovely. (i.e. It *is* lovely.)
• An object complement usually follows the direct object, and its meaning relates to that element. The basic identity between them is shown in parenthesis.
They elected Clinton *president*. (i.e. He is president.)
It made me *angry*. (i.e. I was angry.)
• Complements can be noun phrases (including single nouns), adjective phrases (including single adjectives), pronouns, or certain kinds of subordinate clause (p. 226):
She is *a journalist*. They became *students*.
Arthur is *very happy*. The car's *ready*.
Where's *that*? That's *what I said*.
• When the complement is a noun phrase, it agrees in number with its corresponding element:
The *child* is an *angel* > The *children* are *angels*.
I find your *child* an *angel* > I find your *children angels*.

• Adverbials differ from other clause elements chiefly in that there can be an indefinite number of them in a single clause:
She arrived on the bus / on Thursday / in the rain . . .
• Adverbials can be used in several possible positions in the clause, though they are most common at the end:
Twice I asked him. I *twice* asked him. I asked him *twice*.
• Adverbials express a wide range of meanings, such as manner, place, and time:
I stayed *quietly at home all day*.
• Adverbials perform diverse roles in sentence construction. Some add information about an event; some link clauses together; and some add a comment about what is being expressed.
I walked *quietly*.
The bus was full. *However*, I found a seat.
Frankly, I think it's wrong.
• Adverbials can be adverb phrases (including single adverbs), prepositional phrases, some nouns and noun phrases, or certain kinds of subordinate clause (p. 226):
They ran *very quickly*. They walked *home*.
We walked *in the garden*. She phoned me *this morning*.
I laughed *when I saw you*.
• Some verbs require an adverbial to complete their meaning. These are the S + V + A and S + V + O + A constructions.
The path goes *around the field*. (We cannot say **The path goes*.)
I put the book *on the table*. (We cannot say **I put the book*.)

PHRASES

A phrase is a syntactic construction which typically contains more than one word, but which lacks the subject–predicate structure usually found in a clause (p. 220). Phrases are traditionally classified into types based on the most important word they contain: if this is a noun, for example, the phrase would be called a *noun phrase*; if an adjective, an *adjective phrase*; and so on. Six word classes (§15) – nouns, verbs, adjectives, adverbs, pronouns, and prepositions – are found as the identifying elements (or *heads*) of phrasal constructions. However, there are considerable differences between the syntactic patterns which can occur within each type of phrase, ranging from the very limited possibilities of pronoun phrases to the highly variable patterns found within noun phrases.

• *Pronoun phrases* are restricted to a small number of constructions, and tend not to be recognized as a productive type in English. Examples include *Silly me!*, *You there!*, *she herself*, *we all*, *nearly everyone*, and such relative clause constructions as *those who knew Fred* …They are usually analysed as a minor type of noun phrase.

• *Adverb phrases* are typically found as short intensifying expressions, such as *terribly slowly* and *very happily indeed*. Also common are such time phrases as *quite often* and *very soon*, and constructions of the type *as quickly (as I could)*.

• *Adjective phrases* are usually combinations of an adjective and a preceding intensifier, such as *very happy* and *not too awkward*. Other types include *cold enough* and a wide range of constructions which complement the adjective, such as *easy to please* and *loath to do it*.

• *Verb phrases* display very limited syntactic possibilities: a main verb preceded by up to four auxiliaries (p. 207), as in *may have gone* and *won't have been listening*. However, this limitation does not prevent the verb phrase from expressing a wide range of meanings to do with time, mood, and manner of action.

• By contrast, *noun phrases* allow an extremely wide range of syntactic possibilities, from such simple constructions as *the hat* to such complex phrases as *not quite all the fine new hats which were on sale*. They need to be described separately (see right).

• *Prepositional phrases* are combinations of a preposition plus a noun phrase: *in the back garden*, *beneath the hedge*. They typically perform the role of adverbial in a clause: *I saw it **in the garden*** = *I saw it **there***. They are also adjectival: *the linguist **with the red beard***.

NOUN PHRASE STRUCTURE

The noun phrase (NP) is the main construction which can appear as the subject, object, or complement of a clause (p. 221). It consists essentially of a noun or noun-like word which is the most important constituent of the phrase: *a fat cat*, *the horses in the stable*, *the poor*, *ten Chinese*. Sometimes the noun appears alone in its phrase (*Cats are nice*). More often, it is accompanied by one or more other constituents, some of which are themselves fairly complex syntactic units in their own right. As a result, noun phrases are more varied in their construction than any other kind of phrase in English.

The parts of a noun phrase
No matter how complex a noun phrase is, it can be analysed into one or more of the following four constituents:

• The *head* is the most important constituent, around which any other constituents cluster. It is the head which controls any agreement with other parts of the sentence. Thus we have *His new **book is** interesting* alongside *His new **books are** interesting*, and *The **girl** in the garden saw it **herself*** alongside *The **boy** in the garden saw it **himself***.
• The *determiner* appears before the noun. This constituent decides ('determines') what kind of noun is in the phrase – in particular, whether it is definite or indefinite, proper or common, count or noncount (pp. 208–9). Words such as *a*, *those*, *some*, and *any* are determiners. It is not essential for a noun phrase to have a determiner (for example, proper nouns do not take one), but most noun phrases do, and the commonest determiners (*the* and *a*) are among the most frequent words in the language.

The determiner can be the centre of its own cluster of words which share in the expression of quantity. In the present approach, those which appear before the determiner are called (logically enough) *predeterminers*; they include *all the people*, *twice the cost*, *half the money*. Those which immediately follow the determiner, preceding any adjectives which may occur, are called *postdeterminers*; they are chiefly the numerals (*my three fat cats*, *the second big party*) and a few other quantifying words (such as *many* and *several*).
• The *premodification* comprises any other words appearing between the determiner and the head noun – mainly adjectives or adjective-like words. In the phrase *those lovely old French wooden spoons*, everything before *those* and *spoons* is said to 'premodify' the noun. (In some grammars, the notion of premodification is broader, and includes *everything* in the noun phrase which appears before the head, including the determiner and its satellites.)
• The *postmodification* comprises everything which appears in the phrase after the head. The chief types are prepositional phrases (*the car **in the garage***), finite clauses (*the film **that I saw***), and nonfinite clauses (*the new car **parked outside***). Adverbs and adjectives are also sometimes used to 'postmodify' the noun, as in *the journey **home*** and *something **different***.

GROWING NOUN PHRASES

Buns	are for sale.
The buns	are for sale.
All the buns	are for sale.
All the currant buns	are for sale.
Not quite all the currant buns	are for sale.
Not quite all the hot buttered currant buns	are for sale.
Not quite all the hot buttered currant buns on the table	are for sale.
Not quite all the hot buttered currant buns on show on the table	are for sale.
Not quite all the many fine interesting-looking hot buttered home-made currant buns which grandma cooked on show on the table	are for sale.

Predeterminer	*Determiner*	*Postdeterminer*	*Premodification*	*Head*	*Postmodification*
Not quite all	the	many	fine…currant	buns	which…table

This postcard message shows a number of 'bare minimum' NPs, consisting of a noun only, as well as several Determiner + Noun constructions. The longest example also shows one NP (*the boat*) being used as part of the postmodification of another.

POST CARD

Dear Mum   *Friday*
We're having a smashing time, though the weather's not brilliant. Paul's bought a new jacket to replace the blue monstrosity that (luckily) was pinched on the boat. You'll love the colour this time! And it was half the price!! Now we're off to see some Roman ruins — with brollies, of course. We'll try and phone Sunday morning. Hope you're all well. Paul sends his love.

Kate   X X

Aspects of noun phrase structure

There are so many facets to the structure of the noun phrase that it is not possible to refer to all of them in a general book. No other syntactic unit in English presents such possibilities for structural variation. One consequence of this is that distinctive noun phrase patterns are often part of the stylistic identity of a text, as can be seen in such varieties as popular journalese (p. 380) and scientific writing (p. 372). Another is that several of the meanings expressed by the noun phrase are extremely subtle, requiring a careful consideration of many examples before their function can be consciously appreciated. And even in the 1990s, not all of the rules governing the way noun phrases work are fully understood.

Legal English displays a marked preference for postmodification in the noun phrase, as can be seen in this extract from an insurance agreement. When the structure is presented visually in this way, the meaning is fairly easy to grasp. Without such assistance, the language becomes dense and confusing – and a target of Plain English campaigns (p. 376).

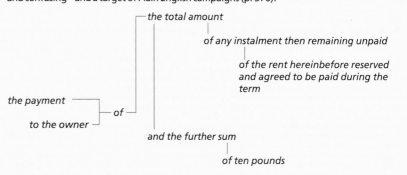

THE ARTICLES

The article system is a good example of the subtle meanings which the noun phrase can express. The contrasts are not easy to define – despite the fact that most features of the system have been intuitively grasped by the time a child is 5 years old.

Three concepts are involved, two of which are familiar from traditional grammar: the *definite article* (the), the *indefinite article* (a or an), and the absence of an article (the *zero article*). The use of these forms affects the meaning of the noun phrase – in particular, allowing us to think of nouns in a *specific* way, referring to individuals (*A/the dog is eating*) or in a *generic* way, referring to a general class or species (*A/the dog is an interesting animal*, *Dogs are nice*).

The definite article
• *The* can refer to the immediate situation or to someone's general knowledge:

Have you fed *the dog*?
He was wounded in *the war,...*

• *The* can refer back to another noun (what is sometimes called *anaphoric reference*):

She bought a car and a bike, but she used *the bike* more.

• *The* can refer forward to the words following the head noun (*cataphoric reference*):

I've always liked *the wines* of Germany.

• *The* can refer to human institutions that we sporadically use, attend, observe, etc.:

I went to *the theatre*.
I watched *the news* on TV.

The indefinite article
• *A(n)* does not presuppose that a noun has been mentioned already. In *The book arrived*, the speaker assumes we know which book is being referred to. In *A book arrived*, no such knowledge is assumed.
• *A(n)* often expresses a general state of affairs, or a notion of quantity:

I'm training to be a *linguist*.
He's scored a *hundred*.
Take this six times a *day*.

The zero article
The article is often omitted in idiomatic usage when talking about human institutions and routines, means of transport, periods of time, meals, and illnesses:

go to bed   in winter
travel by car   have lunch
at dawn   caught
                         pneumonia

A common error of non-native learners of English is to introduce an article in those cases where it is impossible or inappropriate, as in *I shall go to the bed now*, *I have caught a pneumonia*.

THE ORDER OF PREMODIFIERS

Why do you think we make Nuttall's Mintoes such a devilishly smooth cool creamy minty chewy round slow velvety fresh clean solid buttery taste?

This advertising caption from the 1960s probably holds the record for number of adjectives in a single noun phrase. It is of course a highly unusual example – not just because of its length and its use of unexpected word combinations (e.g. *taste* being described as *round* or *solid*, p. 162), but because the adjectives do not display any restrictions on their order. They could be shuffled and dealt out again, and the result would probably be just as acceptable.

The following example shows that not all premodifiers can be used in this random kind of way.

a nice big cardboard box
not
*a big nice cardboard box
*a cardboard nice big box
*a nice cardboard big box

or any of the other possible sequences. This is the kind of grammatical rule that most people never think twice about. However, working out the factors which make one sequence acceptable and others not is an intricate business, and one that is still not entirely understood.

ADJECTIVE ZONES

Examples such as the following suggest that there are four main 'zones' within the premodifying section of a noun phrase, here labelled I, II, III, and IV.

I've got the same big red garden chairs as you.
  I   II   III   IV

IV Words which are usually nouns, or closely related to nouns, are placed next to the head. They include nationality adjectives (*American*, *Gothic*), noun-like adjectives which mean 'involving' or 'relating to' (*medical*, *social*), and straightforward nouns (*tourism brochure*, *Lancashire factory*). Thus we say:

an old Lancashire factory *not* *a Lancashire old factory
a bright medical student *not* *a medical bright student

III Participles and colour adjectives are placed immediately in front of any in zone IV: *missing, deserted, retired, stolen, red, green*. Thus we say:

an old red suit *not* *a red old suit
the red tourism brochures *not* *the tourism red brochures

I Adjectives with an absolute or intensifying meaning come first in the sequence, immediately after the determiner and its satellites: *same, certain, entire, sheer, definite, perfect, superb*. Thus we say:

the entire American army *not* *the American entire army
the perfect red suit *not* *the red perfect suit

II All other adjectives (the vast majority in the language) occur in this zone: *big, slow, angry, helpful*, and all those in the advertising caption above. Thus we say:

a superb old house *not* *an old superb house (with a zone I item)
an old stolen car *not* *a stolen old car (with a zone III item)
an old social disease *not* *a social old disease (with a zone IV item)

There are also signs of 'zones within zones'. For example, we tend to say *a beautiful new dress* not *a new beautiful dress*, suggesting that evaluative adjectives in zone II precede other kinds of adjectives there. We also tend to say *a recognizable zig-zag pattern* not a *zig-zag recognizable pattern*, suggesting that more abstract adjectives precede more concrete ones. But, as the word 'tend' suggests, the rules are not hard and fast.

VERB PHRASE MEANINGS

With only a few verb endings to take into account (p. 204) and a very limited range of auxiliary verbs and sequences (p. 212), the verb phrase would seem to provide the linguist with an easy task of syntactic description. But appearances are deceptive. It is true that the possible patterns of constituents can be described quite quickly, but the meanings which each pattern can convey are extremely difficult to state, being influenced by what else is happening in the sentence, and even by the meaning of particular types of verb. For example, an accompanying adverbial (p. 221) can dramatically alter the period of time to which a verb form refers: *I'm leaving tomorrow* is hours away from *I'm leaving* (said while going through the door). And a verb which expresses a specific action works differently from one which expresses a state of awareness: we can say *I was kicking it* but not **I was knowing it.* Teasing out the various meaning contrasts of tense, aspect, mood, and voice makes the verb phrase one of the most intriguing areas of English syntax.

TENSES

One of the important functions of the verb is to indicate the time at which an action takes place. The term *tense* is traditionally used to refer to the way verbs change their form to express this meaning. On this definition, English has only two tenses – present and past – though traditional grammars would extend the notion to include various kinds of auxiliary verb usage as well (p. 196).

Time is often shown as a line, on which the present moment is located as a continuously moving point. But there is no identity between tense and time. Present and past tenses can refer to all parts of the time line.

Past Time   Present Time   Future Time
            (includes **now**)

PRESENT TENSE

Three uses refer to present time.
• The *state present* is used for timeless statements or 'eternal truths': *Oil floats on water, Two and two make four.*
• The *habitual present* is used for repeated events. There is usually an accompanying adverbial of frequency: *I go to town each week.*
• The *instantaneous present* is used when the action begins and ends approximately at the moment of speech. It is common in demonstrations and sports commentaries: *Smith passes to Brown.*

Three uses refer to other times:

• The *historic present* describes the past as if it were happening now: *I hear you've resigned.*
• In jokes and imaginative writing, a similar use promotes *dramatic immediacy*: *We look outside (dear reader) and we see an old man in the street.*
• With some time adverbials, the present tense helps to refer to a specific course of action in *future time* (see above right): *We leave tomorrow.*

PAST TENSE

Most uses refer to an action or state which has taken place in the past, at a definite time, with a gap between its completion and the present moment. Specific events, states, and habitual actions can all be express-ed with this tense: *I arrived yesterday* (event), *They were upset* (state), *They went to work every day* (habitual).

The past tense is also used for present or future time.
• The *attitudinal past* reflects a tentative state of mind, giving a more polite effect than would be obtained by using the present tense: *Did you want to leave?* (compare the more direct *Do you want to leave?*)
• The *hypothetical past* expresses what is contrary to the speaker's beliefs. It is especially used in *if*-clauses: *I wish I had a bike* (i.e. I haven't got one).
• In indirect speech (p. 230), a past tense used in the verb of 'saying' allows the verb in the reported clause to be past tense as well, even though it refers to present time: *Did you say you had no money?* (i.e. you haven't any now).

FUTURE TENSE?

English has no future tense ending (unlike Latin, French, and many other languages). Rather, future time is expressed by a variety of other means. One of these – the use of *will* or *shall* – is often loosely referred to as the 'future tense'. But this usage changes the meaning of the word 'tense' so that it no longer refers only to the use of verb endings. There are in fact six main ways of referring to future time.

• *Will*, *shall*, or *'ll* followed by the infinitive without *to* (*I'll see you then*) or the progressive form (*I'll be seeing you*). This is by far the commonest use.

• *Be going to*, followed by the infinitive: *I'm going to ask him.* This common informal use (often pronounced *gonna*) usually suggests that the event will take place very soon.
• The present progressive (p. 225), stressing the way a future event follows on from an arranged plan: *The match is starting at 2 p.m.* The happening is usually imminent.
• The simple present tense, often implying definiteness: *I leave soon, Go to bed.*
• The use of *be to*, *be about to*, *have to*, and a few others, all expressing a future action at various removes from the present: *She's to sit here, She's about to leave.*
• The modal verbs (p. 212), which also convey a future implication: *I may/might/could/should travel by bus.*

SHALL OR WILL?

Traditional grammars drew a sharp distinction between the use of *will* and *shall* (p. 194).

• To express *future time*, they recommended *shall* with first persons, and *will* with second and third persons: *I/we shall go, You/he/she/it/they will go.*
• To express an *intention to act*, they recommended *will* with first persons, and *shall* with the others: *I/we will go, You/he/she/it/they shall go.*

On this basis, sentences such as *I will be 20 soon* were condemned as wrong, because (it was said) we cannot 'intend' to be a certain age.

Modern usage does not observe this distinction. Indeed, it may never have existed in the language, but only in the minds of grammarians anxious to impose order on a 'messy' area of usage. The issue is of less relevance today, as *shall* has come to be increasingly replaced by *will* in several varieties. Even in conservative southern British English, it is now rare to find *shall* in the second and third person (*Shall you go?, Mary shall sit there*), and it is becoming less common in the first person. Nonetheless, usage variation remains, as shown by these headlines, both appearing on the same day and ostensibly reporting the same royal remark.

ASPECTS OF ASPECTS

Aspect refers to how the time of action of the verb is regarded – such as whether it is complete, in progress, or showing duration. English uses two types of aspectual contrast, which it expresses with auxiliary verbs: the *perfective* and the *progressive*. Such contrasts were called tenses in traditional grammar (e.g. the 'perfect tense'), but far more is involved than simply the expression of time, and indeed the semantic analysis of aspect has proved to be one of the most complex areas of English linguistics. The examples below illustrate the topic, but by no means indicate the extent of this complexity.

Perfective aspect

This is constructed using forms of the auxiliary verb *have*.

• The *present perfective* is chiefly used for an action continuing up to the present. This meaning of 'current relevance' contrasts with the past tense meaning:

I've lived in Paris for a year (and I still do).
I lived in Paris for a year (but I don't now).

In informal American English, there is a strong tendency to use the past tense instead of the present perfective – a trend which has begun to affect non-US varieties also.

US: Did you eat?
 You told me already.
UK: Have you eaten?
 You've told me already.

• The *past perfective* also expresses 'anterior time', but in an earlier time frame. Thus, *I am sorry that I have missed the train*, put into the past, becomes *I was sorry that I had missed the train*.

Specific events, states, and habitual actions can all be expressed using the perfective aspect.

He *has/had built* a car. (event)
The house *has/had been* empty for years. (state)
He's/'d *done* it often. (habitual)

Progressive aspect

Forms of *be* can be used along with the *-ing* form of the main verb (p. 204) to express an event in progress at a given time. This is the *progressive* (also called the *continuous*) aspect. It is used with both tenses and with both perfective aspects. Non-progressive forms are known as *simple* forms.

Simple	Progressive
They jump	They're jumping
They jumped	They were jumping
They've jumped	They've been jumping
They'd jumped	They'd been jumping

With the progressive, the usual implication is that the activity is taking place over a limited period, and is not necessarily complete. By contrast, the simple aspect tends to stress the unity or completeness of the activity. The contrast can be seen in these sentences:

I live in France. (permanently)
I'm living in France. (at present)

Only a small proportion of all verb phrases appear in the progressive form, and most of those are found in conversation. On the facing page, for example, the text contains 90 verb phrases (excluding the examples), but only a sixth of these use a progressive.

TWO VOICES

The action expressed by a clause can often be viewed in either of two ways.

The dog saw the cat.
The cat was seen by the dog.

This kind of contrast is referred to as *voice*. The first type of construction is known as the *active voice*. The second, which is far less common, is the *passive voice*.

Most verbs which take an object (transitive verbs, p. 212) can appear in both active and passive constructions: *kick, jump, eat, break*, etc. There are just a few exceptions, such as *resemble* and most uses of *have*: *I had a car* does not transform into **A car was had by me*.

The passive is infrequent in speech. In writing, it is more common in informative than in imaginative prose, especially in contexts which demand an objective, impersonal style, such as scientific and official publications. When it is over-used, it tends to attract criticism, especially from those campaigning for clearer forms of English in official documents (p. 376), and many writers have been influenced by their arguments. But passives cannot be dispensed with entirely. They give writers the option of an impersonal style, which can be very useful in contexts where it is irrelevant to state who actually carried out an action. That elements X and Y *were mixed* to form compound Z is usually the important point, not that it was me, Mary, John, or Dr Smith who did the mixing.

HOW TO FORM PASSIVES FROM ACTIVES

• Move the subject (p. 221) of the active verb to the end of the clause, making it the passive agent. Add *by*.
• Move the object of the active verb to the front of the clause, making it the passive subject.
• Replace the active verb phrase by a passive one – usually a form of the auxiliary verb *be* followed by the *-ed* participle (p. 204).

Get can also be used as a passive auxiliary, especially in contexts where we want to focus attention on the (usually unpleasant) event affecting the subject. *I got kicked at the match* reports the perception of a somewhat more vicious event than *I was kicked at the match*. The use of *get* is avoided in formal style, and even in informal style it is much less frequent than *be* (apart from in invective, such as *Get stuffed!*).

Another option is to omit the *by*-phrase agent. Indeed, this phrase is missing in around 80 per cent of passive clauses, usually because the addition of an agent would be to state the obvious: *Jack fought Mike and was beaten (by Mike)*. Sometimes, though, the omission is deliberate, either because the agent is not known (*The car's been stolen*) or because the speaker does not want it emphasized – as when someone returning a damaged library book says, neutrally, *I'm afraid this page has been torn*, rather than adding *by me*.

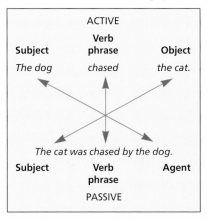

ACTIVE

Subject	Verb phrase	Object
The dog	*chased*	*the cat.*

The cat was chased by the dog.

Subject	Verb phrase	Agent

PASSIVE

This illustration, taken from *The Cambridge Encyclopedia of Earth Sciences*, shows a typical use of the passive in scientific prose. Each sentence has an example, and (as is often the case with captions) two of them have agents (*by*-phrases) expressed.

6.15: *The satellite Starlette launched by the European Space Agency in February 1975. The satellite is a sphere of 250 mm diameter and has sixty reflectors distributed over its surface. Its core is made mainly of uranium giving it a weight of 35 kg and a density of about 18 kg/m³. The satellite is tracked by lasers as a means of determining the Earth's gravity field and tidal deformation.*

MULTIPLE SENTENCES

Up to this point in Part III, most of the sentences illustrated contain only one clause (p. 220): they are *simple sentences*. But many sentences can be immediately analysed into more than one clause: they are *multiple sentences*. In fact, multiple sentences form the majority of the sentences in formal writing, and are common in everyday conversation too. The kind of monologue reported on p. 214, although presenting several problems of analysis, makes it plain that much of the spontaneous character of conversational speech is due to the way it uses multiple sentence constructions. These constructions are often classified into two broad types, both recognized in traditional grammar (p. 192): *compound sentences* and *complex sentences*.

Compound sentences

In compound sentences, the clauses are linked by *coordination* – usually, by the *coordinating conjunctions* (p. 213) *and*, *or*, or *but*. Each clause can in principle stand as a sentence on its own – in other words, act as an *independent clause*, or *main clause*. Tree diagram A (above right) shows the 'balance' between two clauses linked in this way. The same analysis would be made even if one of the clauses had elements omitted due to ellipsis (p. 228). In *I cycled as far as Oxford and Mary as far as Reading*, *Mary as far as Reading* can – once the ellipsis has been 'filled out' – stand as a main clause: *Mary cycled as far as Reading*. 'Main', in this context, has a purely grammatical sense, and does not have its everyday general meaning of 'most important'.

Complex sentences

In complex sentences, the clauses are linked by *subordination*, using such *subordinating conjunctions* as *because*, *when*, and *since* (p. 213). Here, one clause (called the *subordinate clause*) is made dependent upon another (the main clause). This can be seen in tree diagram B (below right). The subordinate clause cannot stand as a sentence on its own. *When Mike dropped the plates* needs some other clause before it can be used.

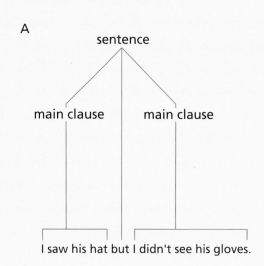

A

I saw his hat but I didn't see his gloves.

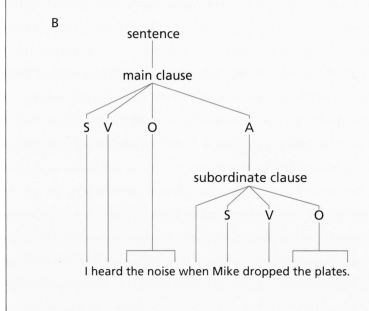

B

I heard the noise when Mike dropped the plates.

The adverbial identity of the subordinate clause in B can be tested using the technique of substitution. The clause *when Mike dropped the plates* can be replaced by an adverb of time, such as *then: I heard the noise then*.

This example shows the importance of clause elements in carrying out the analysis of complex sentences. If one is unable to distinguish between subjects, verbs, objects, complements, and adverbials in single clauses (see p. 221), the prospects of carrying out a successful analysis of a multiple sentence are slim.

ELEMENTS AS CLAUSES

Subordinate clauses can replace the whole of any clause element except the verb. Their grammatical function can always be tested by replacing the clause with a simpler unit whose identity is known, such as a pronoun, adjective, adverb, or noun phrase. A clause as adverbial has already been illustrated above. Here are examples of clauses as subject, object, and complement.

Clause as subject

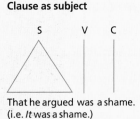

That he argued was a shame.
(i.e. *It* was a shame.)

Clause as object

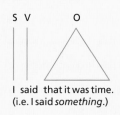

I said that it was time.
(i.e. I said *something*.)

Clause as complement

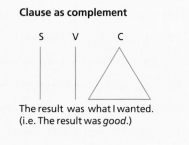

The result was what I wanted.
(i.e. The result was *good*.)

MULTIPLE STRUCTURES

Both compound and complex sentences can contain several instances of coordination or subordination.

- With *multiple coordination*, the analysis is simple, as seen in tree diagram C. The continual use of *and* to build up a long sentence is by no means unusual, as the real-life example on p. 214 suggests.

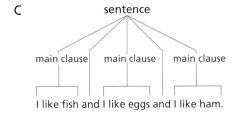

C

I like fish and I like eggs and I like ham.

- With *multiple subordination*, we must take special care to keep the different 'levels' of subordination apart. In tree diagram D, the main clause is *He said [something]*. The first subordinate clause tells us what the speaker said ('We will eat when the cafe opens'), and is therefore the object of the verb *said*. The second subordinate clause tells us when they would eat ('when the cafe opens'), and is an adverbial modifying *eat*.

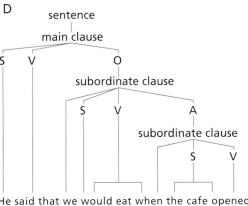

D

He said that we would eat when the cafe opened.

- Several instances of subordination may occur 'at the same level'. The sentence *What I say is what I think* may seem complex at first sight, but in fact it has a simple three-part structure, just like *That is that*, as shown in tree diagram E.

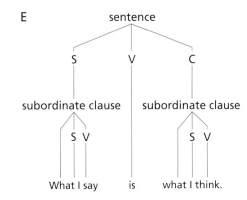

E

What I say   is   what I think.

- Coordination and subordination may of course occur in the same sentence, to produce a *compound-complex sentence*. This possibility is shown in tree diagram F. These are among the most complicated sentence structures to draw, but the sentences these diagrams represent are by no means unusual. A child of 9 could have said the sentence analysed in the diagram, which only goes to show how much grammatical ability we have all unconsciously assimilated without realizing it.

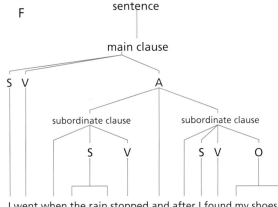

F

I went when the rain stopped and after I found my shoes.

COORDINATION AT OTHER LEVELS

A coordinating conjunction can join any two syntactic units, as long as they have the same status in the sentence. In addition to linking clauses, it can link noun phrases, adjectives, pronouns, and several other forms.

I bought *a paper* and *a book*.
We were *hot* and *dirty*.
It's *them* or *us*.

There is theoretically no limit to the number of units which can be connected in this way.

Coordination seems a simple grammatical matter, but it has some hidden subtleties. To begin with, the different conjunctions express a range of meanings. For example, *and* can convey more than simple addition: in *I ran hard and (therefore) caught the bus*, it expresses 'result'; in *I woke up and (then) got dressed*, it expresses 'time sequence'. When the meaning is one of addition, we may reverse the order of clauses: *I take the bus and she takes the train* can become *She takes the train and I take the bus*. When other meanings are involved, we may not: **I caught the bus and (therefore) I ran hard*, **I got dressed and (then) I woke up*.

Moreover, when two phrases are linked by *and*, they may or may not retain their separate grammatical roles. Compare the following two sentences:

Matthew and Ben are strong.
Matthew and Ben are alike.

The two sentences look the same, but further analysis shows they are different. In the first case, we can say *Matthew is strong and Ben is strong*. Each phrase can be expanded into its own clause. But in the second case, this cannot happen: we cannot say **Matthew is alike and *Ben is alike*. There is something about *alike* which forces the two nouns to work together. Similarly, *Arthur and Joanna have separated* cannot be expanded into **Arthur has separated and Joanna has separated*. Cases of this kind add complexity and interest to what initially seems a straightforward area of English syntax.

MORE AND MORE USES OF AND

There are several idiomatic uses of *and* which are especially common in informal speech and often criticized in writing.

- In such constructions as *I'll try and see him*, *and* is not functioning as a coordinator, but as an informal equivalent of the infinitive particle *to* (p.204): *I'll try to see him*.
- Likewise, in such constructions as *The room was nice and warm*, *nice and* is being used as an intensifying item (similar to *very*), and not as a coordinator. *He was well and truly drunk* is another example.
- By coordinating a word with itself, special meanings are expressed. In *The car went slower and slower*, the sense is one of intensification. In *They talked and talked*, it is continuous action. A particularly interesting usage is found in *There are roses and roses*, meaning 'Everyone knows that some roses are better/worse than others'.

...and then there are roses!

OTHER SYNTACTIC ISSUES

This exploration of English grammar is not intended to be comprehensive, but only to convey some of the interesting issues which arise when we engage in the task of syntactic analysis. The topics so far have related to the analysis of clauses, and to the ways clauses combine into sentences. The remaining pages of Part III deal with issues which go beyond the structure of an individual clause, involving sentences as wholes, and even sentence sequences (p. 232).

Abbreviating the sentence

There are two main ways in which a sentence can be shortened, to avoid saying or writing the same thing twice.

• A *pro-form* can be used – a word which replaces or refers to a longer construction in a sentence. The first process, replacement (or substitution), can be seen in *I've bought a new coat and Mary's bought one too*, where the pro-form *one* replaces the noun phrase *a new coat*. The second process, referring to another construction, can be seen in *The children hurt themselves*, where the pro-form *themselves* refers back to the noun phrase *the children*. Here, *themselves* does not replace *the children*, but simply refers back to it. *The children hurt the children* would mean that some children hurt some other children. When the pro-form has the same meaning (or 'reference') as another construction, but does not replace it, we talk about pro-form *co-reference*.

• *Ellipsis* occurs when part of a sentence is left out because it would otherwise repeat what is said elsewhere. In *I'd like to eat that biscuit, but I won't*, the second clause is elliptical, with *eat that biscuit* being omitted. People usually find the full form of such sentences unnecessary or irritating, and use ellipsis to achieve a more acceptable economy of statement. Conversation dialogues are full of it. If ellipsis were not used, our sentences would become gradually longer as a conversation progressed.

A: Where are you going?
B: To the shops. (i.e. I am going to the shops)
A: Why? (i.e. Why are you going to the shops?)
B: To get some bread. (i.e. I am going to the shops to get some bread)
A: Is John going with you? (i.e. Is John going with you to the shops to get some bread?)

In most cases, the ellipsis refers to something which has previously been said, but sometimes it anticipates what is about to be said: *Don't ask me why, but the shop has sold out of bread* is desirably short for *Don't ask me why the shop has sold out of bread, but the shop has sold out of bread*.

WHAT CAN BE A PRO-FORM?

• Pro-forms used in co-reference are usually definite pronouns (p. 210), such as *she, they, myself, his, theirs, that,* and *such*. We can also use a few definite adverbs of time or space, such as *then, there,* and *here*.

Mat's ill. *He's* got flu.
My hat's red. *Hers* is green.
I'm off to town. See you *there*.

• Pro-forms used in substitution can be either definite or indefinite. They are mostly indefinite pronouns (p. 210), such as *one(s), some, none, either, few, many, several, all,* and *both*. We can also use a few adverbs, such as *so* and *thus*, and the verb *do* plays an important role in such constructions as *do so*.

I have change. Do you want *some*?
Have you seen the new designs? I've bought *several*.
I asked him to leave, and he *did (so)*.

• Most pro-forms replace or refer to some or all of a noun phrase (p. 222); but a few other constructions can be involved. Adverb pro-forms relate to adverbials, as in *Martha went to the shops and I went **there** too*. *Do* relates to a part of the clause containing the verb: *Martha went to the shops and I **did** too* (where *did* replaces *went to the shops*). *So* can replace an object, a complement, an adverbial, or even a whole clause:

A: I'm not feeling well.
B: I thought so. (i.e. I thought that you're not feeling well)

NEVER A TRUER WORD

This extract, from one of the articles written by British humorist Miles Kington for *The Independent* (26 July 1993), relies for much of its impact on the succinct style which the use of pro-forms and ellipsis can convey. The aim of the interview is to obtain advice on how to get through life from 'an expert on clichés'. Because clichés rely greatly on verbosity, and are usually found in full, to see them in an abbreviated, catechism-like form produces a striking stylistic effect.

Q. What is life?
A. Life is what you make it.
Q. What kind of life is it?
A. It is a hard life.
Q. But is it a good life?
A. Yes, if you don't weaken.
Q. How does one get through life?

A. One travels down life's road.
Q. What kind of road is it?
A. A bumpy road.
Q. How do you start?
A. As you mean to go on.
Q. But what kind of start do you need in life?
A. A good one.
Q. How is this acquired?
A. By working hard to get the right qualifications.
Q. What does this involve?
A. Burning the midnight oil.
Q. But not the candle at both ends?
A. Oh, certainly not. At the same time, all work and no play makes a chap a dull boy.
Q. What is the chap's name?
A. Jack.
Q. How do parents contribute to this good start in life?
A. They scrimp.
Q. Is that all?
A. No. They also save.

Q. But what of those who have no scrimping and saving parents, and not even the right qualifications?
A. They must make their own way in life.
Q. By what do they pull themselves up?
A. Their own bootstraps.
Q. To what educational establishments do they later claim to have gone?
A. The university of life.
Q. Is this academy known by any other name?
A. Yes. The school of hard knocks...

Miles Kington

HOW DO WE KNOW WHAT HAS BEEN LEFT OUT?

Faced with an elliptical sentence, there are three ways in which we can work out what has been omitted.

• We can look at the surrounding text. In *I asked for some soup and then for some bread*, the ellipsis in the second clause (*I asked*) can be easily identified just by referring to the words in the first clause.
• We can use our knowledge of English grammar. In a telegram, where the amount paid is based on the number of words used, there is a natural tendency to omit predictable items. These can be restored using our intuition. We automatically read in the auxiliary verbs and prepositions required to

make sense of *John arriving Holyhead station today 3 p.m.* And we deal with newspaper headlines similarly, automatically adding a verb and articles in order to interpret NURSE TO LEAVE, SAYS JUDGE.
• We can look at the situation in which the sentence is used. In conversation, a very common ellipsis involves the omission of the subject and/or auxiliary verb; but there is never a problem deciding what is missing. Simply by observing the situation, we see which people are involved and what the time reference is.

Want a drink?
Serves you right.
You hungry?
Good to see you.
Told you so!

ADDING A COMMENT

People often wish to make a comment, or express an attitude, about what they are saying or the way they are saying it. How does the grammar of the language enable them to do this? The answers to this question require novel terminology, as this issue was never addressed in traditional grammar (p. 192).

Disjuncts

An important role is played by a type of adverbial (p. 221) here called a *disjunct*.

• Some disjuncts convey the speaker's comment about the style or form of what is being said – expressing the conditions under which the listener should interpret the accompanying sentence. In *Frankly (said Jane), Charles should have gone by bus*, Jane is not just saying that 'Charles should have gone by bus', but is adding a comment about how she is making her point – she is 'being frank'. There are many words of this kind, such as *honestly, literally, briefly, strictly,* and *confidentially*.

• Other disjuncts make an observation about the truth of a clause, or a value judgment about its content. In *Fortunately, Charles caught the bus*, Jane is not just saying that 'Charles caught the bus', but that (in her opinion) it was fortunate that he did so. Other words of this kind include *curiously, foolishly, regrettably, undoubtedly,* and *hopefully* (which was arbitrarily singled out for adverse criticism during the 1980s by purist commentators on usage).

Comment clauses

Disjuncts may be words or phrases, and they may even have a clausal character, as can be seen in the sequence *regrettably, to my regret,* and *I regret to say*. When they are clausal, they can be analysed as part of a large number of constructions that have been grouped together as *comment clauses*. These are particularly common in informal conversation, where they are often spoken in a parenthetic tone of voice, with increased speed and decreased loudness.

The rest, *I suppose*, will never be known.
You know, it's time you paid me back.
It's over now, *I'm glad to say*.

Comment clauses express several kinds of meaning:

• *Tentativeness*: I think, I assume, I suppose, I'm told, they say, it seems, rumour has it.
• *Certainty*: I know, I'm sure, it transpires, I must say, it's true, there's no doubt.
• *Emotional attitude*: I'm pleased to see, I'm afraid, I hope, Heaven knows, I'm delighted to say, to be honest, frankly speaking.

• *Asking for attention*: you know, you see, mind you, you have to admit, as you may have heard.

When comment clauses become noticeable in conversation through over-use, it is widely held to be a sign of unclear or evasive thinking. For example, they are often to be heard to excess in the linguistic wriggling of a politician faced by an aggressive interviewer – the 'yes, well, you know, to be honest about this, putting it in a nutshell' response. This usage has led some critics to condemn *all* comment clauses, whatever the context. But this is going too far. These clauses play an important role in conversation, argument, and spontaneous monologue, helping speakers to 'think on their feet', and giving listeners a chance to grasp what is being said (p. 291). The same effects can also be introduced into elegant informal writing, where the judicious use of a comment clause can add personal perspective, strengthen writer-reader rapport, and improve the accessibility of a dense piece of text.

TELLING THE STORY

Alistair Cooke's best-selling *America* (1973) was acclaimed for the way it captured the friendly tone of the original commentary in his television series. One of the stylistic features which contributes to this warmth is the regular use of comment clauses and disjuncts. Here are a few examples (my italics) from the first few pages of his opening chapter.

…my mental picture of the United States, and of such scattered human life as it supported, became sharper but not, *I regret to say*, more accurate.

But I believe that the preconceptions about another country that we hold on to most tenaciously are those we take in, *so to speak*, with our mother's milk…

So I jotted down a long list of such places, most of them, *I should guess*, not much known to tourists or even to the standard history books…

Most people, *I believe*, when they first come to America, whether as travelers or settlers, become aware of a new and agreeable feeling: that the whole country is their oyster.

There are, *in fact*, large regions of the United States that will challenge the hardihood of the most carefree wanderer.

Undoubtedly, all the land mass of the United States has been mapped, and the prospects for a livelihood in any part of it are known.

Fortunately, the broad design was drawn for us, nearly a century and a half ago, by a Frenchman…

REPORTING SPEECH

The usual way in which we report someone's speech is by using a special *reporting clause*, such as *she said, he wrote, they replied* – sometimes adding extra information (*He replied angrily*). The accompanying speech or writing is given in the *reported clause*, which can appear in either of two forms: *direct speech* and *indirect speech*.

• *Direct speech* gives the exact words used by the speaker or writer. They are usually enclosed by quotation marks: *Michael said, 'I like the colour'.* The reporting clause may occur before, within, or after the direct speech. When it occurs in the middle or at the end of the sentence, the order of subject and verb can sometimes be inverted:

'I think,' Michael said, 'that it's time to leave.'
'I think,' said Michael, 'that it's time to leave.'

This inversion is most common when the verb is *said*, and the subject is not a pronoun. *Said she* is literary or archaic, and forms such as **commented he* or **laughed they* are unacceptable. Inversion at the beginning of a sentence is found only in some narrative styles, such as popular journalism: *Declared brunette Lucy …*

• *Indirect speech* (also called *reported speech*) gives the words as subsequently reported by someone. It usually takes the form of a subordinate clause (p. 226) introduced by *that*: *Michael said that he liked the colour*. The conjunction is often omitted in informal contexts: *Michael said he liked the colour*.

This distinction has long been recognized in English grammar. Older grammars used Latin names for the two modes: *oratio recta* (for direct speech) and *oratio obliqua* (for indirect speech). However, the basic distinction does not capture the whole range of stylistic possibilities: mixed and modified forms are used in literature, such as 'free direct speech' and 'free indirect speech', conveying a wide range of dramatic effects (p. 419). And the construction has also been used as a fruitful source of humour (p. 409).

GRAMMATICAL CHANGES

When indirect speech is used, speakers need to introduce grammatical changes to allow for differences between their current situation and the situation they are reporting.

• It is usually necessary to change the *tense forms* of the verbs used in the direct speech (p. 224). In most cases, a present tense becomes past, and a past tense is shifted still further back, by using the perfective aspect (p. 225).

I said, 'I'm leaving'.
I said I was leaving.

I said, 'I saw John'.
I said I had seen John.

The rules governing the correct relationship between the verbs in the reporting and reported clauses are traditionally labelled the *sequence of tenses*. They are actually much more complex than these examples suggest. For example, if the time reference of the original utterance is still valid at the time of reporting, the tense shift is optional.

Mark said, 'Oil floats on water.'
Mark said oil floated on water.
Mark said oil floats on water.

And there are special strategies when it comes to reporting sentences other than statements (p. 218).

'Are you in?' asked Pru.
Pru asked if I was in.

'Sit down,' said Pru.
Pru told me to sit down.

• *Time* and *place* references also need to be altered: for example, *tomorrow* becomes *the next day* or *the following day*, *here* becomes *there*.

I said, 'I saw it here yesterday.'
I said I'd seen it there the day before.

• *Personal pronouns* need to be altered (p. 210). First and second person pronouns have to be changed to third person, unless the original participants are still involved in the conversation.

Pru said to Joe, 'I like your tie.'
Pru said she liked his tie.
(*if the speaker is talking to someone other than Joe*)
Pru said she liked your tie .
(*if the speaker is talking to Joe*)

REPORTING STYLES

Several conventions are used to represent direct speech in fiction. Some authors take great pains to vary the verb of the reporting clause (p. 419), to avoid the repeated use of *said* (see A below). Some use *said* regularly, even in place of other stalwarts (e.g. *asked, exclaimed*) (B). The reporting clause is often omitted, if the identity of the speakers is clear from the context (C). And in drama, the verb of the reporting clause is always absent, with quotation marks never used (D).

A

Jorge could not keep from commenting in a low voice. 'John Chrysostom said that Christ never laughed.'
'Nothing in his human nature forbade it,' William remarked, 'because laughter, as the theologians teach, is proper to man.'
'The son of man could laugh, but it is not written that he did so,' Jorge said sharply, quoting Petrus Cantor.
'Manduca, iam coctum est,' William murmured. 'Eat, for it is well done.'
'What?' asked Jorge, thinking he referred to some dish that was being brought to him.
'Those are the words that, according to Ambrose, were uttered by Saint Lawrence on the gridiron, when he invited his executioners to turn him over, as Prudentius also recalls in the *Peristephanon*,' William said with a saintly air. 'Saint Lawrence therefore knew how to laugh and say ridiculous things, even if it was to humiliate his enemies.'
'Which proves that laughter is some-thing very close to death and to the corruption of the body,' Jorge replied with a snarl…
(Umberto Eco, *The Name of the Rose*, 1983, First Day: Compline)

B

'I'm afraid I missed the UTE conference this year.'
'If that's the one I attended here in '79, then you did well to avoid it,' said Morris Zapp. 'I mean real conferences, international conferences.'
'I couldn't afford to go to one of those,' said Robyn. 'Our overseas conference fund has been cut to the bone.'
'Cuts, cuts, cuts,' said Morris Zapp, 'that's all anyone will talk about here. First Philip, then Busby, now you.'
'That's what life is like in British universities these days, Morris,' said Philip Swallow, presenting Robyn with a glass of rather warm Soave. 'I spend all my time on committees arguing about how to respond to the cuts. I haven't read a book in months, let alone tried to write one.'
'Well, I have,' said Robyn.
'Read one or written one?' said Morris Zapp.
'Written one,' said Robyn. 'Well, three quarters of it, anyway.'
'Ah, Robyn,' said Philip Swallow, 'you put us all to shame. What shall we do without you?'
(David Lodge, *Nice Work*, 1988, Ch. 6.)

C

And she won, she knew she did, because Kurtz spoke first, which was the proof.
'Charlie, we recognise that this is very painful for you, but we ask you to continue in your own words. We have the van. We see your possessions leaving the house. What else do we see?'
'My pony.'
'They took that too?'
'I told you already.'
'With the furniture? In the same van?'
'No, a separate one. Don't be bloody silly.'
'So there were two vans. Both at the same time? Or one after the other?'
'I don't remember.'
'Where was your father physically located all this time? Was he in the study? Looking through the window, say, watching it all go? How does a man like him bear up – in his disgrace?'
'He was in the garden.'
'Doing what?'
'Looking at the roses.'
(John Le Carré, *The Little Drummer Girl*, 1983, Ch. 7)

D

STANLEY (*quickly*). Why are you down here?
McCANN. A short holiday.
STANLEY. This is a ridiculous house to pick on. (*He rises.*)
McCANN. Why?
STANLEY. Because it's not a boarding house. It never was.
McCANN. Sure it is.
STANLEY. Why did you choose this house?
McCANN. You know, sir, you're a bit depressed for a man on his birthday.
STANLEY (*sharply*). Why do you call me sir?
McCANN. You don't like it?
(Harold Pinter, *The Birthday Party*, 1960, Act 2)

SENTENCE INFORMATION

There are many ways in which we can organize the information contained in a sentence, as can be seen from these alternatives:

A mechanic is fixing a car.
There's a mechanic fixing a car.
It's a mechanic that's fixing a car.
It's a car that a mechanic is fixing.
A car is being fixed by a mechanic.

These sentences all express the same basic meaning, but they convey several important differences of style and emphasis. The analysis of these differences is also part of the study of grammar.

Given and new information

There are usually two kinds of information in a sentence. One part of the sentence tells us something *new*. The other part tells us something that we were aware of already (either from previous sentences or from our general knowledge) – in other words, its information is *given*. The distinction between given and new information can be clearly seen in this dialogue:

A: Where did you put your bike?
B: I left it / at my friend's house.

The first part of B's sentence is 'given' (by A); the second part is new.

Given information tells us what a sentence is about; it provides the sentence *theme*. Because the information it contains is familiar, this part of the sentence is not likely to be spoken with any extra prominence (p. 248). New information, on the other hand, provides the point where we expect people to pay special attention, or *focus*. The part of the sentence containing the focus is always spoken in a prominent way.

In most sentences, the theme appears first, and the focus of the message last. But it is possible to bring the focus forwards, so as to emphasize an earlier part of the sentence. This especially happens when we want to state a contrast, as in **The plates** *are new, not the cups.* Conversations make frequent use of emphatic contrasts of this kind.

VARYING THE INFORMATION STRUCTURE

There are several ways in which special attention can be drawn to the theme of a sentence.

Fronting
Fronting occurs when we move to the beginning of a sentence an item which does not usually belong there. This item then becomes the theme, and in such cases it carries extra prominence:

Across the road they ran.
David I said my name was.

Inversion
Here the subject and verb appear in the reverse of their normal order:

Here's Johnny.
Down came the rain.
They were happy and so *was I*.

The verb must be in its simple form (p. 225); we cannot say **Down was coming the rain.*

Cleft sentences
Another way of altering the normal emphasis in a simple sentence is to split ('cleave') the sentence into two clauses, giving each its own verb. The first clause consists of the pronoun *it* and a form of the verb *be*. The second clause begins with a pronoun such as *that* or *who*. These constructions are called *cleft sentences*:

Ted broke the plate.
It was Ted who broke the plate.
It was the plate that Ted broke.

Extraposition
Where the subject or object element is a clause (p. 220), it is possible to change the sentence around so that the clause comes later. The original element is then replaced by the pronoun *it*, which 'anticipates' the following clause:

What you say doesn't matter.
It doesn't matter what you say.

I find reading comics fun.
I find it fun, reading comics.

In examples like these, the clauses have been moved *outside* their normal position in the sentence. The effect is thus said to be one of *extraposition*.

Existentials
Sometimes we want to bring the content of a whole clause to the attention of our listener or reader, making it all new information. To do this, there is a construction in which the first words have no meaning. They seem to act as a theme, because they appear at the beginning of the sentence, but it is a 'dummy' theme. The main means of achieving this effect is to use the word *there* (without giving it any stress) followed by the simple present or past tense of *be*:

Many people are in danger.
There are many people in danger.

Such sentences express the general existence of some state of affairs, and are thus called *existential sentences*. *Be* is not the only verb capable of being used in this way, but others (such as *exist* and *arise*) are rarer and more literary:

There exist several alternatives.
There arose a great cry.

FROM MOSCOW, OUR CORRESPONDENT...

News reporting frequently makes use of variations in information structure in order to capture attention and avoid monotony. The following extracts from radio broadcasts illustrate the use of these techniques.

It was in June that Horace Williams, an unemployed labourer, first met the Smiths.

There were cheers inside the court today when a verdict of not guilty was returned...

In the West Indian city of Georgetown, the final day of the Fourth Test between the West Indies and England has been washed out by rain.

BEYOND THE SENTENCE

In real life, a sentence is rarely used in isolation. Normally, sentences – whether spoken or written – appear in a sequence, such as a dialogue, a speech, a letter, or a book. Any set of sentences which 'cohere' in this way is called a *text* – a term which applies to both spoken and written material (p. 290). The coherence is achieved through the use of a wide range of features which connect sentences, some of which fall well outside the domain of grammar, but they are outlined here because it is not really possible to appreciate the specific role of syntax in connectivity without seeing it in this broader perspective.

• *General knowledge.* We often make a link between sentences because of our general knowledge or expectations about the way the world functions.

The summer was one of the best they had ever had. The vintage was expected to be superb.

Here there is no obvious connection in either grammar or vocabulary to link these sentences. But anyone who knows about wine can readily supply the missing link. Such techniques as inference, deduction, and presupposition are used in these circumstances.

• *Vocabulary.* Often the choice of words is enough to connect two sentences:

Look at that dachshund. He'd win a prize in any dog show.

Because we know that a dachshund is a kind of dog, we have no difficulty in making the relevant connection between the sentences.

• *Punctuation* and *layout.* Graphic and graphological features of a text (p. 257) may be enough to show that sentences, or even paragraphs, are to be connected in a specific way. The use of panels, headings, special symbols (such as bullets), and colour within a text to show how the meaning is organized, provides a particularly clear example – as on the present page.

• *Prosody* (p. 248). Variations in pitch, loudness, speed, rhythm, and pause combine to provide the spoken equivalent of the visual organization and contrastivity of a written text. Question–answer sequences, parenthetic utterances, rhetorical climaxes, and many other features of speech which involve a sequence of sentences are usually signalled through the use of prosodic effects. Several spoken genres, such as radio news bulletins and sports commentaries, are also notable for the way they use prosody to demarcate topics and types of activity.

BEWARE!

A text is a coherent, complete unit of speech or writing. As such it typically consists of many sentences. But it is possible to find a text which contains only one sentence, and a short one at that (p. 216).

GRAMMATICAL CONNECTIVITY

Several aspects of grammar, already discussed in this section with reference to sentence structure, can also be used to connect sentences.

Space and time adverbials (p. 221)	We left Paris on Monday morning. *By the same evening* we were in Rome.
Pronouns and other pro-forms (p. 228)	The children were back in time for dinner. *They* were very tired.
Determiners (p. 207)	A Mercedes was parked in the street. *The* car looked new.
Comparison (p. 199)	Six children took part in the sack race. Jill was easily the *fastest*.
Conjunctions (p. 227)	Several people complained. *And* I did too.
Connecting adverbials (p. 229)	There are several points. *First of all*, we need to know the motive.

TRACING SENTENCE CONNECTIONS

Often several features of grammatical connectivity are present to link a pair of sentences, and in a longer passage the various links combine and overlap in many ways. This can be seen in the following passage, where the specifically grammatical connections have been highlighted. A ∧ symbol indicates a point of ellipsis (p. 228). (Many other links of the same kind are also used to link clauses within sentences, but these are not separately identified.)

The Improbability-proof control cabin of the Heart of Gold looked like a perfectly conventional spaceship except that it was perfectly clean because it was so new. Some of **the** control seats ∧ hadn't had the plastic wrapping taken off yet. **The** cabin was mostly white, oblong, and about the size of a smallish restaurant. **In fact it** wasn't perfectly oblong: **the** two long walls ∧ were raked round in a slight parallel curve, and all the angles and corners of **the** cabin ∧ were contoured in excitingly chunky shapes. **The truth of the matter** is that it would have been a great deal **simpler** and **more practical** to build **the** cabin as an ordinary three-dimensional oblong room, but then the designers would have got

miserable. **As it was the** cabin looked excitingly purposeful, with large video screens ranged over the control and guidance system panels on **the** concave wall, and long banks of computers set into **the** convex wall. In one corner ∧ a robot sat humped, its gleaming brushed steel head hanging loosely between its gleaming brushed steel knees. **It too** was fairly new, but though **it** was beautifully constructed and polished **it** somehow looked as if the various parts of **its** more or less humanoid body didn't quite fit properly. **In fact they** fitted perfectly well, but something in **its** bearing suggested that **they** might have fitted **better**.

(Douglas Adams, *The Hitch Hiker's Guide to the Galaxy* (1979), Ch. 11.)

THE PARADOX OF GRAMMAR

The linguistic literature abounds with metaphors trying to capture the significance of grammar. Grammar is said to be at the very 'heart' of language, at the 'core' of communication. It is seen as the 'key' to our understanding of the way meaning is expressed and interpreted. It has been called the 'skeleton' of narrative and the 'touchstone' of verbal humour. It has been widely hailed as the 'mechanism' which, by manipulating a finite number of grammatical rules, enables us to generate an infinite number of sentences. It dominates the 'milestones' of language learning and acts as a 'yardstick' during the course of language breakdown and recovery (p. 426). There is no doubt, when we read such accounts, that the field of grammar is fundamental, dynamic, relevant, and real.

On the other hand, there is equally no doubt that grammatical study can lack all these attributes. This is the paradox of grammar: how can something which ought to be so fascinating come to be so boring? The historical reasons have been reviewed in earlier pages (p. 190), but even in a positive and optimistic intellectual linguistic climate there is no gainsaying the fact that the relationships of grammar are abstract and at times intricate, and its terminology imposing and at times abstruse. The level of difficulty is probably no worse than that encountered in several other sciences, but the information purveyed by those sciences is established in school curricula in ways that are far in advance of what is as yet available for grammar. The familiarity and accessibility of geography or chemistry is the result of a long pedagogical tradition, in which the selection and grading of information has been tried and tested, and curricula devised which are principled and motivating. Modern approaches to English grammar are not yet in this position, but there is plenty of evidence to show that efforts are being made to improve matters. The examples on this page illustrate just a few of the approaches that are now being used to help people obtain insight into grammatical structure.

GIANT WAVES DOWN FUNNEL

Using sentences which are grammatically ambiguous can motivate an enquiry into the competing structures involved. (Examples from W. H. Mittins, *A Grammar of Modern English*, 1962.)

The only spectators were a woman carrying a small baby and a large policeman.

We saw the Eiffel Tower flying from London to Paris.

A sailor was dancing with a wooden leg.

Bus on Fire!
Passengers Alight!

The airship was about to leave the airport. The last person to go up the gangway was Miss Hemming. Slowly her huge nose turned into the wind. Then, like some enormous beast, she crawled along the grass.

DISCUSSING THE PROBLEM

If teaching grammar is a problem, it can help to bring the children into the discussion at the earliest possible point, using role play, stories, poems, and other genres to focus their attention on a linguistic issue. This poem by Mike Rosen has been much discussed in British secondary schools following its use in a publication written in association with the BBC television series *Language File* (1990).

The teacher said:
A noun is a naming word.
What is a naming word in the sentence
'He named the ship, Lusitania'?
'Named' said George.
'WRONG – it's ship.'

The teacher said:
A verb is a doing word.
What is the doing word in the sentence
'I like doing homework'?
'Doing' said George.
'WRONG – it's like.'

The teacher said:
An adjective is a describing word.
What is the describing word in the sentence
'Describing sunsets is boring'?
'Describing' said George.
'WRONG – it's boring.'
'I know it is,' said George.

TAKING NOTHING FOR GRANTED

One reason why grammar teaching can fail is that the notions being taught take too much for granted. For example, it is not possible to teach a young child the concept of letter order (in spelling) or word order (in sentences) if the basic notion of 'order' is itself not clear. This point was appreciated by Jessie Reid and Margaret Donaldson, who gave it special attention at the beginning of their reading and language programme, *R&D* (1984), aimed at children from around the age of 8.

DRAWING TO A CLOSE

Animation, cartoons, and computer products are just some of the modern ways of putting across a grammatical point. While the sophistication of the software currently lags considerably behind what is available in hardware, the way a child can be motivated to learn about grammatical structure is well demonstrated by the numerous packages which already teach aspects of grammar to special groups, such as language-disordered children (p. 434). Cartoons are also now widely used. The following is an offering from Edward McLachlan to a series of books for British secondary school children by the present author, *Language A to Z* (1991). It accompanies an entry which is attempting to explain to 15-year-olds what a 'comment clause' is (p. 229).

K for an old **K**nife-grinder
stands,
Who wheels his own machine;
And thus the cart before the horse
Is very plainly seen.

L for a brisk **L**amplighter stands,
Who lights the gas, and soon
Our streets will so illuminate,
We shall not miss the moon.

O for an **O**yster-woman stands;
The oysters now begin
To find some one is at the door,
Who's trying to break in.

P for **P**oliceman we shall take,
His number, twenty-five;
And there he's running at full speed,
To catch a thief alive.

PART IV
Spoken and Written English

A message constructed in English grammar and vocabulary may be transmitted in either of two main ways: through speech or through writing. Part IV investigates the technical resources provided by the language under each of these headings. (Stylistic differences in the way spoken and written language are used are considered separately, in Part V.)

We begin with spoken English, the more natural and widespread mode of transmission, though ironically the one which most people find much less familiar – presumably because it is so much more difficult to 'see' what is happening in speech than in writing. Chapter 17 works systematically through the sound system, after providing some general perspective about the subjects of phonetics and phonology and the nature of phonetic transcription. It introduces and classifies vowels and consonants, emphasizing the differences between the way in which these notions appear in speech and in writing. It then goes on to review the way sounds combine into syllables, words, and sentences, and outlines the prosodic resources of the language, which convey such important effects as intonation, emphasis, and tone of voice. The chapter surveys some of the everyday domains in which a knowledge of pronunciation can be useful

or illuminating, and includes a detailed examination of the way sounds can be used symbolically, in a range of contexts which link the poet Keats, breakfast cereals, and the British cartoon character Desperate Dan.

Chapter 18 adopts a similar approach to the writing system, beginning with the topic which is widely regarded as its central domain – the alphabet. Here too some methodological preliminaries are in order, as writing is a subject studied by several fields, including linguists, psychologists, typographers, and graphic designers, and terms and approaches vary greatly. After looking at the history of each letter of the alphabet, we turn to some of the interesting statistical and symbolic properties of letters, paying particular attention to the approach associated with graphologists, and to different kinds of graphic variety and deviance. We then grapple with what is undoubtedly the most notorious aspect of the English writing system: its spelling. The section reviews the reasons for the complexity, discusses the sources of irregularity, and examines possible solutions, including some of the proposed attempts at spelling reform. The chapter then concludes with a close look at the history and present-day use of one of the most neglected aspects of the writing system: punctuation.

◄ Letters from an early alphabet book, *The Amusing Alphabet,* a popular educational approach in Victorian times, promising 'easy steps' to literacy (see also p. 407).

17 · THE SOUND SYSTEM

We are used to seeing the written language as a sequence of letters, separated by small segments of space. This is how we were taught to write. We formed our letters one at a time, then slowly and painstakingly brought them together in 'joined-up' writing. We learned to call five of these letters 'vowels' (A, E, I, O, U), and the others 'consonants'. We may also have learned that letter Y is also 'sometimes' used as a vowel.

Everyone born with the normal capacity to learn acquires the ability to listen and speak long before the ability to read and write. Moreover, when the English alphabet was first devised (p. 258), its letters were based on a consideration of the nature of the sounds in Old English. The origins of the written language lie in the spoken language, not the other way round. It is therefore one of life's ironies that traditionally in present-day education we do not learn about spoken language until well after we have learned the basic properties of the written language. As a result, it is inevitable that we think of speech using the frame of reference which belongs to writing. We even use some of the same terms, and it can come as something of a shock to realize that these terms do not always have the same meaning.

THE ORGANS OF ARTICULATION

The diagram shows the anatomical location of the vocal organs involved in the description of English vowels and consonants. It is not a complete representation of all the vocal organs – the lungs, for example, are not shown.

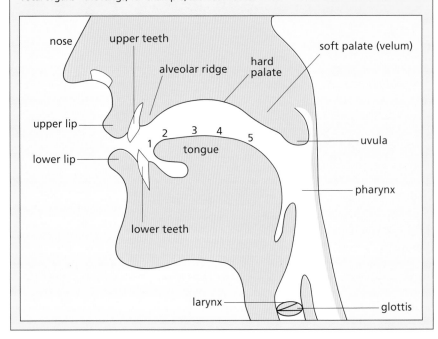

A BASIC PERSPECTIVE

Pronunciation can always be studied from two points of view: the *phonetic* and the *phonological*.

Phonetics
Phonetics is the study of the way humans make, transmit, and receive speech sounds. It is divided into three main branches, corresponding to these three distinctions:

- *articulatory phonetics* is the study of the way the vocal organs are used to produce speech sounds
- *acoustic phonetics* is the study of the physical properties of speech sounds
- *auditory phonetics* is the study of the way people perceive speech sounds

This section gives details of the articulation of vowels and consonants, and makes only passing mention of their acoustic characteristics and the mechanisms of audition. The auditory perspective is more in evidence in the section on prosody (p. 248).

Phonology
Phonology is the study of the sound systems of languages, and of the general properties displayed by these systems. By contrast with phonetics, which studies *all* possible sounds that the human vocal apparatus can make, phonology studies only those contrasts in sound (the *phonemes*) which make differences of meaning within language. When we listen carefully to the way people speak English, we will hear hundreds of slight differences in the way individuals pronounce particular sounds. For example, one person may pronounce /s/ in a noticeably 'slushy' manner, while another may pronounce it in a 'lisping' manner. A

phonetician would be interested in describing exactly what these differences of articulation are. A phonologist, however, would point out that both articulations are 'types of /s/': /set/, no matter how the /s/ varies, it continues to contrast with /bet/, /met/, and other words. There is just one basic unit, or phoneme, involved.

When we talk about the 'sound system' of English, we are referring to the number of phonemes which are used in a language, and to how they are organized. To say there are '20 vowels' in a particular accent means that there are 20 units which can differentiate word meanings: /e/ is different from /iː/, for example, because there are pairs of words (such as *set* and *seat*) which can be distinguished solely by replacing one of these vowels by the other. All the vowels in the list on p. 237 (and all the consonants on p. 242) owe their existence to this principle.

Brackets
To help separate the two ways of looking at pronunciation, the practice has grown up in linguistics of using different kinds of brackets for the two approaches. Square brackets – [ ] – are used when sounds are being discussed from a phonetic point of view – that is, purely as sounds, and regardless of their role in the sound system of the language. Slant brackets – // – are used when sounds are being discussed from a phonological point of view – that is, purely as part of the sound system, and regardless of the particular way they are articulated. For the most part, transcriptions in this book are phonological: they show the phonemes, and use slant brackets, as in /pen/ *pen* and /skruː/ *screw*. When the discussion focuses on points of articulatory detail, however, as in the description of regional differences of pronunciation, we will need to rely as well on a phonetic transcription.

Key
1 tongue *tip*
2 *blade* of the tongue (the tapering part, opposite the alveolar ridge)
3 *front* of the tongue (opposite the hard palate)
4 *centre* of the tongue (opposite where the hard and soft palate meet)
5 *back* of the tongue (opposite the soft palate)

THE VOWELS

A good example of the speech–writing difference is the way we have to re-think the idea that 'there are five vowels' when we begin to discuss speech. There are in fact some 20 or so vowels in most accents of English (the exact number often depending on the way the system is analysed), and their sound qualities can vary enormously from accent to accent. The vowel sounds of American English, for example, are clearly different from those of British or Australian, and the vowels typical of one locality in any of these countries can differ appreciably from those of another. Indeed, vowel differences make up most of the distinctiveness which we associate with a particular accent (p. 298).

The table on this page shows the set of vowels found in English, along with some common transcriptions (for their place of articulation, see p. 240). The most striking feature of a list of this kind is the number of special symbols (part of the *phonemic transcription*) which have to be devised in order to identify each vowel unambiguously. With only five (or six) vowel letters available in the traditional alphabet, extra symbols, combinations of symbols, and diacritic marks are needed to capture all the units in the system, as well as all the variations in vowel quality which distinguish different accents (pp. 240–1).

The vowels in	Gimson	Jones	F&R	Variants
sea, feet, me, field	iː	iː	i	
him, big, village, women	ɪ	i	ɪ	ɩ
get, fetch, head, Thames	e	e	ɛ	
sat, hand, ban, plait	æ	æ	æ	a
sun, son, blood, does	ʌ	ʌ	ʌ	
calm, are, *fa*ther, car	ɑː	ɑː	a	
dog, lock, swan, cough	ɒ	ɔ	a	
all, saw, cord, more	ɔː	ɔː	ɔ	
put, wolf, good, look	ʊ	u	ʊ	ʋ
soon, do, soup, shoe	uː	uː	u	
bird, her, turn, learn	ɜː	ɜː	ʌ (+ r)	ɝ (+ r)
the, but*ter*, so*fa*, about	ə	ə	ə	ɚ (+ r)
ape, waist, they, say	eɪ	ei	e	
time, cry, die, high	aɪ	ai	ay	
boy, toy, noise, voice	ɔɪ	ɔi	ɔy	
so, road, toe, know	əʊ	ou	o	
out, how, house, found	aʊ, ɑʊ	au	aw, æw	
deer, here, fierce, near	ɪə	iə	(i + r)	
care, air, bare, bear	eə	ɛə	(ɛ + r)	
poor, sure, tour, lure	ʊə	uə	(u + r)	

TYPES OF VOWEL

• *Monophthongs* (or *pure vowels*) are vowels with a single perceived auditory quality, made by a movement of the tongue towards one position in the mouth. The first 12 vowel qualities in the above table are all monophthongs.
• *Diphthongs* are vowels where two vowel qualities can be perceived. The remaining eight vowel qualities in the table are all diphthongs. In /aɪ/, for example, the sound begins with an open /a/-type quality and ends with a close /i/-type quality. It is important to note that here we are talking about phonetic diphthongs, not graphic ones: the sounds in *my*, *so*, and *how*, for example, are all diphthongs, even though each has only a single vowel letter.
• *Triphthongs* are vowels in which three vowel qualities can be perceived. The vowels in such words as *player* /pleɪə/, *fire* /faɪə/,

royal /rɔɪəl/, *tower* /taʊə/, and *lower* /ləʊə/ can all be analysed in this way. No new symbols are required, however, as each can be seen as a combination of a diphthong +/ə/.

Often, in the history of English, a vowel has changed its quality. There are two chief possibilities. When a diphthong becomes a monophthong, the sound is said to be *monophthongized*; conversely, when a monophthong becomes a diphthong, the sound is *diphthongized*. An example of the former is the Southern US pronunciation of *my man*, which has become something more like *ma man* (i.e. *my* /maɪ/ has become /maː/). An example of the latter is the British mock-pronunciation of *yes* /jes/ as *yays* /jeɪs/. Indeed, an even more exaggerated form can sometimes be heard, /jeɪəs/, in which case we might say that the vowel has been *triphthongized*.

TRANSCRIBING VOWELS

Several authors have devised sets of symbols for identifying English vowels. The system used in this book is the one introduced by British phonetician A. C. Gimson in *An Introduction to the Pronunciation of English* (1st edn, 1962), which has been particularly influential in the field of teaching English as a foreign language.

• The Gimson system is given in the first column, after a selection of words which illustrate each sound. In several cases there is a wide range of spellings for the same vowel quality – a consequence of the mixed nature of English orthography (p. 274).

Two other vowel transcriptional systems are shown in the table.

• The system used by the British phonetician, Daniel Jones in his pioneering description of Received Pronunciation (p. 365). Gimson (a student of Jones) modified this system in an attempt to show vowel qualities more accurately. The Jones list does not include the use of /ɔə/, which in Jones's day was a common pronunciation in such words as *four*, and distinct from the vowel of *bought*.

• The system used by Victoria Fromkin & Robert Rodman (F&R) in *An Introduction to Language* (1st edn, 1974), a widely used teaching textbook in the USA. It is a simplified version of the influential system devised by John S. Kenyon & Thomas A. Knott in *A Pronouncing Dictionary of American English* (1953), which aimed to provide a standard transcription for the vowels of the main dialects of American English.

• The final column in the table lists a few other symbols which are often seen representing certain vowels. Some are simply typographic variants; some represent a particular sound effect, such as the presence of *r* 'colouring' (p. 245); and /a/ is often used as a simpler alternative to /æ/.

Possible confusibles

The transcriptions use the same symbols in different ways, partly because of different views about the best way to analyse the vowel system, and partly because of the differences between British and American English.

• /a/ in the British systems does not appear as a separate phoneme. In F&R it is used in such words as *dog*, reflecting more directly the way this vowel is articulated further forward in the mouth. This is a major point of possible confusion for British-trained students casually reading an American transcription, for they risk interpreting /lag/ as *lag* instead of *log*. In addition, the same /a/ symbol is used by F&R in such words as *father*, *calm*, and *car*, again reflecting the typical sounds of these vowels in American English, whereas the British systems use /ɑː/ – an important difference between the two sound systems.

• /e/ in F&R refers to the vowel in such words as *say*, whereas the British systems show the diphthongal nature of this sound (p. 239) as /eɪ/ or /ei/. Thus, /met/ refers to *met* in Gimson, but to *mate* in F&R.

• /ʌ/ in the British systems refers only to the vowel in such words as *sun*. In F&R it is also used for the vowel in such words as *bird* (along with a following /r/ consonant).

• /o/ in F&R refers to the vowel in such words as *so*. British students used to a diphthongal transcription would therefore be likely to interpret /kot/ as *cot* rather than *coat*.

• F&R do not have separate symbols for the sounds in such words as *deer*, *care*, and *poor*. These words are analysed as combinations of vowel + /r/, and their different status shown in the table by the use of parentheses.

Describing vowels

All vowels have certain properties in common, which distinguish them from consonants (p. 242).

• From a phonetic point of view (p. 236), vowels are articulated with a relatively open configuration of the vocal tract: no part of the mouth is closed, and none of the vocal organs come so close together that we can hear the sound of the air passing between them (what phoneticians call *audible friction*). The most noticeable vowel quality is therefore [a], said with the mouth wide open. Consonants have a very different method of articulation.

• From a phonological point of view (p. 236), vowels are units of the sound system which typically occupy the middle of a syllable (the nucleus, p. 246), as in *cat* /kat/ and *big* /bɪg/. Consonants, by contrast, are typically found at the edges of syllables, shown also by these examples. (It is reasoning of this kind which explains why letter Y can be described either as a consonant or as a vowel (p. 236). In such words as *yet*, it acts as a consonant, occupying the same position as other consonants (*met*, *set*, etc.). In such words as *my* and *tryst*, it acts as a vowel, occupying the same position as other vowels (*trust*, *me*, etc.).)

• Vowels typically involve the vibration of the vocal cords (*voicing*), and their distinctive resonances are made by varying the shape of the mouth, using the tongue and lips. In English, there are no vowels whose chief characteristic is the use of nasal resonance (*nasal vowels*) – unlike, say, French or Portuguese. English vowels are all *oral vowels*, and take on a nasal quality only when they are being influenced by an adjacent nasal consonant, as in *no*, *long*, and *man*.

The chief task in describing the articulation of vowels, accordingly, is to plot the movements of the tongue and lips. The most widely used method of doing this was devised by Daniel Jones, and is known as the *cardinal vowel* system.

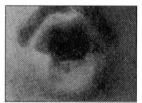
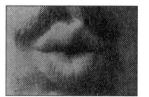

THE CARDINAL VOWEL SYSTEM

The cardinal vowel (CV) diagram was devised to provide a set of reference points for the articulation and recognition of vowels. Its dimensions correspond to the 'vowel space' in the centre of the mouth where these sounds are articulated. The positions of the front, centre, and back of the tongue (p. 236) are represented by vertical lines.

• At the front of the mouth, [a] represents the lowest point that it is theoretically possible for the body of the tongue to reach, and [ɑ] represents the correspondingly lowest point at the back of the mouth. Vowels in the region of [a] or [ɑ] are called *open* or *low* vowels.
• [i] represents the highest point at the front that the body of the tongue can reach while still producing a vowel sound (anything higher, and the tongue would come so near to the roof of the mouth that a consonant sound would result). [u], similarly, represents the highest point at the back of the mouth. Vowels in the region of [i] and [u] are called *close* or *high* vowels.
• Two horizontal lines divide the space between [i] and [a] into equal areas. Vowels made in the region of the higher of these lines, repre-

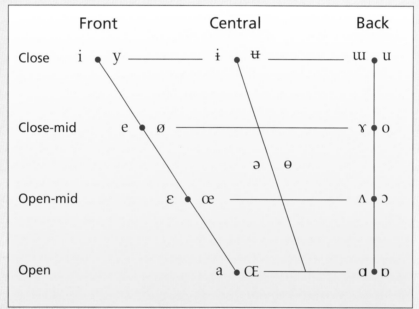

	Front	Central	Back
Close	i • y —————— ɨ • ʉ ɯ • u		
Close-mid	e • ø ———————— ɤ • o		
	ə ɵ		
Open-mid	ɛ • œ ———————— ʌ • ɔ		
Open	a • Œ ɑ • ɒ		

sented by [e] and [o], are called *mid-close* or *half-close*. Vowels made in the region of the lower of these lines, represented by [ɛ] and [ɔ], are *mid-open* or *half-open*. The term *mid* is often used to describe the whole of the area between these two lines.
• The CV diagram also includes information about lip-rounding. In most vowel positions, it is possible to hear a difference in vowel quality depending on whether the lips are *rounded* or *unrounded* (spread), and some languages (though not English) exploit this dimension of contrast quite considerably. Thus, [i] is the high front unrounded vowel, heard in such words as *see*, while [y] is its rounded equivalent, heard often in French (*tu*), and sometimes in regional English (e.g. Scots). The rounded member of a vowel pair is always the symbol on the right in the diagram.

It is important not to confuse the phonetic symbols used to identify the 'cardinal' points on the CV diagram with the phonological symbols used in the actual description of English. Most of the time the symbols correspond quite well, but sometimes they do not. For example, in Received Pronunciation the /iː/ of *see* is very near the [i] point of the diagram (p. 240), and the /uː/ of *shoe* is very near [u]. But the /e/ of *set* is in fact articulated half way between the cardinal values of [e] and [ɛ]; and the /ʌ/ symbol, when it represents the vowels in such words as *does* and *cup*, is reflecting a sound that is much further forward in the mouth than the quality shown in the CV diagram.

The vowel system

A long list of vowels, such as that given on p. 237, is not as informative as a classification which groups them into types, draws attention to the common properties of each type, and notes the features which distinguish one type from another. Becoming aware of the difference between a pure vowel, a diphthong, and a triphthong is a start (p. 239), but there is much more to be said about the way vowels work in English. (The following examples are all from Received Pronunciation (RP, p. 365); regional variants are shown on pp. 240–1.)

A particularly important factor is length (symbolized by [ː]). When we listen to the 12 pure vowels, it is evident that five of them are relatively long in duration, and seven are relatively short. Moreover, in several cases length seems to relate pairs of vowels which are articulated in roughly the same part of the mouth. In the following examples, pairs of words are followed by the same consonant. If each word is given the same amount of emphasis, there is no doubt that the vowel in /siːt/ *seat* is much longer than that in /sɪt/ *sit;* and similar effects can be heard in /fuːd/ *food* vs /gʊd/ *good*, /dɔːn/, *dawn* vs /dɒn/ *don*, and /lɑː(r)d/ *lard* /vs læd/ *lad*. There is also a length difference between /ɜː/ and /ə/, though as the former occurs only in stressed syllables in RP (*bird*, **servant**), and the latter only in unstressed syllables (*above*, *butter*), this is not a contrast which enables a difference of meaning to be expressed.

The contrast between long and short vowels is not just one of length (*quantity*); a different place of articulation (*quality*) is involved. This is why Gimson, for example, in his transcription gives different symbols to these pairs of vowels (/iː/ vs /ɪ/, etc.) – drawing attention to the quality differences between them (p. 237). If length were the only factor, a transcription of /iː/ vs /i/ would suffice.

TYPES OF DIPHTHONG

From the point of view of length, the diphthongs (p. 237) are like long vowels; but the first part of a diphthong in English is much longer and louder than the second. When we listen to the diphthong in /haʊ/ *how*, for example, most of the sound is taken up with the /a/ part, the glide to /ʊ/ being quite short and rapid.

The eight diphthongs are usually grouped into three types, depending on the tongue movement involved.

• The first group ends with a glide towards the [ə] vowel in the centre of the mouth, and are called *centring* diphthongs. They are heard in the words *here* /ɪə/, *air* /eə/, and *sure* /ʊə/. The remainder end with a glide towards a higher position in the mouth, and are called *closing* diphthongs.

• One type of closing diphthong moves in the direction of an [i] quality at the front of the vowel area. These sounds are heard in the words *they* /eɪ/, *cry* /aɪ/, and *toy* /ɔɪ/.

• The other type of closing diphthong moves in the direction of an [u] quality at the back of the vowel area (and thus adds some lip rounding). These sounds are heard in the words *so* /əʊ/ and *how* /aʊ/.

The possibilities are shown in the diagram below. This also shows the two types of triphthong, formed by adding a central glide to the closing diphthongs.

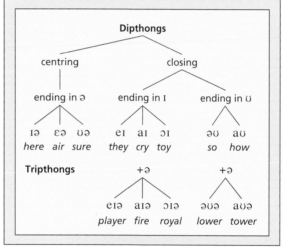

VOWEL FREQUENCY

A study of the frequency of vowels in a sample of conversational RP gave the following results:

	%
/ə/	10.74
/ɪ/	8.33
/e/	2.97
/aɪ/	1.83
/ʌ/	1.75
/eɪ/	1.71
/iː/	1.65
/əʊ/	1.51
/æ/	1.45
/ɒ/	1.37
/ɔː/	1.24
/uː/	1.13
/ʊ/	0.86
/ɑː/	0.79
/aʊ/	0.61
/ɜː/	0.52
/ɛə/	0.34
/ɪə/	0.21
/ɔɪ/	0.14
/ʊə/	0.06

The total for all vowels was 39.21 per cent. Consonant figures are given on p. 242. (After D. B. Fry, 1947.)

DANIEL JONES (1881–1967)

'DJ', as he was known within the profession, originally studied mathematics at Cambridge, and trained as a lawyer, but never practised. He first became interested in language when he took a course in conversational French at the age of 17, and found he had 'some aptitude for getting the pronunciation of French right'. He encountered phonetics after a visit to a language institute in Germany in 1900, studied the subject under Paul Passy in Paris, and gave his first course in phonetics at University College London, in 1907. He built up the Department of Phonetics there, becoming professor in 1921.

Although he researched the phonetics of many languages, his name was chiefly associated with two books, both on English: *An English Pronouncing Dictionary* (1917) and *An Outline of English Phonetics* (1918), both of which (in revised editions) are still used today. The cardinal vowels concept was also developed at that time. By the 1920s, DJ was being recognized as the British authority on phonetics. He served on the BBC Advisory Committee on Spoken English from its foundation (1926), and from 1909 was a strong supporter of the Simplified Spelling Society (becoming its president in 1946). He also served as secretary of the International Phonetics Association from 1927 to 1949, when he retired from university teaching, and was president of the Association from 1950 until his death.

VOWEL LOCATIONS AND VARIATIONS

This table gives a brief description of how each English vowel is articulated, using Received Pronunciation (RP, p. 365) as the reference model. To put this accent in perspective, the table also lists just a few of the hundreds of local and international regional variations which affect each vowel, as well as some of the variations which are found within RP itself. The cardinal vowel diagrams show the RP location of each vowel (in black) and the location of major variants (in red). Diphthongal movements are shown by an arrow; pure vowels by a dot.

Comments about regional variation should be interpreted with caution: to say that an RP vowel is diphthongized (p. 237) in Scots, for example, does not mean that this particular quality is to be found in *all* varieties of Scots. Any major regional dialect area presents a complex phonetic picture, with many variants reflecting differences in age, social background, sex, and other factors. The vowel qualities referred to in the regional variant column, therefore, are intended to be illustrative, not representative: they relate to just one of the accents which are commonly associated with a region. Further details about regional norms can be found in §20, and a historical perspective is given in §7.

Pure vowels

	Vowels	Articulation	Some regional variants		Vowels	Articulation	Some regional variants
	/iː/	Front of tongue raised to slightly below and behind close front position; lips spread; tongue tense; side rims make firm contact with upper molars.	Often diphthongized in RP, with a slight glide from a more central position; noticeable glide [əiː] in several UK accents (e.g. Liverpool, Birmingham, London), and in broad Australian; shorter in Scots.		/ɪ/	Part of tongue nearer centre than front raised to just above half-close position; lips loosely spread; tongue lax; rims make light contact with upper molars.	Centralized variants common (e.g. Scots, Northern Ireland); often replaced by [ə] in RP in unstressed syllables.
	/e/	Front of tongue raised to between half-open and half-close positions; lips loosely spread; tongue tenser than for /ɪ/; rims make light contact with upper molars.	Various diphthongized forms, such as [eɪ] in Cockney, [eə] in refined RP.		/æ/	Front of tongue raised to just below half-open position; lips neutrally open; rims make very slight contact with upper back molars.	More open and centralized [a] variants in N England, Wales; diphthongized [æə] in refined RP; triphthongized in some rural American (*man* /meɪən/).
	/ʌ/	Centre of tongue raised to just above fully open position; lips neutrally open; no contact between tongue and upper molars.	Further back in many older RP speakers; more open and front in Cockney; half-close back in N England, often rounded [ʊ].		/ɑː/	Tongue between centre and back in fully open position; lips neutrally open; no contact between rims and upper molars.	Fronted to [aː] in many varieties, e.g. Liverpool, broad Australian; further back in refined RP ('far back'); shorter in American [r]-pronouncing accents (p. 93).
	/ɒ/	Back of tongue in fully open position; slight, open lip rounding; no contact between rims and upper molars.	No lip rounding in American; lengthened and closer variant in conservative RP (*off* as /ɔːf/ 'orff') and Cockney.		/ɔː/	Back of tongue raised between half-open and half-close positions; medium lip rounding; no contact between rims and upper molars.	Often a triphthong in Cockney (*four* /fɔːʊə/); closer lip rounding in refined RP; length reduced in parts of USA (especially New England).
	/ʊ/	Tongue nearer centre than back, raised to just above half-close position; lips closely but loosely rounded; tongue lax; no firm contact between rims and upper molars.	Little variation, apart from some reduced lip rounding; longer and closer in Scots and some N England accents.		/uː/	Back of tongue raised to just below close position; lips closely rounded; tongue tense; no firm contact between rims and upper molars.	Front rounded variant marked in Scots; centralized and diphthongized in Cockney.

	Vowels	Articulation	Some regional variants		Vowels	Articulation	Some regional variants
	/ɜː/	Centre of tongue raised between half-close and half-open; lips neutrally spread; no firm contact between rims and upper molars.	Closer in Birmingham, Liverpool, Australian; more open in conservative RP; shorter when followed by [r] in Scots, SW England, American; diphthongized in some regional American (*bird* /bɔɪd/).		/ə/	Centre of tongue raised between half-close and half-open; lips neutrally spread; no firm contact between rims and upper molars.	Only in unstressed syllables in RP; replaces /ʌ/ as a stressed vowel in many regional accents; replaced by stronger vowel qualities in Caribbean and other stress-timed accents (p. 249).

Diphthongs

	Vowels	Articulation	Some regional variants		Vowels	Articulation	Some regional variants
	/eɪ/	Glide begins from slightly below half-close front position, moves upwards and slightly backwards towards [ɪ]; lips spread.	Noticeably more open first element in Cockney and broad Australian; monophthongized to [eː] in many British accents; closer start and more central second element in Caribbean (*Jamaica* /dʒamieka/).		/aɪ/	Glide begins slightly behind front open position, moves upwards towards [ɪ]; lips change from neutral to loosely spread; obvious closing movement of the lower jaw.	Considerable variation in first element, both further forward and further back; often centralized, e.g. in Canadian; further back and often rounded in broad Australian; monophthongized to [iː] in some Scots (*die* [diː]) and to [aː], or with a weak glide, in S USA (part of the 'southern drawl').
	/ɔɪ/	Glide begins between back half-open and open positions, moves upwards and forwards towards [ɪ]; lips open rounded changing to neutral.	Closer first element in Cockney; more open in conservative RP; longer first element in S USA.		/əʊ/	Glide begins in central position between half-close and half-open, moves upwards and back towards [ʊ]; lips neutral changing to slightly rounded.	First element more rounded and further back in conservative RP and Dublin; tendency to monophthongize in RP (*goal* [gɜːl]); more open start in broad Australian, and also in Cockney, where the glide is more extensive, with little or no lip rounding.
	/aʊ/	Glide begins between back and front open positions, moves upwards and slightly backwards towards [ʊ]; lips change from neutrally open to slightly rounded; jaw movement quite extensive.	First element fronted in Cockney and broad Australian, and more noticeable rounding on second element; unrounded fronted second element in 'royal family' RP (*house* [haɪs]); monophthongized close rounded vowel in Scots (*house* [huːs]); first element fronted towards mid-open in West Country and Dublin; centralized first element in Canada (p. 342).		/ɪə/	Glide begins in position for /ɪ/, moves backwards and downwards towards /ə/; lips neutral, with slight movement from spread to open.	More open first element in conservative RP; second element sometimes strong in 'affected' RP (*here* /hjɑː/).
	/ɛə/	Glide begins in half-open front position, moves backwards towards /ə/; lips neutrally open throughout.	Closer start in Cockney; much more open in refined RP; centralized long vowel in Birmingham [ɜː]; more open long vowel in Liverpool [ɛː]; closer long vowel in Scots [eː].		/ʊə/	Glide begins in position for /ʊ/, moves forwards and downwards towards /ə/; lips weakly rounded becoming neutrally spread.	Much variation in RP, with more open first element; often monophthongized to [ɔː], so that *sure* appears as [ʃɔː] 'shaw'.

CONSONANTS

The difference between the number of letters and sounds found in English, so dramatic in the case of vowels (p. 237), is far less significant in the case of consonants. There are 21 consonant letters in the written alphabet (B, C, D, F, G, H, J, K, L, M, N, P, Q, R, S, T, V, W, X, Y, Z), and there are 24 consonant sounds in most English accents. The difficulty of transcribing speech is therefore less serious, as most of the written symbols can be assigned individual phonetic values, and the resulting transcription thus looks much more immediately readable than that of vowels. However, because of the erratic history of English spelling, there is no neat one-to-one correlation between letters and sounds. In several cases, one consonant sound is spelled by more than one letter (e.g. *th* in *this*) or one consonant letter symbolizes more than one sound (e.g. *x* in *fox* /fɒks/). There are thus two answers to the question, 'How many consonants are there at the beginning or end of the word *thick?*': 'Two' (in writing); 'One' (in speech, /θɪk/).

Describing consonants

All consonants have certain properties in common, which identify them in contrast to vowels (p. 238).

• From a phonetic point of view (p. 236), they are articulated in one of two ways: either there is a closing movement of one of the vocal organs, forming such a narrow constriction that it is possible to hear the sound of the air passing through; or the closing movement is complete, giving a total blockage. The closing movement may involve the lips, the tongue, or the throat, but in each case the overall effect is very different from the relatively open and unimpeded articulation found in vowels.

• From a phonological point of view (p. 236), they are units of the sound system which typically occupy the edges of a syllable (the margins, p. 246), as in *dogs* /dɒgs/ and *glad* /glæd/. They may also appear in sequences (*clusters*), as these examples show. In fact, up to three consonants may be used together at the beginning of a spoken word in English (as in *string*), and up to four consonants at the end, though not always very comfortably (as in *twelfths* /twelfθs/ and *glimpsed* /glɪmpst/).

• Some consonants involve the vibration of the vocal cords: these are the *voiced* consonants, such as /b/ and /m/. Others have no vocal cord vibration: these are the *voiceless* consonants, such as /p/ and /s/. The distinction is not absolute: depending on where in a word a consonant appears, there may be degrees of voicing. At the end of a word, for example, a voiced consonant typically loses a great deal of its vibration (it is *devoiced*). The /z/ sound at the beginning of *zoo* /zuː/ is much more vibrant than the one at the end of *ooze* /uːz/ (to voice this fully would produce an unnatural buzzing effect at the end of the word).

• An alternative way of capturing the difference between such consonant pairs as /p/ and /b/ is to compare the force with which they are articulated. Voiceless consonants are produced with much greater force than their voiced counterparts, and the terms *fortis* ('strong') and *lenis* ('weak') have come to be used to identify the two types. Thus, /p/, /t/, /k/, /f/, /θ/, /s/, /ʃ/, and /tʃ/ are all fortis consonants; /b/, /d/, /g/, /v/, /ð/, /z/, /ʒ/, and /dʒ/ are all lenis.

• Unlike vowels, some consonants are primarily identified through their use of the nasal cavity. Normally, in English, when we speak we keep the soft palate (p. 236) raised, so that it presses against the back of the throat and allows no air out through the nose. With the three nasal consonants, /m/, /n/, and /ŋ/, however, the soft palate remains lowered (as it is when we breathe), and the result is a series of sounds with a distinctive nasal resonance.

Consonant or vowel

The distinction between consonant and vowel is fundamental, but some sounds sit uneasily between the two, being articulated in the same way as vowels, but functioning in the language in the same way as consonants. /j/ as in *yes* and /w/ as in *we* are like this. /j/ is formed like a very short [i] vowel (as can be heard if we draw out the *y* of *yes*), but it occurs at the beginning of the word, as do other consonants (*yes, mess, best*). Similarly, /w/ is formed like a short [u] vowel, but acts as a consonant (*we, me, see*). These two consonants are therefore sometimes described as *semi-vowels*.

Certain other consonants are also somewhat vowel-like, in that they can be sounded continuously without any audible friction: the three nasals, /m/, /n/, and /ŋ/, /l/ as in *lie*, and /r/ as in *red*. These can all be classed together as (frictionless) continuants or sonorants, within which the four oral items (/l/, /r/, /w/, /j/) are often recognized as forming a distinct group.

CONSONANT FREQUENCY

A study of the frequency of consonants in a sample of conversational RP gave the following results:

	%		%
/n/	7.58	/b/	1.97
/t/	6.42	/f/	1.79
/d/	5.14	/p/	1.78
/s/	4.81	/h/	1.46
/l/	3.66	/ŋ/	1.15
/ð/	3.56	/g/	1.05
/r/	3.51	/ʃ/	0.96
/m/	3.22	/j/	0.88
/k/	3.09	/dʒ/	0.60
/w/	2.81	/tʃ/	0.41
/z/	2.46	/θ/	0.37
/v/	2.00	/ʒ/	0.10

The total for all consonants was 60.78 per cent. Vowel figures are given on p. 239. (After D. B. Fry, 1947, with later corrections incorporated.)

It should be noted that this particular study did not take word frequency into account in the sample analysed. All sounds in the sample were counted, regardless of how many times a particular word was used there. This is why /ð/, in particular, has such a high place in the table: it is largely due to the high frequency of this sound in the definite article (*the*) and demonstratives (*this, that*, etc.).

TRANSCRIBING CONSONANTS

A British and an American transcription system for consonants: A. C. Gimson (1962) and V. Fromkin & R. Rodman (1974) (details on p. 237).

The consonants in	Gimson	F&R	The consonants in	Gimson	F&R
pie, up	p	p	so, us	s	s
by, ebb	b	b	zoo, ooze	z	z
tie, at	t	t	shoe, ash	ʃ	š
die, odd	d	d	genre, rouge	ʒ	ž
coo, ache	k	k	he	h	h
go, egg	g	g	me, am	m	m
chew, each	tʃ	č, tš	no, in	n	n
jaw, edge	dʒ	ǰ, dž	hang	ŋ	ŋ
fee, off	f	f	lie, eel	l	l
view, of	v	v	row, ear (not RP)	r	r
thigh, oath	θ	θ	way	w	w
they, booth	ð	ð	you	j	y

TYPES OF CONSONANT

All English consonants are made with an air-stream from the lungs moving outwards (unlike certain consonants in some other languages, which use other types of air-stream). To differentiate the 24 consonants from each other, phoneticians use a classification based on the place and manner of articulation, in addition to the criteria of whether they are voiced or voiceless and oral or nasal, as described on the facing page. (For the names and locations of the vocal organs, see the diagram on p. 236. For a full description of each individual consonant, see pp. 244–5.)

Place of articulation

We need to know *where* in the vocal tract the sound is made, and which vocal organs are involved. The important positions for English are the following:

- *Bilabial*: using both lips, as in /p/, /b/, /m/, /w/.
- *Labio-dental*: using the lower lip and the upper teeth, as in /f/, /v/.
- *Dental*: using the tongue tip between the teeth or close to the upper teeth, as in /θ/ and /ð/.
- *Alveolar*: using the blade of the tongue close to the alveolar ridge, as in /t/, /d/, /s/, /z/, /n/, /l/, and the first elements of /tʃ/ and /dʒ/.
- *Post-alveolar*: using the tongue tip close to just behind the alveolar ridge, as in /r/ (for some accents).
- *Retroflex*: using the tongue tip curled back to well behind the alveolar ridge, as in /r/ (for some accents).
- *Palato-alveolar*: using the blade (and sometimes the tip) of the tongue close to the alveolar ridge, with a simultaneous raising of the front of the tongue towards the roof of the mouth, as in /ʃ/ and /ʒ/, and the second elements in /tʃ/ and /dʒ/.
- *Palatal*: raising the front of the tongue close to the hard palate, as in /j/.
- *Velar*: raising the back of the tongue against the soft palate, as in /k/, /g/, and /ŋ/.
- *Glottal*: using the space between the vocal cords to make audible friction, as in /h/, or a closure, as in the glottal stop (in some accents).

Manner of articulation

We need to know *how* the sound is made, at the various locations in the vocal tract. Four phonetic possibilities are recognized.
Total closure
- *Plosive*: a complete closure is made at some point in the vocal tract, with the soft palate raised; air pressure builds up behind the closure, which is then released explosively, as in /p/, /b/, /t/, /d/, /k/, /g/, the first elements of /tʃ/ and /dʒ/, and the glottal stop.
- *Nasal*: a complete closure is made at some point in the mouth, with the soft palate lowered, so that air escapes through the nose, as in /m/, /n/, /ŋ/.

- *Affricate*: a complete closure is made at some point in the mouth, with the soft palate raised; air pressure builds up behind the closure, which is then released relatively slowly (compared with the suddenness of a plosive release), as in /tʃ/ and /dʒ/.
Intermittent closure
- *Roll* or *Trill*: the tongue tip taps rapidly against the teeth ridge, as in the 'trilled /r/' heard in some regional accents; a trill in which the back of the tongue taps against the uvula is also sometimes heard regionally and in some idiosyncratic 'weak r' pronunciations.
- *Flap*: a single tap is made by the tongue tip against the alveolar ridge, as in some pronunciations of /r/ and /d/.
Partial closure
- *Lateral*: a partial closure is made by the blade of the tongue against the alveolar ridge, in such a way that the air stream is able to flow around the sides of the tongue, as in /l/.
Narrowing
- *Fricative*: Two vocal organs come so close together that the movement of air between them can be heard, as in /f/, /v/, /θ/, /ð/, /s/, /z/, /ʃ/, /ʒ/, /h/, and the second element in /tʃ/ and /dʒ/. The consonants /s/, /z/, /ʃ/, and /ʒ/ have a sharper sound than the others, because they are made with a narrower groove in the tongue, and are often grouped together as *sibilants*.

CONSONANT COMBINATIONS

The 24 consonants found in RP and many other accents may be used singly or in combination in syllables and words – but only a fraction of the millions of possible combinations actually occur. The table shows the possibilities for three-consonant combinations at the beginning of a word, using data derived from the *English Pronouncing Dictionary*. These are:

s + p + l, r, j
s + t + r, j
s + k + l, r, j, w

In other words, the sequence is /s/ + a fortis plosive + one of the continuants (see above). Outside of this system, there is, in addition, a single example of /smj-/ – the name of a bird, the *smew*. However, of the 12 possible CCC sequences, three (/spw-, stl-, stw-/) do not occur, and /CCj/ and /skl-/ are highly restricted, appearing only with certain vowels.

It is the consonant–vowel combinations which make the table particularly interesting. Is there really no word in the language (using an RP accent) beginning with three consonants and followed by /ɔɪ/? No /splɔɪ-/? /sprɔɪ-/? /strɔɪ-/? Or again, is there no /splaʊ-/? No /skwɑː/? It is fairly easy to check out the possibilities intuitively for short words, though even here it is surprising how many technical or rare words can be found with unusual initial clusters, such as *squamous* and *sclerosis*. Proper names also extend the range somewhat; for example, there seems to be nothing for /straʊ/ except *Stroud* (and thus *strouding*) and *Strauss*. The uncertain status of new loan words (p. 126) and the existence of mixed accents with variant pronunciations (§21) also make it difficult to be absolutely definite that a particular consonant combination does not exist.
(After A. C. Gimson, 1970, 2nd edn of Gimson 1962.)

GAPS? SCHMAPS!

Traditionally, there is no /ʃn-/ initial word cluster in English, but the situation has changed in recent years with the arrival of a number of loan words from German and American Yiddish, and several other /ʃC-/ combinations are now often heard.

schnapps	schlemiel
schnitzel	schmuck
schnorkel	schmaltz
schnauzer	schmo
schnozzle	schlock

	ɪ	e	æ	ʌ	ɒ	ʊ	ə	iː	ɑː	ɔː	uː	ɜː	eɪ	aɪ	ɔɪ	əʊ	aʊ	ɪə	ɛə	ʊə
spl	+	+	+	+	+		+	+					+	+	+					
spr	+	+	+	+	+					+	+		+	+			+			
spj											+									+
str	+	+	+	+	+			+	+	+	+	+		+	+		+	+		
stj											+									+
skl		+	+				+									+				
skr	+		+	+	+					+	+		+	+		+	+			
skj											+									+
skw	+	+			+					+	+	+					+	+		
smj											+									

It is an interesting exercise to try to find examples of all the words marked as possible in the table. A crib is provided on p. 250.

A schnauzer

CONSONANT LOCATIONS AND VARIATIONS

This table gives a brief description of how each English consonant is articulated, using Received Pronunciation (RP, p. 365) as the reference model. To put this accent in perspective, the chief regional and social variations which affect certain consonants are also listed. The diagrams show place of articulation only. As with vowels (p. 240), comments about regional variation are illustrative, not representative, and should be interpreted with caution. For further discussion of variation, see §20; historical developments are summarized on pp. 18, 42.

Plosives

/p, b/

Articulation: Bilabial plosives: soft palate raised; complete closure made by the upper and lower lip; /p/ voiceless, /b/ voiced (and devoiced in word-final position); /p/ fortis, /b/ lenis.

Some regional variants: No important regional variants, though the amount of aspiration (the force of air following the release of /p/) and the degree of voicing can vary.

/t, d/

Articulation: Alveolar plosives: soft palate raised; complete closure made by the tongue tip and rims against the alveolar ridge and side teeth; /t/ voiceless, /d/ voiced (and devoiced in word-final position); /t/ fortis, /d/ lenis; lip position influenced by adjacent vowel (spread for *tee, meat*; rounded for *too, foot*); tongue position influenced by a following consonant, becoming further back (post-alveolar) in *try*, dental in *eighth*; when in final position in a syllable or word, they readily assimilate (p. 247) to /p, k/ or /b, g/ if followed by bilabial or velar consonants.

Some regional variants: In American, and often in informal speech generally, /t/ between vowels is a lenis, rapid tap, resembling [d]; dental in Irish; affricate release as [ts] or [dz] in some urban UK dialects (Liverpool, Cockney) and Irish; /t/ replaced by glottal stop [ʔ] between vowels and before /l/ (as in *bottle*) very noticeable in Cockney, Glasgow English, and urban speech generally; glottal stop increasingly heard in RP, especially replacing /t/ before /n/ (as in *button*) and in final position (as in *shut the gate*).

/k, g/

Articulation: Velar plosives: soft palate raised; complete closure made by the back of the tongue against the soft palate; /k/ voiceless, /g/ voiced (and devoiced in word-final position); /k/ fortis, /g/ lenis; lip position influenced by adjacent vowel (spread for *keen, meek*, rounded for *cool, book*; also, quality varies depending on the following vowel (/k/ in *keen* is much further forward, approaching the hard palate, than /k/ in *car*).

Some regional variants: No important regional variations, apart from some variation in aspiration and voicing (as with /p/ and /b/).

Fricatives

/f, v/

Articulation: Labio-dental fricatives: soft palate raised; light contact made by lower lip against upper teeth; /f/ voiceless, /v/ voiced (and devoiced in word-final position); /f/ fortis, /v/ lenis.

Some regional variants: UK West Country /f/ weakly articulated, approaching [v]; /f/ in *of* often omitted in informal speech (*cup o' tea*), as is the /v/ in auxiliary *have* (*could have*).

/θ, ð/

Articulation: Dental fricatives: soft palate raised; tongue tip and rims make light contact with edge and inner surface of upper incisors, and a firmer contact with upper sideteeth; tip protrudes between teeth for some speakers; /θ/ voiceless, /ð/ voiced (and devoiced in word-final position); /θ/ fortis, /ð/ lenis; lip position depends on adjacent vowel (spread in *thief, heath*, rounded in *though, oath*).

Some regional variants: In Cockney and London-influenced varieties, replaced by labio-dental /f/ and /v/; in Irish, replaced by a dental /t/ and /d/; often omitted in clusters in informal speech (e.g. /kləʊz/ for *clothes*).

/s, z/

Articulation: Alveolar fricatives: soft palate raised; tongue tip and blade make light contact with alveolar ridge, and rims make close contact with upper side teeth; air escapes along a narrow groove in the centre of the tongue; /s/ voiceless, /z/ voiced (and devoiced in word-final position); /s/ fortis, /z/ lenis; lip position depends on adjacent vowel (spread in *see, ease*, rounded in *soup, ooze*).

Some regional variants: UK West Country /s/ weakly articulated, approaching [z]; several deviant forms in speech pathology, especially the use of [θ] and [ð] for /s/ and /z/ respectively (an interdental lisp).

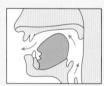

/ʃ, ʒ/

Articulation: Palato-alveolar fricatives: soft palate raised; tongue tip and blade make light contact with alveolar ridge, while front of tongue raised towards hard palate, and rims put in contact with upper side teeth; /ʃ/ voiceless, /ʒ/ voiced (and devoiced in word-final position); /ʃ/ fortis, /ʒ/ lenis, but both sounds laxer than /s/ and /z/; lip rounding influenced by adjacent vowel (spread in *she, beige*, rounded in *shoe, rouge*), but some speakers always round their lips for these sounds.

Some regional variants: No important regional variation; some speakers vary between these sounds and /sj/ or /zj/ in the middle of such words as *issue, casual*; also usage variation with /sɪ/ or /zɪ/ as in *appreciate, ratio*; /ʃ/ and /ʒ/ are themselves alternatives in *version, Asia*, and several other words; /ʒ/ often replaced by /dʒ/ in word-final position (e.g. *garage, rouge*).

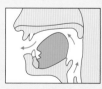

/h/ (followed by [i] vowel)

Articulation: Glottal fricative: soft palate raised; air from lungs causes audible friction as it passes through the open glottis, and resonates through the vocal tract with a quality determined chiefly by the position of the tongue taken up for the following vowel; voiceless with some voicing when surrounded by vowels (*aha*).

Some regional variants: Occurs only in syllable initial position, before a vowel; omitted in many regional accents, and widely considered the chief sign of 'uneducated' British speech; usage variation in initial unaccented syllable (e.g. *an hotel* vs *a hotel*).

Affricates

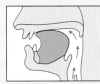

/ʧ,ʤ/ (stop phase only)

Articulation: Palato-alveolar affricates: soft palate raised; for the first element, closure made by the tongue tip, blade, and rims against the alveolar ridge and side teeth; at the same time, front of the tongue is raised towards the hard palate, so that when the closure is released the air escapes to give a palato-alveolar quality; /ʧ/ voiceless, /ʤ/ voiced; /ʧ/ fortis, /ʤ/ lenis; lip position influenced by following vowel (spread for *cheap*, rounded for *choose*), though some speakers always round their lips for these sounds.

Some regional variants: No important regional variation; some RP speakers replace them by /tj/ and /dj/ (in such words as *statue, tune, due*).

Nasals

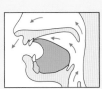

/m/

Articulation: Bilabial nasal: soft palate lowered; a total closure made by the upper and lower lip; voiced, with only occasional devoicing (notably, after [s], as in *smile*); labio-dental closure when followed by /f/ or /v/, as in *comfort*; vowel-like nature allows /m/ to be used with a syllabic function (p. 246), in such words as *bottom* /bɒtm̩/.

Some regional variants: No important regional or social variations.

/n/

Articulation: Alveolar nasal: soft palate lowered; closure made by tongue tip and rims against the alveolar ridge and upper side teeth; voiced, with only occasional devoicing (notably, after [s], as in *snap*); lip position influenced by adjacent vowel (spread in *neat*, rounded in *noon*); much affected by the place of articulation of the following consonant (e.g. often labio-dental closure when followed by /f/ or /v/ (as in *infant*), bilabial when followed by /p/ or /b/); vowel-like nature allows /n/ to be used with a syllabic function in such words as *button* /bʌtn̩/.

Some regional variants: No important regional or social variations.

/ŋ/

Articulation: Velar nasal: soft palate lowered; voiced; closure formed between the back of the tongue and the soft palate; further forward if preceded by front vowel (*sing*, compared with *bang*); lip position depends on preceding vowel (spread in *sing*, rounded in *song*); this is the normal nasal sound before /k/ or /g/ in such words as *sink* and *angry*, despite having only an *n* in the spelling.

Some regional variants: Heard as [ŋg] in Midlands and N England (*singing* as /sɪŋgɪŋg/); ending *-ing* replaced by /ɪn/ in conservative RP (*huntin' and shootin'*) and widely in regional speech (now perceived as uneducated in the UK).

Oral continuants

/l/ (clear [l])

Articulation: Lateral: soft palate raised; closure made by tongue tip against centre of alveolar ridge, and air escapes round either or both sides; voiced, with devoicing chiefly after fortis consonants (as in *please, sleep*); front of tongue simultaneously raised in direction of hard palate, giving a front-vowel resonance in such words as RP *leap* ('clear l'); back of tongue raised in direction of soft palate, giving a back vowel resonance in such words as RP *pool* ('dark l'); lip position depends on adjacent vowel (spread in *leap, peel*, rounded in *loop, pool*); vowel-like nature allows /l/ to be used with a syllabic function in such words as *bottle* /bɒtl̩/.

/l/ (dark [ɫ])

Some regional variants: In RP, clear *l* occurs before a vowel or /j/, and dark *l* in other places, but there is much variation; dark *l* often becomes a back vowel in Cockney, especially with lip rounding, so that *peel* becomes more like [piːo], and this is also heard in some RP, especially London-influenced speech (as in *careful, beautiful*); dark *l* in all positions in some Scots and much American; clear *l* in all positions in some Irish; American uses syllabic /l̩/ where RP has a noticeable vowel (e.g. in *fertile, missile*).

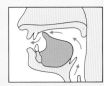

/r/

Articulation: Post-alveolar approximant (or frictionless continuant): soft palate raised; tongue tip held close to (but not touching) the back of the alveolar ridge; back rims touch the upper molars; central part of tongue lowered; lip position influenced by following vowel (spread in *reach*, rounded in *room*); becomes a fricative when preceded by /d/ (as in *drive*); becomes a tap between vowels and after some consonants (as in *very, sorry, three*); voiced, with devoicing after /p/, /t/, /k/ (as in *pry*); lip position influenced by following vowel (spread in *reed*, rounded in *rude*), but some speakers always give /r/ some rounding.

Some regional variants: More variants than any other consonant; major division (p. 307) into accents which use /r/ after vowels (*rhotic accents*) and those which do not (*non-rhotic accents*); tongue tip curled back (*retroflexed*) in much American, South Asian, SW England, the /r/ articulation colouring the preceding vowel (in *bird, girl*); lingual trill or roll against the alveolar ridge in some Scots, Welsh, and may be heard in stylized speech anywhere (as in dramatic declamation); uvular trill or fricative in NE England and some Scots; replacement by /w/ (*red/wed/*) fashionable in England in early 19th century; use as a linking or intrusive sound may attract social criticism (p. 366).

/w/

Articulation: Labio-velar semi-vowel: soft palate raised; tongue in the position of a close back vowel; lips rounded, with greater tension than for [uː] (compare *woos* and *ooze*); voiced, with some devoicing after fortis consonants (*twice, sweet*).

Some regional variants: Several dialects (such as Scottish), and also conservative RP, have a voiceless variant [hw] or [ʍ] in such words as *while*, and this may be contrastive (*Wales* vs *whales*); also common regionally (very noticeable in Cockney) is a strong [w] element replacing a vowel in such words as *door* [dowə]; forms such as *flower* [flawə] may also be heard in modified RP.

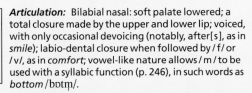

/j/

Articulation: Palatal semi-vowel; soft palate raised; tongue in the position of a front close vowel; lip position influenced by following vowel (spread in *year*, rounded in *you*); greater tension than for [iː] (compare *yeast* and *east*); voiced, with some devoicing after fortis consonants (*pure, huge*).

Some regional variants: Variation between /juː/ and /uː/ in RP after certain consonants, especially /l/ and /s/ (*suit* as /sjuːt/ and /suːt/; *salute* as /saljuːt/ and /saluːt/); /j/ variant now less common, and absent in most regional accents; variation between /sj, zj, tj, dj/ and /ʃ, ʒ, ʧ, ʤ/ in such words as *issue, usual, statue*, and *educate*; also common regionally is a strong [j] element replacing a vowel in such words as *where* [wejə].

SYLLABLES

Vowels and consonants typically do not act alone; there are very few words or word-like noises which consist of only one sound (they include *I, eye, oh, m*). The vast majority of English words contain a combination of vowels (V) and consonants (C), such as CV (*go*), VC (*up*), CVC (*cat*), CCVCC (*stops*), and CCCV (*screw*, p. 243). The combined units are called *syllables*. In the above examples the words each contain only one such unit, and are thus often called *monosyllables*, or *monosyllabic words*. This notion contrasts with words that contain more than one syllable (*polysyllabic words*) – most of the words in the language, in fact. The present sentence contains instances of a two-syllable (disyllabic) word, *despite* /dɪspaɪt/ (CVCCVC), and a three-syllable (trisyllabic) word, *instances* /ɪnstən-sɪz/ (VCCCVCCVC), and the previous sentence has a five-syllable word, *polysyllabic* /pɒliːsɪlabɪk/, which despite its length has a simple syllabic structure (CVCVCVCVCVC).

People know about syllables. 'Not another syllable!'

we may say to someone who is protesting too much. And if we want to emphasize a point, or speak plainly, we may well try to 'put it in words of one syllable'. People are also able to count the number of syllables in a word, by beating out its rhythm. The rule is basically simple: each syllable contains one vowel or vowel-like nucleus. The word *despite* has two such nuclei, so there are two syllables. The word *polysyllabic* has five nuclei, so there are five syllables. However, there are several types of word (notably, those which contain diphthongs or triphthongs, p. 239) where it can be difficult deciding just how many syllables there are. Is *meteoric* four syllables (*me–te–o–ric*) or three (*me–teo–ric*)? Is *several* three syllables or two (*se–ve–ral* or *sev–ral*)? Is *being* two syllables (*be–ing*) or one? Regional accent, speed of speech, level of formality, and context of use can all influence these decisions. For example, the number of syllables we assign to such words can depend on whether they are being spoken spontaneously or read aloud, and on whether they are being said with emphasis, emotion, or equanimity.

A speech bubble from *Comic Cuts*, popular among young British children in the 1940s. The writers have introduced a system of syllable division, presumably believing that this will help children to read.

SYLLABLE STRUCTURE

The structure of English spoken syllables can be summarized as follows:

• Minimally, a syllable consists of a vowel, or a vowel-like sound (see below), which acts as the *nucleus, centre,* or *peak* of the syllable: *I, or, ooh*. Very rarely, a syllable can consist of a consonant: *m, shh*.
• Many syllables have one or more consonants preceding the nucleus. These make up the syllable *onset*: *me, so, play*. Traditionally, they are known as 'open syllables'.
• Many syllables have one or more consonants following

the nucleus. These make up the syllable *coda*: *am, ants, eel*. They are traditionally known as 'closed syllables'.
• Many syllables have both an onset and a coda: *cat, jump*.
• The combination of nucleus and coda has a special significance, making up the *rhyming* property of a syllable: *cat, sat; jump, clump*.

In analysing syllable structure in this way, it is important to look for the pronunciation behind a word's spelling. Although *ooze* ends in a written vowel, it ends in a spoken consonant, and its structure is VC. Similarly, *all* is VC (not VCC),

jumped is CVCCC (not CVCCVC), and *fox* is CVCC (not CVC).

Syllabic consonants
There is one exception to the rule that a syllable must have a vowel as its nucleus. This occurs when certain vowel-like consonants – /l/, /r/, or a nasal – act as the centre of the syllable, as in *bottle* /bɒtl̩/, *bottom* /bɒtm̩/, *button* /bʌtn̩/, and (in those accents which pronounce /r/, p. 245) *perhaps* /pr̩haps/. In each case, the syllabic consonant is shown by a small vertical mark beneath the symbol. In a very slow articulation of these words, the vowels would re-appear, and

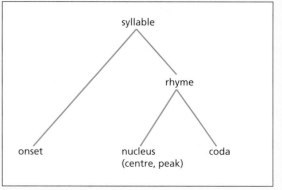

the consonants would revert to their normal coda value (such as /bɒtəl/); but these pronunciations are highly artificial, and would never be heard in usual conversational

speech. (However, there are a few regional accents – in some parts of Wales, for example – where the avoidance of syllabic consonants is normal.)

SYLLABLE BOUND·A·RIES / BOUN·DA·RIES

It is one thing to be able to count the number of syllables in a word. It is quite another to decide where the boundaries between the syllables should go. English is full of cases where alternative analyses are possible.

• There are two syllables in *extra* /ekstrə/, but where should the boundary between them fall? It is unlikely that people would opt for a division between /e/ and /kstrə/,

because there are no syllables in English which begin with the consonant sequence /kstrə/. Similarly, a division between /ekstr/ and /ə/ would feel unnatural. But /ek/ +/strə/, /eks/ + /trə/, and /ekst/ + /rə/ are all possible. People usually prefer either of the first two options here, but there is no obvious way of deciding between them.
• There are two syllables in *standing*, but is the division to be made between *stan* and *ding* or *stand* and *ing*? If we follow our phonetic instinct, and go for two evenly balanced CVC syllables, we will prefer the

former analysis. If we follow our grammatical instinct, and divide between the base form and the inflection (p. 204), we will prefer the latter.
• There are three syllables in *boundary*, but again we have the choice of a division on phonetic grounds (after *n*) or on grammatical grounds (after *d*), preserving a semantic link with *bound*.

Hyphenation points
Some dictionaries add a mark to recommend where a printed word may be hyphenated if it appears at the end of a line. However, these points

do not necessarily correspond to syllabic boundaries in speech. The following examples come from *Webster's Third New International Dictionary*, where the editor is reflecting general publishing practice.

aber·deen·shire   ab·er·do·ni·an
ab·er·rance   abet·tor
abey·ance

There is no division after the *a* or *ab* of *abettor*, for example, because publishers would be unlikely to insert a line-break at those points in the word.

CONNECTED SPEECH

Vowel and consonant segments combine into syllables; syllables combine into words; and words combine into phrases and sentences. But the process of producing connected speech affects the pronunciation of several of these segments in a number of interesting ways. Certain segments have a tendency to run together; extra segments may be added to ensure smoothness of speech; some segments adopt a less clearly defined phonetic form; and some completely disappear. Each of these possibilities has an associated technical label from the domain of phonetics. (Pronunciations shown are those of Received Pronunciation, or RP, p. 365.)

ACOUSTIC EVIDENCE

Several features of connected speech can be seen in this acoustic display of a sentence, using a machine known as a speech spectrograph. Time is displayed horizontally: the utterance lasts for just over two seconds. The acoustic frequency of the speech sounds is displayed vertically, and their intensity is shown by the relative darkness of the marks. The vowels and vowel-like sounds are darkest, and the different vowel qualities can be clearly seen in the changing pattern of black bands (*formants*), which represent varying concentrations of acoustic energy in the vocal tract.

e ni: w eɪ   aɪ t əʊ ldɪm n n tə gəʊ
Anyway,   I told him not to go.

• There is a perceptible pause after *anyway*, but otherwise the words have no silences between them. This is *connected* speech.
• There is elision of /h/ in *him*, and a very rapid running together of sounds at that point. It is difficult to see any vowel in *him*.
• The two /t/ sounds of *not* and *to* have fused into one.
• The vowel of *to* is very short and weak.

ASSIMILATION

Adjacent sounds often influence each other so that they become more alike, or *assimilate*. These effects are more common in rapid speech, but some degree of assimilation will be found in all spoken styles.

• In *anticipatory* (or *regressive*) assimilation, a sound is influenced by the sound which follows it. In the phrase *ten balloons*, /ten/ is likely to be pronounced /tem/, anticipating the following bilabial consonant. In the greeting *good night*, /gʊd/ is usually pronounced /gʊn/, as sometimes shown in writing: *g'night*.
• In *progressive* assimilation, a sound is influenced by the sound which precedes it. The second word in *bridge score* would typically emerge (in RP) as /ʃkɔː/, because of the influence of the palatal element in the preceding affricate (p. 245). Similarly, the second word in *Church Street* would be found as /ʃtriːt/.
• A third possibility is *coalescence* – a reciprocal influence, where two sounds fuse into a single new segment. In *won't she*, the final /t/ and initial /ʃ/ mutually assimilate to produce /tʃ/, resulting in the fused unit, /wəʊntʃiː/.

STRONG AND WEAK FORMS

Nearly 50 words in English can be pronounced in two distinct ways, depending on the degree of force with which they are uttered. They are all words which perform a grammatical function – determiners, pronouns, auxiliary verbs, prepositions, conjunctions, and particles. *Strong* (or *full*) forms are used when the word is said in isolation or is being emphasized. *Weak* forms are normal in connected speech: peripheral vowels (those which are articulated towards the edge of the vowel area in the mouth, p. 238) are replaced by those of a more central quality, and some consonants may be elided. Weak forms are sometimes represented in writing, though not usually very accurately (*bacon 'n eggs, cup o' coffee*).

In the following examples, the strong forms are given on the left and the weak forms on the right.

and	ænd	ən, n
that	ðæt	ðət
his	hɪz	ɪz
from	frɒm	frəm
of	ɒv	əv, v, ə
to	tuː	tʊ, tə
some	sʌm	səm, sm
there	ðɛə	ðə
have	hæv	əv, v, ə
were	wɜː	wə
do	duː	də, dʊ
must	mʌst	məs, məst

In many cases, we need to take note of context. For example, *there* as an adverb of place (*Look over there*) is always strong; but at the beginning of an existential sentence (p. 231) it is always weak (*There's no place like home*). Also, different forms may appear before consonants and before vowels: compare *I must go* (/məs/) and *I must eat* (/məst/), or *for tea* (/fə/) and *for Ann* (/fər/).

ELISION

As speech speeds up, sounds are likely to be left out, or *elided*. This is especially so when clusters of consonants occur. Indeed, some sequences are impossible to articulate naturally without elision. Try *Henry the Sixth's three advisers*. Tongue twisters capitalize on these difficulties.

• Vowels in weak syllables are often elided in informal speech. It is unusual to hear the first vowel in such words as *police*, *tomato*, and *correct*, which routinely appear as *p'lice*, etc. A tip for novice public speakers is to give extra weight to the vowels of their unstressed syllables.
• Consonants in clusters are commonly simplified. We are unlikely to hear all three consonants articulated at the end of the first word in *Acts of Parliament*: /aks/ is normal. Similarly, we will find *next day* /neks deɪ/, *government* /gʌvəmənt/, and *mashed potatoes* /maʃ pəteɪtəʊz/.
• Whole syllables may be elided, especially when there is a repeated consonant, as in British English pronunciations of *library* and *particularly*: /laɪbri/, /pətɪkjʊli/.
• Some words are especially prone to elision, such as *of* before consonants (*cup o' tea, lots o' people*). Other examples include *gonna* (=*going to*), *wanna* (=*want to*), and the weak forms of auxiliary verbs (p. 212).

LIAISON

A sound may be introduced between words or syllables to help them run together more smoothly. The chief example of this in English is the pronunciation of word-final /r/ in RP (and other non-rhotic accents, p. 245). RP speakers pronounce the /r/ in such words as *clear* and *mother* only when there is a following vowel: we find /klɪə/ in *clear question* but /klɪər/ in *clear answer*. This is usually called *linking r*.

Similarly, RP speakers regularly link adjacent vowels with an /r/ even when there is no *r* in the spelling, as in *India(r) and Pakistan* or *media(r) interest*. This *intrusive r* can attract ferocious criticism from conservative RP speakers, when they notice it, on the grounds that there is nothing in the spelling to justify its use (p. 366). It is especially disliked after an open back vowel, as in *law(r) and order, flaw(r) in the argument*, or *draw(r)ing*. (It is hardly ever noticed after a schwa vowel, as in the other examples above, and even the most tub-thumping

critic will be heard using an intrusive *r* in such cases.) The BBC is one of several institutions which have become so sensitive about public reaction to the usage that it warns its presenters of the risks of liaising with *Laura Norder*.

Got one

In Robert Burchfield's *The Spoken Word: A BBC Guide* (1981), there is a clear recommendation about *r* liaison:

In the formal presentation of the news or of other scripted speech:
    Avoid the intrusive *r*.

Some presenters evidently took this advice very seriously, as is seen in this extract from a radio script, where the reader has spotted a case in advance, and has marked his copy of the script so that he does not forget about it.

> PRESENTER: One of the questions we'll be dealing with in today's programme is the future of martial <u>law</u> in Poland. The issue facing the Poles is complex, and to help us debate it we have in the studio two people who have

PROSODY

The sound system enables us to express meaning in speech in both verbal and non-verbal ways. *Verbal meaning* ('what we say') relies on vowels and consonants to construct words, phrases, and sentences. *Non-verbal meaning* ('the way that we say it') makes use of such factors as intonation, rhythm, and tone of voice to provide speech with much of its structure and expressiveness. As the old song wisely says, 'it ain't what you say, it's the way that you say it'. So often, it is the non-verbal meaning which is the critical element in a communication.

Prosodic features

How many 'ways' are there to say things? The chief possibilities are dictated by the main auditory properties of sound: *pitch*, *loudness*, and *speed*. These properties, used singly or in combination (in the form of *rhythm*), and accompanied by the distinctive use of silence (in the form of *pause*), make up the *prosody* or *prosodic features* of the language. This is a much broader sense of 'prosody' than is to be found in poetry, where it refers only to the study of metrical patterning (p. 415).

• The most important prosodic effects are those conveyed by the linguistic use of pitch movement, or melody – the *intonation* system. Different pitch levels (*tones*) are used in particular sequences (*contours*) to express a wide range of meanings. Some of these meanings can be shown in writing, such as the opposition between statement (*They're ready.*) and question (*They're ready?*), but most intonational effects have no equivalents in punctuation, and can be written down only through a special transcription.
• Loudness is used in a variety of ways. Gross differences of meaning (such as anger, menace, excitement) can be conveyed by using an overall loudness level. More intricately, English uses variations in loudness to define the difference between strong and weak (*stressed* and *unstressed*) syllables. The stress pattern of a word is an important feature of the word's spoken identity: thus we find **nation**, not na**tion**; nation**ality**, not **nation**ality. There may even be contrasts of meaning partly conveyed by stress pattern, as with **record** (the noun) and re**cord** (the verb). Stress patterns make an important contribution to spoken intelligibility, and foreigners who unwittingly alter word stress can have great difficulty in making themselves understood (p. 249).
• Varying the *speed* (or *tempo*) of speech is an important but less systematic communicative feature. By speeding up or slowing down the rate at which we say syllables, words, phrases, and sentences, we can convey several kinds of meaning, such as (speeding up) excite-

ment and impatience, or (slowing down) emphasis and thoughtfulness. There is a great deal of difference between *No* said in a clipped, definite tone ('Nope') and *No* said in a drawled, meditative tone ('No-o-o'). And grammatical boundaries can often be signalled by tempo variation, as when a whole phrase is speeded up to show that it is functioning as a single word (*a take-it-or-leave-it situation*).

NINE WAYS OF SAYING YES

No one has yet described all the nuances of meaning which can be conveyed by the intonation system. Even if we restrict the example to a single word (*yes*), and a single context (*Will you marry me?*), it proves difficult to capture everything that is involved. (The accent represented here is RP, p. 365. The direction of pitch movement is shown between two parallel lines, which represent the upper and lower limits of the speaker's pitch range. The commentary indicates the tone's general meaning, and parenthetically remarks on the likelihood of its use in nuptial circumstances.)

low fall
The most neutral tone; a detached, unemotional statement of fact. (Unlikely, though it could be quite a dramatic answer, after tempestuous preliminaries.)

full fall
Emotionally involved; the higher the onset of the tone, the more involved the speaker; choice of emotion (surprise, excitement, irritation) depends on the speaker's facial expression. (Possible, especially if accompanied by other tones of voice, such as breathiness.)

mid fall
Routine, uncommitted comment; detached and unexcited. ('I'm thinking about it.' Wedding bells seem unlikely.)

low rise
Facial expression important; with a 'happy' face, the tone is sympathetic and friendly; with a 'grim' face, it is guarded and ominous. (Neither makes particular sense, in this context, though the speaker might be thinking, 'What's the catch?')

full rise
Emotionally involved, often disbelief or shock, the extent of the emotion depending on the width of the tone. (Unlikely, though it might be used afterwards by the person popping the question, if he/she was not expecting to get a positive answer 'I don't believe you've said yes'.)

high rise
Mild query or puzzlement; often used in echoing what has just been said. (Unlikely, though it might be used to convey 'Are you sure you know what you're saying?')

level
Bored, sarcastic, ironic. (Unlikely. If used, it would have to mean something like 'If I really must' or 'I give up', or possibly, 'Here we go again, the same old routine'.)

fall-rise
A strongly emotional tone; a straight or 'negative' face conveys uncertainty, doubt, or tentativeness; a positive face conveys encouragement or urgency. (The latter is rather more likely than the former, which would be distinctly cagey, in this context. Maybe there are some conditions to be met.)

rise-fall
Strong emotional involvement; depending on the face, the attitude might be delighted, challenging, or complacent. (Very likely. With a bit of breathiness, the speaker can't wait.)

A REALLY INTERESTING HIGH RISE INTONATION[†]

Prosody, and especially intonation, is an important feature of sociolinguistic identity (§§20–21). A well-known example is the way some regional English accents routinely use a rising tone at the end of statements, instead of the falling tone found there in most parts of the English-speaking world. Rising-tone accents, often described as 'musical' or 'lilting', include those typical of Northern Ireland, Wales, and parts of NE England.

In recent years, attention has been drawn to the increasing use of a particular type of rising statement intonation in what are traditionally known to be falling-tone accents. This is the use of the *high rising* contour. Here are some examples of its use, adapted from a recent study of New Zealand English intonation (S. Allan, 1990). The high rising contour is shown by [†].

…It just saves on the wear and tear of all the other clothes[†]
…and it's very rarely we get traffic round here[†]
…the next day we went into Paddy's Market[†]

Although this usage has been noted in several other parts of the English-speaking world, it has certainly been a very noticeable feature of Australian and New Zealand English, at least since the 1960s, and its greater frequency in the latter country suggests that it may well have originated there.

Why is it used? Why should a statement end with an intonation pattern which would normally be associated with the function of a question? Any explanation needs to take into account the descriptive findings of several recent linguistic studies. One such study found:

• Women used it twice as much as men.
• Teenagers used it ten times more often than people over 20, and people in the 20–30 age group used it five times as much as those over 70.
• Working-class people used it three times as much as middle-class people.
• Ethnic minorities used it two to three times more often than members of the majority group. Maori speakers, for example, used up to 50 per cent more such tones than Europeans.

Broadly speaking, two kinds of explanation have been proposed for the phenomenon.

• One hypothesis focuses on the social differences, and suggests that the tone is preferred by the less powerful members of society. It acts as an (unconscious) expression of uncertainty and lack of confidence, perhaps even of subservience and deference. This viewpoint has been particularly debated by linguists in relation to gender: one view argues that women have come to use the tone because of their subservience to men. It is also a widely held view in relation to nationhood. In a Perth (Western Australia) radio programme in 1980, several members of a studio audience expressed the view that Australians used the tone because of their uncertain and still evolving national identity. In 1993 one Australian republican pundit went so far as to predict that the tone would disappear once

the country's new status had been achieved.
• An alternative explanation is that the high rising tone is used as a natural and widespread feature of conversational interaction. A speaker might introduce it for any of several discourse reasons – as an informal check to see if the listener has understood, as a request for empathy or some other form of feedback, or even as an indication that the speaker has not yet finished speaking. One recent phonetic study found that the tone was actually not very common in speech situations of uncertainty, such as the giving of opinions (arguing against the first hypothesis). Rather, it was particularly associated with narratives, especially with those parts of a story where the speaker wished to heighten the interest of the listener. If this explanation is correct, the social trends could be explained by variations in interactive awareness and narrative skills. It will be interesting to see what future, post-republican studies reveal.
(After D. Britain & J. Newman, 1992.)

THE FUNCTIONS OF INTONATION

• **Emotional** Intonation's most obvious role is to express attitudinal meaning – sarcasm, surprise, reserve, impatience, delight, shock, anger, interest, and thousands of other semantic nuances.
• **Grammatical** Intonation helps to identify grammatical structure in speech, performing a role similar to punctuation. Units such as clause and sentence (§16) often depend on intonation for their spoken identity, and several specific contrasts, such as question/statement, make systematic use of it.
• **Informational** Intonation helps draw attention to what meaning is given and what is new in an utterance. The word carrying the most prominent tone in a contour signals the part of an utterance that the speaker is treating as new information: *I've got a new* **pen**, *I bought* **three** *books*.
• **Textual** Intonation helps larger units of meaning than the sentence to contrast and cohere. In radio news-reading, paragraphs of information can be shaped through the use of pitch. In sports commentary, changes in prosody reflect the progress of the action.
• **Psychological** Intonation helps us to organize speech into units that are easier to perceive and memorize. Most people would find a sequence of ten numbers (4, 7, 3, 8, 2, 6, 4, 8, 1, 5) difficult to recall; the task is made easier by using intonation to chunk the sequence into two units (4, 7, 3, 8, 2 / 6, 4, 8, 1, 5).
• **Indexical** Intonation, along with other prosodic features, is an important marker of personal or social identity. Lawyers, preachers, newscasters, sports commentators, army sergeants, and several other occupations are readily identified through their distinctive prosody.

RHYTHM

Features of pitch, loudness, speed, and silence combine to produce the effect known as speech *rhythm*. Our sense of rhythm is a perception that there are prominent units occurring at regular intervals as we speak. In the main tradition of English poetry, this regularity is very clear, in the form of the metrical patterns used in lines of verse. The iambic pentameter, in particular, with its familiar five-fold te-**tum** pattern (*The curfew tolls the knell of parting day*), has given the language its poetic heartbeat for centuries (p. 415).

All forms of spoken English have their rhythm, though in spontaneous speech it is often difficult to hear, because hesitations interfere with the smooth flow of the words. In fluent speech, however, there is a clear underlying rhythm. This is often called a *stress-timed* (or *isochronous*) rhythm – one based on the use of stressed syllables which occur at roughly regular intervals in the stream of speech. It contrasts with the *syllable-timed* rhythm of a language such as French, where the syllables have equal force, giving a marked *rat-a-tat-a-tat* effect.

The history of English is one of stress-timing, though there are signs of the alternative rhythm emerging in parts of the world where English has been in contact with syllable-timed languages, such as India and South Africa. Syllable-timed English, however, is difficult for outsiders to follow, because it reduces the pattern of stress contrast which adds so much to a word's spoken identity. If it is increasing, as some observers suggest, there will be extra problems for the growth of an internationally intelligible standard spoken English (p. 360).

PARALINGUISTIC FEATURES

Prosody does not exhaust all the non-verbal vocal effects available in English. The various cavities of the throat, mouth, and nose can each be used to produce 'tones of voice' that alter the meaning of what is being said. These effects are often called *paralinguistic* – a term which suggests that they play a less central role in the sound system than prosodic features do.

The following examples of paralinguistic effects are accompanied by a gloss indicating the context in which they commonly occur.

• whisper – secrecy or conspiracy.
• breathiness – deep emotion or sexual desire.
• huskiness – unimportance or disparagement.
• nasality – anxiety.
• extra lip-rounding – intimacy (especially to animals and babies).

SOUND SYMBOLISM

It is a fundamental principle of linguistic enquiry that individual sounds do not have meanings. It does not seem to make sense to ask such questions as 'What does [t] mean?' or 'What does [a] mean?' Consonants and vowels are used only to give a distinctive shape to words, and it is these – the words themselves, along with their component morphemes, such as *un-* and *-ness* (p. 128) – which express a meaning. However, there are an interesting number of apparent exceptions to this general rule – cases where native speakers feel that there *is* some kind of meaningful connection between a sound, or cluster of sounds, and properties of the outside world. The phonemenon is known as *sound symbolism*, also called *phonaesthesia* (when focusing on the aesthetic values of sounds) or *onomatopoeia* (when focusing on the use of sound in poetry).

Sound symbolic effects can be studied from various points of view. Which sounds or combinations of sound are most often involved? Some of the most frequently occurring types are illustrated below (the phonetic terminology is explained on pp. 238–43): initial consonant clusters (especially involving /s-/), lateral sounds (either alone, or in a cluster), and plosives (especially in final position) are notable. Then there is the question of how clearly we can identify a symbolic meaning. This is sometimes fairly easy to state, especially when there is a noise to copy in the outside world: *bang, clip-clop, cough, cuckoo, knock, murmur, rat-a-tat, whoosh, yackety-yack, zoom.* But sometimes we can do no more than express a vague feeling that the word is somehow appropriate to the thing, without being able to say why:

- Do *dimple, pimple,* and *wimple* carry over an association from *simple*?
- Is there something in initial /v/ which can reinforce a 'snarling' meaning, as in *venomous, vicious, vile, vindictive,* and *vitriolic*?
- Is there a feeling of shortness in /-nt/, as suggested by *blunt, dent, grunt, pant, runt,* and *stunt* (but not by *front, hunt, mint, pint, rant,* and *tent*)?
- Is there a smallness associated with close vowels and a largeness with open vowels, as suggested by *slit* vs *slot, chip* vs *chop, wrinkle* vs *rumple,* and *wee, titch,* and *little* vs *vast, large,* and *grand* (but not by *big* vs *small* or *huge* vs *dwarf*)?

COMIC ONOMATOPOEIA

Sound symbolic items are of two main kinds: those which are everyday words in the language (see opposite), and those which are special coinages – nonsense words (p. 130) and semi-phonetic renditions of ongoing noises. The latter are particularly common in comic books (for children or adults), where words (usually in full capitals and followed by exclamation marks) identify a remarkable range of noises. The illustration, from a UK children's annual based on an imaginary US character, shows some of these items. As a minor contribution to academic research in this field, the following lines comprise a complete corpus of onomatopoeic exclamatory expressions emanating from objects or events encountered by Desperate Dan in 1990.

bang, blam, blow, boing, boom, bop, chew, chomp, clunk, crack, crash, creak, crump, crunch, heave, hop, kerack, kerash, leap, niff, phft, phllt, phsst, phut, ping, plop, pong, pop, rasp, r-r-ring, roar, rumble, scrub, shatter, slam, slurp, snatch, sparks, splash, split, splooosh, spludge, splurge, squawk, swipe, tear (vb.), tinkle, tug, whiff, whirr, whizz, whoosh, whump, yank, yarf, yelp.

This list excludes the following emotional vocalizations used by Desperate Dan himself, on his journey through life, or by other characters in the stories.

aw, bah, blargh, blurb, eek, gee, giggle, glub, glumph, guffaw, gulp, har, haw-haw, hee-hee, hee-hee-hee, ho-ho, huh, mmm, mumph, oh-oh, oof, ooyah, ouch, shucks, snort, ssshh, ssssshhh, ulp, urrr, waah, wayhay, wow, yah, yahoo, yeeha, yeow, yeuch, yeurgh, yikes, yip-yip, yipes, yowch, yup, zowee.

In traditional grammar, these would be classified as a separate part of speech – interjections (p. 213). However, conventional lists of interjections tend to concentrate on the more genteel examples (such as *oh, ow,* and *tut-tut*), and fail to include the range of bizarre emotional expressions which any comic provides. But then, the characters who make up the various corpora of conversational English (p. 438) tend not to get into such scrapes as those experienced by Desperate Dan.

© D.C. Thomson & Co. Ltd.

CRIB TO THE THREE-CONSONANT COMBINATIONS TABLE (p. 243)

split, splendid, splash, splutter, splosh, splenetic, spleen, splurge, splay, splice.
sprig, spread, sprat, sprung, sprocket, spree, sprawl, spruce, sprain, sprite, sprout.
spume, spurious.
strict, strength, strap, structure, strong, strabismus, street, strata, straw, strew, straight, strike, strove, Stroud.
stew, Stuart.

sclerotin, sclaff (in golf), sclerosis, scleroid.
script, scratch, scrump, scrofula, scream, scrawny, screw, scrape, scribe, scroll, scrounge.
skew, skewer.
squish, squelch, squat, squeeze, squaw, squirm, squamous, squire, Squeers, square.
smew

Attempts at seeing a symbolic meaning running through a cluster of lexical items carry different levels of plausibility. Much depends on which sense and which word class an item represents. *Hush*, for example, carries an implication of suddenness only in its verb use; quite the reverse, as a noun. *Swamp*, likewise, conveys movement only in its use as a verb. To the extent that we have to qualify items in this way, identifying particular senses or word classes, the case for sound symbolism weakens. If a sound is credited with a certain intrinsic meaning, the meaning should exist wherever the sound appears. There are no totally convincing cases of this sort in English, and in each of the categories listed below, the evidence for and against sound symbolism must be carefully weighed. The lists are not comprehensive: a selection has been made from a dictionary, focusing on monosyllabic words but ignoring derived forms (e.g. *floppy* from *flop*), idioms (e.g. *get the chop*), and multiple meanings (e.g. the different meanings of *club*). And in each category, before reaching a conclusion, it is essential to consider the existence of words with the same phonetic shape which do *not* convey the range of meaning suggested. (For other examples of sound symbolism in practice, see pp. 134, 147, 153.)

SOUNDS AND SENSES

Initial consonant clusters with /s–/

• /sl–/ conveys downward movement, direction, or position: *slack, slalom, slant, slash, slaughter, slave, slender, slice, slide, slight, slim, slip, slit, slither, slope, slot, slouch, slow, sluggish, sluice, slump*; often a generally negative association: *slag, slander, slang, slap, sleazy, slime, slink, slob, slop, slosh, sloth, slovenly, sludge, slum, slur, slurp, slush, slut, sly*; words which seem to lack these associations: *slab, slake, slam, sledge, sleek, sleep, sleeve, slick, slogan, slumber*.

• /sn–/ conveys unpleasantness: *snaffle, snafu, snag, snail, snake, snare, snarl, snatch, sneak, sneer, sneeze,* *snide, sniff, snigger, snipe, snitch, snivel, snob, snoop, snooty, snort, snot, snout, snub, snuffle*; words which seem to lack this association: *snack, snap, snip, snooker, snore, snorkel, snow, snuff, snug*.

• /sw–/ conveys smooth or wide-reaching movement: *swaddle, swagger, swallow, swamp* (vb.), *swan* (vb.), *swarm, swat, swathe, sway, sweep, swell, swerve, swift, swill, swing, swipe, swirl, swish, swivel, swoop*; words which seem to lack these associations: *swear, sweat, sweet, swim, swine, switch, swot*.

Laterals

• /–ɜː(r)l/ conveys roundness: *curl, furl, gnarl, pearl, purl, swirl, twirl, whirl,* and *whorl*; also /–r–l/ in *barrel,* *roll, spiral*; words which seem to lack this association: *earl, girl, hurl, snarl*.

• /gl–/ conveys brightness and light: *glamour, glare, glass, glaze, gleam, glimmer, glimpse, glint, glisten, glitter, globe, glossy, glow*; other 'bright' words: *glad, glee, glib, glide, glory*; words which seem to lack or contradict these associations: *gland, gloom, glove, glue, glum, glutton*.

• /–l/ (preceded by a short vowel and single consonant) conveys uncertain or repeated movement, or lack of size, structure, or importance: *babble, bubble, chuckle, couple, cuddle, dabble, dapple, diddle, doodle, dribble, fiddle, freckle, gabble, giggle, gobble, haggle, huddle, joggle, juggle, muddle,* *nibble, niggle, pebble, piddle, piffle, puddle, pummel, rabble, raffle, rubble, rustle, shuffle, snaffle, sniffle, snuffle, snuggle, speckle, squiggle, stubble, tipple, toddle, topple, trickle, twiddle, waffle, waggle, wiggle, wobble, wriggle*; words which seem to lack these associations: *knuckle, riddle, saddle, supple*.

Final consonants

• /–ʃ/ conveys swift or strong movement: *bash, brush, cash, clash, crash, crush, dash, dish* (vb.), *flash, gash, gnash, gush, lash, mash, push, rash, rush, splash, whoosh*; other forceful words: *brash, fresh, harsh, hush* (vb.), *posh, swish*; words which seem to lack these associations: *blush, bush, fish, flesh, marsh, wash, ?Welsh*.

• /–p/ (preceded by a short vowel) conveys suddenness or shortness: *blip, bop, chop, clap, clip, dip, drip, flap, flip, flop, gap, hop, lop, nap, nip, pip, plop, pup, quip, rip, slap, skip, slip, snap, snip, stop, tap, trap, trip, whip, yap, zap, zip*; words which seem to lack these associations: *cap, cup, grip, hip, lap, lip, map, mop, ship, shop, swap, top, wrap*.

• /–b/ (preceded by a short vowel) conveys largeness, or lack of shape or direction: *blab, blob, clobber, club, dab, flab, glob, gob, grab, grub, jab, lob, mob, rub, slab, slob, stab, tub, yob*; words which seem to lack these associations: *bib, cab, crab, crib, cub, fib, hub, job, lab, pub, rib, rob, rub, snob, snub, sob, stub, web*.

THE SOUND OF SWEARING

Given the nature of swearing, and of invective in general (p. 172), we would expect the words involved to be short, sharp, and to the point. Gentle sounds, such as long vowels, nasals, and sonorants (p. 242) are unlikely to be much used, whereas the harsher impact of short vowels, plosives, and high-pitched fricatives should be of great value to anyone wishing to express an insult or curse. Try calling someone a *meem* or a *rahl* as viciously as you can – then compare the result with calling her a *gack* or a *krot*.

The language provides a genuine contrast of this kind in the form of the dual pronunciation of *bastard*: with a short first vowel, the effect can only be vicious; with a long first vowel, it can lose its unpleasantness, and become jocular. Similarly, the use of a long central vowel produces a notable softening of force, in such words as *berk* and *jerk*, as does the use of a nasal before a final /–k/, as in *bonk, bonkers, conk, hunk,* and *lunk*.

The really important sounds are the velar consonants, especially the voiceless ones, and especially when these are used in final position within a word. Also notable is the use of central vowels, such as /ə/, and those at the extremes of the vowel area, such as /ɪ/ and /a/. It is unusual to hear mid-vowels, such as /e/ and /ɔː/, in lexical invective, and front vowels are preferred to back.

Velars
Final /–k/: *bohunk, chink, crook, dick, dink, dork, dreck, dyke, fink, fuck, hick, honk, lunk, mick, prick, puke, punk, schmuck, spick, wank, wick.*
Initial /k–/: *clap, clod, clot, crap, creep, cretin, crone, crud, cunt, kraut.*
Initial and final velar in same word: *cack, cluck, cock, geek, gink, gook, kike, kook, quack, skunk.*
Final /–g/: *fag, frig, hag, hog, lug, mug, nig, pig, shag, slag, wog.*
Medial /g–/: *bugger, dago, nigger.*

Bilabials
Final /–p/: *chump, clap, crap, creep, dope, drip, goop, pimp, poop, sap, twerp, wimp, wop, zip.*

Final /–b/: *boob, slob.*
Initial /p–/: *pig, pimp, piss, poof, poop, prat, prick, puke, punk.*
Initial /b–/: *bitch, bloody, bohunk, bozo, brat, bugger, bum.*

Alveolars
Final /–t/: *brat, clot, dolt, fart, git, nit, nut, prat, shit, slut, tart, tit, twat.*
Final /–d/: *clod, crud, sod, turd, yid.*
Initial /–d/: *damn, dick, dink, dolt, dope, dork, dreck, dyke.*

Fricatives
Final /–s/: *ass/arse, piss.*
Final /–f/: *oaf, poof.*

(Data from popular intuition, supplemented by H. Rawson, 1991.)

LONE WORDS

Forlorn! the very word is like a bell
To toll me back from thee to my sole self!

Apart from raising the tone of the end of this page, these lines from John Keats's *Ode to a Nightingale* (1820) act as a reminder that there are many individual words containing elements about which we have phonaesthetic intuitions, but which defy any simple categorization. It is an interesting linguistic exercise to look for words whose constituent sounds convey semantic associations in this way – such as *ragged, spiky, dawdle, fawning,* and *scrumptious.*

SOUND SYMBOLISM IN PRACTICE

ADVERTISING

In commercial advertising (p.388), the sound a product makes, and the emotion it is claimed to generate in the user, are often given onomatopoeic expression (p. 250): a particular make of car might go *Vr-o-o-m*; a smell of perfume or gravy might evoke *M-m-m-m-m*. Brand names commonly use sound (or letter) symbolism, as the world of breakfast cereals crisply demonstrates, with its *crunchies*, *puffs*, *pops*, and *smacks*. And slogans often rely on it too.

Polo, the mint with the hole.

Taste the tang in Tango. Tingling tang, bubbles – sparkles. New Sparkling Tango.

Bubble Yum. It's so much yum, yum, yum. It's number yum, yum, yum in bubble gum.

Cap'n Crunch [cereal]: the crunch always gives you away.

Who ever heard of a kangaroo with travel sickness?

You'll have to admit, it's not all that common. Wild animals bouncing around, wishing they had something to calm a queasy, travel sick offspring. Proof that, when it comes to motion sickness, Nature really does provide the best defences. And, when you need something to calm your kids' tummies before or during that long journey, why not try a natural, homoeopathic medicine. One whose active ingredients are perfectly safe for everyone and completely without side effects. Like Nelsons homoeopathic Travel Sickness Tablets. They're available from Boots, Sainsbury's, Holland & Barrett, and all good chemists and health stores. So, next time you're off on walkabout take the natural answer to travel sickness. Take Nelsons.

PRIMITIVE POETRY

In some approaches to the teaching of poetry, particular attention is paid to helping children appreciate the sound-symbolic power of words. In the illustrations, a 12-year-old has made up a sound-pattern using invented names for sweets, and a 7-year-old has put down some impressions about the arrival of a fair.

Putting up the fair
Glunk glunk glunk glunk
Lock lock lock lock
Buzz Buzz Buzz Buzz
rolla clatter rolla clatter
Patter Patter
tip tip tip
Wing wang wing wang
bang bong
Clatter clatter
Squeek Squeek
Clug clug clug
bong

Home-Made Sweets

1. Bangles,
   Flix, Slix,
   Tom-Toms, Truffles,
   Popic, Huffles.

2. Flatties,
   Nix, Nax,
   Quaff, Quaff, Quaffles
   Butter Buffles.

3. Nutleys,
   Todd-Todd,
   Lampley's, Luddles
   Lemon Squadlos

(From R. James & R.G. Gregory, 1966.)

The muddy, mucky, murky Mouch

On a small asteroid
in the terrible void
dwells a filthy old slouch,
the vile m-m-m-Mouch.
He sleeps in spaghetti,
looks just like a yeti,
and his grotty green wig
would embarrass a pig.
He enjoys a good splosh
in tomato juice squash,
while from swimming in sludge
he's the colour of fudge.
He gobbles green grottles
swigs pond ooze from bottles
and the stench of his breath
scares all known germs to death.
He's a jumbo-sized pest
falls asleep fully dressed,
and far, far out in Space
he's the last of his race.
The vile m-m-m-Mouch
doesn't run, jump, or crouch,
but squats, gnarled as a gnome,
on his asteroid home.

Wes Magee (1985)

CHILDREN'S LITERATURE

Children's literature is full of sound symbolic words, as these poems illustrate. Onomatopoeic nonsense names also abound. Some rely on 'dark' sounds, full of voiced plosives, nasals, and laterals, such as Spike Milligan's *Bumbley Boo*, Tolkien's *Bilbo Baggins*, or Jonathan Swift's giants, the *Brobdingnagians*. Others rely on 'light' sounds, full of short high vowels and voiceless consonants, such as Dick Bruna's *Miffy* and *Snuffy*, or Swift's midgets, the *Lilliputians*.

The cover of one of Dick Bruna's Miffy books.

Huffer and Cuffer

Huffer, a giant ungainly and gruff
encountered a giant called Cuffer.
said Cuffer to Huffer, I'M ROUGH AND I'M TOUGH
said Huffer to Cuffer, I'M TOUGHER.

they shouted such insults as BOOB and BUFFOON
and OVERBLOWN BLOWHARD and BLIMP
and BLUSTERING BLUBBER and BLOATED BALLOON
and SHATTERBRAIN, SHORTY and SHRIMP.

then Huffer and Cuffer exchanged mighty blows,
they basted and battered and belted,
they chopped to the neck and they bopped
in the nose
and they pounded and pummelled and pelted.

they pinched and they punched and they smacked
and they whacked
and they rocked and they socked and they smashed,
and they rapped and they slapped and they
throttled and thwacked
and they thumped and they bumped and they bashed.

they cudgelled each other on top of the head
with swipes of the awfulest sort,
and now they are no longer giants, instead
they both are exceedingly short.

Jack Prelutsky (1982)

The poetic tradition

In literature, especially in poetry and poetic prose, the phonaesthetic values of sound segments (p. 414) have characterized the genre throughout its history. A short selection of extracts is illustrative:

Batter my heart, three-personed God, for you
    As yet but knock, breathe, shine, and seek to mend;
    That I may rise and stand, o'erthrow me and bend
Your force to break, blow, burn, and make me new…

John Donne, *Holy Sonnets*, 1633

Yet let me flap this bug with gilded wings,
This painted child of dirt, that stinks and stings;
Whose buzz the witty and the fair annoys,
Yet wit ne'er tastes, and beauty ne'er enjoys…

Alexander Pope, *Epistle to Dr Arbuthnot*, 1735

His broad clear brow in sunlight glowed;
On burnished hooves his war-horse trode;
From underneath his helmet flowed
His coal-black curls as on he rode,
    As he rode down to Camelot.
From the bank and from the river
He flashed into the crystal mirror,
'Tirra lirra' by the river
    Sang Sir Lancelot.

Lord Tennyson, 'The Lady of Shalott', 1832

When men were all asleep the snow came flying,
In large white flakes falling on the city brown,
Stealthily and perpetually settling and loosely lying,
    Hushing the latest traffic of the drowsy town;

Deadening, muffling, stifling its murmurs failing;
Lazily and incessantly floating down and down:
    Silently sifting and veiling road, roof and railing;
Hiding difference, making unevenness even,
Into angles and crevices softly drifting and sailing.

Robert Bridges, 'London Snow', 1880

CHARACTER NAMES

In adult humorous literature, personal names and place names are often chosen on the basis of their sound pattern. Comic writers rely greatly on such effects (pp. 89, 147): famous examples include the headmaster *Mr Creakle* in Charles Dickens's *David Copperfield*, the 'hideous fat boy' *Uggug* in Lewis Carroll's *Sylvie and Bruno*, the tutor *Mr Thwackum* in Henry Fielding's *A History of Tom Jones*, the quack physician *Dr Slop* in Laurence Sterne's *Tristram Shandy*, and US academic *Morris Zapp* in David Lodge's *Changing Places*. (For other examples, see pp. 153, 414.)

Much of James Thurber's humour relied on the incongruous use of the sound symbolic power of words, as can be seen in these cartoons from *The Beast in Me and Other Animals* (1949).

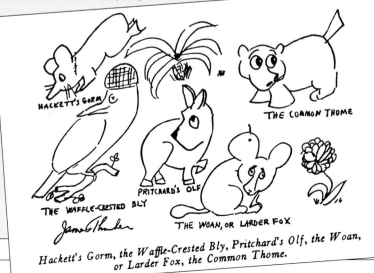

Hackett's Gorm, the Waffle-Crested Bly, Pritchard's Olf, the Woan, or Larder Fox, the Common Thome.

PRONUNCIATION IN PRACTICE

The study of the sound system of English is in principle no more difficult than the study of its writing system, but two factors complicate the task. Most people are unfamiliar with the phonetic terminology required to describe vocal effects; and even after this terminology is understood it is not always easy to relate these descriptions to recognizable sound qualities. Matters are not helped by the fact that we have little conscious recollection of how we learned to talk (unlike the tasks of reading and writing, p. 236), so that the process of speaking and listening seems totally natural and unproblematic. We tend to take pronunciation completely for granted, and notice it only when it becomes distinctive in some way, or when something goes wrong.

One way of sharpening our phonetic sense is to pay particular attention to the special cases where features of pronunciation are drawn to our attention. There are several areas where this is likely to happen. We may notice a child with immature articulation, an adult with a speech handicap, a foreign learner with a marked accent, or a native speaker with a pronunciation idiosyncrasy. A great deal of spoken humour relies on our ability to hear or manipulate sound effects, both verbal and non-verbal (p. 248). We may also find ourselves able to identify specific changes which are taking place in the pronunciation of words, and we will regularly hear letters read out on the radio from people who have made it their responsibility to complain about them. We may also see distinctive pronunciations reflected in the written language, especially when an author has tried to convey the regional or idiosyncratic speech of a character. The examples on this and the facing page illustrate a range of contexts which focus on pronunciation in this way.

For other illustrations of pronunciation in practice, see pp. 86, 91, 406, and 414.

CHANGING HABITS

It is curious how fashion changes pronunciation. In my youth everybody said 'Lonnon' not 'London'.... The now fashionable pronunciation of several words is to me at least very offensive: *contemplate* – is bad enough; but *balcony* makes me sick. (Samuel Rogers, 1763–1855.)

The earlier pronunciation had the stress on the second syllable in each case.

TONGUE-SLIPPING

Analysing slips of the tongue can sharpen our sense of syllable structure (p. 246) and sound categories. The sounds which 'slip' are usually from the same part of the syllable: an onset consonant swops with another onset consonant in *mell wade* (for *well made*); coda consonants are involved in *wish a brush* (for *with*); nuclei are affected in *fool the pill* (for *fill the pool*). Several other such effects can be seen in this children's poem by Rod Hull (1989). They are often referred to as *Spoonerisms*, after William Archibald Spooner (1844–1930), Warden of New College, Oxford, who had many such tongue slips attributed to him (such as *you have hissed all my mystery lessons*).

Ronald/Donald

Ronald Derds (or was it Donald Rerds?)
Was a boy who always wixed up his merds.
If anyone asked him; 'What's the time?'
He'd look at his watch and say, 'Norter past quine.'

He'd spoken like that ever since he was two.
His parents at first didn't know what to do.
In order to understand what he'd said,
His father would get him to stand on his head.

But this didn't work, something had to be done,
So Pa and Ma Derds learnt to speak like their son.

'Mood gorning,' he'd cry, as he chat in his sair.
'Gorning,' they'd answer, without hurning a tair.
And Ron's Mum would say, 'Get a nice brofe of led,'
For Ron to return with a loaf of fresh bread.

Then one special day, young Ronald's voice broke.
He found it affected the way that he spoke.
'Good morning,' he said as he sat in his chair.
'Gorning,' said the others and started to stare.

From that moment on, things just got worse.
The harder they tried, they just couldn't converse.

Ron said to his parents, after a week,
'It's driving me mad, the way that you speak.
I can't understand a word that you say.
You leave me no option, I'm leaving to-day.'

So Ron joined the Navy and sailed to the Barents,
To get as far away as he could from his parents.
And although this story all seems rather sad,
Ron occasionally visits his Dum and his Mad.

ORDERING WORDS

The prosody of the drill sergeant is ingeniously captured in this poem for children by Ray Mather (1989).

Attention   all
            you   words,
GET INTO LINE!
I've had enough of you
Doing what you w
                        ill,
STAND STILL!
There are going to be a few changes
Around here.
From now on
You will do
What I want.
THAT   WORD!
You heard,
Stay put.
Youcomeouttoofast
Or per   ulate
        amb
GET IT STRAIGHT!
You are here to serve me.
You are not at ease

To do as you please.
Whenever I attempt to be serious
You make a weak joke.
Always you have to poke
                              fun.

AS YOU WERE!
Don't stir.
If ever I try to express
My feelings for someone
You refuse to come out
Or come out all wrong
So sense make none they can of it,
Yet you're so good once they've gone!
Well,
I'm in charge now
And you will say what I tell you to say.
No more cursing
Or sarcasm,
Just state my thoughts clearly
Speak what's on my mind.
Got it?
Right,
F
A
L
L   OUT.

PRONUNCIATION IN PRINT

The novels of Charles Dickens (p. 89) provide the best literary collection of data for anyone wishing to examine pronunciation idiosyncrasy. In *Pickwick Papers* (1836–7, Ch. 16), Mr Pickwick describes the speech of Sam Weller as 'somewhat homely and occasionally incomprehensible'. The homeliness can be illustrated from his use of *Wellerisms*, as they have been called – everyday phrases applied to imaginary situations. The incomprehensibility is largely a result of his idiosyncratic use of bilabial and labio-dental consonants.

He wants you particklar; and no one else'll do, as the Devil's private secretary said ven he fetched avay Doctor Faustus. (Ch. 15)

Werry sorry to 'casion any personal inconwenience, ma'am, as the house-breaker said to the old lady when he put her on the fire. (Ch. 26)

Weller also has an interesting prosodic characteristic (which several other Dickensian characters share) of delaying a syllable in a polysyllabic word: *col-lecting*, *hex-traordinary* (both Ch. 13). The hyphen probably represents a lengthened consonant or vowel, but could also be marking a brief pause.

CROSSING ACCENT BOUNDARIES

The fact that people speak in different accents means that, from time to time, there will be ambiguity. A word in one accent will be perceived as a quite different word in another. Usually, context sorts things out – but not always, as the following examples show.

A PEA-SIZED ISSUE

On 10 October 1992, BBC presenter Dave Lee Travis (DLT) was hosting an edition of the Radio 1 competition programme, *Darts*, played between teams from two public houses in different parts of the UK. He asked a team from a pub in Tyrone (Northern Ireland) the following question:

What's the name of the piece of architecture which goes over the top of a door?

The team conferred, and their spokesman (who had a Southern English accent) said what sounded like *lentil*, then paused and corrected it to *lintel*. The incongruity of the first response led to much mirth in the studio, but DLT could not accept the correction, as the rules of the competition allowed only the first answer to be accepted.

   The complaints then started to pour in to the BBC, and by the end of the programme DLT had to issue an apology, and allow the Tyrone pub (which had gone on to lose) another chance to enter the competition at a later date. What had happened?

   /ɪ/ is widely pronounced in Northern Ireland as a more open and centralized vowel, which to outsiders could easily be heard as /e/. Presumably, while the team was conferring, one of the members with a local accent had proposed the correct answer, but pronounced *lintel* as [lentl]. The spokesman (from a different dialect background) at first misheard this as *lentil*, and in the heat of the moment spontaneously

said it aloud. As soon as it was out of his mouth, though, he realized his mistake and corrected it – but by then it was too late. His team had in effect been penalized for giving an answer using a Northern Ireland vowel value spoken in a Southern English accent – though it is hardly surprising that the presenter was unable to recognize it for what it was. Fortunately the production team in the Radio 1 studio recognized the validity of the complaints, as they started to come in from Northern Ireland – otherwise the matter might well have ended up at the European Court of Justice!

HERE TERDAY, GONE TERMORRER

Robert Bridges, in his tract *On the Present State of English Pronunciation* (1913), tells a story to illustrate his disapproval of the standards of English speech current at the time. He is particularly angry at the phonetician Daniel Jones (p. 239), who had drawn attention to the way such words as *for*, *of*, and *to* were normally pronounced with an unstressed vowel [ə] (which Bridges transcribes as *er*):

My friend, the late Dr. Gee, going his round of the hospital wards one day, came to the bedside of a newly-admitted patient. After examining him carefully, and finding little the matter with him, he called for the bed-card, and in his deliberate manner prescribed thereon a diet with a *placebo* to be taken three times a day. The man, frightened by his gravity and silence, feared the worst…and was no sooner left alone than he snatched down the board, and seeing cabalistic signs, and at the foot of them the awful words *ter die*,

and reading them…he saw as he thought his death-warrant; so he whipped out of bed, and fled for his life; to add, no doubt, a new tale to the *terrers* of the hospital.

The point of the story relies on the consequences of the patient's failure to recognize that the two words are written in Latin. He assumes that they are a nonstandard spelling of the English phrase *to die*, and interprets this according to the norms of informal Received Pronunciation. To appreciate the joke, of course, one

must know that the medical Latin for 'three times a day' is *ter die*.

FAXING UP A JUDGMENT

Even the bar is not sacrosanct. Presumably the increased number of accents in the SE of England in which the [æ] and [ʌ] of Received Pronunciation have been pulled in the direction of [a], under the influence of Cockney, explains this story, reported in *The Spectator* on 12 September 1992.

Ever on the search for legal jokes not necessarily connected with the death penalty, I consulted a friend who is still practising. She said a member of her chambers was in court one Monday morning when the judge said, 'I'm afraid we'll have to adjourn this case, I have written my judgment out, but I left it in my cottage in Devon and I can't get it sent here until tomorrow.' 'Fax it up, my Lord,' the helpful barrister suggested, to which his Lordship replied, 'Yes, it does rather.'

The barrister must have pronounced *fax* as [faks] instead of [fæks]. The judge then

interpreted this as a version of [fʌks], with the vowel receiving a more open quality. The whole exchange seems to have taken place using the most judicious of tones.

This cartoon relies on a combination of two accent mismatches. The clerk's RP *now* uses the diphthong /aʊ/, which is phonetically very close to the diphthong used by Cockney speakers in such words as *know*. And his pronunciation of *due*, whether as /djuː/ or /dʒuː/, 'Arriet interprets as the assimilation of *do* + *you* (p. 247), which would be a normal feature of her conversational style.

'ARRIET: "Wot toime his the next troine fer 'Ammersmith?" CLERK: "Due Now." 'ARRIET: "'Course Oi dawn't now, stoopid, or I wouldn't be harskin' yer!"

Through the normal educational process, the chief features of the English writing system become familiar and readily identifiable in a way that the elements of the sound system (§17) are never likely to be. Many children, before they are 3, have been given some informal tuition in letter shapes and sounds, often in the form of a colourful alphabet book (p. 407) bought as a festival or birthday present; and in societies where levels of literacy are high, almost all will have had some systematic teaching – whether from parents, through the media, or in school – by the time they are 5.

Letters attract most of the attention in these early years. This is as it should be, for letters are the main units available for conveying meaning when writing in English. But there is far more to the writing system than learning to recognize individual letter shapes – both 'big' and 'small' – and their associated sounds: punctuation and features of graphic design are important elements of the meaning and identity of a written text; handwriting and typography provide subtle but pervasive dimensions of interpretation; and the rules governing letter combinations ('spelling') promote a standard of intelligible and acceptable communication (p. 272) – though at the expense of presenting young children with a long-term and unprecedented exercise in conscious memorization.

LETTERLAND

Two of the characters from Letterland, an alphabetically populated world devised by British teacher Lyn Wendon to help children learn sound-letter relationships. In Letterland, letter shapes appear as pictographic body shapes, and take on life as people and animals. Stories about the characters explain what sounds they make, and why their sounds vary in different contexts. Teachers who have used the system report that the children enjoy using the story-like language to talk about the sound-letter correspondences, and thus make progress in their metalinguistic skills – an important first step in the acquisition of written language (p. 426).

A Letterland encounter

'The Hairy Hat Man (h) hates noise, so he never speaks above a whisper in words.'

'Sammy Snake loves making a hissing sound – there aren't many hisses he misses!'

'But… when Sammy Snake is next to the Hairy Hat Man in a word we hear a "sh" sound instead. Why? Well, remember what the Hat Man hates? Noise!

So before Sammy Snake can hiss, the Hat Man hushes him up like this: "sh".'

LETTER FRIEZES

The first eight letters of an alphabet frieze published by the World Wide Fund for Nature in 1993: *My Rare Animal ABC Frieze*. A variant of the alphabet book, friezes are better able to capture at a glance the notion of alphabetic sequence, as well as to convey the impression that the alphabet is a fixed and finite set of letters. Designs are invariably eye-catching and imaginative, and in the present case the linguistic content additionally conveys an important environmental message. (Marcus Davies, 1993.)

A BASIC PERSPECTIVE

The study of the linguistic properties of the written language has lagged somewhat behind the study of the sounds of speech. Nonetheless, the efforts of typographers, graphic designers, linguists, psychologists, and others have introduced a number of useful distinctions and terms, some of which are designed to avoid the ambiguity inherent in the apparently simple term, *writing*.

This ambiguity arises in several ways:

• *Writing* can refer to either a process or a result: while we are actively engaged in the process, we are said to be 'writing'; and when we have finished, the product (our composition, or text) is also called (a piece of) 'writing'.
• *Writing* can refer to either an everyday or a professional activity. All literate people, by definition, can write; but only a tiny minority are 'writers' (i.e. *authors*).
• *Written language*, when contrasted with speech, refers to *any* visual manifestation of spoken language – whether handwritten, printed, typed, or electronically generated – and this is how the term is used in the present book. In this sense, private letters, bus timetables, teletext, and books are all examples of 'written text'. On the other hand, when people say 'I can't read your writing', they are referring only to handwritten (not printed or typed) text.

The writing system
Most obviously, writing is a way of communicating which uses a system of visual marks made on some kind of surface. It is one kind of *graphic expression* (other kinds include drawing, musical notation, and mathematical formulae). In an alphabetic system, such as is found in English, the graphic marks represent, with varying regularity, individual speech sounds (or phonemes, p. 236).

The standardized writing system of a language is known as its *orthography*. English orthography consists of the set of letters (the alphabet) and their variant forms (e.g. capitals, lower-case), the spelling system, and the set of punctuation marks. The linguistic properties of the orthographic system can be studied from two points of view, analogous to the distinction used in spoken language between phonetics and phonology (p. 236).

• *Graphetics*, a term coined on analogy with *phonetics*, is the study of the way human beings make, transmit, and receive written symbols. However, unlike phonetics, where a comprehensive methodology for describing the properties of speech sounds has been developed, there is as yet no sophisticated graphic classification, though typographers and printers have developed a limited terminology to handle the most salient features of letter shapes.
• *Graphology*, coined on analogy with *phonology*, is the study of the linguistic contrasts that writing systems express. In particular, it recognizes the notion of the *grapheme*, on analogy with the *phoneme* – the smallest unit in the writing system capable of causing a contrast in meaning. For example, because *sat* and *rat* have different meanings, <s> and <r> emerge as different graphemes; on the other hand, the contrast between *sat* and *sat* is not graphemic, because the graphic difference does not correlate with a change of meaning. Graphemes are usually transcribed in angle brackets. Punctuation marks (such as <.> and <? >) are graphemes also, as are such units as <2>, <&>, and <$>.

GRAPHS

Graphemes are abstract units, and appear in a variety of forms. The grapheme <e>, for example, may appear as E, *E*, e, *e*, or in other forms, depending on such factors as handwriting style and typeface. Each of these possible forms is known as a *graph*. There are thousands of possible physical variations in the shape of graphs.

40 forms of the grapheme <a>.

DIGRAPHS

When two letters represent a single sound, the combination is called a *digraph*. Consonant digraphs include *sh* in *ship* and *gh* in *trough* (*h* is by far the commonest second element); vowel digraphs include *ea* in *bread* and *oa* in *boat*. Some digraphs may be physically joined (*ligatured*), as in æ, œ, ff, though this is unusual in modern practice. There is also the interesting 'split' or discontinuous digraph used to mark long vowels and diphthongs (p. 272), as in *rate* and *cone* (which also illustrate the 'magic e', so-called because its effect operates at a distance, changing a short vowel into a long one: *rat* – *rate*).

Digraphs are an important part of the English writing system, because there are far more phonemes in speech than there are letters in the alphabet (p. 237). There have been many proposals to increase the number of letters so that they are in a one-to-one relationship with phonemes (p. 236), but historically the deficit has been made good by combining the 26 letters in various ways, especially to capture the range of vowel distinctions which exist.

Trigraphs also exist – three letters representing a single sound. Examples include *tch* (*watch*/wɒtʃ/) and the UK spelling of *manoeuvre*, where the *oeu* represents /uː/.

TYPOGRAPHIC TERMS

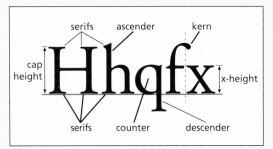

A limited terminology exists to describe the many kinds of typeface and typesetting in regular use. Among the important terms are the following:

ascender A part of a letter which extends above the height of the letter *x*, as in *d* and *h*. It contrasts with a *descender*, a part of a letter which extends below the foot of the letter *x*, as in *y* or *p*.

bold A type with very thick strokes, as seen in **boldface**.

fount The set of characters of the one size of the same typeface, including capitals, lower case, punctuation marks, and numerals; also spelled *font*.

italic Characters that slope to the right, as in *italic*.

justification The arrangement of lines of text so that there are even margins. *Left-justified* setting is standard practice. In *right-justified* setting, the typesetter makes the last character of each line reach the right-hand margin at the same point (by adjusting the spaces between the letters and words). *Unjustified* setting has a 'ragged-edge' right-hand margin (as in this column).

kern The part of a letter which overhangs the body of the type, as in the top part of *f*.

leading /ˈledɪŋ/ The spacing between lines of type. The term derives from the former printing practice of separating lines of metal type by inserting strips of lead between them.

ligature Two or more letters joined together as a single character, as in æ and *ff*.

lower case Small letters, as opposed to any kind of capital letters (*upper case*). (The 'cases' were originally two containers placed one above the other in a printing house: the type for capital letters came from the higher container; the small letters from the lower.) Upper-case letters are divided into *large capitals* and *small capitals* (B vs ʙ). Small capitals are similar in weight and height to a lower-case x. Large capitals are the height of an ascender.

serif A small terminal stroke at the end of the main stroke of a letter. A serif typeface is used in the main text on the facing page. A typeface with no serifs is called *sans serif* /ˈsan ˈserɪf/ (as in this column).

sort A single character of type. A *special sort* is one which the typesetter does not have routinely available in a fount, and which must be formed specially, such as a phonetic character.

superscript A small letter or figure set beside and above the top of a full-size character, as in x^2; also called a *superior*. It contrasts with *subscript*, a small letter or figure set beside and below the foot of a full-size character, as in 3_n; also called an *inferior*.

x height The height of the printing surface of a small letter *x*.

These features would all form part of a graphetic analysis of printed language.
(After J. Butcher, 1992.)

THE ALPHABET

The letter-shapes of the modern alphabet in most cases are part of an alphabetic tradition which is over 3,000 years old. The earliest-known alphabet was the 22-letter North Semitic, which developed *c.* 1700 BC in the Middle East. Several alphabets were based on this model, including the Phoenician, which *c.* 1000 BC was used as a model by the Greeks, who added letters for vowels. Greek in *c.* 800 BC itself became the model for the alphabet used by the Etruscans (a civilization in the Tuscany area of central Italy), and it is from Etruscan that the capital letters of the 23-letter Roman alphabet derived. The Christian era saw the emergence of new styles of writing throughout the Roman Empire, with scribes developing smaller scripts which could be written rapidly and smoothly, and in which the pen remained in contact with the paper as much as possible. The distinctive shapes of several modern lower-case letters arose through the constraints imposed by the need for efficient handwriting.

Old English was first written in the runic alphabet (p. 9), but the arrival of Christian missionaries brought the rapid introduction of the Roman alphabet. The 23 Latin letters were applied to the Old English sound system in a systematic way, with the addition of four new symbols to represent unfamiliar sounds: *æ* (ash), *þ* (thorn), *ð* (eth), and *p* (wynn); also, *g* appeared in a modified form as *ȝ* (yogh). Following the Norman Conquest, the distinctively Anglo-Saxon symbols gradually disappeared, at first because the French scribes preferred more familiar letters, and later because Continental printers did not have the sorts (p. 257) to print the earlier symbols. Ash was replaced by *a*, thorn and eth by *th*, yogh chiefly by *gh*, and wynn by a new letter, *w*. To this alphabet of 24 letters were added, from the late Middle Ages, *v* and *j*, respectively distinguished from *u* and *i*, with which they had previously been interchangeable (p. 41). The result is the 26-letter alphabet known today. One of the distinctive features of this alphabet is its lack of diacritics, apart from the dot over lower-case *i* and *j*, and the occasional use of accents in loan words where a pronunciation would otherwise be unclear (e.g. *resumé, naïve*).

SOME EARLY FORMS OF HANDWRITING

Majuscule
Relatively large letters generally contained within a single pair of imaginary horizontal lines; now usually called *capital letters*. The Greek and Latin alphabets were both originally written in this way.

Minuscule
Relatively small letters whose parts often extend above and below a pair of imaginary horizontal lines; now usually called *small letters* or *lower-case letters*. Minuscule writing was a gradual development, known in Greek from the 7th–8th centuries AD.

Uncial
A form of professional writing used in Greek and Latin manuscripts during the 4th–8th centuries AD. The style consists of large (the name means 'inch-high'), simple, rounded letters. A later development, now known as *half-uncial* or *semi-uncial*, prepared the way for modern small letters. Half-uncial is often found in early manuscripts from the British Isles, where the style of writing developed an 'insular' character of its own.

Cursive
Handwriting in which the characters are joined in a series of rounded, flowing strokes, which promotes ease and speed. Often now known colloquially as 'script' (US) or 'joined-up writing' (UK), it was widely used from the 4th century BC, and eventually replaced uncial and half-uncial as the handwriting norm.

Dual alphabet
The use of capital letters and small letters in a single system. This development took place during the renaissance associated with the reign of Emperor Charlemagne (742–814), as part of the script which was later called *Carolingian minuscule*. Carolingian writing, promoted throughout Europe, was an important influence on later handwriting styles. For example, modern Roman printed letters derive from a classical style, based on the Carolingian, introduced in Italy by humanist printers in the early 15th century.

THE BOOK OF KELLS
Insular half-uncial script, illustrated by this page from the genealogy of Christ, taken from St Luke's Gospel (3.22–26). The text reads: 'facta est tu es filius meus dilectus in te bene conplacuit mihi. et ipse ihs erat incipiens quasi annorum triginta ut putabantur filius ioseph. qui fuit heli...matha...levi... melchi...ianne... ioseph...mathathie... amos...nauum...esli... nagge...maath'

The Book of Kells is a large illuminated volume containing a Latin version of the Gospels. Its date is uncertain, but it was evidently compiled in Ireland over a considerable period of time (with some of the ornamental work left unfinished), probably between the late 7th century and the 9th century. The manuscript is now preserved in the library of Trinity College, Dublin.

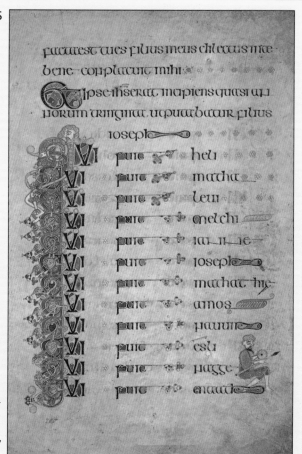

Phonetic terminology used in this section is explained in Chapter 17.

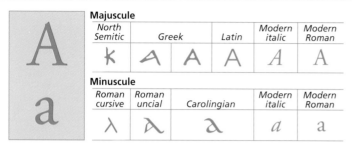

Majuscule

	North Semitic	Greek		Latin	Modern italic	Modern Roman
A	ꓘ	A	A	A	*A*	A

Minuscule

	Roman cursive	Roman uncial	Carolingian		Modern italic	Modern Roman
a	λ	λ	ꝛ		*a*	a

A has been the first letter of the alphabet for the whole of its history. Originally a consonant, *aleph* ('ox'), in the Semitic alphabet, it became the vowel *alpha* in Greek. The lower-case 'open a' is a development of the capital, with the addition of a left-facing loop at the top and a lowering of the cross-bar. The lower-case 'closed a' (*a*) is an italic development from the medieval period.

A/a has both short and long open-vowel values (as in /æ/ *cat* and /ɑː/ *father*), and a range of other pronunciations in specific contexts (such as a closer sound /ɔː/ after *w* or before *l*, as in *water* and *call*). In spelling, it enters into a number of combined forms with other vowels, both separated (*rate*) and adjacent (*say, rain, cause, saw, ear, goat*). It is occasionally doubled, but only in loan words (*aardvark, Aaron*).

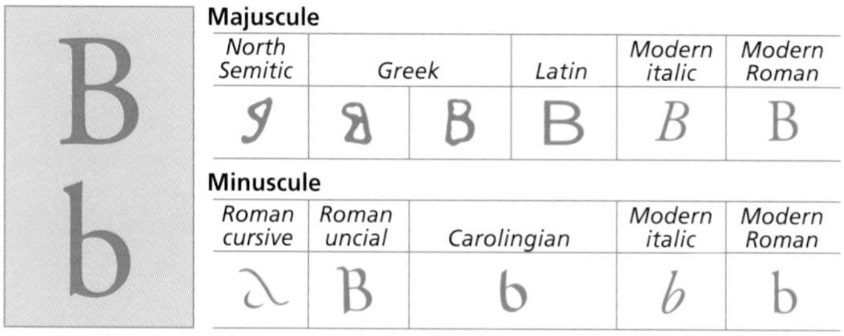

Majuscule

	North Semitic	Greek		Latin	Modern italic	Modern Roman
B	�Ꝗ	𝟖	B	B	*B*	B

Minuscule

	Roman cursive	Roman uncial	Carolingian		Modern italic	Modern Roman
b	λ	B	b		*b*	b

B has been the second letter of the alphabet since Semitic times, where its name was *beth* ('house'). It emerged in the later Greek alphabet as a capital letter with a shape close to its modern form. The lower-case letter developed from a later uncial form.

B/b normally represents the voiced bilabial plosive /b/ (p. 243), but is sometimes silent (*tomb, lamb, debt*). Doubling has been used since the early Middle English period (p. 42) as one way of showing a short preceding vowel (*robbing* vs *robing*).

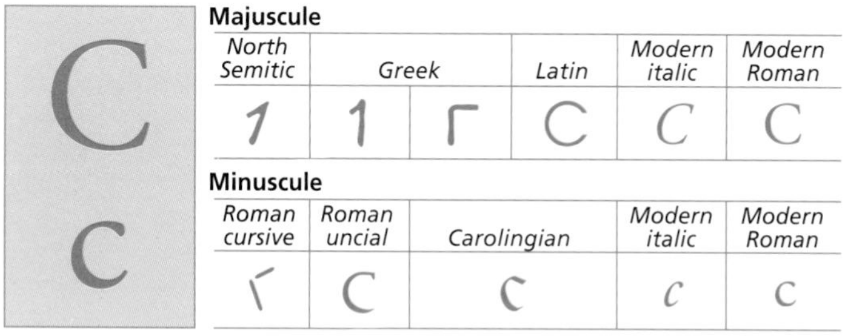

Majuscule

	North Semitic	Greek		Latin	Modern italic	Modern Roman
C	𝟙	𝟙	Γ	C	*C*	C

Minuscule

	Roman cursive	Roman uncial	Carolingian		Modern italic	Modern Roman
c	ꞓ	C	c		*c*	c

C has been the third letter of the alphabet since Semitic times, developing its right-facing curve in the Roman alphabet. The lower-case letter is simply a smaller form of the capital; neither has changed much in shape during the past 2,000 years.

The pronunciation of *C/c* has altered greatly, however: originally representing a voiced sound, as in Greek *gamma*, it became a voiceless velar plosive /k/ in Roman times, and entered Old English with both this 'hard' value, as in *king* (originally spelled *cyning*), and with a palatalized value, /tʃ/, as in *child* (originally spelled *cild*). Under the influence of French, the letter also developed a 'soft' value /s/ before *e* and *i* (*cell, city*). Other sound values include /ʃ/ (*special*), and silence (*muscle*). Both hard and soft doubled forms exist (*occur, accident*). There is some usage variation, both in sound (*Celtic* with /k/ or /s/) and spelling (*connection* vs *connexion, disc* vs *disk*, UK *licence* (noun) vs US *license*).

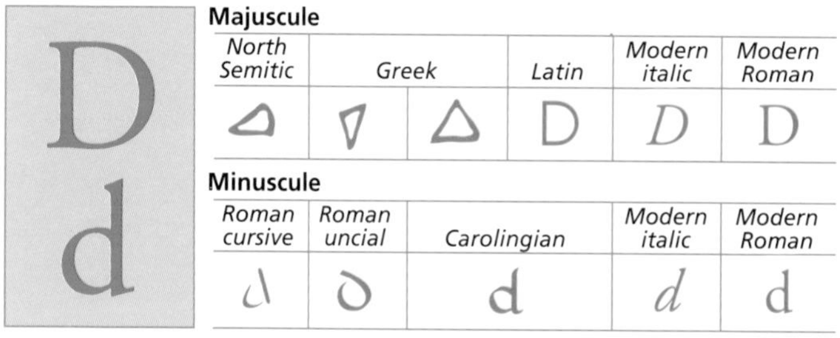

The fourth letter of the alphabet since Semitic times, *D* derives from Greek *delta*. A right-rounded shape appeared in Latin, and this came into English. The lower-case letter is a development of the capital, written rapidly to produce a form with a lengthened upper stroke and a reduced, left-rounded lower element.

D/d typically represents a voiced alveolar plosive /d/, though with devoicing to /t/ when it occurs immediately after a voiceless consonant (*crossed, pushed*, p. 242). It combines with *g* to represent /dʒ/ (*badge*), and is occasionally silent (*handkerchief*). Doubling is one way of showing a short preceding vowel (*bidding* vs *biding*).

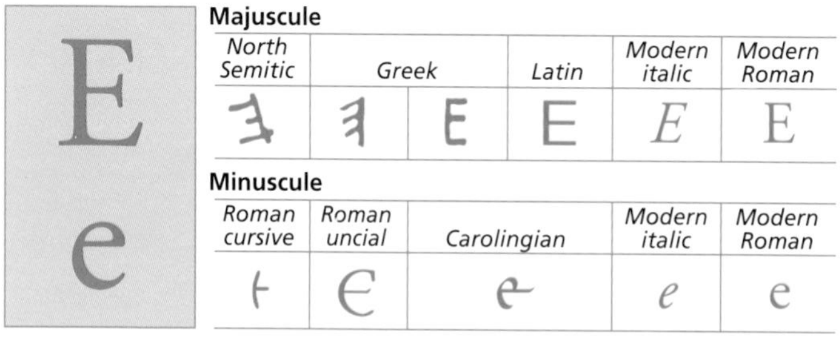

Majuscule

	North Semitic	Greek		Latin	Modern italic	Modern Roman
D	ꝺ	ꝺ	Δ	D	*D*	D

Minuscule

	Roman cursive	Roman uncial	Carolingian		Modern italic	Modern Roman
d	ꝺ	ꝺ	d		*d*	d

E was a consonant symbol in the Semitic alphabet, but was used as a vowel in Greek, one of its shapes emerging in Latin and eventually in English as the capital letter. The lower-case letter developed as a smaller, rounded variant of the capital in cursive style.

E/e represents both short /e/ (*set*) and long /iː/ (*me*) phonetic values, with several other variants (*English, certain, ballet, serious*). It is often combined with other vowel letters, such as *a* (*great, wear, ear*) and *i* (*rein, believe*, p. 272), less often *u* (*Europe*) and *o* (*leopard*), and it is often doubled (*meet, beer*). One of its major functions is to indicate a preceding long vowel, whether adjacent (*die*) or separated (the 'magic e ' in *make, bite*). It may also mark a change in consonant value, as in *teethe* vs *teeth, singe* vs *sing*, and *vice* vs *Vic*. It often has no function, being a silent testimonial to an earlier period of pronunciation history (*have, some, more*). There are several variations in usage (*judg(e)ment, ag(e)ing*) and regional differences, both in spelling (US *ax*, UK *axe*) and sound (*clerk* with /ɜ˞/ (US) or /ɑː/ (UK)).

Majuscule

	North Semitic	Greek		Latin	Modern italic	Modern Roman
E	ꓱ	ꓱ	E	E	*E*	E

Minuscule

	Roman cursive	Roman uncial	Carolingian		Modern italic	Modern Roman
e	ꞓ	Є	e		*e*	e

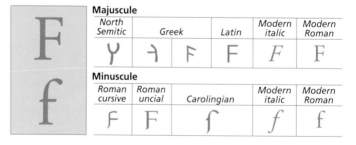

Majuscule

	North Semitic	Greek		Latin	Modern italic	Modern Roman
F	Ꞡ	ꓱ	F	F	*F*	F

Minuscule

	Roman cursive	Roman uncial	Carolingian		Modern italic	Modern Roman
f	F	F	ſ		*f*	f

F, along with *U, V* and *W*, all come from a single symbol used in the North Semitic alphabet. This gave rise to two letters in early Greek, one of which was adapted by the Etruscans and Romans, and given the value of a voiceless labio-dental fricative, /f/. The elongated lower-case form arose later, when scribes began to run letters together in the cursive style.

In Old English, the symbol was at first used for both voiced and voiceless labio-dental fricatives, but once /v/ emerged as a separate phoneme in English (p. 42), *f* was almost entirely used for the voiceless sound (an exception being *of*). There is doubling in many words, indicating a preceding short

vowel (*stuff*, *waffle*). Because other letters also represent the /f/ sound (*cough*, *photo*), there is occasional usage variation (US *sulfur*, UK *sulphur*). An interesting graphic archaism is the spelling of such upper-class surnames as *ffoulkes* and *ffrench*, arising from a medieval practice of representing a capital letter by doubling the lower-case character.

Majuscule				
North Semitic	Greek	Latin	Modern italic	Modern Roman
1	1	Γ	G	*G*	G

Minuscule				
Roman cursive	Roman uncial	Carolingian	Modern italic	Modern Roman
ζ	G	ᵹ	*g*	g

G is found first in the 4th century BC, in a revised version of the Latin alphabet. Previous alphabets had used the C symbol for the voiced velar plosive /g/, and the new letter was a simple adaptation of that, adding a small cross-bar. The lower-case form went through a complex set of changes to produce the modern symbols – the g with a closed lower element (g), often found in print, and the 'open g' of handwriting. An insular variant was found in Anglo-Saxon writing (ᵹ, p. 16), which lasted into early Middle English for the representation of certain palatal and velar sounds until eventually replaced by *gh*.

After the Norman Conquest, *g* is found as both a 'hard' sound, the velar plosive (*go*), and a 'soft' sound (the affricate /dʒ/, used before *e*, *i* and *y*, as in *age*, *gin*, *gym*). French loan words with *g* also often retain a voiced fricative (*rouge*, *genre*). Popular letter combinations include *d* (*ledge*) and *n* (*sing*), and there is frequent doubling (*egg*, *soggy*, *bigger*). It is often silent (*gnome*, *phlegm*, *resign*, *foreign*, *high*) and is famous for its silence in the *-ough* spellings (p. 272). There is some usage variation, both in sound (*rouge* with /dʒ/ or /ʒ/) and spelling (*jail*, *gaol*, and especially in proper names using a 'soft *g*': *Geoff* vs *Jeff*).

Majuscule				
North Semitic	Greek	Latin	Modern italic	Modern Roman
⊟	𝐁	H	H	*H*	H

Minuscule				
Roman cursive	Roman uncial	Carolingian	Modern italic	Modern Roman
⊦	ꜧ	ƕ	*h*	h

H was originally a Semitic letter which came into Latin via Greek and Etruscan to represent the glottal fricative /h/. The lower-case form arose with the development of cursive script. A rounded version, in the uncial style, led to the modern small letter.

H/h is widely used as a combining form in such digraphs as *ch*, *sh*, *th*, and *ph*, but is not doubled (apart from such cases as *ahh!*) unless two syllables come together (*withhold*). It is often silent (*Sarah*, *exhausted*, *rhythm*) and sometimes signals adjacent sound quality (e.g. showing that *c* before *e* in *chemist* is pronounced /k/). It is a major source of usage variation, with several accents not pronouncing *h* initially (p. 244), and some words varying between regions (UK *herb* pronounces the *h*, US *herb* usually does not).

Majuscule				
North Semitic	Greek	Latin	Modern italic	Modern Roman
ᒋ	ᒾ	I	I	*I*	I

Minuscule				
Roman cursive	Roman uncial	Carolingian	Modern italic	Modern Roman
ꞁ	ꞁ	ꞁ	*i*	i

I was a consonant in the Semitic alphabet, represented a vowel in Greek, and came into Latin with both vowel and consonant (*y*) values. The lower-case letter is a smaller form of the capital. The dot was originally a small diacritic, similar to an acute accent, added during the early Middle English period by scribes concerned to distinguish the stroke of an *i* from the otherwise identical strokes (known as *minims*) of adjacent letters (*m*, *n*, *u*).

I/i has a wide range of sound values, both short (*big*) and long (*find*, *ski*); it is sometimes silent (*session*). It often combines as a digraph with *e* (*lie*, *field*), and appears doubled only when syllables become adjacent (*radii*). There is some usage variation with *y* (*gipsy* vs *gypsy*, US *tire* vs UK *tyre*), reflecting a time when *i* and *y* were interchangeable. The choice of the capital *I* for the first person singular pronoun was a standardization introduced by printers in late Middle English, after a period when *i*, *j*, *I*, *y*, and *Y* had all been used for this form.

Majuscule				
North Semitic	Greek	Latin	Modern italic	Modern Roman
ᒋ	ᒾ	I	I	*J*	J

Minuscule				
Roman cursive	Roman uncial	Carolingian	Modern italic	Modern Roman
ꞁ	J	ꞁ	*j*	j

The history of this letter in English dates only from the medieval period. Originally a graphic variant of *i* (a lengthened form with a bottom left-facing curve), it gradually came to replace *i* whenever that letter represented a consonant, as in *major* and *jewel*. The lower-case distinction did not become standard until the mid-17th century, and there was uncertainty about the upper-case distinction even as late as the early 19th century.

J/j is chiefly pronounced as a voiced palato-alveolar affricate /dʒ/ (*jab*), with a fricative or vocalic sound in a few cases, such as foreign names (*Jacques*, *Jung*, *Juan*). It is unusual to find it at the end of a word (*raj*). Many words with initial *j* are from French (*jolly*, *juice*) or Latin (*junior*, *jubilation*), and it is a common letter in personal names (*Janet*, *John*). It is also sometimes used as a nonstandard spelling for the voiced affricate /dʒ/ (*Injuns*, *Roj* = *Roger*).

POOR LETTER H

Tout Contractor (who has been paid a shilling per man, and sees his way to a little extra profit). "Now look 'ere, you two H's! The public don't want yer — nor I don't, nor nobody don't; so just drop them boards, and 'ook it!"

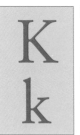

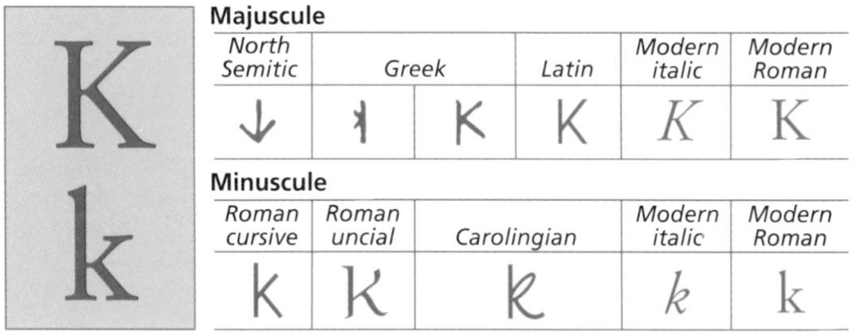

Majuscule

North Semitic	Greek		Latin	Modern italic	Modern Roman
↓	⟨	K	K	*K*	K

Minuscule

Roman cursive	Roman uncial	Carolingian		Modern italic	Modern Roman
k	K	R		*k*	k

K was a Semitic letter which came into Latin via Greek and Etruscan. It was in fact little used in Latin (which preferred *C* and *Q*), and is uncommon in Old English. The letter emerges in Middle English to represent the voiceless velar plosive /k/, which in Old English had been spelled with *c*. The need for the new symbol arose because of the arrival of many French words where *c* had a fricative sound before *e* and *i* (*centre*, *city*), and after a period of uncertainty *k* became used in those contexts where *c* would have had a plosive sound. In this way, Old English words such as *cyning* came to be written as *king*. The lower-case letter arose in handwriting through a simple extension of the upright stroke above the line.

As a result, *K/k* in Modern English is common before *e* and *i*, but less so before other vowels (*kangaroo*), unless it represents a Scandinavian *sk*- word (p. 25), such as *sky*. It is not usually doubled, *ck* being the usual form after short vowels (but note such loan words as *trekking* and *pukka*). It is sometimes silent (*knee*, *know*). It is a common symbol when representing foreign names (*Khrushchev*, *Kaiser*), names of aliens (*Kruls*, *Klingons*), and as a non-standard spelling in trade names (*Kwik-Fit*) or humour (*Keystone Kops*). There is also some usage variation (*disk* vs *disc*, US *check* vs UK *cheque*, US *skeptic* vs UK *sceptic*).

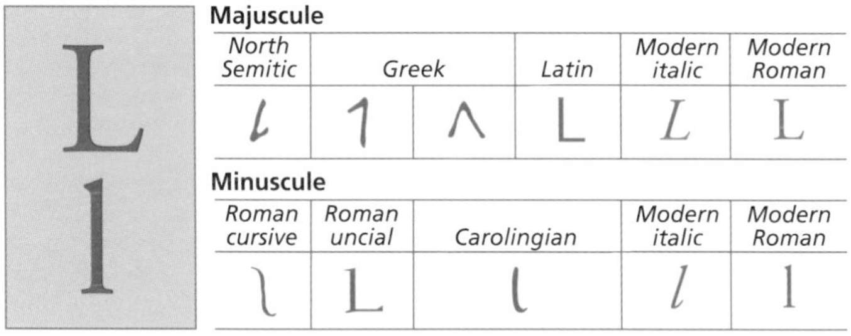

Majuscule

North Semitic	Greek		Latin	Modern italic	Modern Roman
�	⟨	∧	L	*L*	L

Minuscule

Roman cursive	Roman uncial	Carolingian		Modern italic	Modern Roman
↳	L	↳		*l*	l

L was a symbol in the Semitic alphabet, and developed via Greek, Etruscan, and Latin into its modern capital form, with a horizontal line replacing an earlier oblique. The lower-case letter arose in handwriting, when scribes joined *L* to adjacent letters by using an upper loop and turning the horizontal stroke into a curve. These linking features were omitted in the printed form.

L/l represents a voiced alveolar lateral /l/ (*lip*, *pool*), with some variation according to context (p. 245). Other pronunciations may occur in loan words, such as the voiceless lateral in Welsh *ll* (*Llangollen*). The letter is frequently doubled, usually to mark a preceding short vowel (*million*, *well*), but there are many exceptions (such as *welcome*, *until*, with *l* after a short vowel, and *all*, *poll*, with *ll* after a long vowel). *L/l* is often silent (*could*, *chalk*, *folk*), with some variation (*almond* with and without /l/). There is also some written usage variation (US *enroll*, *traveler*, *chili* vs UK *enrol*, *traveller*, *chilli*).

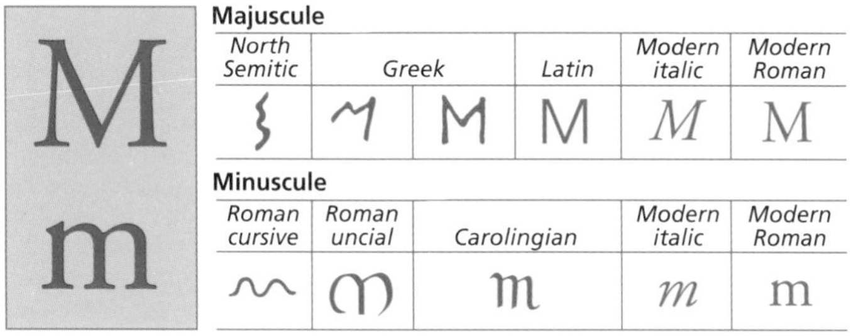

Majuscule

North Semitic	Greek		Latin	Modern italic	Modern Roman
↯	⋀	M	M	*M*	M

Minuscule

Roman cursive	Roman uncial	Carolingian		Modern italic	Modern Roman
∿	⋒	m		*m*	m

M has come from a Semitic letter via the Greek, Etruscan, and Roman alphabets (where it sometimes had four vertical strokes) into Old English. The lower-case letter appeared in a rounded form in uncial style. In medieval

MINIM CONFUSION

In some styles of medieval handwriting, sequences of *m*, *n*, *v/u*, and *i* (with no distinguishing dot, at that time) would appear as an identical series of joined vertical strokes, or *minims*. A sequence of six strokes could therefore be *ium*, *niui*, *inui*, or several other possibilities. The decoding problem is apparent in this extract from a late 7th-century work of Aldhelm (*Carmina Rhythmica*, preserved in a mid-9th century manuscript), notably in such words as *munimine* and *spiramina*.

Heu! tectorum tutamina
Prosternuntur in platea;
Ecce, crates a culmine
Ruunt sine munimine!
Flatus saevi spiramina
Haec fecerunt ludibria.
 Et nisi natalicia
Pauli sancti sollemnia
Tuerentur trementia
Timidorum precordia,
Forsan quassato culmine
Quateremur et fulmine,

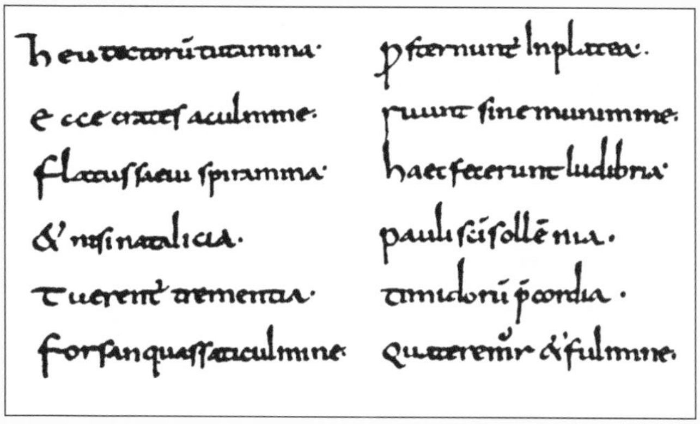

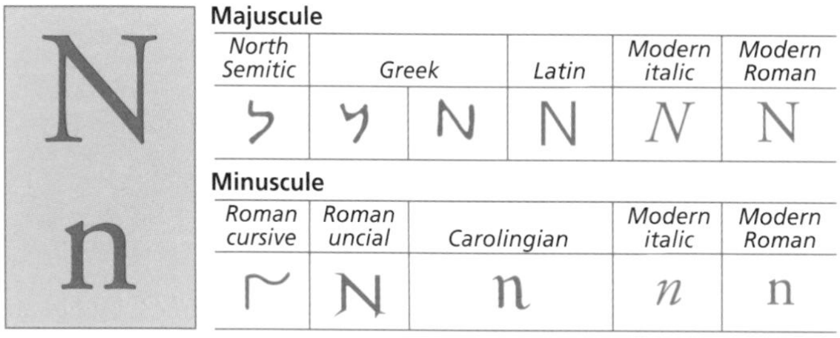

manuscripts, it was common practice to replace *m* by a small stroke over the preceding letter (p. 40), a practice which can still be found in the 17th century.

M/m represents a voiced bilabial nasal /m/, with some minor articulatory variations (p. 245). Doubling is usual after a short vowel (*comma* vs *coma*), but there are many exceptions (*camel* vs *mammal*), especially at the end of monosyllabic words, where a single *m* is usual (*am*, *time*, *seem*), and learning how many *m*s there are in a word remains a source of spelling confusion into adult life (*accommodation*). The letter is silent in a few Greek loan words, notably *mnemonic*.

Majuscule

North Semitic	Greek		Latin	Modern italic	Modern Roman
⅁	⅄	N	N	*N*	N

Minuscule

Roman cursive	Roman uncial	Carolingian		Modern italic	Modern Roman
∼	N	n		*n*	n

N achieved its present-day shape in the Latin alphabet after a history of various angular forms. The lower-case letter resulted from scribal cursive practice. It appears in Old English, and has been used with very little change in form since.

N/n represents a voiced alveolar nasal /n/, with minor variations depending on the following consonant – /ŋ/ before a velar (*ink*), /m/ before a bilabial (*input*). It indicates foreign sounds in a few loan words, such as the nasalized vowel often heard in *restaurant*, and the palatal consonant in *lasagne*. Doubling usually signals a preceding short vowel (*dinner* vs *diner*), but there are many exceptions (*money*, *finish*), especially in monosyllabic words (*an*, *ten*). Spelling difficulties over the number of *n*s in a word are common, as a consequence, especially when *un-* and *-ness* fall adjacent to *n* in a root (*unnecessary*, *openness*). It is occasionally silent (*autumn*, *condemn*), but sounded in derived lexical forms (*autumnal*).

O

Majuscule				
North Semitic	Greek	Latin	Modern italic	Modern Roman
O	O	O	O	O

Minuscule				
Roman cursive	Roman uncial	Carolingian	Modern italic	Modern Roman
o	O	o	o	o

O represented a consonant in the Semitic alphabet, and was used by the Greeks for both a short and a long vowel, these later being distinguished as two symbols, *omicron* ('little *o*' for the short sound) and *omega* ('big *o*' for the long sound). The Romans adopted omicron, giving it both short and long values, and these values were also assigned to the letter when it was used for Old English. The shape has shown hardly any change throughout its history. The lower-case letter is simply a smaller form of the capital.

O/o has a wide range of sound values in Modern English, both short (back quality as in *cot, gone, rocket, lost*; central quality as in *son, love, brother, onion*) and long (diphthongal quality as in *go, oboe, yellow, old*; pure vowel quality as in *do, who, move, shoe*). It is commonly doubled, with both long (*moon*) and short (*good*) values, but there is much regional variation (northern UK *book* /uː/ vs RP /ʊ/). It is occasionally silent (*people*, the second instance in *colonel*). There is also some regional variation in o-forms (US *color, plow, fetus, mustache* vs UK *colour, plough, foetus, moustache*).

P

Majuscule				
North Semitic	Greek	Latin	Modern italic	Modern Roman
Ɂ	ꓓ	Π	P	P	P

Minuscule				
Roman cursive	Roman uncial	Carolingian	Modern italic	Modern Roman
p	p	p	p	p

P was a Semitic letter which came into Greek, Etruscan, and Latin in a variety of forms. It eventually standardized with a rounded upper element. The lower-case letter is a smaller version of the capital, with the additional distinction that the vertical stroke falls below the line of writing.

P/p is usually pronounced as a voiceless bilabial plosive /p/ (*pop*), with minor articulatory variations (p. 244). In Greek loan words it often appears in a digraph with *h* to represent /f/ (*philosophy*). Doubled forms usually indicate a preceding short vowel (*happy, upper*), but there are many exceptions (*lip, drop, proper*), and some regional variations (US often *kidnaping*, UK *kidnapping*). It is silent in Greek loan words before *n, s,* and *t* (*pneumatic, psalm, pterodactyl*), in certain words followed by *b* (*cupboard*), and in a few other cases (*receipt, coup*).

Q

Majuscule				
North Semitic	Greek	Latin	Modern italic	Modern Roman
φ	φ	ρ	Q	Q	Q

Minuscule				
Roman cursive	Roman uncial	Carolingian	Modern italic	Modern Roman
ʮ	q	q	q	q

The location of the distinctive stroke has varied greatly from the Semitic alphabet through Greek and Etruscan to Latin, until a curved 'tail' at the bottom and to the right of the *O* became the standard form. The letter was dropped in Classical Greek, but retained in Etruscan as the representation of /k/ before a *u* vowel, and this practice was taken over in Latin. The lower-case letter developed in scribal writing as a smaller version of the capital, with the tail lengthened below the line and moved to the right, to facilitate rapid

WHEN Q – U = /KW/

In a few cases (all abbreviations) *Q* appears without its accompanying *U*, yet retains the /kw/ pronunciation. The name of this airline is probably the most familiar, /ˈkwɒntəs/, standing for 'Queensland and Northern Territory Aerial Service', but there are several other examples, including *QALY* ('Quality Adjusted Life Year'), *QAMIS* ('Quality Assurance Monitoring Information System'), and *QOMAC* ('Quarter Orbit Magnetic Attitude Control').

cursive script. Old English preferred the spelling *cw* (*cwic* 'quick'), the *qu-* forms not coming into use until after the Norman Conquest. The use of *qu* was further extended in the north of England, remained in Scots in such words as *when* (*quhen*) until Early Modern English, and is still seen today in the occasional surname (*Colquhoun* /kaˈhuːn/).

Q/q represents a velar voiceless plosive /k/, and is usually followed by *u*, representing the bilabial semi-vowel /w/ (*quiz, quack*). It appears without *u* in various transliterated and loan forms (*Iraq, Qin*), and with a silent *u* in Romance loans (*unique, quiche*). There is occasional regional usage variation (UK *cheque, liquorice* vs US *check, licorice*).

R

Majuscule				
North Semitic	Greek	Latin	Modern italic	Modern Roman
ꓷ	ꓷ	P	R	R	R

Minuscule				
Roman cursive	Roman uncial	Carolingian	Modern italic	Modern Roman
ꞁ	R	r	r	r

R appeared in the Semitic alphabet in a variety of forms, and was taken into Greek with a single descending stroke (*rho*). A version with an additional short 'tail' became the basis of the Latin form, with the tail lengthened to avoid confusion with P. The lower-case form arose as a simplified character in handwriting, with the curve and tail smoothed into a single wavy horizontal stroke. The letter appears in Old English.

No other consonantal letter has such a variety of sounds, and is prone to such regional variation. *Rhotic* accents (p. 245) retain a sound value for *r* after a vowel (*far, work*), whereas *non-rhotic* accents do not, unless a vowel follows (*far and wide* – the 'linking *r*' – though this is not heard in all non-rhotic accents). All phonetic qualities of *r* can be heard, such as retroflex *r* in India and the USA, and trilled *r* in Scotland and Wales. Doubling is common (*carry, purr, correct, embarrass*), but there is great inconsistency (*her, stir, harass*), hence the frequency of such spelling problems as the number of *r*'s in *occurrence*. Other common spelling problems involve the vowels which precede *r* in an unstressed position (*alter* vs *altar*). There is also some regional variation (US *center, theater* vs UK *centre, theatre*).

Majuscule					
North Semitic	Greek		Latin	Modern italic	Modern Roman
W	ϟ	Σ	S	S	S

Minuscule					
Roman cursive	Roman uncial	Carolingian		Modern italic	Modern Roman
ſ	S	s		s	s

The Semitic and Greek alphabets had a variety of symbols for sibilant sounds (p. 243), one of which – a rounded form – was taken over by the Etruscans and Romans and eventually entered Old English, usually written in an elongated way. The lower-case letter is simply a smaller version of the capital, though a form resembling an f (but without the cross-bar) came to be used in handwriting in the 17th century, and is found in print especially at the beginning of syllables until the early 19th century.

S/s represents an alveolar sibilant, both voiceless /s/ (*sister, bus*) and voiced /z/ (*is, easy*). Alternations exist, such as *a house* (noun) vs *to house* (verb). A palatal sound is used before certain endings (*session, vision*) and in a few other cases (*sugar*), but /ʃ/ is usually spelled out as the combination *sh*. Doubling is typically voiceless (*hiss, possible*), but there are exceptions (*scissors, dessert*). *S/s* is occasionally silent (*island, corps*). There is some regional usage variation both in sound (US *erase* with /s/, UK with /z/) and spelling (US *defense* vs UK *defence*), as well as some general variation, also in sound (*issue* with /s/ or /ʃ/) and spelling (*focused* vs *focussed*).

Majuscule					
North Semitic	Greek		Latin	Modern italic	Modern Roman
+	X	T	T	T	T

Minuscule					
Roman cursive	Roman uncial	Carolingian		Modern italic	Modern Roman
τ	T	τ		t	t

T was used in the Semitic alphabet, came into Latin via Greek and Etruscan, and entered Old English. The handwritten form in uncial style was a smaller and rounded version of the capital, with a right-curved base. The vertical stroke later became lengthened above the horizontal (forming a cross-bar), in order to distinguish handwritten *t* from *c*.

T/t represents a voiceless alveolar plosive, with some minor articulatory variations (p. 244) and some major regional variants (e.g. dental in Ireland, retroflex in India). In some contexts, it may be pronounced as a fricative /ʃ/ (*patient*) or an affricate /tʃ/ (*picture*), though there is often usage variation with /tj/ (*question*) or /s/ (*negotiate*). Doubling is common, and indicates a preceding short vowel (*bottle, sitting*); this is unusual at the end of a word (*putt*). An important combination is with *h* to represent the voiced and voiceless dental fricatives /θ/ and /ð/ (*thin, this*). The letter is quite often silent (*listen, cabaret, castle, Christmas*). There is occasional usage variation with *-ed* (*smelt* vs *smelled*, p. 204), and *often* is a famous example of a word where the pronunciation of *t* is optional.

Majuscule					
North Semitic	Greek		Latin	Modern italic	Modern Roman
Y	ч	Y	V	U	U

Minuscule					
Roman cursive	Roman uncial	Carolingian		Modern italic	Modern Roman
u	U	u		u	u

The ancestor of *U* is to be found in the Semitic alphabet, eventually emerging in Latin as a *V* used for both consonant and vowel. The lower-case letter developed as a smaller and rounded form in uncial script. In Middle English, both *v* and *u* appear variously as consonant and vowel, in some scribal practice *v* being found initially and *u* medially (p. 41). This eventually led to *v* being reserved for the consonant and *u* for the vowel, though it was not until the late 17th century that this distinction became standard.

U/u typically represents a close back vowel, either long /uː/ (*ruby*) or short /ʊ/ (*put*), though not all accents (e.g. Scots) make this distinction. Other values include (in some accents) a more open vowel /ʌ/ (*cup*), a semi-vowel /w/ (*quick*), and a variant in which /uː/ is preceded by a palatal glide /j/ (*unit, muse*). The letter commonly combines with *o* to give various phonetic values (*south, southern, could, journey*), and is quite often silent (*vogue, quay, build, biscuit*). It is hardly ever doubled (*vacuum, muumuu*, a Hawaiian dress). There is considerable regional variation, both in sound (*duty, tune* US /uː/ vs UK /juː/, *route* US often /aʊ/ vs UK /uː/) and spelling (US *color* vs UK *colour*).

Majuscule					
North Semitic	Greek		Latin	Modern italic	Modern Roman
Y	ч	Y	V	V	V

Minuscule					
Roman cursive	Roman uncial	Carolingian		Modern italic	Modern Roman
u	V	u		v	v

The history of this letter is the same as for *U*. Once a systematic distinction had emerged between the two letters, a larger version of *u* became standard as a capital, and a smaller version of *V* became standard as a lower-case form.

V/v represents a voiced labio-dental fricative /v/, a sound which became phonemic only in the Middle English period (p. 42). Almost all instances of initial *v* are loan words (*valley, Viking*), and in final position the letter is usually followed by a silent *e* (*have, love*). Forms such as *spiv* and *luv* are colloquial and often nonstandard spellings. Doubling is found only in recent coinages (*navvy*), because the doubled *v* was appropriated for *w* in the medieval period; as a result, *v* does not signal preceding vowel length clearly (*love* vs *move*).

The external facade of Bush House, the location of the BBC World Service in the Aldwych, London. The classical architectural style is reflected in the capital letters, which retain the older use of V for U.

Majuscule

North Semitic	Greek		Latin	Modern italic	Modern Roman
Y	Y	Y	V	W	W

Minuscule

Roman cursive	Roman uncial	Carolingian		Modern italic	Modern Roman
—	ɯ	—		w	w

This letter was introduced by Norman scribes in the 11th century as a means of representing /w/, replacing the runic symbol, *wynn*, which had been used in Old English (p. 16). Although its shape is a ligature of two *V*'s, its name is 'double *u*', reflecting the state of affairs in Middle English when *v* and *u* were interchangeable (p. 41). The lower-case letter is simply a smaller version of the capital.

W/w usually represents a voiced bilabial semi-vowel, /w/ (*wig*), and also forms part of digraphs representing several long vowels or diphthongs (*cow, saw, knew, owe*). It combines with *h* in many words, some accents pronouncing this as a voiceless bilabial /ʍ/ (*where, white*). The letter is no longer sounded before *r* (*wreck, wrist*), and there are several other silent forms (*two, answer, Norwich, whole*).

Majuscule

North Semitic	Greek		Latin	Modern italic	Modern Roman
ⱶ	ⱶ	X	X	X	X

Minuscule

Roman cursive	Roman uncial	Carolingian		Modern italic	Modern Roman
X	X	x		x	x

X emerged in the Greek alphabet (*chi*), derived from an earlier Semitic sibilant letter. It came into Latin with the value /ks/, and was used in Old English typically as a variant spelling of *cs*. In Middle English it is found in some dialects with other values, such as /ʃ/ (*xal* for *shall*), and as a spelling for *yogh* (p. 16). The lower-case letter is simply a smaller version of the capital.

Because the English alphabet already contains letters which can represent its sound (*locks, tics, accident*), *x* is often considered an unnecessary letter. It does however have a distinctive visual value, as can be seen from its use as a nonstandard spelling (*pix* for *pictures, sox* for *socks, ax* for *ask*), and from its classical associations (*helix, index, matrix*), which have given it some currency in technical trade names (*Xerox, Unix, Xenix*). It is especially common in final position, usually after a short vowel (*fax*). It also occurs with the sound /z/ (*xerography*), /gz/ (*exit*), and a few other values (*X-ray, luxury*), and is silent at the end of French loan words (*Grand Prix*). There is some usage variation (*inflection* vs *inflexion, Xmas* vs *Christmas*).

Majuscule

North Semitic	Greek		Latin	Modern italic	Modern Roman
Y	Y	Y	Y	Y	Y

Minuscule

Roman cursive	Roman uncial	Carolingian		Modern italic	Modern Roman
y	y	y		y	y

Y is a Greek adaptation of a Semitic symbol, representing a high front rounded vowel (p. 240). In Roman times, it was borrowed to help transcribe Greek loan words into Latin, and given an unrounded value (similar to *i*). It was thus particularly useful in the early history of English: it transcribed the Old English rounded vowel in such words as *cyning* ('king'), and this later enabled Middle English scribes to use it as a replacement for *i*, in cases where there would be minim confusion (p. 261). A further use was as a spelling of

the sounds which were represented by *yogh* (p. 16). A dot was often added above, to distinguish it from Old English letters *thorn* and *wynn* (p. 16). The rounded lower-case letter developed as part of the cursive style, enabling scribes to write it in a single movement. The trunk of the letter was placed below the line, and moved to the right to enable a smoother link to be made with the following letter.

Reflecting this mixed history, modern *Y/y* now represents both the palatal semi-vowel /j/ (*you, yes*) and an *i*-type vowel, whether short (*pyramid*), long (*byte*), or intermediate (*happy*). It is an important element of certain digraphs (*play, they, boy*). There is also some usage variation (*pygmy* vs *pigmy*, UK *pyjamas, tyre* vs US *pajamas, tire*).

Majuscule

North Semitic	Greek		Latin	Modern italic	Modern Roman
I	I	Z	Z	Z	Z

Minuscule

Roman cursive	Roman uncial	Carolingian		Modern italic	Modern Roman
z	z	z		z	z

Z appeared in the Semitic and Greek alphabets, and although it was not needed for Latin the Romans later borrowed the letter to help transcribe Greek loan words, making it the last item in their alphabet. It was little used in Old English, but became more common after the Norman Conquest. However, it was never a popular letter, perhaps because it was difficult to write smoothly in a cursive hand, and *s* was often used instead. The lower-case letter is simply a smaller version of the capital.

Z/z typically represents a voiced alveolar fricative /z/ (*zoo, gaze*), occasionally being used for palatal (*azure*) or palato-alveolar sounds (*Nazi, schizo*). /z/ became a distinct phoneme only in the Middle English period (p. 42). Doubling indicates a preceding short vowel (*jazz, dizzy*), and is often used in a sound symbolic way (*buzz, sizzle*, p. 250). There is an exotic 'feel' to the letter because of its frequent use in loan words from a wide range of languages (*zodiac, zombie, bazaar, mazurka*). It is occasionally silent (*rendezvous*). There is some usage variation, especially in suffixes (*-ise* vs *-ize*), and the name of the letter is itself a source of division (US *zee*, UK *zed*).

The traditional alphabet book (p. 256), with its 'A is for —' formula, always found itself in trouble with such letters as *X*, which are much more commonly used in medial and final position in the word. *X* is more predictably associated with such words as *box* and *fox* – or perhaps, for adults these days, *sex* and *fax* – than with such alphabet-book stalwarts as *xylophone* and *X-ray*.

A frame from *Asterix and Cleopatra*, one of the many books in the Asterix series, by Goscinny and Uderzo.

PROPERTIES OF LETTERS

The letters of the alphabet are the basic elements of the writing system. Like phonemes (p. 236), they have no meaning in themselves: their primary role is to combine into linguistic units, each of the 26 letters, or graphemes (p. 257), playing a contrastive role (e.g. *bit* vs *bet*, *act* vs *art*). Lewis Carroll once invented a game, which he called *doublets*, based on the pairs of words which can be formed in this way. The aim is to change one word into another in a series of steps, as few as possible, each intervening word differing from its neighbours in only one letter. 'Drive *pig* into *sty*' was one of Carroll's own examples: he did it in five steps: *pig – wig – wag – way – say – sty*. Several other word games rely on the linguistic properties of the letters of the alphabet (p. 396), in particular their frequency and their ability to combine.

The linguistic properties of letters are the most obvious. The need to maintain a distinctive graphic form has motivated many of the changes in letter shapes throughout the history of the alphabet, such as the use of the cross-bar in *G* (to preserve a contrast with *C*) or the lengthening of the second leg of *R* (to contrast with *P*). The dot, the English alphabet's sole diacritic (p. 260), began life in this way. However, it becomes more difficult to see the linguistic function of letters when we see them combine. It is much easier to tamper with the written language than the spoken language – the history of English spelling is littered with attempts made by well-meaning individuals to improve the way writing reflects speech (p. 274). Norman scribes were able to introduce spelling conventions reflecting French practice, such as *qu* for *cw* (*queen*) or *c* before *e* (*cell*). And because there was a time when spelling reformers felt that it was important for words to reflect their classical origins, we now have a *b* in *debt*, a *g* in *reign*, and several other such emendations. As a result of these developments, English now often looks like a Romance language, though it does not sound like one.

This is not all bad news, of course. Because the language's history is preserved in the spelling much more than it is in the pronunciation, non-native speakers (especially those with a classical background) who wish to gain only a reading knowledge of English find this relatively easy to achieve. And the semantic relationships between words are often better preserved in their written than in their spoken form: the links between such pairs as *sign/signature* or *telegraph/telegraphy* are straightforward in writing, but by no means so evident in speech.

MORSE AND OTHER CODES

The Morse Code is the best known of the signalling codes devised in the 19th century. Constructed during the 1830s by US artist and inventor Samuel Morse (1791–1872), it is a binary code, in which characters are assigned a distinctive combination of dots and dashes. Morse's choice of individual letter codes was guided by a frequency count of the quantities of type found in a printer's office, the more frequently occurring letters being assigned the shorter dot/dash combinations. In this respect, his system is in principle much more efficient than that used in braille, where dot combinations broadly increase in complexity as one 'descends' the alphabet, or in flag semaphore, where the simpler arm positions are assigned to the opening letters. Thus T, for example, though the second most frequent letter, turns out to have one of the most awkward flag combinations – a fact discovered with arm-aching empiricism by generations of scouts and guides.

LETTER FREQUENCY

This table summarizes the frequency ordering of letters in all the text entries of *The Cambridge Encyclopedia*, totalling 1.5 million words. Column 1 gives the rank order for the book as a whole. Columns 2–6 give the rank orderings for five topic categories. Column 7 gives Morse's original order.

Because it is a general encyclopedia, all topic areas are represented (though not with equal sample sizes), and thus the cumulative total (over 7.5 million letters) is of considerable interest. There are several points to note.

• Only e and v have the same place in each column.

• The second place for a in the cumulative total is unexpected, as previous counts have generally assigned this to t.

• If we calculate a simple measure of difference from the cumulative total (same rank = 0, one rank difference = 1, etc.), we find that politics is closest to the norm (scoring 12 points of difference), literature and religion come next (14), then – strikingly distinct – the science topics, physics (20) and chemistry (26). Morse is even further away (32), for everything after the first seven letters (especially *w*, *p*, and *q*).

• Differences of more than 1 rank place (+ upwards, – downwards) are tantalizing. In literature, the only letters which differ so much are *g* (−2) and *w* (+3); in religion, *a* (−2) and *l* (−2); in politics, *a* (−2), *c* (+3), and *q* (−2), *c* (+3); in physics, *a* (−2), *l* (−2), and *q* (+2); and in chemistry, *i* (+2), *o* (+2), *t* (−2), *c* (+2), *y* (+2), and *j* (−2).

	Cumulative		Literature		Religion		Politics		Physics		Chemistry		Morse Code
e	887,010	e	51,289	e	43,830	e	27,107	e	30,473	e	13,240	e	12,000
a	666,794	a	35,571	t	31,707	t	19,793	t	21,717	i	10,261	t	9,000
t	611,202	i	33,790	i	30,520	i	18,861	i	19,901	a	10,196	a	8,000
i	605,701	t	33,162	a	30,512	a	18,550	a	19,661	o	10,090	i	8,000
n	578,826	n	32,051	n	27,545	n	17,465	n	17,740	t	9,845	n	8,000
o	541,721	o	30,710	o	27,394	o	16,427	o	17,592	n	9,131	o	8,000
r	511,333	r	30,294	s	24,686	r	14,857	s	16,973	s	8,085	s	8,000
s	501,098	s	28,644	r	23,976	s	13,983	r	16,434	r	7,410	h	6,400
l	331,639	h	21,018	h	20,237	h	9,317	c	11,196	l	5,706	r	6,200
h	326,573	l	19,085	d	14,864	l	8,735	h	10,143	c	5,635	d	4,400
d	302,965	d	17,755	l	14,124	c	8,350	l	10,109	h	5,248	l	4,000
c	285,436	c	13,266	c	13,777	d	8,215	d	8,613	d	4,872	u	3,400
m	208,625	u	10,652	m	9,169	m	6,358	m	7,033	m	3,927	c	3,000
u	206,020	m	10,057	u	9,167	u	5,488	u	6,873	u	3,546	m	3,000
f	176,923	f	8,901	f	9,016	p	5,165	p	6,045	p	2,586	f	2,500
p	173,100	p	8,678	p	7,715	f	4,994	f	6,020	f	2,561	w	2,000
g	148,103	w	7,911	g	6,632	g	3,782	g	4,632	y	2,223	y	2,000
b	122,635	b	7,442	b	6,362	b	3,386	y	4,303	g	2,208	g	1,700
y	120,004	g	7,118	w	5,254	y	3,158	b	3,901	b	1,941	p	1,700
w	110,832	y	6,583	y	5,185	w	3,071	w	2,903	w	1,292	b	1,600
v	76,395	v	5,089	v	3,325	v	2,354	v	2,676	v	967	v	1,200
k	42,983	k	2,982	k	1,516	k	745	k	852	x	503	k	800
x	15,860	j	939	j	1,179	x	384	x	759	k	359	q	500
j	12,429	x	814	x	718	z	258	q	658	z	192	j	400
z	11,162	z	705	z	478	j	290	j	361	q	155	x	400
q	9,772	q	326	q	257	q	132	z	360	j	39	z	200
	7,585,141		**424,832**		**396,145**		**221,225**		**247,928**		**122,218**		**106,400**

Semaphore	Letters	Morse	Braille
	A	·–	
	B	–···	
	C	–·–·	
	D	–··	
	E	·	
	F	··–·	
	G	––·	
	H	····	
	I	··	
	J	·–––	
	K	–·–	
	L	·–··	
	M	––	
	N	–·	
	O	–––	
	P	·––·	
	Q	––·–	
	R	·–·	
	S	···	
	T	–	
	U	··–	
	V	···–	
	W	·––	
	X	–··–	
	Y	–·––	
	Z	––··	

Letter distribution

The motivation for George Udny Yule's classic work, *The Statistical Study of Literary Vocabulary* (1944), was to solve a case of disputed authorship (p. 423). As part of this task, he had to answer the question of how much variation might be expected in the vocabulary of different works of the same general type from the same author. He chose some of Macaulay's essays (1825–42) as one sample, and some of Bunyan's works (1678–82) as another, and analysed lists of nouns taken from each, putting each on a separate card. Well into his investigation, he noticed something:

When the work on Bunyan had been finished, I happened on one occasion to have open before me at the same time the first drawer of the Bunyan cards and the first drawer of the cards for the three essays of Macaulay, A, B and C. One can obviously form a rough judgment of the numbers of nouns falling under each initial letter from the distances between guide cards – for my cards 1 inch = 100 cards packed close – and to my surprise it was evident at sight that the distributions of the two authors were quite substantially different. The first and most conspicuous difference simply hit one in the eye, for while in Macaulay the A's were much more numerous than the B's, in Bunyan the B's were more numerous than the A's. Further inspection showed other points of difference. Relative to the vocabulary of Macaulay, E's and I's seemed clearly deficient in Bunyan and W's obviously in excess…The facts seemed so odd, that they called for further investigation.

Yule's first impressions are borne out by his analysis, as can be seen in Table A: the initial letters which show the greatest differences of rank are A, B, E, F, H, I, and W. He then established that there was greater consistency between samples taken from within the same author than from between the two authors. On this basis, he was able to choose a sample 'blind' from either of the authors, allowing its initial letter distribution to predict who had written it, as shown in Table B.

Yule's explanation for his findings was based on a close look at the vocabulary, where he found far more words of Romance origin (p. 126) in Macaulay, especially those which derive from Latin prefixes, such as *ab*, *ante*, *cum*, *contra*, *ex*, *infra*, and *intra*. While Yule stresses that this is by no means 'the whole story', this early exercise in the analysis of style showed the potential of graphological analysis in authorship studies, and helped to found the field of *stylostatistics*.

Table A

1	2	3	4	5	6	7	8	9
	Bunyan		Macaulay			Rank in		Difference of ranks
Rank	Initial	Frequency	Initial	Frequency	Initial	Bunyan	Macaulay	
1	S	256	C	391	A	10	4	−6
2	C	210	S	380	B	5	10	+5
3	P	188	P	338	C	2	1	−1
4	D	153	A	249	D	4	5	+1
5	B	147	D	237	E	16	11	−5
6	R	133	M	209	F	8.5	12	+3.5
7	M	124	R	191	G	14.5	15	+0.5
8	F	112	T	179	H	11	14	+3
9	T	112	I	172	I	14.5	9	−5.5
10	A	111	B	169	J	20	20	—
11	H	110	E	162	K	21	21.5	+0.5
12	W	100	F	150	L	13	13	—
13	L	84	L	122	M	7	6	−1
14	G	72	H	112	N	19	19	—
15	I	72	G	107	O	18	17	−1
16	E	69	W	89	P	3	3	—
17	V	43	O	73	Q	23	23	—
18	O	41	V	64	R	6	7	+1
19	N	40	N	52	S	1	2	+1
20	J	22	J	27	T	8.5	8	−0.5
21	K	18	K	22	U	22	21.5	−0.5
22	U	16	U	22	V	17	18	+1
23	Q	7	Q	14	W	12	16	+4
24	Y	5	Y	8	X	26	26	—
25	Z	1	Z	4	Y	24	24	—
26	X	—	X	—	Z	25	25	—

Table B

1	2	3	4	5	6
	Rank in total			Difference of rank in sample X from	
Letter	Bunyan	Macaulay	Sample X	Total Bunyan	Total Macaulay
A	10	4	12	2	8
B	5	10	6	1	4
E	16	11	15	1	4
F	8.5	12	9	0.5	3
H	11	14	11	0	3
I	14.5	9	16	1.5	7
W	12	16	8	4	8
			Totals disregarding sign	10	37

Columns 2–5 in Table A show the nouns from the Bunyan and Macaulay samples ranked in order of frequency. Columns 6–8 list the rank of each initial letter in the two authors, and Column 9 gives the differences between their ranks in each case. For example, A is 10th in order of frequency in Bunyan but 4th in Macaulay, a difference of 6 points. A positive sign means that the letter is lower in Macaulay; a negative sign, that it is higher. For most of the letters, the distributions are very similar, but there are conspicuous differences in A, B, E, F, H, I, and W.

Who wrote sample X?

These seven test-letters and their rankings (Columns 1–3 in Table B) are then used to identify a text sample, X. The rankings in the sample are shown in Column 4. In Columns 5 and 6 we write down the differences of the ranks in this sample from those in Columns 7 and 8 in Table A (paying no attention to whether it is plus or minus). The sums at the foot of Columns 5 and 6 give a rough measure of the closeness of agreement: the higher the figure, the less the likelihood that this is the author of the sample. In the present case, the authorship is assigned (correctly) to Bunyan.

The table shows letter pair (*digram*) frequencies, using the whole of the text corpus of *The Cambridge Encyclopedia* – over 6 million adjacent character pairs. The figures are raw data, and in thousands (with decimals rounded up). The table should be read from left to right: for example, A was followed by A 400 times, and by B 12,100 times. The symbol [stands for a preceding word space, and] for a following word space: for example, B began a word 75,600 times and ended a word 1,500 times.

The table can be used in a variety of ways, showing both the most frequent and least frequent sequences. The top ten frequencies are: IN, TH, HE, AN, ER, RE, ON, ND, OR, and ES. E is the letter most likely to end a word; J is the least likely. Q is followed by a surprising number of letters, but many of these are due to the presence of abbreviations and foreign names in the encyclopedia.

	A	B	C	D	E	F	G	H	I	J	K	L	M
A	0.4	12.1	24.3	18.1	4.3	6.7	12.3	1.3	22.4	1.7	4.9	79.7	24.5
B	11.0	1.0	1.4	0.3	28.6	0.04	0.02	0.09	7.7	1.0	0.02	12.9	0.2
C	41.9	0.04	5.1	0.06	38.1	0.03	0.02	40.7	21.2	0.005	6.4	11.5	0.7
D	10.6	0.2	0.5	1.9	49.2	0.2	1.6	0.6	30.7	0.2	0.02	1.8	0.9
E	42.9	2.7	31.8	81.3	16.9	8.1	9.1	1.3	7.7	0.2	1.4	32.9	20.7
F	9.5	0.05	0.05	0.05	12.1	5.6	0.1	0.02	15.5	0.03	0.02	6.6	0.03
G	11.1	0.2	0.08	0.5	25.3	0.08	0.9	11.9	10.4	0.01	0.04	5.4	0.8
H	27.5	0.4	3.9	0.3	159.6	0.1	0.07	0.05	41.7	0.006	0.05	1.1	0.8
I	28.4	5.3	53.8	17.0	26.7	7.1	15.0	0.1	1.3	0.2	1.8	27.7	15.5
J	2.4	0.003	0.001	0.005	2.7	0.0	0.001	0.006	0.4	0.005	0.02	0.02	0.009
K	2.0	0.1	0.04	0.06	9.2	0.1	0.2	0.5	5.8	0.02	0.07	0.6	3.3
L	44.0	0.8	1.0	10.2	51.7	2.0	0.9	0.2	40.1	0.03	1.3	31.5	2.3
M	40.8	7.6	0.1	0.07	45.6	0.1	0.05	0.05	25.3	0.005	0.02	0.3	6.4
N	28.7	0.7	26.7	91.8	40.1	3.8	57.6	1.2	25.9	0.5	2.4	3.2	2.1
O	4.4	4.7	11.6	13.9	2.8	69.5	6.4	1.4	5.8	0.3	2.6	25.9	32.7
P	21.7	0.2	0.04	0.03	30.3	0.03	0.008	9.6	11.9	0.007	0.03	13.7	0.9
Q	0.05	0.004	0.004	0.0	0.007	0.001	0.0	0.0	0.08	0.0	0.001	0.003	0.002
R	52.1	2.7	8.6	11.0	97.3	2.4	9.2	1.1	58.3	0.04	7.0	8.5	14.2
S	11.2	0.9	10.2	0.3	48.1	0.9	0.2	21.0	34.5	0.03	2.0	4.2	6.1
T	36.6	0.5	1.5	0.1	76.3	0.3	0.2	161.4	76.0	0.03	0.3	6.4	1.3
U	8.6	6.1	12.9	8.7	8.3	1.1	6.8	0.1	6.5	0.08	1.2	15.4	10.1
V	9.4	0.002	0.008	0.02	43.8	0.006	0.01	0.007	16.5	0.003	0.01	0.06	0.01
W	22.8	0.08	0.2	0.2	14.1	0.1	0.02	16.5	20.6	0.003	0.08	0.7	0.07
X	1.3	0.06	0.9	0.008	1.2	0.5	0.007	0.3	2.6	0.003	0.004	0.05	0.01
Y	2.3	0.3	1.3	1.1	5.1	0.09	0.4	0.1	1.5	0.01	0.06	1.7	2.0
Z	1.9	0.08	0.03	0.02	4.6	0.006	0.02	0.1	1.3	0.0	0.01	0.1	0.02
[	157.5	75.6	86.5	41.7	41.8	68.1	27.0	56.9	113.5	7.8	11.3	39.5	61.1

	N	O	P	Q	R	S	T	U	V	W	X	Y	Z	]
A	139.7	0.5	13.2	0.4	74.6	50.4	77.3	8.1	9.5	3.1	1.3	10.3	1.3	28.4
B	0.2	16.8	0.03	0.007	10.8	2.7	0.5	10.4	0.05	0.08	0.01	15.2	0.004	1.5
C	0.06	46.7	0.03	0.3	9.5	2.6	25.5	9.9	0.007	0.001	0.005	2.4	0.2	19.8
D	0.5	8.7	0.1	0.1	5.4	8.7	0.4	11.0	0.7	0.9	0.003	3.3	0.03	160.5
E	76.4	4.8	9.7	2.3	120.1	82.8	24.1	4.5	11.9	5.4	10.2	5.9	0.7	267.9
F	0.05	28.7	0.03	0.001	16.3	0.7	8.2	4.0	0.005	0.02	0.01	0.3	0.002	68.9
G	4.4	6.9	0.07	0.009	13.5	3.5	1.4	5.8	0.01	0.1	0.02	2.5	0.03	43.3
H	1.7	20.2	0.2	0.1	5.6	1.2	6.7	5.1	0.03	0.3	0.001	4.3	0.04	45.6
I	168.7	42.1	5.8	1.0	19.5	68.0	65.1	2.1	19.0	0.09	1.1	0.09	5.0	7.6
J	0.02	4.2	0.009	0.0	0.01	0.009	0.009	2.4	0.005	0.0	0.0	0.009	0.001	0.08
K	3.4	0.8	0.08	0.001	0.4	3.6	0.1	0.4	0.01	0.2	0.008	0.7	0.0	11.3
L	0.3	27.8	1.5	0.01	0.2	11.6	7.5	10.9	1.9	1.6	0.006	26.4	0.06	55.7
M	0.6	20.1	14.4	0.003	0.1	5.5	0.8	7.1	0.02	0.1	0.02	2.3	0.005	29.0
N	5.4	19.7	0.3	0.4	0.8	28.2	57.0	6.0	2.9	1.2	0.1	6.0	0.5	162.1
O	94.5	9.8	19.2	0.1	84.6	17.3	17.8	36.0	13.1	18.0	1.7	2.1	0.3	45.1
P	0.09	26.2	6.4	0.01	26.3	3.5	5.1	7.3	0.005	0.09	0.002	0.7	0.08	8.7
Q	0.0	0.008	0.0	0.008	0.005	0.006	0.0	7.1	0.001	0.002	0.002	0.001	0.0	2.4
R	15.7	52.6	2.7	0.1	8.0	24.7	23.2	9.3	3.9	0.9	0.1	14.4	0.1	81.8
S	0.6	21.9	13.8	2.9	0.7	21.0	71.0	18.2	0.1	2.3	0.007	4.1	0.05	201.4
T	0.5	51.7	0.2	0.003	31.8	21.0	8.8	17.7	0.1	4.8	0.03	12.6	0.5	100.6
U	25.5	0.7	7.1	0.02	32.7	32.2	18.6	0.08	0.3	0.07	0.4	0.2	0.2	1.8
V	0.03	4.8	0.002	0.0	0.1	0.2	0.02	0.3	0.001	0.0	0.002	0.4	0.0	0.7
W	6.4	11.5	0.06	0.001	3.0	1.7	0.4	0.08	0.008	0.01	0.0	0.3	0.0	9.7
X	0.02	0.3	2.5	0.004	0.08	0.04	2.8	0.3	0.06	0.02	0.05	0.3	0.0	2.3
Y	1.3	2.2	2.2	0.002	1.0	6.6	1.1	0.3	0.02	0.4	0.08	0.02	0.1	88.6
Z	0.02	1.2	0.0	0.003	0.04	0.03	0.05	0.2	0.02	0.03	0.0	0.2	0.4	0.7
[	29.2	111.1	73.1	1.9	45.1	100.1	187.6	21.4	12.5	68.7	0.5	4.7	1.5	0.0

GRAPHEMIC SYMBOLISM

Graphemes, like phonemes, have no intrinsic meaning: it does not make much sense to ask 'What does *m* mean?' or 'What does *e* mean?' The role of graphemes is to combine and contrast, and it is the larger units (the words) which have meaning. However, as with the study of speech, there are an interesting number of cases where we would have to accept that individual letters, and the way they are presented in typography or handwriting, do permit some degree of semantic or psychological interpretation, analogous to that which is found in sound symbolism (p. 250), though the element of subjectivity makes it difficult to arrive at uncontroversial explanations.

GRAPHETIC CONTRADICTIONS

The associations conveyed by the graphic design, especially the choice of typeface, can reinforce or contradict the meaning of the words, as these examples show.

Reinforcing	Contradicting
Olde Tyme Dancing	Modern Alarm Systems
RETREAT	*RETREAT*
ascent	ascent
ADVᴬNCE	ADVₐNCE
UNDERTAKERS	UNDERTAKERS
harmony	harmony

SAY IT WITH XXXX

Despite its low frequency and high redundancy (p. 264), the letter X has more social and technical uses than any other letter in the English alphabet. It is thus more likely to permit sensible answers to the question 'What does X mean?' Here are ten possible responses.

• 'Kisses.' A common use at the end of a letter or a card. This is one of the first functions of the letter *X* that young children learn.
• 'Wrong.' The standard sign for an incorrect answer. No letter value is employed for its opposite, though the tick (√) does bear some resemblance to a V. A related use is the *x-ing out* of a wrongly typed letter or word.
• 'Christian.' Based on the initial symbol of *Christ* in Greek (*khi*), the letter is still widely used as a symbol of Christian identity, partly because of its similarity to the cross. It becomes particularly noticeable at Xmas time.
• 'Adult.' In some countries, formerly used in relation to films and other material on general release but not suitable for children. Pornographic films are also sometimes still rated in this way (up to 'triple-X' level). Censorship boards vary in their use of conventions for this value.
• 'Unknown.' Widely used when a true identity is missing, as in criminal investigations (*Mr X*). There is a similar use in mathematics, where *x* is the first choice for a value to be determined.
• 'Uneducated.' The simplicity of *X* has long made it the symbol to use in place of a signature, for someone unable to write. It continues to have a jocular use, imputing illiteracy to someone ('Put your X here.')
• 'Choice.' Again, the simple clarity of *X* has made it the chosen symbol to express a decision on a ballot paper. In this case, any departure from the norm carries a sanction: the ballot paper is void.

In this case, X means 'right' not 'wrong'.

• 'Location.' *X* has traditionally marked the burial place of a pirate hoard. It is the first-choice symbol in marking any location on a map.
• 'Multiply.' *X* is the only letter which functions as a sign for one of the four basic arithmetical operations. It has a similar use in expressing dimensions (*3x4*), where X is read as 'by'.
• There are also several restricted functions. *X* symbolizes a capture in chess (*RxP* 'rook takes pawn'), a drawn game in UK football pool coupons, a sexual hybrid in horticulture (*Aceras x Herminium*), a male in genetics (*the X chromosome*), magnification in photography (*50x*), and 10 in Roman numerals. A sequence of Xs may take on a specific meaning, such as XXXX – the name of an Australian beer.

Other letters

A few other letters carry associations which go beyond the transiently fashionable or idiosyncratic.

• '*A* is for excellence.' The role of *A* as alphabet opener has been used in many contexts where grading is required, and is now reflected in the language (*I feel A1*, *She's got an A*). The letters *B, C, D, E*, and *F* carry related overtones, especially *B* (*B-movie, B-side*). *E* has a mixed set of uses, being sometimes used as an abbreviation for *excellent* or *Ecstasy*, sometimes for a very low grade or its euphemism (*E for effort*). The connotations of *F*, likewise, are mixed, including failure, loudness (*forte*), sex (vs *M* for *male*), and obscenity (*effing*).
• '*K* is for cornflakes.' In many cases, the symbolic meaning of a letter is evident only if it is in a special typeface. Many advertisers have tried to appropriate letters in this way – most successfully in the case of the cereal manufacturing firm, Kellogg, with its large, red, distinctive initial letter. Their product name, *Special K*, carries this process a stage further. Without this distinctive typography, the letter appears in several other contexts, such as *more KKKK* (used as part of a computer advertisement),

K (kosher, used in food labelling), and *K* or *KKK* (for Ku Klux Klan, used as a terrorizing symbol especially in some of the southern states of the USA).
• '*V* is for victory.' The symbolic role of this letter merged at the end of World War 2, and is still widely used as a hand-sign of success. Its frequency, however, is tiny compared to that of the palm-reversed gesture, widely used in the English-speaking world as a crude symbol of contempt (the *V-sign*).
• '*Z* is for sleeping.' A series of letter *Z*s drifting up from a recumbent figure is the standard graphic way of suggesting that the person is asleep. The language has even adopted this convention in its lexicon: we now *catch some Zs* /zeez/ (US) or say we've been *zedding* (UK). Of course, for those readers who were reared on a certain popular television series, there will be no doubt in their mind that 'Z is for Zorro'.

An awareness of graphic letter symbolism seems to develop very early in life. If young pre-reading children are asked to say what individual letters mean, they will try to make sense of the question, and often give interesting symbolic responses (E. Ferreiro & A. Teberosky, 1983). In addition to 'X is for kisses', there was no doubt in some young English-language minds that 'M is for mummy' or 'McDonalds', 'J is for Jesus', 'K is for cornflakes', 'P is for parking', and 'H is for television' (because of the aerial). There was also a strong trend towards identifying a letter with one's own name: 'C is for Carol' – if your name happens to be Carol. In such cases, the letter is carrying out the function of the ideogram, found in early non-alphabetic systems of writing.

ANALYSING HANDWRITING

An interesting aspect of graphic symbolism is the extent to which individual variations in handwritten letter formation can be reliably interpreted. The psychological study of handwriting has been practised for over a century, the term *graphology* (in a different sense from its later use in linguistics, p. 257) being first used by a French abbot, Jean Hippolyte Michon (1806–81). Graphologists are interested in finding out what handwriting can tell them about character and personality, as well as about a person's suitability for different tasks. In recent years they have been employed in several professional contexts, such as personnel management and marriage guidance, and especially in forensic science, where questions of handwriting identity and imitation (forgery) are critical.

The subject plainly has the potential for scientific development, as such variables as letter size, shape, angle, and connection, line direction and separation, thickness and consistency of strokes, and regularity of letter sequence are all, in principle, capable of precise description. Graphology has however suffered from scepticism generated by the fortune-telling approach to handwriting, often encountered in caravans at agricultural shows and seaside resorts, where characters are told and futures foretold on the basis of a scribbled signature. The subject has also been heavily biased towards the famous or infamous, discerning the basis of success in a signature – but without objective controls: it is not difficult to 'see' such qualities as ambition and dominance in Napoleon's handwriting, when it is evident that the subject is Napoleon.

The field can do better than this, and current research is now much more involved with the handwriting practices of the general population, and with carrying out properly controlled, 'blind' investigations. Still largely untapped are electronic resources, such as computational techniques of magnification, enhancement, and pattern-matching, and more sophisticated methods of quantification.

GRAPHOLOGICAL PRACTICE

Eric Singer's *Manual of Graphology* (1953) contains a series of exercises designed to develop awareness of the distinctive features of handwriting. Here are two of them, which suggest something of the fascination as well as the difficulty of the subject. (Singer's answers are given on page 270.)

1 The word *Dear* has been taken from the opening of 24 letters and cut in two. The task is to match the corresponding pieces.

2 Suppose these are letters applying for a job. Pick a good commercial traveller from among these applicants.

D TALES

Seventeen types of *D*, with feature descriptions and personality interpretations, as analysed by Austrian graphologist Eric Singer in *The Graphologist's Alphabet* (1950). The list is by no means complete, of course. The present author's *D* and *d*, for example, do not fall neatly into any of the categories, though he likes to think that there is a striking resemblance to 5, 8, 9, and 11.

1 Open at bottom *Wants to know himself*

2 Left parts tastelessly exaggerated *Vulgarity*

3 Written in two parts *Individualism, lack of adjustment*

4 Second arc broad, with extended stroke *Underlining of own importance*

5 Block letter *Simplification, intelligence*

6 With claw to left *Egoist*

7 Particular shape *Erotic dreams, lowered resistance to sex excesses and perversions*

8 Stroke extended at top *Enterprise*

9 Upper length extended *Respect for spiritual values, integrity*

10 Open at top and broad, or in two parts *Talkativeness*

11 Simplified with arc to left *Taste*

12 In form of musical notes or keys *Musicality*

13 Open at bottom *Hypocrisy*

14 Stroke to the right *Defensiveness*

15 Enrolled *Secretiveness, family man or woman*

16 Loops *Vanity*

17 Filled with ink *Sensuality*

GRAPHETIC VARIETY

The hierarchical structure of the writing system is most clearly displayed in the domain of typography. Each typeface (e.g. Times) is represented by several alphabets (e.g. roman, bold, italic, upper-case, lower-case), and these consist of letters, punctuation marks, and other symbols. The symbols may then be combined into larger units of text, such as words (which have a spoken language equivalent) and lines (which do not), paragraphs (which have a partial spoken equivalent) and pages (which do not). The visual effect of these larger blocks of text, moreover, is not readily predictable from the graphic properties of individual letters. The complex interaction of typeface, type size, letter and line spacing, colour, and other such variables combine to produce what has sometimes been called *texture* – the dominant visual quality of the typeset text. It is at this level that lower-level decisions about choice of type will ultimately be judged. The point is effectively summarized by Pierre Simon Fournier, a leading 18th-century typographer:

One letter measured singly may seem neither appreciably too big nor too small, but ten thousand composed into printed matter repeat the error ten thousand times over, and, be this never so small, the effect will be the opposite of what was intended. (*Manuel typographique*, 1764–6)

GRAPHETIC DEVIANCE

This advertisement goes out of its way to break standard typographic conventions. The effect is actually achieved by the regular use of only a small set of transformations. In particular, serif and sans-serif features (p. 257) are combined in the same letter, as are angular capital and rounded lower-case features. The greatest visual deviance occurs when all four of these characteristics are used in a single letter, such as *E* and *N*. The technique also relies greatly on a visual ambiguity (a graphic pun) between upper and lower case, as in the case of *B* and *R*.

ABCDEFGHIJKLMNOPQRSTUVWXYZ&
abcdefghijklmnopqrstuvwxyz
ABCDEFGHIJKLMNOPQRSTUVWXYZ&
abcdefghijklmnopqrstuvwxyz
ABCDEFGHIJKLMNOPQRSTUVWXYZ&
abcdefghijklmnopqrstuvwxyz
ABCDEFGHIJKLMNOPQRSTUVWXYZ&
abcdefghijklmnopqrstuvwxyz
ABCDEFGHIJKLMNOPQRSTUVWXYZ&

An elegant Christmas message, sent by the Museum of Promotional Arts, Toronto, Canada in 1992 in its newsletter *Empa*. The typeface is Poetica, devised by Robert Slimbach for Adobe Systems Inc, and modelled on a style of chancery handwriting developed during the Renaissance (p. 41). It is a highly complex type family, with considerable variation and ornamentation, as can be seen from the 58 designs for the ampersand. The type choice and typography are by Ed Cleary of The Composing Room Inc.

To our Readers who observe Christmas:
A HAPPY ONE
&
TO ALL
Best Wishes for 1993.

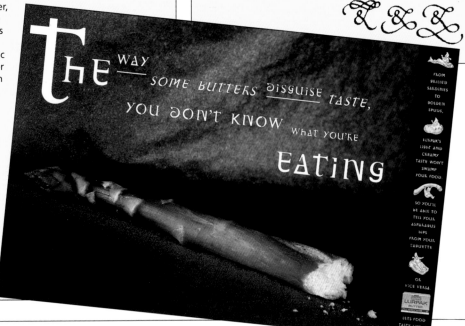

ANSWERS (p. 269)
1 1O, 2V, 3G, 4A, 5U, 6B, 7N, 8H, 9C, 10T, 11D, 12I, 13J, 14E, 15M, 16K, 17P, 18F, 19L, 20R, 21X, 22S, 23Z, 24Y.

2 'I would consider Example 3 the most suitable applicant. He is quick (quick writing), active (quick writing, inclination to the right). He is sociable, enthusiastic and likes to get around (slant to the right, broad writing). He is persuasive (broad writing, clearly shaped and spaced words).'

EXTRA GRAPHIC DIMENSIONS

The choice of typography, including the way a text is laid out on the page, can provide additional dimensions to the meaning conveyed by the words and sentences. In a neutral presentation, such as this paragraph, the typographic design adds nothing to the meaning of the words. Indeed, the whole purpose of the design is to be unobtrusive, so that it does not interfere with sentence meaning. If some typographical feature were to draw attention to itself, it would be a distraction, and the design would, in that tiny respect, have failed. Of course, one must always be prepared for exceptions, such as when an author wishes to make a particular pOINt.

The opposite situation is found when an author wants to make maximum use of the possibilities in graphic design to express a meaning, using features which the purely graphemic elements of the text cannot convey. Because these features (such as colour, type size, and line direction) belong to different dimensions of expression, they permit more than one meaning to be expressed simultaneously, and thus allow such effects as emphasis (when the meanings reinforce each other), irony (when they conflict), atmosphere (when they remind the reader of other aspects of the story), and humour (when they are incongruous). Equally, the writer may have no subtle or profound semantic intentions at all, but wish to use these features simply in the hope that the reader will find them appealing – perhaps elegant, intriguing, charming, clever, beautiful. At this point, the semantic function of the writing system merges with the aesthetic, and linguistics gives way to art (pp. 406, 416).

'Vision and prayer' (1945) is a sequence of 12 short poems by Dylan Thomas. The first six are written in the shape of a diamond; the second six in the shape of an hourglass. The last item in the sequence is reproduced here.

```
  I turn the corner of prayer and burn
     In a blessing of the sudden
    Sun. In the name of the damned
      I would turn back and run
        To the hidden land
         But the loud sun
          Christens down
            The sky.
              I
           Am found
          O let him
       Scald me and drown
      Me in his world's wound.
      His lightning answers my
     Cry. My voice burns in his hand.
    Now I am lost in the blinding
   One. The sun roars at the prayer's end.
```

"Mine is a long and sad tale!" said the Mouse, turning to Alice, and sighing.

"It is a long tail, certainly," said Alice, looking down with wonder at the Mouse's tail; "but why do you call it sad?" And she kept on puzzling about it while the Mouse was speaking, so that her idea of the tale was something like this:—

```
Fury said to
  a mouse, That
        he met
         in the
          house,
           'Let us
            both go
             to law:
        I will
      prosecute
      you.—
        Come, I'll
          take no
            denial;
             We must
              have a
               trial:
                 For
                really
                this
              morning
               I've
              nothing
             to do.'
            Said the
           mouse to
          the cur,
          'Such a
            trial,
            dear sir,
         With no
        jury or
       judge,
      would be
       wasting
        our breath.'
         'I'll be
          judge,
          I'll be
         jury,'
        Said
       cunning
      old Fury:
        'I'll try
         the whole
          cause,
           and
          condemn
          you
           to
          death.'"
```

"You are not attending!" said the Mouse to Alice, severely. "What are you thinking of?"

"I beg your pardon," said Alice very humbly: "you had got to the fifth bend, I think?"

(Lewis Carroll, *Alice in Wonderland*, 1865, Ch. 3.)

The opening lines of *The True Story of the 3 Little Pigs* (1989), told from the point of view of the Wolf. The opening letter sums it all up, really. (Jon Scieszka, illustrated by Lane Smith.)

...verybody knows the story of the Three Little Pigs. Or at least they think they do. But I'll let you in on a little secret. Nobody knows the real story, because nobody has ever heard *my* side of the story.

Some lines from Alfred Bester's science fiction story 'The Pi Man' (1959), showing his use of typography to represent the disturbance in the mind of his protagonist. In an introduction to this story, Bester remarks: 'I've always been obsessed by patterns, rhythms, and tempi, and I always feel my stories in those terms. It's this pattern obsession that compels me to experiment with typography. I'm trying very hard to develop a technique of blending the sight, sound, and context of words into dramatic patterns. I want to make the eye, ear, and mind of the reader merge into a whole that is bigger than the sum of its parts.'

```
            Sometimes

   I          I          I

  am         am         am

        3.14159 +

  from       from       from

  this       other      that

  space      space      space

         Othertimes not
```

```
Foyer
  Bedroom
     Bath            T
     Bath            e
  Living Room        r
Kitchen              r
  Dressing Room      a
  Bedroom            c
   T e r r a c e
```

ENGLISH SPELLING

The two texts on the facing page represent conflicting views about the spelling system. The first is a Victorian saga which suggests that there is so little predictability in English spelling conventions that it is unreasonable to think of them as comprising a 'system' at all. The linguistic ingenuity of this work is so impressive that it is reprinted here in its entirety. The second is an extract from the highly successful *Dr Seuss* series of children's readers, which suggests that there is indeed a highly predictable spelling system, with just a small number of irregular forms causing a disturbance. Supporters of each view would condemn the other text as irrelevant. To chaos theorists, phonic texts are so oversimplified as to be no guide to the realities of reading. To order theorists, poems full of irregularities are no more than a spelling freak show, exercising a ghoulish fascination, but telling us nothing about what is normal.

The truth, evidently, is somewhere in between. But we must not expect to arrive at a definite figure for the amount of irregularity in English spelling. If we include proper names of people and places, and rare foreign loan words (as does the poem opposite), the proportion of irregularity will dramatically increase. If we include lengthy technical terms (such as *trichloroethane*), the proportion will decrease, as most of their syllables are spelled according to quite regular rules. Even if we restrict the question to everyday vocabulary, there are conflicting answers. There seem to be less than 500 words in English whose spelling is wholly irregular; but several of them are among the most frequently used words in the language. Because they are constantly before our eyes, English spelling gives the impression of being more irregular than it really is.

The notion of regularity

Much depends, also, on how the notion of regularity is defined. With only 26 letters to handle over 40 phonemes, the criterion of one letter – one phoneme is plainly too strong. English has never been a 'phonetic language', in that sense. A system which systematically used two letters to write a given sound would also be regular, and English employs this kind of convention a great deal – most clearly in such cases as *sh* for /ʃ/ and *ng* for /ŋ/. Less obvious is the 'magic *e*' rule (p. 42) which lengthens the preceding vowel (*rate* vs *rat*). Though the two vowel letters are, unusually, separated by a consonant, there is a rule here nonetheless, for thousands of words have their vowels lengthened in this way.

Regularity implies the existence of a rule which can generate large numbers of words correctly. A rule which works for 500 words is plainly regular; one which works for 100 much less so; and for 50, or 20, or 10, or 5 it becomes progressively less plausible to call it a 'rule' at all. Clearly, there is no easy way of deciding when the regularity of a rule begins. It has been estimated that only about 3 per cent of everyday English words are so irregular that they would have to be learned completely by heart, and that over 80 per cent are spelled according to regular patterns. That leaves some 15 per cent of cases where we could argue the status of their regularity. But given such statistics, the chief conclusion must be that we should not exaggerate the size of the problem, as some supporters of reform are prone to do. Nor minimize it either, for a great deal of confusion is caused by that 3–15 per cent, and some 2 per cent of the literate population never manage to resolve it (p. 426).

A RULE WITH DEFICIENCIES

One of the most famous spelling rules – '*i* before *e* except after *c*' – is itself famous for its exceptions. The rule was devised as a mnemonic for such words as *receive* and *deceive*, and it also helps in *conceit* and *ceiling*, as well as in a handful of rarer words (*ceilidh*, *enceinte*, *orcein*); but it is far outnumbered by words where *c* is followed by *ie* and words where a letter other than *c* is followed by *ei*.

- *c+ie* ancient, conscience, deficient, efficient, financier, glacier, hacienda, juicier, nescient, science, scient, society, species, sufficient

- *Other+ei* beige, buddleia, cepheid, codeine, deicide, deictic, eider(down), eight, either, foreign, height, heir, leisure, neighbour, neither, protein, reign, seize, seizure, their, weigh, weir, weird.

There are well over 100 such exceptions. The only way to impose a degree of order on this muddle is to relate spellings to grammar and pronunciation. One type of exception involves affixes (*agencies, seeing, niceish, absenteeism, nucleide*); another involves proper names (*Einstein, O'Neill, Leicester*); another involves the way *ie/ei* sequences are sounded – all the words in the first category, for instance, have the *ie* in an unstressed syllable or with a sound other than /iː/, and in the second category, such diphthongs as /eɪ/ play an important role.

WHY THE PROBLEM?

If the spelling system contains such regularity, why is there a problem? The answer is complex, but a major factor is that children are rarely taught *how* to spell. They are made to learn spellings by heart, and are rigorously tested on them, but few attempts are made to explain what it is they have learned. They are not generally told why spellings are as they are, or about how these spellings relate to the way words are pronounced. Without such a perspective, spelling becomes a vast, boring, and time-consuming memory task.

It comes as a surprise to many to realize that there is no simple correlation between reading and spelling ability. Spelling involves a set of active, conscious processes that are not required for reading. It is possible to read very selectively, as when we 'skim' a newspaper. It is not possible to spell selectively: it is a letter-by-letter act. And more things can go wrong when we try to spell. Faced with the word *feep*, there is really only one possible way to pronounce it; but faced with the sounds /fiːp/, there are several possible spellings (such as *feep, feap, fepe, pheep*). The task facing a speller is always greater than that facing a reader.

Learning about the predictable links between spelling and pronunciation is the key to understanding the spelling system. It is never enough to rely on the written language alone. An integrated approach can then act as a framework for the task of mastering the exceptions that history has imposed on the language – but this task seems less formidable once it is accompanied by understanding. If there is a daily battle being fought over spelling in our classrooms, as some suggest, it will be won only if children learn (as wartime generals did) to 'know their enemy'.

---

match	June	picking
catch	July	picked
patch	September	learned
watch	November	reached
fetch	ditch	snatch	everyone
care	infant	tender
careless	darling	gentle
useless	cradle	weak
useful	young	dull
purse	nurse	fur	beak
hammer	too	lunch
bench	tool	buy
blade	stool	beef
wire	fool	cloth
blood	goose	geese	cheese

Some of the words from a page in Group 3 of F. Schonell's *The Essential Spelling List* (1932), which continues to be widely used in schools. The words are those that Schonell found often used in children's writing. The bringing together of words related in grammar or meaning (*care/careless*) is helpful; but it is not possible to see the spelling system when working through words in this way. Regular and irregular spellings (*geese, cheese*) are put side by side with no apparent order.

THE CHAOS

Dearest *creature* in *Creation*,
Studying English pronunciation,
  I will teach you in my verse
  Sounds like *corpse*, *corps*, *horse*
  and *worse*.
It will keep you, *Susy*, *busy*,
Make your *head* with *heat* grow
  dizzy;
  Tear in eye your dress you'll *tear*.
  So shall I! Oh, hear my *prayer*,
Pray, console your loving poet,
Make my coat look *new*, dear, *sew* it!
  Just compare *heart*, *beard* and
  heard,
  Dies and *diet*, *lord* and *word*,
Sword and *sward*, *retain* and *Britain*,
(Mind the latter, how it's written!)
  Made has not the sound of *bade*,
  Say – *said*, pay – *paid*, *laid*, but
  plaid.
Now I surely will not *plague* you
With such words as *vague* and *ague*,
  But be careful how you speak,
  Say *break*, *steak*, but *bleak* and
  streak,
Previous, *precious*; *fuchsia*, *via*;
Pipe, *snipe*, *recipe* and *choir*,
  Cloven, *oven*; *how* and *low*;
  Script, *receipt*; *shoe*, *poem*, *toe*,
Hear me say, *devoid* of trickery:
Daughter, *laughter* and *Terpsichore*,
  Typhoid; *measles*, *topsails*, *aisles*;
  Exiles, *similes*, *reviles*;
Wholly, *holly*; *signal*, *signing*;
Thames; *examining*, *combining*;
  Scholar, *vicar* and *cigar*,
  Solar, *mica*, *war* and *far*.
From 'desire': *desirable* – *admirable*
  from 'admire';
Lumber, *plumber*; *bier* but *brier*;
  Chatham, *brougham*; *renown* but
  known,

Knowledge; *done*, but *gone* and
  tone,
One, *anemone*; *Balmoral*;
Kitchen, *lichen*; *laundry*, *laurel*;
  Gertrude, *German*; *wind* and
  mind;
  Scene, *Melpomene*, *mankind*;
Tortoise, *turquoise*, *chamois*-leather,
Reading, *Reading*, *heathen*, *heather*.
  This phonetic labyrinth
  Gives *moss*, *gross*, *brook*, *brooch*,
  ninth, *plinth*.
Billet does not end like *ballet*;
Bouquet, *wallet*, *mallet*, *chalet*;
  Blood and *flood* are not like *food*,
  Nor is *mould* like *should* and *would*.
Banquet is not nearly *parquet*,
Which is said to rime with 'darky'.
  Viscous, *viscount*; *load* and *broad*,
  Toward, to *forward*, to *reward*,
And your pronunciation's O. K.
When you say correctly *croquet*;
  Rounded, *wounded*; *grieve* and
  sieve;
  Friend and *fiend*; *alive* and *live*;
Liberty, *library*; *heave* and *heaven*;
Rachel, *ache*, *moustache*; *eleven*.
  We say *hallowed*, but *allowed*;
  People, *leopard*; *towed*, but
  vowed.
Mark the difference, moreover,
Between *mover*, *plover*, *Dover*,
  Leeches, *breeches*; *wise*, *precise*;
  Chalice but *police* and *lice*.
Camel; *constable*, *unstable*;
Principle, *disciple*; *label*;
  Petal, *penal* and *canal*;
  Wait, *surmise*, *plait*, *promise*; *pal*.
Suit, *suite*, *ruin*; *circuit*, *conduit*
Rime with 'shirk it' and 'beyond it'.
  But it is not hard to tell,
  Why it's *pall*, *mall*, but *Pall Mall*.
Muscle, *muscular*; *gaol*; *iron*;
Timber, *climber*; *bullion*, *lion*,

Worm and *storm*; *chaise*, *chaos*,
  chair;
Senator, *spectator*, *mayor*.
Ivy, *privy*; *famous*, *clamour*
And *enamour* rime with 'hammer.'
  Pussy, *hussy* and *possess*.
  Desert, but *dessert*, *address*.
Golf, *wolf*; *countenance*; *lieutenants*
Hoist, in *lieu* of flags, left pennants.
  River, *rival*; *tomb*, *bomb*, *comb*;
  Doll and *roll* and *some* and *home*.
Stranger does not rime with *anger*,
Neither does *devour* with *clangour*.
  Soul, but *foul* and *gaunt*, but *aunt*;
  Font, *front*, *wont*; *want*, *grand*,
  and, *grant*,
Shoes, *goes*, *does*.[1] Now first say:
  finger,
And then: *singer*, *ginger*, *linger*.
  Real, *zeal*; *mauve*, *gauze* and
  gauge;
  Marriage, *foliage*, *mirage*, *age*.
Query does not rime with *very*,
Nor does *fury* sound like *bury*.
  Dost, *lost*, *post* and *doth*, *cloth*, *loth*;
  Job, *Job*, *blossom*, *bosom*, *oath*.
Though the difference seems little,
We say *actual*, but *victual*,
  Seat, *sweat*, *chaste*, *caste*; *Leigh*,
  eight, *height*;
  Put, *nut*; *granite*, but *unite*.
Reefer does not rime with 'deafer',
Feoffer does, and *zephyr*, *heifer*.
  Dull, *bull*; *Geoffrey*, *George*; *ate*,
  late;
  Hint, *pint*; *senate*, but *sedate*;
Scenic, *Arabic*, *pacific*;
Science, *conscience*, *scientific*;
  Tour, but *our*, and *succour*, *four*;
  Gas, *alas* and *Arkansas*!
Sea, *idea*, *guinea*, *area*,
Psalm; *Maria*, but *malaria*;
  Youth, *south*, *southern*; *cleanse*
  and *clean*;

Doctrine, *turpentine*, *marine*.
Compare *alien* with *Italian*,
Dandelion with *battalion*,
  Sally with *ally*; *yea*, *ye*,
  Eye, *I*, *ay*, *aye*, *whey*, *key*, *quay*!
Say *aver*, but *ever*, *fever*,
Neither, *leisure*, *skein*, *receiver*.
  Never guess – it is not safe;
  We say *calves*, *valves*, *half*, but
  Ralf!
Heron; *granary*, *canary*;
Crevice, and *device*, and *eyrie*;
  Face but *preface*, but *efface*,
  Phlegm, *phlegmatic*; *ass*, *glass*,
  bass;
Large, but *target*, *gin*, *give*, *verging*;
Ought, *out*, *joust* and *scour*, but
  scourging;
  Ear, but *earn*; and *wear* and *tear*
  Do not rime with 'here', but 'ere'.
Seven is right, but so is *even*;
Hyphen, *roughen*, *nephew*, *Stephen*;
  Monkey, *donkey*; *clerk* and *jerk*;
  Asp, *grasp*, *wasp*; and *cork* and
  work.
Pronunciation – think of *psyche*! –
Is a paling, stout and spiky;
  Won't it make you lose your wits,
  Writing 'groats' and saying *groats*?
It's a dark *abyss* or tunnel,
Strewn with stones, like *rowlock*,
  gunwale,
  Islington and *Isle* of Wight,
  Housewife, *verdict* and *indict*!
Don't you think so, reader, rather,
Saying *lather*, *bather*, *father*?
  Finally: which rimes with 'enough',
  Though, *through*, *plough*, *cough*,
  hough, or *tough*?
Hiccough has the sound of 'cup'…
My advice is – give it up!

Charivarius (G. N. Trenité)

[1] No, you are wrong. This is the plural of 'doe'.

THE ORDER

A climactic moment in
Dr Seuss's *The Cat in the
Hat* (1957).

Then we saw him pick up
All the things that were down.
He picked up the cake,
And the rake, and the gown,
And the milk, and the strings,
And the books, and the dish,
And the fan, and the cup,
And the ship, and the fish.
And he put them away.
Then he said, "That is that."
And then he was gone
With a tip of his hat.
58

The sources of irregularity

The English spelling system is the result of a process of development that has been going on for over 1,000 years. The complications we encounter today are the consequences of the major linguistic and social events which have taken place over this period.

• The origin of the problem lies in the attempt by Christian missionaries to use their 23-letter alphabet for the 35 or so phonemes of Old English (the exact number depending on the dialect and method of analysis). The addition of four new symbols helped (pp. 16, 258), but it still proved necessary to use some letters (such as *c* and *g*) to represent more than one sound, and to represent some sounds by combinations of letters (such as *sc* – the equivalent of present-day *sh*).

• After the Norman Conquest, French scribes introduced several new spelling conventions. A number of Old English forms were replaced, such as *qu* for *cw* (*quick*). The scribes replaced *h* by *gh* in such words as *might* and *enough*, *c* by *ch* in *church*, and *u* by *ou* in *house*. They began to use *c* before *e* and *i* in such words as *city* and *cell*. Because the letter *u* was written in a very similar way to *v*, *i*, *n*, and *m* (p. 261), they tried to ease the reading task in some sequences of these letters by replacing *u* with *o* (*come*, *love*, *one*, *son*) – thereby initiating a set of spelling exceptions once the motivation for the change had passed. By the beginning of the 15th century, English spelling was a mixture of two systems – Old English and French.

• Further complications were caused by the introduction of printing. Many early printers came from the Continent, and brought their own spelling norms to England. For a while, line justification (p. 257) was often achieved by shortening or lengthening words rather than by varying the word spaces. Variation in the final *e* of a word was a common result. A major beneficial effect of printing, however, was to impose order on the many alternative spellings found in manuscripts. Stabilization gradually emerged after Caxton's choice of the London standard as a printing norm (p. 56), and the notion of a 'correct' spelling began to grow.

• Although spelling thereafter was much more stable, pronunciation was not. It is a particular irony that, at the same time as printing was being introduced, the vowel sounds of London speech were undergoing the greatest change in their history. If printing had come a century later, or the Great Vowel Shift (p. 69) a century earlier, the present-day spelling system would be vastly more regular than it has turned out to be. As it is, the spelling of thousands of words now reflects the pronunciation of vowels as they were in Chaucer's time. *Name*, for example, has an *a* because in

HOW DO YOU SPELL...?

We are brought up in a literacy tradition which insists on a definite answer to this question. We expect there to be a single correct spelling for any word in the standard language; and if we do not know what it is, we expect to find an unambiguous answer in a dictionary. However, the reality is somewhat more complex.

A babirusa, babirousa, or babirussa

Alternatives

There are a remarkable number of alternative spellings in Standard English. Some are well known, such as the differences between British and American English (*-our*/*-or*, *-re*/*-er*, consonant doubling, p. 307) and optional *e* (*judg(e)ment*, *ag(e)ing*). The alternations can affect thousands of words – notably, *-ise*/*-isation* vs *-ize*/*-ization*. Other important choices include *e* vs *oe* (*f(o)etus*) or *ae* (*prim(a)eval*) and *-xion* vs *-ction* (*inflection*). The question of whether a word should be hyphenated or spelled (spelt? p. 204) with a capital letter will add thousands more (p. 122).

The pages of an unabridged dictionary will bring to light many examples. Here is the result of a cull of just one page of entries: the beginning of letter *B* in *Webster's Third New International Dictionary*. The symbol * indicates that the alternatives may also be capitalized.

baa / ba
baal-ha-bos / balabos
baalshem / balshem
babacoote / babakoto
babasco / barbasco
babassu oil / babaçu oil
babaylan / babailan /
    babalyan / babalian
babbitt / babbit*
babbittry / babbitry*
babes-ernst / babes-ernest
babirusa / babirousa / babirussa
babu / baboo
babul / babool

There were in addition 19 cases where the only difference between the words was the use of a capital letter: *baal* (*-ism*, *-istic*, *-ite*), *babbittical*, *babbitty*, *babcock test*, *babel* (*-ism*, *-ization*, *-ize*), *babi*, *babinski reflex*, *babism*, *babist*, *babouvism*, *babouvist*, *babylon*, *babylonian*. Including these cases, this page had 32 items with alternative spelling out of a total of 95 entries – a third. Excluding them, we are still left with 14 entries (a remarkable 15 per cent). It will be noted that almost all of these entries are fairly exotic loan words, but they are part of the language nonetheless. It is words like these which present the English spelling system with the biggest modern challenge to its consistency.

Unknowns

There are some words which it seems impossible to spell in an acceptable way. One study collected examples of words with unusual endings, and asked how an *-ed* or *-ing* ending might be added to them.

a(h) polka, verandah, visa, mascara, umbrella, samba, sauna, aroma, balaclava, tiara
e(e) purée, flambé, recce (reconnaissance), frisbee, tree
et parquet, bouquet, beret, duvet, chalet, ballet
i ski, sari, jacuzzi, bikini

The problem is evident. What is the past tense of *samba*? Does it look right to put *They sambaed* or *We're sambaing*? Some write *samba'd* or *samba-ing*. Try the endings with the other words above. Professional writers vary in their decisions: David Lodge has 'her heavily mascaraed eyelids' (*Small World*, 1984, p. 125); Frederick Forsyth has 'So get visa-ed up in Paris' (*The Dogs of War*, 1974, p. 117). Dictionaries are often silent on the point.

Sometimes the addition of an ending produces a conflict of readings (though context makes real ambiguity unlikely): *they skied* (from *ski* or *sky*); *an anoraked figure* (where the spelling suggests a long vowel pronunciation /eɪ/ for the second *a*); *the current arced* (where pronouncing *c* as /s/ before *e* does not hold, leading some writers to prefer *arcked*).

The author of this study concludes by giving a short paragraph containing some of his own preferences. What would you do?

I would rather be in a comfortable verandahed house, sitting pyjamaed in a duveted bed and being fed puréed fruit by a muumuued beauty, than be bivouacked on a sparsely-treed plain, sitting anorak-ed and shivering in the leaden-skied gloom and eating potatoes that were sautéd yesterday before the power cables arc-ed.

(After G. Abbott, 1988.)

Middle English it was pronounced with an /ɑː/ vowel (like that of modern *calm*). The change to /eɪ/ during the 15th century was ignored by the printers. And the same kind of reasoning explains the many 'silent letters' of modern spelling (such as in **k**nee and tim**e**), where the letter ceased to be sounded after the printing conventions had been established.

• Another kind of complication entered the language when 16th-century scholars tried to indicate something of the history of a word in its spelling (p. 66). The *b* in *debt*, for example, was added by people who felt it was important for everyone to know that the word comes from *debitum* in Latin. Similarly, a *b* was added to *doubt* (from *dubitare*), a *g* to *reign* (from *regno*), and (a famous error) an *s* to *island* (thought to come from Latin *insula*, whereas it is Old English in origin). Although only some of the proposals became standard, the ones that survived continue to present modern learners with a problem (especially now that awareness of Latin origins is no longer highly valued). Other aspects of rationalization also had mixed results. The attempt by some reformers to 'tidy up' the spelling was often helpful, but it also increased the number of irregular forms (the *gh* of *night* and *light*, for example, was extended to such words as *delight* and *tight*).

• In the late 16th and early 17th centuries, a new wave of loan words arrived in English from such languages as French, Latin, Greek, Spanish, Italian, and Portuguese (p. 60). They brought with them a host of alien spellings, which greatly complicated the learning of longer words, in particular. Examples include *bizarre, brusque, caustic, cocoa, epitome, gazette, grotto, idiosyncrasy, intrigue,* and *pneumonia*. Many of the items which are the butt of the Victorian spelling critic (p. 273) are loan words in which the foreign spelling has been retained or only slightly modified. The situation continues to the present day, with *intifada, perestroika, squaerial, arbitrageur, becquerel, cajun,* and *chlamydia* just a tiny fraction of the words now in the language which have increased the size of the task facing those who want to master English spelling.

The result of all this is a system which is an amalgam of several traditions, notably Anglo-Saxon, French, and Classical Latin/Greek. However, these are but the chief sources feeding the English habit of borrowing words (and their spellings) from anywhere and everywhere (p. 126). It is said to be one of the strengths of the language that it has such a large and varied lexicon; but this is bought at the expense of an increasingly diversified graphology.

DELIB'RATE MIS-SPELLINGS

GOTCHA Our lads sink gunboat and hole cruiser

A noticeable present-day trend is the use of deviant spelling as part of a trade name or an advertising campaign. The motivation for the distinctive spelling is to provide an unambiguous, identifiable product name which will not be confused with an ordinary word in the language. In the case of slogans, the spelling often aids memorability, as in such famous cases as *Beanz Meanz Heinz* or the Kentucky Fried Chicken line *They're finger-lickin' good*. It remains an open question whether such forms cause serious problems for children when they are learning to spell.

But abnormal spellings are by no means restricted to the world of marketing. They have long been a basis for characterization in literature, where idiosyncrasy and regional background are reflected in distinctive spelling (p. 416). They may also be regularly seen in humour (p. 406) and in journalism, where a headline can be made even more eye-catching if it contains an abnormal spelling.

Certain words and phrases have even developed what might be called 'standard deviance' – accepted ways of writing a colloquial form:

• *Gotcha!* ('Got you!') An accurate portrayal of a colloquial assimilation (p. 247). It has been used as the name of a television play, and most infamously as a headline of *The Sun* newspaper when the British navy sank the *General Belgrano* during the Falklands War.

• *Wot* ('what') A spelling often used to signal an uneducated speaker (p. 400). It has a special place in British post-war memories as part of the exclamatory phrase *Wot, no —*

(e.g. *Wot, no butter?*), used ironically with reference to products in short supply (p. 181).

• *Sez* ('says') An accurate transcription of the way *says* is usually pronounced in spontaneous speech (whether formal or informal).

• *Innit* ('isn't it') A form which represents the elisions (p. 247) found in colloquial speech. Spellings of this kind are sometimes used as a rhetorical device by humorous writers as a light-hearted way of making a persuasive point. Other examples are *dunno* ('don't know'), *yeah* ('yes', and other variants, such as *yup*), *c'mon* ('come on'), *'trif(f)ic* ('terrific'), *nuf(f)* ('enough'), *'em* ('them'), *ya* ('you').

• *Gawd* ('God') A spelling which suggests a distinctive regional or class pronunciation. It is by no means restricted to the representation of uneducated speech, and is often used simply for its stylistic effect: *Oh Gawd* is less serious than *O God*, and would, one imagines, never appear in a liturgical manual, even in prayers of the most supplicative kind. Some forms, indeed, are distinctively upper-class (*gels* 'girls'). The letter *r* often plays an important role in signalling the change of stylistic level, as in *larf* ('laugh'), *lorra* ('lot of'), *luvverly* ('lovely'), *har har* ('ha ha' laughter), *shurrup* ('shut up').

Bob Dylan's 'Gotta Serve Somebody' (1979) illustrates a trend in the lyrics of popular songs to spell words in a colloquial way (*gotta* = '(I've) got to'). Other examples include *wanna* ('I wanna hold your hand') and *gonna* ('I'm gonna sit right down and write myself a letter') – spellings which portray the normal unstressed pronunciation of these verbs (p. 212). Such spellings go well beyond the world of pop music, as seen in the 1980s neologism *wannabee*, a person who 'wants to be' like someone else.

American television cop-star Kojak (Telly Savalas) was known for his catch phrase *Who loves ya, baby?* By no stretch of the imagination could he have said *Who loves you, baby?*

SPELLING REFORM

A concern to eliminate spelling irregularities can be found from the 16th century (p. 66). Hundreds of proposals to reform traditional orthography (TO) have since been devised.

• *Standardizing* approaches, such as New Spelling (see opposite), use familiar letters more regularly (typically, by adding new digraphs, p. 257); no new symbols are invented.

• *Augmenting* approaches, such as Phonotypy (see right) add new symbols; diacritics and invented letters have both been used.

• *Supplanting* approaches replace all TO letters by new symbols, as in Shavian (see facing page).

• *Regularizing* approaches apply existing rules more consistently, or focus on restricted areas of the writing system, as in Noah Webster's changes to US English (p. 82) or those approaches which drop silent or redundant letters, such as Cut Spelling (see facing page).

The chief arguments for and against spelling reform have often been rehearsed. For: children and foreign learners would save vast amounts of time and emotional energy when learning to write; and fewer letters used more systematically would save time and production costs. Against: those who have already learned TO would find it difficult to assimilate a fresh perspective; the many accent differences in World English greatly complicate the choice of a model; and the break in continuity between old and new spelling would build a communicative barrier with the past. However, many of these arguments are academic, as there has never been agreement among reformers about an optimum system. As Isaac Pitman caustically commented: 'we have long known that it is impossible to induce the inventor of any scheme of reformed spelling to support the scheme of any other reformer' (*The Phonetic Journal*, 12 July 1873).

That limited reform is possible was shown by the 16th-century reformers and, later, Noah Webster; and the fact that reform bodies continue to be active testifies to a genuine and widespread concern. But the history of the movement indicates that the disadvantages have generally always outweighed the advantages. A research perspective is prerequisite for progress. We know too little about the way children actually learn and use spelling systems, the kinds of errors adults make with TO, or the nature of compatibility between old and new systems. The strongest argument of the reformers is that English spelling should be allowed to evolve naturally – that there is nothing sacrosanct about print. Their biggest problem remains the question of management: how can any such evolution be organized and implemented?

AN EARLY REFORMER

The enthusiasm and stamina of the 19th-century reformers remains a source of admiration. Here is Isaac Pitman, the inventor of the most widely used British system of shorthand, writing in 1873 about his personal situation as part of a fund-raising proposal to build a new Phonetics Institute in Bath, where he wished to take further his projects on writing reform. 'Phonetics' here does not refer to the modern subject introduced in §17, but to his system of writing and printing words as they are pronounced, which he called *phonography* and *phonotypy*. He writes in his *Phonetic Journal*, a weekly publication 'devoted to the propagation of Phonetic Shorthand, and Phonetic Reading, Writing and Printing'. There is a positively Dickensian description of the present Institute, in which he worked for some 18 years.

The Phonetics Institute is a single spacious room on the third floor above the ground floor of a large building formerly used as a brewery in Parsonage Lane, Bath, and is reached by a dreary staircase of fifty steps. It is exposed to the extremes of heat and cold, being under the roof, and the walls only six inches thick…Close to the street entrance is a slaughter-house, and underneath and round about the building are the necessary appliances for keeping, killing, and cutting up sheep and cows for a large butcher's business. A more unsavory entrance to business premises, I think, does not exist in the city. Although the refuse from the slaughtered animals is usually removed every three or four days, it is sometimes allowed to accumulate for a longer period, and the smell thence arising is extremely offensive. I have occasionally been driven from my desk by its pungency…The dampness of this office has several times been the cause of loss in the damage of books by mildew. The roof is repaired almost every year, yet a violent storm or snow-fall always sends the water through the ceiling…

From the year 1837, when Phonography was invented, to the year 1843, when I gave up my private day-school in order to live for and by the Writing and Spelling Reform, I occupied all my spare time before and after school hours, in extending Phonography through the post, and by traveling and lecturing during the holidays. In this period I gained nothing by my system of shorthand, but spent all the proceeds of my books in extending their circulation. From 1843 to 1861 I labored at the cause from six o'clock in the morning till ten at night,

and literally never took a day's holiday, or felt that I wanted one; and I worked on till 1864 without the assistance of a clerk or foreman. During this period my income from the sale of phonetic books, after paying the heavy expenses connected with the perfecting and extension of 'Phonetic Printing,' did not exceed £80 per annum for the first ten years, £100 for the next five years, and £150 for the next three years. During the first of these periods I was twice assessed for the income-tax. I appealed, and proved that my income was under £100. The commissioners appeared surprised that I should carry on an extensive business for the benefit of posterity.
(*The Phonetic Journal*, 12 April 1873, pp.114–15.)

The British National Anthem, reproduced in cursive Phonotypy in *The Phonetic Journal*, 27 September 1873.

ᴆᴇ NAɀONAL ANꞪEM.

God seu our grešrs Ꞣwin,
loy liv our nobel Ꞣwin,
God seu ᴆe Ꞣwin.
Send her viktoriss,
hapi and gloriss,
loy tu ren over ss,
God seu ᴆe Ꞣwin.

Ꝺ Lord our God ariz,
skater her enemiz,
and mek ᴆem fol.
Ꞣonfound ᴆer politiks;
frsstret ᴆer neviʃ triks;
on ᴆi our hops wi fiks;
Ꝺ! seu ss ol.

Ꞇʃ goisest gifts in stor
on her bi plizd tu por;
loy me fi ren.
Me fi defend our loz,
and ever giv ss hoz,
tu siŋ wiᴆ hart and vois,
God seu ᴆe Ꞣwin.

NEW ALPHABETS FOR OLD

The first verse of a folk poem, shown in four late 19th-century versions.

HOU TU KŪR A KØLD.
(In Fonotipi.)
Wʒn Bidi Broun, a kʒntri dɛm,
az 'tiz bɪ̣ meni tøld,
went tu ðe doktor, (Dreŋ bɪ̣ nɛm,)
for ʃi had køt a køld.

Glosic
HOU TOO CURE A KOALD
Wun Bidi Broun, a kuntri daim,
as 'tiz bei meni toald,
went too dhe doktor, (Drensh bei naim,)
for shee had kaut a koald.

The Scotch Scheme
HOW TOO CURE A COLD
Won Biddy Broun a cuntry dame,
as 'tis by menny told,
went too the doctor, (Drensh by name,)
for shee had caut a cold.

Analogic Spelling
HOW TU CURE A COLD
Wun Biddy Brown, a cuntry dame,
as 'tis by meny told,
went to the doctor, (Drensh by name,)
for she had caut a cold.

Three modern systems of spelling reform are used in this item, an appendix to an article published by the Simplified Spelling Society under the heading 'What might an improved spelling look like?'

Wel, straet in at the deep end!

Menshond abuv wos the revyzed orthografi kauld *Nue Speling* (NS), wich wos sed to be 'moderatli strikt' in uezing egzisting leters, combined with the so-kauld dygrafik prinsipl, to repreezent the sounds of the langwej. Inishali developt by the Sosyeti in 1910, the sistem is shoen in this paragraf in its moest reesent vershun as publisht in *New Spelling 90*.

Dhis paragraf and dhe nekst uez dhe preevyus vurshon ov NS, publisht in 1948. Dhis vurshon iz much strikter in traking dhe soundz ov dhe langgwej, and its ues ov 'dh' for dhe voist 'th' (az in 'then' in tradishonal speling) iz a noetabl feetuer.

U wil aulsoe hav noetist bei nou dhat NS results in a hie degree ov chaenj in dhe look ov wurdz, wich moest peepl fiend disturbing – or eeven repugnant – on furst akwaentans.

By way of contrast, we hav now swichd to *Cut Speling*, a wel thot-out exampl of a posibl partial revision. It is based mainly on th principl of cutng redundnt – and thus usuly misleadng – leters, plus limitd letr substitutions. Th resulting chanje in th apearance of words is not nearly so intrusiv as with NS.

Wethr or not CS or NS as demonstrated here ar found acceptbl, som action is seriusly needd to make english esir to use.

(After B. Brown, 1993.)

THE SHAW ALPHABET FOR WRITERS

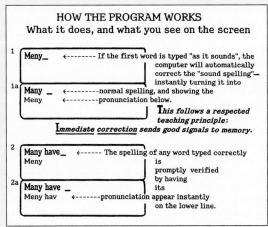

The opening exchanges of *Androcles and the Lion,* by George Bernard Shaw, printed in a special parallel text. The alphabet (often called 'Shavian') was devised by Kingsley Read, who won a competition based on the terms laid down in Shaw's will. The version in traditional orthography omits the apostrophe (Shaw's usual practice). Both extracts are set in type of the same size, but the Shavian one uses a third less space. Writers are recommended to learn the alphabet in pairs, as shown right, the double lines showing their relative height. *Talls* are letters with ascending strokes; *Deeps* have descending strokes. Capital letters are not distinguished. Four words (*the, of, and, to*) are given their own symbols, all shown in the extract.

The headline of a language reform publication from Canada.

MEGAERA [*suddenly throwing down her stick*] I wont go another step.
ANDROCLES [*pleading wearily*] Oh, not again, dear. Whats the good of stopping every two miles and saying you wont go another step? We must get on to the next village before night. There are wild beasts in this wood: lions, they say.
MEGAERA. I dont believe a word of it. You are always threatening me with wild beasts to make me walk the very soul out of my body when I can hardly drag one foot before another. We havnt seen a single lion yet.

The Times Ov Toronto
February, 1989   **$2.00**
Canada's Internasional Nuzepaper
The world's furst nuzepaper tu be printed in the Canadean langwaje.

AMERICAN LITERACY COUNCIL

The Simpler Spelling Board was founded in the USA in 1906, and since 1989 has been called the American Literacy Council, with headquarters in New York City. In a 1993 statement, the Council reaffirms its commitment to attacking what it sees to be the chief cause of English illiteracy: the lack of 'phonic logic and simplicity'. The use of computer technology is now an important aspect of its work.

SoundSpeler is one of the ALC's products, designed as a remedial computer program for those having trouble with literacy. This extract from a promotional brochure illustrates the approach.

HOW THE PROGRAM WORKS
What it does, and what you see on the screen

1 `Meny_` ←-------- If the first word is typed "as it sounds", the computer will automatically correct the "sound spelling"— instantly turning it into
1a `Many _` / `Meny` ←---------normal spelling, and showing the pronunciation below.

This follows a respected teaching principle:
Immediate correction sends good signals to memory.

2 `Many have_` / `Meny` ←------ The spelling of any word typed correctly is promptly verified by having its
2a `Many have _` / `Meny hav` ←-------pronunciation appear instantly on the lower line.

THE SIMPLIFIED SPELLING SOCIETY

This society was founded in Britain in 1908 to promote the idea of planned change in English spelling. It fostered its own revision, called *New Spelling*, a system which brought sounds and spellings closer together by extending the use of digraphs (p. 257). In the 1960s, a version which used extra letters instead of digraphs was introduced into many schools as the *Initial Teaching Alphabet* (i.t.a.). Several other systems have since emerged within the Society, notably the partial-reform approach called *Cut Spelling* (1992). The secretariat of the Society is in London.

The aim of the Society is to bring about a reform of the spelling of English in the interests of ease of learning and economy in writing.

To this end, it:
- encourages the idea that reform is possible;
- fosters debate on reform methods;
- devises, publishes and promotes potential reform schemes;
- persuades and campaigns;
- has a role as an expert organisation on the subject;
- aims to be of benefit to future generations by introducing a consistent spelling.

(From the Society's publications, 1993.)

PUNCTUATION

Punctuation plays a critical role in the modern writing system, yet its significance is regularly underestimated. At least four important functions can be distinguished.

- Its primary purpose is to enable stretches of written language to be read coherently, by displaying their grammatical structure (Part III). Important features here include the use of sentence-ending points, clause-dividing commas, and paragraph-marking indentation.
- It also gives the reader clues about the prosody (p. 248) with which a piece of writing can be read aloud, through such features as question marks, exclamation marks, and parentheses. These are especially important when directly representing the intonation and emphasis of spoken language.
- It may highlight semantic units or contrasts present in the text but not directly related to its grammatical structure. Examples here include the choice of colons vs semi-colons to show the rhetorical structure of a complex sentence, and the use of line divisions and stanzas in poetry.
- It may add a semantic dimension, unique to the graphic medium, which it would be difficult or impossible to read aloud. Examples here include the use of 'scare quotes' to show that a word has a special sense, or capital letters drawing attention to a Very Important Point.

To understand punctuation, a historical perspective is essential. The modern system is the result of a process of change over many centuries, affecting both the shapes and uses of punctuation marks. Early classical texts were unpunctuated, with no spaces between words. The first marks were introduced as a guide to phrasing in an age of oratory, when reading aloud was a prestigious and professional activity. More elaborate and extensive marking is found in later periods, reflecting a wider range of semantic distinctions. Biblical texts, in particular, motivated a special concern to display exact nuances of expression. Standardization gradually emerged after the introduction of printing (p. 56), but punctuation never achieved the same degree of rule-governed consistency as appears in spelling. Two authors might punctuate the same text in very different ways. Some (e.g. Dickens) were very concerned about punctuation, and took great pains to check it when revising proofs; others (e.g. Wordsworth) left the task to their publishers. Scribes and publishing houses have always varied in their practices, and even today punctuation remains to some extent a matter of personal preference.

DOING WITHOUT

One way of sharpening a sense of the role of punctuation is to remove it from a piece of text, and attempt to decode the result. Two variants of an extract from Richmal Crompton's *Just William* are shown below: one with and one without word spaces.

wellmissgrantsintellectualfacelitup
whatabouthiscousindoritatheyreabout
thesameagearenttheybothelevenwell
thetwooftheminwhitesatinwithbunches
ofhollydontyouthinkwouldyoumind
havinghertostayfortheceremony
missgrantalwaysreferredtoherwedding
astheceremonyifyoudonthavehishaircut
forabithemightntlooksobad

well miss grants intellectual face lit up what about his cousin dorita theyre about the same age arent they both eleven well the two of them in white satin with bunches of holly dont you think would you mind having her to stay for the ceremony miss grant always referred to her wedding as the ceremony if you dont have his hair cut for a bit he mightnt look so bad

'Well,' – Miss Grant's intellectual face lit up – 'what about his cousin Dorita. They're about the same age, aren't they? Both eleven. Well, the *two* of them in white satin with bunches of holly. Don't you think? Would you mind having her to stay for the ceremony?' (Miss Grant always referred to her wedding as 'the ceremony.') 'If you don't have his hair cut for a bit, he mightn't look so bad?'

FOUR FUNCTIONS OF PUNCTUATION

Grammar
She had an idea that the son of a gentleman, if he intended to maintain his rank as a gentleman, should earn his income as a clergyman, or as a barrister, or as a soldier, or as a sailor. These were the professions intended for gentlemen. (Anthony Trollope, *The Vicar of Bullhampton*, 1870, Ch. 9.)

Prosody
'What do I mean? Oh, I see. What do I mean? Yes, quite. I ought to have explained that, oughtn't I? It seems that his name isn't Meriwether.' (P. G. Wodehouse, *Service with a Smile*, 1961, p. 86.)

Rhetorical structure
The English are apt to admire men who do not attempt to dominate events or turn the drift of fate; who wait about doing their duty on a short view from day to day until there is no doubt whether the tide is on the ebb or the flow; and who then, with the appearance of great propriety and complete self-abnegation, with steady, sterling qualities of conduct if not of heart, move slowly, cautiously, forward towards the obvious purpose of the nation. (W. S. Churchill, *A History of the English-speaking Peoples*, 1956, Book 6, Ch. 3.)

Semantic nuance
My 'home' was a small mean nasty flatlet in Bayswater, in a big square red-brick block in a cul-de-sac. (Iris Murdoch, *A Word Child*, 1975, p.1.)

HEAVY VS LIGHT STYLES

The following text shows two punctuation styles, whose choice depends more on personal preference and an awareness of contemporary taste than on anything to do with grammar and semantics. In recent years there has been an increasing tendency to use the simpler, 'less cluttered' style. On the other hand, the writing of individual authors represents many positions between these stylistic extremes, and preferences vary between contexts (e.g. informal vs formal letters). The present author, for example, always writes letters in the lighter style, but employs a somewhat heavier style in the present text (e.g. using a 'serial comma' in such sequences as *tall, dark(,) and handsome*).

PO Box 5
Holyhead
Gwynedd
LL65 1RG

1 January 1994

Mr J K Galbraith
AK Tools Ltd
3 The Terrace
London NW3 2PP

Dear Mr Galbraith

Thank you for your letter of 11 December and for the enclosed samples. As with your previous material I have found these to be very

P.O. Box 5,
Holyhead,
Gwynedd,
LL65 1RG.

1 January, 1994.

Mr. J. K. Galbraith,
A.K. Tools, Ltd.,
3, The Terrace,
London, NW3 2PP.

Dear Mr. Galbraith,

Thank you for your letter of 11 December, and for the enclosed samples. As with your previous material, I have found these to be

PUNCTUATION OVER TIME

One of the best ways of becoming aware of how English punctuation has developed is to see what editors do to a text in a series of editions over several hundred years. The following stanzas have all been taken from Chaucer's *Troilus and Criseyde*, Book 3, 119–28 (p. 38) in editions from the early 15th century to the present day (after M. B. Parkes, 1992).

Because the choice of punctuation responds to the sense of a text, an indication of the context of the extract follows, along with a free translation. Two verses previously, Troilus has said he will kill himself if he has failed to please Criseyde; her uncle Pandarus, much moved by his grief, begs her 'for the love of God, to make an end of this, or kill us both at once'. In the first verse of the extract, Criseyde reacts to this plea of Pandarus, who then replies to her. Troilus intervenes again in the second verse.

'Ah, what?' said she, 'by God and by my troth, I don't know what you want me to say.' 'Ah, what?' said he, 'that you have pity on him, for the love of God, and don't make him die.' 'Well then', said she, 'I will beg him to tell me what he has in his mind, for I still do not know what he means.' 'What I mean, O sweet dear heart, kind, lovely and generous?' said Troilus, [is that with your clear eyes you will sometimes look kindly on me…]

I what quod she by god and by my trouthe
I not uat what ȝe wilne that I seye
I what quod he that ȝe han on hym routhe
For goddes loue and doth hym nought to deye
Now thanne thus quod she I wolde hym preye
To telle me the fyn of his entente
Ȝet wist I neuere wel what that he mente

What that I mene o swete herte deere
Quod Troilus o goodly fresshe free

(The earliest surviving copy: Cambridge, Corpus Christi, MS 61, fol. 65.) The most notable feature is the absence of punctuation. The reader is helped only by the way sense units coincide with lines, and by the positioning of *quod* ('said') towards the beginning of a line, providing early warning of a change of speaker – a role also played by the line space at the end of the verse.

I / what (q*uo*d she) by god and by my trouthe
I not nat what ye wylne that I sey
Ey / what (q*uo*d he) that ye haue on hym routhe
For goddes loue / and dothe him nat to dey
Nowe than thus (q*uo*d she) I wolde him prey
To tell me the fyne of his entente
Yet wyste I neuer wel what that he mente

   What that I meane / O swete herte dere
(Quod Troylus) o goodly fresshe free

(1532: W. Thynne, The Workes of Geffray Chaucer newly printed, fol. 187v.) There are two features of punctuation: parentheses around a reporting clause is a common 16th-century practice; and the oblique (*virgula suspensiva*) indicates a brief pause to show a break in the sense (after the exclamatory utterances). No other pauses are marked. The following verse is indented, perhaps to emphasize the switch to a new speaker. The italics in *quod* represent an expanded abbreviation.

I, what (qd she) by God and by my trouth
I not nat what ye wilne that I seie
Eie, what (qd he) that ye haue on him routh
For Goddes loue, and doeth him nat deie
Now than thus (qd she) I wolde him preie
To tell me the fine of his entent.
Yet wist I neuer wel what that he mente.

What that I meane, o swete hart dere
(Qd Troilus) O goodly fresh free

(1598: T. Speght, The Workes of our Antient and Learned English Poet, Geffrey Chaucer, newly printed, fol. 167.) The *virgula suspensiva* has been replaced by a comma, and there is now a point (*punctus*) marking the end of the stanza. In the 1602 edition, Speght adds further punctuation at line endings: colons in lines 2 and 4, commas in 5, 6 and 9, and a point after each qd.

I, what (q*uo*d she) by God and by my trouth
   I n'ot nevir what ye wilne that I seie;
Eie, what? (q*uo*d he) that ye have on him routh
   For Godd'is love, and doeth him nat to deie.
   Now than thus (q*uo*d she) I wollin him preie
   To tellin me the fine of his entente
   Yet wist I nevir well what that he mente.

(1721: J. Urry, The Works of Geoffrey Chaucer, p. 292.) Indentation now shows the rhyme scheme of the verse: lines 1 and 3, lines 2, 4 and 5, and the final couplet. Speaker turns are now indicated by punctuation – a semi-colon and two points. The semi-colon may have been used because of the close grammatical dependency of line 3 on line 2 (*that ye have* is an elliptical object of *seie*). There is a question mark rein-

---

What that I mene, O my swete hertè dere
   (q*uo*d Troilus) godely freshe and fre,

   I, what? (quod she) By God and by my trouth
I n'ot nevir what ye wilne that I seie.
Eie! what? (quod he) that ye have on him routh
For Godd'is love, and doeth him nat to deie.
Now than thus (quod she) I wollin him preie
To tellin me the fine of his entente;
Yet wist I nevir wel what that he mente.

   What that I mene, o my swete herte dere!
(Quod Troilus) o godely freshe and fre!

forcing the exclamation in line 3. Apostrophes now mark an ellipsis (2) and the genitive (4) (p. 283).

(1793: R. Anderson, A Complete Edition of the Poets of Great Britain, i.363.) Punctuation is now being used to give an indication of speech prosody (p. 248). There are exclamation marks in lines 3, 8 and 9, and an additional question mark. The main speech turns are now all marked by points, allowing the semi-colon a role separating the sentence of lines 5–7 into two sense units.

"I, what" (quod she) "by God and by my trouth
   I not nat what ye wilne that I seye:"
"Eye, what" (quod he) "That ye have on hym routh
For Godes love, and doeth hym nat to dey:"
"Now than thus" (quod she) "I woll hym prey,
   To tell me the fyn of his entente,
   Yet wist I never wel what that he ment."

"What that I mean, O my sweet herte dere"
(Quod Troilus) "O goodly, fresh and free,…"

(1810: Alexander Chalmers, The Works of the English Poets from Chaucer to Cowper, p. 252.) Inverted commas now enclose speech turns, as in the contemporary novel, but the parentheses have been retained (perhaps to suggest a parenthetic intonation). The omission of question and exclamation marks (1, 3), and the use of colons instead of points (2, 4) helps to unify the three speeches in the stanza into a single conversational flow – again, as in a novel.

"I! what?" quod she, "by God and by my trouthe,
I not nat what ye wilne that I seye."
"I! what?" quod he, "that ye han on hym routhe,
For Goddes love, and doth hym nought to deye."
"Now thanne thus," quod she, "I wolde hym preye
   To telle me the fyn of his entente.
Yet wiste I nevere wel what that he mente."

"What that I mene, O swete herte deere?"
Quod Troilus, "O goodly, fresshe free,…"

(1957: F. N. Robinson, The Complete Works of Geoffrey Chaucer, 2nd edn, p. 422.) Punctuation is introduced to help the sense wherever possible, both grammatically (marking the parenthetic status of *For Goddes love* or *by God and by my trouthe*) and attitudinally (the exclamatory and interrogative tones in lines 1 and 3). There is standard modern punctuation around the passages of direct speech.

THE DEVELOPMENT OF THE WRITING SYSTEM: A COMPARISON

Emerging linguistic features of handwriting and printing can often best be seen by comparing two versions of a text. This is a page from the manuscript used by the printer for the 1597 edition of a book, *Of the Lawes of Ecclesiastical Politie* (Book 5), written by the English theologian, Richard Hooker (1554–1600). (After M. B. Parkes, 1992.)

The copy, prepared by a scribe, Benjamin Pullen, was corrected and emended by Hooker himself (4, 22, 27). The compositor has marked up the page ready for typesetting, showing the beginning of a new page of print by a pencilled Q12 in the margin (i.e. the twelfth printed page of section Q of the book) and a bracket around the word *coexistence* (21). The manuscript page before this point corresponds to the last 16 lines of the printed text opposite.

Notable features of the manuscript include the use of two types of handwriting. Most of the text uses a script known as Secretary Cursive, distinguished by its prominent, often looped ascenders and descenders (p. 257). There is a raised sign marking a final -*n*, as in *communion* (2). This material is printed in roman type opposite. Quotations and other kinds of special comment are written in the less ornate Humanist Cursive, seen in the bottom ten lines of the page, and printed in italic type opposite (beginning with *This is my bodie*). Later use of underlining within this script (19–20, 23) indicates that the material should be printed in roman type. The inverted commas in the margin highlight an important section of the argument (not a quotation). Points are followed by capital letters, commas are used to mark pauses, and there is a question mark (13). The word-break hyphen at the end of 12 and 17 is a double line.

The printed copy follows the manuscript text quite closely, but several spellings have been altered, and there is a great deal of inconsistency: -ie often becomes -y, as in *body* (32, cf. 1 opposite), *holy* (38, cf. 9), *vertuously* (40, cf. 12), but not in *unnecessarie* (33, cf. 3), *varietie* (41, cf. 13), *certaintie* (44, cf. 18); final -e is sometimes added, as in *holde* (34, cf. 4) and *bee* (34, cf. 4), and sometimes dropped, as in *louing* (37, cf. 13); there are various other vowel and consonant changes, as in *me(a)nt* (35, cf. 5) and *wit(t)* (38, cf. 10). Already we can see an issue over whether there should be an e in *iudgements* (41, cf. 13). Both styles show the use of 'long s' in non-final position (p. 263). In the printed copy, *v* is used initially, *u* elsewhere (2–5), and *I* is used for *J* (8) (p. 260). There is an abbreviation mark in 4 and 13 to help the word fit the narrow measure (compare the full form of *Transubstantiation* in 32). A final e is also added or subtracted to help the justification (p. 257), as in *bloude* (25) vs *bloud* (32), *be* (3) vs *bee* (34).

Punctuation closely follows that used in the manuscript, with occasional variation (e.g. the extra comma after *first* in 45, cf. 19). The printed extract also illustrates a semi-colon (3). The location of the hyphen is sometimes different from modern practice, as in *sanctifi-ed*, (30) and *doub-ted* (43). There is no apostrophe (*Christs*, 20).

Ecclesiasticall Politie.   179

changeth them and maketh them
that vnto vs which otherwise
they could not be; that to vs they
are therby made such instrumēts
as is mistically yet truely, inuisibly
yet really worke our communion
or fellowship with the person of
Iesus Christ as well in that hee is
man as God, our participation also in the fruite, grace and efficacie
of his body and bloud, whereup-
on there ensueth a kinde of Tran-
substantiatiō in vs, a true ʰ change
both of soule and body, an alteration from death to life. In a word
it appeareth not that of all the ancient Fathers of the Church any
one did euer conceiue or imagine other then onely a mysticall
participation of Chrifts both body and bloud in the Sacrament,
neither are their speeches concerning the chaunge of the elements themselues into the body
and bloude of Chrift such, that a
man can thereby in conscience
assure himselfe it was their meaning to perswade the worlde ey-
ther of a corporall Confubstantia-
tion of Chrift with those sanctifi-
ed and blessed elements before we receiue them, or of the like Transubstantiation of them into the body and bloud of Chrift. Which both to our mysticall communion with Chrift are so vnnecessarie that the Fathers who
plainely holde but this mysticall communion cannot easily bee thought to
haue ment any other change of sacramentall elements then that which the
same spirituall communion did require them to holde. These things considered, how should that minde which louing truth and seeking comfort out
of holy misteries hath not perhaps the leasure, perhaps not the wit nor capa-
citie to treade out so endlesse mazes, as the intricate disputes of this cause
haue led men into, how should a vertuously disposed minde better resolue
with it selfe then thus? Varietie of iudgements and opinions argueth obscu-
ritie in those things where about they differ. But that which all parts receiue
for truth, that which euery one hauing sifted is by no one denied or doub-
ted of, must needes be matter of infallible certaintie. Whereas therfore there
are but three expositions made of *This is my body*, the first, This is in it selfe before participation *really and truely the naturall substance of my body by reason of the*
coexistcance

[The right-hand column consists of Latin and Greek marginal notes in italic type, keyed by letters d, e, f, g, h:]

d *Sacramenta quidem quantum in se est siue propria virtute esse non pos-
sunt, nec vllo modo se absentat maiestas mysterijs. Cypr. de Can. c. 7.*
e *Sacramento visibile ineffabiliter diuina se infudit essentia vt esset Reli-
gionis circa Sacramenta deuotio. Idem. c. 6. Inuisibilis sacerdos visibiles
creaturas in substantiam corporis & sanguinis sui verbo suo secreta potess-
ate conuertit. In spiritualibus sacramentis verbi praecipit virtus & seruit
effectus. Euseb. Emisen. hom. 5. de pasch.*
f τὰ σύμβολα τῆς δεσποτικῆ σώματος τε κỳ αἷματΘ· ἀλλα ... εἰσὶ πρὸ
τῆς ἱερατικῆς ἐπικλήσεως, μὸ δε γε ... ἐπικλήσιν μεταβάλλεται ...
... Θεοδο. *Ex quo a Domino dictum est, Hoc
facite in meam commemorationem, haec est caro mea, & hic est sanguis
meus, quotiescunq, his verbis & hac fide actum est, panis iste supersub-
stantialis & calix benedictione solenni sacratus ad totius hominis vitam
salutemq, proficit. Cypr. de can. c. 3 Immortalitatis alimonia datur, a
communibus cibis differens, corporalis substantia retinens speciem sed vir-
tutis diuina inuisibilis efficientia probans adesse praesentiam. Ibid. c. 2.*
g *Sensibilibus sacramentis inest vita aeterna effectus & non tam corporali
quam spirituali transitione Christo vnimur. Ipse enim & panis & caro
& sanguis, idem cibus & substantia & vita factus est Ecclesia sua quam
corpus suum appellat, dans ei participationem spiritus. Ibid. c. 5. Nostra
& ipsius coniunctio nec miscet personas nec vnit substantias, sed affectus
consociat & confederat voluntates. ca. 6. Mansio nostra in ipso est man-
ducatio, & potus quasi quaedam incorporatio. c. 9. Ille est impetre per na-
turam diuinitatis, nos in eo per corporalem eius natiuitatem, ille rursus in
nobis per Sacramentorum mysterium. Hilar. de trin. lib. 8.*
h *Panis hic az ymus cibus verus & sincerus per speciem & sacramentum
nos tactu sanctificat, fide illuminat, veritate Christo cōformat. Cyp. de eam.
e. 6. Non aliud agit participatio corporis & sanguinis Christi quam vt in id
quod sumimus transeamus, & in quo mortus & sepulti & conresuscitatō
sumus ipsum per omnia & spiritu & carne gestemus. Leo de pas. Ser. 14.
Quemadmodum qui est a terra panis percipiens Dei vocationem (id est
facta inuocatione diuini numinis) iam non communis panis est sed Eu-
charistia ex duabus rebus constans terrena & caelesti: Sic & corpora nostra percipientia Eucharistiam iam non sunt corruptibilia spem resurrecti-
onis habentia. Irena. l. 4. c. 34. Quoniam salutaris caro verbo Dei quod
naturaliter vita est coniuncta viuifica effecta est, quando eam comedimus,
tunc vitam habemus in nobis illis carni coniuncti quae vita effecta est. Cyril.
in Iohan. lib. 4. cap. 14.*

PUNCTUATION MARKS

Early English manuscripts present an array of punctuation marks which look very different from those used today. Some have now fallen out of use, whereas others have developed over the centuries into their modern counterparts. A few appear not to have changed at all – but it is always important to take care when considering the function of such marks in a text, as modern values often do not apply. A point, for example, was commonly used to indicate a pause rather than a sentence ending, and different degrees of pause were sometimes shown by varying the height of the point relative to adjacent letters.

The modern punctuation system is extremely wide-ranging, including such features as spaces, indentation, the use of capitals, and a wide range of non-alphabetic graphic cues (such as asterisks and footnote numerals), as well as the traditional 'marks'. There is a great deal of hierarchical organization. Some features identify large units of writing, such as paragraphs and sections; some identify small units, such as words or word parts; some identify units of intermediate size or complexity, such as sentences, clauses, and phrases. Most marks are features that separate – showing the boundaries between grammatical constructions. A few express a meaning in their own right, regardless of the grammatical context in which they occur. These include the question and exclamation marks, the apostrophe, and such special symbols as £, &, @, *, and †.

PUNCTUATION POEMS

A stanza from a 15th-century 'punctuation poem', in which two systems of marks compete (in the manner of a riddle) to give two very different readings of this text about the nature of priests. The 'orthodox' reading is obtained by following the points (*punctus*); the 'unorthodox' reading follows the oblique lines (*virgula suspensiva*). Both are reproduced in the transcription below.

Trvsty . seldom / to their Frendys vniust. /
Gladd for to helpp . no Crysten creator /
Wyllyng to greve . settyng all ye^ir ioy & lust
Only in ye^e pleasour of god . havyng no cvre /
Who is most ryche . wth them ye^ey wylbe sewer /
Wher nede is . gevyng neyther reward ne Fee /
Vnresonably . Thus lyve prestys . parde . /

Reading with points
Trusty. Seldom to their friends unjust. Glad for to help. No Christian creature willing to grieve. Setting all their joy and desire only in the pleasure of God. Having no care who is most rich. With them they will be sure where need is. Giving neither reward nor fee unreasonably. Thus live priests. In the name of God.

Reading with obliques
Trusty seldom / To their friends unjust / Glad for to help no Christian creature / Willing to grieve setting all their joy and desire – only in the pleasure of God having no care / Who[ever] is most rich with them they will be sure / Where need is, giving neither reward nor fee / Unreasonably thus live priests in the name of God /

GRAPHOLOGICAL ARCHAISMS

The present-day punctuation system began to emerge quite rapidly after the introduction of printing (p. 56), though differences from modern conventions continue to be apparent until well into the 19th century. The punctuation of this text of 1766 differs in only minor respects from that used today, but it is notable that these are enough to alter the visual impact of the page quite dramatically. The large dashes, accompanied by a comma or semi-colon, the use of capitals on important nouns (p. 67), and the fairly heavy marking, all contribute significantly to the overall archaic appearance of the text.

AUTHOR's PREFACE.

ARCHÆOLOGY, or an Account of the Origin of Nations after the Universal Deluge; admits of two ways of enquiry,——either beginning at Babel, the place of mankind's difperfion, and tracing them downwards to our own times by the light of records, which is Hiftory, and of natural reafon, which is Inference and Conjecture ; or elfe beginning from our own time, and winding them upwards, by the fame helps, to the firft place and origin of their progreffion ;——both which ways are ufually taken by Hiftorians and Genealogifts, and are equally to be allowed in their manner of proceeding. By the former of thefe methods I have in the following Sections adventured through fome of the darkeft tracks of time, to calculate the Archæology, and to fetch out and put together fome rude ftrokes and lineaments of the ANTIQUITIES of the ISLE of ANGLESEY, from its firft planting to the time of the Roman Conqueft, moftly in an hypothetical way, or a rational fcheme of enquiry.

EXTINCT SYMBOLS

Over 30 obsolete punctuation marks have been identified in early manuscripts, most of them disappearing after the arrival of printing. Here are two of them:

/ The *virgula suspensiva* was widely used in Middle English to mark a brief pause in a text (p. 68). In the 14th century, many writers used the double form, //, to mark a longer pause, or to indicate the beginning of a new paragraph or section.

The *hedera*, or ivy-leaf, is a very old mark, used in classical times to separate words, and in Anglo-Saxon times as a symbol separating major sections of text, or marking the end of a passage. It was often treated very decoratively, and some printers continued to use it in an ornamental role.

MODERN MARKS

Marks that separate constructions

Point (.)
(also called a *period, full point, full stop,* or (Latin) *punctus*)
Chiefly used to identify a sentence ending (typically a statement); in print (and sometimes in type) followed by a wider space than is usual between words; marks an abbreviated word (*A.D.*, though modern practice varies, p. 278); used in such special contexts as times/dates (*8.30, 10.10.94*), money units (*$3.50*), section numbers in a book (*2.2*), and decimal numerals (*5.006*); three points (*suspension* or *ellipsis dots*) show incompleteness or omission (as in the middle of a quotation); also used in question/exclamation marks, colons, and semi-colons.

Semi-colon (;)
First used in the 15th century to mark a pause midway between the colon (longer) and comma (shorter); now identifies the coordinate parts of a complex sentence, or separates complex points in a list; closely corresponds to the conjunction *and*; more common than the colon, and no longer pausally distinct; especially used in formal writing, where several complex ideas need to be interrelated, and lower-level constructions are separated by commas (as in this paragraph).

Colon (:)
Used in 15th-century manuscripts to show a major pause or sense separation; now used mainly to show that what follows is an amplification or explanation of what precedes; also used to introduce examples, and to separate numerical elements, as in the time or date (*5:30*); some people use it after the *Dear X* invocation in a letter; infrequent, and usually restricted to one instance per sentence; first letter of a following sentence often capitalized in US English; often followed by a dash (*:–*) in older printing styles.

Comma (,)
Wide range of uses, marking a sequence of similar grammatical units (words, phrases, clauses), or showing one unit being used inside another; the most frequent punctuation mark, attracting much personal variation; used in early manuscripts, often accompanied by a subscript dot, to show a minor pause or sense change; short semi-circular form, in low position, accompanied early development of printing; no simple rules governing usage, which has built up over several hundred years; no longer corresponds neatly with speech pauses, e.g. a pause after the subject of a sentence (*The chair in the dining room / has a broken leg*) is not reflected by a comma in Standard English; much divided usage, as in the 'serial comma' before a conjunction (p. 278).

Parentheses ( )
(also called *round brackets*)
An alternative to commas, marking the inclusion of a grammatical unit in a sentence; emerged towards the end of the 14th century; in British English colloquially often called *brackets* (though in US and typographic usage this term means *square brackets,* [ ]); *curly brackets,* or *braces* ({ }) also used in scientific writing; pedagogical

aversion to using too many parentheses in one sentence, or to using pairs within pairs; special uses, also showing the use of square brackets, include:

- dates: *Henry VIII (1491–1547)*
- glosses: *H_2O (water)*
- affiliations: *Brown (USA)*
- irony: *young [sic] people*
- authorial comment: *we will **not** go [my emphasis]*
- omitted text: *it is [a] disaster.*

Dash (—)
Used singly to show a comment or afterthought at the end of a sentence, or simply an incomplete utterance; in pairs, has the same function as parentheses; in informal writing, often used randomly to replace other punctuation marks; special uses include signalling a missing word or letter (in crossword puzzle clues), replacing letters in a taboo word (p. 172), and separating elements in dates (*11–11–94*) or page numbers (*15–22*); handwriting makes no regular distinction between dashes with different sizes and functions; print differentiates the hyphen, the *en dash/rule* (–), and the *em dash/rule* (—) (*en* and *em* reflect the width of the letters *N* and *M* in traditional type); *en* dashes usually mean 'and' (as in *Liberal–Labour alliance*) or 'to' (as in *London–Holyhead train*); *em* dashes are often printed with a space on each side.

Inverted commas (' ', " ")
(also known as *quotation marks, quotes,* or *speech marks*)
Derive from the use of a special sign (the *diple*) in the margin of manuscripts to draw attention to part of the text (such as a biblical quotation); printers represented the marks by raised and inverted commas, and eventually placed them within the line; came to indicate quotations and passages of direct speech (hence the alternative names); choice of single vs double quotes is variable; latter are more common in handwritten and typed material, and in US printing; both forms used for speech within speech (*Mike said, 'I heard Fred shout "Yes" just now.'*); US usage prefers placing inverted commas after other punctuation marks; British preference is the reverse; also used for technical terms (*this is known as 'eidetic'*), titles, glosses (Latin *punctus* 'point'), and special senses ('scare' or 'sneer quotes', p. 278).

Hyphen (-)
Marks two kinds of word division: a break at the end of a line, and the parts of a compound word (*green-eyed*); practice varies in the latter use (p. 129), with British English often using hyphens where US English would omit them; usage also varies on where within a word a line-break hyphen should best go: sometimes a contrast in meaning is conveyed, as in *re-cover* ('to cover again') vs *recover* ('get back'); in some early manuscripts, written both with single and double strokes (p. 280).

Space
Separates words and identifies paragraphs (first sentence begins a new line; first word usually indented or extra space separates successive paragraphs); it is a positive feature of

punctuation, as is illustrated by the way a space is treated in computer languages as an individual character.

Marks that convey meaning

Question mark (?)
Chief function to show that the preceding sentence is a question; occasionally found with other roles, such as marking uncertainty (?), irony, or astounded silence:

'We might go in your umbrella,' said Pooh.
'?'

Punctus interrogativus was originally a wavy mark which slanted upwards and to the right above a point, known from the 8th century; may have originated in an attempt to reflect the rising inflection of the speaking voice; upright version introduced by early printers.

Exclamation mark (!)
(also called *exclamation point*)
Punctus exclamativus (or *punctus admirativus*) first appeared in 14th century to show an utterance needed to be read with some exclamatory force; in early manuscripts, appears with two points under a short line, the whole slanting to the right; printers represented it as an upright; in modern usage, may be repeated to show increasing degrees of force (!!!); also used ironically (*The car (!) was waiting*) and as a marker of silent surprise or enlightenment, as in the sequel to the Pooh quotation:

'We might go in your umbrella,' said Pooh.
'!!!!!!'
For suddenly Christopher Robin saw that they might.
(A. A. Milne, *Winnie-the-Pooh*, 1926)

Apostrophe (')
Introduced by early printers as a sign that a letter or letters had been omitted; still used in this way, as in grammatical contractions (*He's, isn't*) and in such words as *o'clock, fish 'n' chips,* and *in '93*; use later extended to distinguish the genitive from the plural in nouns (*dog's, dogs'* vs *dogs*); some usage variation (e.g. *cello* vs *'cello*); some arbitrary uses, unrelated to pronunciation, as when space constraints force elisions (*Stock Market Quot'ns* [for *quotations*] in newspapers). (For the later development of the apostrophe, and contemporary uncertainty about its use, see p. 203.)

twould be nice to be
an apostrophe
floating
above an s
hovering
like a paper kite
in between the its
eavesdropping, tiptoeing
high above the thats
an inky comet
spiralling
the highest tossed
of hats

Roger McGough, 'Apostrophe', 1976.

PART V
Using English

Parts II, III, and IV of this book investigate the structural properties of English: the inventory of elements in vocabulary, grammar, phonology, and graphology which are used to produce meaningful words and sentences. The study of these elements is relatively abstract: we can describe the way a sentence is constructed, or the semantic links between words, or the system of vowels and consonants, without having to say anything about who is using them, or when, or where, or why. Part V turns this approach on its head.

It begins by introducing the notion of discourse (§19), which includes the analysis of larger stretches of speech or writing than the sentence, as well as a study of the factors which facilitate linguistic interaction. This leads to the notion of texts – units of discourse which belong to particular social situations, and whose distinctive linguistic features identify a range of varieties in the language. After a review of the differences between speech and writing and between monologue and dialogue, §20 looks systematically at these varieties, beginning with those which convey geographical information about the user: regional dialects.

The section opens with an international overview – a range of newspaper material illustrating a day in the life of the (written) English language. It then looks in detail at the differences between and within American and British varieties of English, the two chief models of world language use. The three Celtic-influenced dialects of the British Isles are each examined, with particular attention paid to Scots, which has a much richer dialect literature, extending from the Middle Ages to the present, than any other variety of World English apart from Standard English itself. We then follow the same route as in Part I, complementing the historical perspective presented there with contemporary observations on the features of English in Canada, the Caribbean, Australia, New Zealand, and South Africa. We look separately at pidgin and creole Englishes, and also at the emerging range of second language Englishes in India, Africa, South Asia, and elsewhere.

The more we study regional variation, the more we find we cannot make sense of it without taking social variation into account. The next section (§21) therefore looks at what is involved under this heading. It begins with a discussion of two important issues – prescriptivism and gender – which have been referred to at several other places in this book, and then reviews the chief occupational varieties, which provide the clearest examples of distinctive social uses of language. Special attention is paid to the English used in religion, science, the law, politics, the news media, broadcasting, and advertising. The chapter concludes with a brief look at restricted varieties of English, and at some of the new varieties which are emerging as a consequence of the electronic revolution.

Part V ends with an examination of the nature of stylistic deviance and the associated domain of personal linguistic identity. Four broad areas are covered in §22. It begins with an account of the proliferating world of word games, in both spoken and written English. Next it identifies those varieties which are especially likely to break linguistic rules, and looks at the kind of deviance which emerges. The field of verbal humour is found to play a central role in all of this, so the role played by different levels of language structure in jokes and other forms of jocular activity is separately examined. Part V then concludes with a similarly detailed review of the way the various levels of language structure can be used to guide our observation when approaching the most creative domain of language use: English literature.

◀ This sequence of photographs, taken by Jack Chambers in Toronto, anticipates several of the themes of Part V: there is evidence of distinctive regional variety (§20), occupational variety (§21), and creative usage (§22). Canadian identity is suggested by the unusual spelling combination of *tire* (US) and *centre* (UK), and other Canadian expressions can be seen in the *Hydro* office (the publicly owned electricity company), the sign for *take out* food (not *take away*), and the *Kiss 'n' Ride* subway station (where one's spouse drops one off, and gives one a kiss before one takes the underground the rest of the way to work).

19 · VARIETIES OF DISCOURSE

There is a major qualitative difference between studying the components of English structure (as presented in Parts II, III, and IV) and studying the domains of English use. The structural properties of the language are many and complex, but at least they are finite and fairly easy to identify: there are only so many sounds, letters, and grammatical constructions, and although there is a huge vocabulary, at least the units (the lexemes, p.118) are determinate and manageable. None of this applies when we begin to investigate the way English is used: we are faced immediately with a bewildering array of situations, in which the features of spoken or written language appear in an apparently unlimited number of combinations and variations. Sometimes the result is a use of English, or of a feature of English, which is highly distinctive and easily explained, as is often encountered in regional dialects and in some of the more institutionalized areas of language use, such as religion and law. Rather more often, we are faced with usage that is subtle and indeterminate, and which demands detailed and lengthy analysis before we can reach an understanding of what its purpose is and how it works, as is often found in social dialects and in some of the more creative areas of language use, such as humour and literature.

Recent years have seen considerable progress in the study of language in use, and the emergence of several paradigms of enquiry, as people probe the topic from different points of view. Some linguists favour a 'bottom up' approach, studying the way sentences combine into larger units of discourse, and focusing on the role played by specific features of language in facilitating successful interaction. In this approach, whole books might be written on the communicative role of a tiny aspect of language (such as the use of *you know* in conversations). Other linguists work 'top down', beginning with a broadly defined category – such as an area of knowledge (science, politics), a social situation (gender, class), or a communicative genre (poetry, joke) – and examining the range of linguistic features which are found within it. Every conceivable kind of academic enquiry can be found, such as heavily illustrated descriptions of data samples, meticulous statistical or experimental analyses of individuals and groups, ambitious taxonomies, and highly abstract theoretical outlines. The various branches of linguistics that investigate the topic, such as sociolinguistics, stylistics, discourse analysis, pragmatics, and textlinguistics, present a remarkable range of methodologies and emphases. Part V cannot give a comprehensive account of all that goes on under these headings, but a serious effort is made in the following pages to represent the range of approaches which exist, and to give an indication, through the examples, of the complexity which lies behind the apparently simple notion of 'using English'.

GOOD MORNING, GOOD MORNING!

An apparently simple greeting or leave-taking can hide some quite subtle conventions of use. The chief daily greetings (*Good morning/afternoon/evening/night*), along with their regional and colloquial variants (such as Australian *G'day*, informal *'morning*, intimate *night-night*), do not function in identical ways.

• *Good morning* is conventionally used just once between any pair of people. If A meets B for the first time in the office at 9 o'clock, it would be appropriate for each to say *Good morning*. If A meets B again at 9.05, the greeting is not exchanged a second time. Indeed, B would find it distinctly odd if A were to repeat *Good morning*, and might even be upset or puzzled (if A were the boss, did he/she notice me? if B were the boss, is A trying to gain my attention for some reason?). However, the same constraint does not apply to *Good night*. If A meets B on leaving the office at 6 o'clock, then both are likely to say *Good night*. But if A forgets something, returns to the office to get it, and meets B again five minutes later, both may use the exchange again without a problem.

• Consciously deviant uses exist. There are circumstances where *Good morning* may be said in the afternoon, such as when someone sleeps in very late, and arrives in front of the family when mid-day is long gone. Correspondingly, *Good afternoon* can be said in the morning, such as by a sarcastic boss to a late-arriving employee. *Good night* can be said at any time of day, if someone seems about to fall asleep (spoken either by the tired one or by an observer). *Good evening* seems to be the most conventional of all the daily greetings, with hardly any likelihood of hearing it used at other times of day.

• *Good morning*, *Good afternoon*, and *Good evening* may be used as we arrive or as we depart, within the appropriate time frame; but *Good night* can be used only as a leave-taking. Similarly, only the first three can be used as an opening acknowledgement, such as when we arrive at a hotel or telephone a switchboard; even in the middle of the night, *Good evening* or *Good morning* will be used, never *Good night*. On one international television sports link-up, the commentator welcomed the worldwide viewing audience with the words *Hello, good evening, good afternoon, good morning, wherever you are*. He did not use *Good night* – which would have been an open invitation to viewers to switch off!

HELLO, GOOD EVENING, AND WELCOME!

This predictable greeting from British media personality David Frost became a catch phrase in the late 1960s. As a result, it was often used outside its original time frame – the only case the author has encountered of *good evening* being used in the morning.

POTTY THING TO SAY

The Duke of Dunstable, having read all he wanted to read in The Times and given up a half-hearted attempt to solve the crossword puzzle, had left the terrace and was making his way to Lady Constance's sitting-room. He was looking for someone to talk to, and Connie, though in his opinion potty, like all women, would be better than nothing....

He reached his destination, went in without knocking, found Lady Constance busy at her desk, and shouted 'Hoy!'

The monosyllable, uttered in her immediate rear in a tone of voice usually confined to the hog-calling industry of western America, made Lady Constance leap like a rising trout. But she was a hostess. Concealing her annoyance, not that that was necessary, for her visitor since early boyhood had never noticed when he was annoying anyone, she laid down her pen and achieved a reasonably bright smile.

'Good morning, Alaric.'

'What do you mean, good morning, as if you hadn't seen me before today?' said the Duke, his low opinion of the woman's intelligence confirmed. 'We met at breakfast, didn't we? Potty thing to say. No sense in it.' (P. G. Wodehouse, *Service with a Smile* (1961), Ch. 2.)

CONSTRUCTING A DISCOURSE

When we construct a piece of connected speech or writing, whether in monologue or dialogue (p. 294), we are constantly tapping the lexical and grammatical resources of the language to find ways of making our composition flow fluently while at the same time expressing the nuances we wish to convey. The examples on this page illustrate some of the remarkable range of devices which exist for this purpose, and which most adults use and respond to with unselfconscious ease.

57 WAYS OF SAYING NO

Yes and *no* are among the most commonly used words in the language, but they are often insufficient to capture the various degrees of affirmation or disinclination which we may wish to communicate by way of a response. The prosodic features of the language (intonation, in particular) play an important role in adding nuances to these words (p. 248), but our social survival requires linguistic competence in a much more extensive repertoire of responses. Here is a selection of alternatives for *no*, used as a response to a request for, say, the loan of some object. They express a range of emotions from embarrassed reluctance to forthright antagonism.

Inarticulate
Ah
Oh

Apologetic/ Uncomfortable
Alas
Can't help
Do me a favour
Give over
I'm afraid...
Sorry
Unfortunately

Evasive
Any other time...
Ask Arthur
'Bye
Must run
Not right now
Talk to me later
The thing is...
What a pity

Definite (with negative word)
No can do
No chance
No go
No way (José)
Never (in a thousand years)
Not in a million years
Not on your nelly
I should say not

Definite (no negative word)
Are you serious?
Drop dead
Fat chance
Get lost/knotted/stuffed...
God forbid
Hard cheese
I'd rather die
Impossible
Over my dead body
Push off
See you in hell first
Tough titty
Unthinkable
You must be joking
You've had it

Excuses
If it were up to me
I'm right out
It's more than my job's worth
It's not in my hands
Love to, but...

Euphemisms/Clichés
Chance would be a fine thing
Closed for business
Correspondence closed
If wish were father to the deed
Je regrette, mais...
Not my department
Not my remit
The editor regrets...
The umpire's decision is final
Would that it were possible

Parents begin to teach their children to read between the lines in this way at an early age. Here are some of the negative responses used by parents to a request by their 4-year-old for another biscuit.

You've just had one.
It'll be tea time soon.
Ask Daddy.
I haven't heard the magic word yet.

This is saying no without saying *no*.

THE QUEEN OF SHEBA, AND OTHERS

A scene from the British TV series *Yes, Prime Minister* showing the characters Prime Minister James Hacker (left, played by Paul Eddington) and Cabinet Secretary Sir Humphrey Appleby (Nigel Hawthorne).

Some of the most acute observers of the discourse rules of the language are comedians and humorists. Bending and breaking these rules is a comic's stock-in-trade. Here is a list prepared by British newspaper columnist Miles Kington in an honest effort to help tourists and students of English improve their ways of expressing disbelief in each other.

Oh?
Oh, really?
Well.
Well, well.
Well, I never.
Is that so?
How very interesting.
How very, *very* interesting.
Is that a fact?
Who'd have thought it?
You don't say?
Tell me more.
Be that as it may.
With the greatest respect...
That's all very well, but...
I beg leave to differ.
On the other hand...
Is it not possible that...?
If you say so.
I'll believe you – thousands wouldn't.
Well, I'll be...
Well, I'll be damned.
Well, I'll be hornswoggled.
You must be joking.
I have my doubts.
I begin to wonder.
Credibility gap ahead.
A likely story.
A tall tale.
I smell a rat.

Says you.
Some hope.
Pull the other one.
Tell that to the Marines.
Do you think I was born yesterday?
What do you take me for – a fool?
Think I'm wet behind the ears?
Are you trying to teach your grandmother to suck eggs?
Give us a break.
And I'm the Queen of Sheba.
Are you taking the Michael?
Are you extracting the urine?
And pigs can fly.
I should cocoa.
Liar liar, pants on fire!
Same to you, with knobs on.
You're talking through your hat.
You're putting me on.
You're winding me up.
Horsefruit, sailor!
Moonshine!
Baloney!
Fiddlesticks!
Stuff and nonsense!
Codswallop!
What a load of cobblers!
Tosh!
Balderdash!
Mullarkey!
Go and take a running jump!
Get lost!
If you believe that, you'll believe anything.
I bet you say that to all the girls.
That'll be the day.
Don't give me that.

You're asking me to swallow...?
You're going out on a limb here.
You would say that, wouldn't you?
Well, I'm not saying you're wrong.
Well, stranger things have happened at sea.
These are deep waters, Watson.
Much work still needs to be done on this theory.
While in no way doubting the essential veracity of what you say, I am not sure that this is the best moment to announce it, and it might be as well to put it on the back burner for a while, so I am going to recommend that you stall for a time by announcing a public enquiry, or a select committee hearing, or any of the usual delaying tactics, before we ask the media and the public to swallow a lie of quite this enormity...
Are you not being economical with the truth?
...with the actualité?
I can see what you're getting at.
I can see what you're trying to say.
I can see the point.
I see...
I understand...
I'm sure you're right...
Yes, sir...
Yes, Minister...
Yes, Prime Minister...
Of course, Your Majesty...

MICROLINGUISTIC STUDIES

There is only one way to establish the exact function of the various elements which contribute to the organization of discourse, and that is to subject a substantial amount of linguistic data to a microlinguistic analysis. In the case of spoken discourse (p. 291), a recording of reasonable acoustic quality needs to be made, then transcribed with maximum attention to detail, paying particular attention to its pauses, interruptions, false starts, hesitations, and other such features. Ideally, a full prosodic transcription should be included (p. 248), though the level of specialized training required to hear prosodic effects accurately means that this is not always a practical option. Each instance of a particular item of interest is noted – the word *well*, the hesitation noise *er*, the clause *you see* – and its context examined to establish what role it may be playing at that point in the discourse. An immediate intuitive response to the item can be sharpened by manipulating the data in various ways, such as omitting the item to see how this affects the meaning or acceptability of the utterance, or contrasting it with another item. By comparing a large number of instances, the aim is to arrive at an informative classification of uses, and to develop a theory of the organization of discourse which can then be tested against other kinds of utterance. After more than a decade of research, there are now several theoretical frameworks which have emerged in this way.

A SAMPLE TRANSCRIPTION

A few lines illustrating the potential complexity of a discourse transcript, including prosodic features (from J. J. Gumperz, 1982, p. 105). Note the way the speech of the two speakers (B and A) is laid out so that the points of overlap can be clearly seen. For further illustration of intonation contrasts, see p. 248.

[overlapping speech
…   relatively long pause
/   minor boundary marker
//   major boundary marker
ˋ   low falling tone
ˊ   high falling tone
ˇ   falling rising tone
ˆ   rising falling tone
–   level tone
⌐   upward pitch register shift
ˈ   high secondary stress
ˌ   low secondary stress
"   (doubled mark) extra loud
acc   accelerated tempo
dec   decelerated tempo

B: yeh but / sometimes I get wonderin' whether /

   it's ˌall reˌlated // ⌐cause

A: but"ultimately it iṣ / rı̂ght //

   I mean ˈeverybody started out / ˈpeople who were in

   nineteen hundred /

   they did ẹverythin' / rı̂ght //
   acc

B: yeh but ˈthat's thèn / ˌthat's not nôw / ⌐now
     dec   dec

A: ⌐but ˌultimately it

   they it … / so it's ˌall spread out nōw //

DISCOURSE DIRECTION

Some items play a particular role in controlling the direction of movement within a discourse. They signal such broad organizational features as topic identification, change, and exemplification, and such logical relationships as topic contrast and reinforcement. It is never possible to present a truly simple account, as several items have 'fuzzy' meaning (p. 169), and analytical categories (such as evaluating and summarizing) are not always easy to apply consistently. Nonetheless, several studies have provided useful first approximations.

One such approach focuses on lexical phrases (p. 163), recognizing eight types of what it calls *macro-organizers*. These are seen to operate at two levels: *global* features determine the overall shape of the discourse; *local* features mark changes of direction operating in a more restricted way.

Global macro-organizers
Topic markers: let's look at X; what do you think of X?; have you heard about X?; let me start with X
Topic shifters: by the way; let's move on to Y; that reminds me of Y; this is off the subject, but Y
Summarizers: in a nutshell; that's about it; in effect; to cut a long story short; what I'm trying to say is Z

Local macro-organizers
Exemplifiers: in other words; for instance; to give an example; it's like A
Relators: nonetheless; however; and also; it has to do with B; it's the same with B
Evaluators: I think/don't think that C; as far as I can see; seems to me; I'm absolutely certain
Qualifiers: the catch is; it depends on D; that's true but D; this doesn't mean that D
Asides: where was I?; I guess that's beside the point; I'm getting ahead of myself here

The following extract from a meeting between a teacher (T) and a student (S) to talk about a thesis shows the use of several of these organizational features. This exchange is typical of a discourse where serious business is being transacted, and where care needs to be taken (notwithstanding the informal style) with the manipulation of meaning. There are far fewer such features in the more loosely structured language of everyday conversation.
(After J. R. Nattinger & J. S. DeCarrico, 1992.)

T: What I wanted mainly to talk about was ——— Topic marker
your part on the review of the literature.
It seems to me that here you just list things, ——— Evaluator
that here you list all this stuff you read, but
you don't really discuss it.

Clarification ——— S: Huh? I'm not sure what you mean. I do
discuss it…see, in this part here, I talk about it.

T: Well, you sort of do. Here, you say that ——— Qualifier
these theories are the leading ones, in the
current literature these are important.
However, that's not all you need to say here, ——— Relator
you need to say that these are competing
theories, or at least that they are different ——— Qualifier
theories, and also you need to say which you ——— Relator
choose to base your study on. Not only that, ——— Relator
you have to say why you support that one…

Comprehension check ——— you need to say why. OK? Do you see?
Accepting response ——— S: Yeah, I guess so. OK I'll try.

T: OK so (*level intonation*) you need to do ——— Summarizer
more than just list these and tell that they're
important, you need to discuss them more and
say why you're basing your study on a certain
one. OK, now (*falling intonation*)… I also ——— Topic shifter
wanted to talk to you about your hypotheses. ——— Topic shifter
I don't think they are written well enough, ——— Evaluator
they're not quite clear enough. How about ——— Exemplifier
1 and 4? They seem to me to contradict each ——— Evaluator
other.

Accepting response ——— S: Oh yeah, that isn't what I mean… I guess
maybe they do, I guess so.

T: OK so (*level intonation*) you need to state ——— Summarizer
each one more clearly…

OH YES?

Oh is surprisingly frequent in conversation, whether formal or informal, but pinning down its function proves to be extremely difficult. It has little by way of a dictionary meaning which we can hold on to. *Oh!* on its own, as a minor sentence (p. 216), is relatively straightforward: it is an exclamation, expressing a strong emotion whose exact value depends on the choice of intonation and facial expression (p. 248). What is less obvious is why we use *oh* to begin an utterance – sometimes followed by a brief pause, sometimes not.

Does he like opera?
Oh maybe he's too young.

Here the word does not have any exclamatory force. It may be said with very little emphasis, often quite rapidly. In such circumstances it seems to be more like an introductory particle. The question is, what function does this particle have?

In a detailed study of *oh* and related words (e.g. *well, so, now, y'know*), American linguist Deborah Schiffrin argues the case for a discourse function, identifying several types of context in which it commonly occurs. (All the following examples are taken from her recordings of informal conversation, with a summary of preceding context in square brackets, where needed. Transcription conventions are unchanged.

A colon marks a lengthened syllable.)

Correcting oneself

I think it was in seventeen: fifteen, or seventeen fifty five. I'm not sure when. Eh: **oh** I'm wrong. Seventeen seventeen.

Correcting someone else

[How about 'Death of a Salesman'?]
A: Well that was a show, sure.
B: **Oh** that was a movie too.

Requesting clarification

A: Is there anyone you would uh: talk about–
B: **Oh** you mean outside?

Request for elaboration

A: Does she come here or:
B: No we go out to lunch, mostly, I stop over there.
A: **Oh**, where do you like to go?

Suddenly remembered question

Oh listen, I forgot to ask you…

Knowledge re-orientation

A: How can I get an appointment t'go down there t'bring my son on a tour?
B: **Oh** I didn't even know they gave tours!

Unanticipated information

Oh I didn't know that.

Display of recognition

A: We ate at the – we ate at the: eh that Shanty? Seafood Shanty?
B: **Oh** yeh, I've heard that's good.

Receiving new information

A: Hey, Henry, your girl-friend's here!
B: [from living room] **Oh** yeh?

Marking an intense reaction

[Girls' High still has a reputa-tion.]
A: But, like it did?
B: **Oh** yes. Girls' High is still rated. Y'know Girls' High is rated higher than Central.

Some of these uses are easy to recognize, such as the *oh* of surprise (*Oh yeah!* = 'Gosh I never knew that') or bel-ligerence (*Oh yeah!* = 'You wanna make trouble?') or the *oh* of strong intensity (*Oh really?, Oh God!, Oh c'mon!*); others require more reflection before we can consciously identify the nuance; but all of the pro-posed categories occur with some frequency, and any spontaneous conversational exchange of some length will provide copious examples.

Why oh?

Is it possible to find a gener-alization which will apply to all of these *oh*-using con-texts? Schiffrin believes that they are all instances of a single phenomenon – a signal that speakers are preparing to shift their ori-entation to take account of the information they have just received. We use *oh*, in other words, when we become aware that our knowledge is in a state of change, and are prepared to take the new knowledge on

board. It may be a reformu-lation of what we already know, or brand new infor-mation; it may come from other people in the conver-sation or from within our-selves. Either way, we find ourselves faced with the task of replacing one piece of information by another, and the *oh* tells our listener that we are ready to carry this out.

The use of *oh* therefore has an important role in dis-course interaction. Like *well*, and certain other response words, it signals the nature of our participation in the dialogue. It lets our inter-locutor know that we are actively paying special atten-tion to the point which has just been made. It also shows that we are aligning our-

selves towards the other's point of view. To leave *oh* out can make an utterance sound immediately more abrupt or argumentative.

It should therefore be plain why we use *oh* so often in informal (friendly) conversa-tion. The whole point of a conversation is to tell each other things. The state of knowledge of each partici-pant is therefore continually changing. *Oh* marks the points where speaker and hearer are jointly focusing their attention on matters of real concern, where the information content is in the process of change. *Oh* is, in short, a marker of informa-tion management.

(After D. Schiffrin, 1987, Ch. 4.)

PLEASE

The most interesting property about *please* (apart from its 'magical' social role in persuading others to cooperate) is its discourse function. From a structural point of view, *please* is unique.

• It is not easily assigned to any word class: gram-mars tend to call it an adverb (p. 211), but it is like no other adverb. It cannot, for example, be modi-fied by *very*: we can say *very kindly*, but not **very please*.
• It can act as a minor sentence in its own right:

A: Would you like some tea?
B: Please.

• When functioning within a sentence, it is not constrained by the syntactic type (p. 218). It may

occur with statements (*I'd like some pudding, please*), questions (*May I have some pudding, please?*), commands (*Give me some pudding, please*), and moodless clauses (*Pudding, please*).
• It has no easily stateable dictionary meaning. If we were to try to define the 'meaning' of *please* at all, it would have to be in terms of what it *does* – to persuade someone to do something.

Are there any sentences, then, where we may *not* say *please*? That there are many such con-straints can be seen from the following:

• He ate more pudding, please.
• I promise you can have some more pudding, please.
• Would you like some more pudding, please?
• Do you want to come to a party, please?

• Give me more pudding or I'll hit you, please.
• I think you're beautiful, please.

These sentences are, respectively, a narrative state-ment, a promise, an offer, an invitation, a threat, and a compliment. *Please* cannot be used with such sentences, but only with those which are interpretable as a request. The point is not simply a matter of common sense, as can be seen from the errors made by non-native learners of English, who often produce sentences similar to the unacceptable ones above.

In short, *please* is an item whose function is entirely defined by its role in discourse – and more-over, in discourse of a very particular kind (request-ing). More than any other word in English, it is a discourse-identifying feature. (After M. Stubbs, 1983, Ch. 4.)

TEXTS AND VARIETIES

The notion of 'using English' involves much more than using our knowledge of linguistic structure (such as the features described on pp. 286–9) to create and interpret sequences of sentences and conversational interactions. It also involves being aware of the range of situations in which English can be used in a distinctive and predictable way, and of the possibilities available to us when we wish to produce or respond to creative uses of the language.

These situations are enormously varied, and not always easy to define, but we can begin to make sense of them by looking at the communicative products, or *texts*, with which they are associated, and at the linguistic features which define these texts' identity. Prayers, posters, road-signs, lectures, sports commentaries, novels, speeches, interviews, and recipes are all texts, by this account. They each have a particular communicative purpose – easier to state in relation to a road-sign than a novel, perhaps, but a communicative purpose nonetheless. They are also relatively self-contained units of discourse, whether spoken or written, and each to some degree has a definable linguistic identity.

Qualifications such as 'relatively' and 'to some degree' are important, because not all texts have boundaries which are equally easy to identify, or use language which is equally distinctive: for example, the boundaries of written texts are typically more determinate than spoken ones, and (within speech) most sermons have a much clearer beginning and end than most conversations. But when investigating uses of English, it is usually practicable to work with a hierarchy of the following notions: *situations* give rise to *texts*, and texts make use of sets of *distinctive linguistic features*. A particular set of these features, representing a category of text, is known as a *variety*. To take just one example: *O living God* is a distinctive feature (a vocative with *O*, p. 220) of a *prayer* text which is found in a *religious* situation: it is therefore a feature of the variety of *religious language*.

Sociolinguistic and stylistic features

The features which identify a variety are not features of the language as a whole, occurring anywhere the language is spoken or written, in all possible social situations. Variety features depend on the presence of certain factors in the social situation. Classifications of these factors vary, but it is possible to group them into two general types, which give rise to what are here called *sociolinguistic* and *stylistic* features.

• *Sociolinguistic features* relate to very broad situational constraints on language use, and chiefly identify the regional and social varieties of the language (e.g. Canadian, Cockney, upper-class, educated).

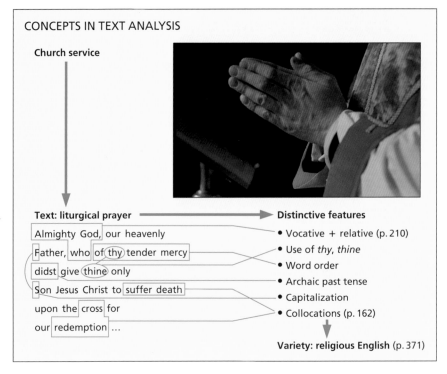

CONCEPTS IN TEXT ANALYSIS

Church service

Text: liturgical prayer → Distinctive features

Almighty God, our heavenly Father, who of thy tender mercy didst give thine only Son Jesus Christ to suffer death upon the cross for our redemption ...

• Vocative + relative (p. 210)
• Use of *thy, thine*
• Word order
• Archaic past tense
• Capitalization
• Collocations (p. 162)

Variety: religious English (p. 371)

They are relatively permanent, background features of the spoken or written language, over which we have relatively little conscious control. We tend not to change our regional or class way of speaking as we go about our daily business, and usually do not even realize that it is there.

• *Stylistic features* relate to constraints on language use that are much more narrowly constrained, and identify personal preferences in usage (poetry, humour) or the varieties associated with occupational groups (lecturers, lawyers, journalists). They are relatively temporary features of our spoken or written language, over which we do have some degree of conscious control. We often adopt different group uses of language as we go through our day (e.g. family, job, religion, sports), and frequently change our speaking or writing style to make a particular effect (as when we put on an accent while telling a story, or play with language in an informal letter, p. 402).

The following pages illustrate many uses of English, manifested in a selection of texts associated with both spoken and written varieties of the language. Chapters 20 and 21 deal with sociolinguistic variation, chiefly of a regional and social kind. Chapters 22 and 23 deal with stylistic variation, with particular reference to occupational and personal factors. But we begin with a review of two very general dimensions which must always be taken into account when considering the characteristics of a language variety: the chosen medium of communication (speech vs writing), and the type of participation involved (monologue vs dialogue).

SPEECH AND WRITING

Spoken and written language display a number of important differences, over and above the obvious distinction in physical form – that speech uses the medium of 'phonic substance', typically air-pressure movements produced by the vocal organs, whereas writing uses the medium of 'graphic substance', typically marks on a surface made by a hand using an implement. These differences are chiefly to do with language use, arising out of the fact that speakers and writers are operating in fundamentally different communicative situations. But there are also several differences in language structure: the grammar and vocabulary of speech is by no means the same as that of writing, nor do the contrasts available in phonology (§17) correspond to those available in graphology (§18).

Writing is sometimes thought to be little more than 'speech written down'. Speech, correspondingly, is often judged by its closeness to writing (p. 236). Neither position is valid. The two mediums, though historically related, function as independent methods of communication. There are few circumstances where we are faced with a genuine choice between speaking or writing. Normally, whenever two people are in earshot, they speak to each other. Only very special circumstances – wicked children passing secret messages in class; partners who are 'not talking' to each other; a jury foreman passing a verdict to a court official; someone who cannot speak or hear (and who is unable to use sign language) – would motivate the enormous trouble of writing down what we wish to 'say'. Conversely, people who are separated by distance in space or time, and who lack electronic means of communication (or the money to use them), have no alternative but to write to each other.

Moreover, the status of the two mediums is not the same. Written formulations, such as contracts, are usually required to make agreements legally binding. Historical documents, ancient inscriptions, original manuscripts, first editions, sacred writings, and other such material are given a kind of respect which is rarely accorded to speech (though archives of recorded sound are beginning to introduce a balance). Above all, written English provides the standard that society values, and its relative permanence and worldwide circulation have given it a very special place within the life of the community (p. 110).

TWO ELECTRONIC EXCEPTIONS TO THE RULE

Speech is normally interactive – but not when talking to a telephone answering machine, where we have to produce a monologue while pretending it is a dialogue (p. 294). This is not something which comes easily to most people – though abilities improve with practice.

Writing is not an interactive medium in the same way as speech, because of the delay in getting the written message to the reader; and in many kinds of writing there is little expectation of a reply (none at all, *pace* the other sense of 'medium', when the writer is dead). But the advent of electronic mail and the fax machine have altered the time parameters dramatically. Questions and answers fly around the world now which are very similar to those that would be used if the participants were talking to each other (p. 390).

DIFFERENCES BETWEEN SPEECH AND WRITING

• Speech is time-bound, dynamic, transient. Is is part of an interaction in which both participants are usually present, and the speaker has a particular addressee (or several addressees) in mind.

• The spontaneity and speed of most speech exchanges make it difficult to engage in complex advance planning. The pressure to think while talking promotes looser construction, repetition, rephrasing, and comment clauses (p. 229). Intonation and pause divide long utterances into manageable chunks, but sentence boundaries are often unclear (p. 214).

• Because participants are typically in face-to-face interaction, they can rely on such extralinguistic cues as facial expression and gesture to aid meaning (feedback). The lexicon of speech is often characteristically vague, using words which refer directly to the situation (*deictic* expressions, such as *that one*, *in here*, *right now*).

• Many words and constructions are characteristic of (especially informal) speech. Lengthy coordinate sentences are normal (p. 226), and are often of considerable complexity. Nonsense vocabulary (p. 130) is not usually written, and may have no standard spelling (*whatchamacallit*). Obscenity may be replaced by graphic euphemism (*f****). Slang and grammatical informality, such as contracted forms (*isn't, he's*) may be frowned upon.

• Speech is very suited to social or 'phatic' functions, such as passing the time of day, or any situation where casual and unplanned discourse is desirable. It is also good at expressing social relationships, and personal opinions and attitudes, due to the vast range of nuances which can be expressed by the prosody and accompanying non-verbal features.

• There is an opportunity to rethink an utterance while it is in progress (starting again, adding a qualification). However, errors, once spoken, cannot be withdrawn (the one exception is when a sound engineer performs wonders of auditory plastic surgery on a tape-recording of nonfluent speech); the speaker must live with the consequences. Interruptions and overlapping speech are normal and highly audible.

• Unique features of speech include most of the prosody (p. 248). The many nuances of intonation, as well as contrasts of loudness, tempo, rhythm, and other tones of voice cannot be written down with much efficiency.

• Writing is space-bound, static, permanent. It is the result of a situation in which the writer is usually distant from the reader, and often does not know who the reader is going to be (except in a very vague sense, as in poetry).

• Writing allows repeated reading and close analysis, and promotes the development of careful organization and compact expression, with often intricate sentence structure. Units of discourse (sentences, paragraphs) are usually easy to identify through punctuation and layout.

• Lack of visual contact means that participants cannot rely on context to make their meaning clear; nor is there any immediate feedback. Most writing therefore avoids the use of deictic expressions, which are likely to be ambiguous. Writers must also anticipate the effects of the time-lag between production and reception, and the problems posed by having their language read and interpreted by many recipients in diverse settings.

• Some words and constructions are characteristic of writing, such as multiple instances of subordination in the same sentence (p. 70), elaborately balanced syntactic patterns, and the long (often multi-page) sentences found in some legal documents. Certain items of vocabulary are never spoken, such as the longer names of chemical compounds.

• Writing is very suited to the recording of facts and the communication of ideas, and to tasks of memory and learning. Written records are easier to keep and scan; tables demonstrate relationships between things; notes and lists provide mnemonics; and text can be read at speeds which suit a person's ability to learn.

• Errors and other perceived inadequacies in our writing can be eliminated in later drafts without the reader ever knowing they were there. Interruptions, if they have occurred while writing, are also invisible in the final product.

• Unique features of writing include pages, lines, capitalization, spatial organization, and several aspects of punctuation. Only a very few graphic conventions relate to prosody, such as question marks and underlining for emphasis. Several written genres (e.g. timetables, graphs, complex formulae) cannot be read aloud efficiently, but have to be assimilated visually.

MIXED MEDIUM

The distinction between the medium of speech and the medium of writing at first sight seems clear-cut: either things are written or they are spoken. In practice, the situation is considerably more complex. When we choose to use either one of these mediums, the reason for our choice may require us to bear in mind the existence of the other, and that then influences the nature of the language we use. The figure below summarizes the chief alternatives which are likely to produce distinctive styles of spoken or written English, and the text illustrates some typical situations under each heading.

TELEPROMPTING

A television presenter facing a teleprompter, also called (from the manufacturers' names) an *autocue* or *autoscript*. The text is typed on rolls of transparent material, and projected as large type, enabling the presenters to read it. It is so positioned that they can see it while facing the camera, conveying the illusion of direct speech to the viewer. Any style of text can be used – informal or formal, monologue or dialogue.

SPEECH

If we choose to speak, we may intend our utterance to be heard immediately. This is the normal state of affairs. But there are several interesting alternatives.

• We may intend our utterance to be heard at a later point in time, as when we use a telephone answering machine (p. 291).
• We may intend that what we say should *not* be heard, as when we speak *sotto voce* ('under our breath'). There are of course two further options here: the genuine *sotto voce*, which our listener does not hear, but which nonetheless makes us feel better for having said it; and the pseudo *sotto voce*, which we intend our listener to hear (usually for jocular purposes). Unintentionally overheard *sotto voce* can lead to trouble for the speaker, though this depends on non-linguistic factors (such as the relative physical build of speaker and listener).
• We may intend our utterance to be written down. If so, there are two further possibilities: we may leave the task of representing what we say to the listener, thus speaking in a relatively 'natural' way (as in some magazine interviews or police statements); or we may speak 'carefully', instructing the writer to ignore non-fluencies and errors (as in letter dictation).

WRITING

If we choose to write, we normally intend that what we have written should be read; and the norm, at least since late classical times, has been for the recipient to read silently. Here too there are several alternatives.

• We may choose to write with the intention that what we have written should be read aloud. If so, we must make a further choice. We may write in such a way that our end-product, when read aloud, will sound like written language. It will be relatively formal and controlled. Those who prepare the text for radio news-readers fall into this category. Alternatively, we may write in such a way that the end-product will not sound scripted, as in those who write material for radio and television drama. The latter are not always successful, of course.
• We may choose to write with the intention that only *some* of what we have written should be read aloud, the rest being ignored. An example of this rather unusual situation can be found in a radio channel's continuity studio, where information of potential interest to the listener (e.g. about the weather, traffic delays) is continually coming in on a television screen or being passed to the presenter in note form. The presenter selects what there is time to incorporate into the running order of the programme. The material arrives in a variety of styles, often highly elliptical, reflecting the ongoing rush of the live broadcast situation.

MIXING

There remain a few situations where speaking and writing are mutually dependent: the language used is partly made up of speaking/ listening activities and partly of reading/writing activities, in proportions that are sometimes difficult to disentangle. There are three chief possibilities, depending on the nature of the addressee.

• We may address ourselves in this mixed way, as when we compile a shopping list simultaneously questioning ourselves about what we want while writing down some of what we say.
• We may address a single listener, as when people work together in a co-authorship situation, jointly poring over a text (an academic paper, a sitcom script) and each contributing suggestions to it.
• We may address a group of listeners, as when a teacher is using the blackboard, keeping up a running commentary to a class while doing so.

In such cases, an audio recording would tell only half the story, as would a photograph of the written work. Both mediums jointly work together to produce a successful use of language.

CLASSIFICATION OF MIXED MEDIUM TEXTS

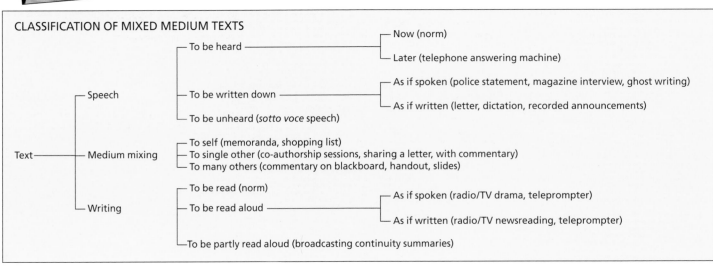

HOW TO LECTURE

Sir Lawrence Bragg (1891–1971), joint Nobel prize-winner with his father at the age of 25, and later Cavendish Professor of Experimental Physics at Cambridge. As resident professor at the Royal Institution (1953–66) he inaugurated the weekly 'schools lectures' for children, and became widely known for the clarity of his own lecturing style. He wrote a number of papers on the topic of lecturing (following in the tradition of Michael Faraday, who was also much interested in the subject, p. 87), and his remarks provide a relevant perspective on the different roles of spontaneous vs scripted speech. His comments on the nature of transcribed spontaneous speech are echoed elsewhere in this book (p. 214).

I feel so strongly about the wrongness of reading a lecture that my language may seem immoderate. I think it is a dreadful thing to do, something out of keeping with all that a lecture should mean. The spoken word and the written word are quite different arts. Though the reader can pause and go back to a passage he has found difficult, the listener cannot do so and may lose the thread of the argument. It is boring in a written account to be repetitious; it is right in a spoken account to put a key idea in several ways to make sure the audience has grasped the point. When a man writes out his lecture he inevitably writes it as if it were to be read, not heard. The ideas follow each other too fast. It is, of course, far easier for the lecturer to read than for him to 'think on his feet' by constructing his sentences on the spot, because he can frame his sentences at his leisure. I realize that many lecturers read their material from a feeling of modesty, thinking they will give a poor rendering if they have no script. While appreciating their reluctance, I am sure they are wrong. I feel that to collect an audience and then read one's material is like inviting a friend to go for a walk and asking him not to mind if you go alongside him in your car. It is easy for the lecturer to deliver well-considered rounded phrases, but the audience has to follow and to think. If someone says, 'I dare not talk. I must write it out,' I am tempted to ask, 'Then why lecture? Why not send a written account to your friends and let them read it comfortably at home; instead of dragging them all out to a lecture hall to listen to your reading the very same thing?'

We come back, it seems to me, to the essential feature of a lecture which justifies bringing the lecturer and his audience together. It is the emotional contact between lecturer and audience. If a lecturer has to find his words as he speaks, he will be automatically restrained from going too fast because he is thinking along with his audience. Every lecturer knows the trick of watching a few sympathetic faces in the audience and of judging (by noting their response) whether he has been successful in making his points or whether he must put things another way. A lecturer who reads is earthbound to his script, but the lecturer who talks can enjoy a wonderful feeling of being airborne and in complete accord with his audience. It is the greatest reward of lecturing.

Footnote

It is my experience that when I have to read a literal transcript of one of my lectures I am quite appalled, even when I have felt that the actual talk was rather a good one. The account taken from the tape-record is ungrammatical, with jerky unfinished sentences and repetitions, and one blushes to read it. I have found that most of my colleagues have had the same experience. There may be some speakers whose language is impeccable in written form, but I am not convinced that the polished talk is necessarily the best. A talk can be 'craggy' and yet very effective, just as a bust in which the artist has thumbed on irregular chunks of clay is often a far more brilliant likeness than one which is carefully smoothed to the finest detail. It is more 'live' just because it leaves more to the imagination it excites.

Advice to Lecturers

OVERLAPS BETWEEN SPEECH AND WRITING

The differences noted between speech and writing on p. 291 are best thought of as trends rather than as absolute distinctions. For example, while it is true that a great deal of speech depends on a shared context, and thus uses many situation-dependent expressions (such as *this/that*, *here/there*), it is not true of all speech. A spoken lecture is usually quite self-contained, except when it refers to hand-outs or board diagrams. On the other hand, such written material as office memos and personal letters regularly depend on a shared context. 'Follow that!', begins one informal letter. 'Have you got one for me too?', begins another.

It is therefore very likely that there are few, if any, absolute differences between speech and writing, and that no single parameter of linguistic variation can distinguish all spoken from all written genres. Rather, the range of potentially distinguishing linguistic features provides a 'pool' of resources which are utilized by spoken and written genres in various ways. The different genres of speech and writing always seem to overlap in the way they use a particular linguistic variable. For example, using the criterion of explicitness of reference mentioned above, one study showed that, while written genres do tend to have high scores (i.e. their reference is less situation-dependent) and spoken genres have low scores (i.e. their reference is more situation-dependent), there were several exceptions. Some kinds of spoken language (public speeches and interviews) had relatively high scores, whereas some kinds of written language (types of fiction, in particular) had relatively low scores. It might be thought that, in a diagram such as the one below, which represents the scores obtained on a single scale, all the written varieties should be above zero and all the spoken varieties below. In practice, an overlapping situation obtains. (After D. Biber, 1988.)

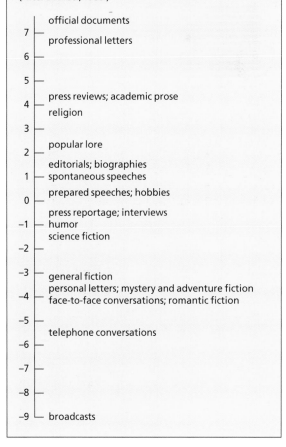

MONOLOGUE AND DIALOGUE

A factor which fundamentally influences the linguistic character of a use of language is the number of participants involved in the activity. Theoretically, the distinction is clear-cut: there is monologue, in which only one person is involved in the linguistic act, and there is dialogue, in which (typically) two people are involved. We would also expect there to be a close correspondence with the two categories of medium (p. 291): monologue is associated with the activities of writing and reading, and dialogue with speaking and listening. As with so many of the theoretical distinctions presented in this book, the outline is broadly correct, but there are several cases where the distinctions become blurred or overlap, and it is these which provide some of the most interesting examples of the way we use language.

We can see how some of these cases arise by paying careful attention to definition. Monologue does not mean that a person is alone, as is typical of most authorial writing – the 'lonely profession', as it has been called. It refers rather to an activity in which the language producer does not expect a response, even though an audience may be present (and even though that audience may, from time to time, respond, as in the heckling which can accompany a political speech). In a monologue, the language is conceived as a self-contained presentation. By contrast, it is of the essence of dialogue that the participants expect each other to respond, and it contains many linguistic features which enable this to happen (most obviously, question forms). The interesting cases, accordingly, are those where the situation imposes special demands or constraints upon the speaker/writer, and interferes with the normal expectations of response.

Not all writers believe that their occupation is a monologue. Laurence Sterne (1713–68) certainly did not:

Writing, when properly managed, (as you may be sure I think mine is) is but a different name for conversation.

(*Tristram Shandy*, 1760–7, Book I)

SPOKEN MONOLOGUE

A great deal of spoken monologue is written English read aloud, as in this example of the Queen's speech at the opening of Parliament – a case where the expectation of response is as near to a theoretical zero point as it is possible to get. (To emphasize the fact that this is spoken language, the transcription makes no use of capital letters. Units of intonation (p. 248) are shown by /; short pauses by .; and longer pauses by -, – and --. For the full transcription, see D. Crystal & D. Davy, 1969, p. 234.)

my government / . reaffirm their support / . for the defence of the free world / - the basic concept / . of the atlantic alliance / – - and they will continue to play their full part / in the north atlantic treaty organization / - and in other organizations / for collective defence / – - they will review defence policy / - to ensure / by relating / our commitments / . and our resources / - that my armed forces / . are able to discharge / their many tasks / overseas / - with the greatest effectiveness . and economy /

WRITTEN DIALOGUE

Questionnaires and registration forms are classically dialogic in form, their whole purpose being to elicit a response. They represent, however, a rather unusual kind of dialogue, with one participant asking all the questions. The extract is taken from the application form enabling people to register under the UK Data Protection Act (1984).

WRITTEN MONOLOGUE

This page.

SPOKEN DIALOGUE

Everyday informal conversation is the archetypal case of spoken dialogue. (Transcription conventions are the same, with the addition of punctuation to show a question, and the use of parentheses to show a response that does not interrupt the speaker's flow. For the full transcription, see D. Crystal & D. Davy, 1975, p. 65.)

A: but er . you're teaching – erm at a grammar school / aren't you? /
B: yes / . yes /
A: well what do you think about sex education / – do you think that er it er I mean . there's been a great hooha about it /
(B: m /)
A: recently / hasn't there? / and erm - er about a film that was made / and so on /
B: mhm / –
A: well what are your views on it? /
A: I find that – with so many of these problems / . marriage / sex education / . as soon as you try and make it . a sort of formal lesson / – the whole thing falls flat / –
B: m /

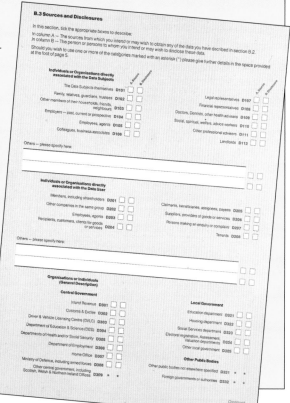

UNEXPECTED FEATURES OF DIALOGUE

When we investigate how dialogues actually work, as found in recordings of natural speech, we are often in for a surprise. We are used to seeing dialogue in contexts where the language has been carefully crafted, such as the script of a play or the conversations in a language teaching textbook. Such dialogues may be very effective for their purpose, but they are usually a long way from what can happen in everyday conversation. The stereotype is that people speak in complete sentences, taking well-defined turns, carefully listening to each other, and producing balanced amounts of speech. The reality is that people often share in the sentences they produce, interrupt each other, do not pay attention to everything that is said, and produce a discourse where the contributions of the participants are wildly asymmetrical. Yet all of this nonetheless produces a perfectly normal, successful conversation.

THE STEREOTYPE

A page from Book 1 of a successful course for foreign learners of English, launched in 1968. The controlled nature of the dialogue appeals to the non-native learner; but there is still a considerable distance between this style of interaction and real conversational English. The writers of the course would be aware of this – it is only Book 1, after all – but it is surprising how many people think that real conversation is like this all the time.

In the whole of this section, which continues for another half a dozen exchanges, Martin speaks 11 times and Jillian 10; he produces 207 words, and she 211. It is a perfectly balanced conversation. There are no interruptions, or speaking at the same time, and the two participants respond carefully to each other. Notwithstanding the content of this passage, their relationship seems safe enough.

Contrast the response pattern of the following extract of dialogue from the author's four-member household around the dinner table, on one of the rare occasions when all were present. The participants are a father (D), a mother (M), a boy (Ben, aged 16), and a girl (Lucy, aged 18):

D (*to Lucy*): Are you going out this evening?

(*to which Lucy 'replies'*)

L: Where did I put my green skirt?

(*to which Ben 'replies'*)

B: Pass the salt, Luce.

(*to which M 'replies', talking to D*)

M: She can never find that skirt.

(*to which Lucy 'replies', to herself*)

L: I think I put it in the wash.

(*to which D 'replies', talking to Ben*)

D: There you are. (*and passes the salt*)

12

JILLIAN   There. There's your father, his wife, his brother and his sister. Good. Hey, Martin, who are those?

MARTIN   Oh, yes. This old woman is my grandmother, and here's her husband, my grandfather. These are very old pictures. Put them on a new page, Jill.

JILLIAN   Very well. Now we have your grandfather and grandmother on this page and their sons and daughters on that page.

MARTIN   Oh, look at this, Jill.

JILLIAN   Wait a minute. I'm still writing. Now, what is it?

MARTIN   Here's that old photograph of us. You are practising tennis and I'm holding your arm. Here, look. It's a very bad photograph of me. Throw it away.

JILLIAN   Don't be silly, Martin. Give it to me, please. Yes, it is a bad picture of you. Why are you opening your mouth? But it's a very good photograph of me. No, don't throw this away. But who's this, Martin? Look at the girl in this photograph. Who is she? Martin, you aren't looking at her. Martin, your face is red.

MARTIN   Oh, I'm sorry, that's Margaret.

JILLIAN   She's very pretty. Is she your cousin?

MARTIN   Er, no. She's an old friend. Put her on a new page in the album,

86

THE REALITY

In many dialogues, the point of conversational turn (when one person stops talking and another one starts) often does not coincide with the end of a sentence. Rather there is a shared expectation that both people will be involved in completing the sentence. This is only likely to be frequent between people who know each other well, and in such circumstances the participants may be totally unconscious that it is happening at all. Twins, for example, regularly complete each other's sentences in this way. Conversely, it can be extremely irritating to be talking to an acquaintance who tries to complete your sentences when you are perfectly capable of finishing them off yourself.

The following extract was based on some of the features observed by US linguist Gene Lerner in a 1991 study of what he called 'sentences in progress'. It is somewhat artificial, in that the various non-fluencies which characterize normal spontaneous speech have been omitted, and the piece has been written to illustrate several features in a short space; but all of the sentence-completing features shown here reflect those which have been observed in naturalistic recordings, and provide a notable contrast with the finished conversational turns of most stage and textbook dialogues.

A: …so he was talking about sentences in progress.

B: Sentences in?

A: Progress. It's where one person starts, and another

B: Oh yes, I see, chips in and finishes it off. I know what you mean. I've got a friend who's always doing it. You're making a point, and then he comes in and finishes it off for you. Uncanny, sometimes, how he's able to anticipate exactly

A: What you're going to say. I know. Some people are almost – almost –

B: Obsessive

A: Yes, obsessive about it. It's as if they can't stop. I must say I find it very irritating. But Lerner's paper isn't about the obsessive types. He's suggesting that joint sentence formulation is quite common in everyday informal conversation, and that there are certain syntactic strategies which promote this kind of collaboration between speakers,

B: Such as…

A: Well, starting a sentence with an if-clause, for instance, especially if you're being a bit hesitant, thinking something out as you go along…

B: The other speaker is likely to chip in and finish it off

A: And the first speaker is happy enough for this to happen, because the point is made, and

B: Even better, the other person is making the point for him,

A: Which is what any conversationalist is happy to have happen. After all, what's a conversation about otherwise, if it isn't about getting your point of view across?

B: And rapport.

A: And?

B: Rapport. R A P

A: P O R T. Oh yes, rapport, of course.

B: Because when you're in an informal situation like that, I imagine this kind of thing isn't by any means restricted to just one pair of utterances. I guess you could keep going more or less

A: More or less indefinitely.

B: Indefinitely, yes.

MONOLOGUE VARIATIONS

There are two possible situations in which someone may choose to engage in a monologue, whether spoken or written: there may be an audience present, or there may be no audience. In each case there are several interesting variations which lead to linguistically distinctive texts. Few have received in-depth stylistic investigation.

Audience present

With an audience present, the likelihood is that the medium will be speech (p. 291), and interruptability provides an interesting basis for classification. Many spoken monologues presented to an audience are in principle uninterruptable (other than by non-linguistic responses, such as applause). Examples include a very formal speech (p. 294), a lecture, and a sermon (in conservative religious traditions). On the other hand, there are several such situations which do permit interruption. The preachers facing many US black congregations are reinforced in their rhetoric by responses from their listeners, and often adopt a questioning style in order to elicit them (p. 371). Political speeches, likewise, regularly play to the audience in this way (p. 378).

An interesting category is the case of an audience which is present but in no position to respond (a 'pseudo-audience'). Examples of these situations include the dentist who carries on a conversation (even including questions!) while the listener's mouth is full of dental equipment, and the adult talking to a prelinguistic infant (or the mother talking to the baby in her womb). It is a moot point whether such events are best described as monologue or dialogue.

Audience absent

Leaving aside the case of literary expression, which can be defended as either monologue or dialogue (p. 294), the notion that there could be monologue without an audience present at first seems somewhat unusual. Why should we say anything at all, if there is no one to hear what we say? Why write anything, if there is no one there to read it? Both speech and writing, however, provide interesting cases where monologic activities do take place.

Speech activities

There is little scientific data on the point, but evidently people do speak to themselves. The author has it on good authority that academics have been known to talk through solutions to their problems while alone (e.g. in the bath). There is also the common case of another kind of pseudo-audience – this time, where no human being is present – though it is debatable whether such uses might not better be called 'pseudo-dialogues'.

There are, for example, people who talk to plants (and who are ready to give reasons for doing so). There are also people who talk to their car – often to condemn it for malfunctioning. Indeed, virtually any object can be addressed as if it were a person. 'Aren't you nice?', someone in a department store was overheard to say to a

dress. (Whether we include animals within this category, or in the same category as the infants mentioned above, presents a further topic for debate.)

Writing activities

Here too we have the unusual possibility of addressing ourselves. The diary is the classic instance. Other examples include making notes while preparing a talk, and note-taking while listening to a talk being given by someone else. That notes are written for the benefit only of the note-taker is evident if ever we try to use another person's material – a situation which will be familiar to any student who has missed a class and tried to catch up in this way. The note-taker's selection of information will have been made with reference to what the writer already knows, and this, along with the elliptical style that comes with writing under a time constraint, limits the possibilities of shared coherence.

Pseudo-audiences for monologic writing activities are also rather unusual. Written examination answers are probably the clearest instances. There has been a dialogue in one direction (the examiner has asked the student a question), but the reply is a monologue (for the student has no expectation of a response – except indirectly, in the form of a grade). Some party-games also provide pseudo-audiences for written language. In one such game, participants each write a sentence about someone else in the room and drop their contributions (anonymously) into a hat. The sentences are then pulled out randomly in pairs and placed in a sequence. In a children's party, the enjoyment comes from the juxtaposition of incongruous activities (such as *Michael has got a new rabbit – Jane's feeling hungry*). In adult parties, rather more risqué incongruities can transpire.

Lastly, there are cases where we can write *as if* an audience is present, because we know that at a later stage one will be. Activities here include preparing a handout for a talk, writing an essay for a tutor, or indexing a book. Indexing has sometimes been described as a task where the compiler is trying to anticipate every possible query about content which future readers of the book might have. Indexers are in effect trying to provide answers to a host of unasked questions – an interesting reversal of communicative priorities. They therefore need to work as if their audience is present – though, without knowing who this audience will be, and without receiving any feedback as to whether their judgments have been successful, the task is a difficult one, requiring exceptional communicative commitment.

FORETELLING

There is also the possibility that we may speak *as if* an audience were present. This can be writing-based, as when we practise a speech before giving it, or an actor rehearses lines, or it can be unscripted, as in the case of talking to an answerphone (p. 291). Television weather-forecasting is probably the most famous example of this second category. The visual material is prepared in advance, but during the broadcast the spoken commentary is spontaneous – with a close eye on the clock, which dictates exactly when the forecast must end. At the BBC, each broadcast has to finish exactly on time, because eight seconds before the forecast ends the next programme starts to run – and cannot be stopped. Woe betide the unfortunate forecaster who launches into a long subordinate clause just before that point is reached. No other form of spontaneous language use presents a speaker with so many constraints in such a short time.

This extract, from a day in a weather-forecaster's life, hints at the difficulties.

8.00 am: Start drawing up symbols maps for the first British Isles forecast which is a detailed forecast for the southern region. Is it going to rain in Margate and not in Brighton? Is it going to be colder to the north of London than in Sussex?…Draw maps for the 9am national broadcast which could be of as little as fifteen seconds duration.

8.30: Engineers arrive to switch on camera…

8.40: Place drawn electronic maps in order to be shown in the bulletin and copy them onto slide file.

8.45: Switch on lights, put in earpiece by which the network director communicates during the broadcast. Get dressed and ready for broadcast. Make sure the countdown clock is working. (We work on a system whereby a digital clock appears on the camera lens counting the seconds down.) Practice broadcast.

8.56.50: South-east broadcast starts – clock counts down.

8.59.20: Cue me to do the broadcast – has to finish exactly at 8.59.50 to link back to the national news at 9am.

9.00: National news followed by first broadcast for the British Isles, lasting just fifteen seconds.

9.04: Switch off lights and prepare maps for 10am broadcast…

(From Bill Giles, *The Story of Weather*, 1990, p. 97.)

DIALOGUE VARIATIONS

One way of classifying dialogues is to examine their symmetry – to see whether the participants are co-equally involved. There may also be variation in the timing of the language contributions relative to each other. The norm is for there to be two participants, who speak in sequence (but with a certain amount of expected overlapping, p. 288). However, several types of dialogic situation depart from this norm in interesting ways.

Symmetrical dialogue

It is possible for people to use language simultaneously, giving the impression of dialogue, but probably with little meeting of minds. If two groups of protesters, both carrying placards expressing their views, were to confront each other, the juxtaposition of written texts would produce a kind of dialogue, but one in which all 'utterances' were on display at the same time.

In speech, any simultaneity is likely to be unintelligible – but this does not stop it happening, as is regularly heard in public political confrontations. Dinner parties also bring up some interesting cases, where a person might end up contributing to two conversations at the same time – introducing remarks into each in sequence, but listening to both at once. It is something which succeeds only when one is either very sober, or very drunk.

A further variation is for a dialogue to depend on a third party, or intermediary. A common example is in foreign-language interpreting and translation, where A has to communicate with B via C. Within a single language, there are also well-known situations where one person (or group) communicates with another via an 'official spokesperson', or (in an apparently rather different domain) a ventriloquist's dummy.

An interesting variant is for a dialogue to be generated using the utterances of a third party. A loud-voiced person in a restaurant may cause a couple at another table to provide their own responses (*sotto voce*) to what is said, creating their own ongoing dialogue stimulated by the outsider's utterances. In François Truffaut's Oscar-winning film, *Day for Night* (*La Nuit Americaine*, 1973), two of the film crew are seen passing a television set which happens to be showing a quiz game about films. They stop to watch, and try to answer the questions ahead of the participants on the screen. They talk to each other while reflecting on their answers, engaging in a dialogue which is, once again, dependent on a third party.

Asymmetrical dialogue

These are the most unusual dialogues of all, as they take place with only one person apparently present. The qualification 'apparently' is important, because of course what happens is that the participant is imagining someone else to be present. In some cases, the missing person is the one who should start the conversation – as in the case of a seance, where people sit waiting for someone to talk to them. In other cases, the missing person is the one who should respond, as when we call uncertainly into the darkness 'Is there anyone there?', and hope that we really are engaged in a monologue after all.

Letters to the press or a radio station perhaps also fall into the asymmetrical category, given that there is only a remote chance that they will be used. In such cases we are trying to make a contribution to a dialogue over which someone else has control. If we do manage to get our contribution published or read out, there is no way of knowing whom we shall end up 'talking to'. Editors and programme presenters are adept in making dramatic juxtapositions of letters in this way.

MULTILOGUES?

If A speaks to one person, it is a dialogue. If A speaks to several people at once, or if several people speak to A at once, the term dialogue hardly seems appropriate. Insofar as each might interpret such a conversation as a series of 'mini-dialogues'. But when there is genuine unison, something else seems to be going on – a 'multilogue'?

In speech, such situations can be found in churches (unison prayer), public meetings (*We want Bill!*), sports grounds (*Come On The Royals!*), and pantomimes (*OH yes he is!*). In writing, unison communication appears in petitions and jointly signed letters. Indeed, in the last case, it is even possible to find several groups of people communicating at once with each other, as when several joint letters to the press, taking different positions, are published side by side.

CLASSIFICATION OF MIXED PARTICIPATION TEXTS

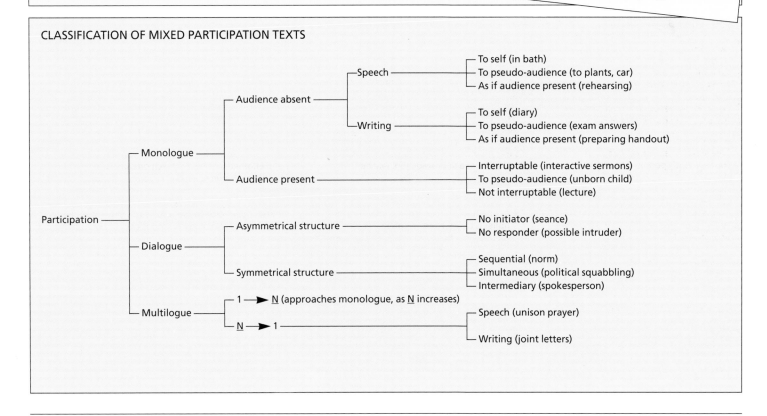

Of all the sociolinguistic and stylistic factors which promote variety in language use (p. 364), the one which people most commonly enquire about is geographical origin. The fact that speech, in particular, can convey such a clear answer to the question 'Where are you from?' exercises a peculiar fascination, and the terms *dialect* and *accent* are a normal part of everyday vocabulary. We readily notice regional differences in the way people talk, and although we may be unable to describe these differences other than in the most vague and impressionistic terms ('guttural', 'musical', 'lilting'), we have no difficulty in responding to them intuitively, laughing at dialect jokes, enjoying dialect literature and folklore, and appreciating the point of dialect parodies (p. 410).

At the same time – and this is the paradox of dialect study – we find it easy to make harshly critical judgments about ways of speaking which we perceive as alien. These attitudes are usually subconscious, of course, but it evidently does not take much to bring them to the surface. Differences of opinion between people of different dialect backgrounds can quickly lead to mutual mockery of each other's speech, and one has to be particularly thick-skinned for this mockery not to hurt. Moreover, disparagement of regional speech readily transmutes into disparagement of the speakers, and newspapers occasionally report disturbing or even catastrophic consequences. Such matters have attracted a great deal of academic study, especially by sociolinguists, but there is still little popular awareness of the problems.

The study of regional linguistic variation has thus more to offer than purely descriptive interest. The more we know about regional variation and change in the use of English, the more we will come to appreciate the striking individuality of each of the varieties which we call dialects, and the less we are likely to adopt demeaning stereotypes about people from other parts of the country, or of the world. An essential first step is to replace the notion that a regional variety is 'only a dialect', because it lacks the prestige of the standard language, with the realization that every dialect is a source of great linguistic complexity and potential. It is not easy to persuade ourselves that a dialect or accent which we dislike or detest is a variety of the English language which deserves as much respect, and has just as much right to exist, as the variety we speak ourselves. But this is the breakthrough demanded by a genuinely democratic dialectology.

ACCENT AND DIALECT

Throughout this book, and especially in this chapter, a systematic distinction is drawn between regional *accent* and regional *dialect*.

• A regional accent refers to features of *pronunciation* which convey information about a person's geographical origin.
Examples:
bath /baθ/ ('short *a*') vs *bath* /bɑːθ/ ('long *a*')
hold /həʊld/ vs '*old* /əʊld/ ('dropping the aitch')
thanks /θaŋks/ vs *thanks* /faŋks/ ('no *th*')
• A regional dialect refers to features of *grammar* and *vocabulary* which convey information about a person's geographical origin.
Examples:
They real good vs *They are really good*
Is it ready you are? vs *Are you ready?*
I'll visit in the fall vs *I'll visit in the autumn.*

• Speakers who have a distinctive regional dialect will have a distinctive regional accent; but the reverse does not necessarily follow. It is possible to have a regional accent yet speak a dialect which conveys nothing about geographical origin, as in the case of Standard English (p. 110). Regional dialects are also typically associated with a range of regional accents – some much 'broader' than others.
Within a country, there may be a prestige or neutral accent which conveys no information about geographical background. The most famous example occurs in Britain, with the accent that has long been called Received Pronunciation, or RP (p. 365). From an international point of view, of course, RP is distinctively regional – perceived as the archetypal British accent, and satirized accordingly.

The Daily Express 28 May 1962

Is an accent so wrong?

by DEREK TYSON

YES, IT TAKES COURAGE TO BE HONEST

BLACKSMITH Harry Speight died a victim of dialect snobbery. He killed himself at 70 because he was ashamed of his Yorkshire accent when he went to live in the South, it was said at the inquest.

His new neighbours are not to be blamed for his death. Responsibility lies partly at least at the door of those who still propagate the theory that a Northern accent is somehow "common," a southern twang correct.

Newspaper headlines (especially in Britain) often focus attention on the problems which can be caused by differences of regional accent and dialect.

REGIONAL ACCOMMODATION

When people with different regional (or social) backgrounds meet, there is a tendency for their speech patterns to become more alike, or *converge*. This process, known as *accommodation*, can be observed in all aspects of language structure, but is especially noticeable in accents. Some people cannot stop themselves unconsciously picking up the accent of the person they are talking to. Less noticeably, when people encounter others with whom they wish to maintain a distance, their language tends to become less alike, or *diverge*. There have been several experimental studies which clearly show both convergence and divergence in action, and which demonstrate the way we unconsciously associate regional variation with psychological and social traits.

In one such study, Anglo-Welsh listeners (p. 334) were asked to rate a dialogue involving two suspects with Welsh accents who were being interrogated by a policeman with an RP English accent. (All roles were being played by actors.) The actors then altered their accents, in one case adopting accents that were *more* like RP (a convergence strategy), in the other case adopting accents that were *less* like RP, and more broadly Welsh (a divergence strategy). The content of the interviews was kept the same throughout. At

no point, of course, was the attention of the listeners drawn to the accent changes: as far as they were concerned, they were listening only to the content of what was being said.

The results were clear-cut. The listeners evaluated the subjects differently, depending on which accent strategy was being employed. In terms of social attractiveness and nationalistic identity, the suspects were rated much more favourably when their accents diverged from that of the policeman. They were also rated as less guilty in this condition, and felt to be deserving of a milder sentence. On the other hand, the divergence condition also attracted some negative ratings, in terms of such factors as intelligence.

This kind of finding is typical of accommodation studies involving regional accents. It seems there is a real danger that we will rate unfavourably people whose accents diverge from our own, and certain groups of people seem especially at risk. For example, it is now well established that immigrant children who are a minority in a school classroom risk being rated as less intelligent or poorer learners. 'He even *sounds* thick' illustrates the stereotype. Needless to say, there is no correlation whatsoever between regional speech distinctiveness and level of intelligence.
(After J. Bourhis, reported in H. Giles, *et al.*, 1991.)

INTERNATIONAL AND INTRANATIONAL

It is inevitable that people traditionally think of dialects as a purely intranational matter – local to the country to which they belong. Historically, the language was restricted to a single geographical area – the British Isles – and for centuries, until the growth of urban populations, the only regional variation which most people would encounter would be that associated with neighbouring communities and the occasional visitor from further afield. Even when English began to move around the world (§7), only a relatively small proportion of the population of each country would travel widely enough for global differences in regional speech to be apparent. All this has changed, especially in the present century. Radio, television, and cinema links, coupled with a vast increase in travelling mobility, have brought a universal awareness that English dialects operate on a world scale. The study of local dialects has thus come to be supplemented by an international approach to dialectology – the study of 'world Englishes'.

REGIONAL TAGS

Although dialects operate both intranationally and internationally, the features which signal regional identity come from the same stock of structural resources. Thus it is not unusual to find the same construction being used in dialects associated with different parts of the world, though not always with the same function. The tag question (p. 218) is one such item.

In Standard English, tag questions agree with the main verb of the clause: in its chief functions, the tag verb changes from positive to negative or vice versa (or adds a corresponding form of *do*), and there is agreement in tense, number, and person. Typical examples are

They're outside, *aren't they?*
It's a Porsche, *isn't it?*
You didn't resign, *did you?*

There are also several other possibilities, expressing a range of attitudes and emphases (e.g. *They're going, are they?*). And there are distinctive falling and rising uses of intonation (p. 248), permitting a contrast between interrogation and direction ('Are you asking me or telling me?').

Invariant tags
In several parts of the world, typically where English is spoken as a second language, an invariant tag construction has arisen – the same form being used regardless of what happens in the preceding clause. Such invariant tags are standard in many languages (e.g. *n'est-ce pas* in French), and their use now seems to be growing in regional varieties of English as a second language, probably because an invariant form avoids the syntactic complexity of the tag construction in the standard language. All the following examples of usage have been observed.

An invariant *is it*, sometimes alternating with *isn't it*, is quite common:

You didn't see him, is it? (Zambia)
You are coming to the meeting, isn't it? (South Asia)
They do a lot of work, isn't it? (Wales)
She's gone to town, is it? (South Africa)
You check out now, is it? (Singapore)
You don't mind, is it? (Malaysia)

He has arrived, isn't it? (Papua New Guinea)
You are tired, isn't it? (West Africa)

An invariant *not so* (compare German *nicht wahr*) is less common, but found in widely separated areas.

He will come tomorrow, not so? (West Africa)
Your children are still schooling, not so? (South Asia)
They're outside, not so? (Papua New Guinea)

This is similar to the use of *no* as a tag, here seen under the influence of Spanish:

Those men were still singing, no? (SW USA, Pueblo)

Such forms are similar to the use of tag words, such as *eh* or *right*, which also show regional variation (p. 342).

Variant tags
Variant tags also diverge regionally, but are more likely to be found within a first language community, where the problem of syntactic complexity is not really an issue (as the constructions are early acquired by children).

He took his car, did he no? (Scotland)
You can't do it, can't you not? (Tyneside)
We never be out, do we? (Ireland)
I'm old enough to get in, amn't I? (Ireland, Scotland)

In addition, there are variations which stem from changing patterns of usage, as one dialect comes to influence another. The use of *ought* and *shall* as tags, for example, is characteristically British, and is avoided in US English. On the other hand, US usages are increasingly heard in the UK.

We ought to help, oughtn't we? (chiefly UK)
We ought to help, shouldn't we? (US, and some UK)

It should perhaps be added that *ain't* is not a regionally distinctive form: it is heard all over the English-speaking world. Its non-standard status arises from social and educational factors (p. 362).

FUNCTIONAL DIFFERENCES

Sometimes it is the function of a tag question which differentiates dialects. In one study of British and American English, *peremptory* and *aggressive* uses of tags are identified as being characteristically British. These have a function which is the opposite of that normally associated with tag questions. Instead of inviting the listener to join the conversation, they freeze the person out. Their force depends on the way they are said. The following utterance (B), spoken mildly, with a low falling tone, is just a slight put-down; spoken more emphatically and with a level tone, it is unpleasantly rude:

A: When will the train arrive?
B: We'll know when it gets here, won't we.

One such use has become a catch phrase, used when someone publicly denies alleged wrong-doing. It originated during a British political scandal of the 1960s (the 'Profumo affair'), when Mandy Rice Davies, told in court that Lord Astor had denied her allegations, remarked: 'Well he would, wouldn't he'.

The aggressive tag is usually spoken more forcefully, and is used after a statement whose truth or falsity the listener could not possibly know. Because the tag implies that 'everyone should know this', the addressee is made to feel an idiot. It is, in effect, a reprimand. Although formerly associated with working-class London speech, the usage is now widespread, but still chiefly British. Examples are taken from British TV series:

A: What are you doing here?
B: I came to finish those letters, didn't I. (*Coronation Street*, 1987)

A: [to a young man on the phone] Is that your brother?
B: It's my dad, innit. (*Eastenders*, 1986)

A: You need to go to your local police.
B: I've done all that, haven't I.
(*Bergerac*, 1986)
(After J. Algeo, 1988.)

NO?

You are coming back on Friday, aren't you? Come back a day earlier, so you can attend Joshi RDC's farewell. He's retiring, no, at the end of the month.

This example, from Upamanyu Chatterjee's novel *English, August* (1988) shows a distinctive use of a particle *no*, which resembles a tag question. It is used thus elsewhere in the novel:

Each of us has his own view of others, no.

However, as a standard tag is used just beforehand, in the first example, *no* cannot be simply a tag. The word seems to be acting more as a marker of emphasis and social solidarity. In most cases it does not require an answer, because the speaker assumes the listener shares the same beliefs. (After J. D'Souza, 1991.)

A DAY IN THE LIFE OF THE ENGLISH LANGUAGE

What would we find if we collected samples of the English language in use all over the world on the same day, talking about the same range of topics? With variations in time-scale and content reduced, would regional variety differences stand out immediately? Would we see clearly the linguistic differences between Britain and the USA, Australia and Canada, South Asia and South East Asia, or between any other locations where the language holds a prestigious place?

In a small-scale attempt to find out, 40 newspapers were collected from all over the English-speaking world on 6 July 1993, and a selection of what they contained is shown on these pages. The results are quite clear, and testify to the outstanding power and universality of the concept of written Standard English. In the vast majority of instances, it is impossible to tell at a glance which paper belongs to which country on purely linguistic grounds. Indeed, we often have to hunt for distinctive linguistic features. We will find them, if we persist – a distinctive lexical item in paragraph 8 on page 3 of one paper, a distinctive US or UK spelling in paragraph 11 of page 2. There will be rather more linguistic consequences arising out of the shared knowledge which editors assume in their readers – concepts unexplained, backgrounds assumed, and terms introduced without gloss. But we can search for many pages before finding something which we could call a distinctively regional use of grammar.

We would certainly find more regional differentiation if we carried out this exercise based on the spoken language, using radio broadcasts and 'vox pop' interviews. We would then hear immediately the many phonological differences which identify regional variety, both segmental and prosodic (§17). We would be much more likely to encounter distinctive grammar, especially in the more informal varieties of local speech. And there would be a marked increase in the amount of local vocabulary – again, especially in more informal contexts. Such a study needs a different medium of presentation than the pages of a book, however. For present purposes, the exercise leaves us with the overriding impression of limited but intriguing diversity, and above all of the unifying power of the standard language.

Emotional fans chase singer's hearse

By CLIFFORD LO

SCREAMING fans broke through police barriers yesterday as the hearse carrying Wong Ka-kui, lead vocalist of rock band Beyond, left the Hongkong Funeral Home in Quarry Bay.

More than 3,000 distraught fans packed the pavements, tram stops and a footbridge outside the funeral parlour in King's Road, yelling "Ka-kui" and singing the band's songs.

"Although Ka-kui isn't here, we hope he can hear our voices and see how we miss him. So we kept yelling his name and singing some of their songs to express our love and support," a 14-year-old girl said.

Another said: "We love Ka-kui forever and his spirit will always remain in our hearts."

Wong, 31, died of a cerebral haemorrhage last Wednesday, six days after he fell from a stage set during a television programme rehearsal in Japan.

There were about 70 police officers, including 40 from the police tactical unit, to control the crowds and traffic yesterday.

But as the hearse left, some fans broke through barriers and chased the vehicle along King's Road between the junctions of Java Road and Healthy Street East.

Fans began to gather at the funeral parlour on Sunday and,

by yesterday morning, there were about 1,500 outside. The number had risen to 3,000 by noon.

Inside the parlour, walls were covered by scrolls, flowers and wreaths – many carrying the words: "A great loss of talent."

Music and radio industry figures, including pop star Aaron Kwok Fu-sing, attended the funeral along with the other members of the band – among them Wong Ka-keung, the late singer's brother.

After a Buddhist ceremony, the coffin was taken to the Chinese permanent cemetery in Junk Bay.

RTHK will screen a half-hour tribute to Wong tomorrow on TVB Jade.

In Japan, there will be a memorial ceremony at a Tokyo temple at the weekend.

It was announced on Sunday that a fund would be set up in commemoration of Wong's contribution to the development of rock music in Hongkong.

A full house attending a memorial concert at the Ko Shan Theatre was told the fund would help pay for budding rock musicians to produce albums.

Money would be raised through the sale of commemorative T-shirts, albums and pictures, and a re-screening of the award-winning film *Cagemen*, in which Wong had a role.

WHERE DID THIS STORY APPEAR?

Is it possible to tell from the language alone the country in which this article appeared on 6 July 1993? The picture, the name of the reporter, and the Chinese name of the dead singer may suggest that we are somewhere in the Far East, but there are millions of people of Chinese ethnic origin in several Western countries, reporters with Chinese names are not unknown in the West, and it is possible that the singer had a cult following anywhere.

A close look at some of the assumptions made by the writer would give us some clues. He assumes we know such places as King's Road and Junk Bay, and what RTHK is. The paper's use of British

spelling (*parlour, programme*) and vocabulary (*pavements, tram,* US *sidewalks, streetcar*) adds a pointer to a British-influenced part of the world (p. 306). But apart from these hints, there is nothing to help us. This article could have been found in many English language newspapers of the same genre, in several parts of the world.

Knowing that the item appeared as the lead article on the front page of the paper would probably settle the matter. Only a Hong Kong paper would be likely to give such prominence to such an item. And, indeed, the paper was the Hong Kong-published *South China Morning Post*.

THE TWO MODELS

One of the first judgments to make, when comparing samples of written English from around the world, is whether the language is British or American English – or some mixture of the two.

The front page of the *Atlanta Constitution* shows several signs of American English. There is a spelling clue in *behavior* (col. 1) and lexical clues in *levee* and *yard* (in the caption – 'garden' in British English). There is a minor grammatical feature in the caption and the political report – *Monday* for *on Monday* – as well as an instance of *toward* (British *towards*). Local knowledge is required to interpret *EDT* ('Eastern Daylight Time').

The business page of *The Plain Dealer*, from Cleveland, Ohio, shows further instances. There is spelling distinctiveness: single -*l*- (pp. 307, 441) in *fueled* (top summary), *traveling* and *traveler* (main article). And there is lexical distinctiveness in the headline (*gas*, British English *petrol*) and lead article: *gasoline*, *self-serve stations* (British *self-service stations*), and *cents*.

THE ATLANTA CONSTITUTION

TUESDAY, JULY 6, 1993

50 CENTS

HOME EDITION

FLOODING ON THE MISSISSIPPI

Is there any end in sight?

Ducking to avoid his clothesline, Cale Coss of LeClaire, Iowa, navigates his yard Monday as the Mississippi River rose to its highest level since 1965. Such scenes were common in Iowa, Illinois and Missouri, where levees broke and National Guardsmen were called in to help with sandbagging. And with another rainy week ahead, many river towns fear that they haven't seen the worst. **See article, Page A8.**

Associated Press

President upbeat for summit

Deficit plan gives U.S. new clout, Clinton say

FROM OUR NEWS SERVICES

President Clinton and his top aides appe optimistic Monday as they prepared for week's seven-nation economic summit claring that Mr. Clinton's domestic policies strengthened his hand.

Mr. Clinton, on his way to Tokyo for the a meeting of the so-called Group of Seven na said his steps toward cutting the U.S. budget mean that other countries now must do their lower trade barriers and stimulate their econo

The president meets today with the s host, Japanese Prime Minister Kiichi Miy The summit itself — involving the leaders of Britain, Germany, France, Italy, Canada a United States — begins at 2:30 p.m. Wed (1:30 a.m. Wednesday EDT).

Mr. Clinton said his predecessors face cism at earlier economic summits about dor to constrain the U.S. deficit. "Your gove deficit is messing up the whole works," he eign leaders told previous presidents. "Do

...*roe* splits doubleheader SPORTS

THE PLAIN DEALER

OHIO'S LARGEST NEWSPAPER Cleveland, Tuesday, July 6, 1993

LATEST SPORTS

HOME DELIVERY DAILY FOR 6 ISSUES (MONDAY-SATURDAY) $1.50. DAILY AND SUNDAY FOR 7 ISSUES (MONDAY-SUNDAY) $2.25. PRICES MAY VARY IN DESIGNATED AREAS.

NEWSSTANDS AND VENDING MACHINES 35¢

The REI
North Coast
Report

Growth in per...

Between 1985 and 1990, Cleveland's per ca... CPI increase by 14.6%. However, fueled by a 38.9% grow... income, Chicago had the greatest difference between income growth and consumer price increases of any Great Lakes metropolitan area.

ANALYSIS BY: **REI:** The Center for Regional Economic Issues, Weatherhead School of Management, CWRU

CPI
10

Chicago   Cleveland   Detroit

Source: U.S. Bureau of Economic Analysis and U.S. Bureau of Labor Statistics

THE PLAIN DEALER

BUSINESS

TUESDAY, JULY 6, 1993

E

■ SMALL BUSINESS/2-E
■ BUSINESS PEOPLE/3-E
■ McCORMACK ON MANAGEMENT/5-E

With gas cheap, Americans driving

By AGIS SALPUKAS
NEW YORK TIMES

With gasoline cheap and plentiful, and expected to stay that way through the summer, Americans who put off trips during the economic doldrums of the last few years are hitting the road again.

The American Automobile Association, based on a survey of 1,500 drivers, predicted last week that travel during the Fourth of July weekend would be up 4% from the same holiday weekend in 1992, with 30 million Americans planning to make trips of 100 miles or more.

Most will pump their own gas at self-serve stations and hunt for bargains at motels. Few said they were worried about the prospect of a gas tax of 4 cents to 5 cents a gallon, which seems likely if the tax bill now before Congress is passed.

Indeed, driving is widely seen as economical, compared with flying. The discounts offered by the airlines are not as steep as they were during a fare war last summer, when ticket prices were slashed by as much as 50%.

As a result, the number of people traveling by airplane is expected to decline 8% from 1992, the survey said.

"There is a new breed of traveler," said Jerry Cheske, the director of public relations for the automobile association. "They shop for vacations much like they shop for a TV or stereo."

The survey also found that more people planned to stay in motels this year: 43%, up from 37% a year ago. Only a quarter said they planned to stay with relatives, down from a third last year.

Few drivers seemed worried about the growing dependence of the United States on foreign oil, which is at an all-time high. About half the oil consumed in the United States in recent months has been from foreign sources.

The dependence on imported oil has jumped this year, up 7.2% in May over the comparable month last year, according to the American Petroleum Institute, a trade group based in Washington.

Of total consumption of 17.1 million barrels a day, imports made up an average of 8.4 million barrels in May. Imports accounted for 49.1% of the oil consumed in May, up from 47.6% in May of last year.

Nationally, the average price for self-serve regular unleaded gas was $1.12 a gallon last week, down 6.1 cents from a year ago, according to the automobile association.

Prices, which have begun to drop recently, are approaching the low levels that prevailed before the invasion of Kuwait by Iraq in August of 1990.

BUSINESS
BRIEFS

INTERNATIONAL

FROM WIRE REPORTS

FIRMS APPROVED: Vietnam has licensed several big U.S. firms including Citibank, General Electric Co. and Philip Morris Cos. Inc. to set up representative offices, a trade official said yesterday. The authorizations last week brought to 12 the number of U.S. firms allowed to operate in Vietnam, the official said. Computer giant ...ational Business Machines Corp.

The spelling of the word *defence* (US *defense*) in the headline of the front page of London's *The Daily Telegraph* signals the British English identity of this paper, as does the spelling of *cancelled* in the first paragraph (US chiefly *canceled*). There is distinctive political vocabulary (*MPs*, *Conservatives*), though the terms are by no means restricted to Britain. *Billion* would be likely to mean different things to British and American readers.

The second extract is from a tourists' advice page from the *Daily Star*. The heading *traveller's cheques* would appear as *traveler's checks* in US English, and a *building society* is a *savings and loan association*. There is a great deal of informal vocabulary and slang in the piece, some of which is distinctively British – such as *high street*, *hole in the wall* (for *cash dispenser*) and *holiday* (US *vacation*). *Cashpoint card*, likewise, is a British usage (= a card for inserting into a cash dispenser).

SPORTS REPORTING

The reporting of national sports in the popular press generally brings regional variety differences out into the open. The two reports (US and UK) shown here (the opening paragraphs only, in each instance) are typical. To provide a linguistic 'translation' of the unfamiliar terms would be of limited value, in such cases, as what is needed is familiarity with the rules of the game, the immediate past history of the event and its players (such as why Pete Schourek is pitching for his life), and to some extent the cultural history of the country (such as the conflict between England and Australia at cricket). Indeed, the British reporter actually refers to historical awareness, at one point. It also helps to have a knowledge of acronyms (*ERA = Earned Run Average*).

FALSE CONTRASTS

It is important not to misinterpret regional trends as absolutes when carrying out linguistic comparisons. The risk is to notice an alien usage in a variety other than our own, and to assume that it is universally used. For example, these extracts from two classified advertising sections suggest that the British use *post* where Americans use *mail*, and the article from an Atlanta (Georgia) paper would confirm the impression, with *mail* rubbing shoulders with a distinctive US grammatical feature (*gotten*). On the other hand, the word *mail* has been used in Britain for centuries (e.g. today's *Royal Mail* and *mail order*), and is now increasingly heard as an alternative to *post*. In the USA, likewise, the word *post* is by no means unfamiliar, as is evident from *post office box* in the article, and the name of the *United States Post Office*, later *Postal Service*.

The English language magazine, *English Today*, published in Britain, has from the outset used a heading for its correspondence column which tries to ensure that no one feels excluded.

The common British view that *auto(mobile)* is American for *car* is wrong, as can be seen from this extract from an advertisement in the *New York Post*. Both words are used in the same ad.

MIXED MESSAGES

These extracts from Australian newspapers provide an illustration of the way the English of a country can be influenced by both British and American models. The locality makes itself felt in such cultural references as *premiers' conference*, *Medicare*, *dollars*, *interstate*, and *federal*. US spellings are seen in *favorable*, *honor*, and *program*, with two prominent examples under *The Age* masthead: *Labor* and *flavor*. On the other hand, there is a use of *towards* (not *toward*) near the end of the political piece. The combination of sources is nicely juxtaposed in the article on the fuel tax, where *truck drivers* (not *lorry drivers*) visit *petrol stations* (not *gas stations*). Distinctive Australianisms are rare in both papers. The extracts have partly been chosen because they do contain some examples: *truckie*, *pom* (beneath the masthead of *The Australian*) and *'roo* (= 'flying kangaroo', a nickname of Qantas Airways). (*Cobra* is a computational acronym – for 'common branding reservation architecture'.)

A similar situation can be found in Canada, where extracts from two papers show *program* and *favor* alongside *theatre*, *fibre optics*, and *manoeuvring*. *Metro* (= the metropolitan area of the city) is also used in the USA. The introduction of a French term in a headline (short for *Caisse de dépôt et placement du Québec*) hints at the bilingual issue which has dominated Canadian politics. (*Univa* is a cultural reference – the trade name of a grocery business in Canada.)

Lexical items specific to Indian English are apparent in these extracts from *Indian Express*. The first story illustrates an item which is regularly used in financial reports: *crore* (= '10 million'). The second illustrates several items of local political vocabulary. *Tiff* here has a somewhat more serious sense than is customary in such phrases as a *lovers' tiff*, where the quarrel is felt to be slight and unimportant. The lack of a definite article before *hotel* at the end of the first item may also be a feature of the distinctive noun usage which is often to be heard in Indian English (p. 360).

THE AUSTRALIAN

TUESDAY JULY 6 1993

70 CENTS

NUMBER 8960

MICROSOFT JOINS PRICE WAR
26 Pages of COMPUTERS starts Page 17

JAPAN
The growing partnership
BUSINESS SPECIAL Pages 8 & 9

Cricket
WHY IT PAYS TO BE A POM
FEATURES Page 11

PM's $109m Medicare backdown

THE AGE

No. 43,085

ER STREET, MELBOURNE. 600 4211 (Classified 604 1144)

TUESDAY 6 JULY 1993

70c

ME MONTHLY
ges of ideas for home & garden
SPECIAL LIFTOUT

LABOR'S BETRAYAL
Philip Chubb on lessons of his TV series

SCOTTISH FLAVOR
More than just haggis

COMPUTERS

Merger's combined reservation system flying high

Cobra keeps flying 'roo a hop ahead

Truckies fill up interstate to beat fuel tax

By LYN DUNLEVY

Truck drivers in Victoria were buying fuel in other states, and roadhouse petrol stations might have to lay off staff following the "bungled" introduction of the State Government's three-cents-a-litre tax, the state Labor leader, Mr Brumby, said yesterday.

Petrol stations in Victoria servicing interstate truck drivers were already losing business since the tax was introduced on petrol and diesel last week, Mr Brumby said.

THE PREMIERS' CONFERENCE

deals privatisation se

the new Commonwealth revenue-sharing formula recommended earlier this year by the Grants Commission.

Yesterday's Loan Council meeting also approved Victoria's application for an extra $3.18 billion in borrowing rights, including $1.08 billion which will be used to fund the next round of about 15,000 redundancies in the state public sector.

The Premier, Mr Kennett, left the conference proclaiming a successful defence of Victoria's Medicare compensation entitlements, but decrying the one-day format of the Premiers' Conference. "This

isn't the way to run the country," he said.

"But I am happy to say that at the end of those discussions the Commonwealth decided to honor the guarantee that was in place, so that will ensure that Victoria is about $45 million better off than when we arrived this morning."

Mr Stockdale said the decision to abolish tax compensation for privatisation of state-owned enterprises had jeopardised Victoria's planned asset sale program.

Previously, states expected to receive compensation from the Federal Government when they privatised a business that previ-

ously paid tax-free profits into state government coffers.

The compensation, in the form of a one-off payment to the state, purported to recognise that a previously tax-free enterprise would, as a private body, begin delivering company tax revenue to the Commonwealth.

Victoria has already received tax compensation for the sale of the State Bank, but could now miss out on tens of millions of dollars worth of compensation it had been expecting from the State Insurance Office and Heatane Gas sales.

Mr Stockdale also said yesterday's decision had produced "a

very dark cloud over the wh issue of microeconomic reforr general, and privatisation in ticular at the state level".

The State Government had c inally requested the tax comp sation issue be put on the miers' Conference Agenda wi view to agreeing on new, f guidelines for its payment, no abolition.

Mr Stockdale, however, sai was satisfied with other aspec Victoria's treatment at the miers' Conference, even th the new Commonwealth rever sharing formula goes so fur towards ending subsidies by toria to Queensland and Wes

---

THE TORONTO STAR Tuesday, .

THE TORONTO STAR

OPINIONS

ry study makes opponents look good

TTAWA — The Conservatives scoffed when Liberal Leader Jean Chretien propsed a $15-billion public works program.

ey snickered when New Democratic Party Leader udrey McLaughlin put forward a $7.5-billion national infrastructure plan.

ow, it looks as if they may have laughed too soon. udy released last week by a government commi-ed task force shows that when a nation cuts its investment in highways, airports, waste dis-al facilities, communication links and other capital ects, it loses its competitive edge.

importance of public investment. Last December, Mulroney announced that the government was committed to developing a high-speed electronic highway, allowing scientists and engineers across the country to exchange vast amounts of information through the use of fibre optics. At the same time, former finance minister Don Mazankowski unveiled a $500 million program of roadbuilding and airport improvements.

It is not yet clear whether Prime Minister Kim Campbell will build on this modest beginning.

She does not have a lot of manoeuvring room, given that she has pledged to get rid of the federal deficit

True Left should favor GST

By Trevor Bartram

HE POLITICAL left, the NDP and Liberals, in its search for support among Canadian voters, has attack the single

B6 THE TORONTO STAR Tuesday, J

Metro's police board rapped over Whitehead, Junger Cases

By Rosie DiManno
TORONTO STAR

Blyth theatre festival off to strong sta

Goldblum character's skepticism refreshing

CANADA S NATIONAL NEWSPAPER

THE GLOBE AND

©1995

Toronto, Tuesday, July 6, 1993

The Globe and Mail, Tuesday, July 6, 1993

REPORT ON BUSINESS

Caisse formalizes hold on Univa

Foreign investment approvals touch Rs 3320.89 crore

NEW DELHI – Foreign investment approvals touched Rs 3320.89 crore during the first five months of this year compared to Rs 530 crore in the whole of 1991 and Rs 3890 crore in 1992, reports UNI.

This unprecedented response by foreign investors to the new industrial policy is also reflected in a total foreign investment of Rs 7610 crore during the post-policy period (August 1991 to May 1993), according to official sources.

More than 90 per cent of these investments have gone to high priority and technology industries. The major share of foreign investment is in setors like power, oil, food processing, chemicals, electronic and electric equipment, telecommunication, transport, industrial machinery and hotel and tourism industry.

Indian Express

INDIA'S ONLY NATIONAL NEWSPAPER

MADURAI NAGPUR PUNE VIJAYAWADA VIZIANAGARAM

LATE CITY

16 PAGES Rs 2.30

Chautala-Bhajan tiff on Kalka polls

NEW DELHI: Samajwadi Janata Party leader Om Prakash Chautala on Monday accused the Haryana Chief Minister Bhajan Lal of misusing the official machinery for campaigning in the Kalka Assembly and urged the Chief Election Commissioner (CEC) to ensure a free and fair election. In a communication addressed to the CEC, Chautala alleged that the Chief Minister and his Congress supporters were threatening the electorate, especially the sarpanches, panches and namberdars of the area to vote for the Congress candidate. The ministers were holding meetings of public representatives and compelling them to toe the official line, failing which they threatened to suspend the development grants to their respective villages, the communication said.

Some of the English-language newspapers published in parts of the world where English has no official status, and is taught as a foreign language. These papers use British or American English as their model, so there is little sign of a 'new English' in their pages. Much of their material, indeed, is syndicated through the international news agencies. However, they do differ linguistically, in that it is usually possible to see the influence of the locality in the way they treat their subject matter. Local terms in such domains as politics and sport are introduced without gloss, and a degree of knowledge of local cultural traditions is assumed. Outsiders reading these papers can therefore find some of the articles extremely opaque, as in the sports report opposite.

THE PRAGUE POST

"The World We Live In and The World Around Us"

Volume 3, Number 27

July 7—13, 1993   25 Kč

Border Pact Blocked

Mečiar Rejects His President's Agreement

by Sophia Coudenhove

Just when an agreement on the contro... Czech-Slovak border seemed... mend that their governments settle the issue of the Czech-Slovak border by July 20. Both promised not to take unilateral action on border policy until this date and provide... said the Czech Republic could to strength...

to enter the Czech Republic from Slovakia, Mečiar continued to insist on more open borders. "We don't need to divide countries and nations with Iron Curtains," he said.

As Germany tightens its refugee policy, a number of Central and Eastern... are following suit,

The Korea Herald

No. 12,376   코리아 헤럴드   LATE CITY EDITION ★★★   SEOUL, TUESDAY, JULY 6, 1993   300 Won Per Copy

Korea to reopen consulate-general in Ho Chi Minh City

HO CHI MINH CITY (Yonhap) — South Korea opens its consulate-general in Ho Chi Minh City Aug. 15 at the same place it abandoned nearly 20 years ago after South Vietnam's communization. Amb. Park Noh-soo said Monday.

Subway construction in Inchon

지하철 1호선 건설 기공

New strike looms as Iraq rejects U.N. arms inspection

Christopher calls refusal a 'bad sign'

By Dilip Ganguly

BAGHDAD, Iraq (AP) — The U...

Al-Ahram
Weekly

No. 124   الأهرام ويكلي   Published in Cairo by AL-AHRAM established in 1875   8-14 July 1993   16 pages   P.T.50

G7 backtrack on Bosnia

Chinese tour

CHINESE Vice-Premier Li Lanqing began official talks in Oman yesterday on economic cooperation and enhancing bilateral relations, as part of a tour of Gulf Arab states and Iran.

The Chinese official assured reporters t... the protocol his... signed with Iran Tu... build a nuclear power... saying the station will... structed under the... sion of the Vienna-ba... ternational Atomic Agency, and will be u... peaceful purposes.

US rejection

THE US renewed its... tion Tuesday of a... offer to put the two li... Lockerbie suspects, a... of blowing up a Pan... flight in 1988 resulting... deaths of 270 people, o... "anywhere in the world... cept the US and Brita... Libyan leader Muam... Gaddafi renewed the off... a recent interview with... Washington Post, but... Department press c... Sandra McCarty said... channel for contact on... Am 103 is the UN Secretary General," alluding to... Security Council resolu... imposing sanctions on Li... for its refusal to turn over... suspects.

Leaders of the seven major industrial powers began their annual economic summit in Tokyo on an upbeat note yesterday after the United States and its major tra...

The G7 summit in Tokyo yesterday achieved a breakthrough by reaching an agreement... term...

...tain also agreed that the G7 should begin a serious dialogue with I...

Mubarak-Assad talks

PRESIDENT Hosni Mubarak flew yesterday afternoon to the Syrian Mediterranean port of Latakia...

Prix de vente 8F   Subscriptions 95F

The Recorder

Balladur opposes GATT to save French farms

by Rod Hayter

France is set to stand by its farmers and go it alone as 118 nations finally appear poised to sign the General Agreement of Tariffs... GATT... Premier Edouard...

Number 19   Place de la Résistance   Tel. 53.83.81.02   July, 1993
47120 Duras   Fax 53.83.76.82

The Monthly

THE DAILY YOMIURI

No. 15453   © (日刊) THE DAILY YOMIURI (1993)   **TUESDAY, JULY 6, 1993**   PRICE ¥120 (¥2,600 a month) — tax included   ★ ★ ★

Tomonohana loses 1st in sumo's top division

Daily Yomiuri

One day after tasting victory for the first time in the makuuchi division, sumo's teacher learned how to lose.

No. 16 maegashira Tomonohana, a former high school teacher making his debut in sumo's top division, fell to No. 11 maegashira Terao on Monday at the Nagoya Grand Sumo Tournament.

Tomonohana notched his first win on Sunday against No. 16 maegashira Hitachiryu, and he held his own early against Terao, trading shoves with the 30-year-old on the tachi-ai. But when Tomonohana tried to move away from Terao, the more experienced rikishi quickly pursued and forced him from the ring. Both wrestlers are now 1-1.

Meanwhile in the makuuchi division's more lofty ranks, the pre-tournament favorites stayed on course for some late—tournament showdowns.

Yokozuna Akebono heads the list of wrestlers at 2-0 after defeating komusubi Takatoriki.

In the day's final bout, Akebono had some trouble dropping Takatoriki, who managed to stay on his feet as the yokozuna landed repeated shots to his face and chest. But eventually his shoving attack broke the komusubi, who fell to 1—1 with the loss.

Others at 2-0 include Takanohana, Wakanohana, Musashimaru and Konishiki.

Ozeki Takanohana found himself in a tough spot against No. 2 maegashira Kotonowaka. The maegashira had an immediate hold on the young ozeki's belt, and kept Takanohana from getting two hands on his own.

Twice Kotonowaka attempted throws that left Takanohana off balance, but both times he recovered. Finally, after nearly a

minute of being held by the maegashira, Takanohana kicked a leg behind Kotonowaka, twisted his belt, and toppled the larger wrestler to the sand.

Wakonohana, facing one of the few rikishi smaller than himself, had little trouble with No. 6 maegashira Mainoumi, who could use none of his tricks against the technically-sound sekiwake. A few pushes from Wakanohana sent Mainoumi off the line and spinning from the ring.

Ozeki Konishiki easily walked out No. 1 maegashira Kirishima to stay unbeaten. The victory gave Konishiki a 16-15 career record against the former ozeki.

Sekiwake Musashimaru once again did his best Akebono imitation, using a slapping attack instead of any holds or throws.

Musashimaru went right at the face of Kitakachidoki, hammering it with repeated slaps as the maegashira struggled to get inside the Hawaiian's reach. The sekiwake continued the assault, un[til] Kitakachidoki started to back up, and fin[i]shed him with a few pushes to the chest.

Still looking for his first victory as [a] sekiwake is Takanonami, who lost to N[o.] 5 maegashira Mitoizumi.

Both wrestlers got belt holds early [and] worked each other around the ring, w[ith] the taller Mitoizumi controlling mos[t of] the action. Takanonami managed to f[end] off Mitzoizumi's first attempts a[t a] throw, but eventually yielded to the [180-] kg maegashira, backing over the rim.

Komusubi Wakashoyo picked u[p his] first win in a brief bout against No. 6[mae]-gashira Daishoyama. Wakashoyo ju[mped] to the side on the tachi-ai, pushed do[wn] Diashoyama's back and tripped the [mae]gashira with his right leg.

No. 1 maegashira Kotonishiki [upped] his record at 1-1 by stopping No. [7 mae]gashira Takamisugi.

This account of the latest stage of a sumo wrestling tournament, taken from the Japanese paper *The Daily Yomiuri*, assumes a high level of lexical awareness. It contrasts with a shorter account of the same tournament reported in the Greek paper, *Athens News*, which carefully adds glosses for the technical terms.

Athens News

Forty-Second Year No. 10583   LEKKA, 23-25, SYNTAGMA   **TUESDAY, 6 JULY 1993**   Price: Hundred and Fifty Drachmae (150 dra)

SUMO WRAPUP

NAGOYA, Japan (AP) — American yokozuna (grand champion Akebono and ozekis (champions) Takanohana and Konishiki won their second victories Monday, second day of the 15 day Nagoya Grand Sumo Tournament.

Sekiwakes (junior champions) Wakanohana and Musashimaru also remained undefeated at 2-0.

Wrestling before 3,800 spectators, Akebono, Japan's first foreign grand champion, coped with skillful dodging by nomusubi (junior champion second class) Takatoriki at the rings' edge and pushed him down. Takatoriki is 1-1. Akebono's real name is Chad Rowan.

Defending champion Takanohana, seeking promotion to sumo's highest rank of yokozuna, downed No. 2 maegashira (senior wrestler) Kotonowaka with a leg trick. Kotonowaka is 1-1.

Ozeki wrestlers can be promoted to yokozuna if they win two consecutive tournaments or compile a record of equal worth. Takanohana won the last tournament with 14-1.

Hawaiian Konishiki grabbed No. 1 maegashira Kirishima's belt and forced him out, handing the former ozeki his second defeat against no victories.

AMERICAN AND BRITISH ENGLISH

As we move away from the formal written English of the press (p. 300) in the direction of the informal spoken language, the differences between regional varieties dramatically increase. In the case of American and British English, the variation is considerable, but there are no accurate estimates for the number of points of contrast, for two chief reasons.

• Recent decades have seen a major increase in the amount of influence the two models have had on each other, especially American on British. The influence of US films and television has led to a considerable passive understanding of much American English vocabulary in Britain, and some of this has turned into active use (as in the case of *mail*, p. 302), especially among younger people. The reverse pattern is less obvious, but British films and TV programmes are seen sufficiently often in the USA to mean that a growth in awareness of UK vocabulary should not be discounted. What were originally fairly clear patterns of lexical differentiation have been obscured by borrowing on a worldwide scale.

• The regional dialect surveys of both countries, several of which have only recently begun to publish their findings, are bringing to light huge amounts of lexical distinctiveness (p. 309). Few of these forms have any literary background or enough breadth of use to warrant their inclusion in general dictionaries, but they do form an important part of the regional pattern, and several of them are retained in educated usage at local level as markers of group identity.

Nonetheless, when we take into account local festivals and folklore, abbreviations, localities, institutional differences (e.g. politics, banking, legal systems, armed forces, sports, honours), local fauna and flora, and everyday slang, the stock of regional differences is likely to be extremely large. In a casual collection made by the author in the 1970s, based solely on available dictionaries and literary works, 5,000 differences were found very easily, and it became apparent that the project was too large for such an informal treatment. A recently published dictionary by David Grote has some 6,500 entries, and deals *only* with British English for American readers. These totals, it must be appreciated, arise because we are dealing not only with different words (lexemes, p. 118), but also different senses of words. UK *chips* (= US *(French) fries*) is not the same as US *chips* (= UK *crisps*) – though American influence has brought both *(French) fries* and *(potato) chips* to Britain.

BEING ENGLISH

Kent The southeastern-most county* or shire* of England,* running from London* to the Channel.* Historically, this is the core of English history, with Dover* the principal access to the continent*, Canterbury* the home of the English Church,* and the Thames* ports on its north border the center of sea power and trading prosperity. It is one of the Home Counties* and is often called the Garden of England both for its agricultural riches and for the lovely rolling hills in the North Downs* that for many are the visual image of England itself, figuring in numberless works of literature.

Terms that British people would take completely for granted are asterisked in this entry from David Grote's *British English for American Readers* (1992), which shows some of the linguistic consequences of using a place-name. It is not unusual to find such terms as *Home Counties* being misapplied. A term such as *county* is also very differently used between the two nations.

The following selection of headwords from the middle of the book illustrates items which Americans would be likely to find distinctively British. Such lists have two kinds of relevance. They inform non-British people what certain terms mean, and they inform British people of the ways in which their usage is distinctive. This last point is important, especially for students of language: it is always easier to identify distinctive forms in varieties other than our own.

jiggery-pokery tricks, fraud
Jock nickname for a male Scot
joint roast meat, especially for Sunday lunch (not marijuana)
jolly as adverb (*jolly good*)
junction intersection
junior school the older section of a primary school
kibosh /kaɪbɒʃ/ ruin, disaster (as in *put the kibosh on*)
kite mark British Standards Institute label
knock-on rugby term
L learner driver
landlord operator of a pub
last call announcing closing time in a pub
Law Society solicitors' association
lay-by highway rest area
lbw cricket term

BEING AMERICAN

American identity is much bound up with home origins. Conversations between two Americans meeting abroad will commonly include an early focus on their home states or colleges, whereas this is unlikely with two Britons (assuming they talked to each other at all). These ties have a linguistic consequence in such matters as awareness of nicknames – a phenomenon which plays a much larger role in the USA than in Britain. Very few British counties have nicknames – and if they do (e.g. *Royal Berkshire*) they do not create a sense of identity. A recent letter from one North Carolinian to another now living in Britain, asking for some information, ended with a postscript which hoped that his request ('from one old Tarheeler to another') would not be too inconvenient. It is inconceivable that someone from Reading in Berkshire would end a letter to a former neighbour now living in Australia as 'one old Royal Berksherian to another'.

In *The American Language* (1919), H. L. Mencken summarizes the linguistic history of the US states, including their various nicknames (p. 152). Here are his remarks on North Carolina (taken from a later edition):

The two Carolinas have been called variously, but *Tarheel State* for North Carolina and *Palmetto State* for South Carolina seem likely to prevail. Of the origin of the former the *Overland Monthly* gave the following account in 1869: 'A brigade of North Carolinians…failed to hold a certain hill, and were laughed at by the Mississippians for having forgotten to tar their heels that morning. Hence originated the cant name.' There are several more flattering versions of the origin of the nickname, but all of these suggest that North Carolinians were known as *Tarheels* before the Confederate War, or, at all events, that some notion of tar was associated with them. The DA [*Dictionary of Americanisms*] offers evidence that they were called *Tarboilers* as early as 1845 …The newspaper of the students at the University of North Carolina has been *The Tarheel* since 1892, and when, in 1922, the state bankers launched a monthly organ at Raleigh it was given the name of *Tarheel Banker*. The other common nickname for North Carolina is *Old North State*; it arose naturally out of the geography and history of the state, and the DA traces it to 1839. *Land of the Sky* is applied to the beautiful mountain country in the far western part of the state; eastern North Carolina is far closer to the bottom of the Atlantic than to the sky.

SPELLING

The spelling differences between British and American English were noted as one of the chief sources of variation in the world press (pp. 80, 300). Several of them are productive, applying to large numbers of words, such as BrE -re, AmE -er (centre / center); BrE -our, AmE -or (colour / color), and BrE -ogue, AmE -og (catalogue / catalog). Many more apply to individual items, including the 100 shown in the following list. An asterisk indicates a usage which is common to both areas in some circumstances; for example, the spelling aesthetics will be found in certain US texts, and inquire is often found in British texts; n. stands for noun. Informal spellings (p. 275), such as nite (night), hi / lo (high/low), and thru (through), are not listed.

British	American
aeroplane	airplane
aesthetics*	esthetics
aether	ether*
amoeba*	ameba
anaemia	anemia
anaesthesia	anesthesia
appal*	appall
archaeology*	archeology

axe*	ax
bale out	bail out
battleaxe*	battleax
boloney	baloney*
B.Sc.*	B.S.
buses*	busses
caesarian*	cesarian
callisthenics	calisthenics
cantaloup	cantaloupe*
carat (gold)*	karat
cauldron*	caldron
cheque	check
chequer	checker
chilli	chili*
cigarette*	cigaret
cissy	sissy*
citrous (adj)	citrus*
connexion	connection*
councillor*	councilor
counsellor*	counselor
defence*	defense
diarrhoea*	diarrhea
disc (not computing)*	disk
doughnut*	donut
draughtsman	draftsman
draughty	drafty
encyclopaedia	encyclopedia*
enquire	inquire*
ensure*	insure
faeces	feces
foetus	fetus*
floatation	flotation*

gaol	jail*
garotte*	garote
gauge*	gage
gonorrhoea	gonorrhea
gramme	gram*
grey*	gray
gynaecology	gynecology
haemo-*	hemo-
homoeopath	homeopath
hosteller	hosteler
inflexion	inflection*
instil*	instill
jeweller*	jeweler
Jnr.	Jr.*
kilogramme	kilogram*
largesse*	largess
leukaemia	leukemia
libellous*	libelous
licence (n.)	license (n.)
liquorice	licorice*
manoeuvre	maneuver
marvellous*	marvelous
mediaeval	medieval*
mollusc*	mollusk
mould*	mold
moult*	molt
moustache*	mustache
M.Sc.*	M.S.
oedema	edema
oesophagus	esophagus
oestrogen	estrogen
offence*	offense

orthopaedics	orthopedics
paediatrician	pediatrician
panellist	panelist
paralyse	paralyze
pedlar*	peddler
plough*	plow
practice (n.)	practise (n.)
premise*	premiss
pretence (n.)	pretense (n.)
primaeval	primeval*
programme (not computing)	program
pyjamas	pajamas
renegue	renege*
sanatorium*	sanitorium
scallywag*	scalawag
sceptical*	skeptical
smoulder*	smolder
snowplough	snowplow
Snr.	Sr.*
storey*	story (building)
sulphur*	sulfur
throughway*	thruway
titbit*	tidbit
traveller*	traveler
tyre	tire
vice (tool)	vise
wilful*	willful
woollen*	woolen

(After M. Benson, E. Benson & R. Ilson, 1986b.)

PRONUNCIATION

There are several regular differences between Received Pronunciation (RP, p. 365) and General American (GA, cf. p. 237), such as the pronunciation of final /-r/ in the latter. In addition, several words have individually different pronunciations.

Item	RP	GA
anti-	'antiː	'antaɪ-, 'antiː
asthma	'asmə	'azmə
ate	et, eɪt	eɪt
capsule	'kapsjuːl	'kapsəl
chassis	'ʃasiː	'tʃasiː
clerk	klɑːk	klɜrk
clique	kliːk	klɪk
data	'dɑːtə, 'deɪtə	'deɪtə, 'datə
derby	'dɑːbi	'dɜːrbi
erase	ɪ'reɪz	ɪ'reɪs
fracas	'frakɑː	'freɪkəs
geyser	'gaɪzə	'geɪzər
gooseberry	'guzbəri	'guːsberi
goulash	'guːlaʃ	'guːlɑːʃ
herb	hɜːb	ɜːrb, hɜːrb
leisure	'leʒə	'liːʒər
lever	'liːvə	'levər, 'liːvər
lieutenant	lef'tenənt	luː'tenənt
medicine	'medsɪn	'medɪsɪn
missile	'mɪsaɪl	'mɪsəl
nephew	'nevjuː, 'nefjuː	'nefjuː
nougat	'nuːgɑː	'nuːgət
progress	'prəʊgres	'prɒgres
route	ruːt	raʊt, ruːt
schedule	'ʃedjuːl	'skedʒuəl, 'skedʒəl
tissue	'tɪsjuː, 'tɪʃuː	'tɪʃuː
tomato	tə'mɑːtəʊ	tə'meɪtəʊ
vase	vɑːz	veɪs, veɪz
wrath	rɒθ	raθ
z	zed	ziː

SHORT AND LONG A

RP has many words in /ɑː/ which are pronounced with /æ/ in GA. They include the following:

advance	mask
after	mast
answer	monograph
ask	nasty
aunt	overdraft
banana	pass
basket	passport
bath	past
blast	pastor
broadcast	path
castle	plant
class	plaster
command	raft
dance	ranch
disaster	raspberry
example	rather
fasten	reprimand
France	sample
giraffe	slander
glass	slant
grass	staff
half	task
last	telegraph
laugh	vast

STRESS DIFFERENCES

There are many words whose stress varies between the two accents. Some of them can be grouped into patterns, such as those ending in -ary/-ory (e.g. secretary, laboratory) or -et (e.g. ballet, beret), which attract stress on the final syllable. Some of the words vary, depending on their sentence position, as in **Princess Anne is a princess**.

This is one of the areas where American influence on British English has been particularly strong, and probably most of the words in the first column can be heard in the UK these days with the American stress pattern, especially spoken by younger people. To a generation of British youngsters reared on episodes of Star Trek, there is only one way of pronouncing frontier (as in 'Space: the Final Frontier'). An asterisk marks words where the stress pattern shown in the other column may also be heard.

RP	GA
address	address*
advertisement	advertisement*
ballet	ballet
cafe*	cafe
cigarette	cigarette
controversy*	controversy
debris*	debris
frontier*	frontier
garage*	garage
inquiry	inquiry
laboratory	laboratory
magazine	magazine
moustache	mustache
premier	premier
princess*	princess
research*	research
reveille	reveille
translate*	translate
valet	valet
weekend*	weekend

CLASSIFYING LEXICAL DIFFERENCES

In describing the lexicon of the two regions, there are *three* distinctions which have to be made: some words (lexemes, p. 118) are found only in American English (AmE), some only in British English (BrE), and some (from either source) have become established throughout the world as part of Standard English (p. 111). While *Congress* and *Parliament* originate in their respective countries, it is no longer very useful to call one AmE and the other BrE, from a linguistic point of view. They are now part of World Standard English (WSE). Similarly, there are many items where the word is part of WSE, though the entity being referred to differs in certain respects from country to country. Many legal terms fall into this category: *jury, juvenile,* and *justice of the peace* are terms in common to both AmE and BrE, but their legal definitions are not. Such items are not the focus of interest on this or the opposite page.

The remaining words represent many different kinds of semantic contrast, and there have been several classifications. One system includes the following important types among its categories (after M. Benson, E. Benson & R. Ilson, 1986b):

• Some words reflect cultural differences but are not part of WSE: AmE *Ivy League, Groundhog Day, revenue sharing*; BrE *A-levels, giro, VAT*. There are no synonyms in the other variety. Several of these words are likely to enter WSE in due course. *Groundhog Day*, for example, received a boost in that direction following its use as the title of a successful film in 1993. Most people in Britain would not have known the tradition before seeing the film.

• Some words are straightforward: they have a single sense, and a synonym in the other variety: BrE *current account* = AmE *checking account*; BrE *estate car* = AmE *station wagon*. If only they were all like that.

• However, they are not, because we have to allow for words which have at least one WSE meaning and one or more *additional* meanings that are specific to either BrE or AmE: an example is *caravan*, which in the sense of 'group of travellers in a desert' is common to both varieties; but in the sense of 'vehicle towed by a car' it is BrE (= AmE *trailer*).

• Some words have one meaning in WSE and a synonym in one or other of the two varieties (sometimes both). Both AmE and BrE have *undertaker*, but only AmE has *mortician*; both have *pharmacy*, but AmE has *drugstore* and BrE has *chemist's*.

• Some words have no WSE meaning, but different meanings in AmE and BrE: AmE *flyover* = BrE *fly-past*; however, BrE *flyover* = AmE *overpass*.

• We also have to remember the effect of frequency. Some words are used in both varieties, but are much more common in one of them: *flat* and *apartment* are used in both, but the former is frequent in BrE and the latter in AmE. Other examples are *shop* vs *store*, and *post* vs *mail* (p. 300).

This set of categories does not exhaust the classificatory possibilities, but it should be enough to suggest caution when working through an apparently simple list of equivalents, as in the examples opposite.

A STRAIGHTFORWARD LEXICAL CONTRAST

Road signs in the USA and UK.

AN IMPOSSIBLE LEXICAL CONTRAST

With hierarchies in organizations (p. 168), it is often impossible to give a precise answer to the question 'What's the equivalent of a – in BrE/AmE?' because there is no one-for-one correspondence between the different ranks, or at best only a partial correspondence. A good example is the hierarchy of university teaching, shown below.

A British *professor* is not exactly equivalent to a US *professor*, because the latter category divides into three levels: *full professor* (the most senior), *associate professor*, and *assistant professor* (the most junior). In the UK, the ranks below professor are *reader*, then *senior lecturer* (though some universities treat these grades as equivalent in salary, but different in function), then *lecturer*. An associate professor is roughly equivalent to a reader, and lower grades of lecturer can be equated with an assistant professor. But it is not possible to identify the AmE equivalent of a senior lecturer, and in the days when tenured positions were serious academic options, there was even less equivalence, as a BrE lecturing post was usually tenured, whereas an AmE assistant professorial position was usually not (but rather, 'tenure-track').

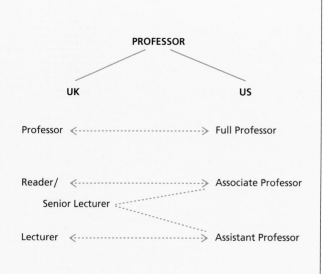

In this list of equivalent lexical items, the 'rules of the road' conventions of Benson, Benson & Ilson (1986b) have been adopted. A solid line indicates that no crossing over into the other variety is possible: the item can be used only in the one variety. The broken line shows that the item can cross: it can be used in the other variety (i.e. it is

WSE). These distinctions can be illustrated as follows:

BrE	AmE
pillar box │	│ mailbox
post ┊	┊ mail
lead /liːd/ │	│ leash
rubbish ┊	┊ garbage

Items with stylistic labels (such as *colloquial*) have no marking.

In the top list, AmE items are given first. In the bottom list, a different selection of items has the BrE version first.

AmE	BrE	AmE	BrE	AmE	BrE
absorbent cotton │	│ cotton wool	candy │	│ sweets	driver's license │	│ driving licence
Administration ┊	┊ Government	car │ (*train*)	│ carriage, waggon	druggist │	┊ pharmacist
airplane │	│ aeroplane	carryall │	│ holdall	dry goods │	┊ drapery, soft goods
allowance │	│ pocket money	casket │	┊ coffin	dump truck ┊	┊ tipper lorry
aluminum │	│ aluminium	catsup │	│ (tomato) ketchup	eighth note │	│ quaver
antenna ┊	┊ aerial	charge account ┊	│ credit account	electric cord │	│ flex
apartment building │	│ block of flats	check │ (*restaurant*)	┊ bill	elementary school │	┊ primary school
Archie Bunker (*colloq.*)	Alf Garnett	checkers │	│ draughts	elevator │	│ lift
ash can │	┊ dustbin	checking account │	│ current account	engineer │	│ engine driver
ass (*colloq.*)	┊ arse	clothespin │	│ clothes peg	emergency cord │	│ communication cord
auto │	┊ car	comforter │	┊ eiderdown	eraser │	│ rubber
baby carriage │	┊ pram	conductor │ (*train*)	│ guard	exhaust fan │	│ extractor fan
back-up │	│ tailback	cookie │	│ biscuit (*roughly*)	expressway │ (*in city*)	│ motorway
baggage ┊	┊ luggage	corn │	┊ maize, sweet corn	fall │	┊ autumn
baseboard │	│ skirting board	cot │	│ camp bed	fanny (*slang*)	┊ buttocks
bathroom │	┊ lavatory, toilet	cotton candy │	│ candy floss	faucet │	┊ tap
bathtub │	┊ bath	county seat │	│ county town	fire department │	│ fire brigade
beltway │	│ ring road	crib │	│ cot	first floor │	┊ ground floor
Big Dipper │	│ The Plough	crossing guard │	│ lollipop man/woman	flashlight │	│ torch
bill │ (*money*)	┊ note	depot │	┊ (railway) station	floor lamp │	│ standard lamp
billfold │	┊ wallet	derby │	┊ bowler (hat)	flutist │	│ flautist
biscuit │	┊ (*roughly*) scone	desk clerk │	│ reception clerk	football ┊	┊ American football
blue jeans │	┊ jeans (*blue denim*)	detour │ (*road sign*)	│ diversion	freeway │	│ motorway
bobby pin │	│ hair grip	dial tone │	│ dialling tone	freight train │	│ goods train
bookstore │	┊ bookshop	diaper │	│ nappy	French doors │	│ French windows
Bronx cheer │	┊ raspberry (*noise*)	dish towel │	│ tea towel	French fries ┊	│ chips
bulletin board │	│ notice board	divided highway │	│ dual carriageway	garbage │	┊ rubbish, refuse
bureau │	┊ chest of drawers	dollhouse │	┊ doll's house	garters │	│ suspenders
caboose │	│ guard's van	dormitory │	│ hall of residence	gasoline │	│ petrol
call-in │ (*program*)	│ phone-in (*programme*)	draft │	┊ conscription	Girl Scout │	│ Girl Guide, Guide
can ┊	│ tin	drapes │	┊ curtains	grade crossing │	│ level crossing

BrE	AmE	BrE	AmE	BrE	AmE
hire purchase │	│ installment plan	nil │	┊ zero, nothing	spanner │	│ wrench
hoarding │	│ billboard	nought │	┊ zero	spirits ┊	┊ (hard) liquor
holiday │	│ vacation	noughts and crosses │	│ tick-tack-toe	sports │ (*school*)	┊ track meet
home help │	│ homemaker	number plate │	│ license plate	spring onion │	┊ scallion
houseman │	│ intern	pancake │	┊ crepe	stalls │	┊ orchestra
ice │	│ ice cream	pants │	┊ underpants	state school │	│ public school
ice lolly │	┊ Popsicle™, ice	paraffin │	┊ kerosene	stone │ (*fruit*)	┊ pit
immersion heater │	┊ hot water heater	patience │ (*cards*)	│ solitaire	stopcock │	┊ valve
Inland Revenue │	│ Internal Revenue Service	pavement │	│ sidewalk	subway │	┊ underpass, tunnel
interval │	┊ intermission	pillar box │	│ mailbox	swede │	│ rutabaga
jelly │	│ Jell-O™	planning permission │	│ building permit	swing door │	┊ swinging door
Joe Public │	│ John Q Public	post ┊	┊ mail	swiss roll │	│ jelly roll
jumble sale │	│ rummage sale	post code │	│ zip code	telegraph pole │	│ telephone pole
jumper │	┊ sweater, pullover	prawn cocktail ┊	┊ shrimp cocktail	telephone box/kiosk │	┊ telephone booth
knave │ (*cards*)	┊ jack	puncture │	┊ flat	terraced house │	│ row house
ladder │ (*hosiery*)	┊ run	pushchair │	┊ stroller	third-party insurance │	│ liability insurance
lead │	│ leash	queue ┊	│ line	tights ┊	│ pantyhose
lemonade │	│ lemon soda	racecourse │ (*horses*)	│ racetrack	trade union │	│ labor union
line │ (*railway*)	┊ track	railway │	│ railroad	trainers │	│ sneakers
lounge suit │	│ business suit	removal van │	│ moving van	transport cafe │	│ truck stop
lucky dip │	│ grab bag	rise │ (*salary*)	│ raise	treacle │	│ molasses
marrow │	│ squash	roundabout │	│ traffic circle	trolley │	│ shopping cart
maths (*colloq.*)	math	rowing boat │	│ row boat	trouser suit │	│ pants suit
mince │	│ ground / chopped meat	sailing boat │	│ sailboat	tube │	│ subway
motorcar │	┊ car, automobile	saltcellar ┊	│ saltshaker	turn-up │ (*trousers*)	│ (trouser) cuff
mudguard │	│ fender	shop assistant │	│ salesclerk	underground │	│ subway
mum, mummy (*colloq.*)	mom, mommy	signal box │	│ signal tower	vest │	│ undershirt
nail varnish │	│ nail polish	signal box │	│ signal tower	waistcoat │	│ vest
newsagent │	│ newsdealer	sleeper │ (*railway*)	│ crosstie, tie	WC	rest room
nightdress ┊	┊ nightgown	slip road │	│ ramp	whisky │	┊ scotch
		solicitor │	┊ lawyer		

There are certain semantic fields (p. 137) where groups of lexical differences cluster. Here is a presentation of the choices to be made with reference to automobiles, adapted from the *Longman Dictionary of English Language and Culture* (1992).

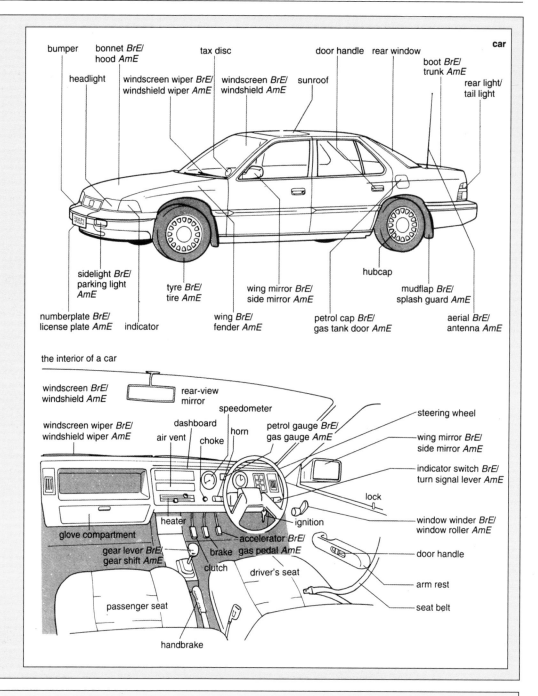

car

bumper
bonnet *BrE*/ hood *AmE*
tax disc
door handle   rear window
boot *BrE*/ trunk *AmE*
headlight
windscreen wiper *BrE*/ windshield wiper *AmE*
windscreen *BrE*/ windshield *AmE*
sunroof
rear light/ tail light
sidelight *BrE*/ parking light *AmE*
tyre *BrE*/ tire *AmE*
wing mirror *BrE*/ side mirror *AmE*
hubcap
mudflap *BrE*/ splash guard *AmE*
numberplate *BrE*/ license plate *AmE*   indicator
wing *BrE*/ fender *AmE*
petrol cap *BrE*/ gas tank door *AmE*
aerial *BrE*/ antenna *AmE*

the interior of a car

windscreen *BrE*/ windshield *AmE*
rear-view mirror
speedometer
steering wheel
windscreen wiper *BrE*/ windshield wiper *AmE*
dashboard
air vent   choke   horn
petrol gauge *BrE*/ gas gauge *AmE*
wing mirror *BrE*/ side mirror *AmE*
indicator switch *BrE*/ turn signal lever *AmE*
lock
heater
ignition
window winder *BrE*/ window roller *AmE*
glove compartment
accelerator *BrE*/ gas pedal *AmE*
door handle
gear lever *BrE*/ gear shift *AmE*
brake
driver's seat
arm rest
clutch
seat belt
passenger seat
handbrake

'THE PLAY WAS A REAL BOMB!'

The question is: did the speaker like it or not? If you are an American reader, you are in no doubt: it was a total disaster. If you are a British reader, you are in no doubt: it was a tremendous success. The point illustrates the need to be careful with idioms, as well as individual words, when crossing the Atlantic. The author recalls a situation where he was at cross-purposes with a US acquaintance who had asked him what someone thought of a book. The response *Hilary was full of it!* was interpreted by the American to mean that she hated it – whereas in BrE the meaning of this idiom is quite the reverse.

It is unusual for there to be an exact idiomatic equivalent between BrE and AmE. Among the exceptions are the following (in each case, the BrE variant is given first):

if the cap/shoe fits, wear it
the lie/lay of the land
to turn on sixpence/a dime
a skeleton in the cupboard/closet
cash on the nail/barrelhead
blow one's own trumpet/horn
off the back of a lorry/truck
put in my two penniworth/two cents' worth.

Most idioms have no easy equivalent, and must simply be interpreted. They include:

BrE
hard cheese! (=bad luck!)
drop a brick (=blunder)
in queer street (=in debt)
a turn-up for the book (=a surprise)
the best of British! (=good luck!).

AmE
right off the bat (=with no delay)
feel like two cents (=feel ashamed)
out of left field (=unexpectedly)
take the Fifth (=refuse to answer)
play hardball (=no holds barred)
a bum steer (=bad advice).

There is a growing awareness of AmE idioms in Britain, and many originally AmE items, such as *ants in his pants* and *a quick buck*, are now commonplace.

GRAMMATICAL DIFFERENCES

There are relatively few grammatical differences between educated BrE and AmE. A leading reference grammar (p. 197) notes regional trends affecting only *c.* 250 points in morphology or syntax, with many of these affecting individual items (e.g. irregular verbs), and very few being general points of syntactic construction. (AmE examples precede BrE in the following paragraphs; for grammatical terminology, see Part III.)

• In the verb phrase, AmE prefers *have* to *have got* for possession (*Do you have the time?* vs *Have you got the time?*); answers also tend to vary (*I don't* vs *I haven't*); AmE prefers such forms as *burned* to *burnt* (p. 441), and there are some special past tense forms (colloquial *snuck out*, *dove*); AmE also sometimes uses a simple past tense where BrE has a present perfect (*I just ate* vs *I've just eaten*); *will/won't* is generally found for *shall/shan't*; there are also differences in the use of tag questions (p. 218).

• In the noun phrase there are some differences of word order (e.g. *Hudson River* vs *River Thames*, *a half hour* vs *half an hour*) and the use of the article (*in the future* vs *in future*, *in the hospital* vs *in hospital*); AmE prefers collective nouns (p. 209) in the singular (*the government is*), whereas BrE allows plural also (*the government are*).

• Clausal patterns sometimes differ, as in AmE *Come take a look* (vs *Come and take*); AmE also makes more use of the subjunctive (p. 216), as in *I asked that he go* (vs *I asked him to go*), and prefers *were* to *was* in such sentences as *I wish she were here*; *different than/from* is more common than *different to/from* (p. 441).

• There are several differences in prepositions (see below) and adverbs, such as AmE *I'll go momentarily* (vs *in a moment*), *real good* (vs *really good*), and *backward* (vs *backwards*).

PARALLEL PREPOSITIONS

AmE	BrE
It's twenty of four.	It's twenty to four.
It's five after eight.	It's five past eight.
It's in back of the building.	It's behind the building.
I'll see you over the weekend.	I'll see you at the weekend.
I haven't seen her in ages.	I haven't seen her for ages.
Mondays we take the bus.	On Mondays we take the bus.
Monday through Friday.	Monday to Friday inclusive.
I looked out the window.	I looked out of the window.
I moved toward the car.	I moved towards the car.
You're on the firing line.	You're on the firing line.
He's got a new lease on life.	He's got a new lease of life.
It caters to all tastes.	It caters for all tastes.
Half the cash goes for clothes.	Half the cash goes on clothes.
She's in heat.	She's on heat.
They live on X street.	They live in X street.

These are some of the ways in which prepositions (p. 213) contrast between AmE and BrE, and given the everyday nature of some of the contexts, it would appear that this is an area of major grammatical differentiation. There are in addition several cases where preferences differ: AmE prefers *round* to *around* in such sentences as *We went round the corner* and *around* to *about* in *They walked about a mile*. *Amongst* is much more likely in BrE, and *atop* in AmE (literary style). Compound prepositions also show some contrasts, such as the AmE preference for *aside from* (BrE *apart from*), *in behalf of* (BrE *on behalf of*), and the informal *off of* and *back of*.

Are prepositions such a major area of differentiation as these examples suggest? A study comparing the distribution of prepositions in two million-word samples of printed text, one BrE and the other AmE (the Brown and LOB corpora, p. 438), found that this was not so.

• The percentage of prepositional occurrences in BrE was 12.34 per cent; in AmE it was 12.21 per cent.
• There were 81 prepositions that occurred in both corpora, accounting for 99.9 per cent of all prepositional occurrences. Just 13 prepositions were found only in BrE, and (coincidentally) just 13 in AmE.
• The distribution of the six most commonly used prepositions

Prepositions occurring only in the AmE corpus		Prepositions occurring only in the BrE corpus	
Preposition	Frequency	Preposition	Frequency
unlike	42	worth	104
pursuant	20	barring	3
excluding	13	less	3
pro	5	failing	2
astride	3	re	2
atop	3	touching	2
involving	3	bar	2
post	3	afore	1
vis-à-vis	2	à la	1
dell'	1	bout	1
infra	1	qua	1
inter	1	vice	1
with-but-after	1	neath	1

(which represent over 70 per cent of all the occurrences) is almost identical in both varieties.
(After D. Mindt & C. Weber, 1989.)

The conclusion is plain: whatever the differences in prepositional usage between the two varieties, as represented in these corpora, they are far outweighed by the similarities. However, in interpreting the figures two points must be borne in mind. These samples are of written English only, and many of the examples above (such as asking the time) are characteristic of speech. The differences are likely to be greater when medium (p. 292) is taken into account. Also, BrE usage is changing under the influence of AmE, as we have seen in other areas of language use (p. 306): *talk with* is now common in BrE (as opposed to *talk to*), and while the British traditionally fill *in* (or sometimes *up*) forms, they now commonly fill them *out*, as Americans do. How far the factor of language change will fundamentally alter the linguistic picture remains to be seen.

Top prepositions	Preposition	AmE	BrE
The rank order of the top six prepositions is identical, with some of the totals being remarkably close.	of	36,432	35,287
	in	20,870	20,250
	to	11,165	10,876
	for	8,992	8,738
	with	7,286	7,170
	on	6,183	6,251
	at	5,375	5,473
	by	5,244	5,724

THE GOTTEN/GOT DISTINCTION

Gotten is probably the most distinctive of all the AmE/BrE grammatical differences, but British people who try to use it often get it wrong. It is not simply an alternative for *have got*. *Gotten* is used in such contexts as *They've gotten a new boat* (='obtain'), *They've gotten interested* (='become') and *He's gotten off the chair* (='moved'), but it is not used in the sense of possession (='have'). AmE does not allow *I've gotten the answer* or *I've gotten plenty*, but uses *I've got* as in informal BrE. The availability of *gotten* does however mean that AmE can make such distinctions as the following: *they've got to leave* ('they must leave') vs *they've gotten to leave* ('they've managed to leave').

PUNCTUATION

Many of the differences which can these days be observed in punctuation stem from different conventions in AmE and BrE. Almost all the set of punctuation marks are shared by the two varieties, but there have been a few exceptions:

• # is used for 'number' in AmE (as in *#12*), but not in BrE (which would write *No. 12*). However, this symbol, often called a 'hash', is increasingly used in BrE because of its role in computational work.
• The raised dot is used for a decimal point in BrE; an ordinary period in AmE.
• A colon plus dash (:–) is very unusual in AmE, but is also now decreasing in BrE.
• Other differences between the two varieties are referred to in the discussion of individual punctuation marks on p. 282.

REGIONAL VARIATION IN AMERICAN ENGLISH

Many of the distinctive features of American English can be established by comparing it with the other major model of English-language use, British English (p. 306); but this exercise is very much an idealization. To make any comparison practicable, we have to work with a single linguistic version from each region, and this is usually (in the case of pronunciation, p. 307) General American and Received Pronunciation. However, as soon as we put external comparison aside, and begin to investigate each dialect as an end in itself, we are faced immediately with a vast amount of variation, some of it regional, some social (p. 362). These pages illustrate aspects of the regional variation which exists.

The scientific study of US regional dialects is over a century old, having begun with the formation of the American Dialect Society in 1889. A series of linguistic atlases was planned, the first of which appeared between 1939 and 1943: *The Linguistic Atlas of New England* (see opposite). Most other areas have now received systematic study, and some, such as the Upper Midwest and the Gulf Coast, have had extensive material published. These studies have established the existence of three broad dialect areas:

• *Northern*: an area not to be confused with the political 'north' of the Civil War period (1861–5). Histori-

cally it is the area of New England, but it now extends west in a narrow northern strip from western Vermont through New York and across all the northern states to the Pacific coast. Dialect studies show that there is an important boundary (roughly along the Connecticut River) separating western and eastern New England. To the east there is a distinctive accent, a major feature of which is the loss of final (postvocalic) *-r* (p. 93).

• *Southern*: the coastal and piedmont areas of Delaware, Maryland, Virginia, the Carolinas, Georgia, the Gulf States, and extending into the eastern part of Texas. In this area also there is frequent loss of final *-r*.

• *Midland*: a very large area extending across almost the whole country, from southern New Jersey and Pennsylvania and northern Delaware, down through the mountainous areas of Virginia, the Carolinas, and Georgia, westward across Tennessee and western Arkansas, then spreading into the whole of the western United States. Northern and Southern dialect sub-regions can be identified. One of the Northern features, shown on the map, is a merger of pronunciation between /ɒ/ and /ɔː/, so that such pairs as *cot / caught* and *don / dawn* sound the same. It is the vast size of the Midland area that accounts for the impression of general uniformity in American English speech.
(After F. G. Cassidy, 1982)

AMERICAN DIALECT ATLASES

The detailed research required to demonstrate the existence of dialect patterns can be seen in these two maps from *A Word Geography of the Eastern United States*, one of the first products of the *Linguistic Atlas of the United States*, which began its survey work in 1931. The survey area covered all the coastal Atlantic states from Maine to Georgia, and included Pennsylvania, West Virginia, and eastern Ohio – an area which at the time contained nearly two-fifths of the US population. Over 1,200 local people were interviewed from a large number of locations. Interviewers spent between 10 and 15 hours with each informant, and obtained data on over 1,000 points of usage.

The maps show the kind of distributional information obtained. The upper map shows a point of grammatical variation: the choice of preposition in telling the time. The use of *of* has been identified as a 'standard' feature of American English, when comparing it with British English (p. 311). The dialect data shows just how much of a simplification that kind of statement can be. The lower map illustrates a point of lexical variation – the several words used for *seesaw*.

Three dialect subdivisions are recognized, providing evidence for the nationwide regions shown opposite. The *Northern* division includes the New England settlement area, upstate New York and the Hudson Valley, NE Ohio, and beyond. The *Midland* division extends south from N Pennsylvania and parts of New Jersey, and west into C Ohio and beyond; its southern boundary swings in an arc from C Delaware along the Blue Ridge Mountains of Virginia, and into the Carolinas. The *Southern* division comprises the southern two-thirds of Delaware, the eastern parts of Maryland, Virginia, and North Carolina, most of South Carolina, and (p. 315) the Gulf States. (After H. Kurath, 1949.)

	South			Mid-land		North				
× regular – fairly common · rare	South Carolina	North Carolina	Virginia Piedmont	Eastern Shore	South Midland	North Midland	Hudson Valley	Upstate New York	Western New England	Eastern New England
quarter to (vs of/till)	–	×	–		·		–	–	–	–
curtains (vs shades/blinds)	·	–	–	–		–	·	–	×	×
piazza (vs porch)	×	×	·			–			×	×
gutters (vs eaves troughs, etc.)	×	×	×	–		–	×	·	–	×
corn house (vs corn crib)	–	·	×	–			·	·	–	–
spider (vs frying pan)	–	–	·	·		·	–	×	×	×
low, loo (vs moo)	×	×	×	×	·	·		–	–	–

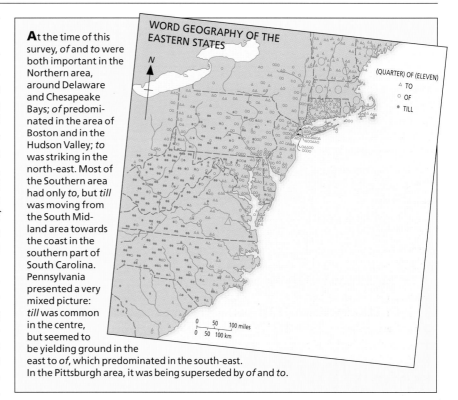

At the time of this survey, *of* and *to* were both important in the Northern area, around Delaware and Chesapeake Bays; *of* predominated in the area of Boston and in the Hudson Valley; *to* was striking in the north-east. Most of the Southern area had only *to*, but *till* was moving from the South Midland area towards the coast in the southern part of South Carolina. Pennsylvania presented a very mixed picture: *till* was common in the centre, but seemed to be yielding ground in the east to *of*, which predominated in the south-east. In the Pittsburgh area, it was being superseded by *of* and *to*.

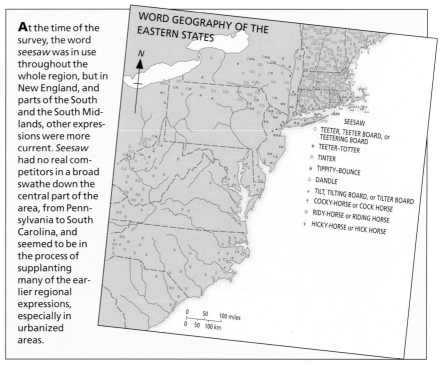

At the time of the survey, the word *seesaw* was in use throughout the whole region, but in New England, and parts of the South and the South Midlands, other expressions were more current. *Seesaw* had no real competitors in a broad swathe down the central part of the area, from Pennsylvania to South Carolina, and seemed to be in the process of supplanting many of the earlier regional expressions, especially in urbanized areas.

◀ **SHARED FEATURES**

Regional dialect divisions are never clear-cut, because of the influence of other (e.g. social) factors. This table shows how some of the words in the Eastern States survey are shared by Northern and Southern areas, but are largely absent in the Midlands. (After H. Kurath, 1949, p. 49.)

DARE

The *Dictionary of American Regional English* is the official dictionary of the American Dialect Society. Based at the University of Wisconsin, Madison, under the direction of Frederic G. Cassidy (1907–), it is a project planned in five volumes, two of which have already appeared (in 1985 and 1991) covering the letters from A to H. The data came from interviews with 2,777 informants in 1,002 communities spread across the 50 states, and was collected between 1965 and 1970. The informants were natives or long-term residents of their communities. The 80 fieldworkers used a questionnaire of 1,847 items dealing with general concerns of daily life, and also made tape recordings. In the final form of the dictionary, use is additionally made of some 7,000 other oral and written sources between the 17th century and the present-day. The illustration shows the entries for the items *chic sale(s)* and *hurting*, along with a computerized map showing the distribution.

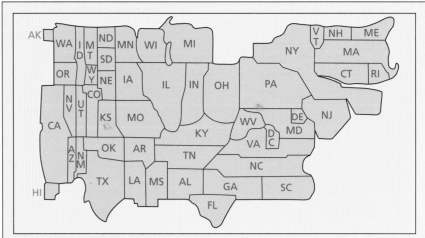

An innovation of the *DARE* study was the use of computers to handle the large quantities of data. It also enabled a US map to be generated which reflects population sizes (and thus the number of communities selected as part of the survey) rather than geographical area. New York and California especially are enlarged through this approach. In using the map to show distributions (see below), a dot is placed on each community which gave a particular response to a question; a blank space means that there was either some other response or no response at all. (For an explanation of state abbreviations and the usual shape of the USA, see p. 312.)

TWO EXAMPLES FROM THE *DARE* MATERIALS

Abbreviations

c	central
cap	capitalized
coll	college
DC	Washington DC
DN	*Dialect Notes*
educ	educated
infs	informants
joc	jocular
LAUM	*Linguistic Atlas of the Upper Midwest*
MD	Maryland
Midl	Midlands
MO	Missouri
n	noun; north(ern)
ne	north-east
NY	New York State
Qq	questions
Qu	question
quot	quotation
s	south(ern)
Sth	south
TX	Texas
usu	usually
Var(r)	variant(s)
w	west(ern)
WELS	*Wisconsin English Language Survey*
WI	Wisconsin

Chic sale(s) n, also attrib Usu cap Also *chick sale(s)* [See quot 1929] **scattered, but chiefly NEast, N Midl, West** See Map *somewhat old-fash, joc*
An outhouse, outside toilet.
   [**1929** Sale *Specialist* [6], There's Chic Sale, Doc Sale's boy / From Urbana, Illinoy, *Ibid* 11, You are face to face with the champion privy builder of Sangamon County.] **1950** *WELS (An outside toilet building)* 5 Infs, **WI**, Chick Sales; 2 Infs, Chick Sale; 1 Inf, Chic Sales; 1 Inf, Chick Sales Classic Palace; 1 Inf, Chick Sale Special. **1962** Atwood *Vocab. TX* 53, *Chic Sale*. **1965–70** *DARE* (Qu. M21b. *Joking names for an outside toilet building*) 119 Infs, **scattered, but chiefly NEast, N Midl, West**, Chic sale(s); **DC**2, **MD**48, Chic sale house; **NY**127, Chic sale special; (Qu. M21a, *An outside toilet building*) Inf **MO**4, Chic sale. [Of all Infs responding to Qu. M21b, 6% were young, 26% coll educ; of those giving these responses, none were young, 50% coll educ.) **1970** Tarpley *Blinky* 149 **ne TX**, *Chick Sales*. [1 Inf] **1971** Bright *Word Geog. CA & NV* 150, *Chic Sale(s)*. [75 Infs, Central and Southern Nevada, scattered in California] **1973** Allen *LAUM* 1.181, Chic Sale. [6 Infs, 2 in Iowa, 4 in Nebraska]

hurting n

1 An ache or pain. **chiefly Sth, S Midl** See Map
   1902 *DN* 2.237 **sIL** [Pioneer dialect], *Hurtn* [sic]. . . A pain. **1917** *DN* 4.413 **wNC**, *Hurtin'*. . . A pain. **1950** *WELS* 1 Inf, **WI**, Hurting. **c1960** *Wilson Coll.* **csKY**, *Hurting*. . . A sort of indefinite ache or pain, like a hurting in the chest. **1965–70** *DARE* (Qu. BB4, *Other words for a pain* . . . *"He's had a _____ in his arm for a week.")* 77 Infs, **scattered, but chiefly Sth, S Midl**, Hurting; GA67, Hurting — [used by] Negroes; (Qu. BB3b) Infs **FL**26, **NH**16, **OH**44, **TN**30, Hurting; (Qu. BB3c) Inf **IN**28, Hurting; **TN**16, Hurtin'. **1965** *DARE* Tape MS61, I had t' go t' the doctor for a hurtin' across my breast. . . When I go t' stoop over, why this hurtin' cumulates across here. **1976** Garber *Mountain-ese* 45 **Appalachians**, *Hurtin'*. . . pain, soreness. I jist kain't do my work no more since I got this hurtin' in my back.

2 in phr *put a hurting on:* To cause a physical mark or pain; see quot.
   1970 *DARE* (Qu. Y11, *Other words for a very hard blow: "You should have seen Bill go down. Joe really hit him a _____.")* Inf **NY**249, Put a hurting on the cat; (QR near Qu. Y35) Inf **NY**249, Put a hurting on the coffee pot; (QR near Qu. AA9) Inf **NY**241, She put a hurtin' on him — in a good sense. [Both Infs Black, male]

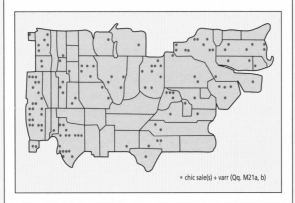

• chic sale(s) + varr (Qq. M21a, b)

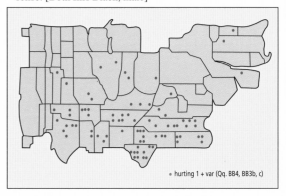

• hurting 1 + var (Qq. BB4, BB3b, c)

APPALACHIAN SPEECH

This story of a raccoon hunt, part of the data collected by a US sociolinguistic study, illustrates some of the features of the Appalachian speech of SE West Virginia – an area that has attracted particular attention because of its supposed conservatism in dialect use. The authors of the study showed that there were certainly several older features still present, but the notion that the dialect is a living example of Elizabethan English, although carrying 'a certain romantic charm', they conclude is too simplistic to be meaningful, as many new developments in grammar and phonology exist alongside the older forms.

Nonetheless, the extract does illustrate some interesting older features. In particular there is the use of the *a-* prefix with *-ing* forms of verbs in certain functions (*a-trying*), which in late Middle English was widely found in Midland and Southern British dialects (p. 50), and which is often used as a literary stereotype of Appalachian speech. There is also evidence of the lack of present-tense subject–verb concord (*we's, I's, he's*). This generalization of the -s form has clear antecedents in Middle English, especially in the varieties used in Scotland (and later Northern Ireland) and northern England, and is found in many parts of England in the Early Modern period (p. 65). A strong case can thus be made for the colonial influence of these areas on the continuing use of these features in this dialect.

…John supposedly had a sack to put the coon in if we caught one. We's gonna try to bring it back alive, so we tromped through the woods 'til along about six o'clock in the morning. The dogs treed up a big hollow chestnut oak, and we proceeded to cut the thing down. It's about three or four inches all the way around. About four foot through the stump. We tied the dogs and cut the thing down. Well, we cut it down and turned one dog loose, and he went down in that thing, way down in the old hollow of the tree and it forked, and we couldn't get up in there so he backed out and he tied 'im. And we's a-gonna chop the coon out if it was in there. I's a kinda halfway thought maybe it just treed a possum or something. Well, I chopped in and lo and behold, right on top of the dang coon. Eighteen pounder, Jack Stern says, kitten coon. I run in with the axe handle down in behind him to kep him from getting out or backing down in the tree. He reached, fooled around and got him by the hind legs and pulled that thing out, it looked as big as a sheep to me. Turned 'im loose, he said 'kitten, Hell.' We had an old carbide light and he turned that over and the lights were…that's all the light we had. And, we had to hunt it then and the dogs took right after the coon right down the holler and the dogs caught it and Jack beat us all down there. Went down there and he's a-holding three dogs in one hand and the coon in the other hand. And they's all a-trying to bite the coon and the coon a-trying to bite Jack and the dogs, and Jack pulled out a sack and it wasn't a dang thing but an old pillow case that Maggie had used, his wife, it was about wore out. So we fumbled around 'ere and finally got that coon in that sack and he aimed to close the top of it and the coon just tore the thing in half, in two, and down the holler he went again. With that sack on him, half of it and we caught that thing, and you know, E.F. Wurst finally pulled off his coveralls and we put that thing down in one of the legs of his coveralls and tied that coon up. He's tearing up everything we could get, we couldn't hold him he's so stout. And I brought that thing home and kept 'im about a month, fed 'im apples and stuff to eat so we could eat 'em. Well, I did I killed him and tried eat that thing, I'd just soon eat a tomcat or a polecat, I wouldn't make much difference. And, that's about the best coon hunt I believe I was on.
(From W. Wolfram & D. Christian, 1976, p. 181.)

MIGHT IT COULD?

The Linguistic Atlas of the Gulf States (LAGS) is a multi-volume project which began publication in 1986, under the direction of Lee Pederson of Emory University, Georgia. Entries in the concordance to the materials are based on over 5,000 hours of tape-recorded speech from over 1,000 interviews conducted by fieldworkers. The inclusion of a great deal of free conversation in the interviews permits a dimension of description which is usually missing in questionnaire responses to specific enquiries.

An interesting example of the range of dialect data brought to light by this project is the use of 'double modals' (such as *will can* or *might could*). In Standard English, modal verbs do not co-occur (p. 212). The double forms are sometimes said to be characteristic of Appalachian speech (and certainly there are antecedents in Middle English, notably in Scotland and northern England, which would support the historical connection hypothesized above). Might it could be a feature?

The combinations, ordered in terms of frequency, are as follows; a remarkable 39 forms use eight different first elements.

might could	219
used to could	124
might can	54
might would	41
used to would	19
used to wouldn't	11
used to couldn't	10
may can	9
might ought to	6
shouldn't ought to	6
might better	3
might have could have	3
might have used to	3
might wouldn't	3
shouldn't have ought to	3
used to used (to) could	3
might couldn't	2
might have would have	2
might will	2

and single instances of:
can might, could might, could used to, may not can, may not ought to, may would, might cannot, might can't, might could've, might have could, might just could, might not can, might not could, might should, might used to, ought to could, shouldn't oughtn't (to), used to used (to) wouldn't, would might, would use to

A *LAGS* computer-generated codemap is shown (right) for the most frequent of these combinations. The map gives social, age, ethnic, and geographical patterns. The age of informants was classified into three broad bands: 13 to 30, 31 to 60, and 61 to 99. The following abbreviations are used: *W* 'white', *B* 'black', *L* 'lower class', *M* 'middle class', *U* 'upper class'.

On the map, each dot represents an informant location. If a double modal form was used, a dot is replaced by a letter or a number. The key to the symbols is shown alongside the map. *A*, for example, is a black, lower-class informant, aged 13 to 30; the figure to the right refers to the number of people in this category who used the form (3 out of 13, in this case). Locator codes on the printout margins have been omitted in this display.

There is evidently a greater concentration of the form in the Lower South, especially stretching from EC Georgia westward to N Louisiana. It occurs relatively infrequently in Tennessee and N Georgia. There is no ethnic difference in the use of the form (23 per cent of whites and 24 per cent of blacks used it). Over-60s are somewhat less likely to use it (22 per cent vs 31 per cent). There is a definite trend with class, with lower-class people using the form most (30 per cent), followed by middle (23 per cent) and upper (14 per cent) classes. There is, however, no evidence for a prevalence of this modal combination in the Appalachian areas. It might couldn't.

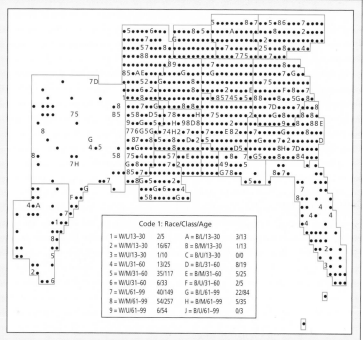

Code 1: Race/Class/Age

1 = W/L/13–30	2/5	A = B/L/13–30	3/13
2 = W/M/13–30	16/67	B = B/M/13–30	1/13
3 = W/U/13–30	1/10	C = B/U/13–30	0/0
4 = W/L/31–60	13/25	D = B/L/31–60	8/19
5 = W/M/31–60	35/117	E = B/M/31–60	5/25
6 = W/U/31–60	6/33	F = B/U/31–60	2/5
7 = W/L/61–99	40/149	G = B/L/61–99	22/84
8 = W/M/61–99	54/257	H = B/M/61–99	5/35
9 = W/U/61–99	6/54	J = B/U/61–99	0/3

URBAN OBSERVATIONS

A great deal of dialectology has been taken up with the speech and subject-matter of rural areas – very often restricted to older people who have lived their whole lives in the same locality. Increasingly, studies are now being made of urban settings, though the mixed nature of the population invariably defies clear linguistic classification.

The map (right) is part of a study of the greater Boston area carried out in the mid-1960s, in which 30 informants responded to 110 test sentences designed to elicit all the vowels and consonants of Boston English. The study concluded that there were at least three sub-dialects in the city: one accent prevailed, typifying most levels of society outside the central area; a second characterized a minority of upper-class speakers, mainly from certain districts (such as Beacon Hill, Back Bay, Milton); and the third occupied districts at the centre of the city (such as South Boston, East Boston, South Cambridge). For example, among the various differentiating features of the city centre subdialect were three consonantal characteristics: the use of a linking /r/ in such sequences as *law and order*, the replacement of /n/ by /l/ in *chimney*, and the use of a flapped [ɾ] for the second /t/ in *potatoes*. (After R. L. Parslow, 1971.)

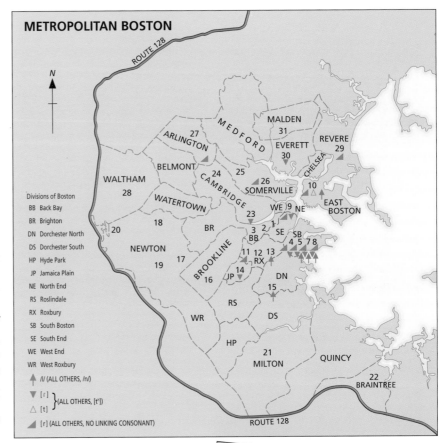

METROPOLITAN BOSTON

Divisions of Boston
BB   Back Bay
BR   Brighton
DN   Dorchester North
DS   Dorchester South
HP   Hyde Park
JP   Jamaica Plain
NE   North End
RS   Roslindale
RX   Roxbury
SB   South Boston
SE   South End
WE   West End
WR   West Roxbury

▲ /l/ (ALL OTHERS, /n/)
▼ [ɾ]
△ [t] } (ALL OTHERS, [tʰ])
◣ [ɾ] (ALL OTHERS, NO LINKING CONSONANT)

CITY TALK

A hint of the complexity to be found in the Chicago area is given in this sketch from a leading US dialectologist, Raven I McDavid, Jr, with several comments about other dialects thrown in for good measure.

Needless to say, we do not always agree on which vowel or consonant we will use, even when we share the whole repertoire. North of Peoria one is likely to find *greasy* with /-s/, further south with /-z/; a person familiar with both pronunciations is likely to consider one more repulsive than the other – depending on which is his pronunciation at home. In metropolitan Chicago the natives of smaller suburban communities are likely to pronounce *fog, hog, Chicago* with the vowel of *father*; in the city itself these words normally have the vowel of *law*...Many Pennsylvanians rhyme *food* with *good*; many highly educated Southerners rhyme *soot* with *cut*. *Roof* with the vowel of *foot* is widespread in the area of New England settlement and some of the areas settled from Pennsylvania; *coop* with the vowel of *do* is almost universal north of the Kanawha River; *root* rhyming with *foot* is characteristic of Yankee settlements...

We even show differences in our grammar. No one in South Carolina, however uneducated, would say *hadn't ought*, which is still current in educated Northern speech, nor would we say *sick to the stomach*, which in the North is almost universal. But many educated Southerners – and I include myself – find a place in conversation for *might could*, *used to could* and *used to didn't*. I have heard the basketball announcer for the Chicago *Tribune* become almost schizoid as he hesitated between *dived* and *dove* (with the vowel of *go*), and there seems to be no regional or social distinction between *kneeled* and *knelt*. Even *ain't* – a four-letter word still taboo in writing despite *Ulysses*, *Lady Chatterly* and Norman Mailer – may be found in educated conversation, especially among the first families of Charleston. When we realize this, we can take calmly the diversity of names for the grass strip between sidewalk and street, the earthworm, the dragon fly or cottage cheese; the debate among New Englanders as to whether a doughnut should be made with yeast; or the fact that the New Orleans poor boy sandwich may be a *hoagy* in Philadelphia, a *submarine* as in Boston, a *grinder* as in upstate New York or a *hero* as in New York City. Only in recent years have people outside Chicago learned that *clout* is our local Chicago name for political influence, a *Chinaman* is a dispenser of such influence, a *prairie* is a vacant lot and a *gangway* is a passage, usually covered, between two apartment buildings...

Yet if we are sometimes bewildered by the differences in American English, we should be comforted to learn that by European standards these differences are very small. We can notice, in fact, that not only are the differences along the Atlantic Seaboard fewer and less sharp than one finds in the much shorter distance between Cumberland and Kent, but that differences diminish as we go west. We owe our relative uniformity of speech to several forces. First, the speakers of the more extreme varieties of British local speech were not the ones who migrated...There was dialect mixture in all of

the early settlements – a situation repeated in the westward movement – so that what survived in each area was a compromise. [(see p. 94) And after referring to traditions of geographical and social mobility, industrialization, urbanization, and general education, McDavid concludes:] All of these forces have combined – and are still combining – to replace local and even regional terms with commercial terms of national use, to eradicate the most noticeable non-standard grammatical features and even to reduce the differences between the pronunciation of one region and that of another. Yet though these forces have reduced some of the regional differences in American English, they have not eliminated them. (R. I. McDavid, 1971.)

THE BLUE RIDGE MOUNTAINS

A 650-mile strand of the Appalachian Mountains, running from Pennsylvania through Maryland, Virginia, and North Carolina to Georgia. Geographically famous for its wooded scenery, it is linguistically well-known as a boundary region between Midland and Southern dialect areas.

ACCENT ATTITUDES

American regional differences are less widespread than, say, in Britain, as Raven McDavid suggests (p. 316), but the ones that do exist seem to attract just as much publicity, fascination, and concern, as appears from this newspaper report from *The Monitor*, published in McAllen, Texas (30 August 1992).

Instructor helping students modify the y'all drawl

GREENVILLE, S.C. – Stories told in David Pence's class often are tragedies on a small stage. If they sound comic, you must not be from around here.

The class is called "How to Control Your Southern Accent."

There was the story of the Southern auto racer, trying to buy clothing in California, who couldn't make the vendor understand that "rice wire" translated to "race wear".

There was the pair of travelers, far from their home in the Piedmont, who ordered "ahss tay." The waitress begged their pardon. "Ahss tay, plaze," they repeated, meaning the cool drink made from steeped tea leaves. The waitress tapped her pencil on the order pad.

"Finally they said, 'Can we have a soda?'" explained Pence, a speech pathologist by day who has taught the evening course at Greenville Technical College for 3½ years.

He smiled in telling the iced tea saga but said accents are not a laughing matter. A student in his first class burst into tears.

"All these handkerchiefs came out," he recalled, as the woman sobbed, "I've been harassed about my accent so much . . . you don't know how upsetting it is."

The encyclopedia of Southern Culture says Southerners are "often schizophrenic about their speech" – proud of its color and expressiveness, but "insecure" about being heard outside their region. Some parents, it adds, try to expunge Southern features from their children's speech.

The goal of Pence's six-week, $65 class is straightforward but hardly simple: to give his students a choice in how they communicate, especially with non-Southerners.

"If people start listening to how you're saying something, instead of what you're saying, then you're losing effectiveness," he said.

But in a region wary that Yankee influences are already spreading like the unkillable kudzu vine, Pence's effort sounds to some like "Gomer Pyle Meets Henry Higgins" – and they hear snickers.

"Go home. We'll never miss you!" declared one of several hate letters he's received. ("I'm from Arkansas; that's considered Southern," Pence protests, his own native twang threading faintly through his speech, like the still-blue seams of jeans bleached to white.)

Another letter writer stormed that he'd rather hear "someone from central Georgia read the phone book than listen to Beethoven. . . . To my mind you are participating in the destruction of a priceless piece of Americana."

An editorial in *The News and Courier* of Charleston, S.C., took note of Pence's class and just chuckled.

"Can y'all stand it?" the newspaper scoffed. Southern speech "has character and resonance that sets it apart from the unaccented, homogenized speech that afflicts most of the nation."

No argument there from Pence. But what about those who don't want their accent to set them apart?

One student told his class she's passed around on the phone whenever she calls her company's New York office. "It's the girl from the South," she hears.

Kathy Young, an executive secretary who's taking the course for the second time, said, "There's no room in the professional world for a hillbilly secretary" – a perception she hears reflected in Northerners' comments and blames on television.

Portrayals of rubes ['country hicks'], from "The Beverly Hillbillies" to the "Dukes of Hazzard" and beyond, have stereotyped those who use any of the 25 or so distinct Southern dialects that researchers have counted. Even Yale- and Oxford-educated Bill Clinton didn't escape the "Bubba" tag in New York.

Pence gave a more positive reason for wanting to control a Southern accent: As major corporations locate in this booming corner of the Sunbelt – BMW, the latest, announced in June it would build a $250 million auto plant outside Greenville – getting and keeping a job depend on being understood.

It was the influx of foreign companies that indirectly led Pence to offer his course.

Typical clients he sees in his private practice are stutterers or stroke patients relearning speech, but a few years ago Pence began offering foreign-born executives help in pronouncing English.

Not long afterward, he said, "I started getting people saying, 'Can you work on my Southern accent?'"

One of these was Nancy Humphries. "In 1987, I was crowned Miss South Carolina," she said, and state pageant officials gave her some advice. "To go to Miss America, they wanted me to have more of a general American accent."

She didn't win the national title but she did land the broadcasting job she wanted. And her Southern accent?

"I turn it on and turn it off," she said from her office at the ABC-TV affiliate in Charleston, WCBD, where she's a reporter and morning news anchor.

"When I'm Nancy I can be Nancy. So I still keep my Southernness. It's just in my professional world that I lose my accent."

Another student of Pence's, 67-year-old Dr. George Grimball, took the class after being named district governor of Rotary International; he knew he'd be making many speeches.

Grimball defended Pence's efforts, despite "criticism from these longtime Confederates." Still, his own success was limited by a schedule that kept him from studying tapes and doing other homework – and by the complexity of his goal to begin with.

"I like the way Southerners talk," Grimball said in a modified version of the rich drawl that Americans heard when South Carolina Sen. Ernest Hollings ran for president in 1984.

(Christopher Sullivan of The Associated Press.)

VARIATION IN BRITISH ENGLISH

Awareness of regional variation in English is evident from the 14th century, seen in the observations of such writers as Higden/Trevisa (p. 35) or William Caxton (p. 56) and in the literary presentation of the characters in Chaucer's *Reeve's Tale* or the Wakefield *Second Shepherd's Play* (p. 58). Many of the writers on spelling and grammar in the 16th and 17th centuries made comments about regional variation, and some (such as Alexander Gil, p. 66) were highly systematic in their observations, though the material is often obscured by a fog of personal prejudices. The scientific study of dialect in England began in the late 19th century. The English Dialect Society was founded in 1873 by W. W. Skeat, and remained active until the launch of the first major work of British dialectology: Joseph Wright's *English Dialect Dictionary* (1898–1905).

The Survey of English Dialects

The next major step was planned in 1946 by Swiss professor Eugene Dieth (1893–1956) and British scholar (later Leeds professor of English) Harold Orton (1898–1975), and became known informally as the Dieth–Orton Survey. A questionnaire of over 1,300 items was developed, and a field survey undertaken between 1948 and 1961 in 313 localities throughout England. It was biased towards rural communities, its topics being the farm and farming, animals and nature, the house and housekeeping, the human body, numbers, time and weather, social activities, and abstract states, actions, and relations. Agricultural communities with a static population were selected, and newly built-up areas avoided. The informants were all locally born, working class, almost all over 60, and mainly men. Responses to the questions (over 404,000 items of information) were transcribed by nine fieldworkers in phonetic transcription, and tape recordings were also made of the unscripted speech of the informants. Much of the material remains in archives, but between 1962 and 1971 the basic material was published in an introduction and four volumes. Then in 1978 the *Linguistic Atlas of England* appeared, containing an interpretation of a selection of the data.

A great deal of other work has since taken place in British dialectology, especially focusing on the speech of urban populations. It has also moved away from the classical model of English dialects, as illustrated in the older rural population, and towards a model which better reflects the more complex sociolinguistic situation of a world of considerable population mobility and rapid social change.

EARLY VARIETY OBSERVATIONS

Commentary
I know not what can easily deceiue you in writing, vnlesse it bee by imitating the barbarous speech of your countrie people, whereof I will giue you a taste...Some people speake thus: the *mell* standeth on the *hell*, for the *mill* standeth on the *hill*; so *knet* for *knit*; *bredg* for *bridg*; *knaw* for *gnaw*...Take heed also you put not *id* for *ed* as *unitid* for *united*, which is Scottish. And some ignorantly write a cup *a wine* for a cup *of wine*: and other like absurdities.
(Edmund Coote, *The English Schoole-Master*, 1597)

It cannot pass my Observation here, that, when we are come this Length from *London*, the Dialect of the *English* Tongue, or the Country-way of expressing themselves, is not easily understood. It is the same in many Parts of *England* besides, but in none in so gross a Degree, as in this Part...It is not possible to explain this fully by Writeing, because the Difference is not so much in the Orthography, as in the Tone and Accent; their abridging the Speech, *Cham*, for *I am*; *Chill* for *I will*; *Don*, for *do on*, or *put on*; and *Doff*, for *do off*, or *put off*; and the like.
(Daniel Defoe, *Tour thro' the whole Island of Great Britain*, 1724–7)

There is scarcely any part of England, remote from the capital, where a different system of pronunciation does not prevail. As in Wales they pronounce the sharp consonants for the flat, so in Somersetshire they pronounce many of the flat instead of the sharp: thus for *Somersetshire*, they say *Zomerzetzhire*; for *father*, *vather*; for *think*, THink; and for *sure*, *zhure*.
(John Walker, *Pronouncing Dictionary*, 1791)

Characterization
Good gentleman, go your gait, and let poor volk pass. And 'chud ha' bin zwagger'd out of my life, 'twould not ha' bin zo long as 'tis by a vortnight. Nay, come not near th'old man; keep out, che vor' ye, or ise try whither your costard or my ballow be the harder. Chill be plain with you.
(Shakespeare, *King Lear*, IV.vi. Edgar, adopting a south-western dialect)

By the mess, ere theise eyes of mine take themselves to slomber, ay'll de gud seruice, or I'll lig i'th'grund for it; ay, or go to death; and I'll pay't as valorously as I may, that sall I suerly do, that is the breff and the long: Marry, I wad full fain hear some question 'tween you tway.
(Shakespeare, *Henry V*, III.ii. Jamy, a representation of Scots)

For other examples of dialect representation in literature, see pp. 331, 348, 353.

OLD LANCASHIRE

This extract from *Tummus and Meary* ('Thomas and Mary') by Tim Bobbin – the pseudonym of John Collier (1708–86) – is an example of the genre of dialect literature which grew up in the 18th century. It appears here in an 1854 edition by Samuel Bamford who considers the account of a century before 'a very imperfect setting forth of the Lancashire dialect' and corrects many allegedly Cheshire forms in it. A translation is given alongside.

Well Mester Cunstable, sed th'Justice, what hanyo brought meh neaw?

Why plyes yur worship, ween meet neaw ta'en a hawse steyler at wur mayin off with' tit as hard as he cud.

Odd! thought I t'mehsel, neaw or never, Tum, spyek for thesel. So aw speek op, an sed, 'That's no true, Mr. Justice, for awr boh gooin foots pace.'

Umph! sed th'Justice, there's no mitch difference as to that poynt. Howdtee the tung yung mon, an speake when theawrt spokken too. Well! theaw mon i'th breawn cwot theaw, sed th'Justice, whot has theaw to say agen this felley? Is this tit thy tit, sesto?

It is, Ser.

Heer clark, bring that book an let's swear him.

Th'clark brought th' book, an th'Justice sed a nomony to th'felley; an towd him he munt tey care o' whot he sed, or he moot as helt be forsworn, or hong that yeawth theer.

Well, Master Constable, said the Justice, what have you brought me now?

Why please your worship, we have just now taken a horse stealer that was making off with it as hard as he could.

Odd! thought I to myself, now or never, Tim, speak for yourself. So I spoke up, and said, 'That's not true, Mr. Justice, for I was but going a foot's pace.'

Umph! said the Justice, there's not much difference as to that point. Hold you your tongue, young man, and speak when you are spoken to. Well! you man in the brown coat you, said the Justice, what have you to say against this fellow? Is this horse your horse, do you say?

It is, Sir.

Here, clerk, bring that book and let's swear him [in].

The clerk brought the book, and the Justice said a speech to the fellow; and told him he must take care of what he said, or he might as likely be forsworn, or hang that youth there.

The rural emphasis of the Survey of English Dialects is well represented by this extract. The question is taken from Book 3 of the Survey, on animals, and the responses shown here are for six counties and the Isle of Man. All transcriptions are in the International Phonetic Alphabet (p. 239).

Abbreviations

Nb Northumberland
Cu Cumberland (now part of Cumbria)
Du Durham
We Westmoreland (now part of Cumbria)
La Lancashire
Y Yorkshire
n.a. not available
n.k. not known

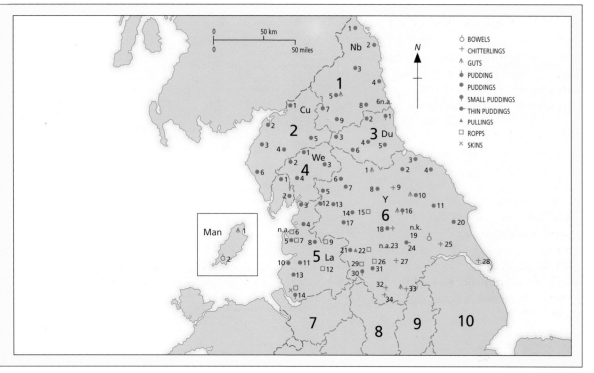

CONSONANT VARIATION

One of the phonological maps from *The Linguistic Atlas of England*, showing the regional distribution of one of the consonants: initial /h/. This has generally been lost in regional speech, but has been retained in three specific rural areas: the far North; an area from East Anglia to N Sussex; and a small area in the South-West.

In these and the following maps, a dot represents the use of a particular form in a locality (numbered in each county). A small cross (x) shows that the fieldworker did not elicit the form. The occurrence of an alternative form in an area is shown by special symbols: ∩ is used for the dropping of /h/ in area 1, and ∧ for the retention of /h/ in area 2. If these symbols are centred on the dot, it means that both forms are found in that locality; if centred on the cross, only the alternative form is found.

Key
OE *hand*, *hond*
OE **h-**
  ∧ h retained
  ∩ h dropped

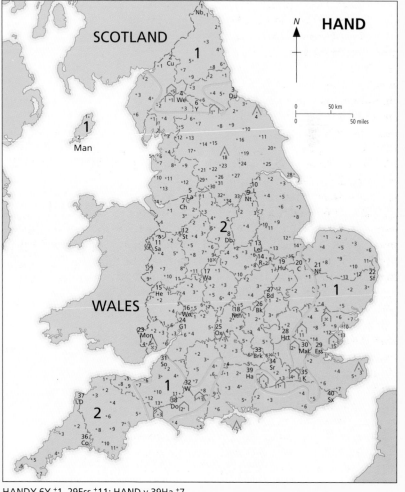

HANDY 6Y +1, 29Ess +11; HAND v 39Ha +7

VOWEL VARIATION

Plotting vowel variation is a much more intricate matter than in the case of consonants, and far more distinctions in phonetic detail are required (p. 238). Vowel maps have always to be interpreted with caution, because of the inevitable uncertainties which accompany impressionistic transcriptions, but clear trends do emerge, as in this example of what happens to /a/ when followed by /r/ and a consonant (in this case, /m/).

A broad distinction can be drawn between those accents which retain some kind of /r/ (generally in the South, West, and far North) and those which do not. Several qualities of /r/-colouring can be distinguished: the symbols show fricative ([ɹ]), retroflex ([ɻ], especially in the South-West) and uvular ([ʁ], in the far North) variants. Front varieties of vowel quality are increasingly likely as one moves away from the South-East, though there are pockets of back vowel quality. Diphthongization occurs in the North-East. Because there are so many variants occurring outside their 'usual' area, a much wider range of symbols for alternative forms is shown on this map than in the case of /h/ (p. 319).

Key
OE *arm*, *earm*
ME **ar + C**

∧ aː
△ aˑ
⊼ aˤː
◹ aʁː
∧ æː
⌂ æˑː
∩ ɑː
⌂ ɑˤː
⍁ ɑˤː
　 əˑː
⋀ əˤː
　 eːʁə
△ ɛə
　 ɛəʁ

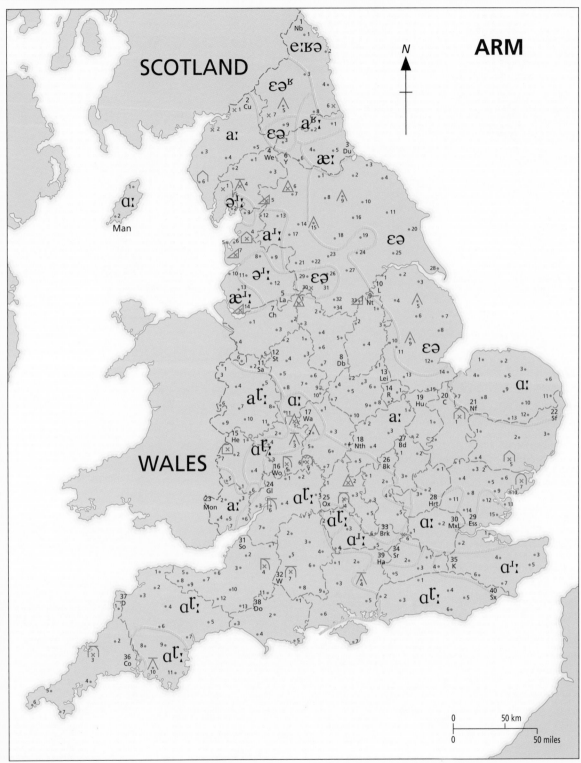

SCOTLAND

WALES

N

ARM

0 ——— 50 km

0 ——— 50 miles

ə͡ᵊ 29Ess 3 under aː:
aɹ 6Y 6, aːɹə 2Cu 2 under aˑː:
aˤɻ 25Ox 3, aˤˑə 26Bk 3 under aˤː:
æə 3Du ⁺3 under ɛə
æˑʁ 1Nb 3 under ɛəʁ
ɑːʁ 28Hrt 3, ɑˑ Man 2 under ɑː:
ɑɹ 15He ⁺7, ɑːɹ 33Brk 3, 34Sr 2/4 under ɑˤː:
ɑːəˤ 34Sr 3/⁺5 under ɑˤː:

ə͡ᵊː 5La3, ə͡ᵊˑɹ 5La 2/11/12, ə̈͡ᵊˑɹ 5La 8 under əˤː:
eəʁ: 1Nb 6, eˑə̈ʁ 1Nb 7
ɛː 6Y ⁺19
ɛːɹə 2Cu 1
ɛə ɹeə 6Y 30
æˤː 25Ox 1
aːɹə 2Cu 2
interpr as r-col: ɹ 5La 9, 6Y 6, 15He 7,

ɽ 25Ox 4, ʁ 1Nb 1/2/4
cons *r* foll r-col Vː ɹ 5La 2/8/11/12, ɽ 25Ox 3/5, 32W 7, 33Brk 1/2, 40Sx 1–6, ʁ 1Nb 3

ARM- 1Nb ⁺5

j- 24Gl ⁺6/7, 31So 3/4, 32W 4/7/8, 33Brk 1/2, 39Ha 7

LEXICAL VARIATION

Some of the maps of the English Dialect Survey (p. 318) show extensive lexical variation. There are nine chief variants noted for *threshold*, for example, and a further 35 alternatives. In the case of *headache*, there is a fairly clear picture. The standard form is used throughout most of the country, but in the North and parts of East Anglia there is a competing regional form, *skullache*. The variant form *head-wark* is found in the far North, with a further variant, *head-warch*, mainly in S Lancashire. Northumberland opts for the more prosaic *sore head*, with *bad head* used in adjacent localities to the south. The Survey also shows the range of words used as premodification (p. 222), where there is an interesting distinction between people who say *a headache* and those who say *the headache*. (For the location of English counties, see p. 143.)

Key

∧ BAD HEAD

∩ HEADACHE
   OE *hēafod + æ ce*
   †c1000

   HEADWARCH
   OE *heafodwærc*,
   ON *hofuðverkr*
   †c1000

⊓ HEADWARK
   †c1350

   SKULLACHE

   SORE HEAD
   OE *sar* + −
   †1549

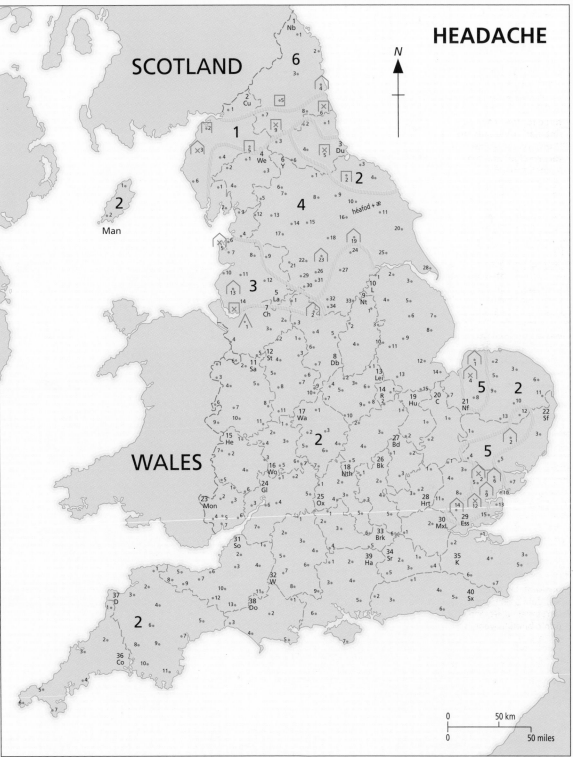

HEADACHE

SCOTLAND

WALES

Man

hēafod + æ

The following pre-modifications were rec:
A (BAD HEAD) 1Nb 7/8, 2Cu⁺2/⁺5/6, 7Ch⁺1
A BIT OF (HEADACHE) 31So 7;
  A (HEADACHE) 7Ch 4/6, 9Nt⁺1/3,
  10L 2/10, 11Sa 4, 13 Lei 7/9, 17 Wa 3/7,
  18Nth 2/4/5, 19Hu 1, 20C 2, 21Nf 2/9,
  22Sf⁺2, 23Mon 5, 24Gl 7, 25Ox 3, 26Bk 3–5,
  27Bd 1–3, 28Hrt 2,
  29 Ess 1/⁺6/8/⁺10/12/13/⁺14, 30MxL 2,
  31So 3/8, 32W 4, 33Brk 5, 34Sr 2, 37 D 9,
  38 Do⁺2, 40Sx 1;

A NASTY (HEADACHE) 16Wo 7;
AN (HEADACHE) 9Nt⁺1, 13Lei 1–6/10,
  14R 1/2, 17Wa 7, 23 Mon 7;
THE (HEADACHE) 1Nb⁺4, 3Du 2,
  5La 5, 6Y⁺2/4/⁺23/24/27/32–34, 7Ch⁺1/3/5,
  8Db 7, 9Nt 4, 10L 8/9/15, 11Sa 1/2/5–11,
  12St⁺9, 15He 1–6, 16Wo 1–6, 17 Wa 1/4–6,
  18Nth 1/3, 19Hu 2, 20C 1, 21Nf 4/7, 22Sf 1/3/5,
  23Mon 1/2/6, 24Gl 1–6, 25Ox 1/2/5/6, 26Bk 2,
  28Hrt 1, 29Ess 2/⁺10/⁺14, 30MxL 1,
  31So 4/6⁺9/13, 32W 3/5/6/8, 33Brk 4,

35K 2, 36Co⁺1/3/5/6, 37D 1/2/5/7/10/11,
  38Do⁺2/3/5, 39Ha 1/3
THE (HEADWARCH) 5La 6/8/10, 8Db 1
A BIT (HEADWARK) 3Du⁺6;
  A (HEADWARK) 2Cu⁺5, 6Y 1/8/10;
  A TERRIBLE (HEADWARK) 6Y 7;
A (SKULLACHE) 29Ess⁺6/⁺14;
  THE (SKULLACHE) 22Sf 4, 29 Ess 5/⁺14
A (SORE HEAD) 1Nb 1–3/⁺4, 2Cu 1;

MORPHOLOGICAL VARIATION

There is a remarkable diversity in the use of the verb *to be* in English dialects, especially in its negative forms. The map shows the range encountered for the first person singular: 16 variants are shown on the map, and a further eight isolated forms listed below. Among the interesting features are: the use of *is*/'s in the North (compare the use of this feature in American dialects, p. 315); *ain't* is widespread in the East Midlands and South-East, with variant forms (*en't*, *yun't*) further west; and forms based on *be* dominate in the South-West.

For comparison, the range of forms recorded in other persons is given below (minor variants in parentheses):

I am: am, are, be, bin, is

you are (sing.): you are, ye are, thou are, thou art, thee art, thou is, you be, you bin, thee bist, (thee be, thou bist, you am)

she is: is, be, bin, (am, bist)

we are: are, am, be, bin, (aren)

they are: are, am, is, be, bin, (aren, at, bist)

she isn't: isn't, 's not, isno', ain't, en't, yun't, idn', inno, bain't, ben't (idn't, binno', byent, 's none, yen't)

they aren't: aren't, 're not, ain't, en't, yun't, anno', bain't, baan't, ben't, byen't, byun't, binno', (amno', inno', in't, isn't, 'm not, 're none)

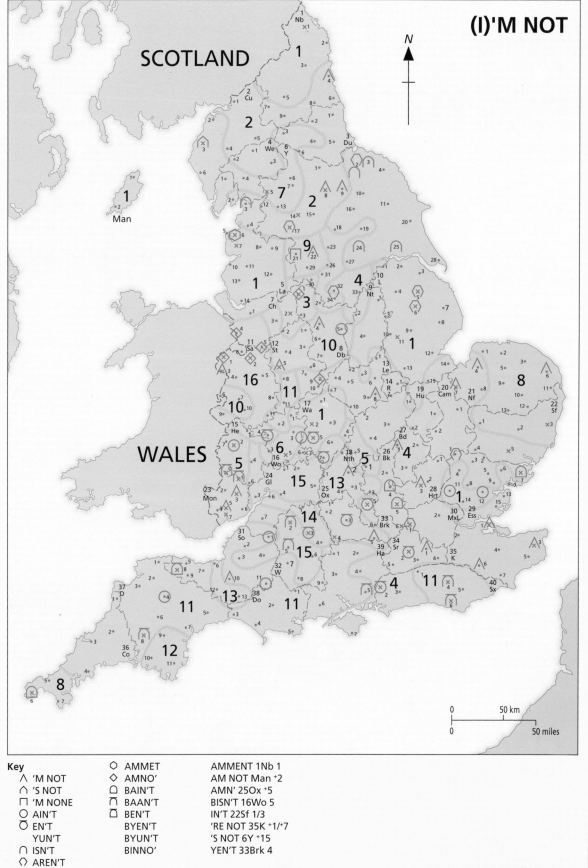

(I)'M NOT

Key

∧	'M NOT
∩	'S NOT
⊓	'M NONE
○	AIN'T
⊖	EN'T
	YUN'T
∩	ISN'T
◇	AREN'T

◇	AMMET
◇	AMNO'
⊓	BAIN'T
⋒	BAAN'T
⊔	BEN'T
	BYEN'T
	BYUN'T
	BINNO'

AMMENT 1Nb 1
AM NOT Man +2
AMN' 25Ox +5
BISN'T 16Wo 5
IN'T 22Sf 1/3
'RE NOT 35K +1/+7
'S NOT 6Y +15
YEN'T 33Brk 4

SYNTACTIC VARIATION

An example of a dialect map showing variations in syntax (p. 214). The word order *give me it* is usual in the North, most of the East, and in a narrow band across the South Midlands; *give it me* dominates in the lower North-West, West Midlands, and South-East, with the prepositional form, *give it to me*, the norm in the South-West, and also occurring in enclaves around the Thames estuary and in East Anglia. The pronoun-less form *give me* is recorded once, in Surrey. This is doubtless one of the forms which would be much more widely represented in an urban dialect survey. (The map summarizes word order patterns only, ignoring the actual choice of pronouns.)

Key

∧ GIVE IT ME
∩ GIVE IT TO ME
⊓ GIVE ME IT

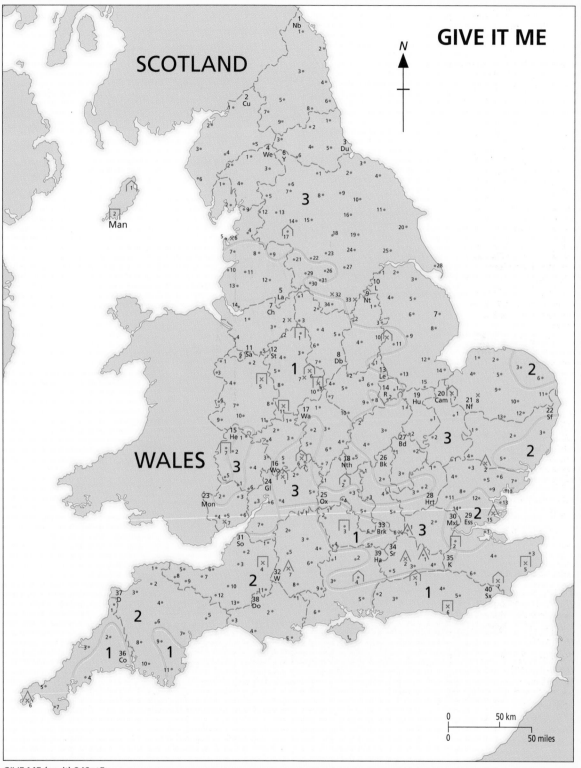

GIVE IT ME

GIVE ME (no *it*) 34Sr ⁺5

DIALECTS OF ENGLAND: TRADITIONAL AND MODERN

The picture which emerges from the kind of dialect information obtained by the Survey of English Dialects (p. 318) relates historically to the dialect divisions recognized in Old and Middle English (pp. 28, 50). This situation is shown below: the map displays 13 traditional dialect areas (it excludes the western tip of Cornwall and most of Wales, which were not English-speaking until the 18th century or later, and the urban area of London). A major division is drawn between the North and everywhere else, broadly following the boundary between the Anglo-Saxon kingdoms of Northumbria and Mercia, and a secondary division is found between much of the Midlands and areas further south. The kind of evidence for these dialect divisions is summarized in the associated table, which gives an impressionistic transcription using normal spelling conventions of eight pronunciation criteria (*rr* refers to the pronunciation of /r/ after a vowel, p. 245). A hierarchical representation of the dialect relationships is shown below. (From P. Trudgill, 1990.)

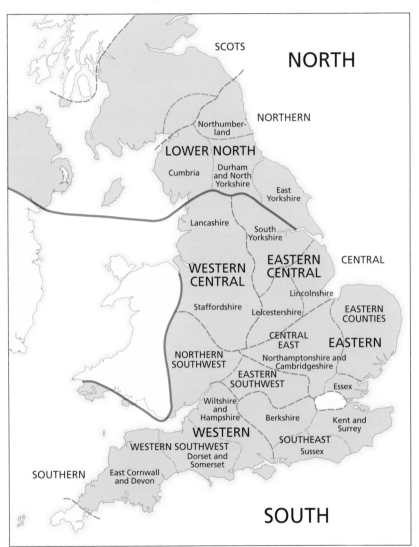

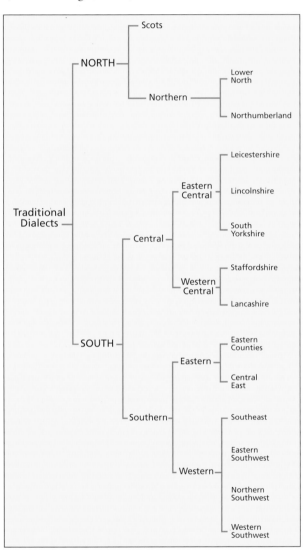

Area	long	night	blind	land	arm	hill	seven	bat
Northumberland	lang	neet	blinnd	land	arrm	hill	seven	bat
Lower North	lang	neet	blinnd	land	ahm	ill	seven	bat
Lancashire	long	neet	blined	lond	arrm	ill	seven	bat
Staffordshire	long	nite	blined	lond	ahm	ill	seven	bat
South Yorkshire	long	neet	blinnd	land	ahm	ill	seven	bat
Lincolnshire	long	nite	blinnd	land	ahm	ill	seven	bat
Leicestershire	long	nite	blined	land	ahm	ill	seven	bat

Area	long	night	blind	land	arm	hill	seven	bat
Western Southwest	long	nite	blined	land	arrm	ill	zeven	bat
Northern Southwest	long	nite	blined	lond	arrm	ill	seven	bat
Eastern Southwest	long	nite	blined	land	arrm	ill	seven	bat
Southeast	long	nite	blined	lænd	arrm	ill	seven	bæt
Central East	long	nite	blined	lænd	ahm	ill	seven	bæt
Eastern Counties	long	nite	blined	lænd	ahm	hill	seven	bæt

Relatively few people in England now speak a dialect of the kind represented on the facing page. Although such forms as *zeven* 'seven' will still be encountered in real life, they are more often found in literary representations of dialect speech and in parodies by comedians or in dialect humour books (p. 410). The disappearance of such pronunciations, and their associated lexicon and grammar, is sometimes described as 'English dialects dying out'. The reality is that they are more than compensated for by the growth of a range of comparatively new dialect forms, chiefly associated with the urban areas of the country.

If the distinguishing features of these dialects are used as the basis of classification, a very different-looking dialect map emerges, with 16 major divisions. Once again, a series of pronunciation criteria illustrate the areas (*gg* represents the use of /g/ after /ŋ/, as in *finger*; *ioo* represents

the use of a very short [u] vowel before [l]), and a hierarchical representation of the dialect relationships is given below. In this analysis, the vowel in such words as *up* ([ʊp] 'oop' in the North, [ʌp] in the South) is considered to be the chief distinguishing feature, and a division between North and South has been made on this basis (from P. Trudgill, 1990). A division using another well-known feature, 'short vs long *a*' (p. 307) would also be possible, though this would make the boundary run somewhat differently in the Midland area. What is plain is that few of the dialect areas coincide with those shown opposite. Moreover, the traditional North–South boundary turns out to be no longer in England, but on the border between England and Scotland, and it is this division which gives rise to the most noticeable dialect distinction in modern British English (p. 328).

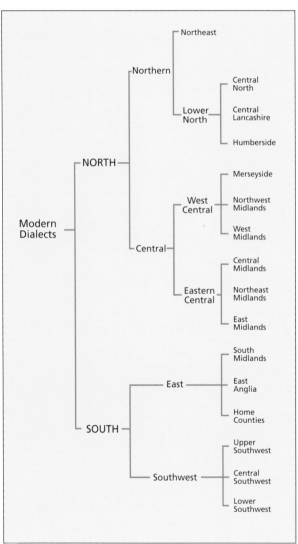

Area	very	few	cars	made	up	long	hill	Area	very	few	cars	made	up	long	hill
Northeast	veree	few	cahs	mehd	oop	long	hill	Northeast Midlands	veree	few	cahs	mayd	oop	long	ill
Central North	veri	few	cahs	mehd	oop	long	ill	East Midlands	veree	foo	cahs	mayd	oop	long	ill
Central Lancashire	veri	few	carrs	mehd	oop	longg	ill	Upper Southwest	veree	few	carrs	mayd	up	long	ill
Humberside	veree	few	cahs	mehd	oop	long	ill	Central Southwest	veree	few	carrs	mayd	up	long	iooll
Merseyside	veree	few	cahs	mayd	oop	longg	ill	Lower Southwest	veree	few	carrs	mehd	up	long	ill
Northwest Midlands	veri	few	cahs	mayd	oop	longg	ill	South Midlands	veree	foo	cahs	mayd	up	long	iooll
West Midlands	veree	few	cahs	mayd	oop	longg	ill	East Anglia	veree	foo	cahs	mayd	up	long	(h)ill
Central Midlands	veri	few	cahs	mayd	oop	long	ill	Home Counties	veree	few	cahs	mayd	up	long	iooll

URBAN GRAMMAR

A great deal of the descriptive and analytical work on British dialects over the years has in fact been concerned with vocabulary and accent (p. 299), rather than with grammar, and as a result many important features of English regional variation have remained undescribed. This page reports on some of the grammatical features which have been found in modern urban dialects, and which will also now be encountered in any area of countryside influenced by the economy of a nearby city.

AUXILIARIES IN READING

The English used by a group of adolescents in Reading, Berkshire (40 miles west of London) displays a number of nonstandard features. One of the main features is a distinctive present-tense use of *do*, which appears in as many as three nonstandard verb forms, alternating with standard forms.

• An *-s* ending occurs with all subjects except third person singular (p. 204):

That's what I does, anyway, I just ignores them.

• A form lacking a suffix occurs with third person singular subjects:

She cadges, she do.

• The form *dos* /duːz/ occurs with all subjects, though mainly as third person singular:

All the headmaster dos now is makes you stand in a corner.

The table below shows the frequency of use of each of these forms as full verb and as auxiliary verb (p. 212), derived from the speech of all (24) speakers in the study. The figures suggest that there is a grammatical rule in this area of usage which Standard English does not share. *Dos* occurs only as a full verb (mainly with third person subjects). *Do* occurs chiefly as an auxiliary verb. *Does* is divided, though occurring chiefly as a full verb, especially with third person singular subjects (as in Standard English).

In other words, the forms of *do* are dependent on different factors in Reading English compared with Standard English. In the latter, they depend only on the subject of the verb (third person vs others), whereas in Reading they also depend on the syntactic function of the verb (whether full or auxiliary). In this respect, the regional dialect is more complex than the standard – clear evidence against the popular view that dialects are in some way 'reduced' or 'simplified' departures from Standard English. (After J. Cheshire, 1982.)

	Full verb			Auxiliary verb		
Subject	*does*	*do* %	*dos*	*does*	*do* %	*dos*
Third singular	50.00	12.50	37.50	33.33	66.67	0.00
Non-third singular	56.80	35.70	7.10	2.10	97.90	0.00

AFFIRMATION IN FARNWORTH

Farnworth is a municipal borough in the Greater Bolton area, just north of Manchester. An analysis of spontaneous speech interviews recorded in the 1970s brought to light an interesting system of negation, including a distinctive use of affirmative and negative particles, with two contrasts under each heading instead of the single *yes–no* contrast of Standard English.

'Yes'
• /aɪ/ *aye* – the normal word for 'yes'.
• /jaɪ/ *yigh* – the word for 'yes' when answering a negative question or contradicting a negative proposition (comparable to the distinction which exists between *doch* and *ja* in German or *si* and *oui* in French).

A: I can't find the scissors.
B: Yigh, they're here.

'No'
/næː, nɛː/ *no* – the normal word for 'no'.
/neː/ *nay* – used when contradicting someone.

A: You know more than you're telling.
B: Nay, by gum! I'm not having that!

Other negative forms
/noːn/ – a negative adverb or pronoun (p. 210):
I'm *noan* going. (='not')
He's gotten *noan*. (='none')
That didn't upset them *noan*.
I *never* eat no dinner. (='not', referring to a single occasion)

Treble and quadruple negatives are common:

I am *not never* going to do *nowt* (='nothing') *no* more for thee.
We could*n't* see *nowt*.
Well I've *not neither*.
He could*n't* get them out *no* road. (='any way')
There were *no* chairs ready *nor nowt*.

A negative verb may also be used with such adverbs as *hardly*, in contrast to Standard English:

I've never hardly done it.
I couldn't hardly eat.

(After G. Shorrocks, 1985.)

PAST TENSES IN TYNESIDE

The area around the R. Tyne, in NE England, and dominated by Newcastle, has a wide range of dialect features, often summed up in the label 'Geordie' (a Scottish nickname for *George*). This dialect area extends throughout Northumberland, and shares several features with southern Scots.

The table shows the past tense and past participle forms (p. 204) of a number of irregular verbs. Most of the features are found in other urban dialects, but there are a few forms which are distinctive to this region. Most of the past participles which actually end in *-en* in Standard English do not occur, but there are four cases, which may be unique to this area, of a nonstandard *-en* use. The verb *treat* is regular in Standard English, but irregular in Tyneside. There are reversals of function in *come*, *run*, *see*, and *shrink*:

I come to see him last week.
They had came to see me.

In this region, also, *gan* is used as an alternative verb to *go*, and *div/divent* are used as forms of *do* when this is an auxiliary verb, especially in tag questions (p. 218):

Ye divent knaa, div ye? (='You don't know, do you?')

The full verb *do* is the same as in Standard English, thus allowing such contrasts as the following:

I do all the work, divent I?

Base	Standard	Tyneside
beat	beat/beaten	beat/beat
bite	bit/bitten	bit/bit
break	broke/broken	broke/broke
come	came/come	come/came
do	did/done	done/done
eat	ate/eaten	ate/ate
		et/etten
fall	fell/fallen	fell/fell
forget	forgot/forgotten	forgot/forgot
		forgot/forgetten
get	got/got	got/getten
give	gave/given	give/give
go	went/gone	went/went
put	put/put	put/putten
ring	rang/rung	rang/rang
run	ran/run	run/ran
say	said/said	sayed/sayed
see	saw/seen	seen/saw
shrink	shrank/shrunk	shrunk/shrunk
	shrank/shrank	shrunk/shrank
sing	sang/sung	sang/sang
sink	sank/sunk	sunk/sunk
speak	spoke/spoken	spoke/spoke
spin	spun/spun	span/spun
swing	swung/swung	swang/swung
take	took/taken	took/took
treat	treated/treated	tret/tret
write	wrote/written	wrote/wrote

(After C. McDonald, in J. Beal, 1988.)

ESTUARY ENGLISH

The 'estuary' in question is that of the R. Thames. The term was coined in the 1980s to identify the way features of London regional speech seemed to be rapidly spreading throughout the counties adjoining the river (especially Essex and Kent) and beyond. It is something of a misnomer, for the influence of London speech has for some time been evident well beyond the Thames estuary, notably in the Oxford – Cambridge – London triangle (p. 50) and in the area to the south and east of London as far as the coast. Nonetheless, the phrase 'estuary English' caught the public imagination, and received considerable publicity, including a front page headline in *The Sunday Times* (14 March 1993):

Yer wot? 'Estuary English' Sweeps Britain

While 'sweeping' may be something of an exaggeration, the spread of the variety has certainly been noticeable in recent years. London-influenced speech can now be heard around three other estuaries – the Humber in the north-east, the Dee in the north-west, and the Severn in the west – at least partly because of the relatively easy rail and motorway commuting networks. With Hull, Chester, and Bristol now only just over two hours from London, the morning and evening transport routes to and from the capital carry many people who speak with an accent which shows the influence of their place of work.

The factors governing the spread of this variety are only partly explained by social mobility and new patterns of settlement. For example, there is the influence of radio and television, and of English media personalities who use a modified form of Cockney, such as Ben Elton and Jonathan Ross. But certainly, after World War 2, thousands of London speakers did move to outside the city, and to the new towns which were being built around the capital. Their move will have caused many to modify their accents, and their numerical presence (as well as their economic standing) may even have influenced the original residents to accommodate (p. 298) in their direction.

Estuary English may therefore be the result of a confluence of two social trends: an up-market movement of originally Cockney speakers, and a down-market trend towards 'ordinary' (as opposed to 'posh') speech by the middle class. There is certainly plenty of anecdotal evidence that many people these days wish to avoid the 'establishment' connotations of Received Pronunciation (p. 365), and try to speak in a way which they perceive to be more down to earth. In the 1993 debate which accompanied the *Sunday Times* report, one leading businessman was explicit about this point. Referring to a 'public school accent' (RP) he commented: 'If you were unlucky enough to have such an accent, you would lower it. You would try to become more consumer friendly'.

A continuum

The phenomenon, as identified in the press, has been perceived as more to do with accent than with dialect, and has been described as a continuum of pronunciation possibilities, with Cockney at one end and Received Pronunciation at the other. But the variety is distinctive as a dialect, not just as an accent, as can be seen from the following selection of features which are becoming increasingly widespread.

DIALECT TRAVELS

The top map shows the distribution of words for a 'food-trough in a cow-house' as recorded to the south of London by *The Survey of English Dialects* (p. 318). It is likely that the older form is *trough*, and *manger* (a more standard term in agricultural writing) has spread into the area from the north. Is there anything to explain the pattern of change?

The bottom map shows the main routes of communication connecting London to population centres along the coast. Each of the three southward movements of *manger* coincides with major road and rail routes – to Dover, Brighton, and Portsmouth. The suggestion is that the spread of a form is accelerated in areas with good communication links, and held back in more isolated areas (p. 54). This pattern may well be being repeated on a nationwide scale, in the case of estuary English.

(After P. Trudgill, 1990, pp. 122–3.)

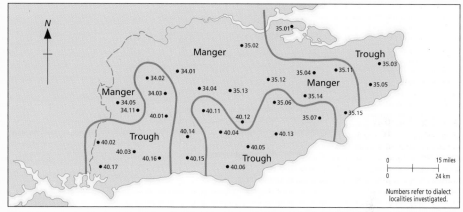

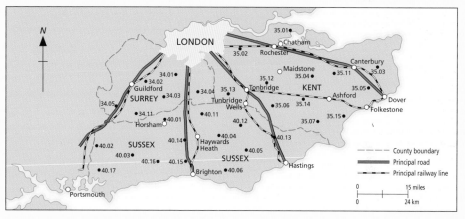

Pronunciation

• The glottal stop in certain positions, especially replacing /t/ at the end of a word or before a consonant (*Gatwick airport*). On the other hand, only those speakers closest to the Cockney end of the continuum would use the glottal stop before a vowel (as in *water*), which is still perceived to be a Cockney feature.

• The replacement of final /-l/ by a short [u] vowel (p. 241), so that *hill* is pronounced [hɪʊ]. Although this feature is common, other features traditionally associated with Cockney speech are much less so, such as the replacement of *th* /θ/ and /ð/ by /f/ and /v/ respectively.

Grammar

• The 'confrontational' question tag (p. 299), as in *I said I was going, didn't I*. Other Cockney tags (such as *innit*) are also sometimes found in jocular estuary speech (or writing, p. 410), which may indicate a move towards their eventual standardization.

• Certain negative forms, such as *never* referring to a single occasion (*I never did, No I never*). Less likely is the use of the double negative, which is still widely perceived as uneducated (p. 194).

• The omission of the *-ly* adverbial ending, as in *You're turning it too **slow***, *They talked very **quiet** for a while*.

• Certain prepositional uses, such as *I got **off of** the bench*, *I looked **out** the window*.

• Generalization of the third person singular form (*I **gets** out of the car*), especially in narrative style; also the generalized past tense use of *was*, as in *We **was** walking down the road*.

Some of these developments are now increasingly to be heard in the public domain, such as on the more popular channels of the BBC, and some have even begun to penetrate the British establishment. Glottalization, for example, will be heard on both sides of the House of Commons, and has been observed in the younger members of the royal family. The publicizing of the trend, however, has provoked a strong purist reaction, and led to a further round of the debate about the safeguarding of standards. What seems to be happening, however, is the gradual replacement of one kind of standard by another – a process which was characterized by several newspaper commentators in 1993 as the linguistic corner-stone of a future classless British society.

VARIATION IN SCOTLAND

Of all the varieties of English which have developed within the British Isles, there are none more distinctive or more divergent from Standard English than some of those associated with Scotland. Indeed, the extent of the divergence in one of these varieties has led to a well-established use of the label, the 'Scots language', and to a spirited defence of all that such a label stands for. It is argued that Scots differs from the regional dialects of England in two crucial ways. It is unique because it was once the variety used, in the late Middle Ages, when Scotland was an independent nation; and it is unique because it has a clearly defined history of its own, with a strong literary tradition beginning in Middle English (p. 52), its own dialect variants (several of which have individual literary histories), its own 'golden age' and period of decline, a modern literary renaissance, and a contemporary sociolinguistic stature which other dialects of British English do not share. There are many more Scottish expressions in current use in Scotland than there are English dialect expressions in current use in any dialect of England. The term 'dialect island' is sometimes used to capture the character of the Scottish situation.

The people of Scotland are generally far more aware of the distinctive character of their speech and writing, take it far more seriously, and argue about standards of usage in it far more forcibly than is the case with speakers of regional dialects to the south. A representation of a regional dialect often appears in print only for jocular or folklore purposes; this is not so in Scotland, where there is in addition a strong and respected tradition of academic linguistic study, societies devoted to the furtherance of Scots as a language, and a growing corpus of written material in one or other of its varieties. For example, Scots has received far more lexicographic description than other regional British varieties, with such major publications as John Jamieson's *Etymological Dictionary of the Scottish Language* (1808, 1825, 4 vols) and the present-day *Scottish National Dictionary* (completed 1976, 10 vols). The Association for Scottish Literary Studies has an active Language Committee. And the Scots Language Society's journal, *Lallans* (p. 333), begun in 1973, presents material in prose which extends the range of the language to well beyond the literary uses to which it has largely been put in recent years (p. 330).

The identity of English in Scotland has become much more than a distinctive regional accent and the occasional habitual feature of grammar and vocabulary. It reflects an institutionalized social structure, at its most noticeable in the realms of law, local government, religion, and education, and raises problems of intelligibility that have no parallel elsewhere in Britain. However, despite these national underpinnings, and the extensive language loyalty, Scots as a language has not so far been able to make inroads into the use of Standard English as the language of power and public prestige, and it has no official existence. Outside certain specialized publications, its public use tends to be restricted to literature and folklore, to a few programmes on radio and television about local issues, and to jocular contexts, such as cartoons and comic strips. At the same time, there have been major publications, such as the translation of the New Testament into Scots. The situation, in short, is complex and unclear. However, even those scholars who debate whether to call Scots a language or a dialect end up by recognizing its special status – for they are faced with no such dilemma in considering the other regional varieties of English in Britain.

LEGAL LANGUAGE DIFFERENCES

Of the 300 entries on law (p. 374) in *The Cambridge Encyclopedia* (1994), 88 of them specify differences between the law in England and Wales and the law in Scotland, with various linguistic consequences.

• Several terms, such as *burglary, covenant, habeas corpus, subpoena,* and *suspended sentence,* do not exist in Scottish law.
• Some semantic fields (p. 157) are structured differently. There is no distinction, for example, between *libel* and *slander,* as the Scottish legal system recognizes only *defamation.* And where the term *minor* exists in England and Wales for a person below the age of 18 years, Scottish law distinguishes between *pupils* (to age 12 for girls and 14 for boys) and *minors* (older children up to 18).
• Several terms in English law have Scottish equivalents, such as:

Scotland	England and Wales
advocate	barrister
arbiter	arbitrator
apprehension	arrest
extortion	blackmail
fire-raising	arson
defender	defendant
interdict	injunction
aliment	alimony
confirmation	probate
culpable homicide	manslaughter
delict	tort

THE BIBLE TRANSLATED

A major step in giving prestige to Scots came with the publication in 1983 of the *New Testament in Scots* by William Laughton Lorimer (1885–1967), which his entry in the *Oxford Companion to the English Language* refers to as 'the greatest achievement of modern Scots prose'. A few lines from the parable of the 'Prodigal Son' convey something of the flavour (though not the stylistic variety) of the translation. For comparison, the same extract is also shown in two other versions, brought together by the journal *English World-Wide* in 1983.

Scots
This, tae, he said tae them: 'There wis aince a man hed twa sons; and ae day the yung son said til him, "Faither, gíe me the faa-share o your haudin at I hae a richt til." Sae the faither haufed his haudin atweesh his twa sons.

No lang efterhin the yung son niffert the haill o his portion for siller, an fuir awà furth til a faur-aff kintra, whaur he sperfelt his siller livin the life o a weirdless waister. Efter he hed gane throu the haill o it, a fell faimin brak out i yon laund, an he faund himsel in unco sair mister. Sae he gaed an hired wi an indwaller i that kintra, an the man gíed him the wark o tentin his swine outbye i the fields. Gledlie wad he panged his wame wi the huils at they maitit the swine wi, but naebodie gíed him a haet…"

Lallans (J. K. Annand, 1982)
And he spak: There dwalt a chiel that had twa sons. And the young ane said til his faither, 'Gie me the bairns' pairt o gear that will be my due.' And he bunced aa that he aucht atween them.

And no lang efter the young son gethert thegither aa his gear and set aff for a fremit land, and there he gaed on the randan. And when he had wared aa hs siller, there was an unco famine in that airt, and he was on his beam-end. And he gaed and fee'd himsel til a fermer in that land, and he was sent intil the fields to fother the grice. And he wad hae likit fine to hae fullt his kyte wi the brock that the grice ate, but he gat nane.

Lowland Scots (J. T. Low, 1983)
Aince mair he said til them: 'There war a chiel had twa sons; and the young ane said til's faither, "Faither, gie me that pairt o the faimily walth that sud faa tae me". Sae noo the faither pairted his guids and gear atween them.

A puckle days later this young ane chynged his pairt intil sillar and left his hame tae gang til a kintra hyne awa. There did he no splairge the hale hypothec in wastrie and cairry-ons. Whan he had gane throu aa, a muckle hership brak oot in that kintra, and he begud tae thole sair scant and want. He gaed and socht wark wi ane o the lairds o that airt; and this chiel telt him tae gang intil his parks tae gie the beasts their mair. He was that sair hungert that he wad fain hae filled his kyte wi the huils that the grumphies war eatan; and naebody gied him onything…'

SOME SCOTS LINGUISTIC FEATURES

The present-day dialect boundary between England and Scotland is one of the most well-defined in Britain. Although there are several features shared with dialects from the north of England – such as some lexical items (e.g. *lass*, *bairn*, *bonny*, *loon*) and some pronunciations, there are many uniquely distinguishing features, found in various distributions north of the border. The following is a selection of features which distinguish Scots from Standard English (SE).

Pronunciation
(See §17 for phonetics terminology.)
• There is the absence of lip-rounding in such words as *stone* and *go*, giving Scots *stane*, *gae*.
• The close back vowel /uː/ is fronted, so that SE *moon* and *use* are heard in several dialects with [y] (as in French *tu*), and written in such spellings as *muin* and *yuise*.
• Final /l/ was replaced by an [u]-type vowel in late Middle English, giving many words to be represented without an *l* in the spelling, as in *saut* ('salt'), *fou* ('full'), *baw* ('ball'). Some spelling systems represent the 'missing *l*' by an apostrophe, as in *fu'*.
• There were several different effects of the Great Vowel Shift (p. 55) in Scottish English, such as the retention of a pure vowel /uː/ in such words as *hoose* ('house') and *doon* ('down').
• Certain vowels have no inherent length, but are long or short depending on the sound which follows them (the *Scottish vowel-length rule*). Close vowels /i/ and /u/ are most affected. For example, /i/ is long in *leave* and *sees*, but short in *leaf* and *cease*. That this is not just a function of longer duration in front of a voiced (lenis) consonant, as in RP (p. 242), is shown by such pairs as *agreed* (long) vs *greed* (short) or *feel* (long) vs *feeling* (short), where the conditioning factor is the grammatical boundary between stem and ending.
• A velar fricative is commonly heard, in such words as *loch* and *nicht* ('night'), and also in *technical*, *patriarch*, *Brechin*, and other -*ch*- items.
• The voiceless bilabial fricative /ʍ/ is widespread, allowing a contrast between *while* and *wile*, or *whales* and *Wales*. In the North-East, the /ʍ/ is replaced by /f/: *fa* ('who'), *fite* ('white'), etc.
• A glottal stop is widely heard in urban accents, in such words as *butter*, and is spreading throughout the country, especially in the speech of younger people.
• Pitch range and direction tends to be wider than in RP, and unstressed syllables are often pronounced with greater emphasis (e.g. *Wednesday* with three distinct syllables).

Grammar
(See Part III for grammatical terminology.)
• Irregular plural nouns include *een* ('eyes'), *shuin* ('shoes'), and *hors* ('horses'). Regularized nouns

THE SUNDAY POST, January 16, 1994.

+ 40

OOR WULLIE
He's aye on cue wi' laughs for you.

Oor Wullie, popular cartoon in *The Sunday Post* since 1936.

© D.C. Thomson & Co. Ltd.

include *leafs*, *wifes*, *wolfs*, *lifes*, etc.
• Two pronoun variants are *thae* ('those') and *thir* ('these'). In Orkney and Shetland, and occasionally elsewhere, the *thou*/*thee*/*ye* distinction is maintained (p. 71). Other distinctive pronouns often heard include *mines* ('mine'), *they* ('these'), *they yins* ('they'), and *yous* ('you' plural).
• Numeral *one* appears in different forms, depending on its position: *ae man* ('one man') vs *that ane* ('that one').
• Distinctive verb forms include *gae* ('go'), *gaed* ('went'), *gane* ('gone'); *hing* ('hang'), *hang* ('hanged'), *hungin* ('hung'); *lauch* ('laugh'), *leuch* ('laughed', past tense form), *lauchen* ('laughed', past participle form); and such other past tenses as *gied* ('gave'), *brung* ('brought'), *tellt* ('told'), *taen* ('took'), and *sellt* ('sold').
• The particle *not* appears as *no* or *nae*, often in contracted forms as -*na* or -*ny*, as in *canna* ('cannot') and *didnae* ('didn't').
• Auxiliary verbs *shall*, *may*, and *ought* are not normally used in speech, being replaced with such forms as *will* (for *shall*), *can* or *maybe* (for *may*), and *should* or *want* (for *ought*, as in *You want to get

out a bit*). Double modals (p. 315) may be heard: *might could*, *will can*, etc.
• The definite article is often used distinctively, as in *the now* ('just now'), *the day* ('today'), *the both of them*, *go to the church* (in a generic sense, SE *go to church*), *they're at the fishing*, *he wears the kilt*, (SE *he wears a kilt*), and before names of chiefs (*Robert the Bruce*).
• Syntactic constructions include several uses of prepositions, such as *the back of 3 o'clock* ('soon after 3 o'clock'), and *from* (*frae*) for *by* in passives (*We were all petrified frae him*). Tag question variations (p. 299) include *Is Mary still outside, is she?* *See* may be used to mark a new topic, especially in Glasgow, as in *See it's daft doing that*.

Vocabulary
A great deal of the distinctiveness of the Scots lexicon derives from the influence of other languages, especially Gaelic, Norwegian (p. 25), and French (p. 46). Gaelic loans, for example, include *cairn*, *capercailzie*, *ceilidh*, *claymore*, *gillie*, *glen*, *ingle*, *loch*, *pibroch*, *sporran*, and *whisky*, and several of these are now part of Standard English. The following are among the lexical items which remain restricted to Scots. It is the tiniest of samples, considering that *The Scots Thesaurus* (1990), for example, lists over 20,000 items.

airt	direction
ay	always
dominie	teacher
dreich	dreary
fash	bother
high-heid yin	boss
janitor	caretaker
kirk	church
outwith	outside of
pinkie	little finger
swither	hesitate

There are also many words which have the same form as in SE, but are different in meaning. Examples include *scheme* ('local government housing estate'), *mind* ('memory, recollection'), *travel* ('go on foot'), and *gate* ('road'), as well as several idioms, such as *to miss oneself* ('to miss a treat') or *be up to high doh* ('be over-excited').

EARLY TRENDS

The anglicization of Scottish writing became noticeable after the joining of the crowns of England and Scotland in 1603 (p. 53), and was increasingly dominant throughout the 17th century. Within a decade, southern English became the printing model, apart from in certain legal or literary texts, and by the end of the 17th century there was little sign of a distinctively Scottish variety in manuscript writing. Southern English speech also became the norm, with the use of 'Scotticisms' attracting fierce criticism from the prescriptive attitudes of 'polite' society which dominated the middle decades of the 18th century (p. 78), and which condemned all instances of what was perceived to be 'unrefined' usage. The 1750s saw the first publication of alphabetical lists of Scottish expressions which educated people ought to avoid, and the arrival in Scotland of elocutionists who taught people how to change their accents towards the London norm.

Popular comic or heroic poems from the earlier periods of Scots continued to be published during this time, and this fuelled a small but continuing poetic output which did much to motivate the revival of the variety, in a more colloquial style, during the 18th century, in the poetry, ballads, and humorous tales of Allan Ramsay, Alexander Ross, and others. Their language was often called 'Doric', because of a supposed parallel between its use of Scotticisms and the features of pastoral Classical Greek poetry. Later, with the advent of Romanticism in literature, provincial linguistic identity came to be even more highly valued. A serious academic interest grew in the vernacular, though it was recognized (but now with regret rather than delight) that Scots was 'going out as a spoken tongue every year' (a much-quoted remark of the Edinburgh judge, Lord Cockburn, in 1838). A further 19th-century development was the rise, as in England, of urban dialects, resulting in a distinction between 'guid Scots', spoken in rural areas, and 'gutter Scots', spoken in the cities, with the speech of working-class Glasgow commonly cited as a prime example.

ANGLICIZATION OBSERVED

The changes which took place in five linguistic variables were examined as part of a study of anglicization in Scotland between 1520 and 1659. A total of 140 texts were examined, representing national public records, official correspondence, personal correspondence, religious treatises, and private records. The rapidity of the process can clearly be seen.

• The marker of the relative clause changed in its spelling from *quh-* (p. 52) to *wh-* in such words as *which* and *who*. In 1520, Scottish writers always used *quh-* spellings; the figures for *wh-* stay low for some 80 years, then dramatically increase, reaching over 80 per cent by 1659.
• The past tense ending changed from *-it* to *-ed*: *intendit* became *intended*. Here too there is a slow start to the change, 5 per cent in 1520, then a sharp increase after 1580, reaching 87 per cent in 1659.
• The indefinite article *ane* changed to *a* or *an*: *ane missive*, *ane oath* became *a missive*, *an oath*. This change is more in evidence at the outset (16 per cent), but by 1659 it still had further to go, having reached only 74 per cent.

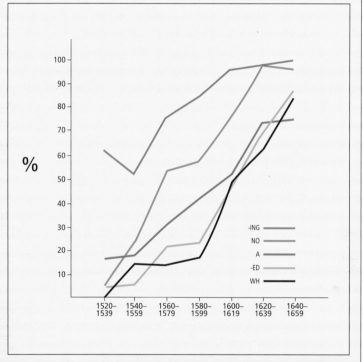

• The negative particles *na* and *nocht* changed to *no* and *not*. These items change very rapidly during the 40 years after 1520, and the rise continues steadily after 1600, so that by 1659 *not* has reached 100 per cent use, with *no* (shown on the graph) just a little behind, at 94 per cent.
• The present participle ending changed from *-and* to *-ing*: *labourand* became *labouring*. This is the most highly anglicized feature of the study. The *-ing* form was already being used in over 60 per cent of cases in 1520, and though its use varies somewhat, the process of replacement is virtually complete by 1600.

It should be noted that these trends are summaries of very complex patterns of usage. It is not a question of, for example, 60 per cent of texts in 1520 using only *-ing* and 40 per cent using only *-and*: usage up to 1600 is highly variable, with authors often using both forms, sometimes even within a single sentence. But after the uniting of the crowns, this kind of variability dies away within two generations. Moreover, the changes took place more rapidly in certain genres: in religious writing, the process is virtually complete by 1600, whereas it is slowest in national public records, which remain conservative even in 1659. (After A. J. Devitt, 1989.)

ROBERT BURNS (1759–96)

The traditional distinctiveness of the English language in Scotland is for many people identified with the writing of Robert Burns, the country's national poet. Born in the Ayrshire village of Alloway, the son of a poor farmer, he read widely as a child, and later was greatly influenced by the popular tales and songs of the time, especially as recalled by his wife's cousin, Betty Davidson.

On his father's death in 1784 he was left in charge of the farm. The birth of an illegitimate child to one of the farm servants, and news of impending twins to a local girl, Jean Armour, whom he wished to marry, brought local church condemnation and the opposition of Jean's father. As the farm went to ruin, his poverty, passion, and despair produced from 1784 a remarkable outpouring of poetry. Looking for money to emigrate to Jamaica, he published in 1786 the now-famous Kilmarnock edition of his poems, which brought such acclaim that he was persuaded to stay in Scotland.

He visited Edinburgh, where he was feted, then travelled widely in Scotland. Early 1788 is known for a short but passionate period of correspondence with 'Clarinda' (Agnes Maclehose). A growing reputation led to his acceptance by Jean Armour's family. He married her in April 1788, and in all they had nine children together. He leased a farm near Dumfries, but succeeded in gaining a more secure appointment as an excise officer in 1789. When the farm began to fail, he left for Dumfries town, where he continued to write. In 1793 the family found a house in Mill Vennel (now Burns Street), and there, three years later, he died.

THE IMMORTAL MEMORY

Bill o' Fare

'Some hae meat and canna eat
And some wad eat that want it:
But we hae meat and we can eat,
And sae the Lord be thankit.'

Cock-a-Leekie

★

Haggis,
warm, reekin, rich wi'
Champit Tatties, Bashed Neeps

Address to the Haggis
Mr A. McPherson

Steak Pie

Tipsy Laird

A Tassie o' Coffee

A page from a typical menu for a Burns Supper, containing the text of the Selkirk Grace.

The Burns Supper is an annual celebration of the art and achievements of the poet. It takes place on the anniversary of the poet's birth, 25 January, or as near to it as is practicable. The first recorded supper took place in Ayrshire in 1801, attended by some of Burns's close friends. Today, the Burns Federation, based in Kilmarnock, has over 300 affiliated clubs.

The basic structure of a Supper is hallowed by tradition. A member of the clergy recites 'The Selkirk Grace'. Dinner is accompanied by the piping in of the haggis, and a reading of Burns's 'Address to the Haggis' – the 'Great Chieftain o' the Puddin-race'. After the dinner, the principal speaker delivers an address to 'The Immortal Memory'. 'The Toast to the Lasses' is proposed by a gentleman speaker, and a lady speaker replies. Various songs and recitations of Burns's work follow, and the evening ends with the company singing 'Auld Lang Syne'. (After N. Marshall, 1992.)

Nae man can tether time or tide;
The hour approaches Tam maun ride;
That hour o'nights black arch the
   key-stane,
That dreary hour he mounts the
   beast in;
And sic a night he taks the road in
As ne'er poor sinner was abroad in.

The wind blew as 'twad blawn its last;
The rattling show'rs rose on the blast;
The speedy gleams the darkness
   swallow'd;
Loud, deep, and lang, the thunder
   bellow'd:
That night a child might understand
The Deil had business on his hand.

The distinctive rhythms of *Tam o'Shanter* (1790), which many critics regard as Burns's masterpiece. Set in Alloway churchyard, it tells of Tam's nightmare meeting with spirits of the other world. It is always a popular item at a Burns Supper.

nae no *maun* must *stane* stone
sic such *taks* takes
'twad blawn would have blown
lang long *Deil* Devil

O my Luve's like a red, red rose
That's newly sprung in June;
O my Luve's like the melodie
That's sweetly play'd in tune.
As fair art thou, my bonie lass,
So deep in luve am I;
And I will luve thee still, my dear,
Till a' the seas gang dry.

Till a' the seas gang dry, my Dear,
And the rocks melt wi' the sun;
O I will love thee still, my dear,
While the sands o' life shall run.
And fare thee weel, my only Luve!
And fare thee weel a while!
And I will come again, my Luve,
Tho' it were ten thousand mile!

Burns is thought to have developed the words of this famous song in 1794 from a street ditty expressing a soldier's farewell to his sweetheart. The haunting melody accompanying the words is *Graham's Strathspey*.

bonie pretty *gang* go *weel* well

Should auld acquaintance be forgot,
And never brought to mind?
Should auld acquaintance be forgot,
And auld lang syne!
   For auld lang syne, my dear,
   For auld lang syne,
   We'll tak a cup o' kindness yet,
   For auld lang syne.

And surely ye'll be your pint stowp!
And surely I'll be mine!
And we'll tak a cup o' kindness yet,
For auld lang syne.

We twa hae run about the braes,
And pou'd the gowans fine:
But we've wander'd mony a weary fitt,
Sin' auld lang syne.

We twa hae paidl'd in the burn
Frae morning sun till dine:
But seas between us braid hae roar'd
Sin' auld lang syne.

And there's a hand, my trusty fiere!
And gie's a hand o' thine!
And we'll tak a right gude-willie
   waught
For auld lang syne.

Burns composed his version of 'Auld Lang Syne' in 1788, adding the third and fourth verses. The first verse and chorus is now an anthem sung at the close of gatherings all over the English-speaking world, and is probably the best-known contribution of Scots to World English. (The melody was composed by William Shield, and forms part of the overture to his opera *Rosina* (1783).)

auld lang syne days of long ago
stowp tankard *twa* two
hae have *braes* meadows
pou'd pulled *gowans* daisies
mony many *fitt* foot
sin' since *paidl'd* paddled
burn stream *frae* from
dine dinner-time *braid* broad
fiere friend *gie's* give us
gude-willie goodwill
waught draught

SCOTS DIALECT AREAS

The map shows the chief dialect areas of Scots, and the counties of Scotland as they existed before the 1975 reorganization of local government in the UK. The Highlands and Hebrides are left blank, as these are the traditional Gaelic-speaking areas, and it is Gaelic rather than Scots which needs to be taken into account when analysing English usage there.

Insular Scots
Orkney and Shetland

Northern
• Caithness, Sutherland, Ross and Cromarty, Inverness
• Nairn, Moray, Banff, Aberdeen (*North-East Scots*)
• Kincardine, E Angus

Central
East Central
• W Angus, Perth, Stirling, Fife, Kinross, Clackmannan (*North-East Central*)
• West Lothian, Edinburgh, Midlothian, East Lothian, Berwick, Peebles (*South-East Central*)
West Central
• W and E Dunbarton, Argyll, Bute, Renfrew, Glasgow, Lanark, N Ayr
South-West
• S Ayr, Wigtown, Kirkcudbright, Galloway, W Dumfries

Southern
• Roxburgh, Selkirk, E/Mid Dumfries

Ulster Scots (p. 337)

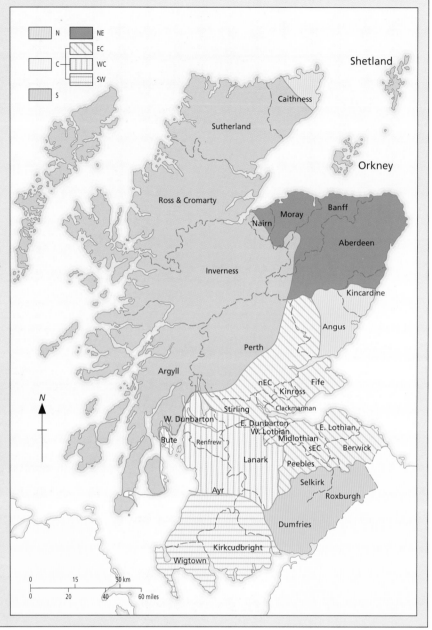

SHETLAND SPEECH

The variety of language used in the Shetland Isles is said to be one of the most distinctive of all Scots dialects. This extract is from a piece of academic writing – a contribution to a symposium on Scots published in the journal *English World-Wide* (1981).

Shetland's 'ain aald language' has its röts awa back ida Norn tongue at wis spokken in Shetland fae aboot da nint tae da seeventeent century. Da Scots fock at cam among wis fae da sixteent century an on brocht der ain leid, an at da lang an da lent da twa languages melled tagidder to mak da tongue we caa Shetlandic. While dis wis gjaan on, anidder wye o spaekin an writin wis shapin da local speech. Dis wis English – ösed by da Kirk, da laa-coorts an ida sköls. (From J. J. Graham, 1981.)

röts roots *ida* in the *fock* folk
at wis that was
brocht brought
da lang an da lent at long last
ösed used *Kirk* Church

Much of the visual identity of this style is due to the choice of spelling (e.g. *da* for *the*). Many Shetlanders, of course, speak a much less distinctive dialect, as seen in this extract from a 64-year-old man's account of the fire festival, Up-Helly-Aa. The language is essentially Standard English, with just the occasional dialect form. (/ marks intonation units, p. 248.)

well / - hit's a procession / a procession of maybe nine hundred guizers / and if you do not ken what a guizer is / that is somebody that dresses up / to pretend to be something else / …in the old days / part of the reason for the festival / was to celebrate the end of the dark days of winter / and the return of the sun / well whatever else has changed / the weather has not changed very muckle / - hit's still the dark days of winter / …and there's nobody now / more than in the old days / blither to see / the return of the sun / even though it's still not very high in the sky / than the Shetlander is (After B. Oreström, 1985.)

blither happier *hit* it
ken know *muckle* much

WRITING *DAVIELY*

One of 75 lexical items expressing tiredness or exhaustion collected by *The Scots Thesaurus* (1990). The meanings vary somewhat in force, from 'languid' and 'weary' to 'totally exhausted' and 'worn out'. Only adjective or adverb uses are shown here, with regional restrictions italicized (for locations, see map above). The retention of the *-it* ending in informal spoken Scots is notable.

hyphen: shows continuity, e.g. *Bnf-Fif* means that the word is also found in the intervening counties
local: usage found sporadically in the stated area

now: usage confined to the stated area, though formerly more widespread

Abd	Aberdeen	Loth	Lothian
Ags	Angus	Ork	Orkney
Bnf	Banff	Pbls	Peebles
Bwk	Berwick	Rox	Roxburgh
C	Central	S	Southern
Cai	Caithness	Sh	Shetland
Dmf	Dumfries	Stlg	Stirling
Fif	Fife	Wgt	Wigtown

bauch, daviely, defait (*now Bnf Abd*), dirt deen (*Bnf Abd*), disjaskit (*local*), doilt, diled (*now Abd*), dowf (*now local Bnf-Fif*), dowless (*now Stlg*), ergh, exowst, fauchled (*now C, S*), fendless (*Sh Cai NE, SW*), forfauchlet, forfochtin, forjeskit (*local Sh-Pbls*), fornyawd, forwandert (*literary*), fusionless, haggit (*now Stlg midLoth*), ha(i)rlt (*now midLoth Bwk*), jabbit (*NE*), jaffled (*SW*), jaskit (*now Sh Ags*), jaupit (*now Bnf-Ags midLoth*), lither (*now Dmf*), lowsed, mated (*Abd*), maukit (*S*), muith (*now Cai*), oorit, pingled, pouskered (*Ags WC*), puggled, socht (*now NE Ags*), taigled (*now local SEC-Rox*), taskit (*now local Ork-Wgt*), tewed (*now Wgt*), thowless, tike-tired, traikit (*now WC Wgt*), trauchled (*NE Ags*), typit (*Bnf Abd*), useless (*Sh-N*), vincust (*Ags*), wabbit (*general, not Sh Ork*), wauch, wauf

THE PRESENT-DAY

We find today a complex dialect picture, which is beginning to be understood through such surveys as *The Linguistic Atlas of Scotland* (from 1975). There is evidently a continuum linking Standard English and Scots in informal speech, and to some extent in writing. At one extreme, people from Scotland may speak a dialect which is to all intents and purposes Standard English, with only a slight Scottish accent indicating where they are from. At the other extreme, a highly distinctive variety may be used, with an extremely localized English vocabulary, pronunciation, and grammar, often coloured by borrowings from Gaelic. In between, Scots features may appear in varying proportions, coloured by regional variations within Scotland, and often with substantial dialect mixing. Certain regions are much more distinctively Scottish, and some have developed their own literatures, notably the north-east, Shetland, and Glasgow. The term 'Doric' continues to be used for rural dialects, especially those in the north-east.

Lallans

In addition, the present century has seen the conscious creation of a 'mainstream' variety of Scots – a standard literary variety, which its proponents maintain can be the basis for a revival of Scots as a whole. This 'Scottish Renaissance', as it is sometimes called, looked to previous literary and dialect usages from the Scottish Lowlands for its distinctiveness. The eclectic variety which emerged, at first seen only in poetry and referred to as 'synthetic Scots', now generally goes under the name of *Lallans* (='Lowlands'). Guidelines for written consistency were formulated, emphasizing differences with Standard English (notably, the *Scots Style Sheet* of the Makars' Club in 1947).

Lallans is noted for its distinctive vocabulary (much of which, because of its historical sources, presents a barrier to the uninitiated, thereby emphasizing its linguistic status). In its grammar and spelling, it shows the marked influence of Standard English, more so than other Scots dialects, and this in itself is a source of controversy among its proponents: for example, in spelling, should 'out' be spelled as *out* or *oot*, or 'was' as *was* or *wes*?

The emergence of Lallans, as with any exercise in language planning, has been controversial, meeting hostility (and attracting such nicknames as 'plastic Scots') from those who find the natural character of regional dialect forms more appealing. It remains to be seen whether this variety can go beyond the literary domain into other stylistic levels, and eventually achieve the kind of prestige which is associated with a standard language (p. 110).

PROMOTING *LALLANS*

An early example from the *Lallans* journal (1977). In this example, the grammar corresponds to Standard English, including the use of *may* (which is not used in Scots, p. 329). (From A. J. Aitken, 1984.)

Scots Literature Competition 1978
The Scots Language Society offers prizes for scrievin in the Scots tongue. There are three clesses: Age 18 and owre wi prizes o £20, £10 and £5; age 12–17 wi prizes o £10, £5 and £2.50; and under 12, prizes o £5, £3 and £2.

Entries maun be original and ne'er afore prentit. They may be (a) Poems up to 60 lines; (b) tales up to 3,000 words; (c) plays that tak nae mair nor 25 meenits to perform. Ilk entry maun be signed wi a byname, and the byname should be prentit on the outside o a sealed envelope, that has inside the entrant's real name and address, and, for them under 18, the date o birth.

scrievin writing *owre* over *wi* with *o* of
maun must *prentit* printed
tak nae mair take no more
meenits minutes *ilk* each

OUR AIN LEID?

The opening sentences of a journal article on Scots, a contribution to a symposium on *Our ain leid?* ('Our own language?') published in the journal *English World-Wide* in 1981. This author uses an orthography which is further removed from Standard English than is usually to be found, but retains some traditional spellings in the interests of intelligibility.

In the upgrowth o a leid ti haill matuirity o lettirs, the staiblishin o an exponent prose is aften deimit a determant stage. A leid may hae a weil-founnit tradeition o hameilt sang, leirit indyte, an ein nerratif prose; but wantan a registir conding for academic screivins, hit maun bide be a 'hauf-leid' (*Halbsprache*: the word o the German leid-scolar Heinz Kloss) at the best…(J. D. McClure, 1981.)

(In the development of a language to full maturity of literature, the establishment of an expository prose is often judged a crucial stage. A language may have a well-founded tradition of domestic song, learned poetry, and even narrative prose; but lacking a register suitable for academic writers, it must remain a 'half-language' (*Halbsprache*: the word of the German language-scholar Heinz Kloss) at best…)

SYNTHETIC SCOTS

Scots must be re-created (really created, for, for literary purposes, it has practically never been) and de-Anglicized.

This comment by Hugh MacDiarmid in 1926 acts as a footnote to his creation of a revived or 'synthetic' Scots, using a range of old and contemporary language sources to produce a vocabulary which became increasingly esoteric as it developed. MacDiarmid (real name Christopher Murray Grieve) was a poet and critic, and a founder-member of the Scottish National Party in 1928. He became the central figure of the 20th-century Scottish Renaissance which flourished between 1920 and 1940, and which provided a major stimulus for later literature in Lallans.

I amna fou' sae muckle as tired – deid dune.
It's gey and hard wark coupin' gless for
    gless
Wi' Cruivie and Gilsanquhar and the like,
And I'm no' juist as bauld as aince I wes.

The elbuck fankles in the coorse o' time,
The sheckle's no' sae souple, and the
    thrapple
Grows deef and dour: nae langer up and
    doun
Gleg as a squirrel speils the Adam's apple.
(From 'A Drunk Man Looks at the Thistle',
1926.)

Hugh MacDiarmid (1892–1978)

fou' drunk *sae muckle* so much *deid* dead
gey very *bauld* bold *aince* once
elbuck elbow *fankles* gets clumsy
sheckle wrist *thrapple* throat *gleg* eager

WELSH ENGLISH

The Welsh, more than any other nation, have a right to feel aggrieved when they reflect on the history of English, for it was their ancestor language which was displaced when the Anglo-Saxon invaders first arrived (§2). Modern Welsh is the direct descendant of the Celtic language which was spoken at the time throughout most of Britain. This language survived for a while in Cumbria, south-west Scotland, Devon, and Cornwall, as well as in Wales, but after the Middle Ages it remained only in the latter two areas, and from the 19th century it is found in Wales alone.

English spread rapidly throughout Wales as a result of the early Norman conquest of the principality, resulting in a very different situation from that presented in other parts of Britain (p. 328). The Statutes which brought England and Wales together (1535, 1542) were far earlier than the Acts of Union passed for Scotland (1707) and Ireland (1800), and a complex set of religious, educational, and economic factors promoted the dominance of English in Wales. Among these was the dissolution of the monasteries, which led to the loss of many centres of Welsh learning. Latin came to be replaced by English as the language of education, and the Tudor grammar schools set up in several Welsh towns taught through the medium of English. In the 19th century, the Industrial Revolution fostered the emigration of Welsh speakers to jobs in England, and later the immigration of English speakers to jobs in the mining and smelting industries of South Wales. The population movements continued to grow in the present century, fuelled by wars and economic recessions. And behind everything, in recent years, there has been the relentless linguistic pressure towards anglicization, stemming from the dominance of English in technology, the media and the economy – as in every other part of the world.

THREE SIGNIFICANT DATES

1284 Following the defeat of Llewelyn by Edward 1, Wales is formally annexed to England, and the Statute of Rhuddlan establishes English law.

1535 The Statute of Wales (commonly known as the Act of Union) imposes English as the official language, requiring 'that all Justices, Sheriffs, Coroners, and all other Officers and Ministers of the Law, shall proclaim and keep the Sessions Courts, Hundred Leets (i.e. local courts), Sheriffs Courts, and all other Courts in the English Tongue…' (20th provision)

1563 An Act of Parliament requires that a copy of the English Bible and the Book of Common Prayer shall be placed alongside the Welsh versions in every church, so that people might 'the sooner attain to the knowledge of the English tongue'.

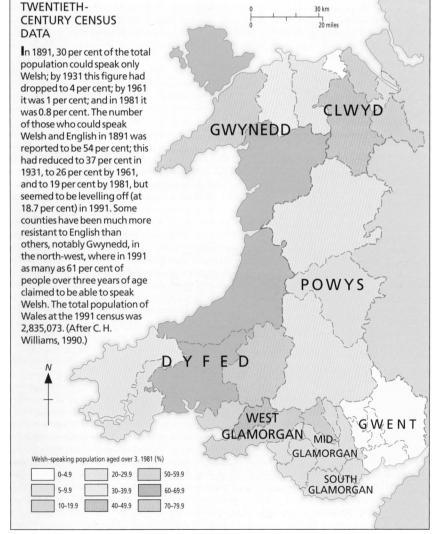

TWENTIETH-CENTURY CENSUS DATA

In 1891, 30 per cent of the total population could speak only Welsh; by 1931 this figure had dropped to 4 per cent; by 1961 it was 1 per cent; and in 1981 it was 0.8 per cent. The number of those who could speak Welsh and English in 1891 was reported to be 54 per cent; this had reduced to 37 per cent in 1931, to 26 per cent by 1961, and to 19 per cent by 1981, but seemed to be levelling off (at 18.7 per cent) in 1991. Some counties have been much more resistant to English than others, notably Gwynedd, in the north-west, where in 1991 as many as 61 per cent of people over three years of age claimed to be able to speak Welsh. The total population of Wales at the 1991 census was 2,835,073. (After C. H. Williams, 1990.)

GWYNEDD　CLWYD　POWYS　DYFED　WEST GLAMORGAN　MID-GLAMORGAN　GWENT　SOUTH GLAMORGAN

Welsh-speaking population aged over 3. 1981 (%)

0–4.9	20–29.9	50–59.9
5–9.9	30–39.9	60–69.9
10–19.9	40–49.9	70–79.9

A BUFFER ZONE

The change in the fortunes of Welsh and English during the present century can be clearly seen in these maps of the linguistic situation in Gwent – a border county in the south-east of the principality. Always the lowest Welsh-speaking area, the percentage of bilingual speakers in the county as a whole has fallen from 5 per cent in 1921 to 2.4 per cent in 1991. (After W. T. R. Pryce, 1990.)

1931

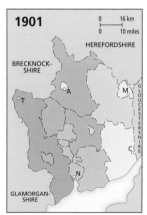

1901

1971

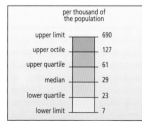

per thousand of the population	
upper limit	690
upper octile	127
upper quartile	61
median	29
lower quartile	23
lower limit	7

Key:
N　Newport
C　Chepstow
M　Monmouth
A　Abergavenny
T　Tredegar

THE REACTION

The statistics show the rapid decline in the number of Welsh speakers in Wales during the present century, and the corresponding growth in the English-speaking population; talk about the 'death' of the language, consequently, has been widespread. Yet there are unmistakeable signs of cultural and linguistic vitality and regeneration which make the future less predictable. The 1991 census showed a significant flattening of the downward Welsh-speaking curve. Unprecedented legal moves (especially the Welsh Language Act of 1967) and media publicity (notably the establishment of a separate TV channel in 1982) have fostered a fresh consciousness and conscience in many monolingual-English Welsh people. More systematic efforts are being made to counter the 'threat' of English (p. 114) by a range of political activities which extend from government debate to terrorism. It is too early to say whether the activities of extremists since the 1960s will diminish the dominance of English or increase it; but English will inevitably be affected to some degree by the process of forging a new and socially realistic bilingualism.

Supporters of Cymdeithas yr Iaith Gymraeg (the Welsh Language Society) protesting in London against the government's proposed legislation for the Welsh language, 1993.

ANGLO-WELSH LITERATURE

Although the term 'Anglo-Welsh' is of recent origin, writing in English by Welsh people can be found from the 15th century, reflecting the emergent bilingualism. The motivation for the label is plain enough – to avoid the ambiguity which would come from using the phrase 'Welsh literature', with its reference to literature written in Welsh – but its application is uncertain and controversial. Must all 'Anglo-Welsh' writers be born in Wales? may they be born elsewhere but with Welsh parents? need they have Welsh parents, and simply have chosen to live in Wales, or chosen to write on Welsh themes? must they be Welsh-speaking? The range of possibilities can be shown by, at one extreme, the Puritan author Morgan Llwyd (1619–59), born in Merionethshire, who lived most of his life in Wales, wrote mainly in Welsh, and was an eloquent preacher in both Welsh and English; and, at the other, the devotional poet George Herbert (1593–1633), of Norman–Welsh ancestry and uncertain birth-place, who probably knew no Welsh, and lived most of his life in England.

The issue has been prominent since the 1920s. Most critics now allow the term a broad application, and include within it anyone who relates to Welsh literary, linguistic, or cultural traditions, but who uses English in order to do so. The question asked by Saunders Lewis (1893–1985) in an influential 1939 pamphlet, 'Is there an Anglo-Welsh literature?' would now be answered by a choir of literary voices: early writers such as W. H. Davies (1871–1940), John Cowper Powys (1872–1963), and Caradoc Evans (1883–1945, whom some call the father of Anglo-Welsh literature), have been supplemented by Emlyn Williams (1905–87), Vernon Watkins (1906–67), Dylan Thomas (1914–53), R(onald) S(tuart) Thomas (1913–), Dannie Abse (1923–), Raymond Garlick (1926–), Meic Stephens (1938–), and the hundreds of authors who since the 1940s have contributed to such lively periodicals as *The Anglo-Welsh Review*, *Poetry Wales*, and *The New Welsh Review*.

A SPACE FOR VOICES

My name is Lowri Dafydd;
Famous for nursing I was.
I rode pillion on a winged horse
Through the high passes of cloud
To come to a queen's palace.
Airy fingers undid the knot
In time's stubborn bandage
About my green eyes.
Who knows how long I stayed?
My pay was the sweet talk
In sun-dusted rooms
Of folk, busy as flowers,
Praising my hands' skill.
When I returned, stars were out
Over my roof, the door fallen
About its hinges, and on the hearth
A cold wind blowing for ever.
(*Lowri Dafydd*, R. S. Thomas, 1958)

I was born in a large Welsh town at the beginning of the Great War – an ugly, lovely town, or so it was and is to me; crawling, sprawling by a long and splendid curving shore where truant boys and Sandfield boys and old men from nowhere, beachcombed, idled, and paddled, watched the dock-bound ships or the ships steaming away into wonder and India, magic and China, countries bright with oranges and loud with lions, threw stones into the sea for the barking outcast dogs; made castles and forts and harbours and race tracks in the sand; and on Saturday summer afternoons listened to the brass band, watched the Punch and Judy, or hung about on the fringes of the crowds to hear the fierce religious speakers who shouted at the sea, as though it were wicked and wrong to roll in and out like that, white-horsed and full of fishes…
(*Reminiscences of Childhood*, Dylan Thomas, 1943)

SOME FEATURES OF WELSH ENGLISH

The distinctiveness of Welsh English varies greatly within Wales, being most noticeable in areas where Welsh is strong (the north-west). There is no universally used standard variety, despite the fact that some features are thought by outsiders to be 'typically Welsh', and used in a stereotyped way in literature and humour. A good example is the tag *look you*, a direct translation from a Welsh tag, which is rarely if ever used by real Welsh English speakers (though you would never guess from listening to Fluellen in Shakespeare's *Henry V*, one of the many famous literary Welsh).

Pronunciation

(For phonetics terminology, see §17.)
• A contrast is not made between /ʌ/ and /ə/: the two vowels of *butter* are identical, unlike RP /ˈbʌtə/.
• Consonants between vowels are often lengthened, as in *money* /ˈmənːi/ and *butter* /ˈbʌtːə/.
• Two Welsh consonants are found: the well-known voiceless *l* sound, as in *Llandudno*), and the velar fricative /x/ (as in *bach*).
• There is no /z/ in Welsh, and in northern dialects several English word-pairs sound the same: *pence* / *pens* are both /pens/. Similarly, the lack of affricates in Welsh results in identity between such pairs as *chin* and *gin*: /dʒɪn/.

Grammar and vocabulary

(For grammatical terminology, see Part III.)
• The tag question *isn't it* is used by some speakers after all pronouns (p. 299): *You're leaving, isn't it?* Another tag is *yes*, especially in colloquial form asking for agreement, *yeah?*
• To express emphasis, the predicate (apart from the first verb) can appear before the subject: *Running on Friday, he is; Fed up I am.*
• There are several Welsh loan-words, such as *eisteddfod* (a type of arts festival), *Duw* ('God', as in exclamations), *del* ('dear', as a term of endearment), and *nain* and *taid* ('grandma', 'grandpa').

IRISH ENGLISH

Ireland, as a geographical part of the British Isles, is usually considered alongside Great Britain when investigating English language use. This makes sense, from a linguistic point of view. It is sometimes forgotten that Ireland was the first of the overseas English-speaking colonies, and that there has been some 800 years of continuous contact between the two nations. Moreover, the issues involved in identifying the kind of variation found today in Northern Ireland overlap considerably with those encountered in the Irish Republic. Both parts of Ireland are therefore dealt with on these pages.

The history of English involvement in Gaelic-speaking Ireland dates from the 12th century, when the country was invaded by Anglo-Norman knights, and English rule was imposed by Henry II. The new settlers, however, were to adopt Irish ways of living, and, despite attempts to halt this trend, the area under English control (known as the 'Pale') was still relatively small by the end of the 16th century. Renewed efforts were then made by the Tudor monarchs to spread English power throughout the country. Plantation schemes encouraged English settlers in the south, and support was given to promote the spirit of the Reformation. The Irish chiefs were defeated in a series of wars during the reign of Elizabeth I, and this was followed by a renewed influx of Protestant settlers, mainly from the Scottish Lowlands (p. 332). James I made available large tracts of land in the north of Ireland, and over 100,000 came to develop plantations there. Further steps to quell Irish rebellion took place in the 17th century, notably Oliver Cromwell's campaign of 1649–50. Then in 1801 the Act of Union made Ireland part of the United Kingdom – a situation which remained until the 1920s, when there was partition between north (Northern Ireland, or Ulster) and south.

The chief linguistic consequence of these events was a steady growth in the use of English, and a corresponding decline in the use of Gaelic, except among the poorer sections of the community. English became the dominant language in the mid-19th century, and the language of prestige. Gaelic was avoided in the home, and became a reason for punishment if children were heard to use it in schools. Today, English is universal, with Gaelic found only in certain rural parts of the west (the *Gaeltacht*) – notwithstanding its status as an official language in the Irish Republic alongside English. Since the 19th century, there have been several attempts to encourage the spread of Gaelic, and it is now an important element of the school curriculum, but these efforts have not affected the dominance of English. Even in the north,

where the political conflict was originally associated with the two languages, nowadays both sides use English.

There is as yet little sign of a regionally distinctive educated standard in Ireland; but there are many cases of words, idioms, and grammatical patterns in informal non-standard speech which are characteristic of the dialects of the area, and which are reflected in a strong regional literature. From a linguistic point of view, Irish English in all its variation is widely referred to as *Hiberno-English*, though the term *Anglo-Irish* has a useful role identifying those varieties in which the phonology, grammar, or vocabulary displays a particularly strong Celtic influence.

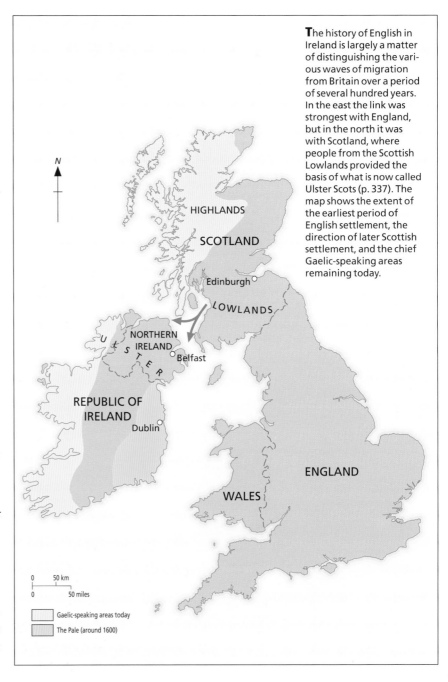

The history of English in Ireland is largely a matter of distinguishing the various waves of migration from Britain over a period of several hundred years. In the east the link was strongest with England, but in the north it was with Scotland, where people from the Scottish Lowlands provided the basis of what is now called Ulster Scots (p. 337). The map shows the extent of the earliest period of English settlement, the direction of later Scottish settlement, and the chief Gaelic-speaking areas remaining today.

HIGHLANDS

SCOTLAND

Edinburgh

LOWLANDS

ULSTER

NORTHERN IRELAND

Belfast

REPUBLIC OF IRELAND

Dublin

ENGLAND

WALES

N

0   50 km
0   50 miles

Gaelic-speaking areas today

The Pale (around 1600)

DIALECT DIVISIONS

As with other English-speaking varieties, Hiberno-English is by no means homogeneous. A major boundary can be drawn, first of all, between the dialects spoken in the southern two-thirds of the island and those spoken further north, in the former province of Ulster (a larger area than the six counties which comprise modern Northern Ireland). Ulster, the more varied linguistic situation, can be divided into two main areas. The dialect spoken in the north-east of the region is known as Ulster Scots or Scotch-Irish, because it displays many features which can be traced back to the speech of the 17th-century immigrants from the Scottish Lowlands. The dialect used elsewhere, known as Mid-Ulster or Ulster Anglo-Irish, displays far less Scots influence, having been largely settled by immigrants from England (chiefly from the west and north-west Midlands).

Within both Ulster and the south, a range of varieties of Hiberno-English can be found. Rural dialects, especially those in the west, display a highly conservative character, much influenced by the speech forms of Gaelic. Urban dialects, especially those of Dublin and Belfast, are more heavily influenced by English, and display many of the nonstandard forms found in the urban dialects of Great Britain. And throughout the country there is an educated variety of Hiberno-English, containing relatively few regional forms – though enough to make such speech 'sound Irish' to outsiders. As heard in the formal language of the national radio station, Radio Telefís Éireann, only occasional items of lexicon (e.g. *taoiseach* /'ti:ʃəx/ 'prime minister') distinguish it from Standard English.

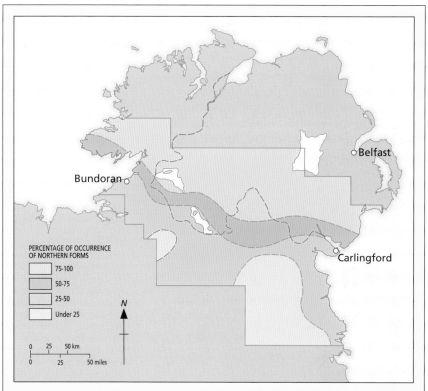

TRANSITIONAL ZONE

The boundary between northern and southern dialect areas in Ireland is usually shown winding its way in a generally south-easterly direction from Bundoran on the west coast to Carlingford Lough on the east. However, this is not a sharply defined boundary line. The map shows a narrow area of mixed northern and southern features co-existing in south Fermanagh, north and central Monaghan, and south Armagh. In the north, for example, the vowel in such words as *horse* is rounded [ɔː]; in the south, it is unrounded [ɑː]; but in this central area it is subject to variation. On the whole, older people who live towards the south of this boundary area use the rounded vowel, whereas younger people use the unrounded one. Similar patterns of variation can be established for several other differentiating criteria, and a conflation of these produces the pattern on the map, which shows the way forms gradually decrease as one moves south. (From M. V. Barry, 1984.)

PRONUNCIATION

Several phonetic features distinguish Hiberno-English from Received Pronunciation (RP, p. 365), some involving subtle contrasts in vowel length, lip rounding, and tongue position. Below is a selection of features heard in the more distinctive accents. (For phonetics terminology, see §17.)

• Words such as *tea* and *key* tend to be pronounced with /eː/ instead of RP /iː/, as reflected in such literary spellings as *tay, Paycock*.
• RP /ɔɪ/ is often pronounced /əɪ/, especially in the south: as suggested by the literary spelling *jine* for *join*.
• There are several differences from RP in open vowels: in particular, words like *path* and *calm* often have a long front /aː/, with a long back /ɑː/ used in *saw* and *talk*.
• /r/ after vowels (p. 245) is kept in such words as *car* and *purse*.
• /t/ and /d/ are usually dental (alveolar in RP), and the RP *th* fricatives /θ, ð/ appear as plosives (*thanks* /t̪aŋks/, *this* /d̪-ɪs/); some pairs of words (e.g. *thin* and *tin*) may therefore sound the same.
• /l/ is always clear (p. 245) in such words as *full* and *field*.
• Some consonant clusters have been influenced by the Gaelic sound system: for example, /s/ may become /ʃ/ before /t,n,l/, as in *stop* /ʃtop/.

IRISH STRESS

A noticeable feature of many Hiberno-English accents is the way the chief stress (p. 248) in a polysyllabic word is often different from its location in RP. Stress patterns seem to be more flexible than in RP, especially in the south, and there is considerable variation, but a few general tendencies have been noted.

• Verbal suffixes attract the stress in words with three or more syllables (*educate, advertise, prosecute*), along with their inflections (*educating, complicated*).
• In polysyllabic nouns, a syllable followed by a consonant cluster tends to attract the stress: *algebra, architecture, character*. This feature is often stigmatized as nonstandard, though such forms as *orchestra* and *discipline* may be heard in educated speech.

The general pattern is one of stress postponement, the primary stress appearing later in the word compared with

RP. Many other words show this pattern (*triangle, safeguard, diagnose*), though there is much variation, especially when people allow their speech to be influenced by American or British models. Many Irish place names also have a final stress, reflecting Gaelic origins, as in *Belfast*, though anglicization to *Belfast* is now common.

Postponed stress is also a noticeable feature of Scots, Caribbean, and Indian English. But the effect has been taken much further in Irish than in Scots English, and something more fundamental seems to be afoot in the case of India and the Caribbean (p. 344). It has also been around in Ireland for a long time, as can be seen from the metrical patterns of pre-20th-century rhyming verse ('So therefore I awaited with my spirits elevated'). The origins of the effect are unclear, but it is thought that part of the answer may lie with the Irish schoolmasters who became early agents of anglicization, and who were often unsure how polysyllabic words should be pronounced. (After D. Ó Sé, 1986.)

IRISH ENGLISH ABROAD

In view of the extensive migrations of the Irish over several centuries, it is not surprising to find evidence of Hiberno-English around the English-speaking world. Signs of its arrival in England can be seen especially in the dialect of Liverpool, and its influence has been found in a number of modern North American dialects and in parts of the Caribbean. It also played an important role in the emergence of the new varieties of English in Australia and New Zealand (p. 352). Patterns of linguistic change are complex, as people are influenced in the way they speak by all kinds of considerations; in particular, it is difficult to be sure of the role that pronunciation features play when a minority dialect emerges in a new linguistic setting. Nonetheless, linguists have pointed to words, constructions, and patterns of discourse in these varieties which can plausibly be argued to derive from Hiberno-English.

- *Youse* ('you' plural), is widespread in Ireland, and is also found in Liverpool, Glasgow, Australia, and many parts of North America.
- Positive *anymore* (as in *He fights a lot anymore*) is in some US Midland dialects. It is found in Ireland, but not in Britain.
- Sentence-final *but* (used adverbially, to mean 'though', as in *I don't want it but*), is common in Ulster, parts of Scotland and Tyneside, and in informal Australian English.
- The construction shown in *Come here till I see you* ('so that I can see you') is used in Liverpool, and often in non-standard Australian English.
- The use of *whenever* to refer to a single occasion (*Whenever I was born, I was given a special present*) is found in Ulster, and is known in New Zealand and parts of Australia.
- The emphatic affirmation *It is so* (as in *A: It's raining. B: It isn't. A: It is so!*) is common in Ireland and in informal Australian English. It may have influenced US English *It is so / too*.
- The Hiberno-English use of *mustn't* where Standard English says *can't* (*He mustn't have seen me, because he drove straight past*) is unknown in most of England (Liverpool is the chief exception), but is common in Australia and the USA.

The British colonies were established by people who represented many dialect backgrounds, and Hiberno-English made its contribution alongside Scots and London English, in particular. The point was noticed by several early travellers. As F. Gerstaecker writes, in his *Narrative of a Journey Round the World* (1853), 'the broad Irish brogue and the London Cockney dialect seemed to strike me everywhere'. (After P. Trudgill, 1986.)

GRAMMAR

The features described earlier on this page are only a few of the distinctive grammatical features found in Hiberno-English. All of the following will also be encountered, though there is considerable geographical and social variation. The verb phrase, in particular, displays a number of idiosyncrasies. (For grammatical terminology, see Part III.)

Verb phrase
- Several features affect verbal aspect, such as a wider use of the progressive form (*Who is this car belonging to?, Who is it you're wanting?*) and the use of the present tense instead of the perfect (*She's dead these ten years*, i.e. 'has been dead'). One of the most distinctive features of Hiberno-English is the use of *after* to express such meanings as recency and completed event: *They're after leaving* (='They've just left'), *They were after leaving* (='They had just left').
- Copula and auxiliary *be* are used in distinctive ways, chiefly expressing contrasts of habitual action and continuity: *be* is found with forms of *do* (*It does be colder at nights*) and also, especially in the north, with an *-s* ending (*I be walking, She bees walking*). Some dialects allow all three patterns: *She's tired, She be tired, She do be tired*.
- Auxiliary usages often vary: *will* for *shall*, *used be* for *used to be*, *amn't* for *aren't*. Forms of *be* may replace *have* with verbs of motion in a past-time context (*He is gone up* for *He has gone up*), as found in earlier English (p. 45), and an interesting parallel with such languages as French.

- There are some distinctive imperative constructions: *Let you stay here a while, Let you be coming up to see me*. The progressive form is common with negatives: *Don't be troubling yourself*.

Other areas
- Definite article: *That's the grand morning, I had a few jars over the Christmas, The wife* (='my wife') *will be expecting me*.
- Prepositions: *till* is often used for *to/until*, as in *It's a quarter till two*; *for ti* can be heard for *in order to*, as in *I went for ti milk the cow*. *On* and *of* are often affected (*You've lost my pen on me, Aren't you a slob of a cat, What age of a man was he?*), and there are some interesting sequences (*If he didn't take the legs from in under me*, i.e. 'He knocked me down'). *From* can be heard in the sense of 'since' in Ulster: *He's been here from he left the Navy*.
- Certain constructions show a Gaelic influence on word order. Cleft sentences (p. 231) of the following kind are typical: *It's meself was the brave singer, Is it out of your mind you are?* There is an interesting double example in *It's thinking I am that it's unyoke him we'd better do* ('I think that we had better unyoke him').
- Some plural pronouns or demonstratives are followed by *is*: *Youse is very funny, Them cars is great, Our'ns is fit for anything*.
- *And* is used as a subordinate clause marker, as in *It only struck me and* (='when', 'while') *you going out of the door*. Sometimes the exact Standard English equivalent is unclear: *How could you see me there and* (='when', 'if', 'seeing that'?) *I to be in bed at the time?*

VOCABULARY

- **T**here is a huge regional lexicon, which includes such items as *blather* talk nonsense; *bold* naughty; *cog* (to) cheat; *delph* crockery; *freet* superstition; *garda* police; *glit* slime; *handsel* New Year's gift; *hogo* bad smell; *insleeper* overnight visitor; *kink* fit of coughing; *mannerly* well-mannered; *widow-woman* widow.
- The suffix *-een* is used as a diminutive form, expressing smallness or familiarity, as in *childreen, girleen*.
- Gaelic influence can be seen in such words as *backy* lame; *bosthoon* clown; *cleeve* basket; *glow* noise; *keerogue* cockroach; *kyoch* diseased; *prockus* mixture; *sleeveen* sly one; *spalpeen* rascal.
- Several Scots words are found in Ulster, such as *clarty* dirty; *greet* weep; *wee* small.

IDIOMATIC EXPRESSION

- **T**he variety has many distinctive idioms, such as *He'd put the day astray on you* ('He would waste your day'), *You'll knock a while out of it* ('It'll last you for a while'), and *He's the rest of yourself* ('He's related to you').
- As with Australian English, there is a great deal of vivid figurative language: *as mean as get out, as often as fingers and toes, as fat in the forehead as a hen, as sharp a tongue as would shave a mouse*. Lengthy, often exaggerated expressions are common: *That I may live long and have my eyesight and never see hide or hair of you again*.
- Proverbial wisdom is widely employed: *Charity is a slap in the mouth, There's a truth in the last drop in the bottle*.

Discourse patterns
The variety is renowned for some of its conversational features.
- Questions in general are rarely answered with a straight *yes* or *no*, but recapitulate the auxiliary.
A: Will you ask John for me?
B: I will / I will not.
- Rhetorical questions are usual: *Now isn't he a fine looking fellow?, What did we want only to get our own?*
- A common practice is to reply to a question by using another question: *A: Can you tell me where's the post office?*
B: Would it be stamps you're looking for?

THE BROADER SCENE

The question of what counts as 'Anglo-Irish' literature is controversial (as in the case of Anglo-Welsh in Wales, p. 335). If it is 'work written in English by Irish writers', as some critics have argued, the definition includes a vast spread of authorship, including Jonathan Swift (1667–1745), Oscar Wilde (1854–1900), W. B. Yeats (1865–1939), and Seamus Heaney (1939–), and a great deal of this writing is in Standard English. However, an important body of Anglo-Irish literature uses Hiberno-English, with varying levels of realism, as part of its medium of expression. The plays of J. M. Synge (1871–1909) and Sean O'Casey (1884–1964), and the novels and short stories of James Joyce (1882–1941), generated particular interest in the literary possibilities of the variety, and this stimulus has been taken up, often with convincing urban realism, in the writing of contemporary authors such as Roddy Doyle.

There is a second way in which Anglo-Irish writers have made a distinctive contribution to the possibilities of English expression: their apparent fascination with language – a force which motivates authors, scholars, and lay people alike. The lay interest in linguistic history and scholarship is difficult to match in the English-speaking world, as is the long-established academic tradition of medieval studies. The fascination can also be seen in the way ordinary people in their everyday conversation, as well as recognized authors in their writing, are prepared to 'play' with the language, manipulating it and embellishing it with figurative expressions and flights of linguistic fancy – a process which reaches its apotheosis in *Finnegans Wake* (p. 134). The exploits of heroic figures are found lyrically recapitulated and reflected in the lives of modern characters, and there is an awareness of folk-history and myth, a strong sense of locality and of the ancient identity of small communities, and a fluency in story-telling – the 'gift of the gab' – which permeates a great deal of Irish literary expression, and adds distinctive colour to its language. Its echoes continue to resound in all English-speaking countries which have Irish settlement as a part of their history.

J. M. Synge

Roddy Doyle

VOICES

CHRISTY [*indignantly*] Starting from you, is it? I will not, then, and when the airs is warming, in four months or five, it's then yourself and me should be pacing Neifin in the dews of night, the times sweet smells do be rising, and you'd see a little, shiny new moon, maybe sinking on the hills.
PEGEEN [*looking at him playfully*] And it's that kind of a poacher's love you'd make, Christy Mahon, on the sides of Neifin, when the night is down?
CHRISTY. It's little you'll think if my love's a poacher's, or an earl's itself, when you'll feel my two hands stretched around you, and I squeezing kisses on your puckered lips, till I'd feel a kind of pity for the Lord God is all ages sitting lonesome in His golden chair.
PEGEEN. That'll be right fun, Christy

Mahon, and any girl would walk her heart out before she'd meet a young man was your like for eloquence, or talk at all.
CHRISTY [*encouraged*] Let you wait to hear me talking till we're astray in Erris, when Good Friday's by, drinking a sup from a well, and making mighty kisses with our wetted mouths, or gaming in a gap of sunshine, with yourself stretched back unto your necklace, in the flowers of the earth.
PEGEEN [*in a low voice, moved by his tone*] I'd be nice so, is it?
CHRISTY [*with rapture*] If the mitred bishops seen you that time, they'd be the like of the holy prophets I'm thinking, do be straining the bars of paradise to lay eyes on the Lady Helen of Troy, and she abroad pacing back and forward with a nosegay in her golden shawl.
(J. M. Synge, *The Playboy of the Western World*, 1907, Act 3.)

Jimmy Sr put down the flask and screwed the top back on it. Then he took the sandwich out of his mouth.
– I'm on me break, he told Bimbo.
Bimbo looked the way he did when he didn't know what was going on.
– I'm entitled to ten minutes rest for every two hours that I work, said Jimmy Sr.
Bimbo still looked lost.
– I looked it up, said Jimmy Sr.
He saw that Bimbo's face was catching up with his brain.
Bimbo stood back from the hatch. Jimmy Sr took a slug of the tea.

– I needed tha', he said.
– Stop messin', will yeh, said Bimbo.
– I'm not messin', said Jimmy Sr. – I'm entitled to me break.
– Sure Jaysis, said Bimbo, – we did nothin' all nigh' except for a few minutes ago.
– Not the point, said Jimmy Sr.
– Not the point at all. I was here. I was available to work.
– Hurry up, will yis!
That came from outside.
– I've five minutes left, Jimmy Sr told Bimbo. – Then I'll sweat for yeh.
(Roddy Doyle, *The Van*, 1991, pp. 279–80.)

Jaysis Jesus *yis*/*yeh* you

A RELIGIOUS FOOTNOTE

No account of contemporary Irish English would be complete without acknowledging the conflict in Northern Ireland, and asking: is there a difference between the way Catholics and Protestants talk in the province? It might be expected that the Catholic population of Northern Ireland would speak English in ways which showed a greater influence of Gaelic (spoken almost exclusively by people whose religion is Catholic), and the Protestant population would show more Scottish features. Doubtless, there are cases where such a contrast exists, but it is unlikely that the community is clearly divided in this way. Language varies in ways that uniforms do not. The amount of contact between the two communities, in such domains as sports and the workplace, makes it likely that there will be many shared linguistic features.

There are however a few unambiguous pointers, arising out of different social or educational practices. For example, children are taught to say *haitch* in Catholic schools, and *aitch* in Protestant ones. And what is *Derry* to Catholics is likely to be *Londonderry* to Protestants. Linguists who have looked for systematic differences in accent, grammar, and vocabulary have found some interesting trends, but few convincing differences.

There is certainly no simple correlation between Gaelicism and Catholicism, or between Scotticism and Protestantism. At the same time, one cannot help wondering about the implications of stories such as the one told by British linguist Loreto Todd. She remarks that the two religious traditions make use of different musical instruments, and that the connotations (p. 170) of the terms therefore differ: *fiddle* suggests Catholic, *flute* Protestant.

The association of *flute* with the Protestant Community is borne out by the song *The Oul' Orange Flute* and the following anecdote related to me by a school inspector. The inspector (Protestant) was visiting a small Catholic school in the Sperrins. He asked the boys if they knew the name for a man who played the piano. All hands shot up and one little boy gave the answer: 'Pianist, sir.' 'Good,' said the inspector, 'and what's the name for a man who plays the violin?' Again, all the children knew. 'Well, now,' said the inspector, 'I'll ask you a hard one. What's the name for a man who plays the flute?' Silence. Not a hand was raised. 'Come on,' urged the inspector, 'surely some boy has heard what a man who plays the flute is called.' One little hand went up. 'Good boy,' encouraged the inspector. 'What is it?' 'Please sir,' said the child, 'at home he would be called an orange bastard.'
(From L. Todd, 1984b.)

CANADIAN ENGLISH

Because of its origins (p. 95), Canadian English has a great deal in common with the rest of the English spoken in North America, and those who live outside Canada often find it difficult to hear the difference. Many British people identify a Canadian accent as American; many Americans identify it as British. Canadians themselves insist on not being identified with either group, and certainly the variety does display a number of unique features. In addition, the presence of French as a co-official language, chiefly spoken in Quebec, produces a sociolinguistic situation not found in other English-speaking countries.

One of the most distinctive characteristics of Canadian English stems from the tension which inevitably exists in such a situation. Both British and American models have supplied the variety with features from the outset, and continue to do so (though with US English tending now to dominate, especially among younger people). The consequence is a sociolinguistic situation of some complexity, with some linguistic features used throughout Canada (or nearly so) and others varying in relation to such factors as age, sex, education, occupation, geographical location, and political viewpoint. Four types of distinctiveness need to be recognized.

• Some features originate within Canada, and are thus independent of US or UK models. A number of them (such as the technical terms of ice hockey) have become part of World Standard English (p. 92).

• Some features originate outside Canada (chiefly US English, UK English, and French), and are used consistently by everyone in a particular region. A national example is the contrast between (federal) *prime minister* and (provincial) *premier*; a regional one, the names of political or cultural institutions in Quebec (e.g. *bloc québecois, caisse populaire*, p. 303).

• Some features can be identified with US English, and are used only by sections of the population.

• Some features can be identified with UK English, and are used only by sections of the population.

It is these last two categories which present real difficulties for anyone wishing to generalize about Canadian English. Or, putting this another way, it is precisely this problem which captures the uniqueness of the Canadian linguistic situation. (See also the photographic collage at the opening to Part V, p. 284).

SPELLING VARIATION

Spellings such as the above, with a US form (*tire*) juxtaposed with a UK form (*centre*) are striking (at least, to a linguist) when they occur, and show that Canadian English cannot be identified with either American or British English. It is important not to overestimate this issue: we may read pages of a Canadian newspaper (p. 303) and not see a comparable instance. However, if we search for instances of words where a spelling choice *is* possible, we will soon find an unusual aggregation of forms.

Moreover, surveys of individual spelling practices have brought to light considerable geographical, occupational, and social variation: for example, in a 1991 report, over 80 per cent of high-school students in Ontario were said to be spelling words like *colour* with -*our*, while over 60 per cent of their counterparts in Alberta were using -*or*. The US model seems to be becoming more widespread in popular publications, and the press on the whole uses US spelling (but see p. 303). British spelling, however, is the norm in learned journals and school textbooks. And juxtapositions of the two models are common in private correspondence: the author has one letter from a Canadian in which *cheque* and *program* (radio, not computer) co-occur, and another from a different correspondent in which *initialed* appears alongside *plough* (p. 307).

Vocabulary
Similarly, both US and UK models provide sources for vocabulary. British *tap* (US *faucet*), *railway* (US *railroad*), and *braces* (US *suspenders*) coexist alongside US *gas* (UK *petrol*), *sidewalk* (UK *pavement*) and *wrench* (UK *spanner*), though usage varies from place to place. Vehicle terms (p. 310) are typically American: *truck, fender, trunk*, etc.

Conflicts over spelling may take place between languages. Thus it is a matter of sociolinguistic identity within Quebec whether one spells the name of the province with or without an accent (*Québec*). The problem facing the airline which is called *Canadian* in English and *Canadien* in French was ingeniously solved through the use of the company logo.

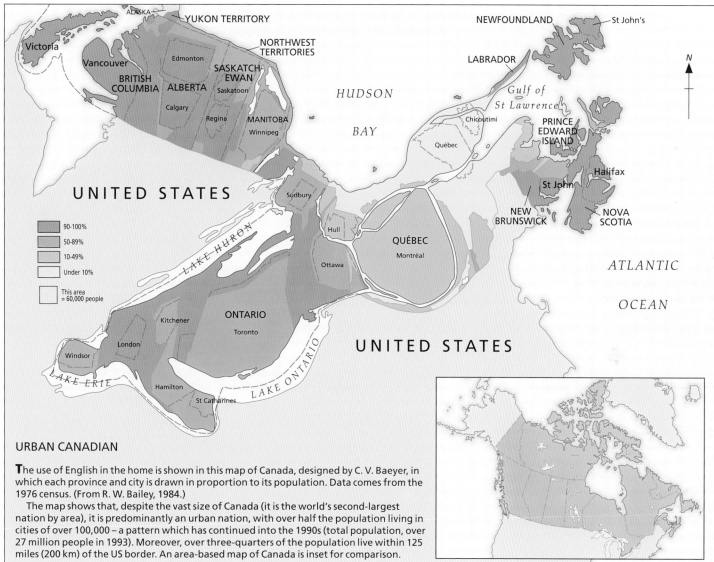

URBAN CANADIAN

The use of English in the home is shown in this map of Canada, designed by C. V. Baeyer, in which each province and city is drawn in proportion to its population. Data comes from the 1976 census. (From R. W. Bailey, 1984.)

The map shows that, despite the vast size of Canada (it is the world's second-largest nation by area), it is predominantly an urban nation, with over half the population living in cities of over 100,000 – a pattern which has continued into the 1990s (total population, over 27 million people in 1993). Moreover, over three-quarters of the population live within 125 miles (200 km) of the US border. An area-based map of Canada is inset for comparison.

PRONUNCIATION VARIATION

It is difficult to generalize about pronunciation patterns, because an already complex system is in a state of change. Canadian accents display features of both US and UK English (p. 307), but preferences are conditioned greatly by such factors as age and social class. The nearness of US English, and the prestige associated with it, impresses some sections of the population, while a concern to preserve a distinct Canadian identity motivates others to maintain as much pronunciation distance from the USA as possible.

Several features are shared with US English, in the speech of most Canadians:

• The pronunciation of /r/ after vowels (p. 245), in such words as *far* and *north*.
• The flapped /d/-like articulation of /t/ in such words as *Ottawa*.
• The use of a strong syllable in such suffixes as *-ary* and *-ory* (*secretary, laboratory*)
• The use of /-əl/ in such words as *fertile, missile*, and *hostile*.
• In addition, several individual words adopt US pronunciations, such as *schedule* with /sk-/ and *tomato* with /eɪ/.

On the other hand, British influence is evident in a number of individual cases:

• /anti/ for *anti-* instead of US /antaɪ/.
• /zed/ for letter *z* instead of US /ziː/.
• The first syllable of *lieutenant* pronounced /lef-/, not /luː/.

• /baθ/ for *bath (a baby)*, not US *bathe* /beɪð/.
• Such words as *tune* are pronounced with initial /tʃuː/ or /tjuː/, not US /tuː/.
• Similarly, such words as *news* are pronounced /njuːz/, rather than US /nuːz/. This is in fact one of the usage issues in the country, with the attention of broadcasters being drawn to the point.

Everywhere, variation is normal: thus in one survey, 68 per cent of adults said *leisure* with /iː/ rather than /e/ (a US preference), whereas 84 per cent said *lever* with /iː/ rather than /e/ (a UK preference). And – notwithstanding the above – younger people, especially those living in the west of the country, often say *lieutenant* in the American way.

TRAWNA

Just one of the various spellings (*Toronna* and *Tronno* are others) which writers have used to capture the fast colloquial pronunciation of the capital city of Ontario, as spoken by many of its inhabitants. These spellings are trying to represent the deletion of /t/ after /n/ (as in *twenty, antidote*, etc.) – a feature Canadian shares with US English (though in fact a similar elision can also be heard in several other varieties). In careful speech, the /t/ is retained, as can be heard routinely in the destination announcements at any Canadian airline terminal.

UNIQUE FEATURES

Canadian English is not solely identified by its unusual distribution of US and UK linguistic characteristics. There are several features which seem to be unique to the variety, and which are often deliberately identified with Canadian speakers in such contexts as joke-telling, satire, and literary characterization.

• In pronunciation, there are two main identifying features – notably the sound of the diphthong /aɪ/ and /aʊ/ before voiceless consonants in such words as *house* and *fight*. The effect has been referred to as 'Canadian raising': the first element of the diphthong is articulated higher and in a more central position than would be heard in RP or nearby US accents, in the area of [ə] (p. 240), so that *out* sounds more like RP *oat* and *isle* more like *oil*. The other chief distinction is the way Canadians pronounce such pairs of words as *cot* and *caught* or *collar* and *caller* with the same short vowel. Such a merger can be heard in some parts of the USA, but not just those bordering on Canada.

• An important characteristic of the vocabulary is the use of many words and phrases originating in Canada itself. These are often borrowings from Native American languages, some of which have entered the variety directly, some through the medium of French. A few have become a part of World Standard English. Examples include *caribou*, *chesterfield* ('sofa'), *kayak*, *kerosene*, *mukluk* ('Inuit boot'), *parka*, *reeve* ('mayor'), and *skookum* ('strong'). Terms reflecting Canadian culture include *riding* (a political constituency), *first nations* (the indigenous peoples), *bannock* (a type of pancake), the *prime minister/premier* distinction (p. 340), and many items to do with fur trading, lumbering, mining, and local fauna and flora. There are around 10,000 distinctive words and senses listed in the *Dictionary of Canadianisms*, though many of these are restricted to certain localities.

• A striking discourse feature is the use of *eh?* as a tag (p. 218), often replacing a tag question, but often with a less specific intent during a narrative sentence: *He finally gets to the garage, eh, and the car's gone.* The form is usually spoken with a rising intonation, and is used by the speaker with various functions, such as checking that the speaker is sympathetically attending, or anticipating a point of special interest in the narrative. A similar form may be heard in several other parts of the world, such as in Scotland, Australia, and Jamaica, though not with such frequency, and usually lacking the narrative function.

EMERGING DIALECTS?

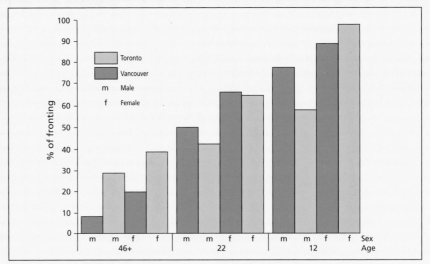

The apparent homogeneity of Canadian speech means that dialectologists have to hunt hard to find any regionally distinctive variant forms. It is likely that the relative lack of variation across most of inland Canada is due to the country's fairly recent history of settlement, and the early dominance of a single group (Ontarians) in the formation of an educated middle class. If so, then as population increases, and other influences intervene (such as the growing 'presence' of the USA, or the growth in immigrants from non-English-speaking language backgrounds), we would expect to find regional variation becoming more noticeable, with changes appearing especially in the cities and in the speech of younger people. Is there any evidence that this kind of change is taking place?

In a study published in 1986, the phonetic quality of the diphthong /aʊ/ (the chief feature of 'Canadian raising') was examined in the speech of middle-class people in Toronto and Vancouver, using samples of people who were 12, 22, and over 46 years of age. The figure shows the chief results.

In younger people, the distinctive centralized element of this vowel was often replaced by one whose quality was either further forward in the mouth (*fronting*), or more open (*non-raising*), or both. These words therefore sounded more like versions of the diphthong common in US English (though not in RP, where the characteristic quality is further back), and thus suggests the growing influence of that variety. Also noteworthy is the fact that the same changes were taking place in Canadian cities over 1,500 miles apart.

Three details of the change, suggested by the data, are important.

• Fronting correlates with age in both cities, and at about the same rate, but with Vancouver adults moving slightly more rapidly than their Toronto counterparts.
• Fronting correlates with sex in both cities, with women the leading innovators. The males in each age group have lower scores than their female counterparts.

• Non-raising (not shown in the figure) is not as noticeable, though it is taking place in both cities. It is more in evidence in Vancouver, especially among 12-year-old girls.

Regional differences
A close examination of the data brings to light two interesting contrasts.

• It is a general expectation of sociolinguistic enquiry that change is more likely to affect younger people. If Vancouver adults are further ahead in fronting than those in Toronto, we would therefore expect Vancouver children to be further ahead than Toronto children – but they are not. It appears that Vancouver adults are being more innovative than their children. How can this be so?
• Although males score less than females, at a given age, they score more than the females in the next higher age group. This applies regularly in the present study, but there is one exception: in Vancouver the 22-year-old women have higher scores than the 12-year-old boys. What has caused Vancouver women to outscore younger males in this way?

A new change
The answer to both these questions is to be found in the emergence of a new sound quality affecting the /aʊ/ diphthong in Vancouver, and found among the younger population. A lip-rounded first vowel element [o] is often being used before voiceless consonants, in words with relatively little stress (such as *about* and *out*). This development seems to be recent and to be 'competing' with fronting and non-raising.

In other words, young people who would otherwise be fronting their diphthongs are not doing so, because they prefer to round them instead. It is not that Vancouver adults (and especially 22-year-old women) are more innovative than the youngsters; it is simply that the youngsters are 'doing their own thing'. Because this change is a recent one, its effects are not so noticeable among older people. And it is not taking place at all in Toronto.
(After J. K. Chambers & M. F. Hardwick, 1986.)

CANADIAN DIALECTS

There is a traditional view that there are no dialects in Canadian English – that it is not possible for Canadians to tell where other Canadians are from just by listening to them – and the term 'General Canadian' has been used to capture this concept. While certainly there is a greater degree of dialect homogeneity in the country compared with, say, the UK, this view is far from the truth. It would be surprising if it were otherwise, given the great size of Canada and the geographical distances separating its communities. The impression of a universally used dialect is due chiefly to the existence of an educated Canadian variety of Standard English, heard across the country through radio and television. At a local level (moving from east to west), several dialect areas have been recognized, and although few signs of regional grammatical variation have yet been identified, there is an appreciable amount of lexical divergence.

• The Atlantic Provinces of New Brunswick, Nova Scotia, and Prince Edward Island, the first part of Canada to be settled (p. 95), have long been recognized as a distinct linguistic region. The area also includes the island of Newfoundland, which has its own dialect identity, often referred to as 'Newfie', and (in common with relatively isolated communities all over the world) a source of national dialect humour. Local words for sea-going and fishing activities are notable, as are weather words such as *tempest* (an ordinary storm) and *trap smasher* (a severe storm). There are many local products, including *grunt* (a type of steamed pudding), *snits* ('dried apple slices'), *larrigan* (a type of footwear), and *water horse* ('salted cod').

• Quebec, dominated by the issue of bilingualism, shows the effects of language contact, with several words which reflect French political and cultural institutions being part of the awareness of the Anglophone population. Loanwords of a more general kind include *caleche* (a type of horsedrawn vehicle), *double window* (a storm window), *whisky blanc* (an alcoholic drink), and *professor* (in the sense of 'school teacher'). In an area where language attitudes are strong, of course, the extent to which Anglophone people are prepared to use words which are perceived to be French in origin varies greatly.

• The Ottawa Valley, a region west of Ottawa along the Ottawa River in Ontario, is known for its history of settlement involving immigrants from Scotland and Ireland. Constructions such as *They're after leaving* will be heard (p. 338), as well as such items as *mind* ('remember'), and they have contributed to a rural image of the area. Canadian raising (p. 342) is heard in words with both voiced and voiceless consonants: for example, *house* as noun and as verb both have /ɔɪ/ (in other parts of the country, only the noun would be affected).

• Southern Ontario, the area originally known as Upper Canada (p. 95), along the northern shore of the lower Great Lakes, is now the most populated part of the country. Its role in Canada's early history produced a number of political and cultural terms which later came into more widespread Canadian use, such as *reeve*, *riding*, *continuation school* ('secondary school'), and *concession* (an area of surveyed land), and it has also developed a great deal of distinctive urban speech. Among its local words are *eavestrough* ('roof gutter') and *dew worm* ('earthworm').

• The Prairies, in Alberta, Saskatchewan, and Manitoba, comprise a huge area with a largely homogeneous dialect fostered chiefly by the communication lines brought by the transport system, especially the railway. The grain, cattle, and oil industries each have their distinctive local vocabulary, such as *Dry Belt* (an arid southern area), *stampede* ('rodeo'), and *oil borer* ('oil driller'). More general terms include *nuisance grounds* ('rubbish dump'), *bluff* (a clump of trees), and *chuck* ('food'). Local native languages have supplied some items, such as *kinnikinik* (a type of smoking mixture) and *saskatoon* (a kind of shrub).

• The Arctic North, covering the Yukon, Northwest Territories, N Quebec, and Labrador, is known for Inuit-derived forms such as *kabloona* ('white man'), *basket sled* (a type of sledge), *fan hitch* (of dog teams), *angakok* ('shaman'), *tupik* (a type of tent), and *chimo* (a drinking toast). Many words from the area have entered Standard English, such as *igloo* and *white out*. The fur trade has also been important: a *factory*, for example, is a fur-trading post, and a *factor* its senior officer.

• The West, in British Columbia, and centred on Vancouver, is separated from the rest of the country by the Rocky Mountains, and this has motivated a high level of north–south movement along the Pacific Coast. As a result, parts of the area – and especially Vancouver itself – are strongly influenced by US English norms. The influence of regional native languages is also present, resulting in such local lexical usages as *keekwillee-house* (a type of earth lodge), *salt-chuck* ('ocean'), and *kokanee* ('land-locked salmon'). There is a distinctive vocabulary to do with local industries, notably mining and forestry (*logging, rigging, yarding, caulk, boom chains, jackladder*), with many of the terms now part of Standard English.

THE ROCK

The dialect of Newfoundland, locally known as 'the Rock', displays many differences from the rest of English-speaking Canada. It was not settled by United Empire Loyalists after the American Revolution, unlike other parts of E Canada (p. 95); and it received large numbers of immigrants from south-east Ireland and south-west England, especially in the first half of the 19th century.

The island's political history and its geographical isolation from the rest of Canada helped to preserve many dialect features from the British Isles. Phonological examples (see §17) include the use of a clear /l/ in such words as *pull*; an extra (*epenthetic*) vowel, as in *film* /fɪlᵊm/; and a plosive replacing the dental fricative, in such words as *this* and *thin* (p. 337). Such distinctive features, in exaggerated form, have formed a stereotype of 'Newfie' speech which is a source of humour on the mainland.

There are also several signs of Hiberno-English grammar (p. 338), such as *yiz* or *youse* as the plural of 'you', inflected *be* (*I bees here*), and perfective *after* (*I'm after losing it*). Among many local words are *scoff* ('large meal'), *praties* ('potatoes'), *bake-apples* (a type of berry), *screech* (a type of rum), *out-port* (a fishing settlement), *bayman* (an inhabitant of an outport), and *Newfs* ('New-foundlanders'), a label sometimes used derogatorily by mainlanders,

In recent decades, there has been a major shift in the status of the island. Newfoundland's important strategic role in World War 2 was followed by a change in its political status (from British dominion to Canadian province) in 1949. Today, as ties with Britain become more distant, and contact with mainland Canada and the USA becomes routine through the media, it is likely that these changes will have far-reaching effects on the character of Newfoundland speech.

CARIBBEAN ENGLISH

Varieties of the English language are used in many of the islands of the Caribbean Sea and in several areas of the adjacent Central and South American mainland, and the label 'Caribbean English' is used, often with more geographical than linguistic accuracy, to refer to its distinguishing properties. The situation is unique, within the English-speaking world, because of the way the history of the region (p. 96) has brought together two dimensions of variation: a regional dimension, from which it is possible to establish a speaker's geographical origins, and an ethnic dimension, in which the choice of language conveys social and nationalistic identity. The interaction between these dimensions has produced a melting-pot of linguistic forms from which several varieties of varying distinctiveness and stability have emerged and now compete for survival. At least six categories of language use need to be distinguished.

• A variety of Standard English (British or American, p. 110) exists as an official means of formal international communication in the area, spoken by an educated minority with any one of a wide range of regional accents. Some have learned this variety as a mother tongue; most have acquired it in school as a second language. The traditional focus on British English is now diminishing in several areas. It is American English which has become the dominant voice of the mass media, and it is the USA which is increasing its role in relation to local economies, especially through tourism. Both models have their supporters and critics.

• Each English-speaking country in the region has to some extent developed its own variety of the standard language, most noticeably through variations in accent and the use of local vocabulary to reflect indigenous biogeography and cultural practices. Many of these varieties show the result of contact with other languages in the region, such as the leading colonial languages (French, Spanish, Portuguese, Dutch, p. 96), local American Indian languages (e.g. Carib, Arawak), and the languages of immigrant groups (e.g. Hindi).

• Because of the shared historical and linguistic heritage of the local peoples, the island varieties have a great deal in common, and the concept of a Standard West Indian English, as used by educated people, and distinct from either British or American English, has begun to emerge. The properties of this variety are gaining in recognition and acceptability, as they come to be used in literary expression and also to be treated more responsibly in schools and examinations.

• The area is chiefly characterized by the use of vernacular varieties known as creoles, some of which are the result of contact with the English language. Traditionally, these have been viewed as dialects of English, often referred to somewhat dismissively by such terms as 'patois'. In recent years, however, with the emergence of several Caribbean countries as independent nations and the growth of a more sophisticated linguistic awareness of the complexity found in creole languages, there has been a tendency to view these varieties as languages in their own right, and to avoid the use of such designations as 'Creole English'. Some supporters of the autonomy of creoles go so far as to suggest that they are varieties of a single language in the region, Creole (also called West Indian Creole or Caribbean Creole), and stress its links with the languages of West Africa (p. 102).

• None of the above varieties has a clearly definable boundary. Within any of the islands, it is possible to find a continuum of language use, with Standard English at one end and a creole language at the other. Within this continuum, the forms used in any one variety may influence those used in an adjacent variety. Thus, some creoles have moved more in the direction of Standard English than others, and educated regional varieties vary in the number of creole features they contain. The nature of this 'creole continuum' has attracted particular attention in recent years, as part of the research programme into the history and processes of creolization. The situation is also characterized by the existence of multidialectism, and by a great deal of code-switching, as people alternate between varieties depending on such factors as the formality and intimacy of the situation.

• Standard English has a limited role as a second language in the region, notably in Puerto Rico (p. 96). English-based creoles, however, are widely used as lingua francas in some of the Spanish-speaking countries, such as Colombia and Nicaragua. It is unclear whether such creoles should be classified along with those of the English-speaking territories, or distinguished from them.

In recent years, West Indian speech has come to be found outside the Caribbean, with large communities of emigrants in Canada, the USA, and Britain, and these new locations have given rise to new varieties. The children of Jamaicans now living in London (many of whom have never been to the West Indies) speak very differently from their counterparts in the Caribbean.

THE CARIBBEAN VOICE

The Caribbean island arc stretches for over 1,000 miles (1600 km), and a wide range of accents is only to be expected. What is surprising is to find that there are so many shared features in the region, resulting in an accent-type which sounds distinctively West Indian to the outsider, though containing many individual differences.

The distinctive prosody (p. 248) of Caribbean English is undoubtedly the feature which has the most unifying force. Syllables tend to be equally stressed, so that a word like *Jamaica* comes out with three roughly equal beats. A consequence of this 'syllable-timed' rhythm is that vowels which would be unstressed in most other English accents are here spoken with prominence, and schwa /ə/ is little used: *bigger* /ˈbiˈga/, *section* /ˈsekˈʃan/, *sofa* /ˈsoːˈfa/, *consequence* /ˈkanˈsiˈkwens/. This rhythmical pattern, widely heard in 'rapping', is the main point of contrast with British or American English accents, and the chief source of intelligibility problems for those unused to this style of speech.

The rhymes in this extract from a poem by West Indian writer, John Agard, illustrate the syllable-timed rhythm of Caribbean speech; the stress on *don* forces the reader to emphasize the second syllable of *Common* in verse 1 and the normally unstressed pronoun *one* in verse 2.

Me not no Oxford don
me a simple immigrant
from Clapham Common
I didn't graduate
I immigrate

But listen Mr Oxford don
I'm a man on de run
and a man on de run
is a dangerous one

I ent have no gun
I ent have no knife
but mugging de Queen's English
is the story of my life

('Listen, Mr Oxford Don', 1985)

The Caribbean islands, showing (a) countries where Standard English is an official language; in these areas, English-based creoles are also widely used; (b) countries where a language other than English is the official language, but an English-based creole is nonetheless spoken. The special standing of US English in Puerto Rico is noted separately (p. 96).

JAMAICA English official
HONDURAS English-based creoles
PUERTO RICO English special status

WHAT'S A *TATU*?

The difficulties facing the Caribbean lexicologist are nicely illustrated by this story from a researcher working on a dictionary of Trinobagian English.

One of the most tangled sets of names I've found started one day on the beach in Mayaro, on the east coast of Trinidad, where I was checking fish names and descriptions. While I was helping a friend's grandchildren make a sand pile, I uncovered a small, fast-moving animal. The children assured me that I could pick it up – 'Is a tatu. Yuh could eat dem.' So I caught it, a white crab-like animal, put it in an empty sweet drink bottle, and took it to the Department of Zoology at the University. There it was identified as *Emerita portoricensis*, a crustacean. But the more I thought I had straightened it out, the more confusion arose.

It turns out that that particular animal is known as *tatu* or *sea tatu* in Mayaro and neighbouring areas, probably because of the similarity of its articulated shell bands and its good digging ability to the land *tatu* (armadillo). It is also known as *kochikong*, an archaic name for the armadillo, and as *sea cockroach*. However, *sea cockroach* in Tobago and northern Trinidad also refers to the chitons *Chiton marmoratus* and *Acanthopleura granulata*. Now these chitons are also known as *pacro*, a word which also refers in some areas to a black or dark brown mollusk which lives on shore rocks and is made into *pacro water*, a local aphrodisiac. Yet another *sea cockroach* is *Sphaeroma* sp., a small many-legged millipede-like arthropod often seen scuttling over rocks and sea-walls. Just to introduce another invertebrate order, the word *tatu* is also used to identify the wasp known as *jep tatu*, *Synoeca surinama*, whose mud nests are built in bands resembling the armadillo's....
(From L. Winer, 1989.)

There are easier ways of earning a living (though they are not usually so engrossing).

SEGMENTAL DISTINCTIVENESS

The following vowel and consonant features will be heard in various varieties of Caribbean English, and some are quite widely represented across the region. (For phonetics terminology, see §17.)

• The /a/ and /ɒ/ vowels merge, so that such words as *pat* and *pot* rhyme, both being pronounced with /a/; /ɔː/ may join them, so that all three words *cat*, *cot*, and *caught* sound the same.
• The /ɪə/ and /ɛə/ diphthongs also merge, so that such pairs of words as *fear* and *fare* sound the same.
• RP /eɪ/ (as in *cake*) is /ɪe/ in some areas (e.g. Jamaica), but otherwise becomes the monophthong /eː/; similarly /əʊ/ (as in

coat) is /ʊo/ in Jamaica, but /oː/ elsewhere.
• RP /θ/ and /ð/ are usually replaced by /t/ and /d/, so that *tin* and *thin*, for example, are both /tɪn/.
• Some varieties pronounce /r/ after vowels in such words as *car* and *hard* (p. 245); this is normal in Barbados and the Virgin Islands, and is also often heard in Jamaica and Guyana.
• Final consonant clusters are commonly simplified, especially if they end in /t/ or /d/: *best* /bes/, *walked* /wɔk/.
• The 'dark' articulation of /l/ in such words as *feel* and *build* (in RP) is widely replaced by a 'clear l' quality (p. 245).
• Consonants are often assimilated or elided (p. 247) to produce such forms as *already* /aːredi/ and *yesterday* /jeside/. Forms such as *ask* /aks/ and *sandals* /slandaz/ show another common feature – metathesis.

GRAMMAR AND VOCABULARY

There are few obvious signs of distinctive grammar in the more standard varieties of Caribbean English, other than those features which betray the influence of a creole variety (p. 346). Linguists have, however, noted high frequencies of certain forms, such as a tendency for *would* to replace *will* (*I would go there tomorrow*), for *get* to be used as a passive (*It get break*, meaning 'it was broken'), and for questions to be marked by intonation rather than by inversion (*You going home?* for *Are you going home?*). It is also likely that research will one day bring to light more subtle patterns of syntax which colour West Indian speech, such as distinctive uses of *if*, *so*, or *well*.

Vocabulary, on the other hand, is as usual a powerful regional differentiator. Each of the islands has a wide range

of distinctive lexical items, often relating to its fauna and flora, or to its folk and religious customs. A few of these items have entered Standard English – for example, *calypso*, *guppy*, *dreadlocks*, *rasta* – but for the most part the vocabulary is regionally restricted. In an informal survey of three lexical projects (Jamaica, Bahamas, Trinidad and Tobago) one researcher found only about 20 per cent of shared vocabulary. For example, a dictionary of Jamaican English (with some 15,000 entries) includes *duppy* ('ghost'), *ganja* ('cannabis'), *susumba* (a type of plant), *sweet-mouth* ('flatter'), and *watchy* ('watchman'). On the other hand, *boar-hog* ('boar'), *roti* (a type of bread), and *congolala* (a type of medicinal plant) are not to be found in this dictionary, but in Trinobagian (Trinidad and Tobago) English. Lexical diversity is a major feature of Caribbean English. (For loan words from French and Spanish, see p. 96.)

CREOLE CHARACTERISTICS

Despite the existence of many political and cultural differences, and the considerable geographical distances separating some of the countries involved, there are striking similarities among the English-based creole languages of the world. This identity can be seen at all levels of language structure, but is most dramatic in relation to grammar. It can be explained, according to the 'creole hypothesis', as a consequence of the way these languages have developed out of the kind of creole English used by the first black slaves in America and the Caribbean. This language, it is thought, was originally very different from English, as a result of its mixed African linguistic background, but generations of contact with the dominant white English population have had an inevitable effect, drawing it much closer to the standard variety. There are certainly many differences between the various Caribbean creoles, and between these and the varieties of Black English Vernacular used in the USA (p. 97) and the English-based creoles of West Africa; but the overall impression is one of a 'family' of languages closely related in structure and idiom.

PIDGINS AND CREOLES

A *creole* is a pidgin language which has become the mother tongue of a community – a definition which emphasizes that pidgins and creoles are two stages in a single process of development.

A *pidgin* is a system of communication which has grown up among people who do not share a common language, but who want to talk to each other, usually for reasons of trade. Such languages typically have a limited vocabulary, a reduced grammatical structure, and a narrow range of functions, compared to the languages from which they derive. They are used only when they need to be, as a 'contact language' in circumstances where communication would not otherwise be possible. They are the native languages of no one.

It has often happened that, within a multilingual community, increasing numbers of people begin to use a pidgin as their principal means of communication. This causes a major expansion of the grammar and vocabulary, and of the range of situations in which the language comes to be used. The children of these people come to hear it more regularly, and in due course some of them begin to use it as a mother tongue. When this happens, the language is known as a *creole*.

The process of *creolization* is the most important linguistic element in the history of the Caribbean, with all the former colonial languages giving rise to creoles. The process of *decreolization* is also apparent, when creoles come into contact with standard languages and are influenced by them (p. 344).

The map shows the distribution of the chief English-based pidgin and creole languages. They cluster in three main areas: the Caribbean, West Africa, and the West Pacific. Most of the Atlantic varieties developed along with the growth in British colonial exploration and trade in the 16th and 17th centuries; the Pacific varieties emerged some time later. (From L. Todd, 1984a.)

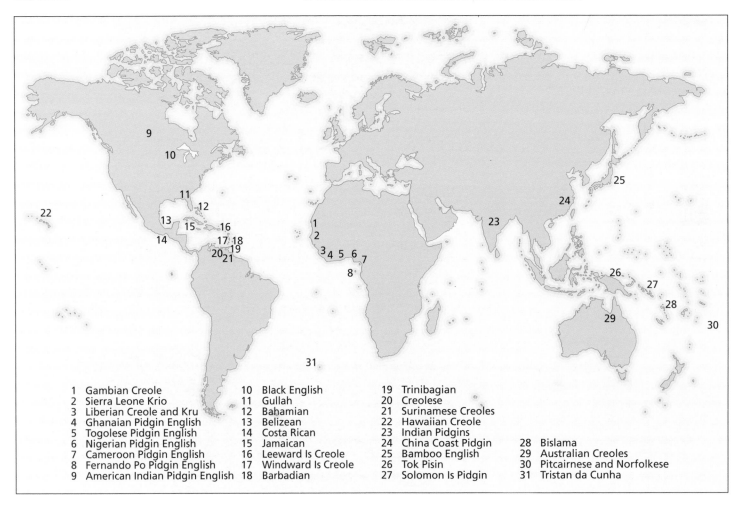

1 Gambian Creole	10 Black English	19 Trinibagian
2 Sierra Leone Krio	11 Gullah	20 Creolese
3 Liberian Creole and Kru	12 Bahamian	21 Surinamese Creoles
4 Ghanaian Pidgin English	13 Belizean	22 Hawaiian Creole
5 Togolese Pidgin English	14 Costa Rican	23 Indian Pidgins
6 Nigerian Pidgin English	15 Jamaican	24 China Coast Pidgin
7 Cameroon Pidgin English	16 Leeward Is Creole	25 Bamboo English
8 Fernando Po Pidgin English	17 Windward Is Creole	26 Tok Pisin
9 American Indian Pidgin English	18 Barbadian	27 Solomon Is Pidgin
		28 Bislama
		29 Australian Creoles
		30 Pitcairnese and Norfolkese
		31 Tristan da Cunha

Carnival in Trinidad

Notting Hill carnival, London

SOME GRAMMATICAL FEATURES

Although Carnival revellers in Jamaica and London have different accents and use different vocabulary, they are firmly linked by a core of common grammar. The grammatical features which distinguish Caribbean creoles from each other are few, and unlikely to interfere with intelligibility – or, at least, no more than we might expect to find between regional dialects anywhere. The following sentence from Jamaican Creole looks very similar when it is 'translated' into Guyana Creole (after L. Todd, 1984a):

Standard English
He used to go to school every day last year, now sometimes he goes and sometimes he doesn't go.
Jamaican Creole
Him go a school every day last year, now sometime him go, sometime him no go.
Guyana Creole
Him a go a school every day last year, now sometime him a go, sometime him naa go.

The following features of creole grammar will therefore be observed in many varieties, though the similarities may sometimes be obscured by regional variations in pronunciation, or (in written form) by different systems of spelling (p. 348). The exact form taken by the various grammatical particles can also vary a great deal. In the following examples, a slightly modified Standard English spelling is used, to permit a clearer focus on the grammatical issues.

Syntax
• There is no concord between subject and verb in the present tense: *She sing in de choir*.
• There are no forms of *be* as copula or auxiliary:

Dem ready, She a nice person.
• Serial verbs are commonly used: *Take it go, He talk say you stupid, Dem go try get it*.
• A verb may be brought to the front of a sentence for emphasis – a common feature of West African languages: *A talk Mary talk make she trouble* ('Mary talks too much and that makes trouble for her').
• Passive constructions are avoided: *De grass cut* (='has been cut'), *Dis record play a lot* (='is played a lot').
• Adjectives are routinely used in adverbial function: *I like it good, She sing real sof'*. The use of the *-ly* ending is rare.

Nouns
• Nouns often do not use *-s* to mark a plural: *two book, dem creature*.
• Particles may be used to mark plurality: *The rabbit dem eat it all, George dem went* (='George and his gang went').
• Possession can be expressed by juxtaposing the noun phrases (*dat man house*) with no 'apostrophe s', or (in Caribbean creoles) by adding a *fi* particle: *De coat a fi me* ('the coat is mine').

Pronouns
• No case distinctions are used in pronouns: *She see he come, take he coat, and go; Carry dat book to she teacher*.
• Several pronouns have alternative forms, such as (for *I*) *mi* and *a*, (for *he*) *im* and *i*, (for *you* plural) *yu* and *unu*, and (for *they*) *de* and *dem*.
• In some varieties (such as Gullah and West African Pidgins) male and female third person pronouns are not distinguished: *so one day Partridge take her head an' stick he head unduh he wing*.
• In Rastafarian speech, *I* is considered a syllable of special, mystical significance, and often appears in unusual contexts, as in West Indian poet Dennis

Scott's line 'Seals every *I* away from light' (*More Poem*, 1982), where there is a play on words between *I* and *eye*.
Verbs
• Past tenses are expressed using the base form without an ending: *Mary go last week*.
• *Did* is often used as a past tense marker with stative verbs: *He did know she name*.
• Particles such as *da, di,* or *a* are used to mark continuous actions: *David a go* ('David is going'), *She da work now* ('She's working now'). In much US Black English the particle is *be*: *Sometime dey be goin' to see her*.
• Completed action is expressed by *done*: *I just done tell dem, We be done washed all dose cars soon*.
• A verb is negated by inserting a *no* particle: *They no want it now*. Multiple negation (p. 194) is used for emphasis: *Ain't nobody found no money in no box*.
• Auxiliary *do* is not used along with a question word: *How they get that?, Why you hit him?*
• Past tense can be expressed using *been* or a variant form: *We been see him* (='we saw him'). This kind of construction is less common in UK West Indian Creole, where *been* tends to be replaced by *did* or *was*.

In addition, creoles are noted for their readiness to create new words using affixes (*no jokifying*) and through conversion (p. 129): *All dis murder and kill mus' stop*. Reduplicated forms are common: *picky-picky* ('choosy'), *one one* ('all alone'), *mess mess* ('wet and sloppy'). There may also be doubling of grammatical items: *only but, or either, dis here, an' plus*, as well as in such constructions as *Bill he gone*. Repetition is frequently an important rhetorical effect: *They jus' eat eat eat, An' it go far far far before we stop it*.

SPELLING

The choice of a spelling system is one of the critical questions facing anyone who works with creole, or who wishes to write in it. Some writers use spellings which are close to Standard English (e.g. writing *car* as *cah*); others try to maximize the differences between the two systems (e.g writing *car* as *caa*). A phonetic-like transcription is not unusual, because of the considerable differences between the creole sound system and that of mainstream accents (e.g. writing *car* as *kaa*). Several variant forms will be found in these pages.

The problem is particularly acute in deciding what symbols to use for vowels. There is a much reduced vowel system, with most Caribbean creole speakers using only 12 phonemes instead of the 20 found in RP. Many spelling alternatives will be found for the /ie/ diphthong, which is a particularly distinctive feature of Jamaican speech: *same* might appear as *siem*, *sehm*, *syehm*, *syem*, *siehm*, and in other ways.

The cardinal vowel diagram (p. 238) shown below summarizes the vowel system generally found in speakers of a Caribbean creole (from L. Todd, 1984a). Each phoneme is accompanied by an example.

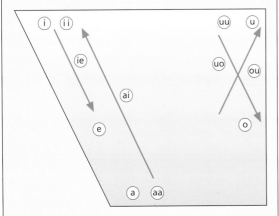

Short vowels	Long vowels	Diphthongs
/i/ *kil* kill	/i:/ *trii* three	/ie/ *biesin* basin
/e/ *dem* they, them	/a:/ *daag* dog	/ai/ *blain* blind
/a/ *mada* mother	/u:/ *duu* do	/ou/ *roun* round
/o/ *op* up		/uo/ *uol* old
/u/ *put* put		

One effect of the reduced inventory is to permit much larger numbers of words which sound the same (homophones) compared to most other British or American accents. Thus /den/ could mean *den* or *then*; /rat/ could be *rot* or *rat*; /la:d/ could be *lord* or *lard*; /tai/ could be *toy* or *tie* (see also p. 345).

The months of the year as spelled in two pidgin languages texts: one in Tok Pisin (Papua New Guinea), the other in Kamtok (Cameroon). There is a great similarity between the pronunciation of these words in the two languages, but (apart from three cases) they certainly look very different.

Tok Pisin	Kamtok	Tok Pisin	Kamtok
Janueri	Janyuari	Julai	Julai
Februeri	Fehrbuari	Ogas	Ohgohs
Mas	Mach	Septemba	Sehptehmba
April	April	Oktoba	Ohktoba
Me	Mei	Novemba	Novehmba
Jun	Jun	Desemba	Disehmba

VOICES

London Jamaican Creole, as recounted by Jennifer Johnson in the short story 'Ballad For You' (from D. Sutcliffe, 1982, p. 24).

There is five gal I want to tell you 'bout. Dem lick head from different part a London; but is one t'ing dough, dem is one an' di same but individual in every sense. Mek a tek dem one by one.

Lightening hail from Guyana an' is a soul-head. Before she buck head wid dem addah gal she couldn't chat a word a bad English; now she pass CSE ina it. Why dem call she Lightening is because when dem sit down ina corner a chat people business, she always miss everyt'ing an' a confuse di issue…

gal girls   *dem lick head* they met up
dough though   *mek a tek* let me take
soul-head soul music fan   *buck head* met up
dem addah those other
a chat discussing

Black Vernacular English, used in a translation of the Gospel of St John (Ch. 3) by Walt Wolfram and Ralph Fasold, but in a spelling which is close to Standard English (from J. C. Baratz & R. W. Shuy, 1969).

It was a man named Nicodemus. He was a leader of the Jews. This man, he come to Jesus in the night and say, 'Rabbi, we know you a teacher that come from God, cause can't nobody do the things you be doing 'cept he got God with him.'

Jesus, he tell him say, 'This ain't no jive, if a man ain't born over again, ain't no way he gonna get to know God.'

Then Nicodemus, he ask him, 'How a man gonna be born when he already old? Can't nobody go back inside his mother and get born.'

So Jesus tell him, say, 'This ain't no jive, this the truth. The onliest way a man gonna get to know God, he got to get born regular and he got to get born from the Holy Spirit…

An extract from a Gullah folk tale, as told by Jane Hunter to a researcher in a field trip in 1971 (from I. Van Sertima, 1976).

Duh Rabbit en duh Patrid, dey was two great fren. So one day Patrid take her head en stick he head unduh he wing, went to Rabbit house.

[Rabbit] say, 'Ol fren, watcha doin?'

Say, 'Oh, I ain't doin nuttin but sittin in duh sun.'

Say, 'Oh, wheahs you head?'

Say, 'Man, I leave my head home fuh my wife to shave.'

All dat time he had his head unduhnea' his wing. Rabbit run in duh house, say, 'Ol Gal,' he say, 'Come on to chop my head off.'

'E say, 'No, Mistuh Rabbit. If I chop yuh head off, you'll die.'

Say, 'No, I won' eidduh, cause Mistuh Patrid leave he head home fuh his wife to shave en so why caan I leave my head fuh you to shave?'

So all his wife, all duh res uh he wife tell him, [he] say, 'If you doan chop my head off, I'll chop you head off.'

So das two fren now. Das why you fren in duh one who gets you, enemy who come en accoshu. Buh if yuh get hurt, it [you] kin get hurt from fren. So he go en bawl his wife, bawl. Duh wife take duh big knife en chop 'e head off 'en 'e chop 'e head off.

So Patrid had a pretty girlfren. Rabbit had a very pretty girl, en Patrid wife wasn' as goodlookin as Rabbit wife. Patrid had a love fuh Rabbit wife, see? En dats duh only way he coulda get Rabbit wife by doin im some haam. So when duh lady gone en chop duh Rabbit head off, Rabbit pitch off yonduh en die.

En duh Patrid take 'e head from unduh-nea' he wing, say, 'Wing, nuh foolin, nuh fun. En wing, no livin, no gettin love.' En den she had two wife, had his wife en duh Rabbit wife.

Patrid Partridge   *fren* friends   *eidduh* either
res rest   *uh* what   *doan* don't
accoshu accost you

Jamaican poet Linton Kwesi Johnson's orthography, seen here in the middle lines of 'Time Come', captures the accent of much Caribbean speech. (From *Dread Beat an Blood*, 1975.)

wi feel bad
wi look sad
wi smoke weed
an if yu eye sharp,
read de vialence inna wi eye;
wi goin smash de sky wid wi bad bad
      blood

look out! look out! look out!

it soon come
it soon come:
is de shadow walkin behind yu
is I stannup rite before yu;
      look out!

but it too late now:
I did warn yu.

TOK PISIN

Tok Pisin is an English-based pidgin, influenced by local Papuan languages, used in Papua New Guinea by around a million people. It has been creolized in some areas. The language has a nationwide presence, being widely seen in advertisements and heard on radio and television. There is also a weekly newspaper written entirely in pidgin, *Wantok* ('Friend').

   The illustration is the last page of an Old Testament story published by a Christian missionary organization in Papua New Guinea. It is from the story of Daniel (*Stori bilong Daniel*), in which *Daraias*, the king of Babylon (*Bebilon*) is persuaded to put Daniel into a den of lions (*hul bilong lion*). On the previous page, the king has just called down to see if God has looked after Daniel.

Glossary
a emphatic particle
amamas be happy (*from Malay*)
antap on top
autim made, put out ('out')
bagarapim ruin, damage ('bugger up')
bekim give back, repay ('back + -im')
biknem praise (big name)
bikpela big ('big + fellow')
bilip believe

bilong indicates possession ('belong')
bosim rule ('boss + -im')
dai die
em he, him
gat get
gutpela good ('good + fellow')
inap can ('enough')
kalabusim imprison ('calaboose + -im')
kam come
kilim kill ('kill + -im')
   -im suffix marks a transitive verb
laik want, like
lo decree ('law')
long indicates location ('along')
mas must
maus mouth
mi I, me
na and
nau now
ol they, them ('all')
olgeta all, entire ('all together')
orait all right, fix
pasim close, fasten ('fast -im')
pastaim in the past ('past time')
pipel people
singautim call, shout ('sing out + -im')
stret straight away
tasol but, however ('that's all')
tokim tell ('talk + -im')
tru very much ('true')
wanpela a, one ('one + fellow')
wok work
yupela you ('you + fellow')

CREOLE TRANSLATIONS

Wilhelm Busch's *Max and Moritz*, first published in German in 1865, has been translated into dozens of languages (including Scots English, (p. 330). Here the opening verse of the 'Fourth Prank' is given in four creole/pidgin translations. A translation into Standard English by Elly Miller is shown for comparison. (From M. Görlach, 1984.)

Fourth Prank
As has frequently been stated
People must be educated.
Not alone the A, B, C,
Heightens man's humanity;
Not just simply reading, writing,
Makes a person more inviting;
Nor does Arithmetic learning
Make a pupil more discerning.
Reason, Wisdom, Moral Thought
Must be equally well taught;
And to teach with erudition
Was Professor Lample's mission.

Jamaican Creole
Badness Nomba Fuor
Ole-time people mek wan rule:
'Learn and study while in school!'
ABC kyan ongle staat
Lov a knallidge in de haat:
Readin, writin, ritmetick
Kyan gi Sietan wan good lick,
Higle smaddy wid no fait
Fine demself a Debbil gate;
Show respeck an lov de wise:
Solomon wi gi yuh prize!
Stody ow fi ondastan
All de ways a Gad an man.
In all learnin, Teacha Lampel
Set de very bes example.
(Jean D'Costa)

Cameroonian
Nᴐmba Foa Kᴐni
Panapu dei, a raitam dᴐng,
'Man mᴐs lɛn fᴐ dis wi grᴐng.'
No bi daso A, B, C,
Mek wi sabi hau fᴐ bi.
No bi ᴐl sɛns dei fᴐ tali
Chinda sabi dis fᴐ Bali.
Man i get fᴐ lisen wɛl
Fᴐ di tru wi papa tɛl.
Pa Matyu, wi katakis,
Sabi ᴐl gut fashᴐn dis.
An i glad fᴐ tich wi tru
Ol ti ting man glᴐt fᴐ du.
(Loreto Todd)

Krio
Nᴐmba Fo
Dɛm kin se, ɛn misɛf gri,
Man fᴐ lan pas ABC.
Wetin go pliz Gᴐd insɛf
Na if wi bɛtɛ wisɛf.
Rayt ɛn rid nᴐto ᴐl o,
Pᴐsin we gɛt sɛns fᴐ no.
Nᴐto arifmitik wan
Pᴐsin fᴐ tray gud wan pan;
I fᴐ gladi fᴐ lisin
We big wan de gi lɛsin.
Ticha Lampel ᴐlwez si
Dat i du dis wit sabi.
(Freddie Jones)

Tok Pisin
Trik Namba Foa
Long ol ples i gat rul
Ol manmeri i mas skul.
Rit na rait na ABC
I save mekim man i fri.
Man i no gat save long ol namba
I gat het olsem kukamba.
Man i no save wok bilong gavman
Em i no man tru, tasol i hapman.
Ologeta samting bilong skul
Man i no save, em i ful.
Na bilong givim gutpela eksampel
Mi tok long wanpela tisa, Lempel.
(Don Laycock)

AUSTRALIAN ENGLISH

Australia is a vast country (the sixth largest in the world by area), with large tracts uninhabited, and nationwide communication dependent on transportation lines or the media. It has a relatively recent history of European settlement (p. 98), with close political ties to Britain, and a pattern of early population growth in which pioneers moved out from a single point (Sydney), retaining their links with central government. The country now has a chiefly urban population, with most people living in the fertile areas near the coast; four cities (Sydney, Melbourne, Brisbane, Perth) account for over half of the population. In all of this there are interesting parallels with earlier developments in Canada (p. 340).

These factors combine to promote an initial impression of Australian English as a variety with little internal variation – an impression (as in Canada) reinforced by the 'single voice' of the country's radio and television and the standard language of the press (p. 110). The point has been emphasized by several commentators – George Turner, for example:

The homogeneity of Australian English is remarkable. It would be difficult to find elsewhere a geographical area so large with so little linguistic variation. (*The English Language in Australia and New Zealand*, 1966, p. 163).

And in the Introduction to *The Macquarie Dictionary* (1981), J. R. Bernard states:

The picture is of a widespread homogeneity stretching from Cairns to Hobart, from Sydney to Perth, a uniformity of pronunciation extending over a wider expanse than anywhere else in the world.

If it is true that there is little or no geographical variation, this would be truly noteworthy in a country which is some 30 times the size of Britain. And there is a certain amount of evidence in support of the view. There seem to be no notable grammatical differences, as one moves from state to state, and only a few regional lexical differences have so far been identified, such as *stroller* (New South Wales) vs *pusher* (South Australia) for a child's push-chair. Language alone, it would appear, says very little about a person's geographical origins. Local people do sometimes try to draw general conclusions from differences they have noted in individual words or speakers; but few are so well-travelled among the informal situations of rural or urban Australia that they can put these differences in perspective. Confident judgments about regional variation depend upon the findings of research in dialectology, and this is still in its infancy in Australia.

It would, however, be a mistake to conclude from impressionistic comparisons with Britain or the USA that there is no variation at all. Even at a purely geo-graphical level, it would be premature to underestimate the extent to which there may be linguistic diversity in the more informal varieties of speech. Regional differences in fauna, flora, climate, and cultural practice are inevitable in a country which extends over 30° of latitude, and these must be reflected to some extent in lexical variation. Also, as with Canada, there have been few studies of the informal speech of urban centres, where local idiosyncrasy is frequently born.

Social variation

Statements about accent uniformity are surprising because they seem to fly against what we know to be the normal state of affairs in language use: social differentiation (p. 364). Such variation undoubtedly exists, as the above authors themselves go on to recognize, and terms such as 'uniformity' must therefore be interpreted with caution – meaning only the absence of variation which can be explained solely on geographical grounds. When social stratification is taken into account, we are faced with a linguistic situation which is more accurately described as one of 'uniformity operating in diversity'.

With hardly any grammatical distinctiveness to point to, it is not surprising that people find the most distinctive feature of Australian English to be its accent. This topic has accordingly attracted considerable study, both to determine its phonetic basis and to see whether it is as homogenous as people sometimes claim. It turns out, in fact, that a great deal of accent variation does exist, and in an influential study of the 1960s, A. G. Mitchell and A. Delbridge classified it into three types. (It should be stressed that there is no sharp boundary between each of these types, which are best thought of as groups of accents.)

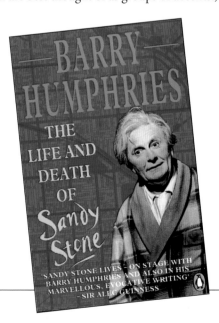

• *Cultivated* An accent, used by about 10 per cent of the population, on which Received Pronunciation (RP, p. 365) continues to exert a considerable influence. In some speakers the accent is very close to educated southern British, with just a hint of its Australian origin in certain vowels and in the intonation. In its most RP-like form, speakers of other varieties tend to think of it as 'affected'.

• *Broad* At the opposite extreme, this accent, used by about 30 per cent of the population, is the one most clearly identified with the notion of an 'Australian twang'. It is heard in many countries in the voices of the characters portrayed by such actors as Paul Hogan and Barry Humphries.

• *General* In between there is a mainstream group of accents used by most of the population.

These variations have provoked not a little controversy in recent years, with the broad Australian accent in particular having its critics and its defenders. There is ongoing debate about whether Australians should be proud of their distinctive speech, and stress its phonetic features, or whether they should aspire to use a more conservative style, associated with the traditional values of educated British speech. The picture has been complicated by a generation of Australian comedians who exaggerate and satirize the broad accent, and whose work has become widely known through the medium of television. When all that most people have to go on is an amalgam of Crocodile Dundee and Dame Edna Everage, it becomes difficult for outsiders to begin to distinguish stereotype from reality.

Comments about accent uniformity in Australia, therefore, need to be seen within a social context. A continuum involving these three types of accent can be found all over the country. There may be no regional basis for distinguishing them (though in the absence of nationwide surveys it is impossible to be sure), but there is probably a social basis, with such factors as sex, age, religion, type of education, and occupation all playing their part, and these areas are currently being investigated by Australian sociolinguists. Another important factor is likely to be country of origin: some 20 per cent of the population now has a background where English is a foreign language.

The sociolinguistic approach (as opposed to one which looks only for regional dialect differences) also relates more clearly to the historical situation of the early decades of settlement. The distance from Britain, coupled with considerable internal population mobility, would have promoted regional homogeneity. At the same time, the great social divisions among the first European settlers – convicts, guards, governors, landowners, free immigrants – would have fostered sociolinguistic diversity. From this point of view, the Australian linguistic scene is not so remarkable after all.

PHONETIC FEATURES

The whole basis for the auditory impression of a distinctive Australian accent lies in the vowel system – and especially in the way diphthongs are handled. The consonant system of Australian English is different only in minor respects from that found in RP, and raises little of regional interest.

• RP /iː/ and /uː/ (as in *see, do*) are heard as diphthongs /əɪ/ and (much less often) /əʊ/, respectively. This effect is marked in the broad accent, and increasingly less so along the continuum from general to cultivated. The effect on /iː/ is particularly striking as a marker of Australian accent.

• RP /eɪ/, as in *say*, is given a more open first element, sometimes fairly front, sometimes further back. It is widely heard in the name *Australia* and in the greeting g'*day* /gədaɪ/. It is this variant which motivates the 'Strine' label for Australian English (p. 410).

• RP /əʊ/, as in *so*, is heard with a much more open and fronted articulation in the broad accent, and to a lesser extent in the general accent. The cultivated accent tends to use the same kind of variation as is heard in RP, with front or back mid-open qualities, more clearly symbolized as /oʊ/ or /ɛʊ/.

• The first element of RP /aɪ/, as in *my*, is given a back, open quality, /ɒɪ/, in the broad and general accents.

• The first element of RP /aʊ/, as in *now*, is produced at the front of the mouth, in broad and general accents, and often raised in the direction of [æ].

• A central vowel /ə/ often replaces /ɪ/ in an unstressed syllable: *hospital* /hɒspətl/, *because* /bɪkəz/.

• Vowels next to a nasal consonant tend to retain the nasality more than in RP: such words as *down* and *now* are often strongly nasalized in the broad accent, and are the chief reason for the designation of this accent as a 'twang'.

The phonetic basis for the three accent types emerges from a consideration of these qualities. The broad accent makes much use of tongue movements which are more open or further forward than the RP norms. The cultivated accent is, literally, 'further back'.

The sources of the Australian accent have also attracted study in recent years. It is assumed that much of its character stems from the speech of the original settlers, most of whom came from the London area, and also from the Midlands and Ireland. For example, some of the distinctive diphthongal qualities of broad Australian speech, with their more open first elements (in such words as *say, so, sigh, sow*), are close to those heard in Cockney English. However, the exact way in which these accents mixed to produce a distinctive accent (noticed as such within 30 years or so of the first settlement) is not easy to establish. (For the distinctive high-rising intonation, see p. 249)

EMERGING REGIONAL DIFFERENCES

Regardless of the view that Australian speech is uniform, if Australians from one state are asked whether people in other states have a different accent, several will say yes. In one report, a speaker from Queensland thought that using /aː/ rather than /æ/ in *dance* showed someone was from Victoria or South Australia. Another cited the word *castle* with /aː/ (as in *New castle, Castlereagh St*) as a Sydney (New South Wales) feature. Is there any truth in such stereotypes? Australian English does preserve the distinction between 'short a' /æ/ and 'long a', as in RP, though the latter is further forward in the mouth (/aː/, not /ɑː/). As this is an important regional marker in Britain (p. 324), might it not also have this function in Australia?

The figure shows the results of a study of these vowels in a group of nearly 50 speakers distributed across five Australian cities. The differences in certain words are very clear, and are striking when *a* occurs before a nasal (as in *dance*). There is a 93 per cent use of /æ/ in such words in the Hobart sample, 42 per cent in Brisbane and Melbourne, 30 per cent in Sydney, and 9 per cent in Adelaide. The word *castle* with /aː/ seems to be especially distinctive in Sydney.

As in Britain, /aː/ is the prestige form, with residents of middle class suburbs and women using a higher proportion of these forms in all cases. The greatest social differences in the study were in Melbourne, and Adelaide, with nearly none in Brisbane – a result which agrees with Australian perceptions of the first two cities as being more sharply stratified by class.

Of course, from the opposite point of view, /aː/ can be seen as the undesirable form, by those who wish to distance themselves from cultivated speech. And insofar as distance from RP (Britain) would be associated with the republican movement, an increasing use of /æ/ is likely as we approach the new millennium. (After D. Bradley, 1991.)

Hobart	%	Melbourne	%	Brisbane	%	Sydney	%	Adelaide	%
graph	100	graph	70	dance	89	dance	60	contrast	29
chance	100	castle	70	castle	67	graph	30	castle	14
demand	90	dance	65	graph	44	chance	20	dance	14
dance	90	chance	40	demand	22	grasp	15	chance	14
castle	40	demand	22	chance	15	demand	10	graph	14
grasp	10	grasp	11	grasp	11	castle	0	demand	0
contrast	0	contrast	0	contrast	0	contrast	0	grasp	0

Percentage of /æ/ in some lexical items (reading style).

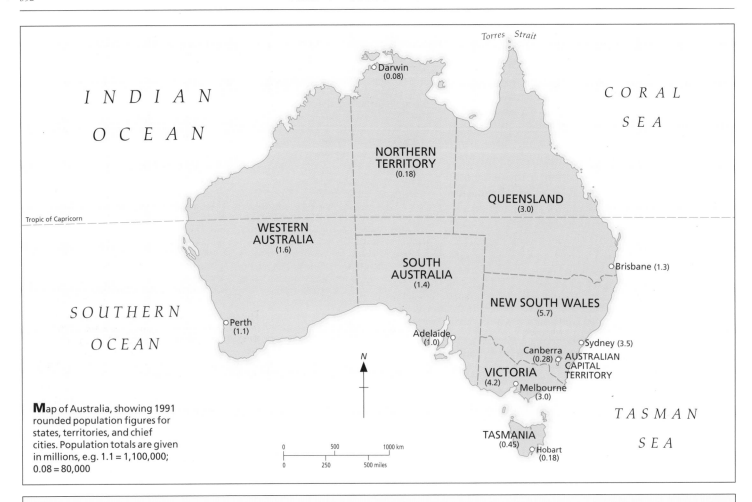

Map of Australia, showing 1991 rounded population figures for states, territories, and chief cities. Population totals are given in millions, e.g. 1.1 = 1,100,000; 0.08 = 80,000

GRAMMAR AND VOCABULARY

There are no clear examples of distinctive regional usage in Australian English grammar – though there are hints of Irish influence in some colloquial forms (about 30 per cent of the population were of Irish origin by 1890). Examples include *youse* ('you'), *mustn't* (='can't'), adverbial *but* (p. 338), some idioms (*Good on you*), word-final *-o(h)*, as in *smoko* ('break'), and the generally vivid rhetorical speech style. Other examples of colloquial word formation, as found in such forms as *arvo* ('afternoon') and *Aussie* ('Australian'), are given on p. 133.

At a lexical level, a very different picture presents itself. It has been estimated that there are over 10,000 lexical items of Australian English origin, some of which have become part of World Standard English (e.g. *flying doctor*, *pavlova*). Many are to do with the biogeography of the region and associated farming or mining practices:

banksia (tree), *barramundi* (fish), *black swan*, *brush* (dense vegetation), *bush* (natural vegetation) and such derivatives as *bushman* and *bushranger*, *galah* (bird), *mallee* (tree), *outback*, *overlander*, *quandong* (tree), *station* ('ranch'), *walkabout*, *waterhole*, *wattle* (tree), *witchetty grub*.

Among many general words are *BYO* ('bring your own', i.e. drink to a restaurant), *footpath* ('pavement'), *frock* ('dress'), *goodday* ('hello'), *lay-by* ('hire purchase'), *paddock* (a field of any size),

and *weekender* ('holiday cottage'). Well-known slang items include *beaut* ('beautiful'), *biggie* ('big one'), *cobber* ('friend'), *crook* ('unwell, irritable'), *dinkum* ('genuine, true'), *do a U-y* ('do a U-turn'), *drongo* ('fool'), *joker* ('person'), *larrikin* ('hooligan'), *poofter* (an effeminate male), *sheila* ('girl'), and *pommy* (an English immigrant, p. 303), along with its derivatives (e.g. *Pommyland*, *whingeing Pom*).

Australian English is famous for its vivid idioms – though many display literary creativity rather than everyday frequency: *bald as a bandicoot*, *scarce as rocking-horse manure*, and *look like a consumptive kangaroo*. Domestic idioms – such as *bring a plate* ('bring some food to share') or *full as a goog* (literally 'egg', i.e. 'drunk') – have been neglected by comparison, though some have been brought to outside attention through television commercials, as in the case of *amber fluid* for 'beer' (known from 1906). There are also important differences in the force of some expressions compared with British English, notably the 'routine' use of *bloody* (p. 173) and *bastard*.

Australian English does not have a great deal of Aboriginally-derived vocabulary (except in place names: see opposite). At the time of European settlement, the Aborigines were nomadic, and contact was occasional; as a result, hardly any native words came into English, apart from some plant and animal names (e.g. *dingo*, *koala*, *kookaburra*, *wallaby*). Among the exceptions are *boomerang*, *corroboree* (a ceremonial dance), and *cooee* (a loud call to attract attention), along with

within cooee ('within earshot'). A similar situation is found in New Zealand with Maori (p. 354).

Variation

The amount of regional lexical variation within Australia is unknown, but is certainly larger than is traditionally thought (p. 350). There are several clear examples, such as *bardi* (a type of grub) in Western Australia, *mainlander* in Tasmania (someone from mainland Australia), and *evening* in Queensland (any time after midday). There are also many unclear examples, such as the regional constraints (if any) governing the choice of *downpipe* and *spouting*, *gumboots* and *wellingtons*, *topcoat* and *overcoat*, or *washer* and *facecloth*.

As in Canada (p. 340), American English (AmE) is making inroads into the British English (BrE) model in varying degrees across the country. It is evident in such words as *caucus* (in politics), *sedan* (BrE *saloon*), *station wagon* (BrE *estate car*), *truck* (BrE *lorry*), and *high school* (BrE *secondary school*). On the other hand, BrE influence is evident in *class* (AmE *grade*), *cinema* (AmE *movies*), *petrol* (AmE *gas*), *boot* (AmE *trunk*), and *tap* (AmE also *faucet*). Spelling is also mixed (*defence* alongside *program*), though there is a traditional preference for British English forms. However, the *Australian Labor Party* uses the AmE spelling, and studies show considerable variation across states and between age groups in such cases as *centre/center* and *colour/color*. The situation is fluid, and looks likely to remain so.

A(NDREW) B(ARTON) PATERSON (1864–1941)

The strains of 'Waltzing Matilda' are enough to bring Australia to mind for most people, and the words (at least of the first verse, along with a simplified chorus) are part of World Musical English, sung lustily by many who would be totally unable to define a swagman, billabong, or coolabah tree. Few people outside of Australia, moreover, are aware of the later verses, or its tragic finale. Written by 'Banjo' Paterson in 1895, it is probably the most widely sung of the genre of bush ballads which formed a major element in Australian literature in the late 19th century. Other famous ballads from Paterson's pen include 'The Man from Snowy River' and the various exploits of Saltbush Bill. A less well-known piece is 'Those Names', reproduced here partly for its distinctive vocabulary and partly for its unusual 'metalinguistic' theme – verbal duelling with place names (p. 12).

WALTZING MATILDA

Oh! there once was a swagman camped in a Billabong,
    Under the shade of a Coolabah tree;
And he sang as he looked at his old billy boiling,
    'Who'll come a-waltzing Matilda with me?'

      Who'll come a-waltzing Matilda, my darling,
      Who'll come a-waltzing Matilda with me?
      Waltzing Matilda and leading a water-bag –
      Who'll come a-waltzing Matilda with me?

Down came a jumbuck to drink at the water-hole,
    Up jumped the swagman and grabbed him in glee;
And he sang as he stowed him away in his tucker-bag,
    'You'll come a-waltzing Matilda with me.'

Down came the Squatter a-riding his thoroughbred;
    Down came Policemen—one, two, and three.
'Whose is the jumbuck you've got in the tucker-bag?
    You'll come a-waltzing Matilda with me.'

But the swagman, he up and he jumped into the water-hole,
    Drowning himself by the Coolabah tree;
And his ghost may be heard as it sings in the Billabong
    'Who'll come a-waltzing Matilda with me?'

billabong an oasis-like old river channel, with no outlet, which usually fills seasonally
billy a tin can used for boiling water or cooking; also called a *billycan* or *billypot*
coolabah a type of eucalyptus tree
jumbuck a sheep (hence the seriousness of the offence)
squatter a major land-holder in the outback
swagman a rural tramp, who carries a rolled blanket with his belongings inside (*swag*)
tucker-bag food-bag

THOSE NAMES

The shearers sat in the firelight, hearty and hale and strong,
After the hard day's shearing, passing the joke along:
The 'ringer' that shore a hundred, as they never were shorn before,
And the novice who, toiling bravely, had tommy-hawked half a score,
The tarboy, the cook and the slushy, the sweeper that swept the board,
The picker-up, and the penner, with the rest of the shearing horde.
There were men from the inland stations where the skies like a furnace glow,
And men from the Snowy River, the land of the frozen snow;
There were swarthy Queensland drovers who reckoned all land by miles,
And farmers' sons from the Murray, where many a vineyard smiles.
They started at telling stories when they wearied of cards and games,
And to give these stories flavour, they threw in some local names,
Then a man from the bleak Monaro, away on the tableland,
He fixed his eyes on the ceiling, and he started to play his hand.
He told them of Adjintoothbong, where the pine-clad mountains freeze,
And the weight of the snow in summer breaks branches off the trees,
And, as he warmed to the business, he let them have it strong –
Nimitybelle, Conargo, Wheeo, Bongongolong;
He lingered over them fondly, because they recalled to mind
A thought of the old bush homestead, and the girl that he left behind.
Then the shearers all sat silent till a man in the corner rose;
Said he 'I've travelled a-plenty but never heard names like those.
Out in the western districts, out on the Castlereagh
Most of the names are easy – short for a man to say.
You've heard of Mungrybambone and the Gundabluey pine,
Quobbotha, Girilambone, and Terramungamine,
Quambone, Eunonyhareenyha, Wee Waa, and Buntijo – '
But the rest of the shearers stopped him:
'For the sake of your jaw, go slow,
If you reckon those names are short ones out where such names prevail,
Just try and remember some long ones before you begin your tale.'
And the man from the western district, though never a word he said,
Just winked with his dexter eyelid, and then he retired to bed.

A SLICE OF PUDDIN'

This is a frontways view of Bunyip Bluegum and his Uncle Wattleberry. At a glance you can see what a fine, round, splendid fellow Bunyip Bluegum is, without me telling you. At a second glance you can see that the Uncle is more square than round, and that his face has whiskers on it.

The opening lines of the 'First Slice' of Norman Lindsay's *The Magic Pudding*, first published in 1918 and since reprinted over 30 times, the fourth edition in colour. Often said to be Australia's most popular traditional children's story, the names of its characters have limited resonance to those living elsewhere, for they reflect the local fauna and flora of the continent (possums, wombats, bandicoots, kookaburras, flying-foxes, wattle gum). The koala bear hero's name, *bunyip*, for example, is taken from a mythical evil being of Aboriginal legend (though leaving its connotations behind). However, this does not detract from the universal appeal of the saga of the inexhaustible Puddin' and the efforts of Bunyip and his friends to protect it from being stolen.

Bunyip lives with his uncle in a small house in a tree, but is forced to leave home to escape the size of his uncle's whiskers:

The trouble was that he couldn't make up his mind whether to be a Traveller or a Swagman. You can't go about the world being nothing, but if you are a traveller you have to carry a bag, while if you are a swagman you have to carry a swag, and the question is: Which is the heavier?

'Why does Bunyip want to be a robber?' This question, asked by a British youngster reared on children's comics in which burglars always go around carrying large bags marked SWAG, illustrates a tiny difference between Australian and British English. *Swag* is countable in AusE, but uncountable in BrE (p. 209).

NEW ZEALAND ENGLISH

New Zealand English is the dark horse of World English regional dialectology. It has long been neglected, mentioned only in passing as part of a treatment of Australian English (p. 350), or assumed by outsiders to be identical with it in all salient respects. During the 1980s, however, this state of affairs began to change, with several studies focusing directly on the variety, and taking into account the unique features of the New Zealand sociolinguistic situation. The results of this interest suggest that there is a great deal that the study of New Zealand English can contribute to our understanding of linguistic variation and change, and – more excitingly – that some of its most distinctive developments have yet to take place.

Several elements in the country's social history (p. 99) have already had linguistic consequences. New Zealand English is different from other first-language varieties around the world in that it has been subject to *four* kinds of pressure. In addition to the problems faced by speakers of many varieties of how to deal with the competing influences of British and American English (p. 107), New Zealanders have to work out how to deal with Australian English and how to handle their linguistic relationship with the Maori (who comprise some 12 per cent of the total population).

• Studies of language attitudes in New Zealand show that British Received Pronunciation (RP, p. 365) is still the most highly rated accent, in terms of such values as educatedness and competence. However, local accents rate more highly than RP in terms of solidarity and social attractiveness.
• There is a real question of whether the people, as New Zealand linguist Allan Bell has put it, are falling 'out of the British frying pan into the American fire'. US accents have been ranked highly in some attitude studies, and there are signs of US influence in pronunciation and vocabulary.
• The question of an emerging variety of Maori English is controversial, and results of studies on listeners' ability to recognize a Maori accent are mixed. However, there has been a major shift of attitude in recent decades, so that items of Maori provenance are now being treated with levels of prominence and sensitivity that have been missing in the past.

With British, American, Australian, local English, and Maori resources all available as input, there is a uniqueness about the New Zealand sociolinguistic situation which makes it more than likely that a distinctive variety will eventually emerge.

PRONUNCIATION

Several features of Australian English accents (p. 351) are also found in New Zealand, such as the tendency to turn /iː/ and /uː/ into diphthongs (as in *mean* /məɪn/, *shoot* /ʃəʊt/), and the use of /ə/ in unstressed syllables (as in *rocket* /ˈrɒkət/. It is unclear whether this similarity stems from a parallel development to what took place in Australia (a 'mixing-bowl' theory, in which several British accents merged) or – politically an unattractive option – whether it is due to the direct influence of Australian English. On the other hand, some of the broader features of Australian pronunciation are not as noticeable in New Zealand.

The threefold distinction between cultivated, general, and broad (p. 351) has been widely used in the analysis of New Zealand speech. The three types are not as perceptible as they are in Australia, but there is certainly evidence of social stratification – for example, in the way some people's accents are close to RP, while others are distant from it. That there must be an emerging New Zealand accent is also suggested, ironically, by the way conservative speakers have come to condemn 'ugly' or 'defective' local speech in the letter columns of the press.

The following are some of the features which have attracted attention. (For phonetics terminology, see §17.)

• /ɪ/ as in *fish* tends to move towards [ə] – a contrast with Australian, where the movement is towards [i]. In popular representations, such as cartoon captions, the difference is often shown in the spelling. New Zealanders often think of Australians as saying 'feesh and cheeps', whereas Australians believe New Zealanders say 'Sudney' for *Sydney*.

• /e/ has a closer articulation, moving towards [i], so that *yes* is heard as 'yis'. Likewise, /a/ is around the position of [ɛ], so that outsiders may mishear *bat* as [ɛt].
• The vowels in such pairs as *here* /ɪə/ and *hair* /ɛə/ vary greatly, and have merged in many speakers, especially in broader accents. One linguist found evidence of this merger in the name of a hairdresser's in downtown Wellington: *Hair Say*. But not everyone in New Zealand would appreciate this pun, as evidently the direction of the merger (whether *here* comes to sound like *hair* or vice versa) is subject to considerable variation.
• /ɑː/ is generally maintained in such words as *castle* and *dance*. It is commonly /æ/ in Australia (p. 351.)
• There is a tendency to maintain the voiceless/voiced contrast between such pairs as *whales* and *Wales*, especially in formal speech. However, it seems to be falling out of use among younger people.
• /l/ is much 'darker' in quality than in RP (p. 245), in all its positions. In final position it is often replaced by a vowel (as in current 'Estuary' English, p. 327).
• Several individual words have local pronunciations. The name of the country is often heard with a short /ɪ/: /zɪlənd/ not (as in RP) /ziːlənd/, though this attracts some social criticism. The first syllable of *geyser* has /aɪ/ not /iː/. *Menu* often has /iː/ not /e/. *English* is often heard without the /g/. *Spectator* is stressed on the first syllable.
• The high rising intonation is a noticeable feature of Australian and New Zealand speech (p. 249). It is said to be more frequently used in New Zealand, and there is speculation that it may have originated there, transferring to Australia via Sydney (which has many New Zealand residents).

VOCABULARY

The existence of a common lexical word-stock between Australia and New Zealand should not be underestimated. Hundreds of 'Australianisms' (p. 352) are known and used in New Zealand. However, many more will not be found, because of the obvious differences in cultural history and biogeography. For example, Australia's penal history brought terms to that country which have played no part in New Zealand's history, and the large 'outback' Australian vocabulary (p. 352) is either irrelevant or differently applied (e.g. *bush* is usually dense forest in New Zealand).

The biggest lexical difference between the two countries is undoubtedly to do with Maori loanwords (see opposite), but there are several other words which have come to be particularly associated with New Zealand (a few have further usage elsewhere). They include: *Aucklander* ('inhabitant of Auckland'), *bach* ('holiday house'), *barnes walk* (a diagonal walk at traffic lights), *chilly bin* ('insulated food/drink box'), *chocolate fish* (a type of sweet), *dwang* ('timber floor strut'), *fizz boat* ('speed boat'), *Golden Kiwi* (the name of the National Lottery), *lamburger* ('burger made from minced lamb'), *section* ('building plot'), *superette* ('small supermarket'), *swannie* (a type of jacket), and *wopwops* (a derogatory term for the suburbs).

Among idioms claimed for New Zealand are *hook your mutton* ('clear out'), *have the wood on* ('have an advantage over'), and *at a rate of knots* ('very fast'). Among discourse patterns is the reply to 'How are you?' – often, 'Good, thanks'.

A few terms of New Zealand origin have become part of World Standard English. The most famous is undoubtedly *All Blacks* (the New Zealand international rugby team), with its chief stress on the first syllable.

REGIONAL VARIATION

There seems to be little clear evidence of regional variation within New Zealand, though local people believe that they can hear such distinctions (e.g. between North and South Island, or West and East Coast), and it may be that such dialects are emerging. However, the few controlled studies of the ability of New Zealanders to identify regional characteristics have not so far shown clear results.

In pronunciation, there is one notable exception. Like Australians, New Zealanders do not pronounce /r/ after vowels; but the 'Southland burr' is found in the speech of those living in the southern part of the country, where such place names as Kelso and Invercargill signal the presence of major Scottish settlement (p. 328). There are now also signs of the use of /r/ after vowels in some young New Zealanders elsewhere, which may be due to the influence of American English.

In vocabulary, several Scottish expressions, such as *slaters* ('woodlice'), have been recorded in the Otago region. There are also sporadic reports of North Island / South Island variants, such as Southern *quarter* (a loaf of bread) vs Northern *half*, and of West Coast region-

alisms, such as *crib* ('miner's lunch') and its derivatives (e.g. *crib tin*). As in other countries, there are probably many local lexical variations waiting to be recorded.

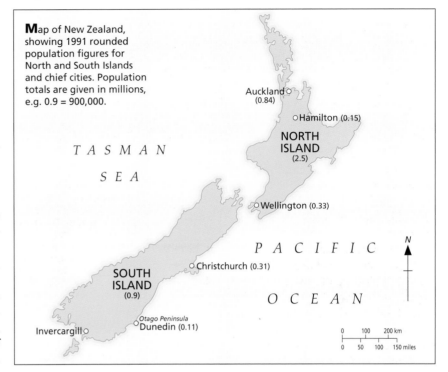

Map of New Zealand, showing 1991 rounded population figures for North and South Islands and chief cities. Population totals are given in millions, e.g. 0.9 = 900,000.

MAORI INFLUENCE

In 1987 the Maori Language Act gave official status to Maori, and led to a much greater public profile for the language, with several consequences for English.

• Maori pronunciation is now increasingly used for words of Maori origin – a policy followed by the New Zealand Broadcasting Corporation. Thus, words spelled with <wh> such as *whanau* , traditionally pronounced as /ʍ/ or /w/ by English speakers, are now being given the Maori sound, /f/. There are several other points of difference, such as the use of initial /ŋ/, as in *Ngaio*, and a long /ɑː/ vowel before /ŋ/, as in *hangi*.
• There are also moves to devise an English

orthography which better reflects the Maori sound system, such as spelling long vowels with a macron or a double letter (as in *Māori* or *Maaori*).
• Maori has also had a small effect on local English grammar. It does not use a plural ending on nouns, and this is increasingly becoming the preferred form in loan words. *Maori* itself is an example (replacing *Maoris*).
• New Zealand has more loan words from Polynesian languages than any other variety of English, but only a handful (such as *kiwi* and *kauri*) are known outside the country. Cultural traditions, fauna, and flora provide important lexical growth points: *hapuku, kahawai, tarakihi* (types of fish), *rata, rimu, maire* (types of tree), *moa, kea, tui* (types of bird). Such words increasingly appear without a gloss in English

publications in New Zealand. As with Australian Aboriginal languages (p. 353), Maori place names are widely used, and some personal names are well known (*Ngaio, Kiri*).

Common loan words include: *aue!* ('oh, alas'), *aroha* ('love, sympathy'), *haere mai* (a greeting), *haka* (a ceremonial dance), *hongi* (the ritual of pressing noses), *huhu* (a type of beetle), *hui* (a ceremonial gathering), *katipo* (a type of spider), *kia ora* ('good health'), *moana* ('lake'), *Pakeha* ('white person'), and *whare* ('house, hut').

There are also several loan words from Samoan in New Zealand English. Examples include *aiga* ('family'), *fale* ('house'), *faamafu* (a type of home-brewed liquor), *talofa* (a ceremonial greeting), *matai* (a titled chief), and *papalagi* ('white man').

VOICES

This sentence from the New Zealand *Metro* magazine (September 1990) does not use glosses or graphic signals to show that the Maori words are anything other than an ordinary part of English:

Maori took seriously what Christians call the communion of saints, a sense of involvement with their dead: they knew their whakapapa many generations back; they mourned together at each marae

gathering; their precious taonga were means by which they communicated with the dead, and the tangi was (and is) for them a time for renewing their place within the whanau, hapu, iwi and waka, giving them their essential dignity and worth.

hapu a tribal division *iwi* tribe *marae* courtyard *tangi* mourning *taonga* heirlooms *waka* war canoe *whakapapa* genealogy *whanau* family

Maori expressions are central to Keri Hulme's Booker prize-winning novel, *The Bone People* (1985). One passage (p. 33) captures the language's resonances especially, when her character thinks her

chest of precious stones has been burgled. (Most of the Maori terms are given rough glosses in the text; a *mere* is a small stone weapon; *pounamu* is greenstone.)

She opens the lid, her heart thudding. On trays in the pale pool of light, a 100 smooth and curvilinear shapes.
   Two meres, patu pounamu, both old and named, still deadly.
   Many stylised hook pendants, hei matau.
   Kuru, and kapeu, and kurupapa, straight and curved neck pendants.
   An amulet, a marakihau; and a spiral pendant, the koropepe.
   A dozen chisels. Four fine adzes.
   Several hei tiki, one especial – so old that the flax cord of previous owners had worn through the hard stone, and the suspension hole had had to be rebored in times before the Pakeha ships came…

SOUTH AFRICAN ENGLISH

The multilingual and multicultural history of South Africa (p. 100) presents a situation without precedent in those parts of the world where English is spoken as a first language. Of all the countries so far reviewed in this chapter, South Africa is the only one where the language is in a minority (used as a mother tongue by about 10 per cent of the population). In addition – and in apparent disregard of this tiny figure – historical, racial, tribal, and political factors have combined to produce a sociolinguistic situation of stunning intricacy, a remarkable array of linguistic proficiency levels, and an unparalleled range of popular stereotypes about English structure and use – few of which have been systematically studied. For example, it is often claimed that people from different tribal backgrounds have different accents when speaking English, or that Coloureds (p. 100) have a different grammar from blacks and whites. It is not known what truth there might be in such claims.

The one factor which tends to unite the countries of southern Africa is the high status of English. It is the preferred language of public use, the media, and school instruction throughout much of the region. This is evidently also the case even in South Africa, where despite its minor rank in terms of first language use there is a much greater degree of language shift towards English than towards the other traditionally co-official language, Afrikaans, especially among the young Afrikaner population. Studies of code-switching indicate this clearly. Over half the pupils in a 1992 investigation into language use in Afrikaans-medium high schools in Pretoria reported that they often used English words when speaking Afrikaans (after V. Webb, 1992). The situation is an interesting reversal of the large-scale borrowing from Afrikaans by English which characterized the early years of language contact in the region.

There is a great deal of evidence supporting the recognition of a distinctive variety of English in South Africa; but this notion is relevant only for those white, Coloured, and Indian native speakers who use the language as a mother tongue. Most of the majority black population speak English as a second language, and thus have more in common with people from those other nations of southern Africa where English has official status (p. 106). English-speaking members of the white population who have Afrikaans as a mother tongue must also be considered in this category, as their variety of English has distinguishing features of its own. For example, mainstream South African English does not have an /r/ after vowels (p. 245), but this consonant is often present in speakers with an Afrikaans background.

When we talk about a variety of South African English, accordingly, we are referring only to those who speak the language as a mother tongue. At the same time, the second-language situation cannot be completely ignored. When first and second language varieties are as closely in contact as they are in South Africa, some mutual influence is bound to take place – a situation which can only intensify in a post-apartheid nation.

M. K. Gandhi (1869–1948), who played a major role in Indian South African politics between 1893 and 1913, noted the early use of 'broken English' by the Indian community. In *Indian Opinion* (30 January 1909) he commented: 'We observe that some Indian youth having acquired a smattering of English, use it even when it is not necessary to do so...'

SOUTH AFRICAN INDIAN ENGLISH

This variety of English illustrates the unusual sociolinguistic complexity which can be encountered in South Africa. It has been called a linguistic 'fossil', preserved by the history of segregation in the country. It dates from the period (1860–1911) when over 150,000 Indians were allowed into Natal, mainly as cheap labour to work on the plantations. Most had no knowledge of English, though a local pidgin (p. 346) involving English (Fanagalo) was in use from early times. From the 1950s, the language came to be taught to Indian children in schools, and within a generation a process of language shift was taking place, with English becoming the first language of the majority. It is now spoken by some 750,000, mainly in Natal.

Because these children were separated by apartheid from British children, their English (at least in informal speech) developed in very different ways from mainstream South African English. It shows some similarities with creole languages (p. 346), but it has come much closer to the standard language, having been much influenced by the model taught in schools.

The result is a variety of English which mixes features of Indian, South African, Standard British, creole, and foreign language learning Englishes in a fascinating way.

• In pronunciation the variety is losing the retroflex consonants typical of Indian languages, but has retained its syllable-timed rhythm (p. 249). It has picked up some features of South African speech (see opposite), such as the raising of short front vowels, but rejected others, such as the rounding of /ɑ/.

• In vocabulary, well over a thousand distinctive items have been recorded in informal speech. There are loan words from Indian languages, such as *thanni* (a type of card game), *dhania* ('coriander'), and *isel* ('flying ant'), and adaptations of many native English words: *future* ('husband/wife-to-be'), *proposed* ('engaged'), *cheeky* ('stern'), and *independent* ('haughty').

Grammar

Undoubtedly the most notable feature of this variety is its syntax. Several distinctive points have been recorded. (For grammatical terminology, see Part III.)

• Reduplication: *fast-fast* (='very fast'), *different-different* (='many and different'), *who-who* (='who' plural).

• Rhetorical use of question-words: *Where he'll do it!* ('He certainly won't do it'), *What I must go?* ('Why should I go?'), *Rain won't make you wet, what?* ('Will rain not make you wet?')

• Pronoun omission: *If you got, I'll take*; *When you bought?*

• Tag questions (p. 218): *He came there, isn't?* (i.e. 'didn't he?').

• End-placed verbs (without the emphasis associated with Standard English): *Customer you got*, *So rude you are.*

• Relative clauses: *I bought the things, which ones you told me*; *Who won money, they're putting up a factory next door* (i.e. The people who won money are...).

• Titles: *Johnny uncle*, *Naicker teacher.*

• Postpositions: *Durban-side* ('near Durban'), *Afternoon-time it gets hot.*

• Final use of some conjunctions and adverbials: *She can talk English but*; *I made rice too, I made roti too* ('I made both rice and roti'); *They coming now, maybe.*

(After R. Mesthrie, 1987, 1993.)

PRONUNCIATION

There is a continuum of accents, as in Australia (p. 350). At one extreme there are many older, conservative speakers, mostly of recent British descent, whose accents remain close to Received Pronunciation (RP, p. 365). At the other extreme, there are broad accents, used mainly by working-class people, often with some Afrikaner background. These are the accents most often satirized as South African. In between, there is a range of mainstream accents which are increasingly to be heard on radio and television. The following features characterize accents towards the broader end of this continuum. (For phonetics terminology, see §17.)

The short front vowels of RP are all raised, and the closest vowel has been centralized:

• /a/ as in *pat* is raised to a mid front position [ɛ], sounding more like *pet*.
• /e/ as in *pet* moves in the direction of /i/, sounding more like *pit*.
• /ɪ/ as in *pit* is centralized, with a value between /ə/ and /ʊ/ (*put*). However, this change depends on the nature of the preceding consonant: it does not apply after back consonants (/k,g,h/); thus there is no rhyme in this variety between *sit* and *kit*.

An ancient piece of wit helps to fix two of these changes in the ear of the outsider: for South Africans, it has been said, *sex* is what you carry coal in, while *six* is needed for procreation.

Two other features are also very noticeable:

• /ɑː/ as in *star* is rounded and raised, so that it resembles /ɔː/, sounding more like *store*.
• Several diphthongs weaken their glides, sounding more like pure vowels: *hair* with [ɛː], *right* and *mouse* with values near to [ɑː].

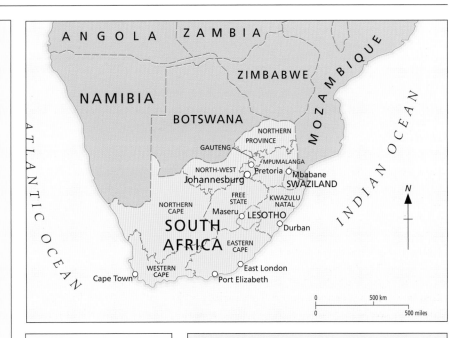

AH BIG YAWS?
Pardon, that is. 'I beg yours?'

This is the title of a humorous guide to South African English ('Guard to Sow Theffricun Innglissh') published in 1972, by Rawbone Malong [Robin Malan]. As with all dialect humour (p. 410), it relies on many of the informal speech patterns which are not in fact regionally distinctive at all (e.g. running together the words *South* and *African* is a perfectly normal feature of all varieties of English). But in its choice of spellings it does capture several of the resonances of this variety of English. To say *Orfficorns* aloud in RP (using conventional spelling values) does produce something which is remarkably close to its target.

Here is Malong's guide to 'peeble's neighms'. In addition to the vowel vari-

ants, the devoicing of final consonants, such as /d/ to /t/, is notable.

Men: Ellbit, Brawn, Chorlz, Claaf, Dayfitt, Jaymce, Grayyim, Gregerree, Jawtch, Hyarrie, Jawn, Pall, Furllup, Rawbit, Ritshit, Rottsa
Women: Dawreen, Daffernee, Alizbiff, Maaibull, Mehrree, Mayphis, Mulldrit, Varlet, Yellsie, Lun, Vellery, Pertreesha.

GRAMMAR

There are no important grammatical variations from Standard English in formal South African speech or writing, but several distinctive constructions are found in colloquial speech. For example, an object noun or pronoun may be deleted: *A: I asked for the car. B: And did you get?; A: Would you like another cup? B: I still have.* Some words may be repeated to express intensity: *now-now* ('immediately'). *Is it?* is widely used as a response tag (*A: They were here recently. B: Is it?*).

Afrikaans may have an influence, as in the use of *must* to mean 'shall' in questions (*Must I translate?*) or the nonstandard use of prepositions (*on the moment, anxious over her*). Speech which is characterized by a great deal of Afrikaans grammar and idiom is often labelled *Anglikaans: I've been rather very ill, I'm busy listening* (='I am in the process of listening'), *I'll do it just now* ('in a little while'), *I'll be by the house* (='at home'). *Yes-no* is an emphatic affirmative. *Jawellnofine* is an interesting construction – a combination of *Ja* ('yes') *well no fine* (*no* here in an affirmative sense), sometimes used to satirize Anglikaans speech.

VOCABULARY

Several words and phrases from South Africa have become part of World Standard English. Some have origins in Afrikaans or local native languages, or are adaptations of Standard English words. They include *aardvark, apartheid, boer, commando, eland, homeland, kraal, rand, spoor, springbok, trek,* and *veld*. Many of the words relating to local fauna, flora, and culture are not known outside the South African context. Local institutions and social groups also fall into this category, often providing opaque abbreviations to the outsider, as in the case of *Bop* ('Bophuthatswana'), *Tuks* ('University of Pretoria'), and *Zim* ('Zimbabwean').

Among the general items found in this variety are: *arvey* ('afternoon'), *bad friends* ('not on speaking terms'), *bakkie* (a type of truck), *bell* ('to phone'), *bioscope* ('cinema'), *bottle store* ('liquor store/off-licence'), *butchery* ('butcher's shop'), *camp* ('paddock'), *dinges* ('thingummy', p. 132), *dorp* ('village'), *fundi* ('expert'), *gogga* ('insect'), *indaba* ('meeting'), *kloof* ('ravine'), *lekker* ('nice'), *putu* (a type of porridge), *robot* ('traffic light'), *verkrampte* ('narrow-minded'), and *voorskot* ('advance payment').A few can also be found in other varieties of English, such as *advocate* ('barrister', e.g. in Scotland) and *shebeen* ('illegal liquor establishment', e.g. in Ireland).

An important source for distinctive vocabulary is the *Dictionary of South African English* (4th edition, 1991), which contains some 4,000 fully-illustrated entries. There is still much to do, in such areas as regional and ethnic lexical variation. Among regional items so far recorded are *bathing box* ('beach hut'), *monkeyface stone*, and *Tablecloth* (the cloud covering Table Mountain), all apparently local to Cape Province. Doubtless hundreds of words, including many invective terms, are also used differently among the various ethnic groups. From those which have already been noted, one word-pair (an appropriate choice for the present book) must suffice as illustration: the facetious coinage *pluralstan*, made by a black journalist for the various bantustans (black homelands), which gave rise to *plurals* ('blacks') and *singulars* ('whites'). The usage is already an archaism.

NEW ENGLISHES: A PRELIMINARY SITTING

The aim of the present chapter has been to review English regional variation, focusing on those countries where it has prominent first-language use – the 'inner circle' of English, as it has been called (p. 107). It is important, however, not to ignore the other two 'circles' identified in §7 – the 'outer circle', consisting of those countries where English has come to play an important role as a second language through a history of colonial contact (such as India and Nigeria), and the 'expanding circle', made up of countries where the importance of English as an international medium has been recognized, but the language has received no special status (such as Japan and Brazil). To systematically survey the 'New Englishes' of these countries is not possible, in the present encyclopedia. Over half the countries in the world have now given English some kind of 'special status' (p. 106), and probably all of them would these days need to be included in considering the role and impact of English as a foreign language. To deal fairly and comprehensively with such a diversity of sociolinguistic situations would take a very large book.

And such a book cannot yet be written. In most countries, no official information is published about how English is taught and how many people speak or write it, and very little academic research is yet available on the nature of local variation in English structure and use. During the 1980s, several academic journals began to publish material on these questions, notably *English World-Wide* (from 1980, subtitled 'A Journal of Varieties of English'), *World Englishes* (from 1982, subtitled 'Journal of English as an International and Intranational Language'), and *English Today* (from 1985, subtitled 'The International Review of the English Language'). Several pioneering collections of essays also appeared, such as *English as a World Language* (see Appendix IV). Nonetheless, the combined efforts of these publications had by 1990 resulted in descriptive data becoming available on only a few dozen topics in a few dozen countries. This is not to demean the valuable progress which has taken place, but many of the articles themselves concluded by stressing their programmatic character, and drawing attention to the need for in-depth descriptive or experimental research. Much of what we know is still outline and impressionistic, apart from in a few countries (such as India) which have a well-established tradition of English language study.

The database required for a systematic approach to world uses of English is inevitably going to be enormous. The first steps in its compilation have actually already begun for a number of countries (p. 438); but no one knows how long it would take to develop such a project on a world scale, or whether such an extension would be practicable. Financial constraints are such that large-scale language projects can easily find themselves left behind by the pace of language change. All scholars may ever be able to do, accordingly, is provide partial portraits of the language, varying in accuracy and depth of detail. At the same time, some subjects are so fascinating that even a partial portrait is well worth painting.

CULTURAL DISTANCE

Cultural distance from the countries of the inner circle inevitably puts pressure on inner-circle linguistic norms. English must change, when it arrives in the countries of the outer and expanding circles, to meet the communicative needs of communities whose social structure involves very different priorities and preoccupations. These changes can affect any area of language structure, but will be most apparent in new vocabulary and styles of discourse. They will also be most apparent in domains of language use whose purpose is to reflect intranational activities, such as local religious events or local politics. For example, in one study of Indian newspapers (see right), the provincial press showed nearly three times as many loan words from local Indian languages in its editorials than did the national press. The leading newspapers of a country tell us more about the norms of World Standard English than they do about regional linguistic identity (p. 300).

MARRIAGE LINES

In the culture of India, religion, caste, colour, region, and economic status traditionally play a major role in marriage arrangements. As a consequence, newspaper matrimonial advertisements are very different in style compared with the equivalent 'lonely hearts' items in the Western press, and use very different vocabulary. More importantly, many items which seem familiar need to be reinterpreted, if their correct sense in the Indian context is to be appreciated.

A cultural reading of the vocabulary brings to light several points of semantic difference.

• *bride with a male child* is a widow or divorcee with a son, mentioned in view of the priority given in Indian society to a male heir, whether natural or adopted.
• *broad-minded* in the West would be likely to mean 'in relation to sexual practices'; here it refers to a readiness to embrace modern values while retaining core values of Indian morality.
• *clean-shaven* indicates that the person is Punjabi, but no longer bearded.
• *divorcee* is a strongly negative term, compared with its modern Western use.
• *fair* means 'relatively light in colour' – that is (unlike in the West), the person is still dark-skinned, though not markedly so; it contrasts with *actually fair-*

complexioned, which is *fair* in the Western sense, and with *wheatish*, which suggests the golden-yellow of ripening wheat.
• *full particulars* would be an astrological reference – a request for a horoscope.
• *good-looking* has to be seen in contrast with other phrases used in this context, such as *exceptionally beautiful*; it suggests 'average' rather than (as in the West) 'above-average'.
• *respectable*, *well-placed*, and *well-established* carry implications of economic standing: a *highly respectable family* is a rich one.
• *stable charactered* and *sincere* suggest loyalty and devotion to a marriage partner, despite a readiness to socialize with the opposite sex.
• *sweet-natured* and *sweet-tempered* hint at the bride's willingness to fit into an Indian joint family.
• *tall* requires reference to a cultural 'ideal' (often made explicit – 155 to 162 cm, or 5 ft 1 in to 5 ft 4 in); the collocation *tall, wheatish, slim* is particularly common.
• *working girl* and *employed girl* have mixed connotations, as some families will accept a bride who is working, whereas others will not.
• *vegetarian* has a less flexible sense than is usual in the West; the norm is to exclude fish and eggs as well as meat. (After V. S. Dubey, 1991.)

☆ Match for Kanyakubja girl MA, B.Ed., PhD scholar, 27, slim, wheatish, 155 cms., belonging respectable U.P. family. Box...(*The Hindustan Times*, New Delhi, 20 June 1981)

☆ Wanted a really beautiful, tall, educated bride (25/26) for a handsome smart highly qualified PhD WBCS Kshatriya groom having own flat with telephone in a posh locality of South Calcutta. Owner of landed properties in Midnapore. Working girls may also write. Beauty is the only consideration. No bar. Box...(*The Statesman*, Calcutta, 15 June 1981.)

NEW NORMS

One reason why the use of English by non-native speakers is so important is that there are so many of them. Probably at least as many people speak English as a second language as speak it as a mother tongue, and both of these totals are likely to be exceeded before long by the number of those speaking it fluently as a foreign language. And when large numbers of people are involved in speaking a language, there is an inevitable tendency to develop fresh local usage – most naturally in vocabulary, but also in pronunciation, grammar, and discourse. New vocabulary can become part of the educated norm quite rapidly. In other areas of usage, change is more erratic, and at first is likely to be found only in colloquial styles among small groups. In the course of time, though, some of these features attract prestige, come to be adopted by educated speakers, and eventually form new local standards – the same process that promoted the development of mother-tongue varieties. The emergence of these non-native Englishes, and the uneasy relationship which exists between them and Standard English, especially in the classroom, is a major feature of the contemporary World English scene.

It is possible to interpret the three-circle model of World English in terms of the way norms of usage manifest themselves. The inner circle can be thought of as 'norm-producing', in the sense that it has given rise to the two leading normative models of Standard English – British and American. Other mother-tongue areas can also act as norms for their local non-native speakers. The outer circle is 'norm-developing', in the sense that the special role of English in these communities is fostering an internal standard of educated usage which has a status and dynamic of its own. The expanding circle, by contrast, is 'norm-dependent', in that speakers of English as a foreign language in a particular country need to look elsewhere for criteria to judge their usage. This set of distinctions is illuminating, as long as we do not interpret the situation to be more clear-cut than it really is. In particular, it still leaves open the question of whether new generations of non-native speakers in a second-language country should look to the external British/American norm or to the emerging second-language norm? And the question of whether autonomous norms can develop in a foreign language situation (such as Japan) remains unresolved.

LEXICAL INNOVATION

Special circumstances can give rise to linguistic innovations of considerable ingenuity. In this panel two such developments, involving substantial lexical idiosyncrasy, are reported from different parts of the world. It is perhaps no coincidence that there are similarities between the sociolinguistic situations of the two countries, Nigeria and Papua New Guinea. Each country is highly multilingual, and a pidgin language plays a major role. It is perhaps not too speculative to suggest that there is something in such situations which might make their speakers more ready to experiment with the standard language and more able (through their wider experience of languages in contact) to introduce new elements to it.

STUFFMAN

Fua will kill my coch. He wans nchang to yang some medicines for his yaourt. My jab don hang biog. She does not wan grub some das.*

At the University of Yaoundé, Cameroon, students are reported to be developing a distinctive variety of English for everyday purposes which is unintelligible to people from outside their group. Whether it is likely to be a long-term feature of the Cameroon linguistic scene is unclear. What is of interest is the way a new variety of English can emerge rapidly out of a mixture of standard languages (both English and French, in this case), pidgins, and local native languages. The variety is described as derogatory, humorous, taboo-orientated, and critical in attitude. Its syntax is largely standard English, though there are several mixed forms and constructions. There are parallels with argot, whether natural or literary (pp. 182, 395).

The lexicon uses all the main processes of word formation (p. 124). There are English and other suffixes, as in *drinkard* ('heavy drinker'), *anglose* ('anglophone'), *chickel* ('chicken'), and *painga* ('pain'). Compounding is seen in *hang pass* ('quit'), *dickoman* ('scholar', from *dictionary*), *sickdie* ('AIDS'), and *paddyman* ('friend'). Clipping is seen in

reto ('restaurant'), *tau* ('thousand'), and *coch* ('room-mate, from French *copain de chambre*). All local languages supply loan words, such as *shark* ('heavy drinker'), *pang* ('trousers', French *pantalon*), *nga* (Nigerian Pidgin 'girlfriend'), *muna* (Douala, 'child'), and *yap* (Bamileke, 'disgrace'). Many words are of unknown origin. (After P. Mbangwana, 1991.)

* *Stuffman*: academically reliable. 'Poverty will kill my room-mate. He needs money to buy some medicines for his cough.' 'My girlfriend is pregnant. She is unable to eat any food.'

2 U 4EVA

10-in a yia older 2-morrow Hapi b/day frm da folks in Pom*

These are the opening words of two birthday greetings from the *Post Courier* of Papua New Guinea. Not all are like this. Some are in Standard English or a local language (e.g. Tok Pisin); but many use a telegraphic code. There are abbreviations, numeral rebuses, phonetic spellings, and other devices (such as *XXX* 'kisses', p. 268).

The style probably began as a way of saving money (the paper charges per line), but its current usage cannot be explained just by rules from a financial grammar. It displays grammatical features from Papua New Guinea English (such as *20 is no teen years* or *Luv and prayer from mum*), and there are signs that its use may be extending to other local contexts. (After S. Holzknecht, 1989.)

* Turning a year older tomorrow / Happy birthday from the folks in Port Moresby

SOUTH ASIAN ENGLISH

The English of the Indian subcontinent – sometimes called South Asian English – provides the most convincing example of the way a 'new English' can develop in the outer circle (p. 107). Or perhaps this should be 'new Englishes', for there are many varieties spoken within the region, in a continuum which extends from pidgin forms of English (known by such names as 'Butler' and 'Babu' English) to educated uses that are indistinguishable from Standard British English and Received Pronunciation (p. 365). There are also several geographical and social subvarieties, influenced partly by the native languages which have been in contact with English, and partly by the highly stratified social system.

Some of these subvarieties have developed over a long period of time, during the period of colonial rule (p. 101). As a result, modern South Asian English has thousands of distinctive lexical items – some deriving from local Indian languages, some new combinations of English words, or English words with new senses. Especially when the subject matter is provincial or specialized, a text such as a newspaper report can be unintelligible to the outsider, and (p. 358) easy to misinterpret.

Pronunciation

The most noticeable feature of the English spoken throughout South Asia is its syllabic rhythm (p. 249), which can be a source of comprehension difficulty for those used to a stress-timed variety, especially when speech is rapid. Also highly distinctive are the retroflex plosives *t* and *d*, (p. 243), though these are often replaced by alveolar plosives in educated speech. Similarly, the traditional use of /r/ after vowels (p. 245) may these days be avoided by younger educated people, especially women. Several sounds have regional variants influenced by local languages, both within and between countries.

Grammar

There are many distinctive usages – though with much social variation. The following are widely encountered, but often condemned as errors by those who speak an English close to the British norm. (For grammatical terms, see Part III.)

- The progressive in 'static' verbs: *I am understanding it, She is knowing the answer.*
- Variations in noun number and determiners: *He performed many charities, She loves to pull your legs.*
- Prepositions: *pay attention on, discuss about, convey him my greetings.*
- Tag questions (p. 218): *You're going, isn't it?, He's here, no?.*
- Word order: *Who you have come for?, They're late always, My all friends are waiting.*
- *Yes* and *no* agreeing with the form of a question, not just its content: *A: You didn't come on the bus? B: Yes, I didn't.*

Problems of identity

Because of the length of the British presence in India, and the vast populations of the countries in the subcontinent, South Asian English has developed to a more distinctive level than in other countries where English has special status. It certainly presents very clearly the problems of identity facing those who use English in such countries – in particular, those in charge of educational programmes, and authors wishing to express their identity.

- In education, should teachers choose Standard English as a model in class, or allow the use of the regional features which the children hear around them?
- In literature, should authors opt for Standard English, which will guarantee them a readership throughout the world, or write according to regional norms which will give them a more authentic and personal voice?

Indeed, some go on to argue, should writers themselves not be making efforts to develop this regional variety into a standard, as inner circle authors have done in the past? The Indian author Raja Rao comments: 'Our method of expression has to be a dialect which will some day prove to be as distinctive and colourful as the Irish or the American…The tempo of Indian life must be infused into our English expression'. However, at the opposite extreme, there are authors who wish to stay with their mother tongue, and not write in English at all. These questions are fiercely and emotionally debated in all parts of the world where there are emerging varieties of second-language English.

South Asia has been the source of several words in World Standard English.

bandana, brahmin, bungalow, calico, caste-mark, chakra, cheetah, cheroot, chintz, chit, chutney, coolie, curry, dacoit, guru, jodhpurs, juggernaut, jungle, juice, mogul, mulligatawny, nirvana, pundit, purdah, rajah, rupee, sahib, tiffin, verandah, yoga

The items shown right are of a more restricted kind, of varying general currency. Many are not known outside the subcontinent, other than through literary work or shared specialized knowledge, as in Indian cuisine or yoga.

The vocabulary has been selected from published lists relating to the individual countries. However, in view of the common cultural history of the region, and the shared contact with several languages (such as Hindi and Sanskrit in the north), these lists are not claiming to be mutually exclusive. Many of the words are likely to be known and used throughout South Asia; but definitive supranational studies of regional variation have yet to be undertaken.

© ICA Förlaget AB, Västerås, Sweden.

Pakistan

affectee someone affected
bearer waiter
boots shoes, tennis shoes
cent percent a hundred per cent
conveyance means of transport (*not archaic*)
eartops earrings
eveninger evening paper
flying coach a type of bus
freeship scholarship
hotel eating house
(*as well as* hotel)
moot meeting
mudguard (car wing/fender)
nook and corner nook and cranny
opticals eyeglasses
thrice three times (not archaic)
tubelight fluorescent light
weekly-off day off

(After R. J. Baumgardner, 1990.)

India

allottee person allotted property
ayah nurse
bandh labour strike
chapatti type of bread
cousin-brother/sister male/female cousin
cow-worship religious practice
crore 10 million
dhobi washerman
Doordarshan TV network
Eve-teasing harassment of women
godown warehouse
goonda hooligan
head-bath hair washing
Himalayan blunder grave mistake
intermarriage marriage between religions or castes
issueless childless
jawan soldier
kaccha road dirt road
lakh hundred thousand
lathi policeman's baton
makan housing
nose-screw woman's nose ornament
paisa 100th of a rupee
panchayat village council
pantry/kitchen car dining car (train)
ryot farmer
scheduled caste lowest Hindu class
stepney spare wheel
swadeshi hotel native restaurant
tiffin room snack shop
wallah one who carries out a particular occupation (as in *policewallah, literature wallah*)

(After B. B. Kachru, 1986.)

The wood and the trees

The old saw of 'not being able to see the wood for the trees' comes persistently to mind when we try to establish what is happening to the English language in the outer-circle nations. Several researchers have now assiduously collected samples from their individual countries, and identified differences from Standard British or American English. They have compiled lists of distinctive words and idioms, and noted points of local usage in grammar and pronunciation. Sometimes the projects have also investigated local patterns of spoken or written discourse, such as the way linguistic distinctiveness emerges in a national literature. But in almost all cases, the point of view has remained stubbornly intranational. The authors are usually mother-tongue inhabitants or long-term residents of the country they are studying. Their accounts tend to be impressionistic or based on few speakers. They are thus guides to individual performance, but not to the underlying system: there is no way of knowing whether a word encountered is a casual error or a stable feature of usage. Nor is it always clear whether what has been observed is also to be found in other territories. As a result, varieties are being postulated for individual countries which may turn out to be chimerical.

This issue has already been mentioned with reference to the subcontinent of India (see opposite), where there are proposals, on the one hand, to establish a supra-national notion of South Asian English, and on the other hand to recognize nation-restricted varieties under such names as Indian, Pakistani, and Lankan English. The question is clouded by non-linguistic considerations. There is often covert political pressure to assert auton-omy: if Country X is thought to have its own variety of English, then why not Country Y? From a linguistic point of view, the matter can be resolved only by detailed comparative research.

The example of Africa

Another clear example of the tension between the two perspectives is in West Africa, where both supranational and national varieties have been proposed. The English used in many of the constituent countries has now received some degree of investigation, and a series of separate varieties has been suggested using such headings as 'Gambian', 'Nigerian', and 'Ghanaian English'. How-ever, authors typically do not provide information about whether the features they have observed in their own country, and think to be distinctive, are also to be found in others.

The answer is not always obvious. Some of these features are unlikely to have supranational distribution, perhaps because a local language is used only within one country, and loan-words from that language into English are therefore less likely to be found elsewhere. Some of the words, moreover, are bound to identify national institutions or practices. But in many cases, there is extensive international overlap. This seems to be especially so in relation to pronunciation and grammar, where we repeatedly encounter similar sound substitutions and syntactic patterns as we move from country to country; but it is also to be found in the lexicon, in the way words are adapted from English in similar ways or taken from one of the pidgin languages used along the coast. A comparison of different projects quickly brings to light examples of the same or very similar words (spelling conventions often differ) crossing national boundaries. The consequences of this complex situation are explored further on p. 362.

Headtie? headkerchief? something else?

LEXICAL COMPARISONS

The following words and glosses are taken from four articles on possible varieties of English in West Africa: in Sierra Leone (SL), The Gambia (GA), Ghana (GH), and Nigeria (N). The articles are very different in style and approach, so a proper comparison is not possible, but the exercise does show the methodological problems which have to be faced before decisions about varieties can be reached.

• There would be no problem if a word appeared in all four lists with exactly the same form and meaning. That would be convincing lexical evidence of a supranational variety. There are no instances of this.

• There are a few instances of words appearing in more than one list, with no change in form and apparently the same meaning (though there are points of possible significant contrast in the definitions):
chop food (SL, GA, GH)
delayance delay (SL, GH)
kola fruit used as a stimulant; a traditional symbol of friendship, social solidarity and 'legal' commitment; also bribery (GA); bribe (N)
lappa a large piece of cloth worn by women from around the waist down to the feet (SL); cloth used as a wraparound skirt (GA)
stranger guest (SL, N)

• Words which *seem* to be in more than one list, but there is a change in form and perhaps a change in meaning:
aunt a female friend of one's parents (SL); *anti* aunt (GA)
head tie a piece of cloth worn round the head by women (SL);
headtie headdress (N);
headkerchief a kind of scarf used by women to cover their hair (GH)

• Words which are in more than one list with a claimed change in meaning:
pepper soup a soup prepared with fresh meat and/or fish and a lot of pepper but usually no oil (SL); soup without meat or fish but high pepper content (N)

• The vast majority of words are in one list only, leaving it unclear whether the word is used in the other areas:
bush meat flesh of wild animals killed for food (GH)
compound house and fenced-in yard (GA)
danfo minibus (N)
next tomorrow the day after tomorrow (SL)
globe electric bulb (N)
palaba disagreeable situation; argument (GA)
rentage rent (SL)
sleeping cloth a piece of cloth of varying size which a person uses to cover himself when sleeping (GH)
slowly-slowly little by little (GA)
yellow fever traffic warden (N)

Thousands of lexicographic questions arise from such comparisons. Is *globe* used for an electric bulb in Ghana? Is a *danfo* a minibus in Sierra Leone? Until such questions are answered, the lexical identity of the region remains unclear. (For a phonological example, see p. 362.)
(After V. O. Awonusi, 1990; I. K. Gyasi, 1991; J. Pemagbi, 1989; E. B. Richmond, 1989.)

Broadening the perspective

The impression of shared distinctiveness described on p. 361 leads inevitably to the view that the different uses of English along the coast may all be manifestations of a single variety of (as it might be called) 'West African Vernacular English' (WAVE). This concept does not of course deny the existence of national or sub-national regional variation. It is only to be expected, according to this view, in much the same way as dialects are recognized within British or American English. But, the argument goes, if a sufficiently large number of the distinctive features observed in the various countries turn out to be held in common, then the idea of a supranational variety becomes plausible. Terms such as WAVE and 'Educated West African English' have been put forward as a way of capturing this commonality.

The argument, of course, cannot stop there. If the perspective is widened further, and East African uses of English are taken into account, other similarities can be noted. The same examples that have been used to illustrate WAVE in one article (e.g. the pluralizing of such nouns as *advices* and *furnitures*) have also been reported in a study of English in Zambia. A reduplicated form such as *quick-quick* ('very fast') in the West has an apparent analogue in *now-now* ('soon') in the East. Phonological changes such as the replacement of /θ/ and /ð/ by /t/ and /d/ are found on both sides of the continent, as are many of the vowel variants and the consequences of syllabic rhythm. Spelling pronunciations also appear to be universal: *houses* as /hɑʊsɪs/, *television* as /televɪʃn/, *limb* as /lɪmb/, *Christmas* as /krɪstmas/. Should this lead us to postulate a variety of 'African English'?

World Second Language English?

The argument continues inexorably, sucking in other parts of the world. It is the case that there are further points of similarity in the way English is used in Fiji, Singapore, and Papua New Guinea. And perhaps in all places where English is taught as a second language we shall find such similarities. Indeed, it would be surprising if it were not so. There are presumably certain idiosyncrasies in English, as in any language, which are likely to pose particular difficulty to learners, wherever it is taught, and it is perfectly possible that some of these difficulties could become institutionalized into local norms in more or less the same way. If so, then what we may eventually need to recognize is a super-supranational concept of World Second Language English, with regional variation arising chiefly from its contact with different native languages and cultures, and primarily reflected in a series of different lexicons.

There is a further dimension to this problem. How shall we cope with distinctive features which seem to cut across the divide between first and second language? For example, consonant cluster simplification (e.g. *wan* for *want*) is widespread both in second-language contexts, such as India, and in first-language contexts, such as some US English accents. It is possible that some of the features currently thought to be of local significance will eventually turn out to be non-standard universals. Is there a Universal Nonstandard English? But this is to engage in science-fiction linguistics. In our present state of knowledge, we are a long way from being in a position to choose between these large-scale scenarios and those where identity is focused upon individual nations. For the moment, the task is to broaden the empirical database of regional variation at a national level – but bearing these broader issues in mind, so that we can ask our empirical questions in the most useful way.

LUGGAGES?

Many nonstandard grammatical features are widely distributed among second-language Englishes. An example is the conversion of an uncountable to a countable noun (p. 209), as in *advices*, *furnitures*, and *luggages*. Such forms have been cited as typical of Nigeria, Singapore, India, and many other places. It is not difficult to see why. Countability is a 'tricky' area of English grammar, posing a problem apparently regardless of the learner's language background.

Several such topics are known to be problematic. For example, there is frequent use of a simplified tag-question (p. 299), in which the many possibilities of Standard English are reduced to a single, invariant form, such as *is it?* or *no?* The preposing of a noun phrase immediately followed by a pronoun (*That girl she's tall*) is recorded in Sri Lanka, Malaysia, Zambia, and elsewhere. The use of the progressive form with such verbs as *have* (*I am having two brothers*) is associated with India (p. 360), but is also cited in other countries, such as Ghana. Even an individual lexical item can vary in the same direction, as in the case of phrasal verbs: *cope up* for *cope* is recorded in Ghana, Kenya, Pakistan, and several other places. The absence of the third person singular ending (*She see me*) goes well beyond second-language use, being typical of creole languages (p. 344) and several dialects of British and American English.

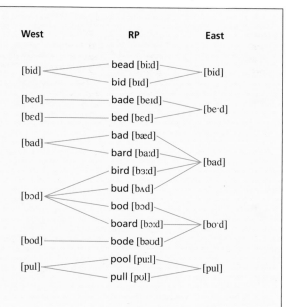

VOWEL COMPARISONS

This diagram proposes vowel systems (p. 238) for West and East African English, shown in relation to the vowels of Received Pronunciation (RP, p. 365). It appears that the two systems are very similar: there are several points of correspondence, notably in the close vowel area. At the same time, various contrasts and points of overlap are predicted, such as *bud* being typically pronounced as /bɔd/ in the West and as /bad/ in the East.

The co-existence of points of similarity and difference allows room for debate over whether we are dealing here with one variety or two. The differences seem to be greater than, say, those distinguishing RP and 'General' American English (p. 307). On the other hand, phonology alone is not a sufficient basis for variety identification. A reasonable decision can be made only when grammatical, lexical, and discourse variations are also systematically (as opposed to anecdotally) taken into account. Given the very large number of variables involved, progress towards this goal is inevitably going to be long-term. (After R. Angogo & I. Hancock, 1980.)

West	RP	East
[bid]	bead [biːd]	[bid]
	bid [bɪd]	
[bed]	bade [beɪd]	
[bɛd]	bed [bɛd]	[beˑd]
[bad]	bad [bæd]	
	bard [baːd]	[bad]
	bird [bɜːd]	
[bɔd]	bud [bʌd]	
	bod [bɔd]	
	board [bɔːd]	[boˑd]
[bod]	bode [bəʊd]	
[pul]	pool [puːl]	[pul]
	pull [pʊl]	

Back to the future

Although this chapter has ostensibly been about regional variation, it has repeatedly had to deal with social issues. A decade of research in sociolinguistics has now made it clear that only a small part of the world's English language variation can be accounted for purely in geographical terms. In addition, any social focus on regional varieties of English makes us re-examine the way we think about language in general. In particular, we are forced to question the apparently neat distinction between a 'first' and a 'second' language. There are several countries where population movement, language loss, divergent language attitudes, and massive shifts in language use have made it difficult to answer the question 'What is your first language?' A large number of people can even be described as 'semilingual', with an uncertain command of more than one language, and unclear as to which of them would best count as a 'mother tongue'. In multilingual countries, a clear distinction between a first language learned from one's parents and a second language learned in school is often difficult to maintain, as both processes may be taking place simultaneously.

The contemporary approach to regional language variety typifies this direction of thinking. The problem for the variety analyst is essentially this: if we encounter a speaker in some second-language country who uses a linguistic form (a word, a sound, a grammatical construction) not known in Standard English, how do we know that this is a genuine, stable feature of a local variety and not simply a casual error on that speaker's part, because of inadequate knowledge of English (p. 361)? One criterion, obviously, will be to see if other speakers use the form, but unless samples are large this does not eliminate the possibility that they may all be making the same error. A more important criterion will be to determine whether the form meets a real need, perhaps reflecting some aspect of the speaker's society (such as ethnic or national identity) which Standard English does not capture. Another will be to see whether it occurs in more formal contexts, such as the written language. Another will be to look at local attitudes to the word: if educated speakers in the community take it for granted, and use it themselves, it is much more likely to be a genuine variety feature than if they are conscious of it and stigmatize it. In each of these cases, we see the need for a broad sociolinguistic perspective.

One conclusion is plain, from the work which has been done to date: the answer to the question 'What are the constraints governing linguistic variation?' is much more complex than was first thought. But at least from these studies it is now much clearer what kinds of constraint are going to be worth investigating on a large scale. It is an important and exciting question to ask, because in answering it we may be seeing the future of the English language. Second language users in the world are increasing much more rapidly than are first language users. It is therefore possible that the kinds of changes we see taking place in the outer (and even the expanding) circle may one day be part of World Standard English.

EXTRATERRITORIAL

The question 'What is your first language?' often receives an interesting answer in the case of well-known writers. Vladimir Nabokov (1899–1977) is a case in point. He was born in Russia, moved to England in 1919, where he studied French and Russian literature, lived in Germany and France from 1922, and emigrated to the USA in 1940. He produced original work and translations in Russian, English, German, and French. The critic George Steiner sums up the 'polylinguistic matrix' of Nabokov's life in this way (in *Extraterritorial*, 1972, p. 7):

the political barbarism of the century made him an exile, a wanderer, a *Hotelmensch*, not only from his Russian homeland but from the matchless Russian tongue in which his genius would have found its unforced idiom… But, whereas so many other language exiles clung desperately to the artifice of their native tongue or fell silent, Nabokov moved into successive languages like a traveling potentate.

Such people, who are uprooted from their mother tongue, 'driven from language to language by social upheaval and war', Steiner characterizes as 'extraterritorial'. It would indeed be difficult to identify the 'first language' (in the sense of a language in which one feels most at home) of the mature Nabokov; and there are other writers, such as Samuel Beckett, who present similar uncertainties. Steiner argues that fluent literary bilingualism in such languages as Latin or French was in fact common in Western literature until the end of the 18th century. At an everyday level, extraterritoriality probably exists to an even greater extent in multilingual societies around the world.

WRITTEN EVIDENCE

The literature of a country often provides early evidence of the way stable features are emerging in a second-language variety. The beginning of Arthur Yap's dialogue poem '2 mothers in a hdb playground' (1981) captures several of the features of Singaporean English. (After J. Platt & K. Singh, 1984.)

ah beng is so smart
already he can watch tv & know the whole story.
your kim cheong is also quite smart
What boy is he in the exam?
this playground is not too bad, but i'm always
so worried, car here, car there.
at exam time it's worse
because you know why?

        kim cheong eats very little.

give him some complan. my ah beng was like that, now he's
different, if you give him anything he's sure to finish it all up.

sure, sure cheong's father buys him
vitamins but he keeps it inside his mouth
and later gives it to the cat.
i scold like mad but what for?
if i don't see it how can i scold?

on saturday, tv showed a new type,
special for children, why don't you call
his father buy some? maybe they are better…

hdb Housing Development Board
What boy is he What place did he get
complan a proprietary vitamin supplement [international]
why don't you call his father buy some? Why don't you ask his father to buy some?
his father your husband

21 · SOCIAL VARIATION

Regional language variation (§20) provides a geographical answer to the question 'Where are you from, in the English-speaking world?' Social language variation provides an answer to a somewhat different question: 'Who are you?' or 'What are you, in the eyes of the English-speaking society to which you belong?' Or rather, it provides several possible answers, because people acquire several identities as they participate in social structure. They belong to different social groups and perform different social roles. A person might be identified as 'a woman', 'a parent', 'a doctor', 'a husband', 'a failure', 'an apprentice', 'a drop-out', 'a lay reader', 'a political activist', 'a senior citizen', 'a *Times* reader', 'a member of the proletariat', 'a respected community leader', or in many other ways. Any of these identities can have consequences for the kind of language we use. Indeed, it is usually language – much more so than clothing, furnishing, or other externals – which is the chief signal of both permanent and transient aspects of our social identity.

Certain aspects of social variation seem to be of particular linguistic consequence. Age, sex, and socio-economic class have been repeatedly shown to be of importance when it comes to explaining the way sounds, constructions, and vocabulary vary (pp. 341, 350, 363). Choice of occupation has a less predictable influence, though in some contexts (such as the world of the law) it can be highly distinctive. Adopting a social role (such as chairing a meeting, or speaking at a wedding) invariably involves a choice of appropriate linguistic forms. And the presence of influential public institutions, such as the monarchy, the established Church, the civil service, broadcasting, and the press, has inevitably given rise to a popular notion of language authority, which can even become explicit through an official language policy.

In all of this, attitudes to social variation vary widely. All countries display social stratification, for example, though some have more clearly-defined class boundaries than others, and thus more identifiable features of class dialect. Britain is usually said to be linguistically much more class-conscious than other countries where English is used as a first language. A highly valued national literature may identify norms of achievement in language use towards which children are taught to aspire. And a particular set of historical circumstances (such as a strong system of privileged education) may make one country, or section of society, especially sensitive to language variation.

U AND NON-U

The most famous debate on the English language and social class took place in the 1950s, following the publication of an article on the subject by British linguist Alan Ross. The article distinguished 'U' (upper-class) usage from 'Non-U' (other kinds of) usage, in terms of its distinctive pronunciation, vocabulary, and written language conventions. It was an impressionistic but perceptive account, and it provoked an enormous public reaction. In 1956 Nancy Mitford edited a collection of light-hearted, satirical essays on the subject called *Noblesse Oblige*, which contained Ross's essay and contributions from herself, Evelyn Waugh, John Betjeman, and others. It went through three printings in a month. Here is Mitford's paraphrase of some of Ross's examples, one of Osbert Lancaster's cartoons from the book, and an endpiece by John Betjeman.

Nancy Mitford

Cycle is non-U against U *bike*.
Dinner: U-speakers eat *luncheon* in the middle of the day and *dinner* in the evening. Non-U speakers (also U-children and U-dogs) have their *dinner* in the middle of the day.
Greens is non-U for U *vegetables*.
Home: non-U – 'they have a lovely *home*'; U – 'they've a very nice *house*'.
Ill: 'I was *ill* on the boat' is non-U against U *sick*.
Mental: non-U for U *mad*.
Toilet paper: non-U for U *lavatory paper*.
Wealthy: non-U for U *rich*.

Modes of address, particularly those used for the nobility, have always been a bugbear to the non-U....Letters to ambassadors whom one does not know should begin *Dear Excellency* and the envelope should be addressed *H. E. The P – Ambassador*....
[In] writing letters to noblemen of very high rank, the rules laid down in the etiquette-books[1] need not always be strictly observed. Thus a Duke addressed by a stranger as *Dear Sir* would not necessarily conclude that his correspondent was non-U; he might be a left-wing gentleman with a dislike of dukedoms. (From A. S. C. Ross, 1956.)

[1] It is, of course, very non-U actually to consult these.

Should be addressed H.E.

HOW TO GET ON IN SOCIETY

Phone for the fish-knives, Norman,
　As Cook is a little unnerved;
You kiddies have crumpled the serviettes
　And I must have things daintily served.

Are the requisites all in the toilet?
　The frills round the cutlets can wait
Till the girl has replenished the cruets
　And switched on the logs in the grate.

It's ever so close in the lounge, dear,
　But the vestibule's comfy for tea,
And Howard is out riding on horseback
　So do come and take some with me.

Now here is a fork for your pastries
　And do use the couch for your feet;

I know what I wanted to ask you –
　Is trifle sufficient for sweet?

Milk and then just as it comes, dear?
I'm afraid the
　preserve's full of
　stones;
Beg pardon, I'm
　soiling the doilies
With afternoon
　tea-cakes and
　scones.

Sir John Betjeman

REQUIESCAT IN PACE?

In England, one accent has traditionally stood out above all others in its ability to convey associations of respectable social standing and a good education. This 'prestige' accent is known as *Received Pronunciation*, or *RP*. It is associated with the south-east, where most RP-speakers live or work, but it can be found anywhere in the country. Accents usually tell us where a person is from (p. 298); RP tells us only about a person's social or educational background.

The ancestral form of RP was well-established over 400 years ago as the accent of the court and the upper classes. The English courtier George Puttenham, writing in 1589, thought that the English 'of northern men, whether they be noblemen or gentlemen…is not so courtly or so current as our Southern English is'. Most people anxious for social advancement would move to London and adopt the accent they found there – though there are famous exceptions, such as Walter Raleigh, who held on to his Devonshire accent.

In due course, RP came to symbolize a person's high position in society. During the 19th century, it became the accent of the public schools, such as Eton and Harrow, and was soon the main sign that a speaker had received a good education. It spread rapidly throughout the Civil Service of the British Empire and the armed forces, and became the voice of authority and power. Because it was a regionally 'neutral' accent, and was thought to be more widely understood than any regional accent, it came to be adopted by the BBC when radio broadcasting began in the 1920s. During World War 2, it became linked in many minds with the voice of freedom, and the notion of a 'BBC pronunciation' grew.

The present-day situation

Today, with the breakdown of rigid divisions between social classes and the development of the mass media, RP is no longer the preserve of a social elite. It is best described as an 'educated' accent – though 'accents' would be more precise, for there are several varieties. The most widely used is that generally heard on the BBC; but there are also conservative and trend-setting forms. The former is found in many older establishment speakers. The latter is usually associated with certain social and professional groups – in particular, the voice of the London upwardly mobile (the 'Sloane Rangers') in the 1980s.

Early BBC recordings show how much RP has altered over just a few decades, and they make the point that no accent is immune to change, not even 'the best'. But the most important observation is that RP is no longer as widely used today as it was 50 years ago. It is still the standard accent of the Royal Family, Parliament, the Church of England, the High Courts, and other national institutions; but less than 3 per cent of the British people speak it in a pure form now. Most educated people have developed an accent which is a mixture of RP and various regional characteristics – 'modified RP', some call it. In some cases, a former RP speaker has been influenced by regional norms; in other cases a former regional speaker has moved in the direction of RP. The 'Estuary English' of the 1990s is a major trend in this respect (p. 327). Regionally modified speech is no longer stigmatized, as it was in Victorian times; it can be a plus feature, expressing such virtues as solidarity and 'down-to-earthness'. A pure RP accent, by contrast, can evoke hostility or suspicion, especially in those parts of Britain which have their own educated regional norms, such as Scotland and Wales.

Nonetheless RP retains considerable status. It has long been the chief accent taught to foreigners who wish to learn a British model, and is thus widely used abroad (by far more people, in fact, than have it as a mother-tongue accent in the UK). This in itself is somewhat surprising, as RP has several features which add to the difficulty of a foreign learner, compared with some regional accents (no /r/ after vowels, several subtly different diphthongs, p. 239). Most learners would find a Scots accent, for example, much easier to pick up. RP has also been valuable as a standard for linguistic research, having received many phonetic and phonological studies, and for convenience I have used it as the baseline for comparative judgments in this book.

But the wind of change is blowing down the estuaries of the world. As British English becomes increasingly a minor dialect of World English, as new second-language norms of pronunciation emerge, and as fewer British teachers of English as a foreign language come themselves to speak RP naturally, it is likely that the special world status accorded to RP in the past will diminish. It will be fascinating to see whether the Royal Family and the British establishment can continue to provide enough prestige to the accent to enable it to survive. It is difficult to see what might take its place, though the British press in 1993 were heralding Estuary English as a possible claimant (usurper, some would say) to the phonetic throne. Phoneticians have already observed glottalization (e.g. of final /t/ in *hot*) in the speech of younger members of the Royal Family. To some observers, this is a sure sign of the beginning of the end.

WHO FIRST CALLED IT RP?

The British phonetician Daniel Jones (p. 239) was the first to codify the properties of RP. It was not a label he much liked, as he explains in *An Outline of English Phonetics* (1918):

I do not consider it possible at the present time to regard any special type as 'Standard' or as intrinsically 'better' than other types. Nevertheless, the type described in this book is certainly a useful one. It is based on my own (Southern) speech, and is, as far as I can ascertain, that generally used by those who have been educated at 'preparatory' boarding schools and the 'Public Schools'….The term 'Received Pronunciation'…is often used to designate this type of pronunciation. This term is adopted here for want of a better. (1960, 9th edn, p. 12)

The historical linguist H. C. Wyld also made much use of the term 'received' in *A Short History of English* (1914):

It is proposed to use the term *Received Standard* for that form which all would probably agree in considering the best, that form which has the widest currency and is heard with practically no variation among speakers of the better class all over the country. (1927, 3rd edn, p. 149)

The previous usage to which Jones refers can be traced back to the dialectologist A. J. Ellis, in *On Early English Pronunciation* (1869):

In the present day we may, however, recognize a received pronunciation all over the country … It may be especially considered as the educated pronunciation of the metropolis, of the court, the pulpit, and the bar. (p. 23)

Even then, there were signs of the future, for he goes on to say:

But in as much as all these localities and professions are recruited from the provinces, there will be a varied thread of provincial utterance running through the whole.

PRESCRIPTIVE ATTITUDES

Prescriptivism is the view that one variety of a language has an inherently higher value than others, and that this ought to be imposed on the whole of the speech community. It is an authoritarian view, propounded especially in relation to grammar (p. 194) and vocabulary, and often with reference to pronunciation (p. 255). The favoured variety is usually a version of the standard written language, especially as encountered in literature, or in the formal spoken language which most closely reflects literary style, and it is presented in dictionaries, grammars, and other official manuals. Those who speak and write in this variety are said to be using language 'correctly'; those who do not are said to be using it 'incorrectly'.

The alternative to a prescriptive approach is the *descriptive* approach associated mainly with modern linguistics, and the one represented throughout this book. As the name suggests, its main aim is to describe and explain the patterns of usage which are found in all varieties of the language, whether they are socially prestigious or not. The approach also recognizes the fact that language is always changing, and that there will accordingly always be variation in usage. Linguists do not deny the social importance of the standard language, but they do not condemn as 'ugly', 'incorrect', or 'illogical' other dialects which do not share the same rules.

Correctness vs appropriateness

There is no difference between the two approaches when it comes to evaluating such cases as *langauge* or *cat the*. As all educated speakers agree that such uses are 'not English', there is no issue, and the notion of 'incorrect' is used happily by both sides. The problem arises only when educated people do *not* all use language in the same way, or when one person varies in usage on different occasions (such as in the case of informal vs formal speech). In these circumstances, linguists do not try to make a value judgment about whether one usage is better than the other. They feel that a notion of absolute correctness is inadequate to explain what is happening in such cases, and work instead with a notion of relative appropriateness – the suitability of a usage to a situation.

For example, any survey of the use of contracted forms (such as *it's*, *won't*) would show that they are widely acceptable in informal speech and writing, but are generally unacceptable in formal writing. Their acceptability evidently depends on the context in which they are used. In answer to the enquiry 'Is it all right to write *it's*?' a linguist would say 'It depends', and go on to explain the impression of informality it conveys, raising the question of whether informality is appropriate to the writing task being undertaken. The same perspective would apply to other examples of colloquial pronunciation, grammar, or vocabulary.

This position has worried those who are concerned with the maintenance of standards of usage. Linguists have been accused of 'not caring about correctness' and of 'getting rid of rules'. Such criticisms they strongly reject, pointing out that the whole thrust of modern linguistics has been to clarify questions of grammaticality, and to identify the structure of the rules which this notion involves. And, from a sociolinguistic perspective, the privileged place of Standard English also looms large – as in the present book.

PRESCRIPTIVE AND PROSCRIPTIVE

A distinction is often drawn between *prescriptive* rules, which recommend usages considered to be acceptable, and *proscriptive* rules, which recommend usages to be avoided ('do's and don'ts'). Popular advertisements for 'remedial' courses start with the latter and move on to the former. The proscriptions are typically illustrated in a speech bubble which contains several examples of usage shibboleths, or in a bold headline warning of the dangers which will befall you if swift action is not taken immediately.

YOUR FRIENDS CAN'T TELL YOU & YOUR BUSINESS ASSOCIATES WON'T
. . . what hampering speech mannerisms may be interfering with your social and financial success

YES   NO
☐   ☐   Are you ever caught in mistakes of grammar or vocabulary? This *instantly* shatters the opinions others may have formed of you based on your true capabilities.

IT'S (NOT) A LAUGHING MATTER

Prescriptive attitudes, because of their extremism, readily lend themselves to satirical treatment. Various 'rules for writing good' were being circulated among US English departments in the 1970s. This one (reprinted in *English Today*) is taken from *The Leaflet* (Fall, 1979), the journal of the New England Association of Teachers of English, identifying contentious issues in grammar, vocabulary, punctuation, and discourse (see also pp. 78, 194).

1 Every pronoun should agree with their antecedent.
2 People like you and I should have no problems with grammatical case.
3 Verbs in any essay has to agree with their subject.
4 It isn't good to be someone whom people realize confuse *who* and *whom*.
5 Nobody should never use double negatives.
6 A writer should not shift your point of view.
7 When writing, participles ought not to be dangled.
8 Join clauses good, like a good writer should.
9 Do not write run-on sentences, it is bad style.
10 Sentence fragments. Watch out for them.
11 In letters themes reports and the like use commas to separate items in a list.
12 If teachers have ever told you, that you don't put a comma before *that*, they were right.
13 Its essential to use apostrophe's properly.
14 You shouldn't abbrev.
15 Always check to see if you have anything out.
16 Take care to never seriously and purposefully split infinitives.
17 Never idly use a preposition to end a sentence with, because that is the kind of thing up with which no right-minded person will put.
18 In my own personal opinion I myself think that authors when they are writing should not persuade themselves that it is all right to use too many unnecessary words; the reason for this is because you should express yourself concisely.

Some people find lists of this kind very funny. Some do not appreciate the joke.

The concept of 'appropriateness' has itself been attacked, usually on the grounds that it is correctness 'in disguise'. However, there is a world of difference between the two concepts. In particular, appropriateness tries to capture a notion of *naturalness* in language use: an appropriate use of language is one which does not draw attention to itself, does not motivate criticism. Informal language on a formal occasion is inappropriate because it stands out, as does formal language on an informal occasion. Both regularly attract criticism, for this reason: the former is stigmatized in such terms as 'uneducated' or 'careless'; the latter as 'talking posh' or 'getting on a high horse'. The best uses of everyday language, by contrast, are those which do not draw attention to themselves, and where the structures do not get in the way of the meaning they are trying to convey. To say that a usage is 'appropriate' in a situation is only to say that it is performing this function satisfactorily.

Prescriptive attitudes play an important part in defining the educatedness of a society, and should not be glibly dismissed. In the case of English, they are the product of over 200 years of social history, and it is probably impossible for anyone to grow up in an English-speaking society without becoming sensitized to some of these attitudes. Even writers who are totally against linguistic pedantry have been known consciously to alter a word order, not because it produces a better style or clearer meaning, but because they feel that the result will be less likely to distract those among their readers who hold strongly prescriptive views. 'I am not in the business of antagonizing my readers', one such writer said, when asked why he had moved an *only* from one sentence position to another. 'It makes for a quieter life', said a radio announcer, in response to a question about his unnatural non-use of intrusive *r* (p. 245).

Probably most people hold a mixture of prescriptive and descriptive views. Linguist-parents have been heard telling off their child for using language they do not like. And prescriptivist-tourists have been heard admiring the properties of dialect nonstandard speech. What is often said to detract most from the prescriptive cause is the aggression with which its case is presented. Its language is invariably highly charged (p. 194), using the metaphors of conflict (defending the language, a battle lost), and strongly condemnatory. At such times, the watchword of 'eternal vigilance' becomes obscured by an apparently eternal intolerance. It is this, more than anything else, which has made linguists so critical of the prescriptive tradition.

EXPLOSIONS

Thomas Hardy (p. 88) was one who had no time for purist critics, especially those who attacked his use of dialect words. This is evident from the following explosion, reported in William Archer's *Real Conversations* (1904):

I have no sympathy with the criticism which would treat English as a dead language – a thing crystallized at an arbitrarily selected stage of its existence, and bidden to forget that it has a past and deny that it has a future. Purism, whether in grammar or in vocabulary, almost always means ignorance. Language was made before grammar, not grammar before language.

And Robert Graves, in *Good-Bye to All That* (1929, Ch. 28), reports a nice anecdote about Hardy which raises interesting questions about the authority of dictionaries (p. 442).

He regarded professional critics as parasites, no less noxious than autograph-hunters, wished the world rid of them, and also regretted having listened to them as a young man; on their advice he had cut out from his early poems dialect-words which possessed no ordinary English equivalents. And still the critics were plaguing him. One of them complained of a line: 'his shape smalled in the distance'. Now, what in the world else could he have written? Hardy then laughed a little. Once or twice recently he had looked up a word in the dictionary for fear of being again accused of coining, and found it there right enough – only to read on and discover that the sole authority quoted was himself in a half-forgotten novel!

Some critics have thought this story to be apocryphal, but it could very well be true, given that there are over a thousand citations from Hardy in the *Oxford English Dictionary*, many his own coinages.

GUILT

In §§201–2 of *The Queen's English* (1869), Henry Alford, Dean of Canterbury, tries to be judicious in his account of prepositions, but finds he cannot escape the metaphor of his own linguistic sinfulness. Feelings of guilt and inferiority are indeed the legacy of the prescriptive tradition – and not even the best-educated are exempt (p. 79).

There is a peculiar use of prepositions, which is allowable in moderation, but must not be too often resorted to. It is the placing them at the end of a sentence, as I have just done in the words 'resorted to;' as is done in the command, 'Let not your good be evil spoken of;' and continually in our discourse and writing.

The account to be given of this is, that the preposition, which the verb usually takes after it, is regarded as forming a part of the word itself. To *speak of*, to *resort to*, are hardly verbs and prepositions, but form in each case almost one word. But let us go on. 'Where do you come from?' is the only way of putting that inquiry. 'Whence come you?' is of course pedantic, though accurate. 'Where are you going to?' is exactly like the other questions, but here we usually drop the '*to*,' merely because the adverb of rest '*where*,' has come to be used for the adverb of motion '*whither*,' and therefore the '*to*' is not wanted. If a man chooses, as West-country men mostly do, to say 'Where are you going to?' he does not violate propriety, though he does violate custom. ... I know, in saying this, that I am at variance with the rules taught at very respectable institutions for enabling young ladies to talk unlike their elders; but this I cannot help; and I fear this is an offence of which I have been, and yet may be, very often guilty.

THE ULTIMATE PRESCRIPTIVISM

The proposed Eleventh Edition of the Newspeak Dictionary (p. 135) reflects the face of totalitarian prescriptivism. Syme, its editor, explains to Winston:

'The Eleventh Edition is the definitive edition,' he said. 'We're getting the language into its final shape – the shape it's going to have when nobody speaks anything else. When we've finished with it, people like you will have to learn it all over again. You think, I dare say, that our chief job is inventing new words. But not a bit of it! We're destroying words – scores of them, hundreds of them, every day. We're cutting the language down to the bone. The Eleventh Edition won't contain a single word that will become obsolete before the year 2050.'

He bit hungrily into his bread and swallowed a couple of mouthfuls, then continued speaking, with a sort of pedant's passion. His thin dark face had become animated, his eyes had lost their mocking expression and grown almost dreamy.

'It's a beautiful thing, the destruction of words. Of course the great wastage is in the verbs and adjectives, but there are hundreds of nouns that can be got rid of as well. It isn't only the synonyms; there are also the antonyms. After all, what justification is there for a word which is simply the opposite of some other word? A word contains its opposite in itself. Take 'good', for instance. If you have a word like 'good', what need is there for a word like 'bad'? 'Ungood' will do just as well – better, because it's an exact opposite, which the other is not. Or again, if you want a stronger version of 'good', what sense is there in having a whole string of vague useless words like 'excellent' and 'splendid' and all the rest of them? 'Plusgood' covers the meaning; or 'doubleplusgood' if you want something stronger still. Of course we use these forms already, but in the final version of Newspeak there'll be nothing else. In the end the whole notion of goodness and badness will be covered by only six words – in reality, only one word. Don't you see the beauty of that, Winston? It was B.B.'s idea originally, of course,' he added as an afterthought. (George Orwell, *Nineteen Eighty-Four*, pp. 44–5.)

GENDER ISSUES

Some of the most important linguistic changes affecting English since the 1960s have arisen from the way society has come to look differently at the practices and consequences of sexism (p. 177). There is now a widespread awareness, which was lacking a generation ago, of the way in which language covertly displays social attitudes towards men and women. The criticisms have been mainly directed at the biases built into English vocabulary and grammar which reflect a traditionally male-orientated view of the world, and which have been interpreted as reinforcing the low status of women in society. All of the main European languages have been affected, but English more than most, because of the early impact of the feminist movement in the USA.

In vocabulary, attention has been focused on the replacement of 'male' words with a generic meaning by neutral items – *chairman*, for example, becoming *chair* or *chairperson* (though not without controversy), or *salesman* becoming *sales assistant*. In certain cases, such as job descriptions, the use of sexually neutral language has become a legal requirement. There is continuing debate between extremists and moderates as to how far such revisions should go – whether they should affect traditional idioms such as *man in the street* and *Neanderthal Man*, or apply to parts of words where the male meaning of *man* is no longer dominant, such as *manhandle* and *woman*. The vocabulary of marital status has also been affected – notably in the introduction of *Ms* as a neutral alternative to *Miss* or *Mrs*.

In grammar, the focus has been on the lack of a sex-neutral third-person singular pronoun in English – a gap which becomes a problem after sex-neutral nouns (such as *student*) or indefinite pronouns (such as *somebody*). The difficulty can be seen in the following sentence, where the blanks would traditionally be filled by the pronouns *he* or *his*:

If a student loses – key, – should report the loss to the bursar.

To avoid the male bias, various alternatives have been suggested, but all have their critics. *He or she* or *she or he* is sometimes used, but this is often felt to be stylistically awkward. In writing, forms such as *(s)he* can be convenient, but this device does not help with *his* or *him*. In informal speech, *they* is widespread after such words as *anyone*, but this usage attracts criticism from those who feel that a plural word should not be made to refer back to a singular one (p. 221). Many writers therefore choose to recast their sentence structure to avoid the problem, for example by turning the singular noun into a plural (*If students lose their key …*). A radical solution, so far unsuccessful, is to invent a completely new pronoun to act as a neutral third person.

NEW PRONOUNS

None of the proposals for a neutral third-person pronoun has attracted much support, though some have had a lease of life in novels and communes.

co (cos, coself), E (*objective* Ir), et (etself), heesh, hesh, hir, hirm, hizer, ho, jhe /ʒiː/, mon, na, ne, person (*in short*, per), po, tey, thon (thons, thonself), xe /ʃeɪ/

DISCOURSE PATTERNS

There is much more to sexist language than single lexical items and isolated grammatical constructions. It involves such considerations as order of mention (**I now pronounce you wife and man*) and worthiness of mention (**Five people were involved in the incident, including two men*). And analysis may reveal a whole framework of thought and belief in operation, often so deep-rooted that it remains unquestioned by females and males alike.

This last prospect is most clearly demonstrated in the language of religion, where a male-dominated conception of God has been handed down from patriarchal times. Along with it has come the attributes which are stereotypically associated with men, such as toughness, coolness, and authority. Missing are attributes such as caring and weeping. God, it seems, could not possibly cry for a lost creation.

British hymn writer and minister Brian Wren has attempted to subvert some of these traditional attitudes by inverting them. 'Bring many Names' (1989) is one of his hymns in which the words reverse the expected stereotypes and introduce fresh resonances and collocations (p. 160).

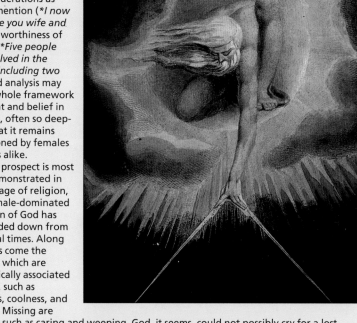

Bring many names, beautiful and good;
celebrate, in parable and story,
　　holiness in glory,
　　living, loving God.
Hail and Hosanna,
bring many names!

Strong mother God, working night and
　　day,
planning all the wonders of creation,
　　setting each equation,
　　genius at play:
Hail and Hosanna,
strong mother God!

Warm father God, hugging every child,
feeling all the strains of human living,
　　caring and forgiving
　　till we're reconciled:
Hail and Hosanna,
warm father God!

Old, aching God, grey with endless care,
calmly piercing evil's new disguises,
　　glad of good surprises,
　　wiser than despair:
Hail and Hosanna,
old, aching God!

Young, growing God, eager still to know,
willing to be changed by what you've
　　started,
　　quick to be delighted,
　　singing as you go:
Hail and Hosanna,
young, growing God!

Great, living God, never fully known,
joyful darkness far beyond our seeing,
　　closer yet than breathing,
　　everlasting home:
Hail and Hosanna,
great, living God!

THE SPEED OF CHANGE

The linguistic effect of these changes in social attitudes has been far more noticeable in writing than in speech – and in certain kinds of writing, in particular. One study (R. L. Cooper, 1984) compared the frequency with which such forms as *he* and *man* were used in half a million words of American English between 1971 and 1979: the frequency fell from around 12 per 5,000 words to around 4 per 5,000 words during that period. Women's magazines showed the steepest decline, followed by science magazines, with newspapers further behind, and congressional records last of all. The trend is likely to continue, and become more pervasive. Publishing companies now usually issue guidelines recommending that authors should avoid sexist language, as do several national bodies.

It will take much longer before we can say whether these changes are having any real impact on the spoken language, with its greater spontaneity. There are conscious controls available for the written language (drafting, re-reading, editing) which are not options in the rush of conversational speech (p. 291). No one knows how long it takes for spoken language to respond to fresh social pressures so that a new usage becomes automatic throughout a community. There are no precedents for the amount of public attention which has been paid to this area of usage, and it is therefore not possible to extrapolate from previous experience of language change. But it is certainly unusual to find a change of such magnitude (affecting an area of grammar, such as the pronoun system) making itself manifest in written language to such an extent within a generation. Until the 1960s, after all, the pronoun system had changed little since Middle English.

EDITING LANGUAGE CHANGE

Several studies suggest that editorial policy is an important element in language change. An example is the way newspapers refer to people by name. If the headline were *Jane/John Smith fights back*, what would the next reference to the person be? There are five possibilities.

• It could use a title: *Ms/Miss/Mrs/Mr Smith said...*
• It could be by their first name: *Jane/John said...*
• It could be by the last name: *Smith said...*
• It could repeat the whole name: *Jane/John Smith said...*
• It could be by a replacement phrase, such as a description or a nickname: *The tall auburn-haired doctor said...*

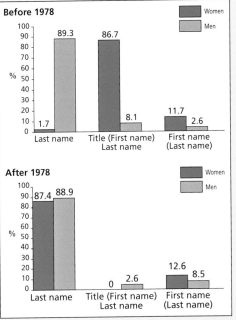

A study of usage over a 20-year period (1966–86) in *The New York Times* and *The Washington Post* saw an important change in editorial practice. In 1978, *The Washington Post* style manual decided that last names alone were to be used as the second reference for both men and women – the third option above. Previously, the use of titles had been by far the commonest way of referring to women. However, after 1978 titled forms totally disappear from the newspaper. The effect of the new policy was immediate. (After R. Fasold, 1987.)

Style manuals do not cover everything, but only what their authors perceive to be the most important patterns. Would a change in editorial policy such as the above have an effect on areas of usage that were not mentioned in the manual? One study examined a minor pattern which was not the subject of an explicit rule: the use of a middle initial in a person's name. Prominent American men are typically identified, on first reference, by a full name including a middle initial; this is much less likely with prominent women. The use of the initial evidently makes an impression of importance: *James H. Smith* sounds more authoritative than *James Smith*. However, after the publication of the style manual the use of middle initials became more equal, even though there was no general policy drawing attention to it. As reporters and editors are unlikely to be conscious of the sociolinguistic significance of this minor feature of usage, the fact that they changed their practices suggests that language planning policy decisions can have a general effect on language awareness. (After R. Fasold, *et al.*, 1990.)

GUIDELINES FOR NONSEXIST USAGE

Many organizations now issue guidelines to their staff on how to avoid sexist language. The following points are adapted from the set of recommendations issued in 1992 to its members by one organization which ought to be among the best-informed on these matters: the Linguistic Society of America. Of particular interest is the way sexist considerations can enter into the use of linguistic examples.

• Avoid so-called masculine generics such as the pronoun *he* with sex-indefinite antecedents or *man* and its compounds (except in unambiguous reference to males).
• Avoid using genuine generics as if they referred only to males (e.g. *Americans use lots of obscenities but not around women*).
• Avoid adding modifiers or suffixes to nouns to mark sex of referents unnecessarily. Such usage promotes continued sexual stereotyping in one of two ways: by highlighting referent sex, modification can signal a general presupposition that referents will be of the other sex (*lady professor, male secretary*), and thus that these referents are aberrant; and conventionalized gender-marking 'naturalizes' the presumptive or unmarked sex of the noun's referents (*stewardess, cleaning lady*).
• Use parallel forms of reference for women and men, e.g. do not cite a male scholar by surname only and a female scholar by first name plus surname.
• Avoid gender stereotyped or demeaning characterizations, e.g. presenting men as actors and women as passive recipients of others' actions. Men are frequently the agents, women the recipients, of violent acts. We recommend that the portrayal of violent acts be avoided altogether, regardless of the sex or species of participants.

The verb *kiss* is sometimes employed as an alternative to verbs which refer to more violent acts; this use, combined with sexist practices in naming participants, results in heterosexist bias as well as sexist bias, e.g. *All the boys kissed Mary*.
• Avoid peopling your examples exclusively with one sex.
• Avoid consistently putting reference to males before reference to females. Not only does this order convey male precedence, in English it will put males in subject position and women in object position.
• Avoid sexist (or otherwise derogatory) content in examples (e.g. *The man who beats his mistress will regret it sooner than the man who beats his wife*).
• Ask yourself whether you have remembered to cite or acknowledge women as well as men whose own research is relevant or whose comments may have helped you. Given traditional views of men's and women's place in intellectual endeavour, there is a danger that ideas advanced by women and adopted by men will be remembered as having originated with men, and that more generally women's intellectual contributions will tend to be underestimated.

OCCUPATIONAL VARIETIES

The term 'occupational dialect' has long been used for the distinctive language associated with a particular way of earning a living. However, such varieties are not like regional or class dialects. Features of language which identify our geographical or social origins, once established, tend not to vary, unless affected by major currents of language change (p. 298). It is very difficult, after moving from one part of a country to another, to change our accent or dialect so as to identify with our new neighbours; and, should we wish to do so, it is even more difficult to change the linguistic indicators of our social background (p. 364).

Occupational varieties of language are not like that. Their linguistic features may be just as distinctive as regional or class features, but they are only in temporary use. They are 'part of the job' – taken up as we begin work, and put down as we end it. The notion, of course, has to allow for people who are 'always on the job' – whose work is so much a part of their personality that it permanently influences their behaviour, linguistically as well as socially. Several of Dickens's characters (p. 89), for example, fall into this category, and it is their propensity to act in this way which is part of his satire. But mostly, when we stop work, we stop using the language of work. To do otherwise (at a party, for instance) usually carries with it an apology – for 'talking shop'.

Any domain could be used to illustrate occupational linguistic distinctiveness, or identity. There are no class distinctions here. Factory workers have to master an array of technical terms and administrative vocabulary (safety regulations, seniority labels, trade union guidelines) in order to carry out their tasks, and in so doing they develop slang and jargon which set them apart from outsiders. The more specialized the occupation, and the more senior or professional the post, the more technical the language is likely to be. Also, the more an occupation is part of a long-established tradition, the more it is likely to have accreted linguistic rituals which its members accept as a criterion of performance. The highly distinctive languages of religion, the law, and central government provide the clearest cases, with grammar, vocabulary, and patterns of discourse affected in far-reaching ways. However, all occupations are linguistically distinctive to some degree, even if all that is involved is a few items of specialized vocabulary. The following pages illustrate the range of distinctiveness which can be found, and presents some of the issues raised by different kinds of occupational language use.

LEXICAL IDENTITY

At its simplest, an occupation can be identified solely by its lexicon (p. 174), as can be seen from this selection of words to do with coal mining, collected in 1849. The list shows how an occupational lexicon is a product of its time: many of the items are no longer current. It also illustrates the way the dimension of occupational distinctiveness interacts with other dimensions of language use. The anonymous author calls his collection 'A glossary of terms used in the coal trade of Northumberland and Durham', suggesting thereby that this is an industry whose vocabulary is prone to regional variation.

barrow-way The way along which the barrow-men put the corves or tubs of coals.
beans A description of small coals, so called from their size.
beater An iron rod, used for stemming or tamping a hole, preparatory to blasting.

bind To hire.
blower A fissure in the roof, floor, or side of a mine, from which a feeder of inflammable air discharges.
boll A coal measure. The coal boll contains 9678.8 cubic inches.
cage A frame of iron which works between slides in a shaft.
cash A soft band.
cathead An ironstone ball.
chaldron The Newcastle chaldron is a measure containing 53 cwt. of coals.
changer and grather A man whose province is to keep the buckets in order, and to change them when necessary.

The notion of occupational variety is not restricted to paid employment: it also includes sports, games, hobbies, character-building, and other types of group activity. Hierarchy is implicit in all occupational groups (in such notions as trainer vs trainee or authority vs neophyte), and this is reflected in the lexicon (p. 118), as can be seen in this diagram listing the terms for non-adult members of the international scout and guide movement in the early 1980s. Age divisions are approximate. Regional dialect variation is apparent.

There is an interesting lexical gap in the third column, where a paraphrase such as 'member of the Boy Scouts of America' has to be used as a heading. The *Language of Scouting* (1981) explicitly points out that a *Boy Scout* is essentially a youth member of a Boy Scout troop, and that on second reference or in informal use the term *Scout* remains its synonym. *Boy* in this context is also semantically more restricted than usual, as all the four lowest age groups have only boys as members. The reason is historical: *boy scouts* was the name used for the original group in US scouting in 1910, and when groups for younger and older boys were added, the name of this first age-group was kept. (After S. Jacobson, 1985.)

		British		American	
		The Scout Association	**The Girl Guides Association**	**Boy Scouts of America**	**Girl Scouts of the United States of America**
Superordinate term		Scout	Guide	—	Girl Scout
Approximate age	6	Beaver		Tiger Cub	Brownie Girl Scout
	7		Brownie Guide		
	8	Cub Scout		Cub Scout	
	9			Webelos Scout[1]	Junior Girl Scout
	10				
	11	Scout	Guide	Boy Scout	Cadette Girl Scout
	12				
	13				
	14				
	15		Ranger Guide	Varsity Scout	Senior Girl Scout
	16	Venture Scout			
	17				
	18			Explorer	Campus Girl Scout
	19				
	20				
	21				

[1] Originally a term, used adjectivally, based on the initial letters of *wolf, bear, lion,* and *scout,* but now short for 'We'll Be Loyal Scouts' (the rank of *lion* having been discontinued in 1967).

RELIGIOUS ENGLISH

By contrast with the lexically distinctive uses of English shown on the opposite page, religious belief fosters a variety in which all aspects of structure are implicated. There is a unique phonological identity in such genres as spoken prayers, sermons, chants, and litanies, including the unusual case of unison speech (p. 297). Graphological identity is found in liturgical leaflets, catechisms, biblical texts, and many other religious publications. There is a strong grammatical identity in invocations, prayers, blessings, and other ritual forms, both public and private. An obvious lexical identity pervades formal articles of faith and scriptural texts, with the lexicon of doctrine informing the whole of religious expression. And there is a highly distinctive discourse identity in such domains as liturgical services, preaching, and rites of passage (e.g. baptisms, weddings, funerals).

Religious English, in short, is probably the most distinctive of all occupational varieties. There are three main reasons.

• It is consciously retrospective, in the way it constantly harks back to its origins, and thus to earlier periods of the English language (or of other languages). People set great store by the accurate and acceptable transmission of their beliefs. Only legal English (p. 374) resembles it in the way texts are subjected to disciplined and periodic reinterpretation.

• It is consciously prescriptive, concerned with issues of orthodoxy and identity, both textual and ritual. This is a reflex of English-language religious history since the Reformation.

• It is consciously imaginative and exploratory, as people make their personal response to the claims of religious belief. These responses range from the highly structured to the totally unpredictable, and from the voluble to the silent. The contrasts can be seen in the tightly structured unison responses of the Roman Catholic Mass, the spontaneous loudness of a pentecostal celebration, and the quiet and meditative atmosphere of a Quaker meeting for worship, fuelled by their founder's admonition: 'let your words be few'.

Commentators on style often point to similarities between religious and legal English – notably in the way historical tradition has sanctioned the use of archaism (p. 185) and ritual dialogue. But the mix of historical and contemporary factors which is found in religion produces an occupational variety that has far more formally identifiable subvarieties than any other use of English.

THE SOUND AND THE FURY

Because of the distinctive character of religious language, and its important place in the history of English, features of this variety have been illustrated in other sections of this book: biblical translation (pp. 59, 64), theological language (p. 403), prayers (p. 163), and hymns (p. 368). A further genre which is highly distinctive, especially in its prosody (p. 248) and use of formulae, is the highly rhetorical, spontaneously composed sermon, heard especially in black Baptist communities within the USA.

The extract from one such sermon, given by the Rev. D. J. McDowell in 1967, shows the oral formulaic character of this genre. There are in fact two main types of formula illustrated: quotations (shown in bold) and the preacher's own verbatim expressions (shown in italics). This preacher has an especially repetitive style: the phrase *The Christ of the Bible* is used 24 times throughout, and *Am I right about it* 15 times – frequent indeed, given that the text of the whole sermon, in this transcription, is only 350 lines long.

The transcription makes use of line breaks which convey the strongly metrical character of the rhythm. It does however exclude the continuous vocal reactions of the emotionally charged congregation. A famous literary example of this genre is to be found in William Faulkner's novel, *The Sound and the Fury* (1946, pp. 310–13). (After B. A. Rosenberg, 1970.)

Keep your hand in God's hand
And your eyes on the starposts in glory
Lord said he would fight your battles
If you'd only be still
You may not be a florist
Am I right about it?
But you must tell them, **that He's the Rose of Sharon**
I know that's right
You may not be a geologist
But you must tell them, **that he's the Rock of Ages**
I know that's right
You may not be a physician
But you must tell them, **that He's the great Physician**
You may not be a baker
But you must tell them, **that He's the Bread of Life**
Am I right about it?
You must tell them
That He's a friend
That stick close t'his brother
He said, 'I'll not cast ya out
In the sixth hour, and in the seventh hour
I didn't know I was turnin' ya out'
If y'keep your hand in God's hand.

A musical transcription of a fragment from this genre of sermon, showing the wide pitch range (p. 248) used by the preacher. With such intonational movement, the speech is almost better described as chant or song.

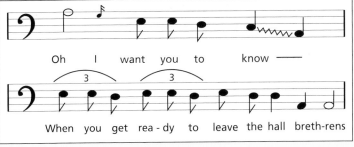

Oh   I   want   you   to   know ——
When   you   get   rea - dy   to   leave   the   hall   breth-rens

SCIENTIFIC ENGLISH

First impressions of the language of science are that its distinctiveness lies in its lexicon. The sheer quantity of technical terms makes this unavoidable: scientific nomenclature comprises most of the English vocabulary (p. 119), and no one understands more than a fragment of it. But this situation should not lead us to ignore the grammatical features of scientific expression. It is possible to grasp the vocabulary of an area of scientific enquiry, yet still have a major difficulty in comprehension because of the way the sentences and discourse have been structured.

DIAGNOSING PLANTS

The bulk of English scientific vocabulary stems from the millions of nameable entities in the field of biology, and the various branches of this science have evolved codes of practice to promote naming consistency. For example, the International Code of Botanical Nomenclature (first published as such in 1952) presents practitioners of this subject with a series of principles, stressing the importance of having only one official name for each type of plant or taxonomic group and avoiding the use of the same name for different plants or groups. Latin is the accepted official language of botanical nomenclature. As with other biological areas, the name of a species is a binary combination of the generic name plus a distinguishing epithet, such as *Fatsia japonica*. However, a large number of terms have come into English as part of a plant's description (an account of its habit, morphology, and periodicity) and diagnosis (an account of its defining features). The figure shows one such set: the chief terms used for describing leaf shapes. (After D. Gledhill, 1989.)

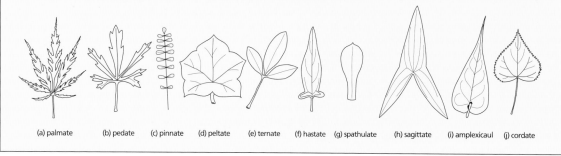

(a) palmate   (b) pedate   (c) pinnate   (d) peltate   (e) ternate   (f) hastate   (g) spathulate   (h) sagittate   (i) amplexicaul   (j) cordate

SOME GRAMMATICAL FEATURES OF SCIENTIFIC ENGLISH

The extract below is from an article in neurolinguistics, chosen because its subject-matter is to do with language (and thus of relevance to the present book) at a point where the issues are anatomical and technological (and thus unfamiliar to all, bar specialists). It is also selected as an example of international scientific English (its authors are French), processed in an English-language journal, and thus likely to avoid stylistic idiosyncrasy.

The paragraph illustrates several features typical of the grammar of scientific English (see Part III for terminology), as well as some lexical characteristics (abbreviations, numerals, special symbols, etc.). The style is lexically quite dense: 62 per cent of the words are lexical (*measured, regional, CBF*, etc.), and only 38 per cent are grammatical (*we, the, during*, etc.). (Compare the much lower figure for the extract on p. 373.) Figure 1 (not shown here) presents visually the information in the second half of the paragraph.

• The style is fairly typical of academic scientific writing.

There are 12 sentences, with a mean of 22.2 words. Sentences range from 8 to 50 words.

• The extract begins with *we*, but this is anomalous within the article as a whole, which uses an impersonal style in over 99 per cent of its clauses. The norm here is the passive, used in two-thirds of the sentences – a widely-quoted stereotype of scientific English syntax (p. 225, but see facing page for another view).

• Noun phrases with complex structure are usual, as in *a transparent removable alignment grid for drawing external landmarks on the skin*.

• There is a compactness of structure, illustrated by the use of parentheses, and the descriptive succinctness of the third sentence.

• There are no features of narrative style, such as sentence-connecting items (e.g. *however, secondly*). The logic governing the order of topics is not supported by linguistic sequencing features (apart from the anaphoric use of *the*, p. 223).

PARTIALLY DISASSEMBLE…

A particularly important aspect of scientific and technological language is the subject-neutral vocabulary which cuts across different specialized domains. In particular, a great deal of scientific work involves giving instructions to act in a certain way, or reporting on the consequences of having so acted. Several lexical categories can be identified within the 'language' of scientific instruction and narrative.

• *Verbs of exposition*: ascertain, assume, compare, construct, describe, determine, estimate, examine, explain, label, plot, record, test, verify

• *Verbs of warning and advising*: avoid, check, ensure, notice, prevent, remember, take care; *also several negative items*: not drop, not spill.

• *Verbs of manipulation*: adjust, align, assemble, begin, boil, clamp, connect, cover, decrease, dilute, extract, fill, immerse, mix, prepare, release, rotate, switch on, take, weigh

• *Adjectival modifiers (and their related adverbs)*: careful(ly), clockwise, continuous(ly), final(ly), gradual(ly), moderate(ly), periodic(ally), secure(ly), subsequent(ly), vertical(ly)

CBF Measurement

We measured the regional CBF during each of the experimental conditions, on the same day, with a 60–75 min interval between measurements. The CBF was assessed using a single photon tomograph (TOMOMATIC 64, Medimatic, Copenhagen) and intravenous injection of Xenon 133 (2200 MBeq). Data were collected from three transverse slices, each of 2 cm thickness, parallel and centred at 1, 5 and 9 cm above the orbito-meatal plane respectively. The in-plane resolution was about 1.7 cm FWHM. During the 4 min data collection PCO_2 was continuously monitored using a cutaneous electrode and a Kontron 634 PCO_2 monitor. The CBF was calculated according to the Celcis *et al.* (1981) algorithm. Correct repositioning of the head was obtained using a transparent removable alignment grid for drawing external landmarks on the skin. Mean CBF was calculated in 20 regions of interest (ROI) by means of pre-definite templates based on anatomical considerations, whose size and localization were adapted to each subject using a custom-made interactive software on a Macintosh II microcomputer with colour monitor. The 20 regions are illustrated in Fig. 1. The two regions in slice 1 (OM + 1 cm) corresponded to the left and right cerebellum. The 16 regions of the mid slice (OM + 5) were labelled as the left and right medial–frontal, anterior–middle frontal, posterior–inferior frontal, superior–middle temporal, posterior temporal–occipital, and medial occipital regions for the cortical rim, and as the left and right lenticular and thalamus subcortical regions. The two regions in the OM + 9 cm slice were labelled as left and right superior frontal–parietal regions. (From P. Celcis, *et al.*, 1991, p. 256.)

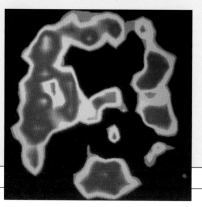

This photograph gives an indication of what the article is about. It is a map of the cerebral blood flow (CBF) seen during a brain scan of one of the subjects in the study. We are looking down on the subject, with the front of the head at the top. The subject was being asked to remember a series of words presented in a list. The map clearly shows the extra activity of several regions of the left hemisphere, indicating its special role in verbal memory tasks.

CLARIFYING CLARITY

When less usual patterns of grammatical structure combine with a high proportion of technical vocabulary, as is often the case in occupational varieties of English, the result is a sharp increase in comprehension difficulty. This is seen most commonly with the language of science, because the breadth of scientific enquiry, with its applications in such domains as medicine and engineering, makes its concerns of daily relevance to millions. When scientific narrative is presented to the general public by professional scientists, it is widely criticized for opaqueness and impenetrability. The persistence of this problem has led to various remedial measures, in the form of science journalism, general reference books (such as this encyclopedia), and communication-aware organizations (such as the Media Resource Service, launched in London in 1985). But, from time to time, science regularly surprises everyone by producing acclaimed exceptions of its own.

Stephen Hawking ▶

TIME UNRAVELLING

One of the best-selling scientific books of the 1980s was Stephen Hawking's *A Brief History of Time*, which was widely commended for the clarity with which it expounded fundamental ideas in 20th-century physics. One reader commented: 'I feel nearer to understanding these matters now than I ever thought I would'. Another said: 'I still haven't fully grasped it, but I feel it's my fault rather than his'. So what is it that makes scientific material, although challenging in content, seem easy to read?

The answer lies in its grammatical and discourse structure. A linguistic analysis by Helen Jenkins of Chapter 4 of the book brought to light a number of central features of textual structure showing Hawking's ability to present his argument transparently and coherently, distributing its information content in ways which make it seem accessible and digestible. Here are some of them. (A comparison should be made with the science text on the facing page.)

Discourse structure
• There is a balance between abstract and concrete points. General discussion alternates with accounts of experiments.
• The problems are explained as they arose over time. We are told how the thinking developed, and seem to learn along with the author.
• The text is visually manageable: Chapter 4 consists of 14 paragraphs, ranging in length from 3 to no more than 12 sentences.
• Most paragraphs begin with a general thematic point, and later sentences elaborate. The theme of the next paragraph then derives from the previous one's elaboration.
• The same tendency is seen in sentences: a new element at the end of one sentence is often picked up as a given element at the beginning of the next (see below: *... one quantum. This quantum ...*)
• The relations between sentences and clauses are often made explicit through the use of connectives (*now, however, so*, etc.). Two out of five sentences are linked in this way.
• Two out of three sentences have a cross-reference back to a preceding sentence or clause (as in the repeated use of *the particle* below). This makes it clear that a given topic is still being discussed, and reduces the scope for vagueness.

Sentence structure
• Chapter 4 has 2,796 words in 11 sentences, a mean of 25.2. Sentences range from 7 to 52 words. This is typical of academic writing. The text on the facing page has in fact a shorter sentence mean. The clarity does not reside here.

• Clauses have short subjects, with most of the information left until after the verb. Such sentences are much easier to understand than the alternative. Compare a recast version of the first sentence below: *The observed rate of emission of radiation from hot bodies is very well explained by the quantum hypothesis.*
• Points of contrast are rhetorically balanced, using such devices as *the more... the less* (see // below).
• Over half the noun phrases consist of a simple determiner plus noun (e.g. *the particle*) or a pronoun alone. There are no strings of the type *low-background, high-sensitivity neutron detectors*, as there are in the article illustrated opposite.
• The other noun phrases are also uncomplicated, typically either compounds (*quantum mechanics, X rays*) or using nontechnical modifiers (*a fundamental, inescapable property of the world*).
• Knowledge of technical terms is not presupposed. In introducing new terms, familiar notions tend to precede new ones (*in certain packets that he called quanta*).
• The passive construction (p. 225) is usually condemned in scientific writing, but 17 per cent of the verb phrases in this chapter are passive (e.g. *were not realized*). The passive can evidently be a helpful way of ensuring a smooth flow of ideas, and is important in allowing objects to receive prominence within clause structure (*Some of the waves of light will be scattered...*).

Lexical density
• The number of items with 'full' lexical meaning (as opposed to grammatical words and other 'empty' forms, p. 372) is relatively low: 48 per cent of all words in the chapter. There are few lexically dense sentences (as in the first sentence below), and many which are lexically light (as in the last). In the extract opposite, the proportion is much higher. (After H. R. Jenkins, 1992.)

Connective	Subject (Theme)	Predicate
	The quantum hypothesis	explained the observed rate of emission of radiation from hot bodies very well,
but	its implications for determinism	were not realized until 1926,
when	another German scientist, Werner Heisenberg	formulated his famous uncertainty principle.
In order to		predict the future position and velocity of a particle
	one	has to be able to measure its present position and velocity accurately.
	The obvious way to do this	is to shine light on the particle.
	Some of the waves of light	will be scattered by the particle
and	this	will indicate its position.
However,	one	will not be able to determine the position of the particle more accurately than the distance between the wave crests of light,
so	one	needs to use light of a short wavelength
in order to		measure the position of the particle precisely.
Now,	by Planck's quantum hypothesis, one	cannot use an arbitrarily small amount of light;
	one	has to use at least one quantum.
	This quantum	will disturb the particle and change its velocity in a way that cannot be predicted.
Moreover,	the more accurately one measures the position // the shorter the wavelength of the light that one needs	
and hence	// the higher the energy of a single quantum.	
So	the velocity of the particle	will be disturbed by a larger amount.
In other words,	the more accurately you try to measure the position of the particle,	
	// the less accurately you can measure its speed,	
and	// vice versa.	

LEGAL ENGLISH

Legal language has a great deal in common with the two varieties already reviewed in this section. It shares with science (p. 372) a concern for coherence and precision; and it shares with religion (p. 371) a respect for ritual and historical tradition. It also shares in the criticisms which these other varieties attract: like science, it is cautioned for its impenetrability; like religion, it is thought wilful in its mystique. Any campaign for Plain English (p. 176) will find much of its fuel here.

The goal of a simplified, universally intelligible legal English has an undeniable appeal, but it has to be pursued wisely if the results are not to raise more problems than they solve. A blanket condemnation of legal language is naive, in that it fails to appreciate what such language has to do if it is to function efficiently in the service of the community. Equally, there are no grounds for blanket acceptance.

Some functions of legal language

Legal language is always being pulled in different directions. Its statements have to be so phrased that we can see their general applicability, yet be specific enough to apply to individual circumstances. They have to be stable enough to stand the test of time, so that cases will be treated consistently and fairly, yet flexible enough to adapt to new social situations. Above all, they have to be expressed in such a way that people can be certain about the intention of the law respecting their rights and duties. No other variety of language has to carry such a responsibility.

That is why legal language has developed such a complex grammatical structure. It has lengthy sentences, because it tries to integrate several relevant issues in a single statement. It is repetitive, because it needs to make clear whether a new point applies to everything which has previously been said or just to a part of it. It goes in for coordinated phrases and long lists of items (*debts, dues, bills, accounts, reckonings…*), in order to reduce the uncertainty about whether the law applies in a particular case.

Legal language depends a great deal on a fairly small set of grammatical and lexical features. For example, modal verbs (e.g. *must, shall, may*, p. 212) distinguish between obligation and discretion. Pronouns (e.g. *all, whoever*) and generic nouns (hypernyms, e.g. *vehicle, person*, p. 166) help to foster a law's general applicability. Certainty can be promoted by explicitly listing specific items (hyponyms): if a law concerns a particular category (such as birds), then its provisions may need to say what counts as a member of that category (does *bird* include *ostrich*, which does not fly?). More than any other variety, legal language has to impose order on the fuzziness of the English lexicon (p. 169).

FOR ETERNITY

Sir William Blackstone (1723–80), whose *Commentaries on the Laws of England* (1765–9) was the first comprehensive description of the principles of English law. Two of his observations place the scope of legal language in its proper perspective.

An Act of Parliament is the exercise of the highest authority that this kingdom acknowledges on earth. It hath power to bind every subject in the land, and the dominions thereunto belonging: nay, even the King himself if particularly named therein. And it cannot be altered, amended, dispensed with, suspended or repealed, but in the same forms and by the same authority of parliament.

What is generally denominated legal language is in reality a mere technical language, calculated for eternal duration and easy to be apprehended both in present and future times; and on those accounts best suited to preserve those memorials which are intended for perpetual rules of action.

WORD-LAW

Legal English has several subvarieties, reflecting its different roles. For example, there is the language of legal documents, such as contracts, deeds, insurance policies, wills, and many kinds of regulation. There is the language of works of legal reference, with their complex apparatus of footnotes and indexing. There is the language of case law, made up of the spoken or written decisions which judges make about individual cases. There is the spoken language of the courtroom, with the ritual courtesies of judges, counsel, and court officials, and the constraints governing what counts as evidence, and what may or may not be said. Legal language is unique in the way its utterances are subject to sanctions, such as a fine or imprisonment for linguistic contempt of court.

A fundamental distinction separates the language of the legislature – the body (such as Parliament or Congress) which institutes a legal text – and the language of the judiciary – the body (the law courts and judges) which interprets and applies that text. A pivotal role is played by the set of constitutional statements, statutes (Acts), and other documents which come from the legislature. In these cases, the words, literally, are law.

Constitution of the United States (1787)

We the People of the United States, in Order to form a more perfect Union, establish Justice, insure domestic Tranquility, provide for the common defence, promote the general Welfare, and secure the Blessings of Liberty to ourselves and our Posterity, do ordain and establish this Constitution for the United States of America.

Article I

Section 1 – All legislative Powers herein granted shall be vested in a Congress of the United States, which shall consist of a Senate and House of Representatives. **• • •**

[and one of the amendments proposed by Congress in 1789]

Article [V]

No person shall be held to answer for a capital, or otherwise infamous crime, unless on a presentment or indictment of a Grand Jury, except in cases arising in the land or naval forces, or in the Militia, when in actual service in time of War or public danger; nor shall any person be subject for the same offence to be twice put in jeopardy of life or limb; nor shall be compelled in any criminal case to be a witness against himself, nor be deprived of life, liberty, or property, without due process of law; nor shall private property be taken for public use without just compensation.

PRECISION AND TRADITION

The need for precision accounts for a great deal of the character of legal language – though ironically the concept of precision is not itself especially precise; rather it is, according to David Mellinkoff, 'loose as water' (*The Language of the Law*, p. 295). As a theoretical aim, its importance is undisputed, because of the demands which legal language has to meet. A comment from a 19th-century jurist, James Stephen, is often quoted, in this respect:

it is not enough to attain a degree of precision which a person reading in good faith can understand, but it is necessary to attain if possible to a degree of precision which a person reading in bad faith cannot misunderstand.

In practical terms, however, legal language seems to be anything but precise – if precision means 'no room for misinterpretation'. A vast amount of what actually goes on in court and in the legal literature is in fact a dispute about the way words are to be interpreted. The law is truly, to quote Mellinkoff again, 'a profession of words'.

The need to anticipate future bad faith, by leaving as few linguistic loopholes as possible, accounts for much of the distinctive structure of legal language. But not everything in legal English can be given a functional justification. A great deal of its stylistic idiosyncrasy, its distance from everyday usage, can be explained only with reference to its origins. The use of legal varieties of Latin and French, after the Norman Conquest (p. 30), introduced a major barrier between the professional lawyer and the ordinary person; and when English eventually became the official language of the law in Britain, in the 17th century, a vast amount of earlier vocabulary had already become fixed in legal usage. The reliance on Latin phrasing (*mens rea, ab initio, certiorari*) and French loanwords (*lien, plaintiff, tort*) was supplemented by ceremonial phrasing (*signed, sealed, and delivered*), conventional terminology (*alibi, negotiable instrument*), and other features which have been handed down to form present-day legal language. As English expanded into new situations around the world (§7), so the syntax and vocabulary of English common law moved with it, accompanied by a respect for tradition and a suspicion of change which invariably resulted in an increased and often unnecessary linguistic complexity. It is in this domain, therefore, that there is a strong case for reform, which these days is argued both from within and from outside the legal profession.

MUCH OBLIGED

The parodists have had a field day with legal language. Here are three of their offerings, the first a piece of dictation by Groucho Marx.

Gentlemen?
In re yours of the 5th inst. yours to hand and in reply, I wish to state that the judiciary expenditures of this year, i.e., has not exceeded the fiscal year – brackets – this procedure is problematic and with nullification will give us a subsidiary indictment and priority. Quotes, unquotes, and quotes. Hoping this finds you, I beg to remain as of June 9th, Cordially, Respectfully, Regards.
(*Animal Crackers*, 1928).

The party of the first part hereinafter known as Jack, and the party of the second part hereinafter known as Jill, ascended or caused to be ascended an elevation of undetermined height and degree of slope, hereinafter referred to as 'hill'.
(D. Sandburg, *The Legal Guide to Mother Goose*, 1978).

In the heels of the higgling
  lawyers, Bob,
Too many slippery ifs and buts
  and howevers,
Too much hereinbefore
  provided whereas,
Too many doors to go in and
  out of.
(Carl Sandburg, 'The Lawyers Know Too Much', *Complete Poems*, 1950.)

But parodists have to yield before lawyers themselves, who have often been highly critical of the language of their own profession (p. 376). (All quotations from R. W. Benson, 1985.)

C. RESTRICTION ON REUSE OF COMPANY NAMES

1912. Restriction on reuse of company names; meaning of 'prohibited name'. Where a company[1] ('the liquidating company') has gone into insolvent liquidation[2] on or after 29 December 1986, a person who was a director[3] or shadow director[4] of the company at any time in the period of 12 months ending with the day before it went into liquidation[5] may not, at any time in the period of five years beginning with the day on which the liquidating company went into liquidation:
  (1) be a director of any other company that is known by a prohibited name; or
  (2) in any way, whether directly or indirectly, be concerned or take part in the promotion, formation or management of any such company; or
  (3) in any way, whether directly or indirectly, be concerned or take part in the carrying on of a business carried on, otherwise than by a company, under a prohibited name,
except with the leave of the court[6] or in the prescribed excepted cases[7].

1 'Company' includes an unregistered company which may be wound up under the Insolvency Act 1986 Pt V (ss 220–229): s 216 (8).
2 For these purposes, a company goes into insolvent liquidation if it goes into liquidation at a time when its assets are insufficient for the payment of its debts and other liabilities and the expenses of the winding up: ibid s 216 (7).
3 For the meaning of 'director' see para 1910 note 3 ante.
4 For the meaning of 'shadow director' see para 1245 note 2 ante.
5 For the meaning of 'go into liquidation' see para 1320 note 9 ante.
6 'The court' means any court having jurisdiction to wind up companies: Insolvency Act 1986 s 216 (5). As to the courts having winding-up jurisdiction see para 1435 et seq ante. As to the mode of application and the procedure see para 2052 et seq post.
7 Ibid s 216 (1), (3). As to the excepted cases see paras 1914–1916 post. As to the penalties and other consequences of contravening these provisions see paras 1917, 1918 post.

COMPANY LAW

This is an extract from a volume (7.2) of the 56-volume *Halsbury's Laws of England* (4th edition, 1988). It is a book of 1,734 pages, the first 234 pages of which are devoted to tables of statutes and cases, the last 110 pages to indexes of company concepts and terms – some 20 per cent of the text. The extract also shows the high proportion of endnotes to text: several pages have a greater proportion of space devoted to notes than to main text, and at one point a note extends over three pages.

The endnotes (shown here as footnotes) identify the points in the semantic structure of the work on which this particular paragraph depends, as well as other points of clarification or illustration. A two-level exposition is typical of this genre of legal language, and is an important device enabling the writer to reduce the structural complexity of the main text.

This is a piece of legal language intended for specialists, and it contains several devices which make it easy to assimilate, such as clear punctuation and indentation. Although a long sentence (154 words, excluding footnotes), it contains a number of formulae (e.g. *whether directly or indirectly*) which would be skimmed over by the experienced reader. The reader who is not a lawyer, of course, has no way of knowing which parts of the text are the 'meat', and which the 'etc. etc.'.

Compared with some examples of legal language which lawyers themselves have attacked, this is a clear piece of writing, despite its syntactic complexity. What is disturbing is when material of corresponding complexity is used without an apology to a lay audience. Then it is time for Plain English sabre-rattling (p. 376).

KNOWLEDGE OF THE LAW

Legal language is made to carry one further, critical burden: it is assumed that everyone knows it. It is a well-established dictum that ignorance of the law is not a valid excuse, if we wish to defend ourselves against a charge of wrongdoing. But knowledge presupposes comprehension. It is this simple fact which has made people feel they have a right to demand clarity from those who draft statutes, and the many kinds of publication (leaflets, notices, official letters, application forms) which stem from them.

Considerable progress has now been made in raising public awareness of these issues, thanks largely to the work of the Plain English Campaign (see opposite). Many complex legal documents have been rendered into a more accessible English, sometimes with an account given of the editing principles involved in the task. This kind of exercise is eminently worthwhile, for it highlights the nature of the problem of legal language in a way that only detailed comparisons can. Whether such analyses gain a sympathetic ear on the part of most law professionals remains to be seen.

• There are problems of a practical nature: those who draft parliamentary statutes, for example, are under considerable pressure just to keep pace with the short-term demands of their occupation, coping with a never-ending stream of Bills that need to be written and revised. The kind of dialogue which will be required in order to determine which plain English proposals are easy to implement and which are contentious is time-consuming and of uncertain outcome. Not everyone agrees on what counts as 'plain' English.

• The reference to 'contentious' also raises problems of a professional kind. 'Simpler' language proposals – and there have been many, each offering its own solution – come from people with varying awareness of legal issues, and may disregard legal distinctions of acknowledged importance. Law-writers have to look beyond the needs of immediate comprehension to anticipate the consequences of having their language tested in the courts (the 'bad faith' argument, p. 375). Drafting takes place against a background of judicial decisions and rules of interpretation which they leave behind at their peril.

The difficulties in the way of change are enormous, and progress will require considerable political will. Even when official enquiries are made into these matters (such as the Renton Report of 1975), there is no guarantee that recommendations will be implemented. But the Plain English case is a plausible one; it needs to be taken seriously, and to be given a detailed response by the legal profession. For behind all the arguments lies a fundamental principle, acknowledged by the Renton Committee: 'the interests of the users should always have priority over those of the legislators' (*The Preparation of Legislation*, 1975, HMSO, p. 149).

LAW OF THE JUNGLE

Not only lay people find the language of statutes difficult, as the following quotations show (after M. Cutts, 1994). 'Supremecourtese', 'parliamentese', 'legalese', 'gobbledygook', 'bafflegab', and 'Fedspeak' are just some of the uncomplimentary labels which surround this variety.

• I have in my time read millions of words from the pens of judges and, despite my professional interest in them, I have rarely failed to experience a sense of defeat or even pain. Sometimes it is as though I saw people walking on stilts; sometimes I seem to be trying to see through dense fog; and always there is that feeling of being belabored with words. (USA: Weissman, quoted in R. W. Benson, 1985.)

• In Britain the drafting of legislation remains an arcane subject. Those responsible do not admit that any problem of obscurity exists. They resolutely reject any dialogue with statute law users. There is resistance to change, and to the adoption (or even investigation) of new methods. The economic cost of statute law is enormous, yet official interest has been lacking. (UK: Lord Renton, 1979.)

• There remains an overwhelming need to achieve much greater clarity and simplicity, and overwhelming scope to do just that. The need is manifest: complexity and obscurity cause massive waste – unnecessary expense for commerce, for professionals, for government and for the public; ... complexity means uncertainty and ignorance in the daily disputes which will never be litigated, where bureaucracies and the economically dominant will usually prevail; complexity brings contempt for the law, for Parliament and for democracy itself. (UK: Richard Thomas, *Statute Law Review*, 1986.)

• I must say that rarely have I come across such a mass of obscurity, even in a statute. I cannot conceive how any ordinary person can be expected to understand it. So deep is the thicket that ... both of the very experienced counsel lost their way. Each of them missed the last 20 words of subsection 8 of section 9 of the Act of 1959. So did this expert tribunal itself. I do not blame them for this. It might happen to anyone in this jungle. (UK: Lord Denning, commenting on *Davy* v. *Leeds Corporation*, 1964.)

Lord Denning

PLAIN ENGLISH

A growing concern about plain English in several countries has drawn attention to the unnecessary complexity of the official language used by government departments, businesses, and other organizations which are in linguistic contact with the public. This concern goes well beyond legal language as such, and includes such matters as the design of application forms and the clarity of instructions on medical labels, but most of their activity relates to material which actually derives from the law. Local government officials, for example, have often defended legalistic phrasing in their publications on the grounds that this reflects the language of the statute on which they are based. And this trend is similarly seen in insurance policies, hire-purchase documents, licences, contracts, guarantees, safety instructions, and many other documents which define our rights and responsibilities.

The plain English movements are a modern phenomenon. In the UK the Plain English Campaign was launched in 1979 by a ritual shredding of government forms in Parliament Square. By 1985 over 21,000 forms had been revised, and a further 15,000 withdrawn. In the USA, President Carter issued an order in 1978 requiring that regulations be written in plain English; the order was revoked by President Reagan in 1981, but it nonetheless promoted a great deal of local legislation throughout the country, and an increase in plain language awareness among corporations and consumers. The annual Plain English awards in the UK continue to attract public interest (p. 176) and have helped to form a climate of opinion which has led many organizations to change their practices.

The campaigners point to enormous savings in time and money which can result from the use of clearer language. They cite cases where unclear letters and instructions have led to so many complaints that staff had to be specially employed to answer them. Another common problem is the return of application forms which have been filled in incorrectly because the instructions were too complex or ambiguous. The Campaign has estimated that sloppy letter-writing alone costs the UK about £6,000 million a year, as a result of mistakes, inefficiency, and lost business.

It is not difficult to see why the Plain English Campaign has had its critics, especially from within the legal profession. 'Doing Lawyers Out of a Job?' ran a press headline after one of its successes. More to the point is the argument that everyday language is itself very prone to ambiguity, and that the more this is used in legal documents, the more there could be problems of interpretation (p. 374). The public, it is argued, needs to have confidence in legal formulations, and such confidence can come only from lawyers using language that has been tried and tested in the courts over many years.

So far, these fears seem to be without foundation: there has been no sudden increase in litigation as a result of the emergence of plain English materials. And although, in view of the undeniable complexity of some of the (non-linguistic) issues involved, there are presumably limits to the amount of clarification which it is practicable to introduce, in the 1990s there are signs of the ultimate accolade, with the institutions of the law themselves using or asking for plain English in order to get their message across. An example is a drafting manual published in the UK by the Law Society in 1990: it is called 'Clarity for Lawyers'.

Chrissie Maher (centre), co-founder of the Plain English Campaign, with colleagues in New York to launch the International Plain English Campaign in 1993.

The Plain English Campaign's gobbledygook monster receives a punch.

POLITICAL ENGLISH

The language of politicians, especially when they are speaking in public, is an interesting mixture of old and new: it displays much of the ritual phraseology and consciousness of precedent which we associate with religion or law (pp. 371, 374); and it makes use of many of the rhetorical and dramatic techniques which we associate with advertising or the media (pp. 380, 388). It is a variety which is much abused. One of society's great paradoxes is that we elect to power people whose language we readily say we do not believe.

But why is this so? What happens to language when people stand up in public to debate the weightiest issues, whether it be on a doorstep, a platform, or the floor of a parliament building? Many ordinary voters know just how clear and helpful individual politicians can be when they consult them on a one-to-one basis in their home locality. Why does everything seem so different when we read the words of these same people in the press, or listen to them in the confrontations now commonly broadcast on radio and television?

The notion of 'confrontation' is probably the key. When two people of different political persuasions confront each other, there is more at stake than grasping the immediate meaning of the words they use. There are questions of identity: does the language conform to that used in the policy statements of their party? There are questions of personal consistency: does the language say the same thing as it did on the previous occasion that the speaker addressed the subject? There are questions of credibility: do the claims made by the language live up to the actions which the speaker has undertaken?

Political questions and answers can rarely be taken at face value, when confrontations happen in public. Politics is not a setting in which the participants are willing to assume (as some maxims of conversational theory assert) that each person is telling the truth, or attempting to communicate in a succinct, relevant, and perspicuous way. On the contrary, most politicians seem to work on the assumption that what their opponent says is a tissue of lies, side-issues, irrelevance, and waffle. They are aware that this is a stereotype, that they are playing a language game; but it is a game with the most serious of consequences, and they play it with no holds barred. They know that their reputations are at stake, if they make (or are perceived to make) a commitment which they cannot deliver. They know that they must speak, often at length and on every conceivable subject, with authority, consistency, and conviction. They know that they must always be on their guard, so that they do not give their opponent a chance to seize on a weakness in the way something has been said. It is only possible to survive such demands by developing a style of language which is at times opaque, inspecific, or empty. If one has not said something, then one cannot be accused of lying. Politics is the world of the half-truth. It is evidently part of the price we have to pay for democracy.

THREE IN ONE

In political speaking, the need for applause is paramount, and much of the distinctive rhetoric of a political speech is structured in such a way as to give the audience the maximum chance to applaud on cue. One widely used technique is an adaptation of an ancient rhetorical structure – the three-part list: X, Y, and Z. These lists are not of course restricted to politics:

signed, sealed, and delivered
Father, Son, and Holy Spirit
Tom, Dick, and Harry
the truth, the whole truth, and
   nothing but the truth
this, that, and the other

Such lists, supported by a strong rhythm and a clear rising + falling intonation sequence (p. 248), convey a sense of rhetorical power, structural control, and semantic completeness. They are widely used in formal writing (as in the previous sentence). And they are especially common in political speeches, where the third item provides a climax of expression which can act as a cue for applause. (*Three-part structures may also operate at sentence level, as in this paragraph.*)
   In an acclaimed study of speech and body language in political speeches, using videotaped data, Max Atkinson found many such instances:

Governor Wallace: and I say segregation now, segregation tomorrow, and segregation for ever.
Norman Tebbit: Labour will spend and spend, and borrow and borrow, and tax and tax.
Tony Benn: and they kill it secretly, privately, without debate.

History and literature provide numerous examples:

Abraham Lincoln: Government of the people, by the people, for the people.
Mark Antony: Friends, Romans, Countrymen …
Winston Churchill: This is not the end. It is not even the beginning of the end. But it is perhaps the end of the beginning.

And even crowds use tripartite sequences:

Lone voice: Maggie, Maggie, Maggie.
Crowd: In, in, in.
(After M. Atkinson, 1984.)

Thatcher: This week has demonstrated (0.4) that we are a
        party united in
        ‾‾‾   ‾‾

↑ purpose

(0.4)

strategy

(0.2)

and re | solve.
        ↓

Audience: | Hear hear   (8.0)
Audience: | x-xxXXXXXXXXXXXXXXxxx-x
(*Conservative Party Conference, 1980*)

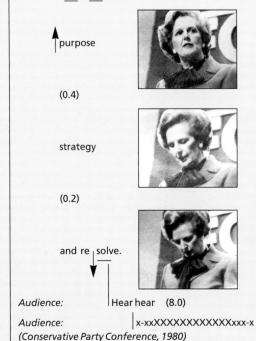

Pauses are shown in seconds or tenths of a second; soft applause is symbolized by x, loud applause by X; an isolated clap is separated by a dash; stressed words are underlined; pitch jumps are shown by arrows; overlapping audience response is shown by vertical alignment.

POLITICAL QUESTIONS

Mr Hirst: Does my right hon. Friend agree that there has been a broad welcome from the business community, which sees the reforms as helping redress the appalling imbalance in business rates north and south of the border? Is he aware that the business community also warmly welcomes the protection which will be given to it during the transitional period of rating reform? Will he contrast the worth of the Government's proposals with the fact the Labour Party will do nothing to reform the rates, and with the rather loopy idea which is circulating in alliance circles that rates should somehow be linked to the profits of a business? (*Hansard*, 1986f, p. 986.)

Mr Maxton: Is the Minister aware that the thousands of people in Glasgow who are waiting for housing improvement grants would be astonished to hear that he is blaming local authorities for failure to provide them? The Government's failure to provide sufficient funds to remove the backlog is the problem. (*Hansard*, 1986f, p. 990.)

THE POLITICS OF EVASION

In the House of Commons, as in other government chambers, the period set aside for MPs to put questions to ministers is a linguistic game *par excellence*. The formal asking of a question is a chance to do several things – to focus public attention on an issue, express identity with a party political line, or cause trouble for the 'other side'. It is a chance to get oneself noticed, settle old scores, or repay a constituency debt. Just occasionally, it is a real question, to which the questioner wishes to receive, and is then given, a real answer.

In a study of oral answers to questions asked in the House during 1986, several points of this kind emerged. Over 40 questions were asked in a session, on average, and over 80 per cent were highly constrained, requiring a 'yes/no' response (p. 218). However, in practice such questions could rarely be acceptably answered by a simple 'yes' or 'no'. There is invariably a hidden text. Parliamentary questions are asked for a reason, which may be little to do with the semantic content of the question and more to do with the kind of confrontation which is taking place. The questioner is expecting an explanation, a defence, a justification. Someone is being put 'on the spot'.

Skilled politicians can resort to several techniques in order to evade an awkward question. They can, for example, ignore the question, decline to answer it, or acknowledge it without answering it; they can criticize the questioner or the question, or play upon its words to make a 'political point'; they can choose to answer just part of the question, repeat an answer to a previous question, or claim that the question has already been answered; they can even respond to the questioner by asking another question themselves. Deuce.

Formal political questioning of this kind has been around a long time in the UK. The first such question was asked in the House of Commons in 1721. And very early on, there are reports of dissatisfaction with the way ministers responded. One study of the history of parliamentary questions (P. Howarth, 1956, p. 35) reports a comment of the Earl of Grafton in the 1770s:

If called upon in Parliament for information which every member in either House has a right to expect they either give no reply or evade the question.

It seems that there are some aspects of language which do not change.
(After J. Wilson, 1990.)

YES, MINISTER?

One of the chief difficulties facing politicians is that the questions they receive are rarely straightforward, but are preceded by a series of often unclear and controversial claims. If they address these points in their reply, they may be accused of trying to avoid the question. But if they fail to address them, they may be accused of accepting the claims as if they were facts. This can be seen in an analysis of one question which was addressed to a cabinet minister during a radio interview.

Well now - when Mr Heseltine protested at the cabinet meeting on December 12th - over the fact that Mrs Thatcher had cancelled this meeting on December 13th - he raised a protest - which as you know - in his resignation statement he said - he said wasn't recorded in the cabinet minutes - and now he's gone back and said that he wants that protest recorded - can you say - as - as a bit of an expert on the constitution - probably more than a bit of an expert - can you honestly say - as a member of the cabinet - that you were happy that Mrs Thatcher allowed proper discussion by all the cabinet in detail of this very important decision for defence?

Elucidating the content of this question brought to light nearly 20 possible issues.

Presuppositions for the validity of the question
• There was a decision on defence.
• The decision was very important.

• The cabinet did not properly discuss the decision.
Assertions about others
• Thatcher cancelled the cabinet discussion.
• Heseltine protested the cancellation.
• Somebody omitted the protest from the record.
• Heseltine resigned over the cancellation.
• Heseltine is demanding his protest be entered in the record.
Attributions about respondent
• You know that some/all of the above assertions are true.
• You are an expert on the constitution.
• You are a member of the cabinet.
Propositions in question
• Thatcher allowed discussion.
• Thatcher allowed proper discussion.
• Thatcher allowed discussion by all the cabinet.
• Thatcher allowed discussion in detail.
Questions to be answered
• Do you agree that some/all of these propositions are true?
• Can you say 'I agree that some/all of these propositions are true'?
• Can you say 'I agree that some/all of these propositions are true' and be honest about it?
Answers
• Yes
• No

But of course, no one would have reached cabinet minister rank who would use such one-word answers by way of reply. What the questioner will receive is better categorized as a 'response' rather than an 'answer'. (After J. Wilson, 1990 and J. T. Dillon, 1990.)

NEWS MEDIA ENGLISH

The world of the media is an area where it is important not to confuse the 'object' with the language. There are newspapers; there is radio; there is television. But there is no such thing as 'a variety' of newspaper language; or of radio language; or of television language. The media reflect all aspects of the human condition, and make available to the public many varieties of language already well known elsewhere, such as those associated with religion, politics, science, and literature, and the more topic-directed aspects of conversation (e.g. discussion, interview, debate, argument, letter). When we apply the notion of a language variety (p. 290) to the media, we have to look within each product (a newspaper, a radio or TV channel) for uses of language which have been shaped by the nature of the medium, or whose purpose is to make use of the capabilities provided by the medium. And here, the communication and presentation of news is dominant.

News reporting

The reporting of news, whether in the spoken or written media, reflects one of the most difficult and constraining situations to be found in the area of language use. The chief constraint is the perpetual battle against the pressures of time and space. Only those who have tried to write something for a newspaper or a radio/TV programme know just how crippling these pressures can be. They are absolutes. To fit a column, 20 words may need to be cut. To fit a radio window, 16 seconds of a script may need to go. There is no argument. If the writer of the original material does not meet the demand, someone else higher up the editorial chain of command will do it instead. Nothing is sacrosanct. Even a letter to the editor can be chopped in half. And there is no comeback. The editor's decision is final.

There is also the constraint imposed by a favoured conception of audience – an awareness of what 'the readership', 'the listener', or 'the viewer' wants. This applies to everything, from the initial judgment about what should be reported to the final decisions about exactly how much should be said about it, where in the medium it should appear, and how it should be written or spoken. Here, too, anyone who has produced material for the media knows how the finished product can differ greatly from what is first submitted. Very Famous Reporters may see their piece appear more or less as they wrote it. This is especially the case with syndicated columns. But the average news report, whether printed or broadcast, is the product of many hands (p. 382).

The shared authorship of news reports is suggested by their reliance on preferred forms of expression, their lack of stylistic idiosyncrasy (even in the reports of named journalists), and their consistency of style over long periods of time. Once a publication or channel has opted for a particular style, it tends to stay with it, and imposes it vigorously on its material. This has particularly been the case with the press. It is not difficult to identify certain features which characterize certain newspapers. That is why it is possible to parody them so easily (and also why news reporting is such a popular topic in English-language student projects). Moreover, the papers themselves are well aware of what they are up to. From time to time a newspaper may even publish a separate collection of material showing off an aspect of its approach. For example, a collection of headlines from the UK newspaper *The Sun* was published as a book in 1993. It was called *Gotcha* (p. 275).

(p. 290) ... (p. 382). ... (p. 275). ... see p. 388. ... see p. 382.

EDITORIAL VARIETY

There are several items in a newspaper whose stylistic identity is conditioned by the medium of expression. The following are examples of linguistically distinctive editorial material, other than news 'stories', found in one paper (*New York Newsday*): editorial comment, comic strips, summaries (e.g. weather, TV, lottery, movie guide, sports results), personal columns (e.g. 'Dear Abby'), wordgames, legal notices, death notices, horoscopes, and letters. Advertising, with its own subvarieties is also a dominant feature of any paper, but is linguistically so different that it requires its own account: see p. 388.

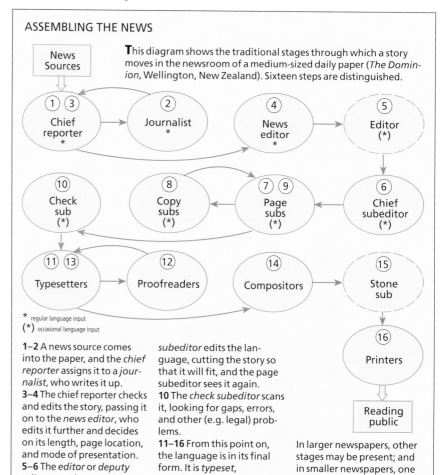

ASSEMBLING THE NEWS

This diagram shows the traditional stages through which a story moves in the newsroom of a medium-sized daily paper (*The Dominion*, Wellington, New Zealand). Sixteen steps are distinguished.

* regular language input
(*) occasional language input

1–2 A news source comes into the paper, and the *chief reporter* assigns it to a *journalist*, who writes it up.
3–4 The chief reporter checks and edits the story, passing it on to the *news editor*, who edits it further and decides on its length, page location, and mode of presentation.
5–6 The *editor* or *deputy editor* may then see the copy, and alter it before passing it on to the *chief subeditor*. This stage is optional.
7–9 The *page subeditor* marks the copy for typesetting and space, including it in a 'dummy' page. The *copy* subeditor edits the language, cutting the story so that it will fit, and the page subeditor sees it again.
10 The *check subeditor* scans it, looking for gaps, errors, and other (e.g. legal) problems.
11–16 From this point on, the language is in its final form. It is *typeset*, *proofread*, and *composed* on the page. Any final cutting to fit the page may be carried out by the *stone subeditor* (a term from the days when pages were composed by hand), and the completed page is sent for printing.

In larger newspapers, other stages may be present; and in smaller newspapers, one individual may combine several roles. These days, journalists often do their own computer typesetting, thus incorporating steps 11–14 into earlier stages of production. For examples of text editing, see p. 382. (After A. Bell, 1991.)

APRIL FOOL!

Probably the most famous journalistic parody of recent years appeared in the UK newspaper *The Guardian* on 1 April 1978. It reproduced the front page of twelve newspapers (clones of those published in the British Isles), said to have been published that day as part of a journalistic merger on the island of San Serriffe – where the custom is evidently to name people and places after concepts in the history of printing. Extracts from four of them are illustrated here. Identity is chiefly conveyed by typography, in the distinctive mastheads and headlines, but several features of each paper's journalistic style is apparent in the texts, showing the range which exists between 'quality' and 'tabloid' language in the British (and San Serriffe) press. Four treatments of a leading story about the Bishop of Bodoni are used as illustration.

After making allowances for the exaggerations which are part of a parody, a comparison with today's papers would show little stylistic difference, despite a gap of over 15 years. Ironically, the exception (typographically, at least) is *The Guardian*, which has since radically changed its house style – a rare event in the history of a newspaper. Over a longer time frame, of course, changes in approach are more in evidence, as can be seen from the 1914 example on p. 383.

SS Mirror

SAN SERRIFFE'S BIGGEST DAILY SALE

Saturday, April 1, 1978

PAGE ONE OPINION

Stuff it bishop

Blimey, pals, what's all this then?

The batty Bishop of Bodoni is at it again!

Cor, strike a light!

Just listen to what the potty prelate has to say about the language riots over on North Island:

" We must approach this problem in a spirit of brotherly love, and try to see all sides of the problem," say the daffy deacon.

Lumme, pals, what a mouthful!

" Brotherly love?"   In a pig's ear!

" Both sides of the problem"?   Don't make me larrff!

The S.S. Mirror says this to the cranky curate:

Can it!

Shut it!

Stuff it up your mitre!

SS GUARDIAN

An unmistakable case of doubt

All men of goodwill throughout our islands will have been heartened by the words of the Bishop of Bodoni. Yesterday he addressed himself to the rioting which has disfigured the face of our North Island, all too recently our South Island. Here is what the Bishop said: " We must approach this problem in a spirit of brotherly love, and try to see all sides of the problem."

Wise words indeed, and words which those who find themselves embroiled in these regrettable events, will do well to recall. To appreciate the value of the … we could do worse than …

called for a …
against all t …
different lig …
will recall …
example s …
14th cent …
subject …
directly …
with it …

The …
of o …
" Flo …
whi …
It …
to …
t …

THE SS TELEGRAPH

SATURDAY, APRIL 1, 1978

Bodoni
Telephone 3524 Ext. 14

Metro
Telephone 3458 Ext. 9

THE BISHOP'S BROTHERLY LOVE

AT FIRST sight, yesterday's remarks by the BISHOP OF BODONI may appear to be little more than common sense. The BISHOP said, of the subversive Communist inspired language riots on North Island " We must approach this problem in a spirit of brotherly love, and try to see all sides of the problem."

Nevertheless, it must be firmly asserted that the BISHOP'S remarks are in fact dangerous, potentially subversive, and possibly treasonous. If, for example, the late EARL MONTGOMERY OF EL ALEMEIN had adopted this particular credo as his watchword when fighting ROMMELL, the Allies might have lost the Second World War. Had the late LORD BADEN-POWELL attempted to see all sides of the problem during the Boer War, the town of MAFEKING would be as yet unrelieved. The DUKE OF WELLINGTON thought little of brotherly love when he took his stand against the late NAPOLEON BONAPARTE. Did the late JULIUS CAESAR EMPEROR OF ROME declare " I Came, I Saw, I Entered Into Fraternal Negotiations"? He did not.

It is true, as the BISHOP reminds us, that the late LORD JESUS CHRIST spoke of brotherly love. There is a time and a place for such sentiment, as the events surrounding the late DAVID and JONATHAN may remind us. But there is an even more urgent place for its opposite and antithesis. Let the deeds of the late SAMSON and his firm stand against the late PHILISTINES be our guides and let the BISHOP take unto him the JAWBONE OF AN ASS rather than imitating one.

TIMES PAST

SS TIMES

Old Printing House Square, Bodoni.   Telephone : Bodoni 1234

WHISPER WHO DARES

It is probably well in matters of ecclesiastical polity for the cautious man to be guided by the Ciceronian dictum, *Omnes artes quae humanitatem pertinent habent quoddam commune vinclum et quasi cognatione quadam inter se continentur*. And if that is admitted it is fair to add, with Pliny, *Ne supra crepidam sutor iudicaret!* (The exclamation mark is ours.) If one were to approach the recent comments of the Bishop of Bodoni with these invaluable aphorisms in mind it would be possible both to admire his words and to take issue with them. " We must approach this problem," the Bishop said, " in a spirit of brotherly love, and try to see all sides of the problem." In that they go to the heart of the dilemma which faces any observer of the dispute between the Flongs and the Phlongs, the Bishop's words will strike a chord. In that they fail to differentiate between the Flong and the Phlong view of the troubles which ravage the island, they are wanting.

In what respect they are wanting is itself a matter of contention and indeed of strife, but it should be clear to anyone with a smattering of history of the North Island that consensus even on so basic a question as the application of brotherly love is often hard to find. " There are the Flongs. There are also the Phlongs." We wrote these words at the beginning of a leading article in 1842 and nothing that has happened in the meantime has caused us to make any marked change in that opinion except, perhaps, that with the passage of time and the sometimes hurtling journey of these islands around the world (for it will be remembered that only a year ago we were in the Indian Ocean) this opinion has acquired an emphasis and an urgency that it did not have before.

The policy of the Government must therefore be even-handed and be seen to be even-handed. In that sense the Bishop's words offer a valuable guide to where immediate priorities should lie. Doubtless he had in mind the Pauline injunction " Let all things be done decently and in order" (1 Corinthians, xiv, 40), although the patristic authorities which could be cited in favour of such a sentiment are many and diverse. The ensuing debate will therefore be followed with keen anticipation although it will not perhaps be altogether surprising if at the end of it the fundamental question remains open. There would be nothing unusual in such an eventuality. Indeed if there is a lesson to be learned from this not entirely unfruitful episode it is probably that open questions admit of greater differences of opinion than closed ones. While it is possible to wish for the closure, it might at the same time be foolhardy to expect it.

JOURNALINGUISTICS

Three aspects of the way news is received, processed, and presented are shown on this page. They are taken from an in-depth investigation of news media language by Allan Bell, a New Zealand sociolinguist who has also worked as a journalist and editor in a daily news service. This combination of personal experience and linguistic training is rare in research into language variety. We do not usually find journalist-linguists, politician-linguists, or priest-linguists. People who are busy earning their living from being the first part of these compounds do not usually have the motivation, opportunity, or training to take up the role of the second. When it does happen, the analysis can provide considerable insight into the mental processes underlying the occupational variety, as well as accumulate a great deal of practical illustration which would not be available to outsiders. The first two examples on this page derive directly from Bell's personal experience. He had access to the teleprinter copy coming into a news office after it had been marked up by the receiving editor and before it was thrown away. And he was able to get hold of both the agency copy and the edited version of the sports story. With the advent of direct screen editing, of course, it is now much more difficult for linguists to observe the stages in the editorial production of a text. There are simply no 'hard copy' printouts to collect.

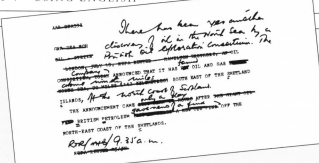

A page of wire copy from Australian Associated Press, with markings by the receiving New Zealand editor.

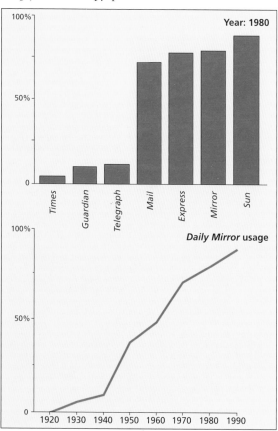

Year: 1980

100%

50%

0

Times · *Guardian* · *Telegraph* · *Mail* · *Express* · *Mirror* · *Sun*

***Daily Mirror* usage**

100%

50%

0

1920 1930 1940 1950 1960 1970 1980 1990

BEFORE AND AFTER

Two stages in a story: the left-hand text is a sports story transmitted by Australian Associated Press–Reuter from Sydney; the right-hand text is the version edited by the New Zealand Press Association. Material is deleted, altered, and added. The commentary below shows the multiple linguistic decisions which the New Zealand editor made in the first paragraph. (For grammatical terminology, see Part III.)

The waterlogged conditions that ruled out play yesterday still prevailed at Bourda this morning, and it was not until mid-afternoon that the match restarted. Less than three hours' play remained, and with the West Indies still making their first innings reply to England's total of 448, there was no chance of a result. At tea the West Indies were two for 139.	Waterlogged conditions ruled out play this morning, but the match resumed with less than three hours' play remaining for the final day. The West Indies are making a first innings reply to England's total of 448. At tea the West Indies were 139 for two, but there's no chance of a result.

* Place adverbial *at Bourda* deleted.
* Time adverbials *yesterday* and *still* deleted.
* Main verb *prevailed* deleted.
* Relative clause *that… yesterday* made a main clause.
* Relative pronoun *that* and associated *the* deleted.
* Cleft structure (p. 231) *it… restarted* replaced by a subject-predicate clause, *the match resumed…*

* Time adverbial *not until mid-afternoon* deleted.
* *resume* replaces *restart*.
* *but* replaces *and*.
* Part of the next sentence added: *less …remaining*.
* Change of finiteness (p. 212): *remained* becomes *remaining*.
* New time adverbial introduced: *for the final day*.

Some features convey more than just semantic content; they also inform about readership. This is seen in the way a determiner (p. 207) is used or deleted in such contexts as *[the] Australian prime minister Paul Keating said …* The top chart shows deletion to be a sociolinguistic feature of newspaper style, typical of British tabloid journalism. The bottom chart shows that this feature has developed during the present century. The *Daily Mirror* made no use of it in 1920, but it had reached 90 per cent by 1990. Why this particular feature should be so salient is unclear, but it is certainly diagnostic of the social stratification which readership analyses have found for these papers.

JOURNALESE

There are several distinctive linguistic features of news reporting. Most relate fairly clearly to the 'who, when, where, what, how, and why' which journalists bear in mind when compiling a story.

* The headline is critical, summarizing and drawing attention to the story. Its telegraphic style is probably the best-known feature of news reporting.
* The first ('lead') paragraph both summarizes and begins to tell the story . This paragraph is also the usual source of the headline, which is written not by the source journalist but by one of the subeditors (p. 380).
* The original source of the story is given, either in a byline (Reuters) or built into the text (*A senior White House official said…*).
* The participants are categorized, their name usually being preceded by a general term (*champ, prisoner, official*) and adjectives (*handsome French singer Jean Bruno…*).
* Other features include explicit time and place locators (*In Paris yesterday…*), facts and figures (*66 people were killed in a bomb blast….*, and direct or indirect quotations (*PM 'bungles', says expert, Expert says PM bungled*).

READ ALL ABOUT IT!

The front page headline and page 6 of London's *The Daily Sketch* for Saturday 11 April 1914. This particular edition has been chosen for its content, which is of historical interest in relation to the development of attitudes towards taboo language, discussed on p. 173. But the page as a whole can be used as an illustration of both the differences and the similarities in the linguistic and typographical treatment of news reporting over a period of 80 years. On the one hand, we find such features as a fuller headline structure, longer sentences (including much greater use of subordinate clauses), and more formal vocabulary than would be found in a paper of a corresponding level today. On the other hand, there are many points of identity, such as the short paragraphs, rhetorical questions, and elliptical headline style.

One Word In Shaw's New Play May Cause A Sensation.

DAILY SKETCH.

No. 1,588.   LONDON, SATURDAY, APRIL 11, 1914.   (Registered as a Newspaper)   ONE HALFPENNY

TO-NIGHT'S "PYGMALION," IN WHICH MRS. PATRICK CAMPBELL IS EXPECTED TO CAUSE THE GREATEST THEATRICAL SENSATION FOR YEARS

"PYGMALION" MAY CAUSE SENSATION TO-NIGHT

Mr. Shaw Introduces A Forbidden Word.

WILL "MRS. PAT" SPEAK IT?

Has The Censor Stepped In, Or Will The Phrase Spread?

Has the Censor interfered?

If not to-night's performance of Bernard Shaw's "Pygmalion" at His Majesty's Theatre may cause one of the greatest sensations of our theatrical history.

If the Censor has not interfered the audience will either laugh immoderately or - well, anything may happen.

Is an expression which hitherto no respectable newspaper has dared to print permissible when uttered on the stage?

Mrs. Patrick Campbell in the new Shaw comedy plays the part of Liza Doolittle, a flower-girl, whom a professor of phonetics turns into a lady.

But before her education is quite complete she uses language which is—at present—barred in drawing rooms, though she has heard her instructor use the word so often that she does not know it is not etiquette to use it.

THE OFFENDING WORD.

And How It Retranslates From The German.

In the German version of the play which has been published in Berlin, though the English version is not yet obtainable, the dialogue, translated quite literally, runs as follows:—

FREDDY (opening the door): Are you going through the Park, Miss Doolittle? In that case might I—
LIZA Am I going? Yes, Muck! (Freddie staggers) I am taking a taxi-cab.

The suburban girl, Clara Eynsford Hill, who has been invited to meet Miss. Doolittle, thinks the expression the very latest thing to use to be in fashion, and bidding good bye to the unconventional professor of phonetics, Professor Higgins (Sir H. Beerbohm Tree), a few minutes later the following conversation takes place:—

CLARA: Such nonsense, all this prudery from Early Victorian days
HIGGINS: Damn'd nonsense!
CLARA: Mucky nonsense
CLARA'S MOTHER: Clara.
CLARA: Haha. (She goes out radiant, conscious that she is thoroughly up-to-date.)

This, it must be understood, is a literal re translation of the German version of Mr. Shaw's play. There is little doubt of the word actually written by the author.

Indeed, it has been the talk of the theatrical clubs of London for days

The Century Dictionary unblushingly defines the shocking word as "very, exceedingly, desperately," and gives examples of its use from Dryden and Swift.

And this evening—unless the Lord Chamberlain and his board of censors have intervened—the most respectable theatrical audience in London will hear the dreadful word fall with bombshell suddenness from the lips of Mrs. Patrick Campbell

Sir Herbert Tree has, by dint of many years' devotion to the cause of drama, built up an audience of theatre-goers at His Majesty's second to none in London.

They have been brought up on Shakespeare, but they are not used to Shaw. Literary men and women will be there, and leaders of Society and drama enthusiasts from Hampstead and the garden cities, middle-class matrons and maidens, all accustomed to hear at His Majesty's only what is wholesome and pure – and Shakespearean.

It will come as a shock to the Upper Circle if they hear Mrs. Pat uttering a word which the

pletive in Mr. Bernard Shaw's new play will serve to increase the complaints against bad language on the stage.

This expression occurs in Shakespeare and the other Elizabethan dramatists. True, but it is difficult to show that the word is used in the sense in which it is used in "Pygmalion."

Not many years ago the Lord chamberlain's theatre license forbad all bad language, even "damns," in plays.

At one time within the memory of living play-going man managers were so afraid of violating the Lord Chamberlain's prohibition that actors dropping in even a 'damn' were fined.

DICKENS'S DEFENCE

When Dickens wrote "Oliver Twist" there was a great outcry against what was called "the revolting language" used by Bill Sikes.

Dickens defended himself on the ground that persons of Sikes's profession and character were not in the habit of using "rose-water language."

But in the dozens of dramatisations of "Oliver Twist" none of the earlier dramatists dared transfer Sike's execrations and swear-words to the stage.

One of the first play licensers to cut every "damn" out of every play that was sent to him was the eminent dramatist and humourist George Colman the younger, author of "The Heir at Law" and other famous comedies for which he got £1,000 apiece.

One of the playwrights out of whose play Colman cut the only two "damns' in it sent to Colman several quotations from that dramatist's own plays, such lines as "Damme! it's the Brazier," "damn his eyes!" "Better be damned than dig," and so on.

Not many years ago, moreover, the name of the Deity was forbidden to be used in any stage play, and any actor daring to interpolate such expressions as "Oh God!" "My God" was either fined or dismissed from the theatre. For the word "God" the word "Heaven"—"Oh Heaven!" "Blessed Heaven grant", etc.—was always substituted. Even in "The Lights o' London," to be revived to-night at the Aldwych, this substitution occurs several times.

For a good while now, however, the word "God" and even the word "Christ" have been used a great deal on the stage, and not merely in passages of anguish or of prayerfulness—when perhaps there might be some excuse—but in passages of lighter or even frivolous import.

IT MUST BE STOPPED.

In a new revue just brought to London there is an episode in which the funny man telephones to Heaven to inquire about certain people who have just died!

He utters certain comic replies from Heaven!

This kind of thing, like the bad language and the naming of the Creator indicated above, must be stopped, together with other forms of "offensiveness.'

THE PLAY IN OUTLINE.

Shavian "Love," Humour And Phonetics.

What of the play that marks the first combination of Shaw and Tree in the history of the modern stage?

Its story is very Shavian, and may be summarised as follows :—

ACT I.

Under the portico of St. Paul's, Covent Garden, at 11.15 p.m. on a very wet summer's night.

A suburban lady and her daughter and several loafers are seeking shelter, as also professor Higgins a professor of phonetics, who is taking notes, and Colonel Pickering, a student of phonetics.

Enter a flower girl, Liza Doolittle. Arguements and recriminations ensue, in which Higgins is suspected of being a police spy.

He clears himself by revealing who he is, and flings Liza a handful of money. Pickering introduces himself and they go off together.

CARDS AS A CURE FOR CURSING.

Clergyman Advocates "Patience" As A Nerve Soother.

A RECREATION FOR WORKHOUSE INMATES.

Is "Patience" a preventative of profanity and can cards cure one of cursing?

Such is the latest problem for earnest thinkers. The Rev. P. Clementi-Smith, a member of the City of London Board of Guardians, is one of those who believe in the virtues of "Patience," that solo card game beloved particularly of our grandmothers.

He says it is an excellent method of keeping people quiet and to prevent them from swearing. His view was apparently endorsed by the majority of his fellows, for the Guardians have decided to ask the Local Government Board to allow inmates of the infirmary at Homerton to play cards.

It seems doubtful if such a sanction will be obtained, for article 127 of the general Consolidated Order (regulations governing the conduct of workhouses, etc.) provides, among other things, that no one shall play cards or other games of chance.

"And a very good rule, too!" was the comment of the master of one of the largest workhouses in London to the Daily Sketch.

THIN END OF THE WEDGE.

Do I think that the inmates should be allowed to play Patience? Certainly not; it would be the thin end of the wedge. In a large class of workhouse the desire to gamble is inherent. It would be impossible to stop them. why, some of them would gamble with their very trouser buttons if they had a chance.

"As things are there doesn't seem to be any particular desire for such a privilege among those in our infirmary. We already provide them with draughts and dominoes, but they rarely touch them."

The master laughed at the suggestion that cards would prevent profanity. "If you play cards yourself" he said, "you ought to know that it would be more likely to increase it. One might as well propose a game of golf as a remedy."

A CRIMEAN VETERAN.

Man Who Fought against Us In The Russian War.

A Crimean veteran—with a difference. A good many people to whom the old man is a familiar figure know that he fought in the Crimean War, but perhaps he is the only one living in England who fought, not for her, but against her.

Mr. Moss Morris, who was 94 this week, fought in South Russia and Finland and was captured and brought to England after the fall of the Finish fortress of Bomarsund in 1854.

The fortress is on an island, and had been bombarded for some weeks by the British Navy. At last the order was given to surrender, and Mr. Morris came to the gates to raise the white flag. As he did so a flying piece of shell tore off the top of his head.

After the signing of peace Mr. Morris was released from the military goal near Portsmouth, and not caring to return to Russia on account of his belonging to the Jewish faith decided to become naturalised.

Until the death of his wife, who was an English woman, last year, Mr. Morris had a small refreshment shop and stall in the Waterloo-road, and walked from there every day twice to and from the Central Synagogue in Great Portland street, where he is a "Minyan man" or paid attendant. This was a total distance of ten miles.

Mr. Morris lives nearer to Great Portland street now, but he is still a keen pedestrian.

SOCIALIST WEDDING.

BROADCASTING

By contrast with most newspapers (p. 380), only a small part of radio and television output is devoted to news and its discussion (current affairs) – as little as 5 per cent, on some channels – but its significance is perceived to be far greater than this small figure suggests. The core element in this output is well-defined: the news bulletin, consisting of a series of items of varying size, often divided into sections (e.g. general, business, sport, weather), sometimes punctuated by advertising, and fitting into a format which may be of any length, but often as short as two minutes. However, it is much more difficult than in a newspaper to draw a clear boundary between a news item proper and its amplification, which can move in the direction of everyday conversation ('vox pop' interviews) and even literature (dramatized documentary).

Analysis of a typical day's radio or television broadcasting brings to light, as with the press, several varieties of language which are in use elsewhere. Indeed, probably all conceivable spoken varieties will be found at some point or other in the broadcasting media. If a use of language is important enough to develop predictable linguistic features, the situations to which they relate are undoubtedly going to be of regular interest to listeners or viewers. In addition, the domain of radio and television drama holds a mirror up to linguistic nature. There are very few constraints on the situations (and thus the language) portrayed in plays – the chief exception being sensitivity to taboo words (p. 172).

The broadcasting media, like the press, have also been responsible for the emergence of varieties of their own – though not as many as might be thought. These media are in a continual search for new ideas and formats, and their fear of the conventional or stereotyped favours the promotion of linguistic idiosyncrasy and eccentricity rather than the preservation of stable and predictable styles. When such styles do emerge, they stand out, as in the case of educational programmes for very young children (whose distinctive prosodic features and simplified sentences are often parodied) or game shows (which regularly fuel the language's stock of catch phrases, p. 178). Weather reporting is one of the best examples, especially on radio, where in its specialized form (such as the BBC's daily shipping forecasts) it is reduced to its bare essentials, as a restricted language (p. 390). But it is the commentary, used in both media, which is probably the most famous and the most distinctive variety to have emerged from the world of broadcasting (see p. 386).

News time in a television studio.

TWO VERSIONS

There is little obvious linguistic difference between the way radio and television present the news, apart from the occasional reference in the latter to what is happening on the screen. Both are highly verbal, and use the same structure of lead-item summaries followed by fuller accounts, and reports from special correspondents. However, the TV version given below is much more succinct and has less complex sentence structure: its headlines use half as many words per sentence as radio (9.6 vs 19.8), and the first few sentences of the main item are a third shorter (15.2 vs 22.2). (/ represents an intonation unit; -, - -, - - - increasing pause length.)

BBC TV, 6 pm News, 7 February 1994
NEWSCASTER: Europe backs air power to lift the siege of Sarajevo /- - after Saturday's mortar attack / European Union foreign ministers / say everything must be done /- John Major calls for immediate effective action /- - but how practical would an air strike be /- the CIA look at the options on computer /- - - here a hoard of machine-guns is uncovered in Liverpool /- the police say they were for criminal not terrorist use /- - - and another security scare for the Prince of Wales /- he says it's breeding that keeps him cool under pressure /-
PRINCE OF WALES: we're not all made like James Bond you know or Indiana Jones /- - -
NEWSCASTER: good evening /- European foreign ministers have called for the immediate lifting of the siege of Sarajevo /- - at a meeting in Brussels today /- they said all means possible should be used / including the use of air power /- John Major has also called for immediate and effective action / to stop the shelling of Sarajevo /- - tomorrow / senior cabinet ministers will hold a special meeting / to discuss the use of air strikes against the Serbs /- from Brussels / our Europe correspondent James Robbins reports /

BBC Radio 4, 6 pm News, 7 February 1994
It's six o' clock /- - the news from the BBC /

with Astley Jones /- - European Union foreign ministers have agreed that all measures / including air power / should be used to lift the siege of Sarajevo /- - John Major has indicated he wants immediate and effective action to stop the bombardment of the city / - MPs were told that Britain was fully prepared to use air power /- if military commanders on the ground / recommended it /- - Merseyside police say weapons / discovered at a house in Liverpool / were probably / not connected with terrorism /- - share prices / have recovered some of the losses suffered this morning / when they plunged in reaction to an interest rate rise / in the United States /- [*two other headlines*] - - - Europe / has edged closer towards authorizing the use of NATO air strikes / to try to break the Serb siege of Sarajevo /- in London /John Major called for immediate / effective / and more muscular action / in the wake of Saturday's devastating mortar attack on a busy market place /- and as European foreign ministers met in Brussels /- France / led the demands for the Serbs to be issued with an ultimatum /- - pull back from Sarajevo / or risk being forced to do so /- - in the event / a slightly less strong form of words was agreed by the ministers /- but the threat of air strikes remains /- - our Europe correspondent Graham Leach / has sent / this report / from Brussels /- - -

RAIN LATER

Two contrasting styles of radio weather forecast (p. 296): the first, informal and conversational, presented before the lunchtime news on BBC Radio 4 on 7 February 1994; the second, formal and formulaic, presented later that afternoon. The duration of the first extract is 1 minute 50 seconds (from a 2 minute 30 second forecast); the second extract is 1 minute 30 seconds (from a 5 minute forecast).

A successful weather forecast is a mixture of fluent spontaneity, controlled informality, and friendly authority.

• The fluency is partly a matter of careful preparation, but is largely achieved through the broadcaster's ability to rely on formulaic phrasing (*with light winds and largely clear skies, blue skies and sunshine, widespread frost*) and on standard sequences of locations (e.g. the areas that form the eastern vs western sides of the country). The number of likely weather situations is really quite limited, in a particular region, and certain combina-

tions of features frequently recur.

• The conversational tone is achieved through the use of informal lexicon (*take a tumble, just a chance, odd rogue shower*), everyday turns of phrase which 'ordinary' people use about the weather (*become a little bit quieter, turn colder*), fuzzy expressions (p. 169) (*more or less, round about*), contracted verbs (*it's, that's, we'll*), and colloquial sentence connection (*anyhow, in actual fact*).

• At the same time, the scientific element in the message is evident in the numerical underpinning (*eight degrees, minus one or minus two*) and the reference to notions which are generally not found in the speech of the amateur (*icy patches on untreated roads, well broken cloud, southwesterly wind*). There is little unqualified precision (meteorology is not an exact science, and its predictions are judicious), but these features combine with a measured and confident tone of presentation to produce an overall impression of authority.

good afternoon / it's still unsettled / although not as much as it was / - and after tomorrow it should become a little bit quieter / although at the same time turn colder / - and I emphasize / - that's after tomorrow / -- anyhow back to the present / - and we more or less have an east-west split / - so we'll start / first of all in the east / with south-east and central-southern England / the Midlands / East Anglia / north-east England / and eastern Scotland / - here most places will be dry / with blue skies and sunshine / - although there's just a chance of an odd rogue shower / - especially in central-southern England and eastern Scotland / -- temperatures will be close to normal / that's around eight degrees in southern areas / and six degrees in the north / -- now during this evening and tonight / with light winds and largely clear skies / temperatures will take a tumble / - and will soon fall below freezing / with frost becoming widespread / - temperatures in actual fact probably bottoming out at round about minus one or minus two / - and in one or two places it'll turn misty for a time / - and there'll also be some icy patches on any untreated roads / --- now for south-west England / Wales / north-west England / western Scotland / and Northern Ireland / - sunny intervals and showers here / the showers heavy in places / -- one or two variations though / for instance in western Scotland / the showers will join forces to begin with / - to give some longer spells of rain or sleet / with snow on the hills / -- generally speaking the showers in most places should tend to become lighter / and more scattered during the afternoon / - temperatures / they'll be close to normal and mostly around seven degrees / --- there'll still be a few light showers around this evening and tonight / but by then most places will be dry / with well broken cloud / -- along the coast / temperatures will only fall to around two or three degrees / but inland / they'll drop below freezing / to give a widespread frost / - although later in the night / increasing cloud and a freshening south-westerly wind / will pick temperatures up again across northern Ireland / the west of Wales / and in south-west England / ...

The highly formulaic character of this forecast, with its specialized vocabulary, reduced grammar, controlled prosody, and cyclical discourse structure, is typical of a restricted language (p. 390). In many ways it resembles the language of commentary (p. 386).

now at ten to six it's time for the shipping forecast / issued by the Met Office / at one seven double oh on Monday the seventh of February / - there are warnings of gales in Viking / North Utsire / South Utsire / Forties / Finisterre / Sole / Fastnet / Shannon / Rockall / and Fair Isle / -- the general synopsis at midday / - low / one hundred and fifty miles west of Bailey / nine eight six / will fill / - new low / expected Bailey / nine eight four / by one two double oh tomorrow / - Atlantic high / a thousand and thirty / expected Trafalgar / a thousand and thirty six / by same time / --- the area forecasts for the next twenty four hours / -- Viking / North Utsire / South Utsire / north-east Forties / -- south-easterly / gale eight / decreasing six / -- occasional rain or snow / moderate / occasionally poor / -- south-west Forties / Cromarty / Forth / Tyne / Dogger / -- southerly four or five / increasing six / perhaps gale eight later / in south-west Forties and Cromarty / - showers then rain / - good becoming moderate / -- ... ...
and now the weather reports from coastal stations / for one six double oh G M T / - Tyree / - south by west four / - recent showers / - nineteen miles / - a thousand and three / - rising slowly / -- Butt of Lewis lighthouse / - south / - three / - twenty four miles / - a thousand and one / - rising more slowly / ...

NORTH AND SOUTH WHERE?

The names of the Meteorological Office sea areas surrounding the British Isles provide British English with some of its most distinctive weather-forecasting lexicon. Most people know at least some of the names by heart, though few could locate more than a handful with any accuracy. It also usually comes as a surprise to see how North and South /uːtˈsɪərə/ are spelled.

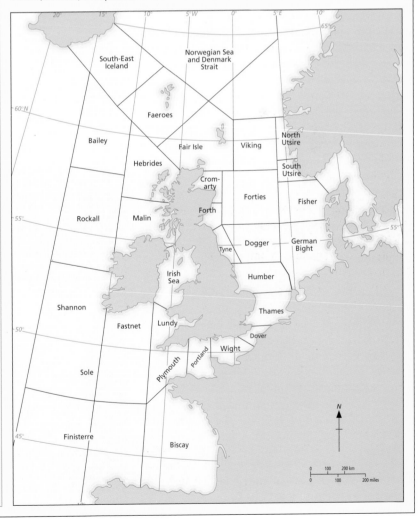

SPORTS COMMENTARY

Commentary is one of the most distinctive of all uses of English. Its roles extend well beyond broadcasting (it will be heard in such varied contexts as fashion shows, race-course meetings, and cookery demonstrations), and within broadcasting its use extends well beyond sporting occasions (it will be heard accompanying such public events as funerals, inaugurations, and processions). But the most frequent kinds of commentary are those associated with sports and games. Here, two elements need to be distinguished: the 'play-by-play' commentary, and the 'colour-adding' commentary. The latter is important, for it provides an audience with pre-event background, post-event evaluation, and within-event interpretation, but there is little to be said about it stylistically: it is conversational in style, and often in dialogue form. Stylistic interest in sports commentary lies chiefly in the play-by-play component.

Because commentary is an oral reporting of ongoing activity, it is unlike other kinds of narrative (which are typically reported in past time). Indeed, it is unlike *any* other kind of speech situation. US linguist Charles Ferguson captured its uniqueness when he described radio sportscasting as 'a monolog or dialog-on-stage directed at an unknown, unseen, heterogeneous mass audience who voluntarily choose to listen, do not see the activity being reported, and provide no feedback to the speaker' (1983, p. 156). If such a strange activity is to survive, and to be successful in maintaining fluency and listener interest, it needs special linguistic features.

Oral formulae

The variety does survive successfully, because of the way language has been adapted to suit the unique circumstances. Its chief feature is a highly formulaic style of presentation, which reduces the memory load on the commentator and thereby helps fluency. The amount a commentator has to remember can be quite considerable, especially in a football match or a horse race, where many participants are involved. There may also be genuine difficulties hindering the commentator from following what is taking place. At such times, the commentary cannot stop. Silence is anathema, especially on the radio. Formulaic language provides a partial solution; it allows the commentator time to think, as this quotation from a horse race illustrates:

it's Fraytas in the lead / followed by as they come round the Canal Turn way over on the other side of the field by Everest /

SULKY RACING

… It was two dollars before and I just think something's wrong with those dividends that are showing up on our screen. They've got Speedy Cheval the favourite but I'm not exactly sure that that's correct but anyway they're in behind the mobile going towards the starting point now for the first heat of the Lion Brown Rising Star Three Year Old Championship just about there.
They're off and racing now.
And one of the best out was Speedy Cheval
(1st cycle)
coming out at number two from El Red
and also Florlis Fella's away fairly well /
a little wider on the track the favourite Race Ruler.
Twilight Time is in behind those.
Breaking up behind is Noodlum's Fella
and he went down
and one tipped out was My Dalrae /
and the driver's out of the sulky.
The horse actually went down on its nose and cartwheeled,

sulky over the top.
They race their way down the far side *(Loop)*
1,600 to go
and El Red stoked up / to go to the lead now.
(2nd cycle)
Race Ruler's going to be caught without cover followed by Speedy Cheval in the trail.
Florlis Fella was next
followed then by Twilight Time.
Little River's got a nice passage / through over on the outside.
Megatrend next along the rail
followed then by Lone Eagle.
About two lengths away is Belvedere.
Belvedere was followed by False Image /
and one buried on the inside of those two was Catarina.
But they race through the straight in a bunch now *(Loop)*
with 1,300 metres left to go.
El Red the leader by two lengths from Speedy Cheval… *(3rd cycle)*

EARLY LEARNING

Josh: Hoyle serves it! Ben Graham cannot get it … over the net and it's twelve eight. Hoyle's lead now.
Ben: Hoyle takes the lead by four.

A typical sportscast (of table tennis)? The only difference is that the commentators are 8-year-old children, and they are playing the game themselves. Like the professionals (p. 387), their speech shows the use of the simple present tense in action verbs, the ellipsis of sentence elements, and other grammatical features of commentary style, as well as a loud and fast prosody marked by

rapid shifts in pitch.
It is quite common for children, while they are playing a competitive game, to give a play-by-play account in this way. This may even happen as a monologue (as in the literary representation opposite). In the study from which the above was taken, spontaneous episodes of this kind lasted from 6 to 22 minutes. The style is not exactly that used by adults, but it is not far from it. What is notable is that such a close stylistic approximation can be achieved by children, presumably just by listening, at such an early age. (After S. M. Hoyle, 1991.)

Presumably the commentator was having some trouble seeing who was in second place, at that point; the formula 'it's X followed by Y' was interrupted by two other formulae ('they come round the Z' and '(way over) on the other side of the field'), giving him time to work out exactly which horse it was.

There are several different kinds of formula. Some are used when starting and finishing a race (*they're off!, and at the post it's* ...). Some introduce a fresh cycle of activity (*into the straight they come; and round the turn it's* ...). Scoring formulae are also important in such games as football, cricket, and baseball (*3–nil; 34 for 3; count of 1 and 1*). On the facing page, an extract from a sulky-racing commentary has been set out in lines (rhythm units) so that the phrasal repetitions and parallelisms can be more clearly seen. Two cycles of activity, and two connecting loops, are shown, as well as a fragment of the preceding colour commentary. (After K. Kuiper & P. Austin, 1990.)

OTHER FEATURES

Sports commentary is not identified by its vocabulary: sporting terms and idioms can be found elsewhere, such as in press reports and everyday chat. Other factors are more distinctive.

• It is extremely fluent, keeping up with the pace of the activities. The rate is steady, and there is little sign of hesitation noises, false starts, comment clauses (p. 229), nonsense words (p. 130), and other features of spontaneous speech (though these may be found in the 'colour' episodes).
• The prosody is suited to the sport, reflecting the atmosphere and drama. Some very unusual prosodies can be heard, and speeds of articulation which differ greatly from everyday conversation (both slower and faster). Some sports (such as horse racing) may be spoken in a monotone, either loudly (as in horse racing) or softly (as in snooker); others make use of wide variations in pitch range (as in football or baseball). A commentator may have a favourite way of 'pointing' a commentary, and idiosyncrasy can be strong.
• Distinctive grammar is seen in the use of the present tense (*he sends it back*); the omission of elements of sentence structure (*Gooch in close*), inverted word order (*over at third is Smith*), and extra modifiers (*The quiet Texan Tommy John delivers* ...; *and Smith, who's scored well this season, runs back* ...). The frequent use of the passive is another 'survival' device: often commentators see a play before they can identify the player, and the passive (perhaps with a tell-tale pause) allows them to delay mentioning the player's name (*His shot is blocked by – Jones*).
• Discourse structure is cyclical (see opposite), reflecting the way most games consist of recurring sequences of short activities (as in cricket, tennis, and baseball) or a limited number of activity options (as in the various kinds of football). In racing, the structure is even simpler, the cyclicity here regularly informing the listener of the varying order of the competitors, with each 'loop' of the cycle introduced by its own formulae (see opposite page). This is a 'state of play' summary, crucial for listeners/viewers who have just switched on – or who have simply lost track of what's happening.

THE COMMENTATOR

Good afternoon and welcome
To this international
Between England and Holland
Which is being played here today
At 4, Florence Terrace.
And the pitch looks in superb condition
As Danny Markey, the England captain,
Puts England on the attack.
Straight away it's Markey
With a lovely little pass to Keegan,
Keegan back to Markey,
Markey in possession here
Jinking skilfully past the dustbins;
And a neat flick inside the cat there.
What a brilliant player this Markey is
And he's still only nine years old!
Markey to Francis,
Francis back to Markey,
Markey is through, he's through,
No, he's been tackled by the drainpipe;
But he's won the ball back brilliantly
And he's advancing on the Dutch keeper,
It must be a goal.
The keeper's off his line
But Markey chips him superbly
And it's a goal
No!
It's gone into Mrs Spence's next door.
And Markey's going round to ask for his ball
    back,
It could be the end of this international.
Now the door's opening
And yes, it's Mrs Spence,
Mrs Spence has come to the door.
Wait a minute
She's shaking her head, she is shaking her head,
She's not going to let England have their ball back.

What is the referee going to do?
Markey's coming back looking very dejected,
And he seems to be waiting . . .
He's going back,
Markey is going back for that ball!
What a brilliant and exciting move!
He waited until the front door was closed
And then went back for that ball.
And wait a minute,
He's found it, Markey has found that ball,
He has found that ball
And that's wonderful news
For the hundred thousand fans gathered here
Who are showing their appreciation
In no uncertain fashion.
But wait a minute,
The door's opening once more.
It's her, it's Mrs Spence
And she's waving her fist
And shouting something I can't quite understand
But I don't think it's encouragement.
And Markey's off,
He's jinked past her on the outside
Dodging this way and that
With Mrs Spence in hot pursuit.
And he's past her, he's through,
What skills this boy has!
But Mr Spence is there too,
Mr Spence in the sweeper role
With Rover their dog.
Markey's going to have to pull out all the stops
    now.
He's running straight at him,
And he's down, he's down on all fours!
What is he doing?
And Oh my goodness that was brilliant,
That was absolutely brilliant,
He's dived through Spence's legs;
But he's got him,

This rugged stopper has him by the coat
And Rover's barking in there too;
He'll never get out of this one.
But this is unbelievable!
He's got away
He has got away:
He wriggled out of his coat
And left part of his trousers with Rover.
This boy is real dynamite.
He's over the wall
He's clear
They'll never catch him now.
He's down the yard and on his way
And I don't think we're going to see
Any more of Markey
Until it's safe to come home.

Gareth Owen, *Songs of the City*, 1985

ADVERTISING ENGLISH

Despite the impact of the glossy format, the memorable image, and the famous personality, it is language which can make or break an ad. If the name of the product is not clearly stated, there is a real risk that we will fail to recall it when the time comes to make our choice in the marketplace. Rare indeed are the ads which are so established that the name can be omitted or hinted at (e.g. using [ʃ] instead of *Schweppes*). Usually the brand name is presented to us in more than one form. In the press, it is likely to be in the main text of the ad (the *body copy*), in the bottom-line summary (the *signature line*), and in the product illustration (if there is one). On television it is also likely to be vocalized. Radio uses sound effects, song, and accents to provide a varied brand-name profile.

It is not easy to draw a clear conceptual boundary around the variety of advertising: political speeches, sermons, and several other uses of language can be said to be 'selling something'. There is also an overlap with announcements, such as births and deaths (a type of prestige advertising?), legal notices, health warnings, and other items whose function is chiefly to inform. But commercial advertising stands out stylistically on several counts. Like literature (p. 412), it can employ other varieties of language in its service: any fragment of the human condition (and a fair amount of non-human) can be found in an ad. Lexically, it tends to use words which are vivid (*new, bright*), concrete (*soft, washable*), positive (*safe, extra*), and unreserved (*best, perfect*). Grammatically, it is typically conversational and elliptical–and often, as a result, vague (*A better deal* [than what?]). It uses highly figurative expressions (*taste the sunshine in K-Y peaches*), deviant graphology (*Beanz Meanz Heinz* p. 275), and strong sound effects, such as rhythm, alliteration, and rhyme, especially in slogans (p. 180). And as the opposite page shows, it can make effective use of word-play (p. 400). (For other examples of advertising language, see pp.199, 219, and 252.)

ADVERTISING GENRES

Commercial advertising is the largest and most visible form of advertising; but by no means the only one. The classified columns of a newspaper include such categories as auctions, automobiles, bargains, careers, entertainment, health and safety, house sales, investments, lost and found, personal, prestige, and situations wanted.

Apart from the major media outlets (daily or weekly press, radio and TV commercials), advertising also employs a vast range of devices and locations to get its messages across: they include billboards, book jackets, bookmarks, carrier bags, catalogues, circulars, flyers, handbills, inserts, labels, leaflets, special merchandise (cups, pens, T-shirts), notices, placards, posters, price tags, programmes, samples, sandwich boards, sportswear, showcards, signs, tickets, tourism brochures, media trailers, vehicle sides, wrapping paper, and classified pages in telephone books.

Common features

Despite the many variations in content and location, advertising is a remarkably homogeneous variety. The most obvious variations, such as use of pictures, colour, and prominence (peak time, front page) are of little stylistic consequence. However, size (and cost) does have an effect in the amount of ellipsis and abbreviation used. For example, crammed into a single line of a three-line narrow-column ad for a mechanic is: *Ford/Merc exp a must. Excel sal/bnfts.* ('Ford / Mercury experience a must. Excellent salary and benefits.') This contrasts with the leisurely style of *We are currently seeking a high calibre salesperson to generate substantial business from UK and European clients ... in an appointments ad* measuring 18 cm x 9 cm.

Another common feature is the use of a restricted range of vocabulary, including idiom, jargon, and other lexical features (§12). The lexical items from the following ads identify their genres, but there is nothing else in the grammar, graphology, or discourse structure to show the difference between them.

- immaculate, views, spacious, landscaped, near shops (p. 170)
- original owner, mint condition, warranty (p. 175)
- hot action, wild with desire, pure pleasure, hungry, relief
- hilarious, for the entire family, blockbuster, near you

Hilarity indeed can be generated by mixing up the lexicons of these different advertising genres.

PUTTING YOUR MOUTH WHERE YOUR MONEY IS

Don't say beer, say Bud.
Don't say brown, say Hovis.
Don't be vague, ask for Haig.
Foster's the Australian for lager.

So, do we? Is it? Or rather, do consumers increasingly use brand names in their language, as a result of advertising slogans of this kind? This intriguing possibility was investigated in a series of studies of the increase in brand-name reference in aspects of US popular culture.

- A sample of 31 best-selling US novels published between 1946 and 1975, and totalling nearly 3 million words, showed that five times as many brand names were being used in the books published in the 1970s (e.g. *Jaws*) compared with those in the 1940s (e.g. *The Street*). *Coca Cola* was the commonest, appearing 59 times across 18 books, closely followed by *Cadillac* (57 times across 16 books), then by *Ford, Buick, Chevrolet*, and *Levi's*.

- A similar study used the scripts of hit plays performed on the New York and London stage during the same 30 years, totalling nearly a million words, and showed over twice as many brand names in the later period. The frequency was over 50 per cent higher in the plays from the USA.
- A third study looked at the lyrics of 256 songs which were hits in the USA in the same period, using a sample of 36,000 words. Only seven different brand names were found, in seven different songs, but all except one were in the 1970s. For example, *Chevy* (car) appears in 'American Pie' (1971) and *Kenworth* (truck) and *Microbus* (car) in 'Convoy' (1975). The exception: *Stetson* (hat) in 'Stagger Lee' (1958).

Apart from the sociological implications, these studies are an interesting demonstration of the effect of one variety of language on others, and thus of a factor which is often ignored in discussing linguistic change. (After M. Friedman, 1985, 1986.)

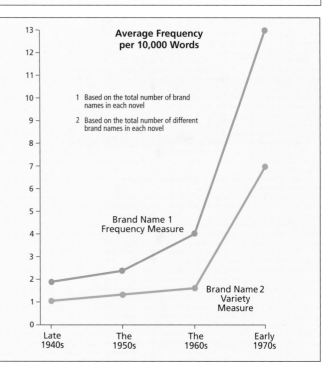

Average Frequency per 10,000 Words

1 Based on the total number of brand names in each novel

2 Based on the total number of different brand names in each novel

Brand Name 1 Frequency Measure

Brand Name 2 Variety Measure

Late 1940s — The 1950s — The 1960s — Early 1970s

REFRESHING SLOGANS

Heineken lager beer is produced under licence in the UK by the Whitbread Beer Company. The slogan *Heineken refreshes the parts other beers cannot reach*, devised by advertising copywriter Terry Lovelock in 1974, generated one of the most interesting linguistic sequences in the history of commercial advertising. The creative brief he received – the single word *refreshment* – led to a fruitful series of striking visual situations (presented in posters and TV commercials), all characterized by the restorative theme 'When something isn't right, Heineken puts it right'.

The early success of the slogan gave it the status of a catch phrase (p. 178), and enabled copywriters to begin playing with its language, knowing that people would readily bring to mind the original version. The chief strategy was to introduce lexical substitutions, *parts* being replaced by words with a similar phonological structure, such as *parrots*, *pirates*, *pilots*, and *poets*. In 1989, the slogan was rested, the restorative situation being supported by the remark 'Only Heineken can do this', but it returned in 1991 as fresh as ever. It is not difficult to imagine what the slogan must have been drinking in the meantime to enable it to do this – nor what new generations of foreign learners (who would not be aware of the original text) need to drink in order to grasp what a sentence such as *Heineken refreshes the poets other beers cannot reach* could possibly mean.

August 1974

September 1988

May 1987

In the case of Sir Les Patterson (p. 350), the entire slogan is taken for granted.

RESTRICTED ENGLISH

In one sense, all linguistically distinctive uses of English are restricted, in that they are more likely to be found in some situations than in others. Only in literature, advertising, and humour (§22) is it possible in principle to disregard all conventions (though of course in practice there may be legal or social constraints, such as those disallowing libel or taboo language). But these general pressures on appropriateness are very different from the tightly constrained uses of English which are described under the heading of 'restricted varieties'. In these cases little or no linguistic variation is permitted. The rules, which often have to be consciously learned, control everything that can be said intelligibly or acceptably.

Restricted varieties appear in both domestic and occupational situations. At home, we can encounter them in a knitting pattern, a cookery recipe, or a book index (p. 296). In the wider community, they are seen in newspaper headlines and in certain types of newspaper announcement, such as birth and death notices or congratulatory messages (p. 359). In more specialized domains, we find the language of shipping forecasts (p. 385), sportscasting scores (p. 386), the numerical formulae of citizen band radio (e.g. 10-4 – 'message understood'), postcodes, zip codes, and the codes of cryptology. Internationally, we can observe restricted varieties in the international language of air traffic control (*Airspeak*) and its maritime equivalent (*Seaspeak*), with Eurolanguage developments for the 1990s prompted by the opening of the Channel Tunnel in the form of *PoliceSpeak* and *Emergencyspeak* (for the emergency services). Other restricted varieties have emerged with the development of electronic systems of communication. EDIFACT, for example, is the international standard for the electronic exchange of goods trading information. It seems likely that this trend will continue.

NAVYSPEAK?

A traditional, restricted language: the British flag signalling code devised by Sir Home Popham in 1803. Each flag combination relates to a separate word in the Admiralty code book. The illustration shows Nelson's famous signal, sent at the Battle of Trafalgar (1805): 'England expects that every man will do his duty'. Ironically, the word *duty* was not listed in the code book, so it had to be spelled out.

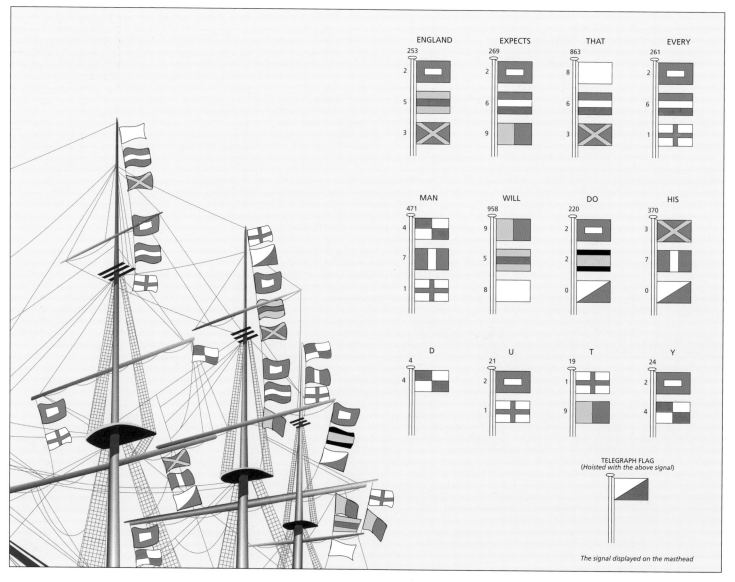

The signal displayed on the masthead

HERALDSPEAK

The confirmation of arms made by Robert Cooke, Clarenceux King of Arms, to Henry Stanley of Sutton Bonington, Notting-hamshire, dated 18 March 1576. The contemporary description shows several of the features of heraldic language, such as a special colour vocabulary (*gules* 'red', *asur* 'blue') and formulaic syntax (*an Egles head golde*).

Golde thre egles legges rased gules on a chief indented asur thre staggs heads caboshed golde and to the creast uppon the healme on a wreath silver and asur an Egles head golde wth thre pellatts and his beake an Egles foote rased gules manteled gules dobled silver

AIRSPEAK

Ground: G-CD expect beacon approach runway 34, descend to altitude 3000 feet, Borton QNH 1015, report reaching
Air: Expect beacon approach runway 34, descending to altitude 3000 feet, Borton QNH 1015, wilco, G-CD
Air: G-CD reaching 3000 feet
Ground: G-CD roger, cleared for beacon approach runway 34, report beacon outbound
Air: Cleared for beacon approach runway 34, wilco, G-CD
(From Civil Aviation Authority, *Radiotelephony Manual*, 1994, p. 96.)
cleared authorized to proceed
descend descend and maintain
G-CD abbreviated callsign of aircraft
QNH altimeter setting
report pass requested information
roger I have received all your last transmission
wilco I understand your message and will comply

KNITWRITE

Knitting patterns present a highly formulaic restricted variety, noted for its sequences of abbreviations which relate to individual words as well as to more complex sets of instructions. Extracts from two patterns are shown below.

Each uses its own set of abbreviations, and follows them scrupulously, but there is a considerable similarity between them, and some abbreviations seem to be standard (e.g. psso). Sentence-level abbreviations vary greatly between patterns, though the syntax of the sentences they refer to is highly restricted. Use of upper-case and lower-case letters seems to be arbitrary. Square brackets are used to set off alternative values, if knitting to larger sizes, according to a key shown at the beginning of the pattern; these are distinguished by punctuation or typography (e.g. bold-face numbers correspond to bold-face columns in the key).

There are certain differences between British and American English (p. 306), which patterns sometimes list as a glossary; for example

BrE	AmE
cast off	bind off
stocking stitch	stockinette stitch
tension	gauge
yarn forward	yarn over

Word abbreviations

alt alternate
beg beginning
cont continue
dec decrease, decreasing
foll following
inc increase, increasing
k, K knit
p, P purl
patt pattern

rem remain(ing)
rep repeat
sl slip
st(s) stitch(es)
st st stocking-stitch
tog together

Phrasal abbreviations

RS right side
tbl through back of loop
WS wrong side
yf yarn forward

Sentence abbreviations

Cr2R Knit into front of second stitch on left-hand needle, then knit first stitch, dropping both stitches off needle together.
KB Knit into back of stitch.
M1 Make a stitch by picking up horizontal loop lying before next stitch and working into back of it.
psso Pass slipped stitch over.
SL1K Slip 1 knitways.
Tw2 Knit next two stitches together but do not drop off needle, then knit the first stitch again, dropping both stitches off needle together.

1st row: K1, Tw2, k5, Cr2R, k5, Tw2, k1.
2nd row: K1, p2, k5, p1, M1, p1, k5, p2, k1. 19 sts.

• • •

Buttonhole row: K1, p1, k1, *yf, k2 tog, rib 4[6:6:6], rep from * twice more, rib 2[0:2:4].

• • •

Neck border: With RS facing and 4 mm needles, starting at left sleeve, (P2, KB1) 4 times, (P2tog) twice, KB1, (P2tog) twice, (KB1, P2) 3 times, KB1, (P2tog) twice, (KB1, P2) 3 times, (KB1) 0 [0, 0, 1, 0, 1, 0] time, (SL1K, K1, psso) 1 [1, 1, 0, 1, 0, 1] time, (inc in next st, SL1K, K2tog, psso) …

COOKWRITE

Parsnip and Apple Soup

Ingredients
6 oz leeks
10 oz parsnips
6 oz cooking apples
1 oz butter
tablespoon cooking oil
scant teaspoon curry powder
1 pt chicken stock
quarter pt milk
salt and pepper

Wash and slice leeks, peel parsnips and cooking apples, slice parsnips, core and slice apples. Melt butter and oil in a heavy pan, and add all vegetables and the curry powder. Cover and cook gently, stir often, and do not let vegetables brown. Add stock and seasoning, bring to boil, and simmer for 25–30 minutes until vegetables are cooked. Puree the soup in a blender, add milk, and reheat.
(From Pam Keating, *Ucheldre Recipes*, 1992.)

RITEWRITE

COLLINS – On July 3, in Liverpool, to MARY (nee Smith) and JOHN, a son (Arthur Hugh).
SMITH - WILLIAMS – On 6 July, at St Mark's Church, Holyhead, Anglesey, JOHN, eldest son of Dr and Mrs Gilbert Smith, of Birmingham, to MARY, only daughter of Mr and Mrs Michael Williams, of Holyhead.
BROWN - on March 8th, peacefully at home in Dublin, aged 68 years, Michael Edward.
SMITH, Jane beloved wife of Mark; adored mother of Mary and John; cherished grandmother of Simon and Peter; devoted sister of Emily. Service Wednesday 10 am at Mount Aran Chapel.

All names are fictitious, but otherwise texts are reproduced exactly.

CHESSWRITE

		6 f3	Nc6
		7 Nxc6	Bxc6
1 e4	h6	8 a4	e6
2 b3	c5	9 Ba3	0h4+
3 Nf3	b6	10 g3	Qf6
4 d4	cxd4	11 Ra2	Bxa
5 Nxd4	Bb7	12 Nxa3	Qc3+

NEW VARIETIES

The electronic age has changed our lives, as communicating human beings. New methods of sending and receiving information enable us to communicate with a bank or supermarket, interrogate a library catalogue or encyclopedia database, or select from a series of menus, as in television data displays (teletext). In each case, we have to learn new conventions of communication – new techniques of accessing or asking, new techniques of reading and assimilating. Interacting with a computer is (at present) not the same as interacting with a human being. And strange things can happen to conversational language when people let an electronic device come between them.

Computer-mediated communication (CmC)

Electronic messages (e-messages) and electronic mail (e-mail) are methods of exchanging letter-like messages on-line. In the former, both sender and receiver are simultaneously logged on to their computers, and the messages occur in real time; in the latter, a message is left in a 'mail box' for later reading. E-mail is a type of delayed dialogue, but unlike the situation of the answering machine a reply is likely, using the same system, some time later. What makes it unusual, in the typology of communication situations, is the delay between stimulus and response, which may be of several days' duration.

The delay between typing, sending, and receiving a message can cause unusual sequences of conversational turns. One study of this phenomenon (D. E. Murray, 1990) found the following example:

T1: THEY HAVE IT RUNNING DOWN AT THE LAB (ON SYS21)
P1: yeah - using lab 'f' for home terminal support i bet!
T1: ALSO ON SYS24. ISN'T IT SOMETHING?
P2: what would be the effect of having the home term with ymon using a high speed modem?
T2: ALEX WAS INTERESTED IN PUTTING IT UP ON SYS54.
HIGH SPEED WOULD MAKE IT REALLY LOOK SWEET.

In this exchange, P's e-message (P1) interrupts T's turn, in which he is telling P where something is operating. P then sends a second e-message (P2). T then replies to both P1 and P2 at once.

Because time is of the essence, errors in typing may not be corrected. The sender usually ignores letter case (p. 257), putting everything into either lower or upper case. Depending on the system used, the computer may print everything out in upper case anyway (as in the above example). When mixed-case programs are available, they are often used inconsistently, because of the extra effort involved. Participants also tend not to use 'time-wasting' formulae such as greetings and farewells, and messages are characterized by space-saving conventions such as ellipsis and abbreviation. Because participants are well aware of the possible time delays, they tend to avoid expressions which would be ambiguous over time (such as *today, this afternoon*). Otherwise, style is very close to that of conversation – and indeed often incorporates emotional expressions and other informalities which one would otherwise find only in intimate face-to-face conversation.

These are very unusual conversations indeed – but they *are* conversations. They are preferred over other methods because they can be the most economical way of sending or receiving information. Also, like the fax machine (p. 291), they do not require the participants to engage in time-consuming rituals of a phatic kind (asking about health, family, weather). In other circumstances, a conversation which omitted such pleasantries would be considered rude.

In systems using a list server, the conversation becomes even more unusual. Here, a message is sent to everyone belonging to a certain group; it is placed on a 'bulletin board', for consultation at any time. We therefore have a one-to-many conversation, in which a single stimulus can elicit many responses, scattered over a period of time, each of which can be read independently. Some responses quickly become out-of-date through the arrival of later messages; equally, later messages can make earlier messages redundant. People who consult bulletin boards often have to process some extremely complex textual tangles.

ONE-WAY DIALOGUE

A page from a teletext transmission, showing some of the features which identify this variety, such as the colour coding of different kinds of information, the succinct sentence structure, and the provision of page connectivity indicators. More is involved than the provision of information in monologue form (p. 294). Jokes and riddles, for example, which are typical of a dialogue situation, may appear on a children's interest page.

DEMOCRATIC CONVERSATIONS

Electronic conversation programs present the linguist with new and intriguing problems. Here is the beginning of a creative writing class which took place at a New York university in 1992, using a program called Daedalus Interchange. The students are each sitting in front of a computer screen, and after they log on, the following message appears on their screen from the course tutor. (Each message is preceded by the name of the sender, omitted here.)

Good morning! Would those of you who attended last night's lecture say something about your impressions of the presentation and the material? Did it change your notion of what Hypertext is and what its possibilities might be? What about its appropriateness for writing autobiography?

The first two student responses are shown here. The omitted punctuation in the second response is unsurprising, given the spontaneity of the response. It is the graphic equivalent of not pausing between sentences. Responses in this medium can be full of typing and spelling errors, with sentences loose and incomplete.

I never really thought of hypertext in a context outside of the classroom. I didn't realize thet it was a medium that could, theoretically, replace books.

Hypertext is a way of life I feel like I belong to a cult. And the only way out is to construct my autobiography.

As more students join in the conversation, the computer screen fills up with a running scroll of electronic messages. Each message is shown in sequence as it comes in. However, as the students are thinking in different ways, and typing at different speeds, new ideas are mixed with responses to old ideas in a nonlinear way. Maintaining a coherent structure in such a seminar can be very difficult for the tutor.

On the other hand, those who have experienced this kind of interchange laud the benefits. There is the obvious point, that it enables people to participate in the same conversation even though

```
G: STORY ARCHERS SCHOOLDAYS WITH LAWYERS. NEED COPY URGENTLY
PAGE 6. DEADLINE THURS. SUGGESTIONS?

C: bring forward story bottomley and dog? a - can you get
pic by thurs?

D: body beautiful staying at green men. try for interview?

G: WHAT DOG?

A: HAVE GOOD PICS BB WITH BLAIR AND ON OWN. BOTTOMLY NO
PROBLEM.

C: pit bull.  bb already spoken to standard (dick says).
check with nina.

D: ade suggests games page. g - shall i ask him to put
something tgether?

G: PUT ADE ON HOLD. CATH PLEASE CALL ME BEFORE 1600 TUES.
```

they may be physically distant from each other. But the new medium has more fundamental implications than this. It appears to encourage participation, in that people do not have to wait until one person has finished talking before they can make their contribution. Even poor typists can make their point (albeit after some delay). It avoids the familiar scenario in which student A is discomfited because student B has made the point A wished to make. In an electronic conversation, A can make the point anyway. For students who tend to be silent in an open class, or who have a quiet voice, or an accent which attracts notice, it can be a way of gaining equality. As one student put it: 'Communicating on the computer is better

for me because I sometimes feel intimidated to speak out loud in front of people. I can put in my thoughts whenever I want to. I don't miss my chance to talk.'

The effect of these programs on learning is as yet unclear. How students make use of the information to which they are exposed, and how they retain salient points faced with a continuously scrolling screen requires research. But from a linguistic point of view, electronic conversations provide an unprecedented multidimensional kind of communication in which such established notions as 'interruption', 'question and answer', and 'conversational turn' do not easily apply. (After S. Rakov, 1993.)

ANSWERSPEAK

Hello. I'm sorry we're not here at the moment, but if you'd like to leave a message you have just under three minutes after the tone. Thank you for calling. *[BEEP]*
Hi. This is Arthur Jones. I'm responding to the letter I got from you this morning. I'm hoping to get to the meeting, but I'll try and reach you later to talk about it – it's 11.30 now – Tuesday – or you can ring me at the office. I'll be there till 5. Thanks. Bye.

The answerphone presents a new kind of conversational situation: delayed single-exchange pseudo-dialogue (p. 296). It is pseudo because in the typical case there is no feedback and no further conversational turn. The situation is also asymmetrical, in two ways. First, the caller may

choose not to speak, thus rejecting the callee's recorded invitation. Secondly, through the monitoring facility the callee can listen to the caller as the message is being recorded and decide whether to cut in, thus turning the situation into a real dialogue.

The recorded message is unusual, as far as telephone linguistic history is concerned. The usual response to a caller is a number or *hello*. Here, neither of these items may be present (the number may be deliberately avoided for security reasons) and instead there is an explanation and a set of instructions. Situational constraints give this message some of the features of a restricted language (p. 390). Limited time makes it very short; and people typically do not include information about how long they are absent, in case they put their home at risk. Some leave messages indicating where a real dialogue can take place, or give

other kinds of instructions. Some dramatize their message, or introduce creative elements (e.g. musical accompaniment), which says more about their personality than about English.

When messages are left, they vary greatly in form. Some people treat the machine as if it were a person, and talk to it in a natural conversational style (introducing their remarks with *Hi* or *Hello* and an identifying formula (*This is …*; *I'm a friend of …*). Some train themselves to leave a precise record of when their message was made. Some find any kind of communication with a machine awkward or impossible, and use a formal style, often highly elliptical and disjointed. Although beginning a message is straightforward, almost everyone finds it difficult to end one. Many messages tail off into silence or uncertainty, or end with an unusual turn of phrase. What is the function of *thanks* in the above example?

22 · PERSONAL VARIATION

English
English of the 1990s
American English of the 1990s
Educated American English of the 1990s
Spoken Educated American English of the 1990s
Spoken Educated Political American English of the 1990s
Spoken Educated Political American English of the 1990s as heard in Speeches
Spoken Educated Political American English of the 1990s as heard in Speeches given by Bill Clinton ...

In a sequence such as this, it is possible to see how the study of English can proceed from the general to the particular. We begin with the language as a whole, the subject-matter of this book. The focus then moves to a particular historical period (§5); a particular medium (§19); a particular region (§20); and a particular social background, occupational variety, and genre (§21). Up to this point we are able to talk about group usages – features of English which would be used by anyone who shared the same background. But the final step moves us in a quite different direction: the domain of personal identity.

It is different because, when we begin to describe the linguistic features which identify an individual, we leave behind the safety-net of predictability, which has guided our study of varieties (p. 290). The distinctive features of political speeches are, to some extent, predictable, as are the features we associate with being educated, being an American, and so on. But there is no way of predicting someone's personal linguistic identity from our knowledge of the way other people use language.

Individual differences

Individuality in language is a complex matter, arising from variations in sex, physique, personality, background, interests, and experience. Physique and physical condition is important, for example, in the way it can influence a person's voice quality (p. 249). Personality plays a part in voice quality too, and, if the graphologists are correct (p. 269), is especially important in relation to handwriting. A particular blend of social and geographical backgrounds, increasingly common in a mobile society, may produce a distinctive accent or dialect. Educational history, occupational experience, and personal skills or tastes (hobbies, leisure pursuits, literary preferences, etc.), will foster the use of habitual words and turns of phrase, or certain kinds of grammatical construction. Also noticeable will be favourite discourse practices – a tendency to develop points in an argument in a certain way, or a penchant for certain kinds of metaphor or analogy. Some people are, evidently, 'good conversa-tionalists', 'good story-tellers', 'good letter-writers', 'good speech-makers'. What actually makes them so is the subject of a fascinating and ancient field of enquiry: rhetoric.

For the most part, individualistic features are unimportant in the act of communication. When we listen to what people are saying, we do not spend much time paying attention to what it is about their language that makes them different. Indeed, differences, once noticed, can get in the way of the meaning. It is not easy to pay attention to someone who has frequent and prominent linguistic idiosyncrasies. A deviant voice quality or pronunciation is a distraction, as is eccentric handwriting, a persistent use of a particular idiom, or a tendency to finish off what someone else is saying (p. 295). Nonetheless, because the chief purpose of language is to share meanings, when we talk or write to each other we try to discount those elements which have no function in that task.

This, at least, is the norm. But there are a number of important cases where individuality in the use of English – a personal *style*, as it is usually called – is considered to be a matter of importance, and worthy of study in its own right. These provide the subject-matter of this chapter.

> **NORMALLY DEVIANT**
> Circumstances can remove all vestiges of linguistic individuality, as is plain from this Victorian observation of Mr Punch's handwriting.

This is before dinner, 7.30. Attested by several witnesses.

This is after the Punch à la Romaine, about the middle of the banquet.

This is with the dessert.

After the Claret.

After the Claret *and* the Port.

During the cigars, whiskey and water.

Before leaving table.

Before getting into bed.

DEVIANCE

In linguistic enquiry, the notion of individual difference – of a linguistic effect which does not conform to a rule or norm – is an aspect of what is commonly referred to as *deviance*. In its extreme form, deviance produces instances of language which are totally unacceptable: *langauge, *[fplat], *cat the, *goodnessness, and *please thanks are all deviant forms at the levels of graphology, phonology, grammar, vocabulary, and discourse, respectively (p. 2). (The asterisk is conventionally used to symbolize this kind of deviant formation.) But there is nothing intrinsically unacceptable about the notion of linguistic deviance. A deviant or strange use of language may be highly effective and widely appreciated – as in any art form.

There are, moreover, different levels of deviance – degrees of departure from the norms which identify the various varieties of English (p. 290), and from the structures they have in common. Slight degrees of deviance will hardly be noticed, or will produce an effect which it may be difficult to pin down. For example, an increased use of a certain kind of vocabulary may become apparent only after a great deal of statistical investigation (as in the case of authorship studies, p. 436). For the most part, though, people who are 'being deviant' or 'strange' are being so for a purpose, and the effects are specific and noticeable. We do not normally equate lexical opposites or twist the language of everyday proverbs; so when we do, it stands out immediately. One of the most famous quotations in the language is George Orwell's 'War is Peace. Freedom is Slavery. Ignorance is Strength.' To explain the purpose and effect of such a dramatic example of norm-breaking would require us to move from a linguistic towards a literary critical world. The purpose of the example here is only to introduce the point that even such a major departure from linguistic normality is by no means uncommon, outside as well as within literature. In everyday speech and writing, Deviance, it seems, is Normal. Strangeness is Familiarity. And familiarity, as everyone knows, breeds content.

DEVIANTLY NORMAL

It would be difficult to think of a clearer case of strange linguistic behaviour than the deliberate use of unintelligible speech; but such cases are by no means uncommon in everyday spoken language. A particularly striking instance (because it turns out to be so widespread, cross-cultural, and international) is the speech of adults talking to babies, where the phonetic structure of words is radically altered, nonsense syllables are introduced, and bizarre (from the point of view of normal adult language) intonation and rhythm patterns used. Moreover, this kind of 'baby-talk' is by no means restricted to talking to babies. It may be heard when people address animals, and even at times between adults on occasions of special intimacy – though in the absence of empirical data, confirmation of this last point will have to be left to the reader's intuition.

Another example is the range of nonsensical expressions which may accompany a moment of sudden emotion. One person was observed to utter an expletive (roughly transcribed as *shplumfnooeeah*, with a crescendo at *fnoo*) when he stood on a broom and the handle came up and hit his head. The poet Robert Southey is on record as swearing by the great decasyllabon *Aballiboozobanganovribo*. Such expressions vary enormously in kind and degree of complexity, and their incidence probably varies greatly in terms of speaker sex, personality, and background; but they are commonplace.

More complex levels of systematic nonsense also exist. The phenomenon of 'scat' singing is a case in point: it reaches its peak in the performances of Ella Fitzgerald and other professional jazz singers, as well as in the duet between Mowgli and Baloo in Walt Disney's *Jungle Book*. But it can be heard at lower levels of creative expertise in many a kitchen or bathroom.

Glossolalia is another interesting domain: 'speaking in tongues' is practised by large numbers of ordinary people as part of their regular religious behaviour. In published glossolalia studies, it is evident that the syllable sequences produced do not add up to a real, unknown, and 'alien' language (what would technically be called *xenoglossia*), but rather to a radically modified form of the speaker's own language, which is used as a sign of spiritual conversion or belief. Some people admit to praying 'in tongues' in private. Here too the data, because of the intimate nature of such occasions, are difficult to obtain.

The same point applies to a further area of linguistic abnormality, the use of hidden or secret languages by criminals. Forms of 'speech disguise' have been studied in many parts of the world, the lexicon of criminal argot attracting especial attention. Cockney rhyming slang also shows similarities (p. 182).

Rather easier to study is the use of secret language by children, where many varieties exist. Large numbers of children experiment with *backslang* (producing a word backwards with a letter-by-letter or syllable-by-syllable pronunciation), and some can reach great speeds of utterance. In *eggy-peggy* speech and in *Pig Latin*, extra syllables are added to each word in a sentence. Such games are found widely across languages, and are not unknown among adults – though adults usually have more time to experiment with versions of the written language (p. 396).

Ella Fitzgerald

TALKING BACKWARDS

One of the first studies of talking backwards in children was published in 1981. It examined an 8-year-old and a 9-year-old who had (quite independently) invented a game of talking backwards, apparently without anyone's help, and had been using it for about a year. Both children had normal forwards speech. The researchers asked each child to 'translate' 100 words into backwards speech, and also a few sentences.

The two children turned out to be very different. Child A reversed the sounds of each word, ignoring the spelling. Child B reversed the spellings, sounding the letters out. The resulting pronunciations were very different. *Size*, for example, would come out as [zais] using A's method, but as [ezis] using B's. Here are some of the words they spoke (in simplified transcription):

	Child A	Child B
nine	nain	enin
guy	aig	jag
boil	loib	ljab
mouse	saum	esuam
bomb	mab	bmab
castle	lesak	eltsak

Talking backwards is one of a large number of language games which children invent at around 7 years of age. It probably stems from the same kind of creative joy which they show in jokes and riddles (p. 407). It is also a skill which, like riding a bicycle, once learned is not lost. The number of closet backwards-talking adults is probably quite large. (After N. Cowan & L. Leavitt, 1982.)

WORD GAMES

Word games played by adults provide the clearest example of the lengths to which people are prepared to go to indulge in strange linguistic behaviour. We take considerable enjoyment from pulling words apart and reconstituting them in some novel guise, arranging them into clever patterns, finding hidden meanings in them, and trying to use them according to specially invented rules. Word puzzles and competitions are to be found in newspapers, at house parties, in schools, on radio and television, and in all kinds of individual contexts—as when a commuter completes a crossword, or a child plays a game of Hangman. One of Britain's most successful television games of the 1980s was 'Blankety Blank', in which people had to guess which word fills a blank in a familiar phrase (p. 162). Another was 'Call My Bluff', where the participants had to decide which of three given meanings correctly defined an unfamiliar word. There are thousands of possibilities, providing an almost inexhaustible series of topics for radio and television game shows, as well as feeding the insatiable demand for new domestic indoor pursuits.

Written medium games

Any aspect of language structure can in principle provide the basis for a game. Most assume literacy: they are based on the written language, and rely on players recognizing the letters of the alphabet (p. 256) and being able to spell. Some are for individuals to play, the fun lying in solving a problem; others are competitive. In 'Word Squares', for example, the aim is to make up words of equal length which read both horizontally and vertically, and sometimes diagonally too. In 'Buried Words', words have to be found within sentences: in a 'find the animals' game, *deer* can be discovered in *The hunters made errors*. In 'Words Within Words', the aim is to make as many words as possible with the letters of a single word. However, to win a competition using this game is more difficult than might at first be thought: one player found 273 words in *psalter*.

Grid games all operate on the principle of building up words using letters on a predetermined network of squares. In 'Word Search', a maze game for one player, the letters are provided in advance, and the words have to be found by moving from one square to the next in any direction. In 'Scrabble®' (see opposite), a game for several players, the words have to be composed from randomly obtained groups of letters. Points are assigned based upon how many letters are used; rarer letters score higher points; and certain squares in the grid are more valuable than others. This is a game which has achieved a special place in the history of

word games, having its own international competitions, and attracting media attention.

At the other extreme, the ordinary crossword puzzle is probably the most familiar and widespread example of a grid game, though the clues which enable the puzzle to be completed rely on much more than purely lexical knowledge. The game is traditionally one for the isolated single player. However, crossword competitions are not unusual, where competitors have to complete a puzzle 'against the clock', or solve a particular set of cryptic clues. The genre is continually developing. Enthusiasts do their best to devise puzzles that are especially ingenious and testing—though 'torturing' would be a better description, bearing in mind the eponyms (p. 155) of some of the great crossword compilers (such as Torquemada and Ximenes—leaders of the Spanish Inquisition).

WORD SQUARES

Word squares involving nine words have been completed, though many of the words are rare, and involve the compiler having to make awkward decisions about the eligibility of proper names, unassimilated loan words, older spellings, compounds, and other unusual coinages (§8).

```
A N G E L S H I P
N O O N E T I D E
G O L D V I L L E
E N D W E L L E R
L E V E L L I N E
S T I L L E N E S
H I L L I N E S S
I D L E N E S S E
P E E R E S S E S
```

CARRY THIS ALLY

Computer programs now do routinely what word-game enthusiasts rack their brains to do. This is an extract from a name anagram generator. A person's name (or any word) is used as input, and the program prints out all possible word sequences (within the limits of its dictionary) using the same letters. The name *Hilary Crystal* produced over 500 such sequences. It is not a very literate program, but some of the words it found are not easily predictable (*catarrh, ashtray, lyrical, rarity*) and some of its choices are pure poetry (*shy altar lyric*).

hay racy trills
hay carry still
hill racy stray
hill scary tray
hilt lay scarry
hit rally scary
ills chary tray
ill ray starchy
ill chary stray
lash try racily
lath rays lyric
lays rat richly
lay rat rich sly
lay tars richly
lily racy trash
lily ray charts
lily star chary
lit racy rashly
racy ray thills
racy tars hilly
rat rays chilly
rat chary silly

rat richly slay
rays chill tray
ray star chilly
ray chart silly
ray chills tray
ray lyric shalt
sat carry hilly
say chill tarry
shy lilac tarry
hay tills carry
hay scary trill
hill racy trays
hilts lay carry
hilt carry slay
icy shall tarry
ill racy rat shy
ill carry hasty
ill chary trays
lash lyric tray
lath ray lyrics
lay list charry
lay silt charry

lay charry slit
lily rats chary
lily ray starch
lily tars chary
lit charry slay
racy slay thrill
racy this rally
rat shy lyrical
rat chary slily
rays rich tally
ray rich lastly
ray tars chilly
ray chart slily
ray chill stray
ray richly slat
say till charry
scar hilly tray
sill chary tray
hay till scarry
hills racy tray
hill carry stay
shy altar lyric

ETYMORPHS

Two examples from a game presented by Ruth Wajnryb in the periodical *English Today* in 1989 – in effect, a combination of 'Call My Bluff' and 'It Pays to Increase Your Word Power' (p. 123). All the reader has to do is decide which definition suits the word.

A **minuend** is:

(a) a North American animal of the fox genus, prized commercially for its fur (via French, from Cree *aminawend*).
(b) in music; a short movement of which there are usually three or four in a sonata (from Latin *minuendum*, required to be brief).
(c) in mathematics, the number from which another is to be subtracted (from Latin *minuere*, to diminish).
(d) a notation in choreography standing for a small end-step in a ballet sequence (from Latin *minus*, less).

A **houri** is:

(a) a Persian measurement of time, based on a glass containing *hur* or sand.
(b) a voluptuously beautiful woman or nymph in the Paradise of Islam (from Arabic *hur*, a woman with dark eyes).
(c) a Scottish variant of *whore*.
(d) a measurement of silk in Thailand, one houri being enough for a basic straight-skirted dress.
(*Answers, if required, are at the foot of p. 399.*)

WORD MAZES

One of the most popular word puzzles: a word maze. In the easy version, a set of words is given in advance and the task is to find them. Words may run forwards, backwards, upwards, downwards, or diagonally, but they are always in straight lines, and they do not skip letters. The same letter may be used in different words. In a more difficult version, the words are not given in advance: one is simply told to 'find the names of ten composers'. The present example allows both: the difficult task is 'Find ten words to do with the rose garden'. After failing this, the easy task is: 'Find the ten words listed at the bottom of p. 399'.

```
Y G L Y V U C M T Y S
G V I F Z H K N S D N
D R X S H E E E E R Y
B I E Q W C T B H U S
L L R E S W R H S K E
H A O B N J E W U Y P
N N U O Y F L K B S R
J R U R M H L B O D P
H O Z G P S I Y B U Z
H H D X O M S S D B O
T T S L A T E P Q W G
```

WHY NOT?

There is no limit to the number of word games. Although the number of linguistic tasks is fairly small, any area of experience can be used to provide the input to a new game. This example uses American presidents, but the exercise could be carried out using any other set of names (of composers, states, monarchs . . .). The task is to find the smallest grid in which all the names can be interlinked, in the manner of a crossword. Gyles Brandreth does it in 527 squares in The *Joy of Lex*, published in 1987. Will his solution stand the test of time? Clinton fits in very naturally in the bottom left-hand corner. However, to fit in Bush, we need two further columns. Why bother? Why not?

President grid (interlinked names): WASHINGTON, JACKSON, FILLMORE, NIXON, CARTER, POLK, TAFT, FORD, MONROE, TYLER, VAN BUREN, HAYES, HARRISON, TAYLOR, GRANT, REAGAN, CLEVELAND, EISENHOWER, and others.

Morris

Rack	Main word	Posn	Pts	CumTot
EGLMMNO	**GNOME**	8Da	20	20
DEJLMST	**JOLTED**	1Ca	42	62
AEIMSSV	**MASSIVE**	K5d	109	171
EEGIPRY	**PEERY**	L1d	33	204
AABEGIS	**JAB**	C1d	33	237
AEGIISZ	**GLAZES**	H10d	51	288
ACHIIIL	**HILI**	2Ga	22	310
ABCIITU	**BISCUIT**	15Fa	12	322
AAAINRT	**TZARINA**	13Ga	36	358
AHNOQST	**QATS**	N10d	50	408
DFHNOO*	**HOOFED**	B10d	56	464
N			−1	
				463

Cappelletto

Rack	Main word	Posn	Pts	CumTot
IINOTT*	**OMITTING**	D1d	68	68
EENOPRW	**POWER**	7Fa	26	94
ADEENUV	**SUAVE**	8Ka	27	121
ADEEINO	**DEPONE**	1Ja	27	148
AIKLRRW	**WARLIKE**	11Ea	28	176
AELORRU	**AUREOLAR#**	M8d	0	176
AELORRU	**LOUR**	B2d	17	193
ACENRUY	**CAY**	10Da	34	227
DENORUX	**OX**	2Na	31	258
DEEFNRU	**UNFREED**	A5d	85	343
G	**DOG**	11Aa	5	348
			+1	
				349

Rack: Letters held by each player prior to each move.
Mainword: Word played at each move.
Posn: Position of first letter of main word played. Board squares are numbered 1 to 15 down and A to O across. Direction of main word: a = across; d = down.
Pts: Points scored for each move.
Cum Tot: Cumulative total score for each player.
\# A play successfully challenged. * A blank tile.
Tile Values: A (1), B (3), C (3), D (2), E (1), F (4), G (2), H (4), I (1), J (8), K (5), L (1), M (3), N (1), O (1), P (3), Q (10), R (1), S (1), T (1), U (1), V (4), W (4), X (8), Y (4), Z (10)

SCRABBLE® CHAMPIONSHIPS

The game of Scrabble® now attracts the kind of specialized interest which traditionally accompanies international chess. Edited highlights from the 1991 World Championship match in London were shown on BBC television, and a book of selected games appeared soon afterwards, showing the move sequences and adding expert commentary.

All games were played with chess-clocks, with each player allowed 25 minutes. Words were allowed only if they appeared in the official dictionaries. Players were not penalized for making an incorrect challenge (i.e. asserting that a word does not exist). An unlimited number of changes were allowed, as long as seven or more tiles were left in the pool of unused letters.

The board shows the end of the first game of the final match between Peter Morris (the eventual champion) and Brian Cappelletto, both of the USA. Next to it is the sequence of plays throughout the game. An extract from the expert commentary is given below. (From G. Brandreth & D. Francis, 1992.)

Moves

6(PM) The obvious move is what Peter actually plays – GLAZES. But this does leave an awkward two I's on his rack. A better move, although scoring slightly less, is ZEA (E3d, 44 points). This would keep the S on Peter's rack – it's well worth taking 7 points less than GLAZES, and hanging on to the S.
6(BC) Brian's actual move of AUREOLAR (M8d) was challenged immediately by Peter. The challenge is upheld, and Brian scores no points on this turn. While AUREOLE, AREOLE and AREOLAR are all valid words, Brian seems to have merged them together to come up with his fictitious AUREOLAR. Potentially the best moves are UREA (6Fa, 26 points) or the very similar URAO (6Fa, 26 points).
7(PM) Peter needs to dump at least two of those I's. His actual play of HILI is excellent, leaving him with ACI.
7(BC) UREA or URAO – both at (6Fa, 26 points) – are still the potentially best moves. Brian's actual play of LOUR has opened up the 3W square at A8. This could be a risk.

GAME LEVELS

Only a few language games are, literally, *word* games – that is, operating within the confines of the orthographic word. Many go well beyond this, operating at levels of sentence and discourse (p. 286). Some examples of each are given below.

Word level

• Turn one word or phrase into another using the same letters (an *anagram*), if possible so that the meaning of the two versions relate or are incongruous.

the eyes > they see
Clint Eastwood > Old West-action
Piet Mondrian > I paint modern
parliament > partial men
astronomers > no more stars
dyslexia > daily sex

• In a word completion game, the task is to complete a partly spelled word. The interest lies in finding unusual letter sequences (p. 266). (*See foot of opposite page for answers, if needed.*)

——U R D
———— U A C
———— A R B
——— K L A ——

Sentence level

• Make a meaningful sentence 26 words long in which each word begins with a consecutive letter of the alphabet. A partial example follows. (*See foot of opposite page for one possible completion.*)

A bronzed cowboy, dancing elegantly for grand hotels in Jersey… would X-ray your zebra.

• Make a meaningful sentence which reads the same in both directions (a *palindrome*). There are several possibilities, depending on whether the word or the sentence as a whole is palindromic. If the latter, either letters or words can be the basis of the construction.

Anna sees nun deified.
I moan, Naomi.
So patient a doctor to doctor a patient so.

• Make a sentence which contains every letter of the alphabet (a *pangram*). This is not difficult to do in long sentences containing several letter duplications. The point of the game is to eliminate as many duplications as possible, ideally ending up with a sentence of 26 letters. Several such sentences have been devised, but they succeed only by using rare loan words (e.g. *cwm, veldt, qoph*), proper names, abbreviations, and a telegraphic style: *Blowzy night-frumps vex'd Jack Q* is one of the more natural ones.

• Make a sentence in which the normal spelling expectancies of the language are constrained. In *univocalics*, only one type of vowel is allowed.

Do not look for lots of good books on London or Oxford school sports.

In *lipograms*, a particular letter or letters is disallowed. This is not a particularly interesting game when using an infrequent letter such as J or X (p. 265); but it becomes intriguing when a common letter, such as E or T, is avoided.

The vowel which is missing in this sentence is the first item listed in the time-honoured sequence of English letters.

• Make a meaningful sentence in which each word begins with the same letter of the alphabet. Here is the opening of 'The Saga of Shrewd Simon Short', to show what can be done at discourse level, if one so wishes:

Shrewd Simon Short sewed shoes. Seventeen summers, speeding storms, spreading sunshine successively, saw Simon's small shabby shop still standing staunch, saw Simon's selfsame squeaking sign still swinging silently specifying: Simon Short, Smithfield's sole surviving shoemaker…

Discourse level

• Make a meaningful dialogue of 26 sentences, so that each participant produces a sentence beginning with a consecutive

letter of the alphabet:
Player 1: Are you in?
Player 2: Believe it!
Player 1: Can I come in, then?
Player 2: Do you want to?
Player 1: Ever ready.
Player 2: Fine.
Player 1: Got any gin?
Player 2: Haven't…

• Make up a poem in which a word or phrase is produced by combining the first letter of each line (an *acrostic*); alternatively, make one up in which a word is produced by combining the last letter of each line (a *telestich*). Some acrostics can be seen just by reading the text; others are constructed as puzzles or riddles ('My first [*i.e. first letter*] is in Rupert and Petra and Paul …').

• In 'Just a Minute', a well-established game on BBC radio, players take it in turns to talk on a given subject for one minute without hesitating, repeating themselves, or deviating from the subject. A chairman awards and subtracts points accordingly.

• In 'Consequences' the aim is to create incongruous juxtapositions by using a simple story-grammar. There are several variants, but the common feature is for a written narrative to be built up item by item on a sheet of paper by the players, each participant not knowing what the previous person has written. The leader provides the story outline, and the players fill in the variables one at a time. Typically, the first player begins by choosing an adjective; the second follows with a male name; the third adds a further adjective; the fourth adds a female name; subsequent players add where they met; what he said to her; what she said to him; the consequence; and what the world said about it. (*Uncertain Fred and doleful Angela met in a sauna…*) Very popular in Victorian times, this game is still played, the spice often resulting from the participants' own names being incorporated into a plot which doubtless becomes increasingly risqué as the evening proceeds.

HANGED AND DRAWN

One of the most popular children's spelling games, known for over a century, is 'Hangman' or 'Gallows'. Player A chooses a word, and shows the number of letters it contains by blanks. Player B has to guess which letters appear in the word. If the guesses are wrong, a figure of a gallows and a hanged man is built up, error by error. If the guesses are right, the correct letters are inserted into the blanks, and no addition is made to the figure. The goal is for B to guess the whole word before the picture of the hanged man is completed. The number of steps in the game varies: the illustration shows 11.

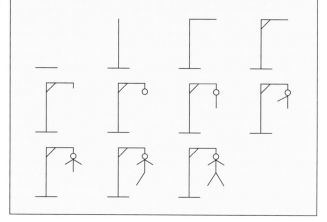

PRIZE-WINNING PALINDROMES

A palindrome by Joyce Johnson from a *New Statesman* Competition of 1967. It is called: 'Headmaster's palindromic list on his memo pad'.

Test on Erasmus
Deliver slap
Royal: phone no.?
Ref. Football.
Is sofa sitable on?
XI – Staff over
Sub-edit Nurse's order
Caning is on test (snub slip-up)
Birch (Sid) to help Miss Eve
Repaper den
Use it
Put inkspot on stopper
Prof. – no space
Caretaker (wall, etc.)
Too many d – pots
Wal for duo? (I'd name Dr O)
See few owe fees (or demand IOU?)
Dr of Law
Stop dynamo (OTC)
Tel: Law re Kate Race
Caps on for prep
Pots – no tops
Knit up ties ('U')
Ned (re paper)
Eve's simple hot dish (crib)
Pupil's buns
T-set: no sign in a/c
Red roses
Run Tide Bus?
Rev off at six
Noel Bat is a fossil
Lab to offer one 'Noh' play – or 'Pals Reviled'?
Sums are not set.

CHRONOGRAMS

A chronogram is a date hidden in a sequence of words, using the conventions of Roman numerals: M (1000), D (500), C (100), L (50), X (10), V (5, also used for U), and I (1). The relevant letters are usually written in capitals, giving an odd mixed-case appearance to the line. Chronograms were commonly used on memorials, foundation stones, tombstones, medals, and title pages to mark the date of an event. They are sometimes seen in Christmas cards. They are not as easy to construct appropriately as it might appear. If, for example, one wished to use the title of this book as a chronogram, it would emerge as:

the CaMbrIDge enCyCLopeDIa of the engLIsh LangUage

which would give a date of appearance of 2458! (=MDDCCCLLLLVIII)

Spoken medium games

Formally constituted games based on speech sounds are less common, though informal word-play, involving riddles, charades, puns and tongue-twisters is common enough, from an early age (p. 395). The reason presumably is that auditory perception and short-term memory cannot cope with the complexities of a multi-dimensional game; it is difficult to conceive of an auditory version of Scrabble®, for instance (p. 397). On the other hand, these very difficulties can motivate a game. 'Chinese Whispers' (or 'Russian Gossip') is an example of a perceptual game, where the participants are arranged in a circle, and a message is passed from one person to the next in a whisper: the fun comes in comparing the original version with the final version. There are also many games in which the object is to remember an increasingly growing list of things to say, or games where we have to recall words from our knowledge of the language ('How many words beginning with W can you say in a minute?'). And there are games which play with the conventions of discourse rules, such as the Victorian circle-game 'Cross Questions and Crooked Answers': the first player whispers a question to the second, who whispers an answer; the second does the same to the third, and so on; when everyone has taken a turn, each person reports the question he or she was asked and the answer he or she received. Some entertaining juxtapositions usually result.

The range and popularity of word games is intriguing. Perhaps their appeal lies in their essentially non-specialized nature. In the world of television games, for example, there are many competitions where to be successful we need to have specialized knowledge, an excellent memory, a special skill, or considerable stamina or strength. To win at such quiz games as 'Mastermind', a period of study and preparation is required. But for language games, the only requirement is that we can speak/listen or read/write. They rely on our knowledge and memory of language, and nothing else.

Our linguistic long-term memory is indeed remarkable. We hear an old record on the radio, and find we can sing the words along with it, even though we might not have heard them for decades, and would have been unable to recall them deliberately five minutes before. Our brains are crammed with fragments of old nursery rhymes, poems learned in school, prayers, local dialect expressions, jokes, advertising slogans, old catch phrases, and much more. And beneath all of this is the solid foundation of the rules of grammar, sounds, and vocabulary laid down in early conversations, and a substantial awareness of spelling expectancies picked up from our reading and writing. It is this combination of skills which makes everyone qualified to play games with English speech and writing.

A UNIQUE UNIVOCALIZER

The Victorian wordsmith, C. C. Bombaugh, devised univocalic poems for each vowel. Here is his offering for *I*: 'The Approach of Evening' (1890).

Idling, I sit in this mild twilight dim,
Whilst birds, in wild, swift vigils, circling skim.
Light winds in sighing sink, till, rising bright,
Night's Virgin Pilgrim swims in vivid light!

DINGBATS®

The aim of this board game, devised by Paul Sellers, and published by Waddingtons in 1987, is to decode a word-puzzle to reveal a well-known phrase or saying. The game cuts across the divide between spoken and written language games, and taps all levels of language awareness. To solve the first card shown you need to see in it a semantic substitution (hyponymy, p. 166), a visual lexical pun (homophony), and an implied lexical pun (*for* vs *four*). The second uses a real word, the logic of spatial prepositions, spelling reversal, and a grammatical pun (noun phrase *back words* vs adverb *backwards*). What 'drives you crazy' (as the game's blurb claims) is the fact that you do not know which of these (and many other strategies) you need to solve a particular puzzle – yet you know you know the answer all the time (see below right).

TWISTING TONGUES (MAINLY)

Tongue-twisters depend for their effect not only on consonant tongue movements, but also on using far-apart vowels (p. 238). Bilabial sequences are often vowel-based (as in *Peter Piper picked a peck of pickled pepper*).

Palato-alveolar/alveolar
If a shipshape ship shop stocks six shipshape ship-soiled ships, how many shipshape ship-soiled ships would six shipshape ship shops stock?
Bilabial
'Are you copper-bottoming 'em, my man?' 'No, I'm aluminiuming 'em with the minimum of aluminium, ma'am.'

MULTI-SYSTEM GAMES

Some word games rely on an interaction with non-linguistic systems–in particular, with numerical values.

• In *alphametics*, a series of semantically related words is given in a puzzle which can be solved only if numbers are substituted for letters. An example is 'Two wrongs make a right', which can be solved if the sentence is treated as an addition sum: WRONG + WRONG = RIGHT. The task is to work out what numerical values need to be assigned to these letters to make them add up correctly. (See foot of page for the answer.)
• In a similar game, numbers are substituted for letters (usually A=1, B=2, etc.), and the 'values' of the words are then compared to see if they convey hidden meanings. People at a party might compute the values of their names and see who is numerically 'related' – having the same value, adjacent values, or separated by a significant round number (such as 100). In earlier times, this technique (known as *gematria*) was used to provide insights into the meaning of life, fuelled by such coincidences as *Jesus* and *Messiah* both scoring 74 (as indeed does the word *English*), or *Bible* and *Holy Writ* being separated by exactly 100.

PUZZLE ANSWERS

Etymorphs (p. 396): (c); (b)

Word Mazes (p. 397): beds, blooms, buds, bushes, greenfly, hybrid, petals, scent, thorn, trellis

Word Completion (p. 398): gourd, bivouac, rhubarb, necklace

Sentence Completion (p. 398): ... knitting lovely mittens nicely on prettily quilted rubber shoes, thought untrained vets ...

Alphametics (above): W = 2, R = 4, O = 1, N = 5, G = 3, I = 8, H = 9, T = 6

Dingbats (left): a time and a place for everything; bend over backwards.

RULE-BREAKING VARIETIES

A readiness to deviate from the norms of language (p. 394) is found in many varieties of English – though by no means all. Indeed, in some situations linguistic strangeness would be unexpected, unwelcome, or positively disallowed. A clear instance is in public legal settings (p. 374), where there are well-established conventions about what we should say and how we should say it (and where, if we do not follow these rules and guidelines, we may be in 'contempt of court'). Many religious situations also depend on linguistic stability and predictability for their identity (p. 371). And the house styles used by publishers promote a standardized presentation which leaves limited scope for linguistic individuality.

On the other hand, there are several situations where it is perfectly in order to be strange, and indeed where the breaking of linguistic rules is seen as a positive and desirable feature of communication. The world of newspaper headings and headlines is a case in point, where telegraphic English (p. 382) is the norm, and where puns, misquotation, and other forms of word play are widespread. But it is probably the world of advertising – both press and television – which provides the best-recognized class of examples (p. 388). Most advertising slogans gain their effect by manipulating the linguistic norms of everyday language. Random examples include deviant rhymes and rhythms (*Drinka pinta milka day*), spellings (*EZLern driving school*), figures of speech (*Kellogg's. That's how you can eat sunshine*), and grammar (the distinctive time adverbial in *Only two Alka Seltzers ago, you were feeling downhearted and low*). The *Heineken* series provides a sophisticated example of the creative use of deviance (p. 389).

DAILY DEVIANCE

If asked to say where linguistic deviance is most commonly to be found, most people would think of literature – poetry, in particular – and they would be right (p. 410). If asked to say which variety of language holds second place, most people would hazard advertising – and they would be wrong. The second prize definitely has to go to a variety which, from a first impression, would not seem to be deviant at all: everyday conversation.

The first impression misleads because most people have a formal idea of conversation – thinking perhaps of the carefully-fashioned dialogues of language teaching textbooks (p. 295). There is indeed little sign of linguistic strangeness there; but that is because the conversational situations presented are typically conventional ones. The participants may not know each other well, or at all, and are invariably shown on their 'best behaviour'. The realities of everyday, natural conversation of the most informal or intimate kind are not presented (p. 295). However, when we take the opportunity to listen to such situations, as everyone can do as participant observers, we quickly encounter evidence of deviant linguistic forms.

Lexical deviance (p. 130) is probably the most widely practised type.

• A group of adults at a party were struck by one speaker's (normal) use of a prefix, *neo-*, mocked him for being hyper-intellectual, and placed *neo-* before all kinds of words for several minutes (*neo-cake, neo-door handles*). After a while, the joke faded, but it returned at the end of the evening, when someone made a further coinage, and a new 'round' of *neo-*isms began.

• During a conversation before dinner, one person, asked if she were hungry, replied *hungry-ish*, which led others to add *-ish* to their responses, and to play with the suffix: *starving-ish*, said one; *I'm ishy as well*, said another.

This kind of 'nonce' lexical creativity (p.130) helps to solve a communication problem or to introduce an element of informality, humour, or rapport into a situation. None of the coinages reach the status of becoming real neologisms – entering the language as a whole.

Phonetic or phonological deviance (§17) is also widely practised, chiefly by putting on 'silly voices'. This is particularly common in joke-telling, but it often has nothing to do with humour (the participants do not laugh), being more a matter of maintaining rapport.

• A man in his mid-twenties enters a room and sees his brother. He addresses him in a high-pitched, larynx-raised, querulous voice, to which the other immediately responds, using a similar voice. Several exchanges are made in this voice, and then they switch into their normal voices. However, from time to time during the meeting they revert to this voice again. At one point a third person in the room, a close friend of both, uses it as well.

Grammatical deviance is less common, and when it occurs is largely an aspect of variety humour (p. 410), adopting a construction which is not part of one's normal way of talking. There is no class restriction here: people who speak Standard English adopt nonstandard constructions, often putting on an alien accent; and people who speak nonstandard English adopt standard constructions, often accompanied by a 'posh voice'. Very often, the constructions (and the accents) are stereotypes, borrowed from television. A famous British example of the 1980s was the use of a *wot* ('what') relative clause, derived from comedian Ernie Wise's weekly account of 'a play wot I wrote'. In the 1990s this is still heard as a grammatical catch phrase (p. 178), but now applied to all kinds of situations (*a car wot I bought*). (For further examples of variety humour, see p. 410.)

KEEP YOUR DISTANCE

The adoption of an alien accent can express social distance rather than rapport. Early in the film *The Third Man* (1949), Holly Martins encounters Major Calloway for the first time, and they do not get on. Martins reflects on Harry Lime's death.

MARTINS: ... Best friend I ever had.
CALLOWAY: That sounds like a cheap novelette.
MARTINS: I write cheap novelettes.
CALLOWAY: I've never heard of you. What's your name again?

MARTINS: Holly Martins.
CALLOWAY: No. Sorry.
MARTINS *as English as possible*: Ever heard of 'The Lone Rider of Santa Fe'?
CALLOWAY: No.
MARTINS *very American*: 'Death at Double X Ranch'?
CALLOWAY: No.

In the film, Joseph Cotten pronounces a drawled [a] for *Ranch*, then follows it up with a mock back RP [ɑː] pronunciation. (Based on the shooting script by G. Greene, 1973, p. 25.)

READ IT ALL ABOUT

Just how universal is linguistic deviance in newspaper headlines – over and above the standard use of telegraphic grammar (p. 382)? An informal survey of the newspapers collected for the 'Day in the Life of the Language' section (p. 300) shows examples of puns, word play, and functional misquotation all over the English-writing world, but with considerable variation in frequency. Usage seems to be influenced more by subject-matter than by region or readership level. It is commonest in humorous columns and satirical diaries, as we might expect, and then in the 'creative' pages of the arts. The sports pages also attract considerable word play. Indeed, in several papers, these are the only sections which provide examples. (Headlines are standardized in lower case; contexts are indicated in parentheses.)

• Word play is less popular in the USA than in the UK. In two New York newspapers, only one example was found in each – and both of these were in the arts sections:

New York Newsday
Bold strokes (*works of art*)
New York Times
Violinists to play so youngsters can string along (*music education*)

On the other hand, word play was more evident in a California paper, sprinkled throughout several sections:

Los Angeles Times
Backin' the saddle again (*local council supports Silver Saddle Casino*)
Pandamonium (*zoo story*)
Unkindest cut of all (*clothing and sport*)
A trying situation (*court case*)

Loan sharks in sheep's clothing (*personal finance*)
Devil's grass: let us spray

Some British and Canadian papers showed word play only in the arts and sport sections:

The Times
Welsh rare hits (*concert review in Wales*)
Familiarity breeds sell-outs (*Ballet review*)
Sisters several times removed (*theatre review*)
Barks worse than their bite (*Review of TV programme about wolves*)
The Daily Telegraph
Minority rites (*TV review of ethnic programme*)
Three ages of woman (*theatre review*)
Souffle can rise to the occasion (*Racehorse called Souffle*)
The Vancouver Sun
Bladerunner (*sport: fencing*)

• British newspapers are much more ready to use word play, and to go in for highly deviant forms. The leader here is *The Sun*. In the quality press, *The Guardian* is traditionally the monarch of intellectual punning, though on the day selected for the survey it provided relatively few examples (and mainly from the arts pages). It was an Australian paper which in fact provided the most examples of all the papers surveyed.

The Sun
Yacht a cheek (*front page: royal yacht costs*)
We're toe in love (*barefoot wedding*)
Kid napper (*device for sending babies to sleep*)
Pain stops play (*cricketer bitten by adder*)
Time marshes on (*renaming of building formerly named after boxer Terry Marsh*)
Nip nip hooray (*firm receives kimono order*)
Pork chop (*meat banned from pub*)
At last we've got 'em by the googlies (*cricket story*)
The Guardian
Out on a wing and a prayer (*front page: air force story*)
Kent expose skinny middle (*cricket*)
The slick and the dead (*tourist spots*)
Where's there a Will? (*Looking for evidence of Shakespeare*)
Pride and prejudice (*TV review of ethnic story*)
Insiders out, outsiders in (*book review*)
The Gospels a-go-go (*religion and discos*)
A suitable case for placement (*social care*)
The Sydney Morning Herald
Tennis suffers from viewers' passing shots (*audience figures*)
Medifraud (*Medicare fraud*)
Did Ming have a Fling? (*review of book on Menzies*)
New low feared at summit (*G7 meeting*)
It's not all Pi in the Sky in HSC maths (*education story*)
Stay composed for music's electives (*education story*)
Famous femme five of film (*review of The Piano*)
California screamin' (*review of jazz group from California*)
A shedentary life (*men's garden sheds*)
Three men and a brasserie (*eating out review*)
Trust in the contents (*review of book on National Trust*)
Spreading nonsense (*review of book on margarine modelling*)
A roo awakening at the table (*gourmet kangaroo meat*)

• It might be thought that second-language situations would be reluctant to use word play, and indeed the papers surveyed from these areas had very little sign of them. But they were not totally absent. We leave the last word with the two items found in the surveyed edition of the **South China Morning Post**:

Top of the pots plus tea for two (*ceramics arts review*)
Manufacturers seek peace of the action (*military technology exhibition*)

a Shedentary LIFE

While women still control the kitchen, some blokes look to the garden shed as the place to find a room of their own. **JON CASIMIR** investigates the shed factor.

STRANGENESS?

Even formal scientific language becomes lexically inventive, from time to time, though not without resistance from the establishment (as in the case of *boojum*, p. 139). Terms such as *quark*, *strange*, and *charmed* have now become part of the accepted terminology of particle physics, as have such metaphors as *slow*, *split*, and *decay*.

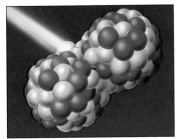

A slow neutron about to split a uranium nucleus.

CREATING

Even swearing can be creative. There are literary precedents in the ritual exchanges (*flyting*) used by Germanic leaders before their battles (p. 12), or in the extravagant invective of the Scottish makars (p. 53). Verbal duelling contests between street gangs or individuals, before or instead of violence, are probably universal, and involve a highly inventive figurative language, in which the taunts subject the participants, their close relatives, and selected parts of their bodies to an increasingly bizarre set of unpleasant circumstances.

First Combatant. " —— ! —— ! —— ! &c." *Bystander.* " Why don't yer answer 'im back ? " *Second Combatant.* " 'Ow can I ? 'E's used all the best words ! "

PPPPS

The nearest we can get to informal conversation in the written language is the informal letter written between people who know each other well. As with conversation (p. 400), this variety is full of usage which at times goes out of its way to break linguistic rules. The most deviant effects are seen in the exchanges between young people, but any informal letter will show some of the following features. The ending of one such letter is provided as an illustration, with the close of a more formal letter brought in for comparison. (For terminology, see §18.)

Graphetic effects
• The writing proceeds in varying directions, often not in straight lines, and sometimes sideways (as in the afterthought shown here). The letter termination may vary in its position, though it is usually in the middle of the page (unlike modern formal letters, which tend to be left-justified, p. 257).
• Informal letters are generally handwritten. Traditionally, typing such letters would warrant a remark or apology, but the use of word processors (whose speed of operation can foster an informal style) has reduced the need for such comments.
• Non-linguistic illustrative material can be included: the illustration shows a tiny face and a couple of kisses.
• Formal letter-writing conventions may be parodied, such as by adding

a 'My Ref/Your Ref' to the opening, or a printed gloss to a signature.
• Coloured paper is often used, of varying sizes, often with decorative designs.

Graphology
• There is an exaggerated use of punctuation, especially of exclamation marks and question marks.
• The formal use of the comma and period is frequently replaced by dashes and continuation dots.
• Punctuation tends to be used inconsistently. In the illustration, the last paragraph begins with three sentences separated by commas; and the third postscript does not use periods.
• Capitalization of varying sizes is used for emphasis, irony, and other purposes.
• There may be a deliberate use of deviant spelling – seen here only in the use of *luv* in the farewell formula and the capitalized mock-name of the visitor.

Grammar
• The style is elliptical. The extract shows omission of subject pronouns (*got to rush*, *Am expecting*), and incomplete sentences.
• Sentences are typically loosely constructed, often linked by a series of *ands* (p. 215).

and look forward to our meeting on the 14th, when I hope we shall be able to resolve all the outstanding matters.

Please let me know if there is anything else I need to do in the meantime.

Yours sincerely

Michael Wilson

M G Wilson <u>Treasurer</u>

Mr T Owen
PO Box 5 Holyhead LL65 1RG

said he'd get me a ticket — and he'd jolly well better had !!! Otherwise there'll be BIG trouble !!

Right, that's it, got to rush. Am expecting the door bell to ring any minute with U-No-HU wanting to come in. Shall I... shan't I?? Read the next exciting episode ...
with biscuits!

Lots of Luv Dee X X

P.S. Did you get to see Freddie ?
P.P.S Don't forget I'll be out on Fri, so if you're ringing, don't.
PPPS Keep taking the tablets !

• The style reflects informal speech in its use of contracted verb forms: *he'd, there'll.*
• No especial attention is paid to niceties of grammatical expression. There may be some highly colloquial constructions, as in *he'd jolly well better had.*

Vocabulary
• Informal abbreviations are common, such as *v* ('very'), *u* ('you'), and – shown here – *Fri* ('Friday').
• There is considerable use of 'basic' vocabulary, such as *get* (used here twice) and *nice*, often criticized in style manuals.
• Writers use a wide range of parochial vocabulary, slang, and semantic allusion, often involving other varieties of the language (as in the references to *episode* and *tablets*).

Discourse
• The lack of pre-planning is shown by the marginal addendum and the repeated postscripts – one of the most widely used informal conventions, allowing great scope for humour.
• Formal opening conventions may be disregarded: *Dear X* can be replaced with *Hi!* or some nickname; the date can be a partial or vague (*Tues p.m.*) or overprecise (*6.07p.m.*); an address can be highly abbreviated (*The Flat*).
• So much information is taken for granted, because of the shared experiences of the correspondents, that most of an informal letter is unintelligible to the outsider – as here.

. . . I read American poems, including, of course, yours, to the University of Wales a week or so ago. And will be broadcasting some soon again. I'll let you know details.
Caitlin sends her love to you & Gene and so do I.
I do hope (again) you can airmail that cabbage back (see asterisk on first page).
Ever,
Dylan

Just finishing final revision of 'Under Milk Wood'. It's quite a bit better. Would you like the ms? or, rather, bunches of the working sheets?
D.

Do you know—I mean, can you get for me—the Hairies' address? I'll send them the crabs of a letter. D.
I'll write fully next time, v soon.

(Dylan Thomas to Oscar Williams, 28 July 1953. From P. Ferris, 1985, p. 908).

The asterisk on the first page referred to a fee which Thomas was owed. *Cabbage* is slang for paper money.

FROM A DRAPER MAD WITH LOVE

Part of the humour in this famous letter stems from the way formal and informal styles of letter-writing are juxtaposed. Mrs Willy Nilly, the postman's wife, has just steamed open a letter from Mr Mog Edwards to Miss Myfanwy Price.

MRS WILLY NILLY From Manchester House, Llaregyb. Sole Prop: Mr Mog Edwards (late of Twll), Linendraper, Haberdasher, Master Tailor, Costumier. For West End negligee, Lingerie, Teagowns, Evening Dress, Trousseaux, Layettes. Also Ready to Wear for All Occasions. Economical Outfitting for

Agricultural Employment Our Speciality, Wardrobes Bought. Among Our Satisfied Customers Ministers of Religion and J.P.'s. Fittings by Appointment. Advertising Weekly in the *Twll Bugle*. Beloved Myfanwy Price my Bride in heaven,

MOG EDWARDS I love you until Death do us part and then we shall be together for ever and ever. A new parcel of ribbons has come from Carmarthen to-day, all the colours in the rainbow. I wish I could tie a ribbon in your hair a white one but it cannot be. I dreamed last night you were all dripping wet and you sat on my lap as the Reverend Jenkins went down the street. I see you got a mermaid in your lap he said and he lifted his hat. He is a proper Christian. Not like Cherry Owen who said you

should have thrown her back he said. Business is very poorly. Polly Garter bought two garters with roses but she never got stockings so what is the use I say. Mr Waldo tried to sell me a woman's nightie outsize he said he found it and we know where. I sold a packet of pins to Tom the Sailors to pick his teeth. If this goes on I shall be in the workhouse. My heart is in your bosom and yours is in mine. God be with you always Myfanwy Price and keep you lovely for me in His Heavenly Mansion. I must stop now and remain, Your Eternal, Mog Edwards.

MRS WILLY NILLY And then a little message with a rubbber stamp. Shop at Mog's!!!

(Dylan Thomas, *Under Milk Wood*, 1954.)

THE EDGES OF LANGUAGE

Religious language has always been a fruitful source of rule-breaking. This is because (to adapt a philosophical aphorism of the 1930s) those who believe in God are continually trying to say what cannot be said. If they choose to operate linguistically at all – as opposed to using glossolalia (p. 395), primitive sounds, or silence – they need to bend language in order to express their sense of something that exists beyond it. In another figure of speech, theists have been described as having to walk along the 'edge' of meaning in an attempt to talk insightfully about spiritual realities; and this metaphor is in fact the title of an influential book on the subject by US theologian Paul Van Buren: *The Edges of Language* (1972).

The search for a special language in religion – a language which breaks away from the norms of expression used elsewhere – is in itself nothing new. Metaphors and paradoxes are found throughout the history of English-speaking Christianity, some (such as *I eat your body*) deriving from its very foundation. John Donne concludes one of his 'Divine Meditations' (XIV) with a series of striking paradoxes:

> Take mee to you, imprison mee, for I,
> Except you enthrall mee, never shall be free,
> Nor ever chast, except you ravish mee.

Expressions of this kind are especially frequent in Christianity, though they can be found in the thought of several religions. Words which in other situations would seem meaningless, absurd, or self-contradictory, are accepted as potentially meaningful in a religious setting.

But figurative language does not stay fresh for ever, and the metaphors of traditional religious expression need to be regularly refurbished, if its message is to stay relevant, meaningful and alive. The devising of new ways of talking about God is always a controversial activity, given the conservative forces within religious expression (p. 368), but it is always there; and the process presents us with a steady flow of fresh language, whose aim is to make people think again about their response to the issues the language conveys. In the communication-aware 20th century, this process of criticism and revision of traditional modes of expression has been particularly noticeable, and has spilled over into several everyday religious contexts in the form of new prayers, hymns (p. 368), biblical translations (p. 59), and semantic allusions. The unexpected collocations (p. 163) of 'Litany for the Ghetto' provide a striking case in point.

TO WHOM WILL YE LIKEN GOD? (ISAIAH 40.18)

Where is the new language, sought by the theologians, to come from? Judging by the examples given in their programmatic statements, it is to be found chiefly in fresh collocations – new juxtapositions of lexical items which suggest ways of talking, and thus of thinking, about God that relate more meaningfully to the present day. Some of these new ways will emerge through intellectual reflection, some through poetic inspiration, some (as in the gender-inspired hymns illustrated on p. 368) from a mixture of the two. They are invariably controversial, attracting criticism both from within religion (for departing too radically from the safe and familiar thinking-grounds of traditional language) and from outside it (for introducing a misconceived mysticism into previously untainted everyday notions).

This poem arose out of a dictionary study of the kinds of collocation which could fuel a new theography (D. Crystal, 1981, 1986). In principle, the whole dictionary is available, from *aardvark* to *zygote*.

Gaardvark

Sometimes I can feel You
    burrowing at night,
    with Your powerful digging claws
    and Your long tubular snout
    and Your long sticky tongue,
Rooting out the ants and termites in my mind.

I'd love to like all creatures great and small,
But that ain't easy, when they're ants.*
We're brought up to hate ants,
To exterminate them with boiling water
Or velly efficient Japanese lemedy
Nippooning them at their last supper.
The earth pig's way is better,
But not so practicable, in Gwynedd.

I wish I could exterminate
    my mind-bending termites
    with the ease of the earth pig,
    but each time I get one
    another hundred come,
Especially in the daytime.

Why don't You burrow in the daytime as well?

I expect You would if I'd let You.
I do mean to let You.
But I forget.

* Or spiders (says my wife).

O God, who hangs on street corners, who tastes the grace of cheap wine and the sting of the needle,

Help us to touch you...

O God, whose name is spick, black-nigger, bastard, guinea and kike,

Help us to know you...

O God, who lives in tenements, who goes to segregated schools, who is beaten in precincts, who is unemployed,

Help us to know you...

O God, who is cold in the slums of winter, whose playmates are rats—four-legged ones who live with you and two-legged ones who imprison you,

Help us to touch you...

(From Robert Castle, 'Litany for the Ghetto', in J. A. T. Robinson, 1967.)

ETERNAL NOW

Paul Tillich is one of several 20th-century theologians who have argued for a radical shift in linguistic consciousness. He says in his book *The Eternal Now* (1963, p. 94):

the words which are used most in religion are those whose genuine meaning is also completely lost... Such words must be reborn, if possible; and thrown away if this is not possible.

The theme is taken up by another theologian, Gerhard Ebeling, in his *Introduction to a Theological Theory of Language* (1972, p. 192):

If the language of faith ceases to be in dialogue with the experience of the world, it has effectively become the language of unbelief.

It is this kind of thought which motivates such radical alternative language as that illustrated on this page.

VERBAL HUMOUR

Much of the linguistic deviance which occurs in informal conversation stems from a humorous use of word play. But word play arises in several different ways. Sometimes it is isolated and unpremeditated, as in the spontaneous wisecrack, quip, or deliberate pun. Sometimes it is pre-planned and structured, as in the lampoon, impersonation, cartoon, and caricature, and in such literary genres as parody and satire. All of these are intentional acts, on the part of the language user. By contrast, humour can arise from an unintentional use of language, resulting in such effects as howlers, misprints, slips of the tongue, and accidental puns. There are also marginal forms of humour, as in teasing and sarcasm, where only the speaker is amused; such exchanges are probably better classed along with ridicule and insult (p. 173). The present section deals only with exchanges which both listener(s) and speaker agree are (in theory, at least) funny.

Jokes

The funny story, or joke, is the archetypal instance of humour. It can be analysed into several components:

• *Speaker floor-taking.* Examples: *Hey, listen to this*; *Can I tell my Kerryman story now?*; *I've got a really awful one.* A preliminary utterance of this kind is not strictly necessary, but it is very common, especially in joke-telling sessions involving several participants.

• *Opening formula.* Examples: *Have you heard the one about the...?*; *There was an Englishman, an Irishman...*; *Knock, knock.* It is evidently important to let listeners know that a joke is about to be told, partly to check that they are in the right frame of mind, and partly to avoid the risk of having the utterance taken seriously. Dead-pan humour often does without this 'warning'.

• *Recitation.* The joke proper, which may be as short as a single sentence (a 'one-liner') or as long as patience permits (the 'shaggy-dog story'). There must be a recognizable climax to the recitation (the 'punch-line'). During the telling, there may be accompanying interaction.

• *Interaction.* This may be informal and random, in the form of groans, feedback noises such as *yeah*, comments (e.g. *I don't think I'm going to like this*), and 'clever' interpolations. It may also be formal, part of the structure of the joke and requiring a response, as in such sequences as the following (see top of facing page):

PARODIC LANGUAGE

Parody is a genre of linguistic imitation which has many purposes: it can be written out of dislike and antipathy, as in a parody of the doublespeak of government spokespeople (p.176), or stem from a spirit of acclaim and delight, as in Anthony Burgess's parody of James Joyce on p. 134. Whatever the motivation, it is critical that the audience recognize that a parody is in fact taking place. A perfect imitation would not be funny, because it would be confused with the real thing. There is a vast difference between parody and forgery. Parody exaggerates, distorts, and aims to be recognizably different – typically by overusing a feature of the original's language or by displacing the content so that it could not have been written in the style used for it.

This poem is an example of the latter. It is on the subject of vacuum cleaners, and is written in Muddle English by Umffrei,

a medieval bard created for the purpose by Bill Nash. It also illustrates a further critical point about parody – that one's appreciation of the joke depends entirely on how well one knows the parodic object. A comparison with p. 36 would not be amiss, at this point – though one should bear in mind Nash's own perceptive comment, which applies to the whole genre of parody:

I have discovered that the most appreciative readers of Muddle English are those who do not know too much about Middle English. Scholars tend to be a little restive, and feel obliged to point out that the grammar, dialect features, and so forth are not strictly consistent or accurate. Indeed they are not, and this is just the parodic point. In parody there has to be a *designed imperfection* . . . that proclaims to the world at large: 'This is a SPOOF. Read in accordance with the rules of SPOOFING. If you don't know the rules, KINDLY LEAVE.'

Vakum Clenere

Ha, vakum clenere, synge thi songe,
A luvsum laye hyt ys, I wene.
Wyth brethynges amorous and stronge
Thow makest mone a mornynge longe
Til al mi hows ys clene.
  Then welcum, welcum, vakum-wight
  That suckest uppe the mucke aright.

A serpente ys thi luvelie necke,
Thi bodie ys a litel bulle;
On duste thow dynest, manye a pecke,
Thow gobblest everie spotte and specke,
Thi beye waxeth fulle.
  Then welcum, welcum, vakum-wight
  That suckest uppe the mucke aright.

Foteless thow farest thurgh mi halle,
Thow grazest on the grittie grownde,
And, grettest wondyrment of alle,
Thi tayle thow pluggest yn a walle,
Yf anye poynte be fownde.
  Then welcum, welcum, vakum-wight
  That suckest uppe the mucke aright.

A derksum closet ys thi den,
Wherin thow liggest stocke-stille
Til hit be Saterday, and then
Thow farest foorth, and alle men
Cryen, wyth gode wille,
  Ha, welcum, welcum, vakum-wight
  That suckest uppe the mucke aright.

(W. Nash, 1992, p. 91.)

COUNTRY LIFF

One of the most popular columns in *Punch* magazine (p. 411) was 'Country Life', a readers' selection of the unintentionally humorous in print – misprints, howlers, and bizarre observations sent in from all over the world.

• At one time he was well up in the first 10 places, but hitting a bride in Wales damaged the suspension and he dropped back. (*Autosport*)
• Volunteers urgently needed to help stroke patients with speech problems. (*Chorlton and Wilbrampton News*)
• He said it is unlikely pollution is the cause and the fish bore no outward signs of disease – 'these fish are perfectly healthy, except that they're dead'. (*Vancouver Sun*)
• Cross-examined by Mr Quinn, witness said that someone called her husband 'an Irish pig'. She said he was not Irish. (*Biddulph Chronicle*)
• A fifteen-year-old Croydon boy has been suspended by his head since last September because of his long hair. (*Times Educational Supplement*)
• The Roman Catholic Archdiocese of New York has joined a group of Orthodox rabbits in condemning the 'Life of Brian'. (From G. Pierce, 1980.)

SPOKEN MISPRINTS

In the British satirical magazine *Private Eye*, there is a column reporting the linguistic howlers made by presenters on radio and television: *Colemanballs*, named after the BBC sports commentator, David Coleman, to whom such blunders were first ascribed. The genre is popular: three collections of the material have now been published. Several items are of little comic value, being simply slips of the tongue or malapropisms (p. 406) which could be found in any pressured speech situation. But each edition also brings to light a gabble of appealing tautologies, anti-climaxes, mixed metaphors, and non sequiturs. Most listeners or viewers would probably not have noticed them at the time they were said: the humour lies in seeing them in the cold light of day, and out of context

• Oh and that's a brilliant shot. The odd thing is his mum's not very keen on snooker.
• Lillian's great strength is her strength.
• Hurricane Higgins can either win or lose this final match tomorrow.
• He and his colleagues are like hungry hounds galloping after a red herring.
• Only one word for that – magic darts!
• The audience are literally electrified and glued to their seats. (From P. Simpson, 1992.)

A: Why is X to do with Y? (e.g. *Why are vampires mad?*)
B: I don't know. Why?
A: Because Z. (*Because they're bats*)

• *Evaluation.* After the joke, there is a reaction, either nonverbal (groans, laughter) or verbal (*That's ancient, Got any more like that?, That's disgusting*), or – most commonly – both. The absence of these kinds of reaction is a sign of failure: the joke is unfunny, inept, embarrassing, out-of-place, or too subtle (*I don't get it*).

Jokes often occur singly, but the occurrence of one tends to provoke others, and long 'joke-capping' sequences can emerge – a kind of friendly verbal duelling (p. 53).

Puns

Puns are the most sharply focused kind of verbal humour: two unrelated meanings are suddenly and unexpectedly brought together in a single word, and the incongruity makes us laugh or groan. A pun may constitute a joke in itself (as is often the case with children's rapid-fire dialogues) or be the punch-line of a much larger joke (as in the shaggy-dog story). Pun-capping sequences are commonplace, too, as in this example, prompted by the arrival of someone who had an arm in plaster (from D. Chiaro, 1992):

Initiator: No 'arm in it, eh Peter?
Participant: Yeah, got to hand it to you . . .
Peter: That's not funny!
Initiator: Put my finger on it have I?
Participant: 'armless enough!

Such sequences rarely last very long, for people quickly get bored with a pun-capping theme, and let it die; but even a well-explored theme can be resurrected later in a conversation, as with the examples of grammatical deviance reported on p. 400.

JOKE FASHIONS

There are fashions in joke telling. A particular object, animal, person, scandal, or TV programme can generate thousands of jokes for a few months, then disappear. Many of the jokes, of course, will turn up again later in some new setting.

Kerryosity (p. 134)

Locality jokes tend to be more permanent in character. Every country has its locale which is used as the butt of humour – usually a rural or isolated spot where the people are supposed to be more stupid than elsewhere. Fortunately, the locals tend to take it in good part, and have their own supply of jokes which they use in return. People from County Kerry in Ireland, for example, do not take it personally when they see themselves lampooned in such collections as Des MacHale's *Bumper Book of Kerryman Jokes* (1981). As the editor of the collection says, 'Kerrymen know they are superior, and no other Irish county could have absorbed in such a good humoured way so many jokes directed against themselves . . . and come back smiling looking for more'. In actual fact, some of the jokes reported are standard, turning up in collections all over the English-speaking world, with appropriate changes of nationality, name, or accent.

Kerry businessman: 'Where's my pencil?'
Secretary: 'It's behind your ear, sir.'
Kerry businessman: 'Look, I'm a busy man, which ear?'

Have you heard about the Kerry kidnapper?
He enclosed a stamped addressed envelope with the ransom note.

First Kerryman: What's Mick's other name?
Second Kerryman: Mick who?

Why do Kerry dogs have flat faces?
From chasing parked cars.

And, from the archive of things Kerrymen are reported to have said about people from other Irish counties:

What do you call an intelligent Mayoman?
Very, very lucky.

How do you save a Galwayman from drowning?
You don't know?
Good.

What's the difference between a Dublin wedding and a Dublin wake?
One less drunk.

Elephants

A: How do you know if there's an elephant in your bed?
B: By the big E on his pyjamas.

A: What should you do if you find an elephant asleep in your bed?
B: Sleep somewhere else!

Owls

A: What do lovesick owls say to each other when it's raining?
B: Too-wet-to-woo!

A: Why are owls cleverer than chickens?
B: Have you ever eaten Kentucky Fried Owl?

Sheep

A: Where do sheep get their fleece cut?
B: At the baaber's.

A: Where do sheep shop?
B: Woolworth's.

Dracula

A: Why is Dracula's family so close?
B: Because blood is thicker than water.

A: How can you join Dracula's fan club?
B: Send your name, address and blood group.

(From K. Wales, *The Lights Out Joke Book*, 1991.)

THE WAY THINGS ARE

The visual story line in a cartoon carries an impact which does not depend on linguistic deviance for its humour. There is generally little word play in the captions or speech bubbles of Garfield, Charlie Brown, Andy Capp, and their fellows. The cartoonist thinks of a comic situation, and the language (if any) follows. Some cartoons, however, arise from the opposite process: the cartoonist selects a linguistic feature, and devises drawings to match. These are three of *101 Things*, devised by Peter Gammond and Peter Clayton – potato-like beings whose existence stems from an idiom containing the word *thing*. We thingk, therefore they are.

25. these things are sent to try us

78. take your things off

82. things have come to a pretty pass

HUMOUR IN STRUCTURE

Any of the recognized domains of language structure and use (§1) can be manipulated in order to provide the input to a joke. The following pages (406–11) illustrate some of the ways in which comic effects can be linguistically categorized.

Graphological humour

Deviation from the norms of spelling, punctuation, layout, and typography (§17) motivates a great deal of written humour, as can be seen in the case of misprints (p. 404), mis-spellings (p. 84), and many graffiti (p. 181). Some jokes in fact work only in the written mode:

- What did one sheep say to the other?
  I love ewe.
- TOO MUCH SEX makes you shortsighted.
- Bakers knead to do it. (p. 409)
- Why did the antelope?
  Nobody gnu.

Phonological humour

Many jokes rely on a deviation from the normal use of sounds, by adding, deleting, substituting, or transposing vowels and consonants. Traditionally recognized genres include tampering with the frequency norms of consonants (*tongue twisters*, p. 399), transposing sounds (*spoonerisms*, p. 254), and using similarities in pronunciation to mix up words (*malapropisms*).

- Patient: Doctor! Doctor! I think I'm a bird.
  Doctor: I'll tweet you in a minute.
- What's the difference between a sick cow and an angry crowd?
  One moos badly and the other boos madly.
- What do you get if you cross a chicken and a bell?
  An alarm cluck.

Some phonological jokes rely on features of connected speech (p. 247) or prosody:

- Teacher: Use the word *antennae* in a sentence.
  Charlie: There antennae sweets left.
- What book tells you about famous owls?
  Who's Whoooo.

This last example also illustrates the phonetic effects which can be introduced into jokes – many of which are difficult to show in writing:

Airline passenger: Where does this door go
  TO-O-O-o-o.

These features are especially important in the silly-sounding names of nonsense verse, which greatly rely on sound symbolism (p. 250).

DO PTELL

Graphological deviance is the basis of the effect in the children's poem by Charles Connell, 'Please Ptell me Pterodactyl' (1985), which takes a spelling exception and turns it into a general rule. Here are the first two verses.

Please ptell me, Pterodactyl
Who ptaught you how pto fly?
Who ptaught you how pto flap your wings
And soar up in the sky?

No prehistoric monster
Could ptake off just like you
And pturn and ptwist and ptaxi
Way up there in the blue.

Some of the strangest plays on words occur in the language of greetings cards. This example, from the Andrew Brownsword Collection (1991), relies on both sound and spelling effects to drive the lexical element underlying the cartoon. The punchline, on the inside of the card, reads simply *Grate* (alongside a picture of a fireplace).

THERE WAS A . . .

Some types of phonological pattern are totally identified with humour – notably the fixed and formulaic rhythms which identify a *limerick*. This example has an ingenious interplay between graphology and phonology, in the manner of Ogden Nash, as well as an opening line which breaks away from the *There was a...*convention:

A girl who weighed many an oz.
Used language I dare not pronoz.
    For a fellow unkind
    Pulled her chair out behind
Just to see (so he said) if she'd boz.

The *clerihew*, named after Edmund Clerihew Bentley (1875–1956), presents another comic rhythm: a verse of four short lines in two couplets. It is always biographical in content.

Sir Humphrey Davy   He lived in the odium
Abominated gravy.   Of having discovered sodium.

This example suggests the origins of the genre. Bentley is said to have devised the form during a boring chemistry lesson.

GNASHISMS

The graphic neologisms of the American humorist, Ogden Nash (1902–71), depend on an interplay between sound, spelling, and meaning. One of his most popular tricks is to take a word which is spelled in an unusual way, find another word which rhymes with it, then respell the latter along the lines of the former, often stretching the pronunciation to fit.

The baby
A bit of talcum
Is always walcum.

The jellyfish
Who wants my jellyfish?
I'm not sellyfish!

There was a brave girl of
    Connecticut
Who flagged the express
    with her pecticut
Which her elders defined
As presence of mind,
But deplorable absence of
    ecticut.

COMIC ALPHABETS

Comic alphabets take each letter in turn, and add a humorous gloss–sometimes in prose, sometimes in poetry–which relates the letter to some character, situation, or saying. They probably arose as a burlesque of the children's alphabet books which were commonplace after the 16th century (of the kind: 'A for an Apple, an Archer and Arrow; B for a Bull, a Bear and a Barrow…'). They rely greatly on alliteration and rhyme, and on the mechanisms of the pun and the riddle (p. 408). Some are phonetic in character, playing with the apparent meanings conveyed by the sounds of the letters; others are graphic, using only the spellings. 'Comic' is not an entirely accurate description. Some were not so much humorous as ingenious–a form of playing with words for its own sake. Also, several of these alphabets had a serious intention, being used as social satire, or as teaching aids (especially for the inculcation of moral values). The classic account of these inventions is Eric Partridge's *Comic Alphabets* (1961).

A SELECTION OF EARLY ALPHABETS

The Comic Alphabet (Nelson, 1876)
A is an ARCHER, alarmed, for an arrow,
Aimed at an antelope, stuck in a sparrow.
B is a BUTCHER, both burly and bluff;
Bob, his big bull-dog is ugly enough.
C is a CAPTAIN, commanding a corps,
Courageous as Cromwell's companions of yore.
D is a DAMSEL, dashingly dressed,
Delighting in pleasing, and doing her best.
E, an ESQUIRE, of course nothing less;
Elegant both in his manners and dress.
F is a FARMER, ploughing his field;
For if he neglects it, no crop will it yield.
G is a GAMBLER, throwing the dice.
Gambling, young folks, is a terrible vice…

The Siege of Belgrade (The Bentley Ballads, 1861)
An Austrian army, awfully arrayed,
Boldly by battery besieged Belgrade;
Cossack commanders cannonading come,
Dealing destruction's devastating doom.
Every endeavour engineers essay
For fame, for fortune – fighting, furious fray:
Generals 'gainst generals grapple – gracious God!
How honours Heaven heroic hardihood!…

The title-page description of *An Alphabet* (1871)
A Beautiful Collection, Delightfully
Etched, Finely Grouped, Highly
Imaginative, Jestingly Knavish,
Ludicrously Mischievous, Notably
Odd, Peculiarly Queer, Recreative,
Sensational, Tittering, Unquestionably
Volatile, Whimsically XYZite (= 'exquisite')

An extract from *The Amusing Alphabet, or Easy Steps to A, B, C*, published in London in the 1850s.

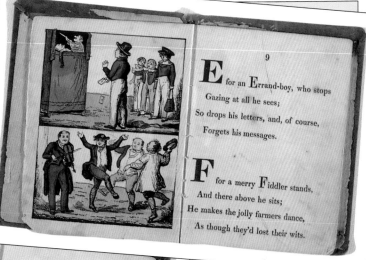

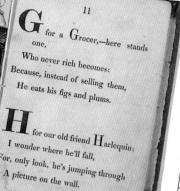

PARTRIDGE'S FAVOURITE

Asked for his favourite comic phonetic alphabet, Eric Partridge compiled the following sequence. (Glosses are in parentheses.)

A for 'orses (hay for horses)
B for mutton (beef or mutton)
C for Thailanders (the Seaforth Highlanders)
D for rent (different)
E for brick (heave a brick)
F for vest (effervesced)
G for the 3.15 (gee-gee – a horse, for the 3.15 race)
H for retirement (age for retirement)
I for an eye (eye for an eye)
J for oranges (Jaffa oranges)
K for restaurant (cafe – pronounced /keɪf/)
L for leather (hell for leather)
M for sis (sister – emphasis)
N for lade (enfilade)
O for there (over there)
P for relief (pee for relief)
Q for flowers (Kew for flowers)
R for moment (half a moment)
S for instance ('s (as), for instance)
T for two (tea for two)
U for nerve (You've a nerve!)
V for l'amour (Vive l'amour!)
W for a shilling (double you for a shilling)
X for the spot (i.e. where the crime was committed)
Y for mistress (wife or mistress)
Z for fun (said for fun – UK pronunciation, /zed/)
Z for breeze (Zephyr breeze – US pronunciation /ziː/)

This version was compiled from several comic alphabet sources. Partridge had plenty of choice, as the range of alternative entries for the letter R illustrates.

R *for crown – dollar – loaf – pint – tick* (all based on Cockney *half*, /ɑːf/)
R *for and his knights* (King Arthur, pronounced /'ɑːfə/)
R *for Askey* (British comedian – or any other well-known Arthur)
R *for seat* (Arthur's Seat, overlooking Edinburgh)
R *for mometer* (our thermometer)
R *for the doctor* (say 'ah' for the doctor)

MORPHOLOGICAL HUMOUR

Under this heading is included all jokes which manipulate the elements of word structure (such as affixes, p. 128), combine elements into novel forms (portmanteaux, p. 131), or divide words in unusual places.

- Why did the matchbox? Because it saw the tin can.
- Did you hear about Robin Hood? He just had an arrow escape.
- What do you call a man with a shovel, sitting at the bottom of a hole? Doug.
- And what do you call a man with a shovel sitting at the bottom of a smaller hole?
  Douglas. [=Doug-less]

Graffiti sequences (p. 181) often play with word boundaries, as in this three-part item:

- BE ALERT! Your country needs lerts.
- No, Britain has got enough lerts now. Be aloof.
- No, be alert. There's safety in numbers.

Most 'Knock knock, Who's there?' jokes are morphological in character. In the first of these two answers, the words are run together; in the second, the words are split in two:

- Egbert.
  Egbert who?
  Egbert no bacon.
- Soup
  Soup who?
  Souperman.

Silly book-titles also rely on making wrong divisions within the author's name, as well as on lexical punning and semantic allusion:

- *Hushabye Baby* by Wendy Bough-Brakes
  Looking After Your Garden by Dan D. Lion

PHONOLOGICALLY MOTIVATED NONSENSE

The bizarre lexical collocations of a great deal of nonsense verse are motivated by rhyme, as in the dénouement of Dennis Lee's 'On Tuesdays I polish my uncle'. (For a further example, see the Dr Seuss extract on p. 273.)

So my dad he got snarky and barked at the shark
Who was parking the ark on the mark in the dark.
And when they got back they had ants in their pants,
Dirt in their shirt, glue in their shoe,
Beans in their jeans, a bee on their knee,
Beer in their ear and a bear in their hair,
A stinger in each finger, a stain in the brain,
A small polka-dot burp, with headache tablets,
And a ship on the lip and a horse, of course,
So we all took a bath in the same tub and went to bed
  early.

LEXICAL HUMOUR

The chief vehicle of lexical humour is the pun (p. 405), often classified into semantic and phonological types. Semantic puns focus on the alternative meanings or applications of a word or phrase. They are especially common in riddles.

- What has four legs and only one foot? A bed.
- When is an ambulance not an ambulance?
  When it turns into a hospital.
- What did the explorer say when he met a koala in the outback?
  I can't bear it.

Phonological puns play upon two different words which sound the same (*homophones*). They are auditory jokes. In some cases, writing them down in traditional orthography either prejudges the answer or gives the game away.

- What's black and white and red all over?
  A newspaper.
- Why did Dracula go to the doctor?
  Because of the /ˈkɒfɪn/. [*coughin'/coffin*]
- Waiter, waiter, what's this? It's bean soup.
  I can see that. But what is it now?

Other categories of lexical humour include the neologism, as in the coinages of Stanley Unwin (p. 131), the use of words with different sense associations (p. 162), and the many kinds of nonsense verse, which break collocations in all directions at once.

SUPERCILIOUS KNOWLEDGE

Mrs Malaprop, a character in Richard Brinsley Sheridan's play *The Rivals* (1775), as played by Beryl Reid. The name is from French, *mal à propos* ('not to the purpose'), and is chosen to capture this character's habit of inappropriately replacing a word or phrase with others of a similar sound and meaning.

Illiterate him, I say, quite from your memory. [*obliterate*]

I would have her instructed in geometry, that she might know something of the contagious countries… and likewise that she might reprehend the true meaning of what she is saying. [*contiguous, comprehend*]

The user of a malapropism has not fully understood a long word, but makes a shot at it, substituting a word which 'sounds right'. The lapse is something which affects everyone, consciously or unconsciously, from time to time.

  Sheridan was not the first dramatist to put such effects into the mouth of a character. An earlier practitioner is Dogberry, in Shakespeare's *Much Ado About Nothing*: O villain! Thou wilt be condemned into everlasting redemption for this. (IV.2)

WHAT'S A VIXEN?*

When children are learning to talk, they often make morphological changes in words, producing creations which are a source of family humour.

Mother (*going through the alphabet*): Say T.
Mary (*age 3½*): T.
Mother: U.
Mary: U.
Mother: V.
Mary: V.
Mother: W.
Mary: Double me.

Marcus (*age 3½, in train, approaching London*): Are we there yet?
Father: No, we're still in the outskirts.
(*Pause*)
Marcus: Have we reached the inskirts yet?

Michael (*age 4, in bedroom*): Don't shut my door, mummy.
Mother: Well I have to close it, darling, because the light will keep you awake.
Michael: No, I don't want you to.
Mother: I'll leave it ajar, then.
Michael: Can you leave it one and a half jars?

Mother: Don't argue!
Hugh (*age 3*): I don't argme.

(From D. Crystal, 1986, p. 208.)

*Oh – a lady vicar. (Mary, age 6)

SYNTACTIC HUMOUR

Riddles also commonly involve syntactic ambivalence, in which one construction is interpreted as if it were another. This is the source of humour in dangling participle constructions (p. 204), and in the genre known as Tom Swifties (see below).

- What kind of animal can jump higher than a house?
  All kinds. Houses can't jump.
- How do hedgehogs make love?
  Very carefully.
- Call me a cab. Sir, you are a cab.
- We're having your mother-in-law for dinner tonight.
  I'd rather have chicken.

Some jokes also rely on syntax in the sense that they have a fixed form. Graffiti chains work in this way, adding variable endings to a fixed opening, or variable openings to a fixed ending: 'X rules…' (p. 181), ' … until I discovered Smirnoff'. Definition one-liners provide a further example: these are all of the form 'An X is a Y who does/is Z'.

- A Romeo is someone who ends all his sentences with a proposition.
- A metronome is a dwarf who lives in the Paris underground.
- A ghost-hunter is someone who keeps fit by exorcising regularly.

DISCOURSE HUMOUR

The vast majority of jokes have a fixed discourse structure. Often, stories are told in threes (p. 378), as in the most famous trio of all, the Englishman, Irishman, and Scotsman. Most riddles use one of a small number of favoured *wh*-question structures (p. 218):

What's the difference between an X and a Y?
Why did the A do B?
What did the X say to the Y?
When is a B not a B?
What do you get when you cross an X with a Y?

There are many types of interactive jokes, such as the music-hall *I say I say I say*, as well as *Knock knock*, *Doctor doctor*, *Waiter waiter*, and other 'emergency' jokes.

- Doctor, doctor, I wake up feeling terrible! My head spins and the room's going round!
  You must be sleeping like a top!

Some discourse jokes break the pragmatic rules of conversation (p. 286), or play with the conventions of sequence and cross-reference. Riddles often turn the tables in this way.

- Constantinople is a long word. Can you spell it?
  I T.
- Good morning doctor, I've lost my voice.
  Good morning Mr Smith, and what can I do for you?

TOM SWIFTIES

This form of word play relies on a combination of grammatical and lexical elements operating in a formulaic sentence structure. A popular game among professional writers, it is known from Victorian times. The modern name comes from a boy's adventure hero, Tom Swift, who would always speak with a following adverb ('said sadly', 'said quietly'), and the genre is based on the humorous development of this construction. Here are some of the ingenious examples which language buffs have submitted for publication in English language periodicals.

Adverbial Swifties
'The results of my electrocardiogram were reassuring', he said wholeheartedly.
  'Can I get you something?' the waitress asked fetchingly.
  'Wouldn't you prefer a poodle?' asked her father doggedly.
  'You can't even look after the plants while I'm away', she said witheringly.
  'Have you seen my ring?', she said engagingly.
  'I prefer to die intestate', he muttered unwillingly.
  'Try that direction', I suggested pointedly.
  'We've no more whiskey', they said dispiritedly.

Verbal Swifties
'What a lovely brook!' Tom babbled.

'I think there's a hole in the road ahead', Sue hazarded.
  'Damn train two hours late again', she railed.
  'But I did repair the boiler', he maintained.
  'What kind of tree? Oh, fir', he opined.
  'Can we get on with the operation?', the surgeon cut in sharply.

Adjectival Swifties
'I am totally disinterested', said the bank manager.
  'That operation has left me feeling quite disfigured', said the accountant.
  'I'm disconcerted', said the conductor.
  'Do you feel disheartened?', asked the cannibal.
  'We've been discharged', said the electricians.

'I'm nonplussed', said the mathematician.
  'I feel unloved', said the tennis ace.

'Do it' types
These phonological puns on an adverbial of manner, using the sexual connotation of 'doing it' as the source of the humour, are very similar to the above.

Accountants do it calculatingly.
Sentries do it haltingly.
Oscar did it wildly.
Little Bo Peep did it sheepishly.
Windsurfers do it standing up.
Doctors do it three times a day after meals.

HE SAID CHOICELY

In *Ulysses* (1922), there is an episode written in the form of a play, in which Joyce often introduces his characters' speech with a parenthetic adverb:

BLOOM (*Coldly.*) You have the advantage of me.

In one sequence, he deals out three Tom Swifties:

A MILLIONAIRESS (*Richly.*) Isn't he simply wonderful?

A NOBLEWOMAN (*Nobly.*) All that man has seen!

A FEMINIST (*Masculinely.*) And done!

VARIETY HUMOUR

The existence of language variety (p. 290) is a major source of humour, in speech and writing, in everyday language and in literature (p. 89), all over the English-speaking world. The regional accents and dialects within a community readily lend themselves to comic exaggeration. If a variety is used as a prestige dialect (a 'standard'), its forms provide an effective means of satirizing the elite group who speak it. Occupational varieties, such as those of the policeman, lawyer, or cleric, are especially vulnerable. And a speech idiosyncrasy, such as a weakly articulated /r/ or /s/, is a gift to the vocal satirist. The funny voices of many US cartoon characters illustrate the point—'It's a wabbit', howls Elmer Fudd, and Bugs Bunny replies with a nasal twang sharp enough to cut steel.

We are most conscious of these effects when they are produced by professional comedians and impressionists; and some 'schools' of comedy have in fact relied heavily on the exaggerated or incongruous use of varieties of English. In the UK, an influential example was the Monty Python TV series of the 1970s, which regularly used situations where people spoke in an unexpected or inappropriate way. A football commentary, for example, might be carried on in the style of the Authorized Version of the Bible. In the USA, the 'Laugh-in' TV series of the 1960s, having established characters with particular vocal styles, would then introduce these styles into situations where they would not usually be found. The mock-German accent of one of the characters, for example, might be encountered in a court of law or a high-class restaurant.

Variations of this kind are part of everyday speech, too.

• A man (with a London accent) is bought a pint of beer in an English pub: he says 'Thanks', but pronounced it in a mock-Irish way, as /taŋks/ (p. 336). His friend responds with a further piece of mock-Irish,"Tis a pleasure, sure and all', and they continue in this vein for a while.
• During a meeting to discuss student applications, an interviewer expresses anxiety that the interviewees won't say very much; 'Ve haf vays off making them tock', says another, lapsing into a mock-German interrogation style.
• A British car-driver finally gets a reluctant engine to fire, and presses the accelerator triumphantly, saying 'We have lift-off', in the mock-American tones of a NASA mission controller.

Casual listening to informal discourse brings to light dozens of such instances each day.

DIALECT BOOKS

Regional dialect books generally rely for their effect on a 'translation' from informal local pronunciation, grammar, or vocabulary into formal Standard English. They can be found all over the English-speaking world (for a further example, see p. 84). The joke lies partly in the re-spelling and partly in the very formal glosses given to highly colloquial speech. Additional glosses are given in parentheses after each example, to aid the foreign reader (or, for that matter, the native one).

The Illustrated Texas Dictionary of the English Language, by Jim Everhart (1968).

slave: the part of a garment covering an arm only. 'Are yew sayin' mah left slave is shorter than mah riot?' (= 'Are you saying my left sleeve is shorter than my right')
wuf: a large doglike carnivorous mammal. 'Who's afraid of the beg, bad wuf?' (= 'Who's afraid of the big bad wolf')
barred (past tense): to receive with the expressed intention of returning the same. 'Who barred mah hat an' didn't brang it back?' (= 'Who borrowed my hat and didn't bring it back?')
sep: to omit or bar. 'Everyone can go in sep yew!' (= 'Everyone can go in except you')

Let Stalk Strine, by Afferbeck Lauder, Professor of Strine Studies, University of Sinny (1965). The title translates as 'Let's talk Australian' (as pronounced in fast speech). *Sinny* is 'Sydney'. To decode the other examples on the title page, say the phrases aloud, and then listen to what you have said: for example, *gloria soame?* 'glorious home'. (*Sex* = 'sacks' – compare *X* below.)

jezz: articles of furniture. As in: 'Set the tible, love, and get a coupler jezz' (= 'Set the table, love, and get a couple of chairs')
X: the twenty-fourth letter of the Strine alphabet; also plural of egg; also a tool for chopping wood.
sly drool: an instrument used by engineers for discovering Kew brutes and for making other calculations. ('slide rule . . . cube roots')
cheque etcher: Did you obtain. As in 'Where cheque etcher hat?' (= 'Where did you get your hat?')

Lern yerself Scouse, by Brian Minard (1972). The title translates as 'Teach yourself Scouse', the dialect of Liverpool. The substitution of *learn* for *teach* is in fact common in many English dialects. 'Where's your sense of humour?' asks the sub-title.

Chairs! Good health! (= 'Cheers')
Eh la, wurz dthe bog? Excuse me, sir, would you direct me to the toilet? (= 'Hey, lad, where's the bog')
Gizzasiggy: Would you be kind enough to give me a cigarette. (= 'Give us a ciggy'—short for *cigarette*)
Upyer pipe! Very well, I have listened to you, but nonetheless I have no respect for your admonishment. (= 'Up your pipe'– not the politest of responses)

Yacky dar, moy bewty! by Sam Llewellyn (1985). The title is a mixture of a Welsh toast (*iechyd da*, 'good health') and a rural greeting ('my beauty', used in addressing horses, rabbits, cars, friends, and all kinds of other worthy recipients. The lady on the cover is saying 'Beg pardon'.

West Country English
Ear voe! Excuse me! (= 'Here you')
Ace? Yes?
Can ee dellus the rawed vor Penzarnce? Please tell me the way to Penzance (= 'Can you tell us the road for Penzance?')
Whoart? I beg your pardon? (= 'What?')

Northern English
Ow do! Excuse me, sir or madam. (= 'How do', short for 'How do you do')
Art ont buzz? Are you travelling by public transport? (= 'Art on the bus?'– short for *art thou*, an archaic singular form of *are you*)
Nay, int caa. No, I am travelling by car. (= 'No, in the car')
A wudn't gan theer if a were thee: I think that is an unwise choice of destination. (= 'I wouldn't go there if I were you')

A VERY PECULIAR PRACTICE

These few pages have tried to characterize the chief linguistic stratagems used in generating humour, but they have been limited in several respects. In particular, it is not possible to use the written medium to capture the dynamics of joke-telling – especially the crucial role played by prosody (p. 248) and by the interaction of face and tone of voice. 'It's the way you tell 'em' is a subject worthy of much greater investigation, but communicating its findings will require a different medium of exposition from the printed encyclopedia. Writing jokes down does something lethal to their humour. Children seem to enjoy reading page after page of such books as *Another 1000 Best Jokes For Kids*, but they do so without a flicker of humour showing on their faces; whereas the same jokes in the playground will elicit raucous laughter. Jokes are not for the individual. There is something very strange about people who tell jokes to themselves, or who read jokes alone – and, it has to be admitted, who study them alone, as the author of these pages has had to do.

CURIOSER AND CURIOSER

Some jokes tell jokes about jokes: they take the language we need to talk about language, and play about with that. This is *metalinguistic* humour, and it is found in catch questions, parodies, and a great deal of nonsense. *Punch's* cartoon captions often made use of it.

• Which word is always spelled wrongly?
  Wrongly.

• What is the longest word in the English language?
  Smiled, because there's a mile between the first and the last letter.

• What two words have the most letters?
  Post Office.

• He walked with a pronounced limp, pronounced
  l, i, m, p. (Spike Milligan)

'Frankly, Wallace, I think you'd better stop telling it. If no one laughs, it may not be a joke.'

Punch has the benevolence to announce, that in an early number of his ensuing Volume he will astonish the Parliamentary Committee by the publication of several exquisite designs, to be called Punch's Cartoons! (24 June 1843)

'Knock, knock. Who's there? Cows go. Cows go who? No, they don't, cows go moo. Knock, knock. Who's there? Little old lady. Little old lady who? Didn't know you could yodel. Knock, knock ...'

PUNCH LINES

We conclude this section with a small tribute to *Punch*, a magazine without equal in the history of humour. Founded by author Henry Mayhew and engraver Ebenezer Landells, it was inspired by the satirical daily, *Paris Charivari*. The name belonged to the puppet-show character, Punch, and was, appropriately enough, selected after a joke – that it was 'nothing without Lemon'. (Mark Lemon was a member of the launch editorial team, and sole editor until 1870, though it was always 'Mr Punch' who signed the editorials.)

The first issue appeared on Saturday 17 July 1841, cost 3d and sold 10,000 copies; the price next went up in 1917, to 6d. After a peak circulation of 175,000 copies in the 1940s, sales declined, and it ceased publication with the issue of 8 April 1992, after 150 years.

The range of its humour was universal, and its impact international. It was often banned in Europe. Kaiser Wilhelm II was so annoyed by it that he put a price on the editor's head. It was also one of the few magazines to have had any kind of permanent effect on the language (and the only one

to be used as a source in the *Oxford Dictionary of Quotations*). It was the first to apply the word *cartoon* to a comic drawing, and the first to use the phrase *a curate's egg* (in a cartoon caption). It gave the name *Crystal Palace* to the 1851 exhibition, and its caption *it's being so cheerful as keeps us going* (from a World War 1 cartoon) became a World War 2 catch phrase.

The *Punch* parodies and cartoons provided a comic commentary on most things – and not least, on language, as can be seen in this book's selection of items out of its pages, from Victorian times to the present-day. With its demise, language enthusiasts lost an unparalleled source of ongoing contemporary (and thus, eventually, historical) illustration about variation and usage in British English. Its revival, in 1996, was therefore a most welcome sociolinguistic event

LITERARY FREEDOM

The peak of personal variation in the English language is to be found in the corpus of speech and writing that goes under the heading of English literature. This is a corpus whose boundaries resist definition. Critics, authors, cultural historians, syllabus designers, and others have often discussed what counts as literature (or Literature), and as the language has spread around the world (§7) so the issue has broadened and become more complex. The notion of 'an' English literature is now much less easy to work with, because it must cope with the claims of a rapidly increasing range of linguistically divergent literatures, qualified by ethnic (e.g. black, creole, African), regional (e.g. Canadian, Australian, Anglo-Irish), and other labels. A similar issue faces the linguist, grappling with the notion of 'an' English language and the claims of 'new Englishes' from around the world (p. 106).

For the linguist, these problems of literary definition and identity provide a clear signal about the uniqueness of this area of language use. Whatever else we might say about literature, there is patently no way in which we can ascribe to literary works the kind of situational identity which can be given to such notions as occupational varieties and regional dialects (§§20–21). Literature transcends this kind of constraint. Authors are free to circle above the language, to swoop down and take from it whatever they wish. The language of literature has no situational restrictions; all structures and all varieties are available to it as a resource. And because there is no theoretical limit to the subject-matter of literature, so there is no theoretical limit to the language variation which authors may choose to employ.

Literary English?

The consequences of this for the linguist are far-reaching. It means that there is no clear notion of 'literary language' to work with – that there is no such thing as a 'variety' of literature. For there to be a variety (p. 288), there needs to be a clear and predictable correlation between features of language and features of a social situation. 'Religious English' exists as a variety solely because there are certain linguistic features which are only to be found in situations that can be described as 'religious' (p. 370). It is simply not possible to take any set of linguistic features and say that they are predictably 'literary'.

This is not to gainsay the fact that, in the history of literature, there have been periods of authorial practice and schools of critical thought which could identify a genre of literary language in this way. At various times – illustrated in poetry by the 16th-century fashion for archaic diction (p. 185), or by 18th-century Augustan notions of classical elegance – authors were prepared to write according to certain linguistic conventions, and their attitudes defined a canon of contemporary literature. The traditional concept of literary 'diction' (p. 419) is one such notion which arose from this outlook. But the present-day consensus is otherwise. Anything that occurs in language, it seems, can now be put to work in the service of literature; and the notion of a clear-cut boundary between literary and non-literary domains turns out to be chimerical. The answer to the question 'What is literature?' is not to be found in the study of its linguistic properties. So there is no separate section called 'literary English' in this book.

OPINIONS

Many authors and critics have thought deeply about the relationship between the medium of their literary expression and the rest of their linguistic experience. The contemporary orthodoxy, stressing the closeness of the relationship, is most often expounded with reference to poetry, which on the surface appears to be the most removed from everyday norms. (For an earlier opinion, see p. 88.)

William Carlos Williams
. . . there can no longer be serious work in poetry written in 'poetic' diction. It is a contortion of speech to conform to a rigidity of line... Speech is the fountain of the line into which the pollution of a poetic manner and inverted phrasing should never again be permitted to drain. (*Selected Letters*, ed. J. C. Thirlwall, 1957, p. 134.)

Robert Frost
To judge a poem or piece of prose you... listen for the sentence sounds. If you find some of those not bookish, caught fresh from the mouths of people, some of them striking, all of them definite and recognizable, so recognizable that with a little trouble you can place them and even name them, you know you have found a writer. (*Selected Letters*, ed. Lawrance Thompson, 1964, p. 113.)

T. S. Eliot
No poetry, of course, is ever exactly the same speech that the poet talks and hears: but it has to be in such a relation to the speech of his time that the listener or reader can say 'that is how I should talk if I could talk poetry'... The music of poetry, then, must be a music latent in the common speech of its time. (*Selected Prose*, ed. F. Kermode, 1975, p. 111.)

Several of the features of conversational speech (p. 286), such as its parentheses, comment clauses (p. 229), and overlapping talk are seen in this extract from 'A Game of Chess', Part 2 of Eliot's *The Waste Land* (1922). (For a further perspective on *said*, see p. 419.)

If you don't like it you can get on with it, I said.
Others can pick and choose if you can't.
But if Albert makes off, it won't be for lack of telling.
You ought to be ashamed, I said, to look so antique.
(And her only thirty-one.)
I can't help it, she said, pulling a long face,
It's them pills I took, to bring it off, she said.
(She's had five already, and nearly died of young George.)
The chemist said it would be all right, but I've never been the same.
You *are* a proper fool, I said.

A LINGUISTIC PERSPECTIVE

Refusing to recognize a variety of 'literary English' need not in any way diminish the central role that literature plays in developing our experience of the language. On the contrary: it can reinforce it, as long as we go on to show how literary experience everywhere makes contact with everyday language use. Authorial voices may be born out of ordinary language (see opposite), but they eventually make a renewal of connection with it, providing a dimension through which we are led to see new meaning in the mundane. Literary examples therefore pervade this book, providing the most frequent category of illustration. They are there for three reasons: to demonstrate the relevance of a linguistic frame of reference in approaching the description of a piece of literature; to show how specific features of language identified through analytic means can be used in creative expression; and to provide ways of increasing a reader's personal response to a text. (An example is the observation on p. 153 about personal name variation in a scene from Shakespeare's *Henry V*, which arose directly out of an analysis of the phonological properties of first names.)

Because these examples are scattered throughout the book, it is difficult to see their common feature – the opportunity that literature offers writers to explore language in individual and unprecedented ways. The present section, therefore, looks specifically at how the notion of personal identity operates in a literary context, citing instances of linguistic freedom at each of the levels of language structure (§1), and drawing attention to those features which occur with some frequency (and which, therefore, are most often cited as features of 'literary language'). However, no attempt is made to bring these observations together into an integrated theory of the analysis of literary style. A whole encyclopedia could be devoted to that task alone.

Although literature cannot be identified *by* language, it is wholly identified *with* it, for it has no other medium of expression. Any of the tools which the study of language has made available can therefore be of value in increasing our awareness of the meaning and effect of the elements which make up a text. But the application of these tools has to be carried out sensitively. The history of stylistics is littered with the intellectual corpses of linguists who have attempted to bludgeon their way into the language of a literary work, without appreciating the critical perspective to which their enquiries need to relate if the relevance of their findings is to be clear. At the same time, the complexity of language is apparent to all who probe it – authors, critics, and linguists alike – and any techniques should be explored which seem capable of providing extra order and illumination in what is, structurally and functionally, the most complex of all areas of language use.

STANLEY: Meg. Do you know what?
MEG: What?
STANLEY: Have you heard the latest?
MEG: No.
STANLEY: I'll bet you have.
MEG: I haven't.
STANLEY: Shall I tell you?
MEG: What latest?
STANLEY: You haven't heard it?
MEG: No.
STANLEY (*advancing*): They're coming today.
MEG: Who?
STANLEY: They're coming in a van.
MEG: Who?
STANLEY: And do you know what they've got in that van?
MEG: What?
STANLEY: They've got a wheelbarrow in that van.
MEG (*breathlessly*): They haven't.
STANLEY: Oh yes they have.
(Harold Pinter, *The Birthday Party*, 1957)

LITERARINESS IN CONVERSATION

How is it possible for features of conversation and other varieties to succeed as poetry? Part of the answer lies in the nature of conversation itself, which analyses have shown to be far more structured and creative than was formerly believed. Not only does it readily admit linguistic deviance (p. 394), it also displays many of the formal features which are traditionally thought to be 'literary', such as metrical rhythm, syntactic parallelism, figurative language, alliteration, and verbal repetition.

The literariness of a conversation is not immediately obvious. Here is a short example taken from a study of conversational repetition and parallelism. Transcribed in a conventional manner, it is difficult to see anything of interest taking place. Laid out differently, several patterns begin to emerge, and a more informed comparison can be made with the crafted conversations of drama. Only the lexical patterns are shown: several other links can be found between certain grammatical words (*I*, *if*), and there are signs of phonological repetition too (p. 415, *in terms of time*, *lot/not*, *just/stuff/much*). (After D. Tannen, 1989, p. 71.)

CHAD   I go out a lot.
DEBORAH   I go out and eat.
PETER   You go out?

    The trouble with ME is
    if   I don't prepare
  and   eat   well,
     I eat   a LOT. ...
Because   it's   not satisfying.
And so if   I'm just eating like   cheese and crackers,
     I'll just STUFF myself on cheese and crackers.
But if   I   fix myself something nice,
     I don't have to eat that much.

DEBORAH   Oh yeah?
PETER   I've noticed that,   yeah

DEBORAH   Hmmm...
   Well   then it works,
     then it's   a good idea.
PETER   It's   a good idea in terms of eating,
     it's not a good idea in terms of time.

PHONETIC FREEDOM

The phonetic properties of English sounds (p. 236) are an important source of special effects, especially in poetry and drama. It is obviously the case that speech sounds have acoustic properties which remind people of noises they encounter in the world; less obviously, they seem to have properties which people often interpret in terms of non-acoustic experiences, such as contrasts of size, movement, or brightness (sound symbolism, p. 250). We readily talk about speech sounds using such aesthetic judgments as 'beautiful' or 'harsh', independently of the dictionary meaning of the words in which they appear, and the term *phonaesthetics* is often used for the study of sounds from this point of view. All aspects of pronunciation are affected, including vowels, consonants, syllables, and prosodic patterns (p. 248), and the effects extend well beyond literature, into such areas as comic names (Mickey Mouse, Donald Duck), tongue-twisters (p. 399), nursery rhyme jingles, advertising slogans (p. 180), and nonsense verse (p. 406). (For phonetics terminology in these pages, see §17.)

MEMORABLE MELODIES

These passages illustrate the symbolic properties of individual sounds, as well as of consonant repetition (alliteration), vowel repetition (assonance), and rhythm.

The moan of doves in immemorial elms
And murmur of innumerable bees
(Tennyson, 'The Princess', 1847)

The Lotos blows by every winding creek:
All day the wind breathes low with mellower tone:
Through every hollow cave and alley lone
Round and round the spicy downs the yellow Lotos-dust is
    blown.
(Tennyson, 'Lotos-Eaters', 1833)

He sipped with his straight mouth,
Softly drank through his straight gums, into his slack long
    body,
Silently.
(D. H. Lawrence, 'Snake', 1923)

Snip-snap and snick-a-snick
Clash the Barber's shears
(Walter de la Mare, 'The Barber's', 1913)

This is the Night Mail crossing the Border
Bringing the cheque and the postal order.
(W. H. Auden, 'Night Mail', 1935)

Sixty-six different times in his fish-slimy kitchen ping, strike,
    tick, chime, and tock.
(Dylan Thomas, *Under Milk Wood*, 1954)

Alfred, Lord Tennyson (1809–92)

W. H. Auden once remarked that Tennyson had the finest ear of any English poet. The first two quotations illustrate his case.

MELODIOUS VELVET

In a *Sunday Times* poll of British readers' favourite words in 1980, *melody* and *velvet* tied for first place. Third was a tie between *gossamer* and *crystal*, followed by *autumn, peace, tranquil, twilight*, and *murmur*, with *caress, mellifluous*, and *whisper* tying for tenth place. The occasion seems to have motivated a poem by John Kitching.

I like to think of words with lovely
    sounds
That I can ease around my Sunday
    tongue –
– Like velvet, melody and young,
Gossamer, crystal, autumn, peace,
Mellifluous, whisper, tranquil, lace,
Caress and silken, willow, mellow,
Lullaby, dawn and shimmer, yellow,
Silver, marigold and golden,
Dream and harmony and olden,
Blossom, champagne, sleep and
    dusk,
Magic, hummock, love and mist,
Darling, laughter, butterfly,
Charity, eiderdown and sky,
And parakeet and rosemary,
Froth, gazebo, ivory,
And syllabub and vacillate,
Mesmerism, echo, fate,
Jacaranda, harlequin
And chrysalis and violin,
Enigma, tart and sycamore,
Pomp, chinchilla, truffle, myrrh,
Bewildered, claret, akimbo, fur,

Flamingo next and celandine,
Ominous, tantalise and wine,
Antimacassar, jewel, skill,
Russet, buckram, delight and thrill,
Clavichord and didgeridoo,
Doppelganger, fractious, zoo.
I don't know what they mean. Do
you?
But I like to have them in my head
And dandle them and handle them
Like Wedgwood china. What finer?

(©John Kitching, 'Sunday Words',
    1980.)

What is it about the phonaesthetics of these words which makes them so attractive? Which vowels and consonants are most involved? It is a useful exercise to stop at this point, and jot down the sounds which strike you as particularly important, before comparing your list with the results of the phonetic survey given below. The task is to notice not only which sounds are frequently used, but also – rather more difficult – which are not used at all.

An analysis of the 81 words listed in the poem shows some clear trends.

• The consonants divide into two types: high frequency and low frequency. Just eight items account for 73 per cent of all consonants (264): /l/ has 41 instances (15 per cent), followed by /m/ (27), /s/ (25), /k/ (23), /r/ (21), /t/ and /d/ (19), and /n/ (18).

If this ranking is compared with that found in conversation (p. 244), the use of /l/ and /m/ is noteworthy.

• There is then a big jump before reaching the low-frequency consonants: /f/ and /b/ (9), /p/ and /v/ (8), /g/ (7), /z/ (6), /ŋ/ (5), /w/ (4), /ʃ/, /tʃ/ and /h/ (3), /θ/, /dʒ/ and /j/ (2). Only /ð/ and /ʒ/ do not occur at all.

• If we group these consonants into types according to their manner of articulation, frictionless continuants are commonest (118: 68 oral, 50 nasal), followed by plosives (85), fricatives (56), and affricates (5). As there are only four oral continuants (/l, r, w, j/) and three nasals (/m, n, ŋ/), but six plosives (/p, b, t, d, k, g/) and nine fricatives (/f, v, θ, ð, s, z, ʃ, ʒ, h/), this distribution is noteworthy.

• Of the 172 vowels, the unstressed vowel /ə/ is commonest (43), showing that words of more than one syllable are preferred. Only 21 words were monosyllables; the largest category (28) was words of three syllables. Most were stressed on the first syllable; and most made use of at least three different manners of consonant articulation.

• The other common vowel was /ɪ/ (38), which occurred over twice as often as the next vowel /a/ (16), followed by /əʊ/ (11), /e/ (10), /iː/, /ʌ/,

and /aɪ/ (9), /ɒ/ (6), /ɑː/ (5), /eɪ/, /uː/ and /ɔː/ (4), /ɜː/ (2), /aʊ/ and /aɪə/ (1). This is close to the vowel rankings of conversation (p. 239).

Is John Kitching's intuition representative of *Sunday Times* readers? Of the 68 vowels and consonants used in the paper's words, only 13 are missing from his top eight consonants and top eight vowels. There is an 80 per cent chance that the readers would like his other words too.

This analysis perhaps explains why a romantic poem about London Underground stations would very likely include *Pimlico* and *Colindale*, which closely reflect these intuitions, and exclude *Goodge Street* and *Wapping*, which do not. Also, why friendly space aliens receive such names as Alaree and Osnomian, why enemy names include Vatch and Triops, and why Klingons are likely to be a mite less aggressive than Kryptons. Also why, if we wanted to create a phonaesthetically correct new word, it would seem advisable to give it three syllables, stress the first, use at least one /m/ and /l/ (preferably both), vary the manner of articulation, and keep most vowels short. We would probably find success with *ramelon* and *drematol*. On the other hand, we could simply settle for *immemorial elms*.

PHONOLOGICAL FREEDOM

With phonology (p. 236), we are not so much listening to the acoustic properties of speech sounds as sensing how these sounds are distributed within words and sentences. The possibility that sounds may have some intrinsic meaning is discounted, and all the attention is focused on how sounds are used contrastively in sequences, pointing to meanings which lie elsewhere (e.g. in grammar or vocabulary). There is thus immense scope in literature for manipulating the phonological status of sounds, whether segmentally (through vowels, consonants, and patterns of syllable structure) or prosodically (through such features as intonation, stress, and rhythm). A distinctive phonological pattern always carries a semantic implication. If I write 'What further thought of fresh desire/Could rouse the deadened mind', the grammar of the text says only that the mind is dead; but the link formed by the alliteration hints that desire may be dead also. This is phonology in action: 'to connect two words by similarity of sound so that you are made to think of their possible connections' (William Empson, *Seven Types of Ambiguity*, 1930). The similarity of sound, in short, prompts a similarity of sense.

THE FORCE OF RHYME

If we stop after the first two lines of this verse from 'Mr Eliot's Sunday Morning Service' (T. S. Eliot, 1920), the impression is altogether august and respectful; not so after the next two lines, with the alliteration (initial-rhyme) forcing us to bring *pustular* and *presbyter* together, and the combination of alliteration and end-rhyme turning the eyes from heaven (*penitence*) to earth (*piaculative pence*).

The sable presbyters approach
The avenue of penitence;
The young are red and pustular
Clutching piaculative pence.

Three verses later, and the effect is found again, but the other way round: connotations of gracelessness and ordinariness are introduced first, with *ham* and *bath*, then transferred through alliteration and end-rhyme to *masters* and *polymath*.

Sweeney shifts from ham to ham
Stirring the water in his bath.
The masters of the subtle schools
Are controversial, polymath.

Such techniques are not modern. Alexander Pope is one who made much use of them. In this extract there is both a reinforcing use of alliteration (*destroy* and *dirty*, *fib* and *sophistry*) and a diminishing use, with *thin* reducing the elevated tone of *thron'd*.

Destroy his fib or sophistry, in vain,
The creature's at his dirty work again,
Thron'd in the centre of his thin designs,
Proud of a vast extent of flimsy lines!
(Alexander Pope, *An Epistle to Dr Arbuthnot*, 1735)

METRICS

Poetic Language is organized into rhythmical units which appear in print as lines (p. 291). What phonological principles govern the way these units are used? In Europe, the traditional study of versification, or *prosody* (a more restricted sense of the term used on p. 249) was based on the rules of Latin scansion. Poetic lines would be analysed into combinations of stressed (/) and unstressed (◡) syllables known as *feet*. Five types were formerly prominent in English verse, as shown in the upper table.

Lines would then be classified in terms of the number of stressed syllables they contained, as shown in the lower table. In theory there is no limit; in practice, most English metrical lines are found to be five feet or less; when they exceed six feet, there is a strong intuitive tendency to break them into two parts.

Combinations of foot-type and line length produced such designations as *iambic pentameter* – the heartbeat of much

English poetry – and analyses in these terms were the staple of traditional metrical studies, which traced the norms of English poetic rhythm and evaluated the way poets deviated from these norms. As a system of description, it worked quite well in giving an account of the regular lines of traditional poetry. But it came to be criticized on several counts. It was often mechanically applied, with students being taught to identify the form of metrical patterns at the expense of their function, or role, in a poem; and it was unable to cope well with lines containing unusual rhythm sequences. Also, with the bulk of modern poetry no longer using such metrical patterns, but working instead with 'free' kinds of verse, the traditional system of description came to be viewed as largely irrelevant. Today, metrists work in several alternative ways, not restricting themselves to the notion of stress, but bringing in other prosodic systems, such as tempo and intonation, and a general concept of rhythmical weight (p. 417).

Name	Syllable type	As in	Example
iamb/iambic foot	◡ /	demand	The curfew tolls the knell of parting day (Thomas Gray)
trochee/trochaic foot	/ ◡	soldier	What of soul was left, I wonder (Robert Browning)
spondee/spondaic foot	/ /	dry dock	*We three* alone in modern times had brought (W. B. Yeats)
dactyl/dactylic foot	/ ◡ ◡	elephant	*This is the* Night Mail crossing the Border (W. H. Auden)
anapest/anapestic foot	◡ ◡ /	disbelieve	*And the things we have seen and have known and have heard* of, fail us (Robert Bridges)

Type	No.	Example
monometer	1	The nursling, Grief, Is dead (Coventry Patmore)
dimeter	2	Wintertime nighs (Thomas Hardy)
trimeter	3	It was the winter wild (Milton)
tetrameter	4	I wandered lonely as a cloud (Wordsworth)
pentameter	5	My name is Ozymandias, king of kings (Shelley)
hexameter	6	When Phoebus lifts his head out of the winter's wave (Michael Drayton)
heptameter	7	Cursed be the social lies that warp us from the living truth! (Tennyson)
octameter	8	What of soul was left, I wonder, when the kissing had to stop? (Robert Browning)

OLD ENGLISH METRE

With some types of poetry, there is a strong expectation that lines should be broken in the middle. This was especially the case in Old English (p. 16), where lines can all be divided into two roughly equal parts, each containing two strongly stressed syllables and a varying number of unstressed syllables. Half-lines are most commonly organized in a trochaic or dactylic pattern (known as *Type A* to Old English metrists – as distinct from four other identified metrical patterns, Types B, C, D, and E). The half-lines are usually sense units, with the two parts linked by alliteration, and the dividing point often emphasized by a change of rhythm.

An extract from *Beowulf* (lines 1113–17) shows the system in operation. Metrical types for each half-line are identified on the right, and the half-lines are separated by a space, as

is conventional in presenting Old English poetry (p. 12). Strong syllables are marked by / and weak by ◡. Syllables where two light syllables are equivalent to a strong syllable are shown by - in the text. A stress level which is intermediate between strong and weak syllables is shown by \. (After D. G. Scragg, 1991, p. 61.)

Bŭgŏn þa to bence   blǽdagandĕ,   A D
fylle gefǽgon;   fǽgĕre gebǽgon   A A
mĕdŏful manig   magas þara   A A
swiðhicgende   on sele þam hean,   D B
Hroðgar ond Hroþulf   A

Then the glorious [Danes] rejoiced at the feast; Hrothgar and Hrothulf, the resolute ones, their kinsmen, drank many a toast courteously in the lofty hall.

GRAPHOLOGICAL FREEDOM

The conventions of the written language are more stable, limited, and perceptible than those of speech, and deviations from written norms are therefore going to be more obvious when they occur. It might be thought that such deviance is unlikely. Operating with a world standard alphabet, a limited range of punctuation marks, fairly strict constraints on capitalization and other typographic options, extremely strict constraints on spelling, and a physical medium – the page – whose edges form an inflexible perimeter, there would seem to be little real freedom for the writer in the area of graphetics and graphology. Yet it is surprising what can be done.

It is the genre of poetry which has tried most urgently and successfully to free itself from the severity of the constraints imposed by its linear medium. Graphological deviance in prose does occur, in both the short story and the novel – most often to convey the prosodic features of conversation, such as variations in loudness and tempo (p. 248). Tales of science fiction and fantasy also regularly manipulate graphological conventions in order to convey a sense of the alien or exceptional (p. 271). And there are some famous cases of deviant usage in the novel, such as the punctuationless end-pages of *Ulysses*. But there is nothing in prose to match the graphic variations which have been used to give visual structure to poetry or to suggest particular modes of oral reading. Nor is there anything to match the remarkable experiments in visual form which have played such a prominent part in 20th-century poetic expression.

'Flight patterns' (John Sewell, 1989)

ONE-DIMENSIONAL DEVIANCE

Some graphological deviance is simple and specific, involving just one dimension of variation, such as spelling, punctuation, or typography. Spelling variation is especially common, being employed by novelists and dramatists trying to represent nonstandard speech (pp. 84, 89), and it can be found in poetry too. Examples include the attempt to mark regional identity, as in Scots or Caribbean poetry (pp. 331, 348), the use of archaic spelling to convey romantic or idyllic associations (p. 185), or the first example below, in which a Cockney accent is suggested chiefly by the omission of /h/. Deviant spelling can also be used simply for fun, as in the graphic deviance of Ogden Nash illustrated on p. 406.

• Then 'ere's to the sons
o' the Widow,
Wherever, 'owever they
  roam.
'Ere's all they desire, an' if
  they require
A speedy return to their
  'ome.
(Rudyard Kipling, *Barrack Room Ballads*, 1892.)

• of course shes right not to ruin her hands I noticed he was always talking to her lately at the table explaining things in the paper and she pretending to understand sly of course that comes from his side of the house and helping her into her coat but if there was anything wrong with her its me shed tell not him he cant say I pretend things can he Im too honest as a matter of fact … (From Molly Bloom's soliloquy in the final pages of James Joyce's *Ulysses*, 1922.)

• When people say, 'I've told you *fifty* times,'
They mean to scold, and very often do;
When poets say, 'I've written *fifty* rhymes,'
They make you dread that they'll recite them too…
(Byron, *Don Juan*, 1819–24)

TWO-DIMENSIONAL DEVIANCE

Concrete poetry is the sub-genre which has tried most dramatically to free itself from the constraints of visual linearity, and to offer alternative representations which do not correspond in any simple way to the linear form of spoken language. These poems are typically two-dimensional (conveying an amalgam of horizontal and vertical messages), though they often make use of a third dimension (such as typographic prominence), and some introduce a fourth (such as colour, or – using animated techniques in television – change in time).

They present many levels of complexity. Some are visually straightforward, written in a form which is simply mimetic of their content. Such 'picture poems' have a long history: a famous example is from the 17th-century poem 'The Altar', by George Herbert, which is designed in the shape of an altar. A recent example is Dylan Thomas's poetic sequence using butterfly and hourglass shapes, one of which is illustrated on p. 271.

The content of a piece of concrete poetry may be extremely simple (such as the repetition of a single word or phrase), akin to abstract art, but it may also be semantically testing. Some poems try to exploit all aspects of the multidimensionality of visual form, and can be read in several directions at once, or impose no single 'correct' direction of reading. There may need to be a considerable intellectual effort to see what meaning(s) the text might yield, and uncertainty over the 'value' of such readings ('What is it saying?') has fuelled controversy over the value of this genre. On the other hand, a critical language for describing the possibilities of variation in visual linguistic form has hardly begun to be developed, so that it would be premature to dismiss nonlinear poems by judging them using criteria which were developed for linear text.

This poem is of a simple but somewhat unusual kind, falling uncertainly between the categories of word play (p. 400) and poetry. 'Palm tree' (1991) is a shaped poem by British academic Gerry Abbott, which can be read in two dimensions: from top to bottom and from bottom to top.

```
                    … sky
                 blue balloon
             a needle that spikes
         dragon with double armed limbs,
 lizard green of ruff or pterodactyl green and leathery of wing
   like flapping umbrellas upraised monstrous and ragged
         those loom where to eye fearful the leading
                   spirals climb
                  naturally but
                  geometrically;
                  chipped badly
                   and askew
                   swivelled
                    capitals
                   Corinthian
                    stacked
                     loftily
                  come next:
                  ringed and
                   fat column
                  a fossilized
                   long trunk
                  mammoth like
                  appears now;
                  one stage is
                  tentacles slow
                  grubbing into
                  oozing liquid:
                  now backwards
                  word by word
                  all this repeat
                 therefore; though
         it was clear really wasn't it …
```

VISUAL FORM

Lines, verse structure, the use of white space, and textual shape define the semantic structure of a poem, and identify the weight to be attached to its various elements. They also control the tempo of a reader's interpretation, and the pace of an oral performance. These variations in visual form offer possibilities which are unavailable in speech. For example, the spatial juxtaposition of ideas on the page can convey shifts of tone, ironic contrast, and other rhetorical meanings. A figurative or abstract graphic shape may be used as an image or icon of a poem's content. And the way the text is structured may signal its relationship to other varieties or its place within a particular poetic tradition.

SIGHT STANZAS

Line and verse division become critical aids to assimilation when a poet offers us a long or complex sentence. They give the text a pattern and cohesion, in a real sense 'making poetic' what might otherwise seem to be a random and indigestible collection of ideas and images. In this extract from William Carlos Williams' 'The Semblables' (1943), the 'sight stanzas' keep the opening sentence of the poem alive and manageable. Without them, it would be difficult to cope with the clausal subject – a sequence of four noun phrases (p. 222), each with complex postmodification – whose verb does not appear until line 27.

These stanzas, however, do not coincide with the main syntactic divisions, producing a series of postulated semantic units which are in tension with the grammatical structure. The challenge to the reader is to find meaning within and between these units. Positional prominence can give dramatic focus to words which would otherwise be unremarkable (such as the monosyllabic *cop* in the last stanza) or suggest new lexical relationships, as is achieved by the foregrounding of *monastery* and *munitions plant*. (After E. Berry, 1985.)

The red brick monastery in
the suburbs over against the dust-
hung acreage of the unfinished
and all but subterranean

munitions plant: those high
brick walls behind which at Easter
the little orphans and bastards
in white gowns sing their Latin

responses to the hoary ritual
while frankincense and myrrh
round out the dark chapel making
an enclosed sphere of it

of which they are the worm:
that cell outside the city beside
the polluted stream and dump
heap, uncomplaining, and the field

of upended stones with a photo
under glass fastened here and there
to one of them near the deeply
carved name to distinguish it:

that trinity of slate gables
the unembellished windows piling
up, the chapel with its round
window between the dormitories

peaked by the bronze belfry
peaked in turn by the cross,
verdigris – faces all silent
that miracle that has burst sexless

from between the carrot rows.
Leafless white birches, their
empty tendrils swaying in
the all but no breeze guard

behind the spiked monastery fence
the sacred statuary. But ranks
of brilliant car-tops row on row
give back in all his glory the

late November sun and hushed
attend, before that tumbled
ground, those sightless walls
and shovelled entrances where no

one but a lonesome cop swinging
his club gives sign, that agony
within where the wrapt machines
are praying...

WEIGHT WATCHING

An effective technique for seeing how these concepts of visual form operate in practice is to rewrite a poem as if it were prose. The prosaic version is generally bizarre and often unintelligible; after attempting to read it, the return to the poetic structure is invariably a relief. When the technique is applied to this passage from T. S. Eliot's 'The Dry Salvages' (1941), it clearly shows the importance of line length and division in controlling the distribution of weight and pace within a text.

And under the oppression of the silent fog
The tolling bell
Measures time not our time, rung by the unhurried
Ground swell, a time
Older than the time of chronometers, older
Than time counted by anxious worried women
Lying awake, calculating the future,
Trying to unweave, unwind, unravel
And piece together the past and the future,
Between midnight and dawn, when the past is all deception,
The future futureless, before the morning watch
When time stops and time is never ending;
And the ground swell, that is and was from the beginning,
Clangs
The bell.

And under the oppression of the silent fog the tolling bell measures time not our time, rung by the unhurried ground swell, a time older than the time of chronometers, older than time counted by anxious worried women lying awake, calculating the future, trying to unweave, unwind, unravel and piece together the past and the future, between midnight and dawn, when the past is all deception, the future futureless, before the morning watch when time stops and time is never ending; and the ground swell, that is and was from the beginning, clangs the bell.

THREE-DIMENSIONAL DEVIANCE

E. E. Cummings, perhaps more than any other poet, has experimented with the aesthetic possibilities of visual form. These items from his most innovative volume, *No Thanks* (1935), illustrate several aspects of his work.

• Poem No. 9 is an example of the way spatial arrangement can create movement, with the arm-like *wingab* sending a ball-like *o* up the left-hand margin to the top of the poem, sweeping up any other *o*'s which happen to get in its way. The 'fanfare' section announcing the president shows alternative readings competing simultaneously so as to convey visually a series of auditory echoes.

• Poem No. 13 has been called Cummings' most famous visual experiment. Irregular spacing, deviant punctuation, and fractured words are used to convey unpredictable movement, with capitalization expressing peaks of activity. The iconicity in the poem is not solely in the grasshopper shape which might be seen in the overall layout, but in the dislocation of letters, which forces the reader's eye to jump grasshopper-like around the poem, searching for coherence. (After R. D. Cureton, 1986.)

```
o pr
gress verily thou art m
mentous superc
lossal hyperpr
digious etc i kn
w & if you d

n't why g
  to yonder s
called newsreel s
called theatre & with your
wn eyes beh

ld The
      (The president The
      president of The president
      of The)president of

      the(united The president of the
      united states The president of the united
      states of The President Of The)United States

         Of America unde negant redire quemquam supp
sedly thr
w
 i
  n
   g
    a
     b
      aseball
```

```
                              r-p-o-p-h-e-s-s-a-g-r
                                     who
a)s w(e loo)k
upnowgath
        PPEGORHRASS
                      eringint(o-
aThe):l
        eA
          !p:
S
                                        a
rIvInG        (r
            .gRrEaPsPhOs)
                              to
rea(be)rran(com)gi(e)ngly
.grasshopper;
```

GRAMMATICAL FREEDOM

There are severe limits on the freedom of writers to deviate from the norms of English grammar, if they want their text to maintain coherence and intelligibility. A sentence such as the following, written by a profoundly deaf 16-year-old about the film *Star Wars* (1977), shows what can happen to grammar when too much deviance is present.

The Star Wars was the two spaceship a fighting opened door was coming the Men and Storm trooper guns carry on to Artoo Detoo and threepio at go the space. The Earth was not grass and tree but to the sand…

Grammatical deviance in literature is not usually so gross, though from time to time – and especially in poetry – we can encounter constructions which strain for intelligibility, as in this parenthesis from E. E. Cummings' *No Thanks* (1935), No. 71:

(the not whose spiral hunger may appease
what merely riches of our pretty world
sweetly who flourishes,swiftly which fails

but out of serene perfectly Nothing hurled
into young Now entirely arrives
gesture past fragrance fragrant;a than pure

more signalling
of singular most flame
and surely poets only understands)

More commonly, a deviant grammatical pattern is there for a fairly obvious reason. In poetry it is typically to satisfy the phonological demands of a line or verse. Rhyme-scheme and metrical structure may license quite marked deviations from normal word order, such as the inversion or deletion of clause elements (p.220), and the addition of extra phrase elements (e.g. the use of auxiliary verb *do* when no emphasis is intended, p. 212). These examples are from Wordsworth's 'Lucy' poems (1799):

Strange fits of passion have I known…
I to her cottage bent my way…
This child I to myself will take…
A slumber did my spirit seal…

Sometimes grammatical deviation is there to add to the archaic tone of a text, using elements of older morphology (*hath, ye, thou, sayest, ungirt*) and syntax. Tennyson's *Morte d'Arthur* (1842) is full of examples of syntactic archaism, such as the use of negative imperatives without *do* (*But now delay not*), adjectives after nouns (*an act unprofitable*), and non-reflexive pronouns (*Where I will heal **me** of my grievous wound*). Comic verse also relies greatly on drastic grammatical variations, both morphological and syntactic, as can be seen in this snippet from Ogden Nash:

Tell me, O Octopus, I begs
Is those things arms, or is they legs?
('The Octopus', 1942)

And it should additionally be recognized that grammatical deviance can account for much of what is generally held to be inept verse, because of the way word order is twisted to fit the metre or rhyme, even to the extent of fracturing the language's most fixed idioms. An example is this offering from William McGonagall:

But, poor soul, he was found stark dead,
Crushed and mangled from foot to head.
(*Poetic Gems*, 1890)

THE STRIKING AND THE SUBTLE

Grammatical deviance can be dramatic. An example is the striking syntactic variation, compounding, and word-class conversion (p. 129) of Gerard Manley Hopkins, as in this example from the sonnet 'No worst, there is none' (c. 1885). *Fall, steep* and *deep* become new types of noun. The second sentence reverses its elements and provides a relative clause without a head (*[those] who never hung there*). And *long* is made prominent by being moved from its normal position after the verb.

O the mind, mind has
    mountains; cliffs of fall
Frightful, sheer, no-man-
fathomed. Hold them cheap
May who ne'er hung there.
    Nor does long our small
Durance deal with that steep or
    deep.

By contrast, Tennyson's famous poem (1842), reprinted below, seems at first to have nothing that stands out grammatically at all, apart from the use of *thy*, the vocative *O*, and the syntactic blends in *O well for …* Yet the regular word order, and its close fit with the verse structure, is deceptive. There is subtle deviance in the use of coordination, as can be seen by first considering the following sentences:

*Sit down and I want a paper.
*Run upstairs but it's raining.
*Take this or I'll look.
*Good for you and it's ready.

None of these is normal in English. An imperative clause cannot be coordinated with an affirmative clause. There is only one type of exception – the conditional sense of *Ask me and I'll do it* ('If you ask me …') – and this sense is not relevant for the poem. Tennyson is not suggesting 'If you break, O Sea …').
   In the poem, the first and last verse both link imperative and affirmative clauses. Similarly, there is unusual linkage between the second verse (a pair of exclamatory clauses) and the third (another affirmative clause).
   The conjunctions seem to provide a steadiness of direction to a text which is being pulled in different ways by the conflicting emotions it expresses. There is grief and incoherence in the first stanza; mixed feelings in the second, as the poet observes those unaffected by loss; an attempt to find calm in the third, by contemplating the stately ships, with the mood quickly extinguished; and anguish in the fourth, along with a coherence lacking at the outset. The syntax reflects these emotions, moving from command to statement, on to exclamation, back to statement and exclamation, and ending with command and statement. Such a diversity of functions could easily result in a text full of erratic, discordant juxtapositions, incompatible with the mood of meditative longing which the words in the body of the text convey. The potential discord is removed by the use of the conjunctions, which provide a smoothness of syntactic linkage, corresponding to the stable metrical beat. (The discord can be artificially introduced by attempting to read the poem with the seven line-opening conjunctions omitted. The text remains grammatical, and there is a viable metre; but the steady rhythm is gone, and the mood is quite lost.) (After E. A. Levenston, 1973.)

Break, break, break,
    On thy cold gray stones, O Sea!
And I would that my tongue could utter
    The thoughts that arise in me.

O well for the fisherman's boy,
    That he shouts with his sister at play!
O well for the sailor lad,
    That he sings in his boat on the bay!

And the stately ships go on
    To their haven under the hill;
But O for the touch of a vanished hand,
    And the sound of a voice that is still!

Break, break, break,
    At the foot of thy crags, O Sea!
But the tender grace of a day that is dead
    Will never come back to me.

LEXICAL FREEDOM

The lexical range of literary English is illustrated on many earlier pages of this book (chiefly in Parts I and II). It defies summary. In drama and the novel it is virtually unrestricted. And even in poetry, where there is a well-established tradition of literary vocabulary (*poetic diction*), the 20th century has seen a remarkable broadening, so that now we are likely to encounter there the whole range of the domestic lexicon, including slang and taboo words, as well as the special vocabulary of regional and social varieties.

As a result, it is no longer so easy to describe the lexical choices in a literary work. We are less likely to encounter well-recognized types of word, such as archaisms (*damsel, yonder, hither, 'twas, quoth*), poetically restricted words (*nymph, slumber, woe, billows, o'er*), or neologisms (as in Hopkins' *lovescape* and *dovewinged*, and in the examples from Shakespeare and Joyce given on pp. 63 and 134). Rather more necessary now is the detailed analysis of lexical items, singly and in combination, to see their contribution to the work as a whole. And a great deal of attention has also been paid to the way deviance operates within restricted lexical structures to create specific meanings – as in the manipulation by Dylan Thomas of such time phrases as *a grief ago* and *all the moon long*.

LEXICAL RANGE

All the moon long I heard, blessed among stables, the nightjars
    Flying with the ricks, and the horses
        Flashing into the dark.
(Dylan Thomas, 'Fern Hill', 1945)

It's no go the picture palace, it's no go the stadium,
It's no go the country cot with a pot of pink geraniums,
It's no go the Government grants, it's no go the elections,
Sit on your arse for fifty years and hang your hat on a pension.
(Louis Macneice, 'Bagpipe Music', 1935)

Paint me a cavernous waste shore
    Cast in the unstilled Cyclades,
Paint me the bold anfractuous rocks
    Faced by the snarled and yelping seas.
(T. S. Eliot, 'Sweeney Erect', 1920)

A barn is not called a barn, to put it more plainly,
Or a field in the distance, where sheep may be safely grazing.
You must never be over-sure. You must say, when reporting:
At five o'clock in the central sector is a dozen
Of what appear to be animals; whatever you do,
    Don't call the bleeders *sheep*.
(Henry Reed, 'Judging Distances', 1946)

Sparkling chips of rock
are crushed down to the level of the parent block.
    Were not 'impersonal judgment in aesthetic
    matters, a metaphysical impossibility', you

might fairly achieve
it.
(Marianne Moore, 'To a Steam Roller', 1935)

'YES', SHE SAID

*a*ccepted, accosted, accused, acknowledged, added, addressed, adjured, admired, admitted, admonished, advised, affirmed… whimpered, whined, whipped out, whispered, whistled, winked, wished, wondered, yattered on, yawned, yelled, yelped.

How many substitutes do novelists find for *said* following direct speech? In a study of 100 novels by 20th-century British and American authors, nearly 600 such substitutes were found. The 'average' novelist uses a range of about 50 such verbs in any one novel.

In N. F. Simpson's poem, these alternatives are scrupulously avoided. *Said* plays a crucial role in identifying the speakers, but it does far more than this. Its reiterated, unemotional ordinariness reinforces the absurdly low-key manner in which the writer is reacting to his bizarre situation. And its very routineness, far from being monotonous, adds increasingly to our sense of the surreal, as the story unfolds.

One of our St Bernard Dogs Is Missing

A moot point
Whether I was going to
Make it.
I just had the strength
To ring the bell.

There were monks inside
And one of them
Eventually
Opened the door.
Oh
He said,
This is a bit of a turn-up
He said
For the book.
Opportune
He said
Your arriving at this particular
As it were
Moment

You're dead right
I said
It was touch and go
Whether I could have managed
To keep going
For very much
Longer.

No
He said
The reason I use the word opportune
Is that
Not to put too fine a point on it
One of our St Bernard dogs is
Unfortunately
Missing.

Oh, dear
I said.
Not looking for me, I hope.

No
He said.
It went for a walk
And got lost in the snow.

Dreadful thing
I said
To happen

Yes
He said.
It is.

To
Of all creatures
I said
A St Bernard dog
That has devoted
Its entire
Life
To doing good
And helping
Others.

What I was actually thinking
He said
Since you happen to be
In a manner of speaking
Out there already
Is that
If you could
At all
See your way clear
To having a scout
As it were
Around,
It would save one of us
Having to
If I can so put it
Turn out.
Ah
I said
That would
I suppose
Make a kind of sense.

Before you go
He said
If I can find it
You'd better
Here it is
Take this.

What is it?
I said
It's a flask
He said
Of Brandy.

Ah
I said.

For the dog
He said.

Good thinking
I said.

The drill
He said
When you find it
If you ever do
Is to lie down.

Right
I said
Will do.

Lie down on top of it
He said
To keep it warm
Till help arrives.

That was a week ago, and
    my hopes are rising all
    the time.
I feel with ever-increasing
    confidence
that once I can safely say
    that I am within what
    might
be called striking distance
    of knowing where,
    within a
square mile or two, to start
    getting down to looking,
my troubles are more or
    less, to all intents and
purposes, apart from frostbite, with any luck once
help arrives at long last,
    God willing, as good as
over.
It is good to be spurred on
    with hope.

(N. F. Simpson, 1977)

DISCOURSE FREEDOM

Evidence of deviance and personal identity is fairly easy to see when the stretch of language being investigated is fairly small (a 'bottom-up' approach to stylistic analysis, p. 286). But as soon as we leave the safe confines of the sentence or stanza, and branch out into such domains as the paragraph, section, scene, act, and chapter, it becomes much more difficult to see distinctive linguistic structure in action. There are comparatively few stylistic studies which have investigated the larger patterns of discourse in essays, short stories, novels, plays, and other genres, and if an analysis succeeds it is usually because it has restricted the scope of its enquiry. Typical topics are novel openings and closings, patterns of textual cross reference, the use of figurative expressions, modes of speech presentation, and the functional role of sentence types. However, there is still a considerable gap between the findings of this kind of enquiry and those which begin 'top down', operating with such notions as characterization, viewpoint, setting, theme, and plot.

S. Dickinson.

We do not play on graves
Because there isn't room;
Besides, it isn't even,
It slants and people come

And put a flower on it,
And hang their faces so,
We're fearing that their
  hearts will drop
And crush our pretty play.

And so we move as far
As enemies away
Just looking round to see
  how far
It is occasionally.

(Emily Dickinson)

WHAT IS IT?

An important feature of the coherence which defines a discourse is the use of the cross-referring properties of pronouns (p. 210). Normally, we expect a pronoun to have a single reference, during the development of a single theme, and from school we are taught in writing to make our pronoun reference clear (p. 191). This poem by Emily Dickinson (1830–86), bends both these conventions.

There is an initial uncertainty over the status of the pronoun *it*. Is this the third person singular inanimate form (as in *it's a computer*)? There is an ambivalence, because there is no clear grammatical antecedent: notionally, the link is with *graves*, but that word is plural whereas *it* is singular. The lack of concord suggests an interpretation as 'empty' *it* (as in *it isn't right*): *it isn't even, / It slants* would then mean 'There's never any evenness on graves; they always slant'. By the end of the poem, we are led to a definite third person reading, but now the reference of *it* seems to have grown, allowing two levels of meaning – beneath the child's wary watchfulness, an adult vision of the inevitable approach of death. Is this sense presaged by the opening use of *it*? The uncertainties of the child seem to be reflected in the uncertainties of the grammar. Faced with death, what is it, that happens?

THAT'S THE QUESTION

According to contemporary thinking in pragmatics, conversation succeeds because we adopt a 'cooperative principle' – a set of rules governing linguistic interaction which everyone recognizes. We assume, for example, that when people ask us a question, they wish us to respond and they intend to pay attention to our answer – for otherwise, why should they have asked it? Someone who asks us a question without giving us time to respond, or who is not interested in our answer, or who asks us a question which we are unable to answer, or which perhaps is impossible to answer, is doing something very strange. If this behaviour keeps up over a series of interchanges, it becomes more than strange: it becomes menacing. It can happen anywhere – in a street, in a bar, between parent and child – and it can be finely crafted as a feature of dialogue in drama. The acknowledged master of this strategy is Harold Pinter. In *The Birthday Party* (1957), Goldberg and McCann are experts at question dominance, eventually reducing the verbally defiant Stanley to inarticulateness.

GOLDBERG: Webber! Why did you change your name?
STANLEY: I forgot the other one.
GOLDBERG: What's your name now?
STANLEY: Joe Soap.
GOLDBERG: You stink of sin.
McCANN: I can smell it.
GOLDBERG: Do you recognise an external force?
STANLEY: What?
GOLDBERG: Do you recognise an external force?
McCANN: That's the question!
GOLDBERG: Do you recognise an external force, responsible for you, suffering for you?
STANLEY: It's late.
GOLDBERG: Late! Late enough! When did you last pray?
McCANN: He's sweating!
GOLDBERG: When did you last pray?
McCANN: He's sweating!
GOLDBERG: Is the number 846 possible or necessary?
STANLEY: Neither.
GOLDBERG: Wrong! Is the number 846 possible or necessary?
STANLEY: Both.
GOLDBERG: Wrong! It's necessary but not possible.
STANLEY: Both.
GOLDBERG: Wrong! Why do you think the number 846 is necessarily possible?
STANLEY: Must be.
GOLDBERG: Wrong!
...
McCANN: What about the Albigensenist heresy?
GOLDBERG: Who watered the wicket at Melbourne?
McCANN: What about the blessed Oliver Plunkett?
GOLDBERG: Speak up, Webber. Why did the chicken cross the road?
STANLEY: He wanted to – he wanted to – he wanted to...
McCANN: He doesn't know!
GOLDBERG: Why did the chicken cross the road?
STANLEY: He wanted to – he wanted to...
GOLDBERG: Why did the chicken cross the road?
STANLEY: He wanted...
McCANN: He doesn't know. He doesn't know which came first!
GOLDBERG: Which came first?
McCANN: Chicken? Egg? Which came first?
GOLDBERG and McCANN: Which came first? Which came first? Which came first?

STANLEY *screams*.

Harold Pinter

FIGMENTAL FACTUALITY

While Adam Munro was changing trains at Revolution Square shortly before 11 a.m. that morning of 10th June, a convoy of a dozen sleek, black, Zil limousines was sweeping through the Borovitsky Gate in the Kremlin wall a hundred feet above his head and one thousand three hundred feet southwest of him. The Soviet Politburo was about to begin a meeting that would change history.

This is the opening of Chapter 2 of Frederick Forsyth's *The Devil's Alternative* (1979). It displays many of the discourse characteristics that we have come to associate with the popular spy novel genre – in particular its attention to verisimilitude. The event described in the paragraph is simple enough: some cars have arrived for a meeting at the Kremlin at a certain time. The rest is 'atmosphere', 'setting' – but of a rather special kind. The technical detail (the exact time, the make of cars, the name of the entrance point) is suggestive of journalistic reporting; but this passage goes well beyond that. As Walter Nash puts it, in his commentary on this text: the stylistic commitment

is to the figment of factuality, to the excitement raised by reference to every boy's own book of little-known facts. Did you know that if you were to stand on the platform of the underground station at Revolution Square, Moscow, the wall of the Kremlin would be exactly one hundred feet above your head and one thousand three hundred feet to the south west of you? Anyone who can tell you that must know what he is talking about; we feel that we are there, in the very thick of things.

In the analysis of literary discourse, it is a useful technique to try to define the obligatory core of action which the text expresses, and then reflect on the reasons for the 'optional' residue. In much popular fiction, the text is mainly residue. Here is another example of Nash's, along with his comment:

Auntie Dier tapped her fingers with impatience as she listened to the ringing tone. Eventually, there was an answer.
'Good morning, Kate!' said the older woman, cheerfully.

This is surely not meant to be read with close attention; dwelling on it provokes mischievous enquiries – do you tap your fingers *patiently*?; when you have dialled your number, what else is there to *listen* to but the ringing tone?; and if you are a character in a short story, using the telephone to speak to another character, is it not reasonable to suppose that an answer will come eventually? Why all this descriptive fuss over a phone call? It could be done quite straightforwardly:

Auntie Dier dialled Kate's number. 'Good morning!' she said.

That, however, misses the major purpose of popstyling, which is to promote constantly the illusion of significant activity on the part of characters who twitch with life – impatient life, cheery life, a tapping, rapping, drumming life that makes an event out of lifting a receiver.

(W. Nash, 1990, pp. 40, 64.)

Frederick Forsyth

FIGURATIVE LANGUAGE

Why should an account of figurative language be placed under the heading of discourse? A clue lies in the traditional designation of this topic – as 'figures of speech' – suggesting that the kinds of semantic contrast involved are of much greater relevance than the study of the written language alone, and hinting that they relate to much wider stretches of language than the individual word or phrase. Also, although the 'classical' accounts of these figures are typically illustrated from literature, there is a much broader tradition, which can be traced back to the subject of classical rhetoric. The literary use of figurative language falls within this tradition, but so does the use made of it by many other varieties, such as advertising, political speaking, journalism, and religion.

The point emerges even more strongly when these features are studied in relation to everyday conversation, where metaphor in particular has been shown to be of great significance. We argue with each other using the terms of battle (*she attacked my views*; *he defended himself*; *I won the argument*). We talk about countries as if they were

people (*America's been a good friend to them*; *France and her neighbours*). We discuss economics in terms of human health (*oil is our lifeline*; *an ailing economy*). And the parties in a political conflict interact as if they were gambling (*showed his hand, what is at stake, how much can they lose*). Often, several conflicting metaphors are available, with the choice revealing much about the chooser. The metaphors of war, for example, include its description as a game (*winner, loser*), as a medical task (*clean up, surgical strike*), as a drama (*villain, plot*), and as violent crime (*rape of Country X*; *Country Y as a victim*).

Metaphor plays a major role in structuring the way we think about the world, though most of these everyday metaphors go unnoticed:

it's difficult to strike a balance
they were flocking to see it
I can't stand that sort of thing
the craze was at its height
did the papers cotton on to it?

These, as George Lakoff and Mark Johnson have succinctly put it in the title of their book on the subject, are among the 'metaphors we live by'.

EXTENDING FIGURES

The minimal case of figurative language is a local, restricted effect in which special meaning is extracted from the linking of two unlike words. The following are some of the chief ways in which this can be done.

- With *metaphor*, the linkage is implicit: *idle hill*.
- With *simile* the linkage is explicit: *drumming like a noise in dreams*.
- With *paradox*, there is the need to resolve a contradiction:

ignorance is strength.
- With *metonymy*, the attribute replaces the whole: *the crown of France*.
- With *oxymoron*, incompatible notions are brought together: *living death*.
- With *personification*, a link is made between the inanimate and the human: *nature spoke*.

In most cases, however, these effects extend beyond an initial pairing of notions. One effect leads to another, and chains of figurativeness arise. Poets in

particular are reluctant to put down a good figure when they find one. In the first example below, the implications of the opening metaphorical link (between *feed* and *heart*) is extended via the words *fare* and *substance* over three lines. In the second, the personification of *nature* in the first line is carried on through the verbs (*care, know, ask*) until the whole stanza is involved.

We had fed the heart on fantasies,
The heart's grown brutal from the fare;

More substance in our enmities
Than in our love;
(W. B. Yeats, 'Meditations in Time of Civil War', 1928)

For nature, heartless, witless nature,
Will neither care nor know
What stranger's feet may find the meadow
And trespass there and go,
Nor ask amid the dews of morning
If they are mine or no.

(A. E. Housman, 'Tell me not here, it needs not saying', 1922)

VARIETY FREEDOM

It is not only the levels of language structure which, singly or in combination, can be used in deviant ways as part of literary self-expression: the complexes of features which define regional and social varieties (p. 290) can also be put to use. A text may begin in one variety, then switch to another, or build up effects by incorporating features of several varieties. This is most evident in the novel, where there is little difficulty in introducing occupational varieties and nonstandard forms of speech as part of the portrayal of character; and some novelists (such as Dickens and Hardy) have a considerable reputation for their ability to capture variety usage in this way (p. 89). By

contrast, it is much more difficult to introduce variety distinctiveness into poetry: the tighter constraints on language imposed by a metrical scheme or verse structure can easily distort the features which it is intended to represent. It is no small feat to introduce even an everyday conversation into a poem (as does T. S. Eliot, p. 412) so that it both retains its naturalness yet permits a line-based structuring which integrates well with the rest of the text. The incorporation of individual lexical items from a recognized regional or social variety is common enough (such as the scientific figurativeness of the metaphysical poets or the religious allusiveness of the romantics), but it is unusual to find in a poem lines which tap the whole range of variety features – in phonology, graphology, grammar, lexicon, and discourse.

NAMING OF VARIETIES

One of the most successful instances of variety freedom in poetry is Henry Reed's 'Lessons of the War' (1946), where two poems, 'Naming of Parts' and 'Judging Distances' (p. 419), rely for their impact on the use of a wide range of features from two occupational backgrounds. The clinical commentary of the army instructor is made to contrast with the reflective tones of the poet in phonology, syntax, vocabulary, idiom, and discourse. In oral performance, the phonological contrast emerges even more clearly when the text is read in two 'voices'.

Naming of Parts

To-day we have naming of parts. Yesterday,
We had daily cleaning. And to-morrow morning,
We shall have what to do after firing. But to-day,
To-day we have naming of parts. Japonica
Glistens like coral in all of the neighbouring gardens,
    And to-day we have naming of parts.

This is the lower sling swivel. And this
Is the upper sling swivel, whose use you will see,
When you are given your slings. And this is the piling swivel,
Which in your case you have not got. The branches
Hold in the gardens their silent, eloquent gestures,
    Which in our case we have not got.

This is the safety-catch, which is always released
With an easy flick of the thumb. And please do not let me
See anyone using his finger. You can do it quite easy
If you have any strength in your thumb. The blossoms
Are fragile and motionless, never letting anyone see
    Any of them using their finger.

And this you can see is the bolt. The purpose of this
Is to open the breech, as you see. We can slide it
Rapidly backwards and forwards: we call this
Easing the spring. And rapidly backwards and forwards
The early bees are assaulting and fumbling the flowers:
    They call it easing the Spring.

They call it easing the Spring: it is perfectly easy
If you have any strength in your thumb: like the bolt,
And the breech, and the cocking-piece, and the point of balance,
Which in our case we have not got; and the almond-blossom
Silent in all of the gardens and the bees going backwards and forwards,
    For to-day we have naming of parts.

STRUCTURING THE RIDICULOUS

In this extract from N. F. Simpson's *A Resounding Tinkle* (1957), a genre of the variety of medicine – the doctor-patient interview – is used to structure an episode in the theatre of the absurd. The technique uses the conventions of this setting to motivate the humour, rather than to poke fun at the conventions themselves. In this respect, it differs from parody (p. 404), which more than any other genre depends for its thrust on the exaggeration of variety features.

SECOND COMEDIAN: It's my feet, Doctor.
FIRST COMEDIAN: What's the matter with your feet?
SECOND COMEDIAN: I was rather hoping you might be able to tell me that, Doctor.
FIRST COMEDIAN: Let me see them. *Second Comedian takes off socks and shoes.*
SECOND COMEDIAN: They're all right now. It's when they suddenly swivel round they catch me. *Second Comedian holds out both legs quite straight in front of him. First Comedian stands over them.*
FIRST COMEDIAN: What are these?
SECOND COMEDIAN: They're my kneecaps, Doctor.
FIRST COMEDIAN: They ought to be much higher up your legs than this.
SECOND COMEDIAN: I can't seem to keep them up, Doctor. *First Comedian goes to wash-basin where he begins washing his hands, while Second Comedian goes into the corner, where the desk conceals him, to undress.*
FIRST COMEDIAN: Eardrums still getting overheated?
SECOND COMEDIAN: Only when I listen to anything, Doctor.

CODE-SWITCHING

This extract, from Walter Scott's *The Antiquary*, displays a regional variety contrast in action: between Southern British English and Scots (p. 328). The English-speaking traveller is complaining to Scots-speaking Mrs Macleuchar about the non-arrival of her coach. In an initial fit of indignation, she switches into English as she tries to evade the issue, then reverts to Scots when she realizes her stratagem will not work. Walter Scott's characters often switch between varieties when it is to their advantage to do so.

'I say, Mrs Macleuchar!'
'I am just serving a customer. – Indeed hinny, it will no be a bodle cheaper than I tell ye.'
'Woman,' reiterated the traveller, 'do you think we can stand here all day till you have cheated that poor servant wench out of her half-year's fee and bountith?'
'Cheated!' retorted Mrs Macleuchar, eager to take up the quarrel upon a defensible ground. 'I scorn your words, sir; you are an uncivil person, and I desire you will not stand there to slander me at my ain stairhead.'
'The woman,' said the senior, looking with an arch glance at his destined travelling companion, 'does not understand the words of action. – Woman,' again turning to the vault, 'I arraign not thy character, but I desire to know what is become of thy coach.'
'What's your wull?' answered Mrs Macleuchar, relapsing into deafness.

DEMONSTRATING IDENTITY

These last pages have illustrated ways in which the chief levels of structural linguistic description can be used to locate features of linguistic deviance that are of literary interest. Some of these features are in widespread use, entering into the definition of literary genres; others are restricted to individuals, forming part of an author's linguistic identity. But in all cases, the identification of potential stylistic features, whether shared or idiosyncratic, has been carried out impressionistically. Certainly, the more we know about the structural possibilities of language, the more we shall spot points of stylistic interest when they arise, and the more we shall be able to explain the nature of the effects; but that first step – the recognition of distinctiveness – is intuitive.

Can the process be made more objective? The present century has seen considerable progress in providing alternative methods for arriving at stylistic decisions, aided by developments in statistics and computing (p. 436). The subject, which has gone under such names as *stylostatistics* and *stylometry*, has now accumulated a large body of analytical procedures, and several classical textual problems of uncertain authorship have been solved.

(Forensic) stylometry

The basic approach is to calculate the frequency and distribution of a small number of linguistic variables in a text, comparing texts of unknown or uncertain authorship with comparable texts whose authorship is known. There are many methodological problems (not least, the question of how words are to be identified and counted, p. 118), but the subject has had several successes. At the turn of the century, the movement to see Francis Bacon's hand in Shakespeare's plays, fuelled by the claims of Ignatius Donnelly and others that a Baconian cipher could be found throughout the Shakespearean canon, was countered by stylometric analyses which showed significant differences in word frequency between the two authors. And more recently there has been the identification by Alvar Ellegård of Sir Philip Francis as the author of a series of pseudonymous 18th-century political letters (the 'Junius letters'). Nor is literature the only beneficiary of these methods. In the legal field, there is now a large body of published material showing how linguistic techniques can be used – though not uncontroversially – to support a claim of identity or difference between samples of speech or writing as part of a case for the defence or prosecution. And this application has generated yet another name for the subject: forensic linguistics.

WHO WROTE TEXT A?

A typical example of stylometry in action is shown in this graph from a 1992 study. The 50 commonest words of narrative (non-dialogue) in two novels by Henry James (c. 191,000 words) and three novels by Jane Austen (c. 237,000 words) were ranked into a combined 'top 50' for both authors. A statistical procedure was then used to determine which of these words would be the most discriminating: 28 were chosen (see list below). For example, all the male pronouns turned out to be used significantly more often in James than in Austen. The third person plural pronouns were higher in Austen, and the two indefinite articles (*a, an*) were very high in James. Connectives and prepositions were also especially differentiating. Of the 28 discriminators selected, only one was lexical (*little*) – this is typical of stylometric studies. The graph shows the results of this comparison. There is a clear clustering of the narratives by Austen on the left and by James on the right.

Text A
An additional text was brought into the study: Text A. This was anonymous, but known to be by one or other of the authors. Would the procedure be able to indicate its provenance clearly? A total of 17 words in Text A was aligned with the 28 known discriminators, and this placed it as shown on the graph. It is perfectly clear that Text A must be by James. (After J. F. Burrows, 1992.)

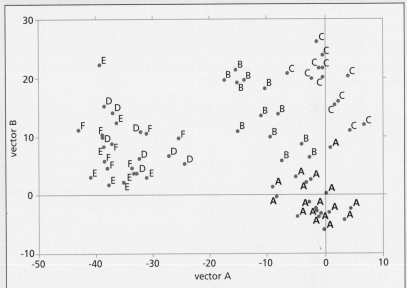

Key: Five narratives by James and Austen (selected segments) and *Text A* (based on the 28 most common 'discriminating word-types' of the five narratives).
A, *Text A*; **B**, *Portrait of a Lady*; **C**, *The Awkward Age*; **D**, *Mansfield Park*; **E**, *Emma*; **F**, *Pride and Prejudice*.

The 50 commonest words in all texts combined, and (right) the 28 most significant discriminators.

1	the	18	that (c)	35	all
2	of	19	not	36	would
3	and	20	for (p)	37	they
4	her	21	but	38	so (av)
5	she	22	him	39	more
6	a	23	said	40	there
7	was	24	be	41	no (ad)
8	to (i)	25	on (p)	42	very
9	had	26	which (rp)	43	their
10	he	27	this	44	them
11	in (p)	28	been	45	if
12	his	29	could	46	herself
13	to (p)	30	an	47	that (rp)
14	it	31	by (p)	48	little
15	with	32	were	49	might
16	as	33	have	50	than
17	at	34	from		

1	this	18	he
2	and	19	not
3	could	20	herself
4	a	21	had
5	be	22	with
6	all	23	from
7	were	24	was
8	if	25	their
9	to (i)	26	his
10	by (p)	27	him
11	an	28	little
12	that (rp)		
13	very		
14	they		
15	no (ad)		
16	them		
17	so (av)		

Abbreviations

ad	adjective	c	conjunction	p	preposition
av	adverb of degree	i	infinitive	rp	relative pronoun

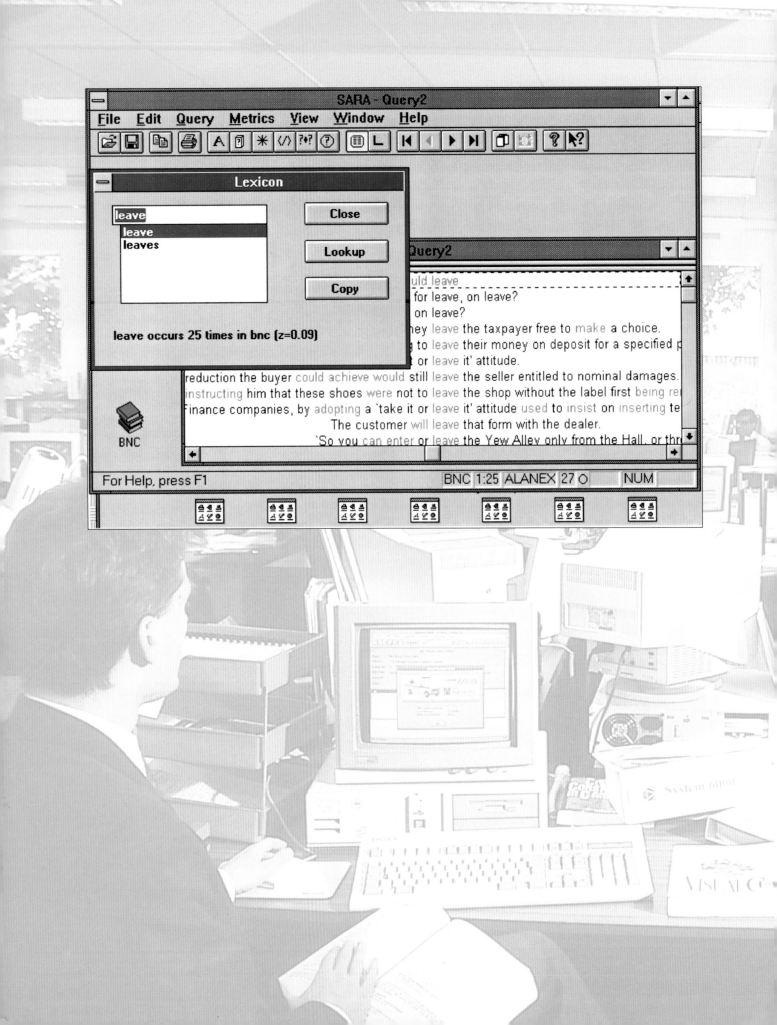

PART VI
Learning about English

Most of this book is devoted to the three foundations on which the study of the English language is built: its history, structure, and use. It is a subject which never ceases to amaze, as we unravel layer after layer of complexity. And it is a subject which seems never-ending, because people are always finding new contexts and applications for this knowledge. It would take another encyclopedia to deal satisfactorily with these larger enterprises; but it would be wrong to leave the present work without giving at least an indication of what they are.

Many fall within the broader subject of applied linguistics – though not all aspects of this subject can be included, because they deal with issues which go well beyond the study of the English language as such. These are chiefly the topics which fall within the area of languages in contact – the nature of foreign (or second) language teaching and learning, questions of translation, interpreting, and bilingualism, and the role of language planning in multilingual situations. Nor does this final section deal with stylistics – a branch of applied linguistics which has already been treated centrally (in Part V).

There remains a subject area that earlier pages have not covered. Some reference needs to be made to how children acquire English as a first language – the spontaneous process of learning to listen and speak (oracy), and the educational process of learning to read and write (literacy). This topic then raises the question of failure – when children do not acquire their language adequately, and when adults lose their command of the language, whether for medical or for other reasons. Major fields of study in their own right, some of the issues dealt with in child language acquisition and language pathology are introduced in §23. The aim is not to explain what these disorders are – a topic which raises issues that, again, go well beyond the study of English – but to show how the study of language disability depends on the information described in Parts II–V of this book if accurate diagnosis and intervention are to take place.

The encyclopedia concludes by looking at the future of English language study. The subject has already benefited greatly from new techniques, especially in computing. In §24 we look at the way these techniques are developing, and at the way corpus studies are advancing our knowledge of the language, especially in lexicography. Dictionaries are given a section to themselves. And we conclude with a brief review of some of the organizations and publications which help to meet the needs of those who find in the English language a source of endless fascination.

◀ **A** screen display (top) using SARA, prototype software currently being developed for use with the British National Corpus (p. 438). In this version, colour is being used to tag different word classes.

The task facing the child acquiring English as a first language can be stated succinctly: to learn most of what is covered by Parts II, III, IV, and V of this book – either as speaker and writer or as listener and reader. Certain sections of Part V, of course are of limited relevance: people do not need to be proficient (as producers or receivers) in all of the enormous range of regional and occupational varieties of English which exist. But everyone needs to acquire a certain minimum ability in the three domains of language structure, interaction and use; and it is often not appreciated just how much this basic proficiency entails. To be an adult, linguistically, means to have acquired the following:

• The 20 or so vowels and 24 or so consonants of a spoken dialect of the language, and over 300 ways of combining these sounds into sequences (such as /s+k+r/ into *scream*, and /m+p+s/ into *jumps*) (§17).
• A vocabulary which can evidently reach 50,000 or more active words, and a passive ability to understand about half as many again (§8).
• At least a thousand aspects of grammatical construction, dealing with all the rules – some very general, some very specific – governing sentence and word formation (Part III).
• Several hundred ways of using the prosodic features of pitch, loudness, speed, and rhythm, along with other tones of voice, to convey meaning: 'it's not what you say, it's the way that you say it' (§17).
• An uncertain (but large) number of rules governing the ways in which sentences can be combined into spoken discourse, both in monologue and dialogue (§19).
• An uncertain (but very large) number of conventions governing the ways in which varieties of the language differ, so that the linguistic consequences of region, gender, class, occupation, and other such factors can be assimilated (§§20–21).
• An uncertain (but even larger) number of strategies governing the ways in which all the above rules can be bent or broken in order to achieve special effects, such as in jokes and poems (§22).

This is already a great deal; but so far all we have produced is an illiterate adult. The task of learning to read and write demands an additional set of skills, involving

---

SUSIE, AT 4½

SUSIE: Oh, look, a crab. We seen – we were been to the seaside.
BABY-SITTER: Have you?
SUSIE: We saw cr – fishes and crabs. And we saw a jellyfish, and we had to bury it. And we – we did holding crabs, and we – we holded him in by the spade.
BABY-SITTER: Oh.
SUSIE: If you stand on them, they hurt you, won't they.
BABY-SITTER: They would do. They'd pinch you.
SUSIE: You'd have to – and we put them under the sand, where the sea was. And they were going to the sea.
BABY-SITTER: Mhm.
SUSIE: And we saw some shells. And we picked them up, and we heard the sea in them. And we saw a crab on a lid. And we saw lots of crabs on the sea side. And I picked the – fishes up – no, the shells, and the feathers from the birds. – And I saw a pig.
BABY-SITTER: Gosh, that was fun.
SUSIE: Yes, and I know a story about pigs.
BABY-SITTER: Are you going to tell it to me?

SUSIE: One – one day they went out to build their houses. One built it of straw, one built it of sticks, and one built it of bricks. And he – the little busy brother knowed that in the woods there lived a big bad wolf, he need nothing else but to catch little pigs. So you know what, one day they went out – and – the wolf went slip slosh slip slosh went his feet on the ground. Then – let me see, er – now I think – he said let me come in, you house of straw. And he said, no no by my hair of my chinny chin chin, I will not let you come in. Then I'll huff and I'll puff, and I'll puff, and I'll blow your house down. So he huffed, and he puffed, and he puffed, and he puffed, and he blew the little straw house all to pieces...

...and so this monologue continues, for nearly two minutes. The story-line, of course, comes from one of her favourite bed-time sagas, and she has evidently been a keen listener. She reproduces several of its phrases very accurately – not only some of the wolf's words, but also some of the story-teller's style, such as *Away went*.... She also dramatizes the narrative, notably in the huffing and puffing sequence, and phrases such as *big bad wolf* are said with long drawn-out vowels (just as adults would say them).

On the other hand, this is definitely Susie's story, not the book's. There are all kinds of partial correspondences, but hardly anything is repeated exactly as it was. She may have learned the events of the story off by heart, and several of its words and phrases, but it is largely her own grammar which is stringing them together.

This transcription does not represent the immaturity of her pronunciation (e.g. *crabs* as /kwabz/). Nor does it clearly show the rather jerky way in which she tells the story. She is also still sorting out some basic points of grammar, especially in the use of irregular verbs: she says *knowed* for *knew*, *we seen* as well as *we saw*, and makes several other errors. But the overall impression we receive from the story, and from the whole dialogue, is one of great competence and confidence. She is having no difficulty keeping her end up in the conversation. A sentence such as *If you stand on them, they hurt you* displays considerable grammatical skill, as well as a mastery of the notion of cause and effect. And she evidently has a wide range of sea-shore vocabulary. It is an impressive performance, for someone who has been alive for only 1,671 days. (From D. Crystal, 1986.)

letter recognition, spelling rules, reading strategies, and writing techniques. And as world literacy studies have repeatedly shown, by no means everyone achieves success in these skills.

The acquisition of a first language is the most complex skill anyone ever learns, and children need a great deal of help if it is to be accomplished successfully. From birth, emerging linguistic awareness needs careful fostering by parents and other caretakers. In school, the nurturing and expansion of linguistic skills needs systematic promotion across the whole curriculum, as well as in the basic area of reading and writing. And for those children who prove to have special needs, there has to be extra help, in the form of special teaching or clinical therapy, using specialists trained in techniques of linguistic intervention. The speed and naturalness with which most children pick up spoken and written language can fool us into underestimating the enormity of the intellectual task which faces them, and thus the enormity of the task facing those who have to solve learning problems when they arise. It is surprising how often we undervalue the work of the teacher of children with special needs in reading or writing, or of the speech therapist/pathologist who has to build up a child's listening and speaking skills from scratch. A moment's reflection about the nature of language, in the light of the breakdown of its components outlined above, should make us think otherwise.

THE LITERACY PROBLEM

It is traditional to think of illiteracy as a problem facing the underdeveloped nations of the world. It can therefore come as a surprise to realize that significant numbers of people have major difficulties with reading and writing in the 'inner circle' (p. 107) of English-speaking countries. Accurate figures are very difficult to obtain, but the estimates are sobering. In the UK, a commonly cited figure is 3–4 per cent of the population, though some surveys suggest twice this amount. In the USA estimates are 10–20 per cent, in Canada 5–20 per cent or more; in Australia 10–15 per cent; and in South Africa, they hover around 50 per cent (whites less than 10 per cent, Asian and coloureds over 30 per cent, and blacks over 60 per cent).

The reason for the variation and uncertainty is largely to do with what is meant by 'being illiterate'. Literacy is not an all-or-none skill, but a continuum of gradually increasing levels and domains of ability. At least five factors are involved:

- learning to read texts of increasing formal difficulty (as in a reading test) with understanding
- learning to read texts from an increasingly wide range of everyday contexts (e.g. road signs, newspapers, medical labels) with understanding
- learning to write (or type) with increasing fluency
- learning to write in response to an increasingly wide range of demands (e.g. letters, forms, questionnaires, computer screen instructions)
- learning to spell.

Someone who was totally illiterate would be unable to perform any of these skills, to any level. But within and between these factors all kinds of possibilities exist. Thus, we find people who can read, but not write or spell; people who can read and write, but with poor spelling; people who can read, but with poor understanding; people who can read only certain kinds of text; and so on. Illiteracy is not a single dimension of difficulty.

Functional literacy

World estimates vary greatly, therefore, depending on whether a notion of absolute literacy is being used to measure the problem, or some concept of 'functional' literacy. In the former case, we have the definition of UNESCO in 1951:

A person is literate who can, with understanding, both read and write a short, simple statement on his everyday life.

In the latter case, we have a corresponding definition of the 1960s:

A person is literate when he has acquired the essential knowledge and skills which enable him to engage in all those activities in which literacy is required for effective functioning in his group and community.

The criterion of functional literacy makes the concept of literacy less arbitrary, but also makes it more demanding. It tries to identify the minimum level of reading/writing efficiency which would be acceptable in the society to which a person belongs. In effect, you are literate only if you can perform the tasks for which society requires you to be literate. To be able to read sentences such as *The cat sat on the mat* does not make you literate, in this sense.

What are the literacy tasks which society makes us perform? One view was put forward in 1970 by the US National Reading Council, which devised a 'survival literacy study'. The test materials were five application forms in common daily use, ordered in an increasing level of difficulty: an application for public assistance; an identification form; a request for a driving licence; an application for a bank loan; and a request for medical aid. The test showed that 3 per cent of Americans could not read the first of these, and 34 per cent could not read the last.

These five areas are of course only a fraction of the literacy demands which modern society makes upon us. There are so many contexts involved, such as road signs, record-keeping, social service pamphlets, time-sheets, tax returns, safety regulations, business agreements, daily newspapers, and medicine labels. It is difficult to generalize about reading problems, when materials are so diverse. A five-word road-sign may or may not pose the same amount of reading difficulty as a five-word medicine label – and doubtless a road sign read when approaching it at 30 mph presents a rather different problem than when approaching it at 70.

Standards of literacy are generally rising, in the developed countries, so that – ironically – it is nowadays much more difficult for illiterate or semi-literate people to achieve an acceptable standard of literacy. A democratic society and a free press presuppose high general literacy levels. There are now more diverse and complex kinds of matter to read, and people are obliged to read more if they want to get on. People who had achieved a basic literacy are thus in real danger of still being classed as illiterate, as they fail to cope with the increased everyday written demands of the media, business, bureaucracy, computing, and the law. Literate society is continually 'raising the ante'.

National literacy campaigns in several English-speaking countries have done a great deal to raise the threshold of public awareness of the problem, and to persuade many who had not previously admitted their difficulties to seek help. Enormous progress has been made since the 1950s, when just under half the world population was thought to be illiterate. However, no one is under any illusion that the problem is beaten. UNESCO has designated year 2000 as the international year for the abolition of illiteracy; but as the millennium approaches it would seem necessary to view this concept as a statement of ongoing intent rather than as one of achievement.

This unusual perspective suggests the difficulty of the reading task for someone who is illiterate.

THE DEVELOPMENT OF GRAMMAR

The learning of grammar is an almost imperceptible process, and it happens so quickly. From the time when parents listen out eagerly for their child's first word to the time when they plead for peace and quiet is a matter of only three or four years – and in that time children master the grammar of the language to an extent which would be the envy of any foreign learner. It is impossible to quantify such matters in any sensible way, but most children, when they attend their first school, give the impression of having assimilated at least three-quarters of all the grammar there is to learn. By making regular tape-recordings every six months or so from around age one, it is easy to see how their grammar grows, and the childish errors they make (as in the case of Susie, p. 426) give an indication of the distance they have left to travel, before they reach adult ability levels.

Stages of grammatical growth

Grammar learning is a continuous process, but it is possible to spot certain types of development taking place at certain stages, as children grow up in English.

• The earliest stage is hardly like grammar at all, as it consists of utterances which are just one word long, such as *Gone, Dada, Teddy,* and *Hi.* About 60 per cent of these words have a naming function, and about 20 per cent express an action. Most children go through this stage from about 12 to 18 months. It is often called a *holophrastic* stage, because the children put the equivalent of a whole sentence into a single word.

• The next stage looks more like 'real' grammar, because two words are put together to make primitive sentence structures. *Cat jump* or *Cat jumping* seems to express a Subject + Verb construction (p. 220). *Shut door* seems to express a Verb + Object construction. Other sequences might be more difficult to interpret (what could *mummy off* mean, in the list opposite?), but on the whole we are left with the impression that, by the end of this stage (which typically lasts from around 18 months until 2), children have learned several basic lessons about English word order.

• The next step is the 'filling out' of these simple sentence patterns – adding extra elements of clause structure (p. 220) and making the elements themselves more complex. The 3-element *Daddy got car* and the 4-element *You go bed now* show this progress, as does (at a more advanced level) *My daddy put that car in the garage.* To get to this point, and to be able to ring the changes on it (such as by asking a question – *Where daddy put the car?*) takes up much of the third year.

WILL'S FIRST 50 WORDS

Most children have a spoken vocabulary of at least 50 words by the age of 18 months. Here is one such list, collected as part of a language acquisition study in the 1980s. In fact it took Will 6½ months to reach his half-century. Notice his liking for repeated items (*quack-quack, beep-beep*). Notice, too, how far *mama* and *daddy* are down his list – contrary to popular belief, these are not usually a child's first words. *Don't throw* is written as two words, but Will pronounced it as if it were a single unit. (After C. Stoel-Gammon & J. A. Cooper, 1984.)

1	uh-oh	26	tick tock
2	alldone	27	ball
3	light	28	go
4	down	29	bump
5	shoes	30	pop-pop (*fire*)
6	baby	31	out
7	don't throw	32	heehaw
8	moo	33	eat
9	bite	34	neigh-neigh
10	three	35	meow
11	hi	36	sit
12	cheese	37	woof-woof
13	up	38	bah-bah
14	quack-quack	39	hoo-hoo (*owl*)
15	oink-oink	40	bee
16	coat	41	tree
17	beep-beep	42	mimi (*ferry*)
18	keys	43	s: (*snake*)
19	cycle	44	ooh-ooh (*monkey*)
20	mama	45	yack-yack (*people talking*)
21	daddy	46	hohoho (*Santa*)
22	*siren sound*	47	bye-bye
23	grrr	48	doll
24	more	49	kite
25	off	50	Muriel

STRINGING WORDS TOGETHER

Here are all the 2-word sentences used by one child, Victoria, at age 1 year 9 months in a single hour. They are in alphabetical order so that her favourite sentence patterns can be more easily seen. Note that most of the patterns correspond to adult word order – but not all (*gone milk, Bluey where*). Incidentally, Ady is the name of her brother, Bluey the name of the dog. (After C. J. Howe, 1976.)

Ady horsie	hat off	my hat
baby bed	hat on	my teddy
baby cry	her coat	my tractor
baby doll	here is	she cold
baby drink	horsie mummy	she hair
baby hat	in there	shut door
baby here	is here	silly hat
baby lie	it gone	that bath
baby like	it off	that car
baby mummy	kiss doll	that hat
Bluey here-y'are	look elephant	that horsie
Bluey where	milk gone	there Bluey
comb hair	more toy	there teddy
come out	mumma back	toy gone
daddy there	mumma drink	waking up
dolly there	mummy off	want on
drink dolly	mummy there	where Bluey
gone milk	mummy toy	where inside
got it	my apple	where there
hat mummy	my bed	you bed

PREPOSITIONAL LIFT-OFF

Eve's use of the prepositions *in* and *on* in 12 samples of her speech, recorded between the ages of 1½ and 2. The graph shows the proportion of occasions when these words were used correctly in a particular phrase – for example by saying *sitting in chair* instead of *sitting chair*. At 1½ the prepositions were used correctly on only 10 per cent of occasions; by 2 it was around 90 per cent. The sudden leap in awareness at around 21 months is dramatic. (After R. Brown, 1973, p. 263.)

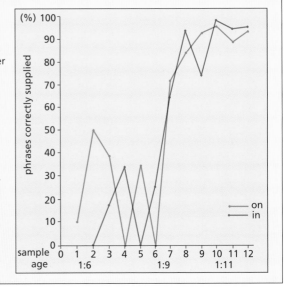

• At around 3 years, sentences become much longer, as children start stringing their clauses together to express more complex thoughts and to tell simple stories. *And* is the word to listen out for at this stage: Susie (p. 426) has long been an expert in using this type of construction. Other common linking words at this stage are *because* (*'cos*), *so*, *then*, *when*, *if*, and *before*. This stage takes six months or so for the basic patterns of clause sequence to be established.

• This takes us towards the age of 4, when children typically do a great deal of 'sorting out' in their grammar. A child aged 3½ might say *Him gived the cheese to the mouses*. By 4½, most children can say *He gave the cheese to the mice*. What they have done is learn the adult forms of the irregular noun and verb, and of the pronoun. As there are several dozen irregular nouns and several hundred irregular verbs, and all kinds of other grammatical irregularities to be sorted out, it is not surprising that it takes children the best part of a year to produce a level of English where these 'cute' errors are conspicuous by their absence. Susie has not yet reached this point.

• And after 4½? There are still features of grammar to be learned, such as the use of sentence-connecting features (p. 232) and complex patterns of subordination (p. 226). The process will continue until the early teens, especially in acquiring confident control over the grammar of the written language – at which point, the learning of grammar becomes indistinguishable from the more general task of developing an adult personal style.

WAYS OF MAKING THEM TALK

One of the problems of trying to establish just how much children know about grammar is to find pictures which will interest them and at the same time make them respond with relevant speech. Here are three well-produced pictures from a photographic colour library, designed to get the child to respond with a preposition. If all goes well, the first picture (clockwise from top) should elicit *in*, the second *on*, and the third *under*. (*Colorcards*, Winslow Press.)

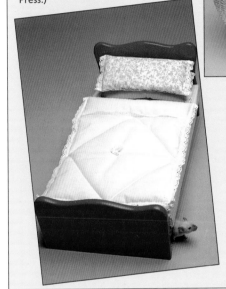

BEING ACTIVE WITH PASSIVES

When do children learn the difference between active sentences (e.g. *The panda chased the monkey*) and passive ones (e.g. *The monkey was chased by the panda*)? Passive sentences (p. 225) are far less frequent, and seem to be more complex in their structure, so it is likely that they will emerge much later in the acquisition process. But how much later?

One way of investigating this question is to devise a set of pictures such as those shown above. If you then say, 'Show me *The panda was chased by the monkey*', you can see whether children point to the right picture. This would be a test of their *comprehension* of the passive. If you then ask 'What happened to the panda?', the child has a chance to respond with 'It was chased by the monkey', or some similar sentence, and you can start compiling data on their *production* of the passive.

In one study using this procedure, 10 children were tested at age 3 to 3½. The group as a whole scored 17 correct out of 30 in the comprehension part of the experiment, but none of them produced any passives at all. A year later, their comprehension total was 26 correct out of 30, and now one or two children were beginning to produce some passives as well – 4 correct responses out of 30. There was very little difference between ages 5 and 6; but from the seventh year, the ability to use passives dramatically increased. The 6-year-olds understood 26 out of 30, and correctly produced 14 out of 30. The 8-year-olds understood 29 out of 30 – near perfect; however their ability to produce passives had not improved greatly – 16 out of 30 – and 20 per cent of the subjects were still producing no passives at all. So it seems that children are well into their ninth year before they approach adult norms of passive production – at least, in this kind of experiment. (After B. Baldie, 1976.)

THE FOUNDATION YEAR

When does the process of language acquisition start? Most people think of the child's 'first word' as the critical point, at around the age of 12 months (p. 428); but that is actually quite late in the process of language learning. Language acquisition is not just a matter of producing sounds and stringing them together into utterances. It is also about being able to perceive sounds and understand the meaning of the utterances other people make. And it is, additionally, about being able to interact with others – how to hold a conversation. By 12 months, children have become quite sophisticated in all three areas.

• Speech perception abilities are in evidence from the first days, with babies responding to different types of sound in predictable ways, such as being able to distinguish between their mother's and other voices before they are a day old. They are able to tell the difference between several pairs of consonants or vowels by about a month, as well as some contrasts in intonation and rhythm, and this ability to discriminate seems to grow steadily during the first year.

• Signs of comprehension emerge between 2 and 4 months, when babies begin to respond to adult tones of voice – such as the difference between angry, soothing, and playful voices. Between 6 and 9 months, the child learns to recognize different utterances in their situations (e.g. *clap hands*; *say bye-bye*). Most games played at this period have a language component to which the baby readily responds. And towards the end of the first year there are clear signs of verbal learning – names of family members, pets, or common objects begin to be acknowledged. Most children know the meanings of at least 20 words by the end of the first year, well before they have come to produce any of them as a first word.

• Similarly, by age 1 children have learned a great deal about the pragmatics of speech (p. 286). The rules governing conversational exchanges begin to be acquired from day 1, as parents react to the baby's noises, changing their way of talking as the type of vocalization changes. Communication games (such as 'This little piggy went to market') or physical movement games such as bouncing (which also have a strong language component) begin to be mutually appreciated. Parental speech style becomes highly distinctive during this time: short sentences, spoken in a wide pitch range and often repeated, maximize the chances for the baby to respond and learn. As a consequence, when a first word finally emerges, it can be integrated immediately into a conversational context with which the child is very familiar.

EARLY WORD GROWTH

Is it possible to be precise about the rate at which children learn early vocabulary? One study examined the first 50 words, in both production and comprehension, of eight subjects between the ages of 9 and 20 months. The results are shown in the figures. By following the growth curves for each child, four important points emerge.

• Comprehension is always ahead of production, with the gap increasing as the child gets older. This gap reaches 5–6 months at the 50-word level.
• The children take on average 2.69 months to get from 10 to 50 words in comprehension; they take 4.8 months to get from 10 to 50 in production – almost twice as long.
• The average rate of lexical acquisition between 10 and 50 words was 22.23 new words per month in comprehension and 9.09 new words per month in production. For some children, this was a steady process; for others, periods of slow growth alternated with spurts.
• The ratio of words understood to words produced is 5:1 at 18 months. This ratio

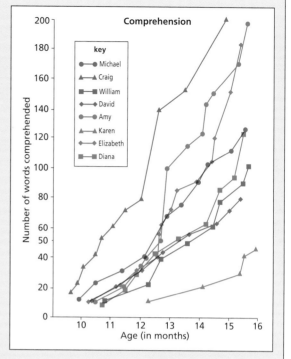

becomes less as children increase their productive vocabulary, and approaches adult norms (p. 123) at around age 3.
• The figures also show the variability in the age of onset of vocabulary learning. Five of the children had produced their first word by 10 months, with the remaining three by 12, 13, and 15 months.

The graph stops at 50 words in production; a total of 100 words is typical after a further two months, 200 by 21 months, and 300 by age 2. But all of this is eclipsed during the third year, when active vocabulary rockets to over 3,000 words. No one has yet studied in detail how this remarkable lexical spurt takes place. (After H. Benedict, 1979.)

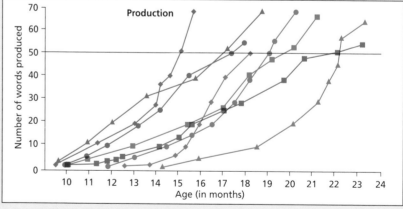

Diagrams of this kind mislead if it is thought that the growth of vocabulary is of a homogeneous kind. A typical 50-item lexicon involves several different types of word, as well as a number of fixed expressions.

• *common nouns*: plant, light, birdie, picture, dummy, ham, cat, rabbit, aeroplane, cheese, juice, book, milk, shoe, clock, car, ear, eye, nose, mouth, stairs, watch (*wrist*)
• *onomatopoeic words* (p. 250): brum, moo, grrr, tick tock
• *proper nouns*: Mummy, Daddy, Jane, Grandad
• *interactive words*: ahh, bye-bye, peepo, yes, ta
• *others*: yum yum, nice, crash, back, poo, out, gone, stuck, up, wee wee, draw
• *frozen phrases*: oh dear, where's it gone?, there it is, Oh God!

(After E. V. M. Lieven, J. M. Pine & H. D. Barnes, 1992.)

SPEECH PRODUCTION

Several stages of development have been distinguished in the first year, when the child develops the skills necessary to produce a successful first word.

• Apart from the cry patterns associated with hunger, pain, and discomfort, the first two months of life display a wide range of primitive vocal sounds reflecting the baby's biological state and activities – as in the 'vegetative' noises heard while eating and excreting. Some of the most basic features of speech, such as the ability to control air flow and produce rhythmic utterance, are being established at this time.

• Between 6 and 8 weeks, there emerge the sounds generally known as *cooing*, produced when the baby is in a settled state. Cooing sounds do not grow out of crying; rather, they develop alongside it, gradually becoming more frequent and varied. They are quieter, lower-pitched, and more musical, typically consisting of a short vowel-like sound, often nasal in quality, and usually preceded by a consonant-like sound made towards the back of the mouth. Strings of cooing noises soon emerge, and the sounds become more varied, as the baby begins to develop a greater measure of control over the muscles of the vocal organs – especially over tongue and lip movements and associated vocal cord vibration (p. 236).

• Between 3 and 4 months, cooing sounds begin to die away, to be replaced by sounds which are much more definite and controlled, often repeated, and produced with wide pitch glides. It is a period commonly called *vocal play*, because the baby seems to take great pleasure in producing these noises, especially those made with the lips, but it is perhaps more accurate to call it a time of vocal practice or experimentation.

• From around 6 months, vocal play gives way to *babbling* – a period of syllable sequences and repetitions which can last most of the second half of the first year. To begin with, the consonant-like sounds are very repetitive (as in [bababababa]), but at around 9 months the babbling moves away from these fixed patterns. The consonants and vowels change from one syllable to the next, producing such forms as [adu] and [maba], and there is a wider range of sounds, anticipating the sounds of the accent of English to be learned. The utterances do not have any meaning, though they often resemble adult words – and of course adults love to 'hear' such words (especially *mummy* and *daddy*) in the baby's vocalizations. But babbling does not gradually shade into speech; indeed, many children continue to babble for several months after they have begun to talk. Babbling is perhaps best summarized as a final step in the period of preparation for speech. The child, in effect, 'gets its

act together'; but it has yet to learn what the act is for – that sounds are there to enable meaning to be communicated in a controlled way. With the production of the 'first word', this final step is taken.

• However, the first word is not the first feature of adult language to be acquired. From as early as 6 months there is evidence that the child is picking up features of the melody and rhythm of the adult language. Certainly by 9 months strings of syllables are often being pronounced in conversation-like ways which adults interpret as communicative. 'He/she's trying to tell us something' is a common reaction to a piece of 'scribble-talk', and such speech-act functions as questioning, commanding, and greeting (p. 284) are ascribed to babbled utterances. The melody and rhythm of often-used phrases, such as *all gone*, are also likely to be heard long before the vowels and consonants are clearly articulated. It is these prosodic features (p. 248) which are the first signs of real language production in children.

SOUND TRENDS

The 2-year-old's words listed on p. 428 are given in normal spelling, which makes them look better than they actually sounded. The process of learning to talk involves a gradual mastery of the vowels and consonants which is certainly nowhere near complete at this age. Indeed, even after children have gone to school, they will be heard sorting out some residual problems, such as difficulties with front fricative sounds (p. 243), /f, v, θ, ð/, words with unusually located consonants (e.g. using /v/ for /b/ at the end of *disturb*), and words with awkward consonant clusters (e.g. saying *string* with /w/ instead of /r/).

There are huge differences between children in the order in which they acquire vowels and consonants; nor, within any one child, does the learning of a sound take place overnight. Some sounds take months before they are used appropriately in all words and in all positions in every word. And there is a considerable amount of personal variation while children are learning a sound: one child used as many as six versions of the word *window* over a period of several weeks until he settled down with one of them.

Although it is not possible to make simple generalizations about the order in which children acquire sounds, certain trends can be observed. In particular, children tend to treat sounds in similar ways: most of them go through such stages as using velar consonants for alveolars (e.g. /gɒg/ for *dog*), dropping unstressed syllables (e.g. /nana/ for *banana*), and simplifying consonant clusters (e.g. /daɪ/ for *dry*). And several studies have proposed a typical order of emergence for consonants, such as this sequence from Pamela Grunwell's *Phonological Assessment of Child Speech* (1987):

/m, n, p, b, t, d, w/ by 2
/k, g, h, ŋ/ by 2½
/f, s, j, l/ by 3
/tʃ, dʒ, v, z, ʃ, r/ by 4½
/θ, ð, ʒ/ after 4½.

PROTO-WORDS

The jump from babbling to speech often has an intermediate step. Short utterances, just one or two syllables long, with a clear melody and rhythm, come to be made in a regular and predictable way. [da:], said Jamie, with a rising melody, one day; and the next day he said it a dozen times. No one was quite sure what it meant to begin with. It sounded as if he was trying to say *that*, but this interpretation did not always fit the situation. It made sense when he said it while pointing at a passing cat. His mother immediately said 'What's that? That's a pussy cat'. But it did not seem to make sense when he said it in an off-the-cuff manner over his mother's shoulder as he was being whisked off to bed. Was it a word or not? As children approach 12 months, they often produce forms where the sounds are clear but the meaning is not: *proto-words*. These are not quite true words, where both the sound and the meaning need to be clear and agreed by both speaker and listener.

INTERVENTION

Learning to speak and listen (p. 430) is a process which usually takes place spontaneously as part of the natural interaction between parent (or other care-taker) and child. It requires no language specialist to intervene in order to achieve success. But special help *is* required in three other contexts of first language acquisition.

• Learning to be literate (p. 427) invariably requires support in the form of teachers and teaching materials which deal with the processes of reading, writing, and spelling. And if children fall seriously behind their peers in acquiring these skills, as in the case of dyslexia, further specialist intervention will be required.
• The natural process of spoken language learning may not take place, for a variety of reasons, and children may become seriously delayed or disordered in their ability to comprehend and/or produce spoken language. Intervention here requires special help in the form of teaching and therapy from a range of professionals who work with language-impaired children.
• A person who has successfully completed the process of learning spoken and written English may lose some or all of that ability, also for a variety of reasons (such as a stroke damaging the language centres of the brain). Here intervention is chiefly in the hands of the speech and language pathologist/therapist.

The world of reading

Learning to read and write involves all aspects of language structure and use – phonology, graphology, vocabulary, grammar, discourse, and variety – but only the first three of these tend to be acknowledged when people talk about educational issues. The traditional controversy focuses on low-level questions: whether reading is best taught by a *phonic* approach, in which letters are brought into correspondence with sounds (a graphology–phonology link), or by a *look-and-say* approach, in which whole words are brought into correspondence with sounds (a lexicon–phonology link). Early reading books are typically evaluated in terms of the type of vocabulary they include and how they portray these sound–spelling relationships. And children's growth in reading skills is also traditionally assessed in this way.

Modern approaches are much more sensitive to the role of grammar, discourse, and variety awareness in the reading process. It is now evident that each of these levels contributes a great deal to success in reading, and also, at a later stage, provides an important foundation for writing.

• A basic principle of early reading is that the language to be read should bear a close relationship to the spoken language used and heard by the child. Children should already know the words they are being asked to read, when they approach the task of reading; and the same principle applies to grammatical constructions. It is now well recognized that traditional readers included many features which were unfamiliar or even alien, and which promoted a 'mechanical' style of reading, where words and sentences were visually decoded but not necessarily understood. Later, of course, reading becomes the main way of introducing children to new words and extending their grammatical abilities. However, with children who have reading difficulties, the principle of maintaining grammatical familiarity stays relevant until well into their teens.

The last three extracts come from a 'beginning reading' corpus of Australian readers, compiled in the 1980s, containing nearly 84,000 words and 2,500 word types. The earlier extracts, from books being used in Britain and the USA at the time, show that this kind of material is representative of a worldwide genre.

Here are three findings from the analysis of this corpus, one linguistic, one social, and one psychological.

• 85 per cent of the sentences were declarative in type (p. 218); median sentence length was five words; and 80 per cent of the words had less than four letters.
• Half of the uses of the word *girl* were accompanied by the word *little*, whereas only a third of the *boy* uses were; about 40 per cent of the instances of *little* were for animals or pets.
• Positive emotions (*good, brave, laugh*) were much more common than negative ones (*bad, scared, cry*); two-thirds of the latter words were uttered by or applied to animals.

The contrast with the extracts from modern texts on the facing page is immediate and striking.
(After C. D. Baker & P. Freebody, 1989.)

BECOMING AWARE

The first step in variety awareness is to become conscious of the nature of written language. Not everything that can be seen can be read. One of the first tasks in the LARR Test ('Language Awareness in Reading Readiness') focuses on this point. The child is shown a picture, such as this bus, and asked to 'circle each thing on the bus that someone can read' (having, of course, previously established that the child knows what the first part of this instruction means). The task is partly to check on whether the child realizes just how inclusive the task of reading is (it includes the

numbers as well as the letters) and also how exclusive it is (it does not include the lion logo). Children who are at the early stages of reading make some intriguing decisions, such as drawing a circle around the whole bus, and drawing one round the capital letters only. Children with reading difficulties may still be uncertain about what reading is all about at much older ages.
(From J. Downing, *et al.*, 1983.)

• Adult written texts vary greatly in the kind of language they present to the reader (p. 292), and children need to be introduced to this enormous range gradually and systematically. Traditional readers offer little by way of variety change. Adults and children talk in the same general way, regardless of topic and setting, and make little use of emotional and evaluative language. The adults are always benevolent and attentive, prepared to follow the child's choice of topic and activity. Participants keep very much to the point of a topic, politely answering each other's questions. All of this is somewhat removed from the unpredictable agendas of real conversation, whether at home, in class, or in the playground (p. 295).

• As the Susie conversation illustrates (p. 426), children have enormous oral language knowledge before they begin to read, and this can be used to help them become familiar with the reading process. However, the discourse structure (§19) of traditional readers is very unlike what children already know. Dialogues such as the one illustrated opposite present a strange kind of conversation, in which the participants talk about the 'here-and-now' of a scene, usually in the present tense, like commentators (p. 386), and rarely about what is absent or past. Most conversational exchanges consist of statements; there are few questions, and even fewer exclamations. The conversational turns are short, often just one sentence or two, with the narrator's intervention constantly stopping the possibility of a real monologue.

The conversations in children's readers are, in short, idealized exchanges, which minimize the complexity of actual oral interaction. It is easy to see why such a genre emerged: it was entirely motivated by the need to maintain graphological simplicity – to keep the words short and the spellings simple. But there is a great deal of research evidence now to show that children can cope with graphological complexity if the reading materials are exciting enough – and this can be seen also at an informal level, in the success of such authors as Roald Dahl (whose complex language is popular even among children of 8 or 9). Certainly contemporary readers, whether in schemes or as 'real books', have made great progress in escaping from the artifice of earlier models. Much more use is now made of techniques of incongruity and humour. And there has been a fresh appreciation of the value of poetry as a means of bringing the reading experience of young children closer to the realities of their world.

SOME MODERN VOICES

'Children are rrreee-volting!' screamed The Grand High Witch. 'Vee vill vipe them all avay! Vee vill scrrrub them off the face of the earth! Vee vill flush them down the drain!'

'Yes, yes!' chanted the audience. 'Wipe them away! Scrub them off the earth! Flush them down the drain!'

'Children are foul and filthy!' thundered The Grand High Witch.

'They are! They are!' chorused the English witches. 'They are foul and filthy!'

'Children are dirty and stinky!' screamed The Grand High Witch.

'Dirty and stinky!' cried the audience, getting more and more worked up.

'Children are smelling of dogs' drrroppings!' screeched The Grand High Witch.

'Poooooo!' cried the audience. 'Poooooo! Poooooo! Poooooo!'

(Roald Dahl, *The Witches*, 1983)

(From *Dr Xargle's Book of Earthlets*, 1988, translated into Human by Jeanne Willis, with pictures by Tony Ross.)

Earthlets have no fangs at birth. For many days they drink only milk through a hole in their face.

When they have finished the milk they must be patted and squeezed to stop them exploding.

Two 'real world' extracts from John Foster's *A Third Poetry Book* (1982).

I'm ten and I'm bored
And I've nothing to do.
I'm fed up with watching
This ant on my shoe.
(John Kitching)

If your hands get wet
in the washing-up water,
if they get covered in flour
if you get grease or oil
all over your fingers

if they land up in the mud,
wet grit, paint, or glue …
have you noticed
it's just then
that you always get

a terrible itch
just inside your nose?…
(Michael Rosen)

Remembering what I had enjoyed when I was young, I remembered what I had missed in children's books, too. The grown ups, apart from a wicked stepmother or uncle, were always flat, peripheral figures with no emotions and no function. The books offered to me in my childhood left out the adult world, and even when they didn't, entirely, they never presented adults as children really see them. Parents and teachers were usually shown as kind, loving, distant figures … not only were they never beastly to children except in a stereotyped, fairy tale way, but they were never beastly to anyone. They were never the uncertain, awkward, quirky, dangerous creatures that I knew adults to be… (Nina Bawden, 1976, p. 8.)

When a novelist talks like this, it is easy to think 'Well it didn't do *her* any harm'. And indeed, many children do learn to read without problems regardless of the reading scheme used. However, there are four facts that will not go away: many people have never learned to read well (p. 427); many children, though having learned to read, do not seem to have enjoyed the experience; the writing levels even of children who *can* read well are nothing to be complacent about; and there has been an enormous falling away of leisure reading in the face of the television and the computer game in recent years. There is therefore continuing urgency in the search for better ways of making the reading experience come alive.

INSUFFICIENT LANGUAGE

Working professionally with something as complex as language (p. 426) requires a great deal of training, even when everything is progressing normally. Language disability introduces a range of extra conditions and factors which immensely complicate the task. The disability may be mild, or moderate, or severe. Its causes may be known (as with deafness and mental handicap) or unknown (as with many cases of stammering and language delay). And it may involve any aspect, or combination of aspects, of language structure and use. A broad-based course of study is therefore essential, including medical, psychological, social, educational, and linguistic components, as well as the fostering of personal clinical and teaching skills.

Under the heading of linguistics, three particular kinds of knowledge are needed, all of which relate (in the case of English language problems) to the subject-matter of this book.

• Before intervention can take place, the specialist needs to have identified exactly what the nature of the language disability is. This requires an analysis of those areas of language that are particularly affected – whether structural (in phonetics, phonology, graphology, grammar, lexicon, discourse) or functional (language in use) (§1). There are no short cuts. Effective intervention presupposes the accurate identification of where the problems lie.

• The target of intervention is to bring the deficient language from where it is to where it ought to be. If a 7-year-old child is speaking like a 3-year-old, there are four years of language learning to be made up. The specialist needs to be aware of the possible paths which can move the child in the required direction, and in particular of the paths which are routinely taken by children who have no language learning problems. A knowledge of the stages of normal language acquisition (p. 428), insofar as these are known, is therefore also a prerequisite of successful intervention.

• The specialist needs to be aware of which teaching techniques and strategies are available and appropriate. What are the best ways of teaching a particular pronunciation contrast, word order, or lexical field? What variations in technique need to be introduced to make them appropriate to a child as opposed to an adult, to a boy as opposed to a girl, or to a person with some additional disability? What teaching material may need to be devised in order to attack a particular problem? To build a knowledge base of this kind, as happened in the history of medicine, takes many professional lifetimes.

Language delay
This child is 4, but his level of speech production is closer to that of a child of 18 months. His comprehension, however, was apparently normal for his age. (A comparison with Susie on p. 426 will suggest the severity of the delay.)

T: now / here's the book / - this is the book we were looking at before / isn't it /
P: teddy bear /
T: there's a teddy bear / yes /
P: teddy a home /
T: you've got one at home /
P: yeah /
T: what do you call him / –
P: a teddy bear /
T: has he got a name /
P: yeah / - he name /
T: what is it /
P: er
T: what's his name / -
P: teddy bear /
T: teddy bear /
P: yeah /
T: does he – do you keep him in your bedroom /
P: yeah / –
T: where in your bedroom does he live /
P: don't know /

Aphasia
This 55-year-old man is recovering from a stroke which has left him with a somewhat erratic speech style, often incomplete, and with little specific content.

T: so did you get wet /
P: no / – no / – it s it seemed / – just about a whole lot of l a bit longer / but it looks as though it might be again / and I shan't
T: it does / doesn't it / m /
P: yeah / yeah / yeah / yeah /
T: you might catch it going home /
P: well / I might do / I'll have to see /
T: what do you think of the weather we've been having /
P: well / it's been very bad / up to now /
T: m /
P: there was about three ooh a bit longer than that / it was very good /
T: yeah /
P: but – but otherwise / no /
T: been awful / hasn't it /
P: yeah / well / there you are / it's the sort of thing you have to leave – you see /

Stammering
This transcription of a man with a fairly severe stammer shows marked abnormalities in grammatical smoothness and rhythm. There is far more to the problem of stammering than the uncontrolled repetition of consonants.

T: and what is your job?
P: I'm a - an - ac -- ac -- count — ant - in local — govern – ment —
T: oh, what does that cover?
P: well - as you — as you prob – ab – ly – know — we look after - the roads and — police - erm housing – and these sort of —
T: and the rates and that kind of
P: yes - and erm - we just – look after the erm money - end of it —
T: yes
P: and I – personally – am an auditor – and – and we look after — the — things like – checking that all income has been banked and – you know this sort of —
T: yes, do you have machines to help or don't you need them?
P: oh yes – we - use a lot of erm – erm - elec — erm elec — tronic aids —

Note: Extracts adapted from P. Dalton & W. J. Hardcastle, 1989, D. Crystal & R. Varley, 1993. Here and opposite: **T** teacher/therapist. **P** pupil/patient. -, –, — represent increasing length of pause. / shows intonation unit. (p. 248)

COMPLEX PROBLEMS, COMPLEX SOLUTIONS

Children with insufficient language to communicate even basic everyday information can benefit from having a highly structured classroom routine of daily activities. This helps them to feel secure, and gives them confidence to concentrate on other work without worrying about what is going to happen to them next. The figure shows a daily diary which was devised to help a child with a severe language disorder that involves major problems of comprehension (Landau-Kleffner syndrome).

William was introduced to a pictorial timetable of daily events each morning. Each day of the week was identified by a colour linked to one important activity; for example, Wednesday was biscuit day, and was coded green because that was the colour of the

(a) Mg | P | | S | D | 1 2 3 4 | | | |

(b) Maggie | Pauline | | playing | Sylvia | Diane | dinner | playing | numbers | t.v. | dancing | book | car | sleeping

(c) Mg | William is talking | William is working | biscuits | Robert is playing | working with Sylvia | Singing with Diane | Jean is eating dinner | Tony is playing | numbers | t.v. | dancing | story book | William is going home | William is sleeping

(d) William is talking with Maggie | William is working with Pauline in the t.v. room | William is drinking milk and eating biscuits | William is playing with Robert on the slide | William and Sylvia are working | William is singing with Diane | Chris and William are eating dinner | James is playing outside with William | Numbers | Faye and William are looking at the t.v. | Jane and Judy and William are dancing | William is reading a book | William is going home in the car | William is sleeping in bed

biscuit tin. Each activity of the day was shown by a line drawing, and a series of drawn boxes showed the sequence of events. As each activity was finished during the day, William would cross out the appropriate box. Over a period of time, the drawings were supplemented by single written words, then by simple sentences, and eventually were omitted, leaving the language to carry out the task of communication alone.

A technique of this kind builds literacy and oracy skills as well as general learning. For example, if something unexpected happens during the day,

the diary can prompt talk about problem solving or cause and effect. By talking about the previous day's diary, past time concepts can be built up. It is typical of the kind of very detailed programming, orientated to the needs of an individual child (or – with rather different materials – adult), which teachers and therapists have to engage in when they are planning remediation, and clearly illustrates the maxim that complex problems (p. 426) demand complex solutions. (After M. Vance, 1991.)

SIGNED ENGLISH

There is no separate section on signing in this book because the linguistic status of the main class of sign languages used by deaf people in English-speaking countries is independent of the structure of the English language. Someone who has learned British Sign Language or American Sign Language, for example, has learned a system of communication whose principles do not depend on the sounds, grammar, or vocabulary of English.

Educationists have however often devised sign languages which do reflect the properties of English, as in the case of *Signing Exact English* in the USA and the *Paget-Gorman Sign System* in the UK. Systems of this kind follow the grammar and vocabulary of English closely, introducing signs which represent affixes as well as words, and following the patterns of word order. Other systems are based on the phonology of English,

providing signs which enable deaf observers to tell which phoneme (p. 237) is being articulated in cases where visual cues are missing (*cued speech*): the distinction between /k/ and /g/, for example, cannot be seen, but it can be signalled by hand gestures towards the throat showing the presence or absence of voicing. And in *finger spelling*, each letter of the alphabet is given its own sign, being made either with two hands (as in the UK) or one (as in the USA).

These systems are invented for educational reasons. In many cases, they can motivate a child to communicate who has made no progress in speaking. Such children are not necessarily deaf; they may simply find signing a clearer or more manageable procedure than the use of the voice. The close correspondence with English grammar is then a benefit, as it can help the transfer to spoken or written language at a later stage.

FINDING THE LEVEL

A critical factor governing the success of intervention is the extent to which T can find a grammatical level that P can understand, and that is also likely to elicit speech in return. If T chooses too advanced a level, such as a normal conversational style, it is likely to confuse P, who has previously failed to learn from participating in such conversations; but if T chooses too easy a level, it will not help P to make progress, and P may additionally not like being spoken to in a 'babyish' way.

In this example, T has chosen a strategy of trying to match his language to the exact stage of grammar that P is trying to

learn – the two-element sentences typical of a child between 18 months and 2 years of age (p. 428). P is 13, and profoundly deaf. T's strategy is to avoid long sentences, breaking the message down into sequences of short, two-part utterances.

Three extracts are given: the first represents a normal adult conversational style, which simply confuses P (the words she understands are in italics); the second shows T using and P responding to 'Stage II talk'; and the third shows P six months later, when her language had made some progress, and they are working on more advanced, three-part sentences. The technique has evidently been successful in this case.

T: *Hello Judith*. Isn't it hot today? It is hot today.
P: *Hello*.
T: *Come in* and sit down. (Pointing to the blackboard) I want you to write this work on that piece of paper.
P: (no response)
T: Just do one page but don't use your book.
P: (looks confused)

T: Hello Judith. Hot today?
P: Hello. Yes, hot. Very hot.
T: Come in. Sit down. (Pointing to the blackboard) Write this.
P: Oh no! How much?
T: One page. On paper. No books.
P: What colour?
T: In blue. In ink. No pencils. Be careful. Good writing.

P: Hello Mr Dennis. How are you?
T: Hello Judith. Very well thanks. Come in now. Sit down here. Look at me. Watch my lips. Please write this. (Points to board)
P: That is hard. In my book?
T: No. Not your book. Write on paper.
P: What title?
T: 'Grammar Work'.
P: What colour?

(From J. E. Williams & D. B. Dennis, 1979.)

We are at the threshold of a new era of English language studies. Until the last quarter of the 20th century, the scientific study of the language had just two broad traditions which prompted the nature of the questions that could be asked and the pace at which they could be answered. The first was a tradition of historical enquiry, fostered chiefly by the comparative studies of 19th-century philology, but also by the editorial and critical concerns of English literature. The second was a tradition of research into the contemporary language, fostered chiefly by the theories and methods of descriptive linguistics. Most of the observations reported in this book come from one or other of these perspectives, and the theoretical framework which has given the book its structure comes entirely from within the latter. Now there is a third perspective to consider, stemming from the consequences of the technological revolution, which is likely to have far-reaching effects on the goals and methods of English language research.

There is no doubt that developments in electronic instrumentation and computer science have already altered the way we look at the language. The vast data-processing capacity of modern systems has made it possible to expect answers to questions that it would have been impracticable to ask a generation ago. The transferring of the *Oxford English Dictionary* (*OED*) onto disk, to take but one example from the 1990s, enables thousands of time-related questions to be asked about the development of the lexicon which it would have been absurd to contemplate before. If you want to find out which words were first attested in English in the year of your birth, according to the *OED* database, you can now do so, and it takes just a few seconds.

A universal impact

All areas of English language study have been profoundly affected by technological developments. In phonetics, new generations of instrumentation are taking forward auditory, acoustic, and articulatory research. In phonology, lexical databases are allowing a new range of questions to be asked about the frequency and distribution of English sounds. In graphology, image scanners are enabling large quantities of text to be quickly processed, and image-enhancing techniques are being applied to obscure graphic patterns in old manuscripts. In grammar, huge corpora of spoken and written English are making it possible to carry out studies of structures in unprecedented detail and in an unprecedented range of varieties. Discourse analyses are both motivating and benefiting from research in

human–computer interaction. And, above all, there has been the remarkable progress made in the study of the lexicon, with the compilation of lexical databases giving rise to an explosion of new types of dictionary.

Other well-recognized areas of English language study have also been affected. The new technology supports sociolinguistic studies of dialect variation, providing computer-generated maps (p. 314) and sophisticated statistical processing. Child language acquisition studies (§23) have since the 1980s seen the growth of a computer database of transcribed samples from children of different language backgrounds (the Child Language Data Exchange System, or CHILDES). In clinical language studies, several aspects of disordered speech are now routinely subjected to instrumental and computational analysis. And in stylistics, there is a computational perspective for the study of literary authorship (p. 423) which dates from the 1960s.

As always, faced with technological progress, the role of the human being becomes more critical than ever. It is not difficult for researchers to be swamped with unmanageable data. The cabinetfuls of slips of paper, whose manual analysis once used to take up so much time, can easily be replaced by unfriendly screen-scrollings of electronic files or boxfuls of unassimilable computer printout. From a position where we could see no patterns in a collection of data, an unlimited number of computer-supplied statistical analyses can now make us see all too many. The age has already begun to foster new kinds of English language specialist, knowledgeable in hardware and software, who help process the findings of their computationally illiterate brethren.

However, there is (as yet) no technological replacement for the sharpened intuition of the informed English language enquirer, who can ask the right question and know where to look for the right answer. Although many of the research findings reported in this book have come from computationally driven research, a great many have come from time-honoured, hands-on methods, using relatively small amounts of data and relatively large amounts of thought. It is a difficult act, balancing the contributions of mind and machine so that they complement and do not supplant each other, and we are only just beginning to learn how to perform it. This final section therefore looks towards the future, by illustrating a few of the areas which are carrying it out successfully. (For other examples of technologically motivated studies, see pp. 247, 267, and 392.)

NASA AND BEOWULF

In the 1970s, the National Aeronautics and Space Administration set up a fund at the California Institute of Technology to apply space technology to terrestrial uses. One such application was the image enhancement of literary manuscripts. Using an electronic camera and image-processing techniques developed for space photography, it proved possible for a team of researchers to decipher most of an erased section of a 14th-century text, and the approach has since been used to examine the most illegible section of the *Beowulf* manuscript (p. 11), the badly damaged folio 179.

The technique uses digital image processing to enhance graphic contrast in very faded areas of the page. Through the use of different kinds of filtering processes, it is possible to equalize the contrast shown in different parts of a letter, to remove irrelevant shading, and to sharpen the edges of strokes.

seðe on hea – hord beweotode
This is line 5 of the recto of folio 179. The top image in the figure, taken before processing, shows an illegible gap between *hea* and *hord* that could take a reading of up to five or six letters (the middle line in both images). Various proposals for filling this gap have been made by editors over the years. They include:

on heaum hæþe 'on the high heath'
on heaðo-hlæwe 'on the war-mound'
on heaure hæðe 'on the grey heath'
on heaum hope 'on the high hollow'
on heaum hofe 'in the high abode'

The digitally enhanced image shows that *heþe* (a spelling variant of *hæþe*) is the most plausible reading. By strongly enhancing the shape of the whole of the second letter, the presence of a middle bar is apparent, eliminating the possibility that the vowel is o. The image also shows an ascender (p. 257) for the following consonant, thus identifying it as þ.

Image enhancement does not by any means solve all graphic textual problems. Providing a better graphic contrast can often do no more than make the existence of a problem easier to see. It will not, for example, solve a problem of whether a reading is due to a letter stroke showing through from the opposite side of the leaf. But even though the technique may not establish a text beyond dispute, it does markedly improve the legibility of what is there, and thus provides editors with a more definite basis for making a judgment.
(After K. S. Kiernan, 1991.)

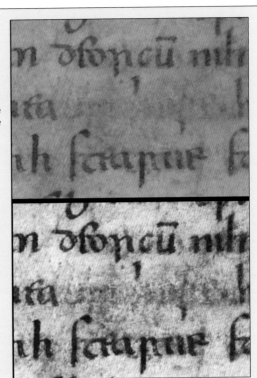

MAKING CONTACT WITH THE TONGUE

One of the problems facing a speech therapist/pathologist working with someone who has a deviant pronunciation is the difficulty of seeing what is happening inside the mouth. An auditory assessment of the problem is a first step, but as there are major limitations on what the ear can discriminate, extra information about what the vocal organs are actually doing is invaluable. The tongue has been a particular focus of attention, as it is involved in the articulation of most English speech sounds (p. 236).

The electropalatograph is a device which enables patterns of tongue contact to be seen. An artificial palate with 64 electrodes is fitted against the roof the mouth, and when parts of the tongue make contact with these electrodes a pattern is displayed on a computer screen or printout. The illustration shows a printed version, in which possible tongue contacts are represented by white ovals, with actual contacts blacked in. The alveolar area of the palate (p. 243) is at the top of the diagram and the velar area is at the bottom. The articulation is three versions of the /s/ sound. (After F. Gibbon, *et al.*, 1990.)

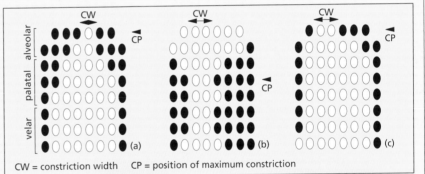

CW = constriction width   CP = position of maximum constriction

• The first palatogram (a) displays the pattern of a normal pronunciation. There is a good alveolar contact on both sides; the groove which produces the sibilant quality of the sound is clearly seen in the middle; and there is contact between the sides of the tongue and the roof of the mouth all the way back to the velum.
• The second (b) is the pattern produced by the patient. There is no contact at all at the front of the mouth, and the sides of the tongue are erratically involved. The point of maximum constriction is in the palatal area, which would give a 'slushy' quality to the /s/.
• After treatment (c), the palatogram shows a much improved pattern. The patient is now making an alveolar contact and a groove in the right place, though the articulation is not yet being made as firmly as it might be.

When the palatograph displays its results on a computer screen, it is possible to divide the screen in two, so that a correct version and the patient's own

version can be simultaneously displayed. By varying the tongue position, a patient can immediately see the pattern of lights change, and thus obtain feedback about tongue movement which can help increase control. This kind of computer-inspired feedback is apparently much appreciated by children with pronunciation difficulties – and by adults too.

THE CORPUS REVOLUTION

Many of the observations in this book have been based on the analysis of language data samples collected together as a *corpus*. Compiling a corpus is very different from the traditional practices of citation-gathering or 'word-watching' which have guided work on dictionaries since the time of Dr Johnson (p. 74). Corpora are large and systematic enterprises: whole texts or whole sections of text are included, such as conversations, magazine articles, brochures, newspapers, lectures, sermons, broadcasts, and chapters of novels. Considerable thought is given to the selection of material so that, in the most general case, the corpus can stand as a reasonably representative sample of the language as a whole (a 'general' or 'standard' corpus).

A well-constructed general corpus turns out to be useful in several ways. It enables investigators to make more objective and confident descriptions of usage than would be possible through introspection. It allows them to make statements about frequency of usage in the language as a whole, as well as comparative statements about usage in different varieties. It permits them, in principle, to arrive at a total account of the linguistic features in any of the texts contained in the corpus. And it provides them with a source of hypotheses about the way the language works. In addition, a corpus which is widely accessible enables researchers in separate locations to collaborate in the analysis of particular problems, and means that results from a range of projects are likely to be somewhat more comparable than if different corpora had been employed.

Corpus characteristics

General corpus designers are to a large extent working in the dark, because it is impossible to predict all the demands which will be made of their products. But three basic principles are clear.

• A general corpus must in principle be large enough to answer the questions likely to be asked of it. A corpus compiled to answer lexical questions, for example, needs to be many times larger than one devised for answering questions about pronunciation or grammar. For work on frequently occurring items, such as auxiliary verbs, fairly small corpora suffice; but for work on the lexicon, even a million words is tiny. There are only about 50,000 different words in a million-word corpus, which is about the size of a good 'concise' dictionary (p. 442).

A CONCRESCENCE OF CORPORA

• The first large corpus of English-language data began to be compiled in the 1960s. This was the *Survey of English Usage*, directed by Randolph Quirk, and based at University College London. It consists of a million words, comprising 200 texts of spoken and written material of 5,000 words each. The texts were transcribed by hand and stored on index cards which were processed manually. In the 1970s the spoken component (nearly half a million words) was made electronically available by Jan Svartvik of Lund University under the name of the *London–Lund Corpus of Spoken English* (see opposite). The whole survey is now computerized.

• The *Brown University Corpus of American English*, based at Providence, Rhode Island, USA, was the first computerized corpus, created in the 1960s by Henry Kucera and W. Nelson Francis. This corpus was also a million words, in 2,000-word samples, and aimed to represent a wide range of genres of published written text in American English produced during a single year.

• The *Lancaster–Oslo/Bergen* (or *LOB*) *Corpus of British English* was compiled in the 1970s, in a British–Norwegian collaboration. It was designed to match the Brown corpus using British English texts.

• The *Collins–Birmingham University International Language* Database (*COBUILD*) was created in the 1980s under the direction of John Sinclair, and designed specifically for lexicography. It used new technology, the optical character reader, to read large quantities of printed text, and accessed much material already available in machine-readable form. The COBUILD dictionary (p. 444) was based on a corpus which eventually reached 20 million words.

• A later initiative from Birmingham is the *Bank of English* project, set up in 1991 with the aim of compiling a corpus of 220 million words to monitor ongoing changes in the language. In this approach, very large amounts of data are collected without being restricted to the size categories of a predetermined design, and the corpus is continually renewed as fresh material becomes available.

• The *Longman/Lancaster English Language Corpus*, developed during the 1980s by Della Summers at Longman with Geoffrey Leech of Lancaster University, is a lexicographic corpus, using material published since 1900 in both British and American English. By the early 1990s it had reached 30 million words of written text, and a spoken component was being developed.

• The *British National Corpus*, a collaboration between Longman, Oxford University Press, Chambers Harrap, the Oxford University Computing Service, the University of Lancaster, and the British Library, with the support of the Department of Trade and Industry was compiled between 1991 and 1994. It consists of 100 million words of British English – 90 million of written text and 10 million of spoken text – sampled from 1960 on. Particular attention has been paid to the internal balance of the corpus, including manuscript materials and ephemera. Its chief components are shown on p. 440.

• The *International Corpus of English*, coordinated by Sidney Greenbaum at University College London, began in the late 1980s with the aim of representing spoken, printed, and manuscript samples of English in countries where it is a first or official second language, each national component being a million running words. By 1991 over 20 countries had agreed to take part, several also planning a national regional corpus. Four specialized corpora are additionally included: written translations into English from languages of the European Union; spoken communication in English between speakers of different nationalities; writing by advanced learners of English; and Euro-English (as used in official publications of the European Union). Its chief categories are shown on p. 441.

ARCHIVES

Several centres now act as archives for different kinds of electronic text relevant to English language work. The *Oxford Text Archive*, for example, focuses on texts in the humanities, and includes the Brown and LOB corpora as well as the corpus of the *Toronto Dictionary of Old English*. Other examples are the *International Computer Archive of Modern English* (*ICAME*) in Bergen, Norway, which acts as a clearing-house for information on corpus studies in English, the *Center for Electronic Texts in the Humanities* at Rutgers and Princeton Universities, USA, and the *Data Collection Initiative* of the US Association of Computational Linguistics.

Several electronic archiving projects are genre restricted. An example is the *English Poetry Full-Text Database*, which began publication in 1992. In its entirety it will contain the works of 1,350 poets from 600 to 1900 in machine-readable form, using the Standard Generalized Markup Language (p. 439) for the coding of its texts. Users can obtain information about bibliography (e.g. source, dates) and text structure (e.g. division into parts, stanzas, scenes), as well as data on individual words and lines within poems, down to the level of specific details about indentation, typographic emphasis, and notes. If you want to know how the word *moon* (or *Moon*) has been used throughout poetic history (at least, in the set of poets and editions represented here), this database will tell you. All kinds of searches and comparisons come to mind – within-text and between-text, within-author and between-author – which this database should now make practicable. As with all database projects, the limitations of the source materials (the poets selected, the editions used) should not be forgotten. But there is no doubt that this kind of compilation will take much of the drudgery out of historical literary stylistics, and set new parameters for research in poetics.

• A general corpus must represent the language as faithfully as possible, within the period of time chosen for study (e.g. the 19th century, the 1980s, post-World War 2). This means maintaining a balance between speech and writing, monologue and dialogue, male and female, and as many other aspects of variation as it is practicable to obtain (Part V). The designer also needs to consider whether only Standard English should be included in the corpus, and whether it should be restricted to just one country, or be moving in the direction of World English (§7).

• A general corpus must be well structured so that it proves easy for researchers to access it efficiently. An example of a popular method of retrieval is concordance listing, in which instances of a key word in its context are shown centrally on the screen (illustrated on p. 424). This is of particular value in lexicography, but it would not be so useful in, say, work on sentence structure, where it is more helpful to see sentence beginning-points or end-points more systematically.

Overcoming difficulties

A large and well-constructed corpus will give excellent information about the frequency, distribution, and typicality of linguistic features – such as words, collocations (p. 160), spellings, pronunciations, and grammatical constructions. But to achieve such results there are several difficulties which the designer needs to overcome.

• Additional information may need to be provided if searches are to be meaningful. In grammatical and lexical research, for example, it is usually necessary to know the grammatical status of a word (its word class, §15), and this means tagging each word in the database with a grammatical label (see below). Being told that there are 500 instances of the word *round* is not as useful as being told how many of these are nouns, adjectives, prepositions, adverbs, and verbs.

• A major problem is the copyright law, which can restrict the public availability of the texts that the designer wants to include. Obtaining permissions is especially difficult in the spoken language, where in certain varieties (such as sports commentary) many people may be involved, and questions of ownership of the material are often untested. Even in literature using classical authors, there are problems: Wordsworth may be well outside a 50-year copyright rule, but the best edition of his work may not.

• Perhaps the biggest problem is the need to encode the language data (whether spoken or written) in a comprehensive and consistent form. Material which comes from many different formats needs to be standardized, which means devising international guidelines for the preparation of machine-readable texts. It is not just the words of the text which need to be encoded. There are many other features which people might want to enquire about, such as paragraph divisions, punctuation, layout, and (in speech) stress, intonation, and pause. It would be frustrating, to say the least, if someone wanted to use a corpus to find out about the use of italics as a marker of emphasis, only to discover that italics had not been included in the coding system. And the more varied the kinds of text to be included (novels alongside bus tickets; sermons alongside telephone calls), the more difficult the descriptive task becomes. The leading project in this area is the Text Encoding Initiative, which began work in the late 1980s. Its aims are to specify a common interchange format for machine-readable texts, to recommend ways of encoding new textual materials, and to document and describe the major existing encoding schemes. For its syntactic framework it uses the Standard Generalized Markup Language developed at Oxford University, and now used by several corpus projects.

WRITTEN MATERIAL

```
' &PUQ;Tell&VVB; me&PNP;,&PUN;"&PUQ; she&PNP; said&VVD;,&PUN;
leaning&VVG; forwards&AV0; with&PRP; a&AT0; smile&NN1; at&AV021;
once&AV022; coy&AJ0; and&CJC; overwhelming&VVG;,&PUN; ' &PUQ;I&PNP;
must&VM0; know&VVI;.&PUN;
```

An illustration of the grammatical tagging used in the British National Corpus. The untagged extract would have read as follows:

'Tell me,' she said, leaning forwards with a smile at once coy and overwhelming, 'I must know.

The tagging codes add information about the grammatical status of the words and identifies punctuation marks. (From G. Leech, 1993.)

SPOKEN MATERIAL

```
B     546 I'm ‖going to BÚRGOS■ ·   547 ‖WEDNESDAY■ ·   548 ‖WEEK■ ·   549 ‖YÈS■
      550 the ‖TÈNTH■ ·
```

```
0101000546 B      I'm<RA*VB+1> ‖going<VA+G> to<PA> B→urgos■<NP> ·
0101000547 B      ‖W→ednesday■<NP> ·
0101000548 B      ‖week■<NC> ·
0101000549 B      ‖y→es■<AS>
0101000550 B      the<TA> ‖t→enth■<JQ> ·
```

An illustration of the tagging used in the London–Lund Corpus (from J. Svartvik, *et al.*, 1982, p.54). The untagged version already looks quite complex, because it includes information about intonation, stress, and pause (p. 248). In the tagged version, the intonation marks which appear above vowels in the original are now adjacent to them, because of the limitations of the computer coding system. Note the limits of the tagging system: for example, the same code, AS, is used for all variant forms of *yes*, so that if you are interested in precisely this point, this corpus would not be informative. All corpus designers must make decisions about how much detail to include, and it is important to be aware what this lowest level of detail is before beginning to use a corpus.

Key to symbols
[■] boundary of an intonation unit
‖ the first prominent syllable in a tone unit
[→] level tone
[↘] falling tone
. brief pause

B speaker B
RA personal, subjective

* indicates a contraction
VB+1 verb *be* first person
VA+G main verb *-ing* form
PA preposition
NP proper noun
NC common noun
AS *yes, yeah, aye,* etc.
JQ ordinal number
TA determiner *the*

THE BRITISH NATIONAL CORPUS

The 90 million words of the written component of the BNC (p. 438) represent a wide range of texts classified according to five selectional features: informative/imaginative, subject field, date, genre, and level. Within each of these categories, texts are classified in the following way:

Informative (70%)
Primary Subject Fields
Natural and pure science (5%)
Social and community (15%)
Commerce and finance (10%)
Belief and thought (5%)
Applied science (5%)
World affairs (15%)
Arts (10%)
Leisure (10%)

Genre
Books (55–65%)
Periodicals (20–30%)
Miscellaneous (published) (5–10%)
Miscellaneous (unpublished) (5–10%)
To be spoken (2–7%)

Level
Specialist (30%)
Lay (50%)
Popular (20%)

Date
1975 – present

Imaginative (30%)
Level
Literary (33%)
Middle (33%)
Popular (33%)

Date
1960–1974 (25%)
1975–present (75%)

The spoken corpus

Spoken language has long been the neglected area of corpus studies. For many years, after corpus work began, the only substantial collection was the London–Lund corpus – just under half a million words derived from the Survey of English Usage (p. 438), the result of thousands of hours of careful tape-listening by teams of researchers. The reason for the neglect is clear: it is relatively easy to scan large quantities of printed text; but no automatic technique has yet been devised for scanning speech and producing a satisfactory transcription.

The BNC contains an orthographically transcribed corpus of 5–10 million words; it covers a wide range of speech variation, and includes a selection of prosodic features (p. 248).

• Some 5 million words represent conversational English, based on a demographic sample of British English speakers in the UK, and varying in terms of age (5 groups), gender, social group (4 groups), and region (12 areas). Around 100 people over the age of 15 were asked to record their conversations using a personal stereo over a period of seven days, keeping a conversation log of such matters as date, setting, and participants. Anonymity and confidentiality were of course guaranteed. Enough material had to be gathered to allow for cases where a recording proved to be unusable (e.g. because inaudible). Over 700 hours of usable material were needed to reach the 5 million word target.

• The context-governed corpus includes all other speech producers, as shown in the figure. It is divided into four main areas, and the distinction between monologue and dialogue (p. 294) is central. The same regional sampling areas were used as in the demographic corpus, though of course some material is not regionally distributed (e.g. parliamentary proceedings). Each monologue text type contains up to 200,000 words, and each dialogue type up to 300,000. The length of text unit within each type varies enormously, from a few hundred words (as in a news broadcast) to several thousand (as in a lecture).

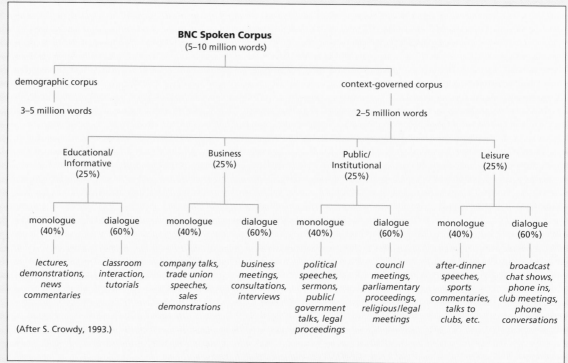

BNC Spoken Corpus
(5–10 million words)

demographic corpus — 3–5 million words

context-governed corpus — 2–5 million words

Educational/ Informative (25%)	Business (25%)	Public/ Institutional (25%)	Leisure (25%)
monologue (40%) — dialogue (60%)	monologue (40%) — dialogue (60%)	monologue (40%) — dialogue (60%)	monologue (40%) — dialogue (60%)
lectures, demonstrations, news commentaries	classroom interaction, tutorials	company talks, trade union speeches, sales demonstrations	business meetings, consultations, interviews	political speeches, sermons, public/ government talks, legal proceedings	council meetings, parliamentary proceedings, religious/legal meetings	after-dinner speeches, sports commentaries, talks to clubs, etc.	broadcast chat shows, phone ins, club meetings, phone conversations

(After S. Crowdy, 1993.)

UNPUBLISHED ENGLISH

This is the most difficult category of written English to cover systematically in a corpus, for it includes a vast amount of ephemeral material (as the publicity appeal indicated), such as informal letters and notes to the milkman. It is by no means socially trivial, for it covers such items as transport tickets, programmes, and bank-notes, and the important linguistic contents of wallets, handbags, filofaxes, and computer notebooks. In theory easy to obtain, it is remarkably difficult to collect in a systematic and representative way. Much of it has been unrecognized in language descriptions to date.

Four main categories are used in this section of the corpus (the examples given illustrate the range of each category, and are not comprehensive):

WANTED
5 MILLION WORDS

Notes to the milkman, postcards, shopping lists, letters to friends and family are all being collected by *Chambers Harrap Publishers Ltd* for their input into a major project on the way we use the English language.

The British National Corpus of Current English is a

Personal: formal and informal letters, postcards, Christmas and birthday cards, self-information items (e.g. shopping lists), diaries, private creative writing, note-taking, newsletters.

Business: letters, faxes, memos, minutes, e-mail, agendas, stock-lists, newsletters, year planners, order forms, notices, flyers, reports, proposals, presentations, information literature.

Institutional: written items from central and local government, law, religion, the forces, politics, charities, leisure bodies, national organizations.

Educational: essays, prospectuses, timetables, notices, course information, lecture notes (from teacher and student), exam papers and answers, minutes, calendars; organizations include schools, higher education and research institutions, libraries, museums, and professional bodies.

THE INTERNATIONAL CORPUS OF ENGLISH

The construction of the British component of this corpus (p. 438), completed in 1992, comprises 500 texts of *c.* 2,000 words, grouped into categories containing a minimum of 10 texts. Other corpora will be very similar in constitution. The material is annotated grammatically at the level of the word (p. 439). A corpus searching and analysis tool, known as ICECUP (the ICE Corpus Utility Program), is under development.

Composition of the Corpus

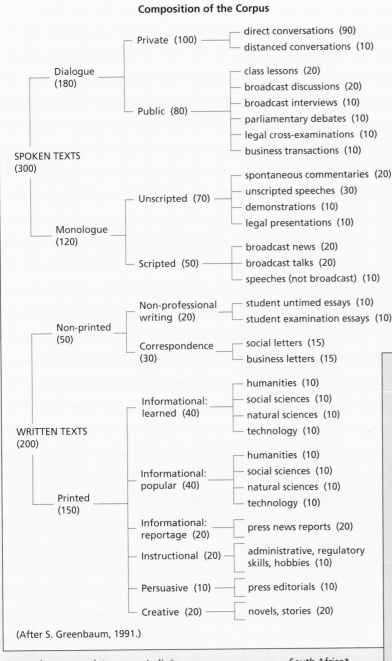

SPOKEN TEXTS (300)
- Dialogue (180)
  - Private (100)
    - direct conversations (90)
    - distanced conversations (10)
  - Public (80)
    - class lessons (20)
    - broadcast discussions (20)
    - broadcast interviews (10)
    - parliamentary debates (10)
    - legal cross-examinations (10)
    - business transactions (10)
- Monologue (120)
  - Unscripted (70)
    - spontaneous commentaries (20)
    - unscripted speeches (30)
    - demonstrations (10)
    - legal presentations (10)
  - Scripted (50)
    - broadcast news (20)
    - broadcast talks (20)
    - speeches (not broadcast) (10)

WRITTEN TEXTS (200)
- Non-printed (50)
  - Non-professional writing (20)
    - student untimed essays (10)
    - student examination essays (10)
  - Correspondence (30)
    - social letters (15)
    - business letters (15)
- Printed (150)
  - Informational: learned (40)
    - humanities (10)
    - social sciences (10)
    - natural sciences (10)
    - technology (10)
  - Informational: popular (40)
    - humanities (10)
    - social sciences (10)
    - natural sciences (10)
    - technology (10)
  - Informational: reportage (20)
    - press news reports (20)
  - Instructional (20)
    - administrative, regulatory skills, hobbies (10)
  - Persuasive (10)
    - press editorials (10)
  - Creative (20)
    - novels, stories (20)

(After S. Greenbaum, 1991.)

Areas where research teams are located:
Australia*
Belgium
Canada*
Caribbean*
Cameroon*
Denmark
Germany
Hong Kong*
India*
Irish Republic*
Jamaica
Kenya*
Netherlands
New Zealand*
Nigeria*
Northern Ireland*
Philippines*
Singapore*
South Africa*
Sweden
Tanzania*
UK*
USA*
Wales
Zambia*
Zimbabwe

* In these areas a national or regional corpus is being planned.

USING A CORPUS

Thousands of researchers now routinely consult corpora, and it is not possible to represent all the kinds of enquiry they make. The following examples have been selected to illustrate some of the basic numerical findings which bear on issues discussed elsewhere in this encyclopedia.

Usage
The Longman/Lancaster Corpus contains these totals for the choice of preposition after *different* (p. 194):

different (total)	14,704
+ from	1,193
+ to	75
+ than	34

Usage books usually state that *from* is the preferred preposition in British English and *than* in American English. However, it turns out that *from* is overwhelmingly the most frequent usage in both varieties. A third of the uses of *than* appear in British texts. (After M. Rundell & P. Stock, 1992.)

Spelling differences between British and American English often do not display a clear-cut pattern (p. 307). The figures below are taken from the LOB corpus of British English and the Brown corpus of American English (p. 438). Even the first example (*color*) has some unexpected variations. The totals for verb forms ending in *-ed* or *-t* confirm that *-ed* forms are definitely preferred in American English, but suggest that something is happening other than just regional difference (p. 204). (Capitalized forms of nouns include totals for both plurals and singulars.)

In the lexical section, when interpreting the figures for such words as *he* and *she*, it should be borne in mind that these corpora were collected in the early 1960s. This illustrates the importance of renewing a corpus at regular intervals, if it is to keep pace with language change. (After S. Johansson, 1980.)

Spellings

	British	American		British	American
COLOR	0	252	BLOKE	5	2
COLOUR	256	2	CHAP	33	6
behavior	9	96	FELLOW	91	86
behaviour	121	3	GUY	15	74
			ATTORNEY	4	77
traveled	0	23	BARRISTER	11	0
travelled	22	4	LAWYER	29	69
traveling	0	19	SOLICITOR	18	6
travelling	23	4			
TRAVELER	0	16	AUTO(MOBILE)	2	104
TRAVELLER	27	5	CAR	343	397
			APARTMENT	21	99
burned	15	42	FLAT	183	80
burnt	11	7			
smelled	0	19			
smelt	4	3			
leaned	33	38			
leant	8	0			

What is real?
Even when the statistics are small, a corpus can provide a useful indication of the way a word is used, as in this list of the nouns used with *real* in the LOB corpus. (From S. Johansson & K. Hofland, 1989, p. 287.)

Lexical sets

	British	American
HE	17,599	19,416
SHE	8,163	6,036
MAN	1,835	2,152
WOMAN	490	471
BOY	338	414
GIRL	459	379
baseball	0	57
cricket	21	3
football	37	36
golf	19	34
tennis	23	16

danger	3	objection	4
difference	2	peace	2
effect	2	power	2
feeling	3	problems	5
interest	2	reason	5
job	2	sense	2
life	3	test	5
love	2	thing	5
man	2	value	2
name	2	world	2

DICTIONARIES

More than any other domain of English language study, the compilation of dictionaries has been aided and stimulated by the availability of computer techniques and electronically stored collections of text (p. 438). The 1980s were, in this respect, a watershed in lexicography. The earlier tradition displayed a continuity of thought and method which can be traced back to Dr Johnson (p. 74). It was a tradition which relied for its success on enormous levels of personal commitment by individual editors and their teams of assistants. At the same time it fostered a level of subjectivism and idiosyncrasy which was noted very early on. Here is Boswell on Johnson:

On Monday, March 23rd [1772] I found him busy, preparing a fourth edition of his folio Dictionary…He would not admit *civilization* but only *civility*. With great deference to him, I thought *civilization*, from to *civilize*, better in the sense opposed to *barbarity*, than *civility*.

It will never be possible to eliminate the subjective element from dictionaries. Unconscious bias can affect the very process of definition writing, as has been pointed out by feminist critics of male-orientated entries. And subjectivity is inherent in the choice of sources for citations. The vast word-totals of computer corpora are impressive, but when broken down into subcategories they can soon seem quite humble. For example, if there is room for only 20 creative texts in a million-word corpus (p. 441), which 20 will the researchers choose? In the past, dictionaries have tended to select the more 'respected' writers, but in a modern dictionary, it could be argued, the writers of crime and popular romance (p. 440) have just as strong a case for inclusion. The arrival of new technology does not diminish the need for editorial decision-making in such matters.

JOYFUL DRUDGERY

It is not always desirable to eliminate the personal element from a dictionary: an element of idiosyncrasy or humour can often make a definition intelligible or memorable. When the Edinburgh firm of W. & R. Chambers eliminated some of the famously whimsical definitions in the 1972 edition of their dictionary, protests from readers persuaded the firm to put many of them back.

double-locked locked by two turns of the key, as in some locks and many novels

éclair a cake, long in shape but short in duration, with cream filling and chocolate or other icing

jay walker a careless pedestrian whom motorists are expected to avoid running down

middle-aged between youth and old age, variously reckoned to suit the reckoner

noose a snare or bond generally, esp. hanging or marriage

petting party (*coll.*) a gathering for the purpose of amorous caressing as an organised sport

---

DICTIONARY GIANTS

The history of lexicography is dominated by the names of three figures: Johnson, Webster, and Murray. The role played by the first two in the Early Modern English period of the language was so significant that it was necessary to take account of it in Part I (pp. 74, 80). Their influence continues today – directly, in the case of Webster, through the series of dictionaries which bear his name; and indirectly, in the case of Johnson, through the tradition which led the Philological Society to sponsor a 'new' English dictionary.

Webster's Dictionary

Webster published his *American Dictionary of the English Language* in 1828. After his death (1843), the rights were purchased by George and Charles Merriam, and later editions have appeared under the name of *Merriam-Webster*. A revision in 1847 was edited by Webster's son-in-law, Chauncey A. Goodrich. Several dictionaries within this tradition appeared in the following decades, via the *Webster's International Dictionary* of 1890 to the *Webster's New International Dictionary* of 1909, with a second edition in 1934. The latest, third edition appeared in 1961, edited by Philip B. Gove, based on a collection of over 6 million citations of recorded usage, and dealing with over 450,000 words. This edition, prepared over a 10-year period, took up 757 editor-years, and proved to be highly controversial. Three supplements have since appeared – of 6,000 words (1976), 89,000 words (1983), and 12,000 words (1986). Outside of this tradition, many other publishers have come to use the 'Webster' name for their dictionaries and word-books.

THE SECOND DICTIONARY WAR

The third edition of the *New International – Webster 3*, as it is often called – appeared in 1961, and caused more lexicographical controversy than at any time since the 19th-century 'War of the Dictionaries' (p. 82). It used a descriptive, not a prescriptive approach (p. 78) and many Americans felt that its descriptivism went too far.

Critics attacked its use of citations from popular (as opposed to literary) sources, such as domestic novels and magazines, and its listing of variant pronunciation forms. Above all, *Webster 3* was said to be in error by not condemning such substandard usages as *ain't*, and by failing to identify colloquialisms through the use of a separate label. By contrast, the many merits of the new edition, such as its fresh approach to definition, and its careful account of variations in capitalization, received hardly any attention in the popular press.

The critics claimed that the editor, Philip Gove, had lost all sense of standards and correctness. The work, as one newspaper put it, 'surrenders abjectly to the permissive school of speech'. Dictionary makers have social responsibilities, it was argued: a dictionary is an authoritative work, and to include a word is to sanction its use. *Webster 3*, it was regretted, gave the all clear to *ain't* and other forms of nonstandard speech.

Gove and his defenders, in turn, attacked the critics for upholding artificial notions of correctness and superiority. Lexicographers did not claim any special authority, they said, but were trying to be detached observers. Linguistic growth and variety was a fact, which ought to be dispassionately recorded in a reference work. It was not the business of lexicographers to make value judgments about the words they encountered.

These arguments did not satisfy those who saw the dictionary as a work whose authority should not be questioned on any account. The controversy, as a result, continued for some time, and the issues it reflected are still with us (p. 366).

THE *OXFORD ENGLISH DICTIONARY*

In 1857 the Philological Society of Great Britain, noting the inadequacies of the English dictionaries then available, resolved to promote a 'New English Dictionary' which would record the history of the language from Anglo-Saxon times. It took over 20 years to launch the project. In 1879, the Society reached an agreement with Oxford University Press, and appointed James A. H. Murray as editor. The aim was to produce a four-volume work in a period of ten years; but after five years, Murray and his colleagues had managed to complete only the section A–ANT: it was 352 pages, and sold for 12s. 6d. (62½p in modern money).

It was evident that the dictionary was a much greater work than had been envisaged. Additional editors were appointed, and the *Oxford English Dictionary* (or *OED*), as it came to be called, was produced in fascicles over the next 44 years, the final section appearing in 1928. It was published in 12 volumes, comprising 15,487 pages and covering 414,825 lexical items. A one-volume supplement appeared in 1933. Work on the dictionary recommenced in 1957, with the appointment of R. W. Burchfield to edit a new supplement. This appeared in four volumes between 1972 and 1986, and included the content of the 1933 work: it added 5,732 pages to the dictionary, and nearly 70,000 further lexical items. But even before the last volume appeared, the task of preparing a second edition had begun.

Murray and his daughters in the Scriptorium in Oxford. The building was constructed in the garden of Murray's house. It was about 50 ft (15 m) long by 50 ft (15 m) wide, and sunk 3 ft (1 m) into the ground to avoid interfering with the next-door neighbour's view. As a result, it was a damp and badly ventilated room, stuffy in summer and cold in winter. One visitor described the building as resembling a 'tool house, a washhouse, or a stable'.

Murray rarely got through the winter without several chills and often pneumonia. A stove warmed the room in the coldest months, but the risk of fire meant it had to be extinguished at night. In cold weather he wore a

thick overcoat, and sometimes sat with his feet in a box to keep away the draught. In such conditions, he worked 80 or 90 hours a week, often for long periods without a break, rising at 5 a.m., and getting through a great deal of work well before breakfast and the arrival of his assistants. He continued this regime until his late 70s, when illness overtook him.

Murray was the son of a village tailor from Hawick, in Scotland. Largely self-educated, he left school at 14, and worked as a bank clerk and teacher before turning to lexicography. His was the plan of the *New English Dictionary*, and he edited more than half of the first edition himself.

The New Oxford English Dictionary Project was established in 1984, under the direction of Timothy J. Benbow. Its aims were to integrate the original *OED* with its supplements, to update the whole work, and to provide a machine-readable version which could produce new editions in both printed and electronic forms.

After a huge keyboarding operation, involving over 170 keyboarders and proofreaders in the USA and UK, the second edition, prepared by J. A. Simpson and E. S. C. Weiner, was published in 1989 as a single 20-volume integrated work, with a further 5,000 lexical items added. The *OED* now consists of 291,627 entries defining over 500,000 items, and using nearly 2½ million quotations.

Other remarkable statistics accompanied the appearance of the work. The five-year task

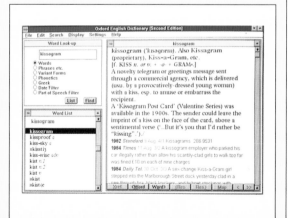

The entry for *kissogram* (see also p. 130).

involved the equivalent of 500 years' labour by the team. For the printed edition, the length of the complete print run was 5,345 miles (8,602 km). Equally impressive, the project made the whole of the first edition available on a single compact disk (CD-

ROM), and in on-line form it can now provide scholars with rapid and precise answers to a host of exciting lexical questions (p. 438). The second edition is now also available in electronic form (see picture above), and a third edition is planned for 2005.

OTHER *OED* EDITORS

▲ Henry Bradley (1845–1923) was appointed as a second editor in 1887, the year letter B was completed.

▲ William Alexander Craigie (1867–1957) was appointed in 1897, and became joint editor in 1901, working on letter Q.

▲ Charles Talbut Onions (1873–1965) became an assistant in 1895 and a full editor in 1914.

▲ Robert William Burchfield (1923–) became editor in 1957, and saw the supplements through to completion in 1986.

INNOVATIONS

An extract from the Reader's Digest two-volume *Great Illustrated Dictionary* (1984), with linguistic information supplemented by encyclopedic data using full colour throughout (the first such use in an English-language dictionary of this size). With many illustrations, the colour is there only for aesthetic reasons, or to give extra clarity to a complex illustration; but in a number of instances the colour is functional – in the case of *dog*, helping to distinguish different breeds.

dog (dog ‖ dawg) *n.* **1.** A domesticated carnivorous mammal, *Canis familiaris*, developed in a wide variety of breeds and probably originally derived from several wild species. **2.** Any of various other animals of the family Canidae, such as the dingo.

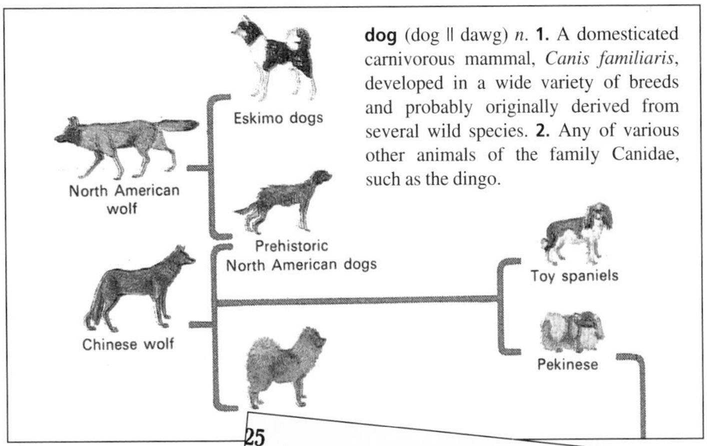
Eskimo dogs
North American wolf
Prehistoric North American dogs
Chinese wolf
Toy spaniels
Pekinese

Part of a page from the *Collins COBUILD English Language Dictionary* (1987). Apart from its technical innovations and the size of its corpus (p. 438), the project broke new ground in lexicographic treatment. It covered the words of the corpus in unprecedented detail and with a range of examples that were fuller and more varied than had previously been usual, in dictionaries of this size. It also paid particular attention to the very common words in the language: for example, over 30 contexts are given for the verb *see*.

It also revised the technique of lexicographic exposition in several ways. The most noticeable feature is the extra column, which contains grammatical notes and data on semantic relationships. The main entries avoid abbreviations, and definitions are written in an everyday prose style. Although this is space consuming (as in the spelling out of such words as 'someone' and 'something'), the sense is thought to be much easier to assimilate. Also, through the use of full-sentence definitional strategies (e.g. 'If you …') a great deal of information is conveyed about how a word is grammatically used.

25 **impair**

immortalize /ɪmɔ̲ːtə⁰laɪz/, **immortalizes, immortalizing, immortalized**; also spelled **immortalise**. If you **immortalize** someone or something, you cause them to be remembered for a very long time, for example by writing about them or making a film. EG *She is immortalised by a very distinguished statue... ...a wondrous event which he had immortalised in verse.* — V+O : USU+A ⇑ commemorate = celebrate

immovable /ɪmu̲ːvəbə⁰l/. **1** Something that is **immovable** is fixed and cannot be moved from its position. EG *...an immovable pillar.* ◊ **immovably.** EG *Each picture was nailed immovably in place.* — ADJ CLASSIF; ◊ ADV

2 If you have a feeling or opinion that is **immovable**, you are firm about it and will not change. EG *...fossilised ways and immovable conservatism... The foundations of personality were immovable.* — ADJ CLASSIF

immune /ɪmju̲ːn/. **1** If you are **immune** to a particular disease, you cannot be affected by it. EG *We are virtually immune to certain diseases.* ◊ **immunity** /ɪmju̲ːnɪti¹/. EG *Babies receive immunity to a variety of infections.* — ADJ CLASSIF : USU PRED; ◊ N UNCOUNT : IF+PREP THEN *to/against*

2 If you are **immune** to something that happens or is done, you are not affected by it. EG *He was immune to the flattery of political leaders... The American economy is proving surprisingly immune to big fluctuations in interest rates.* ◊ **immunity.** EG *This immunity to criticism is built into their whole system nowadays.* — ADJ QUALIT : PRED, IF+PREP THEN *to*; ◊ N UNCOUNT : IF+PREP THEN *to*

3 Someone or something that is **immune** from a particular process or situation is able to escape it or avoid being affected by it. EG *...targets that the West had considered immune from air attack... The fabric of modern society is not immune from decay.* ◊ **immunity, immunities.** EG *He had been granted immunity from prosecution... ...an income tax immunity form... ...the privileges or immunities of citizens of the United States.* • See also **diplomatic immunity.** — ADJ QUALIT : PRED, IF+PREP THEN ⇑ safe = exempt; ◊ N UNCOUNT/COUNT : IF+PREP THEN *from/against* = exemption

immunize /ɪ̲mjə⁴naɪz/, **immunizes, immunizing, immunized**; also spelled **immunise**. If people or animals **are immunized**, they are made immune to a particular disease, often by being given an injection. EG *Everyone who is going abroad will need to be immunized against typhoid.* ◊ **immunization** /ɪ̲mjə⁴naɪze̲ɪʃə⁰n/. EG *...a government programme of immunization.* — V+O : IF+PREP THEN *against* = inoculate; ◊ N UNCOUNT/COUNT

immutable /ɪmju̲ːtəbə⁰l/. Something that is **immutable** will never change; a formal word. EG *Values and attitudes are not immutable, but are likely to change... The view of his time was that all species were immutable, created by God.* — ADJ CLASSIF ⇑ permanent

imp /ɪmp/, **imps**. **1** An **imp** is a small creature in a — N COUNT

Part of a page from the Longman *Dictionary of English Language and Culture* (1992), which aims to give non-native students of English a socio-historical perspective to the lexicon. Such phrases as *Jack and Jill* or *Jack and the Beanstalk* are an important part of native speaker intuitions, but it is traditionally difficult for a learner to find out about them. In many cases, there is lack of awareness even within first-language speakers: for example, *Jackanory* (a TV programme for children) and *Jackie* (a girls' magazine) are little known outside Britain.

jack·al /ˈdʒækɔːl, -kəl‖-kəl/ *n* an African and Asian wild animal of the dog family, which often eats what other animals have killed

jack·a·napes /ˈdʒækəneɪps/ *n* **-napes** [*usu. sing.*] *old-fash* a child who plays annoying tricks

Jack and Jill /ˌdʒæk ənd ˈdʒɪl/ two children in a NURSERY RHYME (=an old song or poem for children):

Jack and Jill went up the hill
To fetch a pail of water;
Jack fell down and broke his crown,
And Jill came tumbling after.

Jack and the Bean·stalk /ˌdʒæk ənd ðə ˈbiːnstɔːk/ also **Jack the Gi·ant-kil·ler** /ˌ· · ˈ·· ˌ··/— a children's story in which a boy, Jack, sells his mother's cow for some magic beans. The mother, in anger, throws the beans out of the window. The next day a very tall bean plant (the **Beanstalk**) has grown up into the clouds. Jack climbs it and finds himself in a strange country outside a GIANT's house. He enters and has to hide from the giant, who sings, "Fee fi fo fum, I smell the blood of an Englishman." Jack robs the giant of a hen that lays golden eggs and a HARP that plays by itself, and escapes down the beanstalk with the giant following. Arriving at the ground first, Jack takes an AXE and cuts down the beanstalk, and the giant falls and is killed.

Jack·a·no·ry /ˌdʒækəˈnɔːri/ a popular British television show in which well-known actors read favourite children's stories

jack·ass /ˈdʒæk-æs/ *n* **1** *infml taboo in AmE* a person who behaves foolishly: *Don't be a jackass – come down off the roof!* **2** *now rare* a male ASS –see also LAUGHING JACKASS

jack·boot /ˈdʒækbuːt/ *n* **1** [C] a military boot which covers the leg up to the knee **2** [*the*] the cruel rule of military men, often used in association with the Nazis in Germany: *living under the jackboot*

jack·daw /ˈdʒækdɔː/ *n* a bird of the CROW family, believed to steal small bright objects

A dictionary which provides cultural perspective is a brave undertaking, because if its range is comprehensive and its definitions are accurate it will inevitably reflect aspects of the less pleasant side of life, and those reflected may take it amiss. As it happens, the day chosen for the special report on World English in Part V (p. 300) was the one when the world press reported that Longman had agreed to withdraw a reference in this book to the amount of prostitution in Bangkok, because of Thai public opinion. The history of lexicography contains several famous cases of this kind, where the aim of the lexicographer to hold a linguistic mirror up to nature has not been appreciated by those who have been mirrored.

borrow

which meaning?

take something from someone and give it back later → ● **BORROW**

give something to someone and get it back later → ● **LEND**

● **BORROW**

to get something from someone which you must give back to them later

1 to borrow money from someone
2 to borrow something such as a car, book, or pen
3 to pay money so that you can borrow and use something for a fixed period
4 words for describing something such as a car, machine, or money that has been borrowed
5 money that is borrowed

1 to borrow money from someone
borrow
take out a loan

borrow /ˈbɒrəʊ ‖ ˈbɑː-, ˈbɔː-/ [*v* I/T]
borrow sth *She needs to borrow some money to pay the doctor.* |
borrow sth from/off *Can I borrow five pounds off you till next week?* | *By the end of the war the Canadian government had borrowed over $5 billion from its own citizens.* | **borrow** *Companies normally expect to borrow at cheaper rates than ordinary people have to pay.* | **borrow heavily** (= borrow a lot of money) *Maxwell had borrowed heavily to finance his business projects.*
borrower [*n* C] *The fall in interest rates is bad news for savers but good news for borrowers.*

take out a loan /ˌteɪk aʊt ə ˈləʊn/ to borrow a large sum of money from a bank or other financial institution [*v phrase*] *We're still paying off the loan we took out to buy our car.* | **take out a loan from** *If you take out a loan from the company you have to pay it back within two years.*

Part of a page from the Longman *Language Activator*™, described as 'the world's first production dictionary'. It is aimed at non-native learners of English who know roughly what they want to say but who are unsure exactly which word to use. In the way it helps them put ideas into words (an encoding function), it resembles a thesaurus (p. 158), and contrasts with the traditional dictionary, which moves from words to meanings (a decoding function).

The *Activator* uses 1,052 key words or concepts, expressing such basic ideas as *big*, *walk*, and *borrow*. Cross-references relate key words (see *which meaning?* in the illustration). Each key word is divided into sections, shown by a numbered menu of meanings. Users select the number which most closely corresponds to the idea they want to express, and go to that section to find the range of items available.

THE WORDTREE®

Entries from *The Wordtree®*, a lexical system first published in 1984 by American scholar Henry G. Burger (1923–). The system lists vocabulary in a way which enables the user to trace any concept backwards towards its causes, or forwards towards its effect. It was devised as a result of the author's dissatisfaction with the current, random ways of codifying vocabulary concepts – the merely alphabetical ordering of the dictionary, and the merely intuitive structure of the thesaurus. He felt that neither met the precision needed by the computer age.

Burger therefore extended into linguistics the 'complementarity' concept of Copenhagen physicists, especially Werner Heisenberg and Niels Bohr – that an analysis of the world in terms of structures (using such notions as 'particles') must not be commingled with its analysis in terms of processes (using such notions as 'radiations').

In common with the thesaurus, Burger's aim is to help a user find an appropriate word; but the approach goes well beyond a work such as Roget's in its organization and scope. It adds a great deal of information about how we can conceptualize the world, and leads the enquirer in a structured way towards a word which is the precise expression of a particular concept. Many interesting questions arise.

• We may know the term *bowdlerize* meaning 'remove the indecent parts of literature'. It is derived from English man of letters Thomas Bowdler (1754–1825), who published an expurgated edition of Shakespeare in 1818. However, few people are aware of its opposite – to put

them in. By using *The Wordtree®* system, the reader is led to *zolaize* (a word which alludes to the controversial reputation of French novelist Emile Zola).

• Because the words in the book are not classified in terms of subjects, parallels emerge which would not normally be apparent, such as the medical use of *percuss* (to tap a person's chest) and the archaeological use of *tunk* (to tap a wall).

The Wordtree® chooses as its basic elements the vocabulary which expresses the notion of process – essentially, the verbs. It limits itself to those verbs which express impact – the transitive verbs (p. 212). Other word classes are listed in relation to these transitives. Following the natural history model, in which organisms are defined binarily into genus and modifier, each verb is defined in terms of two parts: a general activity and a qualifying notion. The latter occurs 'upon' the former – that is, either simultaneously with it, or later than it, but not before it.

Definition is based on the 'lowest common denominator' of the several meanings that each transitive verb usually has. For example, the essence of SWIGGING is fastening. Hence, after that kind of definition, there is a cross-reference to the secondary ('gulping') meaning, to QUAFF. The verb is then alphabetized in the system's 'Index', as shown in the listing from the F pages.

In the other half of the work, the same items are arranged by levels of abstractness in a hierarchy of concepts (which Burger calls a *cladistic*):

PENETRATE & DIVIDE = CUT
CUT & FLAKE = SLICE
SLICE & PICKLE = CALVER

The computerized database provides sources for all the items included. Many are specialized terms or neologisms not always to be found in other dictionaries. By the time the work was first published, after some 27 years of compilation, Burger had found about 24,600 transitive verbs – by his estimation 30 per cent more than in the *Oxford English Dictionary*. The addition of specialized transitives continues, as does the diversification of the system.

From the 'F' section of the Index, showing how the *Wordtree®* system relates FASTEN to other verbs. (How other words, not necessarily verbs, relate to FASTEN appears in the system's Hierarchy, not shown.)

To FASTEN = to HOLD (something) & to STAY (it)........................ ¶12510.

FASTEN upon BINDING = Lash (14788).
FASTEN upon BOLTING = Snib (15217).
FASTEN upon BUNDLING = Nitch (15313).
FASTEN upon CONTRACTING = Swig (12926).
FASTEN upon ENCIRCLING = Hank (12940).
FASTEN upon ENTERING = Latch (12912).
FASTEN upon FILLING = Cotter (12922).
FASTEN upon GROUNDING = Stake (12935).
FASTEN upon HALF-EMBRACING = Embrace (12947).
FASTEN upon INTERSPACING = Norsel (12934).
FASTEN upon INTERSTRATIFYING = Interdigitate (12930).
FASTEN upon INTRUDING = Wedge (20259).
FASTEN upon JOINING = Attach (12914).
FASTEN upon LINKING = Chain (15297).
FASTEN upon MACHINING = Dog (12919).
FASTEN upon METALLIZING Yote (12942).
FASTEN upon MIRING = Bemire (20259).
FASTEN upon PIERCING = Brad (12939).
FASTEN upon PILLARING = Pillory (12933).
FASTEN upon POSITIONING = Moor (12924).
FASTEN upon RAVELING = Enravel (12949).
FASTEN upon RINGING = Parrel (12944).
FASTEN upon SCREWING = Screwfasten (19475).
FASTEN upon SEATING = Barnacle (12921).
FASTEN upon SECURING = Slour (12928).
FASTEN upon SOCKETING = Dop (12945).
FASTEN upon STACKING = Lockstack (12937).
FASTEN upon STRAPPING = Thong (15352).
FASTEN upon STRETCHING = Rack (12917).
FASTEN upon SURROUNDING = Clasp (12943).
FASTEN upon TAUTENING = Drumstretch (12941).
FASTEN upon TRANSVERSING = Toggle (12925).
FASTEN upon TRAVERSING = Bolt (12916).
FASTEN upon TURNING = Belay (12915).
FASTEN upon UPROLLING = Furl (12931).
FASTEN upon WINDING = Bitt (16253).
FASTEN & BECRIPPLE = Headfast (12929).
FASTEN & ENCLOSE = Cope (12923).
FASTEN & FEED = Manger (12950).
FASTEN & FIRM = Fix (12938).
FASTEN & LANGLE = Sidelangle (12946).
FASTEN & ORNAMENT = Brooch (14962).
FASTEN & PATCHWORK = Spotfasten (16708).
FASTEN & RECYCLE = Doublefasten (14001).

FASTENING NUANCES ...... @ Adhere, Bitt, Direct, Enfasten, Impute, Lock, Secure, Tie.
FASTENING CAUSES ...... @ Connect, Control, Possess, Safen, Secure, Shut.
FASTENING EFFECTS ...... @ Exclude, Join, Snug.
FASTENING INSTRUMENTS ...... @ Band, Bolt, Button, Cleat, Hookandeye, Hole, Indent, Knot, Pin, Seal, Sticky, Stitch, Thread, Tie.
FASTENING PREVENTATIVES ...... @ Enlarge, Impermeabilize, Loose, Slick, Stray, Wild.

INDEXING THE DICTIONARY?

Not as silly an idea as it might seem. There are now so many period, regional, and specialized dictionaries that it is often a real problem knowing where to look in order to find some lexical information. In 1973 Richard Bailey proposed that someone should fund an index to the English vocabulary, which would provide a guide to the entry words that are currently treated in different works. Idioms, phrases, proverbial expressions, and suchlike would especially benefit from this approach, as it is always a problem knowing where

to look them up (is *kick the bucket* under *kick* or *bucket*?). Laurence Urdang's *Idioms and Phrases Index* (1983) illustrates the possibilities. A full-scale implementation of this idea is now well within the scope of current technology. The problems remain administrative and financial.

We could extend this idea to include not just whole words but also functional parts of words (morphological elements). The problem may be illustrated thus: how easy is it to find all words containing the root *mobil* in a lexical reference work? There is no problem if the root begins the word (*mobile, mobilize*); but if the root is obscured by

prefixes or is the second part of a compound, it is not easily retrievable (*automobile, immobile, demobilize, immobilize*). A reverse spelling dictionary gives only limited help, in such a case. Behzad Kasravi's *INDEXionary* (1990) is one suggestion towards solving this problem. It lists groups of words alphabetically on the basis of the functional elements they contain. Thus all the lexemes (p. 118) which end in *-archy* are placed together, as are those ending in *-light, -logue,* and so on. The set ending in *-fix* is illustrative.

	fix
af:	fix
cruci:	fix
in:	fix
pre:	fix
suf:	fix
trans:	fix

SOURCES AND RESOURCES

This review of the English language has something of the character of a planetary survey by a passing *Voyager*, straining to see more than its limited methods of investigation allow. At least we have been able to send down frequent probes to find out what is on – and occasionally beneath – the surface. And it is comforting to know that, in this domain of enquiry, 'we are not alone'. Indeed, English proves to be one of the busiest areas of exploration in the linguistic galaxy.

• Some 300 of the explorers are named in the alphabetical list of references in Appendix III. Some 200 others will be found in the further reading section, Appendix IV, which lists a number of general studies of the language, as well as specific studies of the topics dealt with in the 24 chapters of this book.
• The most up-to-date guides to exploratory progress can be found in the periodicals which deal exclusively with the language. There are several journals, of varying levels of technicality, and many of them have informed the topics of this book. Examples include *English World-Wide* and *World Englishes*, the wide-ranging *English Today*, and the lexicon review *Verbatim*.
• It is also invaluable to have the opportunity to talk about the way things are going with fellow explorers. At a professional level, several organizations are devoted to teaching the subject, such as the *National Association for the Teaching of English* (*NATE*) in the UK and the *National Council of Teachers of English* (*NCTE*) in the USA. Bodies concerned with the teaching of English as a second or foreign language (p. 106) include the *International Association of Teachers of English as a Foreign Language* (IATEFL), *Networking English Language Learning in Europe* (NELLE), and *Teaching English to Speakers of Other Languages* (TESOL).
• For the amateur explorer, there are several organizations which are interested in the language as a whole, often in relation to wider issues. The chief example of a broad-based institution is the *English-Speaking Union of the Commonwealth* – a voluntary association which promotes international understanding and friendship through its educational programme. There are also a number of groups concerned with safeguarding standards of English language use: examples here include the *English Academy of Southern Africa* and the British *Queen's English Society*.
• Organizations also exist which cater for explorers with restricted interests. If the territory is dictionaries, there is the *Dictionary Society of North America* and the *European Association for Lexicography*. If it is spelling, there is the *Simplified Spelling Society*. And there are so many 'names' societies that they are best

THE APPEAL OF NAMES – AND A NOMINAL APPEAL

Several countries have societies which are devoted to the study of names, and which publish onomastics journals. Canada has *Canoma, Onomastica Canadiana*, and *Name Gleaner/La Glanure des Noms*; the USA has *Names*, the *American Name Society Bulletin*, and various regional publications; South Africa has *Nomina Africana*; Britain has the *English Place-Name Society Journal* (p. 146), *Nomina*, and *Ainm* ('Name', from Northern Ireland).

In Britain, the Names Society was founded in 1969 by a group of British enthusiasts, with the aim of gathering information about names of all kinds, and putting people who had a special interest in names in touch with each other. It circulated an informal newsletter, and kept published and unpublished data on English names and usage. Though less active in recent years, it continues to deal with enquiries about names through its secretariat.

In the USA, there is the American Name Society, dedicated to naming trends and practices and the history of onomastics. It was founded in 1951, meets annually, and holds several regional meetings. It publishes the *ANS Bulletin, Names*, and an annual report (the Ehrensberger Report) which itemizes the activities of its members. The range of its interests is considerable. A 1992 summary refers to recently published articles on names in relation to Chinese Americans, Jamaica, Shakespeare, baseball players, cemeteries, and cats.

The work goes on, aided now by progress in technology. For example, in 1992 the work of the English Place-Name Society (p. 146) began to be supplemented by a computational research project, the Survey of the Language of English Place-Names, which aims to create a computerized database of English place-name material and to compile a new edition of English place-name elements. The project also anticipates being able to produce a handlist of Old and Middle English words recorded in place names to supplement dictionaries based primarily on literary sources. It is likely that more projects of this kind will try to take advantage of the technological revolution – but only if finances permit.

Funding a future

The organizations mentioned on this page are but some of the bodies, amateur and professional, which have been formed to foster interest and research in the English language. Given the important role of this language in modern times, it is a particular irony that so many of these bodies should be so starved of funding. All amateur organizations struggle to cover their expenses; and all researchers have experienced the frustration of knowing what might be done if only there were funds to do it. English now has both national and international dimensions, and it is surely time for government at both national and international levels to take serious responsibility for fostering the growth of knowledge about its history, structure, and use. This is not an argument for an open cheque book: but there is at least a case for recognizing that the language is now old enough to have a bank account of its own.

Addresses of the organizations mentioned on this page will be found at the end of Appendix III.

dealt with in a separate panel. At an individual level, several of the major lexicography programmes have set up networks of probes in the form of 'word watching' operations, enabling anyone to submit information about new words and uses to a lexicographic database.

A miracle of rare device

When compiling an introductory encyclopedia, fascination has a travelling companion in frustration. English, as any language, is an inexhaustible resource, of great beauty, complexity, and power – and also of temptation. Each topic selected for survey, on our linguistic planetary surface, opens up vast caverns inviting further exploration, and it is painful having to resist their call. Curiosity must yield to discipline, if publishing deadlines mean anything at all. But the caverns remain, measureless, awaiting all who wish to explore.

Appendices

The alphabetical arrangement of Appendices I–III
and V–VII is letter-by-letter.

I · GLOSSARY

This glossary contains a brief definition of all the specialized language terms used in the text of this encyclopedia, along with some of the associated linguistic terminology likely to be encountered by the general reader. The alphabetical arrangement of the glossary is letter-by-letter. Examples are given in italics, with focused items shown in bold face; alternative or related terms within the main text of an entry are given in bold face; *cf.* introduces relevant entries elsewhere in the glossary.

A

abbreviation A reduced version of a word, phrase, or sentence; cf. acronym; initialism; ellipsis.

ablative case An inflection that typically expresses such meanings as 'by/with/from'; cf. case.

ablaut A vowel change that gives a word a new grammatical function (*drink◊ drank*); also called **gradation**.

abstract *see* **concrete**

accent **1** In phonetics, features of pronunciation that signal regional or social identity; cf. dialect. **2** In phonology, a type of emphasis given to a spoken word or syllable. **3** In graphology, a mark above a letter, showing its pronunciation; cf. diacritic.

acceptable Said of any usage that native speakers feel is possible in a language; cf. appropriate; correctness.

accidence Changes in the form of words signalling different grammatical functions (*walk/walking/walked*); cf. ablaut; morphology.

accommodation Adjustments that people make unconsciously to their speech, influenced by the speech of those they are talking to.

accusative case An inflection that typically identifies the object of a verb; also called **objective case**; cf. case.

acoustic phonetics The branch of phonetics that studies the physical properties of speech sounds; cf. phonetics.

acquisition *see* **language acquisition**

acrolect In creole studies, the most prestigious variety of a language, seen in contrast with other varieties; cf. creole; variety.

acronym A word made up out of the initial letters of a phrase (*laser*, standing for *light **a**mplification by the **s**timulated **e**mission of **r**adiation*).

acrostic A poem or other text in which certain letters in each line make a word.

active **1** In grammar, said of language that a person actually uses – as opposed to language that is known but not used (**active** vs **passive knowledge**). **2** In phonetics, said of an articulator that moves (towards an immobile, **passive**, articulator); cf. articulator.

active voice *see* **voice 2**

adjective A type of word identifying an attribute of a noun (*a **red** chair*), expressing contrasts of degree (*redder, reddest*); cf. degree.

adjunct A less important or omissible element in a grammatical construction (*She ran **quickly***).

adverb A word whose main function is to specify the kind of action expressed by a verb (*He spoke **angrily***); other functions include acting as intensifier (***very** big*) and as a sentence connector (***Moreover**, they laughed*).

adverbial Said of words, phrases, or clauses that function as adverbs.

affective Said of the emotional or attitudinal meaning of an utterance.

affirmative A sentence or verb that has no marker of negation (*He's running*); cf. negation.

affix A meaningful form that is attached to another form, to make a more complex word (**un-** + *kind* + **-ness**); cf. infix; prefix; suffix.

affricate Said of a consonant in which a complete closure of the vocal tract is gradually released, as in the opening and closing sounds of *church*.

agent(ive) A linguistic form expressing who or what is responsible for an action (***The man** laughed; **farmer** 'one who farms').

agreement *see* **concord**

alexia *see* **dyslexia**

alliteration A sequence of words beginning with the same sound, especially as used in poetry.

allonym A name an author assumes that belongs to someone else; cf. pseudonym.

alphabet A writing system in which a set of symbols ('letters') represents the phonemes of a language; cf. dual alphabet.

alphabetism *see* **initialism**

alveolar Said of a consonant in which the tongue makes contact with the bony prominence behind the upper teeth ([t], [n]).

ambiguous Said of a word (**lexical ambiguity**) or sentence (**grammatical** or **structural ambiguity**) which expresses more than one meaning.

amelioration A change of meaning in which a word loses an originally unpleasant sense; cf. deterioration.

anacoluthon An unexpected break in a sentence (*John might – Are you listening?*).

anagram A word or phrase formed by changing the order of letters in another word or phrase.

analogy A change that affects a language when regular forms begin to influence less regular forms (children's use of *wented*, on analogy with other past tenses ending in *-ed*).

ananym A name that has been written backwards.

anapaest/anapest A unit of metre consisting of two light beats followed by a heavy beat, as in *understand*.

anaphora A feature of grammatical structure referring back to something already expressed; the pronoun in *When Mary saw John, **she** waved* is **anaphoric**; cf. cataphora.

animate Said of words (especially nouns) that refer to living things, and not to objects or concepts (**inanimates**); cf. gender.

antecedent A part of a sentence to which some other part grammatically refers; in *This is **the cat** which chased the rat, which* refers back to the antecedent *the cat*.

anthimeria In traditional rhetoric, the use of one word class with the function of another, as when *dog* is used as a verb; now called **conversion**.

anthroponomastics The study of personal names; cf. onomastics.

anticipatory *see* **regressive**

antonym A word that is opposite in meaning to another word (*good/bad, single/married*).

apex The tip of the tongue.

aphasia A language disorder resulting from brain damage, which affects a person's ability to produce or understand grammatical and semantic structure; also called **dysphasia**.

aphesis The loss of an unstressed vowel from the beginning of a word (*'mongst*).

aphorism A succinct statement expressing a general truth (*More haste, less speed*).

apico- Said of a sound using the tip (or apex) of the tongue, e.g. 'apico-dental'.

apocope The omission of a final syllable, sound, or letter in a word (the *f* in *cup o' tea*).

apostrophe **1** In graphology, a punctuation mark which signals the omission of letters or numbers (*n't*) or expresses a grammatical contrast (as in *cat's*). **2** In traditional rhetoric, a figurative expression in which an idea, inanimate object, or absent person is addressed as if present.

appellative A personal name used as an everyday word (*a sandwich*).

applied linguistics The application of the theories, methods, or findings of linguistics to the solution of practical problems.

apposition A series of nouns or noun phrases with the same meaning and grammatical status (*Mr Jones, the baker*).

appropriate Said of any use of language considered to be compatible with a given social situation; cf. correctness.

approximant A consonant in which the organs of articulation approach each other, but without closure or audible friction ([l], [j]); also called **frictionless continuant**.

aptronym A name that fits a person's nature or occupation (*Mr Clever, Mr Smith*).

archaism An old word or phrase no longer in general spoken or written use; cf. obsolescent.

areal linguistics *see* **geographical linguistics**

argot Special vocabulary used by a secretive social group; also called **cant**.

article A word that specifies whether a noun is definite or indefinite (*the/a*); cf. determiner; zero article.

articulation The physiological movements involved in modifying a flow of air to produce speech sounds; cf. manner **1**; place of articulation.

articulator A vocal organ involved in the production of a speech sound.

articulatory phonetics The branch of phonetics that studies the way speech sounds are produced by the vocal organs; cf. phonetics.

ascender A part of a letter that extends above the height of the letter *x*; cf. *x*-height.

aspect The duration or type of temporal activity denoted by a verb, such as the completion or non-completion of an action; cf. perfect.

aspiration Audible breath that may accompany the articulation of a sound, as in *pen* [pʰen].

assimilation The influence exercised by one sound upon the articulation of

another, so that the sounds become more alike (*ten* in *ten pounds* becoming /tem/).

associative meaning The sense associations that are not part of a word's basic meaning (*birthday* ◊ presents, party, etc.).

assonance The recurrent use of the same or similar vowels to achieve a special effect.

asterisked form or **starred form** **1** A usage that is not acceptable or not grammatical (**do had gone*). **2** A form for which there is no written evidence (Indo-European **penkwe* 'five').

asyndeton The omission of conjunctions to achieve an economical form of expression (*They ran with haste, with fear*); cf. conjunction; syndeton.

attested Said of linguistic forms where there is evidence of present or past usage.

attribute **1** In phonetics, an identifiable feature of sound sensation, e.g. pitch, loudness. **2** In semantics, a defining property of the meaning of a word (*round* is an attribute of *ball*).

attributive Said of adjectives or other forms that are modifiers of a noun within the noun phrase (*the **big** table*); contrasts with the **predicative** uses (*The table is **big***).

auditory phonetics A branch of phonetics that studies the way people perceive sound; cf. phonetics.

auxiliary language A language adopted by different speech communities for purposes of communication.

auxiliary verb A verb used along with a lexical verb to make grammatical distinctions (*She **is** going/**might** go*); cf. lexical verb; operator.

B

baby talk **1** A simplified speech style used by adults to children. **2** An immature form of speech used by children.

back Said of sounds made in the back part of the mouth ([h]) or with the back part of the tongue ([k], [o]).

back-formation A process of word formation where a new word is formed by removing an imagined affix from another word (*editor* ◊ *edit*).

back slang A type of secret language in which words are said backwards.

base The minimal form of a word to which affixes can be added, e.g. *sad, car*.

basilect In creole studies, a language variety furthest away from the one that carries most prestige; cf. acrolect; creole; variety.

bidialectal Applied to someone who is proficient in the use of two dialects.

bidialectism An educational policy that recommends the teaching of a nonstand-

ard dialect along with a standard one.

bilabial Said of a consonant made with both lips ([b], [m]).

bilingual Said of a person/community with a command of two languages; cf. monolingual.

bisyllable A word with two syllables.

blade The part of the tongue between the apex and the centre; also called **lamina**.

blend The result of two elements fusing to form a new word or construction (*breakfast + lunch = brunch*).

block language The use of abbreviated structures (especially words or phrases, rather than clauses or sentences) in a restricted communicative context, such as a book title or poster.

body language Communication using body movement, position, and appearance, such as facial expressions, hand gestures, and the mutual bodily orientations of speakers; also called **nonverbal communication**.

borrow To introduce a word (or some other linguistic feature) from one language or dialect into another; vocabulary borrowings are usually known as **loan words**.

bound form A minimal grammatical unit that cannot occur on its own as a word, as in *de-* and *-tion*); also known as a **bound morpheme**; cf. morpheme.

bracketing A way of showing the internal structure of a string of elements, as in ((*The girl*) (*ate*) (*a cake*)).

brackets A pair of correlative punctuation marks which typically signals an included, parenthetic unit; cf. parenthesis **1**.

broad Said of a transcription of speech that shows only the major phonetic contrasts; cf. narrow; phonemic transcription.

byname A supplementary name, added to someone's personal name as an aid to identification (*Eric **the Bold***), and sometimes replacing it completely.

C

caesura A break in the rhythm of a line of poetry.

calligraphy The art of beautiful handwriting.

calque *see* **loan translation**

cant *see* **argot**

capital letter *see* **majuscule**

cardinal number The basic form of a numeral (*one, two, three,* etc.); cf. ordinal number.

cardinal vowels A set of reference points, based on auditory and articulatory criteria, used to identify vowels; cf. vowel.

caret A diacritic (∧) used to indicate that something needs to be inserted in a line of manuscript or typed text; cf. diacritic.

caretaker speech The speech of adults when they talk to children; also called **caregiver speech** or **motherese**.

case In an inflecting language, the form of a noun, adjective, or pronoun, showing its grammatical relationship to other words; cf. inflection **1**.

catachresis *see* **malapropism**

catalect Any part of an author's literary work seen as separate from the rest.

cataphora A feature of grammatical structure that refers forward to another unit; (in *John said **this:**, the pronoun is **cataphoric**); cf. anaphora.

cavity An anatomically defined chamber in the vocal tract, e.g. the oral and nasal cavities.

centre/center **1** In phonetics, the top part of the tongue, between front and back, involved in the production of **central** sounds. **2** *see* **syllable**

centring diphthong A diphthong whose second element involves a movement towards the centre of the vowel area; cf. centre **1**; diphthong.

channel A medium selected for communication (e.g. speech, writing).

character A graphic sign used in a writing system, especially one that is not part of an alphabet; cf. logogram.

chiasmus A balanced pattern of sentence sequence in which elements of the first sentence are reversed in the second.

chirography The study of handwriting forms and styles.

chronogram A phrase or sentence in which letters that are also Roman numerals (e.g. C, X) combine to form a date.

circumlocution The use of more words than is necessary to express a meaning.

citation form The form of a linguistic unit when this is produced in isolation for purposes of discussion.

citation slip In lexicography, a written example of a word's usage, on which a dictionary entry will eventually be based.

class *see* **word class**

clause A structural unit smaller than a sentence but larger than phrases or words; cf. dependent; main clause.

clear l A type of lateral sound which has a resonance similar to that of a front vowel of an [i] quality (*leak*); contrasts with a **dark l**, where the resonance is that of a back vowel with [u] quality (*pool*); cf. lateral.

cleft sentence A sentence in which a single clause has been split into two sections, each with its own verb (*It was Mary who arrived*).

cliché An expression which has become so over-used that it no longer conveys much meaning, and is criticized (*a fate worse than death*).

click A sound produced using the velaric air-stream mechanism, as in the noise of disapproval (conventionally written *tsk* or *tut*); cf. velaric.

clipping A process of word formation in which a new word is produced by shortening (*examination* ◊ *exam*); also called **reduction**.

close (adjective) Said of a vowel made with the tongue in the highest position possible without causing audible friction (e.g. [i], [u]); vowels a degree lower are **half/mid-close**; cf. open **3**.

closed **1** In grammar, said of any word class whose membership is limited to a small number of items, e.g. pronouns, conjunctions; cf. open **1**. **2** In phonology, said of a syllable ending in a consonant; cf. open **2**.

closing diphthong A diphthong whose second element involves a movement towards a high vowel position, such as [u]; cf. close; diphthong

closure A contact made between vocal organs in order to produce a speech sound; cf. occlusion.

cluster A series of adjacent consonants occurring at the beginning or end of a syllable (*stray, books*).

coalescence The fusing of originally distinct linguistic units (*would you* in colloquial speech, where the /d/ at the end of *would* and the /j/ at the beginning of *you* coalesce as /dʒ/).

coda Consonants which follow the nucleus of a syllable (*cot, jump*); cf. syllable.

code **1** Any system of signals used for sending messages, often in secret form. **2** A language, or variety of language; cf. variety.

code mixing In bilingual speech, the transfer of linguistic elements from one language into another.

code switching The use by a speaker of more than one language, dialect, or variety during a conversation; cf. dialect; variety.

codify To provide a systematic account of a language (especially of its grammar and vocabulary).

cognitive meaning *see* **denotation**

coherence The underlying functional or logical connectedness of a use of language; contrasts with **incoherence**.

cohesion The formal linkage between the elements of a discourse or text (the pronoun is **cohesive** in *The man left. **He** …*).

co-hyponym *see* **hyponymy**

coinage *see* **neologism**

collective noun A noun that denotes a group of entities (*army, government*).

collocation The habitual co-occurrence (or mutual selection) of lexical items; cf. node.

colon A punctuation mark whose typical function is to express that what follows in the sentence is an expansion of what has preceded.

comma A punctuation mark whose several functions include the separation of a series of clauses or words, and the marking of included units in a sentence.

command *see* **directive**

comment *see* **topic**

comment clause A clause that adds a parenthetic remark to another clause (*The answer, **you see**, is complicated*); cf. clause.

common core The range of linguistic features which would be used and understood by all speakers, regardless of their regional or social background.

common noun A noun that refers to a class of objects or concepts (*chair, beauty*); cf. proper name/noun.

communication The transmission and reception of information between a signaller and a receiver.

communicative competence A person's awareness of the rules governing the appropriate use of language in social situations.

comparative *see* **degree**

comparative linguistics The study of the historical relationship between languages, especially those believed to have a common historical origin; also often called **comparative philology**, or simply **philology**.

complement A clause element that completes what is said about some other element, such as the subject (*That cloud formation looks **strange***); cf. clause.

complex preposition A preposition consisting of more than one word, especially one where a noun or noun phrase is both preceded and followed by single prepositions (*on account of*); cf. preposition.

complex sentence A sentence consisting of more than one clause (especially if including a dependent clause); cf. clause; sentence.

compound Said of a linguistic unit composed of elements that can function separately elsewhere, e.g. a compound word/sentence; usually contrasts with **simple**.

compound-complex sentence In traditional grammar, a sentence which includes both coordinate and subordinate clauses; cf. clause; sentence.

computer language *see* **language 2**

concord A grammatical relationship in which the form of one element requires the corresponding form of another (*She eats*); also called **agreement**.

concordance An ordered list of the words used in a particular text or corpus.

concrete Said of nouns that refer to physical entities (*book, train*); contrasts with **abstract**, which applies to nouns lacking physical reference (*idea, certainty*).

conditional 1 Said of a clause that expresses hypothesis or condition (*If it rains, you'll get wet*). **2** Said of a verb form that expresses hypothetical meaning (*I would walk*).

conjugation In an inflecting language, a set of verbs that show the same inflections (they **conjugate** in the same way); cf. inflection.

conjunct An adverb with a chiefly connecting function, e.g. *however*; also called a **conjunctive adverb**; cf. adverb.

conjunction A word that connects words or other constructions (*cat **and** dog*); classified into **coordinating** (e.g. *and*) and **subordinating** (e.g. *because*) types.

connective/connector An item whose function is to link linguistic units, such as conjunctions and certain adverbs (*moreover*); cf. adverb; conjunction.

connotation The personal or emotional associations aroused by words; cf. denotation.

consonance The repetition of sounds in the same position in a sequence of words; contrasts with **dissonance**.

consonant A speech sound that functions at the margins of syllables, produced when the vocal tract is either blocked or so restricted that there is audible friction ([k], [s], etc.); cf. vowel; semi-vowel.

constituent A linguistic unit that is an element of a larger construction.

constriction A narrowing made in the vocal tract, in order to produce a speech sound.

contact Said of languages or dialects in close geographical or social proximity, which thus influence each other (**contact languages**).

content word A type of word that has an independent, 'dictionary' meaning (*chair, run*); also called a **lexical word**; cf. function word.

context 1 The linguistic environment of an element. **2** The non-linguistic situation in which language is used.

continuant A speech sound made with an incomplete closure of the vocal tract (/l/, /e/, /f/).

continuous *see* **progressive 1**

contour A distinctive sequence of prosodic features (especially tones); also called an **intonation** or **pitch contour**.

contraction 1 A shortened linguistic form attached to an adjacent form (*I'm*), or a fusion of forms. **2** The elision of syllables to keep a line's metre regular; cf. elision.

contrast Any formal difference that serves to distinguish meanings in a language; **contrastive** differences are also known as **distinctive**, **functional**, or **significant**.

contrastive stress Extra emphasis given to a word, in order to draw attention to its meaning (*John bought a **red** car*).

convergence A process of linguistic change in which dialects or accents become more like each other; contrasts with **divergence**.

conversational analysis The analysis of the methods people use to engage in conversation and other forms of social interaction involving speech.

conversational maxims General principles thought to underline the efficient use of a language, e.g. speakers should be relevant and clear; cf. cooperative principle.

converseness A type of oppositeness of meaning, such that one word presupposes the other (*buy/sell*).

conversion A type of word formation in which an item changes its word class without the addition of an affix (*smell* = verb/noun).

cooperative principle A tacit agreement between speakers to follow the same set of conventions ('maxims') when communicating; cf. conversational maxims.

coordinate Said of clauses displaying coordination.

coordination The linking of linguistic units that have the same grammatical status, e.g. two noun phrases (**the cat** and **the dog**); cf. conjunction.

coordinator A conjunction used in coordination, such as *and* or *or*.

copula A verb whose main role is to link other elements of the clause (*It **is** ready*); also called a **linking verb**.

co-reference The use of elements that can be interpreted only by referring to another element in a text.

corpus A collection of language data brought together for linguistic analysis.

correctness An absolute standard of language use deriving from the rules of institutions (e.g. language academies) or respected publications (e.g. dictionaries); cf. appropriate.

correlative Said of constructions using a pair of connecting words (*either/or*).

countable Said of nouns denoting separable entities, as shown by their use with such forms as *a* (*dog, chair*); **count(able)** nouns contrast with **uncountable/non-count** (or **mass**) nouns.

creole A pidgin language that has become the mother tongue of a speech community (through a process of **creolization**).

cryptology The study of how secret messages (**cryptograms**) are constructed, using codes and ciphers (**cryptography**), and then deciphered or decoded (**cryptanalysis**).

cursive A form of handwriting in which separate characters in a sequence have been joined in a series of rounded, flowing strokes.

D

dactyl A unit of rhythm in poetic metre, consisting of one heavy beat followed by two light beats.

dactylology *see* **finger spelling**

dagger *see* **obelisk**

dangling participle The use of a participle, or a phrase introduced by a participle, which has an unclear or ambiguous relationship to the rest of the sentence (*While reading a book, the cat made me jump*); also called a **misrelated participle**; cf. participle.

dark *l* *see* **clear *l***

dash A punctuation mark which typically signals an included unit – such as this one – especially in informal writing.

dative case In inflecting languages, a form that typically expresses an indirect object relationship equivalent to English *I gave the letter **to the girl***; cf. direct object.

decibel A unit (dB) for measuring the relative intensity of sounds, especially in the assessment of hearing loss.

declarative A grammatical construction used in expressing a statement (*The dog barked*); cf. interrogative; statement.

declension In an inflecting language, a set of nouns, adjectives, or pronouns that show the same inflections (they **decline** in the same way); cf. inflection.

decline *see* **declension**

decode 1 To use the brain to interpret an incoming linguistic signal. **2** To convert a secret message into intelligible language; cf. cryptology.

decreolization Change in a creole that makes it more like the standard language of an area; cf. creole.

defective Said of words that do not follow all the rules of the class to which they belong, such as auxiliary verbs, which lack the usual verb inflections.

defining *see* **restrictive**

defining vocabulary A core set of words used to define other words.

definite Said of a specific, identifiable entity or class of entities (*the* car); contrasts with **indefinite** (*a* car); cf. article.

degree A contrast of comparison in adverbs or adjectives; usually identified as **positive** (*big*), **comparative** (*bigger*), and **superlative** (*biggest*).

deixis Features of language that refer directly to the personal, temporal, or locational characteristics of a situation (**deictic forms**) (e.g. *you*, *now*, *here*).

deletion Omitting an element of sentence structure (e.g. *that* in *I said he was ready*).

demonstrative Applied to forms whose function is to distinguish one item from other members of the same class (*this/that*).

denotation The objective ('dictionary') relationship between a word and the reality to which it refers; also called **cognitive/referential** meaning; cf. connotation.

dental Said of a consonant made by the apex and rims of tongue against the teeth.

dependent Said of any element whose form or function is determined by another part of the sentence (in *the red car*, the article and adjective **depend** on the noun); also called **subordinate.**

derivation **1** A major process of word formation, especially using affixes to produce new words (*act*◊ *action*); cf. inflection. **2** The origins or historical development of a language form.

descender A part of a letter that extends below the depth of the letter *x*; cf. *x*-height.

description An objective and systematic account of the patterns and use of a language or variety; cf. prescription.

deterioration A change of meaning in which a word acquires a negative evaluation; also called **pejoration**; cf. amelioration.

determiner An item that co-occurs with a noun to express such meanings as number or quantity (*the, some, each*); cf. article; postdeterminer; predeterminer.

deviance Failure to conform to the rules of the language.

devoiced Said of a sound in which the normal amount of vocal fold vibration (voice) has been reduced; cf. voice **1**.

diachronic *see* **historical linguistics; synchronic**

diacritic A mark added to a symbol to alter its pronunciation value; cf. accent **3**; caret.

diagramming *see* **parsing**

dialect A language variety in which use of grammar and vocabulary identifies the regional or social background of the user; cf. accent **1**; dialectology.

dialect atlas *see* **linguistic atlas**

dialect chain *see* **dialect continuum**

dialect continuum A chain of dialects spoken throughout an area, whose endpoints are not mutually intelligible; also called a **dialect chain.**

dialectology The study of (especially regional) dialects; also called **dialect geography**.

dialogue *see* **monologue**

diction The effective choice of words, especially the vocabulary used by a poet or other writer.

dieresis/diaeresis A diacritic mark (¨) placed over a letter which indicates a change in vowel quality (*naïve*); also called an **umlaut**; cf. diacritic.

diffusion The increased use of a language, or a feature of a language, in a given area over a period of time.

digram A sequence of two adjacent letters; cf. digraph.

digraph **1** A graphic unit in which two symbols have combined to function as one (*encyclopædia*). **2** Any sequence of two letters pronounced as a single sound (*ship, wood*).

dimeter A line of verse containing two units of rhythm (feet).

diminutive An affix with the general meaning of 'little' (*-let*).

diphthong A vowel in which there is a perceptible change in quality during a syllable (*time, road*); cf. monophthong; pure vowel; triphthong.

diphthongization The adding of a diphthongal quality to what was formerly a pure vowel; cf. vowel.

directive An utterance intended to get other people to do (or not do) something (*Sit down*); also called a **command.**

direct object A clause element immediately affected by the action of the verb (*She hit him*); contrasts with a less directly affected (**indirect**) object (*I gave John a letter*).

direct speech The actual utterance spoken by a person; cf. indirect speech.

discontinuous The splitting of a grammatical construction by the insertion of another unit (*Switch the light on*).

discourse A continuous stretch of (especially spoken) language longer than a sentence.

discourse analysis The study of patterns of linguistic organization in discourses; cf. discourse.

disjunction An alternative or contrastive relationship between elements in a sentence (*Either we're early or the bus is late*).

dissimilation The influence sound segments have on each other, so that they become less alike.

dissonance The use of sounds to convey unpleasant effects; cf. consonance.

distinctive Said of a feature capable of making a difference of meaning between otherwise identical forms, e.g. vocal fold vibration; cf. contrast; vocal folds.

distribution The total set of linguistic environments in which an element of language (e.g. a sound or word) can occur.

disyllable A word of two syllables.

ditransitive Said of verbs that take two objects (*give, show*).

divergence *see* **convergence**

dorsal Said of sounds made with the back (**dorsum**) of the tongue ([k], [g]).

double negative A construction in which more than one negative word is used within the same clause (*I didn't say nothing*).

doublet A type of word game in which a series of single-letter substitutions links pairs of words.

dual A grammatical contrast of number in some languages, referring to 'two of'.

dual alphabet The use of capital and small letters in a single system.

dual gender Said of nouns which can refer to either male or female (*artist, cook*).

duration The length of time involved in the articulation of a sound or syllable; cf. long.

dynamic A type of verb that expresses activities and changes of state, allowing such forms as the progressive (*He's running*); cf. state.

dyslexia A language disturbance that affects the ability to read; also sometimes called **alexia.**

dysphasia *see* **aphasia**

dysphemism A use of language that emphasizes unpleasantness (*a horrible dirty day*); cf. euphemism.

E

ear training A technique in phonetics which trains a person's ability to identify speech sounds.

echo utterance A type of sentence which repeats, in whole or in part, what has just been said by another speaker.

-ed form An abbreviated way of referring to the simple past tense form of verbs; cf. past tense.

electropalatograph An instrument which records the contacts made between the tongue and the palate during speech.

elicit To obtain utterances or linguistic judgments from informants.

elision The omission of sounds in connected speech (*bacon' n' eggs*).

ellipsis The omission of part of a sentence (e.g. for economy or emphasis), where the missing element is understood from the context (*A: Where's the book? B: On the table*).

elocution The art of speech training to produce effective public speaking.

embedding Inserting one grammatical unit within another (*The man who left was my uncle*).

emotive meaning The emotional content of a use of language.

empty word A meaningless word that expresses a grammatical relationship (*It's today he goes*); also called a **prop word**; cf. content word.

encode **1** To give linguistic shape to a meaning, as part of communication. **2** To convert a message from one system of signals into another (especially for secrecy); cf. decode.

-en form An abbreviated way of referring to the past participle form of the verb; cf. participle.

enjamb(e)ment The running on of a sentence between two couplets of verse without pause.

epenthesis The insertion of an extra (**epenthetic**) sound in the middle of a word.

epigram A short, witty statement, in verse or prose.

epigraph **1** An inscription on a stone, buildings, coins, etc. **2** A phrase or quotation above a section in a book or on the title page.

epigraphy The study of inscriptions, especially their interpretation in ancient times.

epithet Any item that characterizes a noun and is regularly associated with it (*Ethelred the Unready*).

eponym The name of a person after whom something, e.g. a place, a book title, is named (*Washington, Hamlet*).

equative A clause which relates two elements that are identical in their reference (*Mr Jones is a butcher*).

ethnography of communication The study of language in relation to the social and cultural variables that influence human interaction.

ethnolinguistics The study of language in relation to ethnic groups and behaviour.

etymological fallacy The view that an earlier (or the oldest) meaning of a word is the correct one.

etymology The study of the origins and history of the form and meaning of words.

euphemism The use of a vague or indirect expression in place of one that is unpleasant or offensive (*pass away* for *die*); cf. dysphemism.

euphony A pleasing sequence of sounds.

exclamation An emotional expression marked by a strong intonation in speech or by an exclamation point in writing (*Good grief!*); cf. command; question; statement.

exclusive Said of a first person pronoun (*we*) when it does not include the person being addressed; cf. inclusive.

exegesis An interpretation of a text, especially of a biblical kind.

existential A sentence emphasizing the idea of existence (*There is a book on the table*).

expansion 1 In grammar, the process of adding new elements to a construction, without its basic structure being affected. 2 In child language studies, an adult response to a child which adds grammatical elements that the child has omitted.

experimental phonetics The use of instrumentation and experimental techniques to investigate the properties of speech sounds; also called **instrumental phonetics**.

expletive An exclamatory word or phrase, usually obscene or profane.

expression 1 Any string of elements treated as a unit for analysis, e.g. a sentence, an idiom. 2 All aspects of linguistic form (as opposed to meaning).

expressive 1 Said of a use of language that displays or affects a person's emotions. 2 Said of disorders of language production, e.g. 'expressive aphasia'.

extension In historical linguistics, widening the meaning of a word.

extralinguistic Said of anything (other than language) to which language can relate.

extraposition Moving an element to a position at one end of a sentence (*Working here is nice ◊ It's nice working here*).

eye dialect A way of spelling words that suggests a regional or social way of talking (*Thankee koindly, zur*).

eye rhyme A pair of words that seem to rhyme from the spelling, but have different pronunciations (*come/home*).

F

family A set of languages that derive from a common ancestor (parent) language, and are represented as a **family tree**.

feedback 1 The ongoing reaction speakers receive from their listeners, which helps them to evaluate the efficiency of their communication. 2 The information speakers obtain by monitoring their own speech activity.

feet *see* **foot**

feminine *see* **gender**

field *see* **semantic field**

figurative Said of an expressive use of language when words are used in a non-literal way to suggest illuminating comparisons and resemblances (**figures of speech**); cf. literal; metaphor; oxymoron; simile.

filled pause A vocal hesitation (*erm*).

finger spelling Signing in which each letter of the alphabet is given its own sign; also called **dactylology**.

finite A form of a verb that can occur on its own in a main clause and permits variations in tense, number, and mood (*They ran, He is running*); contrasts with **nonfinite**.

first language The language first acquired as a child (**mother tongue, native language**), or preferred in a multilingual situation.

first person *see* **person**

fixed expression *see* **idiom**

flap A consonant produced by a single rapid contact between two organs of articulation, e.g. the tongue tip movement [r] in *very*.

fluency Smooth, rapid, effortless use of language.

flyting An exchange of curses or personal abuse in verse form.

focal area A region where dialect forms are relatively homogeneous and tend to influence the forms used in adjoining areas; cf. dialect.

focus An element in a sentence to which the speaker wishes to draw special attention (*It was **John** who wrote to me*); cf. presupposition.

folk etymology Altering an unfamiliar word to make it more familiar (*asparagus ◊ sparrow-grass*); also called **popular etymology**.

font or **fount** A complete set of type of a particular design and size.

foot A basic unit of rhythm, especially used in describing poetic metre.

foregrounding Any departure from a linguistic or socially accepted norm, which highlights an element of language.

foreign language A language which is not the mother tongue of a speaker, especially one that has no offical status in a country; cf. second language.

forensic linguistics The use of linguistic techniques to investigate crimes in which language data constitute part of the evidence.

form 1 The outward appearance or structure of language, as opposed to its function, meaning, or social use (**formal** vs notional). 2 The variations in which a linguistic unit can appear (*walk, walks*, etc. are different **forms** of the verb *walk*).

formal *see* **form 1; formality**

formality A scale of language use, relating to situations that are socially careful or correct (**formal**) or otherwise (**informal**).

formant A concentration of acoustic energy, especially distinctive in vowels and voiced sounds.

form class A set of items that display similar or identical grammatical features; cf. word class.

formulaic Said of a sentence that does not permit the usual range of grammatical variation (*Many happy returns*); also called **fossilized** or **stereotyped** sentences, or **routines.**

form word *see* **function word**

fortis Said of consonants made with relatively strong muscular effort and breath force ([f], [p]); cf. lenis.

fossilized Said of any construction that lacks productivity, e.g. idioms (*spick and span*), formulaic utterances (*So be it!*); cf. productivity 2.

free form A minimal grammatical unit that can be used as a word without additional elements; also known as a **free morpheme**; cf. bound form; morpheme.

fricative Said of a consonant made when two vocal organs come so close together that the air moving between them produces audible friction ([f], [z]); also called a **spirant.**

frictionless continuant *see* **approximant**

front Said of sounds made in the front part of the mouth or by the front part (blade) of the tongue ([i] , [t]); cf. back; centre 1.

fronting 1 In phonetics, articulation of a sound further forward in the mouth than is normal. 2 In grammar, moving a constituent from the middle or end of a sentence to the front (***Smith** his name was*).

frozen expression *see* **idiom**

full stop *see* **point**

full verb *see* **lexical verb**

function 1 The relationship between a linguistic form and the other elements of the system in which it is used, e.g. a noun as subject or object of a clause. 2 The role language plays in communication (e.g. to express ideas, attitudes) or in particular social situations (e.g. religious, legal).

functional change 1 In historical linguistics, an alteration in the role of a linguistic feature. 2 In grammar, the use of a word in different grammatical roles (***round** the corner, a **round** table*).

function word A word whose role is largely or wholly to express a grammatical relationship (*to, a*); also called a **form/grammatical/structural word** or **functor**.

functor *see* **function word**

fundamental frequency The lowest frequency component in a complex sound wave, of particular importance in determining a sound's pitch.

futhork/futhark The runic alphabet.

G

gender A way of grouping words into different formal classes, using such labels as **masculine, feminine, neuter, animate**.

generative Said of a grammar that uses a set of formal rules to define the membership of (**generate**) the infinite set of grammatical sentences in a language.

generic A word or sentence that refers to a class of entities (*the Chinese, the rich*).

genitive An inflection that expresses such meanings as possession and origin (*girl's bag, man's story*); also applied to related structures (*the cover of the book*).

genre An identifiable category of artistic (in this book, literary) composition, e.g. the novel.

geographical linguistics The study of languages and dialects in terms of their regional distribution; also called **areal linguistics** or **linguistic geography**.

gerund A noun derived from a verb (a 'verbal noun'), especially as found in Latin grammar, or in grammars based on Latin (*amandum* 'loving').

gerundive An adjective derived from a verb (a 'verbal adjective'), especially as found in Latin grammar, or in grammars based on Latin (*amandus* 'lovable').

ghost form A word originating in an error during the copying, analysing, or learning of a language, which does not exist in the original language.

given *see* **topic**

glide 1 A transitional sound made as the vocal organs move towards (**on-glide**) or away from (**off-glide**) an articulation ([j] in *puny* [pʲuːni]). 2 A vowel where there is an audible change of quality (diphthong, triphthong). 3 A tone involving a change of pitch level.

glossary An alphabetical list of the terms used in a special field.

glossolalia Speaking in tongues, as practised by certain religious groups.

glottal Said of sounds made in the larynx resulting from the closure or narrowing of the glottis, e.g. whisper, creaky.

glottalization An articulation involving a simultaneous glottal constriction.

glottal stop The audible release of a closure at the glottis, e.g. *bottle* as [bɒʔl]).

glottis The aperture between the vocal folds.

goal The entity affected by the action of a verb (*The man kicked the ball*); also called **patient** or **recipient**.

gradable Said of a word (especially an adjective) that can be compared or intensified (*big ◊ very big, bigger*).

gradation *see* **ablaut**

grammar 1 The study of sentence structure, especially with reference to syntax and morphology, often presented as a textbook or manual. 2 A systematic account of the rules governing language in general, or specific languages, including semantics, phonology, and often pragmatics.

grammatical 1 Pertaining to grammar. 2 Said of constructions that conform to the rules of a grammar; those that do not are **ungrammatical.**

grammatical word *see* **function word**

graph The smallest discrete segment in a stretch of writing or print (t, T, *t*, etc.).

grapheme The smallest contrastive unit in the writing system of a language (*t, e, ;, ?*); cf. **contrast**.

graphemics The study of graphemes.

graphetics The study of the visual properties of written or printed language.

graphology 1 The (study of the) writing system of a language. 2 The analysis of handwriting to discover the writer's character.

grid game A visual word game which operates on the principle of building up words on a predetermined grid, as in crossword puzzles.

groove A type of fricative consonant produced when the tongue is slightly hollowed along its central line ([s], [ʃ], etc.)

group *see* **phrase**

H

habitual Said of a form (especially a verb or adverb) expressing repetition of an action (*often*).

half-close/-open *see* **close**; **open 3.**

half-uncial *see* **uncial**

hard palate *see* **palate**

head The main element in a phrase on which other elements depend and which controls the function of the phrase as a whole (*All the new **books** from the library are on the table*).

headword The item that occurs at the beginning of a dictionary entry.

heterographs Words that have the same meaning or pronunciation, but differ in spelling (*bear* vs *bare*).

heteronyms Words that differ in meaning but are identical in either pronunciation or spelling (*threw* vs *through*).

hexameter A line of verse containing six units of rhythm (feet).

hiatus 1 The use of adjacent vowels in different syllables. 2 A break in a sentence that leaves it incomplete.

hierarchy A classification of linguistic units into a series of successively subordinate levels, especially an analysis of sentences into clauses, phrases, words, and morphemes.

high 1 Said of vowels (and sometimes consonants) made by raising the tongue towards the roof of the mouth ([i], [k]). 2 Said of tones that use a relatively high level of pitch range.

historical linguistics The study of the development of language and languages over time; also called **diachronic linguistics** or (with different emphasis) **comparative philology.**

historic(al) present The use of a present tense form while narrating events which happened in the past (*Last week, I'm walking into town …*).

hold To maintain a single position of the vocal organs for a period of time.

holograph A document that is entirely written in the handwriting of its author.

holophrase A grammatically unstructured utterance, usually consisting of a single word, typical of the earliest stage of language learning in children (*dada, allgone*).

homographs Words with the same spelling but different meanings (*wind* = 'air' vs *wind* = 'turn').

homonyms Words with the same form but different meanings (*ear* = 'corn' vs *ear* = 'body part').

homophones Words with the same pronunciation but different meanings (*rode/rowed*).

homorganic Said of sounds made at the same place of articulation ([p], [b], [m]).

hybrid A word composed of elements from different languages (*television*, from Greek and Latin).

hydronymy The study of the names of rivers, lakes, etc.

hyperbole Emphatic exaggeration (*There were millions of people in the cinema*).

hypercorrection A linguistic form that goes beyond the norm of a target variety, because of the speaker's desire to be correct; also called **hyperurbanism**; **overcorrection**.

hypercreolization The development of a kind of creole that is a reaction away from the standard language.

hypernym *see* **hyponymy**

hyperurbanism *see* **hypercorrection**

hyphen A punctuation mark which indicates a division within a word, used chiefly at the end of a line of print or to mark the parts of a complex word.

hypocoristic A pet name (*honey, Bill*).

hyponymy The relationship between specific and general words, when the former is included in the latter (*cat* is a **hyponym** of *animal; animal* is a **hypernym** of *cat;* and *cat, dog,* and *elephant* are **co-hyponyms**).

hypostatize To speak of an abstract quality as if it were human.

hypotaxis The linking of a dependent (**hypotactic**) clause to another part of the sentence using conjunctions (*The boy left when the bell rang*); cf. parataxis.

I

iamb A unit of metre consisting of an unstressed syllable followed by a stressed syllable (*to be*).

iconic Said of signals whose physical form corresponds to features of the entities to which they refer, as in onomatopoeia (*cuckoo*).

ictus The stressed syllable in a unit of metre; cf. metre.

ideogram A symbol used in a writing system to represent a whole word or concept; also called an **ideograph**.

idiolect The linguistic system of an individual speaker.

idiom A sequence of words that is a unit of meaning (*kick the bucket* = 'die'); also called a **fixed** or **frozen expression**.

imagery 1 The use of metaphor, simile, and other figurative language, especially in a literary context. 2 Language that produces clear or vivid mental pictures.

imitation The copying of linguistic behaviour, especially while learning a language.

imperative A grammatical mood expressing a command (*Look!*).

imperfect A tense form expressing such meanings as past duration and continuity, as in Latin *amabam* 'I was loving/used to love'.

impersonal Said of constructions or verbs with an unspecified agent (*It's raining*); cf. agent.

inanimate *see* **animate**

inclusive Said of a first person pronoun that refers to both the speaker and someone else, as when *we* means 'me and you'; cf. exclusive.

incoherence *see* **coherence**

incompatibility A feature of mutually defining items where the choice of one excludes the use of the others (*The ink is **red*** vs *The ink is **blue***).

indefinite *see* **definite**

indention Beginning a line of writing or print further in from the margins than the rest of the passage; also called **indentation**.

independent clause *see* **main clause**

indexical Said of features of speech or writing (especially voice quality) that reveal the personal characteristics of the user, e.g. age, sex.

indicative A grammatical mood that expresses objective statements (*My car is new*).

indirect object *see* **direct object**

indirect question A question as expressed in indirect speech (*He asked if she was in*).

indirect speech A construction in which the speaker's words are made subordinate to a verb of 'saying' (*She replied that she had*); also called **reported speech**; cf. direct speech.

indirect speech act An utterance whose linguistic form does not directly reflect its communicative purpose (e.g. using *It's cold in here* to mean 'Close the window').

inferior *see* **subscript**

infinitive A nonfinite form of the verb, which in many languages acts as the basic form, as in *run, jump*); cf. finite.

infix An affix added within a root; cf. affix.

inflection/inflexion 1 In grammar, an affix that signals a grammatical relationship, e.g. case, tense (*girl's, walked*). 2 In phonetics, change in voice pitch during speech.

informal *see* **formality**

informant Someone who acts as a source of data for linguistic analysis.

-ing form An abbreviated way of referring to the form of a verb when it ends in *-ing* (*running*); cf. progressive.

initialism A word made of initial letters, each being pronounced (*VIP*); also called **alphabetism**.

instrumental phonetics *see* **experimental phonetics**

intensifier A word or phrase that adds force or emphasis (***very** good, **awfully** pretty*).

interdental A consonant made by the tip of the tongue between the teeth ([θ], [ð]).

interjection A class of words with emotive meaning, which do not form grammatical relationships with other clauses (*Gosh!, Yuk!*).

internal evidence Linguistic features in a text that indicate when the work was written.

internal rhyme The rhyming of words within lines of verse.

interrogative A type of sentence or verb form used in the expression of questions (*Who is he?, Are they there?*); cf. declarative.

interrogative word A word used at the beginning of a clause to mark it as a question (***Who** is here?*).

intervocalic A consonant used between two vowels (/p/ in *apart*).

intonation The contrastive use of pitch in speech.

intonation contour *see* **tone group**

intransitive Said of a verb or sentence that cannot take a direct object (*she's going*); cf. transitive.

intrusion The use of sounds in connected speech that do not appear when the words or syllables are heard in isolation, e.g. **intrusive *r*** between vowels (as in *law (r) and order*).

intuition A person's instinctive knowledge of language, which decides whether sentences are acceptable and how they can be interrelated.

invariable word A word that does not undergo any change in structure (*under, but*); cf. variable word.

inversion A reversed sequence of elements (*He is going ↻ Is he going?*).

inverted commas *see* **quotation marks**

irony Language that expresses a meaning other than that literally conveyed by the words (*That's marvellous*, said of poor work).

irregular Said of a linguistic form that is an exception to a pattern stated in a rule.

isochrony/isochronism A rhythmic pattern in which stressed syllables fall at roughly regular intervals (are **stress-timed**) throughout an utterance; cf. stress.

isogloss A line on a map showing the boundary of an area in which a linguistic feature is used.

italic A form of sloped cursive lettering, now used in print with a wide range of functions, such as the marking of titles and cited forms (e.g. *italics*).

J

jargon 1 The technical language of a special field. **2** The obscure use of specialized language.

juncture Phonetic boundary features separating units of grammar, e.g. certain features of pitch, duration, or pause which separate words or sentences.

justification The spacing of words and letters within a line of printed text so that all full lines in a column have an even margin to both left and right (the text is **justified**); text which lacks this evenness is **unjustified**.

K

kenning In the study of Old English vocabulary, a vivid figurative description of an aspect of experience, often expressed as a compound word.

knowledge about language (KAL) In British educational linguistics, the fostering of an increased awareness of the structure and function of spoken and written language by children as they move through the school curriculum; cf. language arts.

koiné The spoken language of a locality that has become a standard language.

L

labial The active use of one or both lips in the articulation of a sound ([f] , [u]).

labialization Rounding the lips while making a speech sound.

labio-dental Said of a consonant in which one lip actively contacts the teeth ([f] , [v]).

labio-velar A speech sound made at the velum with simultaneous lip rounding ([w] , [u]); cf. palate.

lamina *see* **blade; laminal**

laminal Said of a consonant made with the blade (or lamina) of the tongue in contact with the upper lip, teeth, or alveolar ridge ([s], [t]).

language 1 The systematic, conventional use of sounds, signs, or written symbols in a human society for communication and self-expression. **2** A specially devised system of symbols for programming and interacting with computers.

language acquisition 1 The process of learning a first language in children. **2** The analogous process of gaining a foreign or second language.

language arts The areas of an educational curriculum which involve the mastery of skills related to language – chiefly speaking, listening, reading, and writing, as well as related notions such as spelling and nonverbal communication; cf. language awareness.

language awareness An informed, sensitive, and critical response to the use of language by oneself and others; cf. knowledge about language.

language change Change within a language over a period of time; cf. language shift.

language contact A situation of prolonged association between the speakers of different languages.

language delay The failure of a child to learn spoken language (or an aspect of spoken language) at a normal rate.

language disorder A serious abnormality in the system underlying the use of language, whether by children or adults; cf. aphasia; dyslexia.

language loyalty The personal attachment to a language that leads to its continued use in a country where other languages are dominant.

language maintenance The continued use of and support for a language in a bilingual or multilingual community.

language pathologist/therapist *see* **speech and language pathologist/ therapist**

language planning Official intentions and policies affecting language use in a country.

language shift A permanent change in a person's choice of language for everyday purposes (especially as a result of immigrant movement).

larynx The part of the trachea containing the vocal folds; cf. vocal folds.

lateral Said of a consonant in which air escapes around one or both sides of a closure made in the mouth, as in the various kinds of *l* sound; cf. clear *l*; dark *l*.

latinate Applied to any grammar that is based on the terms and categories used in Classical Latin grammar.

law A statement of the predictable relationships (especially in the use of sounds) between different languages or states of a language; cf. sound law.

lax *see* **tension**

leading The white space between lines of type on a page.

lect Any variety of a language that has a functional identity within a speech community, e.g. a regional or social variety.

length *see* **duration**

lenis Said of consonants made with a relatively weak degree of muscular effort and breath force ([b] , [v]); cf. fortis.

lenition A relaxation of muscular effort during articulation.

lento Said of speech produced slowly or with careful articulation.

letter A symbol used in an alphabetic system of writing to represent one or more speech sounds; cf. alphabet; majuscule.

level 1 A major dimension of the structural organization of language, capable of

independent study, e.g. phonology, syntax. **2** In grammar, one of a series of structural layers within a sentence (clause, phrase, word, etc.); also called **rank**. **3** In phonology, a degree of pitch height or loudness during speech. **4** In stylistics, a mode of expression felt to suit a type of social situation (formal, intimate, etc.).

lexeme The smallest contrastive unit in a semantic system (*run, cat, switch on*); also called **lexical item**.

lexical diffusion The gradual spread of a linguistic change through a language.

lexical item *see* **lexeme**

lexical field *see* **semantic field**

lexical verb A verb expressing an action, event, or state; also called a **full** or **main** verb; cf. auxiliary verb.

lexical word *see* **content word**

lexicography The art and science of dictionary-making (carried on by **lexicographers**).

lexicology The study of the history and present state of a language's vocabulary (carried on by **lexicologists**).

lexicon The vocabulary of a language, especially in dictionary form; also called **lexis**.

lexis *see* **lexicon**

liaison The pronunciation of a consonant at the end of a word when the next word begins with a vowel; cf. linking.

ligature A character in which two or more letters have been joined together (*æ*).

lingua franca A medium of communication for people who speak different first languages.

lingual/linguo- Said of any sound made with the tongue.

linguist 1 Someone who is proficient in several languages. **2** A student or practitioner of the subject of linguistics; also called a **linguistician**.

linguistic atlas A set of maps showing the geographical distribution of linguistic terms; also called a **dialect atlas**; cf. dialect.

linguistic change *see* **language change**

linguistic geography *see* **geographical linguistics**

linguistician *see* **linguist 2**

linguistics The science of language; also called **linguistic science** or **linguistic sciences**.

linking A sound introduced between two syllables or words, for ease of pronunciation, as in the English **linking *r*** in *car and bus*; cf. liaison.

linking verb *see* **copula**

lipogram A text from which a specific letter has been omitted throughout.

lip rounding *see* **rounding**

liquid Consonants of an [l] or [r] type.

lisp An abnormal articulation of a sibilant consonant, especially [s]; cf. sibilant.

literal meaning The usual meaning of a word or phrase; cf. figurative.

litotes A figure of speech where something is understated (*Not bad*, meaning 'good').

loan translation A borrowed item in which the parts are translated separately into a new language, as in *superman* from German *Ubermensch*; also called a **calque.**

loan word *see* **borrow**

locative A form that expresses location (*at the corner*).

logogram A written or printed symbol which represents a word (or morpheme) in a language; also called a **logograph** or (in Oriental languages) **character.**

logograph *see* **logogram**

logogriph A word puzzle using anagrams.

logorrhoea Excessive, uncontrolled, incoherent speech.

long Said of a phoneme that contrasts because of its greater duration (the vowel of *beat* compared with *bit*); cf. duration.

look-and-say A method of teaching reading that focuses on the recognition of whole words; also called **whole word**; cf. phonics.

loudness The auditory sensation that primarily relates to a sound's intensity; also called **volume.**

low 1 In phonetics, said of vowels made with the tongue in the bottom area of the mouth ([a] , [ɑ]). **2** Also in phonetics, said of tones that use a relatively low level of pitch range.

lower case *see* **majuscule**

M

main clause A clause that does not depend on any other part of a sentence (*The man arrived* after the bus left); also called an **independent clause**; cf. clause; subordination.

main verb *see* **lexical verb**

major sentence A type of sentence which is highly productive, such as those with a subject plus predicate structure; contrasts with **minor sentence**, where there is a limited productivity, or where the structure lacks some of the constituents found in the major type (*No way*); cf. productivity; sentence.

majuscule A form of writing consisting of letters broadly contained within a single pair of horizontal lines; usually called **capital** or **upper-case letters**; contrasts with **minuscule**, where the letters may extend above and below these lines;

usually called **small** or **lower-case letters**.

malapropism An inappropriate word, used because of its similarity in sound to the intended word (*a paradigm of virtue*); also called **catachresis.**

manner 1 In phonetics, the specific process of articulation used in a sound's production (plosive, etc.); cf. articulation. **2** In grammar, an adverbial answering the question 'how?' (*quickly*); cf. adverbial.

margins Sound segments that form the boundaries of a syllable ([k], [p] in *cup*); cf. syllable.

masculine *see* **gender**

mass Said of nouns that typically express general concepts and lack an indefinite article or plural (*information*); cf. countable.

maxims *see* **conversational maxims**

measure *see* **metre/meter**

medium A dimension of message transmission, especially speech, writing, or sign.

merger In historical linguistics, the coming together of linguistic units that were originally distinguishable.

mesolect In creole studies, a variety between acrolect and basilect; cf. creole; variety.

metalanguage A language used for talking about language.

metanalysis A word deriving from a word-boundary error, as in *a naddre◊ an adder.*

metaphor A figurative expression in which one notion is described in terms usually associated with another (*launch an idea*); cf. figurative.

metathesis Alteration in a normal sequence of elements, especially sounds (*aks* for *ask*).

metonymy A semantic change where an attribute is used for the whole (*crown = king*).

metre/meter A rhythmical verse pattern; also called **measure.**

metrics The study of metrical structure.

microlinguistic Said of highly detailed studies of language data.

mid Said of a vowel articulated between high and low tongue positions (e.g. [e]); cf. close; open **3.**

minim A single downstroke of the pen.

minimal pair Words that differ in meaning when only one sound is changed (*pit/bit*).

minor sentence *see* **major sentence**

minuscule *see* **majuscule**

misrelated participle *see* **dangling participle**

modal A verb that signals contrasts in

speaker attitude (mood), e.g. *may, can*; cf. mood.

modification 1 In grammar, the structural dependence of one element (a **modifier**) upon another. **2** In phonetics, movement that affects the air flow in the vocal tract.

monoglot *see* **monolingual**

monolingual Said of a person/community with only one language; also called **unilingual** or **monoglot**; cf. bilingual; multilingual.

monologue Speech or writing by a single person; contrasts with **dialogue**, where two (or more) people are participants in the interaction.

monometer A line of verse containing a single unit of rhythm (foot).

monophthong A vowel with no detectable change in quality during a syllable (*car*); cf. diphthong.

monosyllabic Said of a word consisting of a single syllable.

monotone Speech using a single level of pitch.

mood Attitudes of fact, wish, possibility, etc. conveyed by a verb (a modal) or clause, e.g. indicative, subjunctive; cf. modal.

morpheme The smallest contrastive unit of grammar (*man, de-, -tion, -s,* etc.); cf. bound form; free form.

morphology The study of word structure, especially in terms of morphemes.

motherese *see* **caretaker speech**

mother tongue *see* **first language**

multilingual Said of a person/community with a command of several languages; cf. monolingual.

mutation A change in the quality of a sound because of the influence of adjacent words or morphemes.

N

narrow Said of a transcription that shows many phonetic details; cf. broad; phonemic transcription.

narrowing In historical linguistics, a type of change in which a word becomes more specialized in meaning (Old English *mete* 'food', now a type of food).

nasality Sound made with the soft palate lowered, thus allowing air to resonate in the nose (**nasals**), e.g. [m], [n], or **nasalized** sounds, e.g. [ã].

native speaker A speaker of a language as a first language or mother tongue; cf. first language.

negation A process expressing the denial or contradiction of some or all of the meaning of a sentence; **negative** forms (**negators**) include *not, un-*, etc.; cf. affirmative.

neologism The creation of a new word out of existing elements (*postperson, linguistified*); also called a **coinage**; cf. blend.

neuter *see* **gender**

neutral 1 Descriptive of the visual appearance of the lips when they are held in a relaxed position, with no spreading or rounding. **2** Descriptive of a lax vowel made in the centre of the vowel area; cf. schwa.

neutralization The loss of a contrast between two phonemes in a particular environment (/t/ vs /d/ is **neutralized** in *stop*).

new *see* **topic**

node In the study of collocations, a lexeme chosen as the central point of a fixed amount (**span**) of language, within which the relationships between lexemes can be studied; cf. collocation; lexeme.

nomenclature A system of terms used in a specialized field.

nominal A noun or noun-like item.

nominalization Forming a noun from some other word class (*redness, my answering …*).

nominative An inflection that typically identifies the subject of a verb; also sometimes called **subjective**; cf. case.

nonce word An invented or accidental linguistic form, used once only (*brillig*).

noncount *see* **countable**

nondefining *see* **restrictive**

nonfinite *see* **finite**

non-native varieties Varieties of a language which have emerged in speech communities where most of the speakers do not have the language as a mother tongue.

nonrestrictive *see* **restrictive**

non-rhotic *see* **rhoticization**

nonsegmental *see* **suprasegmental**

nonstandard *see* **standard**

nonverbal communication *see* **body language**

normative Descriptive of a linguistic rule which is considered to set a socially approved standard of correctness (or **norm**) for language use; cf. prescriptive.

notation *see* **transcription**

notional Said of a grammar whose terms rely on extralinguistic notions, e.g. action, duration, time; cf. form **1.**

noun A word class with a naming function, typically showing contrasts of countability and number, and capable of acting as subject or object of a clause.

noun phrase A phrase with a noun as head (*the tall man in a hat*).

nuclear tone *see* **nucleus**

nucleus The syllable in a tone group that carries maximum pitch prominence (the **nuclear tone** or **tonic syllable**).

number The grammatical category that expresses such contrasts as singular/plural/dual (*cat/cats, he is/they are*).

O

obelisk A typographic symbol (†), whose functions include marking a cross-reference and, when used alongside a personal name, signalling that the person is dead; also called a **dagger**.

object A clause element that expresses the result of an action (cf. direct/indirect object).

objective case *see* **accusative case**

oblique *see* **solidus**

oblique case Said of any case form of a word except the nominative; cf. case; nominative.

obsolescent Said of a word or sense which is dying out; when it no longer has any use, it is **obsolete**.

obstruent Sounds made with a constriction; cf. plosive; fricative; affricate.

occlusion The length of the closure during the articulation of a stop consonant; cf. closure; stop.

octameter A line of verse containing eight units of rhythm (feet).

off-glide, on-glide *see* **glide**

onomastics The study of the etymology and use of proper names; also called **onomatology**; cf. anthroponomastics; etymology; toponymy.

onomatology *see* **onomastics**

onomatopoeia Words that imitate the sounds of the world (*splash, murmur*).

onset The consonants which precede the nucleus of a syllable (*cot, spot*); cf. syllable.

open **1** In grammar, said of a word class with unlimited membership (noun, adjective, adverb, verb); cf. closed **1**. **2** In phonology, said of a syllable that ends in a vowel; cf. closed **2**. **3** In phonetics, said of vowels made with the tongue in the lowest possible position ([a], [ɑ]); vowels a degree higher are **half-open** or **mid-open**.

operator The first auxiliary verb to be used in the verb phrase (e.g. *was leaving, has been going*); cf. auxiliary verb.

opposition A linguistically important contrast between sounds.

oracy Ability in speaking and listening.

oral Said of sounds made in the mouth (as opposed to the nose, **nasal**).

ordinal number A class of numerals (*first*, etc.); cf. cardinal number.

orthoepy The study of correct pronunciation, especially as practised in the 17th/18th centuries.

orthography The study of the use of letters and the rules of spelling in a language.

overcorrection *see* **hypercorrection**

overgeneralization A learner's extension of a word meaning or grammatical rule beyond its normal use (*men➝ mens*); also called **overextension.**

oxymoron A figurative combination of incongruous or contradictory words; cf. figurative.

P

palaeography/paleography The study of ancient writings and inscriptions.

palatal Said of sounds made in the area of the hard palate ([ç], [j]); cf. palate.

palatalization An articulation in which the tongue moves towards the hard palate while another sound is being made; cf. palate.

palate The arched bony structure that forms the roof of the mouth; divided into the **hard palate**, towards the front, and the **soft palate** (**velum**), at the rear.

palato-alveolar Said of a consonant made between the alveolar ridge and the hard palate ([ʃ]).

paleography *see* **palaeography**

palindrome Words or expressions that read the same backwards or forwards (*madam*).

pangram A sentence that contains every letter of the alphabet.

paradigm The set of inflectional forms of a word.

paradigmatic Said of the relationship of substitution between a linguistic unit and other units at a particular place in a structure (*I saw the/my/that/her* (etc.) *car*).

paradox An apparent contradiction that contains a truth.

paragram A play on words by altering a letter, especially in humour (*exorcise* for *exercise*).

paragraph A unit of written discourse between the sentence and the whole text, graphically distinguished either by indention of the first line or by white space preceding and following; cf. indention.

paralanguage Features of speech or body language considered to be marginal to language.

parallelism The use of paired sounds, words, or constructions.

paraphrase An alternative version of a sentence that does not change its meaning.

pararhyme The repetition of the same initial and final consonants in different words (*tail/tall*).

parataxis Constructions joined without the use of conjunctions (*I had tea, eggs …*); cf. hypotaxis.

parenthesis **1** In punctuation, either or both of a pair of round brackets (**parentheses**) to signal an optional, included element of meaning; also called **brackets** in British English. **2** In speech, any construction which can be considered an optional, included element of a sentence.

paronomasia *see* **pun**

paronym A word that comes from the same root as another (*wise/wisdom*).

parsing Analysing and labelling the grammatical elements of a sentence; also called **diagramming.**

participle In traditional grammar, a word derived from a verb and used as an adjective (*smiling face, parked car*); also applied to such nonfinite forms of the verb as *He's smiling* (**present participle**) and *He has smiled* (**past participle**); cf. -*en* form; -*ing* form.

particle A word with a grammatical function, which does not change its form (*to go, not*); cf. inflection.

partitive A form that refers to a part or quantity (*some, piece, ounce*).

part of speech *see* **word class**

passive *see* **voice 2**

past participle *see* **participle**

past perfect(ive) *see* **pluperfect**

past tense A tense form which refers to a time of action prior to the moment of utterance; cf. tense.

patient *see* **goal**

patois A provincial dialect; often used disparagingly.

patronymic A name derived from that of a person's father (*Peterson*).

peak *see* **syllable**

pejoration *see* **deterioration**

pejorative Said of a linguistic form that expresses a disparaging meaning (*goodish*).

pentameter A line of verse containing five units of rhythm (feet).

perfect A verb form typically referring to a past action that has present relevance (*I have asked*); also called **perfective**; cf. aspect; pluperfect.

performative An utterance or verb that performs an action (*promise, baptise*).

period *see* **point**

periphrasis **1** The use of separate words instead of inflections to express a grammatical relationship (**periphrastic**) (*more happy* for *happier*). **2** *see* **circumlocution**

person A grammatical form (especially a pronoun or verb) referring directly to the speaker (**first person**), addressee (**second person**), or others involved in an interaction (especially **third person**).

personal pronoun *see* **person; pronoun**

personification The figurative attribution of human qualities to non-human notions; cf. figurative.

pharynx The part of the throat above the larynx; cf. larynx.

phatic Said of language used to establish atmosphere or maintain social contact.

philology *see* **comparative linguistics**

phonaesthetics/phonesthetics The study of the aesthetic or symbolic properties of sound.

phonation The production of voice through the use of the vocal folds; cf. vocal folds.

phone The smallest perceptible segment of speech sound.

phoneme The smallest contrastive unit in the sound system of a language; cf. contrast.

phonemics The analysis of phonemes.

phonemic transcription A transcription of the phonemes in an utterance.

phonesthetics *see* **phonaesthetics**

phonetic alphabet *see* **phonetic transcription**

phonetician A phonetics specialist.

phonetics The science of speech sounds, especially of their production, transmission, and reception; cf. acoustic/articulatory/auditory phonetics.

phonetic spelling A spelling system that represents speech sounds in a one-to-one way.

phonetic transcription A transcription of all distinguishable phones in an utterance, using special symbols (a **phonetic alphabet**); cf. phone.

phonics A method of teaching reading that trains the recognition of sound values of individual letters; cf. look-and-say.

phonologist A phonology specialist.

phonology The study of the sound systems of languages.

phonostylistics The study of the expressive use of sound, especially in poetry.

phonotactics The specific sequences of sounds that occur in a language (*spr-* is possible in English; *psr-* is not).

phrasal verb A verb consisting of a lexical element and particle(s) (*sit down*); cf. lexeme.

phrase A cluster of words smaller than a clause, forming a grammatical unit (*the tall trees, in a box*); also sometimes called a **group**.

pictogram/pictograph A symbol used in picture writing.

pidgin A language with a reduced range of structure and use, with no native speakers.

pitch The auditory sensation of the height of a sound.

place of articulation The anatomical point in the vocal tract where a speech sound is produced (labial, dental, etc.); cf. articulation.

pleonasm The unnecessary use of words (*in this present day and age*).

plosive Said of a consonant made by the sudden release of a complete closure in the vocal tract ([p], [k]).

pluperfect A verb form that typically expresses the completion of an action before a specific past time (*I had jumped*); also called **past perfect(ive)**.

plural A word form typically expressing 'more than one' in number (*boys, them*).

plurisegmental *see* **suprasegmental**

poetics The linguistic analysis of poetry (and sometimes of other creative language use).

point A punctuation mark that signals the end of an orthographic sentence in statement form; also called a **period** or (in British English) a **full stop**; cf. sentence; statement.

polarity The system of contrast between affirmative and negative in a language; cf. affirmative; negation.

polysemia Several meanings of a word (*plain* = 'dull', 'obvious', etc.); also called **polysemy**; words which have several meanings are **polysemic/polysemous**.

polysemy *see* **polysemia**

polysyllabic Having more than one syllable.

popular etymology *see* **folk etymology**

positive *see* **affirmative**; **degree**; **polarity**

possessive A linguistic form that indicates possession (*my, mine, John's*).

postalveolar Said of a consonant made at the rear of the alveolar ridge; cf. alveolar.

postcreole continuum A related series of varieties that develops when creole speakers are taught in the standard language.

postdeterminer A type of word which occurs after the determiner and before an adjective in a noun phrase (*the three big books*); cf. determiner.

postmodification Items that occur within a phrase after the head (*the man in a suit*); cf. head; phrase.

postposition A word with prepositional function which follows a noun or noun phrase; cf. preposition.

postvocalic Descriptive of a sound which follows a vowel; **postvocalic** *r* is the use of an *r* quality after vowels in certain accents (*car, work*).

pragmatics The study of the factors influencing a person's choice of language.

predeterminer An item that occurs before the determiner in a noun phrase (*all the people*); cf. determiner.

predicate The clause element that gives information about the subject (*He saw a dog*); cf. subject.

predicative *see* **attributive**

prefix An affix added initially to a root (*unhappy*); cf. affix.

prelinguistic Said of child utterances before the emergence of language.

premodification The occurrence of items within a phrase before the head (*the funny clown*); the items themselves are **premodifiers**.

preposition Items that govern and typically precede nouns, pronouns, and certain other forms (*in the box, to me, by running*); cf. complex preposition; postposition.

prepositional phrase A constituent of structure consisting of a preposition plus a following noun phrase.

prescription An authoritarian (**prescriptive** or **normative**) statement about the correctness of a particular use of language; cf. description; normative.

present participle *see* **participle**

present tense A tense form which typically refers to a time of action contemporaneous with the time of utterance; cf. tense.

presupposition The information that a speaker assumes to be already known; cf. focus.

preterite The simple past tense form of a verb (*I saw*).

prevocalic Descriptive of a sound which precedes a vowel.

primary verb A verb which can function either as a main verb or as an auxiliary verb (*be, have, do*); cf. auxiliary/lexical verb.

productivity 1 The creative capacity of language users to produce and understand an indefinitely large number of sentences. **2** The potential of a linguistic rule to produce many instances of the same type; for example, the rule 'add *-s* to form a plural noun' is **productive**, whereas the rule 'change *a* to *e* to make a plural noun' is **unproductive**, being valid only for *man/men*; cf. fossilized.

pro-form An item that substitutes for another item or construction (*so does John*).

progressive 1 In grammar, said of a verb form that typically expresses duration or incompleteness (*He is running*); also called **continuous**; cf. simple. **2** In phonology, said of an assimilation when one sound causes a change in the following sound ([ʃ] ◊ [tʃ] in *did she*); cf. assimilation.

prominence The degree to which an element stands out from others in its environment.

pronominal An item that functions as a pronoun; cf. pronoun.

pronoun An item that can substitute for a noun or noun phrase (*he, who, himself*).

proper name/noun A noun that labels a unique place, person, animal, etc. and lacks the grammatical forms of a common noun; cf. common noun.

proposition A unit of meaning in statement form that is asserted to be true or false (*The cat is asleep*).

prop word *see* **empty word**

proscriptive Said of prescriptive rules that forbid a usage, as in the injunction not to end a sentence with a preposition.

prosodic features *see* **prosody 1**

prosody 1 The linguistic use of pitch, loudness, tempo, and rhythm. **2** The study of versification.

prothesis The insertion of an extra sound at the beginning of a word.

proverb A short, pithy, rhythmical saying expressing a general belief.

pseudepigraphy The false ascription of an author's name to a written work.

pseudonym A fictitious name, especially of an author.

psycholinguistics The study of language in relation to mental processes.

pun A witticism which relies for its effect on playing with the different meanings of a word, or bringing two words together with the same or similar form but different meanings; also called **paronomasia**.

punctuation A set of graphic signs used in written language to separate units in a linear sequence, to indicate when one unit is included in another, or to mark a specific grammatical or attitudinal function (such as possession or exclamation).

pure vowel A vowel that does not change in quality during a syllable; cf. diphthong.

purism The view that a language needs to preserve traditional standards of correctness and be protected from foreign influence.

Q

qualifier A word or phrase that limits the meaning of (**qualifies**) another element (*red car*).

quality The characteristic resonance, or timbre, of a sound.

quantifier An item expressing amount (*all, some, each*).

quantity The relative duration of contrastive sounds and syllables.

question A sentence that asks for information or a response.

quotation marks A punctuation mark which typically signals a piece of direct speech; also called **inverted commas**, or, informally, **quotes**; cf. direct speech.

R

raising The pronunciation of a vowel higher in the mouth than was previously the case.

rank *see* **level 2**

rebus A combination of letters, pictures, and pictograms to make words and sentences; cf. pictogram.

Received Pronunciation The regionally neutral, prestige accent of British English.

recipient *see* **goal**

reciprocal 1 In grammar, an item that expresses mutual relationship (*each other*). **2** In phonology, a type of assimilation in which sounds influence each other; cf. assimilation.

reduction 1 In grammar, the lack of one or more of the normal constituents in a construction (*gone to town*); cf. ellipsis. **2** In phonology, a vowel that becomes central when a word is unstressed ([a] ◊ [ə] as in *he can◊ he c'n go*). **3** In historical linguistics, a narrowing of meaning. **4** *see* **clipping**

redundant Said of a feature that is unnecessary for the identification or maintenance of a linguistic contrast.

reduplication A repetition in the structure of a word, as in such compounds as *helter-skelter*.

reference The relationship between linguistic forms and entities in the world (**referents**); cf. sense relations.

referent *see* **denotation**; **reference**

reflexive A construction or verb in which subject and object relate to the same entity (*She washed herself*).

regional dialect *see* **dialect**

register 1 In phonetics, a physiologically determined range of the human voice, e.g. falsetto. **2** In stylistics, a socially defined variety of language, such as scientific or legal English.

regressive Said of an assimilation when

one sound causes a change in the preceding sound ([t] ↻ [p] in *hot pig*); also called **anticipatory**; cf. assimilation.

regular Said of a linguistic form that conforms to the rules of the language.

relative clause *see* **relative pronoun**

relative pronoun The item that introduces a dependent clause (a **relative clause**) in a noun phrase, referring back to the noun (*the car **which** was sold …*).

release Vocal organ movement away from a point of articulation, especially in plosives; cf. plosive.

repair The correction of a misunderstanding or error made during a conversation.

repertoire The range of languages or varieties that a speaker has available to use.

reported speech *see* **indirect speech**

resonance Air vibrations in the vocal tract that are set in motion by phonation; cf. phonation.

restricted language A highly reduced linguistic system found in narrowly defined settings, such as heraldry or weather reporting.

restrictive Said of a modifier that is an essential part of the identity of another element (*my brother **who's abroad***); also called **defining**; contrasts with **nonrestrictive** or **nondefining,** where the modification is not essential (*my brother, **who's abroad***).

retracted Said of the backwards movement of an articulator, such as the tip of the tongue.

retroflex Said of sounds made when the tip of the tongue is curled back in the direction of the hard palate; cf. palate.

rhetoric The study of effective or persuasive speaking and writing, especially as practised in public oratory.

rhetorical question A question to which no answer is expected.

rhotacism A defective use of [r].

rhoticization The articulation of vowels with *r*-colouring; accents are said to be **rhotic**, if they pronounce /r/ after vowels, and **non-rhotic**, if they do not.

rhyme A correspondence of syllables, especially at the ends of poetic lines.

rhythm The perceived regularity of prominent units in speech.

riddle A traditional utterance intended to mystify or mislead.

roll *see* **trill**

root **1** In grammar, the base form of a word, from which other words derive (*meaningfulness*); cf. stem. **2** In etymology, the earliest form of a word. **3** In phonetics, the furthest-back part of the tongue.

rounding The visual appearance of the lips, permitting contrasts of **rounded** ([u]) and **unrounded** ([i]).

routine *see* **formulaic**

rule **1** A generalization about linguistic structure. **2** A prescriptive recommendation about correct usage.

S

salience The perceptual prominence of a sound.

sans serif *see* **serif**

scansion The analysis of metre.

schwa/shwa An unstressed vowel [ə] made in the centre of the mouth, heard at the end of such words as *after* and *the*.

script *see* **transcription**

second language A non-native language that has an official role in a country; cf. foreign language.

second person *see* **person**

segment A unit whose boundaries can be clearly identified in the stream of speech.

segmental phonology The analysis of speech into phones or phonemes; cf. suprasegmental.

semantic component An element of a word's meaning (*girl* ↻ 'young', 'female', 'human'); also called a **semantic feature**.

semantic feature *see* **semantic component**

semantic field An area of meaning (e.g. colour) identified by a set of mutually defining items (*red, green, blue …*); also called a **lexical field**.

semantic relations *see* **sense relations**

semantics The study of linguistic meaning.

semi-colon A punctuation mark whose typical function is to coordinate clauses.

semi-consonant *see* **semi-vowel**

semi-uncial *see* **uncial**

semi-vowel A sound that displays certain properties of both consonants and vowels (e.g. [l], [j]); also sometimes called a **semi-consonant**.

sense relations The meaning relations between words, as identified by the use of synonyms, antonyms, etc; also called **semantic relations**; cf. reference.

sentence The largest structural unit that displays stateable grammatical relationships, not dependent on any other structure.

serif In typography, a small terminal stroke at the end of the main stroke of a letter; typefaces which lack this feature are called **sans serif**.

shwa *see* **schwa**

sibilant A fricative made by forming a groove along the front part of the tongue, to produce a hissing sound ([s], [ʃ]).

sigmatism **1** Abnormal pronunciation of [s], especially as a lisp. **2** The repetitive use of [s] for effect.

sign **1** A feature of language or behaviour that conveys meaning, especially as used conventionally in a system; also called a **symbol**. **2** A mark used as an element in a writing system; also called a **symbol**. **3** Deaf sign language.

sign language A system of manual communication, especially one used by the deaf.

simile A figurative expression that makes an explicit comparison (*as tall as a tower*); cf. figurative.

simple **1** Said of a tense form that has no auxiliary verb (as in the **simple present** *He runs,* etc.); cf. progressive. **2** Said of a sentence containing one clause; cf. complex sentence; compound.

singular A form that typically expresses 'one of' in number (*dog, It is*).

slang **1** Informal, nonstandard vocabulary. **2** The jargon of a special group.

slant; slash *see* **solidus**

social dialect *see* **dialect**

sociolect A linguistic variety defined on social (as opposed to regional) grounds, such as a social class or occupational group.

sociolinguistics The study of the relationship between language and society.

soft palate *see* **palate**

solecism A minor deviation from what is considered to be linguistically correct.

solidus An oblique stroke typically used to indicate alternatives (*either/or*) or certain kinds of abbreviation (*c/o* 'care of'); also called a **slash**, **slant**, **oblique**, or **virgule**.

sonagraph *see* **spectrograph**

sonorant A voiced sound made with a relatively free passage of air ([a], [l], [n]).

sonority The relative prominence or 'carrying power' of a sound.

sort A special character of type, such as an individual letter, numeral, or punctuation mark.

sound change A change in the sound system of a language, over a period of time; cf. sound law/shift.

sound law A regular, predictable series of sound changes; cf. law; sound change.

sound shift A series of related sound changes; cf. sound change.

sound symbolism A direct association between the sounds of language and the properties of the external world.

sound system The network of phonetic contrasts comprising a language's phonology; cf. phonology.

source language A language from which a word or text is taken.

span *see* **node**

spectrograph An instrument that gives a visual representation of the acoustic features of speech sounds, in the form of a **spectrogram**; also called a **speech spectrograph** or **sonagraph**.

speech The oral medium of transmission for language (**spoken language**).

speech act An utterance defined in terms of the intentions of the speaker and the effect it has on the listener, e.g. a directive.

speech and language pathologist/ therapist A person trained to diagnose, assess, and treat speech disorders; also often called a **speech pathologist/ therapist** or **language pathologist/ therapist.**

speech community A group of people, identified regionally or socially, who share at least one language or variety.

speech defect A regular, involuntary deviation from the norms of speech; also called a **speech impairment**.

speech disorder A serious abnormality in the system underlying the use of spoken language.

speech event A specific act or exchange of speech (greeting, sermon, conversation, etc.).

speech impairment *see* **speech defect**

speech pathologist *see* **speech and language pathologist**

speech perception The reception and recognition of speech by the brain.

speech play *see* **verbal play**

speech processing The stages involved in the perception and production of speech.

speech production The planning and execution of acts of speaking.

speech spectrograph *see* **spectrograph**

speech therapist *see* **speech and language pathologist**.

spelling The rules that govern the way letters are used to write the words of speech; also, a particular sequence of letters in a word; cf. spelling pronunciation/reform.

spelling pronunciation The pronunciation of a word based on its spelling (*says* as /seɪz/); cf. spelling.

spelling reform A movement to make spelling more regular in its relation to speech; cf. spelling.

spirant *see* **fricative**

split infinitive The insertion of a word or phrase between *to* and the infinitive form of the verb in English (*to boldly go*).

splitting One phoneme becoming two as a result of sound change; cf. phoneme.

spondee A unit of rhythm in poetic metre, consisting of two stressed syllables.

spoonerism The transposition of sounds between words, which gives a new meaning (*queer old dean* for *dear old queen*).

spread Said of sounds made with lips stretched sideways ([i]); cf. rounding.

standard A prestige variety, used as an institutionalized norm in a community; forms or varieties not conforming to this norm are said to be **nonstandard** or (pejoratively) **substandard.**

standardization Making a form or usage conform to the standard language.

starred form *see* **asterisked form**

state Said of verbs that express states of affairs rather than actions (*know, seem*); also called **static** or **stative** verbs; cf. dynamic.

statement A sentence that asserts or reports information (*The dog saw the cat*).

static/stative *see* **state**

stem The element in a word to which affixes are attached; cf. root.

stereotyped *see* **formulaic**

stop A consonant made by a complete closure in the vocal tract, as in [t].

stress The degree of force with which a syllable is uttered; syllables may be **stressed** or **unstressed** in various degrees (heavy, weak, etc.).

stress-timing *see* **isochrony**

stricture An articulation in which the air stream is restricted to some degree.

strong form A stressed word form.

strong verb A verb that changes its root vowel when changing its tense (*sing/sang*); also called a **vocalic verb**; cf. weak verb.

structuralism An approach that analyses language (or any human institution or behaviour) into a set of structures.

structural semantics The study of the sense relations between words; cf. sense relations.

structural word *see* **function word**

structure 1 A system of interrelated elements, which derive their (**structural**) meaning from the relations that hold between them. **2** A sequential pattern of linguistic elements, at some level of analysis (e.g. grammar, phonology); cf. level **1**.

stylistics The study of systematic variation in language use (**style**) characteristic of individuals or groups.

stylostatistics The quantification of stylistic patterns; also called **stylometry**; cf. stylistics.

subject The clause constituent about which something is stated (in the predicate) (*The books are on the table*); cf. predicate.

subjective *see* **nominative**

subjunctive A grammatical mood used in some dependent clauses to express doubt, tentativeness, etc. (*Were he here …*); cf. imperative; indicative.

subordinate *see* **dependent**

subordination The dependence of one grammatical unit upon another, as in **subordinate clauses** (*They left after the show ended*); cf. main clause.

subordinator A conjunction used in subordination (*since, because*).

subscript A small letter, numeral, or other symbol set beside and/or below the foot of a full-sized written character; also called an **inferior**; contrasts with **super-script**, which is set beside and/or above the top of a full-sized character; also called a **superior.**

substandard *see* **standard**

substantive A noun or noun-like item.

substitution The replacement of one element by another at a specific place in a structure.

substrate A variety that has influenced the structure or use of a more dominant variety or language (the **superstratum**) in a community; also called **substratum.**

substratum *see* **substrate**

suffix An affix that follows a stem; cf. affix.

superior *see* **subscript**

superlative *see* **degree**

superordinate *see* **hyponymy**

superscript *see* **subscript**

superstratum *see* **substratum**

suppletion The use of an unrelated form to complete a paradigm (*go/goes/going/gone/went*); cf. paradigm.

suprasegmental A vocal effect extending over more than one segment, e.g. pitch; also called **nonsegmental** or **plurisegmental.**

switching *see* **code switching**

syllabic Said of a consonant that can be used alone as a syllable (e.g. /l/ in *bottle*); cf. syllable.

syllabification The division of a word into syllables.

syllable An element of speech that acts as a unit of rhythm, consisting of an obligatory **nucleus** (typically, a vowel) with optional initial and final **margins**; the initial margin is the **onset**, and the remaining element (the **rhyme**) can be divided into a **peak** followed by a **coda.**

syllable-timed Said of languages in which the syllables occur at regular time intervals; cf. isochrony.

symbol *see* **sign 1, 2**

synaesthesia/synesthesia A direct association between form and meaning (*sl-* in *slimy, slug,* etc.).

synchronic Said of an approach that studies language at a theoretical 'point' in time; contrasts with **diachronic.**

syncope The loss of sounds or letters from the middle of a word (*bo'sun*).

syncretism The merging of forms originally distinguished by inflection; cf. inflection.

syndeton The use of conjunctions to link constructions; cf. asyndeton.

synecdoche A figure of speech in which the part is used for the whole or the whole is used for the part (e.g. *wheels* for *car, creatures* for *cats*).

synesthesia *see* **synaesthesia**

synonym A word that has the same meaning (in a particular context) as another word (*a nice range/selection of flowers*).

syntactic Pertaining to syntax; cf. syntax.

syntagm(a) A string of elements forming a unit in syntax.

syntagmatic Said of the linear relationship between elements in a word or construction.

syntax 1 The study of word combinations; cf. morphology. **2** The study of sentence structure (including word structure).

T

taboo Said of a linguistic form whose use is avoided in a society.

tag An element attached to the end of an utterance, especially a **tag question** (*… isn't it?*).

tagging Attaching a grammatical label to a word in a computer corpus to indicate its class; cf. corpus; word class.

tambre/tamber *see* **timbre**

tap A consonant made by a single rapid tongue contact against the roof of the mouth, such as is sometimes heard in the /t/ of *writer.*

target The theoretical position adopted by the vocal organs during the articulation of a sound.

tautology An unnecessary repetition of a word or idea.

telegrammatic/telegraphic Said of speech that omits function words and dependent content words (*Man kick ball*).

telestich An acrostic based on the last letters of words or lines; cf. acrostic.

teletex(t) The transmission of graphic data from a central source to a television screen.

tempo The linguistic use of speed in speech, such as the use of a slow rate to express emphasis.

tense 1 In grammar, a change in the form of a verb to mark the time at which an action takes place (past, present, etc.). **2** In phonetics, *see* **tension.**

tension The muscular force used in making a sound, analysed as strong (**tense**), weak (**lax**), etc.

tetrameter A line of verse containing four units of rhythm (feet).

text A stretch of spoken or written language with a definable communicative function (news report, poem, road sign, etc.).

textlinguistics The study of the linguistic structure of texts.

thematization Moving an element to the front of a sentence, to act as the theme (*Smith his name is*); also called **topicalization**; cf. topic.

theme The element at the beginning of a sentence that expresses what is being talked about (*The cat was in the garden*).

theography The study of the language people use to talk about God.

thesaurus A book of words or phrases grouped on the basis of their meaning.

third person *see* **person**

timbre A sound's tonal quality, or 'colour', which differentiates sounds of the same pitch, loudness, and duration.

time line A hypothetical line used to display the temporal relationships between verb tenses, from past through present to future.

tip (of tongue) *see* **apex**

tone The distinctive pitch level of a syllable.

tone group/unit A distinctive sequence (or contour) of tones in an utterance; also called an **intonation contour.**

tonic syllable *see* **nucleus**

tonicity The placement of nuclear syllables in an utterance; cf. nucleus.

topic The subject about which something is said (*The pen is red*); also called **given** information; contrasts with **comment** (**new** information), which adds extra information about the topic.

topicalization *see* **thematization; topic**

toponymy The study of place names; also called **toponomasiology, toponomastics,** or **toponomatology.**

trade language A pidgin used to facilitate communication while trading.

traditional Said of the attitudes and analyses found in language studies that antedate linguistic science.

transcription A method of writing speech sounds in a systematic and consistent way, from a particular point of view (e.g. phonetic/phonemic transcription, narrow/broad); also called a **notation** or **script.**

transform(ation) A formal linguistic operation (a **transformational rule**) that shows a correspondence between two structures, e.g. active and passive voice sentences; a grammar that uses transformations is called a **transformational grammar**.

transitive Said of a verb taking a direct object (*She saw a dog*); cf. intransitive.

trigraph Three written symbols representing one speech sound (*manoeuvre*).

trill A consonant made by the rapid tapping of one vocal organ against another, as in **trilled** /r/; also called a **roll**.

trimeter A line of verse containing three units of rhythm (feet).

triphthong A vowel containing three distinct qualities (*fire* pronounced as /faɪə/).

trisyllable A word containing three syllables.

trochee A unit of rhythm in poetic metre, consisting of a stressed followed by an unstressed syllable.

turn A single contribution of a speaker to a conversation (a **conversational turn**).

typography The study of the graphic features of the printed page.

U

umlaut A sound change in which a vowel alters because it is influenced by the vowel in the following syllable (**gosi ↻ geese*); cf. asterisked form **2**.

uncial A form of writing (especially found in manuscripts from the 4th to the 8th centuries AD) consisting of large, rounded letters; a later development (**half-uncial** or **semi-uncial**) prepared the way for modern small letters.

uncountable *see* **countable**

underextension The use of a word to refer to only part of its normal meaning, e.g. a child's use of *shoe* to mean only 'own shoe'.

ungrammatical *see* **grammatical 2**

unilingual *see* **monolingual**

univocalic A written composition that uses only one type of vowel throughout.

unjustified *see* **justification**

unproductive Said of a linguistic feature that is no longer used in the creation of new forms, such as the *-th* of *length*, *width*; cf. productivity.

unrounded *see* **rounding**

unstressed *see* **stress**

unvoiced *see* **voiceless**

upper case *see* **majuscule**

urban dialectology The study of the speech patterns used within a modern city community.

usage The speech and writing habits of a community, especially when there is a choice between alternative forms (**divided usage**).

utterance A physically identifiable stretch of speech lacking any grammatical definition; cf. sentence.

uvula The small lobe hanging from the bottom of the soft palate.

uvular Said of a consonant made by the back of the tongue against the uvula, as in the **uvular trill**.

V

variable word A word that expresses grammatical relationships by changing its form (*walk/walks/walking*); cf. invariable word.

variant A linguistic form that is one of a set of alternatives in a given context, as in the plural forms /s/, /z/, /ɪz/.

variety A situationally distinctive system of linguistic expression (legal, formal, etc.).

velar Said of consonants made by the back of the tongue against the soft palate, or **velum**; cf. palate.

velaric Said of sounds, e.g. clicks, when the air has been set in motion by a closure at the soft palate.

velum *see* **palate**

verb A word class displaying such contrasts as tense, aspect, voice, and mood, and typically used to express an action, event, or state (*run, know, want*); cf. aspect; mood; tense **1**; voice **2**.

verbal duelling The competitive use of language, within a game-like structure, with rules that are known and used by the participants.

verbal group *see* **verb phrase**

verbal play The playful manipulation of the elements of language, as in puns, jokes, proverbs, and other forms; also called **speech play**.

verbal noun *see* **gerund**

verbless A construction that omits a verb (*Although angry, he …*).

verb phrase 1 A group of words that has the same grammatical function as a single verb (*has been running*); also called a **verbal group**. **2** In generative grammar, the whole of a sentence apart from the first noun phrase.

vernacular The indigenous language or dialect of a community.

viewdata The interactive transmission of data between a central source and a local television set.

virgule *see* **solidus**

vocabulary The set of lexical items ('words') in a language; also called the **lexicon**.

vocal bands/cords/lips *see* **vocal folds**

vocal folds Two muscular folds in the larynx that vibrate as a source of sound; also called the **vocal cords/lips/bands**.

vocalic Pertaining to a vowel.

vocalic verb *see* **strong verb**

vocalization Any sound or utterance produced by the vocal organs.

vocal organs The parts of the body involved in the production of speech sounds.

vocal tract The whole of the air passage above the larynx; cf. larynx.

vocative A form (especially a noun) used to address a person, animal, etc. (*Excuse me, sir*); in some languages identified by an inflection; cf. inflection.

voice 1 In phonetics, the auditory result of vocal fold vibration (**voiced** sounds, [b], [z], [e]); cf. devoiced; voiceless. **2** In grammar, a grammatical system varying the relationship between subject and object of the verb, especially contrasting **active** and **passive** voices (*The cat saw the dog* vs *The dog was seen by the cat*).

voiced *see* **voice 1**

voiceless Said of sounds made without vocal fold vibration ([f], [p]); also called **unvoiced**; cf. voice **1**.

voice quality 1 The permanent, background, person-identifying feature of speech. **2** A specific tone of voice.

volume *see* **loudness**

vowel 1 In speech, a sound made without closure or audible friction, which can function as the centre of a syllable ([e], [i]). **2** The analogous sign in a writing system.

vowel gradation *see* **ablaut**

W

weak form The unstressed form of a word in connected speech.

weak verb A verb that forms its past tense by adding an inflection (*walk↻ walked*); cf. strong verb.

whisper Speech produced without vocal fold vibration; cf. vocal folds.

white space Any area of the printed page not taken up by type.

whole word *see* **look-and-say**

***wh*-question** A question which begins with a question-word (a ***wh*-word**), such as *why, what, where, how*; cf. question.

word The smallest unit of grammar that can stand alone as a complete utterance, separated by spaces in written language and potentially by pauses in speech.

word class A set of words that display the same formal properties, especially their inflections and distribution (verbs, nouns, etc.); also known as **part of speech**.

word ending An inflection used at the end of a word (*boys, walking*).

word-finding problem Inability to retrieve a desired word, symptomatic of aphasia; cf. aphasia.

word formation The process of creating words out of sequences of morphemes (*un-happi-ness*).

word game Any form of game, puzzle, or competition in which an aspect of language provides the basis of the challenge.

word order The sequential arrangement of words in a language.

X

***x*-height** In typography, the height of the small letter *x*; cf. ascender; descender.

Y

***yes-no* question** A question formed by inversion, typically answered by *yes* or *no* (*Were they there?*); cf. inversion; question.

Z

zero article The non-use of the definite or indefinite article before a noun, where one would normally be found (*in school* vs *in the school*); cf. article.

II · SPECIAL SYMBOLS AND ABBREVIATIONS

Items which are used only in an individual map or transcription are explained along with the illustration.

A	adverbial
acc.	accusative
adj.	adjective
AmE	American English
BNC	British National Corpus
BrE	British English
c.	about
C	[geography] central
C	[grammar] complement
C	[phonology] consonant
Ch.	Chapter
cm	centimetre(s)
CmC	computer-mediated communication
COBUILD	Collins–Birmingham University International Language Database
CS	Chancery Standard
CS	Cut Spelling (Cut Speling)
CV	cardinal vowel
DARE	Dictionary of American Regional English
dat.	dative
E	east(ern)
EAP	English for Academic Purposes
ed(s).	editor(s)
EFL	English as a Foreign Language
EGP	English for General Purposes
EIL	English as an International Language
ELA	English Language Amendment
ELT	English Language Teaching
EMT	English as a Mother Tongue
ENL	English as a Native Language
EOP	English for Occupational Purposes
ESL	English as a Second Language
ESP	English for Special Purposes
EST	English for Science and Technology
F	French
GA	[lexicon] The Gambia
GA	[phonology] General American
gen.	genitive
GH	Ghana

I(s)	Island(s)
ICE	International Corpus of English
ind.	indicative
i.t.a.	Initial Teaching Alphabet
L1	first language
L2	second language
L3	third language
l(l).	line(s)
LAGS	Linguistic Atlas of the Gulf States
LOB	Lancaster–Oslo/Bergen corpus
LSE	London School of Economics
LSP	Language for Special/Specific Purposes
m	metre(s)
Me.	Mercian
ME	Middle English
MIT	Massachusetts Institute of Technology
MnE	Modern English
MT	mother tongue
N	[geography] north(ern)
N	[lexicon] Nigeria
n.	noun
NL	native language
NNL	non-native language
NNV	non-native variety
No.	Northumbrian
nom.	nominative
Non-U	non-upper-class
NP	noun phrase
NS	New Spelling (Nue Speling)
O	Object
OE	Old English
OED	Oxford English Dictionary
ON	Old Norse
p(p).	page(s)
P	patient/pupil
part.	participle
PC	political correctness
pl.	plural
pres.	present tense
RP	Received Pronunciation
S	[geography] south(ern)
S	[grammar] Subject
SE	Standard English
sg.	singular
SGML	Standard Generalized Markup Language
SL	Sierra Leone
subj.	subjunctive
T	therapist/teacher
TEFL	Teaching English as a Foreign Language

TEIL	Teaching English as an International Language
TESL	Teaching English as a Second Language
TESOL	Teaching English to Speakers of Other Languages
TO	traditional orthography
trans.	translation
U	upper-class
UK	United Kingdom
US(A)	United States (of America)
v.,vb.	[grammar] verb
V	[phonology] vowel
vs	versus
W	west(ern)
WAVE	West African Vernacular English
WE	World English
WS	West Saxon
WSE	World Standard English
1	1st person
2	2nd person
3	3rd person
[ ]	enclose phonetic transcription
/ /	enclose phonological transcription
< >	enclose graphological transcription
( )	enclose optional elements
*	[diachrony] hypothetical form
*	[synchrony] unacceptable usage
§	Chapter
∧	ellipsis
/	intonation unit boundary
·	[prosody] increasing
-	pause length
--	

↑	high rising contour
/	stressed metrical syllable
◡	unstressed metrical syllable

PHONETIC SYMBOLS

These symbols are used in the phonological transcription of words throughout the book; for other symbols with these values, see pp. 237 and 243.

Vowels

/iː/	as in *sea*
/ɪ/	as in *sit*
/e/	as in *let*
/æ/	as in *cat*
/ʌ/	as in *cut*
/ɑː/	as in *calm*
/ɒ/	as in *dog*
/ɔː/	as in *saw*
/ʊ/	as in *put*
/uː/	as in *do*
/ɜː/	as in *bird*
/ə/	as in *the*
/eɪ/	as in *day*
/aɪ/	as in *time*
/ɔɪ/	as in *toy*
/əʊ/	as in *know*
/aʊ/	as in *how*
/ɪə/	as in *here*
/ɛə/	as in *there*
/ʊə/	as in *sure*

Consonants

/p/	as in *pie*
/b/	as in *buy*
/t/	as in *to*
/d/	as in *do*
/k/	as in *key*
/g/	as in *go*
/tʃ/	as in *chew*
/dʒ/	as in *jaw*
/f/	as in *foe*
/v/	as in *view*
/θ/	as in *thigh*
/ð/	as in *thy*
/s/	as in *see*
/z/	as in *zoo*
/ʃ/	as in *she*
/ʒ/	as in *rouge*
/h/	as in *how*
/m/	as in *me*
/n/	as in *no*
/ŋ/	as in *sing*
/l/	as in *lie*
/r/	as in *row*
/w/	as in *way*
/j/	as in *you*

III · REFERENCES

Abbott, G. 1988. Mascaraed and muumuu-ed: the spelling of imported words. *English Today* **14**, 43–6.

Adams, D. 1979. *The Hitch Hiker's Guide to the Galaxy.* London: Pan.

Adams, D. & Lloyd, J. 1983. *The Meaning of Liff.* London: Pan and Faber & Faber.

Aitken, A. J. 1984. Scots and English in Scotland. In P. Trudgill (ed.), *Language in the British Isles* (Cambridge: Cambridge University Press), 517–32.

Alford, H. 1869. *The Queen's English.* London: Strahan.

Algeo, J. 1988. The tag question in British English: it's different i'n'it? *English World-Wide* **9**, 171–91.

Allan, S. 1990. The rise of New Zealand intonation. In A. Bell & J. Holmes (eds.), *New Zealand Ways of Speaking English* (Clevedon: Multilingual Matters), 115–28.

Allsopp, J. 1992. French and Spanish loan words in Caribbean English. *English Today* **29**, 12–20.

Angogo, R. & Hancock, I. 1980. English in Africa: emerging standards or diverging regionalisms? *English World-Wide* **1**, 67–96.

Annand, J. K. 1982. Lallans [extract of Bible translation]. *English World-Wide* **4**, 89.

— 1986. *Dod and Davie.* Edinburgh: Canongate Publishing.

Archer, W. 1904. *Real Conversations.* London: William Heinemann.

Armstrong, S. & Ainley, M. 1990. *South Tyneside Assessment of Syntactic Structures.* Ponteland: STASS Publications.

Atkinson, M. 1984. *Our Masters' Voices.* London: Methuen.

Awonusi, V. O. 1990. Coming of age: English in Nigeria. *English Today* **22**, 31–5.

Bailey, R. W. 1984. The English language in Canada. In R. W. Bailey & M. Görlach (eds.), *English as a World Language* (Cambridge: Cambridge University Press), 134–76.

— 1986. Dictionaries of the next century. In R. Ilson (ed.), *Lexicography: an Emerging International Profession* (Manchester: Manchester University Press), 123–37.

Baker, C. D. & Freebody, P. 1989. *Children's First School Books.* Oxford: Blackwell.

Baldie, B. 1976. The acquisition of the passive voice. *Journal of Child Language* **3**, 331–48.

Baratz, J. C. & Shuy, R. W. (eds.) 1969. *Teaching Black Children to Read.* Washington: Center for Applied Linguistics.

Barry, M. V. 1984. The English language in Ireland. In R. W. Bailey & M. Görlach (eds.), *English as a World Language* (Cambridge: Cambridge University Press), 84–133.

Bauer, L. 1983. *English Word-formation.* Cambridge: Cambridge University Press.

Baumgardner, R. J. 1990. The indigenization of English in Pakistan. *English Today* **21**, 59–65.

Bawden, N. 1976. A dead pig and my father. In G. Fox, G. Hammond, T. Jones, F. Smith & K. Sterck (eds.), *Writers, Critics and Children.* London: Heinemann.

Beal, J. 1988. The grammar of Tyneside and Northumbrian English. In J. Milroy & L. Milroy (eds.), *Regional Variation in British English Syntax.* London: Economic and Social Research Council.

Bell, A. 1991. *The Language of the News Media.* Oxford: Blackwell.

Benedict, H. 1979. Early lexical development: comprehension and production. *Journal of Child Language* **6**, 183–200.

Benson, M., Benson, E. & Ilson, R. 1986a. *The BBI Combinatory Dictionary of English: a Guide to Word Combinations.* Amsterdam: John Benjamins.

— 1986b. *Lexicographic Description of English.* Amsterdam: John Benjamins.

Benson, R. W. 1985. The end of legalese: the game is over. *Review of Law and Social Change* **13**, 519–73.

Bernard, J. R. 1981. Australian pronunciation. In *The Macquarie Dictionary* (Sydney: Macquarie Library), 18–27.

Berry, E. 1985. Arbitrary form in poetry and the poetic function of language. In G. Youmans & D. M. Lance (eds.), *In Memory of Roman Jakobson* (Columbia, Mo.: Linguistics Area Program), 121–34.

Biber, D. 1988. *Variation Across Speech and Writing.* Cambridge: Cambridge University Press.

Blair, P. H. 1977. *An Introduction to Anglo-Saxon England,* 2nd edn. Cambridge: Cambridge University Press.

Blake, N. 1969. *Caxton and His World.* London: Deutsch.

— 1992. The literary language. In N. Blake (ed.), *The Cambridge History of the English Language. Vol. 2: 1066–1476* (Cambridge: Cambridge University Press), 500–41.

Bolton, W. F. 1982. *A Living Language: the History and Structure of English.* New York: Random House.

— 1992. *Shakespeare's English: Language in the History Plays.* Oxford: Blackwell.

Bradley, D. 1991. /æ/ and /aː/ in Australian English. In J. Cheshire (ed.), *English Around the World: Sociolinguistic Perspectives* (Cambridge: Cambridge University Press), 227–34.

Brandreth, G. 1987. *The Joy of Lex.* London: Guild Publishing.

Brandreth, G. & Francis, D. 1992. *World Championship Scrabble®.* Edinburgh: Chambers.

Branford, J. & Branford, W. 1991. *A Dictionary of South African English,* 4th edn. Oxford: Oxford University Press.

Bridges, R. 1913. *A Tract on the Present State of English Pronunciation.* Oxford: Clarendon Press.

Britain, D. & Newman, J. 1992. High rising terminals in New Zealand English. *Journal of the International Phonetic Association* **22**, 1–11.

Broadbent, M. 1983. Glossary. In G. Rainbird, *An Illustrated Guide to Wine.* London: Octopus Books.

Brodeur, A. G. 1959. *The Art of Beowulf.* Berkeley, Calif.: University of California Press.

Brown, B. 1993. What might an improved spelling look like? *Newsletter of the Simplified Spelling Society.* London: Simplified Spelling Society.

Brown, R. 1973. *A First Language.* Cambridge, Mass.: Harvard University Press.

Burchfield, R. 1981. *The Spoken Word: a BBC Guide.* London: British Broadcasting Corporation.

Burgess, A. 1973. *Joysprick: an Introduction to the Language of James Joyce.* London: Deutsch.

Burnley, D. 1992. Lexis and semantics. In N. Blake (ed.), *The Cambridge History of the English Language. Vol. 2: 1066–1476.* (Cambridge: Cambridge University Press), 409–99.

Burrows, J. F. 1992. Not until you ask nicely: the interpretative nexus between analysis and information. *Literary and Linguistic Computing* **7**, 91–109.

Butcher, J. 1992. *Copy-editing,* 3rd edn. Cambridge: Cambridge University Press.

Cameron, K. 1961. *English Place Names.* London: Methuen.

Cassidy, F. G. 1982. Geographical variation of English in the United States. In R. W. Bailey & M. Görlach (eds.), *English as a World Language* (Cambridge: Cambridge University Press), 177–209.

— 1985, 1991. *The Dictionary of American Regional English, Vols. 1, 2.* Cambridge, Mass.: Belknap Press.

Celcis, P., Agniel, A., Démonet, J-F. & Marc-Vergnes, J-P. 1991. Cerebral blood flow correlates of word list learning. *Journal of Neurolinguistics* **6**, 253–72.

Chambers, J. K. & Hardwick, M. F. 1986. Comparative sociolinguistics of a sound change in Canadian English. *English World-Wide* **7**, 23–46.

Cheshire, J. 1982. *Variation in an English Dialect: a Sociolinguistic Study.* Cambridge: Cambridge University Press.

Chiaro, D. 1992. *The Language of Jokes: Analysing Verbal Play.* London:

Routledge.

Churchill, W. 1948. *The Gathering Storm*, Vol. 1 of *The History of the Second World War*. London: Cassell.

Cooke, A. 1973. *America*. London: BBC Enterprises.

Cooper, R. L. 1984. The avoidance of androcentric generics. *International Journal of the Sociology of Language* **50**, 5–20.

Corns, T. N. 1990. *Milton's Language*. Oxford: Blackwell.

Cowan, N. & Leavitt, L. 1982. Talking backward: exceptional speech play in late childhood. *Journal of Child Language* **9**, 481–95.

Croft, P. J. 1973. *Autograph Poetry in the English Language*. London: Cassell.

Crowdy, S. 1993. Spoken corpus design. *Literary and Linguistic Computing* **8**, 259–65.

Crystal, D. 1981. Generating theological language. In J-P. van Noppen (ed.), *Theolinguistics* (Studiereeks Tijdschrift, Free University of Brussels, New Series **8**), 265–81.

—— 1984. *Who Cares About English Usage?* Harmondsworth: Penguin.

—— 1986. *Listen to Your Child*. Harmondsworth: Penguin.

—— 1988a. *Rediscover Grammar*. London: Longman.

—— 1988b. *Pilgrimage*. Holyhead: Holy Island Press.

—— 1991. *Language A to Z*. London: Longman.

Crystal, D. & Davy, D. 1969. *Investigating English Style*. London: Longman.

—— 1975. *Advanced Conversational English*. London: Longman.

Crystal, D. & Varley, R. 1993. *Introduction to Language Pathology*, 3rd edn. London: Whurr.

Cureton, R. D. 1986. Visual form in e.e.cummings' *No Thanks*. *Word & Image* **2**, 245–76.

Cutler, A., McQueen, J. & Robinson, K. 1990. Elizabeth and John: sound patterns of men's and women's names. *Journal of Linguistics* **26**, 471–82.

Cutts, M. 1994. *Lucid Law*. Stockport: Plain Language Commission.

Dalton, P. & Hardcastle, W. J. 1989. *Disorders of Fluency*, 2nd edn. London: Whurr.

Davies, M. 1993. *My Rare Animal ABC Frieze*. Godalming: World Wide Fund for Nature.

Devitt, A. J. 1989. *Standardizing Written English: Diffusion in the Case of Scotland, 1520–1659*. Cambridge: Cambridge University Press.

Dickins, B. & Wilson, R. M. 1951. *Early Middle English Texts*. London: Bowes & Bowes.

Dillon, J. T. 1990. *The Practice of Questioning*. London: Routledge.

Donnelly, I. 1888. *The Great Cryptogram: Francis Bacon's Cipher in the So-called Shakespeare's Plays*. London: Sampson Low, Marston, Searle & Rivington.

Downing, J., Ayers, D. & Schaefer, B. 1983. *Linguistic Awareness in Reading Readiness (LARR) Test*. Windsor: NFER–Nelson.

D'Souza, J. 1991. Speech acts in Indian English fiction. *World Englishes* **10**, 307–16.

Dubey, V. S. 1991. The lexical style of Indian English newspapers. *World Englishes* **10**, 19–32.

Dunkling, L. 1974. *The Guinness Book of Names*. Enfield: Guinness Superlatives.

Ebeling, G. 1972. *Introduction to a Theological Theory of Language*. London: Collins.

Ellegård, A. 1953. *The Auxiliary Do: the Establishment and Regulation of its Use in English*. Stockholm: Almqvist & Wiksell.

—— 1962. *Who was Junius?* Stockholm: Almqvist & Wiksell.

Ellis, A. J. 1869. *On Early English Pronunciation*. London: Early English Text Society.

Empson, W. 1930. *Seven Types of Ambiguity*. London: Chatto & Windus.

Fasold, R. 1987. Language policy and change: sexist language in the periodical news media. In P. Lowenberg (ed.), *Georgetown University Round Table on Languages and Linguistics* (Washington, D.C.: Georgetown University Press), 187–206.

Fasold, R., Yamada, H., Robinson, D. & Barish, S. 1990. The language-planning effect of newspaper editorial policy: gender differences in *The Washington Post*. *Language in Society* **19**, 521–39.

Fell, C. E. 1991. Runes and semantics. In A. Bammesberger (ed.), *Old English Runes and their Continental Background* (Heidelberg: Winter), 195–229.

Ferguson, C. A. 1983. Sports announcer talk: syntactic aspects of register variation. *Language in Society* **12**, 153–72.

Ferreiro, E. & Teberosky, A. 1983. *Literacy before Schooling*. London: Heinemann.

Ferris, P. (ed.) 1985. *Dylan Thomas: the Collected Letters*. New York: Macmillan.

Field, J. 1980. *Place Names of Great Britain and Ireland*. Totowa, N.J.: Barnes & Noble; Newton Abbot: David & Charles.

Fischer, O. 1992. Syntax. In N. Blake (ed.), *The Cambridge History of the English Language. Vol. 2: 1066–1476* (Cambridge: Cambridge University Press), 207–408.

Flexner, S. B. 1976. *I Hear America Talking*. New York: Simon & Schuster.

Fournier, P. S. 1764–6. *Manuel typographique*. Paris: Fournier and Barbou; trans. H. Carter, *Fournier on Typefounding*. New York: Burt Franklin, 1973.

Fowler, H. W. 1926. *Modern English Usage*. London: Oxford University Press.

Friedman, M. 1985. The changing language of a consumer society: brand name usage in popular American novels in the postwar era. *Journal of Consumer Research* **11**, 927–38.

—— 1986 Commercial influences in popular literature: an empirical study of brand name usage in American and British hit plays in the postwar era. *Empirical Studies of the Arts* **4**, 63–76.

Fromkin, V. & Rodman, R. 1972. *An Introduction to Language*, 5th edn 1994. New York: Holt, Rinehart & Winston.

Fry, D. B. 1947. The frequency of occurrence of speech sounds in Southern English. *Archives Néerlandaises de Phonétique Expérimentale*, **20**.

Fuller, S., Joyner, J. & Meaden, D. 1990. *Language File*. London: BBC Enterprises and Longman.

Gammond, P. & Clayton, P. 1959. *101 Things*. London: Elek Books.

Garmonsway, A.N. (ed.) 1972. *The Anglo-Saxon Chronicle*. London: Dent.

Gibbon, F., Hardcastle, W. & Moore, A. 1990. Modifying abnormal tongue patterns in an older child using electropalatography. *Child Language Teaching and Therapy* **6**, 227–45.

Giles, B. 1990. *The Story of Weather*. London: HMSO.

Giles, H., Coupland, N. & Coupland, J. 1991. Accommodation theory: communication, context, and consequence. In H. Giles, J. Coupland & N. Coupland (eds.), *Contexts of Accommodation: Developments in Applied Sociolinguistics* (Cambridge: Cambridge University Press), 1–68.

Gimson, A. C. 1962. *An Introduction to the Pronunciation of English*, 5th edn 1994. London: Edward Arnold.

Gledhill, D. 1989. *The Names of Plants*, 2nd edn. Cambridge: Cambridge University Press.

Godman, A. & Denney, R. (eds.) 1985. *Cambridge Illustrated Thesaurus of Chemistry*. Cambridge: Cambridge University Press.

Gonzalez, A. B. 1991. Stylistic shifts in the English of the Philippine print media. In J. Cheshire (ed.), *English Around the World: Sociolinguistic Perspectives* (Cambridge: Cambridge University Press), 333–63.

Görlach, M. (ed.) 1984. *Max and Moritz in English Dialects and Creoles*. Hamburg: Buske.

Gowers, E. 1954. *The Complete Plain Words*. London: HMSO.

Graham, J. J. 1981. Wir ain aald language. Writin ida Shetland dialect. *English World-Wide* **2**, 18–19.

Green, J. 1979. *Famous Last Words: an Illustrated Dictionary of Quotations*. London: Omnibus Press.

Greenbaum, S. 1991. ICE: the International Corpus of English. *English Today* **28**, 3–7.

Greenbaum, S. & Quirk, R. 1990. *A Student's Grammar of the English Language*. London: Longman.

Greene, G. 1973. *The Third Man*. London: Faber & Faber.

Grote, D. 1992. *British English for American Readers*. Westport, Conn.: Greenwood Press.

Grunwell, P. 1987. *Clinical Phonology*, 2nd edn. London: Croom Helm.

Gumperz, J. J. 1982. *Language and Social Identity*. Cambridge: Cambridge University Press.

Gyasi, I. K. 1991. Aspects of English in Ghana. *English Today* **28**, 26–31.

Hancock, I. F. & Angogo, R. 1984. English in East Africa. In R. W. Bailey & M.

Görlach (eds.), *English as a World Language* (Cambridge: Cambridge University Press), 306–23.

Hanks, P. & Hodges, F. 1990. *A Dictionary of First Names.* Oxford: Oxford University Press.

Hanson, J. 1972. *Antonyms.* Minneapolis: Lerner.

Hayakawa, S. I. 1939. *Language in Thought and Action.* New York: Harcourt, Brace & World.

Hill, W. J. & Öttchen, C. J. 1991. *Shakespeare's Insults.* Cambridge: Mainsail Press.

Holzknecht, S. 1989. Sociolinguistic analysis of a register: birthday notices in Papua New Guinea *Post Courier. World Englishes* **8**, 179–92.

Howarth, P. 1956. *Questions in the House: the History of a Unique British Institution.* Oxford: Bodley Head.

Howe, C. J. 1976. The meanings of two-word utterances in the speech of young children. *Journal of Child Language* **3**, 29–47.

Hoyle, S. M. 1991. Children's competence in the specialized register of sportscasting. *Journal of Child Language* **18**, 435–50.

Hughes, G. 1988. *Words in Time: a Social History of the English Vocabulary.* Oxford: Blackwell.

— 1991. *Swearing: a Social History of Foul Language, Oaths and Profanity in English.* Oxford: Blackwell.

Hutton, M. (trans.) 1914. *Agricola and Germania.* London: William Heinemann.

Jackson, C. 1980. *Color Me Beautiful.* Washington: Acropolis; London: Piatkus.

Jacobson, S. 1985. *British and American Scouting and Guiding Terminology: a Lexo-Semantic Study.* (Stockholm Studies in English **62**.) Stockholm: Almqvist & Wiksell.

James, R. & Gregory, R. G. 1966. *Imaginative Speech and Writing.* London: Nelson.

Jenkins, H. R. 1992. On being clear about time. An analysis of a chapter of Stephen Hawking's *A Brief History of Time. Language Sciences* **14**, 529–44.

Jespersen, O. 1933. *Essentials of English Grammar.* London: Allen & Unwin.

Johansson, S. 1980. Word frequencies in British and American English: some preliminary observations. *Stockholm Papers in English Language and Literature* **1**, 56–74.

Johansson, S. & Hofland, K. 1989. *Frequency Analysis of English Vocabulary and Grammar.* Oxford: Clarendon Press.

Jones, C. 1972. *An Introduction to Middle English.* New York: Holt, Rinehart & Winston.

Jones, D. 1917. *English Pronouncing Dictionary.* 14th edn, 1991. Cambridge: Cambridge University Press.

— 1918. *An Outline of English Phonetics.* (9th edn, 1960.) Cambridge: Heffer.

Justeson, J. S. & Katz, S. M. 1992. Redefining antonymy: the textual structure of a semantic relation. *Literary and Linguistic Computing* **7**, 176–84.

Kachru, B. B. 1983. *The Indianization of English: the English Language in India.* Delhi: Oxford University Press.

— 1985. Standards, codification and sociolinguistic realism: the English language in the outer circle. In R. Quirk & H. G. Widdowson (eds.), *English in the World* (Cambridge: Cambridge University Press), 11–30.

— 1986 The Indianization of English. *English Today* **6**, 31–3.

Kasravi, B. 1990. *The Index of the English Dictionary.* Santa Barbara, Calif.: Interbond.

Kastovsky, D. 1992. Semantics and vocabulary. In R. M. Hogg (ed.), *The Cambridge History of the English Language. Vol. 1: The Beginnings to 1066* (Cambridge: Cambridge University Press), 290–408.

Kemp, J. A. 1972. *John Wallis's Grammar of the English Language.* London: Longman.

Kenyon, J. S. & Knott, T. A. 1953. *A Pronouncing Dictionary of American English.* Springfield, Mass.: Merriam.

Ker, W. P. 1904. *The Dark Ages.* Edinburgh: William Blackwood & Sons.

Kermode, F. (ed.) 1975. *Selected Prose of T.S. Eliot.* New York: Harcourt Brace Jovanovich.

Kiernan, K. S. 1991. Digital image processing and the *Beowulf* manuscript. *Literary and Linguistic Computing* **6**, 20–7.

Kington, M. 1993. From the cradle to the grave, you never said a truer word. *The Independent*, 26 July.

Kuiper, K. & Austin, P. 1990. They're off and racing now: the speech of the New Zealand race caller. In A. Bell & J. Holmes (eds.), *New Zealand Ways of Speaking English* (Clevedon: Multilingual Matters), 195–220.

Kurath, H. 1949. *A Word Geography of the Eastern United States.* Ann Arbor, Mich.: University of Michigan.

Lakoff, G. & Johnson, M. 1980. *Metaphors We Live By.* Chicago, Ill.: University of Chicago Press.

Lang, A. (ed.) 1890. *Life, Letters and Diaries of Sir Stafford Northcote First Earl of Iddesleigh*, 2nd edn. Edinburgh: William Blackwood & Sons.

Leacock, S. 1944. *How to Write.* London: Bodley Head.

Leech, G. 1993. 100 million words of English. *English Today* **9**, 9–15.

Lerner, G. H. 1991. On the syntax of sentences-in-progress. *Language in Society* **20**, 441–58.

Levenston, E. A. 1973. A typology of grammatical deviation in poetry. *Scripta Hierosolymitana* (Jerusalem) **25**, 312–26.

Lieven, E. V. M., Pine, J. M. & Barnes, H. D. 1992. Individual differences in early vocabulary development: redefining the referential– expressive distinction. *Journal of Child Language* **19**, 287–310.

Lockwood, W. 1976 Stork. *Fróðskapparit* **24**, 76.

Lounsbury, T. R. 1908. *The Standard of Usage in English.* New York: Harper.

Low, J. T. 1983. In Memoriam: John Thomas Low. *English World-Wide* **4**, 85–91.

Lutz, W. 1987. Doublespeak at large. *English Today* **12**, 21-4.

McArthur, T. 1981. *Longman Lexicon of Contemporary English.* Harlow: Longman.

— 1987. The English languages? *English Today* **11**, 9-13.

— 1992. *The Oxford Companion to the English Language.* Oxford: Oxford University Press.

McClure, J. D. 1981. The makin o a Scots prose. *English World-Wide* **2**, 19–23.

McDavid, R. I. 1971. The language of the city. In J. V. Williamson & V. M. Burke (eds.), *A Various Language: Perspectives on American Dialect* (New York: Holt, Rinehart & Winston), 511–24.

MacHale, D. 1981. *The Bumper Book of Kerryman Jokes.* Dublin: Mercier Press.

McIntosh, A. M., Samuels, M. L. & Benskin, M. 1986. *A Linguistic Atlas of Late Mediaeval English.* Aberdeen: Aberdeen University Press.

MacLeod, I. (ed.) 1990. *The Scots Thesaurus.* Aberdeen: Aberdeen University Press.

Malan, R. 1972. *Ah big yaws?* Cape Town: David Philip.

Maley, A. 1985. The most chameleon of languages: perceptions of English abroad. *English Today* **1**, 30–3.

Marshall, N. 1992. *Chambers Companion to the Burns Supper.* Edinburgh: Chambers.

Mbangwana, P. 1991. Invigorative and hermetic innovation in English in Yaoundé. *World Englishes* **10**, 53–63.

Mellinkoff, D. 1963. *The Language of the Law.* Boston, Mass.: Little Brown & Co.

Mencken, H. L. 1919. *The American Language.* New York: Knopf.

Mermin, N. D. 1990. *Boojums All the Way Through.* Cambridge: Cambridge University Press.

Mesthrie, R. 1987. From OV to VO in language shift: South African Indian English and its OV substrates. *English World-Wide* **8**, 263–76.

— 1993. South African Indian English. *English Today* **34**, 12–16, 63.

Mieder, W. (ed.) 1992. *A Dictionary of American Proverbs.* New York: Oxford University Press.

Mindt, D. & Weber, C. 1989. Prepositions in American and British English. *World Englishes* **8**, 229–38.

Mitchell, A. G. & Delbridge, A. 1965. *The Pronunciation of English in Australia.* Sydney: Angus & Robertson.

Mitford, N. 1956. The English aristocracy. In N. Mitford (ed.), *Noblesse Oblige* (London: Hamish Hamilton), 39–61.

Mittins, W. H. 1962. *A Grammar of Modern English.* London: Methuen.

Mittins, W. H., Salu, M., Edminson, M. & Coyne, S. 1970. *Attitudes to English Usage.* London: Oxford University Press.

Montgomery, M. 1989. Exploring the roots of Appalachian English. *English World-Wide* **10**, 227–78.

Murison, D. 1981. *Scots Saws.* Edinburgh: Mercat Press.

Murray, D. E. 1990. CmC. *English Today* **23**, 42–6.

Nash, W. 1990. *Language in Popular Fiction.* London: Routledge.

— 1992. *An Uncommon Tongue.* London: Routledge.

— 1993. *On Jargon.* Oxford: Blackwell.

Nattinger, J. R. & DeCarrico, J. S. 1992. *Lexical Phrases and Language Teaching.* Oxford: Oxford University Press.

Nevalainen, T. Forthcoming, 1996. Early Modern English lexis and semantics. In R. Lass (ed.), *The Cambridge History of the English Language. Vol. 3: 1476–1776* (Cambridge: Cambridge University Press).

Oreström, B. 1985. *A Corpus of Shetland English.* Stockholm: Almqvist & Wiksell.

Orwell, G. 1946. Politics and the English language. *Horizon*, 13.

Ó Sé, D. 1986. Word-stress in Hiberno-English. In J. Harris, D. Little & D. Singleton (eds.), *Perspectives on the English Language in Ireland* (Trinity College Dublin: Centre for Language and Communication Studies), 97–107.

Palmatier, R. A. 1969. *A Descriptive Syntax of the Ormulum.* The Hague: Mouton.

Parkes, M. B. 1992. *Pause and Effect: Punctuation in the West.* Aldershot: Scolar Press.

Parslow, R. L. 1971. The pronunciation of English in Boston, Massachusetts: vowels and consonants. In J. V. Williamson & V. M. Burke (eds.), *A Various Language: Perspectives on American Dialects* (New York: Holt, Rinehart & Winston), 610–24.

Pederson, L., *et al.* (eds.) 1986. *The Linguistic Atlas of the Gulf States: a Concordance of Basic Materials.* Ann Arbor, Mich.: University Microfilm.

Pemagbi, J. 1989. Still a deficient language? *English Today* **17**, 20–4.

Phillips, K. C. 1970. *Jane Austen's English.* London: Deutsch.

Pierce, G. (ed.) 1980. *Cuttings: the Pick of 'Country Life' from* Punch. London: Elm Tree Books.

Pinter, H. 1960. *The Birthday Party.* London: Methuen.

Platt, J. & Singh, K. 1984. The use of localized English in Singapore poetry. *English World-Wide* **5**, 43–54.

Plummer, C. (ed.) 1892/9. *Two of the Saxon Chronicles Parallel.* (2 Vols.) Oxford: Oxford University Press.

Porter, J. (ed.) 1991. *Beowulf: Text and Translation.* Pinner: Anglo-Saxon Books.

Postman, L. & Keppel, G. 1970. *Norms of Word Association.* New York: Academic Press.

Pryce, W. T. R. 1990. Language shift in Gwent, c. 1770–1981. In N. Coupland (ed.), *English in Wales* (Clevedon & Philadelphia: Multilingual Matters), 48–83.

Quiller-Couch, A. 1916. *On the Art of Writing.* Cambridge: Cambridge University Press.

Quirk, R. 1970. English in twenty years. In *English – a European Language.* (Luxembourg Conference Proceedings.) London: The Institute of Linguists.

Quirk, R., Adams, V. & Davy, D. 1975. *Old English Literature: a Practical Introduction.* Sevenoaks: Edward Arnold.

Quirk, R., Greenbaum, S., Leech, G. N. & Svartvik, J. 1985. *A Comprehensive Grammar of the English Language.* London: Longman.

Rakov, S. 1993. Computers and creative writing. *Computers and Texts* (Oxford University Computing Service) **5**, 11–12.

Rawson, H. 1991. *A Dictionary of Invective.* London: Robert Hale.

Reader's Digest. 1985. *The Right Word at the Right Time.* London: Reader's Digest Association.

Redfern, W. 1989. *Clichés and Coinages.* Oxford: Blackwell.

Rees, N. 1981. *Graffiti 3.* London: Unwin.

Reid, J. & Donaldson, M. 1984. *R&D.* Basingstoke: Macmillan Education.

Renton Report. 1975. *The Preparation of Legislation.* London: Her Majesty's Stationery Office.

Richmond, E. B. 1989. African English expressions in The Gambia. *World Englishes* **8**, 223–8.

Rigg, A.G. (ed.) 1968. *The English Language: a Historical Reader.* New York: Meredith Corporation.

Robinson, J. A. T. 1967. *Exploration into God.* London: SCM Press.

Robinson, M. (ed.) 1985. *The Concise Scots Dictionary.* Aberdeen: Aberdeen University Press.

Ronberg, G. 1992. *A Way with Words: the Language of English Renaissance Literature.* Sevenoaks: Edward Arnold.

Rosenberg, B. A. 1970. The formulaic quality of spontaneous sermons. *Journal of American Folklore* **83** (327), 3–20.

Ross, A. S. C. 1956. U and non-U: an essay in sociological linguistics. In N. Mitford (ed.), *Noblesse Oblige* (London: Hamish Hamilton), 11–36.

Ross, H. E. 1960. Patterns of swearing. *Discovery* (November), 479-81.

Rundell, M. & Stock, P. 1992. The corpus revolution. *English Today* **31**, 21–9.

Sampson, G. 1921. *English for the English.* Cambridge: Cambridge University Press.

Samuels, M. L. 1963. Some applications of Middle English dialectology. *English Studies* **44**, 81–94.

Savory, T. H. 1967. *The Language of Science*, 2nd edn. London: Deutsch.

Sawyer, P. H. 1962. *The Age of the Vikings.* London: Edward Arnold.

Schiffrin, D. 1987. *Discourse Markers.* Cambridge: Cambridge University Press.

Schonell, F. J. 1932. *An Essential Spelling List.* London: Macmillan.

Scieszka, J. & Smith, L. 1989. *The True Story of the 3 Little Pigs!* New York: Viking Kestrel.

Scragg, D. G. 1991. The nature of Old English verse. In M. Godden & M. Lapidge (eds.), *The Cambridge Companion to Old English Literature* (Cambridge: Cambridge University Press), 55–70.

Shorrocks, G. 1985. Aspects of affirmation and negation in the dialect of Farnworth and district. *Journal of the Lancashire Dialect Society* **34**, 20–9.

Simmons, A. & Francis, D. 1991. *OSL: Official Scrabble – Lists.* Edinburgh: Chambers.

Simpson, P. 1992. The pragmatics of nonsense: towards a stylistics of *Private Eye*'s Colemanballs. In M. Toolan (ed.), *Language, Text and Context: Essays in Stylistics* (London: Routledge), 281–305.

Singer, E. 1953. *The Graphologist's Alphabet.* London: Duckworth.

Smith, D. G. (ed.) 1982. *The Cambridge Encyclopedia of Earth Sciences.* Cambridge University Press.

Spillane, M. 1991. *The Complete Style Guide.* London: Piatkus.

Steiner, G. 1972. *Extraterritorial.* London: Faber & Faber.

Stevens, J. (ed.) 1723/1910. *Bede's Ecclesiastical History of the English Nation.* (Everyman's Library edition, No. 479.) London: Dent.

Stoel-Gammon, C. & Cooper, J. A. 1984. Patterns of early lexical and phonological development. *Journal of Child Language* **11**, 247–71.

Strang, B. M. W. 1962. *Modern English Structure.* London: Edward Arnold.

Strevens, P. 1980. *Teaching English as an International Language.* Oxford: Pergamon.

Stubbs, M. 1983. *Discourse Analysis: the Sociolinguistic Analysis of Natural Language.* Oxford: Blackwell.

Sutcliffe, D. 1982. *British Black English.* Oxford: Blackwell.

Svartvik, J., Eeg-Olofsson, M., Forsheden, O., Oreström, B. & Thavenius, C. 1982. *Survey of Spoken English.* (Lund Studies in English **63**.) Lund: CWK Gleerup.

Tannen, D. 1989. *Talking Voices: Repetition, Dialogue, and Imagery in Conversational Discourse.* Cambridge: Cambridge University Press.

Thirlwall, J. C. (ed.) 1957. *Selected Letters of William Carlos Williams.* New York: New Directions.

Thompson, L. (ed.) 1964. *Selected Letters of Robert Frost.* New York: Holt, Rinehart & Winston.

Tillich, P. 1963. *The Eternal Now.* London: SCM Press.

Tipping, L. 1927. *A Higher English Grammar.* London: Macmillan.

Todd, L. 1984a. *Modern Englishes: Pidgins and Creoles.* Oxford: Blackwell.

— 1984b. By their tongue divided: towards an analysis of the speech communities in Northern Ireland. *English World-Wide* **5**, 159–80.

Tolkien, J. R. R. & Gordon, E. V. 1925. *Sir Gawain and the Green Knight.* Oxford: Clarendon Press.

Toon, T. E. 1992. Old English dialects. In R. M. Hogg (ed.), *The Cambridge History of the English Language. Vol. I: The Beginnings to 1066.* (Cambridge: Cambridge University Press), 409–51.

Tournier, J. 1985. *Introduction descriptive à la lexicogénétique de l'anglais contemporain.* Paris: Champion–Slatkine.

Towell, J. E. & Sheppard, H. E. (eds.) 1987. *Acronyms, Initialisms and Abbreviation Dictionary.* 11th edn. Detroit: Gale Research Company.

Trudgill, P. 1986. The role of Irish English in the formation of colonial Englishes. In J. Harris, D. Little & D. Singleton (eds.), *Perspectives on the English Language in Ireland* (Trinity College Dublin: Centre for Language and Communication Studies), 3–7.

— 1990. *The Dialects of England.* Oxford: Blackwell.

Truman, M. 1973. *Harry S. Truman.* London: Hamish Hamilton.

Turner, G. W. 1966. *The English Language in Australia and New Zealand,* London: Longman.

Unwin, S. 1984. *Deep Joy.* Whitby: Caedmon of Whitby.

Van Buren, P. 1972. *The Edges of Language.* London: SCM Press.

Vance, M. 1991. Educational and therapeutic approaches used with a child presenting with acquired aphasia with convulsive disorder (Landau-Kleffner syndrome). *Child Language Teaching and Therapy* **7**, 40–60.

Van Sertima, I. 1976. My Gullah brother and I: exploration into a community's language and myth through its oral tradition. In D. S. Harrison & T. Trabasso (eds.), *Black English: a Seminar* (Hillsdale, NJ: Erlbaum), 123–46.

Vesterhus, S. A. 1991. Anglicisms in German car documents. *Language International* **3**, 10–15.

Wajnryb, R. 1989. Etymorphs. *English Today* **18**, 24.

Wakelin, M. 1986. English on the *Mayflower. English Today* **8**, 30–3.

Wales, K. 1991. *The Lights Out Joke Book.* London: Random Century Children's Books.

Webb, V. 1992. Language attitudes in South Africa: implications for a post apartheid democracy. In M Pütz (ed.), *Thirty Years of Linguistic Evolution* (Amsterdam: John Benjamins), 429–60.

Weekley, E. 1914. *The Romance of Names.* London: Murray.

Wells, J. C. 1989. English pronunciation preferences. London: University College Department of Linguistics.

Williams, C. H. 1990. The Anglicization of Wales. In N. Coupland (ed.), *English in Wales* (Clevedon & Philadelphia: Multilingual Matters), 19–47.

Williams, J. E. & Dennis, D. B. 1979. A partially-hearing unit. In D. Crystal (ed.), *Working with LARSP* (London: Edward Arnold), 214–41.

Wilson, J. 1990. *Politically Speaking.* Oxford: Blackwell.

Winer, L. 1989. Trinbagonian. *English Today* **18**, 17–22.

Wolfram, W. & Christian, D. 1976. *Appalachian Speech.* Arlington: Center for Applied Linguistics.

Wren, B. 1989. *What Language Shall I Borrow?* London: SCM Press.

Wyld, H. C. 1914. *A Short History of English.* (3rd rev edn, 1927.) London: John Murray.

Yule, G. U. 1944. *The Statistical Study of Literary Vocabulary.* Cambridge: Cambridge University Press.

Zupitza, J. (ed.) 1882. *Beowulf* (facsimile). (2nd edition by N. Davis 1959.) London: Oxford University Press.

Addresses of Journals and Societies (see p. 446 and elsewhere)

Ainm Bulletin of the Ulster Place-Name Society, Department of Celtic, Queen's University of Belfast, Belfast BT7 1NN, UK.

American Name Society Prof. W. H. Finke, Romance Languages, Baruch College, 17 Lexington Avenue, New York, NY 10010, USA.

Canadian Permanent Committee on Geographical Names, Room 650, 615 Booth Street, Ottawa, Ontario K1A OE9, Canada.

Dictionary Society of North America Louis Milic, RT-937, Cleveland State University, 1983 East 24 Street, Cleveland, Ohio 44115, USA.

English Academy of Southern Africa, PO Box 124, Wits, 2050, South Africa.

English Place-Name Society Journal Department of English, The University, Nottingham, NG7 2RD, UK.

English-Speaking Union of the Commonwealth Dartmouth House, 37 Charles Street, London W1X 8AB, UK; 16 East 69th Street, New York, NY 10021, USA.

English Today Cambridge University Press, Shaftesbury Road, Cambridge CB2 2RU, UK; Cambridge University Press, North American Branch, 40 West 20th Street, New York, NY 10011–4211, USA.

English World-Wide John Benjamins BV, PO Box 52519, Amsteldijk 44, 1007 HA Amsterdam, The Netherlands; John Benjamins North America Inc, 821 Bethlehem Pike, Philadelphia, Pennsylvania 19118, USA.

European Association for Lexicography Euralex Secretariat, PO Box 1017, DK-1007 Copenhagen K, Denmark.

International Association of Teachers of English as a Foreign Language 3 Kingsdown Chambers, Kingsdown Park, Whitstable, Kent CT5 2DJ, UK.

Journal of the North Central Name Society Edward Callary, English Department, Northern Illinois University, DeKalb, Illinois 60115, USA.

Canadian Society for the Study of Names/Société canadienne d'onomastique Prof. W. P. Ahrens, South 561 Ross Building, York University, 4700 Keele Street, North York, Ontario M3J 1P3, Canada. (Sponsors *Name Gleaner / La Glanure des Noms* and *Onomastica Canadiana*.)

The Names Society Leslie Dunkling, 32 Speer Road, Thames Ditton, Surrey KT7 0PW, UK.

National Association for the Teaching of English, Broadfield Business Centre, 50 Broadfield Road, Sheffield S8 0XJ, UK.

National Association of Teachers of English as a Foreign Language in Ireland PO Box 1917, EIR-Dublin 18, Irish Republic.

National Council of Teachers of English 111 Kenyon Road, Urbana, Illinois 61801, USA.

Networking English Language Learning in Europe Bredestraat 12, NL-6211, HC Maastricht, The Netherlands.

Nomina Council for Name Studies in Great Britain and Ireland, 13 Church Street, Chesterton, Cambridge CB4 1DT, UK.

Nomina Africana Names Society of Southern Africa/Naamkunderverenig-ing van Suideer-Afrika, Dr. L. A. Möller, c/o Onomastic Research Centre, HSRC Private Bag X41, Pretoria 0001, South Africa.

Plain English Campaign PO Box 3, Whaley Bridge, Stockport SK12 7LN, UK.

Queen's English Society 6 Manor Crescent, Guildford GU2 6NF, UK.

Simplified Spelling Society 133 John Trundle Court, Barbican, London EC2Y 8DJ, UK.

Teaching English to Speakers of Other Languages Suite 300, 1600 Cameron Street, Alexandria, Virginia, USA.

Verbatim PO Box 199, Aylesbury, Buckinghamshire HP20 2HY, UK; 4 Laurel Heights, Old Lyme, Connecticut 06371, USA.

World Englishes, Blackwell Publishers, 108 Cowley Road, Oxford OX4 1JF, UK.

IV · FURTHER READING

General

Several books deal systematically with the language as a whole. They include: T. McArthur (ed.), *The Oxford Companion to the English Language* (Oxford: Oxford University Press, 1992); W. F. Bolton, *A Living Language: the History and Structure of English* (New York: Random House, 1982); R. Quirk & G. Stein, *English in Use* (London: Longman, 1990); R. Burchfield, *The English Language* (Oxford: Oxford University Press, 1985); B. Bryson, *Mother Tongue: the English Language* (London: Hamish Hamilton; New York: William Morrow, 1990); and R. Lass, *The Shape of English: Structure and History* (London: Dent, 1987); also, R. McCrum, W. Cran & R. MacNeil, *The Story of English* (London: Faber & Faber, 1986).

Collections of essays include: W. F. Bolton & D. Crystal (eds.), *The English Language* (Vol. 10 of *Sphere History of the English Language*, London: Sphere, 1987) and S. Greenbaum (ed.), *The English Language Today* (Oxford: Pergamon, 1985).

Personal comments on a selection of topics are made in W. Nash, *An Uncommon Tongue: the Uses and Resources of English* (London: Routledge, 1992) and C. Ricks & L. Michaels, *The State of the Language* (San Francisco: University of California Press; London: Faber & Faber, 1990).

Collections of extracts from earlier authors on English include: W. F. Bolton (ed.), *The English Language: Essays by English and American Men of Letters, 1490–1839* (Cambridge: Cambridge University Press, 1966) and W. F. Bolton & D. Crystal (eds.), *The English Language: Essays by English and American Men of Letters, 1858–1964* (Cambridge: Cambridge University Press, 1969). The periodical *English Today* (Cambridge University Press) reviews the field at quarterly intervals.

Part I

A standard textbook on the history of English is A. C. Baugh, now published as A. C. Baugh & T. Cable, *A History of the English language* (London: Routledge & Kegan Paul, 3rd edn, 1978); see also D. Burnley, *The History of the English Language: a Source Book* (London: Longman, 1992); D. Leith, *A Social History of English* (London: Routledge, 1983); T. Pyles & J. Algeo, *The Origins and Development of the English Language* (New York: Harcourt Brace Jovanovich, 3rd edn, 1982); M. L. Samuels, *Linguistic Evolution: with Special Reference to English* (Cambridge: Cambridge University Press, 1972); and B. M. H. Strang, *A History of English* (London: Methuen, 1970).

The period covered by §§2–4 is the subject of A. C. Partridge, *A Companion to Old and Middle English Studies* (London: Deutsch, 1982). For translations of the early Anglo-Saxon texts, see the Everyman Library series (London: Dent; New York: Dutton): *Anglo-Saxon Poetry* (No. 794, ed. R. K. Gordon, 1926), *The Anglo-Saxon Chronicle* (No. 1624, ed. G. N. Garmonsway, 1972) and *The Ecclesiastical History of the English Nation* (No. 479, ed. J. Stevens, 1723/1910). On runes, see R. I. Page, *Reading the Past: Runes* (London: British Museum Publications, 1987). On the Old English period, see B. Mitchell, *An Invitation to Old English and Anglo-Saxon England* (Oxford: Blackwell, 1995); R. M. Hogg (ed.), *The Cambridge History of the English Language. Vol. I: The Beginnings to 1066* (Cambridge: Cambridge University Press, 1992) and M. Godden & M. Lapidge (eds.), *The Cambridge Companion to Old English Literature* (Cambridge: Cambridge University Press, 1991). Standard texts include R. Quirk & C. L. Wrenn, *An Old English Grammar* (London: Methuen, 1955) and B. Mitchell & F. C. Robinson, *A Guide to Old English* (Oxford: Blackwell, 5th edn, 1992). On Middle English, see C. Jones, *An Introduction to Middle English* (New York: Holt, Rinehart & Winston, 1972) and N. Blake (ed.), *The Cambridge History of the English Language. Vol. 2: 1066–1476* (Cambridge:

Cambridge University Press, 1992). On Chaucer, see R. W. V. Elliott, *Chaucer's English* (London: Deutsch, 1974); D. J. Burnley, *A Guide to Chaucer's Language* (Norman: University of Oklahoma Press, 1984); and N. E. Eliason, *The Language of Chaucer's Poetry* (Copenhagen: Rosenkilde and Bagger, 1972, Vol. 17 of *Anglistica*).

The period covered by §5 is dealt with in C. Barber, *Early Modern English* (London: Deutsch, 1976); M. Görlach, *Introduction to Early Modern English* (Cambridge: Cambridge University Press, 1991); and R. Lass (ed.), *The Cambridge History of the English Language. Vol. 3: 1476–1776* (Cambridge: Cambridge University Press, 1995); also N. F. Blake, *Caxton's Own Prose* (London: Deutsch, 1973). On Shakespeare, see W. F. Bolton, *Shakespeare's English: Language in the History Plays* (Oxford: Blackwell, 1992) and N. F. Blake, *Shakespeare's Language: an Introduction* (London: Macmillan, 1983). On the religious linguistic trends of the time, see A. C. Partridge, *English Biblical Translation* (London: Deutsch, 1973) and S. Brook, *The Language of the Book of Common Prayer* (London: Deutsch, 1965); a selection of extracts has been edited by P. Levi, *The English Bible: from Wycliff to William Barnes* (London: Constable, 1974). On the Renaissance, see G. Ronberg, *A Way with Words* (London: Edward Arnold, 1992). On Milton, see T. N. Corns, *Milton's Language* (Oxford: Blackwell, 1990). On *thou* and *you*, see the papers by Quirk, Barber, and Mulholland in V. Salmon & E. Burness, *Reader in the Language of Shakespearean Drama* (Amsterdam: Benjamins, 1987), and Ch. 3 of Ronberg (*ibid.*).

Later periods (§§6–7) are dealt with in the forthcoming volumes of *The Cambridge History of the English Language*: Vol. 4: *1776–Present Day*, S. Romaine (ed.); Vol. 5: *English in Britain and Overseas: Origins and Development*, R. W. Burchfield (ed.); and Vol. 6: *English in North America*, J. Algeo (ed.). S. B. Flexner, *I Hear America Talking* (New York: Simon and Schuster, 1976) is an illustrated history of American words and phrases. On the language of various authors, see the volumes in the Blackwell (formerly Deutsch) *Language Library* (all entitled 'The Language of —'): G. L. Brook on *Dickens* (1970), K. C. Phillipps on *Thackeray* (1978), G. Tulloch on *Scott* (1980), and R. W. V. Elliott on *Hardy* (1984). On Victorian English attitudes generally, see K. C. Phillipps, *Language and Class in Victorian England* (Oxford: Blackwell, 1984).

Issues to do with the historical spread of English around the world are reviewed in R. W. Bailey & M. Görlach (eds.), *English as a World Language* (Ann Arbor, Mich.: University of Michigan Press, 1982; Cambridge: Cambridge University Press, 1984); B. B. Kachru, *The Alchemy of English* (Oxford: Pergamon, 1986); J. Platt, H. Weber & M. L. Ho, *The New Englishes* (London: Routledge & Kegan Paul, 1984); R. Quirk & H. G. Widdowson (eds.), *English in the World* (Cambridge: Cambridge University Press, 1985); and W. Viereck & W.-D. Bald (eds.), *English in Contact with Other Languages* (Budapest: Akadémiai Kiadó, 1986). On attitudes to English, see R. W. Bailey, *Images of English: a Cultural History of the Language* (Cambridge: Cambridge University Press, 1991). The positions in the English Language Amendment debate are presented in several issues of *English Today*: 6 (1986), 11 (1987), and 16 (1988), and in D. Baron, *The English-Only Question: an Official Language for Americans?* (New Haven, Conn.: Yale University Press, 1990).

Part II

On English word-formation generally (§§8–9), see L. Bauer, *English Word-formation* (Cambridge: Cambridge University Press, 1983) and V. Adams, *An Introduction to Modern English Word-Formation* (London: Longman, 1973). On word-history, see G. Hughes, *Words in Time: a Social History of the English Vocabulary* (Oxford: Blackwell, 1988); A. S. C. Ross, *Etymology* (London: Deutsch, 1958); C. T. Onions (ed.), *The Oxford Dictionary of English Etymology* (Oxford: Oxford University Press, 1966); and R. K. Barnhart (ed.), *The*

Barnhart Dictionary of Etymology (New York: Wilson, 1987). Abbreviations are discussed in T. McArthur, 'The cult of abbreviation', *English Today* **15** (1988), 36–42; proper names in D. J. Allerton, 'The linguistic and sociolinguistic status of proper names', *Journal of Pragmatics* **11** (1987), 61–92; nonsense words in A. S. Kaye, 'Whatchamacallem', *English Today* **21** (1990), 70–3. George Orwell's language is the subject of W. F. Bolton, *The Language of 1984* (Oxford: Blackwell, 1984); James Joyce's in A. Burgess, *Joysprick* (London: Deutsch, 1973).

On place names (§10), see K. Cameron, *English Place Names* (London: Batsford, revised 1988); J. Field, *Place-Names of Great Britain and Ireland* (Newton Abbot: David & Charles, 1980); and C. M. Matthews, *Place Names of the English-Speaking World* (London: Weidenfeld & Nicolson; New York: Scribner's, 1972). On personal names, see P. Hanks & F. Hodges, *A Dictionary of Surnames* (Oxford: Oxford University Press, 1988); L. Dunkling & W. Gosling, *Everyman's Dictionary of First Names* (London: Dent, 1983); L. Dunkling, *The Guinness Book of Names* (Enfield: Guinness Superlatives, 1974); and M. Manser, *The Guinness Book of Words* (Enfield: Guiness Superlatives, 1988), Ch. 4.

The following relate to the aspects of the lexicon discussed in §§10–11. On idioms: T. H. Long (ed.), *Longman Dictionary of English Idioms* (London: Longman, 1979) and J. O. E. Clark, *Word Wise: a Dictionary of English Idioms* (London: Harrap, 1988). On taboo language: G. Hughes, *Swearing: a Social History of Foul Language, Oaths and Profanity in English* (Oxford: Blackwell, 1991). On jargon: W. Nash, *Jargon: its Uses and Abuses* (Oxford: Blackwell. 1993). On euphemism: K. Allen & K. Burridge, *Euphemism and Dysphemism* (Oxford: Oxford University Press, 1991) and R. W. Holder, *A Dictionary of American and British Euphemisms* (Bath: Bath University Press, 1987). On Doublespeak, W. Lutz, *Doublespeak: from Revenue Enhancement to Terminal Living* (New York: Harper & Row, 1989). On slang: E. Partridge, *Slang Today and Yesterday* (London: Routledge & Kegan Paul, 4th edn, 1970). On clichés, W. Redfern, *Clichés and Coinages* (Oxford: Blackwell, 1989); N. Bagnall, *In Defence of Clichés* (London: Constable, 1985); and N. Rees, *The Joy of Clichés: a Complete User's Guide* (London: Macdonald, 1984).

Part III

The outline of English grammar in §§13–16 is derived largely from D. Crystal, *Rediscover Grammar* (London: Longman, 1988), which in turn is based on R. Quirk, S. Greenbaum, G. Leech & J. Svartvik, *A Comprehensive Grammar of the English Language* (London: Longman, 1985); see also R. Quirk & S. Greenbaum, *A University Grammar of English* (London: Longman, 1973); S. Greenbaum & R. Quirk, *A Student's Grammar of the English Language* (London: Longman, 1990); G. Leech & J. Svartvik, *A Communicative Grammar of English* (London: Longman, 2nd edn, 1994); and G. Leech, *An A–Z of English Grammar and Usage* (London: Edward Arnold, 1989). A selection of usage issues is discussed in D. Crystal, *Who Cares About English Usage?* (Harmondsworth: Penguin, 1984). The prescriptivism issue is dealt with in J. Milroy & L. Milroy, *Authority in Language* (London: Routledge, 2nd edn, 1991).

Part IV

For an introduction to English phonetics (§17), see A. C. Gimson, *An Introduction to the Pronunciation of English* (London: Edward Arnold, 5th edn, revised by A. Cruttenden, 1994); P. J. Roach, *English Phonetics and Phonology: a Practical Course* (Cambridge: Cambridge University Press, 1983); C. W. Kreidler, *The Pronunciation of English* (Oxford: Blackwell, 1989); J. D. O'Connor, *Phonetics* (Harmondsworth: Penguin, 1971); and E. Couper-Kuhlen, *An Introduction to English Prosody* (London: Edward Arnold, 1986). On accents, see J. C. Wells, *Accents of English* (Cambridge: Cambridge University Press, 3 Vols., 1982). On sounds in writing, see R. Chapman, *The Treatment of Sounds in Language and Literature* (Oxford: Blackwell, 1984).

On the background to the English alphabet (§18), see F. Coulmas, *The Writing Systems of the World* (Oxford: Blackwell, 1989) and D. Diringer, *A History of the Alphabet* (Henley-on-Thames: Gresham Books, 1983). The spelling system is described in detail in E. Carney, *A Survey of English Spelling* (London: Routledge, 1994). On spelling reform, see W. Haas (ed.), *Alphabets for English* (Manchester: Manchester University Press, 1969), and the publications of the Simplified Spelling Society (Birmingham, U.K.). On the history of punctuation, see M. B. Parkes, *Pause and Effect: Punctuation in the West* (Aldershot: Scolar Press, 1992).

Part V

On the study of discourse generally (§19), see M. Stubbs, *Discourse Analysis* (Oxford: Blackwell, 1983); D. Schiffrin, *Discourse Markers* (Cambridge: Cambridge University Press, 1987); D. Tannen, *Talking Voices: Repetition, Dialogue and Imagery in Conversational Discourse* (Cambridge: Cambridge University Press, 1989); and W. Nash, *Rhetoric: the Wit of Persuasion* (Oxford: Blackwell, 1989). The study of varieties is introduced in D. Crystal & D. Davy, *Investigating English Style* (London: Longman, 1969) and R. Carter & W. Nash, *Seeing Through Language: a Guide to Styles of English Writing* (Oxford: Blackwell, 1990). On speech/writing variation, see D. Biber, *Variation Across Speech and Writing* (Cambridge: Cambridge University Press, 1988).

Regional variation (§20) is introduced in the references relating to §7 above, and also in P. Trudgill & J. Hannah, *International English: a Guide to Varieties of Standard English* (London: Edward Arnold, 1982); M. Görlach, *Englishes: Studies in Varieties of English 1984–1988* (Amsterdam: John Benjamins, 1991); and L. Todd & I. F. Hancock, *International English Usage* (London: Croom Helm, 1986). The social perspective is the motivation for J. Cheshire (ed.), *English Around the World: Sociolinguistic Perspectives* (Cambridge: Cambridge University Press, 1991) and J. Cheshire, *Variation in an English Dialect: a Sociolinguistic Study* (Cambridge: Cambridge University Press, 1982).

The classic account of the evolution of American English is H. L. Mencken, *The American Language* (rev. R. I. McDavid, New York: Knopf, 1963); also, T. Pyles, *Words and Ways of American English* (New York: Random House, 1952). The differences between American and British English are reviewed in M. Benson, E. Benson & R. Ilson, *Lexicographic Description of English* (Amsterdam: John Benjamins, 1986); see also J. Algeo, 'British and American grammatical differences', *International Journal of Lexicography* **1**, 1988, 1–31. On British English dialects, see P. Trudgill, *The Dialects of England* (Oxford: Blackwell, 1990); M. F. Wakelin, *English Dialects: an Introduction* (London: Athlone Press, 1972); P. Trudgill (ed.), *Language in the British Isles* (Cambridge: Cambridge University Press, 1984); M. Petyt, *The Study of Dialect* (London: Deutsch, 1980); A. J. Aitken & T. McArthur (eds.), *Languages of Scotland* (Edinburgh: Chambers, 1979); and N. Coupland (ed.), *English in Wales* (Clevedon: Multilingual Matters, 1990).

On other major regional varieties (§20), see on Canadian English: J. K. Chambers (ed.), *Canadian English: Origins and Structures* (Toronto: Methuen, 1975); W. S. Avis, *et al.* (eds.), *A Dictionary of Canadianisms on Historical Principles* (Toronto: Gage, 1967); and R. E. McConnell, *Our Own Voice: Canadian English and How it is Studied* (Toronto: Gage, 1979). On pidgins and creoles: L. Todd, *Modern Englishes: Pidgins and Creoles* (Oxford: Blackwell, 1984); S. Romaine, *Pidgin and Creole Languages* (London: Longman, 1988); J. L. Dillard, *Black English* (New York: Random House, 1972); F. G. Cassidy, *Jamaica Talk: Three Hundred Years of the English Language in Jamaica* (London: Macmillan, 1961); and P. A. Roberts, *West Indians and their Language* (Cambridge: Cambridge University Press, 1988). On English in Australia and New Zealand: P. Collins & D. Blair (eds.), *Australian English: the Language of a New Society* (Brisbane: University of Queensland Press, 1989); W. S. Ransom (ed.), *English Transported: Essays on Australasian English* (Canberra: Australian National University Press, 1970); G. W. Turner, *The English Language in Australia and New Zealand* (London: Longman, 1966); A. G. Mitchell & A. Delbridge, *The Pronunciation of English in Australia* (Sydney: Angus & Robertson, 1965); and A. Bell & J. Holmes (eds.), *New Zealand Ways of Speaking English* (Clevedon: Multilingual Matters, 1990). On South Asian English: B. B. Kachru, *The Indianization of English: the English Language in*

India (Delhi: Oxford University Press, 1983); and P. Nihalani, R. K. Tongue & P. Hosali, *Indian and British English: a Handbook of Usage and Pronunciation* (Delhi: Oxford University Press, 1970).

A general account of issues in social variation (§21) can be found in D. Leith, *A Social History of English* (London: Routledge & Kegan Paul, 1983). See also G. W. Turner, *Stylistics* (Harmondsworth: Penguin, 1973) and N. Fairclough, *Language and Power* (London: Longman, 1989), and the readings in T. Crowley (ed.), *Proper English? Readings in Language, History, and Cultural Identity* (London: Routledge, 1991). A historical perspective is K. C. Phillipps, *Language and Class in Victorian England* (Oxford: Blackwell, 1984). On gender, see J. Coates, *Women, Men, and Language* (London: Longman, 1986). There are several studies of individual varieties. On law, see D. Mellinkoff, *The Language of the Law* (Boston, Mass.: Little Brown, 1963) and W. M. O'Barr, *Linguistic Evidence: Language, Power and Strategy in the Courtroom* (New York: Academic Press, 1982). On Plain English: M. Cutts & C. Maher, *The Plain English Story* (Stockport: Plain English Campaign, 1986). On political language: J. Wilson, *Politically Speaking* (Oxford: Blackwell, 1990). On the media: A. Bell, *The Language of News Media* (Oxford: Blackwell, 1991); R. Fowler, *Language in the News: Discourse and Ideology in the Press* (London: Routledge, 1991); and G. N. Leech, *English in Advertising: a Linguistic Study of Advertising in Great Britain* (London: Longman, 1966).

The different aspects of personal variation (§22) are taken further in the following. On word games: T. Augarde, *The Oxford Guide to Word Games* (Oxford: Oxford University Press, 1984). On humour, D. Chiaro, *The Language of Jokes: Analysing Verbal Play* (London: Routledge, 1992); W. Nash. *The Language of Humour: Style and Technique in Comic Discourse* (London: Longman, 1985); and W. Redfern, *Puns* (Oxford: Blackwell, 1984). On aspects of language in literature: N. F. Blake, *An Introduction to the Language of Literature* (London: Macmillan, 1990); R. Chapman, *Linguistics and Literature* (London: Edward Arnold, 1973); G. N. Leech, *A Linguistic Guide to English Poetry* (London: Longman, 1969); G. N. Leech & M. Short, *Style in Fiction* (London: Longman, 1981); and W. Nash, *Language in Popular Fiction* (London: Routledge, 1990); also, W. van Peer (ed.), *The Taming of the Text:*

Explorations in Language, Literature and Culture (London: Routledge, 1991). On terminology, see J. A. Cuddon, *A Dictionary of Literary Terms and Literary Theory* (Oxford: Blackwell, 3rd edn, 1991) and K. Wales, *Dictionary of Stylistics* (London: Longman, 1989).

Part VI

On child language acquisition, see D. Crystal, *Listen To Your Child* (Harmondsworth: Penguin, 1986); P. Fletcher, *A Child's Learning of English* (Oxford: Blackwell, 1985); and D. Ingram, *First Language Acquisition* (Cambridge: Cambridge University Press, 1989). On literacy, see C. D. Baker & P. Freebody, *Children's First School Books* (Oxford: Blackwell, 1989); H. Graff (ed.), *Literacy and Social Development in the West: a Reader* (Cambridge: Cambridge University Press, 1983); and M. Stubbs, *Language and Literacy: the Sociolinguistics of Reading and Writing* (London: Routledge & Kegan Paul, 1980). On language disability and intervention, see D. Crystal & R. Varley, *An Introduction to Language Pathology* (London: Whurr, 3rd edn, 1993).

Corpora are the subject-matter of K. Aijmer & B. Altenberg (eds.), *English Corpus Linguistics* (London: Longman, 1991). On language and computer technology, see J. Sinclair, *Corpus, Concordance, and Collocation* (Oxford: Oxford University Press, 1991) and C. S. Butler (ed.), *Computers and Written Texts* (Oxford: Blackwell, 1992). On lexicography, see R. R. K. Hartmann (ed.), *Lexicography: Principles and Practice* (London: Academic Press, 1983); R. Ilson (ed.), *Lexicography: an Emerging International Profession* (Manchester: Manchester University Press, 1986); R. W. Bailey (ed.), *Dictionaries of English: Prospects for the Record of our Language* (Ann Arbor, Mich.: University of Michigan Press, 1987; Cambridge: Cambridge University Press, 1989); S. Landau, *Dictionaries: the Art and Craft of Lexicography* (New York: Scribner, 1984; Cambridge: Cambridge University Press, 1989); and G. Stein, *The English Dictionary Before Cawdrey* (Tübingen: Niemeyer, 1985). For the arguments about Webster 3, see J. Sledd & W. R. Ebbitt, *Dictionaries and THAT Dictionary* (New York: Scott, Foresman, 1962). The history of the *OED* is described in K. M. Elisabeth Murray, *Caught in the Web of Words* (New Haven, Conn.: Yale University Press, 1977).

V · INDEX OF LINGUISTIC ITEMS

VI·INDEX OF AUTHORS AND PERSONALITIES

VII·INDEX OF TOPICS

ACKNOWLEDGEMENTS

The publishers gratefully acknowledge the help of the many individuals and organizations who cannot all be named in collecting the illustrations for this volume. Every effort has been made to obtain permission to use copyright materials; the publishers apologise for any omissions and would welcome these being brought to their attention.

The appearance of logos and trademarks in the encyclopedia in no way affects their legal status as trademarks.

Note: Sources and copyright holders for materials used are given in order of their appearance in the volume (page numbers in bold type). The following abbreviations have been used: *b* bottom; *c* centre; *l* left; *r* right; *t* top; *x* text; British Library: by permission of the British Library; Mansell: The Mansell Collection; NPG: reproduced by courtesy of the National Portrait Gallery.

3 Ancient Art & Architecture Collection. **4** By permission of the Syndics of Cambridge University Library. **7** *bl* By permission of the Syndics of Cambridge University Library. **7** *t* & *r* Ancient Art & Architecture Collection. **8** St Edmundsbury Borough Council/West Stow Anglo-Saxon Village Trust. **9** *br* Michael Holford. **10** Ancient Art & Architecture Collection. **11** British Library MS Cotton Vitellius A. xv, fol. 132. *x* Translation reprinted by permission of John Porter from *Beowulf* (Pinner, Anglo-Saxon Books, 1991). **12** Den Phillips. **13** *b* Reproduced by permission of the Dean & Chapter of Exeter Cathedral. **13** *t* Hulton Deutsch Collection. **14** MS 173, f.5r reproduced by permission of the Master and Fellows of Corpus Christi College, Cambridge. **15** *x l* Translation: Everyman's Library, David Campbell Publishers Ltd. **16** British Library MS Cotton Tiberius A. xv, fol. 60v. **17** British Library MS Cotton Nero D. iv, fol. 29. **18** Mary Evans Picture Library. **23** Mary Evans Picture Library. **24** Michael J. Stead. **25** *tr* After P. H. Sawyer *The Age of the Vikings* Edward Arnold 1962. **25** *b* Michael J. Stead. **26** *t* West Country Tourist Board. **27** Mary Evans Picture Library. **30** *t* Taken from the facsimile of Great Domesday Book published by Alecto Historical Editions. **30** *bl, bc* & *br* Hulton Deutsch Collection. **31** *c* City Heritage Services, Southampton City Council. *inset* Joe Low. **32** Peterborough Cathedral Enterprises. **33** Bodleian Library, Oxford MS. Laud Misc. 636, fol. 89v. **34** By permission of the Dean and Chapter of Worcester. **35** Mary Evans Picture Library. **36** British Library, MS Harley 978, fol. 11v. **37** *l* British Library MS Cotton Nero A. x, fol. 95. *r* British Library MS Cotton Nero A. x, fol. 94v. **38** EL 26 c 9f. lr reproduced by permission of The Huntingdon Library, San Marino, California. **40** British Library, MS Royal 17 B. xvii, fol. 11. **41** *t* Michael J. Stead. *b* Crown copyright – reproduced with the sanction of the Controller of Her Majesty's Stationery Office (photographer: A. Bavin). **43** *l* Rex Features Ltd. *r* Michael J Stead. **46** MS 61, fr reproduced by permission of the Master and Fellows of Corpus Christi College, Cambridge. **47** *b* COI. **48** Mansell. **49** Photo-MLC. **50** *b* Frank Lane Picture Agency. **52** *c* Jarrold Publishing. *b* Hulton Deutsch Collection. **53** Mansell. **56** *t* British Library. *c* Mary Evans Picture Library. *b* Mansell. **57** Hulton Deutsch Collection. **58** Brian Tarr Photography. **59** British Library. **61** Mary Evans Picture Library. **62** *t* Andy Fulgoni/Shakespeare's Globe. *b* Hulton Deutsch Collection. **63** Shakespeare Centre Library, Stratford-upon-Avon. **64** British Library. **65** Mary Evans Picture Library. **66** *c* & *b* Pitman Collection, Bath University Library. **67** *c* The Pierpont Morgan Library, New York. MA 457. *b* Hulton Deutsch Collection. **71** Hulton Deutsch Collection. **72** Bodleian Library, Oxford Mal. 754(2). **73** *b* Mansell. **74** Joe Lowe. **76** Mary Evans Picture Library. **77** *b* Reproduced by permission of Punch. **78** Hulton Deutsch Collection. **79** *t* Hulton Deutsch Collection. *c* Department of Manuscripts and Special Collections, University of Nottingham. *r* Hulton Deutsch Collection. **80** Courtesy of the Noah Webster House, West Hartford, CT. **81** *t* & *b* Hulton Deutsch Collection. **82** *t* Hulton Deutsch Collection. *c* Mansell. **83** Mary Evans Picture Library. **84** Mary Evans Picture Library. **86** Reproduced by permission of Punch. **87** The Royal Institution of Great Britain. **88** *t, ct,* & *cb* Mary Evans Picture Library. *b* Mansell. **89** *t* Michael Holford. **90** *b* Ann Ronan/Image Select. *inset* Hulton Deutsch Collection. **92** *b* Courtesy of Plimoth Plantation. **93** Mary Evans Picture Library. **94** *t* Mansell. **95** *b* Kryn Taconis/Magnum. **96** Alex Webb/Magnum. **97** *t* Costa Manos/Magnum. *b* Hulton Deutsch Collection. **98** *t* Mary Evans Picture Library. *cr* Permission granted by the Office of the Official Secretary to the Governor-General, Canberra, Australia. **99** *t* Chris Fairclough Colour Library. *b* Mary Evans Picture Library. *r* British Library. **100** *l* Dave Saunders/TRIP. *r* David Burnett/Contact/Colorific! **101** *tl* Mary Evans Picture Library. *tr* Hulton Deutsch Collection. *b* Syndication International. **104** *t* Marcus Brooke/Colorific! *b* Rick Smolan/Contact/Colorific! **109** *background* NASA/Science Photo Library **111** *clockwise from top* Rex Features; Hulton Deutsch Collection; David Levenson/Colorific!; John Ficara/Woodfin Camp & Assoc./Colorific!; Rex Features; Robert Mass/Sipa Press/Rex Features. **112** *t* Syndication International. *inset* The Lord Quirk, FBA. **113** *t* Michael J. Stead. *c* Trade Promotions Services Ltd. *b* Martin Parr/Magnum. **114** *t* Michael J. Stead. *b* Hulton Deutsch Collection. **115** Hulton Deutsch Collection. **116** Telegraph Colour Library. **118** Tom McArthur & Liz Knox. **119** *r* *Oxford English Dictionary*, Second Edition 1989, by permission of Oxford University Press. **120** Unit 18 Photography. **121** Gale Research Inc. **122** Burt Glinn/Magnum. **123** *t* Mary Evans Picture Library. *bl* Reader's Digest Association Ltd. **124** *l* Vernon Richards/George Orwell Archive: University College London. *r* Mary Evans Picture Library. *x br* Excerpt from 'Politics and the English Language' by George Orwell, Copyright 1946 by Sonia Brownell Orwell and renewed 1974 by Sonia Orwell, reprinted from his volume *Shooting an Elephant and Other Essays* by permission of Harcourt Brace & Company/The estate of the late Sonia Brownell Orwell and Martin Secker & Warburg Ltd. **125** *tl* Mary Evans Picture Library. *tr* National Gallery, London/Bridgeman Art Library, London. *b* Erich Lessing/Magnum. **128** Unit 18 Photography. **129** Jarrold Publishing. **130** *b* Eurotunnel. **131** *l* Hulton Deutsch Collection. *br* Disney. **132** Jennie Gass. **133** *tr* Vibert-Stokes/Ace Photo Agency. *c* & *b* J. C. Davies Photography. **134** NPG. **135** Peter Edwards/NPG. *x* Excerpt from *Nineteen Eighty-Four* by George Orwell, copyright 1949 by Harcourt Brace & Company and renewed 1977 by Sonia Brownell Orwell, reprinted by permission of the publisher/The estate of the late Sonia Brownell Orwell and Martin Secker & Warburg Ltd. **136, 137** *x* G. Hughes *Words in Time: a Social History of the English Vocabulary* Blackwell Publishers 1988. **138** *t* F. Kermode (ed.) *The Tempest* Methuen & Co. **139** *l* Meat and Livestock Commission. **140** Syndication International. **141** *tl* Syndication International. *tc* Jarrold Publishing. *tr* Aerofilms. *cl* Ian Berry/Magnum. *cc* & *cr* Jarrold Publishing. *bl, bc* & *br* Jarrold Publishing. **142** *l* Taken from the facsimile of Great Domesday Book published by Alecto Historical Editions. *r* British Library. **144** *t* Harry Ten Shilling, Shakespeare. *b* NPG. **146** *l* British Library. *r* Mary Evans Picture Library. **147** *t* Jay L. Inge, © National Geographic Society. *b* © Anglo-Australian Observatory (photography by David Malin). **148** *tr* The Bettmann Archive. *cr* National Archives, Washington. **149** *t* Nos 1, 4, 5, & 6 Public Record Office, London (ref. PROB 1/4). *No. 2* Guildhall Library, Corporation of London/Bridgeman Art Library, London. *No. 3* British Library. *b* Crown copyright – reproduced with the sanction of the Controller of Her Majesty's Stationery Office (ref. SC5/Sussex). **150** *l* Hulton Deutsch Collection. *c* Mary Evans Picture Library. *r* London Features. **152** Mary Evans Picture Library. **153** The Kobal Collection. **154** *t* Alan Fearnley. *b* British Library. **155** *tl* & *tcl* Mary Evans Picture Library. *tcr* Peter Newark's Western Americana. *tr, bl, bcl,* & *bcr* Mary Evans Picture Library. *br* Natural History Museum, London. **156** T. McArthur *Longman Lexicon of Contemporary English* Longman Group Ltd 1981. **157** *l* G. Hughes *Words in Time: a Social History of the English Vocabulary* Blackwell Publishers 1988. **157** *r* Fred Mayer/Magnum. **158** Mansell. **159** *tr* Copyright Québec/Amérique International (1992). *x* Dutch (ed.) *Roget's Thesaurus* Longman Group Ltd 1982 &

Kirkpatrick (ed.) *Roget's Thesaurus* Longman Group Ltd 1987. **162** BBC Photography Library. *x br* Academic Press, Orlando, Florida. **163** *x t* *Longman Dictionary of English Idioms*, Longman Group Ltd 1979. *x r* Dylan Thomas 'After the Funeral', from *The Poems* J M Dent. **165** From *Antonyms* by Joan Hanson. © Lerner Publications, Minneapolis, MN. *x br* J. S. Justeson & S. M. Katz 'Redefining antonymy: the textual structure of semantic relation' *Literary & Linguistic Computing* 7 (3) 1992 by permission of Oxford University Press. **166** Unit 18 Photography. *r* *Longman Dictionary of the English Language* Longman Group Ltd 1987. **167** *t* & *b* Telegraph Colour Library. **168** *bl* The Salmon Studio. *br* The Prisoner © ITC Entertainment Group Ltd. **169** *c* Paul Conklin/TCL Stock Directory. *inset* G. Germany/Telegraph Colour Library. **170** Noel Alexander, Tops Property Services/Riley Developments. **171** *bl* Mary Evans Picture Library. *tr* J. C. Davies Photography. *br* E. McLachlan. **173** *tr* & *br* British Library. **174** Cartoon by John Jensen in William Davis *The Corporate Infighter's Handbook* Arrow Books 1986. **176** Bruno Barbey/Magnum. **177** MENCAP. **178** STAR TREK © 1993 by Paramount Pictures. All rights reserved. **179** THE FAR SIDE copyright 1991 FarWorks, Inc. Dist. by Universal Press Syndicate. Reprinted with permission. All rights reserved. **181** *b* © Gyles Brandreth 1978. Extracted from *Graffiti: The Scrawl of the Wild* published by Corgi Books, a division of Transworld Publishers Ltd. All rights reserved. **182** Hulton Deutsch Collection. *x tr* Eric Partridge *Slang: Today and Yesterday* Routledge & Kegan Paul 1933. *x b* P. G. Wodehouse *Service with a Smile* Hutchinson 1961. Reproduced by permission of Random House UK Limited and A. P. Watt Ltd on behalf of The Trustees of the Wodehouse Estate. Eric Partridge *Slang: Today and Yesterday* Routledge & Kegan Paul 1933. Raymond Chandler *The Big Sleep* (Hamish Hamilton 1939) copyright © Raymond Chandler, 1939. Reproduced by permission of Hamish Hamilton Ltd. **183** *x* Eric Partridge *Dictionary of Slang and Unconventional English* Routledge & Kegan Paul 1937. Eric Partridge 'Genesis of a lexicographer', in *From Sanskrit to Brazil* Hamish Hamilton 1952. Copyright © Eric Partridge 1952. Reproduced by permission of Sheil Land Associates. **184** Mary Evans Picture Library. *x b* D. Murison *Scots Saws* (1981) Reproduced by permission of Mercat Press. Extracts from *A Diction-ary of American Proverbs*, edited by Wolfgang Mieder, Stewart A. Kingsbury, and Kelsie B. Harder. Copyright © 1992 by Oxford University Press, Inc. Reprinted by permission. **185** *tr* Reproduced by permission of Punch. *bl* Billett Potter. *cr* © D. C. Thomson & Co. Ltd. *x br* T. S. Eliot *Collected Poems 1909–1962* Faber & Faber Ltd. **186** Giraudon/Bridgeman Art Library. *x* W. Redfern *Cliches and Coinages* Blackwell Publishers 1989. **187** *tl*, *tc* & *tr* Mary Evans Picture Library. *bl* NPG. *br* Mander & Mitchenson. **193** *t* Hulton Deutsch Collection. *inset* Mansell. **195** *tl*, *tr*, *bl*, & *br* Hulton Deutsch Collection. *c* The Royal Library, Copenhagen, Denmark. *x* George Bernard Shaw, Letter to the *Chronicle*, 1892, The Society of Authors on behalf of the Bernard Shaw Estate. W. H. Mittins *et al. A Grammar of Modern English* Methuen & Co. 1962. Ernest Gowers, *The Complete Plain Words* HMSO 1954. Crown copyright is reproduced with the permission of the Controller of HMSO. Barbara Strang *Modern English Structure* Edward Arnold 1962. **196** *c* (copyright) Oxford University Press **197** *x* S. Greenbaum & R. Quirk *A Student's Grammar of the English Language* Longman Group Ltd 1990. **198** Editions Slatkine. **199** South Tyneside Assessment of Syntactic Structures (1988) by Susan Armstrong & Maureen Ainley (courtesy of STASS Publications). **200** *t* Michael J. Stead. **201** Michael J. Stead. **202** Mansell. *x* Reprinted by permission; © 1977 Lisel Mueller. Originally in The New Yorker. **203** *ct* Michael J. Stead. *cc* Telegraph Colour Library. *cbl* Joe Low. *cbr* Michael J. Stead. **204** *l* Reeds Farmers Publishing Library. *r* Michael J. Stead. **205** *l* Telegraph Colour Library. *c* Michael J. Stead. *r* PGC Promotions Ltd. **207** *tl* & *br* Michael J. Stead. *tc* Franco Pace/Rex Features. *bl* David Hurn/Magnum. *tr* Last Resort Picture Library. **208** *b* Netherlands Board of Tourism. **209** *t* Jarrold Publishing. *b* Last Resort Picture Library. *x br* From *The Hitchiker's Guide to the Galaxy* by Douglas Adams. Copyright © 1979 by Douglas Adams. Reprinted by permission of Harmony Books, a division of Crown Publishers Inc. **210** *t* & *b* Michael J. Stead. **211** *b* Paul Willatts Photography. **214** *x* D. Crystal & D. Davy *Advanced Conversational English* Longman Group Ltd 1975. **215** *l* Mansell. *r* Courtesy Good Housekeeping/National Magazine Co. *x* Winston Churchill *The History of the Second World War*, Book 1, Cassell plc.

216 *from top to bottom* Michael J. Stead; Michael J. Stead; Telegraph Colour Library; Michael J. Stead; Michael J. Stead; Michael J. Stead; *bl* Michael J. Stead; **218** *t* Syndication International. *b* Rex Features Ltd. **219** *b* BFI Stills, Posters & Designs. **220** *t* J.S. Library. *bl* Michael J. Stead. *bc* Chris Fairclough Colour Library. *br* Frank Lane Picture Agency. **224** *t* The *Daily Star* 17/4/1985. *b* The *Sun* 17/4/1985. **225** CNES/Groupe de géodesie spatiale. **227** *b* The Royal National Rose Society. **228** Radio Times. *x* The *Independent* 26/7/1993. **230** *x* Excerpt from *The Name of the Rose* by Umberto Eco, copyright © 1980 by Gruppo Editoriale Fabbri-Bompiani, Sonzogno, Etas S.p.A., English translation copyright © 1983 by Harcourt Brace & Company and Martin Secker & Warburg, Ltd., reprinted by permission of Harcourt Brace & Company. David Lodge *Nice Work* Martin Secker & Warburg 1988; Penguin Books 1989. John le Carre *The Little Drummer-Girl* Hodder & Stoughton, 1983. Harold Pinter *The Birthday Party* Faber & Faber Ltd. **231** Stuart Franklin/ Magnum. **232** *t* Michael J. Stead. *x br* From *The Hitchiker's Guide to the Galaxy* by Douglas Adams. Copyright © 1979 by Douglas Adams. Reprinted by permission of Harmony Books, a division of Crown Publishers Inc. **233** *br* D. Crystal *Language A to Z* Longman Group Ltd 1991. *x bl* W. H. Mittins *A Grammar of Modern English* Methuen & Co. 1962. *tr* Reprinted by permission of the Peters Fraser & Dunlop Group Ltd. **243** Colorific! **246** *t* Denis Gifford Comic Collection. **249** Colorific! **250** 'The Dandy', © D. C. Thomson & Co. Ltd. **252** *t* From: *Which?*, January 1992, published by Consumers' Association, London. *bl* A. Nelson & Co. Ltd. *br* R. James & R. G. Gregory *Imaginative Speech and Writing*, Thomas Nelson & Son Ltd 1966. **253** *t* Illustration Dick Bruna, © copyright Mercis b.v., 1970. *br* Copr. © 1948 James Thurber. Copr. © 1976 Helen Thurber & Rosemary A. Thurber. From *The Beast in Me and Other Animals*, published by Harcourt Brace Company. *The Beast in Me and Other Animals* by James Thurber (Hamish Hamilton, 1949) reproduced by permission of Hamish Hamilton Ltd. *x* Wes Magee, 'The muddy, mucky, murky Mouch', © Wes Magee. **254** *x l* Rod Hull *The Reluctant Pote* Hodder & Stoughton 1989. *c* © Ray Mather 1989. **255** *t* Scope Features. *c* Mansell. *bl* Telegraph Colour Library. *br* Reproduced by permission of Punch. **256** *t* Lyn Wendon, Letterland. *b* Source: *My Rare Animal ABC Frieze*, Marcus Davies, WWF UK (World Wide Fund For Nature), 1993. **258** The Board of Trinity College Dublin. **260** Reproduced by permission of Punch. **262** Qantas Airways Ltd. **263** Joe Low. **264** *br* © 1994 Les Editions Albert René/Goscinny – Uderzo. **268** *c* Michael J. Stead. *bl* & *br* Hulton Deutsch Collection. **269** Eric Singer, *A Manual of Graphology* (1953) by permission of Gerald Duckworth & Co Ltd. **270** *c* The Museum of Promotional Arts, Toronto. *b* MD Foods Plc. **271** *r* From *The True Story of the Three Little Pigs* by Jon Scieszka. Copyright © 1989 by Jon Scieszka. Used by permission of Viking Penguin, a division of Penguin Books USA Inc. *x* Dylan Thomas 'Vision and Prayer', from *The Poems* J M Dent. **274** Frank Lane Picture Agency. **275** *tl* Michael J. Stead. *bl* & *br* Rex Features Ltd. **276** *t* Mansell. **277** *x tr* The Society of Authors on behalf of the Bernard Shaw Estate. *bl* American Literacy Council. **278** *x tl* © Richmal Ashbee, reproduced with permission of Macmillan Children's Books. *tr* P. G. Wodehouse *Service with a Smile* Hutchinson 1961. Reproduced by permission of Random House UK Limited and A. P. Watt Ltd on behalf of The Trustees of the Wodehouse Estate. **280** Bodleian Library, Oxford MS. Add. C. 165, fol. 145. **281** Bodleian Library, Oxford Shelfmark G.5.2.Th(2). **282** *l* Pembroke Ms 307 fol. 197v reproduced by permission of the Master and Fellows of Pembroke College, Cambridge. **283** *x br* Reprinted by permission of the Peters Fraser & Dunlop Group Ltd. **284** Jack Chambers. **286** Popperfoto. *x* P. G. Wodehouse *Service with a Smile* Hutchinson 1961. Reproduced by permission of Random House UK Limited and A. P. Watt Ltd on behalf of The Trustees of the Wodehouse Estate. **287** Copyright © BBC. *x r* The *Independent*. **289** Ian Berry/Magnum. **290** Eve Arnold/Magnum. **292** Independent Television News Ltd. **293** Hulton Deutsch Collection. *x* Lawrence Bragg *Advice to Lecturers* Royal Institution 1974. **294** *t* Popperfoto. *bl* Mansell. *br* Reproduced with the permission of the Data Protection Registrar. **295** *c* Geoffrey Broughton *Success with English, Coursebook 1* Penguin Books 1968, copyright © Geoffrey Broughton, 1968. **296** Crown copyright – reproduced with the sanction of the Controller of Her Majesty's Stationery Office. **305** *cr* Telegraph Colour Library. **306** Rex Features Ltd. **308** *t* Michael J. Stead. *c* Tick Ahearn.

310 *Longman Dictionary of English Language and Culture* Longman Group Ltd 1992. **311** *x* D. Mindt & C. Weber 'Prepositions in American and British English' *World Englishes* 8 (2) 1989, Blackwell Publishers. **314** Reprinted by permission of the publishers from *Dictionary of American Regional English*, Vol. I, Introduction and A–C, Vol. II D–H, edited by Frederic G. Cassidy, Cambridge, Mass.: The Belknap Press of Harvard University Press, Copyright © 1988, 1991 by the President and Fellows of Harvard College. **315** *br* M. Montgomery 'Exploring the roots of Appalachian English' *English World-Wide* 10 (1989) 227–78. **316** *b* Art Directors Photo Library. **317** Chris Fairclough Colour Library. **319, 320, 321, 322, 323** University of Leeds. **328** *x* J. T. Low 'In Memorium: John Thomas Low' *English World-Wide* 4 (1983) 85–91. **329** 'The Sunday Post', © D. C. Thomson & Co. Ltd. **330** *br* A. K. Annand *Dod and Davie* Canongate 1986. **331** *l* Mansell. *c* The Still Moving Picture Company. *r* N. Marshall *Chambers Companion to the Burns Supper* Chambers 1992. **332** *A Concise Scots Dictionary* Aberdeen University Press/Chambers 1985. *x b The Scots Thesaurus* Aberdeen University Press/Chambers 1990. *r* J. J. Graham 'Wir ain aald language. Writin ida Shetland dialect' *English World-Wide* 2 (1981) 18–19. **333** Mary Evans Picture Library/Jeffrey Morgan. *x* J. D. McClure 'The makin o a Scots prose' *English World-Wide* 2 (1981) 9–13. *x b* Extracts from Hugh MacDiarmid by permission of Carcanet Press Ltd. **334** *l* C. H. Williams 'The Anglicization of Wales', in N. Coupland (ed.) *English in Wales* Multilingual Matters 1990. Originally published in *Political Geography Quarterly* 3 1984, by permission of the publishers, Butterworth-Heinemann Ltd. ©. *r* W. T. R. Pryce 'Language shift in Gwent, c. 1770–1981', in N. Coupland (ed.) *English in Wales* Multilingual Matters 1990. **335** *t* Jim James/PA News Ltd. *bl* Radio Times. *br* Hulton Deutsch Collection. *x bl* R. S. Thomas 'Lowri Dafydd – Poetry for Supper' from *Selected Poems* Hart-Davis, an imprint of HarperCollins Publishers Limited. *br* Dylan Thomas 'Reminiscences of Childhood', from *Quite Early One Morning* J M Dent. **339** *t* Mary Evans Picture Library. *c* Conor Horgan/Martin Secker & Warburg. *x cr* Roddy Doyle *The Van* Martin Secker & Warburg Ltd 1991. *br* L. Todd 'By their tongue divided: towards an analysis of the speech communities in Northern Ireland' *English World-Wide* 5 (1984) 159–80. **340** *t* Jack Chambers *b* Canadi>n Airline International. **341** *b* Telegraph Colour Library. **342** *r* J. K. Chambers & M. F. Hardwick 'Comparative sociolinguistics of a sound change in Canadian English' *English World-Wide* 7 (1986) 23–46. **344** *x r* By kind permission of John Agard c/o Caroline Sheldon Literary Agency *Listen, Mr Oxford Don* from *Mangoes and Bullets* published by Pluto Press, 1985. **347** *l & r* Rex Features Ltd. **348** *x c* I. Van Sertima 'My Gullah brother and I: exploration into a community's language and myth through its oral tradition', in D. S. Harrison & T. Trabasso (eds.), *Black English: a Seminar* Lawrence Erlbaum Associates Inc. *br* Linton Kwesi Johnson 'Time Come' from *Dread Beat an Blood*. **349** Reprinted by permission of Christian Books Melanesia Inc. *x b* Copyright Helmut Buske Verlag Hamburg 1986. **353** *t, b, & x The Magic Pudding* by Norman Lindsay. © Janet Glad 1918. Reprinted by permission of HarperCollins Publishers Australia. **355** *x br* Keri Hulme *The Bone People* Hodder & Stoughton 1985. **356** Hulton Deutsch Collection. **357** *b* R. Malan *Ah Big Yaws?* David Philip Publishers 1972. **358** Colorific! **359** S. Salgardo/Magnum. **361** Colorific! **362** *br* Michael J. Stead. *b* R. Angogo & I. Hancock 'English in Africa: emerging standards or diverging regionalisms? *English World-Wide* 1 (1980) 67–96. **363** Hulton Deutsch Collection. *x rt* George Steiner *Extraterritorial* Faber and Faber Ltd 1972. **364** *t & b* Hulton Deutsch Collection. *x tr & cr* Reprinted by permission of the Peters Fraser & Dunlop Group Ltd. **367** *x tr* Reprinted by permission of A. P. Watt Ltd on behalf of The Trustees of the Robert Graves Copyright Trust. *br* Excerpt from *Nineteen Eighty-Four* by George Orwell, copyright 1949 by Harcourt Brace & Company and renewed 1977 by Sonia Brownell Orwell, reprinted by permission of the publisher/The estate of the late Sonia Brownell Orwell and Martin Secker & Warburg Ltd. **368** Michael Holford. *x b* 'Bring Many Names' by Brian Wren (b.1936) © 1987, 1989, 1994 Stainer & Bell Limited. **369** *x b* Linguistic Society of America. **370** *t* Penny Tweedie/Colorific! *br* Reproduced by permission of the American Folklore Society from *Journal of American Folklore* 83:327, January-March 1970. Not for further reproduction. **371** *c* The Hutchison Library. **372** *b & x* Reprinted from *Journal of Neurolinguistics* 6, P. Celcis *et al.*, 'Cerebral blood flow correlates of word list learning', pp. 253–72, Copyright 1991, with kind permission from Elsevier Science Ltd, The Boulevard, Langford Lane, Kidlington OX5 1GB, UK. **373** James Sugar/Colorific!. *x b* Reprinted from *Language Sciences* 14, H. R. Jenkins, 'On being clear about time. An analysis of a chapter of Stephen Hawking's *A Brief History of Time*', pp. 529–44, Copyright 1992, with kind permission from Elsevier Science Ltd, The Boulevard, Langford Lane, Kidlington OX5 1GB, UK. **374** *t* Mansell. *b* Art Directors Photo Library. **375** Mary Evans Picture Library. *x b Halsbury's Laws of England*, Vol. 7.2, 4th edn, pp. 1346–7, Butterworths. **376** Rex Features Ltd. **376–7** *x* © Barclays Bank plc. **377** *l & r* Plain English Campaign. **378** *x b* M. Atkinson *Our Masters' Voices* Methuen & Co. 1984. **379** Rex Features Ltd. *x tr* Parliamentary copyright. *b* J. Wilson *Politically Speaking* Blackwell Publishers 1990. J. T. Dillon, *The Practice of Questioning* Routledge 1990. **381** © *The Guardian*. **383** British Library. **384** BBC News & Current Affairs. **386** Chris Fairclough Colour Library. *x cr* K. Kuiper & P. Austin 'They're off and racing now: the speech of the New Zealand race caller', in A. Bell & J. Holmes (eds.) *New Zealand Ways of Speaking English* Multilingual Matters 1990. **387** *x b* 'The Commentator' from *Songs of the City* by Gareth Owen. © Gareth Owen 1985 (ISBN 0 00 184846 1). Used with permission of HarperCollins Publishers Ltd. **388** M. Friedman 'The changing language of a consumer society: brand name usage in popular American novels in the postwar era' *Journal of Consumer Research* 11 (1985) 927–38, University of Chicago Press. **389** The Whitbread Beer Company/Lowe Howard-Spink. **391** *l* copyright © The College of Arms. *r* Telegraph Colour Library. *x tr* Headquarters National Air Traffic Services, Civil Aviation Authority (HQ NATS, CAA). **392** Radio Times. **393** Last Resort Picture Library. **394** Reproduced by permission of Punch. **395** Camera Press London. **397** *cl* SCRABBLE ® game by permission of J. W. Spear & Sons PLC. SCRABBLE is a registered trade mark. *x c & b* G. Brandreth & D. Francis *World Championship Scrabble* ® Chambers. **398** *x c* © *The New Statesman & Society*. **399** DINGBATS ® Copyright © 1994 Paul Sellers. **400** Lumière Pictures Ltd. *x b* Graham Greene *The Third Man* (screenplay) Faber & Faber Ltd. **401** *cr The Sydney Morning Herald*. *bl* AEA Technology. *br* Reproduced by permission of Punch. **402** *x bl* Dylan Thomas *The Collected Letters* Macmillan. *br* Dylan Thomas *Under Milk Wood* J M Dent. **403** Hulton Deutsch Collection. **404** *x cr* W. Nash *An Uncommon Tongue* Routledge 1992. **405** *x l* D. Chiaro *The Language of Jokes: Analysing Verbal Play* Routledge 1992. *c The Bumper Book of Kerryman Jokes* by Des MacHale published by Mercier Press P.O. Box No. 5 Cork, Ireland. *r* K. Wales *The Lights Out Joke Book* Red Fox 1991. **406** *tr* Hulton Deutsch Collection. *tc* Cartoon by E. McLachlan in D. Crystal *Language A to Z Teachers' Book* Longman Group Ltd 1991. *c* © The Andrew Brownsword Collection. All rights reserved. *br* NPG. *x tc* Beaver: The newspaper of the London School of Economics Students' Union. **407** *x r* Eric Partridge *Comic Alphabets* Routledge. Copyright © 1961. Reprinted by permission of Sheil Land Associates. **408** Copyright © BBC. *x bl* Dennis Lee 'On Tuesday I Polish my Uncle', in J. Foster *What a lot of Nonsense* Robert Royce. **410** *t* From J. Everhart *The Illustrated Texas Dictionary of the English Language* (Volume 2), © Copyright Cliffs Notes, Inc., Lincoln, Nebraska, U.S.A. Used with the permission of the publisher. *b* Reproduced by permission of Hamish Hamilton Ltd. **411** *t, l, & r* Reproduced by permission of Punch. **412** *l* Camera Press London. *c* Karsh/Camera Press London. *r* Hulton Deutsch Collection. *x* F. Kermode *Selected Prose of T. S. Eliot* Faber & Faber Ltd. T. S. Eliot *Collected Poems 1909–1962* Faber & Faber Ltd. **413** *x r* Harold Pinter *The Birthday Party* Faber & Faber Ltd. **414** Mansell. *x b* 'Sunday Words' *The Sunday Times* 1980. **416** John Sewell 'Flight Patterns', in J. Foster (ed.) *Another Fourth Poetry Book* Oxford University Press 1989. First published in *The North* 1986. **417** *x l* William Carlos Williams 'The Semblables' from *Collected Poems* Carcanet Press Limited. *tr* T. S. Eliot *Collected Poems 1909–1962* Faber & Faber Ltd. *br* 'o pr' and 'r-p-o-p-h e-s-s-a-g-r' are reprinted from *Complete Poems*, 1904–1962, by E. E. Cummings, edited by George J. Firmage, by permission of Liveright Publishing Corporation and W. W. Norton & Company. Copyright © 1935, 1963, 1991 by the Trustees for the E. E. Cummings Trust. Copyright © 1978 by George James Firmage. **419** *x r* N. F. Simpson. *bl* Reprinted from Henry Reed: *Collected Poems* edited by Jon Stallworthy (1991) by permission of Oxford University Press. T. S. Eliot *Collected Poems*